Marx's Economic Manuscript of 1864–1865

Historical Materialism Book Series

The Historical Materialism Book Series is a major publishing initiative of the radical left. The capitalist crisis of the twenty-first century has been met by a resurgence of interest in critical Marxist theory. At the same time, the publishing institutions committed to Marxism have contracted markedly since the high point of the 1970s. The Historical Materialism Book Series is dedicated to addressing this situation by making available important works of Marxist theory. The aim of the series is to publish important theoretical contributions as the basis for vigorous intellectual debate and exchange on the left.

The peer-reviewed series publishes original monographs, translated texts, and reprints of classics across the bounds of academic disciplinary agendas and across the divisions of the left. The series is particularly concerned to encourage the internationalization of Marxist debate and aims to translate significant studies from beyond the English-speaking world.

For a full list of titles in the Historical Materialism Book Series available in paperback from Haymarket Books, visit:
https://www.haymarketbooks.org/series_collections/1-historical-materialism

Marx's Economic Manuscript of 1864–1865

Edited by
Fred Moseley

Translated by
Ben Fowkes

Haymarket Books
Chicago, IL

First published in 2015 by Brill Academic Publishers, The Netherlands

Published in paperback in 2017 by
Haymarket Books
P.O. Box 180165
Chicago, IL 60618
773-583-7884
www.haymarketbooks.org

ISBN: 978-1-60846-690-0

Distributed to the trade in the US through Consortium Book Sales and Distribution (www.cbsd.com) and internationally through Ingram Publisher Services International (www.ingramcontent.com).

This book was published with the generous support of Lannan Foundation, Wallace Action Fund, and the Marguerite Casey Foundation.

Special discounts are available for bulk purchases by organizations and institutions. Please call 773-583-7884 or email info@haymarketbooks.org for more information.

Cover design by Jamie Kerry of Belle Étoile Studios and Ragina Johnson.

Printed in the United States.

Entered into digital printing June 2025.

Library of Congress Cataloging-in-Publication data is available.

Dedicated to
Phyllis Atwater
and
Andres Guzman
who made this translation possible

Contents

1 Titles in brackets [ ] were added by the MEGA editors.

2 Only a title.

3 Engels gave the title 'Historical Material on Merchant's Capital' (his Chapter 20) to the rest of Marx's Chapter Four.

4 Only a title.

Translator's Note

1. Italics are used for text underlined by Marx.

2. There are no italics for 'v', 'c' and other algebraic symbols in the German text. I have followed this practice.

3. Passages of Marx's manuscript included by Engels in his edition of *Capital* Volume III are enclosed by the symbols < and >. Passages which fall *outside* these brackets were either not included at all by Engels in the published version, or they were modified by him very substantially before inclusion. In other words, where a passage begins with > and ends with < it was either left out by Engels or substantially modified and has been published here for the first time in its original form. I have also added an appendix indicating the page numbers of the passages which were not included in Engels's volume.

4. [and] enclose footnotes by the translator and the editor.

5. Marx's footnotes are given without brackets.

6. ( ) represent Marx's own parentheses; { } represent brackets introduced by Marx within his parentheses.

7. Marx sometimes introduced English words and phrases into his text. I have preserved these if at all possible and have indicated them in footnotes.

8. The page numbers of Marx's manuscript are placed within the text, separated from it by vertical lines, thus: | 1 |. MEGA Volume 4.2 also includes these manuscript page numbers, with the same notation, so matching these numbers is a good way to locate passages from the English translation in the original MEGA volume.

Introduction

*Fred Moseley**

Marx's only full draft of Volume III of *Capital* was written in the *Economic Manuscript of 1864–65*.[1] Marx's 'Book III' manuscript was heavily edited by Engels for the first German edition of Volume III in 1894 (after working on the project off and on for 11 years). A long-standing question in Marxian scholarship has concerned just how much Engels changed Marx's manuscript and whether there are significant differences between the two. Marx's original manuscript was published for the first time in German in 1992 in the *Marx/Engels Gesamtausgabe* (MEGA), Section II, Volume 4.2, but this important manuscript had not been translated into English, until this volume. Therefore, the publication of an English translation of Marx's original manuscript is an important event in Marxian scholarship. English-speaking Marxist scholars can finally compare Engels's Volume III with Marx's original manuscript and evaluate for themselves the significance of the differences. I am very grateful to Ben Fowkes, the eminent translator of Marx's works, for taking on this important task.

This publication of Marx's original Book III manuscript is part of the monumental MEGA project, the comprehensive 110-volume collected works of Marx and Engels (in German) (publication still ongoing).[2] Especially important is Section II, which includes all the economic manuscripts related to *Capital*: the *Grundrisse* (Volumes 1.1–1.2), the *Economic Manuscript* of 1858–61 (*Contribu-*

---

* Professor of Economics, Mount Holyoke College, Massachusetts, USA (fmoseley@mtholyoke.edu). I would like to express enormous gratitude to Regina Roth (a MEGA editor) for all her answers to my many questions about the MEGA over the years. Thanks also to Michael Heinrich for discussions about the MEGA and to Heinrich, Paul Mattick Jr., Tony Smith, and Patrick Murray for helpful comments on a previous draft of this Introduction. These excellent scholars are of course not responsible for the views expressed here. Thanks also to the Amherst College Library for purchasing the full collection of MEGA volumes and making them available to all the Five Colleges. I could not have written this Introduction without consulting these volumes. I also thank Danny Hayward for excellent copy-editing of a difficult text.

1 According to Müller et al. 2002, the *Economic Manuscript of 1864–65* was a complete draft of all three volumes of *Capital*. The draft of Volume II was published in 1988 in MEGA Section II, Volume 4.1. The draft of Volume I has never been found. Müller and his co-authors are the editors of the MEGA volume in which Marx's Volume III manuscript was published (Section II, Volume 4.2).

2 For a history of the MEGA project and a complete list of all the MEGA volumes, see Bellofiore and Fineschi 2009.

tion to a Critique of Political Economy and the *Urtext*) (Volume 2), the *Economic Manuscript of 1861–63* (Volumes 3.1–3.6),[3] the *Economic Manuscript of 1863–67* (Volumes 4.1–4.3), and the manuscripts after 1867, including all the published editions of Volume I, the little-known manuscripts written in the 1870s, and Engels's edited Volumes II and III (Volumes 5–15).[4] All of Marx's manuscripts in Section II have now been published (in German). The editors of the MEGA are to be thanked profusely for so expertly carrying out this extremely important task.

This Introduction will highlight the main differences between Marx's original manuscript and Engels's edited Volume III, in the view of this editor. It is hoped that other Marxian scholars will explore further this important question. The translator Ben Fowkes has very helpfully distinguished in the text between parts of Marx's manuscript that are included in Engels's Volume III (marked off by < and >) and parts of Marx's manuscript not included (by default marked off by > and <) (see Translator's Note #2). Fowkes has also prepared a useful Appendix that lists all the pages in Marx's text that were *not* included in Engels's Volume III.[5]

In comparing Marx's manuscript and Engels's volume, the first point to clarify is that Engels converted Marx's chapters into 'parts' and converted Marx's sections of chapters into chapters and created some chapters and sections of

3 The *Economic Manuscript of 1861–63* was published for the first time in its entirety in German in the MEGA in 1976–82. The English translation was published in 1988–94 by International Publishers, as Volumes 30 to 34 of the 50-volume *Marx-Engels Collected Works*. The manuscript is the second draft of *Capital*, and is the manuscript in which Marx developed for the first time his theory of the distribution of the total surplus-value that would later be presented in Volume III of *Capital*. About two-thirds of this manuscript is what we know as the *Theories of Surplus-Value*, much of which is about the distribution of surplus-value. The other third of the manuscript has been published for the first time in the new MEGA edition, and includes a second draft of Volume I of *Capital* (which is very interesting and important), and, what is most relevant to this volume, approximately 250 pages about material related to Parts 1, 3, and 4 of Volume III. See Dussel 2001b for a detailed textual study of this manuscript, and Moseley 2001b for an introduction to Dussel's book.

4 Each of these volumes also includes a companion volume, called the *Apparat* ('Apparatus'), which presents a wealth of detailed information about the history of the manuscript being published, editorial decisions and variations to these decisions, and further explanatory notes. The MEGA website is: http://mega.bbaw.de/.

5 For further detailed comparisons between Marx's manuscript and Engels's edited Volume III, see Müller et al. 2002 and Vollgraf and Jungnickel 2002. Jungnickel was an editor of Volume 4.2 and Vollgraf is also a MEGA editor. And for an exhaustive comparison (in German) of all the changes Engels made, see the Apparat to Volume 15 (Engels 1894, Volume III).

his own. In the discussion that follows, I will try to make it clear whose chapters I am talking about. This Introduction will discuss each of Marx's seven chapters (Engels's parts) in turn.

I would like to emphasise to begin with what a daunting task Engels faced in editing Marx's manuscript. In the first place, the manuscript was very uneven, with some chapters in close to finished form (Chapters Two, Four, and Seven), while other chapters (most notably Chapter Five and also Chapter One) were very rough – in some parts little more than a collection of notes and quotes. But more importantly, when Engels started this very difficult project, he appears to have had very little knowledge and overall understanding of Marx's Book III.

Engels's scant knowledge of Book III is evidenced by a series of letters between Marx and Engels in April 1868. Engels asked Marx how he explained merchant profit and how the general rate of profit is determined with merchant capital.[6] In order to answer this question, Marx replied with a long and detailed summary of Book III.[7] Unfortunately, Engels's question and Marx's long answer indicate how little Engels understood about Book III at the time. Marx appears to be explaining all this to Engels for the first time. Marx starts off: 'It is proper that you should know the method by which the rate of profit is developed ... In Book III we then come to the conversion of surplus-value into its different forms and separate component parts'.[8]

This letter gives a very clear explanation of Chapters I, II and IV of Marx's Book III, enough to answer Engels's question about merchant profit and also enough to give Engels a basic understanding of these parts for the purpose of editing them. The summary of Chapter III on the falling rate of profit is only three sentences. After Chapter IV (on merchant profit), the summaries of the remaining parts are only a few sentences, perhaps because these chapters were not necessary to answer Engels's question about merchant profit, and/or perhaps because Marx was running out of steam in writing this long substantial letter. Chapter V on interest (which later gave Engels the most trouble) is only a few lines and a bare outline. But this letter appears to be all Engels had to go on in understanding and editing Volume III.

There is no evidence (that I know of) of any further discussions between Marx and Engels in the last 15 years of Marx's life about the contents of his Book III, and certainly no instructions to guide Engels in his editing. Marx

6 Marx and Engels 1988, p. 19; letter of 26 April 1868 from Engels to Marx.

7 Marx and Engels 1988, pp. 20–5; letter of 30 April 1868 from Marx to Engels. This letter provides an excellent summary of Book III, which I highly recommend. To abbreviate, I will refer to this letter in this Introduction as Marx's '1868 letter'.

8 Marx and Engels 1988, p. 21; letter of 30 April 1868 from Marx to Engels.

probably avoided discussing his work on Books II and III with Engels because Engels would have pressured him to finish the books.[9] Indeed, Marx apparently did not even tell Engels directly and in person to edit these remaining books, but instead told his daughter Eleanor to tell Engels.[10] In light of Engels's limited knowledge of Book III before embarking on this enormous editing task and Marx's scant to non-existent instructions about what needed to be done, I think it is quite a remarkable achievement that Engels was able to do as good a job as he did (which does not mean that there are no problems).[11]

The main general difference between Marx's manuscript and Engels's Volume III is that Engels's editing made Marx's manuscript appear to be much better organised and more complete and finished than it actually was, especially Chapter Five and also Chapter One.[12] However, Engels's improved organisation did not change the overall logical structure of Marx's manuscript (the order of the chapters/parts is exactly the same) and does not necessarily change Marx's emphasis or the meaning of specific passages. We will investigate below the extent to which Engels's editing did change Marx's meaning or emphasis.

The first important misleading change that Engels made was the *title* of the book! Marx's title of the *Manuscript of 1864–65* was *Die Gestaltungen des Gesammtprozesses* [*The Forms of the Processes as a Whole*]. We know from the contents of the book that the 'forms' presented in this book are *particular forms of appearance of capital and surplus-value* – profit, average profit, commercial capital and commercial profit, interest-bearing capital and interest, and landed capital and rent. In my view, a better title for Volume III would be *The Forms of Appearance of Capital and Surplus-Value*. That is what Volume III is primarily about.[13]

---

9 This was Engels's explanation to Bebel as to why he knew so little about the state of Marx's Books II and III: '... had I known, I should have pestered him night and day until it was all finished and printed. And Marx knew that better than anyone else'. Marx and Engels 1995, p. 53; letter of 30 August 1883 from Engels to August Bebel.

10 Marx and Engels 1995, p. 39; letter of 24 June 1883 from Engels to Laura Lafargue.

11 It took Engels 11 years to complete the editing and publication of Volume III. Engels sacrificed his own theoretical work to edit Marx's manuscript, and he died of throat cancer one year after the publication of Volume III. Vollgraf and Jungnickel 2002, p. 40, referred to Engels's editorial work on Marx's manuscript as his 'editorial road to Calvary', and this seems like an apt description.

12 Most of the entries in Fowkes's Appendix (which lists all the pages in Marx's manuscript that were not included in Engels's Volume III) are from Chapters One and Five.

13 *Gestaltungen* was translated by David Fernbach in the Vintage edition of Volume III as 'Configurations'. This translation does not capture the concept of *form*, which is very important in Marx's theory and in Book III in particular. Book III is about *forms* – the particular forms of appearance of capital and surplus-value.

Unfortunately, Engels deleted *Gestaltungen* from the title, and changed the title to *Gesammtprozess der kapitalistischen Produktion* [*The Process of Capitalist Production as a Whole*]. This title misses the main point of Marx's manuscript (which Engels maybe did not fully understand, as discussed above). Book III is indeed about capitalist production as a whole, in the sense of the unity of the process of production (Book I) and the process of circulation (Book II). But more precisely, Book III is about the *particular forms of appearance of capital and surplus-value* (profit, average profit, etc.) that develop out of the processes as a whole already theorised.[14]

Vollgraf and Jungnickel argue that pressure from the publisher forced Engels to change the title.[15] It had been so long since the publication of Volumes I and II that a new title was needed that would make a clearer connection to the first two volumes. They also argue that neither Marx's title nor Engels's fit the contents of the book and they suggest a slight variation of Engels's title: *The Process of Capitalist Reproduction as a Whole*. However, I argue that this title does not fit the contents of the book any better than Engels's title. *Gestaltungen* is missing again, and *Gestaltungen* is the key word of the title, because the contents of the book are the forms of capital and surplus-value.

Gestaltungen is a new and unusual term in Marx's manuscripts. To my knowledge, it was not used in Marx's earlier manuscripts and is used only seven times in this manuscript (besides the title),[16] and its full meaning is not entirely clear. The usual translation of *Gestaltungen* is 'forms', i.e., as a synonym for the German word *Form*. But then why didn't Marx simply use the word *Form*? What additional connotation of *Gestaltungen* did Marx have in mind with this unusual choice of words in his title?

An indication of Marx's full meaning of *Gestaltungen* is given in the first paragraph of this manuscript:

---

14 Thanks to Paul Mattick Jr. for clarifying the meaning of Engels's title for me.

15 Vollgraf and Jungnickel 2002, pp. 43–4.

16 See the following pages of the present volume: pp. 49, 308, 359, 433, 715, 895 and 897; Marx 1981 [Engels], pp. 117, 301, 367, 445, 753, 967, and 969. There are also two other later instances in which Marx used the word *Gestaltungen* as the title for his Book III: in a letter to Kugelmann of 13 October 1866 (where it is poorly translated as 'structures'), Marx and Engels 1987, p. 328; and in the Preface to the first German edition of Volume I (also poorly translated as 'configurations'), Marx 1977, p. 93. These later uses suggest that Marx really did intend *Gestaltungen* to be the title of his Book III, but they do not provide any clarification of Marx's full meaning of the word. Thanks to Michael Heinrich for pointing out these other two instances to me.

> What is necessary is rather to discover and present the **concrete forms [*Formen*] which grow out of the process of capital**, considered as a whole ... The **forms [*Gestaltungen*] of capital**, as we develop them in this book, thus come closer, step by step, to the **form [*Form*] in which they appear at the surface of society**, in the everyday consciousness of the agents of production themselves and finally in the action of the different capitals upon each other, namely competition.[17]

Thus we can see that the aim of this book is to present the *concrete forms* (or the particular forms) that grow out of the capitalist process as a whole, as they *appear* on the surface of capitalist society, and in the everyday consciousness of capitalists (and economists).[18] Therefore *Gestaltungen* seems to mean more specifically the *concrete (particular) surface forms of appearance* of capital and surplus-value.

Inwood's *Hegel Dictionary* defines *Gestalt* as follows:

> Objects that have a *Gestalt* ... are thought of as ORGANIC unities, appreciable only as a whole, not by the piecemeal consideration of their parts.[19]

This connotation certainly fits with Marx's theory of the particular forms of surplus-value in the *Manuscript of 1864–65*. All the particular forms of surplus-value are explained on the basis of a unifying principle – they all come from the same source, the surplus labour of workers – and thus they are apprehensible only as an 'organic unity' and cannot be understood by the 'piecemeal consideration of their parts'.

One more point of general introduction: Müller, et al., argue that Marx began writing this manuscript with Chapter Two, and then wrote Chapters One and Three in that order.[20] After Chapter Three, Marx switched to Book II and wrote a complete draft of Book II (published in the MEGA, Section II,

---

17 Marx, this volume, p. 49; Marx 1981 [Engels], p. 117; bold emphasis added, italicised emphasis in the original, and German words in square brackets and italics. This convention will be followed throughout this introduction.

18 In the *Grundrisse*, Marx described these particular forms of surplus-value as 'developments coming out of the germ' of the general form of surplus-value. Marx 1973, p. 310. Another possible translation of *Gestaltungen* is 'formations', which is a process noun like *Gestaltungen*, connoting the process of development of the particular forms of capital and surplus-value.

19 Inwood 1992, p. 108; capitalisation in the original.

20 Müller et al. 2002, p. 18.

Volume 4.11, in 2008), after which he returned to Book III and wrote the remaining chapters in order. Their argument about the backward order of the composition of Chapters One and Two is based primarily on the pagination of the two chapters – Marx originally gave letters rather than numbers to pages in Chapter Two, and then later numbered Chapters One and Two consecutively. However, I will discuss below other reasons that have to do with the *content* of Chapter Two that suggest to me that Chapter Two was written after Chapter One. I don't think it really matters much which chapter was written first, but it is interesting to speculate and it might turn out to be important.

I will now discuss in turn each of seven chapters in Marx's manuscript, starting with Chapter One.

Chapter One

Chapter One ('The Transformation of Surplus Value into Profit') (Engels's Part One) is one of the chapters with the biggest differences between Marx's manuscript and Engels's Volume III. Engels said in his Preface:

> For Part One, the main manuscript could be used only with major limitations. The mathematical treatment of the relationship between the rate of surplus-value and rate of profit (corresponding to our Chapter 3) was introduced in full right at the beginning, while the subject of our Chapter 1 appeared only later and in passing. Two attempted revisions came to the rescue here, each with folio sheets, though even these did not entirely fill the gap. The present Chapter 1 was put together from these drafts.[21]

Marx's 'two attempted revisions' that Engels mentions and that he used as the primary basis of his Chapter 1 were written in 1867–8 and were recently published for the first time (2012) in German in the MEGA, Section II, Volume 4.3; this volume has not yet been translated into English. A translation of this volume into English should be a top priority for Marxian scholarship.[22]

21 Engels 1981a, p. 94.

22 This volume also contains sections on other interesting and important topics, including the effect of turnover on the rate of profit (perhaps written to fill the missing section on this subject in Chapter One of the *Economic Manuscript of 1864–65*), and also an intriguing and heretofore unknown 30-page section on the determination of prices of production, including with unequal turnover times and unequal rates of surplus-value across industries (the only time Marx discussed these important topics).

After the first paragraph of Marx's Chapter One, which is similar to the first paragraph of Engels's Chapter 1, there are four important paragraphs in Marx's chapter that are missing in Engels's chapter. In these paragraphs, Marx argues that the theory of surplus-value presented in the previous two books has determined the magnitude of surplus-value produced by a given capital in a year. If this predetermined magnitude of surplus-value is related to the total capital advanced, instead of variable capital alone (which is the true source of surplus-value), then this magnitude of surplus-value is transformed into 'profit'. The magnitude of profit is the same as the magnitude of surplus-value; the difference is that this predetermined magnitude is viewed subjectively from a different perspective (the capitalists' perspective). Here are excerpts from these missing paragraphs:

> In one year, a capital produces a **certain quantity of surplus-value** … If one now calculates the surplus-value produced in a year … in relation to the *total capital advanced*, which consists of the constant capital advanced plus the variable capital advanced, the surplus-value is transformed into *profit*.
>
> From the point of view of its material, the *profit* … is nothing other than the *surplus-value* itself. Its **absolute magnitude does not therefore differ** from the absolute magnitude of the surplus-value which capital produces during a given turnover time. It is **surplus-value itself, but calculated differently**, or, as it initially appears, viewed subjectively in a different way.
>
> *Profit*, in a material sense, and therefore as an absolute magnitude or quantity, is not at all different from *surplus-value* … e.g. £100[23]

The earlier drafts of this chapter in the *Grundrisse* and the *Manuscript of 1861–63* started off with similar paragraphs.[24]

On the basis of this assumption that the magnitude of profit is equal to the predetermined magnitude of surplus-value, Marx derives in this chapter some

23 Marx, this volume, pp. 49–50.

24 Marx 1973, pp. 745–57 and Marx 1991, pp. 69–70. Marx made the same point in his 1868 letter: 'As a result, *surplus-value* assumes the form of *profit*, **without there being any *quantitative difference*** between one and the other. It is only an illusory manifestation of surplus-value'. Marx and Engels 1988, p. 21; letter of 30 April 1868 from Marx to Engels.

'laws' which have to do with the relation between the rate of surplus-value (S/V) and the rate of profit (S/C+V). These laws are discussed in terms of a single capital and they also apply to the total social capital; the single capital represents the total social capital. In Marx's 1868 letter, he made this point explicitly:

> These laws, moreover, remain *directly* applicable if S/C+V is treated as the relation of the **socially produced surplus-value to the social capital.**[25]

Marx made a similar statement in the first draft of this chapter in the *Manuscript of 1861–63*:

> Just as the surplus value of the individual capital in each sphere of production is the measure of the absolute magnitude of the profit – merely a converted form of surplus value – so is the *total surplus value* produced by the total capital the absolute *measure of the total profit of the total capital*, whereby profit should be understood to include **all forms of surplus value**, such as rent, interest, etc ... It is therefore the **absolute magnitude of value** ... which the **capitalist class can divide among its members under various headings.**[26]

Thus we can see that, at the beginning of Book III, the total amount of surplus-value produced in the economy as a whole in a year is taken as a *predetermined given*.

After these opening paragraphs, Marx launched into a very long footnote (34 printed pages) (pp. 53–81 of this volume), which the MEGA editors brought into the text, and which is a detailed analysis (with many tedious numerical examples) of the *difference* (d) between the rate of surplus-value (s′) and the rate of profit (p′) (d = s′ – p′) and the effects on this difference of changes in constant capital and/or variable capital. But Marx realised in the process of this analysis that it is better to analyse the relation between the rate of surplus-value and rate of profit *directly*, rather than in terms of the difference between them, and that is what he did later in this chapter (as we will see below).[27] Engels (rightfully) did not include any of this long (dead-end) footnote in his Chapter 3.

---

25 Marx and Engels 1988, p. 23; letter of 30 April 1868 from Marx to Engels.

26 Marx and Engels 1991, pp. 98–9.

27 Marx said at one point in this long footnote: 'It is perhaps better to derive the laws **directly** from s′ and p′ than from the **difference** between them'. Marx, this volume, p. 64.

The next section of Marx's manuscript (this volume, pp. 84–92) was given the title 'Cost Price' by the MEGA editors, and contains subject matter related to Engels's Chapter 1 ('Cost Price and Profit') and also Engels's Chapter 2 ('The Rate of Profit').

After this section, there is another long detailed analysis of the relation between the rate of surplus-value and rate of profit (which the MEGA editors gave the title 'The Relationship between the Rate of Surplus-Value and the Rate of Profit', borrowed from Engels), but this time the analysis is in terms of the following equation (which is a much better framework):

$$p' = s' (v / C)$$

where v is variable capital and C is the total capital (C = c + v; c is constant capital). (This equation is included in Engels's Chapter 3, but it is less prominent.) Marx's main (and obvious) point is that the rate of profit depends not only on the rate of surplus-value, but also on the relative proportions of variable capital and constant capital in the total capital. This point was intended as a critique of Ricardo (and classical economists in general), who tended to ignore constant capital and the composition of capital and identify the rate of profit and the rate of surplus-value (or the profit-to-wage ratio). Marx stated during this analysis:

> As can be studied with the Ricardians, etc., it is completely wrong-headed to seek directly to present the laws of the rate of profit as laws of the rate of surplus-value, or vice versa.[28]

> One can therefore see that the movement of the rate of profit can be very complicated and that its analysis is by no means as simple a matter as the political economists have so far imagined.[29]

With the help of Samuel Moore, Engels condensed Marx's 44 printed pages of detailed numerical examples into 20 pages in his Chapter 3, which he gave

28 Marx, this volume, p. 95.

29 Marx, this volume, p. 124. Marx had presented an earlier critique of Ricardo on this point in the *Economic Manuscript of 1861–63* (Marx and Engels 1989b, pp. 9–18), which Marx summarised as follows: 'It has already been shown in some detail that the laws of surplus value – or rather the rate of surplus value – ... do not so directly and simply coincide with, nor are they applicable to, the laws of profit, as Ricardo supposes. It has been shown that he wrongly identifies surplus value with profit ...' Marx and Engels 1989b, p. 60.

the title 'The Relationship between the Rate of Profit and the Rate of Surplus-Value'.

This equation seems to imply that the rate of profit will always vary directly with the variable capital. However, Marx realised in the course of this exploratory analysis that this 'law' is valid *only if the wage rate per worker is assumed to remain constant*, so that variable capital serves as what Marx called an 'index' of the *number of workers employed*, which changes *only* if the number of workers changes. With this assumption, a change of variable capital will leave the rate of surplus-value unaffected and will change the rate of profit in the same direction. However, if variable capital changed as a result of a *change in the wage rate per worker*, then (assuming a constant working day) the rate of surplus-value would also change and would vary *inversely* with variable capital, and thus the rate of profit might also vary inversely to variable capital, and this 'law' would no longer be valid. Therefore, in Marx's further analysis of this 'law', he generally assumed that the wage rate remains constant and thus v serves as an index of the number of workers employed.

On the other hand, Marx emphasised in these pages that *constant capital is different* in this respect. With respect to effects on the rate of profit (the crucial point here), it is *irrelevant* whether a change of constant capital is due to a change in the *quantity* of means of production or to a change in the *prices* of the means of production (analogous to the wage rate); in both cases, the change of constant capital does not affect the rate of surplus-value and thus the rate of profit will always vary inversely to a change of constant capital.

Marx expressed this key difference between the effects of changes of variable capital and constant capital on the rate of profit in the following important passages in this section of Chapter 1:

> This shows precisely the special **organic relationship** that the **variable capital** has with the movement of the capital as a whole and its valorisation, as well as its **distinction from the constant capital.** The latter, to the extent that the creation of value comes into consideration, is important only on account of the value that it has. It is **quite immaterial** here, as far as value formation is concerned, whether a constant capital of £1,500 represents 1,500 tons of iron at £1 a ton or 500 tons at £3. The **quantity of actual material** is **completely unimportant** for the formation of value and its **influence on the rate of profit.** The rate of profit is inversely related to it, whatever relationship the increase or decrease in the exchange-value of the constant capital has to do with the **material elements**, the **use-values**, which it represents.

> The situation is **completely different** in the case of **v**. What is important is not the value which it has, the labour which is objectified in it, but that this value is an **index** of the total labour that it sets in motion, and which is not expressed in it.[30]

And in the concluding paragraphs of Chapter One, Marx stated again:

> If we consider the **influence of c on the rate of profit**, the reasons why c falls are **entirely irrelevant**, although differences between the causes for a fall have a very evident impact on the prices of commodities. What is of *decisive importance*, however, is whether v changes because a smaller or larger number of workers is technologically required for the production of the same value; whether, therefore, the decrease or increase in v is an **index** of the amount of labour set in motion ... or v rises or falls because the *wage* rises and falls ...[31]

Engels included the first passage above in his Chapter 3 (p. 144), but did not include the second concluding paragraph, and this omission weakens this important point.

After the second paragraph just quoted, Marx stated in a brief preview of his Chapter Two (which unfortunately Engels also did not include) that what has been analysed in Chapter One as *changes* over time in a given capital will be analysed in Chapter Two as *differences* between capitals (different proportions of constant capital and variable capital) in different industries at the same time.

> It should finally be remarked that what we have presented here as movements of different constituents of the same capital over a period of time could just as well be presented as *differences between different capitals in various areas of investment lying alongside each other in a spatial sense* and that what has been presented so far ***will be utilised in this latter form in the next chapter***.[32]

The important point about the different effects on the rate of profit of *changes* in variable capital and constant capital is also applied in Chapter Two to the different effects on the rate of profit of *different proportions* of constant capital and variable capital across industries.

---

30 Marx, this volume, p. 106; Marx 1981 [Engels], p. 144.

31 Marx, this volume, p. 143.

32 Marx, this volume, p. 143.

After this long section on the rate of profit and the rate of surplus-value, the rest of Marx's Chapter One is very similar to Chapters 5, 6, and 7 of Engels's Part One. Marx's Section 3 ('Economy in the Use of Constant Capital') becomes Engels's Chapter 5, Marx's Section 4 ('The Effect of Changes in Raw Material Prices') and Section 5 ('Release and Tying-up of Capital, Depreciation and Appreciation, Revaluation and Devaluation of Capital') become Engels's Chapter 6, and Marx's Section 7 ('Profit (as it appears to the bourgeois)') becomes Engels's Chapter 7, now with a less informative title ('Supplementary Remarks'). Engels's chapters are somewhat condensed, with fewer and shorter examples and some material rearranged, but I do not find any significant differences in the content and meaning.

Marx's Section 6 was only a title ('The Influence of Changes in Circulation Time, its Shortening and Lengthening'), and Engels wrote his short Chapter 4 ('The Effect of the Turnover on the Rate of Profit') on this subject and moved its location up in front of the chapters mentioned in the last paragraph, perhaps because Marx's 1868 letter suggests this earlier location. The main point of this chapter is not controversial – that the annual rate of profit varies inversely with the turnover time of capital (e.g., a reduction of turnover time would increase the annual rate of profit). When Engels wrote his Chapter 4 in the 1880s, Marx had already discussed in Volume II the effect of turnover time on the quantity of advanced capital, and the effect of turnover time on the rate of profit follows from this earlier analysis. Engels discussed in his chapter examples of reductions in turnover time due to railroads, steamships, and the Suez Canal.

Chapter Two

Chapter Two ('The Transformation of Profit into Average Profit') is the pivotal chapter in Marx's Book III, in which he presented his theory of the general rate of profit and prices of production (i.e., the infamous 'transformation problem'). This chapter is the beginning of Marx's theory of the distribution of surplus-value, and it has to do specifically with the division of the total surplus-value into average amounts for each industry, so that each industry receives the same general rate of profit on the capital invested in that industry. And this theory of the distribution of surplus-value takes as a presupposition the total amount of surplus-value produced in the economy as a whole in a year that is to be distributed across individual industries, which has been determined by the prior theory of the production of surplus-value in Volumes I and II. The presupposed total annual surplus-value (S) is used to determine the general rate of profit (R

$= S / C$), and the general rate of profit is then a prerequisite in the determination of prices of production ($P_i = (C_i + V_i)(1 + R)$). In Marx's main numerical example in this chapter, the total annual surplus-value is 110 and the total capital advanced is 500, so that the general rate of profit is 22 percent.[33]

Chapter Two (Engels's Part 2) is of course very controversial, and many (myself included) have wondered whether Marx's original Chapter Two was significantly different from Engels's Part 2. But this turns out largely not to be the case. Chapter Two in Marx's manuscript is much better organised and more finished than Chapter One, and Engels's Part Two is almost the same as Marx's Chapter Two, with very little editing. Marx's Chapter Two is divided into five sections with titles, which Engels converted into his Chapters 8–12.

Geert Reuten has argued that Engels's editing of Chapter Two 'polished away most of Marx's worries' that Marx expressed in Section 3 (Engels's Chapter 10) about his theory of prices of production presented in Section 2 (Engels's Chapter 9).[34] But in comparing the two texts, I find no evidence to support this conclusion and Reuten provides no specific examples. Marx's Section 3 is almost identical to Engels's Chapter 10. I find no worries expressed in Marx's Section 3 that were polished out by Engels. In Fowkes's Appendix to this volume, which lists all the passages in Marx's manuscript that were not included in Engels's Volume III, there are no entries for Section 3 of Chapter Two (i.e., Engels's Chapter 10).

However, there are a few significant passages that are in Marx's manuscript, but are missing in Engels's volume. The first important set of passages that are missing in Engels's Part Two (Chapter 8) are several intermittent paragraphs between pp. 200 and 205 in this volume that have to do mainly with unequal turnover times of different capitals, which is another source of unequal rates of profit besides unequal compositions of capital.[35] Engels's omission of these paragraphs obscures this important further complication in Marx's theory of prices of production.

---

33 In Marx's 1868 letter: 'This rate of profit, expressed absolutely, can be nothing but the *surplus-value* produced (annually) by the *capitalist class* in relation to the total of *social* capital advanced'. The result is a kind of '*capitalist communism*' in which each capital gets 'a fractional part of the total surplus-value proportionate to the part of the total social capital that it forms'. In Marx's numerical example in this letter, the total annual surplus-value = 100 and the total capital = 500, so that the general rate of profit = 20 percent. Marx and Engels 1988, p. 23; letter of 30 April 1868 from Marx to Engels.

34 Reuten 2009.

35 The reader can use the translator's indicators of > and < to identify the missing paragraphs in these pages; see Translator's Note #3.

The second important passage that is missing in Engels's Part Two is three paragraphs that should be in Engels's Chapter 9. This omission was first pointed out by Alejandro Ramos.[36] The passage is missing from p. 263 of Engels's Chapter 9 (it should be in the middle of the page, after the paragraph that begins 'In Volumes 1 and 2 ...'),[37] and it presents a concise algebraic formulation of the determination of the value and price of production of commodities and the conditions under which value is > than, < than, or = to price of production. An excerpt from the missing passage:

Value = Cost Price + surplus-value	V = K + s
or profit as identical with surplus-value	or = K + p
cost price = value – surplus-value	or K = V – s
price of production = cost price + profit	P = K + p′
calculated according to the general rate of profit = p′ ...	

Since V = K + s or p, and P = K + p′, V = P when s = p′, > P when p′ < s, and < P when p′ > s.[38]

The important point here is that the *cost price* component (K) *is the same* in the determination of both value and price of production in all these formulations. The only possible difference between value and price of production is the second component – whether surplus-value is > than, < than, or = to profit. This very clear passage provides important new evidence that *the cost price is supposed to be the same* in the determination of both values and prices of production in Marx's theory, as I and others have argued.[39] In other words, there are not two cost prices in Marx's theory, one equal to values and the other equal to prices of production, but *only one cost price*, which is the *actual* cost price (the sum of the actual constant capital and variable capital advanced to purchase means of production and labour-power consumed in production), which in turn is equal to the prices of production of the inputs. Thus, according to this interpretation and contrary to the traditional interpretation, Marx did *not* 'fail to transform the inputs' because the inputs (the cost prices) are not supposed

36 Ramos 1998.

37 The page reference here and in future references to Engels's edited text is to the Random House edition of 1981. For the purpose of clarity, the reference will be given as Marx 1981 [Engels].

38 Marx, this volume, pp. 275–6. Please note that Marx is using p′ here to stand for the *amount* of profit, not the *rate* of profit (which is different from Chapter One).

39 Wolff, Roberts, and Callari 1982; Ramos 1998; Moseley 2016.

to be transformed (as is commonly alleged), but are instead supposed to be the *same magnitude* (K) in the determination of both values and prices of production.[40]

Another important passage that is missing in Engels's Part Two is at the very end of Marx's Chapter Two as one of four 'Supplementary Remarks'. Engels included Marx's other three 'supplementary remarks' in his Chapter 12, but did not include a very important one which is entitled 'Transition from Chapter One to Chapter Two'. This supplement obviously belongs at the end of Chapter One, but it was written at the end of Chapter Two. Instead of relocating this supplement at the end of his Part One, Engels chose not to include it, which I think was unfortunate.

One important difference between Marx's Chapters One and Chapter Two is that in Chapter Two the relative proportion of variable capital and constant capital is discussed throughout in terms of the concept of the *organic composition of capital*. The three related definitions of the *technical* composition of capital, the *value* composition, and the *organic* composition are presented in the opening pages of Chapter Two and these concepts are utilised throughout the chapter. However, in Chapter One, these concepts are not used at all, even though the relative proportion of variable capital and constant capital also plays a crucial role in this chapter, as we have seen above. It appears that Marx gained greater clarity about these concepts while working on Chapter Two, and he wrote this summary of Chapter One and transition to Chapter Two in terms of these concepts.

It is worth quoting this important supplement in full:

> *Supplement to the Transition from Chapter One to Chapter Two of this Book*
>
> We have considered the subject under three aspects: (1) *a change in the mode of production* and as a result in the composition of capital; (2) no change in the mode of production, a change in the *value relation* between constant and variable capital, involving no change in the relative amounts of these elements of capital but a *change in the value* of the commodities which enter into the formation of the constant and variable capital; and (3) a change in the mode of production and in the value of the elements of constant and variable capital, or of one or other of them etc.
>
> What was considered here as a *variation* within the **organic composition** of *a single* capital can equally appear (make itself felt) as a *difference*

40 I have discussed this important passage further in Moseley 2016, Chapter 4, Section 4.3.

> between the **organic compositions** of *the capitals of different spheres of production.*
>
> *Firstly*: instead of a *variation* in the **organic composition** of *one and the same* capital, a *difference* in the **organic composition** of *different capitals.*
>
> *Secondly*: an alteration in the **organic composition** of capital as a result of a *change in the value* of the two parts of *the same* capital – *a difference in the value of the machinery, raw material etc. applied* on behalf of capitals in different trades. This is **not true for variable capital**, since we assume *an equal* wage in the *different* trades. The difference in the *value* of different days of labour in different trades has nothing to do with the matter in hand. If the labour of a goldsmith is dearer than that of a labourer, the surplus time of the goldsmith is of greater value than that of the peasant in the same proportion.[41]

It is clear in this passage that the organic composition of capital across industries may be different for *two reasons*: both because of differences in the technical composition of capital and also because of differences in the values of the means of production. The reason that differences in the value of the means of production are included in Marx's definition of the organic composition of capital is that such differences *have the same effect on the rate of profit* as different technical compositions of capital, as discussed above.

But variable capital is different. Variable capital per worker (or wages per worker) is assumed to be *equal* across industries, because, unlike constant capital, unequal wages across industries have a *different effect* on the rate of profit than unequal quantities of labour employed across industries, as Marx discussed at length in both Chapter One and Chapter Two (and as we discussed above).

Ben Fine and Alfredo Saad-Filho have offered a different interpretation of Marx's concept of the organic composition of capital, according to which the organic composition differs across industries for *only one reason* – because of unequal technical compositions of capital *only*, and *not* because of unequal values of the means of production.[42] Their interpretation is contradicted by Marx's very clear summary of Chapter One (discussed above) and also by the transition to Chapter Two (just discussed) and indeed by Marx's discussion throughout Chapter Two. For example, another clear statement that the organic composition of capital in different industries may be different for these *two reasons* is

41 Marx, this volume, pp. 317–18.

42 Fine 1983 and Saad-Filho 1993.

the first sentence of Section 2 of Chapter Two in Marx's manuscript (which is the first sentence of Chapter 9 of Engels's Volume III).

> At any one given time, the organic composition of capital depends on **two factors**: firstly, on the **technological proportion** between the labour-power and the means of production applied, and secondly, on the **price of those means of production** in the different spheres of production.[43]

Finally, this supplement to Chapter Two is one of the main pieces of textual evidence that leads me to think that Marx wrote Chapter One before Chapter Two, contrary to Müller et al. (as mentioned above). If Chapter One had not yet been written when Marx wrote this supplement at the end of Chapter Two, why wouldn't he write this supplement in Chapter One (to be written next) where it belongs? It seems more plausible to me that Marx realised after first writing Chapter One and then writing Chapter Two that this summary and transition from Chapter One to Chapter Two was necessary, so he wrote this transition at the end of Chapter Two, intending to relocate it later.

Also, the same conclusion is suggested by the fact that the concept of the organic composition of capital, which Marx developed and used extensively in Chapter Two, is not mentioned at all in Chapter One. If Chapter One had been written after this Supplement to Chapter Two, it seems likely that Marx would have used the concept of the organic composition of capital explicitly in Chapter One, especially in the concluding paragraphs of Chapter One discussed above (which are about the ratio of constant capital and variable capital without this ratio being called the organic composition of capital). The fact that he did not use this concept in Chapter One suggests to me that he wrote Chapter One before he developed the concept in Chapter Two.

A final piece of evidence for this interpretation is the beginning of Chapter Two. In the first few pages, Marx wrote a detailed summary of the main points of Chapter One, including points that Marx had not hitherto discussed in his previous manuscripts. For example, assuming a constant rate of surplus-value, the rate of profit will vary as a result of changes in constant capital or variable capital and the proportion between them (discussed extensively in Chapter One, as we saw above, and not before); and also the 'tie-up and release' of capital. These details suggest to me that Marx had recently written Chapter One and these details were fresh in his mind as he started Chapter Two.

43 Marx, this volume, pp. 265–6; Marx 1981 [Engels], p. 252.

Chapter Three

Chapter Three is of course the chapter in which Marx presents his famous theory of the falling rate of profit ('The Law of the Tendential Fall in the Rate of Profit with the Advance of Capitalist Production'),[44] and like Chapter Two is also very controversial. Engels made the following changes to Marx's Chapter Three, which are of varying degrees of significance.

In the first place, Marx's chapter was not divided into any sections, and Engels divided his Part Three into three chapters, the well-known Chapters 13, 14, and 15, with Chapters 14 and 15 further divided into sections. The titles of the chapters and sections were also added by Engels. This structure of course makes Marx's manuscript look more organised and more complete than it actually was, but it does not necessarily change its meaning or emphasis.

Secondly, Engels left out an important footnote from early in his Chapter 15, which states clearly that the rate of profit (the ratio of the total surplus-value (or profit) to the total capital advanced) is independent of the division of the total surplus-value into industrial profit, interest, and rent.

> $$\textit{Rate of Profit} = \frac{\textit{Surplus-value}}{\text{Capital Advanced}} \ldots$$
>
> If profit = P, industrial profit = P′, interest = Z and rent = R, P = P′ + Z + R. And it is clear that whatever the absolute magnitude of P may be, P′, Z and R may rise or fall in proportion to each other, independently of the magnitude of P or a rise or fall in P. The reciprocal displacement of P′, Z and R **amounts to no more than a change in the distribution of P** under its different headings.[45]

Marx had already emphasised this point earlier in his Chapter Three, and Engels included this passage in his Chapter 13,[46] so perhaps Engels thought that this footnote was redundant.

Another change made by Engels was to relocate five pages from the middle of his Chapter 15 (pp. 350–5 in this volume) to the end of his Chapter 13 (pp. 332–8 in Engels's Volume III), and Engels also added two pages of his own in the middle of these pages (pp. 334–5), which are marked as an addition. The relocation of these pages makes some sense, since these pages are primarily

44 We can see that Engels abbreviated Marx's title by deleting the last phrase.

45 Marx, this volume, p. 346.

46 Marx, this volume, pp. 322-3; Marx 1981 [Engels], p. 320.

about an increase in the *mass* of profit in spite of a decrease in the *rate* of profit, and this subject is also discussed in the preceding pages in Chapter 13. Again, this relocation is not necessarily inconsistent with Marx's intentions.

Geert Reuten has argued that Engels's relocation gives more weight to Chapter 13, which Engels entitled 'The Law as Such', and thus gives the impression that Marx concluded that the rate of profit would definitely decline over the long run as a secular trend, instead of fluctuating between periods of decline and periods of increase, without a definite trend over the long run (the latter is Reuten's interpretation).[47] I agree in part, but I think that the additional weight given to Chapter 13 and to the 'Law as Such' interpretation by this relocation is minor and hardly noticeable. And, as mentioned, this relocation makes sense in that the topic of the relocated pages is the same as the end of Chapter 13 to which it is joined.

Reuten has also pointed out that Engels inserted the following important sentence towards the end of the relocated text that he did not mark as an insertion:

> In practice, however, the rate of profit will fall in the long run, as we have already seen.[48]

This sentence clearly gives the impression that Marx concluded that the rate of profit would definitely decline in the long run; but this is a misleading impression, as Reuten argues, because the sentence was written by Engels, not Marx. On the other hand, the end of Marx's title of Chapter Three ('... with the Advance of Capitalist Production'), which Engels deleted, seems to suggest a long-run secular decline.

Vollgraf and Jungnickel have noted another misleading modification that Engels made in his Chapter 15, in the last paragraph of Section 1.[49] Marx stated in parentheses that the centralisation and concentration of capital would cause a 'shake' [*Klappen*] in capitalist production if there were not counteracting tendencies.[50] Engels removed the parentheses and changed the mild word *Klappen* to the stronger *Zusammenbruch* [collapse or breakdown].[51] Vollgraf and Jungnickel argue that this one change encouraged the 'breakdown' theorists of the Second International (e.g., Kautsky).

47 Reuten 2002.
48 Marx 1981 [Engels], p. 337.
49 Vollgraf and Jungnickel 2002, p. 62.
50 Marx, this volume, p. 350.
51 Marx 1981 [Engels], p. 337.

Heinrich has argued that the section of Marx's chapter that Engels turned into his Chapter 15 ('Development of the Law's Contradictions') is no longer systematic, but is only a 'large mass of remarks, additions, and argumentative approaches, in unelaborated and incomplete form'.[52] This description is accurate for the last 10 pages of this section, which Engels turned into his Section 4 of Chapter 15, entitled 'Supplementary Remarks', since these pages are indeed a few remarks presented in non-systematic fashion. However, the first three sections of this chapter are systematic in the sense that they are all various aspects of the tendency of the rate of profit to fall. Section 1 makes three main points: the relative proportions of industrial profit, interest, and rent may have been different from the overall rate of profit; a decrease in the rate of profit may be accompanied by an increase in the mass of profit; and the decline in the rate of profit is not due to reduced exploitation, but to a decline in the number of workers employed. The main point of Section 2 is that the development of the productivity of labour in capitalism has two main effects – an increase of surplus labour per worker and a decrease in the number of workers employed – and these two effects in turn have opposite effects on the rate of profit. Section 3 presents a sketch of a pioneering theory of capitalism's boom-bust cycle, which follows directly from Marx's theory of the falling rate of profit. If capitalist crises are caused by a falling rate of profit, then a recovery from crises requires above all else a restoration of the rate of profit to previous higher levels. Furthermore, if the underlying cause of a falling rate of profit is an increase in the value composition of capital (the ratio of constant capital to variable capital), then a restoration of the rate of profit requires a reduction in the value composition of capital, which is typically accomplished during capitalist depressions by the *devaluation of capital* that results from widespread bankruptcies of capitalist enterprises. Thus Marx's theory not only predicts recurring capitalist crises, but also predicts that a precondition for recovery from crises is the devaluation of capital and widespread bankruptcies. The sketch of a theory of capitalist cycles in this section is certainly a long way from a complete theory, but it was way ahead of all other economic theories at the time (which barely even recognised capitalism's tendency toward crises), and I think remains today a useful and unique framework within which to analyse capitalism's boom-bust cycles. Heinrich misses Marx's important theoretical achievement in these pages.[53]

52 Heinrich 1996–7, p. 459.

53 This chapter also contains eloquent summaries of the '*barriers* to capitalist production' (e.g., 'capital itself'; i.e., the main motive and purpose of capitalist production is the valorisation of capital).

Heinrich has also argued that Engels changed a key phrase in Section 3 of Chapter 15 in such a way as to change Marx's meaning into its opposite. Marx stated that a closer analysis of the phenomenon of the overaccumulation of capital (i.e., of crises) 'belongs to the study of the apparent movement of capital, where interest capital etc. and credit etc. will be examined in more detail'.[54] This is an important statement by Marx – that a more complete theory of crises requires more than the falling rate of profit; the role of credit and debt must also be incorporated.

Engels changed Marx's phrase just quoted to the following: 'its closer analysis follows later'.[55] Heinrich argues that the meaning of Marx's phrase is that a further analysis will come *after this book*, but the meaning of Engels's phrase is that a further analysis will come later *in this book*. However, the subjects that Marx explicitly referred to in his phrase – interest capital and credit – were in fact included later in Marx's Book III of *Capital* (Chapter Five in Marx's manuscript and Part Five in Engels's Volume III, to be discussed below), and of course Engels knew this since he was editing Marx's manuscript, and Chapter Five was giving him fits. Therefore, Engels's phrase in this case is accurate, although it is unfortunate that Engels leaves out the specific topics of 'interest capital' and 'credit' that 'follow later' in this book. This later discussion in Chapter Five is still a long way from a complete theory of crises, but it is an extensive discussion of interest-bearing capital and interest and credit. While working on Chapter Three, Marx may not have intended to write so much about the credit system in this book, but he ended up writing quite a lot about the credit system, and that is what Engels was dealing with and referring to in this phrase.

Chapter Four

Marx's Chapter Four ('The Transformation of Commodity Capital and Money Capital into Merchant's Capital (Commodity-Dealing Capital and Money-Dealing Capital)') presents his theory of merchant profit (i.e., how merchant capital receives a share of the total surplus-value produced, even though merchant labour does not directly produce value and surplus-value), and presents his modified theory of prices of production to include merchant profit and the

54 Marx, this volume, p. 360.

55 Heinrich is quoting from the International Publishers edition of Volume III, p. 251. In the Vintage edition of Volume III, Fernbach translates Engels's phrase as 'we shall study it in more detail below'. Marx 1981 [Engels], p. 359.

distinction between wholesale prices and retail prices of production, with the assumption again that the total surplus-value is pre-determined and does not change.

> Since mercantile capital does not itself produce any surplus-value, it is clear that the surplus-value that accrues to it in the form of the average profit forms a portion of the surplus-value or surplus labour produced by the *productive capital* as a whole.[56]

Thus, in moving from Chapter Two to Chapter Four, the total surplus-value remains the same (as determined in the prior volumes) and the total capital increases with the addition of merchant capital. Thus the general rate of profit is reduced, which allows merchant capital to receive its share of the total surplus-value. In Marx's main numerical example in this chapter, the total surplus-value = 180 and the total social capital is increased from 900 to 1000, and thus the general rate of profit is reduced from 20 percent to 18 percent.[57]

Marx had previously written an initial exploratory draft of this chapter towards the end of the *Economic Manuscript of 1861–63*,[58] so he was able to write the second draft of this chapter in fairly finished form. Marx's chapter is divided into sections (with titles) that Engels converted into chapters in his Part Four. There are a few changes of terminology and notation, but nothing of significance. In several places, Engels changed Marx's term 'productive capital' into 'industrial capital',[59] but this does not indicate that Engels was altering Marx's concepts of productive and unproductive capital; Engels clearly accepted Marx's assumption that only productive capital (capital invested in the sphere of production) produces value and surplus-value.[60]

---

56 Marx, this volume, p. 390; Marx 1981 [Engels], p. 395.

57 In the numerical example in Marx's 1868 letter, the total surplus-value remains = 100 and the total social capital is increased from 500 to 600, so that the general rate of profit is reduced from 20 percent to 16⅔ percent. Marx and Engels 1988, p. 24; letter of 30 April 1868 from Marx to Engels.

58 In a part of the manuscript which was published for the first time in 1980 in Volume 3.5 of the MEGA and translated into English in Volume 33 of the *Marx-Engels Collected Works* (published in 1991).

59 Compare this volume, pp. 376, 385, and 395 with Marx 1981 [Engels], pp. 379, 389, and 396. Marx's concept of *industrial capital* was a more general concept that included commodity capital and money capital as well as productive capital.

60 For example, in Volume II, Engels added two sentences in Chapter 8 which criticised 'Political economy since the time of Adam Smith' for failing to make the distinction

Engels also added a title to Marx's final section (p. 421 in this volume; Engels's Chapter 20: 'Historical Material on Merchant's Capital'). Other than these minor examples, Engels's Part Four is almost the same as Marx's Chapter Four and I find nothing more to comment on.

Chapter Five

Chapter Five ('The Division of Profit into Interest and Profit of Enterprise (Industrial or Commercial Profit). Interest-Bearing Capital') is the longest chapter in Marx's manuscript (250 pages). This chapter explains interest as part of the total surplus-value, with the assumption that the total surplus-value is taken as a pre-determined given amount (determined by the prior theory of the production of surplus-value in Books I and II) and this total does not change as a result of its division into profit and interest.

Engels said in his Preface that Chapter Five gave him 'the major difficulty' in preparing Marx's manuscript for publication. However, when looked at more closely, it becomes clear that almost all of the difficulty was in the last half of Marx's chapter (pp. 598–692) (which became Engels's Chapters 30–5), and this last half is the least important part of this chapter (consisting in large part of excerpts of parliamentary reports). The first four sections of Marx's Chapter Five (which became Engels's Chapters 21–4) are about interest-bearing capital and interest and the division of the total surplus into profit and interest, and are the most important sections in this chapter for the main subject of this volume (the distribution of surplus-value and the particular forms of capital and surplus-value, including interest). These sections are in almost finished form (Engels said 'basically completed')[61] and Engels made no important changes, besides converting sections into chapters. The main conclusion of these four sections is that there is no 'general law' of the determination of the rate of interest, and thus that there is no general law of the division of the total surplus-value into profit and interest. Instead, Marx argued, the rate of interest is determined by the accidental relation between the supply and demand for loanable funds on the money market, which vary a lot over the cycle of expansion and contraction.

---

between productive capital and capital in the sphere of circulation (Marx 1978 [Engels], p. 247). These sentences are not marked as Engels's insertion, but Rolf Hecker, one of the MEGA editors, informs us that Engels did insert them (Hecker 2009, p. 22).

61 Engels 1981a, p. 95.

There are no subsections with titles for the first 98 pages of Section 5 ('Credit. Fictitious Capital') of Marx's Chapter Five. There are only three subsections marked with Roman numerals. The MEGA editors added titles to these subsections in the text (but not in the contents page), using Engels's titles of his chapters. Engels converted the first 50 pages of Section 5 of Marx's Chapter Five into his Chapters 25 through 29, and these pages also did not require much editing.[62] Chapters 27 ('The Role of Credit in Capitalist Production') and 29 ('Bank Capital's Component Parts') are taken almost directly from Marx's manuscript. Engels did more editing revisions in his Chapters 25 ('Credit and Fictitious Capital'), 26 ('The Accumulation of Money Capital ...'), and 28 ('Means of Circulation and Capital ...'), but there do not appear to be any substantial changes of meaning, with one possible exception in the first sentence of Chapter 25, to be discussed below.

Engels said in his Preface that his main difficulties were with the rest of Section 5 (pp. 598–692). Engels made six chapters out of these pages (Chapters 30 through 35). There are substantial rearrangements and relocations of the text, but by and large Engels's edited version follows Marx's manuscript fairly closely. Engels said in his Preface that he tried three times to make this large part of Section 5 into more coherent chapters, but he finally gave up; and these failed attempts to improve this part of Section 5 were one of the main reasons for the long delay in the publication of Volume III (this part of Section 5 will be discussed further below).

Finally, the last section of Chapter Five (Section 6: 'Pre-Bourgeois Relations') is taken with very few changes by Engels for his Chapter 36 (Engels: 'completed in full').[63]

Heinrich has argued that Engels's improved organisation of Section 5 'shifted the emphasis' in this chapter from interest-bearing capital (Marx) to credit (Engels).[64] I tend to agree with Heinrich on this point. Engels's improved organisation makes Section 5 look more like a theoretical work than a set of research notes, and thus implicitly places more weight on this section. It also gives the misleading impression that all of Section 5 belongs in this book

62 The title of Section 5 is Marx's title, but is somewhat misleading. By 'fictitious capital' Marx meant stocks and bonds, which are legal claims to ownership and/or to future profits, not real capital in the sense of the value of capital invested in capitalist enterprises. But not many of the 250 pages of Section 5 are about fictitious capital in this sense. Instead, almost all of this section is about bank loans to industrial capitalists and merchant capitalists.

63 Engels 1981a, p. 96.

64 Heinrich 1996–7, p. 461.

on competition and the distribution of surplus-value, but most of it does not belong (see below).

Vollgraf and Jungnickel have criticised Engels for making a misleading alteration in Section 2 of Chapter Five of Marx's manuscript: Engels omitted cursive brackets around the following sentence, which they argue transformed a 'crutch for thought' into a 'penetrating triviality'.[65]

> {Where a given whole – such as profit – is to be divided between two people, the first thing that matters is of course the *size* of the whole to be divided, and this, the magnitude of *profit*, is determined by the average rate of profit.}[66]

I argue that this sentence in brackets is not a 'crutch for thought' nor a 'penetrating triviality', but is instead an important methodological remark (Marx often put his methodological remarks in brackets). This sentence is related to the fundamental assumption on which the whole of Marx's theory of the distribution of surplus-value in the *Economic Manuscript of 1864–65* is based, including Chapter 5 on interest – that the total surplus-value (the 'whole') is determined prior to its division into individual parts, including the division into profit and interest. According to Marx's logical method, the total surplus-value (as determined in Volumes I and II) is used to determine the general rate of profit ($R = S / C$), and then the general rate of profit is used to determine the average profit in each industry ($\pi_i = R\ C_i$), and finally this average profit is divided into profit of enterprise and interest in each industry ($\pi_i = \pi_{ie} + int_i$) (this last step is what Marx was talking about in the passage quoted: π_i is determined prior to its division into π_{ie} and int_i). I am glad that Engels included this important methodological comment, although he should have left the brackets.

The main interpretive issue with respect to Chapter Five has to do with the long Section 5 on the credit system (Engels's Chapters 25–35) and the logical relation between the credit system and the rest of Marx's Chapter Five and Book III as a whole. The following is my interpretation:

In April 1858, toward the end of his work on the *Grundrisse*, Marx wrote the following outline of his 'book on capital' in a letter to Engels, in which 'Credit' is the third section, after capital in general and competition:

65 Vollgraf and Jungnickel 2002, p. 50.

66 Marx, this volume, p. 463; Marx 1981 [Engels], p. 482.

> *I. Capital* contains *four sections*:
> a) ***Capital in general*** (this is the *subject-matter of the first part*).
> b) ***Competition***, or the action of the **many capitals** upon one another.
> c) ***Credit***, here capital as the general principle confronts the individual capitals.
> d) *Share capital* as the most highly developed form (turning into communism) together with all its contradictions.[67]

I argue that this very clear outline remained the basic logical structure of Marx's theory of capital in all the later drafts of *Capital*, including the *Economic Manuscript of 1864–65*. Capital in general has to do primarily with the production of surplus-value and the determination of the total amount of surplus-value produced in the economy as a whole, and competition has to do primarily with the distribution of surplus-value and the division of the pre-determined total amount of surplus-value into particular forms and individual parts. The *Grundrisse* is almost entirely about the section on capital in general (except for a few incidental remarks).[68] The *Economic Manuscript of 1861–63* started out in the section on capital in general (a second draft of the theory of the production of surplus-value; what later became Parts 2–4 of Volume I), but Marx's work on this manuscript moved progressively into an initial exploration of the particular forms of surplus-value (average rate of profit, rent, interest, merchant profit) and the distribution of surplus-value and thus into the section on competition.[69] And the *Economic Manuscript of 1864–65* (presented in this volume) consists mostly of the section on competition; it develops more fully the theory of the distribution of surplus-value begun in the *Manuscript of 1861–63*, except for Chapters 1 and 3 (profit and the falling rate of profit), which belong to the section on capital in general.[70,71]

From this perspective, the interpretive issue is: does Section 5 of Chapter 5 on the credit system belong to the section on competition or to the section on credit? In my view, almost all of Section 5 belongs to the later section on credit. Just the common name suggests this conclusion. This conclusion is also suggested by the first section of Marx's Section 5:

---

67 Marx and Engels 1985, p. 298; letter of 2 April 1858 from Marx to Engels.

68 Moseley 2011.

69 Moseley 2009.

70 Moseley 2002.

71 Some authors have argued that Marx abandoned this logical framework after encountering difficulties in the *Economic Manuscript of 1861–63*; e.g., Vollengraf and Jungnickel 2002 and Heinrich 1996–7. This interpretation is discussed in the concluding section.

> It is **outside the scope of our plan** to give an analysis of the **credit system** and the instruments this creates (credit money, etc.)[72]

This statement seems to suggest that Section 5 on the credit system does not really belong in this chapter or this manuscript, which is mainly about competition and the distribution of surplus-value.

Heinrich has noted that Engels added a key word to Marx's first sentence of Section 5, which he argues significantly changes its meaning.[73] Before the word 'analysis' [*Analyse*], Engels added the word '*eingehende*', which has been translated as 'exhaustive' or 'detailed'. Heinrich argues that Engels's added adjective suggests that Section 5 on the credit system *does* belong in this chapter to some extent, but not a complete consideration of the credit system; more details would come later.

Engels may have thought that Marx's second sentence justified his additional adjective:

> Only a few points will be emphasised here, which are necessary to characterise the capitalist mode of production in general.[74]

This sentence suggests the possibility that at least part of Section 5 on the credit system *does* belong in this chapter (but 'only a few points') because these points are 'necessary to characterise the capitalist mode of production in general'. Unfortunately, Marx did not clearly specify which topics discussed in Section 5 on the credit system are necessary to characterise the capitalist mode of production in general, and which topics are not necessary and belong instead to the later section on the credit system.

In my view, there are only a few parts of Section 5 that could be considered as 'necessary to characterise the capitalist mode of production in general'; most of Section 5 is not necessary in this general sense. The main part that is about such general points is presented in five pages early on in Section 5 (pp. 535–40), which Engels turned into his Chapter 27 with the title 'The Role of Credit in Capitalist Production' (there is no title in Marx's manuscript; the MEGA editors added Engels's title to their volume). I think this chapter provides the kind of broad general statements about credit that Marx had in mind by 'necessary to characterise capitalism in general'. These pages discuss the following important

72 Marx, this volume, p. 500; Marx 1981 [Engels], p. 525.

73 Heinrich 1996–7, pp. 461–2.

74 Marx, this volume, p. 500; Marx, 1981 [Engels], p. 525.

aspects of the role of credit in capitalism: (1) it reduces the costs of circulation (less gold and silver required) and the time of circulation (related to Chapter One of Book III); (2) it is necessary 'to bring about the equalisation of the profit rate or the movement of this equalisation, on which the whole of capitalist production depends' (related to Chapter Two of Book III); (3) it leads to the development of joint-stock companies (which Marx optimistically characterised as 'the abolition of capitalism within capitalism'); and in the most general terms (4) it accelerates the development of the productive forces in capitalism, and therefore also intensifies the contradictions in capitalism, especially the contradiction of recurring crises ('credit is the principal lever of overproduction and excessive speculation'), and with crises the 'dissolution' of capitalism.[75]

These important pages are not marked off in the manuscript in any way, and are immediately preceded by 25 pages of excerpts from parliamentary reports on the causes of the economic crisis of 1847 (most of which were included by Engels in his Chapter 26). This striking juxtaposition of very concrete analysis and broad general theory illustrates the unevenness of Section 5.

A second topic discussed in Section 5 that could be considered 'necessary to characterise capitalism in general' are discussions in Engels's Chapters 25 and 29 about the *concentration of loanable money capital in the hands of banks*, so that bank loans represent in a concrete form the capital of the capitalist class as a whole as distinguished from individual capitalist borrowers (industrial capitalists or merchant capitalists). We saw above that Marx expressed this same idea in his 1858 outline of the four sections of his theory in his descriptor for section c) on credit: 'capital as the general principle confronts the individual capitals'. Marx also expressed the same idea in the *Grundrisse* (probably written a few weeks or months before the April 1858 letter): bank loans function as 'capital in general' in relation to concrete, particular capitals.[76]

A third topic that could be considered 'necessary to characterise capitalism in general' is discussions of the *quantity of money under the credit system*

75 Marx commented humorously that this 'dual character' of the credit system gives to its spokesmen the dual character of both 'swindler and prophet'. This volume, p. 540; Marx 1981 [Engels], pp. 572–3. Marx repeated this point in two paragraphs in Section 6 of Chapter 5 on 'Pre-Bourgeois Relations': 'Banking and credit, however, therefore, become the most powerful lever for driving capitalist production beyond its limits, and one of the most effective vehicles for crises and swindling ... Finally, there can be no doubt that the credit system will serve as a powerful lever in the course of the transition from the capitalist mode of production to the mode of production of associated producers'. This volume, p. 709; Marx 1981 [Engels], pp. 742–3.

76 Marx 1973, p. 449.

(Engels's Chapters 28, 33, and 34). The main point of these discussions is that the 'law' of the quantity of money in circulation that Marx derived in Chapter 3 of Volume I still applies:

> It has already been shown, in our consideration of simple money circulation, that if the velocity of circulation and an economical use of the means of payment are assumed, the quantity of money really circulating is simply determined by the prices of the commodities and the number of transactions. **The same law applies to the circulation of notes.**[77]

This important general statement was relocated by Engels from material corresponding to his Chapter 31 to his Chapter 33 (p. 655). The next five pages in Engels's Chapter 33 elaborate on this general statement and emphasise that banks do not have the power to increase the quantity of bank notes in circulation *beyond what is needed for the circulation of commodities*, and these pages are taken from several different places in Section 5 of Chapter Five.[78]

Engels added the following key sentence at the beginning of a paragraph in these pages without marking it as an insertion:

> It already emerges from this that it is in no way in the power of the note-issuing banks to increase the number of notes in circulation, **as long as these notes are exchangeable at any time against metal money.**[79]

Engels marked the rest of this paragraph as his insertion, thus leaving the erroneous impression that this first sentence was written by Marx. This sentence is an accurate statement about Marx's theory – that the laws of the quantity of money in circulation also apply to bank notes *as long as bank notes are convertible into gold or silver at legally fixed rates* – and it was good for Engels to remind readers of this important institutional context of Marx's theory of the quantity of money. However, he should not have implicitly attributed this sentence to Marx.[80]

---

77 Marx, this volume, p. 589; Marx 1981 [Engels], p. 655.

78 See MEGA, Section II, Volume 15, Apparat, pp. 963–4, for details about where in Marx's manuscript these pages in Engels's Chapter 33 come from. Thanks to Regina Roth for informing me about this source.

79 Marx 1981 [Engels], p. 656.

80 The problem was compounded by the Fernbach translation of the Vintage edition of Engels's Volume III, which explicitly attributed the unmarked first sentence of the paragraph to Marx by name.

However, all three of these general topics together account for only a small part of the 175 pages of Section 5. Much of Section 5 has to do instead with various *critiques of the classical economists' theories of money and capital and credit*, rather than a systematic presentation of Marx's own theory. Most of Marx's discussion of the quantity of money under the credit system mentioned in the previous paragraph occurs in the context of critiques of the classical economists. A brief summary of some of these critiques include: as mentioned above, Engels's Chapter 26 consists almost entirely of excerpts from parliamentary reports on the views of the classical economists on the causes of the crisis of 1847 (pp. 324–44);[81] Engels's Chapter 28 is a critique of Tooke's and (especially) Fullarton's confusion between money as means of circulation and money as capital (pp. 349–60); and Engels's Chapters 30–32 are mostly about the failure of the classical economists to distinguish between money capital (in the sense of banks' loanable money capital) and real capital (invested in productive enterprises) (pp. 368–422). The rest of Section 5 (pp. 422–65) consists mostly of more excerpts of statements by economists and bankers from parliamentary reports on the crises of 1847 and 1857, which Marx entitled critically 'The Confusion', and which Engels converted with considerable editing into his Chapters 33, 34, and 35 (placing a few quotations in other chapters), without including 'The Confusion' in the title.

In light of all this material on the critique of the classical economists, I think that a better title for most of Section 5 would be 'Theories of Money and Capital and Credit', similar to Marx's earlier 'Theories of Value' and 'Theories of Money' in the *Contribution to a Critique of Political Economy*, and his 'Theories of Surplus-Value' in the *Manuscript of 1861–63*, which belong at the ends of chapters or in a later volume ('Volume IV' of *Capital*). Engels remarked that in order to make all this material into more coherent chapters, he 'would have to go through the whole of the literature in this field',[82] which is perhaps what Marx was planning to do.

Marx may have intended at the outset of Section 5 to limit his discussion of the credit system to those topics which are 'necessary to characterise the capitalist mode of production in general', but in fact Section 5 goes way beyond such general topics, and is almost entirely about much more concrete topics and Marx's critiques of the classical economists' theories of money, capital, and credit. Earlier in Section 2 of Chapter Five, Marx commented that 'short term fluctuations in the money market **fall outside the scope of our discus-**

81 Pages in parentheses in this paragraph refer to this volume.

82 Engels 1981a, p. 95.

sion'.[83] But there are many pages in Section 5 of Chapter Five which are about precisely 'short term fluctuations in the money market'.

I think that the main reason for Marx's diversion into these more concrete aspects of the credit system is that he was especially interested in understanding economic crises in capitalism, and the role of credit in crises (as we saw above), and the specific crises of 1847 and 1857 that he had experienced. So he read and took notes on the parliamentary reports on these specific crises, even though logically this concrete analysis belongs at a lower level of abstraction and thus to a later volume. In addition, Marx also commented earlier in Section 2 of Chapter 5 that 'nothing is more amusing' than to read these parliamentary reports and the statements of economists and bankers who 'chatter back and forth' without understanding the fundamentals of money and credit in capitalism.[84] I think this was part of what Marx was doing in much of Section 5 – he was amusing himself criticising these economists, who had no clue! Many of his comments on the economists in this section are humorous or satirical. While working on this section, Marx mentioned in a letter to Engels the 'utter nonsense' in these reports and said that he intended to write a critique of these reports in a later paper.[85] This intention was partially realised in Section 5, even though it is logically out of place in this volume.

Perhaps the few 'general' parts of Section 5 mentioned above belong to a kind of *transition* between the section on competition and the section on the credit system. Marx had suggested such a transition earlier in the *Manuscript of 1861–63* in the following passage:

> Credit is both the result and the condition of capitalist production and this provides a convenient **transition** from **competition** between capitals to capital as **credit.**[86]

However that may be, my conclusion is that almost all of Section 5 does *not* belong to the section on competition, and thus does not belong in Book III. Competition is primarily about the distribution of surplus-value, i.e., about the division of the total surplus-value into individual parts, including its division into interest and profit; and Section 5 is not about the determination of interest or the rate of interest or the division of the total surplus-value into profit and

83 Marx, this volume, p. 461; Marx 1981 [Engels], p. 480.
84 Marx, this volume, p. 467; Marx 1981 [Engels], pp. 485–6.
85 Marx and Engels 1987, pp. 185–6; letter of 19 August 1865 from Marx to Engels.
86 Marx and Engels 1989a, p. 435.

interest. That determination had already been accomplished in the first four sections of Marx's chapter (Engels's Chapters 21 to 24), especially Section 2 (Engels's Chapter 22). As we have seen, in these earlier sections Marx argued that there is 'no general law' that determines the rate of interest, and thus that there is no general law that determines the division of the total surplus-value into interest and profit. Instead, the rate of interest is determined by the accidental relation between supply and demand in the loanable funds market. Therefore, there is nothing left to investigate concerning the general laws of the rate of interest and the division of the total surplus-value into interest and profit, since there are no such general laws. Most of Section 5 belongs to the later section on the credit system and some parts of it could perhaps be considered a transition from the section on competition to the section on credit.

Heinrich has argued that *Capital* is supposed to be a general abstract theory of capitalism that is applicable to more or less all capitalist economies; therefore, including all the material about the banking institutions of nineteenth-century England in Engels's Volume III gave the impression that the English banking institutions were generalisable to all capitalist economies.[87] That may be true (I don't really think so), but I don't think that was Engels's intention. I don't think Engels had this distinction between general and historically specific in mind while he was editing Marx's manuscript. Engels was not trying to decide what material goes in Volume III and what material does not. Instead, he was trying to figure out the best way to include *all* the material Marx wrote, and this was difficult because Marx's Section 5 was so uneven and unorganised. Engels said in his Preface: 'In this way I finally managed to introduce into the texts *all* of the author's statements that were in any way pertinent to the matter at hand'.[88] Therefore, the ultimate blame for this problem, if there is a problem, should go to Marx, who wrote all this historically specific content in Section 5. But I don't think this is a problem in the first place. It just needs to be recognised that most of this material belongs to the later section on the credit system, and that it would have been better and logically more correct and consistent to move this more concrete section to the end of the book, or perhaps to another book altogether, as Marx planned.

87 Heinrich 1996–7, pp. 462–3.

88 Engels 1981a, p. 96; Engels's emphasis.

Chapter Six

Chapter Six ('The Transformation of Surplus Profit into Ground Rent') is another long chapter, but is much more finished than Chapter Five. Marx had already written extensively on this subject in the *Economic Manuscript of 1861–63*,[89] so he was able to write a fairly complete chapter in this manuscript, although there were a few incomplete topics, to be discussed below.

Rent is analysed in this chapter as a part of the total surplus-value that is appropriated by landlords because of their monopoly ownership of the land. As in the previous chapters and the other individual parts of surplus-value, the total amount of surplus-value is taken as a pre-determined given magnitude in the theory of rent. This total amount of surplus-value is 'split' into profit and rent, and rent does not enter into the equalisation of profit rates across industries.

> The analysis of *landed property* in its various historical forms lies outside the scope of the present work. We are concerned with it only in so far as a portion of the *surplus-value* that capital produces falls to the share of the landowner.[90]

Marx divided Chapter Six on rent into three sections: (a) Introduction; (b) Differential Rent; and (c) Absolute Rent. In the manuscript, Marx actually wrote section (c) (pp. 737–97 of this volume) before section (b) (pp. 798–883).[91] Section (c) was not subdivided by Marx, but Engels subdivided it into three chapters: Chapters 45 ('Absolute Rent'), 46 ('Rent of Buildings. Rent of Mines. Price of Land') and 47 ('The Genesis of Capitalist Ground-Rent'). The contents of these three unmarked subsections in Marx's manuscript that Engels turned into chapters were quite distinct (as Engels's chapter titles suggest), but there were no headings or even extra line spaces in Marx's manuscript to mark the transitions from one topic to another.

The long section (b) on differential rent was well structured, but it was also not explicitly divided into subsections. The first implicit subsection is about the 'first form of differential rent' (due to unequal fertilities of land) (this volume, pp. 806–23) and the second implicit subsection is about the 'second form of differential rent' (this volume, pp. 824–83) (due to unequal

89 Marx and Engels 1989a, pp. 250–550.

90 Marx, this volume, p. 713; Marx 1981, p. 752.

91 See Marx, this volume, p. 737 for an explanation of this structure.

capital investments). The discussion of the second form was in turn subdivided into three clearly marked 'cases' with titles (prices of production constant, decreasing, and increasing; for the last case there is only a title). And the first two cases are in turn subdivided into three or four variants (the productivity of the additional capital constant, decreasing, and increasing). The main question throughout this detailed analysis of the second form of differential rent is the following: *what are the effects of additional capital accumulation in agriculture on the amount of surplus profit*[92] *produced in agriculture*, and thus on the amount of rent and the structure of differential rent across lands of unequal fertility and productivity?

Engels turned this long section into seven chapters: his Chapters 38–44. Except for this division into chapters, Engels made very few changes in the content of what Marx wrote. He changed some of the numbers in Marx's tables in order to eliminate fractions and make them clearer. The main addition was that Engels wrote the first half of his Chapter 43 ('Differential Rent II – Third Case'; pp. 847–50) because Marx only had a title for this case.[93] Engels's first half of Chapter 43 also included a helpful detailed recapitulation of the seven variants analysed by Marx for the first two cases, with different and more realistic tables, and the six variants for Engels's third case. Engels's main conclusion is that in 10 of the 13 variants he considered, additional capital investment in agriculture resulted in an *increase* in the total rent of landlords, which 'explains the amazing vitality' of landlords. On the other hand, the other three variants explain why this vitality 'is gradually approaching its end', due to the more fertile lands in North and South America, Russia, etc., being brought into cultivation.[94]

The rest of Engels's Chapter 43 is Marx's own conclusion of his analysis of differential rent II,[95] which is much more theoretical and complicated, and is focused on the second variant of the first case (constant price of production, declining capital productivity). Marx's main conclusion is that the necessity to pay rent creates an 'artificial barrier' for the investment of capital in agriculture,

---

92 Surplus profit is profit that is greater than the average rate of profit due to lower than average costs of production. In non-agricultural industries, surplus profit is temporary and is generally eliminated by competition among capitals. But in agriculture, surplus profit that is due to unequal natural fertility cannot be competed away and thus becomes the basis for ground-rent.

93 Marx, this volume, p. 864.

94 Marx 1981 [Engels], p. 859.

95 Marx, this volume, pp. 864–83; Marx 1981 [Engels], pp. 860–71.

which requires an 'earlier and more rapid rise' in the price of agricultural goods 'in order thereby to guarantee the increased supply … that has become necessary'.[96]

Just before this conclusion, Marx inserted the following detailed outline of his chapter on rent:[97]

> *Rent should be discussed* under the following headings:
>
> A1. The *concept of differential rent* as such. The example of water-power. Then the transition to agricultural rent proper.
>
> A2. *Differential rent I*, arising from the varying fertility of different tracts of land.
>
> A3. *Differential rent II*, arising from successive capital investments on the same land. This should be *divided further* into:
>
> (a) differential rent with the *price of production stationary*,
>
> (b) differential rent with the *price of production falling*,
>
> (c) differential rent with the *price of production rising*,
>
> and (d) *the transformation of surplus profit into rent.*
>
> A4. The influence of this rent on the *rate of profit.*
>
> B. *Absolute rent.*
>
> C. *The price of land.*
>
> D. *Final considerations on ground-rent.*

We can see that the basic structure of this outline is the same as in Marx's draft that he was working on, in the sense that differential rent comes before absolute rent, and differential rent is subdivided into 'first form' and 'second form', and the second form is in turn subdivided into three cases. The 'price of land' (a short draft of which was included in the section of the manuscript on absolute rent, as mentioned above) is given a section of its own. The remaining topics of this outline (A3(d), A4., and D) remained to be written.

The planned subsection on 'the transformation of surplus profit into rent' (A3(d)) would have been interesting. This topic has to do with the actual historical conditions that determine how much of the surplus profit produced in agriculture by additional capital investment is in fact transferred from capitalist farmers to landlords, which depends on the class conflict between capitalist farmers and landlords. The long discussion of the second form of differential rent in this manuscript assumed that all the surplus profit produced in agricul-

96 Marx, this volume, p. 875; Marx 1981 [Engels], p. 870.

97 Marx, this volume, p. 864; Marx 1981 [Engels], p. 860.

ture was transferred as rent to landlords, without considering the conditions under which the transfer of this surplus profit from capitalists to landlords is actually made.[98] It appears that this final subsection would have discussed these concrete historical conditions.

A4 ('The influence of this rent on the rate of profit') is an important topic and it is unfortunate that Marx did not write a draft of this section. But we can infer from Marx's theory of surplus-value and rent (as part of the total surplus-value) that the effect of rent on the rate of profit would be as follows: The existence of rent means that at least part of the surplus profit produced in agriculture is appropriated by landlords and as a result does not enter into the equalisation of the general profit rate across all industries in the economy. Thus the general rate of profit that is equalised across industries and that determines prices of production is modified for a second time (it was modified earlier in Chapter Four to take commercial profit into account). In this second modification, rent appropriated by landlords is subtracted from the gross surplus-value in the numerator of the general rate of profit.

The precise magnitude of the modified rate of profit depends on how much of the surplus profit produced in agriculture is appropriated by landlords and how much (if any, as a residual) goes into the equalisation of the profit rate across industries. If landlords are able to appropriate the whole surplus profit, then differential rent would have a maximum effect on the general rate of profit that is equalised across industries (i.e., it would be reduced by a maximum amount), because none of this surplus profit goes through the equalisation process. On the other hand, if capitalist farmers are able to keep part of the surplus profit for themselves, then this surplus profit would go into the equalisation process and thus the general rate of profit would be reduced by a smaller amount.

In the section on absolute rent, Marx briefly discussed the influence of absolute rent on the rate of profit,[99] and the effect of differential rent is the same – the effect depends on who gets the surplus profit produced in agriculture: capitalists or landlords. In Marx's numerical example in this discussion, he assumes that all the surplus profit is appropriated by landlords and that the general rate of profit that is equalised across industries is reduced from 20 percent to 15 percent.

98 Marx stated in the beginning of his analysis of differential rent II: 'Let us start by considering simply the formation of *surplus profit* in the case of differential rent II, without troubling ourselves yet about the ***conditions*** under which this surplus profit can be transformed into ground-rent'. Marx, this volume, p. 832; Marx 1981 [Engels], pp. 815–16.

99 Marx, this volume, pp. 750–2; Marx 1981 [Engels], pp. 896–8.

So we can see that a fair amount of work remained to be done on Chapter Six, but that the basic structure of the chapter and Marx's theory of absolute and differential rent were clear and mostly settled. Engels's editing certainly made the logical structure of this chapter much more apparent to the reader, but this logical structure was implicit in Marx's manuscript and was made explicit by his outline toward the end of the chapter, which Engels followed.

Marx's theory of rent was clearly a significant advance over Ricardo's theory of rent in three important respects: Marx's theory explained the possibility of absolute rent on the basis of the labour theory of value; his analysis of differential rent was much more detailed and thorough than Ricardo's; and his analysis of differential rent did not depend on the 'ridiculous and arbitrary' assumption of declining productivity in agriculture.[100] On his advances over Ricardo's theory of rent, Marx remarked in this manuscript:

> From this we can see the very complicated combinations to which differential rent can always give rise, and particularly when Form II is taken together with Form I, whereas Ricardo for instance deals with the matter quite one-sidedly and 'in simple terms'.[101]

Chapter Seven

Chapter Seven is another chapter in Marx's manuscript that was close to being publication-ready. Marx had written a first draft of much of the material in Chapter Seven in his previous *Economic Manuscript of 1861–63*,[102] so Chapter Seven in the *Economic Manuscript of 1863–65* was a second draft and close-to-final form. It is at times eloquently written and presents a kind of summary of Marx's theory of the production and distribution of surplus-value presented in the three volumes of *Capital*. This chapter (part) is seldom discussed in the literature, but I think it is very important.[103]

The main point of Chapter Seven (and indeed of Book III as a whole) is that all the different forms of surplus-value come from the same source – the surplus labour of workers – and thus that the total amount of surplus-value

100 Marx 1985, p. 397; letter of 2 August 1862 from Marx to Engels.

101 Marx, this volume, p. 834; Marx 1981 [Engels], p. 817.

102 Marx 1989b, pp. 449–541.

103 An important exception is Murray 2002.

is determined logically prior to the division of this total surplus-value into individual parts, i.e., its division into profit, interest, and rent, which also depend on other factors. For example:

> *Profit* (profit of enterprise plus interest) and *rent* are but characteristic forms assumed by particular portions of the *surplus-value* in commodities. The size of the *surplus-value* sets a *quantitative* limit to the parts into which it can be divided.[104]
>
> We thus have an absolute limit for the value component that forms surplus-value and can be broken down into profit and ground-rent; this is determined by the excess of the unpaid portion of the working day over its paid portion, i.e. by the value component of the total product in which *this surplus labor* is realised.[105]

However, this is not the way it looks to capitalists and economists. Instead, each individual part of surplus-value appears to them to have its own source and determinants. And then the total surplus-value appears to be determined by *adding up* these mutually independent individual parts. This distorted, inverted misunderstanding of the relation between the total surplus-value and its individual parts was a characteristic feature of what Marx called 'vulgar economics'.

Because of its almost complete condition, Engels made very few substantive changes in his Part Seven. Marx's manuscript had five sections, which Engels turned into chapters. One misleading rearrangement that Engels made has to do with the order of the three fragments with which Engels began his Part Seven. For complicated reasons that have to do with the fact that Marx actually wrote these fragments while working on Chapter Six, and also unclear pagination by Marx, Engels did not realise that his fragment #3 was supposed to go at the beginning of Chapter Seven (Marx referred in the beginning of Chapter Seven to the page in Chapter Six and said that 'the passage should be transferred here'),[106] and his fragments #1 and #2 were supposed to go five pages into the chapter. Engels's mis-location makes it appear as if Marx's manuscript is more disjointed than it was and makes it harder to follow Marx's argument. Engels's fragments #1 and #2 are in their proper location

---

104 Marx, this volume, pp. 898–9; Marx 1981, p. 971.

105 Marx, this volume, pp. 923–4; Marx 1981, p. 999.

106 See Marx, this volume, p. 884.

in this volume (pp. 888–90) and fragment #3 remains in Chapter Six where it was written.[107]

The main substantive change in Chapter Seven was a key phrase added by Engels to Marx's text, which comes five pages from the end of Section 1 ('The Trinity Formula'). Engels's insertion is in square brackets and bold type in the second line below:

> We have already demonstrated, in connection with the simplest categories of the capitalist mode of production [**and in commodity production in general**] the *commodity* and *money*, the mystificatory character that transforms the social relations for which the material elements of wealth serve as bearers in the course of production into properties of these things themselves (*commodities*), and still more explicitly transforms the relation of production itself into a thing (*money*).[108]

Marx's sentence makes it clear that the beginning of his theory in Part One of Volume I of *Capital* is about the capitalist mode of production (the 'simplest categories' of the capitalist mode of production). Engels's insertion suggests that Part One is also about commodity production in general (i.e., applies to all commodity producing societies). Marx's next sentence might provide some justification for Engels's insertion:

> All forms of society participate in this distortion, in so far as they involve commodity production and monetary circulation ...[109]

This sentence appears to mean that the 'distortion' of perception discussed in Part One, although derived on the basis of the capitalist mode of production, also applies to all commodity-producing societies, and perhaps this is what Engels meant by his insertion. However, Engels argued elsewhere (including in his Preface and his Supplement to Volume III) that Part One of Volume I applies to 'simple commodity production' as the historical presupposition of capitalism,[110] and Engels's interpretation has been followed by Kautsky and

---

107 The fragment to be transferred is the second half of the very long paragraph on pp. 764–7 of this volume; the fragment begins: 'Since vulgar economics ...' For further details on Engels's mistake, see Vollgraf and Jungnickel 2002, p. 48.

108 Marx, this volume, p. 894; Marx 1981 [Engels], p. 965.

109 Marx, this volume, p. 894; Marx 1981 [Engels], p. 965.

110 Engels 1981a and 1981b; see also Engels's 1857 review of Marx's *Introduction to a Contribution to the Critique of Political Economy*: Engels 1970.

Meek and others. There is no textual justification for this pre-capitalist 'simple commodity production' interpretation of Part One either in this manuscript or elsewhere.[111]

The paragraph just discussed is the beginning of a remarkable five-page summary of all the 'distortions of perception' of vulgar economics that are caused by capitalist production and that have been discussed in the three volumes of *Capital*: production relations among people appear as exchange relations among things; the productive power of labour appears as the productive power of capital; surplus-value is transformed into profit and appears to come from constant capital as well as variable capital and from circulation as well as production; surplus-value is divided into profit and interest and interest appears to come from money capital by itself. Surplus-value is further divided into profit and rent, and rent appears to come from the fertility of the land. But, according to Marx's theory, all these forms of appearance of surplus-value come from the same source: the surplus labour of workers.[112]

Conclusion

The main conclusions that I draw from this comparison of Marx's *Manuscript of 1864–65* and Engels's Volume III of *Capital* are the following: (1) Marx's manuscript was very uneven, with Chapters Two, Four, Six, and Seven close to being ready for publication, but Chapter One and Chapter Five, Section 5, still very unfinished and mostly just research notes; (2) Engels's editing makes Marx's manuscript look much more complete and organised than it actually was (especially Chapters One and Five), but he mostly did not change the content of what Marx wrote (with a few exceptions, as discussed); (3) Engels changed the title of Marx's manuscript, and left out the key word *Gestaltungen* [forms], which is the main subject of Marx's manuscript – the particular forms of appearance of capital and surplus-value; (4) Engels left out one of Marx's 'supplements' to Chapter Two, which was intended as a transition from Chapter One to Chapter Two, and which clarified the meaning of Marx's key concept of the 'organic composition of capital' – that variable capital is an index of the quantity of labour employed, but constant capital depends on both the quantity and the price of means of production employed; (5) Engels left out several

111 See Arthur 1997 for a further discussion of Engels's interpretation of Part One of Volume I.

112 The first draft of this sweeping summary of the three volumes of *Capital* is in the *Economic Manuscript of 1861–63*. Marx and Engels 1989b, pp. 482–6.

paragraphs in Marx's Chapter Two that had to do mainly with unequal turnover times of different capitals, which is a further complication of Marx's theory of prices of production; (6) Engels left out another key paragraph in Chapter Two that clarified the meaning of 'cost price' in Marx's theory – that the cost price is the same in the determination of both values and prices of production – which implies that Marx did *not* fail to transform the cost price from values to prices of production in his theory of prices of production; (7) Engel's organisation of Chapter Three and a key sentence inserted by Engels (without marking it as such) left the possibly misleading impression that Marx definitely concluded that the rate of profit would fall in the long-run; (8) Section 5 of Chapter Five is the part of Marx's manuscript that Engels worked on the most and changed the most. Engels's improved organisation made Marx's Section 5 look more like a finished chapter than it actually was. It also gave the misleading impression that all of Section 5 on the credit system belongs in this book on competition and the distribution of surplus-value, even though most of it does not belong.

Engels tried hard to organise the disorganised Section 5 as best he could, but in my view he tried too hard to include all of this section in his Volume III. Much of Section 5 was just research notes on parliamentary reports on the economic crises of 1847 and 1857 and other aspects of the financial system in England, interwoven with criticisms of the classical economists. Most of this more concrete material does not belong to the subject of competition and the distribution of surplus-value (the particular forms of surplus-value), which is the main subject of Book III. Instead this more concrete material belongs to the later analysis of the credit system. It would have been better if Engels had separated out this more concrete material on the credit system and relocated it at the end of his Volume III, or perhaps not included it at all and saved it for a later volume. Perhaps Engels did not fully understand Marx's logical distinction between competition and the credit system, in which case this option would not have occurred to him. If Engels had not tried to include all this material, his Volume III could have been published several years earlier.

To say that a large part of Marx's manuscript was close to being 'publication-ready' does not mean that the theory presented in this manuscript was a complete theory of capitalism and that no further work needed to be done. There were (and are) a number of important points that remained to be developed further, which included: (1) obviously Marx felt that more work was needed on the relation between the rate of profit and the rate of surplus-value, because Marx returned to this subject in his *Manuscript of 1875* (MEGA, Section II, Volume 14); (2) a more complete discussion of his theory of prices of production, including a clarification of the determination of the cost price in this theory (which has turned out to be the most controversial issue in the century-long debate over the 'transformation problem') and also taking into account unequal turnover times across industries;[113] (3) a more complete theory of the trends and cycles of the rate of profit and their relation to crises;[114] (4) with respect to commercial capital, a more complete theory of modified prices of production (and wholesale prices and retail prices) is needed, taking into account the operating costs of commercial capital; (5) the credit system requires much more analysis, and especially the role of the credit system in economic crises; (6) a more complete theory of rent is needed, which would include the historical conditions that affect the actual transfer of the surplus profit in agriculture into differential rent II.

In spite of this long list of important further tasks that remained to be done, in my view the basic logical structure of Marx's theory (capital in general – competition – credit system) was settled in Marx's mind and is logically sound. All this remaining work would take place within this basic logical structure, and would not involve any fundamental changes in this structure.

Müller, et al., and Heinrich have argued that Marx encountered difficulties in the *Economic Manuscript of 1861–63* in maintaining the logical distinction between capital in general and competition and that he abandoned this logical structure thereafter.[115] I have argued, to the contrary, that Marx did not encounter these difficulties in the *Manuscript of 1861–63* and did not abandon this logical structure after that.[116] The main aspect of Marx's logical structure of capital in general and competition is the production of surplus-value and the distribution of surplus-value – i.e., the determination of the total surplus-value prior to its division into individual parts. Marx definitely did not abandon this fundamental quantitative premise of his theory after 1863, and thus did not abandon the logical structure of capital in general and competition.

The main textual evidence to support this conclusion is the *Economic Manuscript of 1864–65* itself, which we have just reviewed. This manuscript is about the particular forms of surplus-value and the individual parts into which the

113 As mentioned in footnote 21, Marx wrote a short preliminary draft of this latter topic in the *Economic Manuscript of 1867–68*, published in the MEGA, Section II, Volume 4.3, which has not yet been translated into English, and which should be very interesting.

114 I concur with Reuten's conclusion regarding Marx's theory of the rate of profit: 'I guess that anyone studying Chapters 13–15 of Marx's *Capital* III … cannot but be impressed by the conscientious and thorough exhibition of that theory up to the minutest detail … It may also appear a very realistic theory … Nevertheless, that theory is insufficient and must be developed further'. Reuten 1997, p. 170.

115 Müller et al. 2002, pp. 16–17; Heinrich 1989, pp. 68–72.

116 Moseley 2002 and 2008.

total surplus-value is divided, and the quantitative premise for the entire book is the prior determination of the total surplus-value. This quantitative premise is repeated in all the chapters of this manuscript, including in the concluding Chapter Seven on 'Revenue', in which Marx's logical structure – the whole of surplus-value is determined prior to its parts – is contrasted with the opposite logical structure of 'vulgar economics' – the parts of surplus-value are determined prior to and independent of the whole and the whole is determined by adding up the parts.[117] Therefore, it is clear Marx did not abandon the logical structure of capital in general (production of surplus-value) and competition (distribution of surplus-value) after 1863.[118]

Vollgraf-Jungnickel and Heinrich conclude that, because of the many changes that Engels made to Marx's manuscript, Engels's Volume III should not be considered as Volume III of Marx's *Capital*.[119] I think this conclusion is too drastic; it seems to miss the point that the main subject of Marx's Volume III is the distribution of surplus-value and the particular forms of surplus-value, and that Marx's theory of the distribution of surplus-value is by and large faithfully and accurately presented in Engels's Volume III, with a few exceptions discussed above. In this most important respect, Engels's Volume III should be considered Marx's Volume III (with the caveats noted). However, I agree with these authors that future research concerning Volume III should focus primarily on Marx's manuscript, published here in English for the first time.

It is my hope that the publication of this English translation of Marx's *Manuscript of 1864–65* (at long last) will stimulate further research on all the remaining tasks listed above, in order to further develop Marx's theory for twenty-first-century capitalism. The basic logical structure is in place – the prior determination of the total surplus-value by surplus labour. Our task is to further develop Marx's theory in relation to the incomplete topics outlined above, especially concerning the distribution of surplus-value and the credit system and, ultimately, economic crises.

---

117 See Moseley 2002 for a review of Marx's many statements of this fundamental quantitative premise throughout Volume III.

118 Additional important textual evidence to support this interpretation is Marx's 1868 letter, which has been discussed in a number of places in this Introduction, and in which the prior determination of the total surplus-value is clearly assumed (= 100 in Marx's numerical example) in the summaries of Parts I, II, and IV (the main parts summarised in this letter) (Marx and Engels 1988, pp. 20–5; letter of 30 April 1868 from Marx to Engels).

119 Vollgraf and Jungnickel 2002, pp. 68–9; Heinrich 1996–7, pp. 464–5.

MARX'S ECONOMIC MANUSCRIPT OF 1864–1865

Translation

The Economic Manuscript of 1864–1865

Karl Marx

Capital

|1| Book Three

Forms [*Gestaltungen*][1] of the Process as a Whole

1 [*Gestaltungen* is a difficult word to translate into English; see pp. 4–6 of the Introduction for a discussion of the meaning of *Gestaltungen*. Engels deleted the word *Gestaltungen* from his title. *Gestaltungen* also appears in the first paragraph. Editor]

< CHAPTER ONE

The Transformation of Surplus-Value into Profit >

1) Surplus-Value and Profit

We have seen that the production process, considered as a whole, is a unity of the processes of production and circulation. This point was examined more closely when we considered the circulation process as a process of reproduction (in Chapter Four of Book Two).[1] < It cannot be the purpose of the present book to make general reflections on this 'unity'. What is necessary is rather to discover and present the concrete forms [*Formen*] which grow out of the process of capital, considered as a whole. (In their actual movement, capitals confront each other in certain concrete forms, for which both the shape of capital in the direct production process and its shape in the process of circulation appear merely as particular aspects of their movement. The forms [*Gestaltungen*] of capital, as we develop them in this book, thus come closer, step by step, to the form [*Form*] in which they appear at the surface of society, in the everyday consciousness of the agents of production themselves and finally in the action of the different capitals upon each other, namely competition.)[2] >

We may presuppose any period of time we like as the unit of measurement for the turnover of capital, but for the reasons discussed earlier when we looked at capital in general, the *year* would be appropriate as such a unit. In one year, a capital produces a certain quantity of surplus-value. For convenience of estimation we take the number 100 as our standard of measurement (unit of measurement) of the magnitude of a capital, as indeed we did earlier, with the result that the rate of surplus-value is expressed as a percentage. If one now calculates the surplus-value produced in a year (or in any other specific circulation period) in relation to the *total capital advanced*, which consists of the constant capital advanced plus the variable capital advanced, the surplus-value is transformed into *profit*.[3] The *rate of profit* is the ratio of the annual surplus-value

1 [This process was examined in Chapter Four of Marx's 1865 manuscript for what he called 'Book Two' of *Capital*. When Engels published Book Two as Volume II in 1885, this chapter became 'Part Three'. Translator]

2 [The next four important paragraphs were not included in Engels's Volume III; see pp. 8–9 of the Introduction for a discussion of these paragraphs. Editor]

3 The surplus-value produced during a given period of circulation (one may take for example a

to the total capital, a ratio which is similarly usually expressed as a percentage. For example, let a given capital consist of £400 constant and £100 variable capital and let the annual surplus-value come to £100. If we consider this £100 as the offspring of the total capital advanced, £500, we are looking at it under the *profit* category. |2| The annual *rate of profit* would be expressed by the ratio 100/500 = 1/5 = 20 percent, and we should say that the rate of profit of the capital amounted to 20 percent a year.[4]

(Later on in this chapter we shall have to give further details and determine how the annual rate of profit is related to the daily profit and hence also to the daily rate of surplus-value.) (Here, of course, we shall only be dealing with the average day.)

From the point of view of its material, the *profit* (in the shape in which it directly confronts us here) is nothing other than the *surplus-value* itself. Its absolute magnitude does not therefore differ from the absolute magnitude of the surplus-value which capital produces during a given turnover time. It is surplus-value itself, but calculated differently, or, as it initially appears, viewed subjectively in a different way. The surplus-value is by its nature related to the variable part of the capital, and it is therefore calculated in relation to this, i.e., to the part of the capital which causes the surplus-value to originate through exchange with the price of labour, from which it arises in reality. Circulation time, differing as it does from production time, only comes into consideration here as a barrier to the creation of surplus-value. As *profit*, in contrast, surplus-value is not related to, and therefore not measured against, a part of the capital advanced, but rather the total amount of capital, without regard to the very different roles which the various constituents of capital play in the creation of surplus-value and the production of commodity values as such.

Profit, in a material sense, and therefore as an absolute magnitude or quantity, is not at all different from *surplus-value*. It is nevertheless a changed form of the latter, and we shall therefore investigate the significance and importance of this *simple alteration of form* immediately after the present discussion. In contrast to this, in the *rate of profit* – or its relative magnitude, i.e., its magnitude as compared with the magnitude of the capital advanced – the surplus-value

---

year, a week, a day as the unit of measurement), if measured against the *total capital advanced*, is called the *profit*.

4 Here we consider the surplus-value of £100 not in relation to the £100 of variable capital, hence a fifth of the total capital from which it arises, but in relation to the five-fifths (5/5) of which the total capital consists, hence with regard to the total capital advanced.

receives not only a new conceptual expression but also a new *numerical expression, which differs* from its original shape. The profit is the same as the surplus-value in terms of its magnitude, but the rate of profit is from the outset *of a different magnitude from the rate of surplus-value.* The numerical expression of the same magnitude, e.g., the £100 of surplus-value in the above example, naturally changes according to whether it is expressed in proportion to a smaller or a larger number; whether 100 is measured against 100 or 100 against 500. It amounts to 100 percent in relation to 100 and only 20 percent in relation to 500.

< Let us call the surplus-value s, the constant capital c, the variable capital v, and the total capital C (= c + v).

We know from our previous investigation that the rate of surplus-value is equal to the *ratio of the surplus-value to the variable capital* = s/v. The rate of profit, in contrast, is equal to the *ratio of the surplus-value to the total capital,* hence = s/C, in other words = s/(v + c). > The rate of surplus-value |3| and the rate of profit can therefore only be *identical* in magnitude *in a single case,* that is when the constant capital = 0, hence the capitalist advances nothing apart from wages, and presents the worker with neither the raw material nor the means of labour, such as tools, machinery, buildings, etc. In that case, the variable capital forms the total capital. The surplus-value then undergoes absolutely no transformation. If we posit the constant capital, c, equal to 0, then s/(c+v) = s/(0+v) = s/v and since s/(c+v) = s/C, in this case s/v also = s/C. Hence the ratio of the surplus-value to the variable capital is the same as its ratio to the total capital, so the rate of surplus-value = the rate of profit. This single case, in which the difference of magnitude between the rate of surplus-value and the rate of profit disappears, is only worth mentioning, as far as capitalist production is concerned, for the sake of theoretical completeness. If it occurs at all in practice, it is at most an exception, on a very insignificant scale, in entirely isolated spheres of production or in conditions in which the subordination of labour to capital is still hidden beneath forms belonging to earlier modes of production. Profit and surplus-value, hence also the rate of profit and the rate of surplus-value, are identical, to the extent that the whole of the capital advanced is identical with the capital laid out directly in wages. In the investigation that follows, it is always assumed that the constant capital is > 0, greater than zero, in other words that at least a part of the capital is advanced by the capitalist in raw materials or machinery, etc., or both together. Surplus-value is converted into profit only to the extent that this is the case, and this is the only situation we are investigating in this chapter.

Hence although in this first form of profit the mass of profit is quantitatively identical with the mass of surplus-value, and profit and surplus-value therefore are only distinguished notionally (conceptually), the *rate of profit* is from the outset also quantitatively distinct from the *rate of surplus-value*, since the latter = s/v and the former = s/(c+v), in other words s/C.

It follows from this that the *rate of profit is always expressed as a smaller percentage than the rate of surplus-value*. A given magnitude is naturally expressed in a smaller or larger ratio to a third magnitude, in inverse proportion to the ratio in which the latter is itself smaller or larger.

Since, however, the total capital, c+v, is always larger than the part laid out in labour, v, the ratio of the surplus-value to the total capital, s/c+v, in other words the rate of profit, is always smaller than the ratio of the surplus-value to the variable capital, s/v, in other words the rate of surplus-value. It is clear that s/c+v is always < than s/v if c > 0.

As long as the dividend remains the same and the divisor increases, or, and this is the same thing, the numerator of a fraction remains the same and the denominator increases, the quotient declines or the value of the fraction falls. The *same* numerical quantity, the *surplus-value*, appears in the rate of profit and the rate of surplus-value as the numerator or dividend, but the denominator or divisor is greater in the rate of profit than in the rate of surplus-value. Thus, in the above example, where the total capital of 500 = 400 (c) + 100 (v) and the surplus-value = 100, |4| the rate of surplus-value = 100/100 or 100 percent, whereas the rate of profit, which is 100/(400 + 100) = 100/500 = 1/5, is only equal to 20 percent. The rate of profit is therefore expressed in this case in a five times smaller percentage figure than the rate of surplus-value; it is expressed in a ratio which is five times smaller.

And in general: s(c + v) < s/v. The rate of profit, p′, is smaller than the rate of surplus-value, s′. In other words, p′ < s′.[5] In general: as soon as c > 0, C or c + v > v and therefore p′ or s/(c + v) < s/v. If we posit the rate of surplus-value, s/v, as s′ and the rate of profit, s/(v + c), or s/C, as p′, s′ is always = p′ + sc/v(v + c) and p′ = s′ – sc/v(v + c), or the rate of profit is always smaller than the rate of surplus-value in the ratio sc/v(v+c).[6] Or, since v + c = C, the total capital, the difference = sc/vC.

5 s/v = s′ or the rate of surplus-value; s/C = s/c + v = p′, the rate of profit: s/c + v < s/v. This is self-evident; the only question here is merely one of algebra, to find the specific ratio, i.e., expressed in the numbers c, v and s, in which s′ > p′.

6 This formula is of general application, as can be seen from the following: there are here only two possible cases, either c = 0 or c > 0. If we first posit c = 0, the equation s′ = p′ + sc/v(v + c) becomes s′ = p′ + s × 0/ v(v + 0 = p′ + 0/v^2 + 0 = p′ + 0, or s′ = p′, which is in fact the case, if c = 0, if no constant capital exists, hence what was investigated in the text finds no application. If, on the other hand, c does not = 0 but is > 0, it is clear from the outset that the two equations 1) s′ = p′ + sc/v(v+c) and 2) p′ = s′ – sc/v(v+c) are identical. It is therefore a matter of indifference which of the two equations we investigate. Let us take the first one, and place on both sides

That is to say, the difference between the rate of surplus-value and the rate of profit is equal to the product of the surplus-value and the constant capital divided by the product of the variable capital and the total capital.

[FOOTNOTE][7]

(The expression sc/vC = s/v × c/C. The expression sc/vC = the difference between the rate of surplus-value and rate of profit, = d or = s′ – p′. Therefore s′ – p′ = sc/vC or s′ – p′ = s/v × c/C. But since s/v = s′, we have: s′ – p′ = s′ × c/C or (s′ – p′)/s′ = c/C. In words, *the difference between the rate of profit and the rate of surplus-value is related to the surplus-value exactly as the constant capital is related to the total capital*, or, the larger c/C is, the larger is (s′ – p′)/s′, that is to say, the ratio of the difference between the rate of surplus-value and the rate of profit and the rate of surplus-value. Moreover, the expression sc/vC = c/v × s/C. But s/C = s/(c + v) = p′, or the rate of profit. s′ – p′ therefore = c/v × p′. It therefore follows that (s′ – p′)/p′ = c/v. In words, *the difference between the rate of surplus-value and the rate of profit is related to the rate of profit as the constant capital is related to the* |5| *variable capital*. It must now be possible to derive the relation between the rate of profit and the rate of surplus-value directly from these two ratios. The equation (s′– p′)/s′ = c/C yields the result that (s′ – p′): s′ = c: C, or (s′ – p′) × C = s′c. And the equation (s′ – p′)/p′ = c/v yields (s′ – p′): p′ = c: v, hence (s′ – p′)v = p′c. We therefore have these two equations:

$$(s' - p')C = s'c, \text{ and } (s' - p')v = p'c.$$

Accordingly:

$$\frac{(s' - p')}{(s' - p')} \times \frac{C}{v} = \frac{(s')\,(c)}{(p')\,(c)}, \text{ or } \frac{C}{v} = \frac{s'}{p'}, \text{ or } \frac{p'}{s'} = \frac{v}{C}.$$

the values of s′ and p′. s′ = p′ + sc/v(v + c) gives, if we replace p′ with its value, namely s/(v + c), [the following expression:] s/(v + c) + sc/v(v + c); and if we similarly replace s′ with its value, we get: s/v = s/(v + c) + sc/v(v + c); or, s/v = (s)v/(v + c)v + sc/(v + c)v; or s/v = s(v + c)/v(v+c), in other words s/v, which = s/v. In the above example, where s/v = 100/100 and s/(v + c) = 100/500, the difference between the rate of profit and the rate of surplus-value is according to the formula 400/500, which is 4/5 and in fact 100/100 – 100/500 or 1 – 1/5 = 4/5.

7 [This footnote extends for 28 pages in the manuscript, and the MEGA editors thought it more convenient to insert it into the main text. I have followed their example; the long footnote ends on p. 81 of the present volume. Translator]

Expressed in words, *the rate of profit is related to the rate of surplus-value as the variable capital is related to the total capital.* If the constant capital = o, the total capital = the variable capital. In that case, v/C = v/v, hence p′ = s′, since p′/s′ = v/C and v/C = v/v. As we noted previously, not only profit and surplus-value, but the rate of profit and the rate of surplus-value, are identical when c = o, that is to say there is no constant capital at all. Once c becomes greater than o, C, or c + v, is greater than v, and therefore p′ or s/(c + v) is greater than s′ or s/v, and indeed the more c rises above o, or, in other words, the more the constant capital increases and accordingly the more the difference between the total capital and the variable capital grows, the smaller the proportion expressed by the rate of profit in comparison with the rate of surplus-value. It already follows from the formula s′ – p′ = sc/vC that s′ – p′ = o when sc/vC = o, or sc/(v{v + c}) = o. This is the case when c = o. But s′ – p′, that is to say the excess of the rate of surplus-value over the rate of profit, grows when sc/vC grows, and falls when sc/vC declines. Since there is absolutely no difference between s′ and p′ when c = o, the difference will be reduced the more c approaches zero, i.e., the smaller the constant capital, and it will grow the more c moves away from o, i.e., the larger the constant capital. The composite ratio s/v × c/C, or s/C × c/v determines s′ – p′, i.e., if we look at the expression in the form s/v × c/C, or s′ × c/C, it depends on the rate of surplus-value and the ratio of the constant capital to the total capital. Hence if the rate of surplus-value, s/v, is given, the distinction between the rate of profit and the rate of surplus-value depends on c/C, i.e., on the *ratio of the constant capital to the total capital.* The bigger the value of c/C, i.e., the greater c is in proportion to C, hence to c + v, the bigger the constant capital in proportion to the total capital, and the smaller the rate of profit as compared with the rate of surplus-value, or the bigger the difference between the rate of surplus-value and the rate of profit. On the other hand, the expression also has the form s/C × c/v, but s/C = p′, and therefore = p′ × c/v × s′ – p′ = p′ × c/v. If p′ is taken to be constant, s′ – p′ will rise and fall with c/v, i.e., it will grow as c/v grows, and therefore the larger c is in proportion to v, and it will decline as c/v gets smaller, i.e., the smaller c is in proportion to v. The difference between the rate of profit and the rate of surplus-value is greater *the larger the constant capital in proportion to* the variable capital, and it is smaller, the smaller the constant capital is in proportion to the variable capital, which also means *the larger the variable capital in proportion to the constant capital. The points developed* in this paragraph can certainly be deferred until Chapter Two.)[8]

8 [Engels renamed Marx's 'Chapters' as 'Parts'. Hence Chapter Two became Part Two of Volume III in Engels's published version. Translator]

As we have already seen, the difference between the rate of profit and the rate of surplus-value is $sc/(v\{v + c\})$. If $sc/(v\{v + c\}) = 0$ {which is the case when $c = 0$} the rate of profit has reached its maximum, i.e., it will then fall along with the rate of surplus-value. It rises and falls in an inverse ratio to the expression $sc/(v\{v + c\})$ or sc/vC. The greater this difference, the smaller the rate of profit, i.e., the greater the difference between it and the rate of surplus-value, and the smaller this difference, the greater the rate of profit, i.e., the smaller the difference between it and the rate of surplus-value.

It must therefore be possible to determine the rise and fall of the rate of profit by analysing the conditions under which $sc/v(v + c)$ rises and falls. $s/v \times (c/\{v + c\}) = s' \times c/(v + c)$. *If* s', *the rate of surplus-value, is given*, the movement of the rate of profit depends on the movement of $c/(v + c)$. The greater $c/(v + c)$, the greater is $s' \times c/(v + c)$; the smaller $c/(v + c)$ the smaller is $s' \times c/(v + c)$. $c/(v + c)$ is greater, the greater c is in proportion to $v + c$ or C; hence *the greater the constant capital is in proportion to the total capital*, and it is smaller, the smaller c is in proportion to the total capital C. The magnitude of the rate of profit thus stands in an inverse ratio to the relative magnitude of the constant capital, that is to say the proportional part it constitutes of the total capital. However, the relative magnitude of c, compared with $c + v$, may rise when c rises while $v + c = C$ remains unchanged. This rise is then associated with a reduction in the variable capital v. Or c may remain unchanged while $v + c$ declines. Here too, since c remains unchanged, v, the variable capital, must decline. The difference between this and the case first mentioned is that in the former the total capital remains unchanged, while its constant part grows at the expense of its variable part, whereas in the latter case the total capital declines, as a result of a decline in the variable capital. It is clear that whether the constant capital grows to a greater degree than the variable capital, or the variable capital declines to a greater degree than the constant capital, the result must in both cases be the same: a fall in the rate of profit. And vice versa. *The magnitude of the rate of profit* thus rises and falls *in an inverse relation* to the proportional magnitude of the constant capital, and *in a direct relation* to the proportional magnitude of the variable capital.

If, on the other hand, $c/(v + c)$, hence the ratio of the constant capital to the total capital, hence also the ratio of the constant to the variable capital, is a given factor, |6| the rate of profit will rise and fall *alongside the rate of surplus-value*. For, taking the expression $s' \times (c/\{c + v\})$, if $c/(c + v)$ remains unchanged, the expression can only change when s' changes, and its numerical value is greater, the greater s' is, and smaller, the smaller s' is. In this case, however, the rate of profit increases in absolute terms at the same time as the difference between it and the rate of surplus-value increases, and similarly with a movement in the opposite direction. Assume now that c/(c + v) = 2/3, so that the constant capital forms 2/3 of the total capital:

If we have 200 c + 100 v + 100 s, the rate of surplus-value = 100 %. The *difference* between the two is 66⅔. But if we have 200 c + 100 v + 200 s, the rate of surplus-value = 200 %, a *difference* of 133⅓. Furthermore, if we have 200c + 100v + 300s, the rate of surplus-value = 300 %, a *difference* of 200. The rate of profit = 33⅓ in the first case, 66⅔ in the second, and 100 in the third.

Here, the rate of profit grows *in the same proportion as the rate of surplus-value*: while the one grows from 100 to 200 to 300, the other grows from 33⅓ to 66⅔ to 100 = (3 × 33⅓); at the same time the difference between the rate of profit and the rate of surplus-value increases progressively. Let us now take the opposite case:

If we have 200c + 100v + 300s, the rate of surplus-value = 300 %, and the rate of profit = 100 %. Then with 200c + 100v + 200s, the respective percentages will be 200 and 66⅔, and with 200c + 100v + 100s, they will be 100 and 33⅓. The difference falls from 200 to 133⅓ and finally to 66⅔.

[Here are six more cases.]

c		v		s	Rate of surplus-value	Rate of profit	*Difference*
200	+	100	+	50	50	16⅔	33⅓
200	+	100	+	25	25	8⅓	16⅔
200	+	100	+	10	10	3⅓	6⅔
200	+	100	+	5	5	1⅔	3⅓
200	+	100	+	3	3	1	2
200	+	100	+	1	1	⅓	⅔

Here the rate of profit declines in proportion with the decline in the rate of surplus-value, first by a third, then by two-thirds. But the *difference* between the rate of surplus-value and the rate of profit also declines at the same time, instead of rising as it did before.

|7| This is therefore a law of general validity. If the ratio of the constant capital to the total capital, c/(c + v), or c/C, remains unchanged, the absolute (numerical) magnitude of the rate of profit rises and falls in direct relation to the rate of surplus-value, but also the difference between the rate of profit and the rate of surplus-value grows when the rate of surplus-value grows, and

declines when the rate of surplus-value falls; i.e., the *difference* between the two rates moves in the same direction as the rate of surplus-value does.

It is therefore evident that the rise and fall in the difference between s′ and c/(c + v) does not necessarily require a reduction in the *absolute magnitude* of p′, the rate of profit, but may be associated with an increase in the latter. Incidentally, merely by inspecting the formula s′ × (c/{c + v}) we can see that if s′ increases, the difference, s′ × (c/{c + v}), must increase, and that it will fall when s′ falls, although it is to be assumed in advance that, given that c/(c + v) remains unchanged, the absolute magnitude of the rate of profit must move in a direct ratio with the movement of s′. The question we must ask is: does a twofold movement of this kind (a difference of such a nature between the movement of the absolute numerical value of p′ and its proportional magnitude) take place only when c/(c + v) is constant, and s′ variable, or does it also happen when s′ is constant and c/(c + v) variable?

Before we answer this question, it must be noted that the rate s′, or s/v, can remain constant even if s and v change, but this must then take place in the same proportion, so that s/v always retains the same magnitude, s′, presupposed as constant, whatever changes take place in s or v. If s and therefore also v both become smaller, falling from 200 and 100 and then to 100 and 50, but the proportion always remains 50% or ½ (100/200 = 50/100 = 1/2), then c + v cannot remain constant unless c grows to the same extent as v declines. For example:

	c		v		s	s′	s	p′
I	300	+	200	+	100	50	100	20
II	400	+	100	+	50	50	50	10
III	450	+	50	+	25	50	25	5

In these three cases, the *rate of surplus-value* remains constant at 50%. The *surplus-value* itself, as well as the *variable capital*, fall by half as we go from I to II, and by half again from II to III. The *rate of profit* is in the first case 20%, in the second 10% and in the third 5%. If we reversed the process, the rate of profit would rise. The formula s/v × (c/{c + v}) evidently remains the same if it is multiplied or divided by x: xs/xv × (c/{c + v}), or if s/x is divided by v/x and multiplied by c/(c + v). It is therefore not affected by any changes in the magnitude of the surplus-value and the variable capital which are not accompanied by simultaneous changes in the ratio s/v or s′. But this would be incorrect, if c + v did not |8| remain unchanged, and instead c rose to the extent that v declined and vice versa, since C, i.e., the sum of c + v, was assumed to remain constant. Hence, as we have already shown, the rate of profit falls with the growth of c and rises with a fall in c. The decline in the rate of profit corresponds exactly to the reduction in surplus-value and in variable capital.

The *variable capital declines* in these proportions: 200, 100, and 50. The *surplus-value* likewise: 100, 50, and 25. The *rate of profit* likewise: 20, 10, and 5, while the rate of surplus-value, s′, remains unchanged at 50%. This case is important for capitals of equal size but different organic composition, assuming an *equal rate of surplus-value*, i.e., an equal level of exploitation of labour.

In case I, the *difference* between s′ and p′ is 50 – 20 = 30, in II it is 50 – 10 = 40, and in III it is 50 – 5 = 45. If the fall in the rate of profit, while the rate of surplus-value remains constant, is caused by a fall in the magnitude of the variable capital and in surplus-value, this difference rises and falls in the opposite direction to the rise and fall in the rate of profit.

Finally we have the case where s and s′ are both constant, hence not only is the ratio s/v constant, but the numbers which express this ratio are the same. In this case, s′ × c/(c + v) will only change if c/(c + v) changes. But since s/v is constant and s is constant, v is also constant. There can therefore only be a change in c, the constant capital, to cause C to rise or fall. For example:

c	v	s′	s	p′	Difference between s′ and p′
300	200 + 100	50	100	20	30
200	200 + 100	50	100	25	25
100	200 + 100	50	100	33⅓	16⅔
50	200 + 100	50	100	40	10
50	200 + 100	50	100	40	10
100	200 + 100	50	100	33⅓	16⅔
200	200 + 100	50	100	25	25
300	200 + 100	50	100	20	30

The rate of profit increases in direct proportion to the reduction in the constant capital (hence there is a *relative* increase in the variable capital) and it falls in direct proportion to the increase in constant capital. The difference between s′ and p′ declines with the rise in the rate of profit, which corresponds to the reduction in constant capital and therefore the relative increase in the variable capital; while the difference between s′ and p′ increases with the growth in constant capital and the corresponding decline in the rate of profit. In both these cases, there is either a growth in total capital combined with an increase in constant and therefore a proportional reduction in variable capital, or a reduction in total capital as a result of the reduction in constant capital, which corresponds to a proportional (relative) increase in the variable capital.

|9| It will now be appropriate to bring together what has been developed so far in this note in schematic form.

We shall use the following symbols:

c = constant capital
v = variable capital
C = c + v, i.e., = total capital
s = surplus-value
s′ = rate of surplus-value
p′ = rate of profit
d = the difference between the rate of profit and the rate of surplus-value, i.e., = s′ – p′.

I) $s' = s/v$; $p' = s/(v + c)$ or $p' = s/C$. $s' = p'$, when $c = 0$; (p′ is then at a maximum). If $c > 0$, $s' > p'$ and therefore $s' - p'$ is always a positive quantity. $d = s' - p' = s/v - s/(v + c) = s(v + c)/v(v + c) - s(v)/(v + c)v$. Hence $d = s(v + c - v)/v(v + c) = sc/v(v + c) = s \times (c/\{v + c\}) = sc/C$. (As soon as $c > 0$, C, or $c + v$ will be $> v$ and therefore p′ or $s/(c + v)$ will be $< s/v$ in other words $< s'$.)

It is equally possible to express d as sc/vC, i.e., d = the product of the surplus-value and the constant capital divided by the product of the variable capital and the total capital. *This is the general expression for d or* s′ – p′.

II) $s' - p' = s'c/C$. Therefore $s' - p'/s' = c/C$ or $d/s' = c/C$; i.e., *the difference between the rate of surplus-value and the rate of profit is in the same ratio to the rate of surplus-value as the constant capital is to the total capital.* The numerical value of d/s′ rises and falls in the same ratio as does the expression c/C. c/V or $c/(c + v)$ may however increase when c *rises, while* C remains unchanged. In that case c must increase at the expense of v, in other words the rise in C corresponds to an absolute fall in v. Or c/C may increase in magnitude *when* c *remains unchanged and* C *falls* (or, and this amounts to the same thing, when both quantities fall but c falls less than C.) In that case the reduction in C must arise from a reduction in v, corresponding to the relative increase in c. C may also increase, with v remaining unaltered absolutely, but then c would have to grow absolutely, hence increasing in relation to v. For example:

c	v	
200	100	Here c/(c + v) = 200/300 = 2/3 = 40/60
300	100	Here c/(c + v) = 300/400 = 3/4 = 45/60
400	100	Here c/(c + v) = 400/500 = 4/5 = 48/60

In the above case, then, where the increase in C arises from an increase in c, the expression c/C grows with the growth of the denominator, instead of getting less with this growth. Here the denominator increases proportionally less than the numerator, although by the same absolute amount. This is a consequence of the ratio law: *a ratio of less inequality*, such as c/(c + v), is increased by adding any quantity to both its terms.

III) sc/vC = c/v × s/C; s/C = s/v + c = p′; hence s/C (c/v) = p′ (c/v). Therefore: s′ = p′, in other words d = p′ × c/v; d/p′ = c/v. Thus d/p′ = c/v, or, in words, *the difference between the rate of surplus-value and the rate of profit is related to the rate of profit as the constant capital is related to the variable capital.*

|10| IV) It was shown in II) that d/s′ = c/C. Hence s′/d = C/c and s′/p′ = C/v. It was shown in III) that d/p′ = v/c and p′/d = v/c, or s′/p′ = C/v. *Hence* p′/s′ = v/C. Or, in words, *the ratio between the rate of profit and the rate of surplus-value is the same as the ratio between the variable capital and the total capital.*

Let us take the following as an example:

	c	v	s	s′	p′
(1)	400	100	100	100	20
(2)	800	200	200	100	20
(3)	1,000	500	250	50	16⅔.

In (1), p′/s′ = v/C, i.e., 20/100 = 100/500. (20/100 = 1/5 and 100/500 = 1/5.)
In (2), p′/s′ = v/C, i.e., 20/100 = 200/1,000. (200/1,000 = 2/10 = 1/5. And 20/100 = 1/5.)
In (3), p′/s′ = v/C, i.e., 16⅔ / [50] = 500/1,500. (500/1,500 = 1/3.)

$p' = (s' \times v)/C$. (In actual fact the total amount of surplus-value = s′, the rate of surplus-value, multiplied by v, the amount of variable capital.)

V) If d, which = $(s' \times c)/C$ or = $s/v \times (c/\{v + c\})$, increases, so too does the excess of the rate of surplus-value over the rate of profit, and in the same proportion, and if it declines, so too does the latter, and in the same proportion. Since the rate of profit is at its maximum when it is the same as the rate of surplus-value, $p' = s'$, or when the difference between them = o (when d = o), the more d approaches zero, i.e., the smaller d becomes, the larger will the rate of profit be, and, conversely, the more d diverges from zero, i.e., the larger d becomes, the smaller will it be. An investigation of the circumstances in which $s'v/C$ increases and diminishes must therefore yield more precise laws governing the rise and fall of the rate of profit.

It follows in any case from Law IV above, $p'/s' = v/C$, that the *rate of profit is greater*, the greater the variable capital is in proportion to the total capital, hence also, conversely, it is smaller, the *greater the constant capital is in proportion to the total capital,* and therefore that the rate of profit *rises and falls* in a direct *ratio* with the *proportional magnitude of the variable capital,* and in an *inverse ratio with the proportional magnitude of the constant capital.* Moreover, since according to Law II, $d/s' = c/C$, i.e., the difference between the rate of surplus-value and the rate of profit is related to the rate of surplus-value as the constant capital is related to the total capital, it is clear that the ratio between this difference and the rate of surplus-value *moves in the opposite direction* to the rate of profit.

VI)

$$d = \frac{s' \times c}{C} \left(\text{or } \frac{s' \times c}{c + V} \text{ or } \frac{s}{v} \times \frac{c}{c + v}\right)$$

If s′ *is given,* the magnitude of d depends on the magnitude of c/C or $c/(c + v)$, and thus moves in the opposite direction to the magnitude of p′. The greater |11| v is in comparison with C, the greater is $c/(c + v)$, [while] the greater c is in comparison with c + v, hence the greater the *constant capital is in comparison with the total capital,* the more does the rate of profit move in the opposite direction, a point which was already developed under V).

However, $c/(v + c)$ can increase if c *grows while* c + v, *or* C, *remain constant.* But since C = c + v, c cannot grow and C remain constant unless v declines to the same degree as c increases. Here, therefore, there is a positive decline in variable capital.

c/(v + c) can increase if C *grows, but the proportional increase in* c *is more rapid.* This is in turn only possible when the variable capital does not grow as quickly as the constant capital, hence *declines in comparison with the latter.*

c/(v + c) can increase if c *remains constant,* but v + c or C declines. If, however, c remains constant and v + c declines, this reduction must have its origin in a reduction in the amount of variable capital.

Hence if *s′ is given, the rate of profit rises and falls in an inverse ratio to the proportional magnitude of the constant capital, and in a direct ratio to the proportional magnitude of the variable capital.* This is the law we developed under headings IV and V.

VII) d = (s′× c)/C. If c/C is given, the *rate of profit* rises and falls *in an inverse ratio to the rate of surplus-value,* although in terms of its *absolute magnitude* it rises and falls with it. The rate of profit rises or falls absolutely in a direct ratio to s′, [and] d, the difference between s′ and p′, increases when the rate of profit grows, and declines when it declines.

VIII) s′, i.e., s/v, *can remain constant* although s *and* v *vary,* provided that they vary to the same degree, since s/v (= s′) is a constant magnitude according to our assumption. If s, and therefore also v, becomes smaller, either C declines, because v has declined, or, if C remains constant, c would have to increase as much as v has declined. The converse is also true if s and v become larger. In that case, C will grow because v grows, or, if C remains constant, c would have to decline as much as v has increased. *Here, the rise and fall in the rate of profit corresponds exactly with the rise and fall in the magnitude of the surplus-value and the variable capital, while* s′, *the rate of surplus-value, remains constant. But the difference, d, moves in the opposite direction to the rate of profit or the surplus-value.* If the change in p′ is determined by the change in s′, d will rise and fall in the same direction as p′; if, on the other hand, the change in p′ is determined by changes in s and v, d will move in the opposite direction to p′.

|12| **IX**)

$$d = s'\left(\frac{c}{c+v}\right) \text{ or } \left(s' \times \frac{c}{C}\right) \text{ or } \frac{s}{v}\left(\frac{c}{c+v}\right).$$

If both s′ and s are constant, a single glance will tell us that v is also constant, since otherwise s/v = s′ would be impossible. Here, therefore, a change is only possible if the magnitude of c/(c+v) or c/C changes. But since the absolute magnitude of v is constant, this is only possible through a change in the magnitude of c. If c falls, so also does C, since v is of a fixed magnitude. In that case, v still rises relatively, because c has fallen. Or C grows, because c grows, and in that case although the numerical value of v remains constant, it falls relatively because there is an increase in c. The rate of profit increases in a direct ratio to the decline of the constant capital, hence the *relative increase in variable capital*, and *it falls in a direct ratio to the increase in the constant capital and therefore the relative decline in variable capital.* The difference between s′ and p′, namely d, rises with the growth in the constant capital and falls with its decline. It therefore moves in the *opposite direction to the rate of profit*, whereas the situation in VII was that both moved in the same direction.

The main laws we have derived are therefore as follows:

1) $p'/s' = v/C$. *The ratio between the rate of profit and the rate of surplus-value is therefore the same as the ratio of the variable capital to the total capital.* It rises and falls directly as the proportional magnitude of the variable capital. (It is assumed here that s′ is a given quantity.) (It follows from $p'/s' = v/C$ that $p' = (s' \times v)/C$. Since the rate of profit, p′, = $(s' \times v)/C$, it rises and falls directly as the variable capital does. If the ratio v/C is constant, the rate of profit rises and falls directly as s′, the rate of surplus-value.)

2) If s′ and s, i.e., the rate of surplus-value and the surplus-value, are given quantities, *the rate of profit will rise and fall in an inverse ratio to [changes in] the proportional magnitude of the constant capital* (compared with C, the total capital). The difference, d, between s′ and p′, i.e., *between the rate of surplus-value and the rate of profit, rises and falls in the same direction as [changes in] the constant capital*, hence in the opposite direction to the level of the rate of profit. (Compare no.V with this.)

3) If s′ is given, *the rate of profit varies in an inverse ratio to the proportional magnitude of the constant capital.* (Doesn't this case in fact come under number 2 above?)

4) If the *ratio of the constant capital to the total capital is constant, the absolute magnitude of the rate of profit rises and falls in direct relation to the magnitude of the rate of surplus-value. But the difference* between *the rate of surplus-value and the rate of profit also rises and falls in direct relation to rises and falls in the rate of profit.*

5) If s′, i.e., s/v, is given, and remains unchanged, while s *and* v vary, *the rate of profit rises and falls* in exactly the same degree as the *surplus-value and the*

variable capital vary. But the *difference between the rate of surplus-value and the rate of profit* rises and falls in the *opposite* direction to the [changes in the] rate of profit. The difference lessens as the rate of profit increases, and increases as the latter is reduced.

|13| It is perhaps better to derive the laws directly from s′ and p′ than from the difference between them.

$$1)\ s' = \frac{s}{v};\ p' = \frac{s}{c+v} \text{ or } \frac{s}{C};\ \frac{p'}{s'} = \frac{s/C}{s/v} = \frac{vs}{sC} = v/C. \text{ Hence } \frac{p'}{s'} = \frac{v}{C}.$$

So p′ = s′ × v/C. If s′ is constant, [p′] is directly determined by v/C; if v/C is constant it is determined by s′.

p′ = s′× v/C. s′ × v is equal to s, the mass of surplus-value, for this = the product of the rate of surplus-value × the magnitude of the variable capital. s′, the rate of surplus-value, can remain constant while s rises or falls; for s′ to remain constant all that is needed is that the numerical value of s/v – of this ratio – should remain constant; the numbers which constitute its numerator and denominator do not need to remain constant. If s′ remains constant, s will rise or fall in line with the rise or fall of v; i.e., according to the increase or decline in the variable capital. (One can see that s′v/C = s/C by replacing s′ with its value. sv/vC = s/C.) For example, if the rate is 100% and the variable capital = 100, s = 100 at that rate. If it is 1,000%, s = 1,000, etc.

It therefore follows from p′ = s′v/C that (1) *if* s′ *is constant* the magnitude of p′ depends on the variations in v/C, i.e., it depends on *the ratio of the variable capital to the constant capital*, or, in other words, on the proportional magnitude of the variable capital. v/C can vary either because v varies or because C varies. If they both vary simultaneously, the effects of this variation would cancel each other out, if they vary *by the same proportions*. Therefore this case does not come into consideration here. If, on the other hand, they vary in different proportions, these variations will paralyse each other to the extent that they coincide. Where they do not, this is shown by an excess variation of either v or C, but not by a simultaneous variation of both of them. We have already noted that if equal quantities are added to v and C, the expression v/C becomes larger, because v/C is a ratio of less equality.[9] For our case, therefore, it is sufficient to assume either that v varies and C is constant, or that v is constant and C varies. If v *varies*, i.e., if it increases or decreases, while C remains constant, the constant part of C (c) must decline as much as v increases, and vice versa; the reason for this is that, as C is the same as v + c, and v is varying, C cannot remain constant

9 [The last five words were written in English by Marx. Translator]

unless every variation in v is counteracted by an opposite variation in c, so that the *overall total* of c + v remains unchanged, with one of its parts losing what the other one gains, and vice versa. In short, all that has taken place is a change in the way the total amount, C, is distributed between its components. |14| It is assumed that s′, the rate of surplus-value, remains constant. If v increases, the *surplus-value* will also increase, as well as the rate of profit, *given a constant rate of surplus-value;* if v declines, the rate of profit will also decline, if the rate of surplus-value remains the same. Hence if s′ and C are both constant, the rate of profit will rise and fall in *direct* ratio to the *magnitude of the surplus-value*, which, on our assumption, since s′ is given, rises and falls in direct ratio to, or is entirely dependent upon, the absolute *increase or decline in the variable capital*, compared with the constant capital, and its *proportional* increase compared with the total capital C.

Now assume the converse, that v/C *varies*, with v *constant and* C *variable*. If v is constant, C, because it is v + c, can only vary because of a variation in c. In the first case that was considered, c did vary, but its variations were only a result of the variations in v. *The magnitude of value remained the same*, and c rose or fell to the extent that v rose or fell, but in the opposite direction. (Increases or reductions in variable capital are thus expressed by *increases or reductions in constant capital*. And since the rate of profit moves in *the same direction* as the variable capital, it must move in the *opposite direction* from the constant capital. This, however, only applies to the *direction* of the movement. The general law that p′: s′ = v: C cannot be reformulated in opposite terms to apply to the constant capital. The constant capital rises and falls by *the same magnitude of value* as does the variable capital; but not in the same *proportion*. The proportion in which it rises or falls depends instead on the original ratio c/C or c/v.) Variations in v, on the other hand, are now only relative, i.e., they are the result of variations in c, which rises or falls. The latter cannot remain the same, since on our assumption C varies and v remains constant. If c declines, v increases relatively. And in general the numerical value of v/C increases when the denominator grows smaller. In that case, therefore, the variable capital grows in proportion to the constant capital and therefore in proportion to the total capital. For example, let s′ = 100%; c = 400, v = 100; and C = 500. The rate of profit, p′, is therefore 100/500 = 20%. If c is now reduced by 100, c + v = 400 and p′ = 100/400 = 1/4 = 25%. It is the same as if C had remained 500, but either the *rate of surplus-value* had risen from 100% to 125% or the *variable capital*, and therefore the total surplus-value, had risen from 100 to 125, with the rate of surplus-value remaining constant. Here, then, the *rate of profit* rises, although s′ (100%), and s (100), remain constant, [because] the same surplus-value, s, is calculated on a smaller total capital, or because the variable capital, although unchanged absolutely, has grown relatively to the constant capital and therefore to the *total capital.*

Conversely, if C grows because c grows, so that C (the C that has grown) = C + x, or = (c + x) + v, the *rate of profit* falls, because v/C has fallen, because its denominator has risen, and C′ = v/(C + x). Here the variable capital has declined in relation to the constant capital and therefore the total capital as well, and, assuming s′ and s remain constant, s/C′ < s/C. |15| In one case, therefore, p′ rises, and in the other case it falls. This is because in the first case the total capital is reduced by the decline in constant capital, and in the second case the total capital is increased by the rise in constant capital. The rate of profit therefore rises and falls in inverse ratio to the movement of the constant capital and the variation in the total capital caused thereby.

In both cases it is assumed that s′, *or the rate of surplus-value, remains unchanged.* But in the first case, where the total capital is constant and the variation proceeds from v, the rate of profit changes because the *surplus-value changes in absolute numerical terms.* This change corresponds to a change in the profit rate in the same direction, and itself follows an absolute change in the *magnitude of the variable capital.* In the second case, where the total amount of capital changes, and the variation proceeds from c, while v remains constant, not only s′, the *rate of surplus-value*, but also s, *the absolute numerical amount of surplus-value*, remain constant. The *rate of profit* changes, and indeed in *the opposite direction*, because there is a change in the *magnitude of the constant capital* and through this and owing to this a change in *the total capital.* [In algebraic terms:]

$$\frac{s}{C} < \frac{s}{C} - x \text{ and } \frac{s}{C + x}, \text{ or } \frac{s}{c + v} < \frac{s}{(c - x) + v} \text{ and } > \frac{s}{(c + x) + v}.$$

Two laws have therefore emerged. First, that where the *rate of surplus-value* and the *magnitude of the total capital* remain unchanged the rate of profit changes in a direct ratio to the magnitude of the *variable capital* and the corresponding *magnitude of the surplus-value*; and second, that where the *rate of surplus-value and the amount of variable capital remain unchanged*, and therefore also the *magnitude of the surplus-value* remains unchanged, the rate of profit changes in the *opposite direction* to the change in the *magnitude of the constant capital* and the corresponding change in the *magnitude of the total capital* caused by that change in the magnitude of the constant capital.

If the change in the magnitude of the total capital were caused not by an increase in the constant capital but by an increase in v, this would fall under the first law. For example, c = 600, v = 200, C = 800; s′ = 100, s = 200. In this case, p′ = 200/800 = 1/4 = 25%. If now v is increased from 200 to 400, with s′ remaining the same, we should have: C = 1,000, s = 400, and p′ = 400/1,000 = 4/10 = 40%. In other words, p′ would have increased from 25% to 40%. If now, conversely, v is reduced to 100, and C therefore falls by that amount, we should have: C = 700, s = 100, and p′ = 100/700 = 1/7 = $14\frac{2}{7}$%. In the first case, p′ grows although C has increased, and in the second case p′ declines, although C has declined; in the first case because the surplus-value has increased along with the increase in the variable capital, and in the second case because the surplus-value has declined along with the decline in the variable capital.

It is assumed in this connection that wages remain unaltered, hence that *variations in the numerical magnitude of the variable capital* do not arise from *variations in the wages of a constant quantity of workers*, but rather express differences in the mass of labour employed, at the old wage. This last point should be borne in mind in the course of the whole of the investigation in this chapter.

|16| (2) The next case to be examined is covered by the expression $p' = \frac{s' \times v}{C}$.

Here $\frac{v}{C}$, i.e., the ratio of the variable capital to the total capital, is constant, and the level of p′ depends *directly on the changed magnitude* of s′. If s′ increases, $\frac{s' \times v}{C}$ increases, and also p′; if s′ falls, $\frac{s' \times v}{C}$ falls, hence p′ falls. Therefore, at a given magnitude of the total capital, and a given ratio of the variable capital to the total capital (hence in general a given proportion between the components of capital), *the rate of profit will rise and fall in a direct ratio to the rise and fall of the rate of surplus-value*. For example, c = 400, v = 100, and C = 500. If the rate of surplus-value = 100, p′ = 100/500 = 20%. If the rate of surplus-value = 50, s = 50 and p′ = 50/500 = 1/10 = 10%. If s′ = 200, s then = 200, and p′ = 200/500 = 2/5 = 40%. On the assumption that the *variable capital* is a given quantity (and C is as well), the *magnitude of the surplus-value* depends exclusively on the *rate of surplus-value*, while the rate of profit, on the other hand, depends exclusively on the *magnitude of the surplus-value*, since C is a given quantity.

(3) In the expression $p' = \frac{s' \times v}{C}$, both s′ and v may vary, while only C remains constant. In this case, either s and v vary in *the same* direction or they vary in *opposite* directions. Let us first assume that they vary in the same direction, so that when the variable capital grows, the rate of surplus-value also grows. (This case is actually absurd and unacceptable, except where the growth in v is only relative, being derived from a reduction in c, which means that C cannot remain constant but must decline. What is absurd about this is the

necessary assumption that more labour is needed to set in motion the same quantity, or a smaller quantity, of constant capital, and that the labour has therefore become more unproductive yet the rate of surplus-value has risen. The case is of course possible if there is *an absolute increase in the length of the working day*; for the necessary labour may increase, and yet the surplus labour may increase in a still higher degree.) If v increases so that it becomes v + x, while C remains constant, the rate of profit will increase in this proportion, if s′ remains constant. It will increase still more if s′, instead of expressing an aliquot part of v, expresses a greater aliquot part of v + x. The surplus-value would increase here because more variable capital was applied and at a higher rate. This increased surplus-value, or $\frac{s+x}{C}$, is greater than $\frac{s}{C}$. The opposite will be the case if s′ and v both decline, but this case does not offer any new insights of any kind.

However, assume now that s′ and v vary in opposite directions. Assume that v increases, i.e., more workers are employed, because the labour has become more unproductive, and therefore the rate of surplus-value delivered by each individual worker has lessened. Here v and s′ increase in opposite directions. We are not therefore assuming that v denotes *more money* for *the same quantity of labour* or *the same number of workers*. Only to the extent that a larger v = more workers does this correspond to a larger amount of surplus-value, because the *number* of workers exploited by the same capital has increased. Therefore s will grow, and along with s, p′. Because s′ falls, however, each individual worker paid by v will deliver a smaller quantity of surplus labour or surplus-value. To that extent s will decline, and therefore p′ will also decline. Whether this results in an increase, a reduction, or neither, will depend on whether the increase in the number of workers constituted by v balances out the fall in s′, or is smaller and is therefore outweighed by the fall, or is larger, and therefore outweighs it. |17| If, on the other hand, there is a fall in the number of workers employed and at the same time the rate of surplus-value increases (whether relatively or absolutely), both effects will similarly counterbalance each other if they are of equal magnitude; or, if the reduction in surplus-value produced by the reduction in the number of workers is greater than the increase in the same produced by the increase in the rate of surplus-value, the *surplus-value and with this the rate of profit will fall*. And vice versa.

If, therefore, C is constant, and s′ and v are variable, the opposing movements of s′ and v will cancel each other out if they are of equal magnitude. If they are not equal, one must predominate, and to the extent that it does, it will push the movement to one side or the other, either towards a reduction or an increase in surplus-value. In both cases the rate of profit will simply follow the movement of the surplus-value, which is determined by the contrary variations in its two component elements, the *number of workers employed, and the degree of exploitation of the workers employed.*

(4) Finally, we have the case where in the expression $p' = \frac{s' \times v}{C}$ all three elements vary. Our first task is then to examine the matter as if C were fixed. The variations in $s' \times v$ either cancel each other out, or, if that does not happen, they move in *one single* direction, whether towards an increase or a reduction in s and therefore p′. Once this point is settled, in line with the argument developed *under* (3), it is the same as if $s' \times v$ were a given quantity, say a, and the expression $p' = \frac{s' \times v}{C}$ changes into the one examined earlier, in which s′ and v are constant and C varies. This case therefore also offers no new area for investigation and we only mention it for the sake of completeness and in order to prove how very complex are the movements through which the rate of profit is ultimately determined, and how much they overlap and are intertwined with each other.

We observed previously that if c > o, if the total of C > v, in other words if the whole of the capital is not laid out exclusively in wages, the difference between s′ and p′, which we shall call δ, is always equal to $\frac{s' \times c}{C}$ or $\frac{s}{v} \times \frac{c}{c+v}$, whatever numerical value these letters may represent. It should not be thought that this difference follows a uniform law in all cases. On the contrary, *if* s′ *is constant* and the rate of profit changes, whether as a result of a change in the magnitude of v (and a corresponding change in c), which also implies a change in s, or as a result of a change in the magnitude of the total capital resulting from a change in the magnitude of c, while the variable capital and therefore the surplus-value remain the same, δ (the difference between s′ and p′) will rise and fall in the opposite direction to p′, growing when p′ declines and declining when p′ grows. It is easy to see the reason for this. δ = s′ – p′. Since s′ is constant, s′ – p′ will become smaller when p′ increases, and larger when p′ decreases. If p′ were as large as s′, s′ – p′ would be = o, in other words the difference between them would disappear completely. But the closer p′ gets to o, the larger is the difference s′ – p′. The larger p′ becomes, |18| the smaller is the difference s′ – p′, and the smaller p′ becomes, the larger is the difference s′ – p′.

The movement of δ (the difference s′ – p′) takes a different course when v/C, the ratio of the variable capital to the total capital, is constant, and the change in the rate of profit therefore proceeds exclusively from a change in the magnitude of s′, the rate of surplus-value. Although in this case the rate of profit not only rises and falls in the same direction as the rate of surplus-value, but does so in exactly *the same ratio*, hence s′ and p′ rise and fall simultaneously to the same degree, the difference between s′ and p′ increases and declines simultaneously with the reciprocal rise and fall of the two quantities, following therefore a law which is exactly contrary to the one just mentioned, in which δ rose and fell in an inverse ratio with p′. The reason for this is that s′ is in its very nature greater than p′, since $\frac{s}{v} > \frac{s}{v+c}$. If two quantities, a and b, a being greater than b, increase in a given proportion (but not *by the same* numerical amount) the difference between them grows in the same proportion as the numerical increase, and if, conversely, both quantities diminish in the same proportion, the difference between them diminishes in the same proportion. Take for example the numbers 3 and 9, and double them repeatedly:

	Numbers		Difference
We have:	9	3	6
	18	6	12
	36	12	24

And then the converse, dividing by 2:

	Numbers		Difference
	36	12	24
	18	6	12
	9	3	6

In the first case, the difference increases as the numbers increase from 6 to 12 and then to 24, and in the second case, the difference diminishes as the numbers diminish from 24 to 12 and then to 6.

It can be seen from this that differences between p′ and s′ of very divergent amounts can result from the different combinations in which the rate of profit rises or falls.

In order to illustrate what has been said here, we shall repeat in schematic form the examples already given earlier in this note:

|19| **I)** *The case where* v/C *is constant, and only* s′ *is variable.*

c	v	s	s′	p′	δ (difference between s′ and p′)
200	100	100	100	33⅓	66⅔
200	100	200	200	66⅔	133⅓
200	100	300	300	100	200
200	100	300	300	100	200
200	100	200	200	66⅔	133⅓
200	100	100	100	33⅓	66⅔

II) *The case where* s′ *is constant,* v, s *and* c *are variable and* C *is constant.*

c	v	s	s′	p′	δ (difference between s′ and p′)
300	200	100	50	20	30
400	100	50	50	10	40
450	50	25	25	5	45
450	50	25	25	5	45
400	100	50	50	10	40
300	200	100	50	20	30

Finally, we have

III) *The case where* s′, s *and* v *are all constant, while* c *is variable and* C *rises and falls with* c.

c	v	s	s′	p′	δ (difference between s′ and p′)
300	200	100	50	20	30
200	200	100	50	25	25
100	200	100	50	33⅓	16⅔
50	200	100	50	40	10

(cont.)

c	v	s	s′	p′	δ (difference between s′ and p′)
50	200	100	50	40	10
100	200	100	50	33⅓	16⅔
200	200	100	50	25	25
300	200	100	50	20	30

|20| The laws already developed above about the divergent relations between the rate of profit and the rate of surplus-value, or the divergent movement of the difference between them, depending on whether s′ is constant or variable, emerge very clearly from the above tables.

Case I. If (a – b) = δ, the difference between them, 2(a – b) = 2δ or 2a – 2b = 2δ; and n(a – b) = nδ, or na – nb = nδ. In this case a and b both increase by multiplication by the same factor, 2, or n, but δ increases in the same proportion as their own increase. The greater n, the greater the growth of a, b, and also their difference, δ. Conversely, if a – b = δ, (a – b)/n = δ/n or a/n – b/n = δ/n. They decline in the same proportion; but the difference between them also declines in the same proportion as their decline. The larger n is, the smaller do a and b become, and the smaller does their difference, δ, become, i.e., the smaller does the difference between the rate of surplus-value and the rate of profit become.

This first case applies when s′ is variable, because only in this case is (a – b) multiplied or divided by n. If s′ is constant, on the other hand, it is only b (the subtrahend) which is multiplied or divided. The difference therefore follows a completely different course in this case.

Case II. If (a – b) = δ, a – (b + n) = (δ – n) or δ′. The larger the number n by which b grows, the smaller is δ′ or (δ – n). Conversely, if b declines by n, a – (b – n) = δ + n or δ′, in other words, the larger the number n by which b falls, the larger is δ + n or δ′. The difference therefore increases in an inverse relation to the growth in the rate of profit, i.e., it falls when the latter rises and rises when the latter falls.

We have seen that the *rate of profit*, or p′, = $\frac{s}{C} = \frac{s' \times v}{C}$, since s = s′v. If for example s′ = 50% = ½, and the variable capital = 100, then the surplus-value = half a hundred = 50.

It results from the above proposition, (1) that p′/s′ = v/C; (2) that if s′ is constant p′ will rise and fall directly as does v/C. If C is constant, it will rise and fall directly as v, and if v is constant it will, conversely, rise and fall as C changes in consequence of changes in c; and (3) that if v/C is constant (in which context v and C can well vary, hence C does not need to be a capital of an unchanging magnitude, only the proportion v/C needs to be fixed) p′ will rise and fall directly as s′ does.

To the extent that the movement of p′ depends on v and therefore on the ratio v/C, or on s′, we have a strictly mathematical expression. For what is involved here is not only an increase in a certain direction but an increase of a definite proportion.

Firstly: p′/s′ = v/C. For example, c = 400, v = 100, and s = 100. Here C = 500. v/C = 100/500 = 1/5 and so the 20% of p′ divided by the 100% of s′ = 20/100 = 1/5.

Secondly: v/C constant. This can be, for example, 1/5. If v = 200, C will be 1,000, and v/C = 200/1,000 = 100/500 = 1/5. If the surplus-value is then 100, in other words 50%, p′ will be 50/1,200 = 5/120 = 1/24. If the surplus-value is 100%, p′ will be 100/1,200 = 1/12. The rate of surplus-value, or s′, has doubled, and so has the rate of profit, from 1/24 to 1/12. The opposite movement takes place if s′ falls from 100% to 50, because p′ will then decline from 1/12 to 1/24 or from 8⅓% to 4⅙%.

|21| Finally we have the *third* case, where s′ *is constant* and p′ rises and falls directly as v/C does. And indeed, it is assumed in this case that C is constant and v varies.

Let C = 1,000, v = 200, and s′ = 100. In this case, s = 200 and p′ = 200/1,000 = 2/10 = 1/5 = 20% and v/C = 1/5.

As against this, if C = 1,000, v = 400 and s′ = 100, s = 400, p′ = 400/1,000 = 4/10 = 2/5 = 40% and v/C = 2/5.

And if C = 1,000, v = 300 and s′ = 100, s = 300, p′ = 300/1,000 = 3/10 = 30% and v/C = 3/10.

And if C = 1,000, v = 150 and s′ = 100, s = 150, p′ = 150/1,000 = 15/100 = 3/20 = 15% and v/C = 3/20.

We see here how, as a result of changes in v, v/C rises from 1/5 to 2/5, etc, and falls from 3/10 to 3/20 in exactly the same ratio as p′ rises and falls.

In all these three cases, where there is either a *direct ratio*, as in (1) p′/s′ = v/C, or, as in (2), p′ rises and falls as s′ does, if v/C is constant, or, as in (3) p′ rises and falls as v (or s) does, if C is constant, not only is the direction of growth or decline precisely determined, but also the precise mathematical exponent of this variation.

In a fourth case, in contrast, *where* s′ *is constant, and the variation in* v/C *proceeds not from* v *but from* C, *as a result of a change in* c, we have it is true been able to determine the direction, namely that p′ varies inversely with the variation in the constant capital, but the exact numerical relation is missing, and a precise formula must be given for this, because we have, in fact, established four exact mathematical laws on the movement of the rate of profit, and two laws on the movement of the difference between s′ and p′.

Once the fourth case is found (i.e., formulated precisely) we know from the third case how p′ rises and falls when s′ is constant, and with C constant the change in v/C proceeds from a change in v (admittedly, a change in c must correspond to this variation in v, as its consequence); we know from the fourth case how p′ behaves when s′ is constant, v is constant and the change in C proceeds from c. It will then be easy to discover how matters stand when s′ varies, v varies, C varies, and also c varies, or, in other words, how the |22| rate of profit varies with capitals which diverge in absolute magnitude because they are composed of v and c in different proportions, and are valorised at various rates of surplus-value.

To get a better understanding of these questions, we should like to look again at case (3), which has already been dealt with. We shall examine this from another angle, in which it is assumed that C remains constant. Because C remains constant, the variation in v must be counterbalanced by an equal and opposite change in c. Or, in so far as the variations come into consideration, the case does not differ from that in which c varies (i.e., the variation proceeds from c and the variation in v is merely a consequence of the variation in c.) This same *third case* can therefore be treated as *the fourth case*, as a case in which p′ changes as a result of variations in c, but the *magnitude of* C *remains the same*. We shall then see how the relationship is expressed differently and, when this has been found, we can investigate further how this is modified when C does not remain constant, but, because v is constant, variations in c must necessarily bring about variations in C.

The difference in the relationship (its inversion) between the determination of p′ by v or c is clear from the outset, since the surplus-value derives from the variable capital: s′ = s/v and s = vs′. If s′, the rate of surplus-value, is a given quantity, its magnitude depends exclusively on the magnitude of v; it rises and falls in an exact proportion with the magnitude of v. If, on the other hand, v is given, its magnitude depends exclusively on s′, and its rise and fall is exclusively determined by the rate of surplus-value. If they both need to be determined, s is determined by its product (s = vs′, which yields v: $\sqrt{s} = \sqrt{s} : s'$). Therefore, since s arises exclusively from the variable capital and is determined solely by *the magnitude of the variable capital* (v) and its percentage increase or growth (s′), it is clear that the magnitude of the rate of profit stands in a direct proportion to the magnitude of v, for the rate of profit is a *proportion* of s, the magnitude of which is determined exclusively by v. If c were = 0, v would = C and s/C would = s/v, i.e., the rate of profit would = the rate of surplus-value, p′ = s′. A difference between p′ and s′ – hence the transformation of s′ into p′ – is produced by the entry of constant capital into the equation, since the constant capital, by being added to v, the variable capital, produces a C, a total capital, which differs from the variable capital, and therefore produces an s/C, or p′, which differs from s/v or s. By being added to v, it reduces the rate of profit in comparison with s′, and it does this more or less to the extent of its magnitude. The change in the magnitude of c therefore always has an opposite impact on the magnitude of p′, and it only has an impact on p′ to the extent that it produces a C which differs from v, and in the proportion to which it produces that difference. It cannot stand in a direct relation to p′ because in fact it stands in *no* relation to s or s′, and its increase or diminution therefore can never affect their substance or magnitude but only the manner in which this magnitude is calculated.

|23| The rate of profit increases in the proportion to which the reduction in c raises the ratio v/C, and the rate of profit decreases in the proportion to which the increase in c reduces the ratio v/C. However the actual proportion in which the rise and fall of c has an impact on v/C depends on the original ratio of c or v to the total capital, and therefore on the original ratio of v to c.

[The following table shows this.]

	c	v	s	s′	p′	C	c/C	v/C	p′/s′
I)	600	300	150	50	16⅔	900	16/24	8/24	8/24
II)	900	300	150	50	12½	1,200	18/24	6/24	6/24
III)	300	300	150	50	25	600	12/24	12/24	12/24

p′/s′ varies in exactly the same proportion as v/C. The changes in v/C proceed here from the changes in C, which proceed in turn from changes in c. First c increases from 600 to 900, and p′ *falls*; then c falls from 900 to 300 and p′ rises. p′ therefore rises and falls in an *inverse* or opposite direction to the change in the magnitude of c; but the absolute proportion in which c grows absolutely does not determine the numerical relation in which p′ passes through this opposite movement. This numerical relation precisely follows the change in v/C, which is produced by the change in c. From I) to II) c increases by *50%*, from 600 to 900, and C increases from 900 to 1,200, or by 33⅓% as a result of this increase. (This takes place because c was originally ⅔ of C.) Through the 50% increase, one-third of C is added to C, in other words c's growth by 50% produces an increase on C's part of 33⅓%, because c/C was = 2/3. If this ratio had been different, so also would the impact on C. If for example c had been = ⅕ C, an increase of c by 50 % would only have increased C by 1/10 of its original amount, i.e., by 10 %. (This original ratio of c: C is determined by (or expressed in) the original ratio of c/v. In case I) c/v was 600/300 = 2: 1. Here c = 2v, hence C = 3v; v = C/3 and therefore c = 2(C/3) = 2/3 C, as noted previously. c = av. C = v(a + l). $v = \frac{C}{a+1}$ and $c = \frac{a(C)}{a+1.}$).

On the other hand, while an increase of c by 50 % leads to an increase of C by 1/3 or 33 1/3 %, p′ falls only half as much as C increases, namely by 1/4 or 25 %. v/C, instead of being 300/900, is now 300/(900 + 300), hence instead of being v/C it is $\frac{v}{C + \frac{1}{3}C}$. 300/900 = 1/3 and 300/1,200 = 1/4. 1/3 = 4/12 and 1/4 = 3/12. Thus the rate of profit falls by 1/4 or 25 %. Since v was originally 1/3 C, not C = 4v. Hence v/4v = 1/4. And therefore p′ falls.

|24| (If v remains constant, the growth of c {by a particular percentage} or the decline of c {by a particular percentage}, by δ, must always transform C into C + δ, where δ expresses the absolute magnitude by which c rises or falls. But δ = c/x, where x represents any whole number or fraction {always positive of course}. In other words, c + δ = c + c/x. To what extent c/x is expressed in C depends on the original proportion of C/c. If this original proportion = r, C/c = r, or C = rc, or c = C/r, hence c/x = C/rx. The change in c which turns it into c + or – c/x, or δ, is expressed in terms of C as an increase of C to C + C/rx, if there is an increase, or C – C/rx, if there is a decrease. C + C/rx or C – C/rx is the new magnitude of C′, or the total capital C increased or decreased by δ. v/C becomes v/C′, and $v/C' = \frac{v}{C + C/_{rx}}$ or $\frac{v}{C - C/_{rx}} = \frac{v}{C + \delta}$ [or] $\frac{v}{C - \delta}$; in one case $\frac{v}{c + \delta}$ falls and p′ also falls to the same degree, in the other case it increases.)

As we have said, it is only the change in magnitude, which the change in c brings about for C and thereby for v/C, that affects the ratio p′/s′ and therefore the absolute magnitude of p′. If v is constant, an increase in c must always produce an increase in C, and a decrease in c must bring about a reduction in C. The degree to which C increases or decreases, as compared with its original magnitude, depends |25| on the original ratio of c/C. Any change in c (positive or negative) can be expressed as an increase or decrease of c by c/x. Hence c becomes c + c/x (or c – c/x). C itself therefore increases in one case and decreases in the other by c/x. But how much this quantity c/x is, calculated on C (or what is the percentage by which C increases or decreases through the addition or subtraction of c/x) depends on the ratio c/C. If c/C = 1/4, 4c = C, or c = C/4. c/x is then C/4x. So if C increases or decreases by c/x, it increases or decreases by C/4x. And we then get $C' = C \pm C/_{4x}$. Then v/C becomes $\frac{v}{C \pm C/_{4x}}$.

$$\left(\frac{v}{(4xC \pm C)/4x} = \frac{v}{C(4x \pm 1)/4x}\right)$$

The degree to which this ratio v/C′ diverges from v/C progressively or regressively determines the proportion by which p′ rises or falls.

c	v	s′	s	p′
800	200	50%	100	10%
1,000	200	50%	100	8⅓%

Let C now grow by ¼. Since c = 800, c/4 = 200. c grows by 25%, from 800 to 1,000. The original ratio of c/C was 800/1,000 = 8/10 = 4/5. Hence c/C = 4/5 and c = 4/5 C. ¼ c (the proportion by which c grew) is therefore 4⁄20 C = ⅕ C. In other words, C grows by 20%, because c has grown by 25%. We now have, instead of C, C′, = C + ⅕ C. C was 1,000, ⅕ C was 200, and therefore C′ = 1,200. v/C now becomes v/C′, or instead of 200/1,000 it becomes 200/1,200 = 2/10. Instead of being ⅕ C, v/C now becomes 200/1,200 = 2/12, or ⅙ C. ⅕ = 6⁄30 and ⅙ = 5⁄30. It has fallen by ⅙ because C has increased by ⅕, and ⅕ = v, hence v/5v has become v/6v. ⅙ is 16⅔%. And p′ was originally 10%. It is now 100/1,200 = 1⁄12 or 8⅓%. The difference between 10% and 8⅓ is however 16⅔%.

|26| To summarise the above, v/C can vary [in the following conditions] (and if s′ is given p′ depends on these variations, since $p' = \frac{s' \times v}{C}$).

(1) Firstly, C *remains constant* and v varies, increasing or decreasing, but then, since C is constant, c must vary in the opposite direction. (α)

C changes and c *remains constant*. Then the increase or decrease of C must make v/C smaller or larger, since C = c + v. (β) In (α) when v increases and c decreases to the same extent, v/C grows, and p′ also grows, in the same numerical proportion. The converse applies when v decreases and c increases to the same extent.

In (β), if v increases, v/c + v becomes v′/c + v′ (if v + δ = v′). In this case, v/(c + v) increases because $\frac{v + \delta}{c + (v + \delta)}$, a lesser ratio, increases by adding the same number to both its parts.

Assume that c = 300, v = 100, s′ = 100, s = 100 and p′ = 25%. Let v grow from 100 to 300. Then v/C moves from 100⁄400 to 300⁄600. Instead of ¼ it becomes 3⁄6, or ½, which = 2⁄4. v/C has doubled. Looking at the rate of profit, it has now become 300⁄600 = 50%. Thus the rate of profit has also doubled. Assume now that s′ was 50%, so that s was 50 in the first case. 50⁄400 = 5⁄40 = ⅛ = 12½%. In the second case, s becomes 150, and 150⁄600 = 15⁄60 = 5⁄12 = ¼, hence again twice as much as in the previous case. As long as s′ remains the same, s must increase in the same proportion as v. In the first case, it becomes $^{300}/_{600}$ instead of $^{100}/_{400}$; in the second case, it becomes $^{150}/_{600}$ instead of $^{50}/_{400}$. And vice versa.

|27| (2) Secondly (α) C *remains constant* and c increases and decreases; v moves in the opposite direction, and the case falls under 1 (α). But it should be noted that if the movement of p′ is compared with the movement of c, we get an inverse proportion, the numerical value of which will be determined in the immediately following calculations.

(β) C *changes*, increasing and decreasing in a certain proportion with the rise and fall of c. The proportion in which the rise and fall of c causes it to move depends on the original ratio c/C. In both cases, $\frac{v}{c+v}$ or $\frac{v}{C}$ becomes $\frac{v}{(c+x)+v}$ or $\frac{v}{C'}$, or also $\frac{v}{(c-x)+v}$ or $\frac{v}{C'}$. The exact numerical ratio by which p′ decreases or increases inversely with the increase or decrease effected by changes in c depends on the relation between v/C′ and the original ratio, v/C.

The situation can be summarised in this way:

$p' = \frac{s'v}{C}$. If s′ is constant, C *is either constant or not.*

(α) *If* C *is constant*, v cannot increase or decrease without an equal and opposite decrease or increase in c. From this angle, it is also a matter of indifference whether one views the change in magnitude as proceeding from v or from c. For if s′ is given the magnitude of s depends entirely on the magnitude of v, and if C is given the magnitude of s/C = p′ depends exclusively on s, so here there is a direct ratio between p′ and the change in magnitude of v, and an inverse ratio to c, as previously explained.

(β) *If* C *changes* and v remains constant, there are two further constants, s′ and s, since s′ = s/v and s = (s/v) × v. In this case C increases or decreases as a result of changes in c. Although v has the same magnitude in absolute terms, its proportional, relative magnitude in comparison with C increases or decreases, not because it changes itself but because c and therefore C change. But this *relative* fall or rise in v as compared with C has the same effect as if v's actual numerical magnitude had altered. If C increases, v/C decreases, hence (s′ × v)/C, or p′, also falls, and if C decreases, v/C increases, etc. The extent to which changes in the magnitude of c have this inverse impact on p′ depends on how far they modify the ratio v/C.

|28| (γ) A change in C while c remains constant is only possible as a result of a change in the magnitude of v, leading to a rise or fall in C. The magnitude of v/C, and therefore of p′, alters in a direct ratio with increases or reductions in v. Nevertheless, it is not correct to say, as under (α), where the denominator

remains the same, that v/C rises and falls in exactly the same numerical proportion as v.

Assume first that C is constant and s′ is constant. For example, let c = 400, v = 100, s′ = 100, s = 100, and p′ = 20. If c becomes = 300, v = 200, s′ = 100, and s = 200, p′ will then be = 40%. If c becomes = 450, v = 50, s′ = 100, s = 50, and p′ = 10%. In the first case v/C = 100/500 = 1/5; in the second case v/C = 200/500 = 2/5; and in the third case v/C = 50/500 = 1/10, and p′ moves in exactly the same numerical proportion as v/C.

Assume now that C is variable, c is constant and s′ is constant, as in the following example:

(1) c = 400, v = 100, C = 500, s′ = 100, s = 100, p′ = 20%
(2) c = 400, v = 200, C = 600, s′ = 100, s = 200, p′ = 33⅓%
(3) c = 400, v = 300, C = 700, s′ = 100, s = 300, p′ = 42 6/7%
(4) c = 400, v = 50, C = 450, s′ = 100, s = 50, p′ = 11 1/9%

In the first case, v/C = 100/500, so v = ⅕ C.
In the second case, v/C = 200/600, so v = ⅓ C.
In the third case, v/C = 300/700, so v = 3/7 C.
In the fourth case, v/C = 50/450, so v = 1/9 C.

Here the changes in v/C are admittedly reproduced exactly by the numerical changes in p′. But this probably happens because s′ = 100, so that s = v.

Let us therefore set s′ at 50% in the above example. [Now the result is:]

(1) c = 400, v = 100, s′ = 50%, s = 50, p′ = 10%
(2) c = 400, v = 200, s′ = 50%, s = 100, p′ = 16⅔%
(3) c = 400, v = 300, s′ = 50%, s = 150, p′ = 21 3/7%
(4) c = 400, v = 50, s′ = 50%, s = 25, p′ = 5 5/9%

[In case (2)] v/c = 200/600; v/C = ⅓ v = ⅓ C. Since s′ is here exactly half the size it was previously, p′ is also exactly half its previous figure. But in (1) v = ⅕ C, in (2) v = ⅓ C, in (3) v = 3/7 C, and in (4) v = 1/9 C.

However, p′ does not grow from ⅕ to ⅓, i.e., from 20% to [33⅓%], and from ⅓ to 3/7, i.e., to 42 6/7%, and so on.

|29| Since v alters C here, either increasing or reducing it, it to a certain extent counteracts its own effect, and therefore the numerical ratio established under (α) is no longer appropriate here; instead, one always has to see how far the addition of equal quantities to the numerator and the denominator alters v/C. To the extent that this is the case, p′ is in its turn altered.

Since changes in v/C only directly determine p′ because with a given s′ the magnitude of s depends on the magnitude of v, hence rises and falls with v, it is clear that it must always be presupposed that v represents a particular number of labour processes (taking a given amount of labour-time) and that the variations in v, its rises and falls, do not derive from any increase or reduction in the amount of payment for the *same* quantity of labour, for otherwise we should arrive at the absurd result that p′ increases because s decreases, and decreases because s increases. But this result would also contradict our presupposition. We have assumed in considering v/C that s′, the rate of surplus-value, is constant. (It is true that if there is a change in the length of the working day wages may rise and yet s′ may remain constant, as we showed earlier. But in this case, while the value expression of v rises, s remains the same, and its proportion to v remains the same. Changes in the value of c would then have to be brought into the calculation. We shall return to this case later on. It could be said, namely, that when wages rise or fall it cannot be assumed, as previously, that there was a change in s′, and that v/C remained constant. For if s′ changes in this manner {i.e., because it represents *a different quantity* of labour, rather than a smaller or larger degree of exploitation of a variable capital of the same amount of value} v also changes. This case needs to be examined separately; whatever the result of this, once a change in the value of labour has taken place, a definite ratio of v/C emerges.) (Here it is assumed in our investigation that v = a definite quantity of necessary labour, so that it expresses more labour when it increases, and less labour [when it declines].)

|30| I shall now examine the following series of questions:

(1) the question raised earlier, as to how far v/C remains constant when s′ changes;

(2) the differences between the laws that govern the level of the rate of surplus-value and those that govern the rate of profit which derive from the general laws on the rate of profit, and the incorrect theories (in Ricardo, etc.) which follow from the confusion between these laws.

(3) *Economy in the use of constant capital*, in order to reduce the relative magnitude of c and thus raise p′.

(4) The influence of *changes in the price of constant capital*, particularly raw material, *in changing the magnitude of* p′. Before discussing the above questions under these various headings, |31| of which (2) and (3) in fact merely require the application of the general laws on the rate of profit, it should also be noted that, in examining the ratio v/C, if v and C vary in the same proportion, and in general if v and c vary in such a way that the ratio between them and therefore also the ratio v/C remains constant, any change in magnitude is

irrelevant to the determination of p′, since what is important for the latter is not the absolute magnitude of the capital but its specific composition.

[END OF LONG FOOTNOTE.

THE MAIN TEXT STARTS AGAIN HERE.]

We shall later get to know the importance of this law for grasping otherwise inexplicable phenomena, and we shall see in the eighth and ninth chapters[10] how political economy has vainly exhausted itself in the hunt for an explanation. As simple and so to speak tautological as the law is, it remains more or less impossible for political economy to grasp it, because it does not provide a pure treatment of surplus-value in its pure form.

|6|[11] The initial result here is this: the *rate of surplus-value* expresses the actual degree of exploitation of labour, the actual proportion in which capital appropriates labour without an equivalent, unpaid labour, whereas the *rate of profit*, if it is to count as a measure of the exploitation of labour, always presents this *proportion* as much smaller than it is; it expresses it downright falsely. Thus, in the above case, the exploitation amounts to 100 percent, i.e., over the whole year the worker must work for the capitalist for nothing half the time; the rate of profit, however, only amounts to 20 percent, hence judging by that proportion the worker only works for no return for 1/6 of his time. It can be seen straight away how much the ignorant confusion and lumping together of the rate of profit and the rate of surplus-value by twaddling statisticians and sycophantic economists must facilitate the task of prettifying apologists.

It follows from the nature of the *rate of profit*, as the ratio of the surplus-value to the total amount of capital advanced, (s)/(c + v), that *equal rates of surplus-value* may *be expressed in different rates of profit*. Let us assume that the variable capital is 100 and the surplus-value is similarly 100, so that the rate of surplus-value = 100 percent. If the constant capital = 400, v + c or C (the total capital) = 500. Thus the ratio of s/C = 100/500 = 1/5 = 20 percent. If the constant capital is 500, then 100/600 (s/C) = 1/6 = 16 ⅔ percent, and if it were 200, s/C would be = 100/300 = 1/3 = 33 ⅓ percent. Here the same rate of surplus-value of 100 percent

10 [As noted earlier, Marx's manuscript, which became Volume III, was divided into seven chapters. The eighth and ninth chapters were presumably envisaged as part of the *Theories of Surplus-Value*, which was intended to form Volume IV. Translator]

11 [Pages 6 to 8 occur twice because Marx wrote his long footnote (which we number 6) on the lower half of manuscript pages 6 to 8, then used the whole of pages 9 to 30. Translator]

is expressed in different rates of profit of 20, 16 ⅔, and 33 ⅓ percent, and with a continuing change in the magnitude of the constant capital could be expressed continuously in various other rates of profit.

Conversely, while equal rates of surplus-value can be expressed in different rates of profit, equally the *same rate of profit can be expressed in different rates of surplus-value.* (*Different rates of surplus-value can be expressed in the same rate of profit.*)

If the variable capital = 100, the surplus-value = 100, and the constant capital = 400, the rate of surplus-value amounts to 100 percent and the rate of profit 20 percent. If the variable capital = 100, the surplus-value = 50, and the constant capital = 150, the rate of surplus-value = 50 percent, and the rate of profit = 50/250 = 1/5 = 20 percent. Finally, if the variable capital = 50, the surplus-value is 100 and the constant capital = 450, the rate of surplus-value comes to 200 percent (100/50 = 2/1) and the rate of profit will be 100/500 = 1/5 = 20 percent. And thus we should always have the same rate of profit of 20 percent, |7| behind which the very different rates of surplus-value of 100, 50 and 200 percent lie hidden. And, as in the first case, this could be varied indefinitely. It is particularly important to bear this in mind when one is comparing the rates of profit in *different countries* (where it is possible that the exploitation of labour may differ considerably).

∴

Three important laws result from the determination of the *rate of profit.*

1) The *rate of profit always expresses the actual degree of exploitation of the worker as less than it is.* The rate of surplus-value = s/v; the rate of profit = $\frac{s}{c + v}$. $\frac{s}{c + v} < \frac{s}{v}$; $\frac{s}{v}$ is the limit, which s/(c + v) approaches the smaller c becomes, but it never arrives at this limit except when c = 0, hence $\frac{s}{c + v} = \frac{s}{0 + v} = \frac{s}{v}$. This implies that the capitalist advances only wages but *no* means of production, a case which is generally impossible in the capitalist mode of production.

2) *The same rate of surplus-value can be expressed in the most varied rates of profit.* In this case s/v is constant; s/(c+v) is variable, because c varies. For example, s/v = 100/100 = 1/1 = 100 percent. In another example, the variable capital is set equal to 100, the surplus-value = 100 and the product is 200, equal to the realised labour of x workers. If the constant capital set in motion by these x workers = 200, the total capital will be = 300, and the rate of profit = $\frac{100\ (s)}{200\ (c) + 100\ (v)}$ = 100/300 = 1/3 = 33⅓ percent. If the constant capital = 400, s/(c + v) = $\frac{100\ (s)}{400\ (c) + 100\ (v)}$ = 100/500 = 1/5 = 20 percent; if c = 900, s/(c + v) = $\frac{100\ (s)}{900\ (c) + 100\ (v)}$

= 100/1000 = 1/10 = 10 percent and so on. The same rate of surplus-value (and the same quantity of surplus-value) of 100 percent is therefore expressed in rates of profit of 33⅓, 20, and 10 percent, or any other rate, according to the variation in c.

Law No. 2 can also be expressed like this: *the most varied rate of profit can represent the same rate of surplus-value.*

3) *The same rate of profit can express different rates of surplus-value.* What is constant here is s/(c + v), the rate of profit; what is variable is s/v; it is clear, however, that s/(c + v) can only remain constant with appropriate changes in c. Assume that s/(c + v) = 10 percent. If we have s = 50, v = 100 and c = 400, s/(c + v) = 50/(400 + 100) = 50/500 = 10/100 = 1/10 = 10 percent. If we assume that s = 25, v = 100, and c = 150, then s/(c + v) = 25/(150 + 100) = 25/250 = 5/50 = 1/10 = 10 percent. The same rate of profit expresses in one case a rate of surplus-value of 50 percent and in the other case 25 percent. Here it is not just s which is variable but c too. This is the prerequisite for keeping s/(c + v) constant while s/c is variable. *The same law: different rates of surplus-value can be expressed in the same rate of profit.*

Fourth law: assuming that all other circumstances remain the same, the rate of profit rises and falls with the rise and fall in the rate of surplus-value. That is, s/(c + v) becomes larger when s/v increases, and it becomes smaller when s/v diminishes; assuming that the ratio between v and c remains the same. For example, s/v = 50/100 = 50 percent. If c = 400, s/(c + v) = 50/400 + 100 = 50/500 = 5/50 = 1/10 = 10 percent. If we posit a rise in the rate of surplus-value to 100 percent, then s/(c + v) = 100/(400 + 100) = 1/5 = 20 percent; if we posit the converse, that the rate, s/v, falls from 50 to 25 percent, then s/(c + v) = 25/(400 + 100) = 25/500 = 5/100 = 1/20 = 5 percent. If here the rate of surplus-value is 50 percent, the rate of profit will be 10 percent; if the rate of surplus-value falls to 25 percent, the profit rate will fall to 5 percent. That is to say, the rate of profit rises and falls with the rate of surplus-value, all other circumstances remaining the same.

From these four laws, it follows automatically that the laws for the rate of surplus-value (which determine its movement) cannot be applied directly to the rate of profit.

|8| We have illustrated the movement of surplus-value sufficiently in Volume I. The rate of surplus-value will therefore be assumed as given/constant in what follows. Three further remarks need to be made:

1) It is now clear why a simple lengthening of labour-time (extensive or intensive) raises the *rate of profit* even when the worker is paid for the excess hours of labour, and indeed receives extra pay for overtime; that is, when he receives an equivalent for himself of a part of the excess labour-time and only a

part of it represents surplus-value for the capitalist. An increase in the quantity s in $s/(c + v)$ always takes place where c remains the same. (The same can be said of a quicker turnover.)

2) A simple reduction in the value of c (that is to say the constant capital laid out in the production of a given mass of products) will cheapen the commodity, i.e., each aliquot part of the mass of products, P. If these commodities re-enter into the reproduction of the worker as provisions, the impact of this is a reduction in the value of labour-power, hence an increase in the *rate of surplus-value* while the working day remains (intensively and extensively) the same. The same factors (reduction in the value of c), which, independently of any movement in s/v, i.e., the rate of surplus-value, produce an alteration in the rate of profit $s/(c + v)$, can react back to alter s/v. What was true above of the reduction in the value of c is also true of an increase in its value. It can raise the relative value of labour-power and therefore reduce s/c.

3) Case 2) is interesting in its application to the means of nourishment, when the (material) elements of v and c simultaneously change their value.

[(2) Cost Price][12]

|31| *Surplus-value*, as previously discussed, is nothing other than *unpaid labour*, which is realised [*realisiert*] in the commodity, and, after the sale of the commodity, in money. And the *rate of surplus-value* is nothing other than the ratio or the degree in which unpaid labour is related to paid labour. But the part of capital which is exchanged for labour is *variable* capital, and thus surplus-value and the rate of surplus-value are by their nature related to variable capital, and it would not alter this relation in any way if the constant capital, c, were equal to 0.

On the other hand, the surplus-value stands in a ratio to the total capital advanced (even if the rate of surplus-value does not) and this ratio is *numerically different* from the ratio in which it stands to the part of the capital from which it arises through the latter's exchange for labour. Means of production are needed in order to appropriate labour, and their value precisely forms the value of the constant capital. Leaving aside the technical need for the material elements of the constant capital, < it has already been shown that it is precisely the possession of these means of production in the hands of the non-workers which converts workers into wage-labourers, non-workers into capitalists > and

12 [Title added by the MEGA editors. Translator]

the means of production and subsistence as such into capital. The means of production, or constant capital, can be regarded from a double viewpoint. On the one hand they are the necessary condition for the production of commodities, as means of production; but on the other hand, constant capital, just like variable capital, is only an *advance* made in order to create surplus-value. This is because for the capitalist the production of commodities is never an end in itself but always only a means to acquire money, i.e., surplus-value. (Whether this is realised in commodities or money it is always inscribed in the capitalist's brain under the heading of money.) Constant capital does not produce surplus-value, but it is the instrument needed to squeeze surplus-value out of the variable part of the capital. Constant capital is a condition of production necessary to employ variable capital, and it forms a part of the *advances* of the capitalist just as much as does variable capital. < The surplus-value, from wherever it may derive, is an *excess* over and above the total capital advanced. > If the commodities are sold at their value, their price, less the price of the means of production incorporated in them, equals the surplus-value, or, in other words, the surplus-value represents the *excess* of the value of the product over the price of all its ingredients, labour included. It was seen earlier that $c + v + s$ comes out in the final result as $(c + v) + s$. This excess over the total capital advanced, which constitutes surplus-value, *stands in a ratio* with *the total capital*. In order to compare its magnitude with the total capital, to calculate its relative magnitude, s/C, or the surplus-value taken over the total capital as a percentage, obviously offers itself, just as the surplus-value did in relation to the variable capital. But since s/C is a different magnitude from s/v (the rate of surplus-value), it is rightly fixed as a specific category with a specific name. < We thus obtain the *rate of profit* as distinct from the *rate of surplus-value*: the latter is surplus-value calculated in relation to v, i.e., the part of the capital from which it originates, and the former is the same |32| surplus-value, calculated in relation to the total capital. The one is s/v, the other is $s/(v + c)$, or s/C. > In both cases it is the surplus-value whose magnitude is *measured*. The difference lies not in the surplus-value itself, but in the standard of measurement which is applied to determine its magnitude. Surplus-value divided by variable capital = s' (rate of surplus-value). Surplus-value divided by the total capital = p' (rate of profit). < The rate of surplus-value, as measured against the variable capital, is called *the rate of surplus-value* and the rate of surplus-value, as measured against the total capital, is called *the rate of profit*. These are two different standards for measuring the same quantity, > which therefore express *completely* different ratios or relations of the same thing, since the difference in standards of measurement implies that the ratios or relations are themselves different.

< It is the transformation of surplus-value into profit that is derived from the transformation of s' into p', the rate of surplus-value into the rate of profit, not the other way round. In actual fact the rate of profit is the historical starting-point. Surplus-value and the rate of surplus-value are, relative to this, the invisible essence to be investigated, whereas the rate of profit, and hence the surplus-value in its form as profit, is a visible surface phenomenon [*Erscheinung*]. > What is actually present, and forces itself onto our attention, as something distinct from the rate of surplus-value is the *rate of profit*, while there is initially absolutely no difference between *surplus-value* and *profit*, either in magnitude or in any other way.

< As far as the individual capitalist is concerned, it is evident enough that the only thing that interests him is the ratio of the surplus-value – or the *excess value* which he receives from selling his commodities – to the total capital advanced for the production of those commodities, whereas not only is he not interested in the specific ratio of this excess value to the particular constituents of his capital, it is in his interest to bamboozle people about these particular ratios and inner connections. >

M-C-M′ forms the movement of capital, and in it the second M′ is bigger than the first. Thus £100 – C – £110. The difference of 10 between M′ and M is the surplus-value, and the ratio in which 100 is used for the production of more money, or in which the sum of value of 100 has been valorised, is the ratio of this surplus-value of 10 to the total capital advanced of 100, is in other words *the rate of profit*. Hence $10/100 = 10\text{p.} = v/C = p'$.[13]

The surplus-value therefore represents the realised [*realisiert*] excess (the excess realised in money) of the value *of the product over* the value of the *capital advanced* or over the *price of the ingredients of production*, and the ratio of this excess to the value of the capital advanced is the *rate of profit*.

If the total product existing in commodity form is converted into money and the capitalist withdraws from this amount of money another amount which is equal to the value of the capital advanced for the production of the commodities – hence withdrawing 100 from the 110 – the remainder is equal to 10, being the surplus-value obtained, and the ratio of 10/100, of this surplus-value to the total capital advanced, = the rate of profit.

In calculating surplus-value as rate of profit, it is related not just to the part of the means of production whose value appears again in the product, |33|

13 [Here, where the movement of capital is under investigation, M represents 'money', and C represents 'the commodity', although in other contexts C represents 'the total capital advanced'. Translator]

because its use-value separate from the product, its use-value in its old form, has been extinguished, but simultaneously to the part of the constant capital which has not been consumed, namely the fixed capital which is preserved in the production process, the value of which continues to exist after the deduction of an average depreciation [*Dechet*], only to lose another part of its value in a new production process. We explained previously that the rate of profit always expresses a smaller proportion of the valorisation than is contained in the surplus-value, in other words that in this *measurement of surplus-value* the level of exploitation of labour is represented as being much smaller than it is in reality. This lesser proportion becomes yet smaller through the fact that the surplus-value is calculated on the total capital advanced, not just on the part of the capital which is consumed in the course of production and the value of which is therefore transferred to the product.

The *value of the capital advanced*, both the constant and the variable capital, and both the fixed and the circulating, the consumed and the unconsumed part of the constant capital, represents the total value of the capital advanced as opposed to the *excess of value* (which is how the surplus-value now appears). (This is to be distinguished from the *cost of production*, as we shall see later.) Only one part of the fixed capital, which = the depreciation, enters into production. And the value or price of this part of the capital is the *cost price*. The surplus-value is therefore the excess of the price of the commodity over and above its *cost price*, or the *excess of the value of the commodity* over and above the *value of the capital consumed to produce it*. (Whereas in the *rate of profit* it is by no means merely the cost price, but also the unconsumed part of the capital which is included as the standard of measurement. In actual fact the whole of the fixed capital is advanced for production. It must be advanced all at once. Although only an aliquot part of the value of the machinery, for example, is transferred to the product, the whole of the machinery is needed to produce the product. The total value of the machinery must therefore be advanced for production, although it is only transferred to the product piece by piece in a series of turnover periods.)

The objective character [*Bestimmung*] of the *cost price* of the commodities is that it is the *total value* of the *capital* consumed for and in production, hence the part of the *value of the commodities* which *replaces* the constant and variable capital consumed in producing them. From the subjective standpoint of the capitalist the *cost price* is the part of the commodity value for which he has paid, or must pay, an equivalent, which replaces the capital he has advanced, and here, where all that is involved is the *value* of the capital, it is the part of the commodity value, which costs him, or has cost him, money. But the surplus-value is the *excess quantity* over and above this *cost price*.

It therefore follows that the *cost price of the commodities is less than their value*. If the cost price of the commodity were equal to the value of the commodity, the capital would not be valorised, in other words it would not create any surplus-value. If the capitalist sells the commodity *at its value*, he receives for it the portion of value contained in the commodity relating to the constant capital that has been consumed, the portion of value relating to the wage of labour, and finally the portion of value in which *unpaid labour* has been realised. The capitalist has paid no value in return for this unpaid labour, no equivalent, and it therefore *costs him nothing*, and precisely for that reason it creates surplus-value for *him*. For the worker *the cost of this surplus-value is naturally his own labour*. The whole of the product, viewed from the angle of its value, is nothing other than *objectified* labour. But it is only the part of this objectified labour for which the capitalist pays an equivalent which forms the *cost price* for him; the other part of the commodity in which *unpaid* labour has been objectified, hence a *portion of value* which the capitalist *sells* although he has *not* paid for it, forms surplus-value, *the excess of the price of the commodity over its cost price*. It costs him nothing. If we include in c only the part of the objectified labour whose value, as in the case of raw material and accessories, enters entirely into the product, alongside the part of the fixed capital which enters into the product as depreciation, the value of the product = (c + v) + s; or, since c + v = the value of the capital consumed in production (v is consumed for the capitalist by the payment of wages), it equals the portion of value of P, the product, which costs the capitalist money, and for which he has paid or must pay an equivalent, it equals *the price he himself has to pay for the product*, the cost price of the product. In that case, the *value of the commodities* = c + v, or *the cost price of the product* + the surplus-value, or the part of the value of the product appropriated by the capitalist without equivalent. The *value* of the commodity includes its surplus-value, i.e., the unpaid labour contained in it, just as much as it does the paid labour, but the *cost price* of the commodity excludes its surplus-value, which precisely for that reason represents an *excess* over exactly that cost price. If we call the cost price of the commodity K, its surplus-value S, and its value W, then W = (c + v) + s, and c + v = K, hence W = K + S, hence K = W – S and S = W – K. The value of the commodity is therefore necessarily greater than its cost price; the magnitude of the value is greater the larger the ratio of the surplus-value to the capital advanced, or the larger the unpaid part of the labour objectified in the commodity.

Hence although nothing can emerge from production which did not previously come into it, so that there can be no more value in the commodity than has entered into it in the production process – partly in the form of objectified labour, partly in the form of living labour – while on the other hand the value of the commodity is only realised, i.e., only takes on the money form, without its magnitude having been altered, in circulation; and although accordingly no *surplus-value* can arise through the sale of the commodity (this only appears to happen to the extent that one person sells his commodity *beneath* its value and another sells it *above* its value) it is nevertheless true that 1) an excess of value over the cost price is created in production, and 2) this excess of value over the cost price is realised in circulation. |34| How this excess over the cost price is created has been exhaustively presented in the first section, which deals with the production of surplus-value, and there is therefore no need to come back to it here.

Since the value of the commodity is greater than its cost price, or K < W, it is clear that if a commodity is sold *beneath* its value and *above* its cost price, a part of the surplus-value continues to be realised in its sale price. If the sale price, P, is > K < W, the commodity will still continue to be sold at a profit. Its sale price continues to yield an excess over and above its cost price – a portion of value for which the seller has not paid an equivalent, or, in other words, a part of the surplus-value contained in it continues to be realised. A great number of prices lie in the middle, between K and W, i.e., between the commodity price which only replaces the value of the capital consumed in it and the commodity price which is = to its value, hence is an equivalent for the total amount of labour, paid and unpaid, contained in it. The greater the difference between W and K, = S, i.e., the greater the excess of the value of the commodity over its cost price or the greater the surplus-value contained in it, the greater is the number of possible prices between W and K. A commodity can therefore be sold *beneath* its value at a profit, and it can be sold profitably at very *different prices between its value and its cost price*, although the rates of profit will differ greatly. It follows from the law that the *cost price* of a commodity is less than its *value* – and precisely the excess of the *value* of the commodity over and above its *cost price* constitutes the *profit* it yields – it follows that commodities can be sold at a profit *beneath* their value. As long as an excess over the cost price is realised by the sale, a profit is realised, without the buyer's needing to pay the whole difference between the value and the cost price of the commodity. This provides the whole of the margin within which profit can rise and fall, a margin which is determined by the difference between the value of the commodity and its cost price, between the total amount of labour and the quantity of paid labour which is contained in it.

The law that the capitalist *can sell* commodities *beneath their value at a profit* explains a number of phenomena of competition, and in particular it also explains the main phenomenon, namely the *formation of a general rate of profit*, which is only made possible by the fact that some commodities are sold *beneath* their value, and others *above* their value.

This last circumstance is important for two reasons: it explains phenomena of competition which would otherwise be incomprehensible, particularly to the economists, who confuse cost prices with values.

It can even be seen as a law that the industrial capitalist does not realise the whole of the surplus-value but rather leaves it to his brethren in commerce, etc., to realise a part of it. The distribution of profit among the different classes is connected with this law.

(Only one more remark needs to be made here: if commodities are sold, perhaps for reasons of competition, etc., above their cost prices but significantly beneath their value – or if commodities are in general sold *beneath* their value – this does not change in any way the quantity of surplus labour which has been embodied in those commodities, or the quantity of surplus-value they contain. But in that case a part of this surplus-value is not then realised by the capitalist who has extracted it {even when he has pocketed all of it he has to share it in part with pensioners, bankers, etc}. A part of the surplus labour {hence of the labour in general} which is objectified in the commodity is unpaid. The benefit devolves upon the buyers of the commodity; the worker himself may turn out to be one of those buyers.)

The *excess* of the price (of the value) of the commodities over their *cost price* – measured against the *total capital advanced or applied* to produce them (= the part of the capital *consumed* in their production + the part of the fixed capital which has not been consumed) forms the *rate of profit*. This is the form which appears as s/(c + v) or s/C. With this, the surplus-value itself acquires the transformed form of *profit*. Surplus-value, as |35| an *excess* over the *cost price* (= the price of the total amount of constant and variable capital consumed in production) appears as an excess over a certain sum of money: in this form the essential difference between constant and variable capital, and thereby the conceptual relation between surplus-value and variable capital, is extinguished and wiped out. As parts of a *single* sum of money – the cost – they differ only quantitatively. Qualitatively they are the same. In the *rate of profit* the excess is also calculated in relation to the undifferentiated total value of the capital, and in the money expression of this total value all parts of the capital are themselves only sums of money of an identical kind. If for example the surplus-value of a capital of £1,000 is 200, this is represented in a sale price of the commodities of £1,200 which is an excess of 200 over the cost price of 1000. These £200 would then = 20 percent. But if perhaps there exists apart from the depreciation of the constant capital contained in the £1,000 a sum of £1,000 of constant capital which has, it is true, been employed, but remains unconsumed, hence is *fixed* capital, the excess is calculated on 2,000 and the rate of profit is only 10 percent.

We have seen that this rate, whether of 20 percent or of 10 percent, is smaller than the rate of surplus-value, or at least that its magnitude is numerically *different*. In actual fact we proceed in and from this *rate of profit*, and not from the rate of surplus-value. (In our investigations into the rate of profit we have left out of consideration the unconsumed part of the fixed capital. This should be mentioned right at the outset, so as to make the difference between s′ and p′ yet more striking, but for the rest it needs to be set = 0 for the first investigations in order not to complicate matters. This can be achieved more easily if, for instance, it is supposed that the whole fixed capital is used up in one year, the time for which the rate of profit is calculated.) Although the inner ground, hence the secret, hidden first principle of the rate of surplus-value, can only be discovered by analysis, absolutely no specific relation between surplus-value (or the excess of price over the cost price) and any particular constituent of the capital advanced can be perceived. It appears as the fruit of the whole of the capital. The surplus-value presents itself to us as something that springs forth equally from all parts of the capital. 'The capitalist', says Mr. Malthus, 'expects an equal profit on all parts of his capital'. In fact, in the above example, where there is £1,000 of unconsumed fixed capital + 800 of consumed constant capital (raw material, ancillary material and depreciation of the machinery), + 200 [variable capital], hence (1,000 + 800 + 200) + 200 surplus-value, a surplus-value of 100 percent appears as a profit of 10 percent, which derives equally from the fixed capital employed, the raw material and the labour bought with the 200. The only difference, which is still somewhat visible, is that between fixed and circulating capital, not between constant and variable capital, and indeed the first difference appears because the circulating capital enters entirely into the cost price of the commodities, |36| whereas only the depreciation, wear and tear of the fixed capital enters into this cost price, although the whole of the fixed capital forms part of the total value of the capital advanced, on which the rate of profit is calculated. This difference between the portion of the capital which enters entirely into the cost price and the other portion, which only enters in part into the cost price but enters in its entirety into the calculation of the rate of profit, necessarily fixes attention on the difference between fixed and circulating capital, and indeed in such a way that this difference has a vital effect on the calculation and determination of the profit or the surplus.

As a result, however, the variable capital disappears into the circulating capital and confronts *fixed capital*, or the fixed constituent of capital, under this category, *together* with raw materials and ancillary materials, and is *identified* with the latter. The contrast between fixed capital and the circulating capital which consists of raw materials etc., as *constant* capital, on the one hand, and the capital laid out in labour as variable capital is thereby *extinguished*. These differences between capitals, which arise purely and simply from circulation, conceal the organic difference, the relation of variable and constant capital, and thereby hide the *secret of surplus-value*.

Let us take up the aforementioned example once again. We have 1,000 (unconsumed fixed capital) + 800 constant + 200 variable capital (cost price). We have 200 surplus-value, that is to say the amount by which 1,200 exceeds 1,000. Every part of this capital has an equal yield of 10 percent. Of the excess of 200 only £20, or 10 percent, falls to the lot of the £200 of variable capital, because 2,000: 200 = 200: 20. Since the variable capital of 200 only yields 20, or 10 percent profit, just as the 400 raw materials, etc., yield 40, the organic connection between the surplus-value and the variable capital is obliterated and the *excess* of 200 has lost its character of being surplus-value. It has become just as mysterious as the 40 profit yielded by the £400 of raw materials and the 100 profit yielded by the buildings, the machinery, etc.

If the rate of surplus-value is expressed in the *rate of profit* as a numerical quantity of a very different magnitude, in *profit* – and the surplus-value is abstracted as profit from the rate of profit – the *form of surplus-value* (although not its absolute magnitude) is transformed and its conceptual determinateness [*Bestimmtheit*] is extinguished; it is given a form in which its original source is extinguished and thus the whole relation is *mystified* and *externalised* [*veräusserlicht*].

We have seen that the particular forms of capital (fixed and circulating) which arise from the circulation process submerge, as it were, the organic differences between constant and variable capital, and, along with these, the nature of surplus-value. The way the immediate production process is entwined with the circulation process – and the transformation of surplus-value into profit proceeds from the concrete unity of both processes – also contributes in many respects (apart from the point just mentioned) to mystify the surplus-value which has been transformed into profit. Surplus-value, as *profit*, is from the outset determined as the self-valorisation yielded by the total capital in the course of a specific period of circulation, e.g., a year.

|37| < Even though the excess of the value of the commodity *over* its cost price arises in the immediate production process, it is only in the circulation process that it is realised, and it takes on the appearance [*Schein*] of deriving *out of* the circulation process the more easily in that in the world as it actually is (the

world of competition, on the actual market), it depends on market conditions whether or not this excess is realised and to what extent. It needs no further elaboration here that, if a commodity is sold above or below its value, there is simply a different distribution of the surplus-value. This different distribution, the different ratio in which various individuals divide up the surplus-value, in no way affects either the magnitude or the character of the surplus-value. Not only is the actual circulation process the scene of the transformations we considered in the second book,[14] the latter also coincide with actual competition, the purchase and sale of the commodities above or below their value, so that, for the individual capitalist, the surplus-value that he himself realises depends just as much on this mutual cheating as on the direct exploitation of labour.

In the circulation process, labour-time is restricted by the circulation time, which has an impact on the amount of surplus-value that is realised in a specific period. Other aspects > which do not belong to the immediate production process < also intervene with decisive effect. Both processes (the immediate production process and the circulation process) constantly run into one other and intertwine, and in this way their distinguishing features are continuously blurred. In the circulation process, as we have already shown, the production of surplus-value, and of value in general, assumes new characteristics. Capital passes through transformations. Finally it steps, as it were, from its inner organic life into its external relations where it is not capital and labour that confront each other, but on the one hand capital and capital, and on the other hand individuals as simple buyers and sellers once again. Circulation time and labour-time cut across each other's paths, and both appear to determine surplus-value in the same way. The original form in which capital and labour confront each other is disguised and relations apparently independent of this come into the picture; surplus-value itself does not appear as having been produced by the appropriation of labour-time, but as the excess of the sale price of the commodities over their *cost price*, which readily presents itself as their proper *intrinsic* value, with the result that profit appears as an excess of the *sale price of the commodities over their immanent value*.

It is true that the nature of surplus-value persistently impresses itself on the capitalist's consciousness in the course of the immediate production process, as we were shown by his greed for other people's labour-time, etc., when we were considering surplus-value as such. However: (2)[15] Under the heading of

---

14 [Volume II of *Capital*, as later published by Engels. Translator]

15 [This is the order of points 1 and 2 in Marx's manuscript. It is reversed in the published version. Translator]

costs, which include not only wages but the price of raw material, the depreciation of the machinery, etc., the extortion of unpaid labour (surplus labour) appears simply as an *economy* in the payment for one of the articles that comprise these costs; simply as a lesser payment for a certain quantity of labour, an economy similar to that made when raw material is bought more cheaply or the wear and tear of machinery is reduced. The extortion of *surplus labour* then loses *its specific* character (its specific relation to surplus-value), a process which, as we showed in Volume I, Chapter 4,[16] is greatly furthered and facilitated by the representation of *the value of labour-capacity* [*Arbeitsvermögen*][17] in the form of *wages*. On the other hand: (1) The immediate process of production is itself simply an evanescent moment, which is constantly passing over into the process of circulation, and vice versa, so that any inkling of the nature of surplus-value (of the profit made in it) which dawns more or less clearly on the capitalist in the production process, appears at most as an equally valid moment alongside the movement that is independent of the production process and derives from the sphere of circulation, a movement that capital possesses independently of its relation to labour. These phenomena of circulation are even adduced by modern economists (such as Ramsay, |38| Malthus, Senior, Torrens, etc.) as direct proofs that capital in its material existence, independently of the social relation in which it is capital, is an autonomous source of surplus-value *alongside* labour and *independently* of labour.

Since all sections of capital appear equally as sources of the *excess value* (the profit), the capital relation is mystified.

Yet the way in which surplus-value is transformed into the form of profit by way of the rate of profit is only a further extension of that inversion of subject and object which already occurs during the production process. We saw in that case how all the > social < productive forces of labour present themselves as productive forces of capital. On the one hand value, i.e., the past labour that dominates living labour, is personified in the capitalist; on the other hand the worker conversely appears as mere objectified labour-capacity, a commodity. This inverted relationship necessarily gives rise, even in the actual production process, to a correspondingly inverted conception [*Vorstellung*] of the situation, a transposed consciousness, which is further developed by the transformations and modifications of the circulation process proper.

16 [In the later editions of Volume I of *Capital* this passage is located in Chapter Nineteen. Translator]

17 [Engels replaced *Arbeitsvermögen* with *Arbeitskraft* [labour-power] wherever the word occurred. Translator]

As can be studied with the Ricardians, etc., it is completely wrong-headed to seek directly to present the laws of the rate of profit as laws of the rate of surplus-value, or vice versa. In the mind of the capitalist, of course, these things are not distinguished.

In the expression s/C, or p' >

> (which is very much externalised [*veräusserlicht*] by the fact that s appears as the *excess of the sale price of the commodity* {which is realised in circulation and appears to derive from circulation} *over the cost price of the commodity*, a price in which the organic difference between its various constituents vanishes, so that the surplus-value appears to come just as much from circulation as it does from production, and perhaps more so; and to the extent that it derives from the latter, no specific relationship can be perceived between it and a particular portion of the capital, namely the variable capital)[18]

< surplus-value is measured against the *value* of the total capital advanced for its production, of which one part is completely consumed in this production, while another part is only *employed*. In fact, the ratio s/C expresses the *degree of valorisation* of the whole of the capital advanced; i.e., it is viewed in accordance with the conceptual, inner connection and the nature of surplus-value: it shows how the degree of variation in the variable capital is related to the magnitude of the total capital advanced.

In itself, the *magnitude of the value* of the total capital stands in no inner relationship with the amount of surplus-value, at least not directly. As far as its material elements are concerned, the total capital minus the variable capital, i.e., the constant capital, consists of the material conditions for the realisation of labour: the material of labour and the means of labour. In order that a definite quantity of labour may be realised in commodities, and therefore also form value, a definite quantity of the material and means of labour is required. In order to add a definite quantity of living labour a definite quantity of the means of production is required. There is a definite *technological* [*technologisch*] *proportion* between the amount of the means of production and the amount of labour required to add a definite quantity of living labour, a proportion that depends on the particular character of the labour added. There is also therefore a definite proportion between the amount of surplus-value or surplus labour

---

18 [Marx separated this passage from the running text with large bold parentheses. Translator]

and the mass of means of production. If for example 6 hours of labour a day are *necessary* for the production of the worker's wage, the worker has to work for 12 hours in order to realise 6 hours of surplus labour and create a surplus-value of 100 percent. In 12 hours he consumes or utilises twice as much |39| in the way of means of production as he does in 6 hours. But this does not mean that the surplus-value he adds in 6 hours stands in any direct relationship to the value of the means of production he consumes, uses, in these 6 or 12 hours. He delivers, for example, a definite quantity of the product in one hour, in 12 hours he delivers 12 times this quantity and in the product of the 12 hours 12 times as much of the means of production are consumed as in the product of one hour. But the *value* of these means of production is completely immaterial here; what matters is the amount technologically necessary. Whether the raw material or the instrument of labour is cheap or dear is a matter of complete indifference, as long as it possesses the use-value required and is present in the technologically prescribed proportion for the living labour it has to absorb. But if I know that x lb. of cotton – the amount that is spun in an hour – costs y shillings, I naturally also know that 12x lbs. of cotton = 12y shillings, and I can then calculate the ratio of the surplus-value to the value spun in 12 hours just as well as the ratio to the value spun in 6. But the relation of living labour to the *value* of the means of production comes into view here only in so far as y shillings serves as the name for x lb. of cotton; because a definite quantity of cotton has a definite price, and conversely, therefore a definite price can serve as an index for a definite quantity of cotton, as long as the price of cotton does not change. If I know that in order to appropriate 6 hours of surplus labour I have to have the workers perform 12 hours of labour, hence spin cotton for 12 hours, and I know the price of the quantity of cotton required for 12 hours of labour, there exists in this roundabout way a relationship between the *price of the cotton* (as an index of the quantity needed) and the surplus-value. But I can never argue conversely from the *price* of the raw material to the *quantity* of raw material that can be spun in one hour but cannot be spun in 6. There is thus no inner, necessary relationship between the *value of the constant capital* and the *surplus-value*, nor, therefore, between the value of the *total capital* (which = the value of the constant and the variable capital) and the *surplus-value*.

If the nature of the surplus-value, and its ratio to the variable capital, and also its magnitude, are known, the *rate of profit* expresses no more than what it in fact is, *an alternative measurement of surplus-value*, its measurement in terms of the value of the total capital, instead of the value of that part of capital from which it directly derives by way of its exchange for labour. In actuality, however (i.e., in the world of phenomena), things are the other way round. The surplus-value is given, but it is given as an *excess of the sale price of the commodity over its cost price*, whereby it remains a matter of mystery whence this excess emerges – from the exploitation of labour in the immediate production process, from fraud and deception in the circulation process, or from both. What is then given is the *ratio of this excess to the value of the total capital*, or the *rate of profit*. > What was first given was the absolute excess of the sale price of the commodity over its cost price, or C – K = S (the surplus-value), in other words the *excess*. The second step is then to calculate this excess of the sale price over the cost price, or to measure it against the value of the total capital advanced. < This calculation is very important and obvious, since this is the way in which we find a figure for the ratio in which the total capital has been valorised, or its *degree of valorisation*. > It will then be possible to establish the nature of the excess by working backwards from this rate of profit. Thus in the above example, if the excess = 200, the rate of profit = 10 percent and the part of the capital laid out in wages = 1/10 of the total capital, the part of the excess that belongs to the part of capital laid out in wages is 20, |40| the part for the raw material is 40, etc. < But if we start from the rate of profit, we can never establish any specific relationship between the excess and the part of capital laid out in wages, and we shall see in a later chapter the amusing capers cut by Malthus when he tries in this way to penetrate through to the secret of surplus-value and its specific relationship to the variable part of capital. What the rate of profit as such shows is rather a uniform relationship of the excess to equally important parts of the capital, which from this point of view displays absolutely no immanent distinctions apart from that between fixed and circulating capital. Even *this distinction* only arises because *the excess is calculated in two ways*: first as a *simple quantity: the excess over and above the cost price*. In this first form the circulating capital enters the cost price in full, while the fixed capital enters only to the extent of its depreciation. *Secondly: from the point of view of the relationship of this excess value over the cost price to the total value of the capital advanced*. In this calculation – or in this relationship – the value of the entire fixed capital enters as much as does the entire value of the circulating capital. In both measurements, therefore, the circulating capital enters the calculation in the same way each time, whereas the fixed capital is involved in the first case in a different way from the circulating capital, in the second case in the same way. Thus the distinction between circulating and fixed capital suggests itself here to us as the only one.

We might say, in Hegelian fashion, that the excess is reflected back into itself from the rate of profit, or, to speak differently, that the excess, which is characterised more specifically by the rate of profit, appears as an excess which capital produces over and above its own value, either annually or in some definite period of circulation.

Thus even if the rate of profit is *numerically* different from the rate of surplus-value, while surplus-value and profit are in fact the same and even *numerically* identical, profit is still for all that a *transformed form of surplus-value*, a form in which its origin and the secret of its existence are veiled and obliterated, > *externalised.* < In point of fact, the reverse is the case: profit is the form of appearance of surplus-value, and the latter can be sifted out from the former only by analysis. In surplus-value, the relationship between capital and labour is laid bare. In the relationship between capital and profit, i.e., between capital and surplus-value as it appears on the one hand as an excess over the cost price of the commodity realised in the circulation process and on the other hand as an excess determined more precisely by its relationship to the total capital, *capital appears as a relationship to itself*, a relationship in which it is distinguished, as an original sum of value, from another new value which it posits. It appears to consciousness as if capital creates this new value in the course of its movement through the production and circulation processes. But how this happens is now mystified, and appears to derive from occult qualities that are inherent in capital itself.

The further we trace out the realisation process [*Verwirklichungsprozess*] of capital, the more will the capital relationship be mystified and the less will the secrets of its internal organism lie open to view.

In the chapter we have just completed, the rate of profit is taken as numerically different from the rate of surplus-value; profit and surplus-value on the other hand are treated as *numerically identical magnitudes*, different only in form. In the next chapter we shall observe the further development of the process of externalisation by which *profit* presents itself as a magnitude *distinct* from surplus-value in a *numerical* respect as well. >

A characteristic distinction of form between profit and surplus-value takes place: the former is a *transformed* form of the latter, in which it can no longer be directly recognised.

|41| *Supplement to 6, which has just been quoted* (*from my notebook*)

<The general form of capital is M – C – M′; i.e., a sum of value is cast into circulation in order to draw out of it a greater sum of value. The process that creates this greater sum of value is capitalist production; the process that realises it is the circulation process of capital. The capitalist does not produce the commodity for its own sake, or for its use-value or his own personal consumption. The product with which the capitalist is in fact concerned is not the material product, but the *excess of value of the product over the value of the capital consumed in it.* The capitalist advances the total cap-

ital without regard to the qualitative differences in the role its components play in the production of surplus-value. He advances them all uniformly, not only in order to reproduce the capital advanced, but to produce an excess of value over and above it. He can only exploit labour, i.e., convert the value of the variable capital he advances into a higher value through the exchange with living labour, by simultaneously advancing the conditions for the realisation, for the reproduction, of this labour – raw material and machinery – by transforming a sum of value he has appropriated into this form of the conditions of production, just as he is in any case only a capitalist at all, can only undertake the process of exploiting labour, because as the owner of the conditions of production he confronts the worker as the mere owner of labour-capacity.

It is a matter of indifference to the capitalist whether he regards himself as advancing the constant capital in order to make a profit out of the variable capital, or advancing the variable capital in order to valorise the constant capital; whether he lays out money in the form of wages in order to give a higher value to his machines and raw material, or advances money in machinery and raw material in order to be able to exploit labour. Although only the variable part of the capital creates surplus-value, the condition for its creation is that the other parts of the capital, labour's conditions of production, are advanced as well. Since the capitalist can exploit labour only by advancing constant capital, and since he can valorise the constant capital only by advancing variable capital, both of them coincide in his mind, the more so in that the actual level of his profit is determined not by the ratio of the surplus-value to the variable capital but by its ratio to the total capital; not by the rate of surplus-value, but by the rate of profit, which, as mentioned previously, can remain *the same* and nevertheless express *different rates of surplus-value*.

The cost of the product includes all the constituents of its value which the capitalist has *paid for*, or for which he on his part has cast *equivalents* into production. These costs must be replaced in order that the capital may be maintained or reproduced in its original magnitude.

The value contained in the commodity is equal to the labour-time it has cost to produce it, and in its total amount it consists of paid and unpaid labour. The costs of the commodity for the capitalist consist in contrast only of the portion of the objectified labour he has paid for. The surplus labour contained in the commodity costs the capitalist nothing, although it costs the worker his labour just as much as paid labour does, and although it creates value, or enters into the commodity as a value-constituting element, just as much as paid labour does. The profit of the capitalist derives from the fact that *he has something to sell which he hasn't paid for*. This profit consists precisely in the excess of the value of the commodity over its cost price, i.e., in the excess of the total amount of labour contained in the commodity over the quantity of paid labour contained in it. >

∴

[The Relationship between the Rate of Profit and the Rate of Surplus-Value][19] |42| For 1) and 2). Conclusion to the note.

[THE FOLLOWING LONG NOTE BY MARX HAS BEEN TRANSPOSED INTO THE MAIN TEXT FOR EASE OF REFERENCE.]

Since the rates of surplus-value are the same, the amounts of surplus-value can only be the same if the variable capitals are the same. In that case the difference can only arise out of a difference in the magnitude of the constant capital.

1) 400c + 100v + 100s. s′ = 100%, p′ = 20%.
2) 300c + 100v + 100s. s′ = 100%, p′ = 25%.
3) 500c + 100v + 100s. s′ = 100%, p′ = 16 ⅔%.

$\frac{100}{500}, \frac{100}{400}, \frac{100}{600} = \frac{1}{5}, \frac{1}{4}, \frac{1}{6}$

The *rates of profit are inversely proportionate to the magnitudes of the total capitals advanced.*

100/500: 100/400 = 400: 500. (100/500 × 500 = 100 and 100/400 × 400 = 100.)

If the rate of surplus-value is the same, the amount of surplus-value depends on the magnitude of the variable capital advanced; if we call the amounts of surplus-value in examples one, two, and three (100s, 200s, and 50s) s^1, s^2, s^3, and the amounts of variable capital (100, 200, 50), similarly v^1, v^2, v^3, then $s^1 : s^2 : s^3 = v^1 : v^2 : v^3$.

But since the rate of profit p′ = s/C = s/(c + v), in every situation where the total capital advanced = C^1, C^2, C^3, p′ in equation 1) = s^1/C^1, in equation 2) = s^2/C^2, and in equation 3) = s3/C^3. Therefore if $C^1 = C^2 = C^3$, the rates of profit in equations 1, 2 and 3 are $s^1/C: s^2/C: s^3/C$.

But $s^1/C: s^2/C: s^3/C = s^1: s^2: s^3$ (e.g., $s^1/C: s^2/C = \frac{s^1/C}{s^2/C} = s^1/C \times C/s^2 = s^1/s^2$). And $s^1: s^2: s^3 = v^1: v^2: v^3$; therefore $s^1/C: s^2/C: s^3/C = v^1: v^2: v^3$, *or the rates of profit are related*

19 [Title added by the MEGA editors. Translator]

to each other as the magnitudes of the variable components of capital. In this case, the rates of profit are related to each other as the respective surplus-values are. This is not the case, however, if the total capitals C^1, C^2, C^3 are of *unequal* magnitude.

Let us take three further examples:

1) 400c + 100v + 100s; s′ = 100%; p′ = 20%
2) 400c + 50v + 50s; s′ = 100%; p′ = 11⅑%
3) 500c + 100v + 100s; s′ = 100%; p′ = 16⅔%.

The variable capitals v^1 and v^3 are equal here, and so is the rate of surplus-value, but p′ for 1) = 20%, and p′ for 3) = 16⅔%. Moreover, v^2 = half of v^1 and also half of v^3; the rate of surplus-value remains the same, but p′ for 2) = 11⅑%, which is greater than half of p′ for 1) and still greater than half of p′ for 3).

The total capitals C^1, C^2, and C^3 are related as 500: 450: 600 = 50: 45: 60 = 10: 9: 12.

Let us take the case where the *rate of surplus-value* is equal in different capital investments of equal magnitude, but the *magnitude of the variable capital is not equal*:

1) 400c + 100v + 100s
2) 300c + 200v + 200s
3) 450c + 50v + 50s.

In all three cases, s′ = 100%.

Let us however assume that 1) 400c + 100v + 100s changes into 3) 450c + 50v + 50s. s′ = 100%; p′ = 50/450 = 5/45 = 1/9 = 11⅑%. 50: 450 = x: 500; x = (500×5)/45 = 55⁵⁄₉.

p′/s′ = v/(c + v).
1) If c = 0, v/(c + v) = v/v = 1. Hence p′/s′ = 1. Hence p′ = s′.
2) If c = v, v/(c + v) = v/2v = 1/2. Hence p′/s′ = 1/2. Hence p′ = 1/2 s′.
3) If c > v, c = v + δ. Hence v/(c + v) = v/(δ + v + v) = v/(δ + 2v); v/(δ + 2v) < v/2v. Hence p′/s′ < 1/2; hence p′ < 1/2s′.
4) If c < v, c = v − δ. Hence v/(c + v) = v/(v − δ + v) = v/(2v − δ); v/ 2v − δ) > v/2v > 1/2. Therefore p′/s′ > 1/2; hence p′ > 1/2s′.

Since the rate of profit, p′ = s/(c + v) and the rate of surplus-value, s′ = s/v, it follows that $s' - p' = s/v - s/(c+v) = \frac{s(c+v) - sv}{v(c+v)} = \frac{sc + sv - sv}{v(c+v)} = \frac{sc}{v\,(c+v)} = c/v \times s/(c+v)$

= c/v × p′. Or: s′ – p′ = p′; therefore s′ = p′ + p′; s′ = 2p′; p′ = s′/2; p′ = 1/2s′. Hence s′ – p′ = c/v × p′.

1) Hence if c = v, s′ – p′ = 1 × p′ = p′. *Or if constant capital = variable capital the difference between the rate of surplus-value and the rate of profit = the rate of profit.* Take, for example, 250c + 250v + 250s. s′ = 100%, p′ = 50%. The difference = 50% = p′. s′ – p′ = 250/250 × 50%. If however we have 250c + 250v + 125s, s′ = 50% and p′ = 25%. The difference = p′. s′ – p′ = 250/250 × 25% = 25%.

2) If, in the fraction c/v, c is greater than v, c/v is an improper fraction. *c/v × p′ is therefore > p′.* Hence *if constant capital > variable capital, the difference between the rate of surplus-value and the rate of profit is greater than the rate of profit.*

s′ – p′ > p′. Therefore s′ > 2p′; therefore p′ < s′/2. Take, for example, 400c + 100v + 100s. s′ = 100%, p′ = 20%. s′ – p′ = 80% which is greater than p′ (= 20%).

3) Finally, if, in the fraction c/v, v is greater than c, c/v is a proper fraction, *hence c/v × p′ < p′. Therefore if variable capital > constant capital, the difference between the rate of surplus-value and the rate of profit is smaller than the rate of profit.*

Take, for example, 100c + 400v + 400s. s′ = 100%. p′ = 400/500 = 4/5 = 80%. s′ – p′ = 20% which is less than p′. s′ – p′ = 100/400 × 80% = 1/4 × 80% = 20%. *Finally: s′– p′ < p′; therefore s′ < 2p′; therefore p′ > s′/2.*

4) If c = 0, c/v = 0/v = 0; hence c/v × p′ = 0 × p′ = 0. Therefore s′ – p′ = 0; therefore s′ = p′. (As previously, when s/(0 + v) = s/v.)

p′/s′ = v/(c + v). 1) If c = 0, v/(c + v) = v/ (0 + v) = v/v = 1/1. Hence p′/s′ = 1/1 or p′ = s′.

2) p′ × (c + v) = vs′. Take, for example, 400c + 100v + 100s. p′ = 20%. s′ = 100%, 100/100 × 100 = 20/100 × 500. 100 = 100.

∴

This formula, p′/s′ = v/(c + v) expresses only the relative magnitudes of the rates of profit and surplus-value. It is possible for the ratio of the rate of profit to the rate of surplus-value to rise or fall in the opposite direction to the magnitude of the rate of profit and the rate of surplus-value.

I) First example: 400c + 100v + 100s. s′ = 100%. p′ = 20%. p′: s′ = 100v: 500C = 20: 100.

II) Second example: 400c + 150v + 50s. 50/550 = 1/11. s′ = 33⅓%, p′ = 9 1/11%. p′: s′ = *150v: 550C = 15: 55 = 3: 11* and 9 1/11: 33⅓ = 3: 11 (3 × 33⅓ = 11 × 9 1/11)

∴

In this example no. II, the amount of labour-power [*Arbeitskraft*] applied and the time during which it is applied remain the same. The increase in variable capital from 100 to 150 simply expresses a rise in the price of labour-power. The surplus-value falls by the same amount, namely by 50. The rate of surplus-value therefore falls from 100% (in example I) to $33\frac{1}{3}$% (in example II) and the rate of profit falls from 20% to $9\frac{1}{11}$%. But the ratio between the rate of profit and the rate of surplus-value increases: $s' = 33\frac{1}{3}\%$, $p' = 9\frac{1}{11}\%$. $p' : s' = 9\frac{1}{11} : 33\frac{1}{3}$, $150 : 550 = 15 : 55 = 3 : 11$. $9\frac{1}{11} : 33\frac{1}{3} = 3 : 11$. $p' = 150/550 = 15/55 = 3/11 = 27\frac{3}{11}\%$, $s' = 100\%$.

Example III: 400c + 150v + 150s.

∴

[END OF THE NOTE]

[THE TEXT NOW CONTINUES]

1) $p' = s/C$. It follows from this under *all* circumstances that if C remains unchanged, p′ will increase or decline directly as s does, and vice versa, for the magnitude of every fraction rises and falls in direct proportion to the numerator and in inverse proportion to the denominator.

2) The expression $p' = s/C$ is however the same as $p' = s' \times v/C$ and therefore: $p' : s' = v : C$. Or, in words, the rate of profit is related to the rate of surplus-value as the variable part of the capital is related to the total capital. This proposition is in general self-evident. If the rate of surplus-value = 50%, it would be ½ v. But if $v = \frac{1}{5}$ C, it is $\frac{1}{10}$ C; if $v = \frac{1}{3}$ C, it would be $\frac{1}{6}$ C; if $v = \frac{1}{10}$ C, it would be $\frac{1}{20}$ C. In the first case $v/C = 1/5$ and $p'/s' = 10/50 = 1 : 5$, in the second case $16\frac{2}{3}$% or 1/6, and in the third case 5%, or 1/20. (See also the examples given previously.)

There is nevertheless an apparent exception to these laws.

The maximum level of p′ occurs when $p' = s'$, and this is the case when $v = c$ and therefore v also = C, hence $s/v = s/C$ or $s/(v + c) = s/(v + o) = s/v$. Hence $p'/s' = v/C$; as the proportional magnitude of $v : C$ varies, so does the proportional magnitude of p'/m' and therefore p′ is larger, since it increases in magnitude the closer it approaches s′. (This must admittedly be compared with what was said earlier about difference.)

If s′ is constant, the more p′ approaches s′, the greater it becomes, and the more it diverges from s′ the less it becomes.

Hence it becomes greater, the greater v is in comparison with C, and it becomes smaller, the smaller v is in comparison with C.

It is however possible that v may rise because s′ declines and v may increase because s′ falls.

For example, assume that 100 workers are employed, each of them receiving 24s. a week = £1. 4s. Multiplying by 100 (£100 + 400s.) = (£100 + £20) = £120. And the [rate of] surplus-value would be 100%, so that the worker's total product would be 48 shillings and the total product of the 100 would be £240.

Assume now that such a cheapening of provisions takes place that necessary labour falls by ⅙. 24 shillings a week makes a daily wage of 4 shillings and a total value of 48 shillings a week, because each individual makes 8 shillings a day. Multiplied by 100 that gives 800 shillings = £40. ⅙ of 4 shillings makes 4/6 a day and $\frac{4 \times 6}{6}$ or 4 shillings a week. Multiplied by 100 that gives 400 shillings = £20.

Assume that these people continue to work 12 hours a day as before and that no change has taken place in the raw material or the machinery in their sphere of production. (The cheaper provisions might come from abroad, for example.) The variable capital then falls from £120 a week to 100 and the surplus-value rises from 100 to 110. The rate of surplus-value equally rises from 100% |43| to 110%. According to Law 1, p′ must have grown, since in the equation p′ = s/C there has been an increase in s, and C has remained the same (the people continue to work six 12-hour days under the same conditions of production). On the other hand, since, according to Law 2, p′/s′ = v/C, and since v has fallen from 120 to 100, while C has remained unchanged, v has fallen both absolutely and in relation to C. Hence p′ must have declined.

Let us, inversely, posit the case in which the provisions the workers consume (or some of their most important provisions) rise in price because it becomes increasingly difficult to produce them, and as a result the workers have to work ⅙ of a day more, for 7 hours instead of 6, in order to reproduce their labour-capacity. In this case the daily wage rises from 4 to 4 4/6 shillings and over a week to 24 + 4/6 × 6 shillings, or to 28 shillings. The surplus-value per individual would fall from 6 to 5 hours or from 24 to 20 shillings. The weekly wage for 100 workers would be £100 + 800 shillings = £140. Hence variable capital now = £140 instead of £120. And the surplus-value is 100 instead of 120. The surplus-value has fallen by £20, the rate of surplus-value from 100% to 71 3/7%. Here v has grown from 120 to 140 and s′ has declined from 100 to 71 3/7%, while s has fallen by 20. According to Law 1, therefore, since s has fallen, and C has remained constant, p′ must have fallen; but according to Law 2, since p′/s′ = v/C, and v has risen in proportion to C, p′ must have risen. So this is the problem. And whatever the solution, it is clear that the law by which p′/s′ = v/C is either false or requires modification in certain circumstances.

In the first case, the surplus-value grows because the number of workers remains the same and the *rate of surplus-value* increases; in the second case, [it declines] because the *rate of surplus-value* declines and the number of workers remains the same. Both cases result from a change in the *rate of surplus-value* while C remains the same.

But this is wrong. C does not remain the same, because v is one of its elements. Only c has remained the same. In the first case, because the variable capital declines, C similarly declines, or v/(v + c); v + c declines because v declines. In the second case, C grows because v grows, or v/(v + c) grows[20] because v grows.

Assume that the constant capital = £480. Then we have the following starting-point:

c	v	s	s′	p′
480	120	120	100	20
480	100	140	140	24⁴⁄₂₉
480	140	100	71¹⁄₇	16⁴⁄₃₁

(In any case, this is an example of constant capital remaining constant while variable capital and surplus-value undergo change. But the magnitude of the total capital changes along with the variable capital.)

The law that the rate of profit rises and declines in direct proportion to v/C, if there are no countervailing circumstances, implies that a certain portion of v, 100 for example, is the purchase price of a *certain number of working* capacities [*Arbeitsvermögen*], or the wage for a certain number of workers, so that if 100 is the wage for 100 workers, 200 is the wage for twice as many, etc. Since s = s′v, and with s′ remaining constant, s′v or s will rise and fall in direct proportion to v, which expresses the number of workers employed and is therefore the *index* for the total amount of labour set in motion by the capital, C. Let s′ = 100%, for example. Then the worker works half the labour-time for himself and half for the capitalist, *gratis*. If a worker's weekly wage is = £1, £100 represents the weekly wage of 100 workers. And if £1 is the expression in money of half a week

20 [The expression '(v + c)' appears at this point. It has been removed as it renders the passage nonsensical. Translator]

of objectified labour, £2 is the total amount in which the worker's working week is objectified. £100 is therefore the index of a mass of labour of 100 complete working weeks, objectified in £200; £200 is the index of a total amount of labour of twice as much, the working weeks of 200 workers, objectified in £400, etc.

If the working day is not given, one cannot conclude from the rate how long it is and how large therefore the surplus-value is. Take for example ⅓. If the necessary labour-time is three hours, and the surplus-value is one hour, then the rate is ⅓, and if the necessary labour-time is 6 and the working day is 18, then a rate of 6/18 = 1/3; but in the first case the surplus-value = the expression in money of one hour, and in the second case = the expression in money of 12 hours. In order to know the *magnitude of the surplus-value* the length of the working day must be known as well as the rate of surplus-value. But if the variable capital is given, e.g., £450, and if I know that £450 = the wage (e.g., the weekly wage) of 450 workers and I also know how much average labour is represented by £1, its expression in money, e.g., 6 hours a day,[21] then I know that s′ = 50%, that the complete day = 12 hours and that £450 sets in motion the labour of 450 12-hour working weeks.

< This shows precisely the special organic relation of the variable capital to the movement of the capital as a whole and its valorisation, as well as |44| its distinction from the constant capital. The latter, to the extent that the creation of value comes into consideration, is only important on account of the value that it has. It is quite immaterial here, as far as the creation of value is concerned, whether a constant capital of £1500 is 1500 because it represents 1500 tons of iron at £1 a ton, or 500 tons at £3 a ton. The quantity of actual material in which its exchange value is represented is completely unimportant from the point of view of the formation of value and its influence on the rate of profit. The rate of profit is inversely related to it, whatever relationship the increase or decrease in the exchange-value of the constant capital has to the material elements, the use-values, which it represents.

The situation is completely different in the case of v. What is important is not the value which it has, the labour which is objectified in it, but this value as an *index* of the total labour which it sets in motion, and which is not expressed in it. The difference between this total labour and the labour expressed and therefore paid for in the variable capital, i.e., the part that creates surplus-value, grows greater in proportion as the labour contained in the variable capital grows smaller. > Let a working day of 12 hours = £1. If the necessary labour =

21 [The words 'in 4' have been omitted here. Translator]

10 shillings, then the surplus labour = 10; if the former = 8 then the latter = 12, if the former = 14, the latter = only 6, and so on.

If then the magnitude of value of the variable capital ceases to be an index of the mass of labour that it sets in motion, and the standard of measurement of this index itself alters, the law that the rate of profit increases or declines in direct proportion to changes in the proportion of the variable capital to the total capital no longer operates.

It is assumed, as always in our investigation, that the value of money does not alter, and that therefore a specific quantity of labour-time or a specific quantity of labour continues to be materialised [*materialisiert*] in a specific quantity of money. If previously 100 workers were paid every week with £100 and now for example only 80 workers are paid; if, furthermore, the working day remains the same, £100 would now set in motion the labour, paid and unpaid, of 80 workers, two-tenths less than previously, and since the expression in money of the whole of a worker's labour (given the length of the working day) remains the same, the product of one worker continues to = £2, and the product of the 80 workers = £160. Hence the surplus-value only amounts to £60, precisely because the value of the variable capital, or the value of the necessary workers, has increased. If £100 of surplus-value is to be produced according to this measurement, 100 workers must be paid, and since one worker now costs 100/80 = 10/8 = £1¼, 100 would cost (100 + 100/4) = £125. But the 100 workers would only produce £200, hence only £75 of surplus-value. 60: 100 = 100: x, thus £166⅔ must be laid out in order to produce a surplus-value of £100. A worker receives 25 shillings and produces 40. The ratio of his unpaid to his paid labour = ⅗ or 60%. Previously it was 100%.

(If, in contrast to this, the working day was previously 10 hours, hence ½ a day was 5 hours, and it now becomes 12 hours long, the ratio would be different, as previously developed in Volume I, Chapter IV.[22] Then an increase in variable capital would also indicate a larger *total quantity of labour*, although it would not perhaps grow in the same ratio as the variable capital; it might grow in a yet larger ratio. The result would be in accordance with these proportions.)

|45| The value of labour-capacity, or the average wage, is paid on the basis of the foregoing assumptions.

Thus for the *same number of workers* to cost more variable capital (presupposing that *the working day remains the same* and that no extra hours are worked) the prices of the necessary food supplies must increase or the pro-

22 [See Chapter 19 of later editions of Volume I of *Capital.* Translator]

ductivity of labour must have fallen in the branches that produce them. The converse is true when a smaller amount of variable capital sets the same number of workers in motion. In the former case there is a fall in *relative surplus-value*, and in the latter case it rises; in the former case the necessary labour-time grows longer, in the latter case it is shortened.

If the same *numerical* amount, e.g., £100, sets in motion a tenth smaller amount of labour than previously, and therefore costs £110 rather than the previous £100, the growth of the variable capital corresponds not to an increase but to a fall in the rate of profit; in the opposite case, if 100 expresses a tenth larger amount of labour set in motion than it did previously, the reduction from 100 to 90 (or relatively speaking, according to the number of workers employed) will correspond not to a fall but to an increase in the rate of profit.

But if the following are given: 1) *the rate of surplus-value;* 2) *the length of the working day;* and 3) *an unchanged value of money*, so that a specific amount of money is the expression of a *specific amount* of objectified labour-time, the general law holds, that p′: s′ = v/C and that the rate of profit produced by a capital under otherwise identical circumstances depends on the relative magnitude of the capital employed by it. If the rate of surplus-value and the working day are given, the *amount of surplus-value* depends on the magnitude of the variable capital, i.e., on the number of workers set in motion by it. But the rate of profit is determined by the ratio of the surplus-value to the capital as a whole. It is therefore determined just as much by the rate of surplus-value as by the number of workers exploited simultaneously by the same capital.

Let us take up our earlier example once again.

	c	v	s	s′	p′
I)	400	100	100	100	20
II)	400	80	120	150	25
III)	400	120	80	66⅔	15⁵⁄₁₃

Firstly: in case II) the rate of profit grows although the *value* of the variable capital declines in proportion to that of the constant capital, and in case III) the rate of profit declines although the value of the variable capital increases in proportion to that of the constant capital. This only apparently contradicts the law, because the *magnitude of value* of v does not express an increase in its function as variable capital but the reverse. This is the first thing to be noted.

Secondly: in case II) s′ grows by 50%, and s by 20%, but the rate of profit only grows by 20%; it grows as s does, but not as s′ does. The value of v falls by ⅕ or 20%. In case I v forms ⅕ of the total capital, in case II ⅙. Hence if the value of v were to remain the index of the same amount of labour that has been set in motion, with s′ remaining unchanged, s would = 80 and p′ would = 16⅔%. There would therefore have been a fall of 3⅓%, compared with case I, which is exactly the same as the fall in the proportion of variable capital, namely ⅙ (because 3⅓% is ⅙ of 20%).

We should therefore have to bring into the calculation a ⅙ fall in the rate of profit in line with the proportional reduction in v (in relation to C) of ⅙. On the other hand, s′ does not stay unchanged, but grows from 100% to 150%, hence by 50%. So we have on the one side an increase in the rate of surplus-value by 50%, or ½, and on the other a reduction in the rate of profit by ⅙.

If the ratio between v and C were the same in II as in I, i.e., if v = ⅕ C, instead of = ⅙ C, C would = 5 × 80 = 400 and c would = 400 − 80 = 320.

In the latter case, we should have $^{120}/_{400}$ = $^{12}/_{40}$ = $^{6}/_{20}$ = $^{3}/_{10}$ = 30%. But there is only 25%, and the difference between 30 and 24 = 6. However, six is ⅕ of 30, in other words the increase in the rate of profit which would have taken place in other circumstances is paralysed to an extent of 20% through the fact that the magnitude of the variable capital has fallen by ⅕. Whatever the reason for a fall in the *value of the variable capital*, the rate of profit falls to the extent that the constant capital (or indirectly C) grows in comparison with the variable capital.

On the other hand, this is cancelled out in the present case by the growth of the surplus-value resulting from the rise in its rate. If s′ had remained the same, s would = 80 and $^{8}/_{48}$ = ⅙ = 16⅔%. The increase in the rate of profit therefore does not correspond to the growth in the rate of surplus-value because the former is to a certain degree paralysed by the fall in the ratio between v/C and p = s′ × v/C. The one increases, the other declines. If the number of workers were now 20 instead of 80, we should get:

	c	v	s	s′	p′
II)	400	20	180	900	over 42%.

But here s′ rises to 900% while p′ has not yet doubled, on account of the relative increase in the value of c and hence in the value of C in relation to v.

The situation is inverted in *Case III:* v grows from 80 to 120, hence by ½ or 50%. Whereas in II the ratio is v/C = 80/480 = 1/6 or 16⅔%, and thus [the rate of profit becomes] $^{12}/_{52} = ^{6}/_{26} = ^{3}/_{13} = 23^{1}/_{13}$%. On the other hand, in II s falls from 120 to 80, or by ⅓ (since $^{120}/_{3} = 40$), and the rate of surplus-value falls from 150% to 66⅔%, a fall of 83⅓%.

For example III it would be better to use quantities which allow simpler percentage figures to be derived:

Let II be as follows:

c	v	s′	s	p′
400	100	100	100	20

And let III be:

400	160	25	40	$7^{1}/_{7}$

In II, therefore, v/C = $^{100}/_{500}$ = ⅕ = 20%, and in III it = $^{16}/_{56} = ^{8}/_{28} = ^{4}/_{14} = ^{2}/_{7} = 28^{6}/_{7}$%. The rate of surplus-value falls from 100 to 25, by ¾ or 75%, surplus-value falls by $^{6}/_{10}$. The fall in the rate of profit is not quite so large, because it is to a certain extent paralysed by the relative fall of c, if compared with v.

|46| Case 2 [the length of the working day] has now been fully examined. What has to be added is that in this case the rate of surplus-value changes and as a result there is a change in the *magnitude of the value* of the variable capital, while the *constant capital* remains the same, as does the mass of labour set in motion. The *total capital* does however undergo a change in magnitude as a result of the *increase or the reduction of the variable capital while the magnitude of the constant capital remains unchanged.* We assume here that not only the rate, but also the quantity, of surplus-value is changeable.

It has also to be added that the effect of a change in the magnitude of the *value* of the variable capital while the number of workers employed, and the *length of the working day*, remains the same, could be entirely or partially paralysed by a contrary motion on the part of the constant capital.

For example:

	c	v	s	s′	p′
I)	400	100	100	100	20
II)	520	80	120	150	20
III)	280	120	80	66⅔	20

Here p′ remains unchanged in I, II, and III, although in II the rate of surplus-value and the surplus-value grow as compared with I, and the *value of the constant capital* declines, while in III as compared with I and II the rate of surplus-value falls, the surplus-value falls and the *value of the constant* capital increases. These movements are however balanced out in II by the relative rise in the value of the constant capital and in III by the relative fall in the value of the constant capital.

One can see here how the movements cancel each other out, or, if not completely, as in the present case, at least to a certain extent, so that their impact remains restricted and is not measured by the degree to which one movement is greater than the other. In the present case, however, c is not constant. If it were constant, no mutual compensation of this kind would be possible.

|47| In looking at Case 3 we do not need to repeat all the rubbish in the long note, but only to 'fix' a number of points left undetermined and vague by investigating them from a new angle.

Since p′ = s/C and s/C = s′v/C or = s′ × v/C, it follows that p′ = s′ × v/C.

We previously proceeded by assuming that s′ was constant and v/C were variable, and then that v/C was constant and s′ was variable, and the corresponding changes in the magnitude of p′ were then derived under these presuppositions.

I: p′ = m′ × v/C. *If we take* s′ *as constant*, changes in v/C can be considered from two main aspects.

α) C is constant; β) C varies along with the variations in v, c, or v and c.

α) What had first to be investigated was this: with s′ constant, in other words a constant rate of surplus-value, what variations of v/C are permissible without removing this constancy of the rate of surplus-value (presupposing that C remains constant)?

In order to answer this question it is necessary first to look more closely at s′. The rate of surplus-value (s′) = s/v. A simple variation in v therefore does not remove the constancy of s′, if s varies in the same proportion as v does. If there is a doubling of v, or the variable capital, s must double as well, in other words ns/nv leaves unchanged the ratio s/v, or s′. Similarly $\frac{s/n}{v/n}$ = s/v = s′. Thus a variation in v does not necessarily cancel out the constancy of s′.

The question then has to be asked, whether a *unilateral* variation in v is possible without cancelling out the constancy of C. That is positively impossible. If v alone varies, c is constant. Hence v becomes v – δ, where δ represents any particular number or ratio. But since C = c + v, it becomes in one case C = c + (v + δ) and in the other case = c + (v – δ). In one case it increases, in the other case it declines.

Exactly the same thing applies to a unilateral variation in c, if v remains unchanged. C must grow smaller or larger as a result. For the rest, variations in c are in themselves irrelevant to s/v or s′, and we can never say *prima facie* how far they are possible. The size of c has nothing to do with s/v or s′, in other words the rate of surplus-value.

If the value of v or c changes, C can only remain constant when their respective values change in opposite directions, so that their overall sum = C remains the same, although the proportion in which C is divided between these different headings may change to any extent one may postulate.

A further question arises: this simultaneous and mutually compensatory change in opposing directions does not make it impossible for the capital to remain constant, but is it compatible with the presupposition that the surplus-value, or s/v, remains constant?

|48|	c	v	s	s′		p′
I)	400	100	50	50%	=	10%
II)	450	50	25	50%	=	5%
III)	300	200	100	50%	=	20%

Is this a possible schema? Let us assume that a change takes place in productive power, which enables 50 workers to produce not only what previously required 100 workers but also one-eighth more than this, in other words 12½%. Assume that this occurs in a branch of industry whose product does not form part of the workers' means of subsistence, hence has no influence on the value of variable capital or, and here this is the same thing, assume that this cheapening of the commodity does not have a direct impact on v, or has no impact at all, because this cheapening, if it enters into the worker's consumption, is paralysed by the rise in the cost of another article which enters into it to the same degree. All this is possible (entirely disregarding the practical situation in which the cheapening of the means of subsistence does not have a direct impact because the state of demand does not allow this.)

Thus II) is possible if, on the one hand, there is a reduction in the number of workers employed as a result of technological improvements, and with this a fall in the value of the variable capital as well, and on the other hand this reduced number sets in motion an amount of constant capital, c, which has risen to the extent of the reduction in value of the variable capital, v. In this case we have the following presuppositions: *a reduction in the number of workers* and in proportion to this a reduction in variable capital while the wage and the division of the working day into paid and unpaid labour remain the same. *An increase takes place in the value of the constant capital*, because given that the value of its components, of the raw material, etc., remains roughly the same, an amount of constant capital is set in motion by the smaller number of workers which is greater than the amount of capital released from the variable part by the dismissal of the other workers. In this case, *the growth in the amount of constant capital* indicates *an increase in its material elements*, given that the *value* of its components has not changed. This may be because more raw material, etc., has been used up, it may be because the newly introduced machinery, which makes it possible for 50 to produce as much as 100 did previously, is so much bigger that it adds 50 to the constant capital under the heading of depreciation, accessory materials, etc. In each case, the increase in the value of c is an *index* of its *material expansion*. This is a possible scenario.

Would it be possible to cheapen the means of subsistence to such an extent that the workers only needed to work half as much necessary labour-time, and therefore that the variable capital which previously amounted to 100 is now 50? The rate of surplus-value, or s′, could only remain unchanged if a proportional cheapening of the surplus labour corresponded to this reduction in necessary labour-time, hence the whole of the working day of the employed worker now came to 50 + 25 as opposed to previously 100 + 50, hence a relative shortening of the working day had taken place. Since it is assumed that *50* represents the same number of workers as previously, only the value of v has fallen, and not the number of workers it sets in motion, no technological change has therefore occurred, and it sets the same quantity of the means of production in motion as previously. However, because a constant capital of 400 must rise to 450, this is only possible if a rise in the price of the means of production or of part of them has taken place to the extent of 50 out of 400 or 12½%. This is |49| possible, although here, as under the previous assumption, the increase in the value of c in exactly the ratio in which v falls is a mere coincidence and conceptually a matter of complete indifference. (*To be sure*, all these hypotheses become essential and important as soon as these various ratios are calculated in percentages as ratios *between different capitals* which are either of equal magnitude, or, if unequal, belong to different spheres of production, and they therefore also need to be examined exhaustively.)

It is to be noted that on this assumption the change in the value of c does imply a *change in the quantity of its material elements. The quantity remains the same*, under unchanged technological conditions, hence there is *simply a change in the value of the mass of the means of production which have remained technologically constant.*

In both cases the surplus-value has fallen from 50 to 25. For the relation of the surplus-value to the total capital it is absolutely irrelevant whether the 400c has grown to 450c on account of a *material expansion* in its constituents with *prices remaining the same*, so that the greater value of c indicates the presence of more raw material, added machinery, etc., or whether c has remained unchanged technologically, hence also in the quantity of its material constituents, but its *value* has increased, so that the 450c refers to the same mass of constant capital as the 400c did previously.

As far as the variable capital is concerned, on the first assumption it falls from *100 to 50*, because the same number of people can now be bought with 50 as could previously be bought with 100, owing to a cheapening of the means of subsistence by a half, or, and this is the same thing, a reduction in the necessary labour-time by a half. If they now work the same number of hours as before, the *rate of surplus-value* would have to rise, which contradicts the above assumption. We therefore assume that they only work half as long as before, so that if the expression in money of their total working day was previously 150 it is now 75. In this case, therefore, just as much as in the other one, where it was assumed that the *number* of workers was reduced by a half, s only falls by a half, because v only sets in motion half as much labour as before: in the previous case 50 workers worked for perhaps 16 hours and in the present case 100 work for 8 hours. Although the *change in the value of* v takes place here for entirely different reasons, the function of v changes in the same manner. If it were assumed that the working day remained *constant*, it would be impossible for s′ to remain constant under the given conditions.

Is a third combination also possible, with c rising to 450, v falling to 50 and s′ remaining the same? It seems not. In both cases the surplus-value falls from 50 to 25, C remains constant, and the [rate of] profit therefore falls from 50/500 or 10% to 25/500 or 5%.

The most important results to come out of this investigation are the following two remarks:

Firstly: with an alteration in productive power, which either shortens or lengthens the labour-time necessary for the worker's maintenance, the amount of surplus-value, hence also s′ or s/v, can only remain constant if in the one case the surplus labour is reduced in the same proportion as the necessary labour, and in the other case it is increased in the same proportion, hence if in the one case the *working day* (the sum total of the necessary and surplus labour together) is shortened and in the other case is lengthened, in a specific manner, through these proportional variations.

Secondly: from the point of view of the ratio of the surplus-value to C it changes absolutely nothing whether variations in the value of c are the result of oscillations in the value of its constituent elements, or technological changes, or changes in the quantity of its material elements, their value remaining constant, in other words whether the change in value indicates a change in the technology or can be described as purely nominal. (Although this makes a great deal of difference to the *prices of the commodities* and although if a larger or smaller v given *a technological relation which remains constant* indicates *more or fewer workers*, corresponding to which c must increase or decline in quantity {hence also in *value*, other circumstances remaining the same}; similarly if the labour becomes more or less productive, so that in the same labour-time, or, as the case may be, with the same number of workers, work is conducted on a greater or smaller quantity of c. In this situation the change in c is organic, whereas if there is a change in the value [of c] thanks not to a change of the above kind but to a change in its own costs of production, it appears to that extent to be non-organic.)

|50| If we now make a comparison between II and III, or also between I and II in the schema indicated above, it seems necessary *prima facie* to concede in advance the abstract correctness of the schema, for if

		c	v	s	
a)	I)	400	100	50	can be distributed in this way
	II)	450	50	25	why cannot
b)	II)	450	50	25	a *movement in the opposite direction*
	I)	400	100	50	also be possible? Such an inverted movement would not differ in principle from:
c)	II)	450	50	25	
	III)	300	200	100.	

The whole distinction between the movements b) and c) is nothing more than an arbitrary numerical inversion.

Nevertheless, the matter is not quite as simple as it appears. Does the inverted movement involve a (technological) worsening in the conditions of production in one of the cases, which would also be associated with a fall in the amount of constant capital? Movement b) therefore (hence also c)) by no means results obviously from a).

< In agriculture and the extractive industries, where a decline in productivity and a consequent increase in the number of workers employed is easy to comprehend > under certain circumstances < this process – within the confines of *capitalist production* and on its basis – is linked not with a decline but with an increase in constant capital > and its value. In *different* countries or specific branches of agriculture which differ from others, < it would be by no means unusual if more workers, hence a bigger variable capital, were employed > and this greater mass of drudgery < worked with less expensive and less plentiful means of production > or indeed with more *constant capital* or the same amount, although its *value would have fallen*.

The same thing applies to the other case, in which the number of workers, 200, is the same as before, but their wage has doubled. In this case, s could only stay the same if the length of the surplus labour became greater in proportion to that of the necessary labour, hence the working day as a whole were longer, and the value of the same amount of constant capital fell from 450 to 300.

In both cases, both in a) and now in b) and c), where there has been a *shortening or a lengthening of the working day*, there is a new difficulty (which arises where the necessary labour-time, in other words the time required for the reproduction of labour-capacity, is shortened or lengthened). If, that is to say, the total working day is shortened, less constant capital will be utilised, if everything remains the same technologically, and if, inversely, the working day is lengthened (in order to extract the same rate of surplus-value) more constant capital will be required. Admittedly, one could if one wished assume that there was a rise in the value of the raw material, etc., in short a rise in the value of c, despite |51| the reduction in a physical sense in the extent of the means of production of which it consists, and that in b) and c) the opposite happened, the value of c fell, although more of the means of production were required. It can be seen that this leads to a series of very complex preconditions, which may possibly coincide, but if they did so the coincidence would be highly absurd and inelegant.

(In the final version of this story, therefore, we only need to concentrate on the theoretical aspect. For the investigation itself it is of course necessary to go into all these details, but they should definitely not be inflicted on the reader.)

In the cases b) and c), there is therefore each time a doubling of the surplus-value along with the variable capital, in one case because the number of workers has increased and the working day has remained the same, and in the other case because the working day is lengthened while the number of workers has remained the same. (Hence on each occasion the specific function represented by variable capital increases only as an index of the mass of labour set in motion by it.) In both cases, therefore, because C remains constant there is an increase in s/C and accordingly in the rate of profit.

β) Let us now assume that C changes at the same time as the change in v/C, while, as previously, s′ is assumed to be constant.

The ratio s/v, or the magnitude of s′, has nothing directly to do with C, since if C = v, hence c = 0, s/v would not need to be affected. Because of this, we can proceed from changes in C which derive from changes in the magnitude of c.

But before we look at this we must note the following: if C grows, but v and c both grow to the same degree, so that v/C remains unchanged, the rate of profit, or p′, remains the same. For example:

c	v	s	s′	p′
400	100	100	100%	20
n.400	n.100	n.100	n.100%	20
400/n	100/n	100/n	100%	20

For example: c = 400,000, v = 100,000, s = 100,000, p′ = 20%, C = 500,000 instead of 500 and the profit is 100,000 instead of 100. (Because s is now 1,000 times as large as it was before.) And the case is the same if both diminish equally and thereby C does as well.

It emerges from this that if the composition of the capital remains the same, the ratio between v and c, and similarly s/v, that is to say the *rate of profit*, the *amount of profit* (which is identical with the amount of surplus-value) rises and falls in direct proportion to the magnitude of the capital advanced.

Now back to our case:

	c	v	s	s′	p′	C
I)	400	100	100	100%	20	500
II)	500	100	100	100%	16⅔%	600
III)	300	100	100	100%	25%	400

As we go from I) to II) c rises from 400 to 500, hence by a quarter, and C rises from 500 to 600, by ⅕. If c = ⅘ C, ¼ c = 4⁄20 C, which is ⅕ C. If c grows by ¼, C grows by ⅕ (since v is assumed to be constant). The surplus-value, which was ⅕ of C, has now to be calculated on 6⁄5 C. The ratio ⅕ C: 6⁄5 C is 1: 6. The rate of profit has fallen in an exact proportion to the increase in C through the increase in c: 20⁄6 = 3⅓ and 20 − 3⅓ = 16⅔, the rate of profit of II. It is entirely irrelevant whether 400 C rises to 500 C because the *value* of the constant capital grows by ⅕ or because the amount of labour signified by 100v sets in motion ⅕ more constant capital as a result of changes in the technology of the labour process, while the value of the aliquot parts of the constant capital has remained the same.

II to III is the inversion of *I to II*. In this case, c falls from 500 to 300, or by ⅖ (or 40%), either because the same amount of constant capital which previously cost 500 now only costs 300 as a result of a change in the value of its constituents, or because the same amount of labour sets in motion a smaller quantity of constant capital while the value of the latter remains the same, as for example when less Indian than American cotton is spun in the same period of time. For whatever reason, as we go from II to III, c falls by ⅖ (40%) and since it was originally (in II) ⅚ C, it falls in the ratio ⅚: ⅖. 10⁄30 = ⅓ C. The new C, C′, is therefore = C − ⅓ C, or ⅔ of the C of II, and in fact C′ = 400, whereas C in II was 600. There is a fall of 33⅓% in C. Instead of (s/6) × 100, we now have (s/3) × 100. But since (s/6) × 100 = 16⅔%, (s/3) × 100 = (2 × 16⅔%) = 33⅓%; exactly the percentage by which C has fallen as a result of the contraction of c.

|52| Let us now look at the case where changes in C result from changes in v. *Fewer workers* are required to work on the same quantity of constant capital, as a result of a change in the technology of the process. This coincides with the case just mentioned, where more c is needed while its value remains the same, because the same number of workers sets in motion more of the means of production.

	c	v	s	s′	p′
I)	400	100	100	100%	20%
II)	400	80	80	100%	16⅔%
III)	400	120	120	100%	23$\frac{1}{13}$%

The result in relation to p′ is exactly the same as in the previous case, when c rose from 400 to 500 and C consequently rose from 500 to 600, while v remained unchanged. v falls from 100 to 80, i.e., by ⅕ or 20%. C falls from 500 to 480, i.e., by $\frac{1}{25}$ or 4%. Since v = ⅕ C originally, a fall of ⅕ in [v] is a fall of $\frac{1}{25}$ in C. ($\frac{1}{25}$ × 500 = 20), or 4%. This fall in [C] is very insignificant. It amounts to 4%, while the fall in v and therefore in s amounts to 20%. In fact, $\frac{100}{600}$ (the case on the previous page) = $\frac{80}{480}$.

The fall in the rate of profit is the same as when c rises from 400 to 500; but here the profit declines by 20%, whereas in the previous case it remained 100.

In the first case the rate of profit falls because in v/C, C grows as a result of the growth in [c]; in the second case the rate of profit falls because in v/C, C declines as a result of the fall in v, but v falls to a much greater degree. C falls by $\frac{1}{25}$ and v by ⅕, i.e., by $\frac{4}{25}$ more. If C had remained unchanged, and only v had fallen, this would be $\frac{80}{500}$ = 16%. Now, however, it is 16⅔, hence ⅔% more.

100/600 = 1/6. 80/480 = 1/6. 100/500 = 1/5. 80/400 = 1/5. The ratio between v/C and s/C is therefore the same in both cases, although in one case C has increased in size, and in the other it has become smaller, in one case c has risen and v remained constant, and in the other case c has remained constant and v has fallen, and in one case the amount of surplus-value has remained constant, while in the other it has fallen by 20%.

In one case s/C becomes s/C′, or s/(C + x) = 100/(500 + 100). In the other case s/C becomes s′/C′, or (s – x)/(C – y) = (100 – 20)/(500 – 20). Although s and C have changed by the same numerical amount, this comes to ⅕ of s and $\frac{1}{25}$ of C. s is therefore reduced 5 times more than c, since $\frac{5}{25}$ = ⅕.

The question is whether this transition from I to II is feasible when 100 (v) does not fall to 80 (v) because fewer workers handle the same amount of constant capital, hence the figure 80 is not an index of less labour set in motion, but because the same number of workers receives a wage of 80 instead of 100 owing to a cheapening of the means of subsistence, etc.

How could the rate of surplus-value remain the same in this case, namely 80? This would only be possible with a *shorter working day*. The surplus labour would have to fall to the same degree as the necessary labour. In this case the amount of surplus-value would fall as previously by ⅕ or 20%, just as the variable capital had done.

Without *a shortening of the working day of this kind*, it would be impossible, given that the rate of surplus-value stays the same, for v to fall in *value* in consequence of a change in the price of the necessary means of subsistence and {consequently a change in the length of the time of labour necessary for maintaining the labourers' labouring power}.[23]

From II to III 80 rises to 120, i.e., by 40%, thus 120 (v) is an indication either that 50% more labour has been set in motion in order to handle the same amount of constant capital, or that the wage of labour (the value of labour-capacity) has risen to 120 because the means of subsistence have become dearer. |53| 80 (v) has risen to 120 (v), so that if the wage of labour remains the same the 120 is an indication that 50% more labour has been set in motion. 400 (c) may express a greater amount of constant capital, hence its *price has fallen*. If 80 (v) corresponded to 400 (c), now 120 corresponds to 600 (c). With a fall in the price of c, 400 (c) could indicate the same amount of the material constituents of the constant capital as 400. If however no such fall in the price of c takes place, the movement from II to III would only be possible if ½ more workers were necessary as a result of worsening productivity in order to set in motion the same amount of constant capital. In that case the rate of profit would rise because the product would involve twice as much labour, and therefore also twice as much surplus labour. (The commodity would however *be very much dearer.*) < (*For later investigation, how this case is related to ground-rent.*) >

If, in contrast to this, the increase from 80v to 120v is not an indication that ½ as much labour again has been set in motion, but that wages have increased by 50%, so that 120v does not indicate more labour than 80v, s′ could only remain constant given the condition that the surplus labour, and thus the whole of the working day, was lengthened by ½. If *the working day remains the same* this is impossible.

We have now analysed α and β. A third case, γ, would also be possible, in which C, the total capital, neither remains constant, nor, as previously assumed, increases, either because v is variable and c is constant, or because v is constant and c is variable. The third case is C variable and both v and c variable. Here it should first be noted that if c and v vary in the same proportion, the amount of surplus-value and therefore the amount of profit would vary as the total capital increased or declined, but the *rate of profit* would remain unchanged, because

23 [The passage in brackets was written in English. Translator]

it is given by v/C. For $v/C = \frac{v}{v+c}$ and $\frac{nv}{nv+nc} = \frac{n}{n}\left(\frac{v}{v+c}\right) = \frac{v}{C}$. Similarly, $\frac{v/_n}{v/_n + c/_n} = \frac{1/_n(v)}{1/_n(v+c)} = \frac{1/_n\ (v)}{1/_n\ v+c} = \frac{v}{C}$. If we leave aside this case, in which v and c, and therefore also v and C, vary to an equal degree – and indeed in a single direction, so that they decline or increase in the same ratio – we can now investigate the matter further.

What is the situation when they vary equally in *opposite directions*, with the result that v grows as much as c declines, and vice versa? This case is *impossible*, since it is presupposed that C is variable. If now each reduction or increase of, for instance, v, corresponds to an inverse contraction or expansion on the part of c, C remains unchanged. Thus this case is excluded, by the nature of things. Equal variation along with simultaneous variation in the total capital is possible only if the variation takes place in the same direction for both v and c.

We now therefore have to assume the following: *a variation in* v *and* c *of unequal magnitude*. This *variation of unequal magnitude* is again possible in two ways. It may take place in the same direction or in different directions.

|54| Thus we have:

	c	v	s	s′	p′	C
I)	400	100	100	100%	20	500
II)	500	200	200	100%	28⁴⁄₇%	700
III)	600	150	150	100%	20%	150
IV)	600	160	160	100%	21¹⁄₁₉	760
V)	600	120	120	100%	16⅔	720
VI)	300	400	400	100%	57¹⁄₇%	700

This paradigm can be *viewed* as one wishes both as unequal variation in the *same* direction (growth and decline) and in *opposite directions*.

Compared with I), which is the starting-point, all five rows demonstrate a growth in c and v in unequal proportions, hence an unequal variation in the same direction.

If, however, we compare II with III, or IV, or V, there is *variation* in different directions.

Although, as compared with I, there is increase in both v and c in all the others, the result is very different.

In II, compared with I, the rate of profit grows from 20 to 28⁴⁄₇. Here the total capital grows from 500 to 700, by ⅖ or 40%. C grows by ⅕ or 20%, and v grows by 100%. If c remained constant and v alone grew by 200, the total capital would grow to 600, hence only by ⅕ or 20%. The rate of profit would have grown by 40%. If v remained constant and c alone grew by ¼, the total capital would similarly be 600, or it would only have grown by ⅕ (since it was originally 500), but the rate of profit would have fallen to 16⅔%. As things stand, v *is doubled, while* C only grows by ⅖, the former grows by 100%, the latter by only 40%.

As we go from I to II, p′ grows by 70%.[24]

In I, the ratio of v/C was 100/500 = 1/5 = 20%. And p′ changes accordingly. In II, the ratio of v/C is 200/700 = 2/7 = 28 4/7. There is a doubling of v, but the rate of profit does not double, because C increases by 2/7.

The best way of grasping the matter is this. [c] grows by ¼, from 400 to 500. If v also grew by only ¼ it would increase from 100 to 125. We should then have: v = 125, c = 500, C = 625. And 125/625 = 1/5. That is to say, v/C would remain unchanged. The rate of profit therefore is unaffected by the variation from 100/500 to 125/625. It would continue to be 20%. But let us from now on think of c as constant and look at the case where v grows from 125 to 200. Since 200 − 125 = 75 this gives an increase of 75, i.e., ⅔, or 60%.[25] At the same time, however, C, which is 625, also increases by 75, because C = c + v and (c + v + 75) = C + 75. The ratio is 200/700, or (125 + 75)/(625 + 75) = 200/700 = 2/7 or 28 4/7%.

Therefore[26] this case, like I and II, where both c and v increase (with C variable), but v grows more rapidly than c, can be reduced to the case handled previously, in which C *grows as a result of an increase in* v *while* c *remains constant*. For insofar as c and v grow equally, p′ remains unchanged because the ratio v/C is unchanged. The effect only begins from the point at which the growth of v ceases to be paralysed by the growth of c.

|55| *Let us take the contrary case, in which* v *and* c *increase in the same direction, but* c *increases more rapidly than* v.

If we compare III with I, we find that c grows from 400 to 600, v from 100 to 150 and the total capital from 500 to 750. Here the growth is equal, because 400: 600 = 100: 150 (2: 3 = 10: 15). p′ therefore also remains unchanged, comparing I with III, although the total capital has grown from 500 to 750.

If we compare I with V, we find that c grows from 400 to 600, hence by ½ or 50%, v however only grows from 100 to 120, hence by ⅕ or 20%.

---

24 [This seems to be a mistake. A 70% increase would give a rate of profit of 34%, not 28 4/7%. Translator]

25 [This should be 66⅔%. Translator]

26 [Either Marx or Engels drew a line in ink to the left of this paragraph and added the number '1'. Translator]

If c also only grew by 20% the ratio would be 480: 120 and v/C = 120/600 = 1/5 would be 20%. No alteration would have taken place. Up to this point, therefore, there has been no change. It begins now, however, at the point where 120/(480 + 120) = 120/600, has to be treated as the original v/C. Instead of this v/C, or 120/600, we now get: v/(C + 120), or v/(v + (c + 120)) = v/720 = 120/720 = 1/6 or 16⅔%. The ratio falls from 1/5 to 1/6.

This[27] case is therefore the one treated earlier, where C grows as a result of the *growth of* c, v *remaining constant*, for to the extent that v grows equally with c, p′ remains unchanged, because it is v/C. The effect [on the rate of profit] first begins from the point at which the growth of c is no longer paralysed by the growth of v, where v, therefore, can be assumed to be constant, as previously.

The[28] same thing takes place when v and c, instead of growing unequally, decrease unequally. We therefore arrive at this general rule: *if the total capital varies*, while at the same time the *variable and the constant capital change* in magnitude, and indeed in *the same direction*, hence both increase, or both decline, an impact on the rate of profit first begins from the moment at which the equal rise or fall of c and v ceases, hence the growth of C occurs only through a unilateral increase in c or v, with v or c remaining constant. These cases therefore fall under the categories previously examined.

One more case remains to be discussed, in which c and v vary in *opposite directions* and *unequally*.

Comparing first II and III, here c rises from 500 to 600 and v falls from 200 to 150, i.e., c rises by ⅕ and v falls by ¼. But what is involved *here* is not the *ratio* between them but their respective *magnitudes*. [c] rises by 100 and v falls by 50. If we posited a fall of 100 in v, we should have c = 600 and v = 100, hence C = 700, and the total capital would be 700 just as it was in II.

But the matter can also be investigated by proceeding from the part of capital which undergoes the lesser increase or reduction. v falls by 50 and c rises by 100. If we posited that c rose only by 50, we should have: 550c, 150v, and total capital 700, as in II. The case would therefore coincide with that examined earlier, in which C was constant and therefore v and c varied in opposite directions, and in which it was shown how the rate of profit was affected by whether v or c increased or declined.

Up[29] to this point, therefore, the case coincides with that examined earlier. From this point onwards, C becomes variable, and v remains constant at 150.

---

27 [The same as above, with the number '2'. Translator]

28 [The same as above, with the number '3'. Translator]

29 [The same as above, with the numbers '3' and '4'. Translator]

Only c varies, growing from 550 to 600, hence by 50, which results in a rise of the total capital from 700 to 750. Therefore, where C is variable, and v and c vary *in opposite directions and unequally*, the case initially comes down to a situation in which they vary inversely but equally, hence C remains constant. When the point is reached at which C becomes variable, the third case comes into play, in which C varies as a result of a unilateral movement by c or v. |56| One can therefore see that all cases in which C is variable and there is at the same time an unequal variation in v and c, whether in the same direction or in opposite directions, can be reduced to cases previously examined.

One more case remains to be examined: would it not be possible for the ratio v/C, looking at it in numerical terms, to remain unchanged, in that the numerical values of v and c have not changed, but their significance has changed?

For example, v/C = 100/500 = 100/(400 + 100). 100 may express an increase in wages for, say, half as many workers as before, or it may express a reduced wage for twice as many workers as before; moreover, 400 may express the value of, say, half as much constant capital (viewed in material terms) if its value has risen, or perhaps twice as much, if its value has fallen. The same expression, 100/(400 + 100) or the same numerical expression of v/(v + c) or v/C could accordingly express very different situations.

Firstly: 100/(400 + 100), where 100 is the wage of 100 workers and 400 is the value of a certain quantity of raw material and machinery, etc., which is turned into money by the 100 workers in the production process.

Secondly: the number 100 cannot represent *more or fewer* workers than before unless there has been a change in wages. This is also true of the ratio of the surplus-value to the variable capital, or s′, which is presupposed as constant in this investigation. It is of course possible if *the length of the working day changes*, so that, if 100 = 100 – x workers, the surplus labour of the individual worker and therefore the overall working day grows in the same ratio. In this case, c (400) would have to remain the same if the number of workers had fallen but the amount of labour set in motion remained the same, or the reverse.

It is possible for 100 to be the index of more or fewer workers than originally, when it set 100 workers into motion, as assumed, given *a change in the length of the working day* and an unchanged s′. Let us say that the 100 worked 10 hours, 5 of which were surplus labour. They would then work a total of 1,000 hours, 500 of which would be surplus labour. If 100 were the wage for 150 instead of a hundred workers, each worker would receive ⅓ less. The workers would work only 3⅓ hours for themselves instead of 5, and therefore 6⅔ instead of 5 for their master. But for s′ to remain the same, the working day would have to be shortened from 10 to 6⅔ hours. In that case there would be less raw material used and less depreciation, etc. This would mean a fall of the same extent in c, and since the number 400 remains the same, the 400 would represent less raw material, etc., hence c would have become to that extent more expensive. Conversely, if the working day were lengthened as a result of a rise in wages, c would have to become larger in the same ratio, 400 would therefore be the index of a correspondingly greater amount of the material elements of c, which would therefore have to undergo a corresponding reduction in their price. This corresponds exactly to the movement in the opposite direction ... But this is an irrelevance here.

What[30] is important for the investigation is this: the assumption that v/C, or 100/(400 + 100), although the numerator and the denominator *remain unchanged numerically* (just as, inversely, the ratio v/C remains *unchanged*, although the numerator and the denominator alter, but proportionately) *nevertheless expresses a different situation*, s′ remaining constant, implies that the following has occurred:

A change in the length of the working day; or an inverse movement of wages and the value of constant capital, whereby each of these changes goes exactly neck and neck with the other.

But what then? Then the *surplus-value* at any rate must change, since it is *determined by the absolute number of hours*. If only 3⅓ hours of surplus labour are delivered, the surplus-value will be smaller than if 5 are delivered, and if 8 hours of surplus labour are delivered (even though the 8 hours of surplus labour are balanced by 8 hours of necessary labour, hence the extra 3 hours are matched by 3 hours of necessary labour) the surplus-value will be larger than if 5 hours are delivered. In this case of course v/C is unchanged from the point of view of value, but s changes, because the working day, and therefore also s/C, will have changed in line with s, and this changes in line with the length of the working day.

This case is also possible when there is a change in s′, but not in the working day. If s′ changes, however, so does s, and indeed to the same extent as v (insofar as it is an index). In this case, s/C is in turn different, although 100/(400 + 100) or v/C has not changed nominally.

|57| If in developing the above argument we have spoken of a *constancy* of C, the *total capital*, what is to be understood by this is the *sum of value* which is formed by the part of the capital laid out in wages and the means of production.

Given a certain technological relationship, as for example when £100 is the index of 100 days of spinners' labour, raw material, ancillary materials and

30 [The same as above, but the line covers four paragraphs and the number is '6'. Translator]

machinery (in some cases no raw material) is required in a certain proportion, say a definite quantity of value of £400.

The total capital in this case is 500. And at every given moment every capital has to be divided into c and v, which are related to each other in a certain proportion, as for instance where c = 4v, or v = 1/4. If then c + v = C, c = 4/5 C and v = 1/5 C; taking them together, c + v = 4/5 + 1/5 = C.

This ratio is therefore given. If it changes, the changes can themselves in turn be in a fixed ratio, so that the constant magnitude C is never differently distributed.

For example, 400 c and 100 v; from this, c/(v + c) = 100/500 = 1/5. v = 1/5 C and c = 4/5 C. If c is 500 and v 100, c/(v + c) = 100/600 = 1/6. v = 1/6 C and c = 5/6 C. If v continues to be represented here by 100, c = 500, and a total capital of 600 is required instead of one of 500. At the same time, this new ratio can again be expressed as a constant, per 100.

The first proportion for a capital of 100 is 80c and 20v. The second proportion for a capital of 100 is 83⅓ and 16⅔. If in the first case 5 × v = 100 are to be applied, 5v = 400 is necessary, and in the second case 5 × v = 83⅓ makes 5v = 500 necessary.

Any further development of these proportions belongs to Chapter Two of this book. But we want to assemble here some essential conclusions from what has been developed so far, as soon as we have investigated the situation in case II where s′ is assumed to be variable rather than constant as it has been so far.

(*On the numerical expression of the effect an increase in the magnitude of* C *by growth in* c *with* v *remaining constant has on* p′.) The effect is *the reverse* of that exerted on the magnitude of v/C. Let us assume now that c changes by plus or minus δ. Let δ = c/r. Let c, on the other hand, = C/n. c = C/n, c/r = C/nr. δ (which is plus or minus) therefore = C/nr. Instead of the expression v/C one therefore has $\frac{v}{(v) + (c + \delta)} = \frac{v}{C'} = \frac{v}{C + {}^{C}/_{nr}}$. The greater is nr, the smaller is C/nr, and the smaller is nr, the greater is C/nr. $\frac{v}{C + {}^{C}/_{nr}} = \frac{v}{{}^{Cnr + C}/_{nr}} = \frac{vnr}{C(1 + nr)} = \frac{(v)}{(c)} \cdot \frac{(nr)}{(1 + nr)} = \frac{(v)}{(C)}\frac{(nr)}{(1 + nr)}\ \frac{v}{C}$ will grow here in proportion to nr/(1 + nr). The larger nr is, the *larger* is nr/(1 + nr), hence the larger also is $\frac{(v)}{(C)}\frac{(nr)}{(1 + nr)}$ and hence the greater the fall in the rate of profit which is brought about by the increase in c. And the smaller nr is, the smaller is $\frac{nr}{1 + nr}$, the smaller is $\frac{(v)}{(C)}\frac{(nr)}{(1 + nr)}$, and the smaller accordingly is the fall in the rate of profit. Therefore, because r = the ratio of the increment to c, or is equal to the growth of c, and n = the ratio of c to C, it follows that the larger the increment to c and the larger the original ratio of c to C (and therefore to v), the greater the fall in profit, etc.

|58| II) It has been assumed so far that s′ is constant and v/C variable (despite this variability, C itself may either be *constant* or *variable.*)

This has now to be investigated on the assumption that s′ is variable. It was already apparent in our previous investigation that certain variations in v/C were incompatible with a constant s′, and it will now appear that certain variations in s′ are incompatible with a constant C. This is not a surprise, since s′ = s/v, hence there is an inner relation between s′ and v, and therefore this inner relation also exists *indirectly* with c. There are only two cases to be investigated: either the rate of surplus-value rises or it falls.

We should first look into the conditions under which v/C can be constant, with s′ variable.

If wages (v) fall, the rate of surplus-value grows (*provided that the length of the working day remains the same*) and v/C remains unchanged if c rises to the same extent as v falls. Since C = v + c, if (v − δ) is compensated for by (c + δ), one then has C = v + c + δ − δ or C = v + c, which means that C is unchanged.

It is to be noted in general that C remains unchanged if c plus or minus δ is compensated for by v minus or plus δ.

v/C remains unchanged when v/C is replaced by vn/Cn or (v/n)/(C/n)

	c	v	s	s′	p′	C	
I	400	100	50	50%	10%	500	v/C = 100/500 = 1/5 = 20%
II	480	20	20	100%	4%	500	v/C = 20/500 = 1/25 = 4%

In this case, when we compare II with I, C remains constant; but the ratio v/C is very different. In I it is 20, in II it is only ⅕ of that, namely 4%. But the variable capital has also fallen by 80% while the constant capital has risen by 80. 480/20 = 24/1. The constant capital is now 24 times as large as the variable capital; hence the total capital is 25 times as large.

If the rate of surplus-value had not risen by 50%, becoming 100% instead of 50%, the surplus-value would only have been 10 and the rate of profit would have been 10/500 = 1/50 = 2%. As a result of the rise in the rate of surplus-value, the rate of profit stands twice as high as it would have done if s′ had remained constant.

The rate of profit always rises as a result of rises in the rate of surplus-value, and it always falls as the latter falls; thus in the above example the rate of profit stands 50% higher than it would have done without this increase in s′. But this effect of s′ is concealed because the rate of profit falls for other reasons, namely the reduction in variable capital and the increase in constant capital, and indeed it falls to a much greater degree than it rises as a result of the rise in s′.

If the working day remains constant at the level indicated in I, 100 + 50 will be the expression of the total value which 100 workers can deliver. If the same number of workers continues to be employed, they now (in II) cost only 20v, so that while necessary labour-time was 10 hours before and surplus labour-time was 5 hours, they now work only 2 hours of necessary labour-time and 13 hours of surplus labour-time. But since the value expression for the same number of workers remains the same, v is now 20 and s is 130, so that we arrive at 20 + 130 = 150. In that case:

	c	v	s	s′	p′	C	
II	480	20	130	650%	26	500	v/C = 1/25

Here the rate of profit rises because the rate of surplus-value grows from 50% to 650%, hence 13 times, or by 1,300%. The rate of profit rises from 10 to 28,[31] therefore 2⅘ times, 280%. The variable capital, on the other hand, has fallen by 80% and the constant capital has risen by 20%, so that v compared with C is only 1/25. Here the rate of profit rises with the rate of surplus-value, although not by any means in the same proportion as the rate of surplus-value, which more than outweighs the fall of the rate of profit arising from the fall in the variable capital and the growth in the constant capital.

One can see here that both a *rising and a falling* rate of profit can be accompanied by a *rising rate of surplus-value*. Equally, it can both *rise and fall* along with a *falling rate of surplus-value*.

For example:

	c	v	s	s′	p′	C		
I	600	200	200	100	25%	800	v/C = 1/4	= 25%
II	500	400	300	75%	33⅓%	900	v/C = 4/9	= 44%
III	600	200	100	50%	12½%	800	v/C = 200/800 = 1/4	= 25%

31 [The new rate of profit would appear to be 26%, as indicated in the table. Translator]

|59| If we compare III with I, we find that the rate of surplus-value falls by 50% and the rate of profit along with it, because there are no countervailing circumstances present. Between I and II, in contrast, we find a rise in the rate of profit, despite the fall in the rate of surplus-value.

We should like now to take up again from the beginning the whole discussion about the *movement of the rate of profit* when the *rate of surplus-value* is increasing. We start first with the simplest case, *where* c remains *unchanged*, and the whole of the alteration which takes place proceeds exclusively from s′. We shall assume at the same time that the *working day* is given, and that it is therefore a matter of *relative* surplus-value, in which every movement in necessary labour-time is complemented by an inverse, opposite movement in surplus labour-time.

If the whole working day is 12 hours, for example, one worker will work 72 hours in the week. Assume that the monetary expression of these 72 hours is £2. In that case wages + surplus-value = > £2. If the necessary labour-time is ½ the working day, the wage = £1 and the surplus-value = £1. If only a quarter of the day is necessary labour, the wage = 10 shillings, or £½, and the surplus-value = £1½. If the necessary labour is ⅔ of the whole day, the wage will be £1½ and surplus-value £½. This applies to the individual worker. The whole of the variable capital = the wage of the individual worker × the total number of workers set in motion by that capital. And what is true for the working day of the individual worker also applies to the overall total of the working days of the workers employed simultaneously. Hence, on the above assumption, if a hundred workers are employed by one capital, the monetary expression of their total product can never be more than £2 × 100 = £200. If, in line with the above assumption, the wage of the individual worker is £1 (i.e., the necessary labour-time = *the whole of the working day*), the total amount of variable capital = 1 × 100 = £100, and the surplus-value is the same, 100. In general the following always applies:

	Wage		Surplus-value		Total
100	(1	+	1)	=	2(100) = 200
100	(1½	+	½)	=	2(100) = 200
100	(½	+	1½)	=	2(100) = 200

This is the distribution of the individual working day multiplied by the number 100, which is here the number of workers simultaneously employed by capital A or capital B.

|60| Proceeding on this basis, we shall now assume that s′ rises or falls:

Case II 1) A)

	c	v	s	s′	p′	C	v/C
a)	400	200	200	100%	$33\frac{1}{3}$%	600	$^{200}/_{600} = \frac{1}{3}$ or v/C $= ^{55}/_{165}$
b)	400	150	250	$166\frac{2}{3}$%	$45\frac{5}{11}$%	550	$^{150}/_{550} = \frac{3}{11}$ or v/C $= ^{45}/_{165}$
c)	400	100	300	300%	60%	500	$^{100}/_{500} = \frac{1}{5}$ or v/C $= ^{33}/_{165}$

If we read this table in descending order, starting with a) and passing through b) to c), s′ rises from 100% first to $166\frac{2}{3}$% and finally to 300%, while the surplus-value itself goes up from 200 to 250 and then to 300. Here the *surplus-value* grows by the same amount as the variable capital diminishes, and since this reduction in the magnitude of v, c remaining unchanged, causes a fall in (v + c), C, the total capital, also falls. There is also a continuous fall in v/C. The law here turns out to be the opposite of the law previously developed: where the fall in v/C results from a fall in the value of v and a corresponding increase in the value of s, this means not a fall but a rise in surplus-value.

(Incidentally, if in case b) – assuming an equal rate of surplus-value – v/C were 1/3, as it was in a), the variable capital would be $^{550}/_{3} = 183\frac{1}{3}$ and the surplus-value and the rate of profit would also be higher.)[32]

Nevertheless, although v/C constantly diminishes, because v is falling, C also diminishes: in a) it was 600, in b) 550 and in c) 500. The reduction of v in relation to c is therefore paralysed to a certain extent by the simultaneous decline in C.

The movements of v, s, s′ and p′ occur at very different rates.

If we now look at s/C, which is what determines the rate of profit, p′, we get the following sequence:

32 (*Although the total capital falls from 600 to 550 and then to 500, it increases in comparison with* v. 200/600 = 55/165, while 150: 550 = 45/165, etc. The total amount of the capital advanced declines as a result of the diminution in v, but at the same time C, despite falling, increases in comparison with v. Since C is greater than v, a decline by the same amount will reduce v more than C.)

a) 200/600 = s/C
b) 250/350 = s/C
c) 300/500 = s/C

It is clear here that the rate of profit grows not only because s grows by the same amount as v decreases, but because the fall in v also reduces C, hence v/C grows for two reasons, because s grows absolutely and because C declines. If C remained constant, we should have:

a) 200/600
b) 250/600
c) 300/600

and the rate of profit would change from 33⅓% for a) to 41⅔% for b) and 50% for c). The rate of profit would be determined exclusively by the growth in s; the fact that it is now larger is a result of the reduction in C caused by the fall in v.

|61| If we now invert the order in which we look at the same paradigm, we find that s′ falls, hence s′ falls by the same amount as v rises, and accordingly the growth of v is accompanied by a fall in s′ and p′. v grows in relation to C, but at the same time C increases absolutely, and therefore s/C falls for two reasons: because s falls and because C increases.

Hence if all other circumstances remain the same, i.e., the change in s′ is not accompanied by any change in the magnitude of the constant capital, the rise in s′ will be accompanied by a fall in v by the same amount as s increases, the total capital will fall through the reduction in v, and s/C, or the rate of profit, will double. The rise in s′ is determined, first by the *increase in surplus-value*, and second by the fall in *the total capital advanced* (C).

Let us now assume that c does not remain constant, but that the change in v is accompanied by a change in c. We assume first that the changes proceed in the same direction, hence when v falls c also falls, and vice versa.

Case II 2) B)

	c	v	s	s′	p′	C	v/C	s/C
a)	400	200	200	100	$33\frac{1}{3}$	600	$200/600 = 1/3$ (or $v/C = 63/189$)	$200/600 = 1/3$
b)	300	150	250	$166\frac{2}{3}$	$55\frac{5}{9}$	450	$150/450 = 5/9$ (or $v/C = 105/189$)	$250/450 = 5/9$
c)	250	100	300	300	$85\frac{5}{7}$	350	$100/350 = 2/7$ (or $v/C = 54/189$)	$300/350 = 6/7$

If we look at this sequence from a) to c), we find that c moves in the same direction as v, *falling*; and if we look at it in reverse, from c) to a), we find that it also moves in the same direction, *rising*.

Let us choose the first alternative (in examining the reverse direction all we would need to do is to invert the argument). The rate of profit rises here much more rapidly than it did in case II 1) A), where c remained constant. Here C falls much more rapidly, from 600 to 450 and then to 350. The change in s′, and therefore also in s, is the same, since the variable capital is *originally of the same magnitude* as was assumed in the previous paradigm. The change in the value of c has as a result the greater effect. Apart from this, paradigm B) does not differ from paradigm A) in its underlying assumptions. C falls continuously, and more rapidly than v. v/C grows here, because though v falls, C falls still more quickly. s/C grows for three reasons, first because s grows; second because C declines owing to the fall in v, and finally C also declines owing to the fall in c. To the extent that it is caused by the decline in v, since C = c + v, the decline in C, i.e., the total capital, is a decline which is caused by the growth in s′, which corresponds to the decline in v. The fall in C, in contrast, to the extent that it is caused by a change in the value of c, is prima facie independent of the movement of s′ and belongs to the case examined earlier, in which C declines as a result of the reduction in c, and s/C, or the rate of profit, thereby increases. This would be the case even if s did not also grow.

The same line of reasoning can be applied inversely, when we read paradigm II 2) B) from c to a.

|62| Let us now assume that c and v change in opposite directions:

Case II 3) C)

	c	v	s	s′	p′	C	v/C	s/C
a)	400	200	200	100	$33\frac{1}{3}$	600	$\frac{200}{600} = \frac{1}{3}$ (or $\frac{91}{273}$)	$\frac{1}{3} = \frac{91}{273}$
b)	500	150	250	$166\frac{2}{3}$	$38\frac{6}{13}$	650	$\frac{150}{650} = \frac{3}{13}$ (or $\frac{63}{273}$)	$\frac{5}{13} = \frac{105}{273}$
c)	600	100	300	300	$42\frac{6}{7}$	700	$\frac{100}{700} = \frac{1}{7}$ (or $\frac{39}{273}$)	$\frac{3}{7} = \frac{117}{273}$

We see first of all, when we read down from a to c, that the *rate of profit* continues to grow, although, with the rise in c, the total capital grows from 600 to 650 and then from 650 to 700, for which reason v/C declines very quickly, from 91/273 to 63/273 then down to 39/273. But as a result of the increase in s′, expressed by the reduction in v, s increases more rapidly than C grows as a result of the increase in c. Relatively, then, C falls in relation to s, although it increases absolutely. And for that reason, the rate of profit also grows. If one makes a comparison, however, with the series of profit rates in II 1) A) and II 2) B), one sees that the rate of profit falls in comparison with both of them, although the movement of s′ is the same. The rise in s′ and the corresponding rise in s is therefore paralysed in part by the increase in c and therefore in C.

If we now look at the sequence in reverse, we find that the total capital, C, falls from 700 to 650 to 600 as a result of the *decline* in c. Despite this real reduction in C, s/C = p′ falls because s′ also falls, v as a result grows and thus we have a double effect, *firstly* through the fall in s and secondly because C grows in relation to v, hence its lessened reduction is paralysed through the reduction in c.

In the first case we have a *growth in the rate of profit* accompanying a *rise* in the value of the *constant capital* and therefore of the total capital, and an increase in surplus-value, and in the second case we have a *fall* in the rate of profit accompanying a *fall in* c *and therefore in the total capital,* because s′ falls still more quickly and therefore v increases and s declines.

In any case, movement in opposite directions has a paralysing effect on s′ and c. The rate of profit may therefore remain *the same* while the *rate of surplus-value rises*; it may indeed *fall* instead of *rising*. Both these cases are presented in the paradigm that follows:

|63| **Case II 4) D)**

	c	v	s	s′	p′	C	v/C
a)	400	200	200	100	⅓ = 33⅓ %	600	200⁄600 = ⅓ = 60⁄180
b)	600	150	250	166⅔	⅓ = 33⅓ %	750	150⁄750 = 3⁄15 = 1/3 = 60⁄180
c)	1100	100	300	300	¼ = 25 %	1200	100⁄1200 = 1⁄12 = 15⁄180

Comparing b) with a), the rate of profit *remains the same*, although the rate of surplus-value rises from 100 % to 166⅔ %. Comparing c) with b), the rate of profit *falls* from 33⅓ % to 25 %, although the [rate of surplus-value] rises from 166⅔ % to 300 %. Reading back from c) to b), *the rate of profit rises*, although the rate of *surplus-value* falls, while from b) to a) the rate of profit remains unchanged although the rate of *surplus-value* falls.

This shows that the rate of profit may rise, fall or remain unchanged while *the rate of surplus-value rises*; that the rate of profit may rise, fall or remain unchanged while *the rate of surplus-value falls*; and finally that the rate of profit may rise and fall while the *rate of surplus-value remains unchanged*. This has already been demonstrated, under case I), above.

The effects examined under Case II 4) D) result from the fact that, reading from a) to c), s/C either remains unchanged or falls, because either the growth of s is paralysed by the growth of C, or, however, the growth of s is not only paralysed by the growth of C, but an excess growth of C takes place, which is unaccompanied by any increase in s. In the present paradigm, v declines very considerably in comparison with C, a reduction which is caused, not by any growth in s′, but by an increase in c.

In all our previous examples, v/C changes along with s′; only in the case introduced in the following paradigm can v/C remain constant in spite of the change in s′. This situation, involving an increase or reduction in v, as a result of the increase or reduction in s′ and therefore in s, = ± δ, is only possible when c increases or declines by ± δc/v in line with the increase or reduction of ± δ in v. For example, when v declines from 200 to 150, as in b) of the [following] paradigm, c grows by – δc/v, hence as δ = – 50, v = 150 and c = 400, c grows by – δc/v = – 50.400/200 = – 50.2 = – 100. And since c = 400, c – 100 = 300. In fact v/C = 150/450 = 3/9 = 1/3.

This is how we shall alter paradigm D) in the next case, in which connection it should be noted that c always grows by ± δc/v when ± δ expresses the increase or reduction in v as a result of a change in s′:

|66|[33] II 5) E)

	c	v	s	s′	p′	C	v/C
a)	400	200	200	100	33⅓	600	200/600 = ⅓
b)	300	150	250	166⅔	55⁵⁄₉	450	150/450 = ⅓
c)	200	100	300	300	100%	300	100/300 = ⅓

Here the rate of surplus-value varies considerably, as also does the size of the capital employed, but v/C remains constant. In fact – with this *particularity excepted*[34] – we have the same case as before, with c and v rising and falling together, only here in such a manner that v/(v + c) or, in other words, v/C, remains unchanged, since the complete expression of the formula is as follows:

$$\frac{v \pm \delta}{(v \pm \delta) + (c \pm {}^{\delta.c}/_{v})} = \frac{v}{v + c} = \frac{v}{C}$$

This is the only situation in which v/C can remain constant while s′ is changing. So far, then, we have had three different configurations of v/C: 1) it changes and s′ *remains constant*; here v grows and declines in line with the *number of workers employed*, since the proportion of the surplus-value to the capital employed, hence the *relative surplus-value*, remains unchanged; 2) it changes and s′ *is variable*; here the change in v proceeds from a change in its value, since *the same number* of workers costs either more or less; and 3) it remains *constant* and s′ is variable. This is only possible when the numerical relation of the *change in the value* of the constant part of the capital to the *change in the value* of the variable capital is such that v/C remains unaltered.

It can be seen that this third formula is also applicable when v grows while its value remains unchanged, because the number of workers has increased, and c grows, whether because its value increases or because the amount of constant capital set in motion by the increased number of workers increases, because the formula

$$\frac{v \pm \delta}{(v \pm \delta) + (c \pm {}^{\delta.c}/_{v})}$$

33 [Marx moved straight from '63' to '66' in his pagination of the manuscript. Translator]

34 [The words in italics were written in English by Marx. Translator]

contains absolutely nothing to indicate whether v grows for the first or the second reason. The only thing that comes into question here is its growth as such.

For v/C to be constant while s′ changes, as above, the assumption is that the *capital* is in fact the same, and the proportions are the same, for 200: 400 = 150: 300 = 100: 200. It is in fact the same example, but with the presupposition that the same quantity of labour (v + s) sets in motion a constant capital of 400 in one case, 300 in another and 200 in the third; a decline in productivity is assumed, in other words it is assumed that the value of c undergoes transformations independently of v.

|67| Before we make any further exploration of the *circumstances* in which the various formulae with a variable s′ are applicable or have any meaning, we must first note that so far we have assumed that the *working day is a given factor*. In contrast to this, if, with *no change in* the intensity of labour, an increase or a reduction in s′ takes place, because the working day has been lengthened or shortened, it cannot be said that the *total amount of variable capital and surplus-value* is always = a, a constant magnitude, but rather that this *total itself changes*.

IV

	c	v	s	s′	p′	C	v/C
a)	400	200	200	100	$33\frac{1}{3}$ or $\frac{1}{3}$	600	$\frac{200}{600} = \frac{1}{3} = \frac{13}{39}$
b)	450	200	250	125	$38\frac{6}{33}$	650	$\frac{200}{650} = \frac{4}{13} = \frac{12}{39}$
c)	400	200	250	125	$41\frac{2}{3}$	600	$\frac{200}{600} = \frac{1}{3} = \frac{13}{39}$
d)	350	200	250	125	$45\frac{5}{11}$	550	$\frac{200}{550} = \frac{4}{11}$
e)	400	200	150	75	25	600	$\frac{200}{600} = \frac{1}{3} = \frac{13}{39}$
f)	350	200	150	75	$27\frac{3}{11}$	550	$\frac{150}{550} = \frac{3}{11}$

This paradigm contains all the possible cases in which the variable capital, the number of *workers employed* and the workers' wages remain the same, hence there is no change in the magnitude of the variable capital, but the surplus-value grows or declines because the *absolute length of the working day* is increased or reduced.

Moving from a) to b), c grows by ⅛, because ⅛ more labour is set in motion (although for the same wage, with the same variable capital), and it is presupposed that the value of c remains constant. In any case, the change in the *value* of c is a fact independent of the lengthening of the working day and therefore of the increase in surplus-value. With no change in technology more c is required because more labour is set in motion. (The ratio is not the same, of course, because the amount of fixed capital does not increase in the same proportion as the amount of labour employed.) Increases take place in s′, s and p′. Comparing e) with b), the opposite assumption is made, that as s′ and therefore also s declines, there is a fall in the constant capital, because the amount of labour employed has fallen. There are falls in both s′ and p′.

In c) it is assumed that the *total value of* c remains constant, despite its increased amount, which is only possible on the assumption that the *value of* c falls, for example through a cheapening of the raw material, etc. On this assumption surplus-value increases, and profit grows even more; they both grow still more strongly when, as assumed in d), c falls instead of increasing or remaining the same. In f) the *reduction in surplus-value* is bound up with the decline in constant capital, because less of it is *worked on*. When this case is compared with a), therefore, there is a fall in p′.

Let us now contemplate this case of a change in absolute surplus-value and therefore in the *total sum of variable capital and surplus-value*, when we leave out of account all changes in the value of c which are not explained by the *increase or decline* in its own magnitude, or at least do not allow c to grow in the same proportion as v + s because fixed capital does not grow in the same proportion. The same thing applies inversely to a reduction in v + s. The change which C then undergoes is caused by the change in c, but this is effected by a change in s′, that is to say here in the *amount of labour employed*. This is the change in c effected by the change in s′ itself, which can be counteracted by an independent change in the value of c. Here we have the cases in [table] IV [above], where a rise in c and consequently in C with v remaining constant corresponds to a rise in the rate of profit, and a reduction in c corresponds, conversely, to a fall in that rate. But here c rises only because s rises.

Every fall in c which does not result from a reduction in the amount of c employed, because less surplus labour-time is worked, increases the *rate of profit* to that extent.

|68| We shall now assemble together the results of the previous discussion in tabular form, and draw some general conclusions.

A) s′ constant.

I) C *taken as constant.*

	c	v	s	s′	p′	v/C	C
a)	400	100	50	50%	10	1/5 = 20%	500
b)	450	50	25	50	5	1/10 = 10%	500
c)	300	200	100	50	20	2/5 = 40%	500

The fact that C remains constant has no effect on the investigation.

II) C *taken as variable.*

II) 1)

	c	v	s	s′	p′	C	v/C
a)	400	100	100	100%	20%	500	1/5
b)	500	100	100	100%	16⅔	600	1/6
c)	300	100	100	100	25%	400	1/4

Here v is *constant,* c *variable.*

p′ rises and falls in inverse proportion to the changes in the magnitude of C produced by changes in c, and therefore in v/C.

II) 2)

	c	v	s	s′	p′	C	v/C
a)	400	100	100	100	20%	500	1/5 = 78/390
b)	400	80	80	100	16⅔	480	1/6 = 65/390
c)	400	120	120	100	23 1/13	520	3/13 = 90/390

Here c is *constant,* v *variable.* p′ is determined by v/C; it is affected directly by variations in v. It is affected twice over, since v/C = v/(v + c).

II 3) When C is variable, v and c increase either in proportion, or in the same direction but not uniformly, or in opposite directions but not uniformly.

II 4) The expression v/C may remain identical (i.e., the numerator and the denominator may continue to be of the same magnitude) but it may express entirely different situations.

Our initial supposition, namely A I) above, in which C is assumed to be constant, has significance for the investigation in that where the opposite movements of v and c *paralyse* each other, which must to a certain degree be the case wherever they move in opposite directions, the *total capital* remains constant, hence case A I) is valid.

Suppositions II and III are useful for our investigation in the same way.

B) s′ taken as variable.

III 1) *s′ variable while the working day remains constant.*

	c	v	s	s′	p′	C	v/C
a)	400	100	50	50	10%	500	1/5 = 20%
b)	480	20	130	650	26%	500	1/25 = 4%

III 2)

	c	v	s	s′	p′	C	v/C
a)	400	200	200	100	33⅓%	600	1/3 = 55/165
b)	400	150	250	166⅔	45¾%	550	3/11 = 45/165
c)	400	100	300	300	60	500	1/5 = 33/165

Here p′ rises *in an inverse relation to* the decline in v/C and in a direct relation to the rise in s/C, and indeed for two reasons, because s grows and because C declines owing to the change in v.

III 3)

	c	v	s	s′	p′	C	v/C	s/C
a)	400	200	200	100	33⅓	600	1/3 = 21/63	1/3
b)	300	150	250	166⅔	55⁵⁄₉	450	1/3 = 21/63	5/9
c)	250	100	300	300	85⁵⁄₇	350	2/7 = 18/63	1/3

A rise[35] of v/C combined with a fall in v, because C falls owing to the fall in c, etc. *Here c, v and s′ all vary in the same direction.*

∵

In this particular case s/C increases because s rises and C declines owing to the fall in v and c. And vice versa.

III 4)

	c	v	s	s′	p′	C	v/C	s/C
a)	400	200	200	100	33⅓	600	1/3 = 91/273	1/3 = 91/273
b)	500	150	250	166⅔	38⁶⁄₁₃	650	3/13 = 63/273	5/13 = 105/273
c)	600	100	300	300	42⁶⁄₇	700	1/7 = 39/273	3/7 = 117/273

c and v vary in opposite directions. v/C declines, p′ increases; s increases more rapidly as a result of the increase in s′ caused by the reduction in v than C does as a result of the increase in c. p′ increases, although c grows and v declines.

35 [Clearly, this should read 'fall'. Translator]

III 5)

	c	v	s	s′	p′	C	v/C	s/C
a)	400	200	200	100	1/3 = 33⅓	600	1/3 = 60/180	1/3 = 33⅓
b)	600	150	250	166⅔	1/3 = 33⅓	750	3/15 = 36/180	1/3 = 33⅓
c)	1100	100	300	300	1/4 = 25%	1200	1/12 = 15/180	1/4 = 25%

Here v/C declines owing to the increase in C which results from the increase in c. The two opposite movements paralyse each other in a) and b), so that p′ is unchanged. In case c), p′ declines despite the increase in s. And vice versa.

III 6)

	c	v	s	s′	p′	C	v/C
a)	400	200	200	100	33⅓	600	1/3
b)	300	150	250	166⅔	55 5/9	450	1/3
c)	200	100	300	300	100%	300	1/3

This is the only case where v/C remains constant while s′ varies.

C) Changes in s′ with variations in the working day.

IV)

	c	v	s	s′	p′	C	v/C
a)	400	200	200	100	33⅓	600	1/3
b)	400	200	250	125	41⅔	600	1/3
c)	400	200	150	75	25	600	1/3
d)	450	200	250	125	38 6/13	650	4/13
e)	350	200	250	125	45 5/11	550	4/11
f)	350	200	150	75	27 3/11	550	4/11

|69| It follows from the above, first of all, that there can be no greater error than to regard the laws that regulate the rates of surplus-value and profit as identical.

If the *working day* is given, the value of constant capital remains unchanged and the rate of surplus-value varies, the law of relative surplus-value is dominant, i.e., rises and falls in the rate of surplus-value derive from rises and falls in wages, or variable capital, and they are inversely related to them. The rate of profit will then vary accordingly, as shown in Table III 2), although even then the rate of profit is determined not only by changes in s, the surplus-value, but also by variations in C, since C = c + v, whether c is constant, grows or falls with v.

But it has also been shown that the rate of profit can rise or fall while s′ *remains constant*, therefore where these rises and falls certainly cannot be explained by *a movement in s′ which does not exist*. It is also clear that with s′ *variable and the working day constant*, a stationary, falling or rising p′ can correspond to a *falling* s′, and that a rising, falling or stationary p′ can correspond to a *rising* s′. Hence the movements of s′ can be paralysed or eliminated (*over-reached*) by movements of C in the opposite direction.

Lastly, it has been seen that *variations in* s′ *combined with unequal working days* can provide, in the first place, different combinations of profit rates, and that a *constant* s′ combined with unequal working days can also provide *unequal profit rates* because of differences in s.

The rate of surplus-value is not determined simply by the *ratio* between surplus-value and variable capital, or the *ratio* between surplus labour and necessary labour. *Surplus-value* itself is determined by the *rate of surplus-value, the length of the working day and the number of workers employed by the variable capital.* These are the initial requirements for the rate of profit. But there is an additional determinant, which often works in the opposite direction: the relation of v and c both to each other and to C.

It has been shown that the formula p′/s′ = v/C *ceases to be correct when the rise or fall of* v *expresses a change in the value of the variable capital and not in the quantity of labour set in motion by it.*[36]

It has also been shown that the great multiplicity of combinations [between v and c] and the difficulty in working them out also results from the fact that the *value* of constant capital can rise or fall either because the same amount of the means of production appreciates or depreciates; or, on the other hand, because *the amount itself falls* while the value of its constituent

36 [The next two important paragraphs were not included in Engels's Volume III. Editor]

elements remains the same. Each of these movements can cut across the other. If we consider the influence of c on the rate of profit, the reasons why c falls are entirely irrelevant, although differences between the causes for a fall have a very evident impact on the prices of commodities. What is of decisive importance, however, is whether v changes because a smaller or larger number of workers is technologically required for the production of the same value; whether, therefore, the decrease or increase in v is an index of the amount of labour set in motion (assuming that the length of the working day is given, for v would be able to set more labour in motion with fewer workers, and vice versa) or v rises or falls because the *wage* rises and falls, and a *change in the value* of the variable capital takes place, with the result that the same number of workers costs more or less, and these variations in v are therefore not a direct index of the quantity of labour set in motion by it. Each of the movements of v can cut across the other, in the same direction or in opposing directions. For example: v may fall from 100 to 30 instead of 50, because only half as many workers are required, but at the same time this smaller number of workers cost less than they did previously, etc. One can therefore see that the movement of the rate of profit can be very complicated and that its analysis is by no means as simple a matter as the political economists have so far imagined.

It should finally be remarked that what we have presented here as movements of different constituents of the same capital over a period of time could just as well be presented as *differences between different capitals in various areas of investment lying alongside each other in a spatial sense*, and what has been presented so far will be utilised in this latter form in the next chapter.

|70| 1) *Absolute* (*not only relative*) *movements* of c, which proceed directly from movements of v [take place for the following reasons]:

either differences in v express differences in the amount of labour set in motion as a result of a change in s′ associated with an altered length of the working day, to which different amounts of c correspond, all other circumstances remaining the same;

or the same v (as an index of the same quantity of labour) may set in motion more or less of the means of production than before owing to a technological change, involving an increase or reduction in the productive power of labour, which thereby causes a change in the amount of c, a change which must also find expression in a change in the value of c, all other circumstances remaining the same.

2) *Relative movements of* c, which proceed from movements in v, can be defined as all movements in which c (the *value expression* of c) remains constant (for whatever reasons) and v, for whatever reasons, increases or declines.

In this case, a relative rise and fall in the proportional magnitude of c, whether compared with v or C, corresponds to this positive increase or reduction in [v].

3) *Finally there can be absolute movements in* c, *independently of movements in* v. These are changes in the value of the constant capital which are either derived from *economies in the utilisation of the means of production*, or produced by independent *changes in the value of those means of production* themselves. We now want to fit in a discussion of these last-mentioned circumstances as the final part of this section.

∵

Let s = v/r (v can be either a fraction or a whole number. E.g., if s′ = 100%, s = v, hence r = 1; if s′ = 50%, r = 2 or s = v/r; if s′ = 300%, r = 1/3, then v/(⅓) = 3v, etc.) It follows that if v = C/n, and s = v/r, and v = C/n, s or v/r = C/nr, where r indicates the ratio of s to v and n indicates the ratio of v to C. It is clear that if r, and therefore s′ and s, are given, the smaller n, the greater will be C/nr, and the greater n, the smaller will be C/nr.

∵

Realisation of surplus-value. We remarked at the beginning of this chapter that commodities can be sold at a profit *beneath* their value. Assuming that the cost price of the commodity is covered, this is only possible because *a part of the surplus-value* (or profit) *is not realised in the sale price*. Two things are now possible. Either the part of the surplus-value not realised in one commodity is realised in another commodity, so that if one is sold beneath its value the other is sold above its value (as we shall see when we discuss *prices of production*); or no such compensation takes place. For the worker, from whom a specific quantity of surplus-value has been extorted, it is a matter of complete indifference whether his own capitalist, or another one, realises part of that surplus-value. Its non-realisation would only be of interest to him if the commodity which had been cheapened in this way entered into his own consumption, and the cheapening *thus* achieved did not have an impact on his wages or his employment.

|71| (3) < Economy In The Use Of Constant Capital

In the present investigation, as in that of fluctuations in the price of raw materials > to be dealt with in (4)[37] < we proceed from the assumption that > the surplus-value and < the rate of surplus-value are given. > In the meantime, there is one more important point to be stressed:

Absolute surplus-value, or < *an extension of surplus labour* and hence of the *working day*, with the variable capital remaining the same and thus the same number of workers being employed at the same nominal wage, causes a relative *fall* in the value of the constant capital compared with the total capital and the variable capital, and *thus raises the rate of profit*, quite apart from the rise in the rate of surplus-value and the growth in the mass of surplus-value. (It is immaterial here whether the > surplus labour, < 'overtime', is paid or not.) The volume of > the part of constant capital which consists of < *fixed capital* (factory buildings, machinery, etc.) remains the same, whether work continues for 16 hours or for 12. The extension of the working day requires no new expenditure on this, the most expensive portion of the constant capital. (The value of the fixed capital, moreover, is now reproduced in a shorter > turnover period, so that when a comparison is made between profits made by capitals of a given magnitude in a certain turnover period, < the time for which it has to be advanced in order to make a certain profit > is shorter in the case where the fixed capital is advanced for a longer period than where it is advanced for a shorter period).[38] < The lengthening of the working day is therefore > profitable < even if the overtime is paid and, naturally only up to a certain point, this is true even if the overtime is paid at a higher rate than normal working hours. > The development < of fixed capital in the modern industrial system was therefore

37 [This refers to the next section of the manuscript, part of which became Chapter Six in the published version of Volume III. Translator]

38 > The *circulation time* during which the value of the machinery and other constituents of the fixed capital is reproduced, is determined in practice not by its actual duration but by the quantity of labour-time during which it serves as means of production, and in general by the dimensions or the length of the labour-process in the course of which it functions and is used up. If the workmen work for 18 hours instead of 12, this gives 3 more days a week, 1½ working weeks in one week, and 78 in 52 weeks. In 5 years that comes to 390 weeks, hence 7½ years. If the overtime is unpaid and the normal surplus time = two hours, 30 out of the 36 hours (3 days) would have to be paid. Thus the workers give one out of the two weeks for nothing, and one out of two years. Thus the *valorisation* of the machine is *doubled* and this is obtained in *half* the time that would otherwise be necessary. <

> one of the main stimuli < for profit-mad capitalists to prolong the working day.[39]

The situation is different when the working day remains constant. Here one solution is to increase the number of workers and with them also to a certain degree the amount of fixed capital – buildings, machinery, etc. – so as to exploit a greater mass of labour (for we ignore here any deductions from wages or depression of wages below their normal level). Alternatively, if the intensity of labour is to be increased, labour productivity increased, and relative surplus-value produced in any way, then *the mass of this part of the constant capital applied* will have to grow in those branches of industry that use raw materials, since more raw materials, etc., are worked up in a given space of time. Secondly, the amount of machinery set in motion by the same number of workers will have to grow, and this too is a part of constant capital. A growth in surplus-value is therefore accompanied by a growth in constant capital > or < the growing exploitation of labour by an increase in the price paid for the conditions of production > in < which labour is exploited, i.e., by greater outlays of capital. The rate of profit is thereby reduced on the one hand, even if increased on the other. > This is what causes the drive towards overtime and the lengthening of absolute labour-time, whatever the given level of development of the forces of production.

Equally, the costs of superintendence are less for 500 people who work 18 hours per day than for 750 people who work 12 hours in the same concern.

< 'The expense of working a factory 10 hours almost equals that of working it 12'. (*Factory Reports. Appendix* 1849 (1), p. 37, n. 10.) > 'There are certain expenses upon a mill which go on in the same proportion whether the mill be running short or full time, as for instance rent, rates and taxes, insurance against fire, wages of several permanent servants, deterioration of the machinery, with various other charges upon a manufacturing establishment, *the proportion of which to profits increases as the production decreases*'. (*Factory Reports* 1863 (1), p. 19.)

While on the one hand the mere lengthening of labour-time produces a *relative reduction* in the costs of the fixed capital (of this part of the constant capital), on the other hand labour-time is often *prolonged* in order to make savings on this or that outlay. 'The bleachers point to part of their processes being chemical processes, and that they cannot, therefore, be as regular as purely mechanical works are, that it is a trade of sudden demand for the

---

39 < 'As in all factories there is a very large amount of fixed capital in buildings and machinery, the greater number of hours that machinery can be kept at work the greater will be the return'. (*Reports of the Inspectors of Factories* [referred to from now on as *Factory Reports*] 1858 (2), p. 8.) >

completion of goods for immediate shipment etc. But multiplied appliances have, and can, overcome the first two of these objections, and they are thus *reduced to a question of outlay*'. (*Factory Reports* 1863 (1), p. 54.)

|72| < As already emphasised in the analysis of co-operation, the division of labour and machinery, the *economy in the conditions of production* which characterises > work < (production) on a large scale arises in essentials from the way that these conditions function as conditions of *social and socially combined labour*, hence as *social* conditions of labour. They are consumed *in common* in the production process, by the *collective worker*, instead of being consumed in fragmented form by a mass of unconnected workers or workers directly co-operating only to a small degree. > If we look for example at a < large factory with one or two central motors, the costs of these motors do not grow in the same proportion as, > e.g., their horse-power and therefore their possible sphere of action; the costs of the driving machinery do not grow < in the same proportion as the number of working machines to which it imparts motion; the body of the working machinery does not increase in cost in proportion to the rising number of tools, its organs as it were, with which it functions. The concentration of the means of production also saves on all manner of buildings, > not only for the machinery itself, but for the storage of the raw materials, the semi-manufactured and the manufactured materials, etc. < The same is true of expenses for heating and lighting, etc. > A given number of receptacles do not become dearer in the same proportion as the area they cover grows, or as they assist in the storage of a greater amount of products, etc.[40] < Other conditions of production also remain the same, whether they are used by many people or by few.

But all these economies, arising from the concentration of the means of production and their employment on a massive scale, presuppose as an essential condition the *conglomeration and co-operation of the workers*, the social combination of labour. They thus arise as much from the social character of labour as surplus-value does from the surplus labour of each individual worker taken in isolation. Even the constant improvements that are possible and necessary here arise solely from the social experiences and observations that are made possible and promoted by the large-scale production of the combined collective worker.

The same applies also to the second major aspect of the economical use of the conditions of production. By this we mean the transformation of the *refuse of production*, its so-called *waste products*, back into *new conditions of*

40 Fourier 1829, pp. 6–8.

production, either in the same branch of industry or in another branch; the processes by which this refuse is sent back into the cycle of production and thus consumption (productive or individual). This branch of savings – with which we shall deal somewhat more closely later on > just as we shall also deal with the first aspect mentioned, the savings on fixed capital < – is the result of social labour on a large scale. It is the resulting massive scale of these waste products that makes them into new objects of trade and therefore new elements of production. These waste products, quite apart from the service that they perform as new elements of production, reduce the cost of raw material to the extent that they can be resold, for this cost always includes the *normal* wastage, i.e., the average quantity that is lost in the course of processing. To the extent that the costs of this portion of constant capital are reduced, the rate of profit is correspondingly increased, with a given magnitude of variable capital and a given rate of surplus-value. > (If the variable capital is given, and the rate of surplus-value, the amount of surplus-value is also given, hence the length of the working day too, since v + s is the expression in money of the labour-time contained in the two taken together.)

< It is only as the waste products of *production in common*, and hence of production on a large scale, that they acquire this importance for the production process and remain bearers of exchange value. *If surplus-value is a given factor*, profit can only be *increased* > (and also *reduced* by a movement in a contrary direction) to the extent that it is possible to reduce < the *value* of the constant capital required for the production of the commodities in question. In so far as the constant capital is involved in the *production* of the commodities, all that matters is its use value, not its exchange value. > If the *level of production*, i.e., a specific level of technological development, is given, < the amount of labour that the flax in a spinning mill can absorb depends not on its *value* but on its *quantity*. In the same way, the assistance that a machine gives to > e.g., 100 workers < depends not on its *value* but on its *use value* as a machine. At one stage of technological development a bad machine may be expensive, at another stage a good machine may be cheap.

The increased profit that a capitalist obtains through a fall in the cost of cotton and spinning machinery, for example, is the result of *an increase in labour productivity*, and indeed not in the spinning mill, but rather in the production of machines > and the cultivation of flax, etc. < A smaller amount of expenditure on the conditions of labour, > on the constant part of the capital, the existing value of which alone reappears in the product, but is not increased, < is needed in order to > materialise < a given quantity of labour and thus appropriate a given quantity of surplus labour. The costs of appropriating a certain quantity of surplus labour therefore fall.

|73| We have already discussed > the *economies* < brought about because the collective worker – the socially combined worker – employs the means of production in common in the production process. > Here it is of course assumed that the opportunities provided in this way are utilised in an appropriate manner. A further reduction in the value of the constant capital or saving on the outlay of capital which arises < from the *reduction of the circulation time* (the *development of the means of communication* being the decisive material aspect here) > will be considered in a later section of this chapter. In a subsequent section of the same chapter we shall undertake a special investigation of the influence exerted by fluctuations in the price of raw materials, etc., on the rate of profit. < Here, however, we must firstly dwell on the economies that arise from the continuous improvement of machinery > perhaps by the use of improved material, e.g., iron instead of wood, but in particular 1) < through the cheapening of machinery through the improvement of machine-building in general, so that even if the value of the fixed part of constant capital constantly grows with the development of labour on a large scale, it in no way *grows to the same degree*[41] and 2) through the special improvements that enable machinery that is already installed to operate more cheaply and efficiently, e.g., improvements to steam boilers, etc., which we shall discuss later on in more detail. (Everything that reduces the depreciation of machinery, and of fixed capital in general, during a given period of circulation and production, not only cheapens the individual commodity, since each individual commodity reproduces its aliquot part in the depreciation in its price, but also reduces the aliquot outlay of capital for this period. *Repair work* and the like, to the extent that it is needed, counts as part of the *original costs* of the machinery. Its reduction, as a consequence of the machinery's greater durability, reduces the price of the machinery proportionately.)

For all economies of this kind, > what was said of those of the other kind is still partially true: < they can only be applied by the *combined worker* and often only by work on a still larger scale. They demand a still greater combination of workers directly in the production process.

On the other hand: *the development of the productive power of labour in one branch of production*, e.g., of iron, coal, machines, buildings, etc., which may in turn be connected with new developments in the field of intellectual production, or the natural sciences and their application, appears as the condition for a *reduction in the cost* (the value) *of the means of production in another branch of production*. This is self-evident, for the commodity that emerges from one

41 See Ure on advances in factory construction, etc. [Ure 1836, pp. 62–3. Translator]

branch of industry as a product enters another branch as means of production. Its cheapness or otherwise depends on the *productivity of labour* in the branch of production of which it is the product, and is at the same time a condition not only for the cheapening of the commodities into the production of which it enters as means of production, but also for the *reduction in value* of the constant capital > of which it forms an element in another branch of production < and therefore for an increase in the *rate of profit*. >

Although the level of the rate of profit does not directly correspond here to the *degree of direct exploitation* of the worker directly employed by the capitalist, as is the case with the rate of surplus-value, and although here our earlier statement that *economies in the conditions of production* are exclusively a result of the *social* function of the means of production or their function as means of production of the worker in a social sense, < the characteristic feature of this kind of *economy in constant capital*, which proceeds from the progressive development of industry, is |74| that here the *rise in the rate of profit* for one branch of industry depends on the development of *labour productivity* in another. The benefit that accrues here to the capitalist is once more the *product of social labour* > although not, as in the case of surplus-value, or even the case of the previously mentioned economy in the use of constant capital, the product of < *the workers whom he directly exploits*. The development of labour productivity can always be reduced in the final analysis to the social character of the labour that is employed, to the division of labour within the society, and to the development of intellectual labour. (The *natural sciences*, etc.) What the capitalist makes use of here is the *social division of labour*, the division of labour > operating by and large over the whole of the society. It is the development of the productive power of labour in a Foreign Department,[42] < the department that provides the capitalist with the means of production, *which raises capital's rate of profit* (because it causes the value of the constant capital applied by the capitalist to fall relatively > even if not absolutely).

< A different form of increase in the rate of profit arises not from *economy in the labour* by which constant capital is produced, but rather from *economy in the employment of constant capital*. By the concentration of workers and their co-operation on a large scale, constant capital is spared. The same buildings, heating and lighting equipment, etc., cost relatively less for production on a large scale than on a small scale. > The costs of a part of the machinery, etc., rise similarly. For example, the cost of a steam boiler does not rise in proportion to its horsepower. < Although its absolute value rises, its relative value

42 [In English in the manuscript. Translator]

falls, in relation to the scale of production and the magnitude of the variable capital set in motion or the amount of labour that is exploited. The economy that a capital makes in its own branch of production, e.g., in spinning, rests directly on *economies in labour*, i.e., in reducing the paid labour of its own workers to the absolute minimum; the economy previously mentioned, however, consists in the *greatest possible appropriation of unpaid alien labour* in the most economical fashion, i.e., in operating at the given scale of production with the lowest possible costs. > This kind of economy, too, is dependent either on the < exploitation of the productivity of social labour > outside this particular branch of production, i.e., on the productivity of the labour employed in the production of the constant capital – or on < economy in the use of constant capital, which either directly facilitates saving through co-operation, the social form of labour within the particular branch of production, or makes production of the machinery, etc., possible on a scale at which its exchange-value does not increase to the same degree as its use-value.

Two points have always to be borne in mind here: if the value of c were 0, we would have $p' = s'$, and *the rate of profit would be at its maximum.* > This is point number one. < Secondly, however, what is important for the direct exploitation of labour itself is by no means the value of the means of exploitation applied, whether that of the fixed capital or that of the raw and ancillary materials. As directors and absorbers of labour – as media in and through which the labour and therefore also the surplus labour is objectified, the *exchange-value* of these machines, buildings, raw materials, etc., is completely irrelevant. The only thing that matters here is on the one hand the quantity of these means of exploitation *technologically* required for a certain quantity of labour (for combination with a certain quantity of living labour), and on the other hand > their efficiency, the need for which in the case of the machinery goes without saying (which is the first thing one thinks about) < but which also plays its part in relation to the quality of the raw material, etc.

(((The rate of profit depends in part on the quality of the raw material > compare for example East Indian and American cotton. < There is firstly little waste (I mean here *refuse*) hence a smaller amount of raw material is needed to absorb the same quantity of labour. This is one item. The working machine also meets with less resistance. In part this even affects surplus-value and the rate of surplus-value, > presupposing, that is, that the worker is paid the *value of his labour-capacity*. [With bad raw material] he needs more time to work up the same quantity. < There is also a very significant effect on the reproduction and accumulation of capital, which, as explained previously, depends still more on the *productivity* than on the *amount of labour applied*.)))

The fanaticism the capitalist shows for economising on the means of production is now comprehensible. (Nothing is to be lost; there must be no waste and the means of production may only be consumed in the manner required by the production itself, etc.; all these requirements depend partly on the skill and training of the worker and partly on the discipline exerted by the capitalist over the combined workers > which in a higher state of society would be viewed as self-direction and appropriate behaviour, etc.) < The same fanaticism is also expressed inversely in the form of *skimping on the elements of production*, which is a major way of lowering the value of the constant capital in relation to the variable and thus of increasing the rate of profit (in this connection, we also have the sale of these elements of production above their value – in so far as this value reappears in the product – which is an additional important aspect of fraud.) These phenomena, however, pertain to competition and do not concern us here. >

We should also add the following to the above themes of *'economy in the use of fixed capital', 're-use of waste products', 'introduction of improvements'*, etc.: *reduction in the wastage of raw material* and in the *deterioration of fixed capital* (hence also repairs to fixed capital). The first is achieved by *employing better machines and implements*, e.g., the saw instead of the axe, etc., the second by *improving the raw material used in the fixed capital*, iron instead of wood, etc.

|75| < It must be noted how this *rise in the rate of profit* brought about by *a reduction in the value* (expense) *of the constant capital* is completely independent of whether the branch of industry in which it takes place produces luxury products, means of subsistence that enter the consumption of the workers, or means of producing such means of subsistence. This last circumstance would be important only inasmuch as it affected the *rate of surplus-value*, which depends essentially on *the value of labour-capacity*, i.e., the value of the worker's customary means of subsistence. Here, on the contrary, surplus-value and the rate of surplus-value are presupposed as given. How the surplus-value is related to the total capital – and this is what determines the *rate of profit* – depends under these circumstances exclusively on the value of the constant capital and in no way on the *use-value* of the elements of which this consists.

The relative *cheapening of the means of production* (which naturally does not exclude a growth in their absolute value, considering that the *absolute scale* on which they are applied increases extraordinarily with the growth of labour productivity and the growing *scale* of production that accompanies it) and economy in the use of constant capital, from whatever aspect they are viewed, are in part the exclusive result of the fact that they function, are consumed, as the *common* means of production of the *combined workers*, so that this economy itself appears as a *product* of the social character of *directly productive labour*, but they are also the result of the *development of labour productivity* in those spheres that provide capital with its means of production, so that even if labour as a whole is considered vis-à-vis capital as a whole, and not merely the workers employed by capitalist A vis-à-vis this capitalist A, this economy is again the product of the development of the productive forces of social labour, and the distinction is simply that capitalist A, instead of profiting directly from the productivity of labour in his own workshop, makes use of the productivity of labour in other firms. > Yet despite this fact about the source of *economies in constant capital* < it still appears to the capitalist as a requirement completely alien to the worker, which is absolutely no concern of his, and which he has nothing at all to do with. Nevertheless, it always remains very clear to the capitalist that the worker certainly does have something to do with whether he buys more or less labour for the same amount of money (for this is how the transaction between capitalist and worker appears in his consciousness). To a still higher degree than is the case with other powers immanent [*immanent*] in labour, this *economy in the use of the means of production*, this method of attaining a given result with the least possible expense, appears as *a power inherent in capital* and a method specific to and characteristic of the capitalist mode of production.

This way of conceiving things is all the less surprising in that it corresponds to the semblance [*Schein*] of the matter and since the capital relation actually does conceal the inner connection thanks to the complete indifference, externality [*Äusserlichkeit*] and alienation [*Entfremdung*] between the worker and the conditions of production of his own labour.

Firstly, the *means of production* which comprise the constant capital > considered from the point of view of their *value* < simply represent the *capitalist's money* (as the body of the Roman debtor represented the body of his creditor, according to Linguet), and they are connected to him alone, while the worker, in so far as he comes into contact with them in the actual process of production, deals with them only as *use-values for production*, means and materials of labour. The decrease or increase in this value is therefore a fact, which affects his relationship to the capitalist as little as whether he works with copper or with iron. (The capitalist, of course, likes to conceive things differently, as we shall see later, as soon as there is an *increase in the value* of the means of production and hence a decline in the rate of profit.) *Secondly*: in so far as these means of production are at the same time a *means for exploiting* |76| *labour* in the capitalist production process, the relative cheapness or otherwise of these *means of exploitation* concerns the worker as little as a horse is concerned with whether it is controlled with a cheap or an expensive bit and bridle. Finally: as we have already seen, the worker in fact treats the social character of his work, its combination, as something alien to him, and its conditions of realisation as the property of another, and he would be completely indifferent to the wastage of this property if he were not himself forcibly compelled to economise on it. (Things are different, for example, in factories that belong to the workers themselves, as in Rochdale.) It need hardly be mentioned that in as much as the *productivity of labour* in one branch of production appears as a *cheapening* and an *improvement* of the means of production in another (and to that extent serves to increase the rate of profit) this general connection of social labour appears as something *completely alien to the workers*, something that simply concerns the capitalist, in as much as he alone *buys and appropriates* these means of production. That he buys the product of labour in a different branch of production with the product of the workers in his own branch of production and therefore only has the product of other workers at his disposal to the extent that he has appropriated the product of his own workers without giving anything in return, is a situation that is fortunately concealed by the circulation process, etc.

A further aspect, moreover, is that since production on a large scale developed first in the *capitalist form*, the profit-mania on the one hand, and the need to produce the commodity as cheaply as possible on the other (because of sale and competition) give this *economy* in the use of constant capital the appearance of something peculiar to the capitalist mode of production and therefore make it seem a function of the *capitalist*.

Just as the capitalist mode of production promotes on the one hand the development of the productive forces of social labour, so on the other hand does it promote *economy* in the *use* of constant capital.

Yet there is more to this than the alienation and indifference that the worker, as the bearer of living labour, has towards the economical use of the conditions of his labour. The contradictory and antithetical character of the capitalist mode of production leads it to count the *squandering of the life and health of the worker, the depression of his conditions of existence*, as itself an *economy in the use of constant capital*, and hence a means for *raising the rate of profit*.

Since the worker spends the greater part of his life in the production process, the conditions of this process are in part conditions of his life process, of his active life, his conditions of life, and economy in these conditions of life is a method of increasing the profit rate. In the same way, as we saw previously, overwork, the transformation of the worker into a beast of burden, is a method which lies at the basis of the self-valorisation [*Selbstverwertung*] of capital – it is a method of accelerating the production of surplus-value. This economy extends to forcing the workers to huddle together in confined spaces – which amounts to saving on buildings –; crowding of dangerous machinery[43] and failure to provide means of protection against the resultant dangers; neglecting to carry out precautionary measures in works (branches of production) the very nature of which is unhealthy; failing to install adequate measures of protection in mines, etc., in order to save on expenditure, etc. Not to speak of the absence of all provisions that would make the production process humane and comfortable for the worker. From the standpoint of the capitalist this would be a senseless and purposeless waste. Capitalist production is in general thoroughly wasteful of *human material*, just as its way of distributing its products (through trade), and its manner of competition, make it very wasteful of material resources, so that it loses on one side of the account what it gains on the other.

As capital has the tendency to reduce the direct *employment of living labour to necessary labour*, and constantly to shorten the labour-time necessary for the creation of a product by exploiting the social productivity of labour, hence economising as much as possible on living labour (i.e., the labour it directly *applies*), so also it has the tendency to apply this labour, which has already been reduced to its necessary amount, under the *most economical conditions*, i.e., to reduce to the absolute minimum the exchange-value of the constant capital applied. If the value of commodities is determined by the necessary labour-time contained in them and not simply by labour-time as such, it is capital that first makes a reality of this mode of determination and immediately goes on continually to reduce the labour socially necessary for the production of a commodity. The price of the commodity is therefore reduced to a minimum through reducing to a minimum each part of the labour required to produce it.

We have to make the following distinction, in connection with this economy in the use of constant capital: if the *mass* of the capital applied grows, and *with it also the sum of capital value*, this first involves simply the concentration of more capital in a single hand > *the application of a greater amount of the same capital.* < It is precisely this greater mass employed by one capital, which generally corresponds also to an absolutely greater, if also a relatively smaller number of employed workers, that permits *economies in constant capital*. If we take the individual capitalist, we see a growth in the *size of his necessary capital outlay* (we are speaking here of fixed capital) but in relation to the mass of material to be worked up and the amount of labour to be exploited, its value undergoes a relative *decline*.

43 [In English in the manuscript. Translator]

We shall now elaborate on this with some brief illustrations. We begin with what is really the end, *economies in the conditions of the worker's life, i.e., economies in the conditions of production*, in so far as these > simultaneously react (impact) upon the worker's *conditions of existence and life*.

|77| <*Economies at the Expense of the Workers* (*Economies in the Conditions of Production at the Expense of the Producers.*)

Coal Mining. Neglect of the Most Necessary Outlays.

'Under the competition which exists among the coal owners and coal proprietors in each district for the supply of their several markets, *no more outlay is incurred* than is sufficient *to overcome* the most obvious physical difficulties; and under that which prevails among the labouring colliers, who are ordinarily more numerous than the work to be done requires, a large amount of danger and of exposure to the most noxious influences will gladly be encountered for wages a little in advance of the agricultural population round them, in an occupation, in which they can moreover make a profitable use of their children. This double competition ... is quite sufficient to cause a large proportion of the pits to be worked with the most imperfect drainage and ventilation; often with ill-constructed shafts, bad gearing, incompetent engineers; and ill-constructed and ill-prepared bays (recesses in which it is hewn) and roadways; causing a *destruction* of life and limb, and health, the statistics of which would present an appalling picture'.[44]

On an average, 15 men were killed in the English coal mines every week [at the time in question]. During the 10 years concluding with 1861, about 10,000 people were killed,[45] mostly by the sordid avarice of the owners of coal mines,

---

44 'The *First Report of the Children's Employment Commissioners in Mines and Collieries etc., 21 April 1842*' [*Westminster Review*, vol. 38, July–October 1842, 1.5., p. 102. Translator].

45 < According to the report *Coal Mine Accidents* published on 6 February 1862, 8466 persons were killed in the 10 years ending with 1861 (*Coal Mine Accidents* 1862, p. 8). But this number is far too small, > because: 'In the early part of the existence of the inspection (which began in 1850) when the districts were so extensive, and the requirements of the act of Parliament not fully known to the managers of the collieries ... a considerable number of accidents and deaths were not reported'. (Note by John J. Atkinson, Inspector of Mines, *Coal Mine Accidents* 1862, p. 5.) The very circumstance that, despite the great and still continuing butchery, the number of accidents has dropped sharply since the system of inspection was established, shows the natural tendency of capitalist exploitation.

who for example only have one shaft sunk, so that there is no escape if the shaft gets blocked, or other circumstances make a sudden flight necessary. > (Capitalist production is, to a certain degree, if we abstract from the whole process of circulation, and the superfetations of competition, most economical of *realised labour*, labour realised in commodities. It is a greater spendthrift than any other mode of production, of men, of living labour, a spendthrift not only of flesh and blood, but of brains and nerves. It is, in fact, only by the greatest waste of individual development that the development of general men is secured in those epochs of history preceding the socialist constitution of mankind.)[46]

'Sollte diese Qual uns quälen,
Da sie unsre Lust vermehrt,
Hat nicht Myriaden Seelen,
Timur's Herrschaft aufgezehrt?'[47]

< If in fact the whole of the economising we are discussing here arises from the *social character of labour*, it is *this directly social character* of labour which produces this waste of workers. The question raised by Factory Inspector R[obert] Baker is very pertinent here:

'The whole question is one for serious consideration, in what way *this sacrifice of infant life occasioned by congregational labour* can be best averted?' (*Factory Reports* 1864 (1), p. 157). > (See also the same source on early marriages, *Factory Reports* 1864 (1), p. 156.)

|78| < Under this heading belong the suppression of all precautionary measures as to the safety, comfort and health of the workers. As in the coal mines, so in the factories proper a great part of the *casualty lists* of the wounded and dead of the industrial army stem from this (see the biannual *Factory Reports*). Also *insufficient space*, and lack of ventilation, etc. >

---

46 [The passage in parentheses is in English in the manuscript. Translator]

47 [This quatrain from Goethe's poem 'An Suleika', from the collection *Westöstlicher Diwan*, was a favourite with Marx. It appears several times in his works. There are many English verse translations. Alexander Rogers's 1890 version is perhaps most appropriate here:
Should his shrill complaint torment us?
Since it has increased our joy?
Did not Timur's harsh dominion
Myriads of souls destroy?
Translator]

Factory Reports (*Biannual.*)

It must first be remarked that not all accidents are reported on, although this is prescribed by law. The official statistics therefore understate the reality. 'I have reason to fear that no notice is given of many that the law requires (namely accidents) to be reported'.[48]

The attention of the inspectors was first directed to the subject of the fencing of machinery by a letter of 10 June 1853 from the Secretary of State. The Act of 1844 prescribes fencing [on the following grounds]:

'… the lives of factory operatives, being spent in the midst of dangers, tend to render them in some measure insensible to risk, and as they cannot be at all times alive to the consequences of a false step, they ought, as far as practicable, to be protected from the chance of accidents arising out of their own indiscretions'. (*Factory Reports* 1856 (1), p. 44.) 'Another fruitful source of preventible accidents is in setting machinery in motion without any previous notice, for while it is standing there will be hands and fingers doing something or nothing among the wheels. It would be so very easy to give some understood signal, that I beg earnestly to recommend its adoption in all mills in which such practice is not already carried out, for many accidents continue to arise for want of this precaution' (ibid.)

'One good effect of *legislation upon the subject of the fencing of machinery* is to be found in the fact that no new machines ever leave the premises of the engineer now, in which all outside wheels are not 'well and securely fenced' by iron casings; the ends *of the old frames are a mass of complicated wheels*, in the new ones *not a wheel* can be touched, nor in many frames can one even be seen; and I trust the time is not far distant when an engineer will as rarely erect *mill-gearing* which he has not "well and securely fenced", by some appropriate and sufficient means'. (*Factory Reports* 1856 (1), p. 56.)

In his official report for the half year which ended on 31 October 1853, *Leonard Horner* writes this:

'There exists a continued *resistance among a considerable number of millowners* to a compliance with those enactments which require horizontal shafts to be securely fenced, notwithstanding that the danger of leaving them exposed has been proved, and continues to be proved, by serious and fatal accidents; notwithstanding that they are aware that a sufficient fencing need not in the least degree interfere with the free working of the machinery; that it does not involve more than a moderate outlay'.[49] In the same report, under the date of

48 *Factory Reports* 1856 (1), p. 6 (L. Horner.)

49 *Factory Reports* 1856 (1), p. 4.

31 January 1854, Horner relates that he 'did, in obedience to the instructions of Lord Palmerston', circulate a circular, 'directing the attention of mill-owners to the enactments of the law that require horizontal shafts to be securely fenced', adding that 'I have been made the object of very acrimonious attacks by a section of influential mill-owners in my district'.[50]

Furthermore: 'I have heard some millowners speak with inexcusable levity of some of the accidents; such for instance as the loss of a finger being a trifling matter. A working man's living and prospects depend so much on his fingers, that any loss of them is a very serious matter to him. When I have heard such inconsiderate remarks made, I have usually put this question: "Suppose you were in want of an additional workman, and two were to apply, both equally well qualified in other respects, but one had lost a thumb or a forefinger, which would you engage?" There was never a hesitation as to the answer'.[51] These manufacturing gentlemen, says Horner, have 'mistaken prejudices against what they have heard represented as a pseudo-philanthropic legislation'.[52]

|79| Sir John Kincaid, at that time Factory Inspector for Scotland, *remarks in the same report for October 1855*:

'A considerable portion of the occupiers of the unfenced works still intend to fence, but there are others of them who are "waiting to see what is done at Manchester"'. He now comments: 'Every factory has quantities of old iron lying about, which is readily convertible to such purposes ... in the extensive ... establishment of Messrs. Gordon of Arbroath, in which about 500 workers are usually employed, and where they have fenced efficiently with 181 strap hooks at the average cost of 1s. each, making in all £9. 1s. Their engines are of 110 horse power. Had they, without fencing, joined the Manchester Association at 2s. per horse power, which is the call already made upon its members, the expense to

---

50 Ibid.

51 *Factory Reports* 1856 (1), pp. 6, 7. The extent to which the *unpaid magistrates*, themselves composed of manufacturers, parsons, country squires, etc., uphold the interests of the manufacturers, can be seen for example from the remarks of Lord Chief Justice Campbell with regard to a judgment by one of them, against which an appeal had been made to him: 'It is not an interpretation of the Act of Parliament, it is a repeal of the Act of Parliament'. (*Factory Reports* 1856 (1), p. 11.) A large number of cases have been tried, which has given the other millowners a renewed excuse for postponing the execution of the law. (*Factory Reports* 1856 (1), p. 35.)

52 *Factory Reports* 1856 (1), p. 15. When they have been found responsible by a court for accidents caused by their neglect of the legal requirements (receiving very small fines as a result) these gentlemen sometimes demonstrate their magnanimity by refusing to pay the fine until the Inspector has taken out a distress warrant against them. (Ibid, p. 16.)

Messrs. Gordon would have been £11, while the lives and limbs of their workers would have been left without the protection provided by law'.[53] He adds this quotation (*Factory Reports* 1856 (1), p. 46 n.):

'At a meeting of the Committee of Management of the *National Association for the Amendment of the Factory Law*, held at Manchester on the 27th. of March 1855, it was moved by Joseph Simpson, Esq. of Manchester; seconded by Edmund Birley Esq. of Preston, and unanimously resolved: That the recommendation of the Report to raise immediately a sum of not less than £5,000 be immediately carried into execution, and that an additional contribution of one shilling per nominal horsepower from each mill occupier (making a total contribution of 2s. per nominal horse power) be at once called for, to enable the Committee to carry out the recommendation to defend, at the cost of the Association, all *cases of prosecution* (the object was to prove that killing for the sake of profit is no murder) which they may consider fairly to come within the sphere of the Association'.

The *International Statistical Congress* was held *at Paris in September 1855*. Its proceedings were regulated by a Commission appointed by the French government, composed of [Eugène] Rouher, Minister of Agriculture, Commerce and Public Works, President; Baron Charles Dupin, Vice-President, and other similar official humbugs. The *Programme of this Commission* states, with relation to the accidents in manufactories and similar establishments: 'It is certain that the greater number of these sources of accidents could be removed by the adoption of precautions skilfully arranged, by strict internal regulations, but above all by an effective inspection of industrial establishments etc'. (*Programme*, p. 107.)

'This (the above-mentioned judgment by Lord Campbell)[54] is the third occasion upon which a deliberate judgment has been pronounced by a Superior Court upon the scope and intention of s.21 of 7 Victoria c.15'.[55] 'The law', say the Inspectors in self-defence against the angry reproaches of the |80| manufacturers, 'imposes upon us the responsibility of carrying out its provisions, and the still more serious responsibility of enforcing that security which has been provided for protecting the poor and defenceless operatives from the danger to which their daily labour exposes them'.[56] In their *Joint Report* (for the half year up to 31 October 1855) the Inspectors also give us, so to speak, the history of the Association which the millowners of Manchester, etc., set up in 1854 against the implementation of the 1844 Act. The circular which [Leonard] Horner issued at

53 *Factory Reports* 1856 (1), pp. 45, 46.

54 [See above, n. 51. Translator]

55 *Factory Reports* 1856 (1), p. 107.

56 *Factory Reports* 1856 (1), pp. 107, 108.

the beginning of 1854, on the instructions of the Home Minister, was provoked by the rapid multiplication of accidents, accompanied by the circumstance that for the whole of the decade between 1844 and 1854 the millowners had not taken the slightest notice of the precautionary measures prescribed by the 1844 Act. It was announced to the factory-owners that the matter of fencing would now be taken seriously, and that the Inspectors (in accordance with the 1844 Act) would pursue them in court for damages (maximum £20, minimum £5) for industrial accidents caused by unfenced machinery. In response to this the worthy gentlemen founded the Defence Association, an organised conspiracy to put down and paralyse the law for the protection of the limbs and bodies of the 'defenceless operatives'.

In the first half year of 1855, 'a caution ... was addressed by the Manchester Association of Factory Occupiers to the several factory occupiers in the U.K.', as a result of which 'many persons ... continued to expose their workpeople to imminent danger', and have 'hitherto declined to fence their horizontal shafts in any manner whatever ... The recommendations and caution issuing from a combination deriving very powerful influence from their numbers and their wealth, and still more from their station, *many prominent members of the association being themselves Justices of the Peace, and as such charged with administering the law in their respective districts*, have produced ... an effect much to be deplored. For instance, they exhort their brother mill-occupiers not to fence their horizontal shafts; and they tell them that if the Inspectors take proceedings against any member, they, the association, 'undertake to protect [their] members from improper prosecutions and legal proceedings instituted or promoted by the factory inspectors or by other parties'. In the case of the proceedings against Messrs. Cumming, of Bolton ... Mr. Earle stated that he appeared as solicitor to the *National Association of Factory Occupiers*, to conduct the defence; and in the case of Messrs. Cheetham, the same gentleman repeated the same statement. Thus a committee of millowners sitting in Manchester decides that the prosecution is improper before the merits of the case have been brought out by a judicial investigation'.[57]

'On the 3rd. of April last (1855) a report was, according to their printed proceedings, received by the Manchester association from its Deputation to the Secretary of State, which report, as afterwards adopted and published by the association, contained these words: "Sir G[eorge] Grey particularly referred to the proposal (which he remarked had emanated from the trade, and not from the Government or the Inspectors) for the adoption of rectangular hooks, and

57 *Factory Reports* 1856 (1), pp. 110, 111.

trusted that by some such compromise the wishes of the trade might be met, seeing that in some districts such hooks had been adopted". The report thus dealt with this most reasonable suggestion: "The deputation beg to caution the trade against the adoption of any compromise, whether of hooks or otherwise. They anticipate an attempt to *divide* the union of the trade upon this point"'.[58]

|81| 'Seeing that this caution was addressed and sent to the mill-occupiers of the United Kingdom in a circular from the Manchester association soliciting a remittance of money from each firm; seeing that in this circular appeared the following announcement: "With these views the deputation are of opinion that a fund of not less than £5,000 should be immediately raised, and they suggest that all cases of prosecution which the committee of management may be of opinion can be legitimately dealt with by the association shall be *defended by*, and the *penalties or damages paid out of the funds of, the association*"; seeing that such were among the ostensible objects for which factory occupiers were solicited to join the combination and contribute to its funds an *assessment of "two shillings per nominal horsepower"*, it is not surprising that so many, especially in the immediate neighbourhood of Manchester, should have obeyed the precepts and followed the example of the associated mill-occupiers, and should have continued to refuse to fence the horizontal shafts in their factories, or to "adopt any compromise, whether of hooks or otherwise". In the special report of 7 August 1855, however, they withdrew one of the principal objects for which mill-occupiers had been solicited to enrol their names and contribute their money. They say, namely, that "they do not intend to pay damages or penalties in any case whatever"'.[59]

Mr. [William] Fairbairn, an 'eminent civil engineer of Manchester', was brought forward by the defendants on several occasions of legal proceedings in the case of unfenced horizontal shafts, in order to give false evidence and untruthful opinions in favour of the economy and the injured freedom of 'Capital'.[60] What a miserable *parvenu*!

In the same Blue Book, Leonard Horner bears witness to the fury of these fellows: 'From the time that in obedience to the instructions of Lord Palmerston (then Home Secretary) I issued the circular letter of the 31st. of January 1854, as my colleagues did in their respective districts, directing the attention of mill-owners to the enactment of the law that requires horizontal shafts to be

---

58 *Factory Reports* 1856 (1), p. 111.
59 *Factory Reports* 1856 (1), pp. 111, 112.
60 *Factory Reports* 1856 (1), p. 112.

securely fenced, I have been made the object of very acrimonious attacks by a section of influential mill-owners in my district. Not only have I been publicly charged with harshness and unfairness in the administration of the law, in a memorial presented to you last June (1855), but I have been singled out from my colleagues as having prompted Lord Palmerston to issue the instructions complained of etc'.[61]

The Factory Inspectors have the following remark to make in their Joint Report for the Final Half Year of 1855 in regard to the *degree of exactitude of the General Return of Accidents in Factories*, which is attached to every half-yearly report:

'On the subject of the General Return of Accidents we may mention that the statements are sent to us immediately after the accident, and therefore in many *cases before the final result*, whether fatal or otherwise, is known. Hence it follows that *the number of fatal accidents* may have really been greater than the returns indicate'.[62]

|82| The rabble of < factory-owners, however, did not rest until they had obtained a judgment from the Court of Queen's Bench to the effect that the Act of 1844 did not prescribe > 'fencing of horizontal shafts above seven feet from the floor', and according to the circular of 3 March 1856 the Factory Inspectors, on the instructions of the Home Secretary [Sir] G[eorge] Grey, were obliged to inform the factory-owners of 'the amount of fencing which they had been authorised to accept as a compliance with the spirit of the provisions of the Act etc.' The matter then took its course, and in Horner's district 'many mills were advancing towards the same end' (namely the construction of fencing, which many mills in the other districts had already carried out) 'until the Bill introduced into Parliament by Col. Wilson Patten, to alter the law relating to the fencing of mill-gearing, paralysed the proceedings of many, and, in a great measure, suspended the fencings which were in progress in each of our districts'.[63] They declared that the bill would make all of this effort nugatory. This is what the Inspectors say in their Joint Report about accidents during the half year ending April 1856: 'They show an increase over the previous half year of 79 accidents, which include three additional deaths; and the circumstances under which several of the deaths and mutilations took place, leave no reason to doubt that they would have been prevented had either of the fencing precautions, recommended by your predecessor and by yourself, been adopted'.[64]

61 *Factory Reports* 1856 (1), p. 4.

62 *Factory Reports* 1856 (1), p. 113.

63 *Factory Reports* 1856 (2), pp. 3, 5.

64 *Factory Reports* 1856 (2), p. 4.

The Bill introduced by that pig Wilson Patten for the 'further amendment of the laws relating to labour in factories ... is looked upon as putting the subject in abeyance for the present, and, should it pass into law, it is expected by many to operate practically as a release of the factory occupiers from their present liability to fence securely the shafts, whether upright, oblique, or horizontal, by which the motion of the first moving power is communicated to machinery etc'.[65]

It is also remarked here, in regard to the milder interpretation of the law by the Court of Queen's Bench, cited above:

'The list of serious and fatal injuries caused by shafts upwards of seven feet above the floor, which is annexed to our joint Report for the present half year, in continuation of the lists which accompanied the four preceding half-yearly reports, continues to prove that mere height above the floor is no true safeguard against accidents'.[66]

Further remarks on the manufacturers' plausible grounds of excuse:

'The suggestion, too, that these shaft accidents are attributable, not to the insecurity of the shaft, but to the want of proper and ordinary care and foresight on the part of the sufferers, who are maimed or killed by their own headstrong wilfulness, gross negligence, or perverse disobedience of orders, and the like –, seems hardly reconcilable with the fact which the periodical returns have disclosed, that several of the victims, and some in my own district, have been men in the prime of life, in the full enjoyment of all their faculties, familiar from their childhood with factory machinery, and, therefore, thoroughly alive to the dangers of unfenced shafting; men too who have been promoted above their fellows to situations of trust and responsibility, as overlookers, foremen, or spinning-masters, on account of their superior skill, carefulness, intelligence, attention and steadiness. And it seems not unreasonable to require that these men, when engaged in any occupation |83| which would bring them close to an horizontal shaft while revolving, the dangers of which, though they are familiar with them, *no caution on their part can at all times* enable them to escape, should be protected from injury by every contrivance which can be applied to that part of the shaft with which their occasional employment would otherwise necessarily bring them into contact'.[67] 'It is frequently said, indeed, of the sufferer who has sustained injuries from an unfenced shaft, that it was not his business – his ordinary occupation – to do that which brought him into

65 *Factory Reports* 1856 (2), pp. 21, 22 (Howell's Report).
66 *Factory Reports* 1856 (2), p. 22.
67 *Factory Reports* 1856 (2), pp. 22, 23.

contact with the revolving shaft, and the like. But, practically, the thing must be done, and quickly, by somebody; in the great majority of cases it does not appear to be the "ordinary occupation" of anybody, because it does not *occupy any one person's sole time and attention*; but, at the same time, it does appear to be the occasional occupation of anybody, or of everybody; for, as the moving power is not stopped to render the shaft harmless, and as the job must be done on the spur of the moment, the person who happens at the instant to be nearest at hand, and at leisure, does it. Hence the common excuse, "It was not his business", so far as I have been able to test its value, is tantamount to saying "It was nobody's business", seeing that for the purpose of these shaft accidents, the right man, whose proper business it would be to do that which is always done by the wrong man, seems – if he be not altogether an imaginary personage – at any rate to discharge these dangerous duties vicariously, and never to be forthcoming at the right time in the right place, notwithstanding the precision and regularity which characterise the factory system in all its other details'.[68]

In the same Blue Book, Sir John Kincaid, who was then Inspector for Scotland, cites various cases, and continues:

'I have quoted the foregoing cases, which have happened since the first of January last, because they occurred in factories, in which the provisions of the law with regard to fencing had been fully complied with, for the purpose of showing how much the factory operations need all the protection which the Legislature has enacted for the safety of their lives and limbs, when they are liable to accidents so numerous and so appalling as those I have just quoted, which were caused by other portions of machinery which the law does not require to be fenced'.[69]

In the second half of 1856 the bourgeois < managed to put through the above-mentioned Bill for the 'amendment of the Factory Law', with the help of the hypocrite Wilson Patten – a sort of fellow who, like all religious people, is always ready to do the dirtiest work at the bidding of the knights of the purse. The 'amendment' consisted in this, that in fact it *withdrew all special protection from the workers* and referred them to the ordinary courts in case of an accident caused by the masters' machinery. Moreover, a very cunningly concocted arbitration clause left it open to the Factory Inspector, if he was a scoundrel or subject to bourgeois influence, to deprive the workers even of this recourse. One needs to read the following remarks of the Factory Inspectors on the new Act to be able to judge the spirit of a legislation under the domination of Capital.

68 *Factory Reports* 1856 (2), p. 23.

69 *Factory Reports* 1856 (2), p. 31.

This is what they say about the 'Act passed in the last session of Parliament' in their *Joint Report for the half year ending on 31 October 1856*:

'Under the new Statute, a young person performing, in his *"ordinary occupation"*, an act which brings him in contact with unfenced mill gearing, may still be compensated, as he would have been had this Statute not been passed, either by summary proceedings before magistrates, or by an action at law, for the bodily injuries he may have sustained; but if a young person be ordered, by the manager or other person in authority, to do an act, not in the course of his "ordinary occupation", but which he dare not refuse to do, which brings him in contact with unfenced mill gearing, and he is injured thereby, he seems to us to have no redress. Thus the persons whose "ordinary occupation" brings them near to mill gearing, and who are consequently well acquainted with the dangers to which their employment exposes them, and with the necessity of caution, are *protected by the law, while protection has been withdrawn from those who may be obliged, in the execution of special orders, to suspend their "ordinary occupation" and to place themselves in positions of danger, of the existence of which they are not conscious*, and from which, by reason of their ignorance, they are unable to protect themselves, but who, on that very account, would appear to require the especial protection of the Legislature'.[70]

Hence the first 'improvement' made was to remove from one category of youthful factory worker not only administrative protection but the ordinary protection of the law (i.e., through the ordinary courts).

With regard to the other categories of factory worker the Inspectors were more or less provoked by the Act of 1856, says the Report, '*to prejudice or impair, by a previous reference to arbitrators* acting under the very imperfect powers given to them by the Factory Act of 1856, the right of children, young persons, and women, injured by unfenced mill gearing'.[71] That is to say, as soon as the Inspector – in the case of an accident – had submitted to arbitrators the question whether the gearing was dangerous and ought to be fenced, and the arbitrators had decided for the millowner, the right of redress through the customary judicial route was closed off to the victims of capitalist avarice.[72] The Inspectors make this point in more detail: 'If an inspector should unwarily give rise to an arbitration under the Factory Act of 1856, and if the arbitrators, looking at such machinery, should be of opinion that it was from its position harmless, and should adjudge, that it need not be fenced, and if a young person should

70 *Factory Reports* 1857 (1), p. 3.
71 *Factory Reports* 1857 (1), p. 4.
72 Ibid.

afterwards, in the course of his "ordinary occupation" suffer a similar injury etc., the loss of an arm, from such machinery remaining unfenced, it is presumed that, even though the sufferer should be able to prove, by legal evidence, and in a court of law, that he had sustained this injury by reason of the shaft not having been securely fenced, that the injury would not have been inflicted if the shaft had been so fenced, and that it did not occur through his own disobedience, negligence or misconduct, still we apprehend that the *formal though extrajudicial award of two arbitrators*, appointed under the authority of an Act of Parliament, and acting in pursuance of its provisions, though of no real value ... in determining a matter of fact, and to *whose arbitration he was no party, – would* |85| *materially damage the plaintiff's case before a jury, if not destroy his right of action altogether*'.[73]

Now hear how they have devised the rules for this arbitration which, although he was no party to it 'would materially damage the plaintiff's case before a jury, if not destroy his right of action altogether'.

This is in reality an invention designed to secure the mill-occupiers by way of such arbitrations against damages for death and other accidents incurred by their workmen from their unfenced machinery.

'In the Appendix, note 3, page 23, will be found *a list of 16 serious accidents* during the half year, caused by a particular class of mill gearing, viz. horizontal shafts, not being securely fenced; and of these it will be seen that *6 were fatal*. We are clearly of opinion that mill gearing of this class *is in all cases liable* to cause bodily injury to the persons employed, inasmuch as it has already, in many cases, caused serious and fatal injury, and that it can in all cases be well and securely fenced, inasmuch as in every variety of case it has been well and securely fenced. To accomplish this, the Factory Act of 1856 empowers us to designate this class of *mill gearing not as mill gearing but as machinery*, and to serve upon the occupier of the factory a notice that we deem this so-called machinery to be dangerous, whereupon he must either comply with the requirements of this notice, or deny the fact and refer the disputed point to *arbitration*'.[74] 'If the occupier of a factory, after having received the notice, desire to submit the question to arbitration, he must appoint a person "*skilled in the construction of the kind of machinery to which the notice refers*", and the inspector must thereupon appoint another person similarly qualified, and *these two arbitrators* are then directed to "*proceed to examine the machinery alleged to be dangerous*". If they cannot agree, they are required to appoint a

---

73 Ibid.

74 *Factory Reports* 1857 (1), p. 5.

third arbitrator similarly qualified, and *the decision of two of the said arbitrators*, whether it is "*necessary and possible*" to fence the said machinery, is *binding and final*. **The notice is issued** (by the Inspectors) **because danger is, from experience, known to exist; and the opinion** whether danger exists or not is to be pronounced by *arbitrators skilled in the construction of machinery but having no power to compel the appearance of the witnesses who can prove the danger and the practicability of removing it, to examine them on oath*, or to conduct their inquiry to a satisfactory conclusion, under the same guarantees for securing the ends of justice under which *ordinary references to arbitration* of matters in dispute between individuals are conducted ... *The powers given to arbitrators in all ordinary judicial references are withheld from the arbitrators who are*, by the Factory Act of 1856, *to determine this question, which affects the lives and limbs of those who are least able to protect themselves*'.[75] These powers, that is to say, are contrary to the Arbitration Clauses of the Common Law Procedure Act, 1852; for in this case the arbitrator has 'full power to compel the attendance of witnesses and to examine them upon oath subject to the penalties of perjury etc'.

|86| Firstly, the arbitration proceeds here under conditions which render it nugatory in advance. Secondly, it is entrusted to civil engineers and machine-builders, fellows who *in the first place* neither understand nor wish to understand the issues, and *in the second place* always take sides with the manufacturer against the worker because they are customers of the manufacturer and fellow-bourgeois. The wretched Fairbairn is an example.

[Four further points:] *Firstly*: 'This is in reality a question which requires for its solution *not the opinion of professional engineers, but the evidence of intelligent and observant men* who are daily employed in factories. An engineer would undoubtedly be entitled to deference in expressing an opinion whether any obstruction would arise to the action of machinery from any particular mode of fencing, but the *prevention of accidents is no part of his professional business*. It was truly remarked by Mr. Cubitt, principal engineer at the works of Rothwell and Company, that "the engineer's part is done when the engine is fixed and the gearing put in proper working condition; the fencing or guarding it is at the discretion of the mill-owner". *Engineers and machine makers*, who, as *skilled in the construction of machinery*, are the class of persons from whom the arbitrators must be chosen, have really no familiar personal knowledge of the way in which shaft accidents occur. The safest guides to the discovery of danger, and of the best means of averting it, are the persons who pass their lives

75 Ibid.

in factories among the machinery (after it has been turned out of the workshop of the engineer or machine maker), who have to adjust the straps on the drums, who witness, and occasionally in their own proper persons experience, the bodily injuries inflicted by horizontal shafts, the position of which is so elevated as to render them apparently harmless to the scientific looker on'.[76] 'In fact, engineers and machine makers look only to the construction and working of the machinery, which is their business, and not to the prevention of accidents, which is not their business'.[77]

Secondly: they turn what is a clear matter of fact into a *matter of opinion*. 'We (the Inspectors) have repeatedly reported that fencing of different kinds, as metallic or wooden casing, parallel rods, and rectangular hooks, has been very extensively applied by millowners in various part of the United Kingdom, and in every variety of circumstance, with complete success. *The secure fencing of mill gearing is therefore not a matter of opinion for the speculations of men of science, but it is a plain matter of fact*, to be proved, like any other matter of fact, *by evidence before a tribunal* armed with all the powers necessary for eliciting the whole truth'.[78] And precisely because it is a matter of fact to be proved by evidence, 'these arbitrators are not to take evidence, but simply to look at the machinery'. (*Factory Reports* 1857 (1), p. 7.) Quite apart from the fact that the dogs are not appropriate for the task, their 'defective tribunal' has been legally 'divested of the ordinary powers of an arbitrator to satisfy the demand of justice'. (ibid.)

Thirdly: the fellows are themselves manufacturers, understrappers of manufacturers, or their customers.

'It, moreover, appears to us, that engineers and machine makers ought to be considered *as disqualified to act as factory arbitrators, by reason of their connection in trade with the factory occupiers, who are their customers*; for, however unquestionable their integrity, we conceive that a question involving *the safety of the operative* cannot be determined *impartially* by an arbitration, *while the arbitrators are required to be exclusively selected from a class so intimately connected with the party refusing to fence the machinery*, which we know from experience to be dangerous'.[79]

Fourthly: the Inspectors declare that in order not 'to take away the right of damages' from the workers by such arbitration, which is a right the latter would be otherwise legally entitled to enforce, they have 'refrained from giving, under

76 *Factory Reports* 1857 (1), pp. 5–6.
77 *Factory Reports* 1857 (1), p. 6.
78 Ibid.
79 *Factory Reports* 1857 (1), pp. 7–8.

the Factory Act of 1856, *any notice which would call into action the imperfect extrajudicial kind of arbitration* provided by that Statute; and although *all provision for* ***preventing*** *accidents* from horizontal shafts has thus been *practically repealed* by the Factory Act of 1856', they have 'taken care not to compromise any right, which still remains to the injured person, to *compensation* ***after*** *the accident has befallen him*'.[80] '*The safeguards which the operatives ... possessed have been virtually withdrawn*'.[81]

|89|[82] In their report for the half year ending on 30 April 1857, the Inspectors say (in their Joint Report):

'We regret that we cannot report a more general adoption of means that have been repeatedly recommended, and found in practice to afford, at a trifling cost, sufficient protection from accidents from unfenced horizontal shafts; and we particularly call your attention to facts mentioned in the Appendix No. 3, in the cases Nos. 6 and 13, that, after serious accidents had occurred from unfenced horizontal shafts, strap-hooks or rods had been fixed up in the factories in which the accidents had occurred, which, had they been previously adopted, would have prevented these sad calamities'.[83]

In the *Report for the half year ending 31 October 1858*, Inspector R[obert] Baker writes that, in his district, there was:

'an increase of accidents of 21 per cent over the half year ending in April last'.[84] 'Of those (accidents) that happened by machinery, 30.1 per cent were occasioned by unfenced gearing wheels, which might have been rendered secure without prejudice to the works; 2.2 per cent by the shuttle of looms flying from the raceboard and injuring contiguous workpeople; 3.2 per cent from the pulleys and shafts of machinery; and 1.2 per cent from the horizontal line shafting and drums. All these (36.7 per cent) I consider to have been *avoidable* accidents; and *in one instance the feelings of the sufferer were aggravated*, and I think an outrage was committed, *by the refusal of the mill occupier to pay the injured person's wages during his absence for cure*'.[85]

'As has been shown again and again in these reports, two things are eminently dangerous to all labour connected with *machinery moved by mechanical power*; the one almost invariably destroys fingers, the other, life. The first is the ingathering parts of machine-gearing wheels; the second, the strap and drum

80 *Factory Reports* 1857 (1), p. 7.
81 *Factory Reports* 1857 (1), p. 8.
82 [Marx passed straight from 86 to 89 in his pagination. Translator]
83 *Factory Reports* 1857 (2), p. 3.
84 *Factory Reports* 1858 (2), p. 61.
85 *Factory Reports* 1858 (2), p. 62.

upon the line shafting. Yet the former can be remedied by an inexpensive casting, which has now become so well understood that few new machines are sent out without them; the latter by a rectangular piece of crooked iron suspended from the ceiling under each drum, and so placed as to catch the strap when falling off the drum, so that it never lies on the shaft at all. *Under these circumstances, it is melancholy to find that so large a percentage of the accidents which I have now the regret to record, should have arisen from original causes, and might have been prevented by a nominal outlay, but which, by the recent change in the law, it is now very difficult to effect when entreaties fail* ... When the shuttle is flying across the raceboard of the loom with great speed, a very slight interrupting body will cause it to leave its bed at such an angle as to make it almost certain to reach the eye or temple of a neighbouring worker. The weavers work in "alleys" or "gates", as they are called, and stand parallel to each other; hence the facility with which the shuttle of one loom may injure the worker of another. I have been informed by a certifying surgeon connected with a public infirmary in a town where powerlooms are numerous, that at least two eyes are destroyed in that town every year from this cause alone. This is another form of accident which is avoidable either by the proper application of a piece of wire netting so as to catch the shuttle within the radius of its flight, or by a threepenny invention of an ingenious mechanic near Wigan, a drawing of whose plan will be found with others in Appendix 5'.[86]

One reason for the danger: 'the complicated machinery, moving with vast speed, *often in a very contracted space*, among which people are employed'.[87] In his *Report for the half year ending 30 April 1859*, R. Baker says: 'I regret to say that the accidents have slightly increased. Last half year they amounted to 1 to every 340 persons; this, to 1 to every 321 persons ... *Twenty two* per cent happened by unfenced gearing wheels, which is less than the average number from this cause. But as all such gearing ought to have been fenced, I have directed "Notices of Dangerous Machinery" to be served etc.'[88]

In spite of the impact of the amended law of 1856, there was a reduction in the number of accidents (fatalities, etc.) involving machinery. This is the best proof of the need to keep a sharp eye on capital and its tendency to sacrifice human lives. 'By a comparison of all the accidents reported to all the Inspectors for the half years ending 31 October 1845 and 30 April 1846 with the half years ending with October and April 1858 and 1859, the gross diminution of accidents

86 *Factory Reports* 1858 (2), p. 64.

87 *Factory Reports* 1859, p. 3.

88 *Factory Reports* 1859, p. 37.

is equal to 29 per cent, notwithstanding an increase of workers of 20 per cent, at the lowest estimate'.[89]

Whereas there was 1 accident per 261 persons in the cotton mills, 1 per 348 in wool, 1 per 389 in flax, 1 per 2,251 in silk and 1 per 424 in worsted, |90| in the factories of Nottingham (not yet under the Factory Law at that time) the proportion in 1859 was 1 per 27, and in Birmingham it was 1 per 34; in Birmingham too there was no legal protection or necessity for fencing machinery.[90]

Mr. [Robert] Baker, Inspector for Lancashire, Staffordshire, Derbyshire, etc., wrote as follows in 1861:

'I very much regret to report to you 549 accidents, 10 of which were fatal. For the half year ending with October 1860, the number was 551. What they would have amounted to during the past half year, had all the mills been at work, I scarcely like to contemplate. Of these accidents, nearly 39 per cent happened to children and young persons when cleaning what is now defined to be "mill gearing" when in motion. I assure you that this number of accidents, half year by half year, has given me great uneasiness, not only on account of the sufferings of those who have been subject to them, but on account of the loss of their means of future livelihood in many instances. But so long as the law was indefinite about the terms "mill gearing and machine gearing", and there appeared to be no remedy for any neglect of precautionary fencing excepting through a *notice almost inoperative* on account of certain legal technicalities and interpretations, there remained nothing for it but to entreat and suggest, that millowners would fence the gearing of their old machinery in the same simple and *effective manner as new machinery is now fenced when sent out from the machine makers' shops*. The judgment, however, in the case of Holmes v. Clarke, reported in the Law Journal for May 1861, has, I hope, defined "mill-gearing" sufficiently clearly to enable me to act more effectively where entreaties fail'.[91] 'In the case of Holmes v. Clarke ... the plaintiff was a factory worker employed by a cotton spinner, against whom he brought an action at the Liverpool Assizes in August 1860, for the loss of his arm by the wheels of a machine in his factory in 1857. The jury who tried the cause gave the plaintiff £200 damages, against which the defendant appealed to the Court of Exchequer'. This court, however, rejec-

89 *Factory Reports* 1860 (2), p. 55.

90 *Factory Reports* 1860 (2), pp. 54–5. 'Nottingham, where a large number of persons, and especially of children, are employed amongst machinery, which is not protected by the law'. (ibid.)

91 *Factory Reports* 1861, p. 30.

ted the appeal.[92] 'By this decision it may be hoped that the question of what is "mill-gearing" is settled, and that little children and ignorant young persons ... may be preserved from the serious mutilations which unfenced gearing wheels have so long occasioned; and that the mill occupiers will forthwith do that which it is reasonable and proper they should do, and *ought to have done long ago*, viz. fence in all the toothed wheels of their machinery, so as to save their workpeople's limbs and lives, and themselves from the major as well as minor actions to which they will be henceforth subjected, if they do not'.[93] The manufacturers, however, were still not content, and they appealed from the Court of Exchequer to the *Court of Queen's Bench*, by which 'all the judges being present, both the former decisions were confirmed, and the mill-occupiers may therefore now be assured, not only of a statutory, but of a moral obligation on their part to fence all dangerous machinery amongst which their work people are employed'.[94]

These laws for the fencing of machinery do not apply to printing works, bleaching and dyeing works and lace factories.[95]

< So much for *economy in the means of protecting* the lives and limbs of the workers (including many children and young persons in all the big industries) from the dangers that directly arise from their *use of machinery*.

It is well known how much *economy* on space and therefore on buildings, etc., results in crowding workers together in cramped conditions. A further factor is *economy in the means of ventilation*. These two things, together with long working hours, produce a great increase in chest and lung diseases and consequently increased mortality. The following illustrations are taken from the *Sixth Public Health Report, 1863*, an official Blue Book published by order of Parliament. The report was compiled by [Dr.] John Simon, a member of the 'Medical Department of the Council Office', and was published in London in 1864.

Just as the combination of workers and their cooperation is what permits the use of machines on a large scale, concentration of the means of production and economy in their use, so this *working together en masse in enclosed spaces*, which is a source of growing profit for the capitalist, is at the same time a cause of early death, an accelerated decline, and a *squandering of the worker's life and health*, if it is not counteracted by, on the one hand, shorter working hours, and on the other hand, special precautionary measures.

92 *Factory Reports* 1861, p. 31.

93 *Factory Reports* 1861, p. 33.

94 *Factory Reports* 1862 (2), p. 17.

95 *Factory Reports* 1862 (2), p. 15.

The official English Health Report for 1863 puts forward the following rule, backed up with a mass of statistics:

|91| *'In proportion as the people of a district are attracted to any collective indoor occupation, in such proportion, other things being equal, the district death rate by lung diseases will be increased'.*[96] The cause is 'bad ventilation'. 'And probably in all England there is no exception to the rule that in every district which has a large indoor industry, the increased mortality of the workpeople is such as to colour the death-return of the whole district with a marked excess of lung-disease'.[97] The [mortality] statistics laid before Parliament with regard to the indoor industries investigated in 1860 and 1861 show that while about 100 deaths by phthisis and other lung diseases are occurring in various agricultural districts of England among men aged from 15 to 55, there occur, on similar masses of population, in Coventry 163 such deaths, in Blackburn and Skipton 167, in Congleton and Bradford 168, in Leicester 171, in Leek 182, in Macclesfield 184, in Bolton 190, in Nottingham 192, in Rochdale 193, in Derby 198, in Salford and Ashton-under-Lyne 203, in Leeds 218, in Preston 220 and in Manchester 263.[98] There is a yet more striking example given in the following table for the age-group between 15 and 25, *with regard to districts where only one sex pursues indoor industry*, so that the death rates of the sexes may be compared:[99]

96 *Public Health* 1864, p. 23.
97 Ibid.
98 *Public Health* 1864, pp. 24–5.
99

District	**Nature of principal industry pursued in district**	**Death rate by phthisis and other lung diseases between 15 and 25 per 100,000 of each class referred to.**	
		Male	**Female**
Berkhamstead	Extensive female employment in straw plaiting	219	578
Leighton Buzzard	Ditto	309	554
Newport Pagnell	Extensive female employment in lacemaking	301	617
Towcester	Ditto	239	577
Yeovil	Extensive female, with some female, employment in glove making	280	409

In the silk industry districts > of Leek, Congleton, and Macclesfield, < where the participation of males is higher, their mortality is also significant. The fact that the death rate here from phthisis, etc., is worse for both sexes, shows, as the Sanitary Report says: '*the atrocious sanitary circumstances* under which much of our silk industry is conducted'. And this is the same silk industry in which, as previously indicated, the worthy manufacturers demanded – and to a certain degree obtained – exceptionally long working hours from children under 13 years of age on account of the particularly healthy conditions in their establishments. >

In 1863 the House of Lords ordered an investigation of the sanitary circumstances of three very large London industries, those in which the *female dressmakers* (including dressmakers, milliners and various other workers of articles of dress), the *tailors* and the *printers* are employed. The inquiry concerning dressmakers was made by Dr. [William] Ord, the other two inquiries by Dr. Edward Smith.

According to the census of 1861 (volume II, published in 1863), there were in London:

District	**Nature of principal industry pursued in district**	**Death rate by phthisis and other lung diseases between 15 and 25 per 100,000 of each class referred to.**	
		Male	**Female**
Leek	Extensive employment, more female than male, in *silkwork*	437	856
Congleton	Ditto	566	790
Macclesfield	Ditto	593	890
Standard Northern Districts	Agriculture	331	333

(*Public Health* 1864, p. 24.)

	Males	Females	Total
Tailors	22,301	12,377	34,678
Dressmakers, milliners etc.		54,870	54,870
together			82,944
Shirtmakers, Sempstresses		28,074	
Printers	13,803	134	13,937[100]

|92| < 'Probably no industry which has yet been investigated has afforded a worse picture than that which Dr. Smith gives of tailoring: "Shops", he says, "vary much in their sanitary conditions, but almost universally are overcrowded and ill ventilated, and in a high degree unfavourable to health ... Such rooms are necessarily warm; but when the gas is lit, as during the day-time on foggy days, and at night during the winter, the heat increases to 80 degrees and even to upwards of 90 degrees, causing profuse perspiration, and condensation of vapour upon the panes of glass, so that it runs down, streams or drops from the roof, and the operatives are compelled to keep some windows open, at whatever risk to themselves of taking cold". And he gives the following account of what he found in 16 of the *most important West End shops*: "The largest cubic space in these ill-ventilated rooms allowed to each operative is 270 feet, and the least 105 feet, and in the whole average only 156 feet per man. In one room, with a gallery running round it, and lighted only from the roof, from 92 to upwards of 100 men are employed, where a large number of gaslights burn, and where the urinals are in the closest proximity, the cubic space does not exceed 150 feet per man. In another room, which can only be called a kennel in a yard, lighted from the roof, and ventilated by a small skylight opening, five to six men work in a space of 112 cubic feet per man"'.[101] And 'in those atrocious workshops which Dr. Smith describes, tailors work generally for about 12 or 13 hours a day, and at some times the work will be continued for 15 or 16 hours'.[102] > One therefore also finds [the following contrast in death rates]:

100 *Census* 1863.

101 *Public Health* 1864, pp. 25–6.

102 *Public Health* 1864, p. 28.

Number of persons of all ages employed in the industries respectively	*Industries to be compared as to their effect to health*	*Death rates per 100,000 men employed in the respective industries at the undermentioned ages*		
		25–35	35–45	45–55
958,265	Agriculture in England and Wales	743	805	1,145
22,301 men and 12,377 women	London tailors	958	1,262	2,095
13,803	London printers	894	1,747	2,367[103]

|93| < What is true of tailoring is true also of the printers, among whom lack of ventilation, foul air, etc., is worsened by night work. Their customary working day lasts for 12 to 13 hours and sometimes 15 to 16 hours. ([There is] 'great heat and foulness which begin when the gas-jets are lit ... It not infrequently happens that fumes from a foundry, or foul odours from machinery or sinks, rise from the lower room, and aggravate the evils of the upper one. The heated air of the lower rooms always tends to heat the upper by warming the floor, and when the rooms are low, and the consumption of gas great, this is a serious evil, and one only surpassed in the case where the steam boilers are placed in the lower room, and supply unwished-for heat to the whole house ... As a general

103 *Public Health* 1864, p. 30. < It should be noted, and indeed it was noted by Dr. John Simon, Chief Medical Officer, and author of this report, that in the age-group 25–35 the mortality of both tailors and printers in London was under-reported, > because in both industries London employers receive from the country large numbers of youths and young adults (probably up to 30 years of age) as apprentices and 'improvers'. They swell 'the *number of hands*' on which the London industrial death rates have to be reckoned, but they do not contribute in like proportion to the '*number of deaths*' in London, because their stay in London is only temporary; if they fall ill during their stay, they return to their country homes, where, if they die, their deaths would be registered. This influence affects still more the earlier ages, and renders the London death rates for those ages quite valueless as measures of the industrial insalubrity. (Ibid.)

Public Health 1864, pp. 26 and 28.

expression, it may be stated that universally the ventilation is defective, and quite insufficient to remove the heat and the products of the combustion of gas in the evening and during the night, and that in many offices, and particularly in those made from dwelling-houses, the condition is most deplorable'.) 'In some offices, especially those of the *weekly papers*, [there will be] work, in which boys of between 12 and 16 equally take part, for almost uninterrupted periods of 2 days and a night at a time; while, in other printing offices, which lay themselves out for the doing of "urgent" business, Sunday gives no relaxation to the workman, and his working days become 7 instead of 6 *in every week*'.[104]

We have already devoted some attention to the dressmakers and milliners, in the context of overworking.[105] In his official report, Dr. Ord says that the rooms, even though they are better during the day, are overheated, foul and unwholesome during the hours of artificial lighting. In thirty-four dressmaking establishments of the better sort (not of the class worked by middle-men) Dr. Ord found that the average allowance of cubic feet to each worker was only in four cases more than 500, in four other cases from 400–500, in seven others from 200–50, in four others from 150–200, and in nine others only from 100 to 150. The largest of these allowances would but be scanty for continuous work, unless the space were thoroughly well ventilated ... Even with good ventilation the workrooms tend to become very hot and close at night on account of the number of gas-jets required for the proper lighting up of the work ... And here is Dr. Ord's note concerning an establishment which he visited of the lower or middle-man's class: 'One room, area in cubic feet 1280; persons present, 14; area to each, in cubic feet, 91.5. The women here were weary-looking and squalid; their earnings were stated to be 7s. to 15s. a week, and tea. Hours from 8 a.m. to 8 p.m. The small room into which these 14 persons were crowded was ill ventilated. There were two moveable windows and a fireplace, but the latter was blocked up, and there was no special ventilation of any kind'.[106]

---

104 *Public Health* 1864, pp. 26 and 28.

105 [See Marx 1976, pp. 364–5. Translator]

106 < *Public Health* 1864, p. 27. The same report remarks with regard to *overwork* among dressmakers, etc.: 'The overwork of young women in fashionable dressmaking establishments does not, *for more than about four months of the year*, prevail in that monstrous degree which has on many occasions excited momentary public surprise and indignation; but for the *indoor hands* during these months, it will, as a rule, be of full 14 hours a day, and will, when there is pressure, be, for days together, of 17 or even 18 hours. At other times of the year the work of the indoor hands ranges probably from 10 to 14 hours; and uniformly the hours for outdoor hands are 12 or 13. For mantle-makers, collar-makers, shirtmakers, and various other classes of needle workers (including persons who work at the sewing-

The Chief Medical Officer remarks in his official report that '*it is practically impossible for workpeople to insist upon that which in theory is their first sanitary right, the right that whatever work their employer assembles them to do, shall, so far as depends on him, be, at his cost, divested of all needlessly unwholesome circumstances*; |94| and ... while workpeople are practically unable to exact that sanitary justice for themselves, they also, notwithstanding the presumed intentions of the law, cannot expect any effectual assistance from the appointed administrators of the Nuisances Removal Acts'.[107] 'Doubtless there may be some small technical difficulty in defining the exact line at which *employers shall become subject to regulation*. But ... in principle the sanitary claim is universal. And in the interest of myriads of labouring men and women, whose lives are now needlessly afflicted and shortened by the infinite physical suffering which their mere employment engenders, I would venture to express my hope, that universally the *sanitary circumstances of labour* may, at least so far, be brought within appropriate provisions of law, that the *effective ventilation* of all indoor workplaces may be ensured, and that in every naturally insalubrious occupation *the specific health endangering influence* may as far as practicable be reduced'.[108] >

---

machine) the hours spent in the common workroom are fewer – generally not more than 10 to 12 hours; but, says Dr. Ord, the regular hours of work are "subject to considerable extension in certain houses by the practice of taking work away from houses of business, to be done after hours at home; both practices being, it may be added, often compulsory"'. (*Public Health* 1864, p. 28.) Dr. John Simon remarks in a note to page 28 of the report that 'Mr. Radcliffe, the Hon. Secretary of the Epidemiological Society, who had a great deal of opportunity to check the health of milliners and dressmakers in first class houses of business, found that out of every 20 girls who called themselves "quite well" only one was genuinely healthy; the rest exhibited in various degrees evidence of depressed physical powers, nervous exhaustion, and numerous functional disorders thereupon dependent. He attributes these conditions to, in the first place, the length of the hours of work – the minimum of which he estimates at 12 hours a day out of season – and secondly ... to crowding and bad ventilation of workrooms, gas-vapours, insufficiency or bad quality of food, and inattention to domestic comfort'. >

107 *Public Health* 1864, p. 29.

108 *Public Health* 1864, p. 31. > We have not mentioned the industries which are unhealthy by their very nature, and in which no precautionary measures whatsoever have been taken against the 'specific health-endangering influences'. The condition to which the worker has been reduced in industries such as mirror-making, etc., where the most frightful blood-poisoning and so on is rife, is shown for example in the fact that he himself regards his exposure to blood-poisoning, etc., owing to which his wages are a little higher, as a privilege, and to some extent himself resists the imposition of precautionary measures, seeing them as a way of reducing his wage! One can see from the following table, borrowed

|95| Economy in the Use of Constant Capital. < Economy on Buildings. Economy of Power. Economy in the Machinery of Transmission. Improvements, etc. >

Economy in expense and additional capital.

'It will occasionally be necessary to adjust or repair the machine; this is done with greater ease by a workman accustomed to machine-making than by one who merely directs its motion. Now, since the good performance of machines and their duration depend to a very great extent upon the care given to immediately correcting every irregular vibration, the tiniest imperfection in their parts is seen as soon as they appear; it is evident that the expenditure arising from wear and tear and the need to repair the machinery is considerably reduced by installing the appropriate workman right on the spot. But in the case of a single tulle loom, this would be too expensive a plan. The conclusion that directly follows from this is that it could only be applied by an establishment composed of

---

from the Sixth Sanitary Report (p. 31), how phthisis and other diseases of the lung (chronic lung diseases, here usually not phthisical but irritative and inflammatory) break down the worker in the prime of life in the districts where miners, metal-forgers, cutlers and potters follow their respective industries. In these districts the death rate by *lung disease of men* aged from 45 to 65 is from 2½ to 8 times as high as in healthy agricultural districts:

Deaths per 100,000 by phthisis and other lung diseases

Place	**Men aged 45–55**	**Men aged 55–65**	**Mean of the two columns, reduced for facility of comparison to the scale of the Standard Group, taken as 100**
Redruth	1499	2360	4823/8
Penzance	975	1157	266½
Wolstanton	1173	1811	373
Stoke-on-Trent	1309	1787	387
Wolverhampton	763	1430	274
Birmingham	1169	1907	384½
Aston	697	1290	2483/8
Sheffield	1205	1912	3895/8
Reeth	1391	3214	5755/8
Alston	2069	4400	8085/8
Abergavenny	628	1305	2415/8
Merthyr Tydfil	898	1582	310
Standard Northern Districts	322	477	100

a number of such looms; in the latter case the whole of the time of one workman could be occupied in keeping the looms in order and making whatever repairs happened to be necessary. If this principle of economy is applied consistently, one is bound of necessity to double and treble the number of machines, in order to employ the whole time of 2 or 3 workmen in this kind of work'.[109]

With development, machinery becomes cheaper, in part relatively, in comparison with its force,[110] and in part absolutely, but this cheapening is at the same time bound up with a massive concentration of machinery in a single workshop, so that its value increases in proportion to the living labour employed, although the value of its individual components diminishes. *Economies of power* may be obtained, so that for example the same central machine has a reduced consumption of coal, etc., whether through improvements in the construction of the steam boiler or through improvements in the transmission machinery which lessen the amount of friction, thereby reducing the resistance the motive force has to overcome. In that case, *a larger amount of working machinery* can be driven by the same *central machine* with transmission machinery which is more expensive, but not *in the same proportion*. In order to make use of these *economies*, however, there has to be an *increase in the quantity of machinery employed*.

'The facilities resulting from the employment of self-acting tools have not only *improved the accuracy and accelerated the construction of the machinery* of a mill, but they have also *lowered its cost and increased its mobility* to a remarkable degree. At present a throstle frame, made in the former manner, may be had complete at the rate of 9s. 6d. per spindle, and a mule-jenny at about 8s. per spindle, including the patent licence for the latter. The spindles in cotton factories *move with so little friction that one horse power* will drive 500 on the fine hand mule, 300 on the mule-jenny, and 180 on the throstle; this power includes all the subsidiary preparation machines such as for carding, roving etc. A power of 3 horses is adequate to drive 30 large looms and their dressing machines'.[111]

|96| *Prime Motors*. In his report for *October 1852*, Leonard Horner quotes from a letter sent to him by James Nasmyth, the eminent civil engineer, of Patricroft, which contains the following passage, among others:

---

109 Babbage 1832, Chapter 22 [quoted here from Babbage 1833, pp. 280–1].

110 [In English in the manuscript. Translator]

111 Ure 1836, pp. 62–3. Cf. the following quotation from [John] Baynes: 'Each real and mechanical horsepower will drive 450 self-acting mule spindles with preparation, or 200 throstle spindles, or 15 looms for 40 inches cloth, with winding, warping and sizing'. (*Factory Reports* 1858 (2), p. 59.)

'It would not be very easy to get an exact return as to the increase of performance or work done by the identical engines to which some or all of these improvements have been applied; I am confident, however, that ... from the same weight of steam-engine machinery, we are now obtaining *at least* 50 per cent more duty or work performed on the average, and that, as said before, in many cases, the *identical steam engines* which, in the days of the restricted speed of 220 feet per minute, yielded 50 horse power, are now yielding upwards of 100'.

'The fact that the nominal horse power of the steam engine is but an index of its actual force, will be further evident upon a comparison of the horse power and machinery employed in 1850 and 1856. In the former period the factories of the U.K. employed 134,217 nominal horse power to give motion to 25,638,716 spindles and 301,445 looms. The number of spindles and looms in 1856 was respectively 33,503,580 of the former and 369,205 of the latter, which, reckoning the force of the nominal horse power required to be the same as in 1850, would require a force equal to 175,000 horses, but the actual power given in the Return for 1856 is 161,435, less by above 10,000 horses than, calculating upon the basis of the Return of 1850, the factories ought to have required in 1856'.[112]

'We formerly had 75 carding engines, now we have 12 doing the same quantity of work ... Our estimated saving in waste is about 10 per cent in the quantity of cotton consumed'.[113]

'When our yarn goes to the manufacturers it is so much better by the application of our new machinery, that they will produce a greater quantity of cloth and cheaper than from the yarn produced by old machinery'.[114]

[Here is a statement by a manufacturer about his] newly built (1863) cotton-spinning factory in Manchester:

< 'As regards the improvements made in machinery, I may say in the first place that a great advance has been made in the construction of mills adapted to receive improved machinery ... In the bottom room I double all my yarn, and upon that single floor I shall put 29,000 doubling spindles. I effect a saving of labour in the room and shed of at least 10 percent; not so much from any improvement in the principle of doubling yarn, but from a *concentration of machinery under a single management*; and I am enabled to drive the said number of spindles |97| by one single shaft, a saving in shafting, compared with what other firms have to use to work the same number of spindles, of 60

112 *Factory Reports*, 1857 (1), pp. 14–15.

113 *'Improvements in Manchester factories'*, in *Factory Reports* 1864 (1), p. 108.

114 'Statement by another Manchester manufacturer', *Factory Reports* 1864 (1), p. 109.

percent, in some cases 80 percent. There is a large saving in oil, and shafting, and in grease ... With superior mill arrangements and improved machinery, at the lowest estimate I have effected a saving in labour of 10 percent, a great saving in power, coal, oil, tallow, shafting and strapping etc'.[115] >

As previously remarked, the cost of the steam engine does not increase exactly in proportion to its horse power. The consumption of coal, etc., also does not rise in the same proportion as the power of the steam engine, since great savings can be made by alterations to the steam boiler. Moreover, the cost of the preparatory machines, for example those for cleaning, opening, and carding the cotton, etc., does not rise in proportion to the increase in their productive capacity. Many advantages can be derived merely from concentrating the machinery under one single management (often in one single room). Similarly, innumerable small economies are possible in shafting, strapping, oil, grease, etc. There are therefore some advantages to be gained by *combining* together factories which spin with those which weave, or, for example, by combining the extraction of iron with the manufacture of iron objects, etc.

With all machines, we need to distinguish between 'the work expended and the useful work performed' (Lefrançois). 'If the action of the motive force were entirely transmitted to the tool, both quantities of labour would be equal to each other. But it is not so, nor can it be so. Take the grinding tool, for instance: the axle of the pedal rubs against its bearings, the axles of the wheels rub against their bushes, the continuous transmission belt is stiff and does not roll on the wheels without resistance; and the resistance from the wheels of the tool itself is still greater. The whole machine is subject to a considerable amount of vibration and even the surrounding atmosphere feels the effect of this. *Each of these resistances uses up a certain amount of work, which increases as the distance from the point of application increases, at the expense of the motive force*. (Hence it is important for *economies of power* or the *greater utilisation of a given power* that this distance be *reduced*, something which is achieved by *concentrating all the machinery* in the same place.) This *unproductive consumption of work takes place with all machines*. (What is important, therefore, is to reduce this to a *minimum*: the absolute minimum would be if unproductive consumption = 0. This cannot be attained. But there is a constant approach to the minimum. Hence also a constant improvement of machinery from this point of view.) It can be concluded from this that with all machines driven by a uniform motive force, *one must distinguish between two parts of the motor's mechanical action*; one part is swallowed up by the passive resistances which unceasingly

115 *Factory Reports* 1864 (1), pp. 109–10.

re-emerge, the other has the job of producing the expected useful effect. *How these two parts are related is in general the natural measure for the degree of perfection arrived at by machines whose movement is uniform*'. 'It is essential *to distinguish* between the *mechanical work* (i.e., the application or effort of the motive force) *which is applied by the motor* in order to keep a machine running continuously *at an unvarying speed*, and the work needed *to bring the machine from a state of rest to this unvarying speed.* |98| Owing to the inertia of matter, all the movable parts of the machine, on emerging from the state of rest, oppose resistance to this motion, and this resistance continues until the machine has arrived at *the unvarying speed demanded by the nature of the work to be performed.* It follows from this *that until this speed has been attained the motor must produce an excess quantity of work*, which may in certain cases exceed *by many times the amount of power necessary for the maintenance of the speed of operation once it has been attained.* But whereas the work consumed by the other resistances is lost for ever, *a machine collects and preserves, stores away, as it were, the work which has been done to overcome the inertia of the moving parts*. This stored-up work becomes the *vital force of the machine*, and in a certain sense it comes to the assistance of the *motive force* when an *unforeseen increase in resistance* makes it necessary to develop a level of work superior to that which the motor has at its disposal at that time. Finally, when the action of the motor has completely ceased and the machine is so to speak left to its own devices, *the vital force* supports and maintains the machine's motion until the resistances have completely consumed the mechanical work it represented'. (Lefrançois.)[116]

Therefore, since a definite *excess expenditure of motive power* is needed to bring machinery into motion, which however reproduces itself as the machinery's own vital force, it is clear that the longer the machinery is kept in motion, the more this in turn compensates for the extra expenditure of power. This is *yet another factor leading to the extension of the working day*. (This should be inserted above.)

|99| < *Economies Arising from the Re-Utilisation of the Refuse of Production*

The general conditions for this re-utilisation are: *the massive presence of this refuse*, a thing which results only when labour is carried on on a large scale; *the improvement of machines*, which allows materials that were previously unusable in this form to be shaped into a form suitable for new production; and

116 [Lefrançois n.d., Chapter 2, pp. 140–3. Translator]

scientific progress, especially in *chemistry*, which discovers the useful properties of such waste products.[117] > Refuse emerges not just from production, but from consumption (by *individuals*), and this can re-enter production, as for example natural waste products, rags, etc. These must first be *collected together* in order to be usable once again as elements of production. A consideration of this is not relevant here. It is enough to say in this connection that there is still *much profligacy* to be seen in the bourgeois, or rather the capitalist régime.

< It is necessary to distinguish this *re-utilisation of the refuse of production*, whereby it enters as an element of production into the same production process or into the production process of another sphere of production, from *economies in the creation of waste*, i.e., *reduction of refuse to a minimum*, and the maximum direct *exploitation of all the raw and ancillary materials that enter the production process*. We shall consider this point first.

[*Reduction in Waste*]

Reduction in waste depends in part on the quality of the machinery used. E.g., oil, soap, etc., are saved in proportion to the better polishing of the machine components. This concerns the *ancillary materials*. In part (and this is the most *important* thing) it depends on the quality of the *machines* and tools that are used whether a *greater or lesser part of the raw material fails* to re-enter the production process *as refuse*. Finally, this depends on the *quality of the raw or semi-manufactured material itself*. > As far as the semi-manufactured materials are concerned, these fall into the previous category. < As far as the *raw material* is concerned, this depends in part on the development of the extractive industries and of agriculture, by which these raw materials are produced (thus it depends on the *progress of civilization* in the true sense), but also partly > on the degree of care and ingenuity which has gone into the < processing which the raw material undergoes before it serves as raw material in a factory. >

[*Savings in*] *the sawing of wood*: the [introduction of the] machine (in fact a colossal razor) which cuts or shaves the veneer, as compared both with the earlier cylindrical sawing machine, in which a number of saws were inserted, and with the handsaw, and still more with the axe and the knife.

---

117 < Of course, great economies of this kind can also be found in the small-scale, almost horticultural agriculture carried on in Lombardy and the south of China. In general, however, agricultural productivity is obtained in this system only at the cost of a great prodigality in human labour-power withdrawn from other spheres of production. > (Cf. Ramsay [1836, p. 337.])

The Transformation of Wheat into Flour and Bread

< 'Parmentier has shown that in a relatively short space of time, i.e., since the age of Louis XIV, the art of milling has been very much improved in France, so that the new mills can supply up to half as much again in the way of bread from the same quantity of flour. The annual consumption of wheat |100| in Paris was calculated originally at 4 *setiers* for each inhabitant, later at 3, then 2, while today it is only 1½ *setiers*, or approximately 342 lbs. ... In the Perche, where I have lived for a long while, the crudely constructed mills, with their millstones of granite and trap rock, have been rebuilt in line with the rules of mechanics, which have advanced so much in the last thirty years. Good millstones from La Ferté have been installed, the grain has been milled twice over, the bolter has been converted to circular movement, and the amount of flour produced from the same quantity of wheat has been increased by a sixth. It is therefore easy to explain the immense disproportion between the daily consumption of wheat among the Romans and among ourselves: the reason lies entirely in the inadequacy of their procedures in milling and bread preparation. This is how the remarkable state of affairs reported by Pliny (XVIII, XX. 90) should also be explained ... Flour was sold in Rome at 40, 48 or 96 *as* per *modius*, depending on quality. These prices, so high in proportion to present-day grain prices, are to be explained by the imperfection of milling methods, which were then still in their infancy and gave rise to considerable extra costs'.[118] >

'The *aerated bread* (of Dr. Dauglish, which is made without yeast) first came into use in London in March 1849. Certain difficulties, described by Dr. Dauglish (p. 528) and arising chiefly from the large cost of distribution from one centre at a remote part of the metropolis, caused the experiment at Bermondsey to be discontinued in the early part of 1861. The process has since been carried out successfully at Portsmouth, Dublin, Leeds, Coventry, and Bath. A model bakery on an improved plan is now completed at Islington etc'.[119] 'In introducing a system which necessitates the use of well-constructed, roomy, cool bakehouses above ground, Dr. Dauglish, Mr. Nevill and others who carry on the baking business on a large scale, confer a great benefit on those whom they employ'.[120]

'By the *new* process (Dr. Dauglish's) there is a clear extra yield of five 4 lb. loaves for every sack of flour more than the same flour would yield by fermentation. This, when bread is selling at 6d. per 4 lbs., will be equal to 2s.6d. per sack. This arises in consequence of the new process causing no degradation or injury

---

118 Dureau de la Malle 1840, pp. 280–1.

119 *Report relative to the Grievances* 1862, pp. lxi–lxii.

120 *Report relative to the Grievances* 1862, p. lxiv.

to the flour, similar to what takes place in the process of fermentation, and no loss of flour as in the process of kneading. There is then the further fact, that the flour for the aerated bread is ground and dressed coarser than ordinary flour. The quality or alimentary value is therefore also improved to the extent of from 3 to 4 shillings per sack. If the American process of preparing the flour be practised, then there will be a gain beyond that resulting from coarse grinding and dressing equal to 2s. per sack. Making a total gain by the new process of 7s.6d. per sack'.[121]

Dr. Dauglish's system 'does away entirely with fermentation, and with all those chemical changes in the constituents of the flour which are consequent upon it. It avoids the loss consequent on the decomposition of the portion of starch or glucose consumed in the process of fermentation estimated at from 3 to 6%. This loss may be estimated at about at least £1,500,000 in the total quantity of bread made annually in the U.K. It reduces the time requisite to prepare a batch of dough for the oven from a period of from 8 to 12 hours |101| *to less than 30 minutes* ... It has the recommendation of absolute and entire cleanliness, the human hand not touching the dough or the bread from the beginning of the process to the end ... It will effect an immense saving in the material from another source, namely, by preventing the sacrifice of at least 10% in the nutritive portion of the grain, hitherto lost as human food by the method of grinding and dressing necessary in the preparation of flour for making white bread by fermentation ... there is also the important result of the proportion preserved (the cerealine), being a most powerful agent in promoting the easy and healthy digestion of food. This agent is retained uninjured by the aerated bread process, but is destroyed by the process of panary fermentation'.[122]

'It is the *chemical* part out of which all the difficulties and uncertainties arise, and which has presented the only obstacle in the way of the bread manufacture participating in that marvellous progress of the industrial arts, which is the distinguishing feature of the present age, and its taking that position as a manufacturing institution which its magnitude and importance really deserve'.[123]

The point being made here is that 'the chemical changes in the substance of the dough ... result in the alcoholic fermentation of the transformed starch or glucose, whereby these bodies are broken up into *alcohol* and *carbonic acid*,

121 *Report relative to the Grievances* 1862, Appendix, Dr. Dauglish's evidence, nos. 534–6.

122 *Report relative to the Grievances* 1862, no. 550.

123 *Report relative to the Grievances* 1862, no. 542.

which latter is the only product desired, but which cannot be obtained without the previous transformation or degradation, more or less, of the constituents of the flour'.[124]

'The yeast acts directly upon the glucose or grape sugar contained in the flour, breaking it up into alcohol and carbonic acid'.

'About 1846, Mr. Bentz, an American, invented a machine for removing the outer seed-coat of the wheat grain (previous to grinding), without injuring the grain itself, by which he proposed to save that highly nutritious portion of the internal coat of the grain, which, adhering to the bran, in the ordinary process of grinding is torn away and lost to human consumption. It is stated that by this means 90% of fine white flour was obtained from the grain, instead of about 74 or 75, as by the old method. Trials were conducted in the French government bakeries. The experiments were successful as to the obtaining the extra quantity of the flour, but as soon as this flour was subjected to the ordinary process of fermentation, the bread, much to the astonishment of the parties conducting the experiments and of the inventor himself, was brown instead of white. The invention therefore did not go into practical operation. But on 9 June 1856 a French chemist, Mr. Mège Mouriès, presented the results of his investigations to the Academy of Sciences, and they have been reported on since that time by Messieurs Dumas, Pelouze, Payen, Peligot and Chevreul. Before the publication of Mouriès' researches, the nutritious substance attached to the bran was considered by chemists to be a portion of the *gluten of the* grain, but it now proves not to be gluten at all, but chiefly a new nitrogenous body, analogous to gluten, which the discoverer has named "cerealine", with a portion of another well-known nitrogenous body, "vegetable caseine"'. M. Mouriès has this to say about the properties of cerealine: 'It is *soluble in water*, and *insoluble in alcohol*. It acts as a *ferment* on starch, dextrine, glucose, or grape sugar. It alters gluten extremely, and gives to the altered matter a brown colour. Its peculiar action, when brought into contact, in the process of fermentation, with the ordinary constituents of fine white flour, is the true cause of the dark brown colour |102| imparted to the bread made from flour in which the cerealine was retained. (This is why Mr. Bentz failed.) M. Mouriès, having satisfied himself as to the properties of cerealine, adopted a method by which its peculiar action was neutralised, and then made bread by the ordinary process of fermentation, in which the whole of the bran contained in the internal coat of the grain was allowed to remain. The result was a loaf having merely an orange colour instead of the dark brown colour which always results

124 *Report relative to the Grievances* 1862, no. 543.

when the bran contained in the internal coat of the grain is used in bread made by the ordinary method ... In Dauglish's process, in which the fermentative changes are never allowed to take place, bread made from wheaten meal, from which only the coarsest bran has been separated, is entirely free from the dark brown colour.

By the method of grinding and dressing necessary in the preparation of flour for making white bread by fermentation, about 392 lbs. of flour are obtained from 504 lbs. of wheat, the remaining 112 lbs. being lost to human consumption in the form of bran, pollard etc., which is used chiefly in feeding cattle, and about *2 % waste by evaporation and dust in grinding.* About a quarter of this bran, pollard, etc., which is rejected, *consists of the hard siliceous external coat of the grain*, which is wholly indigestible, and therefore not a desirable substance to retain as food. The remaining three quarters consists of the *internal coat*; this, however, instead of being indigestible, proves to be the most valuable alimentary substance in the whole grain. According to the experiments of the French government, an extra yield of 10 % to 15 % was obtained when the whole of the nutritive portion of the grain was made into flour. This corresponds with the results given above of grinding 504 lbs. of wheat. Three quarters of the 112 lbs. lost = 78 lbs., which amounts to 13½ % of the 504 lbs. But take the lower figure of 10 %. If we apply this to the estimated annual consumption of wheat in this country – 30,000,000 quarters. – we get a saving of 3,000,000 quarters., an addition to human consumption of that amount. In money value, at 50s. a quarter., this is equal to £7,500,000. From this must be deducted the value of that number of quarters as bran etc., which would amount to about £1,000,000, leaving as net gain for human consumption a value of £6,500,000. It has already been shown that the destruction of nutritive matter by the ordinary process of fermentation in bread making amounts in money value to at least £1,500,000 per annum. The national gain, therefore, in the consumption of wheaten bread, if my process of bread making became universal, would amount to £8,000,000 yearly'. In addition to this, the investigations of M. Mouriès have shown 'that *the internal coat of the wheaten grain* is an infinitely more *important alimentary substance* than its mere bulk would indicate. It had long been known to be exceedingly rich in plastic or tissue-forming elements, and these were supposed to be chiefly gluten ... But it belongs to the class of bodies known as catalytic agents (solvents), which by simple contact have the power of determining definite chemical changes. This substance, named by its discoverer *cerealine*, has a most powerful solvent action, in the presence of warmth and moisture, *on gluten and starch*, and promotes the easy and healthy digestion of those matters when taken as food. It is the true solvent prepared by nature for the gluten of wheat for its assimilation in the system. It is to be found in minute particles in most flours ... The aerated bread process affords the means of incorporating the whole of it (with the customary grinding and dressing of wheat for fine flour part of it gets lost) and of thus securing the whole nutritive and chemical value of the wheaten grain'.[125]

|103| The 'special alimentary value of the cerealine' is completely destroyed by 'the process of fermentation'.[126]

'By the aerated bread process the gas is obtained from the water with which the dough is formed, and which is supersaturated with carbonic acid gas previous to its being mixed with the flour. This is effected by taking advantage of the known law that water will absorb its own bulk of carbonic acid, whatever the density, with great readiness, when agitated with it. The water which has been made to hold in solution the necessary quantity of carbonic acid gas is incorporated in a closed apparatus, under pressure, with the flour; and the gas being then allowed to escape, the minute bubbles of gas, in escaping, distend the dough into a perfect sponge, even more perfect than that which is obtained by fermentation, since every atom of water yields its atom of gas, not only between the particles of starch and their gluten coat, but also within the substance of the coat itself, rendering that porous'.[127]

'The time required for making a sack of flour of 280 lbs. into dough = 26 minutes ... One boy is capable of drawing the dough from one sack of flour into loaves in 15 minutes, as fast as they can be weighed and placed in the oven ... In a little more than *40 minutes*, therefore, a baker can rely upon having his dough ready for and placed in the oven, and this with a certainty which is nearly mathematical; whilst by the process of *fermentation it requires from 8 to 12 hours*, and is subject to many vicissitudes and much uncertainty'.[128]

'All our loaves are baked separately, and are consequently crusty all over. There is an advantage in that to the consumer, as the crust of a loaf baked separately is more easily digested by persons of delicate digestive powers than the crumb of a batch loaf; it is more perfectly cooked. This mode of baking also gives us *another advantage* over the ordinary baker of batch bread. Our Paris loaves are baked in 45 minutes, and our tin loaves in one hour and 5 minutes. *It does not take the heat out of the oven so much.* We are able to have batches following each other all day continuously; less fuel is consequently consumed. We can bake 84 sacks of flour converted into bread with 1 ton of coals. A baker baking 2 sacks a day estimates the cost of coal at 1s. per sack. If our ton costs us

125 *Report relative to the Grievances* 1862, nos. 559–71.

126 *Report relative to the Grievances* 1862, no. 572.

127 *Report Relative to the Grievances* 1862, nos. 577–9. The apparatus is described in no. 580.

128 *Report Relative to the Grievances* 1862, nos. 582–5.

20s., our fuel costs us a little less than 3d. per sack. Our carbonic acid costs us 9d. to 10d. per sack; the yeast costs the baker from 3d. to 1s. Our actual cost of converting flour into bread, when we are in fair operation, with our machinery perfectly employed, is 3s. per sack, namely: *labour*, 1s., *carbonic acid gas, fuel for oven and steam engine, dusting, salt, gas for lighting etc.*, 2s. *Together*: 3s. The ordinary baker estimates his costs at 4s. per sack'.[129]

'I have spoken of the national gain (at least 10 % upon the amount of wheaten grain converted into flour for human food) arising from our being able to *grind* **coarser**, *and dress through larger sieves*; so coarsely that if the flour were made into bread by the process of fermentation, it would be unsaleable ... A few *other economical advantages: no loss from flour dust*, all our work with the flour being done in hermetically sealed vessels. We are never subject to *the losses by fermentation*. Sometimes, in an ordinary baking, a whole batch is ready to go into the oven, and it cannot go in; it is spoilt in the process of fermentation. Again, those who carry on the ordinary baking business on a large scale are under great difficulties *during great changes of temperature*, not only as to the *quality*, but also as to the *quantity* of the bread to be made. A sudden accession of cold leads to a considerable increase of consumption, and vice versa. In providing for this, if they make too little bread it leads to loss of custom, if too much, to loss of bread. As the process requires from *8 to 12 hours*, they cannot meet these contingencies rapidly as they occur. By our process – *2 to 3 hours* – we can make our bread as we require it; *we can bring our production round to the hour or the minute*. We thus put an end to *the great obstacle ... hitherto in the way of the baking* |104| *business being carried on on a large scale*' (instead of as a small handicraft, as is mostly the case in London at present).[130]

Professor Johnston, Professor of Chemistry in the University of Durham, published a paper in *Blackwood's Magazine* for June *1847*, which was later issued as a pamphlet; a pamphlet was also issued in London in *1846* by an anonymous physician, entitled *Instructions for Making Unfermented Bread*. In the latter pamphlet attention [was] drawn to the fact that Dr. Thomas Thompson, Professor of Chemistry at the University of Glasgow, in *an essay for the supplement to the Encyclopedia Britannica, published in 1816*, proposed that *as the only purpose served by fermentation in bread making* was the *generation of the carbonic acid required to raise the dough*, this end could be attained by the use of carbonate of soda and muriatic acid, and that by thus avoiding the waste consequent upon fermentation *a considerable economy* would be effected. He

129 *Report Relative to the Grievances* 1862, nos. 590–2.

130 *Report Relative to the Grievances* 1862, nos. 593 and 594.

estimated the saving at 13%. Apart from the fact that the 'mode of raising bread by the use of muriatic acid and bicarbonate of soda is liable to introduce small quantities of arsenic', there were also all sorts of other objections to the idea.[131]

In Professor Johnston's pamphlet it is shown, among other things, that:

'A thousand pounds of the *whole meal* (*containing the whole bran*) and a thousand pounds of *white flour*, contain, respectively, the following ingredients:

	Whole meal	*Fine flour*
Muscular matter	*156 lbs.*	*130 lbs.*
Bone material	*18*	*9*
Fat	*28*	*20*
Total in each	202 lbs.	159 lbs.

Taking the three ingredients together, the whole meal is a third more valuable for fulfilling *all* the purposes of nutrition than the fine flour'. He therefore recommends *brown bread*, which contains the whole bran, 'particularly for the feeding of the young, the pregnant, and those who undergo much bodily fatigue'.[132] Nevertheless, it proved impossible to persuade people to adopt the practice of eating whole meal instead of white bread. Philanthropists and economists tried to introduce 'whole meal' bread into Unions, prisons and the houses of the poor. '*But the results were not satisfactory*. In fact, it has been found that only a very small minority of persons living in large towns (*and especially among the poor and ill-nourished*) are capable of eating whole meal bread without its producing so much irritation in the alimentary canal as to lead to far greater waste in the system than if the bread had been *minus* that extra quantity which the materials of the bran added to it ... The *silicious covering* and *woody fibre* forming the *outer coat of the wheat grain are wholly and entirely indigestible*, and *their presence in the food acts as a powerful purgative*, causing much nutritive matter to pass away with the excretions, which would otherwise be absorbed into the circulation to nourish the body ... Hence it would appear that by the *American process of preparing flour* (patented by Dr. J.E. Brown), and the *aerated bread process for making that flour into bread*, we

131 *Report Relative to the Grievances* 1862, nos. 596 and 597.

132 *Report Relative to the Grievances* 1862, no. 597.

have for the first time the means of securing for perfect human food the whole of the nourishment offered by the wheaten grain'.[133]

'The investigations of M. Mouriès', says Mr. [Hugh] Tremenheere in the *Report on the Grievances of the Journeymen Bakers*, 'have received a further confirmation after an elaborate inquiry. A report made by Colonel Favé, in the name of a Commission issued by the Minister of Commerce, confirms, after the most exact experiments, the deductions previously laid before the Academy by M. Mouriès, relative to the extra available produce of flour from wheat, resulting from the process of grinding described above. Subsequently to this report, the new process was, by order of the Préfet of the Seine, tried in the "Boulangerie de Scipion", in which the bread is made for the hospitals of Paris, the result of which was the conclusion that it would effect a saving of no less than 45 days' consumption, if [introduced] generally throughout France. "These advantages, it is known, are equivalent to 45 days' consumption in France" (p. 147 of the work cited in the footnote). M. Chevreul, on presenting the Memorandum to the Academy, gave the following table as embodying the results established by M. Mouriès:

	1 **Percentage yield of flour from wheat**		2 **Yield in bread from flour obtained by the methods indicated in column 1**	
1)	Following M. Mouriès' method	82	First class bread	109–110
2)	Maximum with normal methods	70	First class bread	92
3)	Method giving bread of standard quality	75	Standard bread, inferior to the first two types	100'.[134]

|*105*| ***To be inserted into the section on savings in the use of fixed capital, etc.***

< As we said earlier, these savings are the result of the fact that the conditions of labour have been applied on a large scale, in short, that they serve as conditions of directly social, *socialised* labour, of direct *cooperation within the production process*. This is firstly the only condition on which mechanical and chemical

133 *Report Relative to the Grievances* 1862, nos. 598–600.

134 *Comptes Rendus*, vol. 54, no. 7, 24 February 1862, p. 445. Memorandum presented by M. Mége Mouriès, 'On wheat and wheaten bread'.

discoveries can be applied, *without increasing the prices of commodities*, and that is always the *conditio sine qua non*. Next, it is only with production on a large scale that we can have the *economies* that arise from *communal (productive) consumption*. Finally, however, it is only the *experience of the combined worker* that discovers and demonstrates how inventions already made can most simply be developed, and what are the particular *practical frictions* arising from the implementation of the theory that need to be overcome, etc.

(*Incidentally*, we must distinguish between *universal labour* and *communal labour*. They both play their part in the production process, and merge into one another, but they are each different as well. Universal labour is all *scientific work*, all *discovery*, all *invention*. It has as its condition partly the cooperation of contemporaries, but partly also the work of the predecessors. *Communal labour*, however, simply involves the *direct cooperation* of individuals).

All this receives confirmation from certain facts that have frequently been observed:

(1) The great difference in *cost between the first construction of a new machine*, and *its reproduction*, for which one should refer to Ure and Babbage.[135]

(2) The much greater cost that is always involved in an enterprise based on new inventions, compared with later establishments that rise up on its ruins, *ex suis ossibus*.[136] The extent of this is so great that the first owners generally go bankrupt, and it is only their successors who flourish, because they obtain cheaper premises, etc. It is therefore generally the most worthless and wretched kind of money-capitalist who draws the greatest profit from all the new developments of the universal labour of the human spirit and its social application by combined labour. >

'The expenses which are always attendant upon *the introduction of any new process* will prevent its full economy being felt in the reduction of price until it is *pretty generally* adopted'.[137]

Here is what Dr. Dauglish says about the experiences of the first firm (Messrs. Peek, Frean and Co., of Dockhead, Bermondsey) to make bread for sale under his patent, in March 1859:

'As the process necessitates the employment of carefully made and somewhat costly machinery, in order to supply the increasing demand economically, and at the same time to ensure a remunerative return upon the capital employed, it is necessary to *conduct the manufacture on a somewhat extensive*

135 *See Ure and Babbage, etc* [Ure 1836, pp. 62–3; Babbage 1833, pp. 377–8].

136 [Emerging from their bones. Translator]

137 *Report relative to the Grievances* 1862, Dr. Dauglish's evidence, no. 586.

scale, and to sell to and distribute the bread among consumers with the greatest facility and with the least possible expense. It *could not be expected that the best mode of effecting this should be arrived at all at once*. The method of sale and distribution from one large bakery, placed at the extreme limit of the metropolis, adopted by the wealthy firm who held the extensive licence to work the patent in London, involved a system of agencies so costly and so difficult of management that it not only absorbed the legitimate profits arising from the manufacture, but it proved so inefficient that the public could never depend upon a regular supply of fresh bread daily at stated hours, a condition absolutely essential to render permanent and to cultivate public patronage'.[138]

|*106*| ***The Preparation of Flax. (Saving on waste.)***

'I apprehend that the chief reasons why both the English and many of the Irish farmers, especially in the south of *Ireland*, have been unwilling to grow flax to the extent which might have been expected of them, are:

(1) the difficulty *in dry seasons* of getting their flax scutched in the country, there being in some districts comparatively few *steam scutch mills*;

(2) *the great waste, to call it by its gentlest name, which has taken place at the little water scutch mills*;

(3) the *distance of the grower from any adequate market* after his flax has been prepared'.[139]

< 'The waste in cotton is comparatively small, but in flax very large. The efficiency of water steeping and of good machine scutching will reduce this disadvantage very considerably ... We see now, flax, scutched in Ireland in a most shameful way, and a large percentage actually lost by it, equal to 28 or 30 per cent, > which would be saved if there were scutch mills conducted by firms whose principles would not allow this devastation of fibre, and who would have the means of putting up all the most valuable machinery'.[140]

'Very few growers of flax know the nature of this textile; are not aware what treatment will preserve and increase its spinning capabilities; and how much the natural oil, called the nature of the flax, is required for making the flax what it ought to be. *Only in Brabant and Flanders* have these points been matters of study and [there they] are comprehended. Here and in Ireland we have found *water-steeping*, but in all *other parts of Europe dew retting*, which produces serious mischief to the spinning qualities of the fibre. Hence the great loss to

138 *Report Relative to the Grievances* 1862, no. 528.

139 *Factory Reports*, 1864 (1), p. 139.

140 *Factory Reports*, 1864 (1), p. 142.

the English grower and spinner; since *dew retted flax* does not yield more than from *12 to 14 lbs.* of clean flax to the *100 lbs. of steeped straw*, and this yield will not give more to the spinner than from *23 to 33 per cent*, seldom up to 50 per cent of scutched flax, whilst water steeped flax will yield from 16 to 26 per cent, and in the hackling from 50 to 75 per cent'.[141]

Herr Friedländer of Breslau has invented three kinds of machine for the more economical treatment of flax:

(1) A small *beetling* or *bruising* machine of 5 or 6 hammers. Its price is £35. It will beetle *12 to 15 hundredweight* of straw per day. Hand beetling in the Belgian fashion (which is the model fashion extant) would not do more than 100 lbs. per man per day;

(2) A *scutching* machine, which costs £40.

(3) A machine for separating the chip from the very short fibre, which has hitherto been made into *nail bagging*, and for bringing that into *tow*, of which yarns may be spun into from 10 to 14 lea. This costs £120. (We shall say more of this machine in the immediately following section, in which we discuss the utilisation of waste products.)[142]

R. Baker says this, in his Report for 31 December 1863:

'May we not then hope to see within a very short space of time, *perambulating scutching machines along with the threshing machines* which traverse our country roads, visiting our farmers for the double purpose of threshing the corn which has been harvested, and scutching the flax, in districts where there are no permanent rettories. A farmer would only have to prepare a steep pool in some field, 12 to 18 feet broad and 3½ feet deep, to be filled with soft water during rainy seasons, in which to steep his flax as soon as he had notice of the probable advent of the scutcher, and then he may be as certain of his flax crop being prepared for the market as his corn crop, and at a comparatively small expense; and without being obliged to sell it at a diminished price on account of his distance from such machines, or of having to use it for thatch as is done in one county in England. Or such perambulating flax machines might be taken to any convenient railway station periodically, to which the neighbouring flax could be brought, and there it might be scutched and distributed to different markets. In this way the greatest difficulty to flax growing would be overcome'.[143]

(To *ret* = to roast flax; *beetle* = mallet, pestle; *chip* = splinter, cutting, waste; *bagging* = sacking; to *scutch* = to winnow, beat flax; *tow* = oakum.)

---

141 *Factory Reports*, 1864 (1), p. 141.

142 *Factory Reports*, 1864 (1), pp. 140–1.

143 *Factory Reports*, 1864 (1), p. 143.

|107| Re-utilisation of the refuse of both individual consumption and production.

< As the *capitalist mode of production* extends, so also does the utilisation of the *refuse left behind by production and consumption*. Under the heading of production we have the waste products of industry and agriculture, under that of consumption we have both the excrement produced by man's natural metabolism, and the form in which articles of consumption survive after use has been made of them. Refuse is therefore in the chemical industry the by-products which get lost if production is only on a small scale; in machine-building the iron filings which fall off in the course of the process, but then are re-inserted into the iron foundries or forges to serve once again as raw materials for iron production. > The use of rags in the manufacture of paper. This is partly connected with the *natural metabolism* and partly with the *industrial transformation* of objects. < This is of the greatest importance in *agriculture*.

The *increase in the cost of raw materials*, of course, provides a stimulus for the utilisation of waste products. >

We shall now give a number of examples from different branches of production.

Aerated water. 'In aerated water making, *the sulphuric acid* is simply used to generate *carbonic acid gas* from *carbonate of lime* in a separate and distinct vessel ... the gas so generated is received into a gas holder for use, whilst the *sulphate of lime* formed in the generator, in which any arsenic that might possibly be in the sulphuric acid is retained, is afterwards thrown away or used for *making* (artificial) *manure*'. (Dr. Dauglish)

The Preparation of Flax. Oakum. < 'I have been informed with respect to some of the *scutch mills* in Ireland that the *waste* made at them has often been used by the scutchers to burn on their fires at home, and yet it is very valuable; > for even the short *shove* (batch) has been mixed with tar and made into *lights for night burning*. But the *short fibre* which falls with the shove is capable of being put to spinning purposes; and the *tow* particularly, one hundredweight of which usually falls to a ton of flax. I believe, however, that there is now a considerable improvement in the economy of these matters'.[144]

'The *tow cleaning machine* (namely Friedländer's machine, previously mentioned, for separating the chip from the very short fibre, which has hitherto been made into nail bagging, and for bringing that into tow, of which yarns may be spun into from 10 to 14 lea) costs £120 ... The *tow machine* is of the utmost

144 *Factory Reports*, 1864 (1), p. 140.

importance for cleaning the coarsest refuse and rendering it equal to *jute*, and thus an immense amount of fibre burnt and lost, or spun into nail bagging, will be brought into spinning of from 8 to 14 lea'.[145]

< As for *cotton waste*, we shall come back to this very soon in the following paragraph, in dealing with fluctuations in raw material prices. >

Woollen industry. < 'It was once the common practice to decry the preparation of waste and woollen rags for re-manufacture, but the prejudice has entirely subsided as regards the "*shoddy*" trade, which has become an important branch of the *woollen trade of Yorkshire*, and doubtless the "cotton waste" trade will be recognised in the same manner as supplying an admitted want. *Thirty years* since, woollen rags, viz. pieces of cloth, old cloth[es] etc., of nothing but wool, would average about £4 4s. per ton in price; within the last few years they have become worth *£44 per ton*, and the demand for them has so increased that means have been found for utilizing the fabrics of cotton and wool mixed by destroying the cotton and leaving the wool intact, and now thousands of operatives are engaged in the manufacture of *shoddy*, from which the consumer has greatly benefited in being able to purchase cloth of a fair and average quality at a very moderate price'.[146] >

'The efforts of the majority of the *West Riding manufacturers* have been chiefly directed to the production of a cheap cloth ... The demand for cheap goods has given an immense impulse to this kind of manufacture, the economy of which consists not so much in improved machinery and labour-saving processes, as in the employment of an inferior staple and woollen rags, brought again, *by powerful machinery*, to the original condition of wool, and then either spun into yarn for inferior cloths, or mixed with new wool, and spun into yarn for better kinds of cloth. This manufacture prevails nowhere to so great an extent as in England, although it is considerable in Belgium'.[147]

'What then' (in 1862) 'is the quantity of remanufactured wool admitted into woollen fabrics on an average of all districts? It has been estimated to me as *one third*, i.e., a third [consists of] Shoddy, Mungo, Brakes, Noils and other descriptions of remanufactured wool'.[148]

Silk: 'Thus we see that the imports of raw and waste silk in 1862 do not vary very much from those of 1839, but have decreased rather than increased, whilst the import of *knubs and husks* has doubled, and of foreign thrown [silk] has

---

145 *Factory Reports*, 1864 (1), p. 141.
146 *Factory Reports*, 1864 (1), p. 107.
147 *Factory Reports* 1856 (1), p. 64.
148 *Factory Reports* 1863 (1), p. 81.

diminished by nearly a half; and the conclusion seems evident, that while we have lost none of our manufactures of the best quality, we have cheapened the *wearing of silk goods* by the use of *a kind of silk* which is comparatively valueless elsewhere. In other words that we have relied upon our own skill and ability more and more every year, and have brought our *dressing machinery* to greater perfection'.[149]

|108| *Chemical example.* Hydrochloric acid (Cl H), 'is very often used in medicine, and in many branches of the chemical industry, in particular for the production of chlorine. When mixed with nitric acid it produces *aqua regia*, or gold refiner's liquid, which is used in the refining of gold. One hundredweight of hydrochloric acid costs 3 to 4 thalers. It occurs in immense quantities as a *by-product* of the manufacture of soda. It generally contains ferrous impurities and is therefore yellow in colour'. (Schödler.)[150]

|109| (4) The Effect of Changes in Raw Material Prices

In the following paragraphs, as previously, it is assumed that *surplus-value is constant*; at any rate < it is assumed that there is *no change in the rate of surplus-value*. This is a necessary assumption, if we are to investigate the situation

149 Ibid., p. 131. The following table is from p. 130:

		Raw silk and waste lbs.	Knubs and husks lbs.	Foreign thrown lbs.
1839	Import	9,788,738		225,268
	Export	103,304		12,660
	Remainder	9,085,434		212,608
1850	Import	4,942,407	1,747,242	469,527
	Export	557,310	13,019	75,190
	Remainder	4,385,117	1,734,223	394,337
1856	Import	7,382,672	2,015,216	853,015
	Export	1,438,598	662,944	841,553
	Remainder	5,944,074	1,952,272	11,462
1861	Import	8,710,681	3,318,224	124,574
	Export	4,096,784	93,520	82,780
	Remainder	4,613,897	3,224,704	41,794

150 [Schoedler 1852, p. 239. Translator]

in its pure form. (It would be possible, at a *constant rate of surplus-value*, for a certain capital to employ a greater or lesser number of workers as a result of a contraction or expansion which the variations we are considering might bring about. In that case, the *amount of surplus-value* might change while the *rate of surplus-value remained constant*. This is however a side-effect, which we shall not consider here.) If the variations, whether they are improvements in machinery, etc., or fluctuations in raw material prices, simultaneously affect the *number* of workers employed by a given capital, or else the *level of wages*, we simply have to combine (1), the effect that the variation in *constant capital* has on the profit rate, and (2), the effect that the *variation in wages* has on the profit rate. The result is then immediately given.

It should in general be noted – as in the previous case – that if variations occur, brought about either by *economies in the use of constant capital*, or by *fluctuations in raw material prices*, and do not affect *wages in any way* (hence do not affect the *rate and quantity of surplus-value*), they nevertheless do affect the *rate of profit*, one way or the other.[151] It is therefore completely immaterial here – as distinct from what we found in considering surplus-value – *what the spheres of production were* in which these changes take place; whether the branches of industry in which they occur produce means of subsistence or constant capital for the production of those means of subsistence, whether they produce for the workers *or not*. The argument developed here is equally valid when these changes occur in luxury production, by which we mean all production that is not required for the reproduction of labour-capacity.

Raw material also includes ancillary materials such as indigo, coal, etc. Moreover, if we are examining machinery under this heading, its own raw material consists of iron, wood, leather, etc. The price of a machine is therefore affected by fluctuations in the prices of the raw materials of which it consists (the materials of which it is constructed). To the extent that its *price is increased* by increases in the price either of the raw material of which it consists or the ancillary material which is required for its operation (and is consumed by it) the rate of profit declines in proportion to this. And vice versa. > (It is possible that the same materials, e.g., in a machine factory, may be constituents both of the machines themselves and of the material they work on. It is possible that these materials may also be an element in the workers' means of subsistence. It would be pointless to examine all these complications more closely here.) < In the investigations which follow we shall confine ourselves directly to *fluctuations in the price of that raw material* which actually goes into the process

151 [This phrase is in English in the manuscript. Translator]

of production of the commodity, and not consider the raw material of machines or the ancillary materials required in their use. The only point we want to note here is that *natural riches* in the shape of iron, coal, wood, etc., the main elements in the construction and use of machinery, appear here as *a natural fruit borne by capital* and form an element in the determination of the rate of profit that is independent of the *high or low level of wages*.

|110| Since the rate of profit = s/C, or s/(v + c), it is clear that everything that gives rise to a change in the magnitude of c (and therefore of C), if s and v and their reciprocal relationship remain constant, also brings about a change in the rate of profit. *Raw material*, however, forms a major component of constant capital. (Even in branches of industry that do not use any raw material of their own, there is still raw material in the form of ancillary materials or the components of the machinery, etc., and so fluctuations in its price still influence the rate of profit – to that degree.) If the price of the raw material *falls*, by δ for example, s/C, or s/(v + c) becomes ${}^{s}/_{v + (c - \delta)}$. The rate of profit therefore rises. And vice versa. If the price of the raw material rises, s/C, or s/(v + c) becomes ${}^{s}/_{C + \delta}$ or ${}^{s}/_{v + (c + \delta)}$, and the rate of profit therefore falls. As long as *other circumstances remain the same, the rate of profit therefore rises and falls in the opposite direction* to the price of the raw material. This shows among other things how important raw material prices are for industrial countries, even if variations in raw material prices were not accompanied by fluctuations in the product's orbit of sale (hence *quite apart from the relationship between supply and demand*.) It also has the further result that *foreign trade* has an impact on the *rate of profit*, irrespective of any effect that it has on wages by cheapening the necessary means of subsistence, to the extent that it affects the prices of the raw and ancillary materials *used in manufacturing or in agriculture*. The fact that any understanding of the *nature of the rate of profit* and its *specific difference* from the *rate of surplus-value* has been so completely lacking is responsible for a situation in which on the one hand those economists, such as for example Torrens, who on the basis of practical experience stress the influence of the prices of raw materials on the rate of profit, give this an entirely false theoretical explanation,[152] while on the other hand those economists who hold firmly to the general principles, such as Ricardo, fail to recognise the influence of such things as world trade on the rate of profit.[153]

One can therefore understand how important the abolition or reduction of import duties on raw materials is for the manufacturers. To let in raw materials

152 [Torrens 1821, pp. 28–9. Translator]

153 [Ricardo 1821, pp. 131–8. Translator]

as freely as possible was already a principal doctrine of the system of protection in its more rational presentations. This was, alongside the repeal of the Corn Laws, the main preoccupation of the English free-traders, who were above all concerned '*that the duty on cotton wool should be repealed*'.

To give one example of the importance of *changes in price*, not just for raw materials proper, but for an ancillary material, we may take flour (a material which is of course also a major food-stuff): > 'Flour is an ingredient most extensively used in the manufacture of cotton'. (The damned manufacturers themselves brought this point forward during the Anti-Corn Law agitation.) < 'Great manufacturers, thoughtful, calculating men of business, have said that *ten hours' labour* would be quite sufficient, *if the Corn Laws* were repealed'.[154] > They gained the repeal of the duty on cotton as well; but as soon as the Corn Laws had been repealed, they furiously opposed the Ten Hours' Bill, and after the Ten Hours' Bill had been passed |111| they attempted a general reduction in wages.

'As long ago as 1837 the following statement was made upon this subject by an authority of deservedly high reputation:

"In the third place, the cost of *dressing the warps*, a process necessary for preparing them for the loom, *is only one half* (in America) *what it is in England*. This arises partly from *cheap flour*".[155]

"*Question 5381: What do you suppose is the increased cost to your manufactory arising from the duty on flour?* I should think we pay in *Duty* on flour £600 to £700 per annum"'.[156]

'Estimate of the Flour used in the Cotton Manufactures of Great Britain

	lbs.
50,000 power looms, on heavy goods, at 250 lbs. fine flour	12,500,000
50,000 power looms on light goods, at 156 lbs. fine flour	7,800,000
250,000 handlooms, at 83 lbs. fine flour	20,750,000
	41,050,000

154 *Factory Reports* 1849 (1), pp. 97–8.

155 [Greg 1837, p. 115. Translator]

156 Evidence of Mr. William Graham to the *House of Commons Committee on Manufactures, Commerce and Shipping, 1853*, quoted in *Factory Reports* 1849 (1), p. 322.

	lbs.
41,050,000 lbs. at 35s. per 280 lbs.	256,562
1/3 more in bleaching etc.	85,521
	£342,083

£342,083 has been the *annual* cost for the last 10 years of flour used by the British manufacturer. By returns of the price of flour on the Continent during the same period, it is clear that the *English manufacturers have been paying a tax in this single item of above* £170,000 a year. It cannot now be less than £200,000 a year, and we could name one firm who pay £1,000 per annum *in this item, which they would not pay, were their manufacture on the Continent or in America*'.[157]

|112| (To the extent that the release and tying-up, as well as the appreciation and depreciation of capital, are connected either with the development of machinery {and the development of the productivity of labour in general} or with fluctuations in the prices of raw and ancillary materials, we shall only deal with these at a later point; they are therefore excluded from our present discussion.)

< The value of the raw material (and the same is true of ancillary material) *enters entirely* and at a single stroke into the value of the product of which it is the raw material or the ingredient, whereas the machinery, and the fixed capital in general, enters into the product only to the extent of its depreciation, and only gradually. It follows from this that the *price of the product* is affected to a much higher degree by the *price of the raw material*, even though the *rate of profit* is determined by the total amount of capital *employed*, irrespective of how much of this is consumed or not. It is clear (even if this is mentioned only in passing, as we are still assuming here that the commodities are sold at their value, not yet being concerned with the price-fluctuations brought about by competition) that the expansion or contraction of the market depends on the *price of the individual commodity* and stands in an inverse relation with the *expansion and contraction* of that price. In actual fact, therefore, it happens that a rise in the price of the raw material does not lead the price of the manufactured product to rise in the same proportion as that of its ingredients,

157 [Greg 1837, p. 115. Translator]

or to fall in the same proportion when the price of the raw material falls. The rate of profit thus falls more sharply in the one case, and rises more sharply in the other, than would be the case if the commodities were sold at their value. Moreover, the size and value of the machines employed grows as the productivity of labour develops, but not in the same proportion as the productivity of the machinery, or the labour, increases. On the other hand, in branches of industry that use raw materials, i.e., wherever the object of labour is already the product of earlier labour, the increasing productivity of labour is expressed precisely by the proportion in which *a certain amount of labour absorbs a greater quantity of raw material*, hence in the increasing mass of raw material which is transformed into products, worked up into commodities, in an hour of labour, for example. In proportion, therefore, as the productivity of labour develops, the value of the *raw material* forms an ever greater component of the *value of the commodity*, not only because *it enters into it as a whole*, but because in each *aliquot part of the total product* the part formed by the depreciation of the machinery and the part formed by newly added labour both constantly decline. As a result of this falling movement a *relative growth takes place* in the *component of value* constituted by the raw material, provided that this growth is not paralysed [*paralysiert*] by a corresponding *decline in value* on the part of the raw material, which arises from the increasing productivity of the labour applied in its own creation.

Moreover, since the *raw and ancillary materials*, just like *wages*, *form* components of the *circulating capital*, and must therefore be constantly and completely *replaced* out of each sale of the product, whereas as far as the machine is concerned it is only the depreciation (that is to say, the reserve fund for the depreciation) that has to be replaced, |113| in which connection the proportions in which this occurs are in no way particularly important, e.g., it may happen over a year from the proceeds of the sale of the commodities, we see here again (and this is connected with the release and tying-up of capital) how a rise in raw material prices may restrict or curtail the entire *reproduction process*, since the *price obtained by the sale of the commodity* either does not suffice to replace all of its elements. > (The composition [of the capital] is a technologically given fact. For instance, over the week the prime motor requires a specific amount of power, of spindles and looms, of raw material {*with a constant working day*} and finally a specific number of workers operating a specific number of machines, e.g., four for each horse power. A rise in the price of the raw material throws the value relationship between the various constituents entirely out of kilter {this is a matter to be dealt with in the next section}) < in other words it makes it impossible to continue the process on a scale that corresponds with its technological basis, so that for example only a part of the machinery can be employed or it cannot be allowed to work for the same period of time as before, > so that either fewer days a week are worked or fewer hours are worked during the day.

< The *raw material costs* resulting from waste, finally, vary *in direct proportion to the fluctuations in the value of the raw material.* They rise when it rises, and they fall when it falls. >

(To the extent that the *fluctuations in the price* of the raw material and the ancillary materials affect the *process of reproduction*, this matter will be dealt with in the next paragraph.)

We shall now give some individual examples to clarify what has just been discussed.

Cotton is one of the most striking examples of how much the development of a branch of industry depends on raw material prices. We shall start with cotton, and the influence the invention of Whitney's cotton gin had on cheapening this commodity.

|*114*| *Waste*

< 'The price now given for waste, and its re-introduction in the factory in the shape of cotton waste, go some way to compensate for the difference in the loss by waste, between Surat cotton and American cotton, about 12½ per cent. The waste in working Surat cotton being 25 per cent, the cost of the cotton to the spinner is enhanced one fourth before he has manufactured it. The loss by waste used not to be of much moment when American cotton was 5d. or 6d. per lb., for it did not exceed ¾d. per lb., but it is now of great importance when upon every lb. of cotton which costs 2s. there is a loss by waste equal to 6d'.[158]

'One source of considerable loss arising from an advance in the price of the raw material would hardly occur to any one but a practical spinner, viz., that from waste. I am informed that when cotton advances, the cost to the spinner of the lower qualities especially, is increased in a ratio beyond the advance actually paid, because the waste made in spinning coarse yarns is fully 15%; and this rate, while it causes a loss of ½d. per lb. on cotton at 3½d. per lb., brings up the loss to 1d. per lb. when cotton advances to 7d'.[159] >

|*115*| *Fluctuations in the Price of Raw Material and in the price of the article*

'From all parts of my district I hear of the great disadvantages under which the cotton factories are now; and for a long time past have been working

158 *Factory Reports* 1864 (1), p. 106.

159 *Factory Reports* 1850 (2), p. 17.

from the high price of the raw material. This more particularly applies to those mills in which the *coarser yarns* are spun and the heavier fabrics are manufactured; because, in them, the *raw material forms so much greater a proportion of production, than it does in the finer qualities*. The *disproportion between the advance on the raw material* and that *on articles manufactured* from it *since May 1848* (up to 1850) will be seen from the following comparative statement of the prices of American cotton, and of some of the principal articles manufactured from these qualities at the two periods:

Prices of Cotton in Liverpool in the Middle of May in Each Year, Taken from the Circular of an Eminent Broker

Description of cotton		Year	Price per lb.	Being an advance of
Bowed and Mobile:	*Ordinary*	1848	3¼ to 3¾d.	
		1850	6¼ to 6⅝	nearly 84%
	Good	1848	4⅝ to 5	
		1850	7½ to 7½	nearly 56%
New Orleans:	*Ordinary*	1848	3¼ to 3¾	
		1850	6 to 6¾	about 82%
	Good	1848	5½ to 5¾	
		1850	7¾ to 7¾	about 38%

The following statement of the prices of yarns and manufactured goods from a gentleman in Manchester, on whose accuracy perfect reliance may be placed.

Description of the article		Year	Price per lb.	Being an advance of
No. 20 Water Twist	*Common Quality*	1848	6½d.	
		1850	8d.	about 30⅔%
	First Quality	1848	7¼d.	
		1850	9¾d.	about 34½%
No. 30 Mule Twist	*Common Quality*	1848	6½d.	
		1850	9½d.	about 46%
	First Quality	1848	8d.	
		1850	11d.	about 37½%

Description of the article		Year	Price per lb.	Being an advance of
No. 40 Mule Twist	*Common Quality*	1848	7⅛d.	
		1850	10½d.	about 47⅕%
	First Quality	1848	8¾d.	
		1850	12d.	about 37%
			Per piece	
⅞ 72 reed Printing Cloth	29 yards	1848	4s. 9d.	
		1850	6s.	about 26½%
¾ 66 reed T Cloth	24 yards	1848	6s. 6d.	
		1850	7s.	about 7¾%
¾ 66 reed Long Cloth	36 yards	1848	8s.	
		1850	8s. 9d.	about 9⅓%
6/4 40 reed Jacconets	20 yards	1848	3s. 8d.	
		1850	4s. 7d.	about 25%'[160]

|116| (The raw material forms the biggest element in the value of the cheapest sorts of product {semi-manufactures}, and it is those which suffer the greatest loss in value when the price of the raw material rises, and have the greatest gain when the price falls. It also follows from this that more of the superior types is spun when the price of the raw material rises).[161]

The prices do not fall in proportion to the fall in raw material prices, because demand increases; and, inversely, demand falls as raw material prices rise.

'The advance that has taken place in the manufactured articles must have materially lessened the consumption of all heavy goods, such as fustians, and those fabrics that are used by the working classes; for they know the rapid and extensive effect of even a moderate increase in price on articles consumed by them'.[162]

160 Leonard Horner's report, in *Factory Reports* 1850 (2), pp. 15–16.

161 *Factory Reports* 1850 (2), pp. 16–18.

162 *Factory Reports* 1850 (2), p. 17.

Cotton

Description		*Year*		
		1 May 1853	*1 May 1854*	*1 May 1855*
Boweds	Ordinary	5⅜d.	4½d.	4¾d.
	Middling	5⅞	5⅛	5¼
	Fair	6⅜	6¼	5⅞
Mobile	Ordinary	5⅜	4⅝	4⅞
	Middling	5⅞	5⅛	5 5/16
	Fair	6⅜	6¼	5⅞
New Orleans	Ordinary	5½	4⅝	4⅞
	Middling	6	5¼	5⅜
	Fair	6¾	6½	6⅛

Yarns	1 May 1853	1 May 1854	1 May 1855
20s Water, common	8¼d.	7⅞d.	7¾d.
20s Water, best Wigan quality	9	8⅞	8¾
30s Mule, common	9	8½	7¾
30s Mule, best	10	9½	8¾
40s Mule, common	9⅝	8⅞	8½
40s Mule, best	10½	10	9¾

Goods	1 May 1853	1 May 1854	1 May 1855
30 in. T. Cloths, 4 lbs.	3s. 4d.	3s. 2½d.	2s. 11½d.
36 in., 60 reed, 50 yards. 9 lbs. 10 oz. to 9 lbs. 12 oz.	10s. 3d.	9s. 4d.	9s. 2d.
36 in., 72 reed, 25 yards. 5 lbs. 12 oz. to 5 lbs. 14 oz.	7s. 0d.	6s. 0d.	6s. 0d.[163]

163 *Factory Reports* 1856 (1) (Report of L. Horner), pp. 28–9.

'The above tables were accompanied with the following remarks, dated 12 December 1855:

"Towards the *end* of May 1855, a large advance took place in cotton without a corresponding advance in yarns. The "middling" and "fair" qualities of cotton are the best to judge by, as they are best understood and correspond with the statements of yarn and cloth also. This statement will clearly show the effects of dear provisions and other disturbing causes in 1855"'.[164]

|117| Examples to show that the price of yarn does not fall in proportion to that of the raw material. Spring 1845. Heyday of the cotton industry.

'I have heard too, from persons possessing the means of accurate information *of profits* arising from the *low price of cotton* and the *disproportionately high price of yarn*, which indicates a very high state of prosperity. I have heard, however, that it is the spinners who have been the most prosperous, and that *where the manufacturer had to buy his yarn*, he has not been able to obtain a remunerating price for his cloth. Towards the end of October I heard, for the first time since the revival of trade, of mills, where they weave only, working short time; a sure proof that the selling price of the manufactured article had been for some time considerably under the cost of its production'.[165]

Prices of Cotton, Yarn and Tissue, 1863

In the following table, 'the price of Surat cotton, which has now taken the place of the great bulk of the American formerly consumed' is set against 'the price of ordinary Orleans, also quoted'.

		Price per lb.	Advance
1855	Ordinary Orleans	4s. ⅞d.	
1863	Average price of Dhol fair cotton	1s. 9¼d.	nearly 300%
1855	Best Water twist	8¾d.	
1863	N. 20s. water twist	2s. 0¾d.	about 64%

164 *Factory Reports* 1856 (1), p. 29.

165 *Factory Reports* 1846 (1) (L. Horner), p. 13.

'Average price of N. 30s. mule twist in 1863, 2s. 1⅝d., being an advance upon the 38s. mule twist since 1855 of 190%. Average price of N. 40s., mule twist in 1863, 2s. 3⅞d., being an advance upon the price of the best 48s. mule twist, since 1855, of 180%. The two last returns show in as striking a manner as the first return quoted from Mr. Horner's report that the price of yarn follows at a considerable distance a rise in the price of cotton'.[166]

And vice versa. If we compare the price of cotton in 1855 with that in 1850, we find:

	Price per lb.	Reduction since 1850	As against	Price per lb.	Reduction since 1855
Bowed and Mobile			*N. 20s. water*		
Ordinary	4¾d.	24%	*twist, common*	7¾d	about 3%
Fair	5⅞d.	21%			
New Orleans					
Ordinary	4⅞d.	18%	*N. 20s. water*		
Fair	6⅛d.	20%	*twist, best*	8¾d.	about 10%[167]

|*119*| ***Improvement of Machinery***

'It frequently happens that great additions are made to the machinery and to the productive powers of the establishment without any increase of the moving power already existing in a factory; neither have I any means of distinguishing what proportion of the increase (of the factory system) indicated by these returns is to be ascribed to an absolute increase of trade from that which arises from the gradual extension of the factory system to employments and processes not formerly embraced by it'. (*Factory Reports* 1852, p. 38.)

< 'The rapid strides with which improvement in machinery has advanced within these few years have enabled manufacturers *to increase production without additional moving power*. The *more economical application of labour* has been rendered necessary by the diminished length of the working day, and in most well-regulated mills an intelligent mind is always considering in *what manner production can be increased with decreased expenditure*. I have before

166 *Factory Reports* 1864 (1) (A. Redgrave), p. 102.

167 *Factory Reports* 1864 (1), pp. 101–2.

me a statement, kindly prepared by a very intelligent gentleman in my district, showing the number of hands employed, their ages, the machines at work, and the wages paid from *1840* to the present time. In October *1840* his firm employed 600 hands, of whom 200 (⅓) were under 13 years of age. In October 1852, *350* hands were employed, of whom 60 (⅙) only were under 13 years of age; the *same number of machines*, within very few, were at work, and the same sum in wages was paid at both periods'. (*Factory Reports* 1863 (1), A. Redgrave's report, pp. 58–9.) >

(What he means here by 'more economical application of labour' is the employment of *fewer workers*, whose productivity and intensity of labour has been raised. In the above case 250 out of the 600 workers were dismissed, and among those dismissed there were 140 children less than 13 years old.)

'There are ... many simple mechanical contrivances whereby the shafting can be properly oiled, without the mechanic being placed in jeopardy. Some of these contrivances are said to lubricate the parts much better than could be done by the periodical oiling of the mechanics, and as *they have been invented with a view to economise oil*, and ... fulfil that purpose, and as they require the attention of the mechanic only at long intervals, when the requisite filling with oil and other details can be done while the machinery is standing, the employment in a dangerous situation of any person to oil mill-gearing while in motion appears altogether inexcusable'. (*Factory Reports* 1854 (2), p. 42.)

'At one of the flax-spinning factories in my district, occupied by Mr. Gordon Stuart, at Balgonie mills in Fifeshire, a water-wheel has recently been erected, with a vertical axle, on the plan of the turbine of Fourneyron, constructed so as to bring out that form of wheel best adapted to the height of all and quantity of water; so that *a very great addition to the work* formerly driven by two breast-wheels is obtained from the same spinning machinery at Balgonie mills'. (*Factory Reports* 1847, p. 41.)

|*120*| *Improvements of Machinery*

'It frequently happens that great additions are made to the machinery and to the productive powers of the establishment without any increase of the moving power already existing in a factory'. (*Factory Reports* 1852, p. 38.)

'Changes in the system of working the steam engines ... < The public are little aware of the vast increase in *driving* power which has been obtained by such changes of system and improvements as I allude to. The *engine power* of this district lay under the incubus of timid and prejudiced traditions for nearly 40 years, but now we are happily emancipated. During the last 15 years, but more especially in the course of the last 4 years, (*since 1848, therefore*) some very important *changes have taken place in the system of working condensing steam engines* ... The result of such changes ... has been to *realise a much greater amount of duty or work performed by the identical engines*, and that again at a *very considerable reduction in the expenditure of fuel* ... For a great many years after the introduction of steam-power into the mills and manufactories of the above-named districts, the velocity at which it was considered proper to work condensing steam engines with a 5 feet stroke was restricted by "rule" to make 22 revolutions of the crank shaft per minute. Beyond this speed it was not considered prudent or desirable to work the engine; and as *all the mill gearing* (especially the *first motion wheels*) *were made suitable to this 220 feet per minute speed of piston*, this slow and absurdly restricted velocity ruled the working of such engines for many years. However, at length, either through fortunate ignorance of the "rule", or by better reasons on the part of some bold innovator, a greater speed was tried, and as the result was highly favourable, others followed the example, by, as it is termed, "*letting the engine* away", namely, by so *modifying the proportions of the first motion wheels of the mill gearing* as to *permit the engine to run at 300 feet and upwards per minute*, while the mill gearing generally was kept at its former speed, as best suited to the requirements of the work ... This "letting the engine away", > namely, allowing it to run at as high a speed as kept within the bounds of safety in respect to strength of the rim of the fly-wheel [now results in] < almost universal "speeding" of engines, because it was proved that not only was there *available power gained from the identical machines*, but also as *the higher velocity of the engine yielded a greater momentum in the fly-wheel the motion was found to be much more regular*'. Hence one obtained '*more power from a steam engine by simply permitting its piston to move at a higher velocity* (*pressure of steam and vacuum in the condenser remaining the same*). For example, suppose any given engine yields 40 horse power when its piston is travelling at 200 feet per minute. If by suitable arrangement or modification we can permit this same engine to run at such a speed that its piston will travel through space at 400 feet per minute (pressure of steam and vacuum, as before said, remaining the same), we shall then have just *double* the power exerted by such an engine at 400 feet per minute > to what we had when it was restricted to 200 feet < and as the pressure of steam and vacuum is the same in both cases, the strain upon the parts of this engine will be no greater at 400 than at 200 feet speed of piston, so that the risk of "breakdown" does not materially increase with the increase of speed. All the difference is, that *we shall in such case consume steam at a rate proportional to the speed of the piston*, or nearly so; and there will be some *small* increase in the wear and tear of the "brasses" or rubbing parts, but so slight as hardly to be worth notice. > After it was proved by examples that by simply "letting the engine away" at a higher speed *the amount of work performed by the identical engine* increased in proportion ... the traditional 220 feet speed of the piston became a matter of history. < But in order to obtain an increase of power from the same engine by permitting its piston to travel at a higher velocity it is requisite either to "*fire up hard*", that is to *burn more coal per hour under the same boiler*, or to *employ boilers of greater evaporating capabilities*, i.e., *greater steam-generating powers*. This accordingly was done, and *boilers of greater steam-generating or water-evaporating power* were supplied to the old "speeded" engines, and *in many cases nearly 100% more work was got out of the identical engines* ... About 1842 the *extraordinary economical production of power* as realised by the engines employed in the mining operations of Cornwall began to attract attention; and *as competition in the spinning trade forced manufacturers to look to "savings" as the chief source of profits*, the remarkable *difference in the consumption of coal per horse-power per hour*, as indicated by the performance of the *Cornish pumping and crank engines*, as also the extraordinary economical performance of Woolf's *double cylinder engines*, began to attract greater attention to the subject of *economy of fuel* in this district, and as the Cornish and double cylinder engines gave *a horse-power for every 3½ to 4 pounds of fuel per hour*, while the generality of *cotton mill engines were consuming 8 or 12 pounds per horse per hour*, so remarkable a difference induced mill-owners and engine-makers in this district to endeavour to realise, by the adoption of similar means, such extraordinary economical results as were proved to be common in *Cornwall and France*, where *the high price of coal* had compelled manufacturers to look more sharply to such costly departments of their establishments. The result of this *increased attention to economy of fuel* has been most important in many respects. *Firstly:* many *boilers, the half of whose surface had been in the good old times of high profits* (before 1842!!!) *left exposed to the cold air, began to get covered with thick blankets of felt, and brick and plaster*, and other modes and means whereby to *prevent the escape of that heat from their exposed surface which had cost so much fuel to maintain. Steam pipes* began to be "*protected*" in the same manner, and *the outside of the cylinder of the engine felted and cased in with wood* in like manner. Next came the use of "*high steam*", namely, instead of having the *safety-valve loaded so as to blow off* at 4, 6, or 8 lbs. to the square inch, it was found that *by raising the pressure to 14 or 20 lbs.*, and admitting only a fraction of a cylinder full, a very decided economy of fuel resulted; in other words, the work of the mill was performed by a very *notably reduced consumption of coals*, and so *"lapped valves"* and *"cut off" apparatus* became quite the rage, and those who had the means and the boldness *carried the increased pressure and "expansion system"* of working to the full extent, by employing *properly constructed boilers* to supply steam of 30, 40, 50, 60 and 70 lbs. to the square inch; pressures which would have frightened an engineer of the old school out of his wits. But as the economic results of *so increasing the pressure of steam as to work expansively* > (i.e., to set more machinery in motion simultaneously) < soon appeared in the most unmistakable £. s. d. forms, the use of high-pressure steam boilers for working condensing engines became almost general. Those who took a radical attitude to these arrangements for reducing the consumption of fuel adopted the *Woolf engines*, which are employed in most of our mills lately built, engines on which there are *two cylinders to each*, in one of which the high-pressure steam from the boiler *exerts or yields power by its excess of pressure over that of the atmosphere*. Instead of the said *high-pressure steam being let pass off at the end of each stroke free into the atmosphere, it is caused to pass into a low-pressure cylinder* of about 4 times the area of the former, and after due *expansion passes to the condenser*. The economic result obtained from engines of this class is such that the consumption of fuel is at the rate of from 3½ to 4 lbs. of coal per horse per hour; while in the engines of the old system the consumption used to be on the average from 12 to 14 lbs. per horse per hour. By an ingenious arrangement, the Woolf system of double cylinder or combined low and high pressure engines has *been introduced extensively to already existing engines*, whereby their performance has been increased *both as to power and economy of fuel*. The same result has been in use these 8 or 10 years, by having a *high-pressure engine* so connected with a *condensive engine* as to enable the *waste steam of the former* to pass on to and work the latter. This system is in many cases very useful. It is not easy to get an exact return as to the increase of performance or work done by the identical engines to which some or all of these improvements have been applied; I am confident, however, that could we obtain an exact return the result would show that from the same weight of steam-engine machinery we are now obtaining *at least 50%* more duty or work performed on the average and that in some cases the identical steam engines which in the days of the restricted speed of 220 feet per minute yielded 50 horse power, are now yielding upwards of 100. The very economical results derived from the employment of high-pressure steam in working condensing steam engines, together with *the much higher power required by mill-extensions from the same engines*, has *within the last 3 years* (since 1850) led to the adoption of *tubular boilers*, the tubular boilers yielding a much more economical result than those formerly employed in generating steam for mill engines'. (Letter of James Nasmyth, civil engineer, Patricroft, near Manchester, to Leonard Horner, in *Factory Reports* 1852, pp. 23–7.)

|121| [5] *Release and Tying-up of Capital. Depreciation and Appreciation, Revaluation and Devaluation of Capital*

The phenomena under investigation in this section require for their full development the credit system and competition on the world market, the latter forming the very basis of the capitalist mode of production, > which in any case needs the world market as its sphere of action. < These more concrete forms of capitalist production can (1) only be depicted after the general nature of capital has been understood, and (2) it is outside the scope of this work to present them – they belong to a possible continuation. Yet the phenomena listed in the heading to this section can still be discussed here in general terms. They are both inter-related and related to *the rate and in part the mass, of profit.* And this reason alone justified a brief account of them, because they produce the *appearance* [*Schein*] that not only the *rate of profit* but also the *mass of profit* (which is in fact identical with the *mass of surplus-value*) can increase and decrease independently of, or at least *side-by-side with* the movement of surplus-value, whether of its mass or its rate.

Should the release and tying-up of capital on the one hand, and its depreciation and appreciation on the other, be regarded as *distinct* phenomena?

The first question that arises is what is it that we understand by the release and tying-up of capital? Depreciation [*Depreciation*] and appreciation [*Appreciation*] for their part are self-explanatory. They have no other meaning than that the existing capital increases or decreases in value as a result of general economic conditions of whatever kind, since what is involved here is not the fate of one single private capital, i.e., that the value of the capital advanced to production rises and falls *independently of its valorisation by the surplus labour it employs.* >

< This appreciation or depreciation may affect either constant or variable capital or both, and in the case of constant capital it can relate either to the fixed or the circulating part, or both.

In considering constant capital we have to consider the following: raw materials and ancillary materials (*semi-finished products* also belong here), machinery and other forms of fixed capital. Raw and ancillary materials can be thrown in together here.

In previous sections we considered variations in the prices (the values) of the raw material with regard to their influence on the rate of profit, and we put forward the general law that the rate of profit varies inversely with the value of the raw material. This law is unconditionally correct, other things being equal, for capital which is newly engaged in a business, and where the investment of capital, the transformation of money into productive capital, takes place for the first time.

But, apart from this newly invested capital, a large part of the active capital is located in the sphere of circulation, while another part is to be found in the sphere of production. One part exists as a commodity on the market and has to be transformed into money, another part exists as money (in whatever form) and has to be transformed back into conditions of production. A third part, finally, exists within the sphere of production, partly in the original form of means of production, raw materials, ancillary materials, semi-finished articles, machinery and other forms of fixed capital, finally as products on which work has already started but is not yet complete. Here the impact of appreciation or depreciation depends very much on the respective proportions of these components. Let us *initially*, to simplify matters, leave all machinery and fixed capital out of account, and consider only the part of the constant capital that consists of raw and ancillary materials, semi-finished articles and commodities on the market in their finished form.

|122| If the price of a raw material rises – cotton for example – the price of cotton goods rises as well: both semi-finished goods such as yarn, which are produced with cheaper cotton, and finished products such as cloth, etc. And cotton that has not yet been worked up, but is still in the warehouse, rises in price, as does the value, finally, of the cotton that has already entered the process of manufacture. As the retrospective expression of more labour-time, this cotton adds a higher value to the product which it enters into as an ingredient than it possessed originally and than the capitalist paid for it.

Thus if an increase in the price of raw material takes place with a significant amount of finished goods already present on the market, at whatever stage of completion, the value of these commodities rises and there is a corresponding *increase* in the value of the *available capital*. This appreciation can compensate the individual capitalist, or the whole of a particular sphere of capitalist production – even more than compensate perhaps – for the fall in the rate of profit that accompanies the raw material's rise in price. > The same is true for the supplies of raw materials and semi-finished articles the producer has available to hand, lying in the warehouse. < Without going into the detailed effects of competition here, we may remark for the sake of completeness that (1) if there are substantial stocks of raw material in the warehouse they will counteract the rise in the price of the raw material, and (2) if the semi-finished or finished goods weigh heavily on the market, they may prevent the prices of these goods from rising in proportion to the prices of their raw materials.

The reverse is the case with a fall in the price of raw material which, generally speaking,[168] would raise the rate of profit. The commodities on the market,

168 [These two words are in English in the manuscript. Translator]

supplies of raw material and finally the semi-finished articles and articles just started are all depreciated.

The smaller the amount of stock to be found in the production sphere and on the market at, for example, the end of the business year, at the time when raw materials are supplied afresh, the more clearly does the effect of fluctuations in raw material prices depicted in the previous section come into view.

Our whole investigation has proceeded from the assumption that *price fluctuations*, the rise and fall of prices, are an expression of real *fluctuations in value*. But since we are dealing here with the effect that these price fluctuations have on the rate of profit, etc., it is actually a matter of indifference what their basis might be. The present argument is just as valid if prices rise or fall not as a result of fluctuations in value but rather as a result of the intervention of the credit system, competition, etc.

Since the rate of profit = the proportionate *excess* of the value of the product over the *value of the capital advanced*, an increase in the rate of profit that arose from a depreciation of the capital advanced would involve a loss, while a reduction in the rate of profit that arose out of an appreciation of the capital advanced could well involve a gain.[169]

|123| As far as the other portion of constant capital is concerned, machinery and fixed capital in general, the price increases [*Appreciation*] that take place here, particularly affecting buildings, land, etc., cannot be explained without the theory of ground-rent, and therefore do not belong here. The following points, however, are of general importance for falls in price [*Depreciation*]:

(1) The constant improvements which rob existing machinery, factory installations, etc., of a part of their use-value, and therefore also their exchange-value. This process has a particularly forceful effect in the period when new machinery is first introduced, before it has reached a certain degree of maturity, and where it thus constantly becomes outmoded before it has had time to reproduce its value. This is one of the reasons for the unlimited extension of working hours, and work based on alternating day and night shifts, to enable the value of the machinery to be reproduced without too great costs having to be borne for wear and tear. If the short working life of the machines (their short life-expectancy) were not counterbalanced in this way, they would transfer too great a portion of their value to the product as depreciation [*Dechet*], so that they would not even be able to compete with handicraft production.[170] (2) Once machines, factory buildings, or any other kind of fixed

169 > *Cf. the sophistical passage on capital and profit* < [in Malthus 1827, p. 86].

170 < *Examples for this in Babbage, among others.* The usual expedient – the reduction of the

capital have reached a certain degree of maturity, so that they remain unchanged for a considerable length of time, at least in their basic construction, improvements in the reproduction of this machinery, of these factory buildings, etc., [lead to a similar fall in value]. Their value falls, not because they are superseded, or, at least, to a certain degree antiquated by newer and more productive machinery, etc., but because they can be more cheaply reproduced than when they were first produced. This is one of the reasons why large enterprises often flourish only under their second owners, after the first have gone bankrupt and the second owner is therefore able to begin the process from the outset with smaller costs.[171]

It is particularly apparent in the case of agriculture that the same causes that raise the price of the product, also raise the *value of the capital* since this itself consists in part of that product, such as cattle, etc. And vice versa.[172]

The *variable capital* has still to be mentioned.

In as much as the *value of labour-capacity* rises because the value of the means of subsistence required for its reproduction rises, or conversely falls, because the value of these means of subsistence falls (and the appreciation and depreciation of the variable capital can mean nothing more than these two cases), and assuming that the working day remains constant, an appreciation of this kind means a fall in surplus-value, and a depreciation means a rise. > We investigated this point in examining earlier the reasons for the rise and fall of surplus-value, and there is therefore no need to consider it here. < However, other circumstances can also be linked with this, such as the release and tying-up of capital, which we have not yet investigated and should now indicate in brief.

|124| *If wages fall*, owing to a fall in the *value of labour-capacity* (though this may even be associated with a rise in the actual price of labour), a portion of the capital previously laid out in wages is *set free*. There is a release of *variable* capital. For capital that is newly invested, this has simply the effect of enabling it to function at an increased rate of surplus-value. The same quantity of labour is set in motion with less money than before, and in this way the unpaid labour is increased in proportion to the paid labour. But for capital that was already invested earlier, not only does the rate of surplus-value increase, but on top of this a portion of the capital previously laid out on wages is set free.

---

wage – is also employed here, and thus the impact of this constant depreciation is quite different from what Mr. Carey dreams of in his harmonic brain. >

171 < *Examples* need to be given. >

172 *Ricardo* [1821, Chapter 6, pp. 123–4].

This was formerly tied up and formed a portion constantly deducted from the proceeds of production which was laid out in wages and had to function as variable capital if the business was to continue on the old scale. This portion now becomes available and can therefore be used as a new capital investment, whether to extend the same business or to function in another sphere of production.

By the *tying-up* of capital we mean that, out of the *total value of the product, a certain additional proportion* must be transformed back into the elements of constant or variable capital, if production is to continue on its old scale. By the *release* of capital we mean that a part of the *total value of the product*, which previously had to be transformed back into either constant or variable capital, becomes available, and is *superfluous* if production is to be continued within the limits imposed by the old scale. This release or tying-up of capital is different from the *release or tying-up of revenue*. If the annual surplus-value of a capital C = x, for example, the cheapening of those commodities that enter the consumption of the capitalist may render $x - a$ sufficient to procure the same amount of enjoyment, etc., as before. > Since $x - a + a = x$, a part of the revenue, a, is set free and can now serve either to expand the capitalist's consumption or to be transformed back into capital (for accumulation). And vice versa. If $x + a$ is required in order to continue with the same mode of life, either this expenditure must be restricted or else a portion of income = a that was previously accumulated must now be spent as revenue.

In the above case, then, if £500 was originally required to set 500 workers in motion for a week, and now only £400 is required for this, and if > the surplus-value = s = 250, it was $^{250}/_{500}$ previously and is now $^{250}/_{400}$. It has therefore risen from 50% (500: 250 = 2: 1 = 100: 50) to 62½%. < And this is the only effect for someone making a new investment with a variable capital of 400. But at the same time £100 > or 1/5 of the capital previously tied up has been set free and this can again be valorised as capital, whether in the same investment or another one.

And vice versa, if previously £400 of variable capital was required and now £500 is needed to exploit the same quantity of labour. To simplify the example, let us assume that the surplus-value = 100%. Hence the 500 workers in the first example originally cost 500 and produced £500 of surplus-value. The value of their total product = 1,000 and the rate of surplus-value = 100% (500: 500). As a result of the depreciation of the variable capital, 400v + 600s = £1,000, so that < now the rate of surplus-value = 150%. It has risen by 50%. In addition, £100 has been set free and can be used to exploit labour again. The same labour, therefore, is not only more profitably exploited, but also *more* workers are exploited at the higher rate owing to the release of the £100, and with the same total amount of capital, 400 + 100, as before.

Now the other way around. If we take it that the original division of the product, with 500 workers employed, was 400v + 600s = 1,000, the rate of surplus-value = 150%. If 500 workers are employed every week with £400, £4 employs 5 workers, or 1 worker receives 16s. a week (500 workers at 16 × 500s. = 16 × £25 = £400). If, as a result of the appreciation of the capital, 500 workers cost £500, the weekly wage of 1 worker will be £1 and £400 will only be able to set 400 workers in motion. If the same number of workers as before are set in motion, we have 500v + 500s = £1,000. And the rate of surplus-value would have fallen from 150 to 100, hence by a third or 33⅓%. For newly invested capital, the only effect of this would be that the rate of surplus-value would have fallen by a third, and therefore, with other circumstances remaining the same, the rate of profit would have fallen correspondingly. (If for example c = 2,000, we have:

	c		v	s	s′	p′
(1)	2,000	+	400	600	150	25%
(2)	2,000	+	500	500	100	20%.)

|125| For the capital already operating, on the other hand, the effect is a dual one. With £400 of variable capital, only 400 workers can be utilised, and this is at a rate of surplus-value of 100%. The 400 workers produce only s/400, whereas previously they produced s/500. > Because the value 500 workers deliver = £1000, the value 1 worker delivers is £2, and the value 400 deliver is £800. Thus v will be 400, s will be 400 and the rate of surplus-value will be 100% instead of the previous 150%. And if everything else remains the same, < where 500 workers set in motion a constant capital of 2,000, one worker sets £4 in motion, and 400, £1,600. > If the remaining £400 are divided in the same proportions, so that one worker sets in motion £4, 80 workers will set in motion 4 × 80 = £320.

The total constant capital = £1,920 c and the 480 workers cost £480. 1,920 c + 480 v = 2,400. (This calculation is wrong in relation to the constant capital, as the exact proportion is not given here. For the present investigation, however, this is unimportant.) The formula would now be:

c	v	s	s′	p′
1,920 +	480	480	100	20%.

The same capital of £2,400, under conditions which are still too favourable, would produce 20% instead of 25%. But that is not all. If production is to be continued on the same scale in the old business – and this is necessary to avoid stopping part of the machinery, or working short time, or, generally, carrying on the business on a falsely contracted scale – since on our assumption no change has taken place in the technological [*technologisch*] distribution of the capital – 500 workers must continue to be employed in order to set in motion a constant capital of 2,000. Hence £500 of variable capital must be laid out instead of £400; in other words, £100 more must be engaged as variable capital in order to continue production on the former scale, < and this is possible only because capital that was formerly available is now tied up, in that part that was supposed to be accumulated now serves simply to fill the gap, or, alternatively, a part of the income that was to be spent as revenue is > converted into an integral part of the old capital without its setting in motion any increment of labour. Using the earlier data, the formula would then be as follows:

	c	v	s	s′	p′
(II)	2,000	500	500	100	20%

500v is now needed in order to produce 500s, whereas previously only 400v was needed to produce 600s. The outlay of capital has increased, and since the previous situation was:

	c	v	s	s′	p′
(I)	2,000	400	600	150	25

the increased outlay of capital produces less surplus-value. This is a result of the tying-up of the capital. < More capital is needed in order to set in motion *the same number* of workers, and at the same time the surplus-value that each of these individual workers supplies is reduced.

The advantages that arise from the release of variable capital and the disadvantages that arise from the tying-up of additional variable capital both exist only for capital that is already in operation and thus reproduces itself in conditions that have been given. For newly invested capital, the advantage or disadvantage is confined to this, that there will occur a rise or fall in the rate of surplus-value, and a corresponding change in the rate of profit. >

(What is peculiar about the example introduced here is the contrast between the fall in the rate of surplus-value from case I to case II, which is 1/3 or 33⅓%, and what happens to the rate of profit, which falls from 25 to 20%, or by ⅕ = 20%. *The rate of profit* and *the rate of surplus-value* therefore do not fall *in the same proportion*. In order to explain this, one must bear in mind the following:

	c	v	s	s′	p′
(I)	2,000	400	600	150	25
(II)	2,000	500	500	100	20

|126| Comparing (II) with (I) we find that v rises from 400 to 500, i.e., by ¼ or 25%. If the surplus-value remained the same, 400: 600 = 500: 750. Hence s would have to be 750, and then p′ would be $^{750}/_{2500}$ = 30%. As a result of the rise in variable capital, with s′ remaining the same, p′ would rise from 25 to 30%, in other words by 5, which is ⅕ of 25, hence 20%. In actual fact the profit on 2,400 was 600 and ⅕ of 600 is 120. {(100 + 20) × 5 = 500 + 100 = 600}. If the profit grows by ⅕ or 20% it grows from 60 to 600 + 120, which is 720. But the 500, instead of producing a surplus-value of 750 produce only 500 {the £500 represents not 625 workers but only 500, hence ¼, or 25%, fewer} which is ⅓ less, since 3 × 250 = 750. If s were 750, p′ would be 30%. ⅓ less = $^{30}/_{3}$ = 10%. The rate of profit therefore remains 20%. The falls in the rate of profit and the rate of surplus-value respectively are not expressed in the same numerical ratio, because there is a change not only in the ratio s/v but also in v/c and therefore in v/(v + c) or v/C. v becomes v + δ or v′ and therefore v/C (= v/{v + c}) becomes v′/(v′ + c). Instead of $^{400}/_{2,000+400}$ we have $^{500}/_{2,000+500}$. C does admittedly grow as compared with v, but only because v grows as compared with c. Under the old conditions, the workers would only receive £320. They would therefore only produce a surplus-value of 480. Therefore:

c	v	s	s′	p′
2,000	320	480	150	[$20\frac{20}{29}$]

It is to be noted that s only falls from 600 to 500, hence only by ⅙, while s′ falls by ⅓.)

< The release and tying-up of variable capital that has just been investigated is a result of the *depreciation* and *appreciation* of variable capital. *Variable capital* can also be set free if the development of productivity leads to a reduction in the number of workers required to set the same amount of constant capital in motion, with the rate of wages remaining the same. (*Conversely*, additional variable capital may be tied up if more workers are required to set the same amount of constant capital in motion, owing to a worsening in productive conditions.) If a portion of the capital earlier applied as variable capital is now applied in the form of constant capital, however, or vice versa, hence if there is only a different distribution of the component elements of the same capital, then although this certainly has an influence on the rate of surplus-value and the rate of profit, it does not come under the heading of the tying-up and release of capital which we are considering here. >

(Continuing with the example cited earlier:

	c	v	s	s′	p′
(I)	2,000	400	600	150	25%
(II)	2,000	500	500	100	20%

When we compare (II) with (I), the rate of s rises from 100 to 150, hence by 50%, or when we compare (I) with (II) it falls from 150 to 100, hence by 33⅓%. The rate of profit, in contrast, rises from 20% to 25%, hence by 25%, or, comparing (I) with (II), falls from 25% to 20%, or by 20%. The rates of profit and surplus-value therefore do not rise and fall in the same proportion. Assume now that C, = 2,000 + 400, = 2,400, remains unchanged, and the same for v, while only s′ changes. Then we should have:

	c	v	s	s′	p′
(II′)	2,000	400	400	100	$16\frac{2}{3}$.

Now a third of 25 = $\frac{25}{3}$ = $8\frac{1}{3}$ and 25 – $8\frac{1}{3}$ = $16\frac{2}{3}$. On the other hand, half of $16\frac{2}{3}$ = $8\frac{1}{3}$ and 16 + 8 + ($\frac{2}{3}$ + $\frac{1}{3}$) = 25. In this case, therefore, one sees that p′ would rise and fall in exactly the same proportion as s′. (But this case is impossible on our assumption. It would only be possible if for example *there was a reduction in labour-time*, so that the total value produced by the 500 workers, instead of being 1,000, became merely 800. Or, as a result of technological change, the £400 represented only 400 workers instead of 500. In that case, if labour-time remains the same, 500: £1,000 = 400: £800. At the same time, however, each worker's wage would rise from £$\frac{4}{5}$ to £1. Then the case would be possible.)

|127| Let us now imagine a further change in (II):

	c	v	s	s′	p′
(II″)	1,900	500	500	100	$20\frac{5}{6}$

In this example, the value of c has fallen by 100, while the value of v has risen by 100. As a result, c + v = C remains unchanged. And the only change in s/C takes place in s, which, comparing I with II″, has fallen by $\frac{1}{6}$, while if we compare II″ with I it has risen by $\frac{1}{5}$. $\frac{1}{6}$ of 25 = $\frac{25}{6}$ = $4\frac{1}{6}$. 25 – $4\frac{1}{6}$ = $20\frac{5}{6}$. And similarly $\frac{1}{5}$ of $20\frac{5}{6}$ = 4 + $\frac{5}{30}$ = 4 + $\frac{1}{6}$ and $20\frac{5}{6}$ + $4\frac{1}{6}$ = 25. Here, therefore, we see that when C remains constant the different rates of profit in II″ and I resulting from a change in c are in both cases in exact proportion with s, which has fallen from 600 in I to 500 in II″. The ratio between s′ in I and s′ in II″, however, only has an impact on the rate of profit to the extent that it is expressed in the difference between s/C in I and s/C in II″. Here there is no change in C, but there is a change in the ratio of v to c, and therefore in s/v. Hence instead of getting a rate of profit of $16\frac{2}{3}$%, we get one of $20\frac{5}{6}$, because as a result of the diminution in c to the same extent as v increases, this increase is expressed only in a larger s (comparing II″ with II′) but not in a larger C. The difference $20\frac{5}{6}$ – $16\frac{4}{6}$ = $4\frac{1}{6}$ is a consequence of this fact. Or $4\frac{1}{6}$ = (16 + $\frac{4}{6}$): 4, hence = $\frac{1}{4}$ of 16 + $\frac{4}{6}$, *a difference of 25%* between II″ and I′. Hence there is a divergence of 25% from the exact way p′ (II″) and p′ (I′) are related to s′ (II″) and s′(II′).

Finally we come to II‴:

c	v	s	s′	p′
2,000	500	500	100	20

Since c increases by 100 in comparison with II″, or remains unchanged in comparison with II′ and I, while v grows by 100, we get the formula $^{v+100}/_{C+100}$. C grows from 2,400 to 2,500, by 1/24, hence by 4⅙%. Let us compare II‴ with II″. If II″ is compared with II‴, the rate of profit falls from 20⅚ to 20, in other words from $^{125}/_{6}$ to $^{120}/_{6}$, from 125 to 120, or from 25 to 24, hence by 1/25 = 4%. If II‴ is compared with II″, on the other hand, p′ rises from 20 to 20⅚, in other words from $^{120}/_{6}$ to $^{125}/_{6}$ or from 24 to 25, hence by 1/24 = 4⅙%, exactly the proportion in which C falls in II″ as compared with C in II‴. The difference accounted for by the rise of C in II‴ or in II therefore amounts to ⅚, which is 4⅙% as a proportion of 20 and 4% as a proportion of 25.

Thus the whole of the difference between (I) and (II), or (I) and (II‴) has been accounted for. Instead of being 16⅔ – as it would be if the p's behaved in exactly the same way as the s's, as they do in II′ (the difference between p′I and p′II would then be 25 – 16⅔ = 8⅓) – p′II is 20, in other words 3⅓ more, so that the difference between it and p′I is only 5 instead of 8⅓. For 4⅙ would then be added to the 16⅔ to account for the rise of s from 400 to 500, and 16⅔ + 4⅙ = 20⅚. On the other hand, ⅚ is then again deducted to account for the rise of C in II by 1/25 as compared with C in I. This leaves 20, or, if we consider the addition to 16⅔, namely 4⅙, it leaves 4⅙ – ⅚ = 3⅓, and this is exactly the difference between p′ in II and p′ in II′, i.e., between p′ as it actually is and p′ as it would be if the p's behaved in exactly the same way as the s's, which is only possible when C and therefore c and v remain unchanged.

|128| < Constant capital can also be tied up or released as a result of the appreciation or depreciation of its material elements. Apart from this, constant capital can be tied up (without a part of the variable capital being transformed into constant) only if the productivity of labour increases, hence the same amount of labour produces a larger product, and therefore sets more constant capital in motion. (The same result may occur if there is a decline in productivity, as in agriculture for example, so that the same amount of labour needs more means of production to produce the same product, e.g., a greater amount of seed, drainage, etc.) Constant capital can be released (without any depreciation) if owing to improvements, the harnessing of natural forces, etc., a constant capital

of lesser value is technologically able to perform the same service as a constant capital of greater exchange value did earlier.

We saw in examining the circulation process how, after commodities are transformed into money, are sold, this money must in turn be transformed back into the material elements of capital in the proportions that are required by the specific technological character of the sphere of production in question. *Ignoring wages*, i.e., variable capital > which must be paid every week or at some other specific interval, < the most important element in all branches of production is *raw material* (including the ancillary materials which are particularly important in branches of production which do not involve any raw material proper, as with mining and the extractive industries in general) since the portion of the price which must replace the wear-and-tear of the machinery as long as the machinery is still at all serviceable enters the account more in an ideal sense, i.e., it does not very much matter whether it is paid for and replaced today or tomorrow, or at any particular point in the capital's turnover time. If the price of the raw material rises, it may be impossible to replace it completely out of the value of the commodity after wages, etc., have been deducted. Violent fluctuations in raw material prices thus lead to interruptions, major upsets and even catastrophes in the reproduction process. It is particularly agricultural products proper, whose raw materials belong either to the plant or the animal kingdom, which are most subject to these fluctuations in value (quite apart from the impact of the credit system, which we are not examining here). The same quantity of labour may here be expressed in very diverse amounts of use-value, depending on uncontrollable natural conditions, favourable or unfavourable seasons of the year, etc., and a particular quantity of these use-values will accordingly have very different prices. If a value x is expressed in 10 lb. of a, the price of 1 lb. of a is $x/100$; if it is expressed in 1,000 lb. of a, the price of 1 lb. is $x/1{,}000$; and so on. (See Book I, Chapter Seven.)[173] This is therefore one element in the price fluctuations of raw materials. A second element is this – and we mention it here only for the sake of completeness, |129| since competition and the credit system both still lie outside the orbit of our discussion – that it is in the nature of the case that vegetable and animal products, whose growth and production are subject to certain organic laws involving naturally determined periods of time, cannot suddenly be increased in the same degree as, say,

173 [This refers to what Marx originally planned as 'Chapter Seven' of Volume I of *Capital*. This was not included in the versions published during his lifetime, but it was later discovered and published in German in 1933. The passage referred to here is printed in translation in Marx 1976, pp. 957–9. Translator]

machines and other fixed capital, coal, etc., which, assuming the requisite natural conditions, can be added at the shortest notice in an already industrially developed nation. It is possible, therefore, and indeed unavoidable in a situation of developed capitalist production, that the production and extension of the portion of constant capital which consists of fixed capital, machinery, etc., may run significantly ahead of the portion consisting of raw materials (vegetable and animal, ancillary materials included), so that the demand for these raw materials, etc., grows more quickly than the supply, and their *prices* therefore rise. This rise in prices leads to the following changes, (1) that these raw materials are supplied from a greater distance, because the rise in their price can cover higher transport costs; (2) that their production is expanded (although in the nature of things the volume of products may actually increase perhaps a year later); and (3) that all kinds of surrogates are now employed that were previously unused, and more economical use is made of waste products, etc. When the price-rise begins to have a marked effect on the expansion of production and supply, the turning-point has generally already been reached, at which demand falls as a consequence of the continuing increase in the price of the raw material and all the commodities it enters into as an ingredient, bringing about a reaction in its turn on the price of the raw material. Apart from the convulsions that achieve this effect by devaluing capital in various ways, still other circumstances come into play, which we must now go on to mention.

First of all, however, one thing should be clear from what has already been said: the more capitalist production is developed and the greater accordingly the means for a sudden and uninterrupted increase in the portion of constant capital that consists of machinery, etc. – the more rapidly accumulation proceeds (as in times of prosperity) – the greater is the *relative overproduction* of machinery and other forms of fixed capital and the more frequent the *relative underproduction* of raw materials (vegetable and animal) and the rise in their prices previously described, leading to a corresponding collapse. The more frequent, therefore, are those revulsions which have their origin in these violent price fluctuations of one of the elements of the process of reproduction. > (Many other elements of the crisis do not belong here.)

|130| < When these high prices collapse, because their rise has provoked a decline in demand as well as an extension in the scale of production, and the sourcing of supplies from locations of production (regions) that were previously drawn on far less or not at all, and consequently a situation in which the supply of raw materials overtakes the demand, overtaking it in particular under the former high prices, the result should be considered from different aspects. The sudden collapse in the price of raw materials places a check on their reproduction, and in this way the *monopoly* of the supplying country or countries,

which produce under the most favourable conditions, is re-established, perhaps with certain limitations, but anyhow re-established. The impulse that was given may indeed cause the reproduction of the raw materials to proceed on an expanded scale, particularly in those countries that possess a monopoly in this production. But the *basis* on which production proceeds as a result of the expanded machinery, etc., and which must now be regarded as the new normal basis, as a new point of departure, has been very much extended thanks to the events of the previous turnover cycle. Among some of the secondary sources of supply, however, reproduction has suffered a serious check. One only needs to run one's finger down the export tables for the last 30 years (up to 1865) to see how Indian cotton production has risen whenever there has been a shortfall in American production and then suddenly suffered a more or less lasting check. In periods when raw materials become dearer, the industrial capitalists get together and form associations to regulate *production*. This was the case for instance in 1848 in Manchester, after the rise in cotton prices, and similarly for the *production* of flax in Ireland, etc. As soon as the immediate impulse has passed by, the general principle of competition 'to buy in the cheapest market' again naturally rules supreme, instead of the principle aimed at by those associations, which is to favour production in suitable markets, in order to develop their productive capacity, irrespective of the immediate, present price at which these countries can supply the product. Once again, it is left to 'prices' to regulate supply. Any idea of a common all-embracing and far-sighted control over the production of raw materials – a control which is by and large entirely incompatible with the laws of capitalist production and therefore always remains a pious wish or is confined to exceptional common steps in moments of great immediate danger and perplexity – gives way to the belief that supply and demand will regulate each other. The capitalists' superstition about this matter is so crude that in their reports even the factory inspectors repeatedly throw up their hands in sheer astonishment. The alternation of good and bad years, of course, does bring cheaper raw materials round again. Apart from the immediate effect this has in extending demand, its impact on the rate of profit, as already mentioned, also serves as a stimulus. And the process depicted above, with the production of raw materials being gradually overtaken again by the production of machinery, etc., is then repeated once more on a larger scale. Any actual improvement in the raw material, so that not only the required quantity was supplied, but also the required quality, for instance cotton from India, would necessitate a regular and steady rise in European demand over a long period (quite apart from the internal economic conditions in which the Indian producer is placed.) The sphere of production of raw materials is thus expanded or intensified in fits and starts, before being violently contracted once more, etc. This can all be studied very well, as indeed can the spirit of capitalist production in general, from the cotton famine, a situation in which a raw material that is one of the most essential elements of reproduction was in part completely lacking. Prices can also rise in a situation of full supply, if this is full only |131| under difficult conditions. Alternatively there may be a genuine lack of raw material. In the cotton crisis the latter situation originally prevailed.

The more we look into the history of production in the most recent period, the more closely do we approach, particularly in the key branches of industry, an always recurring dearth and consequent depreciation of the raw materials (plants, etc.) The above arguments are illustrated by the following examples taken from the *Reports of the Inspectors of Factories*.

(The moral of the tale, which can also be extracted from other discussions of agriculture, is that the bourgeois system[174] runs counter to a rational agriculture, or that a rational agriculture is incompatible with the bourgeois system {even if, technologically speaking, it promotes its development} and needs either the touch of the small private cultivator or the control of the associated producers.) >

***1857 and 1858.* (*Cotton and Wool*)**

Factory Report (by R. Baker) *for the half year ending 31 October 1858*: < 'The state of trade is better' but the *'cycle of good and bad times diminishes as machinery increases*, and *the changes from the one to the other happen oftener, as the demand for raw materials increases with it'*. >[175] < 'At present, confidence is not only restored after the panic of 1857, but the panic itself seems to be almost forgotten. Whether this improvement will continue or not *depends greatly upon the price of raw materials*. There appear to me evidences already, that in some instances the maximum has been reached, beyond which their manufacture becomes gradually less and less profitable, till it ceases to be so altogether. If we take, for instance, the *lucrative years in the worsted trade of 1849 and 1850*, we see that the price of English combing wool stood at 1s. 1d. and of Australian at between 1s. 2d. and 1s. 5d. per lb., and that on the *average of the ten years from 1841 to 1850*, both inclusive, the *average price of English wool* never exceeded 1s. 2d. and of Australian wool 1s. 5d. per lb. But that in the commencement of the disastrous year of 1857, the price of Australian wool

174 [Here, as elsewhere, Marx refers to the 'bourgeois system', while the version published by Engels speaks of the 'capitalist system'. Translator]

175 *Factory Reports* 1858 (2), p. 56.

began with 1s. 11d., falling to 1s. 6d. in December, when the panic was at its height, but has gradually risen again to 1s. 9d. through 1858, at which it now stands; whilst that of English wool, commencing with 1s. 8d., and rising in April and September 1857 to 1s. 9d., falling in January 1858 to 1s. 2d., has since risen to 1s. 5d., which is 3d. per lb. higher than the average of the 10 years to which I have referred'.[176] >

< 'This shows, I think, one of three things, – either that the bankruptcies which similar prices occasioned in 1857 are forgotten; or that there is barely the wool grown which the existing spindles are capable of consuming; or else, that the prices of manufactured articles are about to be permanently higher'.[177] >

< 'And as in past experience I have seen *spindles and looms multiply both in numbers and speed in an incredibly short time*, and our exports of wool in France increase in an almost equal ratio, and as both at home and abroad the age of sheep seems to be getting less and less, owing to increasing populations and to what the agriculturalists call "a quick return in stock", so I have often felt anxious for persons whom, without this knowledge, I have seen embarking skill and capital in undertakings, wholly reliant for their success on a product which can only be increased according to *organic laws*'.[178] >

< 'The same *state of supply and demand* of all raw materials ... seems to account *for many of the fluctuations in the cotton trade* during past periods, as well as *for the condition of the English wool market in the autumn of 1857*, with its overwhelming consequences'.[179] >

Cotton trade. (1858) < 'Since the hours of labour in factories have been fixed, the amounts of consumption (of the raw materials), produce, and wages in all textile fabrics have been reduced to a rule of three ... I quote from a recent lecture delivered by ... the present Mayor of Blackburn, Mr. Baynes, on the cotton trade, who ... has reduced the cotton statistics of his own neighbourhood to the closest approximation:

"Each real and mechanical horsepower will drive 450 self-acting mule spindles with preparation, or 200 throstle spindles, or 15 looms for 40 inches cloth, with winding, warping and sizing > (size = *Schlichten*). < Each horse-power in spinning will give employment to 2½ operatives, but in weaving to 10 persons, at wages averaging full 10s. 6d. a week to each person ... The average counts of yarn spun and woven are from 30s. to 32s. twist, and 34s. to 36s. weft

176 *Factory Reports* 1858 (2), pp. 56–7.
177 *Factory Reports* 1858 (2), p. 57.
178 Ibid.
179 *Factory Reports* 1858 (2), p. 61.

yarns; and taking the spinning production at *13 ounces per spindle* per week, will give 824,700 lbs. yarn spun per week, requiring 970,000 lbs. or 2,300 bales of cotton, at a cost of £28,300 ... The total cotton consumed in this district (within a five-mile radius around Blackburn) *per week* is 1,530,000 lbs., or 3,650 bales, at a cost of £44,625. This is one eighteenth of the whole of the cotton spinning in the U.K. and one sixth of the whole of the power-loom weaving". Thus we see that, according to Mr. Baynes' calculations, the total number of cotton spindles in the U.K. is 28,800,000, and that supposing these to be always working full time, the annual consumption of cotton ought to be 1,432,080,000 lbs. But as the import of cotton, less the export in 1856 and 1857 was only 1,022,576,832 lbs., there must necessarily be a deficiency of supply equal to 406,503,168 lbs. Mr. Baynes ... who has been good enough to communicate with me on this subject, thinks that an annual consumption of cotton based upon the quantity used in the Blackburn district would be liable to be overcharged, owing to the difference, not only in the counts spun, but in the excellence of the machinery. He estimates the total annual consumption of cotton in the U.K. at 1,000,000,000 lbs. But if he is right, and there really is an excess of supply equal to 22,576,832 lbs., supply and demand seem to be nearly balanced already, without taking into consideration those additional spindles and looms which Mr. Baynes speaks of as getting ready for work in his own district, and, by parity of reasoning, probably in other districts also'.[180]

1849–50. Heyday of the worsted trade. The number of persons employed in this trade was 29,246 in *1838*, 37,060 in *1843*, 48,097 in *1845*, and 74,891 in *1850* (all of them in Yorkshire, but particularly in the West Riding). In the same district there were: 2,768 power looms in *1836*, 11,458 in *1841*, 16,870 in *1843*, 19,121 in *1845* and 29,539 in *1850*.[181] >

Suspicions had already begun to be raised in October 1850 as to whether this prosperity of the worsted trade would last. Inspector Saunders, in his report for the period ending on 30 April 1851, quotes from a report by the then sub-inspector [Robert] Baker about *Leeds* and *Bradford*: 'The state of trade is, and has been for some time, very unsatisfactory. The *worsted spinners* are fast losing the profits of 1850, and, in the majority of cases, the manufacturers are not doing much good. I believe, at this moment, that there is more woollen machinery standing than I have almost ever known at one time, and the flax spinners are also turning off hands and stopping frames. The *cycles of trade*, in fact, in the textile fabrics, are now *extremely uncertain*, and I think we shall

180 *Factory Reports* 1858 (2), pp. 59–61.

181 *Factory Reports* 1851 (1), p. 60.

shortly find it to be true ... that there is no comparison made between the producing power of the spindles, the quantity of raw material, and the growth of the population'.[182]

|*132*| [*The Cotton Famine and its Background*]

< *The high tide of the cotton trade was in 1845. Cotton prices were very low.* This is how Leonard Horner describes the period in his report:

'For the last eight years I have not known so active a state of trade as has prevailed during the last summer and autumn, particularly in cotton spinning. Throughout the half year I have been receiving notices every week of *new investments of capital in factories, either in the form of new mills being built,* of the few that were untenanted finding occupiers, of enlargements of existing mills, of new engines of increased power, and of manufacturing machinery'.[183]

1846 (*Cotton trade*) 'For a considerable time past I have heard from the occupiers of cotton mills very general complaints of the depressed state of their trade ... Within the last 6 weeks several mills have begun to work short time, usually 8 hours a day instead of 12; this appears to be on the increase ... *There has been a great advance in the price of the raw material,* and ... there *has been not only no advance in the manufactured articles,* but ... *prices are lower than they were before the rise in cotton began.* From *the great increase in the number of cotton mills within the last 4 years,* there must have been, on the one hand, *a greatly increased demand for the raw material,* and, on the other, a *greatly increased supply in the market of the manufactured articles;* causes that must *concurrently* have operated against profits, supposing the supply of the raw material and the consumption of the manufactured article to have remained unaltered; but, of course, *in a greater ratio* by *the late short supply of cotton,* and *the falling off in the demand for the manufactured articles* in several markets both home and foreign'.[184]

A rising demand for raw material naturally goes hand in hand with an excess supply of finished goods on the market.

In the district of *Bradford etc.* there were in 1836 only 318 mills; in 1846 there were 490. 'All have contributed, more or less, during the last 10 years, to the overstocking of the market, to which a great part of the present stagnation of

182 *Factory Reports* 1851 (2), p. 52. (Worsted goods are made from long wool; much the greater part are mixed fabrics, cotton and worsted being mixed in different proportions. Goods made either wholly or in part of Alpaca wool also fall under this category.)

183 *Factory Reports* 1846 (1), p. 13.

184 *Factory Reports* 1847 (L. Horner), p. 10. (This report was officially issued for the half year ending 31 October 1846.)

trade must be attributed ... The great increase of mills ... does not however afford, by any means, a full estimate of the increased trade carried on. A large proportion of the mills at work in 1836 have had considerable additions made to them; and *in machinery alone there have been improvements*, which have caused a very large increase in the quality of goods manufactured. This is perhaps true most of all for the flax-spinning machinery ... The depression naturally results from such a rapid increase of mills and machinery'.[185]

October 1847. Monetary crisis. (8% discount.) Railway bubble etc. However:

'Mr. Baker enters into very interesting details respecting *the increased demand*, in the last few years, for cotton, wool, and flax, owing to the extension of these trades. He considers the *increased demand for these raw materials*, occurring, as it has, *at a period when the produce has fallen much below an average supply*, as almost sufficient even without reference to the monetary derangement, to account for the present state of these branches. This opinion is fully confirmed by my own observations, and conversation with persons well acquainted with trade. Those several branches were all in a very depressed state, while discounts were readily obtained at and under 5 per cent. *The supply of raw silk* has, on the contrary, been abundant, the prices moderate, and the trade, consequently, very active, till ... the last 2 or 3 weeks, when there is no doubt the monetary derangement has affected not only the persons actually engaged in the manufacture, but more extensively still, the manufacturers of fancy goods, who were great customers to the throwster. *A reference to published returns shows that the cotton trade has increased nearly 27 per cent in the last 3 years. Cotton* has consequently increased, in round numbers, from *4d. to 6d. per lb.*, while *twist, in consequence of the increased supply, is yet only a fraction above its former price*'.[186] 'The *woollen trade* began its increase *in 1836*, since which time Yorkshire has increased its manufacture of this article by *40 per cent*, but Scotland exhibits a yet greater increase. The increase of the *worsted trade* is still larger. Calculations give a result of an increase of upwards of *74 per cent* within the same period. The consumption of raw wool has therefore been immense. *Flax* has increased since 1839 about 25 per cent in England, 22 per cent in Scotland, and nearly 90 per cent in Ireland; the consequence of this, in connection with bad crops, has been that the *raw material has gone up £10 a ton*, while the *price of yarn has fallen 6d.* a bundle'.[187]

185 *Factory Reports* 1847, p. 30.

186 *Factory Reports* 1848, p. 30.

187 *Factory Reports* 1848, pp. 30–1.

1849 and the last months of 1848. Revival. 'The *price of flax*, which has been so low as to almost guarantee a reasonable profit under any future circumstances, has induced the manufacturers to carry on their work very steadily. The *woollen* manufacturers were exceedingly busy for a while in the early part of the year ... I fear that consignments of woollen goods often take the place of real demand, and that periods of *apparent prosperity*, i.e. *of full work*, are not always periods of legitimate demand. In some months the *worsted* trade has been exceedingly good ... At the commencement of the period referred to, *wool was exceedingly low*: what was bought by the spinners was well bought, and no doubt in considerable quantities. When the price of wool rose with the spring wool sales, the spinner had the advantage, and the demand for manufactured goods becoming considerable and imperative, they kept it'.[188]

'If we look at the variations in the state of trade which have occurred in the manufacturing districts of the kingdom for a period now of between 3 and 4 years, I think we must admit the *existence of a great disturbing cause* somewhere ... May not the *immensely productive power of increased machinery* have added another element?'[189]

In November 1848, May 1849 and during that summer up to October 1849 trade improved continuously. 'The *worsted stuff trade*, of which Bradford and Halifax are the great hives ... has been one of the most active; *this trade has never before reached anything like the extent to which it has now attained* ... Speculation, and *uncertainty as to the probable supply of cotton wool*, has ever had the effect of causing greater excitement, and more frequent alterations in the state of that branch of manufacture, than any other. There is at present an accumulation in stock, of the coarser kinds of cotton goods, which causes anxiety on the part of the smaller spinners, and is already acting to their detriment, having caused several of them to work their mills short time ... > The *increased price* of the *raw material* has lessened ... the inclination in some fine spinning mills to work the long hours previously practised with adult men'.[190]

|133| < *April 1850.* Continued revival. The exception is the 'great depression in a part of the cotton trade attributable to the scarcity in the supply of the raw material' precisely of the 'branches which spin low numbers of cotton yarns, or manufacture heavy cotton goods ... A fear is entertained that the increased machinery built recently for the worsted trade may be followed with a similar reaction. Mr. Baker computes that in the year 1849 alone the worsted looms

188 *Factory Reports* 1849 (2), p. 42.

189 *Factory Reports* 1849 (2), pp. 42–3.

190 *Factory Reports* 1850 (1), pp. 64–5.

have increased their produce 40 per cent and the spindles 25 or 30 per cent and they are still increasing at the same rate'.[191]

October 1850. 'The high price of cotton continues ... to cause a considerable depression in this branch of manufacture, especially in those descriptions of goods in which the *raw material constitutes a considerable part of the cost of production*. In consequence of this, many powerlooms and a good deal of spinning machinery is unemployed. *The great advance in the price of raw silk* has likewise caused a depression in many branches of that manufacture'.[192] >

29 September 1850. General Annual Meeting at Belfast of the Royal Society for the Promotion and Improvement of the Growth of Flax in Ireland. The 10th Annual Report by the Committee of this society states among other things: 'The yield (of flax) has not proved so large in some localities ... Notwithstanding this, however, the brisk demand and high prices for the fibre have so well remunerated the farmers, especially when contrasted with the low rates for other kinds of agricultural produce, as to ensure a greatly increased breadth being sown next year'.[193]

< *April 1853. Prosperity.* 'At no period during the last 17 years that I have been officially acquainted with the manufacturing districts of Lancashire have I known such general prosperity; the activity in every branch is extraordinary'. (Report by Leonard Horner.)[194]

October 1853. Depression in the cotton trade. 'Overproduction'.[195]

30 April 1854. '*The woollen trade*, although not brisk, has given full employment to all the factories engaged upon that fabric; and a similar remark applies to the *cotton* factories. The *worsted* trade was generally unsettled during the whole of the last half year'. Disturbance in *flax* by reason of the diminished supplies (of flax and hemp) from Russia (on account of the war).[196]

1859. Jute and flax. The trade in the *flax* districts (in Scotland) is still depressed ... the raw material being scarce, as well as high in price; and the inferior quality of the last year's crop in the Baltic, from whence come our principal supplies, will have an injurious effect on the trade of the district; *jute*, however, which is gradually superseding flax in many of the *coarser fabrics*, is

191 *Factory Reports* 1850 (2), p. 54.
192 *Factory Reports* 1851 (1), p. 14.
193 *Factory Reports* 1851 (1), p. 33.
194 *Factory Reports* 1853, p. 19.
195 *Factory Reports* 1854 (1), p. 13.
196 *Factory Reports* 1854 (2), p. 37.

neither unusually high in price, nor scarce in quantity, and ... about one half of the machinery in Dundee is now employed in jute spinning.[197]

'Owing to the *high price of the raw material, flax spinning is still far from remunerating, and while all other mills are going full time*, there are several instances of the stoppage of flax machinery ... > Even so, a large business continues to be carried on in that department. < *Jute spinning* ... is in a more satisfactory state, owing to the recent decline in the price of the material, which has now fallen to a very moderate point'.[198]

1861–4. Cotton famine. The biggest example of an interruption in the process of reproduction caused by the want and consequent high price of the raw material.

1860. 'With respect to the state of trade, I am happy to be able to inform you that, notwithstanding *the high price of raw material*, all the textile manufacturers, with the exception of silk, have been fairly busy during the past half year ... In some of the cotton districts hands have been advertised for and have emigrated thither from Norfolk and other rural counties ... There appears to be, in every branch of trade, *a great scarcity of raw material*. It is ... the want of it alone, which keeps us within bounds. *In the cotton trade*, the erection of new mills, the formation of new systems of extension, and the demand for hands, can scarcely, I think, have been at any time exceeded. Everywhere there are new movements in search of raw material. > The establishment of the *Cotton Supply Association of Lancashire* has induced [the foundation of] a *Flax Supply Association* at Belfast. At a meeting held by the Chamber of Commerce in December last, it was stated by the president "that for 5 years, ending with 1853, the average importation of flax, with the flax crop of Ireland added, amounted to 113,409 tons per annum, and for the last 5 years ending with 1858 it was only 101,672 tons, showing a diminution of 12,000 tons per annum, with an increased annual value of exports of £1,000,000"'.[199]

< 1860. October. 'The state of trade in the cotton, woollen, and flax districts has been good; indeed in Ireland it is stated to have been "very good" for more than a year now; and that it would have been still better but for the high price of raw material. The flax spinners appear to be looking with more anxiety than ever to the opening out of India by railways, and to the development of its agriculture, for a supply of flax ... commensurate with their wants etc'. > ('Labour was also in short supply', by the way.)[200]

197 *Factory Reports* 1859, p. 19.
198 *Factory Reports* 1860 (1), p. 20.
199 *Factory Reports* 1860 (2), p. 57.
200 *Factory Reports* 1860 (3), p. 37.

< *April 1861.* 'The state of trade is at present depressed ... *A few cotton mills are running short time*, and many silk mills are only partially employed. Raw material is high. In almost every branch of textile manufacture it is above the price at which it can be *manufactured for the masses of the consumers*'.[201]

|134| *October 1861. Overproduction in 1860.* 'Trade has been for some time in a very depressed state ... It is not improbable indeed that during the winter months many establishments will be found to work very short time. This might, however, have been *anticipated ... irrespective of the causes which have interrupted our usual supplies of cotton from America* and our exports, short time must have been kept during the ensuing winter in *consequence of the great increase of production during the last three years*, and the unsettled state of the *Indian and Chinese markets*'.[202]

Overproduction in 1860. 'It has taken between two and three years to absorb the overproduction of 1860 in the markets of the world'.[203]

'The depressed state of the markets for cotton manufactures in the *East*, early in 1860, had a corresponding effect upon the trade of Blackburn, in which 30,000 powerlooms are usually employed almost exclusively in the production of cloth to be consumed in the East. There was consequently but a limited demand for labour for many months prior to the effects of the cotton blockade being felt'.[204] 'Fortunately, the *growing scarcity of the raw material*, and the *slow but steady advance* in *the price of manufactured goods*, operated so far beneficially, that they preserved many of the spinners and manufacturers from being involved in the common ruin. *Stocks increased in value so long as they were held*, and there has been consequently nothing *like that alarming depreciation in the value of property* which might not unreasonably have been looked for in such a crisis'.[205]

Cotton Waste. Surat Cotton. Influence on Wages. Improvements in Machinery. Making up of Raw Material by using Size. Effect of this Size on the Workers. High Counts of Yarn. Fraud by the Manufacturers.

'A manufacturer writes to me thus: "As to estimates of *consumption per spindle*, I doubt if you take sufficiently into calculation the fact that when cotton is high

---

201 *Factory Reports* 1861, p. 33.

202 *Factory Reports* 1862 (1), p. 19.

203 *Factory Reports* 1864 (1), p. 127.

204 *Factory Reports* 1863 (1), pp. 28–9.

205 *Factory Reports* 1863 (1), p. 30.

in price, every spinner of ordinary yarns (say up to 40s.) (principally 12s. to 32s.) will raise his counts [200] as much as he can, that is, will spin 16s. where he used to spin 12s., or 22s. in the place of 16s., and so on; and the manufacturer using these fine yarns will make his cloth the usual weight by the addition of so much more size. The trade is availing itself of this resource at present to an extent which is even discreditable. I have heard on good authority of a cloth weighing 8 lbs. which was made of 5¼ lbs. cotton and 2¾ lbs. size; and of another cloth weighing 5¼ lbs. of which 2 lbs. was size. These were ordinary export shirtings. In cloths of other descriptions as much as 50 per cent of size is sometimes added; so that a manufacturer may and does truly boast that he is getting rich by selling cloth for less money per pound than he paid for the mere yarn of which they are composed'".[206]

'I have also received statements that the *weavers* attribute increased sickness to *the size* which is used in dressing the warps of Surat cotton, and which is not made of the same material as formerly, viz. *flour*. This *substitute for flour* is said, however, to have the very important advantage of increasing greatly the weight of the cloth manufactured, making 15 lbs. of the raw material to weigh 20 lbs. when woven into cloth'.[207]

'The earnings of the weavers are much *reduced* from the employment of *substitutes for flour as sizing for warps*. This sizing, which gives weight to the yarn, renders it hard and brittle. Each thread of the warp in the loom passes through a part of the loom called a "heald", which consists of strong threads to keep the warp in its proper place, and the hard state of the warp causes the threads of the heald to break frequently; and it is said to take a weaver 5 minutes to tie up the threads every time they break; and a weaver has to piece these ends at least 10 times as often as formerly, thus reducing the productive powers of the loom in the working hours; > and time so lost cannot under any circumstances be recovered'.[208]

Influence of the [cotton] famine and the inferior material on wages etc. Experimenta in corpore vili.[209]

< 'In Ashton, Stalybridge, Mossley, Oldham etc. the reduction of time has been fully one third, and the hours are lessening every week ... *Simultaneously*

206 *Factory Reports* 1864 (2), p. 27.

207 *Factory Reports* 1864 (1), p. 63.

208 *Factory Reports* 1864 (1), pp. 42–3.

209 [Experiments on a worthless body. Translator]

with this diminution of time there is also a reduction of wages in many departments'.[210] >

April 1861. 'During the early part of the year a strike which had commenced among the power-loom weavers in some parts of Lancashire adjoining my district spread to Ashton, Stalybridge, Glossop, and their neighbourhoods. The strike had its origin from the announcement made by certain manufacturers that they would reduce the rate of wages in some cases by 5%, in others by 7½%. To this the leaders of the operatives objected, and they proposed that the rate of wages should be retained, or that a lesser deduction should be made, and that the factories should be worked short time. After one month the operatives had to give way ... < In addition to the reduction of wages to which the operatives at last consented, many mills are now running short time'.[211]

April 1862. 'The sufferings of the operatives since the date of my last Report have greatly increased; but *at no period of the history of manufactures*, have sufferings so sudden and so severe been borne with so much silent resignation and so much patient self-respect'.[212]

'The proportionate number of operatives wholly out of employment at this date appears not to be much larger than it was in 1848, when there was an ordinary panic, of sufficient consequence to excite alarm amongst the manufacturers, so much so as to warrant the collection of similar statistics of the state of the cotton trade in *Manchester*, as |135| are now issued weekly ... In *May 1848*, the proportion of cotton operatives out of work in Manchester out of the whole number usually employed was 15%, on short time 12%, whilst 70% were in full work. On the 28th. May of the present year (1862), of the whole number of persons usually employed 15% were out of work, 35% were on short time, and 49% were working full time ... In other places, Stockport for instance, the averages of short time and of non-employment are higher, whilst those of full time are less'.[213] > (Because particularly fine numbers[214] are spun in Manchester.)

October 1862

The small fry among the cotton manufacturers. < 'I find by the last return to Parliament that there were 2,887 cotton factories in the U.K. in 1861, *2,109* of them being in my district. I was aware that a very large proportion of the 2,109 factories in my district (Lancashire and Cheshire) were small establishments,

---

210 *Factory Reports* 1862 (1), pp. 12–13.

211 *Factory Reports* 1861, p. 23.

212 *Factory Reports* 1862 (2), p. 10 (A. Redgrave).

213 *Factory Reports* 1862 (2), p. 16.

214 ['Grades'. In English in the manuscript. Translator]

giving employment to few persons, but I have been surprised to find how large that proportion is. In 392, or 19%, the steam engine or water wheel is under 10 horsepower; in 345, or 19%, the horsepower is above 10 and under 20; and in 1,372 the power is 20 horses and more. The above are the proportions in my district, and I assume that the proportion for the rest of the kingdom would be as nearly as possible the same. *A very large proportion of these small manufacturers* – being more than a third of the whole number – were operatives themselves at no distant period; they are men without command of capital, which has been invested in their trade etc. The brunt of the burden then would have to be borne by the remaining two thirds'.[215] >

Number of Unemployed (Lancashire and Cheshire)

< '*Number of operatives on full time* 40,146, or 11.3%; *short time* 134,767, or *38%*, *unemployed* 179,721 or *50.7%*. If we subtract the returns for Manchester and Bolton, where there is principally fine spinning > a department less affected than the other branches, < the situation was even worse, namely: full-time operatives 8.5%, *short time* 38%, *unemployed* 53.5%'.[216] >

Influence of the quality of the raw material on wages. < '*Working up good or bad cotton* makes a material difference to the operatives. In the *earlier part of the year*, when manufacturers were endeavouring to keep their mills at work by using up all the moderately priced cotton they could obtain, much bad cotton was brought into mills in which good cotton was ordinarily used, and the *difference to the operatives in wages* was so great that many strikes took place on the ground that they could not make a fair day's wages at the old rates ... in *some cases, although working full time, the difference in wages from working bad cotton* was as much as one half'.[217]

April 1863. 'During the present year there will not be full employment for much more than one half of the cotton operatives in the country'.[218] >

Influence of Surat cotton on wages, etc. < 'A very serious objection to the use of Surat cotton, as manufacturers are now compelled to use it, is that the speed of the machinery must be greatly reduced in the processes of manufacture. For some years past every effort has been made to increase the speed of machinery, in order to make the same machinery produce more work; and the reduction

215 *Factory Reports* 1863 (1), pp. 18–19.
216 *Factory Reports* 1863 (1), pp. 19–20.
217 *Factory Reports* 1863 (1), p. 27.
218 *Factory Reports* 1863 (2), p. 14.

of the speed becomes therefore a question which affects the operative as well as the manufacturer; for the chief part of the operatives are paid by the work done; for instance, *spinners* are paid per lb. for the yarn spun, weavers per piece for the number of pieces woven; and even with the other classes of operatives paid by the week there would be a diminution of wages in consideration of the lesser amount of goods produced. From inquiries ... and statements placed in my hands of the earnings of cotton operatives during the present year ... there is a diminution averaging 20% upon their former earnings. In some instances the diminution has been as much as 50%, calculated upon the same rate of wages as prevailed in 1861'.[219]

'The sum earned depends ... upon the nature of the material operated upon ... The position of the operatives in regard to the amount of wages is very much better *now* (*31st. October 1863*) than it was this time last year (1862). *Machinery* has improved, the material is better understood, and the operatives are able better to overcome the difficulties they had to contend with at first. I remember being in a sewing school at Preston last spring, when two young women, who had been *sent to work at a weaving shed the day before, upon the representation of the manufacturer* that they could *earn 4s. per week*, returned to the school to be re-admitted, complaining that they could not have earned 1s. per week. I have been informed of "*self-acting minders*" ... men who manage a pair of self-acting mules, earning at the end of a *fortnight's full work* 8s. 11d., and that from this sum was deducted the *rent of the house*, the manufacturer, however, *returning half the rent as a gift* (What a generous fellow!)[220] The minders took away the sum of *6s. 11d.* In many places the self-acting minders ranged from *5s. to 9s.* per week, and the weavers from 2s. to 6s. per week during the *latter part of 1862*'.[221] 'At the present time a much more healthy state of things exists, although there is still a great decrease in the earnings in most districts'.[222]

'There are several causes which have tended to the reduction of earnings, *besides the shorter staple* of the Surat cotton and its dirty condition; for instance, it is now the practice to mix "waste" largely with Surat, which consequently increases the difficulties of the spinner or minder. The threads, from their shortness of fibre, are more liable to break in the drawing out of the mule and in the twisting of the yarn, and the mule cannot be kept so continuously in motion. In some cases the spinners are required to spin weft on twist mules,

219 *Factory Reports* 1863 (2), p. 13.

220 [The whole of this passage has an exclamation mark in the margin. Translator]

221 *Factory Reports* 1864 (1), pp. 41–2.

222 *Factory Reports* 1864 (1), p. 43.

which is said to make a difference of 2s. 6d. per week to the spinner. Then, from the great attention required in watching the threads in weaving, many weavers can only mind one loom, and very few can mind more than two looms'.[223]

'In *many instances* ... there has been a *direct reduction of 5, 7½ and 10% upon the wages of the operatives* ... In the majority of cases the operative *has to make the best of his material*, and to earn the best wages he can at the ordinary rates'.[224]

'Another difficulty the weavers have sometimes to contend with is that they are expected to produce *well finished cloth from inferior materials*, and are *subject to fine* for the flaws in their work'.[225]

The wages were utterly wretched, even with full-time working. > (Now, in October 1864, with the fresh crisis, they are again at rock bottom.) < The cotton operatives, etc., were ready to do all the public works, drainage, road-building, etc., they could be 'used' for, so as to get *relief* (which was in fact a form of relief for their employers) from the town authorities. The bourgeois dogs[226] were always on the watch. If starvation wages were offered and the operative was unwilling to accept them, the Relief Committees struck him off the list. This was a golden age for the bourgeois dogs in the sense that |136| the workers either starved or had to work at the price most profitable for the bourgeoisie, with the Relief Committees acting as their watchdogs. At the same time these bourgeois dogs hindered emigration as far as possible, in a secret understanding with the government, partly so as to keep their 'capital' in readiness (this capital which existed in the flesh and blood of the workers), partly to make sure of the *rents* they extorted from the workers for their dwellings.

'The Relief Committees acted with great strictness upon this point. If work was offered, the operatives to whom it was proposed were struck off the lists, and thus *compelled* to accept the offer. When they objected to accept work ... the cause has been that *their earnings would have been merely nominal*, and the work exceedingly severe'.[227]

The *cotton operatives* showed themselves to be ready for every sort of labour they were put to under the *Public Works Act*. 'The principle upon which industrial employments were organised varied considerably in different towns, but even in those places in which the outdoor work was not absolutely a *labour test*

223 *Factory Reports* 1864 (1), p. 42.
224 *Factory Reports* 1864 (1), p. 43.
225 Ibid.
226 [In the published version: 'bourgeoisie'. Translator]
227 *Factory Reports* 1864 (1), p. 97.

the manner in which labour was remunerated by its being paid for either at the exact rate of relief, or closely approximating the rate, it became in fact a labour test'.[228] 'The *Public Works Act* of the last Session (1863) was intended to remedy this inconvenience, and to enable the operative to earn his day's wages as an independent labourer. The purpose of this Act was threefold: firstly, to enable *local authorities* to borrow money of the Exchequer Loan Commissioners (for this they needed the sanction of the President of the Poor Law Board); secondly, to facilitate the improvement of the towns of the cotton districts; thirdly, to provide work and remunerative wages to the *unemployed operatives*'. So far (up to the end of October, 1863) £883,707 has been applied for under this Act, and 'authorised by the Poor Law Board to be borrowed for various public local purposes'.[229] (Mainly for drainage, street-paving, water reservoirs and sewers, etc.)

Mr. Henderson, the chairman of the Blackburn Relief Committee, wrote to Factory Inspector Redgrave on the subject of the outdoor operatives as follows: 'Nothing in my experience, during the present period of suffering and distress, has struck me more forcibly or given me more satisfaction, than the cheerful alacrity with which the unemployed operatives of this district have accepted of the work offered to them through the adoption of the Public Works Act by the Corporation of Blackburn. A greater contrast than that presented between the cotton spinner as a skilled workman in a factory, and as a labourer in a sewer 14 or 18 feet deep, can scarcely be conceived. (For this they earned an average of 4 to 12 shillings a week, though the latter figure, a 'large sum of money', often had to suffice for a family of man, woman and six children, so that the municipal philistines profited twice over: firstly they received cheap loans for improving their urban pigsties, and secondly they paid the workers *below the standard rate of wages*.) Accustomed as he has been to a temperature all but tropical, to work at which agility and delicacy of manipulation availed him infinitely more than muscular strength and to double and sometimes treble the remuneration which it is possible for him now to obtain, his ready acceptance of the proffered employment involved an amount of self-denial and consideration the exercise of which is most creditable. In Blackburn the men have been tested at almost every variety of out-door work: in excavating a stiff heavy clay soil to a considerable depth, in draining, in stone-breaking, in road-making, and in excavating for street sewers to a depth of 14, 16 and sometimes 20 feet. In many cases while thus employed they are standing in

228 *Factory Reports* 1864 (1), p. 69.

229 *Factory Reports* 1864 (1), p. 70.

mud and water to the depth of 10 or 12 inches, and in all they are exposed to a climate which, for chilly humidity, is not surpassed ... even if it is equalled, by that of any district in England'.[230]

'*The conduct of the operatives* has been almost blameless ... their readiness to accept and make the best of out-door labour'.[231] >

Bad yarn means bad wages for the weavers. Competition from stone-breaking.

April 1864. (As soon as the crisis broke out again, in *September 1864*, the workers were again thrown out of work everywhere by these scoundrels.)

< 'Complaints are occasionally made in different districts of the scarcity of hands, but this deficiency is chiefly felt in particular departments, as for instance of *weavers* ... These complaints *have their origin* as much from *the low rate of wages* which the hands can earn *owing* to the *inferior qualities of yarn used* as from any positive scarcity of workpeople even in that particular department. Numerous differences have taken place during the last month between the masters of particular mills and their operatives in respect to wages. Strikes, I am sorry to say, are but too frequently resorted to'. 'The effect of the Public Works Act is *felt as a competition by the millowners*' (this applies particularly to work in the quarries: in the stone quarries of the Bacup district the demand for labour grew so steeply as a result of the Public Works Act that 'many factory operatives earned 4s. to 5s. per day at stone getting') and, consequently, 'the *local committee at Bacup has suspended operations*, for although all the mills are not running, yet a scarcity of hands has been experienced'.[232]

Experimentum in corpore vili[233]

'Although I have given the > very reduced full-time < actual earnings of the operatives in several mills, it does not follow that they earn the same amount week by week. *The operatives are subject to great fluctuation, from the constant experimentalizing of the manufacturers upon different kinds and proportions of cotton and waste in the same mill, the "mixings"* as it is called *being* frequently changed; and the earnings of the operatives rise and fall with the quality of the cotton mixings, sometimes they have *been within 15% of former earnings*, and then *in a week or two, they have fallen from 50 to 60%*'.[234] Inspector Redgrave goes on to give actual lists of wages; the following examples will be sufficient:

230 *Factory Reports* 1864 (1), pp. 91–2.

231 *Factory Reports* 1864 (1), p. 69.

232 *Factory Reports* 1864 (2), pp. 9–10.

233 [Experiment on a worthless body. Translator]

234 *Factory Reports* 1864 (1), pp. 50–1.

Family of 6, 2 of them employed as *weavers, 4 days a week*, 6s. 8d.; *twister*, 4½ days a week, 6s.; family of 4, *weavers*, 5 days a week, 5s. 1d.; *slubber* (family of 6) working 4 days, 7s. 10d.; *weaver*, 7 in the family, 3 days, 5s. and so on. Redgrave continues: 'The above returns are deserving of consideration, for they show that *work would become a misfortune in many a family, as it not merely reduces the income*, but brings it so low as to be utterly insufficient to provide more than a small portion of their absolute wants, were it not that supplemental relief is granted to operatives when the wages of the family do not reach the sum that would be given to them as relief if they were all unemployed'.[235]

|137| 'In no week since *the fifth of June 1863* (until the 31st. December 1863) was there more than *two days, seven hours, and a few minutes* employment for all the workers'.[236] >

The total amount of relief. < From the time the crisis began, up until 25th. March 1863, nearly £3,000,000 was 'expended by the Guardians, the Central Relief Committee, and the Mansion House Committee'.[237]

'In a district in which the finest yarn is spun ... the spinners suffer an indirect reduction of 15% in consequence of the change from South Sea Island to Egyptian cotton ... In an extensive district, in many parts of which waste is largely used as a mixture with Surat, the spinners have had a *reduction* of 5%, and have lost from 20% to 30% in addition, through working Surat and waste. The weavers are reduced from 4 looms to 2. In 1860 they averaged 5s. 7d. per loom, in 1863 only 3s. 4d. The *fines* which formerly varied from 3d. to 6d. (for the spinner) on American, now run up to from 1s. to 3s. 6d'. In one district where Egyptian cotton was used, mixed with Surat: 'the average of the mule spinners ... which in 1860 was 18s. to 25s. is now 10s. to 18s., caused, in addition to the inferior cotton, by the reduction of the speed of the mule to put an extra amount of twist in the yarn, which in ordinary times would be paid for according to list'.[238]

'Although the Indian cotton may (in some mills) have been *worked to profit* by the manufacturer, it will be seen (see the *wage-list for October 1863* on p. 53) that the operatives are sufferers compared with 1861, and if the use of Surat be confirmed, the operatives will want to earn the wages of 1861, which would *seriously affect the profits of the manufacturer*, unless he obtain compensation either in the price of the raw cotton or of his products'.[239]

---

235 *Factory Reports* 1864 (1), p. 53.

236 *Factory Reports* 1864 (1), p. 121.

237 *Factory Reports* 1864 (1), p. 13.

238 *Factory Reports* 1864 (1), pp. 43–4, and cf. pp. 45–50.

239 *Factory Reports* 1864 (1), p. 105.

House rent and *emigration*. 'The rent is frequently *deducted from the wages of operatives, even when working short time, by the manufacturers whose cottages they may be occupying*. Nevertheless, the value of this class of property has diminished, and houses may be obtained at a reduction of from 25% to 50% upon the rent of the houses in ordinary times; for instance a cottage which would have cost 3s. 6d. per week can now be had for 2s. 4d. per week, and sometimes even for less'.[240]

The 'master' was of course against emigration, partly because 'looking forward to the recovery of the cotton trade from its present depression' he wanted to 'keep within his reach the means whereby his mill could be worked in the most advantageous manner'. In addition, 'many manufacturers are owners of the houses in which operatives employed in their mills reside, and some unquestionably expect to obtain a portion of the back rent owing'.[241] >

State of Health. Harmful influence of Surat. Good influence of the open air, etc.

|151|[242] [6] The Influence of Changes in Circulation Time, its Shortening or Lengthening (and also changes in the means of communication connected with this) on the Rate of Profit

|153| [7] Profit (as it appears to the bourgeois)

< We assume, as throughout this chapter, that the mass of profit *appropriated* in each particular sphere of production is equal to the sum of the surplus-value produced by the total capital applied in this sphere. The bourgeois, however, will not conceive profit as identical with surplus-value, i.e., with unpaid surplus labour, because:

(1) In the process of circulation, he forgets the production process. The *realisation* [*realisieren*] of the *value* of the commodities – in which the *realisation of their surplus-value* is included – is regarded by him as the *making of this surplus-value*.

(2) We have shown that, assuming the same *degree of exploitation of labour*, and ignoring all modifications introduced by the credit system, as also all

240 *Factory Reports* 1864 (1), p. 57.

241 *Factory Reports* 1864 (1), p. 96. Mr. Bernal Osborne, M.P., said in a speech to his electors on 22 October 1864 that the workers of Lancashire had behaved, and were still behaving, like the Stoic philosophers of ancient times. Not like sheep?

242 [There is a gap in the pagination between 138 and 150, and 152 was left blank. Translator]

mutual swindling and cheating among the capitalists themselves, as also any advantageous choice of markets, the *rate of profit* can be very different according to whether raw materials are purchased cheaply or less cheaply > (in which connection the evaluation and choice of raw materials of the correct *quality* is very important) < according to whether the machinery employed is productive, suitable and cheap; whether the overall arrangement of the production process in its various stages is more or less satisfactory, with wastage of material avoided, and administration more or less simple and effective, > and finally whether there is order or disorder, regularity or its absence. < In short, given the *surplus-value* that accrues to a certain variable capital, > i.e., for a given capital, e.g., 100, that is laid out in wages, < it depends very much on the *business acumen of the individual,* either the capitalist himself or his manager, whether this same surplus-value is expressed in a higher or lower rate of profit, and therefore whether it delivers a *larger* or a *smaller* amount of profit. The *same surplus-value of 1,000*, the product of £1,000 of *wages*, may involve £9,000 of constant capital in concern A, and £11,000 in concern B. In case A we have $p' = {}^{1,000}/_{10,000}$ $= 1/10 = 10\%$. In case B we have $p' = {}^{1,000}/_{12,000} = 1/12 = 8\tfrac{1}{3}\%$. In the first case > each thousand of the total capital gives 100, in the second case it gives only $80 + 10/3 = 83\tfrac{1}{3}$. < The *total capital* produces *more profit* in case A than in case B, because the rate of profit is higher, although the *variable capital advanced* (£1,000) and the surplus-value that is extracted from it (£1,000) are the same in both cases, and there is thus in each case an equal exploitation of the same amount of labour. This *variation in the way the same mass of surplus-value is presented,* or the variation in the rate of profit and therefore in the *profit itself,* with *the same exploitation of labour,* may also stem from other sources; it can also arise purely and simply from differences in the *business skill* with which the two concerns are conducted. And this circumstance *misleads* the capitalist by convincing him that his profit is due not to the exploitation of labour, but at least in part also to other circumstances independent of this, such as his own individual activities, etc. >

(Since the magnitude of the surplus-value is entirely irrelevant to what we have just been examining, and it is only necessary to assume that it is of a *given* magnitude, the above analysis is equally valid when surplus-value is replaced by average profit, hence when each capitalist participates only proportionately in the total surplus-value produced by the total capital. In the cases considered here, things are depicted differently: namely in the sense that at a given *market price of the commodities* and with a *given degree of exploitation* of labour, any *saving in cost prices* depends on the skill and attention of the individual.)

As Dr. Dauglish says in his evidence previously mentioned, 'the *actual profits* on working such bakeries will vary according to the localities in which they are placed, and the *amount of administrative talent and business capacity of the* ***manager***'. (*Report Relative to the Grievances* 1862, evidence, p. 122.)

|154| < The arguments developed in this chapter (which is Chapter One of Book Three) show the incorrectness of the view (see Rodbertus)[243] according to which (in distinction from ground-rent, where the land area can remain *the same*, for example, while the *rent* rises) a change in the magnitude of the capital can remain without effect on the proportion between capital and profit, and therefore on the rate of profit, because if profit (the mass of profit) grows, so does the mass (the magnitude) of the capital on which it is calculated, and vice versa.

This is true in only two cases. Firstly, if, other things being equal, and in particular the rate of surplus-value, there is a depreciation or an appreciation of the material (the commodity) in which the money exists. (The same also applies to a merely nominal appreciation or depreciation of tokens of value, as long as other factors remain the same.) In this case, if the total capital, C, = £100 and the profit = £20, and, e.g., gold depreciates or appreciates by 100%, in the first case the same capital that was previously worth £100 would be worth £200, and in the second case what was previously worth £100 would be worth £50. But in the first case a profit that was previously £20 would be worth £40 (i.e., it is expressed in this amount of money) and in the second case it would be £10 instead of £20. In both cases $^{40}/_{200} = {}^{10}/_{50} = {}^{20}/_{100} = {}^{1}/_{5}$. In both cases there would nevertheless be in fact *no change in the magnitude of value* of the capital, but simply a change in the *monetary expression* of the same value and surplus-value. The rate of profit, s/C, could not be affected.

The other case is when there is a *real change in the magnitude of value*, but this change is not accompanied by any kind of change in the ratio v: c, or v/c, i.e., when the rate of surplus-value is constant and the ratio of the capital invested in labour (the variable capital, taken as an index of the labouring power[244] set in motion) to the capital invested in the means of labour remains the same. Under these conditions, whether we take *C* or *nC* or C/n, e.g., 1,000 or 2,000 or 500, the profit will be in the first case (at a rate of 20%) = 200, in the second case = 400 and in the third case = 100, but $^{200}/_{1,000} = {}^{400}/_{2,000} = {}^{100}/_{500} = {}^{1}/_{5}$. That is to say, the *rate of profit* remains unchanged here because the *composition of the capital remains the same* and is not affected by the change in its magnitude. Hence the *increase or decrease in the mass of profit* simply indicates *an increase or decrease*

243 [Rodbertus 1851, p. 125. Translator]

244 [These two words are in English in the manuscript. Translator]

in the mass of capital applied, an increase or decrease in the *magnitude* of the capital applied.

In the first case there is simply an *apparent* change in the magnitude of the capital applied; in the second case there is a *real* change in magnitude, but no change in the *relative magnitudes of the components of the capital*, i.e., *variable and constant capital*. Leaving aside these two cases, the change in the magnitude of the capital invested is either *the result* of a prior change in the value of one of its components, and thus a change in their relative magnitude (as long as the *surplus-value* does not itself change with the variable capital); or else this change in magnitude is the *cause* of a change in the relative magnitude of its components (as with large-scale operations, the introduction of new machinery, etc.) In all these cases, therefore, a *change in the magnitude* of the capital applied must be accompanied by a *simultaneous change in the rate of profit*, as long as other things remain equal.

An *increase in the rate of profit* always stems from a *relative* or *absolute* increase in the surplus-value in relation to its costs of production, i.e., it is *increased* in relation to the capital advanced, or there is a *reduction* in the difference between the rate of profit and the rate of surplus-value.

Fluctuations in the rate of profit that are independent of organic changes in the components of capital or independent of the absolute magnitude of the capital are possible if the *value* of the capital advanced, whatever might be the form – fixed or circulating – in which it exists, rises or falls as a result of an increase or decrease in the labour-time necessary for its *reproduction*, an increase or decrease that is independent of the capital already in existence, since the value of any commodity – thus also of the commodities of which capital consists – is determined not by the necessary labour-time it itself contains, but by the *socially* necessary labour-time required for its *reproduction*. This reproduction may differ from the conditions of its original production by taking place under easier or more difficult circumstances. If the changed circumstances mean that twice as much time, or, conversely, half as much time, is required for the reproduction of the same capital, then, given an unchanged value of money, this capital, if it was previously worth 100 thalers, would now be worth 200, or if 250 originally, now 125. If this increase or decrease in value affects all parts of the capital equally, the profit is also expressed accordingly in twice or only half the number of thalers. If it is only the *monetary value* of the capital advanced that rises or falls (as a result of an alteration in the value of gold) the monetary expression of the surplus-value will rise and fall in the same proportion. The rate of profit will remain unchanged. >

|155| < CHAPTER TWO

The Transformation of Profit into Average Profit

(1) Different Compositions of Capital in Different Branches of Production and the Resulting Variation in Rates of Profit

In the previous chapter we showed, among other things, how the *rate of profit* may undergo variation (may alter), either rising and falling, while *the rate of surplus-value stays the same*. In this chapter > the rate of surplus-value will always be assumed to be a constant, given magnitude. < We also assume that the degree of exploitation of labour, i.e., the rate of surplus-value, and the length of the working day, is *the same*, is equally long, in all the spheres of production among which social labour is divided *in a given country*. As far as the many variations in the exploitation of labour between different spheres of production are concerned, Adam Smith has already shown exhaustively how they cancel each other out through all kinds of compensations, either real or accepted by prejudice, and how they therefore do not need to be taken into account in investigating the general conditions, as they are only *apparent* and evanescent. Other distinctions, for instance in the level of wages, depend in large measure on the distinction between simple and complex labour that was mentioned already > in the introduction, < and although they make the lot of the workers in different spheres of production very unequal, they in no way affect the degree of exploitation of labour in these various spheres. Finally, although the equalisation of wages and working hours > and hence of the rate of surplus-value < between *different spheres of production* and even between different capital investments in one and *the same sphere of production* > *in the same country* comes to grief on < all kinds of local obstacles, > these are nevertheless reduced by < the advance of capitalist production and the subordination of all economic relations to this mode of production. Important as the study of frictions of this kind is for any special examination of wages, they are still accidental and inessential as far as the general investigation of capitalist production is concerned, and can be > excluded < (left out of account). In a general analysis of the present kind it is assumed throughout that actual conditions correspond to their concept [*Begriff*], or, and this amounts to the same thing, that actual conditions are depicted only in so far as they express > (represent) < their own general type.

The distinctions between *rates of surplus-value* in different countries and hence between different *national levels of the exploitation of labour* are completely outside the scope of our present investigation. The object of this chapter is simply to present the way in which a *general rate of profit* is arrived at within one particular country. It is clear, however, that in comparing different *national* rates of profit one need only combine what has been developed earlier with the arguments to be developed here. One would first consider the variation between national rates of surplus-value and then compare, on the basis of these given or constant rates of surplus-value, how national rates of profit differ. In so far as their variation is not the result of differences in national rates of surplus-value, it must be due to circumstances in which, as in our presentation in this chapter, surplus-value is assumed to be constant everywhere.[1] >

< We showed in the previous chapter that if the rate of *surplus-value* is taken as constant, the rate of profit yielded by a particular capital can rise or fall as a result of circumstances that increase or decrease the value of one or another portion of the constant capital, and thereby affect the ratio between the constant and variable components of the capital as a whole. We also noted that circumstances which lengthen or shorten a capital's circulation time may affect the rate of profit in a similar way. It was also apparent, finally, that the amount of profit or the profit itself as opposed to the rate of profit, was identical with the amount of surplus-value, with surplus-value itself, and that profit as such – as opposed to the rate of profit – was therefore not affected by the fluctuations in value just mentioned. These only modified the *rate* in which a given *surplus-value*, and hence also a *profit of a given magnitude* was expressed, i.e., its *relative* **magnitude**, its magnitude compared with the magnitude of the capital advanced. In so far as these fluctuations in value led to the tying-up or the release of capital, both the rate of profit and profit itself could be affected by this indirect route. However, this was true only of capital already invested, not of new capital investments; and, moreover, the expansion or contraction of *profit* itself was always dependent on the extent to which *more* or *less* labour could be set in motion > a larger or smaller number of workers employed < as a result of these fluctuations in value, i.e., the extent to which a greater or lesser mass of *surplus-value* could be produced with the same capital, at the same rate of surplus-value. Far from contradicting the general law or forming an exception to it, this *apparent* exception was in actual fact only a *special case of the general law's application.*

|156| It was shown in the previous chapter that, given a constant degree of exploitation of labour, the rate of profit *alters* with changes in the value of the

---

1 > 'The remaining value or overplus will in each trade be in proportion to the value of the capital employed'. (Ricardo 1821, p. 84.) <

components of the constant capital, as well as with changes in the capital's circulation time [*Circulationszeit*]. From this it follows naturally that *rates of profit* in different spheres of production that exist simultaneously alongside one another will *differ* if, other things remaining equal, either the circulation times of the capitals invested differ, or the *value relation* between the components of these capitals differs in different branches of production. What we previously viewed as *changes that took place over time in the same capital* are now considered by us as distinctions between capital investments that exist alongside one another in different spheres of production.

We have now to investigate: (1) *differences* in the *organic composition of capitals*; and (2) differences in their circulation time or their *turnover*.

For this whole investigation, when we speak of the composition (and also the circulation time) of capital in a specific branch of production, it should be clear enough that we always mean the normal, average situation for capital invested in this branch of production, and refer always to the average of the total capital in the sphere in question, not to chance differences between individual capitals invested there.

|157| Since we also assume that the rate of surplus-value and the working day are constant > (disregarding any variations in them) < a certain quantity of variable capital will mean a certain quantity of labour-capacity [*Arbeitsvermögen*] set in motion and therefore a certain quantity of labour set in motion. Thus if, e.g., £100 expresses the weekly wage of 100 workers, thus indicating 100 units of labour-power [*Arbeitskraft*], then $n \times$ £100 expresses the wages of $n \times$ 100 workers and £100/n the wages of 100/n workers. The variable capital serves here, as always when wages are taken as constant, as an *index* of the mass of workers set in motion by a certain total capital; variations in the magnitude of the variable capital applied therefore logically serve as *indices* of variations in the mass of labour-power applied. If £100 represents 100 workers per week and thus > assuming the length of the working day is given < 6,000 hours of labour, then £200 represents 12,000 hours of labour and £50 only 3,000.

By *organic composition* of capital we mean the ratio between its passive and its active component, between *constant* capital and *variable* capital. Two relationships are involved in this organic composition, which are not of equal importance, even though they may in certain circumstances produce the same effect.

The first relationship has a *technological* basis, and is to be taken as given and constant at *a particular stage of development of productivity*. A certain *quantity of labour-power* – represented by a certain number of workers – is required to produce a certain volume of products in a day, for example, and this act of production involves putting a *definite mass of means of production*, namely machinery, raw material, etc., in motion and consuming them productively. A definite *number of workers* corresponds to a *definite quantity of means of production*, and thus a *definite amount of living labour* corresponds to a definite amount of *labour already realised in the means of production.*[2] > <This *proportion* can *vary greatly* between different spheres of production and often between different branches of one and the same industry, although it may also happen to be *the same* > *or roughly the same* < *in branches of industry* that are very far apart.

The proportion just mentioned constitutes the actual basis of the organic composition of capital.

But it is also possible for the proportion to be the same in *two* (different) *branches of industry*, for the proportion between *variable* and *constant* capital to be the same, in so far as variable capital serves simply as an index of labour-power, and constant capital as an index of the volume of means of production that the labour-power sets in motion. Certain operations carried out on copper and iron, for example, [may] involve the same proportion between labour-power and the means of production. But because copper is dearer than iron, the *value relationship* between variable and constant capital will be different in each case, and so there will be a difference in the proportion in which a given quantity of capital, e.g., £100, is divided into variable and constant capital, hence there will be a *difference in their composition*. The distinction between *technological composition* [*technologische Zusammensetzung*] and the mere value ratio between the components shows itself in every branch of industry by the way the *value ratio* may change while the *technological composition remains constant*, while, with a changed *technological composition*, the *value ratio* may remain the same; the latter, of course, happens only if the change in the ratio of the quantities of variable and constant capital applied is paralysed by a contrary change in their values. Variable capital is assumed to be simply an *index of a definite amount of labour-power, a definite number of workers or a definite mass* of living labour that has been *set in motion*. We saw in the previous chapter how changes in the *magnitude of value* of the variable capital may possibly represent nothing but a *higher or lower price for the same amount of labour*, but here, where the rate of surplus-value and the working day, and the *wage for a certain labour-time* are all taken as constant, this does not apply. This is not the case, however, with *constant capital*. A difference in its magnitude may be simply an *index* for [a change in] the amount of the means of production set in motion by

---

2 > The proportion prevailing in the cotton industry as given in the Factory Reports should be introduced here.

a certain quantity of labour-power; but it may also arise from a *difference in the value* that the > material, etc., < has set in motion in one sphere of production as compared with that in the other spheres. Here, therefore, these two aspects both come into consideration.

The following fundamental point should also be noted:

Assume that £100 is the weekly wage for 100 workers. Assume that the working day is 10 hours, hence the working week is 60 hours. Assume further that the rate of surplus-value, > or the degree of exploitation of labour < is 100%. In that case, the workers work 30 of these 60 hours for themselves and 30 gratis for the capitalist. The £100 in wages actually embodies only 30 working hours of the 100 workers, or a total of 3,000 hours, while the other 3,000 hours that they work are embodied in the £100 of surplus-value, or profit, that the capitalist tucks away. Even though the wage of £100 does not express the value in which the week's work of 100 workers is objectified, it still indicates (since the rate of surplus-value and the length of the working day are given) that 100 workers are set in motion by capital > and with these 100 workers 6,000 hours of labour or 100 working weeks of 60 hours. < The capital of £100 indicates this for two reasons. Firstly, because it indicates the number of workers set in motion, since £1 = 1 worker per week, i.e., £100 = 100 workers; the second reason is this: owing to the fact that each worker, set in motion at the given rate of surplus-value of 100%, performs as much labour again as is contained in his wage, i.e., £1, this wage, which is the expression of half a week's labour, sets a whole week's labour in motion, and similarly £100, though it contains only 50 weeks' labour, sets in motion 100 weeks'. There is therefore a very fundamental distinction to be made here between the variable capital, or the capital laid out on wages to the extent that its value, the *sum of wages paid*, represents a definite *quantity of objectified labour*, and the variable capital to the extent that its value is *simply an index of the mass of living labour that it sets in motion*. This last is always greater than the labour contained in the variable capital and is thus also expressed in a higher value than its own; in a value that is determined on the one hand by the number of workers that this variable capital sets in motion and on the other hand |159| by the quantity of surplus labour they perform.

Considering variable capital in this way, we arrive at two conclusions:

If a capital invested in a sphere of production A (the spinning of cotton, for example) spends only 100 in variable capital against 600 in constant, for each 700 of total capital, while in sphere of production B 600 is spent in variable capital and only 100 in constant, then that total capital A of 700 sets in motion a labour-power of only 100, thus under our above assumptions only 100 working weeks, or 6,000 hours of living labour, while the total capital of 700 in sphere B sets in motion 600 working weeks and therefore 36,000 hours of living labour.

The capital of £700 in A would therefore absorb or appropriate only 50 working weeks or 3,000 hours of surplus labour, while that in B would appropriate 300 working weeks or 18,000 hours. The variable capital > (unlike the constant capital) < is not only an index of the labour it itself contains, but also, at the same time, of the excess or surplus labour that it sets in motion over and above that amount. At the same degree of exploitation of labour, the profit would be $100/700 = 1/7 = 14\frac{2}{7}\,\%$ in the first case, and $600/700 = 85\frac{5}{7}\,\%$ in the second: a rate of profit six times as high. Not only that, but the actual profit in this case would itself be six times greater, 600 for B as against 100 for A, as six times as much living labour has been set in motion with the same capital, and so, since the degree of exploitation of labour is the same in both cases, six times as much surplus labour, i.e., six times as much surplus-value, and thus six times as much profit. > It would change absolutely nothing < if in sphere A it was not £700 but £7,000 that had been applied to carry on the business, as against a capital of only £700 in sphere B. In that case, the £7,000 of capital in A would use £1,000 of variable capital > (since the ratio of its organic composition would remain 1v to 6c, $^{1v}/_{6c}$, in other words $v = 1/7\ C$ and $c = 6/7\ C$) < and thus employ 1,000 workers for a week = 60,000 hours of living labour, of which 30,000 hours would be surplus labour. But A would still, as before, set in motion only a sixth as much living labour > (hence also only a sixth as much surplus labour) < as B > and with the same absolute value, e.g., 1,000, would therefore absorb only a sixth as much surplus labour, hence produce only a sixth as much surplus-value and therefore also < only a sixth as much profit. If we consider the rate of profit, [A would receive] $^{1,000}/_{7,000} = 100/700 = 14\frac{2}{7}\,\%$, against the $600/700$ or $85\frac{5}{7}\,\%$ > of the capitalist in production branch B who is working with only £700. < With equal amounts (aliquot parts) of capital, such as 100, 1,000, etc., the rates of profit are different, since at an equal > (identical) degree of exploitation of labour < the masses of surplus-value and therefore profit that are produced are positively different as a result of the different masses of living labour set in motion.

|160| The same result follows in fact if the technological relations in production sphere B are the same as in A, but the *value* of the mass of constant capital applied is greater or less than in A. Let us assume that both capitals employ £100 as variable capital and thus use 100 workers for a week to set in motion the same quantity of machinery and raw material, but that this quantity is dearer > or cheaper < in case B than in case A. In this case, £100 of variable capital would correspond, e.g., to £200 of constant capital in A and £400 in B. At a rate of surplus-value of 100 %, then, the surplus-value produced in both cases is £100. The amount of profit produced with the same number of workers, 100, receiving the same payment, is also the same, £100. But in A, $^{100\ \text{Profit}}/_{200c\,+\,100v} =$

$^{100}/_{300} = {}^{1}/_{3} = 33^{1}/_{3}\,\%$, while in B $^{100}/_{500} = {}^{1}/_{5} = 20\,\%$. In actual fact, if we take a definite aliquot part of the total capital in both cases, in case B only £20 of each £100, or a fifth, forms the variable capital, while in case A £$33^{1}/_{3}$ of each £100, or a third, forms the variable capital. > The quantities of living labour that are set in motion by equal amounts of capitals A and B are therefore different, because variable and constant capital enters into the composition of the capitals in different proportions. < B in fact produces less profit for each £100 because it sets less living labour in motion, hence less surplus labour. The difference in the *rate of profit* is thus reduced here again to a difference in the *mass of profit* – because *mass of surplus-value* – produced for each 100 units of capital invested.

The distinction between this second example and the first is simply this: the equalisation of A and B in the second case would require no more than a *change in the value of the constant capital*, either in A or B, with the technological basis remaining the same; in the first case, on the other hand, the *technological composition* itself differs between the two spheres of production and would have to be transformed in order for such an equalisation to occur. >

Since the result is in practice the same, when we refer to the *organic composition* of capital we always mean the proportion in which the total amount of capital invested in different spheres of production is divided into, or consists of, constant and variable capital viewed in terms of percentages.

Thus if we look at the total capital [invested in different spheres of production, we get the following result:]

(1) Sphere of Production C: consists of c and v; rate of surplus-value: s′
(2) Sphere of Production C′: consists of c′ and v′: rate of surplus-value: s′
(3) Sphere of Production C″: consists of c″ and v″: rate of surplus-value: s′

The rate of surplus-value is the same in all three cases. Differences in the magnitude of C, C′, and C″ are irrelevant. In all three cases we take an *equal* portion of the total capital, say 100. If $v > v'$ and $v'' > v'$, since each pair (whether $c + v$, $c' + v'$, or $c'' + v''$) = 100, $c' > c$, and $c' < c''$. Since the |161| degree of exploitation of labour remains the same, $p > s'$ or p' of the second sphere of production, and s' or $p' > s''$ or p'' of the third sphere, since $v > v'$ and $v' > v''$, hence also the equal increment of v or s is greater than the increment of v′ or s′, and the latter is greater than the increment of v″ or s″. Hence s or p is greater than s′ or p′ and s′ or p′ is greater than s″ or p″. Hence:

$$\frac{p}{c+v} > \frac{p'}{c'+v'} \text{ and } \frac{p'}{c'+v'} > \frac{p''}{c''+v''}.$$

< Differing organic compositions of capitals are thus independent of > whether the amount of differently composed capital applied is in one sphere of production $n \times 100$, in another $mn \times 100$ and in yet another $\frac{1}{5}n \times 100$. < The only question is always what is the percentage of variable capital in relation to the constant capital.

Capitals of different magnitudes reduced to percentages, or, and this is exactly the same here, *capitals of the same size*, operating with the same working day and the same degree of exploitation of labour, thus produce *very different amounts of surplus-value, and therefore of profit*. This is because their variable portions differ according to the differing organic composition of capitals in different spheres of production, which means that different quantities of living labour are set in motion, and hence also different quantities of surplus labour or unpaid labour, which forms the substance of surplus-value and therefore of profit, > which is identical with surplus-value, considered quantitatively, < are absorbed or appropriated (or realised) by those capitals. Equal-sized portions of the total capital in different spheres of production embody sources of surplus-value of unequal size, and the only source of surplus-value is living labour. At any given level of exploitation of labour, the mass of labour set in motion by a capital of 100, and thus also the surplus labour it will appropriate, depends on the size of its variable component. If a capital, whose percentage composition is 90 constant and 10 variable, or $\frac{9}{10}$ c and $\frac{1}{10}$ v, were to produce just as much surplus-value or profit, at the same level of exploitation of labour, as a capital consisting of 10 constant and 90 variable, it would be as clear as day that surplus-value and hence value in general had a completely different source from labour, and with this any rational basis for political economy would fall to the ground. If we take £1 as the worker's weekly wage, and the working week as 60 hours, > and the surplus labour or unpaid labour contained in these 60 hours as 30 hours, with the result that < the rate of surplus-value is 100%, it is readily apparent that the total value of the product a worker can supply in a week is £2. Therefore 10 workers cannot supply more than £20, and as £10 of this £20 has to replace the wages, these workers, under these conditions, cannot create a surplus-value greater than £10. However, 90 workers whose total product was £180 and whose wages were £90 would create a surplus-value of £90. > Looking at the two different capitals, the profit on one would be 10, on the other 90 < and the rate of profit would be in the one case $\frac{10}{100} = 10\%$ and in the other $\frac{90}{100} = 90\%$. If it were to be otherwise, value and surplus-value would have to be something other than materialised [*materialisierte*] labour. Since capitals of equal size in different spheres of production, are, when considered in percentage terms, unequally |162| divided into a constant and a variable element, and set in motion unequal amounts of living labour, hence producing different amounts of surplus-value or profit, *the rate of profit*, which consists precisely of the surplus-value calculated as a percentage of the total capital, *is different in each case.*

But if capitals of *equal size* in different spheres of production, and thus of different size *taken by percentage*, grow with *unequal profit rates* as a result of differences in their organic composition, it follows that *the profits of unequal capitals* in different spheres of production cannot stand *in proportion to their respective magnitudes*, in other words that profits in different spheres of production are not *proportional to the magnitude of the capitals that are respectively applied.* For if profits did increase in proportion to the size of the capital applied, this would imply that the percentage of profit was always the same, and that therefore *capitals of equal size had the same rate of profit in different spheres of production*, despite their varying organic composition. It is only *within the same sphere of production*, where the organic composition of capital is therefore given, or between different spheres of production with *the same organic composition of capital* > (which are therefore not two *different* spheres with regard to their organic composition) < that the mass of *profit* stands in direct proportion to *the mass of capital applied.* > (Here, as we are considering the *total* capital applied in an individual sphere of production, or in different spheres of production which nevertheless belong together from the point of view of their organic composition, we disregard the distinction in organic composition according to the *scale of operations* in one and the same sphere of production, which was emphasised at the end of Chapter One of Book III.) < If the profits of *unequal capitals* were *in proportion to their size*, this would mean nothing other than that *capitals of equal size yielded equal profits*, > whatever their organic composition < or that the *rate of profit* was the same for all capitals, whatever their size. > (But if the *rate of profit* is the same, so also are the *profits* for capitals of the same size, but unequal organic composition.)

< The above argument assumes that commodities are sold at their *values*. The value of a commodity is equal to the value of the constant capital contained in it, plus the value of the variable capital reproduced in it, plus the increment on this variable capital, the surplus-value produced > or the surplus labour appropriated in the process of production. < Given an equal rate of increment, its mass evidently depends on the mass of the variable capital. The value produced by a capital of 100 would be in the one case, (I) £90c + 10v + 10s = 110; and in the other case, (II) £10c + 90v + 90s = 190. If commodities are sold at their values, the product of (I) = 110, 10 of which represents surplus-value or unpaid labour, and the product of (II) = 190, of which 90 represents surplus-value or unpaid labour. (This is particularly important when national rates of profit |163| are compared with one another. Assume that in a European country the rate

of surplus-value, or s′, is 100%, i.e., the worker works half the day for himself and half the day for his master; assume also that in an Asian country the rate of surplus-value = 25%, i.e., the worker works $\frac{4}{5}$ of the day for himself and $\frac{1}{5}$ for his master. Assume at the same time that the organic composition of the national capital is 84c and 16v, while in the Asian country, where little fixed capital, machinery, etc., is used, and apart from that relatively little raw material is productively consumed by a given amount of labour-power in a given amount of time, the organic composition is 16c and 84v. We should then have the following calculation:

	c	v	s′	s or p	p′
In the European country	84	16	100%	16	16%
In the Asian country	16	84	25%	21	21%

In the European country the rate of profit is only 16%, whereas it is 21% in the Asian country, thus 5% higher, an increase of over 25% > (since 20 is a 25% larger number than 16, it is, namely, larger by $\frac{16}{4}$) < although in the European country the degree of exploitation of labour = 100% and in the Asian one only 25%, hence it is 4 times as great in the European country as it is in the Asian one. Carey, Bastiat, and their like would draw precisely the opposite conclusion.[3] > This interpolation belongs in a later section of the book.)

We saw earlier (in dealing with the process of circulation) that *equally large* capitals may produce *unequal values* (over a given period) because fixed and circulating capital enter in unequal proportions into the *constant capital*, or, in other words, because the whole of the constant capital, and the part of the constant capital which can only be replaced to the extent that it suffers wear-and-tear, may enter into the products of capitals of equal size in different proportions.

One can now see that capitals of equal size may produce *values of unequal magnitude* (over a given period) because they *produce surplus-values, and*

3 [Several paragraphs between now and the end of this section, that are mainly about the important subject of unequal turnover times as another factor that causes unequal rates of profit (besides unequal compositions of capital), were left out in Engels's Volume III. The reader can use the translator's indicators of > and < to identify the missing paragraphs in the following pages. Editor]

therefore profits, at unequal percentages in proportion to their variable component.

This is what follows when we put these two propositions together:

Capitals of equal size may produce *values of unequal magnitude* in different branches of industry, and yet they may produce *surplus-values and therefore profits of an identical magnitude*, in percentage terms; and capitals of equal size in different branches of industry may produce *values of the same magnitude*, and yet produce *unequal surplus-values and therefore profits*.

Assume that $s' = 100\%$, and $C = 12{,}000$, 6,000 of which is fixed capital, machinery, etc., 5,000 is raw material, etc., and 1,000 is *a quarter of a year's* wages (about 83 workers). The profit would be 1,000. If there is a depreciation of one-sixth in the fixed capital over 12 months, in 3 months this would be $^{1{,}000}/_{4} = 250$. We assume that over the same 3 months £5,000 of raw material has been worked up. Thus the product = £250 depreciation of constant capital + £5,000 raw material used up by the constant capital + £1,000 wages + £1,000 profit or surplus-value. Total: £7,250. The rate of profit will be $^{1{,}000}/_{12{,}000} = {}^{1}/_{12} = 8\frac{1}{3}\%$ (Over the year it will be 16%, as when the profit is 4,000 the amount of capital will have grown in the same proportion to make up for the depreciation.)

Assume that another capital contains only 3,000 of fixed capital, etc., 8,000 of raw material, etc., 1,000 wages as previously, and all other elements are the same as before. Then depreciation would be 500 over the year, and $^{500}/_{4}$ in 3 months $= {}^{250}/_{2} = 125$. Hence the value of the product = 125 depreciation + £8,000 raw material, etc. + 1,000 wages + 1,000 surplus-value = 10,125. The rate of profit would be $^{1{,}000}/_{12{,}000} = 8\frac{1}{3}\%$ as in the previous case.

Conversely, if in the second case we had 5,000 of fixed capital, a depreciation of 250, raw material, etc., of 6,500 and wages of 500, the value of the product would be:

$$\frac{c}{250 + 6500} + \frac{v}{500} + \frac{s}{500} = 7{,}750,$$ the same value as in the first case.

The rate of profit, in contrast, would be $^{500}/_{12{,}000} = {}^{1}/_{24} = 4\frac{1}{6}\%$. (This case plainly shows the irrelevance of the proportion between fixed and circulating capital for the rate of profit.)

|164| Apart from the differing proportions of variable to constant capital, hence < besides the different masses of labour, and therefore, of surplus labour, < set in motion by capitals of the same size in different spheres of production > other things being equal (i.e., the rate of surplus-value remaining the same, as also the length of the working day, in which context working days may be of different length in appearance alone because this is compensated for by vari-

ations in intensity, etc.) – leaving aside this reason for different rates of profit in different spheres of production – < there is a further source of inequality between rates of profit: *the variation in periods of circulation* or *turnover* of capitals of equal size, or, and this is the same thing, capitals of unequal size viewed in percentage terms, in the different spheres of production. > It will be recalled from Book Two that here circulation time includes production time, since every phase capital passes through from the transformation of money into the material elements of capital up to the reconversion of the product into money (and therefore also up to the realisation of the surplus-value) forms a phase of its overall circulation, or turnover. The extent to which circulation time has an impact on the rate of profit is a question we do not wish to examine here in detail (since Book Two, which is devoted to discussing this, has not yet been written). Since the rate of profit is determined by the amount of profit which is made during a *given period*, if capital A needs, say, 2b of time to realise a profit, p, and capital B, which is the same as A in its monetary value or magnitude, produces p in 1b of time, we have:

	Time	Profit
Capital B produces in	b	p
Capital B produces in	2b	2p
whereas A produces in	2b	p
and A produces in	b	p/2
and 2 capitals A produce in	b	p

It therefore follows that in one case twice as much capital is required as in the other in order to produce the same profit if the *circulation time*, in which the profit p is realised, is twice as long in one branch of industry as in the other, and vice versa.

< *Differences in turnover time* are thus a further reason why capitals of equal size do not produce equally large profits in equal periods of time, and why rates of profit thus vary between the different spheres. >

(The influence of circulation time can be viewed in two ways: to the extent that capital is engaged in this process it cannot be used to absorb fresh surplus-value. The process of accumulation therefore does not proceed at the same rate. This does not, however, make for any difference in the *actual* rate of profit. It belongs rather to the capitalists' *grounds for reciprocal compensation*.

On the other hand, a *larger mass of capital is necessary* to exploit *the same mass of labour*. For example, assume there are two capitals with variable and constant components divided *in the same proportion*, and one of them produces 10% at the end of the first year, the other the same; but capital II cannot yet realise this, but uses up half of its previous yield and produces 5% in the first half of the year. As the end of one and a half years, both capitals, each of them of say £1,500, have produced £150 of profit. But since capital I turned over at the end of the first year, it can exploit its profit again at the beginning of the second year. For capital II, in contrast, £500 of extra capital was needed. In actual fact, therefore, capital II needs a C of 1½, whereas capital I needs only a C of 1, in order to produce £150 in 1½ years. Hence the rate of profit differs in each sphere.)

|165| < The *proportion in which the capitals are composed of fixed and circulating elements*, on the other hand, does not in any way affect the rate of profit, taken by itself. It can only affect it either if this differing composition conditions (or coincides with) a differing ratio between the *variable and constant portions*, in which case the variation in the rate of profit is due to *this* difference and not to the different ratio between *fixed and circulating capital*; or alternatively if the varying ratio between the fixed and circulating components involves a difference in the *turnover time* it takes to realise *a certain profit*. If capitals exhibit different proportions of fixed and circulating capital, this always has an influence on their turnover time and gives rise to differences in it; but it does not follow from this that there is any difference in the turnover time in which the same capitals realise a certain profit. Though A might always have to convert a greater portion of its product into raw material, etc., while B uses the same machinery, etc., for a longer time, both have regularly committed a portion of their capital to the extent of their production; the one in raw material, i.e., *circulating* capital, the other in buildings, etc., i.e., *fixed capital*. A is constantly transforming a portion of its capital from the product form into the money form, and from this back into the form of raw material; while B uses part of its capital as an instrument of labour for a longer period of time without these changes. If they both employ the same amount of labour, and sell during the course of the year products which although of unequal value (because only the depreciation of the fixed capital enters into B's product, while the whole of the value of the circulating capital enters into A's product) nevertheless contain the same amount of surplus-value, their rates of profit will be *the same*, since the profit is calculated on the total capital advanced, whether consumed or not, despite the differences in their composition in terms of fixed and circulating capital, and although their *total circulation time* differs. The two capitals realise equal profits in equal *circulation times*, although they require different *circula-*

tion times to turn over *completely*. (The differences in circulation time are only significant in themselves to the extent that they affect the mass of surplus-value that *the same capital* can appropriate and realise in a *given time*.) Thus if an unequal composition of circulating and fixed capital does not necessarily go together with *an inequality in circulation time*, which in turn means an unequal rate of profit, it is evident that in so far as the latter does occur, this does not arise from the unequal composition of circulating and fixed capital, but rather from the way the latter simply indicates that in certain cases there is an inequality in circulation time which affects the rate of profit. >

Finally, and this point is actually already included in the above analysis, the proportion in which the *constant capital* itself is divided into *circulating* and *fixed* components is in itself completely irrelevant to the determination of *rates of profit*.

The constant capital consists of, on the one hand, machinery and other fixed components, and on the other hand of raw materials and ancillary materials. In some branches of industry the fixed capital is very insignificant, and relatively speaking = 0, while the circulating part of the constant capital, in particular the raw material, forms almost the whole of it, as for instance in tailoring, shoemaking, etc., where the work is conducted largely in craft fashion, and the amount of labour-power employed is very significant. (As industry develops, bringing with it the introduction of machinery and other installations needed for production on a large scale, the mass of fixed capital increases everywhere.) In the banking business, the circulating capital, which consists of money, etc., is very large, while the fixed capital = 0 (relatively speaking) and also the labour-power (the variable capital) applied is relatively insignificant. (We shall see in the next section, however, that this sort of capital, and trading capital [*Handelscapital*] in general, needs to be treated *separately*.)

In the mining and fishing industries, in the extractive industries in short, the raw material = 0, although in part the ancillary materials may fulfil this role, as for example in the mining industry the consumption of coal, etc. *Fixed capital*, on the other hand, is very important. The same is true of *cattle-raising*, as well as the *transport industry*, in which raw material does not exist (except in the form of ancillary materials). But the ratio between variable and constant capital can vary very greatly here. The ratio of applied labour-power (hence of variable capital) to constant capital is, e.g., relatively low in railway transport; it is much more significant in the mining industry, in some branches of which it is extremely high, and it is still higher in the fisheries. In various branches of industry where either fixed capital is relatively non-existent, |166| or, conversely, circulating capital is relatively non-existent (because no raw material is used, for example), more labour-power may be applied in proportion to the constant capital (more in some branches, less in others) than it is in *manufacture* and *agriculture* proper, where the constant capital is composed of fixed and circulating constituents in very varied proportions, if only in a number of subdivisions.

In agriculture proper the *seed* is the *raw material*, the *manure etc*., is the ancillary material, and both together form the circulating part of the constant capital, while working cattle, the instruments of labour, buildings, irrigation and drainage channels and other productive installations form a fixed capital of very different degrees of fixedness. The fact that the seed, etc., is not sold but immediately separated from the product and incorporated afresh in the production process no more deprives it of its character of being a part of the capital advanced than does the fact that machinery is not sold as a whole, but only its depreciation, deprive it of its character as capital. The actual act of sale is absolutely unnecessary. Every part of the product is transformed into capital, if only for accountancy purposes, and it figures as such in the account books, although in reality it is directly re-used for reproduction. Incidentally, this point becomes increasingly evident with the further development of agriculture, because *trading in seed and the production of seed* becomes a special branch of agriculture and therefore also openly enters into the product as a *purchased element*. The same applies to *manure*. The more agriculture is conducted in a capitalist fashion, the more do all these elements emerge *openly* as parts of capital, having the character of *invested capital* – simply particular material forms of capital. Even in the early part of the eighteenth century, by the way, one finds that both in England and in France, in discussions of the running of large estates, and in calculations about the number of workers required, by theorists and by farmers themselves and other practical people, that *seed*, etc., is *brought into the account as an outlay*, and indeed as a *major outlay*.[4]

< *Thus the differing proportions* of circulating and fixed capital, of which *constant capital is composed*, in the different branches of industry, do not have any bearing in themselves on the rate of profit; what is decisive is the ratio between the variable capital and the constant, while the *value of the constant capital*, and thus its relative magnitude in relation to the *variable*, is absolutely independent of the fixed or circulating character of its components. We do find, however, in practice – and this may lead to incorrect conclusions – that where fixed capital is strongly developed, this is simply an expression of the fact that production is pursued on a large scale and therefore that *constant capital* is very

---

4 *Examples need to be brought in here against the views of Rodbertus*. [Marx discussed Rodbertus's views on this question in the 1861–63 Manuscript, published in English in MECW 31, 1989, pp. 279–96. Translator]

much predominant over *variable*, in other words that the living labour-power applied is small in comparison with the volume of means of production that it sets in motion.

We have shown, therefore, that in different branches of industry *different profit rates* prevail, corresponding to the different organic composition of capitals. and, within the previously indicated limitations, corresponding also to their different circulation times, and that it is only for capitals of *the same organic composition* – assuming equal circulation times – that the law holds good, as a general tendency, that *profits stand in direct proportion to the size of the capitals*, and therefore that *capitals of equal size yield equal profits in the same period of time*. The above argument is true on the same basis as our whole investigation so far: that commodities are sold at their *values*. There is no doubt, however, that in actual fact, ignoring inessential, accidental circumstances that cancel each other out, no such variation exists between different branches of industry, and it could not exist without abolishing the entire system of bourgeois production. The *theory of value* thus appears to be incompatible with *the actual movement*, incompatible with the actual phenomena of production, and it might seem that we must abandon all hope of understanding these phenomena.

It has emerged from the first chapter that *cost prices are the same* for the products of *different spheres of production* if equal portions of capital are advanced in their production, no matter how different the organic composition of these capitals might be. In the *cost price*, the distinction between variable and constant capital is abolished *for* the capitalist. For him, a commodity which he must lay out £100 to produce costs the same whether he lays out 90c + 10v or 10c + 90v. In each case it cost him £100, neither more nor less. *Cost prices* are the same for capitals of equal size in different spheres however much the *values* and *surplus-values* that are produced may differ. This *equality* in cost prices forms the basis for the competition between capital investments by means of which an average profit is produced.

|167| (2) Formation of a General Rate of Profit (Average Profit) and Transformation of Commodity Values into Prices of Production

>

First, these introductory remarks need to be made for a better understanding of what follows:

< At any one given time, the organic composition of capital depends on two factors: firstly, on the technological proportion between the labour-power and the means of production applied, and secondly, on the price of those means of

production in the different spheres of production. As we have seen, this must be considered in percentage terms. We express the organic composition of a capital that consists of four-fifths constant and one-fifth variable capital by using the formula 80c, 20v, where c represents the constant, and v the variable, part of the capital. We also assume for the sake of comparison an unchanged rate of surplus-value, any will do, but say 100%. The capital of 80c + 20v then yields a surplus-value of 20s, which makes a *rate of profit* on the total capital of 20%. The actual *value* of the product depends on how large the fixed part of the constant capital is and on how much of it goes into the product as depreciation. But since this fact is *completely immaterial* as far as the *rate of profit* is concerned, and thus also for the present investigation, we shall assume for the sake of simplicity that in all cases the constant capital enters as a whole into the annual product of these capitals. > (The reader can construct for herself or himself examples in which only the depreciation is included, which would mean that a much smaller part of the value of the constant capital went into the annual product.) < We shall also assume that capitals in different spheres of production annually realise the same amount of surplus-value in proportion to the size of their variable components; and we shall ignore for the time being the differences that may be produced here by *variation* in circulation times. (We shall return to this point later.)

Having made these assumptions, let us now take five different spheres of production, each with a different organic composition for the capital invested in them, approximately as follows:

		Rate of surplus-value	Surplus-value	Value of product	Rate of profit
I	80c, 20v	100%	20	120	20%
II	70c, 30v	100%	30	130	30%
III	60c, 40v	100%	40	140	40%
IV	85c, 15v	100%	15	115	15%
V	95c, 5v	100%	5	105	5%

We now have very different rates of profit in different spheres of production with a uniform exploitation of labour, rates which correspond to the differing organic composition of the capitals in those different spheres.

The total sum of the capitals applied in the five spheres is 500; the total sum of the surplus-value produced by them is 110, and the total value of the commodities produced by them is 610. If we treat the 500 as one single capital, so that I, II, III, IV and V simply form different portions of it (as for instance a *single* combined cotton mill will have different proportions between variable and constant capital in its various departments, e.g., in the cotton-cleaning room, the carding room, the spinning room, and the weaving room, etc.) and the total product of 610 is simply divided up under the headings I to V, the average composition of the capital of 500 would be 390c + 110v, or in percentages 78c + 22v. Treating the capitals of 100 as each simply a fifth of the total capital, its composition would be this average one of 78c + 22v; in the same way the average surplus-value of 22 would accrue to each of these capitals of 100. The average rate of profit would thus be 22%, and, finally, the price of each fifth of the total product produced by this capital of 500 would be 122 > if, as we assumed, the value of the constant capital entered as a whole in the annual product of each of the capitals I to V. The fact that this is not the case is, as already mentioned, a matter of indifference because the rate of profit is calculated on the whole of the capital advanced and not on the part of it consumed in the course of production (although this circumstance should not be forgotten when we come to determine the price of production later on), hence, other things remaining equal, how much of the constant capital sinks the whole of its value in the product and how much of it enters into the product only as depreciation is irrelevant to the rate of profit. Assuming, however, that the constant capital in every case enters in its entirety into the product, the product of each 100, hence of each fifth of the total capital advanced, would have to be sold at 122.

|168| < Yet in order not to arrive at totally incorrect conclusions, we must not assume that all cost prices are = 100.

With 80c + 20v, and a rate of surplus-value (s′) of 100%, the total *value* of the commodities produced by capital I would be 80c + 20v + 20s = 120, assuming the entire constant capital enters into the annual product. This may well be the case in some spheres of production, with certain capital investments, but hardly where the ratio of constant capital to variable capital = 4:1. In considering the values of the commodities produced by each different capital of 100, therefore, we must take into account the fact that they differ according to the different composition of the constant capital in terms of its fixed and circulating components, and that the fixed components of different capitals may themselves become worn out either faster or more slowly > and thus need to be replaced more quickly or more slowly, < thus adding unequal quantities of value to the product in the same period. This is immaterial, however, as far as the profit rate is concerned. Whether in the total capital 80c + 20v the 80c gives up the whole of its value to the annual product, or 50, or 5, and whether the annual product is accordingly 80 + 20 + 20s = 120 or 50 + 20 + 20 = 90 or 5 + 20 + 20 = 45, in all these cases the excess of the value of the product over its cost price, > i.e., over the part of its value which replaces no more than the worn out constant capital and the variable capital advanced < is 20, and in all these cases the 20 has to be calculated on a capital of 100 > since the rate of profit = $^{\text{surplus-value}}/_{\text{total capital advanced}}$, not $^{\text{surplus-value}}/_{\text{cost price}}$ or $^{\text{surplus-value}}/_{\text{capital consumed}}$. The proper place for this discussion is part 1 of this chapter. However, the point needs to be emphasised here, partly to make it clear why in our example different capitals produce commodities of different values irrespective of differences in the amount of surplus-value, partly to make it possible to grasp that the precise extent to which in the following examples the constant capital enters, or does not enter, into the product, is completely immaterial for the matter under consideration here. Thus: <

		Rate of surplus-value	Surplus-value	Rate of profit	Value of commodities	Cost price
I	80c, 20v	100%	20	20%	90	70 (40 raw material, 10 depreciation)
II	70c, 30v	100%	30	30%	111	81
III	60c, 40v	100%	40	40%	131	91
IV	85c, 15v	100%	15	15%	70	55
V	95c, 5v	100%	5	5%	20	15

If we treat capitals I to V as a single total capital, we see that their composition = 390c and 110v, which is 78c and 22v in percentage terms; and the average surplus-value per 100 = 22. If this surplus-value were evenly distributed among capitals I to V, we should arrive at the following commodity prices:

		s′	Surplus-value	Value of commodities	Price of commodities	Rate of profit	Divergence betw. price and value
I	80c, 20v	100%	20	90	92	22%	+2 over value
II	70c, 30v	100%	30	111	103	22%	–8 under value
III	60c, 40v	100%	40	131	113	22%	–18 under value
IV	85c, 15v	100%	15	70	77	22%	+7 over value
V	95c, 5v	100%	5	20	37	22%	+17 over value

Taken together, the commodities are sold at 2 + 7 + 17 = 26 over their value and –18 –8 = –26 under their value, so that the divergences of price from value indicated above cancel each other out when the surplus-value is distributed evenly, i.e., through adding *the average profit of 22 on 100* to the *respective cost prices* of the commodities I to V. To the same extent that one section of commodities is sold above its value, another is sold below it. And it is only because they are sold at these prices that the rates of profit for capitals I to V are equal at 22 percent, irrespective of their differing organic compositions. The prices that arise when the average of the different rates of profit is drawn from the different spheres of production, and this *average profit* is added to the *cost prices* of these different spheres of production, are *prices of production*. Their prerequisite is the existence of a *general rate of profit*, and this presupposes in turn that the profit rates in each particular sphere of production |169| are average profit rates. These particular rates are s/C in each sphere of production and can only be developed from the *value* of the commodity. In the absence of such a development the general rate of profit (and hence also the production price of the commodity) remains a meaningless and irrational conception. Thus the *production price* of a commodity equals its cost price + the percentage price added to it in accordance with the general rate of profit, that is to say it is its cost price + the average profit.

> In actuality however < *very different profit rates* prevail in the different branches of production as a result of differences in the organic composition of the capitals invested in them, and as a result, therefore, of the circumstance that according to the different percentage share of the variable part of the capital in a total capital of a given size very different amounts of labour are set in motion by capitals of equal size, and that therefore also very different amounts of surplus labour are appropriated by these capitals, or very different amounts of surplus-value are produced by them. These different rates of profit > in the different spheres of social production < are balanced out by *competition* to give a *general rate of profit* which is the *average* of all the different rates. The profit that falls to a capital of a given size according to this general rate of profit, whatever its organic composition, we call the *average profit*. That price of a commodity which is equal to its *cost price plus the average profit* on the *capital applied* in its production (not simply the capital consumed in its production) is its *price of production*. Thus although the capitalists in the different spheres of production get back the portions of capital (the capital *values*) consumed in the production of their respective commodities (by selling their commodities, in other words by transforming them back into money), they do not recover > (one might say *cash in* instead of recover) < the surplus-value and hence the profit that is produced in their own sphere in a given period,

but only the amount of surplus-value and hence of profit that falls to the share of each *aliquot* part of the total capital, when evenly distributed, from the *total surplus-value or total profit* which is produced within a given period by the *total social capital* in all spheres of production taken together. For each 100 units, every capital advanced, whatever may be its composition, draws in the profit that accrues to 100 units as an *n*th part of the total capital: a profit of *n*. Here, as far as profit is concerned, the various different capitalists are in the position of mere shareholders in a joint-stock company, in which the dividends are evenly distributed for each 100 units, and hence are distinguished, as far as the individual capitalists are concerned, *only according to the relative size* of the capital that each of them has put *into the common enterprise*, according to his relative participation in the common enterprise, according to the *number of shares he holds*. While the proportion of *the commodity price* that replaces the parts of the capital that are consumed in the production of the commodities, and with which these capital values must be bought back again – while this portion, the *cost price*, is completely governed by the *outlay* within each respective sphere of production, the other component of the commodity price, *the profit that is added* to the cost price, is governed not by the mass of profit that is *produced* by this specific capital in its specific sphere of production, but by the mass of profit that falls on average to *each capital invested*, as an aliquot *part* of the total social capital invested in *production as a whole*, during a given period of time.[5] If a capitalist sells his commodities at their *price of production*, he recovers money according to the *value* of the capital that he consumed in their production and adds a profit to this in proportion to the capital he *advanced* as a mere aliquot part of the total capital. His *cost prices* are specific. But the *profit added* to this cost price is independent of his particular sphere of production, it is a simple average per 100 units of capital advanced. > The cost price depends on the specific costs of a particular line of business; but the profit on top of this cost price depends on the total profit realised by the total social capital invested in every sphere of social production.

|170| Thus the way to handle the five examples given in our previous illustration is as follows: < let us suppose that the five different capital investments belong to a single person. The amount of capital (variable and constant) that is *consumed* in the production of the commodities in each investment I – V would be given, and this share in the value of commodities I – V would at first glance form a portion of their price, since this is the price required to replace the por-

5 Cherbuliez [1841, pp. 70–2].

tion of the capital advanced that is necessary for reproduction but has been consumed. These *cost prices* would be different for each kind of commodity I – V and would thus be fixed differently by the proprietor. As far as the different masses of surplus-value or profit produced in I – V were concerned, however, the capitalist might very well count them all as profit on the total capital of 100 that he advanced, so that a definite aliquot part would fall to each capital of 100. The cost prices would therefore be different for each of the commodities produced in the individual investments I – V; but the *share* of the commodity prices that arose from the profit added per 100 units of capital would be the same. The total price of the commodities I – V would thus be equal to their *total value*, i.e., *the sum of the cost prices I – V + the sum of the surplus-value or the profit produced in the five spheres of production*; in point of fact, therefore, it would be the *monetary expression for the total quantity of labour, dead + added, contained in commodities I – V*. And in the same way, *the sum of the prices of production for the commodities produced* in the society itself – taking the totality of all branches of production – *is equal to the sum of their values.* >

(It might appear that a difficulty arises here: if one takes capitals I – V, both the constant and the variable part of these capitals may well be *bought*, they may enter into these capitals from other spheres of production, and so it could be said that the production price of one sphere < goes into the cost price of another. But if the *sum of the cost prices* of all commodities in a country is placed on one side and the *sum of the profits or the surplus-values* on the other, we can see that the calculation comes out right. Take for example a commodity we shall call A. Its cost price may contain the profits of B, C, D, E, just as the profits of A may in turn go into E, F, G, etc.[6] If we make this calculation, the profit of A will be absent from its own *cost price*, and the profits of B, C, D, E will be absent from their *cost prices* > as also will those of *E, F, G*, etc. < Considering the calculation as a whole, to the same extent that the profits of one sphere of production go into the cost price of another, to that extent these *profits have already been taken into account* for the *overall price* of the commodities, and they cannot appear on the profit side a second time. They appear on this side only because the price of the commodity in question does not enter into the *cost price* of another commodity.

6 > None of them includes his own profit in his cost price. And so if there are n spheres of production, the cost price of all of them taken together is k [the symbol for the cost price] – np, p being the sum of profits made by all of them together. <

If p goes into the cost price of a commodity for the profits, and apart from this a further p_1 is to be found on the profit side, the total profit P = p + p_1. The total cost price of the commodity, discounting all portions of the price that count towards profit, is then the cost price less p. If this cost price p = k, evidently k + P (or p + p_1) = C, i.e., the total value of the commodity. We saw earlier in dealing with surplus-value that the product of any capital can be treated as if one part simply replaces constant capital, while the other only represents surplus-value. If this calculation is made for the whole society, for the total social product, we have to make certain rectifications, since, considering the whole society, the profit contained in the price of flax, for instance, cannot figure twice, as both part of the price of the linen and simultaneously as the profit of the flax spinners.

|171| There is no distinction between profit and surplus-value when the surplus-value of A, for instance, goes into the constant capital of B. As far as the *value of the commodities* is concerned, it is completely immaterial whether the labour contained in them is paid or unpaid. This shows only that B pays the surplus-value of A. In the total account, A's surplus-value cannot figure twice.

The distinction is rather this: that apart from the fact that the price of the product of capital B, for example, diverges from its *value*, because the *surplus-value* realised in B is greater or less than the *profit* added to the prices of B's commodities, *the same* situation also holds for the commodities that form the *constant* part of B and its *variable* part. As far as the constant portion of capital is concerned, it is itself equal to the cost price + the surplus-value, hence it is now equal to cost price + profit and this profit can again be greater or less than the surplus-value whose place it has taken. As for the variable capital, the average daily wage is admittedly always equal to the number of hours the worker must work in order to produce his necessary means of subsistence; but the number of hours is itself distorted by the fact that the production prices of the primary necessities diverge from their values. However this is always reducible to the situation that whenever too much surplus-value goes into one commodity, too little goes into another, and the divergences from *value* that obtain in the cost prices of the commodities therefore cancel each other out. With the whole of > this bourgeois shit < the general law prevails as the dominant tendency > only in a very complicated, and very rough way.

< Since the general rate of profit is formed by the average of the various *different rates of profit* on each 100 units of capital advanced over a definite period of time, say a year, the distinctions produced between the different capitals by the *differences in circulation time* are also obliterated. But these distinctions play a decisive role for the *various different rates of profit* in the

various spheres of production, by means of whose average the general rate of profit is formed.

In our previous illustration of the *formation of the general rate of profit*, every capital in every sphere of production was taken as 100, and we did this in order to make clear the percentage differences in the rates of profit and hence also the differences between the values of the commodities that are produced by capitals of equal size. It should be understood, however, that the actual masses of surplus-value that are produced in each *particular sphere of production* depend on the *magnitude* of the capitals applied, since the composition of the capital is given in each of these given spheres of production. Yet the *particular rate of profit* of a *particular sphere of production* is not affected by whether a capital of C, m × C or xm × C is applied, > where C represents a total capital of 100, m represents a specific coefficient of C, and x a coefficient of undetermined magnitude. If the profit rate of C = p′, it is p′ for m × C and for xm × C. For C (= a capital of 100) p = p′, i.e., the rate of profit = the profit. (For example, if 10 is the profit on 100, this = a 10% *rate of profit*.) Thus p is the profit on C, mp is the profit on mC, and mxp is the profit on mxC, but

$$\frac{m\,p}{m\,C} = \frac{x\,m\,p}{x\,m\,C} = \frac{p}{C} \text{ and since } \frac{p}{C} = p', \frac{m\,p}{m\,C} \text{ and } \frac{m\,p\,x}{m\,x\,C} \text{ similarly} = p'.$$

< However, since the rates of profit in the *various spheres of production* differ, in that very different masses of surplus-value and therefore profit are produced according to the proportion that variable capital forms in the total, it is evident that the *average profit* per 100 units of social capital, and hence the average or *general rate of profit*, will vary greatly according to the *respective magnitudes of the capitals invested in the various spheres*. For example, if the rate of surplus-value for all capitals, A, B, C and E, is 100%, and the variable capital per 100 in capital A is 25, in B 40, in C 15 and in E 10, we should have the following result: >

(I)	A's	surplus-value or profit per 100 total capital	= 25
	B's	ditto	= 40
	C's	ditto	= 15
	E's	ditto	= 10
			90,

an average rate of profit, therefore, of 90/4 = 22½%. If 300 is invested in A, 100 in B, 200 in C and 100 in E, the general rate of profit will be:

(II)	A	300	75
	B	100	40
	C	200	30
	E	100	10
		700	155

This would give $22\frac{1}{7}$%. If, finally, the picture were as follows:

(III)	A	200	50
	B	300	120
	C	1,000	150
	E	4,000	400
		5,500	720

This would give $13\frac{1}{11}$%.

> Firstly, therefore, where the capitals invested in A to E are assumed to be of equal magnitude, namely 100 each, the general rate of profit in (I) = $22\frac{1}{2}$%, in (II) = $22\frac{1}{7}$% and in (III) it is only $13\frac{1}{11}$%. < The masses of surplus-value produced in (I), (II) and (III) vary according to the different sizes of the total capitals respectively invested in A, B, C, and E. What is important here, therefore, is not just the difference *in rates of profit in the various spheres of production*, from which an average is drawn, |172| but the *relative weight* which these different rates of profit assume in the formation of the general rate of profit. But this depends in turn on the *comparative magnitude* of the capital invested in each particular sphere of production, or on what *aliquot* part the capital invested in each particular sphere forms of the total social capital. > It is clear, for example, that if, out of a total social capital of 10,000, yielding a rate of surplus-value of 100%, half belongs to a sphere where the variable capital is $\frac{1}{10}$, and the other half to a sphere where it is $\frac{1}{5}$, the total profit of one on 5,000 would be 500 and of the other on 5,000 would be 1,000. Taken together this would be 1,500 = 15%. If, on the other hand, the variable capital made up $\frac{1}{2}$ of the one half and $\frac{1}{5}$ of the other half, there would be a profit of 2,500 on one sum of 5,000 and 1,000 on the other. Together that is 3,500, giving a rate of profit of 35%. < It must naturally make a great deal of difference whether it is a greater or a lesser part of the total capital that yields a higher or a lower profit rate. And this depends in turn upon whether more capital is invested in the sphere in which the variable capital is larger or the sphere in which it is smaller, in relation to the total capital. It is the same as in the case of the average profit per 100 that a money-lender

makes if he lends out different capitals at different rates of interest, e.g., 6, 5, 4, or 3 %. The average rate is completely dependent on how much of his aggregate capital he respectively puts out at [these] different rates.

The general rate of profit is therefore determined by two factors:

(1) the organic composition of the different capitals in the various spheres of production, hence by the *different rates of profit*.

(2) the *distribution of the total social capital* between these different spheres, hence by the relative magnitude (comparing one sphere with another) of the capitals invested in each particular sphere, and therefore at a particular rate of profit, i.e., the relative amount of the total social capital

swallowed up by each particular sphere of production, > or the relative magnitude of the (specific) area taken up by each one.

< In books one and two [of *Capital*] we were only concerned with the *values* of commodities. Now a part of this value has split away as the *cost price*, on the one hand, while on the other, the *production price* of the commodity has also developed, as a transformed form of value.[7] >

(If we know, for example, that the capital advanced = 500, that the average profit over a given period = 10 %, that ⅕ of the 500 consists of *fixed capital*, of which 10, say, goes into the commodity as wear-and-tear, and that 400 = the circulating part of the constant capital + the variable part of the capital, we know that the production price of the commodity = 10 (Wear-and-tear) + 400 (consumed capital) + 50 (profit) = 460. This price of 460 yields a profit of 50, or 10 %, on the total capital of 500 which was advanced during the period in question.) As we have seen, the *cost price* is always lower than the *value* of the commodity. The *production price* can be *lower than, higher than, or equal to* the value of the commodity. The value of the commodity is equal to the value of the capital consumed to produce it plus the surplus-value. If we take the cost price as equal to the value of the capital advanced in the production of the commodity, as we did in our original analysis of cost price (*in chapter one*), we arrive at the following equivalences:

Value = Cost Price + surplus-value	$V = K + s$
or profit as identical with surplus-value	or $= K + p$
cost price = value – surplus-value	or $K = V - s$
price of production = cost price + profit	$P = K + p'$
calculated according to the general rate of profit = p′.	

7 [The next four paragraphs, which are important, were not included in Engels's Volume III; see pp. 18–19 of the Introduction for a discussion of these paragraphs. Editor]

Since $K = V - s$ and $V = K + s$, the value of the commodity is always > than the cost price.

P will be >, <, or = V according to whether the surplus-value or profit of each particular sphere of production is greater than, less than, or equal to the average profit determined by the general rate of profit.[8]

Since $V = K + s$ or p, and $P = K + p'$, $V = P$ when $s = p'$, $> P$ when $p' < s$, and $< P$ when $p' > s$.

< If we take it that the *composition of the average social capital* is $80_c + 20_v$ and the annual rate of surplus-value $s' = 100$ percent, the average annual profit for a capital of 100 is 20 and the average annual rate of profit is 20 percent. For any cost price, k, of the commodities annually produced by a capital of 100, their price of production will be $k + 20$. In those spheres of production where the organic composition of capital is $(80 - x)_c + (20 + x)_v$, the surplus-value actually created within this sphere (or the profit produced within it) $= 20 + x$, i.e., more than 20, and the value produced, $k + 20 + x$, is more than $k + 20$, or more than its price of production. In those spheres where the organic composition of capital is $(80 + x)_c + (20 - x)_v$, the surplus-value or profit created is $20 - x$, i.e., less than 20, and therefore the *value* is $k + 20 - x$, i.e., less than the price of production, which is $k + 20$. Leaving aside any eventual differences in circulation time, the production prices of commodities would be equal to their values only in cases where the composition of capital was by chance precisely $80_c + 20_v$.

The specific degree of development of the social productivity of labour differs from one particular sphere of production to another, being higher or lower according to *the quantity of means of production set in motion* by a *certain quantity of labour*, thus by a *specific number of workers*, once the working day is given. Hence its degree of development depends on *how small a quantity of living labour is required* for a certain quantity of means of production. We shall therefore call capitals > whose composition differs from the average composition of the social capital (differing therefore for example from the composition $80_c + 20_v$ if this is the composition of the average capital in a given society) < in that they contain a greater percentage of constant capital than the social average, and thus a lesser percentage of variable capital, capitals of *higher*

8 [Marx actually has the inequalities backwards in this sentence. With K the same for both value and price of production, price of production is > or < value according to whether the surplus-value in each sphere of production is < or > the average profit determined by the general rate of profit. Marx gets it right in the next sentence. Editor]

composition than the social average. Conversely, we shall call capitals marked by a relatively smaller share of constant capital, and a relatively greater share of variable, capitals of *lower* composition, capitals whose composition lies *below* the social average. Capitals of *average* composition, finally, are capitals whose composition is the same as that of the average social capital. If m and n are constant magnitudes and m + n = 100, and x is any variable magnitude one cares to choose, and the *composition of the average social capital* = $C^m + V^n$, capitals of the form $C^{m+x} + V^{n-x}$ are of *higher* organic composition, whereas capitals of the form $C^{m-x} + V^{n+x}$ are of *lower* organic composition. The value of the commodities produced by the former would be less than their production price, and for the latter the production price of the commodities would be less than their value. Only for those capitals whose composition coincided by chance with the social average (= $C^m + V^n$) would the value of the commodities produced by them be equal to the price of production. (In applying this calculation to specific cases, of course, we must bear in mind that the ratio between c and v may diverge from the general average not just as a result of a difference in technical composition, but also simply because of a *difference in the value* of the elements of constant capital.)

The development given above also involves a modification in respect to the determination of the *cost price* of commodities.[9] It was originally assumed that the *cost price* of a commodity equalled the *value* of the commodities *consumed* in its production. But since the *production price* of a commodity enters as a cost price into forming the price of another commodity, and since the production price of a commodity can diverge from its value, the cost price of a commodity can also stand *above or below the portion of its total value* which is formed by the value of the means of production going into it. It is necessary to bear in mind this |174| modified significance of the cost price, and therefore to recall that if the *cost price* of a commodity is equated with the *value* of the means of production consumed to produce it, it is always possible to make an *error*. Our present investigation does not require us to go into further detail at this point. It still remains correct that the cost price of commodities is always smaller than their value. For even if a commodity's *cost price* may diverge from the *value* of the means of production consumed in it, this past *error* is a matter of indifference to the capitalist. The cost price of the commodity is a given prerequisite, independent of his production, while the result of that production is a commodity that contains *surplus-value*, and therefore an *excess value* over and above its cost price. Otherwise – practically speaking – the proposition that

9 [The last part of this key sentence from 'in respect to ...' was in English. Translator]

the *cost price* of the commodity is less than its *value* has now been transformed into the proposition that its *cost price* is less than its *price of production*. For the total social capital, where *price of production = value*, this assertion is identical with the previous one. Even though it has a different meaning for the particular spheres of production, the basic fact remains that, taking the social capital as a whole, the *cost price* of the *commodities* that this produces is less than their *value*, or than the *price of production which is identical with this value*. The *cost price* of a commodity simply depends on the quantity of *paid* labour it contains, while its *value* depends on the total quantity of labour it contains, whether paid or unpaid; the *price of production* depends on the sum of paid labour and a certain quantity of unpaid labour which is determined independently of its own particular sphere of production.

The *prices of production* of the commodities in every *particular* sphere of production may undergo *changes of magnitude*, either (1) because while the *value of the commodities remains the same* (so that *the same quantity of dead and living labour* goes into their production afterwards as before) there has been a change in the general rate of profit independently of the particular sphere in question, or (2) because while the general rate of profit has remained the same there has been a *change in value* either in the particular sphere of production itself as a result of technological change, or as a result of a change in the value of the commodities that go into its constant capital as formative elements, or, finally, (3) by the common action of these two circumstances.

For all the great changes that constantly occur in the actual rates of profit in particular spheres of production (as will appear later) a genuine change in the *general rate of profit*, one not simply brought about by exceptional economic events, is the final outcome of a whole series of protracted oscillations, which require a good deal of time before they are consolidated and balanced out to produce a change in the general rate. In all periods shorter than this, therefore, and even leaving aside fluctuations in *market prices*, a change in the *prices of production* is always to be explained *prima facie* by an *actual change* in commodity values, i.e., by a change in the total sum of labour-time needed to produce the commodities. (We are not at all referring here to mere changes in the monetary expression of the same values.)[10]

---

10 See Corbet > on how the up and down movement of particular rates of profit – which is however during a certain greater or lesser number of years equalised to become the general rate of profit (the *average* for instance of the profits in one trade during ten years being equal to the average profit in all the other trades) – is one of the forces behind the development of the division of labour in modern society. [Corbet 1841, p. 174.] <

It is clear on the other hand that, taking the total capital as a whole, the *sum of the values* of the commodities produced by it (or their *price*, expressed in *money*) = the value of the constant capital + the value of the variable capital + surplus-value. Assuming a *constant* level of exploitation of labour, the profit rate can only change here, with *the mass of surplus-value remaining the same*, either if the value of the constant capital changes, |175| or if the value of the variable capital changes, or if both change. All these result in a change in C, thereby changing s/C, the general rate of profit. In each case, therefore, a change in the general rate of profit assumes *a change in the value of the commodities* which enter as formative elements into the constant capital, the variable capital, or both simultaneously.

Or the *degree of exploitation of labour would have to change*, with the *value of the commodities remaining the same*, which would then result in a change in the general rate of profit.

Or again, the degree of exploitation of labour remaining the same, the *sum of labour applied* relative to the constant capital would have to change as a result of technological changes in the labour process. But technological changes of this kind would always have to show themselves in, and therefore be accompanied by, a *change in the value of the commodities* whose production would now require either more or less labour than previously.

We saw in the first chapter how surplus-value and profit are identical, seen from the point of view of their *mass*. But the *rate of profit* is from the very beginning different from the *rate of surplus-value*, though at first this appears simply as a different *way of calculating* the same thing. Given however that the rate of profit can rise or fall, with the rate of surplus-value remaining the same, and that all that interests the capitalist in practice is *the rate of profit*, this circumstance also from the very beginning completely obscures and mystifies the real origin of surplus-value. *The difference in magnitude*, however, was only between the *rate of surplus-value* and the *rate of profit*, not between the *magnitude of surplus-value* and the *magnitude of profit*. Because the rate of profit measures surplus-value against the *total capital* and the latter is its *standard*, surplus-value itself appears in this way as having arisen from the *total capital* and *uniformly* from all parts of it, so that the essential and organic distinction between constant and variable capital is obliterated in the concept of *profit*. In actual fact, therefore, *surplus-value* denies its own origin in this, its transformed form, which is *profit*; it loses its character and becomes *unrecognisable*. For all that, the distinction between *profit* and *surplus-value* relates to a *qualitative* change, a *change of form*, while any actual *difference in magnitude* at this initial stage of the transformation exists simply between the *rate of profit* and the *rate of surplus-value*, and not yet between *profit* and *surplus-value* as such.

It is quite a different matter as soon as a *general rate of profit* is established, and with this an *average profit* corresponding to capital of a given magnitude invested in the various spheres of production.

It is now purely accidental if the surplus-value actually produced in a particular sphere of production, and therefore the profit, coincides with the profit contained in the commodity's sale price. Profit and surplus-value themselves, and not just their rates, are as a *rule* generally *different in magnitude*. At a given level of exploitation of labour, the mass of surplus-value that is created in a particular sphere of production is now more important for the overall average profit of the social capital, and thus for the capitalist class in general, than it is directly for the capitalist within each particular branch of production. It is important for him only in so far as the quantity of surplus-value created in his own branch intervenes as a co-determinant in regulating the average profit, a process which takes place invisibly behind his back. He does not see it, he does not understand it, and in fact it does not interest him. The actual *difference in magnitude* between profit and surplus-value in the particular spheres of production (and not merely between the rate of profit and the rate of surplus-value) now completely hides the true nature and origin of profit, not only for the capitalist, who has here a particular interest in deceiving himself, but also for the worker. With the transformation of values into prices of production, the basis for determining value is now removed from sight. The upshot is this: in the case of a simple transformation from surplus-value into profit, the portion of commodity value that forms this profit confronts the other portion of value as the commodity's *cost price*, and the capitalist already loses grip of the concept of value, because he does not have to deal with the *total labour* that the production of the commodity cost, but only the part of the total labour that he has *paid for* in the form of *means of production*, living or dead, so that profit appears to him as something |176| standing outside the immanent value of the commodity. But what happens now is that this idea is completely confirmed, reinforced and ossified in that the *profit added* to the cost price is not actually determined, if the *particular* spheres of production are taken separately, by the limits set by their own value formation, but on the contrary established entirely from outside.

This inner connection is revealed here for the first time, as we shall see in the later historical chapters. All economics up till now has either *violently* made abstraction from the distinctions [we have made] so that it could retain the determination of value as its basis, or else it has abandoned, along with this determination of value, any kind of solid foundation for a scientific understanding, so as to be able to retain those distinctions which obtrude themselves on the phenomenal level. This confusion on the part of the theorists shows better than anything else how the practical capitalist, imprisoned in the competitive struggle and in no way penetrating the phenomena that it exhibits, cannot but be completely incapable of recognising, behind the semblance [*Schein*], the inner essence [*Wesen*] and the inner form of this process.

All the laws governing the rise and fall of the rate of profit, developed in Chapter One > may now be viewed from a double aspect < and have in fact the following double significance:

(1) On the one hand they are *laws about the general rate of profit*. Given the many different causes that lead the profit rate to rise or fall, as indicated in Chapter One, it might be believed that the general rate of profit would have to change every day, so to speak. But as the movement of one sphere of production is cancelled out by the movement of another, the forces mutually counteract and paralyse each other. *The direction towards which these changes tend* is a point we shall develop later on. But this process is slow: the suddenness, many-sidedness, and uninterruptedness of the changes in particular spheres of production leads to a situation in which they partly cancel each other out successively (today up, tomorrow down), they remain local (by which I mean that they remain confined to the particular sphere of production in question) and the various local changes reciprocally neutralise each other. Changes take place within each particular sphere of production, departures from the general rate of profit, which on the one hand balance each other out over a certain period of time and hence do *not* react back on the general rate, while on the other hand they do not react back on it because they are cancelled out by other simultaneous local fluctuations. Since the general rate of profit is determined not only by the average rate of profit in each sphere, but also by the distribution of the total capital between the various particular spheres, and since this distribution is constantly changing, we have again a constant source of change in the general rate of profit – but a source of change that also becomes paralysed, in part, given the uninterrupted and all-round character of this movement.

(2) Within each sphere there is room for shorter or longer periods in which the profit rate in that sphere rises, falls and rises again, etc., before this movement is consolidated for a sufficient time to affect the general rate of profit > to alter its composition < and therefore to have more than local effects, > i.e., effects which are restricted to a particular sphere of production. < Within these spatial and temporal limits, therefore, the laws governing the movement of the rate of profit developed in Chapter One of this book similarly continue to apply.

The theoretical opinion regarding the first transformation of surplus-value into profit to the effect that each portion of capital yields profit in a uniform way[11] now becomes a *practical state of affairs*. However the capital may be composed, whether it sets in motion only ¼ dead labour and ¾ living labour, or ¾ dead labour and ¼ living labour, whether in one case three times as much surplus labour is absorbed or surplus-value produced as in the other – with the same level of exploitation of labour and ignoring individual differences – which we have already discounted, because > the differences in organic composition considered here < are those of spheres of production as a whole – in both cases it yields the same profit. The individual capitalist (or the whole gang of capitalists in a particular sphere of production) whose vision is a restricted one, |177| is right to believe that his profit does not derive just from the labour employed *by him* or employed *in his own branch*. This is quite correct as far as his average profit goes. How much this profit is mediated by the overall exploitation of labour by capital as a whole, i.e., by all his capitalist brothers, is a complete puzzle (a mystery) to him, the more so in that even the bourgeois theorists, the political economists, have not yet solved it. Saving of labour – not only the labour necessary to produce a specific product, but also the number of workers employed – and a greater use of dead labour, appears as a quite correct economic operation and seems on the face of it not to affect the general rate of profit and the average profit in any manner. So how could living labour be the exclusive source of profit, since a reduction in > – a doing away with – < living labour does not undermine profit, in fact under certain circumstances it appears to be the immediate source of an increase in profit, at least for the individual capitalist?

If the *portion of the cost price* which represents constant capital rises or falls, this is the portion that comes out of the sphere of circulation and goes into the *process of production* of the commodity either enlarged or reduced from the outset. But say that the workers employed produce more or less in the same period of time, hence the quantity of labour required in a given sphere of production for the production of a certain amount of commodities changes, the part of the price that represents the value of the variable capital may remain *the same* (given that the number of workers remains the same) and thus go into the cost price of the total product with the same magnitude. But each of the *individual commodities* whose sum comprises the total product now contains more or less labour (paid and therefore also unpaid), i.e., also more or less of the outlay for this labour, a greater or smaller portion of the wage. The total paid by the capitalist in wages remains the same, but this is different when

11 Malthus. ['The capitalist generally expects an equal profit upon all the parts of capital which he advances' (Malthus 1836, p. 268).]

calculated on each item of the individual commodity. There is thus a change in this part of the commodity's cost price. It does not matter whether the cost price of the individual commodity now rises or falls as a result of such changes > in its cost price, produced by *changes* < *in value*, either its own or the value of its commodity elements (or alternatively the cost price of the sum of commodities produced by a capital of a given size). If the average profit is 10 percent, for example, it remains 10 percent, even though this 10 percent, viewed as a profit on the individual commodity, may represent a very different magnitude as a result of the *change in the cost price* of the individual commodity brought about by the *change in value* we have just mentioned.[12]

As far as the *variable capital* is concerned – and this is the most important thing, since it is the source of surplus-value and since everything that conceals its position in the capitalist's enrichment mystifies the entire system – the situation is cruder, or at least this is the way it appears to the capitalist. A variable capital of £100, say, represents 100 workers. If these 100 workers, with a given working day, produce a product of n commodities, 1 commodity (ignoring the portion of the cost price that the constant capital adds) = £$^{100}/_{n}$, since £100 = $n \times C$ (the commodity). Let us now assume a change in the productivity of labour; if this doubles, the same number of workers produces twice as many commodities in the same time as they formerly took to produce the original number. In this case (so far as the cost price consists of wages) one commodity now costs £$^{100}/_{2n}$, since £100 = $2n \times C$. If productivity were reduced by a half, so that the same quantity of labour which previously produced nC now produces only $^{n}/_{2}$ C, 1C would now be equal to £$^{200}/_{n}$, since £100 = $^{n \times C}/_{2}$. The changes in the labour-time required for the production of the commodities, and therefore in their value, now *appear* – with regard to the cost price, and therefore also to the price of production – as a *different distribution* of the same *wages* over more or fewer commodities, according to whether more or fewer commodities are produced in the same labour-time for the same wages. What the capitalist sees, and therefore the political economist as well, is that the part of the *paid* labour that falls to each item of the commodity changes with each individual article; what he does *not* see is that this is also the case with the *unpaid* labour contained in each article, and the less so, as the average profit is in fact only accidentally limited by the unpaid labour absorbed in his own sphere. The fact that the value of commodities is *determined* by the labour they contain now continues to percolate through only in this crude and naive form.

12 Corbet ['Profit is always the same, whatever be price; keeping its place like an incumbent body on the swelling or sinking tide' (Corbet 1841, p. 20)].

|178| (3) The Equalisation of the General Rate of Profit through Competition. Market Prices and Market Values. Surplus Profit.

In some of the spheres of production the capital employed has a *mean* or *average composition*; i.e., a composition exactly or approximately the same as *the composition of the average social capital.*

In these spheres, the *production prices* of the commodities produced coincide with their *values* (either exactly or with very slight divergences). > Here, therefore, the *monetary expression* of value coincides with the *total amount of money*. It is the same as the price of production. < If there were no other way of arriving at the mathematical limit, it could be done as follows. *Competition* distributes the social capital between the various spheres of production in such a way that the *prices of production* in each of those spheres > (disregarding the question of how large a portion of the fixed capital goes into these prices for wear-and-tear) < are equal to the prices in the spheres of mean composition, i.e., k + p, > where k is the cost price, but a *variable* magnitude, and p is a constant magnitude, namely is equivalent to the magnitude of the < percentage profit in that sphere (which in the sphere of mean composition coincides with the surplus-value). The rate of profit is thus the same in all spheres of production, because it is adjusted to that in those branches of production where the average composition of capital prevails. The sum of the profits for all the different spheres of production would then be equal to the sum of surplus-values, and the sum of the prices of production for the total social product would then be equal to the sum of its values. It is evident, however, that the equalisation between spheres of production of different composition > (whether these differences are based simply on differences in the ratio between constant and variable capital, or also arise from variations in circulation time) < must always seek to adjust these to the spheres of mean composition, whether these correspond exactly to the social average or just approximately. Between those spheres that approximate more or less to the social average there is again a tendency to equalisation, which seeks a possibly ideal mean position, i.e., a mean position which does not exist in reality. In other words, it tends to shape itself around this ideal as a norm. In this way there prevails, and necessarily so, a tendency to make production prices into mere transformed forms of value, or to transform profits into mere portions of surplus-value that are distributed, not in proportion to the surplus-value that is created in each particular sphere of production, but rather in proportion to the amount of capital applied in each of these spheres, so that equal amounts of capital, no matter how they are composed, receive equal shares (aliquot parts) of the totality of surplus-value produced by the total social capital. >

What we have said so far amounts to this: < for capitals of mean or approximately mean composition, the price of production coincides exactly or approximately with the value, and the profit coincides with the surplus-value they produce. All other capitals, however they might be composed, seek to adjust themselves to the capitals of mean composition. But since the capitals of mean composition are equal or approximately equal to the average social capital, it follows that all capitals, whatever the surplus-value they themselves produce (with the level of exploitation of labour remaining constant), seek to realise, in the prices of their commodities, not this surplus-value but the *average profit*, hence they seek to transform these prices into *prices of production*.

On the other hand, it can be said that wherever an *average profit* is established, hence a *general rate of profit*, and however this result might have been brought about, this average profit can be nothing other than the profit on the average social capital, the total sum of profit being equal to the total sum of surplus-value. It can also be said that the prices produced by adding this average profit to the cost prices can be nothing other than the values which have been transformed into *prices of production*. It would not change anything if for whatever reason capitals in certain spheres of production were not subjected to the process of equalisation. The average profit would then be calculated on the portion of the social capital that was involved in the equalisation process. It is clear enough that the average profit can be nothing other than the totality of the surplus-value distributed between the masses of capital in each sphere of production in proportion to their size. It is the sum total of the realised *unpaid* labour, and this totality is represented similarly in the *totality of commodities and money* which accrues to the capitalist class.

|179| The really difficult question here is this: how does this equalisation of profits or this establishment of a general rate of profit take place, since it is evidently a result and cannot be a point of departure?

It is clear first of all that an assessment of commodity values, e.g., in money, can only be a result of exchanging them, and that, if we presuppose such an assessment, we have to view it as a result of *real exchanges of one commodity value against another*. But how is this exchange of commodities at their actual values supposed to have come about?

Let us assume to start with that all commodities in the various spheres of production were to be sold at their actual values. What would happen then? According to our above arguments, *very different rates of profit* would prevail in the various spheres of production. It is, *prima facie*, a very different matter whether commodities are sold at their values (i.e., whether they are exchanged with one another in proportion to the value contained in them, at their value price) or they are sold at prices which make their sale yield equal profits on equal amounts of the capitals advanced for their respective production. (If capitals which set in motion unequal quantities of living labour are to produce unequal amounts of surplus-value, this presupposes, at least to a certain degree, that the *level of exploitation of labour* or the *rate of surplus-value* is the same, or that the distinctions that exist here are balanced out by real or imaginary (conventional) grounds of compensation. This assumes competition among the workers and an equalisation that takes place by their constant migration from one sphere of production to another. A general rate of surplus-value of this kind – as a tendency, like all economic laws – is presupposed by us as *theoretical* simplification; but in practice it is an actual presupposition of the capitalist mode of production, even if inhibited to a greater or lesser extent by practical frictions that produce more or less significant local differences, such as the settlement laws for agricultural labourers in England, for example. In theory we assume that the laws of the capitalist mode of production develop in their pure form. In reality, this is only an approximation; but the approximation is all the more exact, the more the capitalist mode of production is developed, and the less it is adulterated by, or entangled with, survivals of earlier economic conditions).

The whole difficulty arises from the fact that commodities are not exchanged simply as *commodities*, but as the *products of capitals*, which claim shares in the totality of surplus-value in proportion to their magnitude, demanding equal shares for equal sizes. And the *total price* of the commodities that a given capital produces in a given period of time has to satisfy this demand. The total price of these commodities, however, is simply the sum of the *prices of the individual commodities*, which form the product of the capital in question.

The salient point will best emerge if we consider the matter as follows. Let us suppose that the workers themselves are in possession of their respective means of production, and exchange their commodities with each other. Then these commodities would not be the products of capital. The value of the means and material of labour applied in the different branches of production would vary according to the technological nature of their work; similarly, ignoring the unequal *value* of the means of production applied, different masses of these means of production would be required for a given amount of labour, since one worker might require say an hour to finish a certain commodity, while another might take a day, etc. Let us further assume that these workers work on the average for the same length of time, taking into account the adjustments that arise from the varying intensity, etc., of the work. Firstly, then, two workers would both have replaced their *outlays*, the cost prices of the means of production they had consumed, in the commodities that formed the products of their respective day's labour. These outlays would vary according to the technological nature of their branch of labour. Secondly, they would both have created an equal quantity of *new value*, namely the working day added to the means of production. (This would comprise their *wages + the surplus-value*, the surplus labour over and above their necessary requirements, though the result of this would belong to themselves.) If we express ourselves in 'capitalist' terms, they would both receive the same wages plus the same profit, which would be equal to the value expressed for instance in the product of a ten-hour working day. > But the *value* of their commodities would be different. < Commodity I, for instance > which is how we shall describe the product of worker number one < might contain a greater share of value in relation to the means of production applied to produce it than commodity II; and in order to introduce all possible distinctions straight away, commodity I might also absorb more living labour than commodity II for its production. |180| The values of these commodities I and II would therefore be very different. So too the sums of commodity value that are the respective products of the work performed by workers I and II over a given period of time. *Profit rates* would also be very different for I and II, if we give this name here to the ratio of the surplus-value to the total value laid out on means of production. The means of subsistence which I and II consume every day in the course of production, and which substitute for wages in this example, here form the portion of the means of production advanced which we would elsewhere call variable capital. But the *surplus-values* would be the same for both I and II, given the same working time, or, more precisely, since I and II each receive the value of the product of one working day, they therefore [after the deduction of the value of the constant elements advanced] receive *equal values*, one part of which can be viewed as a replacement for the means of subsistence consumed in the course of production, the other as the additional surplus-value on top of this. If worker I has higher outlays, these are replaced by the greater portion of the value of his commodities that replaces the constant part; and he therefore again has a greater part of his product's total value to transform back into the material elements of this constant part, while II, if he receives less for this, has also that much less to transform back. > (If both of them wanted to change their branch of production, I would as a result have more value at his disposal than II, but this has nothing to do with the present question. In any case, permanence of occupation is more in accordance with our general presuppositions here than changes of this character.) < Under these conditions the *difference in rates of profit* would be a matter of indifference, just as *for the present-day wage-labourer* it is a matter of indifference in what *profit rate* the quantity of surplus-value squeezed out of him is expressed, and just as in international trade the differences in *profit rates* between different nations are completely immaterial as far as the exchange of their commodities is concerned.

The exchange of commodities at their *values* – or at approximately these values – thus calls for a much lower stage [of development] than exchange at *prices of production*, for which a definite degree of capitalist development is necessary.

(Whatever may be the ways in which the prices of different commodities are first established or fixed in relation to one another, their movement is subject to the *law of value*. Where the labour-time required for their production falls, prices fall; and where it rises, prices rise as long as all other circumstances remain the same.)

Apart from the way in which the law of value governs prices, > i.e., the domination exerted over the *movement of prices* by the *law of value*, < it is also quite apposite to view the values of commodities not only as theoretically prior to the prices of production, but also as historically prior to them. This applies to those conditions in which the *means of production belong to the worker*, conditions which are to be found in the ancient and the modern world, among *peasant proprietors* and *handicraftsmen*.

(This agrees, moreover, with the opinion we expressed previously, that the development of products into commodities *arises* from exchange between different communities, and not between the members of one and the same community.)

This is true not only for this condition [mentioned above] but also for conditions based on slavery and serfdom, as long as the means of production involved in each branch of production can be transferred from one sphere to another only with difficulty, and the different spheres of production relate to each other, to a certain degree, like foreign countries or communities.[13]

If the prices at which commodities exchange for each other are to correspond approximately to their values, nothing more is needed than (1) that the exchange of different commodities ceases to be purely accidental; and (2) that, in so far as we are dealing with the *direct exchange of commodities*, these commodities are produced on both sides in relative quantities that approximately correspond to mutual need, something which is learned from the reciprocal experience of trading and which therefore arises precisely as a result of continuing exchange, or, as far as *selling* is concerned, no natural, artificial or accidental monopolies enable one of the contracting parties to sell above value, or force them to sell cheap, below value. By 'accidental' monopoly we mean the monopoly that accrues to buyer or seller as a result of the accidental state of supply and demand.

13 [Engels added the word 'communist' before 'communities'. Translator]

It is assumed that commodities from different spheres of production are sold at their value; this presupposition naturally means no more than that their value is the centre of gravity around which their prices turn and at which their constant rise and |181| fall is balanced out. Besides this, however, there is always a *market value* (of which more later) as distinct from the individual value of particular commodities produced by the different producers. The individual value of some of these commodities will stand *below* the market value (i.e., less labour-time has been required for their production) while the value of others will stand *above* it. *Market value* is to be viewed, on the one hand, as the *average value* of the commodities produced in a particular sphere, and, on the other hand, as the individual value of commodities produced under *average conditions* in the sphere in question, and forming the *great mass* of its commodities. Only in extraordinary situations do commodities produced under the *worst conditions*, or alternatively *exceptionally favourable* ones, govern the market value, which forms in turn the centre around which market prices fluctuate – these being the same for all commodities of the same kind. If the *supply of commodities* at the *average value*, > which it would be better to *regard* as < the *mean value of the mass* that lies between the two extremes, satisfies the customary demand, the commodities whose *individual* value stands below the *market price* will realise a *surplus profit*, i.e., more value, while those whose *individual value* stands *above* the market price will be unable to realise a part of the surplus-value which they contain. It is of no assistance to say that the sale of commodities produced under the worst conditions proves that they are required to meet the demand. If the price were *higher* than the *mean market value* in the case assumed, the demand would be less. At a given price, a species of commodity can only take up a certain area of the market; this area remains the same through changes in price only if the higher price coincides with a smaller quantity of commodities and a lower price with a greater quantity. If the demand is so strong, however, that it does not contract when the price is determined by the value of the commodities produced in the worst market conditions, it is these that determine the market value. This is possible only if demand rises above the usual level, or supply falls below this. Finally, if the *mass of commodities produced* is greater than can be sold (or are required) at *mean market values*, the *market value* is determined by the commodities produced under the best conditions. These commodities may be sold completely or approximately at their *individual value*, for instance, in which connection it may happen that commodities produced under the worst conditions may fail even to realise their cost prices, while those produced under average conditions realise only a part of the *surplus-value they contain*. What we have said here of *market value* holds also for the *price of production*, as soon as this takes the place of market value. The *price of production* is regulated in each sphere, and regulated too according to circumstances which vary. But it is again the centre around which the daily market prices revolve, and at which they are balanced out in definite periods.[14]

In whatever way prices are determined, the following is the result:

(1) The *law of value* governs their movement, in so far as *reduction or increase* in the labour-time needed for their production makes the price of production rise or fall.[15]

(2) The *average profit*, which determines the prices of production, must always be approximately equal to the *amount of surplus-value* that accrues to a given capital as a *particular part of the total social capital*. Suppose that the *general rate of profit*, and *hence the average profit*, is expressed in a monetary value that is higher than that of the *actual average surplus-value*. As far as the capitalists are concerned, it is all the same whether they charge one another 15 percent or 10 percent as the rate of profit. The one percentage covers no more actual commodity value than the other does, since the exaggerated level of its monetary expression is *reciprocal*. For the workers, however (we assume that they receive their normal wages, hence the exaggeration of the average profit does not result in an actual *deduction* from the wage, but expresses something completely different from surplus-value) the increase in commodity prices resulting from this rise in the average profit must correspond to an increase in the price of the variable capital. In actual fact, a general *nominal* increase of this kind in the profit rate, and hence in *average profit*, over and above the level given by the proportion of the *actual surplus-value* to the *capital advanced*, is not possible unless it brings with it an *increase in wages* and similarly an increase in the prices of those commodities which form the *constant capital*. The same applies to a *decrease* [in the profit rate]. Since it is only the total value of the commodities that regulates the total surplus-value, |182| while this in turn regulates the *level of average profit* and hence the *general rate of profit* (as a general law, or as dominating the fluctuations) it follows that the *law of value* regulates *production prices*.

What competition brings about, first of all in *one sphere*, is the establishment of a uniform *market value* and *market price* out of the various individual values

---

14 See Ricardo on the determination of the prices of production by those working under the worst conditions. [Ricardo 1821, pp. 60–1.]

15 It is in this sense that Ricardo, who certainly feels that his prices of production differ from the values of the commodities, says that: 'the inquiry to which he wishes to draw the reader's attention relates to the effect of the *variations* in the *relative* value of commodities, and not in their *absolute* value'. [Op. cit., p. 15.]

of commodities. But it is only the competition of capitals in *different spheres* that brings forth the *production price* that equalises the *rates of profit* between those spheres. The latter process requires a higher development of the capitalist mode of production than the former.

In order that *commodities* from the same sphere of production, of the same type and the same *quality* (an *approximation* to this is assumed), may be sold at their *value*, two things are necessary:

First, the different individual values must be equalised to give *one single* social value, the *market value* presented above, and this requires competition among the producers of the *same type* of commodity, as well as the presence of a *market* on which they all offer their commodities. > (The concept of a *market* needs to be developed in general outline in the section on the circulation process of capital.) < For the market price for identical commodities (which though they are identical are produced in circumstances coloured by characteristics which differ according to the individual) to correspond to the *market value*, and not to diverge either by rising above it or falling below it, it is necessary for the pressures that the various sellers exert on each other to be strong enough to throw onto the market the quantity of commodities that is required to fulfil the given social need, i.e., the quantity for which the society is capable of paying the *market value*. If the mass of products exceeds this need, the commodities will have to be sold *below* their market value, and conversely, if the mass of products is not large enough, or if the pressure of competition among the sellers is not strong enough to compel them to bring this mass of commodities to the market, they will have to be sold *above* their market value. If the market value changes, the conditions under which the whole mass of commodities can be sold will also change. If the market value falls, the social need is on average expanded (here this always means the need which is able to pay for itself), and within certain limits the society can absorb larger quantities of commodities. If the market value rises, the social need for the commodities contracts and smaller quantities are absorbed. Thus if supply and demand regulate the market price, or rather the divergences of market price from market value, the *market value* in turn regulates the relationship between demand and supply, and the centre around which fluctuations in demand and supply make the market price oscillate.

If we consider the matter more closely, we see that the same conditions that obtain for the *value of the individual commodity* reproduce themselves here as conditions for the *value of the total amount of any one type of commodity*; we see how capitalist production is, right from the start, mass production, and how even what is produced in smaller amounts by petty producers in other, less developed modes of production is (at least as far as the major commodities are concerned) concentrated and agglomerated together on the *market* and brought to sale in the same way: as the *common product* of a whole branch of production, or of a bigger or smaller contingent of such a branch.

(Let us note here, but merely in passing, that the '*social need*' which governs the principle of demand is for its part essentially conditioned by the *relationship of the different classes* and their respective *economic positions*; in the *first* place, therefore, particularly by the proportion between the total surplus-value and the wage, and secondly by the proportion between the various parts > or categories < into which surplus-value is itself divided. Here again we can see how absolutely *nothing* can be explained by the relationship of demand and supply, before the *basis* has been developed on which this relationship comes into play.)

|183| Even though both commodities and money are unities of exchange-value and use-value, [we saw earlier how] in the course of buying and selling both determinations [*Bestimmungen*] were distributed in a polarised way at the two extremes, so that the commodity (the seller) represented use-value and money represented exchange-value.[16] It was one precondition for the sale that the commodity should have use-value, and thus satisfy a social need. The other precondition was that the quantity of labour contained in the commodity should represent *socially necessary labour*, so that the individual value of the commodity (and its *sale price*, which is the same thing under this assumption) should coincide with its social value.[17]

Let us now apply this to the mass of commodities present on the market and forming the product of an entire sphere.

The matter will be represented most easily if we conceive the entire mass of commodities as a *single* commodity, and regard the sum of the prices of the many identical commodities as *a single price* (i.e., we add them together to form a single price). What we said of the individual commodity now applies word for word to the mass of commodities of a certain branch of production which are to be found on the market. The fact that the individual value of a commodity agrees with its social value is now realised in, or subsequently determines, the fact that the total quantity contains the socially necessary labour involved in its production and that the value of this mass equals its *market value*. Let us now assume that great quantities of these commodities are produced in something like the same normal social conditions, so that this value is also

---

16 See K. Marx, *Zur Kritik der politischen Oekonomie, Heft I*, Berlin, 1859, pp. 26–8 [MEGA II/2, pp. 128–30; MECW 29].

17 Op. cit., [pp. 3–16] [MEGA II/2, pp. 107–17; MECW 29].

the individual value of the individual commodities making up this mass. If now a relatively small portion of them are produced in *worse* conditions, and another portion in *better* conditions, so that the individual value of the one part is greater than the mean value of the great bulk of the commodities, and that of the other part less than this mean, these two extremes will cancel each other out, and as a result the average value of the commodities at the extremes will be the same as the value of the mass of average commodities. The *market value* will then be determined by the value of the commodities produced under average conditions. > The *average value* of every aliquot part of the whole mass of commodities will then in fact be equal to the individual value of the commodities produced under average conditions,[18] and < the value of the overall mass of commodities will be equal to the actual sum of values of all individual commodities taken together, both those produced in *average* conditions, and those produced in *better* or *worse* ones. In this case, the *market value* or *social value* of the mass of commodities – the necessary labour-time they contain – is determined by the value of the great middling mass.

Now assume on the contrary that the value of the commodities produced under worse conditions is not balanced out by the value of those produced under better conditions, so that the part of the total quantity of commodities produced under worse conditions forms a relatively significant quantity, both vis-à-vis the average mass and vis-à-vis the opposite extreme. In this case it is the mass produced under the *worse conditions* that governs the *market*, or social, value.

Let us finally assume that the mass of commodities produced under conditions which are *better* than the *mean* significantly exceeds that produced under worse conditions and is itself of significant magnitude in relation to that produced under average conditions. In that case the market value would be regulated by the part produced under the most favourable |184| conditions.[19]

18 Loc. cit.

19 The controversy between Storch and Ricardo in connection with ground-rent (a controversy only in so far as the subject is concerned, as neither party paid any attention to the other) over whether market value (in their terms rather market price or price of production) is governed by commodities produced under the least favourable conditions (Ricardo) or the most favourable (Storch) is thus resolved in this way, that both are right and both are wrong, and also that both have entirely left the average case out of account. (Compare Corbet on cases where the price is always regulated by commodities produced under the best conditions.) [Corbet 1841, pp. 42–4]. And compare this: 'It is not meant to be asserted by him' (Ricardo) 'that two particular lots of two different articles, as a hat and a pair of shoes, exchange with one another when *those two particular lots* were pro-

We leave aside here the situation where the market is over-supplied, in which case it is always the portion produced under the most favourable conditions that governs the *market price*; here we are not dealing with *market price* in so far as this differs from *market value* but simply with the *various determinations of this market value* itself.

Strictly speaking (though this is of course only approximately true in actual practice and is modified there in a thousand ways) in case I the market value of the entire mass, as governed by the average values, is equal to the sum of its individual values; although for the commodities produced at the two extremes this value is expressed as an average value imposed on them. (Those producing at the worst extreme must then sell their commodities *below* their individual value, while those at the best extreme sell theirs *above* it.)

In case II, the masses of value produced at the two extremes do not balance each other out. Instead, it is rather those produced under the worst conditions which decide the issue. Strictly speaking, the *average* price or *market value* of each individual commodity or quantity of commodities, calculated as an aliquot part of the total mass, is now determined by the total value of this mass, which is arrived at by adding together the values of the commodities produced under various different conditions, and by the aliquot part of this value, which, > again as part of the total mass of commodities, < falls to the share of the individual commodity. The *market value* obtained in this way is not only *above* the individual value of the favourable extreme, but also above that of the middle stratum of commodities; but it would always remain less than the individual *value* of the commodities produced at the unfavourable extreme. How close it would be to this, or whether it would ultimately coincide with it, depends completely on the volume of the commodities produced at the unfavourable extreme in the sphere of commodities in question. > (We disregard demand here; if demand is fairly strong, < but not *predominant*, it is the *individual value* of the unfavourably produced commodities that governs the market price.)

Finally, if the commodities produced at the favourable extreme are greater in quantity (if demand is weak in relation to supply, the favourably situated part, whatever its size, forcibly makes room for itself by drawing the price towards its individual value), not only compared with the other extreme, but also with the

duced by equal quantities of labour. By "*commodity*" we must here understand "*description of commodity*", not a particular individual hat, pair of shoes, etc. The *whole labour* which produces all the hats in England is to be considered, to this purpose, as *divided among all the hats*. This seems to me not to have been expressed at first, and in the general statements of this doctrine'. (*Observations* 1821, pp. 53–4.)

middle conditions, the *market value* falls below the average value. The market value can never coincide with the *individual* value of the commodities produced under the most favourable conditions, except under an unfavourable constellation of supply as compared with demand. The *average value*, calculated by adding the sums of value at the two extremes and in the middle, here stands *below the middle value* and, while being nearer or further from it according to the relative place taken by the favourable extreme, regulates the *market value*.

This *abstract* establishment of market value is brought about by competition among the buyers, assuming that the *demand* is strong enough to absorb the whole mass of commodities at the values established in this way.

And here we come to the other point.

To say that a commodity has use-value is to assert that it satisfies some kind of social need. As long as we were dealing only with an individual commodity, we could |185| presume that the need for this specific commodity was already included in the price, without having to go in any further detail into the *quantitative* extent of the need which had to be satisfied. But the quantity is a vital factor, as soon as we have on the one hand the product of a whole branch of production and on the other the social need. It now becomes essential to consider the *volume*, hence the quantity, of this social need.

In the determinations of market value given previously we assumed that the *mass of commodities produced remained the same*, was *a given*, and that the only change that took place was in the proportion between the components of that mass, which were produced under different conditions, and therefore that the *market value* of the same mass of commodities was regulated differently. > The general production may remain the same, and still there may be changes in the market price produced by accidental variations in the amount of commodities offered upon the *market*, exhibited for sale. These details do not fall within the limits of our observations.[20] < Let us take this mass to be the customary quantity supplied. If the demand for this quantity now also remains that customary, the commodity is sold at its market value > however regulated according to the variable composition of the elements forming the aggregate supply.[21] < The mass of commodities not only satisfies a need, but it satisfies this need to its 'social' extent. If, however, the quantity supplied is less than the *demand*, or alternatively more, the market price will vary from the market value. In the first case, if the quantity is too small, it is always the commodit-

20 [The last two sentences are in English in the manuscript. Translator]

21 [Again in English. Translator]

ies produced under the worst conditions that govern the market value, while if it is too large, it is always those produced under the best conditions; hence it is one of the two extremes that determines the market value, despite the fact that the proportions produced under the different conditions, taken by themselves, would lead to a different result. If the difference between the demand for the product and the quantity produced is more significant, the market price will diverge more significantly from the market value, either upwards or downwards. This difference between the quantity of commodities produced and the quantity of those commodities which would be sold at their market value can arise for *two* reasons. Either the former quantity itself changes, becoming either too little or too much, so that reproduction would take place on a scale different from that which regulated the given market value. In this case it is the *supply* that has changed, even though the demand remains the same, and in this way we have relative overproduction or underproduction. Alternatively, however, the *supply*, i.e., the *reproduction*, remains the same, but demand rises or falls, something which can happen for various reasons. Even though the *absolute* size of the supply remains the same here, its *relative* size varies, i.e., there is a variation in its magnitude *compared* with, or measured against, the need. The effect is the same as in the first case. Finally, if changes occur on both sides, but either in the opposite direction, or else in the same direction but not to the same degree, if, in a word, bilateral |186| variations take place, which nevertheless affect the *proportion* – the proportion between the two sides – the end result must still amount to one of the two cases considered above.

The real difficulty in pinning down the general concepts of supply and demand is that we seem to end up with a tautology. Let us first take *supply*, the product which is actually on sale in the market (or can be delivered to it: so as not to get involved in completely useless details, we refer here to the mass of the annual production or reproduction in each particular branch of industry and ignore therefore the greater or lesser capacity that various commodities possess for being withdrawn from the market and, as to their consumption, held over to a future year, etc.) This annual production or reproduction is firstly expressed as a *definite quantity*, in measure or number, according to whether the commodity is measured continuously or discretely; it is not just use-values that satisfy human needs, but use-values which are available on the market on a *given scale*. Secondly, however, this quantity of commodities has a definite *market value*, which can be expressed in the market value of the commodity or in the measure that serves as the unit. There exists no necessary connection between the *quantitative volume* of commodities on the market and their *market value*, since some commodities, for example, have a generically high value, others a generically low one, so that a *given sum of value* may be expressed (represented) in a very small quantity of the one kind and a very large quantity of the other kind. Between the quantity of the commodities > (use-values, *articles*) < on the market and the *market value* of those articles there is only this one connection: on a given basis of labour productivity the *production of a particular quantity of articles requires a particular quantity of social labour-time* in every particular sphere of production, even though this proportion varies greatly from one sphere of production to another, and has no intrinsic connection with the usefulness of the articles or the particular character of their use-value. All other things being equal, if quantity *a* of a certain species of commodity costs a labour-time of *b*, quantity *na* costs a labour-time of *nb*. In so far as a society wants to satisfy its needs, and to have an article produced > which satisfies a social need, < it has to pay for it. In actual fact – since commodity production presupposes the division of labour – the society purchases these articles > in advance by applying to their production < a certain quantity of the *labour-time it has to dispose of*, > hence a certain *quantity of the labour-time* a given society has at its disposal. < The section of society whose responsibility it is under the division of labour to spend its labour on the production of these particular articles must receive an equivalent in social labour represented in those articles that satisfy its needs. *But* there exists no necessary > and definite < connection (simply a fortuitous one) between on the one hand the *total quantity of social labour* that is spent on a particular article > (what is involved here is not the *labour-time* necessary to produce a particular number of commodities, or quantity of a commodity, e.g., a house, or a quartal of wheat, but the *relevant part of the total labour-time* the society spends to produce houses or wheat) < and therefore between the *proportion* that the production of this article assumes in the total production, and on the other hand the *proportion* in which the society demands satisfaction |187| of the need appeased by that particular article. Even if an individual article, or a definite quantity of one kind of commodity, may contain simply the *social labour* required to produce it, and as far as this aspect is concerned the *market value* of this commodity represents no more than the *necessary* labour, > if *too much* of the commodity in question is produced, if more is produced than is required under the given conditions of social need, < a part of the society's labour-time is wasted, and the mass of commodities in question then represents on the market a *much smaller quantity of social labour* than it *actually contains*. (Only when production is subjected to the genuine, *prior* control of society will society establish the connection between the *amount* (*the extent*) *of social labour-time* applied to the production of particular articles, and the *scale* of the *social* need to be satisfied by those articles.) These commodities, if they are not in fact completely unsaleable, must therefore be got rid of at *less* than their market value. The converse applies, if the *amount of social labour spent to produce a particular kind of commodity* is too small for the *specific social need which the product is to satisfy*. But if the *volume of social labour* spent on the production of a certain article corresponds in scale to *the social need to be satisfied*, so that the amount produced corresponds to the customary measure of production and reproduction, the commodity will be sold at its *market value*. The exchange of commodities at their value > or the *sale* of commodities at their value, which is only another form of the same thing < is the rational, natural law of the equilibrium between them; this is the basis on which the divergences have to be explained, and not the converse, the law should not be derived from the divergences. >

> Well. < Let us now examine the other aspect, *demand*.

Commodities are bought as *means of production* or as *means of subsistence* > (in the narrower sense) < (it makes no difference that some kinds of commodity may serve both these ends), they are bought to go into either *productive* or *individual consumption*. There is therefore both *demand* from *producers* (here capitalists, as we assume that the *means of production* are *transformed into capital*) and from *consumers*. |188| Both of these at first appear to assume a *given volume of social needs* on the demand side, to which *definite quantities of social production* in the various branches of industry are to correspond. If for example the cotton industry is to carry on its annual reproduction at a given level, it requires the usual amount of cotton, and as far as the annual expansion of reproduction > consequent upon the accumulation of capital < is concerned, other things being equal, an additional quantity of cotton will be required, and so on. With regard to the means of subsistence, the working class must find at least the same amount of necessary provisions available, even if perhaps somewhat differently distributed among various kinds of provision, if it is to go on living on the average in its customary manner; and taking the annual growth of population into account, it also needs an additional quantity. The same is also true for the other classes, with varying degrees of modification.

It appears, therefore, that there is a certain quantitatively defined social need on the demand side, which requires for its fulfilment *a definite quantity* of an article on the market. But the *quantitative determination* of this need is completely *elastic* and *indefinite*. Its fixedness is an illusion [*Schein*]. If means of subsistence were cheaper or money wages higher, the workers would buy more of them, and a 'greater social need' for these kinds of commodity would appear, not to mention those paupers, etc., whose 'demand' is *below* the narrowest limits of their needs. If cotton, on the other hand, became cheaper, the capitalists' demand for cotton would grow, more excess capital would be put into the cotton industry, and so on. (It must never be forgotten in this connection that the demand for *productive* consumption, on our assumptions, is the capitalist's demand, and that his true purpose is the *production of surplus-value*, so that it is only with this in mind that he produces a particular kind of commodity. On the other hand, this does not prevent the capitalist, in so far as he is present on the market as a buyer, of cotton for instance, from being the representative of the *need* for cotton, just as it is completely unimportant for the seller of cotton whether the buyer transforms it into > calico or gunpowder, < or whether he uses it to stop up his own and the world's ears. And yet the capitalist's purpose exerts a great influence on the kind of buyer he is. His need for cotton is modified fundamentally by the fact that all it really clothes is his need to make a profit.) The extent to which the need for commodities as *represented* on the market – i.e., *demand* – is *quantitatively* distinct from a *genuine* social need is of course very different for different commodities; what I mean here is the *difference* between the quantity of commodities that are demanded and the quantity that would be demanded at other *money prices* or under different *financial conditions* (living conditions) affecting the buyers.

|189| Nothing is easier to understand than the inadequacies of demand and supply and the consequent divergence of *market prices* from *market values*. The real difficulty lies in determining what is to be understood by a *coincidence of demand and supply.*

Demand and supply coincide if they stand in such a relationship that the mass of commodities produced by a certain sphere of production can be sold at their *market value*, neither above nor below it. This is the first thing we are told.

The second thing is that when commodities can be sold at their market value, demand and supply coincide.

If demand and supply coincide, *they cease to have any effect*, and it is for this very reason that the commodity is sold at its *market value.* >

As soon as demand and supply coincide, they paralyse each other, just as when, say, centrifugal force and centripetal force are at work uniformly and with equal strength, they have no effect at all, and phenomena taking place in these conditions < must be explained otherwise than by the operation of these two forces. The truly immanent laws of capitalist production clearly cannot be explained in terms of the interaction of demand and supply (not to mention the deeper analysis of these two social motors[22] which would not be appropriate here), since these laws are realised in their pure form only when demand and supply *cease to operate, i.e., when they coincide*. In actual fact, demand and supply *never* coincide, or if they do so it is only *by chance*

22 [Again in English. Translator]

and therefore of zero scientific importance (it should be considered as not having happened). Why then does political economy assume that they do coincide? In order to treat the phenomena it deals with in their law-like form [*gesetzmässige Gestalt*], the form that corresponds to their concept [*Begriff*], i.e., to consider them *independently* of the *appearance* [*Schein*] produced by the movement of demand and supply. And, in addition, to order to discover the real *tendency* of their movement and to define it to a certain extent. For the disproportions are contrary in character, and since they constantly follow one another, they balance each other out in their character as opposites, in their mutual contradiction. Thus if there is no single individual case in which demand and supply actually do coincide, their disproportions still work out in the following way – and the result of a *divergence in one direction* is to call forth a *divergence in the opposite direction* – that supply and demand always coincide if a greater or lesser period of time is taken as a whole > (a greater or lesser time in which the capital turns over) < but they coincide only as the *average of the movement* that has taken place and only through the *constant movement of their contradiction*. Market prices that diverge from market values balance out on average to become market values, since the departures from those values cancel each other out as pluses and minuses, when their average is taken. And this average figure is by no means of merely *theoretical* importance. It is, rather, *practically* important for capital, the investment of which is calculated over the fluctuations and compensations of a more or less fixed period of time.

|190| The relationship between demand and supply thus explains on the one hand simply the *divergences* of market price from market value, while on the other hand it explains the *tendency* for these divergences to be removed, i.e., for the *effect of the demand and supply relationship to be cancelled*. (The exceptional case of commodities which have prices without having any value will not be considered here > and even in this case it has to be decided *what* exactly determines the *demand*. This can in turn only be explained by the demand and supply relationship.) < Demand and supply can cause the *cancellation* of the effect that their *disproportion* produces in very different ways. If demand falls, for example, and with it the market price, this can lead to a withdrawal of capital and thus a reduction in supply. But it can also lead to a fall in the *market value* itself as a result of inventions which shorten the necessary labour-time; this would also bring the market value into line with the market price. Conversely, if demand rises, so that the *market price* rises above the market value, this can lead > production to become overcrowded,[23] until < the

23 [Again in English. Translator]

market price falls; alternatively it may lead to a rise in prices which forcibly drives down demand. It may also lead, in one or another branch of production, to a rise in the *market value* itself for a shorter or longer period, because part of the products must be supplied under worse conditions during this time to cover the demand.

If demand and supply determine the *market price*, the reverse also applies: market price, and at a further remove market value, determine demand and supply. As far as demand is concerned, this is self-evident, since it moves in the opposite direction to price. But the same is also true of supply. For the prices of the means of production that go into the commodities supplied determine the *demand* for those means of production, and *therefore* also the supply of the commodities which have to be supplied to meet the demand for those means of production.

On top of this confusion – the determination of price by demand and supply, and the determination of demand and supply by price – > is the further point that < demand determines supply, and, conversely, supply determines demand, production determines the market, and the market determines production.[24]

---

24 The following 'subtlety' is sheer stupidity: 'Where the quantity of wages, capital, and land, required to produce an article, are become different from what they were, that which Adam Smith calls the *natural price* of it is also different, and that price, which was previously its natural price, becomes, with reference to this alteration, its market price; because, though *neither the supply, nor the quantity wanted may have been changed*' (both of these change here, precisely because the *market value*, or, as Adam Smith has it, the *price of production* changes as a result of the change in value) 'that supply is not *now* exactly enough for those persons who are able and willing to pay *what is now* the *cost of production*, but is either greater or less than that; *so that the proportion between the supply, and what is with reference to the new cost of production the effectual demand*, is different from what it was. An *alteration in the rate of supply* will then take place if there is no obstacle in the way of it, and at last bring the commodity to its new natural price. It may, then, seem good to some persons to *say* > (namely, it may seem good to *say* so to some imbeciles who do not understand that in the case alluded to the *alteration in the cost of production* had produced an *alteration in the state of demand*, or in the proportion of demand and supply, and that the change so produced may result in a changed state of supply, which would prove the exact contrary of what the imbecile wants to prove, viz., [it] would prove that the *alteration in the cost of production*, instead of being regulated by the proportion of demand and supply, did on its part regulate that very proportion) < that, as the commodity gets to its natural price by an alteration in its supply, the *natural price is as much owing to one proportion between the demand and supply, as the market price is to another*, and, consequently, that the *natural price*, just as much as the *market price*, depends on the *proportion that demand and supply bear to each other* ... "The great principle of demand and supply is called into action to determine what Adam Smith calls

Even the ordinary economist (see the footnote) understands that without some kind of change in supply and the quantity wanted, the relationship between the two can change as a result of a *change* in the *market value* of the commodity. Even he has to concede that, whatever the market value may be, *demand and supply must always be in an equal relationship* if the market value is to emerge, i.e., '*the supply must be equal to the effective demand, which is prepared to pay the market value*', in other words it is not the relationship between demand and supply that explains market value, but it is the opposite, namely the market value explains their up and down oscillations. > They themselves admit (see the concluding sentence of the quotation in the footnote) that with < two *different natural prices* of the same commodity, at different times, *demand and supply can and must coincide*, if the commodity is to be sold at its *natural price*. > Since in both cases *demand and supply* do coincide – < hence there is no *difference* in this relationship, but rather a *difference* in the magnitude of the *natural price* itself – the latter is evidently *determined independently of supply and demand*, and can certainly not be determined by them.

|191| If a commodity is to be sold at its market value, i.e., in proportion to the *socially necessary* labour contained in it, the *total quantity* of social labour which is consumed to produce *the whole amount of that commodity*, must correspond to the quantity of the social need for it, i.e., to the social need with money to back it up. Competition, the up-and-down of market prices, corresponding to the up-and-down of the variations in the proportion between demand and supply, constantly seeks to reduce to that standard the total quantity of labour employed on commodities of all descriptions.[25]

In the relationship of demand and supply for commodities we have firstly a repetition of the relationship between buyer and seller, between commodity and money (use-value and exchange-value); and secondly the relationship of producer and consumer (although both may be represented by third parties, in the shape of merchants). As far as buyer and seller are concerned, it is sufficient simply to put them face to face with each other as individuals to create

---

natural prices, as well as market prices". [Malthus 1820, p. 75]. > This *proportion, however, if we still mean* by "demand" and "natural price" what we meant just now, when referring to Adam Smith, *must always be a proportion of equality;* for *it is only when supply is equal to the effectual demand,* that is, *to that demand which will neither more nor less than pay the natural price,* that the *natural price is in fact paid;* consequently, there *may be two very different natural prices,* at *different times, for the same commodity,* and yet the *proportion, which the supply bears to the demand, be in both cases the same, namely the proportion of equality*'. (*Observations* 1821, pp. 60–1.)

25 [This sentence is in English in the manuscript. Translator]

the relationship. Three persons are enough for the complete metamorphosis of a commodity, and hence for the whole process of sale and purchase. A transforms his commodity into B's money by selling B the commodity and he then transforms his money back into commodities which he buys with this money from C. > To present the process it is enough to have the three persons A, B and C. < The entire process takes place between these three parties. > This is number one. *Secondly*: < in dealing with money we assumed that commodities were sold at their values; there was no reason at all to consider prices that diverged from values, as we were concerned simply with the changes of form that commodities undergo when they are turned into money and then transformed back from money into commodities again. As soon as a commodity is in any way sold, and a new commodity bought with the proceeds, we have the entire metamorphosis before us, and it is completely immaterial here > where we are considering them *as such* < whether the realised price of the commodity stands *above* or *below* its value. The commodity's *value* remains important as the basis, since any rational understanding of money has to start from this foundation, and *price*, in its general concept, is simply monetised value. In dealing with money as means of circulation, moreover, we did not assume simply one metamorphosis by a single commodity. We considered rather the way these metamorphoses were socially intertwined. Only in this way did we come to the circulation of money and the development of its function as means of circulation. But however important this framework is for the transformation of money to enable it to function as means of circulation and for the altered form that it assumes as a result, as far as the transaction between individual buyers and sellers is concerned it is completely immaterial.

When we consider supply and demand, on the other hand, the supply is equal to the sum of commodities provided by all the sellers or producers of a particular kind of commodity, and the demand is equal to the sum of all buyers or consumers (individual or productive) of that same kind of commodity. These totals, moreover, act on one another as unities, as aggregate forces. Here the individual has an effect only as part of a social power, as an atom in the mass, and it is in this form that competition brings into play the *social* character of production and consumption.

(The side that is temporarily *weaker* in competition is also that in which the individual operates independently of the mass of his competitors, and often against them, illustrating precisely in this way the dependence of one on the other, whereas the *stronger* side always acts towards its opponent as a more or less united whole. If, for example, demand is greater than supply for this particular kind of commodity, one buyer outbids the others – up to a certain limit – and thus *raises the price* of the commodity above its market value for everyone, while the sellers, on the other hand, all seek to sell at a high market price. If, the converse is true, |192| if the supply is greater than the demand, A will start to unload his goods more cheaply and the others will have to follow, while the buyers work *together* to depress the market price as far as possible below the market value. Each is only concerned with the *common* interest as long as he obtains more *with* it than he would *against* it. And this unity of action ceases as soon as one entire side or other weakens, when each individual independently tries to extract what he can. If one seller produces *more cheaply* and can get rid of more of his product and carve out a bigger share of the market by selling below the current market price or market value, he does so, and the action thus begun gradually forces the others to introduce the cheaper form of production and thereby reduces the *socially necessary labour* to a new standard level. If one side has the upper hand, each of its members profits; it is as if they had a joint monopoly to exert. As for the weaker side, each member can try for his own part to be stronger (e.g., he may try to be the one operating with lower production costs) or at least he may endeavour to come off as well as possible, and here it is a case of devil take the hindmost, even if this action ultimately affects not only him but the whole group of which he is a part.)[26]

Demand and supply imply the transformation of value into *market value*, and in so far as they proceed on the basis of capitalist production, the *commodities* are the products of capital, and imply capitalist *processes of production*, hence conditions that are much more intricate than the mere sale and purchase of commodities. Here it is not simply a question of the formal conversion of commodity value into *price*, i.e., a mere change of form; what is involved are specific *quantitative* divergences of market prices from market values and, at a further remove, from prices of production. For simply buying and selling, it is enough that *commodity producers* confront one another as such. A further analysis of demand and supply requires one to depict the various different classes and sections of classes which distribute the total social revenue among themselves and consume it as such, thus making up a demand created out of revenue; while it is also necessary to understand the overall configuration of the capitalist production process if one is to comprehend the demand and supply generated among the producers as such.

---

26 'If each man of a class could never have more than a given share, or aliquot part, of the gains and possessions of the whole, he would *readily combine to raise the gains*'; (he does this whenever the proportion of demand and supply is favourable to his side) 'this is *monopoly*. But where each man thinks that he may any way increase *the absolute amount of his own share*, though by a *process which lessens the whole amount*, he will often do it: this is *competition*'. (*An Inquiry* 1821, p. 105.)

In capitalist production it is not simply a matter of extracting, in return for the mass of value thrown into circulation in one form, an equal mass of value in another form – whether in the form of another commodity or of money – but rather of extracting for the capital advanced in production *the same surplus-value or profit* as any other capital of the same size, or a profit proportionate to its size, in whatever branch of production it may be applied. The problem therefore is to sell commodities (and this is a minimum requirement) at prices which deliver the average profit, i.e., at *prices of production*. This is the form in which capital becomes conscious of itself as a *social power*, in which every capitalist participates in proportion to his share in the total capital of the society. *Firstly*, capitalist production as such is indifferent to the particular use-values > of the *commodities* < it produces, in fact to the specific character of its *commodities* it produces in general. All that matters in any sphere of production is to produce *surplus-value*, to appropriate a definite quantity of unpaid labour or the product of that labour. And it |193| lies in the very nature of wage-labour subjected to capital that it is indifferent to its own specific character; it must allow itself to be metamorphosed according to the needs of capital, and to be transferred from one sphere of production to another. *Secondly*, one sphere of production really is as good or as bad as any other; each would be a failure if the commodity it produced did not satisfy some kind of social need.

If commodities were sold at their *values*, however, this would mean very different *rates of profit* in the *different spheres of production*, as we have already explained, according to the differing organic composition of the masses of capital applied in them. Capital is withdrawn from one sphere and thrown into another. This constant emigration and immigration between the different spheres according to whether the profit rate is rising or falling, this constant redistribution of capital, produces, in brief, a relationship between supply and demand such that the *average profit* is *the same* in the various different spheres, and values are therefore transformed into *prices of production*. Capital succeeds in bringing about this equalisation to an extent that varies according to how advanced capitalist development is in a given national society; i.e., the more the conditions in the country in question are adapted to the capitalist mode of production. As capitalist production advances, so also do its requirements become more extensive, and it subjects all the social conditions within which the production process takes place to its specific character and its immanent laws.

This constant equalisation of ever-renewed inequalities is accomplished the more quickly, (1) the more mobile capital is, i.e., the more easily it can be transferred from one sphere to another; and (2) the more rapidly the labour can be thrown from one sphere to another and from one *local* point of production to another. The first of these conditions implies completely free trade within the society and the removal of all monopolies other than *natural* ones, i.e., monopolies that arise from the capitalist mode of production itself. It also presupposes the *development of the credit system*, which concentrates together the floating social capital as an inorganic mass vis-à-vis the individual capitalist. It further implies the *subordination* of the various spheres of production to *capitalists*. (This last point is already contained in our assumption, if it is supposed that we are dealing with the transformation of values into prices of production in all spheres of production that are exploited in a capitalist manner; and yet this equalisation comes up against major obstacles if several substantial spheres of production are pursued in a non-capitalist fashion, these spheres being interposed between the capitalist enterprises and entwined with them.) A certain density of population is also important. The second condition involves: the abolition of all laws that prevent workers from moving from one sphere of production to another or from one local seat of production to any other; indifference of the worker to the content of his work; the greatest possible reduction of work in all spheres of production to simple labour; the disappearance of all prejudices of trade and craft among the workers; and also, in particular, *the subjection of the worker to the capitalist mode of production, etc.* Further details on this > fall outside our limits because they < belong to our treatise '*On Competition*'.[27]

|194| From what has been said so far, we can see that each individual capitalist, just like the capitalist species of each particular sphere of production, participates in the *exploitation of the entire working class* by capital as a whole, and in the *level of this exploitation*; not just in terms of general class sympathy, but in a direct economic sense, since, taking all other circumstances as given, including *the value of the constant capital advanced*, the *average rate of profit* (i.e., in percentage terms) depends on the *level of exploitation* of labour as a whole by capital as a whole. The average rate of profit coincides with the average surplus-value that capital produces, say, for each 100 units, and as far as surplus-value is concerned, what has been said above is evident enough from the very start, while in the case of average *profit* the additional aspect, which is one of the determinants of the rate of profit, is the *value* of the capital advanced. In actual fact, the *particular* interest that one capitalist or capital in a particular sphere of production has in *exploiting* the workers he directly employs is confined to the possibility of taking an *extra cut*, making an excess profit over and

27 [Marx evidently intended to make a separate investigation later on of 'more concrete' forms of capitalist production, including competition. Translator]

above the average, either by exceptional *overwork*, by reducing wages below the average, or by exceptional productivity in the labour applied. Apart from this, a capitalist who employed *no variable capital at all* in his sphere of production, hence *not a single worker* (in fact an exaggerated assumption) would have just as much of an interest in the exploitation of the working class by capital and just as much derive his profit from unpaid surplus labour as would a capitalist who employed > no constant capital but < only variable capital (again an exaggerated assumption) and therefore laid out his entire capital on wages. With a given working day, the *level of exploitation* of labour depends on the general *intensity* of labour, while with a *given intensity* it depends on the length of the working day. How high the rate of surplus-value is depends on the *level of exploitation* of labour, and thus, for a given mass of variable capital, the *size of the surplus-value* and consequently the *amount of profit* depend on this. (The *special interest* possessed by the capital of one sphere {as distinct from the total capital} in the exploitation of the workers directly employed by it is paralleled by the interest of the *individual capitalist* {as distinct from his sphere} in the exploitation of the workers *personally* exploited by him.)

Each particular sphere of capital, however, and each individual capitalist, has the same interest in the *productivity of the social labour* applied by the total capital. For two things are dependent on this. Firstly, the mass of use-values in which the average profit is expressed; this is important for two reasons, as it serves both as the *accumulation fund for new capital* and as the *revenue fund for consumption*. Secondly, the *value level of the total capital advanced* (both constant and variable) which, with a given size of surplus-value or profit for the entire capitalist class determines the *rate of profit*, or the profit on a particular quantity of capital. The *specific productivity* of labour in one *particular* sphere, or in one *individual concern* in this sphere, interests the capitalist *species* of this sphere in only one respect: in so far as it enables the *species* of this particular sphere to make an *extra profit* in relation to the total capital, or enables the individual fellow of this sphere to make an *extra profit* in relation to the capitalists of his own *species*.

|195| We thus have a mathematically exact demonstration of > why the capitalists are birds of a feather, and < why, no matter how little love is lost between them in their competition with one another, they are nevertheless united by a real freemasonry vis-à-vis the workers, i.e., the working class.

The *price of production* includes the average profit. And what we call *price of production* is in fact the same thing that Adam Smith calls 'natural price', Ricardo 'price of production' or 'cost of production', and the Physiocrats '*prix nécessaire*' (none of these people explained the difference between price of production and value). We call it the price of production because in the long run it is the condition of supply, the condition for the reproduction of commodities, in each particular sphere of production.[28] We can also understand why those very economists who oppose the determination of the *values* of commodities by *labour-time*, by the quantity of labour contained in them, always prattle about the *price of production* as the axis around which market prices oscillate. They do so, because the price of production is already a completely externalised [*veräusserlicht*] and at first sight *irrational* [*begriffslos*] *form* of commodity value, a form as it *appears* [*erscheint*] *in competition*, hence is present in the consciousness of the 'vulgar man of capital', and consequently also in that of the vulgar economist.

> *Surplus profit* <.

α) We saw in the course of our argument how *market value* (and everything that was said about this applies *mutatis mutandis*[29] *to the price of production*) involves a surplus profit for those producing under the best conditions in any particular sphere of production. Excluding all cases of crisis > or of incipient crisis < (or of overproduction in general) this holds good for all *market prices*, no matter how they might diverge from *market values* or *market prices of production*. The concept of *market price* means that *the same* price is paid for commodities, even if these are produced under very different individual conditions. (We say nothing here about surplus profits that result from *monopolies* in the customary sense of the term, whether they are artificial or natural.) >

β) But in addition to the mode of producing a *surplus profit* indicated under α) < a surplus profit can also arise if certain spheres of production opt out of the transformation of their commodity values into prices of production and therefore avoid *the reduction of their profits to the average profit*. In the chapter on *ground-rent* we shall have to consider the further formation [*Gestaltung*] of these two forms of surplus profit indicated under headings α) and β).

|196| (4) The Effects of a General Increase or Reduction (Fall) in Wages on the Prices of Production of the Different Commodities

Assume that the average composition of the social capital is $C^{80}\ V^{20}$, and the profit (P) is 20%. In this case, the rate of surplus-value = 100%. A general rise in wages – all other circumstances being supposed to remain the same[30] – is a

28 (See Malthus) [1836, pp. 77–8.]
29 ['With the necessary changes'. Translator]
30 [In English in the manuscript. Translator]

fall in the rate of surplus-value. For the average capital, *profit* and *surplus-value* coincide. Say that wages rises by 25%. The same mass of workers, whom it previously cost 20 to set in motion, now cost 25. We then have, instead of C^{80} V^{20} P^{20}, C^{80} V^{25} P^{15}. Since the labour set in motion by the variable capital produces a value sum of 40, the excess, P, = 15, if V rises from 20 to 25. A profit of 15 on 105 = $14\frac{6}{21}$% > since 15: 105 = $14\frac{6}{21}$: 100. < The new average rate of profit would therefore be $14\frac{6}{21}$%. The *price of production* of the commodities produced by the average capital would not have changed, since value coincides here with production price. The increase in wages would therefore involve a decline in profit, but no change in the value or the price of the commodity.

Previously, when the average rate of profit was 20%, the cost price of the commodities was K + 20, where K is a variable magnitude differing according to the value of the means of production that go into the commodities and according to the amount of depreciation that the fixed capital employed in their production surrenders to the product. Now the cost price is K + $14\frac{6}{21}$.

Let us first take a capital whose composition is lower than the original composition of the average social capital C^{80} V^{20} (which has now been changed into $C76\frac{4}{21}$ $V23\frac{17}{21}$), for example $C^{50}V^{20}$. If we assume for the sake of simplification that the entire fixed capital goes into the annual product as depreciation the production price of the annual product = 100 + 20 = 120. A wage rise of 25% means that > for *the same number of workers* or the same amount of labour set in motion < there is a rise in variable capital from 50 to $62\frac{1}{2}$. If the annual product were sold at the former cost price of 120, the relationship would be as follows: C50 $V62\frac{1}{2}$; C + V = $112\frac{1}{2}$; Profit = 20. Now, however, the new average profit is $14\frac{6}{21}$%. Since a capital of 100 gives $14\frac{6}{21}$%, a capital of $12\frac{1}{2}$ gives a profit of $\frac{75}{42}$ or $1\frac{33}{42}$. Thus if the average profit on 100 is $14\frac{6}{21}$, on $112\frac{1}{2}$ it is 14 + $\frac{6}{21}$ + 1 + $\frac{33}{42}$ = 15 + $\frac{12}{42}$ + $\frac{33}{42}$ = 15 + $\frac{45}{42}$ = 16 + $\frac{3}{42}$. Thus it is 16 + $\frac{3}{42}$%. The production price of the same quantity of commodities (all other circumstances being supposed unchanged) is therefore $112\frac{1}{2}$ (K) + $16\frac{3}{42}$ = 128 + $\frac{21}{42}$ + $\frac{3}{42}$ = 128 + $\frac{24}{42}$ = 128 + $\frac{4}{7}$. As a result of the wage rise of 25% the price of production of the same quantity of the same commodity has risen from 120 to $128\frac{4}{7}$. > That is the same as if it had risen from 100 to $107\frac{1}{21}$, i.e., by $7\frac{1}{21}$, by over $7\frac{1}{21}$%.

|197| < Let us now, conversely, take a sphere of production with a higher composition than the average capital, e.g., C^{92} V^{8}. The average profit, on our original assumption, is 20, and if we again assume > in order to simplify the case < that the entire fixed capital > (hence the circulating + the fixed portion of the constant capital) < goes into the annual product, the price of production of the commodity is also 120.

As a result of the rise in wages by 25%, the variable capital grows from 8 to 10, i.e., by $\frac{1}{4}$ > although the number of workers is the same < and the amount of labour is the same > (assuming the length of the working day remains constant). < The outlay for the same quantity of commodities now amounts to 102 instead of 100.

The profit, however, has fallen from 20 to $14\frac{6}{21}$ or $14\frac{2}{7}$. But the ratio $100 : 14\frac{2}{7} = 2 : \frac{2}{7}$. Hence $100 : 14\frac{2}{7} = 102 : 14\frac{4}{7}$.

The profit that now accrues to 102 is therefore $14\frac{4}{7}$. And the total product is therefore sold at $102 + 14\frac{4}{7} = 116\frac{4}{7}$. The production price has thus fallen from 120 to $116\frac{4}{7}$, i.e., by $3\frac{3}{7}$. > And $120 : 116\frac{4}{7} = 100 : 97\frac{1}{7}$; this makes a fall of $3\frac{1}{7}$ on 100, hence a fall of $3\frac{1}{7}$% in the price of production as a result of a rise in wages of 25%.

If we call the cost price K in case I, before the increase in wages takes place, and we call the profit P, and then in case II we call the cost price K′, we have the following results:

I *Before* the increase in wages, the *price of production* = K + 20; *after* the increase in wages the price of production of the same quantity of commodities $= K + 10 + 20\ (5 + \frac{5}{7}) = (K + 10) + 14\frac{2}{7}$. Instead of K + 20, therefore, the price becomes $K + 24\frac{2}{7}$.

II *Before* the increase in wages, the *price of production* = K′ + 20; *after* the increase in wages it is $K' + 2 + (P - 5\frac{5}{7}) = (K' + 2) + 20 - 5 + \frac{5}{7} = (K' + 2) + 14\frac{2}{7} = K' + 16\frac{2}{7}$.

< The result of the wage rise of 25% is thus as follows:

(I) for *capital* of an average social composition the *commodity's price of production remains unchanged*;

(II) for capital of a *lower* composition the *price of production rises*, although not in the same ratio as the profit has fallen;

(III) for capital of a *higher* composition the *price of production falls*, though again not in the same ratio as the profit.

Since the production price of commodities produced by the average capital has remained the same, namely equal to the value of the product, the *sum* of production prices for the products of all capitals has also remained the same, namely equal to the sum of values produced by the total capital, since the rises on the one hand and the falls on the other balance out at the level of the socially average capital, viewed from the angle of the entire capital of the society.

|198| If the production price for commodities in example I rises, while it falls in example II, this *opposite* effect which is produced by the fall in the rate of surplus-value or the general rise in wages already shows that there can be no corresponding *compensation in prices* for the rise in wages, since in example II the fall in the price of production can in no way compensate the capitalists for the fall in their profit, while in example I the rise in *price* still does not prevent

a fall in profit. In each case, rather, both where the price rises and where it falls, profit is the same as for the average capital, whose price remains *unchanged.* It is the same for both I and II, a fall in the average profit of a quarter, a fall of 25%. It follows from this that if the price did not rise in example I and fall in example II, I would be sold at *less than* the new, lower, average profit, and II at *more than* this. It is of itself clear that according to whether $\frac{1}{2}$, $\frac{1}{4}$, $\frac{1}{5}$, $\frac{1}{10}$, $1/n$ or $1/xn$ out of every 100 units of capital are laid out on labour > (consist of variable capital) < a rise in wages will necessarily have a very different effect on a capitalist who lays out a tenth of his capital on *wages* from its effect on one who lays out a half. The rise in the price of production on the one hand and its fall on the other, according to whether the capital involved has a *lower* or *higher* composition than the social average, is only *accomplished* by the process of *equalisation* towards the new, lower, *average profit.* > It is clear that when values are transformed into prices of production (and a general rate of profit and an average profit corresponding to this process becomes established) they become *prices of production* (namely K + P, where K is a variable and P is a given magnitude which equals the average profit determined by the general rate of profit) by *falling* in the case of capitals of *lower* composition, i.e., those which employ more than the average percentage of variable capital, while in the case of capitals of *higher* composition they become prices of production by *rising*. *Conversely*, once *prices of production* are established and become a basic condition of the movement, a fall in average profit *raises* the *prices of production* of the commodities produced by capitals of lower composition, and lowers the prices of commodities produced by capitals of *higher* composition.

< How then would the prices of production of commodities produced by capitals that diverge in contrary directions from the socially average composition be affected by a *general fall in wages*, with a corresponding *general rise in the rate of profit*, and hence in *average profits*?

We have simply to turn the above example round to obtain the result (something which Ricardo does not investigate). >

|199| It is better to abandon these lousy little digits and make a fresh start with a new example.

< I. *Average capital* C^{80} V^{20} = 100; rate of profit 20%; rate of surplus-value 100%. If wages fall by a quarter, the same constant capital will be set in motion by V^{15} instead of by V^{20}. We then have C^{80} V^{15}. A profit of 25 on a total capital of 95 becomes a profit of $26\frac{6}{19}$ on 100 and the new composition of 100 is $C84\frac{4}{19}$ $V15\frac{15}{19}$ Profit $26\frac{6}{19}$. The amount of profit is 25 (since the quantity of labour produced by V remains unchanged, and is simply distributed differently between capitalist and worker). The price of production *created* by the total capital of 95 = 120, exactly the same as the price created previously by the *total*

capital of 100. But the surplus-value has risen from 20 to 25, and if the rate of surplus-value was 100% previously, it is now *$166\frac{2}{3}$ %* (it has risen by $1\frac{2}{3}$). The rate of profit on 95 is now 25, hence the rate of profit on 100 is $26\frac{6}{19}$. > (Here the constant capital increases because a *greater* mass of the means of production is employed with an amount of variable capital which is smaller in terms of its value.)

< II. *Below average composition. Originally C^{50} V^{50}*. Becomes C^{50} $V^{37\frac{1}{2}}$. > The *production price of the same* quantity of commodities falls from 120 to $110\frac{10}{19}$. < Since wages fall by a quarter, or 25%, V falls by $\frac{50}{4}$ = $12\frac{1}{2}$, hence to *$37\frac{1}{2}$*. We therefore get $37\frac{1}{2}$ for V and 50 for C. If we apply to this the new rate of profit of $26\frac{6}{19}$%, we get 100: $26\frac{6}{19}$ = $87\frac{1}{2}$: $23\frac{1}{38}$. > Hence because all other circumstances are the same, and on the assumption made previously, < the same mass of commodities that previously cost 120 now costs $87\frac{1}{2}$ + $23\frac{1}{38}$ = $110\frac{10}{19}$; a fall in price of almost 10.

III. *Higher composition*. Originally C^{92} V^{8}. Becomes C^{94} V^{6}. > The *production price of the same quantity of commodities* rises by $3\frac{5}{19}$, from 120 to $123\frac{5}{19}$, < V falls as a result of the fall in wages from 8 to 6, namely by 2 or a quarter = 25%. > If 100 gave a profit of $26\frac{6}{19}$%, 96, which is the total capital now before us, gives $25\frac{5}{19}$. Hence the *same quantity of commodities* which previously had a production price of *120* has now, *after* the fall in wages, a price of 98 (K′) + $25\frac{5}{19}$ (P) = $123\frac{5}{19}$.

< We can thus see how it is only necessary to pursue the same chain of reasoning as before in the reverse direction, *mutatis mutandis*, in order to demonstrate that a general fall in wages = a general rise in surplus-value, in the rate of surplus-value, and, all other things being equal, the rate of profit (even if in a different proportion). It results in a *fall in production prices* for the commodity products of capitals of *lower than average* composition and a *rise in production prices* for the commodity products of capitals of *higher than average* composition. This is exactly the *opposite result* to the one we found in examining a general rise in wages.[31]

---

31 It is extremely curious that Ricardo (whose method of development is naturally very different from the one in the above text, as he did not understand the adjustment of values to production prices) did not once consider this latter possibility, only examining the first case, namely a *rise in wages* and the influence of this on the production prices of commodities. [Ricardo 1821, pp. 36–41]. And the *servum pecus imitatorum* [slavish breed of imitators] did not even succeed in making this quite self-evident and indeed *tautological* practical application.

|200| In both cases, that of a rise in wages and that of a fall, the working day is assumed to remain the same, and so are the prices of all *other commodities*. (A fall in wages is thus only possible here either if wages stood *above* the *minimum* or if they are now to be forced down *below the minimum*.) How the matter is affected if the rise or fall in wages derives from a change in the *values* and *hence* in the *production prices* of the commodities that customarily go into the workers' consumption will in part be further investigated below, in the section on *ground-rent*. The following points, however, have to be made here once and for all:

If the rise or fall in wages results from a change in the value of the necessary means of subsistence, the only modification of the process analysed above occurs when the commodities whose changes in price serve to increase or lessen the variable capital also enter as *constituent elements* into the constant capital and hence do not simply affect wages. But in so far as they do only affect wages, the above argument contains all that needs to be said.

In dealing with the question treated in this section, we have assumed that the establishment of a general rate of profit, an average profit, and consequently the transformation of values into prices of production is a given fact. All that has been asked is how a general rise or fall in wages affects the *production prices of commodities*, prices we have assumed as given. This is a very secondary question compared with the important themes dealt with in this chapter. Yet it is the only question Ricardo deals with which is relevant here, and as we shall see in a later chapter, he deals with it only in a one-sided and inadequate manner.

|201| (5) The Capitalist's Grounds for Compensation

It has been said that competition equalises profit rates between the different spheres of production to produce an average rate of profit, and that this is precisely the way in which the values of products from these various spheres are transformed into prices of production. This happens, indeed, by the continuous transfer [of capital] from one sphere into the other.[32] Something that must be considered here, however, is the *succession* of years of prosperity and dullness in a given branch of industry, during certain epochs, and the oscillations of profit that these involve. This continuous emigration and immigration

32 [Marx wrote the next two sentences, and the subsequent paragraph, in English. Translator]

of capital from, and to, the different spheres of production, is constantly acting, and constantly trying, to reduce profits to the common and general level by an alternation of ups and downs equalising each other within a certain time.

This movement of capitals is always caused – proximately – by the stand of the market prices which swell the profits in one sphere *over*, and [cause them to] sink in another *under*, the common level of profits, or under the average profit. (Apart from the mercantile capital, with which we have in fact nothing to do *as yet*, and which, as you may see in the general sudden speculations in favourite articles, allows a very [rapid][33] supply, and very sudden withdrawal of capital from a given business – all other investments of capital, whether in manufacture, or agriculture, or mines, etc., offer – although in very different degrees – difficulties to the sudden transfer, in whatever direction that transfer may take place – of capital, because of the fixed capital, etc. Besides, experience very soon shows that if the cotton industry for instance offers very high profits at one time, it offers very small ones at another, and that, taking a cycle of years, the average profits are very nearly approaching those made in other industries. Well, the capitalists learn by experience to take the average view of the different branches of industry.)

What competition does *not* show, however, is the determination of values that governs the movement of production; it does not show the values behind the price of production. It exhibits rather the following phenomena: α) *firstly*, average profits that are independent of the organic composition of the capitals in the various spheres of production, i.e., independent of the mass of *living labour appropriated in a given sphere of exploitation*; β) *secondly*, rises and falls in the *prices of production* as a result of changes in the wage level – a phenomenon which *prima facie* completely contradicts the *value relationship* of the commodities; γ) *thirdly*, oscillations in market prices that reduce the average market price of a commodity over a given period of time, not to its *market value*, but rather to a *market price of production* that diverges from this market value and is something very different. All these phenomena, α), β), γ), *seem* [*scheinen*] to contradict both the *value relation* determined by labour-time, and the nature of surplus-value as consisting of unpaid or *surplus labour*. In competition, therefore, everything *appears* [*erscheint*] upside down. The finished configuration of economic relations, as these are visible on the surface, in their actual existence, and therefore also in the notions [*Vorstellungen*] which the bearers and agents of these relations have about them, is very different from

33 [Marx wrote 'soon'. Translator]

their *inner configuration*, which is *essential* but concealed, and is their invisible core, and from the *concept* [*Begriff*] corresponding to it. It is in fact the very reverse of this. As soon as capitalist production has reached a certain level of development, the equalisation between the various rates of profit in individual spheres which produces the general rate of profit does not just take place through the interplay of attraction and repulsion in which market prices attract or repel investment capital. Once *average prices* and the production prices corresponding to them have been established for a certain length of time, it enters the *consciousness* of the various individual capitalists that *certain differences* are balanced out in this equalisation, and so they take these into account in their *calculations amongst themselves*. These differences are actively present in the capitalists' view of things, and are taken into account by them as *grounds for compensation*.

The basic notion in this connection is that of average profit itself, the idea that capitals of equal size must yield *equal profits* in the same period of time. This is based in turn on the idea that capital in each sphere of production has to participate *according to its size in the total surplus-value extorted from the workers by the total social capital*; or that *each particular capital* should be viewed simply as a fragment of the total capital, and each capitalist in fact as a shareholder in the total enterprise, partaking in the overall profit in proportion to the size of his share.

This notion is then the basis of the *capitalists' calculations*, for example that a capital which has a more infrequent turnover, either because the commodity in question remains in the production process for a longer period or because it has to be sold on more distant markets, still, by raising its prices, charges the profit it would otherwise lose and in this way compensates itself. Another example is how capital investments that are exposed to greater risk, as in shipping, for instance, receive indemnification through increased prices. (In actual fact, once capitalist production is fully developed, and with it the *insurance system*, the risk is the same for all spheres of production.[34] But those more endangered then pay higher insurance premiums.) In practice this always boils down to the situation that any circumstance that makes one capital investment less profitable and another one more so (and all these investments are supposed to be equally necessary, if kept within certain limits)[35] is invariably taken into account as a valid *motive for compensation*, without there being any need for the constant repetition of the activities of competition in order to demonstrate

34 See Corbet [1841, pp. 100–1.]

35 [This parenthesis is in English in the original. Translator]

the justification for including such motives or factors in the calculations. The capitalist simply forgets – or rather he no longer sees, since competition does not *show* this to him – that all these grounds for compensation that make themselves felt in the *reciprocal calculation of commodity prices* by capitalists in different branches of production are simply related to the fact that they all have an equal claim on the *common booty*, the total surplus-value, in proportion to their capital. It *appears* [*scheint*] to them, rather, that the profit which they pocket is *something different* from the *surplus-value* they extort; that the *grounds for compensation* do not simply equalise their participation in the total surplus-value, but that they actually *create profit*, since profit seems to derive simply from the *addition to the cost price of the commodity* made with one justification or another. >

|202a| Supplement on Prices of Production

< The price of production of a commodity can vary for only two reasons:

Firstly: a change in the rate of profit, namely the average rate of profit. This is possible only if the *average rate of surplus-value* itself alters, or the average *ratio of this rate* to the capital advanced.

In so far as the *rate of surplus-value* does not rest on the depression of wages *below* their > minimum < or a rise *above* it – and movements of this kind are never more than oscillations – it can occur only because the value of labour-capacity has either fallen or risen, > the former when the reproduction of the means of subsistence has become cheaper, the latter when it has become dearer. < Both of these are impossible without a change in the productivity of that labour which produces the means of subsistence, i.e., without a change in the *value* of the commodities consumed by the worker.

Alternatively there may be a change in the *ratio* between > this average rate of surplus-value and the constant capital of the society. < Since this change does not arise from the rate of surplus-value, it must proceed from a change in the constant capital. The mass of this, in its technological [*technologisch*] aspect, is increased or reduced in proportion to the variable capital, and the sum of its value then rises or falls with the growth or decline in the mass itself; > in this case, therefore, a change takes place in the mode of production. < If the same amount of labour is required to set more constant capital in motion, it has become more productive, and vice versa. Thus a change has taken place in the productivity of labour and a change must have occurred in the value of certain commodities. Hence if the *production price* of a *commodity changes as a result of a change in the general rate of profit, its own value* may well remain unaffected. However, there must have been a *change in its value relative to other commodities*.

Secondly: the general rate of profit remains unaltered. In this case the production price of a commodity can change only because *its own value* has altered; because less or more labour is required for it to be reproduced, whether because of a change in the productivity of the labour that produces the commodity in its final form > (if less labour is needed to produce, e.g., 1 lb. of yarn, less necessary labour is needed, hence less wages and costs are reduced accordingly) < or in that of the labour producing those commodities that go towards producing it.

Price of production, as we have already shown, is k + p′ > (p′ being the average percentage of profit, and k being an indeterminate magnitude, being different in the different spheres of production, and always equal to the value of the commodities consumed in the production of the commodities and the wages paid for their production.) < It is clear that this price of production can remain *the same*, however much the value of the commodities may change. > However much the value of k changes, p′ remains the same rate. If k = 100, and p′ = 10 %, k + p′ = 110 = k + ⅒ k. If the value of k falls to 50, the price of production = k + p′ = k + ⅒ k = 55.

< All changes in the price of production of a commodity can ultimately be reduced to a change in value, but not all changes in the value of a commodity need find expression in a change in the price of production, since this is not determined simply by the value of the particular commodity in question, but rather by the value of all commodities. A change in commodity A, therefore, may be balanced by an opposite change in commodity B, so that the general proportion remains the same. >

|202b| Supplement concerning the Transition from Chapter One to Chapter Two of this Book[36]

We have considered the subject under three aspects: (1) *a change in the mode of production* and as a result in the composition of capital; (2) no change in the mode of production, a change in the *value relation* between constant and variable capital, involving no change in the relative amounts of these elements of capital but a *change in the value* of the commodities which enter into the formation of the constant and variable capital; and (3) a change in the mode of production and in the value of the elements of constant and variable capital, or of one or other of them, etc.

36 [This important Supplement was not included in Engels's Volume III; see pp. 16–18 of the Introduction for a discussion of this Supplement. Editor]

What was considered here as a *variation* within the organic composition of *a single* capital can equally appear (make itself felt) as a *difference* between the organic compositions of *the capitals of different spheres of production*.

Firstly: instead of a *variation* in the organic composition of *one and the same* capital, a *difference* in the organic composition of *different capitals*.

Secondly: an alteration in the organic composition of capital as a result of a *change in the value* of the two parts of *the same* capital – *a difference in the value of the machinery, raw material, etc., applied* on behalf of capitals in different trades. This is not true for variable capital, since we assume *an equal* wage in the *different* trades. The difference in the *value* of different days of labour in different trades has nothing to do with the matter in hand. If the labour of a goldsmith is dearer than that of a labourer, the surplus time of the goldsmith is of greater value than that of the peasant in the same proportion.

|*152*| < ***The Production Price of Commodities of Average Composition***

We have already seen that the *divergence of prices of production from values* arises for the following reasons:

(1) because the *average profit* is added to the *cost price* of a commodity, rather than the *surplus-value* contained in it;

(2) because the price of production of a commodity that diverges in this way from its value enters as an element into the cost price of other commodities, which means that a divergence from the *value* of the means of production consumed in a commodity may already be contained in the *cost price*, quite apart from the divergence that may arise from the difference between average profit and surplus-value.

It is therefore possible for the *cost price* to diverge from the *value* of this component of the production price of *commodities* that are produced by capitals of average composition. Let us assume that the average composition is 80c and 20v. It is possible now that, for the actual individual capitals that are composed in this way, the 80c may be greater or less than the value of c, the constant capital, since this c is composed of commodities whose *prices of production* are different from their *values*. The 20v can similarly diverge from its value, if commodities whose prices of production differ from their values > enter into the wage of labour. < The workers must work for a greater or lesser amount of time in order to buy back these commodities (to replace them) and must therefore perform more or less necessary labour than would be needed if the prices of production of their necessary means of subsistence did coincide with their values.

Yet this possibility in no way affects the correctness of the principles put forward for commodities of average composition. The quantity of profit that falls to the share of these commodities is equal to the quantity of surplus-value contained in them. With regard to a capital of 80c and 20v the important thing as far as the determination of surplus-value is concerned is not whether these figures are the expression of actual values, but rather what their mutual relationship is; i.e., that v is one-fifth of the total capital and c is four-fifths. As soon as this is the case, as assumed above, the surplus-value v produces is equal to the average profit. On the other hand, because it is equal to the average profit, the price of production = cost price + profit = k + p = k + s, which is equal in practice to the commodity's value. In other words, an increase or decrease in wages in this case leaves k + p unaffected, just as it would leave the commodity's value unaffected, and simply brings about a corresponding converse movement, a decrease or increase, on the side of the profit rate. If an increase or decrease in wages did affect the price of the commodity in this case, the profit rate in these spheres of average composition would come to stand below or above its level in other spheres. It is only in so far as the price remains *unaltered* that the spheres of average composition maintain the same level of profit as the others. It is therefore the same in practice as if the products of these spheres were sold at their *actual values*. For if commodities are sold at their actual values, it is clear that, *all other circumstances remaining the same*, a rise or fall in wages calls forth a corresponding rise or fall in *profit* but no change in the commodity's value, and that *under no circumstances* can a rise or fall in wages ever affect the *value* of the commodity, but only the *size of the surplus-value*. >

|203| < CHAPTER THREE

The Law of the Tendential Fall in the General Rate of Profit > with the Advance of Capitalist Production

< Once wages are given, a variable capital, of £100, for example, represents a definite number of workers set in motion; it is an index of this number. Say that £100 provides the wages of 100 workers for one week. If these 100 workers perform as much necessary labour as surplus labour, they work as much time for themselves every day for the reproduction of their wages as they do for the capitalist, i.e., for the production of surplus-value. Their total product would then be equal to £200 and the surplus-value they produced would amount to £100. The rate of surplus-value, s/v, would then be 100/100 = 100 percent. Yet, as we have seen, the *rate of surplus-value* > and thereby also the level of exploitation of labour (which could however vary in line with changes in the length of the normal working day) < would be expressed in very *different rates of profit*, according to differences in the scale of the constant capital c and hence the total capital C, since the rate of profit = s/C.

£ £

$$\text{If } c = 50 \text{ and } v = 100,\ p' = \frac{100}{150} = 66\tfrac{2}{3} \text{ percent}$$

$$\text{If } c = 100 \text{ and } v = 100,\ p' = \frac{100}{200} = 50 \text{ percent}$$

$$\text{If } c = 200 \text{ and } v = 100,\ p' = \frac{100}{300} = 33\tfrac{1}{3} \text{ percent}$$

$$\text{If } c = 300 \text{ and } v = 100,\ p' = \frac{100}{400} = 25 \text{ percent}$$

$$\text{If } c = 400 \text{ and } v = 100,\ p' = \frac{100}{500} = 20 \text{ percent}$$

$$\text{If } c = 500 \text{ and } v = 100,\ p' = \frac{100}{600} = 16\tfrac{2}{3} \text{ percent}$$

And so on.

The same rate of surplus-value, therefore, and an unchanged level of exploitation of labour, would be expressed in a *falling rate of profit*, as the value of the constant capital, and hence of the *total capital* grows along with the increase in the constant capital's material volume > (if not to the same extent to which it represents a greater mass of the means of labour).

|204| < If we further assume now that this gradual change in the composition of capital does not just characterise certain individual spheres of production, but points to changes in the composition of the total capital belonging to a given society, hence involves changes *in the average organic composition* of the social capital, its necessary result would be a gradual fall in the *general rate of profit*, assuming that the rate of surplus-value, or the level of exploitation of labour by capital, remains the same. Moreover, it has been shown to be a law of the capitalist mode of production that its development does in fact involve a *relative decline in the relation of variable capital to constant*, and hence also *to the total capital set in motion*. This means, in other words, that the same *number of workers* (the same labour-power) is set in motion by a *capital of the same amount of value*, by a variable capital of a given magnitude of value, as a result of the specific methods of production that develop within the capitalist mode of production, and that a constantly growing mass of the means of labour, machinery and fixed capital of all kinds, and raw and ancillary materials, is set in motion or productively consumed, worked up, in the same period of time, hence also a constant capital of an ever-growing extent is also set in motion. This progressive relative reduction of the variable capital in proportion to the constant capital, and hence in proportion to the total capital, is identical with a progressively *higher* organic composition of the social capital, a higher average organic composition of capital. It is just another expression for the progressive development of the *social productivity of labour*, which is shown by the way that the growing use of machinery and fixed capital generally enables *more raw and ancillary materials* to be transformed into products *in the same time*, i.e., with less labour. There corresponds to this *growing volume of constant capital* – although this expresses only at a certain remove the growth in the actual mass of use-values which the constant capital consists of in material terms – a continual *cheapening of the product*. Each individual product, taken by itself, contains a smaller sum of labour than at a lower stage of development of production, where the capital laid out on labour stands in a far higher ratio to that laid out on the means of labour. The hypothetical series we constructed at the opening of this chapter therefore expresses the actual tendency of capitalist production. With the progressive decline in the variable capital in relation to the constant capital, this tendency leads to a rising *organic composition* of the total capital, and the direct result of this is that the rate of surplus-value, with the level of exploitation of labour remaining the same or even rising, is expressed in a *constantly falling general rate of profit*. (We shall show later on why this fall does not present itself in such an absolute form, but rather more in a *tendency* to a progressive fall.) The progressive tendency for the *general rate of profit to fall* is thus simply the expression, peculiar to the capitalist

mode of production, of the progressive development of the *social productivity of labour*, > given a constant level of exploitation of labour or even a rising level of exploitation (whether this is more intensive or more extensive). < This does not mean that the rate of profit may not fall temporarily for other reasons as well, |205| but it does prove that it is a self-evident necessity, deriving from the nature [*Wesen*] of the capitalist mode of production itself, that as it advances the general rate of surplus-value must be expressed in a *falling general rate of profit*. Since the mass of living labour applied continuously declines in relation to the mass of the objectified labour that it sets in motion, i.e., the productively consumed means of labour, the part of this living labour that is unpaid and expressed in surplus-value must always stand in an ever-decreasing ratio to the value of the total capital applied. But this ratio between the surplus-value and the total capital applied constitutes the *rate of profit*, which must as a result constantly be in decline.

Simple as this law appears from the above analysis, not one of the previous writers on political economy has succeeded in discovering it, as we shall see later on. These economists perceived the phenomenon, but tortured themselves with their contradictory attempts to explain it. And given the great importance that this law has for capitalist production, one might well say that it forms the mystery around the solution of which the whole of political economy since Adam Smith revolves and that the difference between the various schools since Adam Smith consists in the different attempts made to solve it. If we consider, on the other hand, how previous political economy has fumbled around with the distinction between constant and variable capital, but has never managed to formulate this in any definite way; how it has never presented surplus-value as something separate from profit, nor profit in general, in its pure form, as distinct from the various constituents of profit which have attained an autonomous position towards each other (such as industrial profit, commercial profit, interest, ground-rent); how it has essentially never analysed the differences in the organic composition of capital, and hence has not analysed the formation of the general law of profit either – then it ceases to be a puzzle that political economy has failed to find this puzzle's solution.

We are deliberately putting forward this law before depicting the decomposition of profit into various categories which have become mutually autonomous. This independence of this presentation from the division of profit into various portions, which accrue to different categories of person, shows from the outset how the law in its generality [*Allgemeinheit*] is independent of that division and of the mutual relationships of the categories of profit deriving from it. Profit, as we speak of it here, is simply another *name* for surplus-value itself, only now depicted in relation to the total capital, instead of to the variable capital from which it derives. The fall in the rate of profit thus expresses the falling ratio between *surplus-value itself* and the total capital advanced; it is therefore independent of any *distribution of this surplus-value* we may care to make among the various categories.

We have seen that at one stage of capitalist development, when the constant capital = 50, the variable capital = 100 and the surplus-value is 100, a rate of surplus-value of 100 percent is expressed in a rate of profit of 66⅔ percent, while at a higher stage of development, where the constant capital = 400, the same rate of surplus-value is expressed in a rate of profit of 20 percent. What applies to different successive stages of development in *a single* country applies also to *several different* countries that find themselves in differing stages of development *at the same time*. In the undeveloped country, where the composition of capital is as first mentioned, the general rate of profit would be 66⅔ percent, while in the country on the second, much higher level of development it would be 20 percent. (The distinction between the two national rates of profit |206| could disappear, or even be reversed, if for example in the less developed country labour was less productive, and accordingly a greater quantity of labour was expressed in a smaller quantity of the same use-value, hence a greater exchange-value was represented in less use-value, so that > owing to the lower productivity of labour < the worker would have to spend a greater portion of his time in reproducing his own means of subsistence or their value, leaving a smaller portion for producing surplus-value, thus providing less surplus labour. If the worker in the less advanced country, instead of working half the day for the capitalist as in the advanced countries, worked for only a third of the day for the capitalist, then, under the conditions indicated above, the same labour-power would be paid 133⅓ and would provide a surplus of only 66⅔. To the variable capital of 133⅓ there would correspond a constant capital of 50. The total capital advanced would therefore be 183⅓ and the surplus-value would be 66⅔. This would give a rate of profit of 66⅔ divided by 183⅓, in other words a little more than 36 percent.)

Since we have not so far investigated the various components into which profit is divided, so that these do not yet exist for us, the following point is anticipated here simply to avoid any misunderstandings. When a comparison is made between countries at different levels of development, and particularly between countries of developed capitalist production and those where labour is not yet really[1] [*real*] subsumed [*subsumiert*] under capital, although

1 [Marx may have meant to write 'formally' here, which would fit with his description of exactly the same situation in the 1861–63 manuscripts (MEGA (2) II/3.6, p. 2155.1–41; MECW 34, 1994, p. 118.) Translator]

the worker is in reality exploited by the capitalist (in India, for example, where the ryot operates as an independent peasant farmer, and his production is therefore in reality *not* subsumed under capital, although the money-lender may well extort from him in the form of interest not only his entire surplus labour, but even – to put it in capitalist terms – a part of his wages), it would be quite wrong to seek to measure differences in national rates of profit by differences in national rates of interest. Interest here includes both the entire profit and more than the profit, whereas in countries where capitalist production is developed it expresses an aliquot part of the total surplus-value. Moreover, in the former case the rate of interest is predominantly determined by factors such as the level of advances by money-lenders to the big landowners who are the recipients of ground-rent, which have nothing at all to do with profit but rather express the extent to which the money-lender himself appropriates the ground-rent.

In countries where capitalist production stands at different levels of development and between which the organic composition of capital consequently varies, the rate of surplus-value (this one factor which determines the rate of profit) may be higher in a country where the normal working day is shorter than in one where it is longer (greater).

Firstly, if the English working day of 10 hours is equal to an Austrian working day of 14 hours, on account of its higher intensity, 5 hours of surplus-value in England may represent a higher *value* on the world market than 7 hours in Austria, given the same division of the working day. *Secondly* a greater part of the working day may form surplus labour in England than in Austria.

The law of the *falling rate of profit*, as expressing the same or even a rising rate of surplus-value, means in other words: taking any particular quantity of average social capital, e.g., a capital of 100, an ever greater portion of this is represented by means of labour and an ever lesser portion by living labour. > The reason for this is that as the total amount of added living labour falls, the *unpaid* part falls, and < the *portion of value* in which it is expressed falls in relation to the value of the total capital advanced. Alternatively, an ever smaller part of the total capital laid out is converted into living labour, hence the total capital absorbs ever less surplus labour in relation to its size, even though the *ratio* between the *unpaid* and the *paid* part of the labour applied may at the same time be increasing. The relative decline in the variable capital and the increase in the constant capital, even while both portions grow in absolute terms, is simply another expression for the increased productivity of labour. For example, let a capital of 100 be laid out in ⅘ constant |207| and ⅕ (= 20) variable capital (= 20 workers). The rate of surplus-value is 100 percent, hence the workers work half the day for themselves and half the day for the capitalist.

In a less developed country $\frac{1}{5}$ (= 20) might be laid out in constant capital, and four times as many workers would be required in order to set in motion this four times smaller amount of constant capital. But these workers might need two-thirds of the working day for themselves and work only one-third of the day for the capitalist, instead of half the day. They produce, as before, a value of 120 (assuming a working day of the same length) (just as the 20 workers produced a value of 40). But they need two-thirds of this 120 for themselves and they leave only one-third for the capitalist. In this case the situation is as follows: 20c + 80v + 40s. And the rate of profit is therefore 40 percent. This rate is thus as large again as in the first case, even though the rate of surplus-value was 100 percent in the first case, and only 50 percent in the second. In the first case the equally large capital appropriates the surplus labour of only 20 workers, whereas in the second case it appropriates that of 80 workers. > Yet the level of exploitation of labour in the first case is much greater than in the second.

Expressed precisely, the composition of capital is 80c 20v in the first case and $15 + \frac{15}{19}$ c $84 + \frac{4}{19}$ v in the second. A surplus-value of 100 percent gives a profit of 20 percent in the first case, and a surplus-value of $33\frac{1}{3}$ percent gives ...

But here is a better example, without fractions: suppose we have 80c, 20v, 20s and 100 percent s′. The 20 here = 20 workers. Suppose now that 60 workers are needed to set in motion a c of 20. Their total product is 120, given the same working day as the 20 had. But they work only one-third of the time for their master, and two-thirds for themselves. Hence v is 80 and s is 40. The composition of the capital will be 20c + 80v, with s = 40, and s′ = 50 percent. In the first case, p′ = 20 percent, in the second case p′ = 40 percent. The rate of profit is therefore twice as high in the second case as in the first, although in the first case the rate of surplus-value was twice as high as in the second. But the mass of surplus-value is greater where one-third of the day of 60 workers is appropriated by a capital of the same size as the capital which in the other case swallowed up half the day of 20 workers. Assume that the working day is 12 hours long. A half of this is 6 hours, and a third is 4 hours. 20 × 6 = 120 hours, but 60 × 4 = 240, exactly twice as much. Hence although the level of exploitation of labour is much greater in case I than in case II, the rate of profit is twice as high in case II as in case I. The level of exploitation in case I is 100 percent, while in case II it is 50 percent.

< The law of a progressive falling ratio of the rate of profit, or of the mass of surplus labour appropriated *relatively* to the mass of materialised labour put into movement by it, in no way excludes[2] an increase in the absolute

2 [These three lines were written in English by Marx. Translator]

mass of the labour set in motion and exploited by the social capital, hence also in the *absolute mass* of the surplus labour appropriated by it; just as little does it exclude the capitals under the command of individual capitalists from commanding a growing mass of labour and hence of surplus labour, the latter indeed even if there is *no* increase in the number of workers under their command.

|208| If we take a *given* working population, of two million for example, and further assume that the length and intensity of the average working day is given, as well as wages, and hence also the relationship between necessary and surplus labour, the total labour of these two million workers always produces the *same* magnitude of value, and the same thing is true of their surplus labour, as expressed in surplus-value. But as the mass of constant (fixed and circulating) capital set in motion by this labour grows, there is a fall in the ratio between this magnitude and the value of the constant capital, which grows with its mass, even if not in the same proportion. This ratio falls, and with it the *rate of profit*, even though capital still commands the same mass of living labour as before and absorbs the same mass of surplus labour. The fall in the ratio is not the result of a fall in the mass of living labour but rather of an increase in the mass of already objectified labour that it sets in motion. The reduction is relative and not absolute, and it has in fact nothing at all to do with the *absolute magnitude* of the labour and surplus labour set in motion. The fall in the rate of profit does not arise from an *absolute* decline in the variable component of the total capital but simply from its *relative* decline in comparison with its constant component.

What holds when the amount of labour and surplus labour is at a constant level holds also when the *number of workers* is growing, and when, accordingly, under the given assumptions, the mass of labour under capital's command is growing in general, and its unpaid portion, surplus labour, is growing in particular. If the working population rises from 2 to 3 millions and the amount of variable capital laid out on wages similarly becomes 3 million instead of 2, while the constant capital rises from 4 million to 15 million, then under the given assumptions (working day and rate of surplus-value constant) the mass of surplus labour and surplus-value still rises by a half, by 50 percent, from 2 to 3 million > and the *mass of surplus labour*, the *mass of surplus-value*, grows in the same proportion. < It is none the less the case, however, that despite this growth of 50 percent in the *absolute* mass of surplus labour and hence surplus-value, the ratio of > this increased mass of (1) < variable capital to constant > and (2) surplus-value to the total capital < would fall, > the first from 2: 4 or 1: 2 to 3: 15 or 1: 5 and the second, if the surplus labour is 100 percent, from 2: 6 to 3: 18. In spite of this falling ratio between variable and constant capital, and between surplus-value and the value of the total capital advanced, the *absolute mass* of the surplus-value absorbed by the total social capital would have grown by 50 percent alongside the growth in the working population. The *profit* (to be distinguished from the rate of profit), calculated on the social capital, is however only another category for the surplus-value, and the *mass of profit*, its *absolute magnitude*, is therefore, looked at from the angle of society, equal to the *absolute magnitude of the surplus-value*. < The absolute magnitude of the profit or the absolute mass of profit would therefore have risen by 50 percent, despite the enormous decline in the ratio between this profit and the total capital advanced, i.e., despite the enormous decline in the *general rate of profit*. The *number of workers* employed by capital, |209| i.e., the *absolute mass* of labour set in motion by it, hence the *absolute mass* of the *surplus labour* absorbed, appropriated by it, hence the mass of surplus-value it produces, hence the *absolute magnitude* or *mass of the profit produced by it*, **can** therefore grow, and *progressively so*, despite the *progressive fall in the rate of profit*. This not only *can* but *must* be the case – discounting temporary fluctuations – on the basis of the capitalist mode of production.

The capitalist *production process* is essentially, and at the same time, *a process of accumulation*. We have shown how, with the progress of capitalist production, the *value* that must simply be produced and maintained rises and grows, even if the labour-power applied remains constant. But as the social productivity of labour develops, so the *mass of use-values produced* grows still more, and the *means of production* form a portion of these. The additional labour, moreover, which has to be appropriated in order for this additional wealth to be transformed back into capital, does not depend on the value but on the *mass of these means of production* (including means of subsistence), since the worker is not concerned in the actual [*wirklich*] labour process with the *value* of the means of production but with their *use-value*. Accumulation itself, however, and the concentration of capital it involves, is simply a material means for *increasing*, for *heightening*, *productivity*. And this growth in the means of production entails a growth in the working population, the creation of a surplus population of workers that corresponds to the surplus capital, and indeed constantly exceeds its usual requirements. A momentary excess of surplus capital over the working population it commands has a double effect. On the one hand the increase of wages will attenuate the destructive influences that decimate the offspring of the workers, and provide a stimulus to marriages, while on the other hand by using methods that create relative surplus-value it creates an artificial redundancy of population, which is in turn the hotbed for an actual increase in the population, as misery creates population within capitalist production.[3] It thus follows from the very nature of the capitalist accumulation process – which is one aspect of the capitalist process of production – that the increased mass of means of production designed to be turned into capital finds a correspondingly increased and even excessive working population ready for exploitation. As the processes of production and accumulation advance, therefore, the mass of *surplus labour* that can be and is appropriated *must* grow, and with it too the *absolute mass of profit* appropriated by the social capital. But the same laws of accumulation and production mean that *the value of the constant capital* increases *along with its mass*, and progressively more quickly than that of the *variable* portion of capital which is converted into, exchanged for, living labour. The same laws, therefore, produce both a *growing absolute mass of profit*, which the social capital appropriates, and a *falling rate of profit*.

We entirely leave aside here the fact that with the progress of capitalist production and the corresponding development of the productivity of social labour and the *proliferation of branches of production* and hence of products, the same *amount of value* represents a progressively rising mass of use-values and satisfactions.

|210| The course of the development of capitalist production and accumulation requires increasingly large-scale labour processes. Hence the growing concentration of capitals (accompanied at the same time, though in lesser degree, by a *growth in the number* of capitalists, > in other words an increase in these *points of concentration*) < is both one of its material conditions and one of the results it itself produces. The progressive expropriation of the more or less immediate producers goes hand in hand with this, in a relationship of reciprocity. Accordingly it is a matter of course for the individual capitalists, since they have command over increasingly large armies of workers (no matter how much the variable capital > the capital laid out in wages < may fall in relation to the constant capital > the capital laid out in the means of labour) < that *the mass of surplus-value they themselves appropriate* and hence the *mass of profit* they appropriate grows along with and despite the fall in the *rate of profit*. The reasons > and agencies < that concentrate (centralise) massive armies of workers under the command of individual capitalists are the same reasons as also swell the amount of machinery, buildings and in general fixed capital applied, as well as the raw and ancillary materials, in a growing proportion as compared with the mass of living labour employed.

3 [The second half of this sentence was written in English by Marx. Translator]

The only other thing that needs to be mentioned here is that with a given working population that remains the same, if the rate of surplus-value grows, whether by prolongation or intensification of the working day or by reductions in the *value* of wages as a result of the developing productivity of labour, the absolute *mass of surplus-value* and hence the *absolute mass of profit* will grow, whatever be the relative diminution in the variable capital exchanged against labour in respect to the constant capital existing in the form of fixed and circulating capital, etc.[4]

The same development of the productivity of social labour, the same laws that are evident in the relative fall in variable capital as a proportion of the total capital, and the accelerated accumulation that follows from this – while on the other hand this accumulation also reacts back to become the starting-point for a further development of productivity and a further relative decline in the variable capital in relation to the constant capital – this same development is expressed, leaving aside temporary fluctuations, in the progressive increase in the total labour-power applied and in the progressive growth in the *absolute mass of surplus-value* and therefore in *the absolute mass of magnitude of profit.*

How, then, should we present this double-edged law of a *decline in the rate of profit* coupled with a simultaneous *increase in the absolute mass of profit* arising from the same causes? A law based on the fact that under the given conditions the mass of surplus labour and hence surplus-value that is appropriated grows, and that viewing the total capital as a whole, or the individual capital simply as a piece of the total capital, profit and surplus-value are identical in magnitude?

Let us take an aliquot part of the capital, say 100, as a basis for reckoning the profit rate. This 100 represents the average composition of the total capital, say 80c + 20v. We saw in Chapter Two of this book how the average rate of profit in the various branches of production is determined not by any one particular composition of capital but rather by its average social composition.

With the relative decline in the variable portion as compared with the constant, and hence also as a fraction of the total capital of 100, the *profit rate* falls if the level of exploitation of labour remains constant, or even if it rises: there is therefore a fall in the *relative magnitude of surplus-value*, i.e., in its *proportion to the value of the total capital of 100 that has been advanced.* But it is not only this relative |211| magnitude that falls. The *amount of surplus-value, or profit,* produced (appropriated) by the total capital of 100 also falls in absolute terms. At a rate of surplus-value of 100 percent, a capital of 60c + 40v produces a mass of surplus-value and hence profit of 40; as soon as the composition

4 [Marx wrote the words following the comma in English. Translator]

becomes 70c + 30v, > and assuming that the rate of surplus-value or the level of exploitation of labour remains the same, the mass of surplus-value and profit falls by 10, i.e., by a quarter of 40, i.e., by 25 percent, and with a composition of 80c + 20v it falls, as compared with the original capital, and under the same assumptions, from 40 to 20, i.e., by a half or 50 percent. < This fall bears on the *mass of surplus-value* and therefore of *profit*, and it follows from the fact that because the total capital of 100 sets in motion less living labour in general, it also sets in motion less surplus labour and hence produces less *surplus-value*, > which is nothing other than materialised surplus labour, < with the level of exploitation remaining the same. Whatever aliquot part of the social capital, i.e., whatever part of the capital of average social composition, we take as the *standard for measuring surplus-value*, – and this is the case with any calculation of profit > and this calculation corresponds to the nature of profit – hence assuming that a capital of average social composition is used as the measuring standard for the percentage calculation of profit – < a *relative fall in surplus-value* is always identical with an *absolute fall*. The rate of profit falls from 40 percent to 30 percent and then to 20 percent in the above cases because the mass of surplus-value and therefore profit produced by the capital in question falls from 40 to 30 to 20 in absolute terms. Since the size of the capital against which we measure the surplus-value is constant at its given level of 100, a fall in the ratio of the surplus-value to this magnitude, which itself remains constant, can only be another expression for the decline in the *absolute magnitude* of the surplus-value and the profit. This is in fact a tautology. But the reason for this decline, as has been shown, lies in the nature of the development of the capitalist process of production.

On the other hand, however, *the same* reasons that produce an absolute decline in surplus-value and hence profit on a capital of each hundred, thus also in the rate of profit reckoned as a percentage, bring about a growth in the *absolute* mass of the surplus labour, surplus-value and therefore profit produced and appropriated by the social capital > (or also by the individual capitalists). < How can this be explained, what is it dependent on, or what conditions are involved in this apparent contradiction?

Whereas any aliquot part of the social capital, say 100, and hence any capital of 100 of average social composition is a *constant magnitude* and with a decline in the variable part of this given magnitude the surplus-value and therefore the profit declines in absolute terms – or a decline in the rate of profit coincides here with a decline in the absolute amount of the profit, precisely because the capital against which this is measured is a constant magnitude – the *total magnitude* of the social capital, in contrast, just like that of the capital to be found in the hands of the individual capitalists, is a *variable* magnitude, which must *vary* in a given *inverse* proportion to the variable part of a slice of capital of a given magnitude, e.g., a capital of 100, if it is to fulfil the conditions we have presupposed.

When the percentage composition of the capital of 100 was 60c + 40v, the surplus-value or profit on it was 40 and therefore the rate of profit was 40 percent. Let us assume that at this level of composition the total capital was one million. The total surplus-value and therefore the total profit would then amount to 400,000. If the composition were later to become 80c + 20v, the surplus-value or profit on each 100 would be 20, if the level of exploitation remained the same. But the absolute mass of the surplus-value or profit grows, as we have shown, despite this decline in the rate of profit or decline in the production of surplus-value by each capital of 100, say by a tenth, from 400,000 to 440,000, for example > (the numerical relation is here completely unimportant and therefore arbitrarily chosen here). < This is possible only if the total capital that corresponds to this new composition has grown to 2,200,000. The |212| mass of the total capital set in motion has risen to 220 percent of its initial value, whereas the rate of profit has fallen by 50 percent. If the capital had simply doubled > it would have been impossible for it to have produced an absolutely greater mass of surplus-value and profit. For 2 million at 20 percent produces no more than 400,000, hence no more than 1 million produces at 40 percent. < Had it grown by less than this, it would have produced less surplus-value or profit than the capital of 1,000,000 did previously at 40 percent, although at its earlier composition it would only have had to grow from 1,000,000 to 1,100,000 for its surplus-value to grow from 400,000 to 440,000.

(Here we can see asserting itself the law we developed earlier, according to which the relative decline in the variable capital, and thus the development of the social productivity of labour, means that an *ever greater amount of total capital* is required in order to set the *same quantity of labour-power* in motion and to *absorb* the same amount of *surplus labour*. In the same proportion as capitalist production develops, therefore, there also develops the possibility of a relative *surplus working population*, not because the productivity of social labour declines, but rather because it increases, hence not from an absolute disproportion between labour and the means of subsistence, or the means of producing those means of subsistence, but rather from a disproportion arising from the capitalist exploitation of labour, the disproportion between the progressive growth of capital and the relative decline in its need for a growing population.)

A fall of 50 percent in the rate of profit is a fall of a half. If the mass of profit is to *remain the same*, therefore, a capital of 100 must double, since $100 \times 1 = 200 \times \frac{1}{2}$. The multiplier that indicates the growth in the total capital must be the same as the divisor that indicates the fall in the rate of profit. > If one factor is multiplied by the same number by which the other is divided, the product remains unchanged. < If the rate of profit falls from 40 percent to 20 percent, the total capital must rise in *the opposite direction* from 20 to 40, if the result is to remain the same. > The number 40 is divided by 2 and the capital is multiplied by 2. If the number falls from 40 to 30 the capital must grow in an inverse proportion from 30 to 40, i.e., by one-third, in this case from 1 million to 1,333,333$\frac{1}{3}$. < If the profit rate had fallen from 40 to 8, the capital would have to grow in the ratio 8: 40, i.e., by five times. A capital of 1,000,000 at 40 percent produces 400,000, and a capital of 5,000,000 at 8 percent also produces 400,000. This is necessary if the product (the resultant) is to remain *the same*. If it is to grow, on the other hand, the capital must grow in a *higher inverse proportion* than that in which the profit rate > or the surplus-value or profit produced per 100 < falls > as a result of the higher composition of the average capital, or, and this is the same thing, the diminishing proportion of variable capital as calculated on the capital of 100. < In other words, if the *variable component of the total capital* is not just to remain *the same* but to grow, even though there is a fall in the amount of variable capital which forms an aliquot part of each 100 of the total capital, the total capital must not only grow in the same inverse ratio in which the variable capital per 100 diminishes, but more. It must grow so much that in the new composition it requires not only the former amount of variable capital, but still more than this. If the variable part of the capital falls from 40 to 20, the total capital must not only rise from 100 to 200, it must rise to more than 200 if it is to require a variable capital of more than 40.

|213| Even if the exploited mass of the working population remains *constant* and it is only the length and intensity of the working day that increases, the mass of capital applied must still rise, since it must rise even if the same mass of labour is to be employed under the former conditions of exploitation with an altered composition of capital.

Thus the same development in the social productivity of labour is expressed, as the capitalist mode of production advances, in two ways: on the one hand in a progressive tendency for the *rate of profit to fall*, and on the other in a constant growth in the absolute *mass of the surplus-value or profit* appropriated; so that, by and large, a relative decline in the variable capital corresponds to an absolute increase in surplus-value and profit. This twofold effect, as explained, can be expressed only by a *growth in the total capital* that takes place more rapidly than the fall in the rate of profit, > and in the opposite direction. < In order to apply an absolutely greater variable capital at a higher composition, or with a reduction in the variable capital as compared with the constant capital, the total capital must grow in the same proportion as the raising of the composition. > (Hence the flexibility provided by the *surplus population*, since a growing amount of capital is necessary, as a result of the rising productivity of labour, to employ the same amount of labour-power, and still more a growing amount.) < If the variable capital forms only a sixth of the total capital instead of a half, as formerly, the total capital must grow from say 200 to 600, hence it must triple, in order to employ the same amount of labour-power, in other words to employ a variable capital of the previous magnitude; but if it is to employ double the labour-power, the total capital must rise to 1,200, whereas previously it only needed to rise to 400 to achieve the same result.

Previous economists, not knowing how to explain the law of the falling rate of profit, invoked the *rising mass of profit*, the growth in the *absolute amount of profit*, whether for the individual capitalist or for the social capital as a whole, as a kind of consolation, but this was also based on mere truisms and imagined possibilities.

It is a tautology to say that the *mass of profit* is determined by two factors, firstly by the rate of profit and secondly by the amount of capital that is applied at a given rate of profit. The fact that the mass of profit may possibly grow, therefore, despite a simultaneous fall in the rate of profit, is only an expression of this tautology and > does not prove the necessity of this connection, < since it is equally possible for the capital to grow without any growth in the mass of profit, and, indeed, the capital might even grow while the mass of profit falls. 25 percent on 100 gives 25, > 500 at 5 percent also gives 25, although the capital has now increased fivefold, while 1,000 at 2 percent gives 20, hence less by one-fifth than the original mass of profit, although the capital has now increased tenfold.[5] But if the same reasons that make the profit rate

5 *Cf. Ricardo*. If the profit rate is given, the gross amount of profit will depend on the magnitude of the capital advanced, and therefore the accumulation too, to the extent that this is determined by the rate of profit. If the total amount of capital is given, the gross amount of profit will depend on the level of the rate of profit. A small capital with a high rate of profit can therefore yield a greater gross profit than a larger capital with a low rate of profit. Let us suppose the following:

(1)

		Capital	*Rate of profit*	*Gross profit*
100		10%	10	
	× 2	200	10/2 = 5%	10
	× 3	300	10/2 = 5%	15
	× 1½	150	5%	7½

(2)

Capital	Rate of profit	Gross profit
100	10%	10
2 × 100 (200)	$^{10}/_{2\frac{1}{2}}$ = 4%	8
2½ × 100 (250)	4%	10
3 × 100 (300)	4	12

(3)

Capital	Rate of profit	Gross profit
500	10%	50
10 × 500 = 5,000	1	50
3,000	1	30
10,000	1	100

If the multiplier of the capital and the divisor of the rate of profit are the same, i.e., the magnitude of the capital increases in the same proportion as the fall in the rate of profit, the total amount of gross profit remains unchanged. 100 at 10% = 10 and 200 at $^{10}/_{2}$ or 5% = 10. Therefore if the rate of profit falls in the same proportion as the capital accumulates (grows) the gross profit remains unchanged.

If the rate of profit grows more rapidly than the capital, the total amount of gross profit declines. 500 at 10% = 10. But 6 × 3,000 at $^{10}/_{10}$ or 1% = 30.

Finally, if the capital grows more quickly than the rate of profit declines, the gross profit increases, although the rate of profit falls. 100 at 10% = 10, but 3 × 100 at 4% = 12.

< 'We should also expect that, however the *rate of profits of stock might diminish* in consequence of the accumulation of capital on the land, and the rise of wages, yet that the *aggregate amount of profit would increase*. Thus supposing that, with repeated accumulations of £100,000, the rate of profit should fall from 20 to 19, to 18, to 17 percent, a constantly diminishing rate, we should expect that the whole amount of profits received by those successive owners of capital would always be progressive; that it would be greater when the capital was £200,000, than when £100,000; still greater when £300,000; and so on, *increasing, though at a diminishing rate, with every increase of capital*. This progression, however, is only true for a certain time: thus 19 percent on £200,000 is more than 20 on £100,000; again 18 percent on £300,000 is more than 19 percent on £200,000; but after capital has accumulated to a large amount, and profits have fallen, *the further accumulation diminishes the aggregate of profits*. Thus suppose the accumulation should be £1,000,000, and the profits 7 percent. The whole amount of profits will be £70,000; now if an addition of £100,000 capital be made to the million, and profits should fall to 6 percent, £66,000 or a diminution of £4,000 will be received by the owners of stock, although the whole amount of stock will be increased from £1,000,000 to £1,100,000' (Ricardo 1821, pp. 124–5.) Indeed, it is assumed here that the capital

fall also promote accumulation, i.e., the formation of additional capital, and if all additional capital also sets additional labour in motion and produces additional surplus-value; if, on the other hand, the very fact of the fall in the rate of profit means a growth in the former capital in proportion to the increase in the constant capital, then the entire process ceases to be a mystery. We shall see later on[6] how people resorted to deliberately falsifying their calculations in order to swindle away the *possibility* of a reduction[7] in the *mass of profit* together with a decline in the rate of profit.

|214| We have shown how the same reasons which produce a *tendential fall in the general rate of profit* > (= a proportional reduction in variable capital as compared with the total capital = a proportional reduction in surplus-value as compared with the value of the capital advanced) < imply an accelerated accumulation of capital and hence a growth in the absolute magnitude or the *total mass* of the surplus labour (surplus-value, profit) appropriated by it. Just as everything is expressed upside down in competition, and hence in the consciousness of its agents, so too is this law – I mean this inner and necessary connection between two apparently contradictory phenomena. It is evident > (not forgetting the proportions explained above) < that a capitalist controlling a large amount of capital will make more profit > i.e., more money (money being used here merely as an independent expression of value) < than a smaller capitalist making apparently 'high' profits.[8] The most superficial examination of competition also shows that, under certain circumstances, if the bigger capitalist wants to make more room for himself on the market and expel the smaller capitalists, as in times of crisis, etc., this situation is in practice used by the bigger capitalist to drive the smaller ones from the field, i.e., a deliberate reduction in the rate of profit takes place. Commercial capital in particular, which we shall discuss in more detail later, also exhibits phenomena that allow

grows from 1 million to 1,100,000, hence by $\frac{1}{10}$ or 10 percent, while the rate of profit falls from 7 to 6, i.e., by $\frac{1}{7}$ or $14\frac{2}{7}$ percent. *Hinc illae lacrimae!* ['This is the reason for those tears'.]

6 [This refers to the projected fourth volume of *Capital*. Translator]

7 [Marx wrote 'reduction' here. Engels changed this, no doubt correctly, to 'increase'. Translator]

8 > If the rate of profit is given, the amount of profit depends altogether on the size of the capital advanced. This is simply an application of the principle that, assuming the equalisation of the rate of profit to form a general rate of profit, capitals of equal size yield profits of equal amounts, hence a larger capital yields more profit than a smaller one. But whether the rate of profit is in general high or low depends in fact on the total quantity of labour employed by the aggregate capital of society, on the *proportional* quantity of *unpaid* labour employed, and, lastly, on the proportion between the capital employed in labour and the capital merely reproduced as a condition of production. <

the fall in profit to be seen as a result of the expansion of business, and hence of the capital concerned, etc. (We shall give the proper scientific expression for this false conception later on. > Adam Smith with his lowering of the rate of profit by the growing competition of the capitals, springing from their accumulation, etc.)[9] < Similar superficial considerations arise from comparing the rates of profit that are made in particular[10] trades, according to whether they are subject to the regime of free competition or monopoly. The entire shallow conception that thrives in the heads of the agents of competition can be found in Professor Roscher, who says that this reduction in the rate of profit is 'both more advantageous and more humane'.[11] Here the decline in the rate of profit appears as a *result* of the increase of capital and the capitalists' consequent calculation that a lower rate of profit will enable them to tuck away a greater mass of profit. The whole thing (with the exception of Adam Smith, on whom more later)[12] is based on a complete failure to conceptualise [*Begriffslosigkeit*] what the general *rate of profit* actually is and on the crude idea > which underlies this < that prices are determined by *adding* a more or less arbitrary quota of profit onto the commodity's actual value. Crude as these notions are, they are a necessary product of the inverted [*verkehrt*] way in which the immanent laws of capitalist production present themselves within competition.

If we consider the enormous development in the productive powers of social labour, e.g., over the last thirty years alone, compared with all earlier periods, and particularly if we consider the enormous mass of fixed capital involved in the overall process of social production, quite apart from machinery proper, then instead of the problem that occupied previous economists, namely the problem of explaining the fall in the rate of profit, we now have the opposite problem of explaining why this fall is not greater or faster. > If we take for example a capital composition in which the variable capital forms ⅛ of the total capital, and a rate of surplus-value of 100 percent, we should have 87½ c + 121½ v and s would be 12½. The rate of profit (including interest, rent and all other forms of surplus-value) would also be 12½. < Counteracting influences must be at work, checking and delaying the effects of the general law and giving it simply the character of a *tendency*, which is why we have described the fall in the general rate of profit as a *tendential fall*. The most general of these factors are as follows:

---

9 [Smith 1999, Book 1, Chapter IX, p. 190].

10 [Marx has 'peculiar' here. Translator]

11 *See the passage in Roscher, that donkey* [Roscher 1858, p. 192.]

12 [Again a reference to the projected fourth volume. Translator]

|215| (1) *A more intense exploitation of labour,* i.e., *an increase* in surplus labour or surplus-value, particularly by the *prolongation of the working day* and the *intensification of labour.* > Everyone who is familiar with the development of modern industry knows this. The legislation on the *normal working day* provides the best and the most thorough commentary on the subject. < There are many aspects [*Momente*] to the *intensification* of labour that involve a growth in the constant capital as against the variable, i.e., *a fall in the rate of profit,* such as when a single worker has to supervise a *greater amount* of machinery, etc. Here, as also with most procedures that serve to produce relative surplus-value, the same reasons that bring about a rise in the *rate of surplus-value* can produce a fall in the *amount* of surplus-value, taking the magnitude of the total capital applied as given. But there are other aspects of this *intensification,* as for example the accelerated speed of the machines, which, where raw material is being treated, use up more of it in the *same* time, but although they wear out the machinery more quickly this does not affect the ratio of their value to the price of the labour that sets them in motion. In particular, however, it is the *prolongation of the working day,* this discovery of modern industry, which increases the amount of surplus labour appropriated without making any essential change in the ratio of the labour-power applied to the constant capital it sets in motion, and in fact rather reduces the constant capital in relative terms. It has already been shown, moreover, and this forms the real secret of the tendential fall in the rate of profit, that the procedures for producing relative surplus-value are based, by and large, either on transforming as much as possible of a given amount of labour into surplus-value or on spending as little as possible labour in general in relation to the capital advanced; so that the same reasons that permit the *level of exploitation* of labour to increase make it impossible to exploit *as much labour* as before with the same total capital. > *The same number of workers* is exploited to a greater degree, but a *smaller number of workers* is exploited by *the same* capital. < These are the counteracting tendencies which, while they act to bring about a rise in the *rate of surplus-value,* simultaneously lead to a fall in the *mass of surplus-value* produced by a given capital, hence a fall in the *rate of profit. Female and child labour* should be mentioned here, in so far as the whole family has now to supply capital with *a greater quantity of surplus labour* than before, even if the total sum of their wages increases, which is by no means always the case. Everything that promotes the production of relative surplus-value by the simple improvement of *the methods* > *with which the same amount of capital is applied* < as in agriculture, [has the same effect]. Here there is a rise in the volume of the product in relation to the labour-power applied, but the *constant capital applied* does not grow in proportion to the *variable capital,* > to the extent that the latter

can be considered as an index of labour-power (number of workers). < The *same thing* takes place if the productivity of labour (irrespective of whether its product goes into the workers' wages or into the *elements of constant capital*) is freed from restraints on commerce, restrictions which are arbitrary or have become irksome in the course of time, and generally from fetters of any kind, without any initial impact on the proportion of variable to constant capital. |216| It might be asked whether these factors that inhibit the fall in the profit rate, although in the final instance they always accelerate it further, include the temporary, but ever repeated *increases in surplus-value* that appear now in one branch of production, now in another, raising them about the general level for the capitalist who makes use of inventions, etc., before they are universally applied. This is indeed the case.

The *mass of surplus-value* that a capital of a given size produces is the product of two factors, the *rate of surplus-value* and the number of workers employed at that rate. With a *given rate of surplus-value*, therefore, it depends on the *number of workers*, and with a given number of workers it depends on the rate of surplus-value, > or, in other words, on the composite relation between the *absolute magnitude of the variable capital* and the *rate of surplus-value*, or the relation between the paid and the unpaid portion of the labour. < Now we have seen that the same factors that increase the *rate of relative surplus-value* lower the *amount of labour-power applied* on average. It is clear, however, that this effect can be *greater* or *less*, depending on the specific proportions in which this antithetical movement takes place, and that the tendency for the profit rate to be reduced, in particular, is attenuated by the increase in the rate of absolute surplus-value that stems from the prolongation of the working day. >

While the *mass of surplus-value* itself is determined by two factors, the absolute *magnitude of the variable capital* (the number of workers) and the *rate of surplus-value* (the division of the mass of labour into paid and unpaid) the *rate of profit is determined* by the relation between the *mass of surplus-value* and the *value* of the total capital advanced, hence it is determined essentially by the *relative* proportion of the variable capital – at a given rate of surplus-value – to the constant capital and therefore to the total capital.

< In connection with the *profit rate*, we have found that to a *fall in the rate*, resulting from a rise in the mass of total capital applied, there corresponds in general an *increase in the absolute magnitude or mass of profit*. Taking the total *variable* capital of the society as a whole, the *surplus-value* it produces is the same as the *profit* it produces. > A twofold development occurs here: < a rise in the *absolute mass* of the surplus-value and a rise in its *rate*, the first because the absolute number of workers applied by the society has grown, and the second because the level of exploitation of this labour has increased. But with respect

to a capital of a given magnitude, e.g., 100, the rate of surplus-value can grow while the *average mass of surplus-value* falls, since the *rate* is determined by the ratio in which the *variable* portion of the capital is *valorised*, while the mass is determined by the *proportional magnitude* of the variable capital compared with the total capital.

The *rise in the rate of surplus-value* – particularly since it takes place under circumstances in which, as mentioned above, there is no increase in the constant capital as against the variable capital, or no relative increase, > i.e., an increase in the level of exploitation of labour – < is a factor by which the mass of surplus-value and therefore the *rate of profit* is determined. It does not annul the general law. But it has the effect that this law operates more as a *tendency*, i.e., as a law whose absolute implementation is > paralysed, < held up, retarded and weakened by counteracting factors. However, as |217| the same factors that increase the rate of surplus-value (and the prolongation of the working day is itself a result of large-scale industry) tend to reduce the amount of labour-power employed by a given capital, the same factors tend both to *reduce the rate of profit* and to *retard* the movement in this direction. If one worker is compelled to do work that it would be rational for *two* to perform, and if this happens under circumstances in which this one worker replaces three, the one worker will now provide as much surplus labour as two did before, and to that extent the *rate of surplus-value* will double. But the one worker will not supply as much surplus labour as three did before, and this leads to a fall in the mass of surplus-value. Its fall is however compensated for, or limited, by the rise in the rate of surplus-value. If the entire population is set to work at the increased rate of surplus-value, the mass of surplus-value rises, even though the population remains *the same*. Still more is this the case with a growing population; and even though this growth is linked with a *relative* fall in the amount of labour-power as compared with the size of the total capital, the fall is still moderated or halted by the *higher rate of surplus-value*.

Before we leave this point, it should be stressed once again that the rate of surplus-value can rise while the *capital remains constant*, although its mass falls, because the mass of surplus-value is equal to the *rate times the number of workers*, but the rate is never calculated on the total capital but only on the variable capital advanced. In fact it is calculated on *each* working day counted individually. Once there is a *given capital* of a *given value*, however, the rate of profit can never rise or fall without a similar rise or fall in the *mass of surplus-value*.

(2) *A reduction of wages below their value*. We simply make empirical reference to this point here, as, like a number of other things that might be brought into this investigation, it has in fact nothing to do with the general analysis of

capital, but has its place in an account of competition, which is not dealt with in this work. It is none the less one of the most important factors in stemming the tendency for the rate of profit to fall.

(3) Everything is relevant here that has been said in Chapter One of this book about the causes that raise the rate of profit while the *rate of surplus-value remains constant*, or at least raise it independently of any change in the rate of surplus-value. In particular, therefore, the fact that, if we view the total capital as a whole, the *value of the constant capital* does not increase in the same proportion as its material volume. For example, the quantity of cotton that a single European spinning operative works up in a modern factory has grown to a most colossal extent in comparison with that which a European spinner used to process with the spinning-wheel. But the *value* of the cotton processed has not grown in the same proportion as its mass. It is the same with machines and other fixed capital. > (Here too there are in turn counteracting factors, such as a rise in the prices of various vegetable and animal materials, coal, etc.) < In short, the same development that raises the mass of constant capital in comparison with variable reduces the value of its elements, as a result of the higher productivity of labour, and hence prevents the value of the constant capital, even though this grows steadily, from growing in the *same degree* as its material volume, i.e., the material volume of the means of production that are set in motion by the *same* amount of labour-power. In |218| certain cases, the mass of the constant capital may increase without any alteration at all in its value. Indeed, it may even move in the opposite direction and become smaller.

Also related to what has been said is the *depreciation of the existing capital* that goes hand in hand with the *development of industry*. This too is a factor that steadily operates to delay the fall in the rate of profit, even though in certain circumstances it may reduce the *mass of profit* by reducing the *mass of capital* that produces profit. We see here once again how the same factors that produce the tendency for the rate of profit to fall also *moderate* the realisation [*Verwirklichung*] of this tendency.

(4) The *relative surplus population*, the creation of which is inseparable from, and accelerated by, the *development of labour productivity*, which is expressed in the *decline in the rate of profit*. The more the capitalist mode of production is developed in a country, the more strikingly does this relative surplus population obtrude. This is in turn a reason why the more or less purely formal subsumption of labour under capital persists in many branches of production, and indeed it lasts longer than would seem at first sight to correspond to the general level of development; this is a result of the cheapness and quantity of available or dismissed wage-labourers, and of the greater resistance (or difficulty) that some branches of production by their nature offer to the replacement

of *predominantly* manual labour by machines. *Furthermore*, new branches of production open up, particularly in the field of luxury goods, which precisely take the relative surplus population as their basis, a population often made available owing to the preponderance of constant capital in other branches of production; these base themselves in turn on a preponderance of the *element of living labour*, and only gradually pass through the same trajectory as the other branches of production. In both cases variable capital forms a significant proportion of the total. Now since the general rate of profit is formed by the equalisation of the rates of profit in the various particular branches of production, here again the same reasons that produce the tendential fall in the rate of profit also produce a counterweight to this tendency, which to a greater or lesser degree paralyses its effect.

(5) In so far as foreign trade cheapens on the one hand the elements of constant capital and on the other the necessary means of subsistence into which variable capital is converted, it acts to raise two elements of the rate of profit, the *rate of surplus-value* and the *value of constant capital*. It has a general effect in this direction in as much as it permits the *scale of production* to be expanded. > But it is exactly from this angle that < it accelerates the fall in variable as against constant capital, and therefore the *fall in the rate of profit*, while it also thereby accelerates accumulation. And similarly, whereas the expansion of foreign trade was the basis of capitalist production in its infancy, it becomes the product of the capitalist mode of production as this progresses, created through the inner need of this mode of production for an ever-extended market. Here again we can see the same duality of effect. (This aspect of foreign trade was completely overlooked by Ricardo.)[13]

There is a further question, the specifics of which actually lie beyond the limits of our investigation: is the general rate of profit raised by the higher profit rate made by capital invested in foreign or colonial trade?

|219| Capital invested in foreign trade can yield a higher rate of profit, firstly because it competes with commodities produced by other countries with less developed production facilities, so that the more advanced country sells its goods *above* their value, even though still more cheaply than its competitors. In so far as the labour of the more advanced country is valorised here as labour of a higher specific weight > just as within a country when a manufacturer employs a new invention which has not yet come into general use < the profit rate rises, since labour that is not paid at its higher specific weight is nevertheless sold as such. The same relationship may hold towards the country to which

13 [See Ricardo 1821, pp. 136, 137–8 and 413. Translator]

goods are exported and from which goods are imported: i.e., such a country gives more labour in return than it receives, even though it still receives the goods in question more cheaply than it could produce them itself. In the same way, a manufacturer who makes use of a new invention before this has become general sells more cheaply than his competitors and yet still sells above the *individual* value of his commodity, valorising the specifically higher productivity of the labour he employs as *surplus labour*. He thus realises a surplus profit. As far as capital invested in the colonies, etc., is concerned, however, the reason why this can yield higher rates of profit is that the profit rate is generally *higher* there on account of the lower degree of development, and so too is the exploitation of labour, through the use of slaves, etc. Now there is no reason why the higher rates of profit that capital invested in certain branches yields in this way, and brings home to its country of origin, should not enter into the equalisation of the general rate of profit and hence *raise* this in due proportion, unless monopolies stand in the way. (Adam Smith is right here, as against Ricardo.)[14] There is in particular no reason why this should not be so when the branches of capital investment in question are subject to the laws of free competition. What Ricardo has in mind, on the other hand, is this: the commodities are sold within the country, and in them the higher return is realised. This gives the favoured spheres of production at most a temporary advantage over the others. As soon as we take our leave of the money form, however, this semblance [*Schein*] vanishes. The privileged country receives more labour in return for less, even though this excess is pocketed by a certain class, just as in the exchange between labour and capital in general. Thus in as much as the profit rate is higher because it is generally higher in the colonial country, favourable natural conditions there may enable it to go hand in hand with lower commodity prices. An *equalisation* still takes place, but not an equalisation to the *old level*, as Ricardo believes.

But this same foreign trade develops the capitalist mode of production, and hence promotes a decline in variable capital as against constant at home, though it also produces overproduction in relation to the foreign country, so that it again has the opposite effect in the further course of development.

We have shown in general, therefore, how the same causes that bring about a *fall in the general rate of profit* provoke countereffects that inhibit this fall, delay it and in part paralyse it. These effects do not annul the law, but they weaken

14 'They contend, that the *equality of profits* will be brought about by the general rise of profits, and I am of opinion, that the profits of the favoured trade will speedily submit to the general level'. (Ricardo 1821, pp. 132, 133.)

its impact. If this were not the case, it would not be the fall in the general rate of profit that was incomprehensible, but rather the relative slowness of this fall. The law operates therefore simply as a tendency, whose impact is decisive only under certain particular circumstances and over long periods.

|220| Before we proceed any further, we should like to repeat again two points that have already been developed repeatedly, in order to avoid any misunderstanding.

Firstly, the same process that leads to the cheapening of commodities as the capitalist mode of production develops leads to a change in the organic composition of the social capital applied in commodity production, and leads as a result to a fall in the rate of profit. Thus the reduction in the relative cost of the individual commodity, or even in the part of this cost that represents the wear and tear of the machinery, should not be confused with the rising *value* of the constant capital compared with the *variable*, even though, conversely, any reduction in the relative cost of the constant capital, with the volume of its material elements remaining the same or increasing, acts to increase the *rate of profit*, i.e., acts to reduce proportionately the value of the constant capital, compared with the variable capital that is applied on a scale which declines progressively.

Secondly, the fact that the *additional living labour* contained in the individual commodities which together compose the product of capital stands in a declining ratio to the materials of labour these contain and the means of labour consumed in them; the fact, therefore, that a *declining quantity of additional living labour is materialised in them*, because less labour is required to produce them as social productivity develops, is a fact which does not affect the proportion in which the *living labour* contained in those commodities is divided between *paid* and *unpaid*. On the contrary. Even though the total amount of the additional living labour contained in it falls, the unpaid part still grows in proportion to the paid part, either by a direct reduction or a proportionate fall in the paid part; for the same mode of production that reduces the total mass of additional living labour in a commodity is accompanied by a rise in absolute and relative surplus-value. The tendential fall in the rate of profit is linked with a tendential rise in the rate of surplus-value, i.e., in the level of exploitation of labour. Nothing is more absurd, then, than to explain the fall in the rate of profit in terms of a rise in wage-rates, even though this too may happen by way of exception. Only when the relationships that form the rate of profit have been understood will statisticians be able to undertake genuine analyses of wage-rates in different epochs and countries. > The profit rate falls, although the rate of surplus-value remains identical or rises, because variable capital falls in proportion to constant capital, and therefore in proportion to the total capital, as a result of the development of the productivity of labour. < It therefore does not fall because labour becomes less productive but rather because it becomes more productive. > It does not fall because the worker is less exploited but because he is more exploited, whether through an increase in absolute surplus time or relative surplus time.

< The above five points could also be supplemented by a sixth one, though we cannot go into it more deeply on the basis of what has been developed so far: as capitalist production advances, hand in hand with an accelerated amount of accumulation, one portion of capital is considered simply to be interest-bearing capital and is invested as such. This is not in the sense in which any capitalist who loans out capital is content to take the interest, while the industrial capitalist pockets the entrepreneurial profit. Nor does it affect the level of the general rate of profit, for this = interest + profit of all kinds + rent, its distribution between these particular categories being a matter of indifference. It is rather in the sense that these capitals, although invested in large productive enterprises, simply yield an interest, great or small, after all costs are deducted. This is the case with railways, for example. These do not therefore enter into the equalisation of the general rate of profit, since they yield a profit rate less than the average. If they did enter into this process, the average rate would fall much lower. Theoretically speaking it is possible to include them, and we should then obtain a profit rate lower than that which seemingly exists and is really decisive for the capitalists, since it is precisely in these undertakings that the proportion of constant capital to variable is at its greatest.

|221| We saw in Chapter One of this book that the rate of profit always expresses the rate of surplus-value lower than it actually is. We have now seen that even a rising rate of surplus-value tends to be expressed in a falling rate of profit. The rate of profit would only be equal to the rate of surplus-value if c, the constant capital, were = 0, i.e., if the total capital were laid out on wages. A falling rate of profit, then, expresses a falling rate of surplus-value only if the *value* of the constant capital and the amount of labour-power that this sets in motion remains *unchanged*.

(Ricardo, while claiming to be dealing with the *rate of profit*, actually deals only with the *rate of surplus-value*, and this only on the assumption that the working day is a *constant* magnitude, both intensively and extensively.)

A fall in the rate of profit and accelerated accumulation are simply *different* expressions of the *same* process, in so far as both express the development of productivity. Accumulation in turn accelerates the fall in the profit rate, in so far as it involves the concentration of workers on a large scale and hence a higher composition of capital. On the other hand, the fall in the profit rate again accelerates the concentration of capital and the expropriation of the smaller capitalists, > the expropriation of those who are relatively speaking more or less direct producers. < In this way there is an acceleration of accumulation – so far as its mass is concerned – although the *rate* of accumulation falls.

On the other hand, however, to the extent that the *rate of profit*, i.e., the *rate of valorisation of the total capital*, is the stimulus to capitalist production (in the same way as the valorisation of capital is its sole purpose), a fall in this rate retards the formation of new, independent capitals and thus appears as a threat to the development of the capitalist production process. (This fall promotes overproduction, speculation and crises, and produces a redundancy of capital alongside the redundancy of labour or the relative surplus population.) Thus economists like Ricardo, who take the capitalist mode of production as absolute, feel here that this mode of production creates a barrier for itself and seek to ascribe the barrier not to this mode of production but rather to nature (in the theory of rent). What is important in their horror in the face of the falling rate of profit is the feeling that the capitalist mode of production comes up against a barrier in the development of the productive forces, which in itself has nothing to do with the production of wealth; but this *characteristic* barrier in fact testifies to the *restrictiveness* and the solely historical character of this mode of production. It demonstrates that this is not an *absolute* mode of production for the production of wealth but rather comes into conflict at a certain stage with the latter's further development.

(Of course Ricardo, etc., consider only industrial profit, within which they include interest. Yet the *rate of rent* also has a tendency to fall, even though its absolute *value* grows and it may even grow in relation to industrial profit.) (See Edward West, who put forward the law of ground-rent before Ricardo.)[15] > If there is a fall in s/C, i.e., p′, the rate of profit, although s and p rise, but nevertheless fall relatively to C, which grows much more rapidly < (taking C here as the total social capital) it is absolutely no contradiction if, s = p (p being the industrial profit) + i (interest) + r (rent), hence $s/C = {}^{p+i+r}/_{C}$, the three relations, p/C, i/C and r/C all fall, although r increases in relation to i and p, or p increases in relation to i, or both at once. > The relationship between the parts of s may change in proportional terms, but s/C can never become smaller as a result of changes in the proportional relationship between p, i, and r, the components of s. Firstly, if s grows, p, i, and r can grow despite a fall in s/C on account of the *relative* fall of s as compared with C, and secondly, this

15 [Edward West, *Essay on the application of capital to land, with observations shewing the impolicy of any great restriction of the importation of corn*, London, 1815. Translator]

relative fall of s as compared with C may be accompanied by a change in the relative magnitude of p/C, i/C and r/c, which may each rise or fall reciprocally at the cost of the other two. < If the rate of profit falls from 50 to 25 percent, as for example when, given a rate of surplus-value of 100 percent, a capital of 50c and 50v changes to become 75c and 25v, then in the first case a capital of 1,000 will give a profit of 500 and in the second case a capital of 4,000 will give 1,000. s or p will have doubled, while p′ has fallen by half. Now if, out of the original 50 percent, 20 was profit, 10 interest and 20 rent, we should have p/C = 20 percent, i/C = 10 percent, and r/C = 20 percent. So if the proportions remain the same after the rate has fallen to 25 percent, we now have p/C = 10 percent, i/C = 5 percent and r/C = 10 percent. If p′ (or p/C) now falls to 8 percent and i′ (or i/C) to 4 percent, r′ will rise to 13 percent. The proportionate size of r would have risen against p and i, but p′ would still remain unchanged. On both assumptions the sum total of p, i, and r would have risen, since this is now calculated on a capital four times larger. Incidentally, Ricardo's assumption that industrial profit (plus interest) *originally* accounted for the entire surplus-value is > *nonsense* < both historically and theoretically. It is rather the progress of capitalist production which (1) gives industrial and commercial capitalists the entire profit, in the first instance, for later distribution, and (2) *reduces* rent to the surplus over and above profit. On this capitalist basis rent then grows once more, as a portion of profit (i.e., of surplus-value considered as the product of the total capital), but not the specific portion of the profit pocketed by the capitalist.[16] >

|222| < Assuming the necessary means of production, i.e., a sufficient accumulation of capital, the creation of surplus-value faces no other barrier than the working population, if the *rate* of surplus-value (the level of exploitation of labour) is given; and no other barrier than this level of exploitation of labour if the working population is given. And the capitalist production process essen-

16 > *Rate of Profit* = $\frac{\textit{Surplus-value}}{\text{Capital Advanced}}$. This rate of profit can fall, even though the ratio of industrial profit to interest may rise, for example, or vice versa. If profit = P, industrial profit = P′, interest = Z and rent = R, P = P′ + Z + R. And it is clear that whatever the absolute magnitude of P may be, P′, Z and R may rise or fall in proportion to each other, independently of the magnitude of P or a rise or fall in P. The reciprocal displacement of P′, Z and R amounts to no more than a change in the distribution of P under its different headings. Moreover either $\frac{P}{C}$, $\frac{Z}{C}$, or $\frac{R}{C}$, the rates of industrial profit, interest and rent, may *rise* even though there is a fall in $\frac{P}{C}$, the general rate of profit. [This important footnote was left out of Engels's Volume III. It should be on p. 351 of Marx 1981 [Engels], at the end of the first paragraph. Editor]

tially consists of this *production of surplus-value*, represented in the *surplus product* or the aliquot portion of *commodities* produced in which *unpaid labour is materialised* [*materialisiert*]. It should never be forgotten that the production of this surplus-value – and the transformation of a portion of it back into capital, or accumulation, forms an integral part of the production of surplus-value – is the *immediate purpose* and the *determining motive* of *capitalist production*. The latter should therefore never be depicted as something that it is not, namely as production whose immediate purpose is consumption, or the production of means of enjoyment for the capitalist, > who is the *producer*, the head of production; < this would be completely to ignore its specific character, as expressed in its entire inner pattern.

It is the *extraction* of this surplus-value which forms the *immediate* process of production, and this, as we have said, faces no other barriers than those just mentioned. As soon as the amount of surplus labour it has proved possible to extort has been materialised in commodities, the *surplus-value has been produced*, > and its absolute mass is limited only by the number of workers who are at the capitalist's disposal. < But this production of surplus-value is only the first act in the capitalist production process, and its completion only brings to an end the immediate production process itself. Capital has absorbed a given amount of *unpaid labour*. With the development of this process as expressed in the fall in the profit rate, the mass of surplus-value thus produced swells to monstrous proportions. Now the total mass of commodities, the *total product*, must be *sold*, both the portion that replaces constant and variable capital and the portion that represents surplus-value. If this does not happen, or happens only partly or only at prices that are less than the *price of production*, then although the worker is certainly exploited, his exploitation is not *realised* as such for the capitalist and may involve the partial or complete loss of his capital or a merely partial realisation of the surplus-value that has been extorted. The conditions for *immediate* exploitation and for the realisation of that exploitation are not identical. Not only are they separate in time and place, they are also conceptually separate. The former is restricted only by the society's productive forces, the latter by the *proportionality between the different branches of production* and by the society's *power of consumption*. And this is determined neither by the absolute power of production nor by the absolute power of consumption but rather by the power of consumption on the basis of *antagonistic conditions of distribution*, which reduce the consumption of those who form the bedrock of society to a minimum level, restricted within more or less narrow limits. The conditions of realisation are also restricted by the drive for accumulation, the drive to expand capital and to produce surplus-value on a larger scale. This is the law governing capitalist production, arising from the constant revolutions in the methods of production themselves, from the depreciation of the existing capital which is always associated with this, from the general competitive struggle and the necessity to improve production and extend its scale, > on pain of death, < merely as a means of self-preservation. The market, therefore, must continually be extended, so that its relationships and the conditions governing them assume ever more the form of a natural law independent of the producers and become ever more uncontrollable. The internal antagonism seeks to resolve itself by extending the external field of production. But the more productivity develops, the more it comes into contradiction with the narrow basis on which the relations of consumption rest. It is in no way a contradiction, on this *contradictory basis*, that redundancy of capital is associated with a growing *relative surplus population*; for although the mass of surplus-value produced would rise if these were brought together, this would equally heighten the *contradiction* between the conditions in which this surplus-value is produced and the conditions in which it is realised.

|223| Once a certain rate of profit is given, the gross profit, the mass of profit, always depends on the magnitude of the capital advanced. But accumulation is then determined by the part of this mass that is transformed back into capital. This part, since it is equal to the gross profit *minus* the revenue consumed by the capitalists, will depend not only on the value of the total profit but also on the cheapness of the commodities the capitalist can buy with it; commodities which go partly into his own consumption, his revenue, and partly into his constant capital. Wages are here taken as *given*, and the rate of profit as well.

The *mass of capital* that the worker sets in motion, and whose value he maintains and reproduces by his labour, is completely different from the value he adds – the surplus-value. If the mass of capital is 1,000 and the labour added is 100, the capital reproduced is 1,100. If the mass is 100 and the labour added is 20, the capital reproduced is 120. The rate of profit is 10 percent in the first case, and 20 percent in the second. Nevertheless, more can be accumulated out of 100 than out of 20. Thus the stream of capital (leaving aside its devaluation as a result of a rise in productivity), or its accumulation, flows on in proportion to the impetus that it already possesses and not in proportion to the rate of profit. It is possible to have a high rate of profit even if labour is unproductive, if this is based on a high rate of surplus-value and the working day is very long; this is possible because the workers' needs are very slight and the average wage is very low, even though labour is unproductive. The scantiness of the minimum wage corresponds to a lack of energy on the workers' part. In both cases, capital accumulates slowly, despite the high profit rate. The population is stagnant, and the product requires a great deal of labour-time, although the wages the workers are paid are small.

The rate of profit does not fall because the worker is less exploited, but rather because less labour is generally applied in relation to the capital invested. >

If a capital of 1,000 is made up of 500c and 500v, and s' is 50 percent, s is 250 and p' is 25 percent.

If a capital of 1,000 is made up of 750c and 250v, and s' is 50 percent, s is 125 and p' is 12½ percent. In this second case, however, the living labour applied is less than in the first case, if we assume that the wage of one worker is £25 a year. In the first case, £500 pays the wages of 20 workers, while in the second case £250 pays the wages of 10. The same capital employs 20 workers in the first case, and only 10 in the second. In the first case the ratio between the amount of capital and the number of working days is 1,000: 20, in the second it is 1,000: 10. Corresponding to each of the 20 workers in the first case there is a sum of £50 of invested capital (constant and variable taken together), because 20 × 50 = 2 × 500 = 1,000. In the second case £100 of capital corresponds to one worker, because 100 × 10 = 1,000. Nevertheless, in both cases the same proportion of the capital is laid out for the wage of one individual worker.

(To say that there is one worker for an invested capital of 50, in one case, and one worker for 100c in the other, hence only half a worker for a capital of 50, is the same thing as to say that there is an invested capital of 50 for one worker in one case, and 50 × 2 = 100c for one worker in the other case.)

< If a falling rate of profit coincides with a rise in the mass of profit > (because the accumulation of capital [is] quicker than the fall in the rate of profit) < a greater part of the annual product of labour is appropriated by the capitalist *under the category of capital*, and a smaller part under the category of *profit*, relatively speaking. Hence the fantasy of the cleric Chalmers to the effect that the smaller the mass of the annual product the capitalists spend as capital, |224| the greater the amount of profit they swallow up. The Established Church, of course, comes to their aid here, by making sure that a large portion of surplus produce is consumed instead of being capitalised. The confounded cleric confuses cause and effect. The mass of profit certainly does grow, even at a smaller rate of profit, as the capital laid out increases. > In addition to this there is an increase in the quantity of use-values represented by this smaller proportion. < But this brings about a simultaneous concentration of capital, since the conditions of production now require the use of capital on a massive scale. It also leads to the swallowing-up of small capitalists by bigger ones and the 'decapitalisation' [*Entcapitalisierung*] of the former. This is once again the divorce of the conditions of labour from the producers, raised to a higher power. These smaller capitalists still count among the producers since their own labour still plays a role. The work done by a capitalist generally stands in inverse

proportion to the size of his capital, i.e., to the degree to which he is a capitalist. This process of divorce of the conditions of labour from the producers (which would soon shake[17] capitalist production if counteracting tendencies were not constantly at work alongside this centripetal force, in the direction of decentralisation) > forms the *concept* of *capital* and of *primitive* accumulation, subsequently appearing as a *constant process* in the *accumulation* of capital, before it is finally expressed here as the *centralisation of the capitals that already exist* in a few hands and the *decapitalisation* > (this is what distinguishes it from *expropriation*) < of *many*.

(*The primitive accumulation of capital* involves the centralisation of the conditions of labour. In it, the conditions of labour assert their independence vis-à-vis the workers and labour itself. This historical act is the action by which capital originated. It is the *historical process of divorce* which transformed the conditions of labour into capital and labour into wage-labour. In this way the foundations of capitalist production were brought into existence.

The accumulation of capital on the basis of capital itself therefore presupposes the relationship of capital and wage-labour. On an ever-increasing scale it reproduces the divorce [of the conditions of labour from the producers] and material wealth's assertion of autonomy [*Verselbstständigung*] vis-à-vis labour.

The concentration of capital. The accumulation of large-scale capital by the destruction of smaller capital. Attraction. Decapitalisation = *the dissolution* of the intermediate links between capital and labour. It is merely the highest degree and the highest form of the process which transforms the conditions of labour into capital, for capital is multiplied and reproduced on an expanded scale, and finally separates the capitals which have been formed at many points in society from their possessors and centralises them in the hands of the bigger capitalists. With this most extreme form of antagonism, production is transformed into social production, even if in an estranged [*entfremdet*] form. Labour is social and the instruments of production are used in common in the real labour process. As *functionaries* of the process which simultaneously develops this social production and thereby accelerates the development of the productive forces, the capitalists become superfluous to the degree that they draw the benefits from this as representatives of society and puff themselves up as the *proprietors* of this social wealth and the *commanders* of social labour. They are in the same position as the feudal lords, whose exactions became

17 [Marx's word 'shake' [*Klappen*] was changed by Engels to 'breakdown' [*Zusammenbruch*], thereby encouraging a breakdown theory of crisis. Editor]

superfluous to the degree that their services became superfluous with the rise of bourgeois society, turning into anachronistic and inappropriate privileges as they hastened towards their doom.)[18]

|225| < The law that the *fall in the rate of profit* occasioned by the development of productivity is accompanied by an *increase in the mass of profit* is also expressed in this way: the *fall in the price* of commodities produced by capital is accompanied by a rise in the *amount of profit* contained in them and realised by their sale.

Since the development of productivity and the higher composition of capital corresponding to it leads to the setting in motion of an ever greater amount of means of production by an ever smaller amount of labour, each aliquot part of the total product, each *individual commodity* or each specific individual *element* of the total quantity of commodities produced absorbs less living labour, and also contains less objectified labour in terms of the depreciation of the fixed capital applied, > and also in terms of the *instruments of labour and the living labour* it replaces (in whose place it steps) *taking all these together*. < Each individual commodity therefore contains a smaller sum of labour objectified in means of production and > living < labour newly added in the course of production. The *price of the individual commodity therefore falls*. The amount of profit contained in the individual commodity may still increase for all that, if the rate of absolute or relative surplus-value rises. It contains less newly added labour, but the unpaid portion of this labour grows as a proportion to the paid part. But this only takes place within certain definite limits, and with the enormous *absolute* decrease, in the course of the advance of production, of the amount of living labour newly added to the individual commodity, the unpaid labour, the surplus labour, contained in it undergoes an *absolute* decline, no matter how much it may have *grown* in relation to the *paid* portion. The *amount of profit on each individual commodity* becomes very much reduced as labour productivity develops. Similarly, a fall in the *rate of profit* occurs, despite the rise in the rate of surplus-value, which is slowed down only by the cheapening of the elements of constant capital and the other circumstances adduced in Chapter One of this book, which increase the rate of profit alongside a given, and even a falling, rate of surplus-value.

If there is a fall in the *prices* of the individual commodities whose sum makes up capital's total product, this means nothing more than that a given quantity of labour is realised in a greater mass of commodities, so that each individual

---

18 [Most of the next 12 paragraphs were relocated by Engels to the end of his Chapter 13 (Marx 1981 [Engels], pp. 332–8). Editor]

commodity contains *a smaller quantity of labour* than before. This is the case even if one part of the constant capital, e.g., raw material, *rises* in price. With the exception of isolated cases (for example when the productivity of labour cheapens all the elements of constant and variable capital *to the same extent*) the rate of profit will fall, despite the higher rate of surplus-value: (1) because even a greater unpaid portion of the smaller total sum of newly added labour is less than a smaller aliquot unpaid portion of the greater total sum added previously, and (2) because the higher composition of capital is expressed, in the case of the individual commodity, in the fact that the whole portion of this commodity's value that represents newly added labour falls in comparison with the portion of value that represents raw materials, ancillary materials, and the wear and tear of the fixed capital. This change > (variation) < in the proportion between the various components of the individual commodity's *price*, the decline in the portion of the price that represents newly added labour, and increase in the portions of the price that represent previously objectified labour – this is the form in which the decline of the variable capital as against the constant is expressed in the individual commodity. This decline takes place in absolute terms for a given amount of capital, say 100, and for each individual commodity as an aliquot part of the capital reproduced. Even so, the rate of profit, if calculated simply on the price elements of the individual commodity, > and therefore from its standpoint, would be expressed *higher* than it is *in reality*. For in the individual commodity the |226| constant capital figures only from the point of view of its wear and tear. It is only the part that is *consumed* that counts, not the part *applied*. And the total amount of commodities produced contains no more than the total amount of wear and tear of the constant capital. (If we call this wear and tear, the amount by which the value of the constant capital has lessened {or, in other words, the amount that has gone into the product} ΔC, as opposed to C, which is ΔC + the part of C that has not been consumed but *applied* in the production process (C + ΔC = C′), the actual rate of profit is then represented as $\frac{s}{\Delta C + C' + V}$, which therefore = $\frac{s}{\Delta C + c' + v} = \frac{s}{C}$ (C being the *total* capital advanced {constant and variable}) whereas if it were considered purely in terms of the amount and price of the commodities would appear as $\frac{s}{\Delta C + v}$ or as $\frac{s}{C - c'}$.)

The *part of the price* of the individual commodity (or even the total amount of commodities during a particular circulation period) which represents the constant capital also does not rise in as great a proportion to the part of the price which represents newly added living labour as the constant part of the total capital rises in proportion to its variable part. Conversely, in proportion as the absolute total magnitude and total value of this part of the constant capital increases, one part of the constant capital – the part that consists of fixed capital – the *depreciation* it gives up to the individual commodity and the commodities produced during a single circulation period has a tendency to *decline*. This shows once again how important it is in dealing with capitalist production not to look at the individual commodity in isolation as a commodity and nothing else but to see it as the product of the capital advanced and in its relationship with the total capital from which it issues. This point also applies to the whole mass of commodities produced during a single circulation period.

Although the *rate of profit* must now be measured by comparing the quantity of surplus-value produced not only to the part of the consumed capital that is reproduced in the commodities but to that part of the capital plus the part of the capital that has not been consumed but rather applied, continuing to serve the process of production, the *quantity of profit* cannot be any greater than the quantity of profit or surplus-value contained in the commodities themselves, which has to be realised through the sale of those commodities.

An increase in the productivity of industry leads to a fall in the prices of the individual commodities. Less labour is contained in them, both paid and unpaid. The same labour produces three times the product, for example; hence two-thirds less labour is contained in the individual product, and since the amount of profit can be nothing other than a portion of this quantity of labour contained in the individual commodity, the *amount of profit* on the individual commodity must decline (even when the rate of surplus-value increases. This is valid within certain limits, as remarked earlier). In *all* the cases the *amount of profit* on the total number of individual commodities, in other words the whole product, does not fall *below* the original amount of profit, once the capital employs the *same number of workers* as before (this can also happen if *fewer* workers are employed, but with a longer working day and more surplus labour). This is because the number of products then increases in the same ratio as the amount of profit on the individual product declines. The *total amount of profit* remains *the same*, as long as the rate of exploitation remains the same and the same number of workers is employed, however the profit is *divided* among the mass of commodities (the *total sum of the commodities*). There is no change either in the amount or in the division of that amount between the workers and the capitalist. The *amount of profit* can only rise in these cases: when *the same* quantity of labour is performed but the *relative magnitude of the surplus labour* is increased (in such a way that the *unpaid* portion of the labour grows while the overall quantity of labour remains the same; the former can to a certain degree keep the quantity of surplus labour constant or even cause it to rise despite an absolute fall in the total quantity of labour), or when the number of workers employed increases while the level of exploitation remains the same.

Or, finally, the two tendencies operate side by side. In all these cases – which presuppose, however, |227| an increase in constant capital at the expense of variable and an increase in the magnitude of the total capital invested – the individual commodity contains a smaller *amount of profit* (and the rate of profit falls, even if this is only calculated on the *commodity* itself); a given quantity of additional living labour is contained in a *larger quantity of* commodities; the *price* of the individual commodity falls, and the amount of profit contained in it also falls. (Looking at this from an abstract point of view, the rate of profit can remain *the same* when the *price of the individual commodity* falls as a result of an increase in the productivity of labour and therefore a simultaneous increase in the *number* of these lower priced commodities. This happens for example when the increase in the productivity of labour acts *evenly* and *simultaneously* on *all* the constituents of the commodities, so that the *total price* of the commodity would fall in the same proportion as the productivity of labour increases, while the *proportions* between the different components of the price of the commodity may remain *the same* (remain constant), *fall*, as previously investigated, or rise, if the increase in the rate of surplus-value was associated with a significant depreciation in the components of the constant capital.)[19]

(When one looks only at the *prices of the individual commodities* in themselves, or when one merely measures the labour in respect of the quantity of the [commodities] produced by it, the investigation always goes astray. Everything depends on the magnitude of the total capital laid out. Even if we analyse the price of an individual commodity, as for example if the price of an ell of yarn falls from 3s. to 1⅔s.; if we know that 1s. represents the yarn, ⅓s. represents wages and ⅓s. represents profit, we do not know whether the total amount of profit has remained the same or not. It depends on whether the magnitude of the capital advanced has or has not grown.)

The phenomenon – which derives from the nature of capitalist production – that with a growth in the productivity of labour the price of the individual commodity or a given quantity of commodities *falls*, the number of commodities *increases*, the *amount of profit* and the *rate of profit on the individual commodity* generally falls, but the *amount of profit on the total number of commodities increases*, is a phenomenon which presents itself on the surface merely as follows: *a fall in the amount of profit* on the individual commodity, a fall in its *price*, a rise in the *amount of profit* on the *increased total number of commod-*

19 [Engels added a key sentence here ('In practice, however, the rate of profit will fall in the long run'. Marx 1981 [Engels], p. 337), which seems to suggest a more definite conclusion than Marx's manuscript. Editor]

ities produced by the social capital, or indeed by a single capitalist considered individually. This is conceived in such a way that the capitalist, of his own free choice, adds less profit on each individual commodity, but finds compensation for this from the increased number of commodities he produces. This view rests on the notion of 'profit upon alienation' which is in turn for its part taken from the mode of thought characteristic of *merchant's capital or commercial capital*.

We saw previously, in Chapter Six of Volume I,[20] that the growth in the amount of commodities, and the cheapening of the individual commodity, which goes hand in hand with the rise in the productivity of labour, does not as such affect the *ratio between the paid and the unpaid labour* contained in the individual commodity, despite the fall in its price (except where the commodity has a determining impact on the price of labour-power).

Since everything presents itself wrongly, that is to say inversely, in competition, the individual capitalist can imagine that:

(1) he reduces his *profit* on each individual commodity by cutting down its price, but makes an increased profit on account of the *greater amount of commodities* he sells (here he confuses the greater amount of profit which comes from increasing the amount of capital advanced even at a lower rate of profit.)

(2) he sets the price of the individual commodity and determines the price of the total product by *multiplication*; whereas the original process was one of *division* (see Chapter Six of Volume I)[21] and the multiplication only takes place subsequently and depends for its correctness on that previous division. All the vulgar economist in fact does is to translate the queer notions of the capitalist who has been deluded by competition into a seemingly more theoretical, more generalised language and to endeavour to demonstrate the correctness of these notions.

The fall in *commodity prices* and the rise in the amount of profit on the increased quantity of cheapened commodities is in fact merely another expression for the law developed above of the *fall in the rate of profit*, accompanied by a rise in the *amount of profit*. (This point about commodity prices should therefore be placed immediately after the statement of the law as a form of the latter, merely expressed differently.)

20 [This is a reference to a chapter Marx originally intended for Volume I, but did not include in the published version. It was discovered later among his manuscripts. English translation: Marx 1976, Appendix, 'Results of the Immediate Process of Production', pp. 948–1084, here p. 959. Translator]

21 [Marx 1976, p. 957. Translator]

The investigation of how far a falling rate of profit can coincide with rising prices does not belong here, nor does our previous discussion of this point in connection with the production of relative surplus-value. The capitalist who applies the improved mode of production sells *below* the market price, but *above* his |228| own individual production price (thus the *rate of profit* rises for him until competition has balanced this out; the second requisite, the growth of the capital laid out, proceeds hand in hand with this period of adjustment. If the capital is not large enough at the outset to employ the whole of the previous mass of workers, or an even greater mass, under the new conditions, if, in other words, the total capital has not risen sufficiently to produce the *same amount of profit or a greater amount*, this will still happen in the way we have described.)[22]
>

< The development of the social productivity of labour is reflected in two ways – firstly, in the size of the productive forces already produced, the scale of the conditions of production in both value and mass, in so far as these are the conditions for new production to take place, i.e., in the absolute magnitude of the productive capital already accumulated; secondly, in the relatively low proportion of capital, out of the total, that is laid out on wages, i.e., in the relatively small amount of living labour that is required to reproduce and valorise a given capital, and for mass production. This presupposes at the same time the concentration of capital.

As far as *the living labour applied* is concerned, the development of productivity again takes a double form.

Firstly, there is an increase in surplus labour, i.e., a shortening of necessary labour-time, the time required for the reproduction of labour-power. Secondly, there is a decline in the total amount of labour-power (the number of workers) applied to set a given capital in motion.

These two movements not only go hand in hand; they mutually condition one another, and are phenomena that express the same law. But they affect the *rate of profit* in *opposite directions*. Profit = surplus-value, and the rate of profit $= \frac{\text{the surplus-value}}{\text{the total capital advanced}}$. But the surplus-value, as a total amount, is determined firstly by its rate and secondly by the mass of labour that is applied at this rate at any one time, or, and this comes to the same thing, by the magnitude of the variable capital. One of these factors, the rate of surplus-value, is rising; the other factor, the number of workers > by which this rate is multiplied < is falling (relatively and absolutely). In so far as the development of productivity reduces the paid portion of the labour applied, it increases the surplus-value by raising

22 [End of the paragraphs that Engels relocated to the end of his Chapter 13. Editor]

its rate; but in so far as it reduces the total quantity of labour applied by a given capital, it reduces the numerical factor by which the rate of surplus-value has to be multiplied, and hence also its amount. Two workers working for 12 hours a day could not supply the same surplus-value as 24 workers each working for only 2 hours, even if they were able to live on air and hence scarcely needed to work at all for themselves. Thus the compensation for the reduced number of workers provided by a rise in the level of exploitation of labour has certain limits which can certainly not be overstepped; this can therefore check and retard the fall in the rate of profit, but it cannot cancel it out.

We have seen that as the capitalist mode of production develops the rate of profit falls, while the mass of profit rises together with the growth in the mass of the functioning capital. Once the rate is given, the absolute amount by which the capital grows depends on its existing magnitude. But if this magnitude is given, the *proportion* in which it grows, its *proportionate growth*, its rate of growth, depends on the rate of profit. |229| A rise in the productivity of labour (which moreover always goes hand in hand with the *depreciation* of the existing capital, as already mentioned) can only *directly* increase the *magnitude of value* of the capital, hence only help to increase the *exchange-value of the existing capital*, to the extent that it increases the *part of the value of the annual product that is transformed back into capital*, by *raising the rate of profit*. In so far as labour productivity is concerned this can come about (since this productivity is as such not directly relevant to the *value* of the existing capital) only to the extent that it either involves a rise in *relative surplus-value* or else reduces the *value of the constant capital*, in other words cheapens either the commodities that go into the reproduction of labour-power or the elements of constant capital. Both of these, however, involve a *depreciation* of the existing capital, and both of them go hand in hand with a *reduction* in the variable capital relative to the constant capital. Both processes condition the fall in the profit rate, and both retard it. Furthermore, in so far as the higher rate of profit causes an increased demand for labour, it provides the stimulus for an increase in the working population > (or an absorption of the surplus population) < and hence in the exploitable material > – the quantity of labour – of which the value of capital consists.

< *Indirectly*, however, the development of labour productivity, by increasing the mass and diversity of the use-values in which the same *exchange-value* is represented, and which form the material substratum, the physical basis, of this capital, the material ingredients of which both components of capital, constant and variable, consist. The same capital and the same labour create more elements that can be transformed into *capital*, quite apart from their exchange-value. These things can serve to absorb additional labour, hence

surplus labour, and thus to create additional capital. The mass of labour that capital can command does not depend on its value but rather on the mass of raw and ancillary materials, machinery, fixed capital in all its forms, and the means of subsistence of which it is composed, whatever their exchange-value may be. Since the mass of necessary and surplus labour applied thus grows > (and the stimulus to the increase of the working population considered earlier goes hand in hand with this) < the value of the capital reproduced and of the surplus-value added to it grow as well.

Yet these two aspects involved in the accumulation process cannot just be considered as existing quietly side by side, which is how Ricardo treats them; they contain a contradiction, and this finds expression in contradictory tendencies and phenomena.

There are contradictory agencies simultaneously in operation here.

Simultaneously with impulses towards a genuine increase in the working population, which stem from the increase in the portion of the annual product that functions as capital, we have those agencies that create a relative surplus population.

Simultaneously with the fall in the profit rate, the mass of capital grows, and this is associated with a depreciation of the existing capital, which stops this fall and gives an accelerated impulse to the accumulation of capital *value*.

|230| Simultaneously with the development of productivity, the composition of capital becomes higher, in other words there is a relative decline in its variable as against its constant portion.

These various influences sometimes tend to exhibit themselves side by side, spatially; at other times one after the other, temporally; and at certain points the conflict of contending agencies breaks through in crises. These crises are never more than momentary, violent solutions for the existing contradictions, violent eruptions that re-establish the balance that has been disturbed.

To express this contradiction in the most general terms, it consists in the fact that the capitalist mode of production tends towards an absolute development of the productive forces irrespective of exchange-value and the surplus-value (profit) this contains, and irrespective of the social relations within which capitalist production takes place; while on the other hand its purpose is to maintain the current exchange-value of the existing capital and to valorise it to the utmost extent possible (i.e., to achieve an accelerated increase in its exchange-value). In its specific character it is directed towards the exchange-value of the existing capital and towards the greatest possible increase of this value. The methods through which it attains this end involve a decline in the profit rate, the depreciation of the existing capital, and the development of the productive forces of labour at the cost of the productive forces already produced.

The periodic depreciation of the existing capital, which is a means, immanent to the capitalist mode of production, to delay the fall in the rate of profit and to accelerate the accumulation of capital value and the formation of new capital, disturbs the given conditions in which capital's process of circulation and reproduction takes place, and is therefore accompanied by sudden stoppages and crises in the production process.

The relative decline in the variable as against the constant capital, which goes hand in hand with the development of the productive forces, gives a stimulus to the growth of the working population, while it continuously creates an artificial surplus population as well. The accumulation of capital, from the point of view of value, > receives a shock (shocks itself owing to the falling rate of profit) < but this serves to accelerate the accumulation in terms of use-value, which in turn sets in motion an accelerated accumulation in terms of value.

Capitalist production constantly strives to overcome its immanent barriers, but it overcomes them only by means that set up the barriers afresh and on a more extensive scale.

The true barrier to capitalist production is *capital* itself. It is the fact that *capital* and its self-valorisation appear as the starting and finishing point, the purpose of production; that production is production only *for* capital, and not the reverse, i.e., that the means of production are not simply means for the expansion and formation [*Gestaltung*] of the pattern of life *for* the society which is formed by the producers. The *barriers* within which the capital values which rest on the basis of the impoverishment and expropriation of the great mass of the producers are able to maintain and valorise themselves therefore come constantly into contradiction with the methods of production that capital must apply to its purpose and which set its course towards an *unrestricted* expansion of production, production as an end in itself, towards an unlimited development of the social productive powers of labour. The means – the unconditional development of the productive forces of social labour – comes into persistent conflict with the restricted end, the valorisation of the existing capital. If the capitalist mode of production is therefore a historical means of developing the material powers of production and creating a corresponding world market, it is at the same the constant contradiction between this, its historical task, and the social relations of production that correspond to it.

|231| As the *profit rate falls*, the *capital-minimum* grows. This minimum is the level of concentration of the means of production in the hand of the individual capitalist he requires to make any productive use at all of labour; it is needed both to exploit labour and to ensure that the *necessary labour-time* spent on the production of commodities does not overstep the average *labour-time socially necessary* for the production of those commodities. Concentration grows at

the same time, since within certain limits a large capital with a lower rate of profit accumulates more quickly than a small capital with a higher rate of profit. This growing concentration leads in turn, at a certain level, to a new fall in the rate of profit. The mass of small, fragmented capitals are thereby forced into risky adventures: speculation, credit swindles, share swindles, and the resulting crises. The so-called plethora of capital is always basically reducible to a plethora of that capital for which the fall in the profit rate is not outweighed by its mass – and this is always the case with fresh offshoots of capital that are newly formed – or to the plethora in which those capitals which are incapable of acting independently are at the disposal of the directors of the great business branches in the shape of credit. This plethora of capital arises from the same causes that stimulate the production of a relative surplus population and it is therefore a phenomenon that complements the latter, even though the two things stand at opposite poles – unoccupied capital on the one hand and an unemployed working population at the other.

Overproduction of capital > (= plethora of capital) < and not of individual commodities (although this overproduction of capital always involves the overproduction of commodities) is nothing more than *over-accumulation of capital*. To understand what this over-accumulation is (a closer investigation of it will form part of > our consideration of the *apparent movement of capital* in which interest capital, etc., and credit, etc., will be examined in more detail) < we have only to take it as an *absolute*. When would the overproduction of capital be absolute? And indeed we refer there to an overproduction which does not just extend to this or that or a few major areas of production, but is rather itself absolute in scope, so that it involves all fields of production.

There would be an *absolute* overproduction of capital as soon as the amount of additional capital that could be employed for the purpose of capitalist production became equal to 0. But the purpose of capitalist production is the *valorisation* of capital, i.e., the production of *surplus-value, of profit, the appropriation of surplus labour*. Thus as soon as capital has grown in such proportion to the working population that neither the absolute labour-time that this working population supplies nor its relative surplus labour-time can be extended (the latter would not be possible in any case in a situation where the demand for labour was so strong, and there was thus a tendency for wages to rise); where, therefore, the *expanded capital* produces only the *same mass of surplus-value* as before < or even *less* – we are speaking here of the absolute mass, not the rate of profit – than capital did before it grew, < there will be an *absolute overproduction of capital*; i.e., the original C, with the addition of ΔC, would produce only P (this represents the total amount of profit produced by C), or even $P - x$. In both cases there would even be a sharp and sudden fall in the general rate of profit, but this time on account of a change in the composition of capital which would not be due to a development in productivity, but rather to a rise in the *money value* of the *variable capital* and a corresponding decline in the proportion of *surplus labour* to the labour objectified in the *variable capital*.

|232| In actual fact, the situation would take the form that one portion of the capital would lie completely or partially idle (since it would first have to expel the capital already functioning from its position, to be valorised at all) while the other portion would be valorised at a lower rate of profit, owing to the competition of the unoccupied or semi-occupied capital > even though this competition exists only potentially. The fact that a portion of the additional capital might take the place of the old, and that the old capital might thus take up a position within the additional capital, would be a matter of indifference here, as the old capital sum would be on one side of the account, the additional capital on the other. >

We should have here, under the above assumption,

(1) on one side of the account $C + \Delta C$,
(2) on the other side, instead of $C + P$,
$C + \Delta C\ (+ P + 0)$
or $C + \Delta C\ (+ P - \Delta C.)$

In both cases, even in case (1), $C + \Delta C$ is applied at a loss in comparison with the original C. In case (2) this is clear from the outset. We therefore need only examine case (1).

Since, under our assumption, $C + \Delta C$ or C' does not provide more profit than $C = C' - \Delta C$ did previously, it is clear that C provides less profit than before. For if $C + \Delta C$ yielded no more than P, as for example < if 1,000 yielded 100 but 1,500 similarly yielded no more than 100, the yield from 1,000 would in the second case be only $66\frac{2}{3}$. The valorisation of the old capital would have fallen absolutely. Under the new circumstances the capital of 1,000 would not yield more than a capital of $666\frac{2}{3}$ did earlier.

It is clear, however, that this kind of actual devaluation of the old capital would not take place without a struggle, but that the additional capital ΔC could not function as capital without a struggle. That competition which results from the overproduction of capital would not cause the rate of profit to fall. Rather the reverse: since the reduced rate of profit and the overproduction of capital spring from the same situation, a competitive struggle would not be unleashed. The capitalists already functioning would let the portion of ΔC that was already in their hands lie more or less idle, so as not to devalue their own original capital themselves or to constrict its place in the field of production, or else they would apply it so as to shift the idleness of the additional capital onto the more recent interlopers and onto their competitors in general, even at a temporary loss.

The part of ΔC that was in new hands would attempt to find a place for itself at the cost of the old capital, and would partly succeed in this, forcing a portion of the old capital either to lose its value completely or to evacuate its former place, to take the place of the additional capital that was employed only partially or completely idle.

Whatever the circumstances, one part of the old capital would *lose its value completely*, entirely ceasing to function as capital, ceasing to valorise itself. As to which section of the capital was particularly subject to this process of annihilation, this would be decided in the course of the competitive struggle. As long as everything goes well, |233| competition acts, as is always the case when the general rate of profit is established, as a practical fraternity of the capitalist class, so that they all share in the common booty in proportion to the size of the portion that each puts in. But as soon as it is no longer a question of the division of profit, but rather of who is to bear the loss, each seeks as far as he can to restrict his own share and saddle it on someone else. For the class as a whole, the loss is unavoidable. But how much each individual member has to bear, the extent to which he has to participate in it, now becomes a struggle of enemy brothers. The opposition between the interest of each individual capitalist and that of the capitalist class as a whole now comes into its own, in the same way as competition was previously the instrument through which the identity of the capitalists' interests was asserted in practice.

How then is this conflict to be resolved? How are the relations corresponding to a 'healthy' movement of capitalist production to be restored? The method of resolution is already implicit in the way in which the conflict is stated. It involves this, that capital should be destroyed. > In *Case 1* what is destroyed is the portion ΔC of the new total capital of C + ΔC, in *Case 2* it is a portion greater than ΔC of the new total capital of C + ΔC. < As our depiction of the conflict has shown, this loss is by no means uniformly distributed amongst all the independent individual capitalists > who go to make up the total capital. < Its distribution is decided instead by a competitive struggle in which the loss is divided very unevenly and in very different forms according to the particular advantages or positions that have already been won, in such a way that one capital lies idle, another is destroyed, a third experiences only a relative loss or a temporary depreciation, and so on.

Under all circumstances, however, the balance will be restored by the *annihilation of capital* to a greater or lesser extent. This will also extend in part to the *material substance of capital*; i.e., part of the means of production, fixed and circulating capital, will not function and operate as capital, and a part of the productive effort that was begun will come to a halt. Even though, as far as this aspect goes, *time* affects and damages all means of production (except the land), what we have here is a far more intense actual destruction of means of production. The major destructive effect here is simply that these means of production cease to be active as means of production, i.e., a shorter or longer disruption occurs in their *function* as means of production.

The chief disruption, and the one possessing the sharpest character, would occur in connection with capital in so far as it constitutes *exchange-value*, i.e., in connection with *capital values*. The portion of capital value that exists simply in the form of future claims for a share in surplus-value and profit, in other words promissory notes on production in their various forms, suffers depreciation simultaneously with the fall in the revenues on which it is reckoned. A portion of ready gold and silver lies idle and does not function as capital. Part of the commodities on the market can complete their process of circulation and reproduction only by an immense reduction in their prices, i.e., a depreciation of the capital they represent. The value of fixed capital suffers more or less the same depreciation. Added to this |234| is the fact that since certain price relationships are assumed in the reproduction process, and govern it, this process is thrown into stagnation and confusion by the general fall in prices. This disturbance and stagnation > is made more acute by the < development of money as a means of payment, which runs alongside the development of capital and depends on those presupposed price relationships, and by the chain of payment obligations at specific dates. It is sharpened still further by the credit system which has also developed at the same time, and the whole thing leads to severe crises, sudden losses of value, actual stagnation and disruption in the reproduction process, and hence an *actual decline in reproduction.*

But other agencies come into play at the same time. Stagnation in production itself deprives part of the working class of employment, and hence places the employed workers in conditions where they have to accept a fall in wages, even beneath the average; an operation that has exactly the same effect for capital as if relative or absolute surplus-value had been increased. Periods of prosperity for the workers provide a stimulus to marriage and reduce the decimation of their offspring, factors which, however much they might involve a *real* increase in the population, do not involve any *increase in the population actually working*, but do have the same effect on the relationship between the workers and capital as if the number of workers actually active had increased. The fall in prices and the competitive struggle, on the other hand, impel each capitalist to reduce the *individual* value of his total product below its *general value* by employing new machinery, new and improved methods of working and new forms of combined labour. That is, they impel him to raise the productivity of a given quantity of labour, to reduce the proportion of variable capital to constant and thereby to > *make population redundant*, < i.e., to create an artificial surplus population. Moreover, the depreciation of the various elements of capital, to the extent that this relates to constant capital, itself involves a rise in the rate of profit. The mass of constant capital applied grows as against the variable, but not its *value*. The stagnation in production that has occurred increases the need for an expansion of production, within the limits set by capitalism.

And so we go round the whole circle once again. One part of the capital that was depreciated by the cessation of its function now regains its old value. And apart from that, with expanded conditions of production, an extended market and increased productivity, it would pass through the same vicious circle one more time.

Even under the most extreme assumption that might be made, *absolute overproduction of capital* is not *absolute overproduction*, it is not *absolute overproduction of the means of production*. It is an overproduction of the means of production only in so far as these function *as capital*, and hence have to produce an additional value in proportion to the value that has expanded together with their mass, i.e., *have to valorise their value to a greater extent*.

|235| It is still overproduction, since the capital is unable to exploit labour at the level of exploitation that is required by the 'healthy' and 'normal' development of the capitalist production process, at a level of exploitation that at least increases the *mass of profit* along with the growing mass of capital applied; that therefore excludes a situation in which the rate of profit falls to the same degree as capital grows > $(C + \Delta C - P + 0)$, < or even falls more quickly than this > $(C + \Delta C - P - x)$.

The genuine overproduction of capital is never identical with the cases examined above; it is not absolute but rather purely relative

< Overproduction of capital never means anything other than *overproduction of the means of production* – means of labour and means of subsistence – that can *function* as capital, i.e., can be applied to exploiting labour *at a given level of exploitation*; a given level, because a *fall in the level of exploitation* below a certain point produces disruption and stagnation in the capitalist production process, crises and the destruction of capital. It is no contradiction that this *overproduction of capital* is accompanied by a greater or smaller *relative surplus population*. > (A fall in this relative surplus population is itself an aspect of the crisis, since it brings nearer the fall in the absolute overproduction of capital we have just examined.) < The same causes that have raised the productivity of labour, increased the mass of products (commodities), extended markets,

accelerated the accumulation of capital in terms of both *mass* and value, and lowered the *rate of profit*, have produced, and continue constantly to produce, a *relative surplus population* [of workers] who are not employed by this *surplus capital* on account of the low level of exploitation of labour at which they would have to be employed, or at least on account of the *low rate of profit* at which they could be employed at a given level of exploitation.

If capital is sent abroad, this is not because it absolutely could not be employed at home. It is rather because it can be employed abroad at a higher rate of profit. But this capital is *absolute surplus capital* for the employed working population and for the country in question. It exists as such *alongside the surplus population*, and this is only an example of how the two things exist side by side and reciprocally condition one another.

On the other hand, the fall in the profit rate that is bound up with accumulation necessarily gives rise to a competitive struggle. Compensation for the fall in the profit rate by an increase in the mass of profit is possible only for the *total capital* of a society and for the big capitalists who are already established. New and independently functioning additional capital finds no compensatory conditions of this kind ready made; it must first acquire them, and so it is the fall in the profit rate that provokes the competitive struggle between capitals, and not the reverse. This competitive struggle, moreover, is accompanied by a temporary rise in wages and a further temporary fall in the profit rate which also derives from this circumstance. The same thing is evident in the *overproduction of commodities*, the overstocking of markets. Since capital's purpose is not the satisfaction of needs but *the production of surplus-value, profit*, and since it attains this goal only by methods that determine the mass of production by reference exclusively to the yardstick of production, and not the reverse, there must be a constant tension between the restricted demands of consumption on the capitalist basis, and a production that is constantly striving to overcome these immanent barriers. Moreover, capital consists of commodities, and hence overproduction of capital involves overproduction of commodities. Thus we have the singular phenomenon that the same economists who deny overproduction of commodities |236| admit overproduction of capital. If it is said that there is no general overproduction, but simply a disproportion between the various branches of production, this again means nothing more than that, *within* capitalist production, the proportionality of the particular branches of production presents itself as a process of passing constantly out of and into disproportionality, since the interconnection of production as a whole here forces itself on the agents of production as a blind law, and not as a law which, being grasped and therefore mastered by their combined reason, brings the productive process under their common control. Countries where the capitalist mode of production is not developed are also required to consume and produce at a level that suits the countries of the capitalist mode of production. If it is said that *overproduction* is only *relative*, this is completely correct; but the whole capitalist mode of production is only a *relative* mode of production, whose barriers are not absolute, but only absolute *for it, on its basis*. How else could there be a lack of demand for those very goods that the mass of the people are short of, and how could it be that this demand has to be sought abroad, in distant markets, in order to pay the workers back home the average measure of the necessary means of subsistence? It is because it is only in this specific, capitalist context that the surplus receives a form in which it is in part able to be consumed by its possessors and in part able to be transformed back into capital for them. If it is said, finally, that the *capitalists* have only to exchange their commodities among themselves and consume them, then the whole character of capitalist production is forgotten, and it is forgotten that what is involved is the *valorisation of capital*. In short, all the objections raised against the *existing phenomena of overproduction* (phenomena that remain impervious to these objections) come down to the assertion that the *barriers to capitalist production* are not barriers to production in general, and are *therefore* not barriers to *this specific, capitalist* mode of production. But the contradiction in this capitalist mode of production consists precisely in its tendency towards the absolute development of productive forces that come into continuous conflict with the *specific conditions of production* in which capital moves.

It is not that too many means of subsistence are produced in relation to the existing population. On the contrary. Too little is produced to satisfy the mass of the population in an adequate and humane way.

Nor are too many means of production produced to employ the part of the population that is capable of working. On the contrary. What is produced is firstly too great a section of the population which is in fact *not* capable of working, which owing to its situation is dependent on the exploitation of the labour of others or on kinds of work that can only count as such within a miserable mode of production. Secondly, not enough means of production are produced to allow the whole working population to work under the most productive conditions, so that their absolute labour-time is limited by the mass and effectiveness of the constant capital applied during that labour-time.

Periodically, however, too much is produced in the way of means of labour and means of subsistence, too much for them to be able to function as means for exploiting the workers at a *specific rate of profit*. Too many commodities are produced for the value and the surplus-value contained in them to be valorised under the conditions of distribution and consumption given by capitalist production, and to be transformed back into new capital. That is to say, it is impossible to carry out this process without constantly repeated explosions.

It is not that too much wealth is produced. But from time to time too much wealth is produced in its capitalist, *antagonistic* form.

|237| The barriers to the capitalist mode of production show themselves as follows:

(1) in the way that the development of labour productivity gives rise to a law, in the form of *the falling rate of profit*, that at a certain point confronts this development itself in the most hostile way and has constantly to be overcome by way of crises.

(2) in the way that it is the *appropriation of unpaid labour*, and the *proportion between this unpaid labour* and objectified labour in general > that appears as its barrier < instead of the proportion between production and social needs, the needs of socially developed human beings. Barriers to production therefore arise at a level of expansion which appears to be inadequate from the standpoint of social needs. Production stops, not at the point where needs are satisfied, but rather where the production and realisation of profit impose this cessation.

If the rate of profit falls, on the one hand we see exertions by capital to ensure that the individual capitalist raises the *individual* value of his commodities above[23] their *average social value*, by using better methods, etc. (the market price, affording the small profit, being then to be considered as a determinate magnitude); on the other hand we have swindling and the facilities afforded to swindlers, by the frantic attempts at securing this or that new line of production, of outlay of capital, of adventures, to secure some kind of *surplus profit* independent of, and towering above, the general level.[24]

The *rate of profit*, i.e., the *proportional* increase in capital, is important for all new *offshoots of capital* that organise themselves independently. And if capital formation were to fall exclusively into the hands of a few existing big capitals, for whom the mass of profit outweighs the rate, the animating fire of production would be totally extinguished. It would cease blazing. The *rate of profit* is the driving agency in capitalist production, and nothing is

23 [Engels replaced 'above' with 'below' here, but it is clear from a passage in the 1861–63 manuscripts that Marx did intend to write 'above': 'The capitalists sell it *above* the value it costs them, and *below* the value it costs society'. (MEGA [(2)] II/3.5, p. 1659.15–16); English translation: MECW 33, 1991, p. 129. Translator]

24 [The passage from 'the market price' to the end of the paragraph was written in English but is printed here with some slight modifications for grammatical reasons. Translator]

produced save what can be produced at a profit. Hence the anxiety of the English economists over the decline in the rate of profit. The fact that Ricardo is disquieted by the mere possibility of this is a precise demonstration of his deep understanding of the conditions of capitalist production. What other people reproach him for, his lack of concern for 'human beings' and his exclusive concentration, when considering capitalist production, on the development of the productive forces, whatever sacrifices of human beings and capital *values* it may cost, is precisely his most significant contribution. The development of the productive forces of social labour is capital's *historical* mission and justification. For that very reason, it unwittingly creates the material conditions for a higher mode of production. What disturbs Ricardo is the way that the rate of profit, which is the stimulus of capitalist production and both the condition for accumulation and its driving force, is endangered by the development of production itself. And the quantitative relation is everything here. In actual fact, the underlying reason is something deeper, about which he has no more than a suspicion. What is visible here in a *purely economic manner*, i.e., from the bourgeois standpoint, within the 'limits of the capitalist understanding', from the standpoint of capitalist production itself, is its barrier, its *relativity*, the fact that it is not an *absolute* but only a historical *mode of production*, corresponding to a specific and limited epoch in the development of the material conditions of production.

|238| Since the development of labour productivity is far from uniform in the various branches of industry, and, besides being uneven in degree, often takes place in opposite directions > since the productivity of labour is to such a degree bound up with natural conditions that it may fall while the *social* productivity of labour is increasing (the whole investigation of the extent to which *natural conditions* influence the productivity of labour independently of the development of the *social* forces of production, and often in opposition to them, belongs to our consideration of *ground-rent*) < it so happens that the average profit (= surplus-value) is necessarily very far below the level one would expect simply from the development of productivity in the most advanced branches of industry. And if the development of productivity in different branches of industry does not just proceed in very different proportions, but often also in opposite directions, this does not arise simply from the anarchy of competition and the specific features of the bourgeois mode of production. The productivity of labour is also tied up with *natural conditions*, which often become less productive in the proportion to which productivity rises – to the extent that the latter depends on social conditions. We thus have a contrary movement in these different spheres > so that the productivity of labour rises in one place while it falls in another. < We need only consider

the influence of the seasons, for example, on which the greater part of the raw materials depend, as well as the exhaustion of forests and coal and iron mines, etc.

If the *raw material* – a part of constant capital – steadily grows in mass along with the productivity of labour, this is not the case for the fixed capital – buildings, machinery, lighting heating installations, etc. Even though the machinery, as its bulk increases, becomes more expensive in absolute terms, it becomes cheaper relatively speaking. If five workers produce ten times as many commodities as before, this does not mean that the outlay on constant capital increases ten-fold. Even though the value of *this portion* of constant capital grows with the development of productivity, it is far from growing in the same ratio.

We have already called attention several times, > particularly in this section, < to the distinction between the *relationship of constant capital to variable*, as this is expressed in the *fall in the rate of profit*, and the *relationship between the components of capital* as it presents itself – with the development of labour productivity – with respect to the *individual commodity* and *its price*.

The *value of a commodity* is determined by the total labour-time contained in it, both *past* and *living*. > If *a smaller amount of living labour is added*, in order to transform a larger amount of raw material (or in general any object of labour, such as in the mining industry) into the product, (leaving the *raw material* out of the equation: the mere object of labour which is not *raw material* is worthless in any case) it follows that the difference between the part of the value added to the individual commodity by the new constant capital (fixed capital and ancillary materials) and the part of the value added by the old constant capital is less than the difference between the new, smaller amount of labour and the old surplus labour replaced by it. (If the differences were the same, the commodity would *not* become cheaper, even though the labour most recently added was more productive. Under rational conditions of production, not regulated by profit, the new method would even in this case be better and more productive.) It is not possible to add as a condition of labour a greater amount of past labour than the living labour that has been saved. But it is to be noted in regard to the individual commodity or the mass of commodities produced during a particular turnover time that it is sufficient that the *wear and tear* which the fixed part of the constant capital gives up to it is less than the living labour it replaces. Moreover, although there is a significant increase in the *absolute value of the ancillary materials employed* – their value as a *part of the constant capital laid out relatively to the capital laid out in wages* – in relative terms, referring to the total quantity of commodities produced, with regard to the proportion of the lower productivity of labour which affects the individual commodity required by the individual worker himself given the lower productivity of labour under the now antiquated relations of production, they have *economised* on this. A *smaller amount of the value* of these materials has entered into the individual commodity. There is a decline, a decrease, in the *portion of value* |239| added by this part of the constant capital to the individual commodity or to the mass of commodities produced in a given turnover time or also in the *total reproduction time of the capital,* although this *component of the value of the constant capital* has grown in relation to the *value of the variable capital.* There is absolutely no contradiction here, since the same productivity of labour increases the *mass of commodities* and *reduces* the labour that produces them, hence lessening the variable capital. Nor is a contradiction involved in the fact that the same *amount of value* (of this part of the constant capital) distributed over *an increased mass of commodities* is reduced in proportional terms, whereas it is increased in proportion to a *smaller amount of value* (the variable capital) or *a smaller amount of living labour* (even in the individual commodity). The requirement always remains, however, that the *part of the value* which enters into the individual commodity as wear and tear, as a depreciation of the fixed capital, and as *an equivalent value* to the ancillary materials consumed in it must be smaller than the difference between the productivity of the *new,* most recently added labour and that of the old labour. Nevertheless, this does not exclude the possibility that an equally large or even a larger quantity of constant capital might be consumed, might enter as a constituent of the value of a given total amount of commodities, e.g., the number of pounds of twist which are produced in a given period of time, say a day, than was previously expended in the form of wages. Only a smaller quantity in respect of the individual commodity. This however implies that the same *amount of commodities,* using the old process, would have used up a larger *total amount* of living labour + a larger part of the value of the constant capital. Assume that ¼n workers produce exactly as much as n workers produced previously. Then the amount of commodities produced remains the same. But ¾ of the living labour has been saved. There is an increase in the amount of constant capital added, but (after deduction of the old constant capital) it grows by less than ¾, and thus the total value of the constant capital has grown as a proportion to the amount laid out in wages (even the wear and tear may have grown as well), although in respect to the commodities it has grown to a lesser degree than the amount of living labour has been reduced. Nevertheless, the total capital laid out is *absolutely larger* than it was previously, but it is in a *smaller* proportion to the *mass of commodities* produced. In relation to the variable capital, the total capital has grown both absolutely and relatively. If the *raw material rises,* this rise must be counterbalanced by the replacement of part of the remainder of the constant capital which enters into the commodity and of the added living labour. In this case the commodity continues to be cheaper, but the rate of profit falls because the ratio of the value of the total capital to the variable capital grows still more. The greater the increase in fixed capital resulting from the increase in the productivity of labour, the greater the portion of the capital that has not been consumed or *the longer* the turnover period during which the reproduction process of this portion of the constant capital runs its course.

< In competition, the *growing minimum amount* of capital needed as productivity increases *appears* in the following way: as soon as the new invention has been introduced generally, smaller capitals are in future excluded from this line of business. Only when *mechanical inventions* in the various spheres of production are *in their infancy* can they be operated by smaller capitals. Very large undertakings, on the other hand, where the proportion of constant capital is extraordinarily high, such as railways, *do not yield the average rate of profit*, but only a portion of this, *interest*. If this were not so, the general rate of profit would sink still lower. On the other hand, it is only here that this big capital (share capital) finds a direct field of employment.

The growth of capital, i.e., the *accumulation* of capital, involves a reduction in the rate of profit only in so far as this growth brings with it those changes in the ratio between the organic parts of capital that were considered above. Yet despite the constant and daily transformations in the mode of production, a greater or smaller part of this total capital, now one, now the other, continues to accumulate for a certain length of time *on the basis of a given* |240| *average ratio of these components*, so that its growth does not involve any organic change and is thus no cause for a fall in the rate of profit. > During certain periods, < it is owing to this constant enlargement of capital and expansion of production goes forward continuously > in certain branches of industry without an accompanying change in the ratio between its organic components – i.e., on the basis of methods of production that remain the same – < that the rate of profit does not decline in the same measure as the total social capital increases.

The increase in the absolute number of workers, despite the relative decline in the variable capital laid out in wages, does not take place in all branches of production, nor does it take place evenly in the branches where it does. In agriculture, the decline in the element of living labour may be absolute.

It is simply the *needs of the capitalist mode of production*, moreover, that lead the number of wage-labourers to increase absolutely > while the number declines relatively < despite this relative decline. For this mode of production, labour-power is superfluous the moment it is no longer necessary to employ it for 12 to 15 hours a day. A development in the productive forces that would reduce the absolute number of workers, thus enabling the whole nation to accomplish its entire production in a shorter period of time, would produce a revolution, because it would deprive the majority of the population of its income. Here the *specific barrier* to capitalist production appears once again, and we see that it is in no way an absolute form for the development of the productive forces (and the creation of social wealth) but rather collides with it at a certain point. One aspect of this collision is presented by the periodic crises that arise when one or another section of the working population is made superfluous in its old employment. The barrier to capitalist production is the *surplus time of the workers*. The absolute surplus time that the society gains is of no concern to capitalist production. The *development of productivity* is important to it only in so far as it increases the surplus labour-time of the worker, not in so far as it *lessens the labour-time needed for material production as such*. In this way it moves in a contradiction.

We have seen how the growing accumulation of capital involves its growing concentration. Thus the power of capital grows, in other words the autonomy of the social conditions of production, as personified by the capitalist, is asserted more and more as against the actual producers. Capital shows itself more and more to be a *social power* (with the capitalist as its functionary), a power that no longer stands in any possible kind of relationship to what the work of one particular individual can create. It is instead an *alienated* [*entfremdet*] *social power which has gained an autonomous position*, and confronts society as a *thing*, and as the power that the capitalist has through this thing. The contradiction between the *general social power* into which capital has developed and the *private power of the individual capitalists* over these social conditions of production develops ever more blatantly, while this development also contains the *solution to this situation*, in that it simultaneously converts the conditions of production into general, communal, social conditions. This transformation is brought about by the development of the productive forces under capitalist production and by the manner and form in which their development is accomplished.

No capitalist voluntarily applies a new method of production, no matter how much more productive it may be or how much it might raise the rate of surplus-value, if it *reduces the rate of profit*. But every new method of production of this kind makes |241| commodities cheaper. At first, therefore, he can sell them above their price of production, perhaps above their value. He pockets the difference between their costs of production and the market price of the other commodities, which are produced at higher production costs. This is possible because the *average* socially necessary labour-time required to produce these latter commodities is *greater* than the labour-time required with the new method of production. His production procedure is *ahead of* the social average. But competition makes the new procedure universal and subjects it to the general law. A *fall in the profit rate* then ensues – firstly perhaps in *this* sphere of production, and subsequently equalised with the others – a fall that is completely independent of the capitalists' *will*.

It should also be noted at this point that the same law prevails even in those spheres of production whose products do not enter either directly or indirectly into the workers' consumption, or into the conditions of production of their means of subsistence; i.e., it prevails even in those spheres of production in which no cheapening of commodities can increase *relative surplus-value* and make labour-power cheaper. (In fact a cheapening of constant capital in any of these branches may increase the *profit rate*, if the level of exploitation of labour remains the same.) As soon as actual proof is provided that these commodities can be produced more cheaply, those capitalists who operate under the old conditions of production must sell their product *below* its price of production; the *value* of their commodities has fallen because they need more labour-time to produce them than is socially necessary. In short – and this *appears* as an effect of competition – they must also introduce the new mode of production which reduces the ratio of variable capital to constant.

The application of machinery reduces the price of the commodities produced with that machinery owing to various factors, which can always be reduced to the decline in the quantity of labour absorbed by each individual commodity; but in addition to this there is the reduction in the portion of value that goes into the individual commodity as wear and tear on the machinery. The slower the machinery's depreciation, the less labour is required to reproduce it. The quantity and value of capital which consists of machinery (and fixed capital in general) are increased as against the capital which exists in the form of labour. >

Jones on accumulation and the fall of profit. < '*All other things being equal*, the power of a nation to save from its profits varies with the *rate of profits*, is great when they are high, less, when low; but as the rate of profit declines, *all other things do not remain equal* ... A *low rate of profit* is ordinarily accompanied by a *rapid rate of accumulation*, relatively to the numbers of the people, as in England; and a *high rate of profit* by a *slower rate of accumulation*, relatively to the numbers of the people, as in Poland, Russia, India, etc'. (Jones 1833, p. 50.)

Jones is right to stress that despite the falling rate of profit the '*inducements and faculties to accumulate*' increase. Firstly, on account of the growing relative surplus population. Secondly, because as the productivity of labour grows, so does the *mass of use-values represented by the same exchange-value*, i.e., the *material substratum* of capital increases. Thirdly, because of the *increas-*

ing diversity of branches of production. Fourthly, through the development of the credit system, joint-stock companies, etc., and the consequent ease with which the possessor of money can transform it into capital without having to become an industrial capitalist. *Fifthly,* the growth in needs and the mania for enrichment. *Sixthly,* the growing mass of investment of fixed capital, and so on.

|242| The main facts about capitalist production are these:

The concentration of the means of production in a few hands, which means that they cease to appear as the property of the immediate workers and are transformed on the contrary into *social powers* of production, even if at first as the private property of capitalists. The latter are trustees of bourgeois society, and they pocket all the fruits of this trusteeship.

The organisation of labour itself as social labour: through cooperation, division of labour and the association of labour with natural science.

On both these counts the capitalist mode of production abolishes private property and private labour, even if in *antithetical* forms.

The establishment of the world market. >

An example of the differences in the ratio of constant to variable capital.

'Price of cotton cloth in the island of Java. The cotton, in the seed, is sold by the picul (about 133 lbs.). Not above ¼ or ⅕ of this weight ... is cotton; and the natives, by means of rude rollers, separate at the expense of one day's labour about $1^1/_4$ lbs. cotton from the seed. In this stage worth between 4 or 5 times its original cost; and the prices of the same substance, in its different stages of manufacture, are, for one picul:

Cotton in the seed ...	2 to 3 dollars;
clean cotton	10 to 11 dollars;
cotton thread	24 dollars;
cotton thread died blue ...	35 dollars;
good ordinary cotton cloth ...	50 dollars.

Thus the expense of spinning in Java is 117 percent on the value of the raw material ... the expense of spinning cotton into a fine thread is, in England, about 33 percent'. (Babbage 1832, pp. 165–6.)

Owen on the growth of productivity in England between 1792 and 1817 (see Notebook XVIII, p. 1143).[25]

25 [This is a reference to an extract Marx made from a French translation of a book about Robert Owen (Macnab 1821, pp. 128–30). It is printed in full in MEGA (2) II/3.5, p. 1866 (English translation: MECW 33, 1991, pp. 351–2.) Translator]

If the capital applied is C and the rate of profit is r, the accumulation will be Cr. And it is clear that Cr will increase if the factor C grows more quickly than the factor r declines.

< The tremendous productive power, in proportion to the population, which is developed within the capitalist mode of production, and – even if not to the same degree – the growth in capital *values* (not only in their material substratum), these growing far more quickly than the population, contradicts the basis *on behalf of* which this immense productive power operates, since this basis becomes ever narrower in relation to the growth of wealth; and it also contradicts the *conditions of valorisation* of this swelling capital. Hence crises. >

|243| CHAPTER FOUR

The Transformation of Commodity Capital and Money Capital into Commodity-Dealing Capital and Money-Dealing Capital or into Merchant's Capital

< *Merchant's* or *trading capital* is divided into two forms (sorts), *commercial capital* and *money-dealing capital*, which we shall go on to distinguish in enough detail as is needed in order to analyse capital in its basic inner structure. This is all the more necessary in that modern economics, and even its best representatives, lump trading capital and productive capital directly together and in fact completely overlook trading capital's characteristic peculiarities.

1 Commodity-Dealing Capital (Commercial Profit)

a) The movement of *commodity capital* has been analysed in Chapter Three of Volume II. Taking the social capital as a whole, one part of this is always on the market as a *commodity*, waiting to pass over into money, even though this part is always composed of fresh elements, and elements of varying magnitude; another part is on the market as money, waiting to pass over into commodities. Capital is always involved in this *movement* of transition, this metamorphosis of form. In as much as this function of circulating capital acquires *independent life* as a *special* function of a special capital and is fixed by the division of labour as a function that falls to a particular species of capitalist, *commodity capital* becomes *commodity-dealing capital* (commercial capital.)

We have already explained in Volume II (*'Costs of Circulation'*)[1] the extent to which the *transport industry, warehousing* and *the dispersal of goods in a distributable form* (retailing) should be viewed as production processes that continue within the process of circulation. These incidents in the circulation of commodity capital are sometimes confused with the functions peculiar to commercial capital (*commodity-dealing capital*); they are sometimes linked

---

1 [This refers to sections 2 and 3 of Chapter Six of Volume II. English translation: Marx 1978, pp. 214–29. Translator]

in practice with the specific functions *peculiar* to this capital, although with the development of the *social* division of labour the function of commercial capital also *exists in a pure form*, i.e., separately from those real functions and independent of them. For our purpose, where what matters is to define the specific difference of this special form of capital, we can therefore ignore those functions. In so far as capital that functions exclusively in the circulation process, and especially commercial capital, sometimes combines part of those functions with its own, it does not appear in its *pure* form. We only have this pure form once those functions have been discarded and removed,

|244| We have seen how the existence of capital as *commodity capital*, and the *metamorphosis* that it undergoes as commodity capital within the sphere of circulation, on the market – a metamorphosis that breaks down into buying and selling, the transformation of commodity capital into money capital and of money capital into commodity capital – forms a phase in industrial capital's reproduction process and thus in its production process as a whole; but that at the same time, in this function as *circulating* capital, it is distinguished from its own existence as *productive* capital. These are two separate and distinct forms of existence of the same capital. One part of the overall social capital is always to be found in this form as *circulating* capital on the market, in the course of this metamorphosis, although for any individual capital its existence as commodity capital and its metamorphosis as such forms only a *point of transition*, ever vanishing and ever repeated, a *transitional stage* towards the continuity of its production process; although, accordingly, the elements of commodity capital to be found on the market are constantly changing, since they are constantly being withdrawn from the commodity market and just as constantly returned to it as the new product of the production process.

Commercial capital, then, is nothing but the *transformed form of a portion* of this circulating capital which is always to be found on the market, in the course of its metamorphosis, and is perpetually confined to the sphere of circulation. We say here *one portion only*, because another part of the buying and selling of commodities always takes place directly between the industrial capitalists themselves. We shall completely *ignore* this other portion of the circulating capital in the present investigation, since it contributes nothing to the theoretical definition or to our understanding of the specific nature of commercial capital, and was moreover exhaustively dealt with for our purposes when we examined the circulation process of capital previously.

The dealer in commodities, like any other *capitalist*, first appears on the market as the representative of a certain sum of money that he advances as capital, i.e., which he seeks to transform from x (the original value) into x + Δx (this sum advanced plus the profit on it). As he is not just a capitalist, but specifically a commodity dealer, it goes without saying that his capital has to appear on the market originally in the form of *money capital*, since he does not produce any commodities himself but simply deals in them, facilitates their movement; and in order to deal in them, he must first buy them, and be therefore the possessor of *money capital*.

Let us assume that a commodity dealer has £3,000 that he valorises as trading capital. Say that he uses this £3,000 to buy, for example, 30,000 ells of linen from a linen manufacturer (One ell costs 2s.) He sells these 30,000 ells, so that if the average annual rate of profit is 10 percent he makes a profit of 10 percent, after deducting all his incidental expenses, or, in other words, by the end of the year he has transformed his £3,000 into £3,300. *How* he makes this profit is a question we shall go into only later. Here we want first of all to consider *just the form* of his capital's movement. He keeps buying linen for £3,000 and he keeps selling it again. He constantly repeats this operation of *buying in order to sell*, M – C – M′, the simple form of capital, when it is completely restricted to the circulation process, and not interrupted by the interval of the production process, which lies outside his own movement and function.

What then is the relationship between this *commodity-dealing capital* and *commodity capital* as a mere form of existence of industrial capital?

As far as the linen manufacturer is concerned, he has realised the *value* of his linen with the merchant's money, thus completing the first phase in the metamorphosis of his *commodity capital*, its transformation into money; and, all other circumstances remaining the same, he can now transform the money back into yarn, coal, wages and so on, as well as into his own continuing expenditure on the means of subsistence (the consumption of his revenue). Apart from this expenditure of profit as revenue, he can now continue the reproduction process with the rest.

But although the metamorphosis of the linen into money, its sale, has taken place *for him*, it has not yet happened for the *linen itself*. This is still on the market as before in the shape of *commodity capital*, its destiny being to complete its first metamorphosis by being sold. With respect to *this commodity capital itself*, nothing has happened except a change in the person of its owner. As far as its own function is concerned, its position in the process, it is still commodity capital. But now it is a *saleable commodity*; it is in the hands of the merchant instead of those of the producer. The function of *selling it*, i.e., of facilitating by this operation the first phase of its metamorphosis, has been taken over from the producer by the merchant and transformed into his *special business*, whereas previously it was a function the producer himself had to perform after he had completed the function of producing it.

|245| Let us assume that the merchant does not succeed in selling his 30,000 ells in the interval that the linen producer takes before putting a further 30,000 ells on the market, at a value of £3,000. The merchant cannot buy these again, since he still has the 30,000 unsold ells in stock and has not yet transformed them back into money capital. There is now a stoppage, an interruption in the reproduction. (Either that, or the linen producer has additional money capital at his disposal, with which he can > purchase more yarn, coal and labour, and thus < continue the process of production, independently of the sale of the 30,000 ells. But to make this assumption would not alter things at all. As far as the capital advanced in the 30,000 ells is concerned, its reproduction process is and remains interrupted.) Here we thus have palpable evidence that the operations of the merchant are nothing more than those operations that must always be performed to transform the producer's commodity capital into money, operations which accomplish the functions of commodity capital in the circulation and reproduction process. If selling were the exclusive business of a mere agent of the producer, instead of being performed by an independent merchant, and purchase likewise, this connection would not be obscured for one moment.

Commercial capital, therefore, is absolutely nothing more than the *commodity capital* of the producer which has to go through the process of transformation into money and has to perform its function as commodity capital on the market; only instead of being an incidental operation carried out by the producer himself, this function now appears as the *exclusive operation* of a particular *set* of capitalists, the merchants, and acquires an autonomous position as the business of a particular capital investment.

This is in any case evident in *commodity capital's specific form of circulation*. The merchant buys a commodity and later sells it: M – C – M′. In simple commodity circulation, or even in *commodity circulation* as this appears as a circulation process of industrial capital, C′ – M – C, the circulation is effected in such a way that *the same piece of money* changes hands twice. The linen producer sells his commodity, the linen, transforming it into *money* with the result that the buyer's money passes > out of the hands of the merchant < into the producer's hands. He buys yarn, coal, labour, etc., with *this same money*, so that *the same money* is again expended by him in order to transform the value of the linen back into the commodities that form its elements of production. > (However, to the extent that M – C – M′ is the general form of capital, so that for example the linen producer first lays out money to buy the elements of production of the linen, then he makes sure that these elements enter into the production process, and finally transforms the product of this process, the linen, back into money, it is not *the same* commodity which is bought and sold.

The commodity is bought in the form of the means of production, it is sold in the form of the product; it is therefore a commodity that has undergone *a change*, it has been changed as a result of passing through the production process.) < But it is a different matter with the movement of commercial capital > for example the capital of the linen dealer. < With his £3,000 he buys 30,000 ells of linen; he sells *the same* 30,000 ells in order to recover his money capital (£3,000 plus profit) from the sphere of circulation. Here it is not *the same pieces of money* that change place twice, but rather the same *commodity*; it passes from the hands of the seller into those of the buyer, and from the hands of this buyer, who has now become a seller, into those of another buyer. It is sold twice; > (we disregard here the repetition of this process through the interposition of a *series of merchants*); < and it is precisely through this repeated sale, the double change of place of the same commodity, that the return of the money advanced by the first buyer for the purchase of the commodity is mediated. In the case C′ – M – C, the same money's double change of place makes it possible for the commodity to be alienated in one shape and appropriated again in another shape. In the other case, M – C′ – M, the double change of place of *the same commodity* makes it possible for the money advanced to be withdrawn from circulation again. All this shows precisely that the commodity has not yet been definitively sold when it passes from the hands of the producer into those of the merchant, and that the latter is only continuing the *operation* of sale – or the facilitation of the commodity capital's function. It also shows at the same time how what was C – M for the productive capitalist – simply a function of his commodity capital > or of *his* capital as circulating capital < – is M – C – M′ for the merchant, a particular valorisation of the money capital he had advanced. One phase of the commodity's metamorphosis, M – C, now exhibits itself, with respect to the merchant, as M – C – M′, i.e., as the evolution of a specific kind of capital.

|246| The merchant > (the dealer in linen, for example) < definitively sells the *commodity*, the linen, to the consumer, whether this is an industrial consumer (e.g., a bleacher) or an individual who wants the linen for his own private use. In this way the capital he has advanced returns to him (with a profit) and he can begin the operation afresh. If his money had circulated as means of payment, so that he only had to pay for it say six weeks after the receipt of the linen, then, if he had sold the linen before this time, he could have paid the linen producer without himself having to advance any money capital. If he had not sold the linen, he would have had to advance the £3,000 six weeks after the purchase, instead of immediately; and if he had sold the linen below the price at which he bought it, because of a fall in its market price, he would have had to replace the missing amount from his own capital; > and the same thing would occur if he were only able to sell part of it.

< What, then, gives *commercial capital* the character of an *independently functioning capital*, whereas > as long as it remains in the hands of the producer or < is sold by the producer himself it obviously appears as no more than a particular form of his capital at a particular phase in its reproduction process, during its stay in the circulation sphere?

Firstly, the fact that the *commodity capital* accomplishes its definitive *transformation into money*, and its first metamorphosis, its function on the market that falls to it *as commodity capital*, in the hands of an agent distinct from the producer, and that this function of commodity capital is facilitated by the operations of the merchant, by his sales and purchases, which thereby take on the shape of a *specific business*, separate from the other functions of capital and hence *autonomous*. It is a particular form of the *social division of labour*, such that one part of the function which has to be performed in a particular phase of the capital's reproduction process, here the phase of circulation, appears as the exclusive function of a specific *agent of circulation* distinct from the producer. But this does not mean that this *special business* necessarily appears as the function of a *special capital*, different from industrial capital which is going through its reproduction process and independent of it; it does not appear like this in practice when trading is pursued simply by > those who sell on commission, < travelling salesmen or other direct agents of the industrial capitalist. A second aspect must also be involved.

This second aspect enters the scene in this way. The *circulation agent*, the merchant, *advances money capital* (whether his own or borrowed is irrelevant here) in this transaction. What presents itself for the capital involved in its reproduction process simply as C – M, the transformation of commodity capital into money capital or *a simple sale*, takes the form of M – C – M′ for the merchant, the purchase and sale of the same commodity, > and hence as the reflux of money capital < so that the money capital he parted with on the purchase returns to him through the sale.

It continues to be C – M, the transformation of commodity capital into money capital, that presents itself to the merchant as M – C – M (in so far as he advances capital for purchasing the commodity from the producer); it continues to be the first metamorphosis of the commodity capital, even though the same act may present itself for a producer or for the industrial capital in the course of its reproduction process as M – C, the transformation of money back into commodity (the means of production), i.e., as the second phase in the metamorphosis. (For the linen dealer[2] C – M was the first metamorphosis of the

2 [Engels has 'linen producer' here. Translator]

commodity capital, its transformation into money capital. For the merchant, this act takes the form M – C, the transformation of his money capital into commodity capital. If he now sells the linen to the dyer (printer), this in turn represents M – C for the dyer, the transformation of money capital into commodity capital, or the second metamorphosis of his commodity capital; but for the merchant it is C – M, the sale of the linen that he has bought. In point of fact, however, it is only now that the *commodity capital* that the linen manufacturer has produced is definitively sold; the merchant's M – C – M, in other words, simply represents a mediatory process for the C – M > of the linen which is passing through its reproduction process. < Let us assume, alternatively, that the same linen dealer now buys yarn, coal, etc., with a part of the value of the linen he has sold. For him, therefore, this is M – C. But for the merchant who sells the yarn, coal, etc., it is M – C – M, the resale of the coal, yarn, etc.; and with regard to the coal and yarn themselves, with regard to these commodity capitals, it is simply its definitive sale, C – M, the completion of its first metamorphosis. Thus whether the merchant buys from the industrial capitalist or sells to him, his M – C – M, the circuit of his capital, only ever expresses what with respect to the commodity capital itself, as a particular form of existence of the capital which is involved in its reproduction process C – M, is simply the completion of its first metamorphosis. The M – C of the commercial capital is M – C only for the industrial capitalist, and not for the commodity capital he has produced. It is only a transition of the commodity capital from the hands of the industrialist into those of the agent of circulation; and it is only the commercial capital's C – M that is the definitive C – M for the functioning commodity capital. M – C – M is nothing but two C – M's performed by the same commodity capital, it consists of two successive sales which between them simply make possible its final and definitive sale).

|247| Thus *commodity capital* assumes in *commercial capital* the form of an *independent variety* of capital in the following way: the *merchant* advances money capital that is valorised as capital, and functions as capital, *only* because it is *exclusively* engaged in facilitating the metamorphosis of commodity capital, by making it fulfil its function as commodity capita, i.e., its transformation into money. It does this through the constant purchase and sale of commodities. This is its exclusive operation; this *activity that mediates* the circulation process is the exclusive function of the money capital with which the merchant operates. By way of this function he transforms his money into money capital, puts his M forward as M – C – M′, and by this same process he transforms *commodity capital* into *commercial capital.*

If we are considering the reproduction process of the total social capital, *commercial capital*, in so far as it exists in the form of *commodity capital*, and as long as it does so, is evidently nothing other than the part of the productive capital which is still on the market and is engaged in its process of metamorphosis and now exists and functions as commodity capital. Thus is only *the money capital advanced by the merchant*, the money capital exclusively designed for buying and selling, which therefore never assumes any other form that that of commodity capital and money capital, never assumes that of productive capital, and always remains penned into capital's circulation sphere – it is only this money capital that has now to be considered with regard to the overall reproduction process of capital.

Once the producer, the linen manufacturer, has sold his 30,000 ells to the merchant for £3,000, he uses the money thus released to buy the means of production he needs, and his capital goes back again into the production process. His production process continues, it goes forward without a break > as a process of reproduction. < As far as he is concerned the transformation of his commodity into money has taken place. But this transformation has not taken place for the *linen itself*. It has not yet been transformed back into money, it has not yet gone into either productive or individual consumption as a use-value. The linen dealer now represents the same commodity capital on the market as the linen producer originally represented there. For him the process of metamorphosis has been *shortened*, but only to be taken in hand by the merchant.

If the linen producer had had to wait until his linen really ceased to be a commodity, i.e., until it had passed to its final buyer, the industrial or individual consumer, his *reproduction process* would have been *interrupted*. Or, in order not to interrupt it, he would have had to restrict his operations, transform a smaller part of his linen, his product, into yarn, wage-labour, etc., in short into the elements of the production process, and retain a greater part of this as a monetary reserve. In this way, one part of his capital would be able to be present on the market as a commodity, while another part was re-transformed into productive capital, so that when this latter part entered the market as a commodity, the other part would return as money. > Even when *trade* enters the picture this *division* of his capital continues to be necessary. < But without the former the part of the circulating capital that exists in the form of a monetary reserve would always have to be greater in proportion to the part employed within the production process, and the scale or the reproduction process would accordingly be restricted. Instead of this, the producer can now apply a greater part of his capital in the actual production process, leaving a smaller part as a monetary reserve.

In this new situation, another part of the social capital, in the form of commercial capital, is always to be found in the circulation process. It is never employed for any other purpose than buying and selling commodities. There thus seems to be only a change in the persons that have this capital in their hands.

If, instead of buying linen for £3,000 with the intention of selling it again, the merchant were himself to apply this £3,000 productively, the society's productive capital would be that much greater. However, the linen producer would then have to keep a larger part of his capital as a money reserve, and so would the merchant now turned industrial capitalist. If the merchant remains a merchant, on the other hand, the producer saves time in selling which he can apply to supervising the production process, while the merchant has to spend his entire time selling. >

|248| (In its independent form, *commercial capital* is always originally money capital. It has been acquired in the money form, through being handed on, etc., since the merchant does not produce, hence the product is never in his possession in its original *commodity* form, but only in its transformed form as *money*.)

< If the commercial capital does not overstep its necessary proportions, we can assume the following:

(1) As a result of the *principle of the division of labour*, the capital which is *exclusively* concerned with buying and selling is *smaller* than it would be if the industrial capitalist had to conduct the *entire* commercial part of his business himself. (And besides the money that has to be laid out on the purchase of commodities, this capital also includes the money laid out for the workers needed to pursue the merchant's business, as well as for the merchant's constant capital, warehouses, expenditure on transport, etc.)

(2) Because the merchant is exclusively concerned with this business, not only is the producer's commodity converted into money sooner, but the *commodity capital itself* goes through its metamorphosis more quickly than it would in the hands of the producer.

(3) Taking commercial capital as a whole in relation to industrial capital, a single turnover of commercial capital can correspond not only to the turnovers of several capitals in one sphere of production, but also to the turnovers of a number of capitals in different spheres. The former is the case if the linen dealer, for example, after he has used his £3,000 to buy the product of a linen producer and sold this again before the producer in question puts the same quantity of goods on the market once more, buys the product of another linen producer, or several other linen producers, and sells this also, thus facilitating the *turnovers* of various capitals in the same sphere of production. The latter is the case if the merchant, after selling the linen, now buys silk, for example, and thus facilitates the turnover of a capital in another sphere of production.

It should generally be noted that the *turnover* of the productive capital is restricted not just by the *circulation time*, but also by the *production time*. The *turnover* of commercial capital, in so far as it deals with just one particular kind of commodity, is not restricted by the turnover of a single industrial capital, but rather by the turnover of all industrial capitals in the same sphere of production. After the merchant has bought and sold one producer's linen, he can buy and sell that of another, before the first puts his commodity on the market again. The same commercial capital can thus successively facilitate the different turnovers of various capitals invested in a sphere of production, so that *its turnover* is not identical with the turnovers of one individual industrial capital and hence does not replace only the monetary reserve that this particular industrial capitalist had to keep to himself. Naturally, the turnover of commercial capital in one sphere of production is restricted by the overall production in that sphere > the total production of linen, for instance, forms its limit. < But it is not limited by the limit of production or the turnover time of an individual capital in the same sphere, in as much as the latter is determined by its production time. Assume that A supplies a commodity that takes three months to be produced. After the merchant has bought and sold it, say in one month, he can buy and sell the same product as supplied by another producer. Or, after he has sold one farmer's wheat, for example, he can buy and sell a second farmer's with the same money, and so on. The turnover of his capital is limited by the amount of wheat he can successively buy and sell in a given time, say a year, but the turnover of the farmer's capital, quite apart from the time it takes to sell it, is limited by the time needed to produce it.

The turnover of the same commercial capital can just as easily mediate the turnovers of capitals in various spheres of production. |249| To the extent that the same commercial capital serves in different turnovers to transform various commodity capitals successively into money, and thus buys and sells them in a series, it performs the same function, as money capital in relation to commodity capital, that money does in general vis-à-vis commodities as a result of the number of times it circulates in a given period.

The *turnover* of commercial capital is not identical with the turnover or > the number of reproductions < of *a productive capital of the same size*; it is equal, rather, to the sum of the turnovers of a number of such capitals, whether in the same sphere of production or in different ones. The more quickly the commercial capital turns over, the *smaller* it > is in relation to the mass of the productive capital. And the slower its turnover, the greater is < the portion of the total money capital that figures as commercial capital. The less developed production is, the greater is the sum of commercial capital in proportion to the amount of *commodities put into circulation in general* (although it is smaller *in absolute terms*). (In undeveloped conditions of this kind, therefore, the greater part of money capital proper is in the hands of merchants, so that their wealth constitutes *monetary wealth* as far as others are concerned.)

(The velocity of circulation of the money capital advanced by the merchant depends on two things: on the speed with which the production process is repeated and the various production processes are linked together, and on the speed of consumption.)

The turnover described above does not require the commercial capital just to buy the commodities for £3,000 and then to sell them. The merchant rather performs both movements *at the same time*. His capital is then divided into two parts, the first consisting of commodity capital and the second of money capital. He buys from one person, and thereby transforms his money into commodities. He sells to other people and thereby transforms another part of the commodity capital into money. On the one hand his capital flows back to him as money capital, while on the other hand this money capital is simultaneously transformed into commodity capital, or flows back to him as commodity capital. The greater the part existing in one form, the smaller that existing in the other. This fluctuates and is balanced out. If the use of money as means of circulation is combined with its use as means of payment and the credit system that grows up on this basis, there is still a further reduction in the money capital portion which forms *mercantile capital* in relation to the volume of transactions that this mercantile capital performs. If I buy £1,000 worth of wine which is to be paid for in three months and I sell this wine before the end of the three months, not a single farthing has to be advanced for *this* transaction. In this case, moreover, it is as clear as daylight that the *money capital* that figures here as *mercantile capital* is nothing but productive capital itself in its form as *money capital*, its return to itself in the form of money. (If the producer who has sold commodities at three months' credit for £1,000 can get the bill {that is to say, the promissory note} discounted by a banker, this does not alter the matter in any way, and has nothing to do with the capital of the dealer in commodities.) If the market price of the commodity were to fall in the meantime by a tenth, say, not only would the merchant not receive any profit, but he would get only £3,000 – £300 back, in other words £2,700, instead of £3,000. He would have to put up another £300 in order to pay. This £300 functions simply as a reserve for settling the difference in price. But the same thing holds for the manufacturer. If he had himself sold while prices were falling, his return would be £2,700 instead of £3,000, and he would not be able to begin production again on the same scale without reserve capital.

The linen dealer buys linen from the manufacturer for £3,000; the latter spends £2,000 > or any other aliquot part < on the purchase of yarn; he buys this yarn from the yarn dealer. The money with which the manufacturer pays the yarn dealer is not the linen dealer's money, for the latter has received *commodities* to this amount in exchange. It is his own capital in money form. In the hands of the yarn dealer, this £2,000 now appears to be *mercantile capital* (*returned* mercantile capital), but how far is it really this, as distinct from £2,000 as the money form shed by the linen and assumed by the yarn? If the yarn dealer has bought on credit and sells before his payment falls due, this £2,000 does not contain a farthing of *mercantile capital* as distinct from the money form which productive capital itself assumes in the course of its process of circulation. In so far as it is |250| not simply a form of productive capital which happens to be found, in the shape of commodity capital or money capital, in the hands of the merchant, *commodity capital* is nothing but the *portion of money capital* that belongs to the merchant himself, and is circulated in the purchase and sale of commodities. This portion represents, on a *reduced scale*, the portion of the capital advanced for production that always had to exist as a money reserve, a *means of purchase*, in the hands of the manufacturer, and always had to circulate as his money capital. This portion is now to be found, *reduced*, in the hands of the merchant capitalists; as such it functions exclusively in the circulation process.

> Apart from the portion of the productive capital which constantly has to exist as money for current expenditure < another part constantly has to circulate in the market as a means of purchase, for the sake of the whole capitalist class, to ensure the continuity of the reproduction process of the total capital. > This portion constitutes *mercantile capital.* < The quicker the reproduction process and the more developed the function of money as means of payment, i.e., the *credit system*, the smaller it is, *relatively speaking*.[3]

---

3 So that he can classify commercial capital as productive capital, Ramsay confuses it with the transport industry and calls it (namely commerce) 'the transport of commodities from one place to another'. (Ramsay 1836, p. 19.) See Say [1817], pp. 14 and 15. S.P. Newman says the following: 'In the existing economical arrangements of society, the very act, which is performed by the merchant, of standing between the producer and consumer, *advancing* to the former *capital* and receiving *products* in return, and then handing over these products to the latter, receiving back capital in return, is a transaction which both facilitates the economical processes of the community, and adds value to the products in relation to which it is performed'. (Newman 1835, p. 174.) Manufacturer and consumer save time and money by his (the merchant's) intervention. This service requires an outlay of capital and labour and must, '*since it adds value to products*, for the *same products in the hands of consumers are worth more than in the hands of producers*'. (This is fundamentally wrong. The use value of a commodity is

Mercantile capital is nothing but capital functioning within the circulation sphere. The circulation process is one phase in the reproduction process as a whole. But in the process of circulation, no value is produced, and thus also no surplus-value. The same mass of value simply undergoes *changes in form*. Nothing in fact happens except the metamorphosis of commodities, which has nothing to do with the creation or alteration of value as such. If a surplus-value is realised on the sale of the commodity produced, this is because it already existed in the commodity. With the second act, therefore, the exchange of the money capital back into commodities, no surplus-value is realised. (What happens here is rather that surplus-value begins to be realised by the exchange of money for labour.) Quite the contrary. In as much as this metamorphosis costs circulation time – a time during which capital does not produce anything – hence does not produce surplus-value either – it restricts the creation of value, and the surplus-value, as expressed in the rate of profit, will actually vary inversely with the length of the circulation time. *Mercantile capital* thus creates neither value nor surplus-value, at least not directly. In so far as it contributes towards shortening the circulation time, it can indirectly help the productive capitalist increase the surplus-value he produces. In so far as it helps to extend the market and facilitates the division of labour between capitals, thus enabling capital to operate on a bigger scale, its functioning promotes the productivity of productive capital and its accumulation process. In so far as it *reduces circulation time*, it raises the ratio of surplus-value to the capital advanced, hence it increases the rate of profit. And in so far as a smaller part of capital (money capital) is confined to the circulation sphere of the commodities, it increases the portion of capital directly employed in production.

greater in the hands of the consumer than it is in those of the producer, because it is only here that it is at all realised. The value in use of the commodity only becomes realised by passing into the sphere of consumption. In the hand of the producer it exists in a latent form only. But I do not pay [for] a commodity twice over, first its value in exchange and secondly its value in use. By paying its value in exchange, I appropriate its value in use. Its *value in exchange* is not augmented by passing from the producer to the consumer.) '[*S*]*trictly be considered an act of production*'. (Newman 1835, p. 175.) (See the passages from Corbet, etc., quoted at the start of the note in Chapter One of Book One.) [Marx quoted passages from Corbet 1845, in a part of the 1863–65 Manuscript, covering Book One of *Capital*, which has not been preserved. Translator]

|251| (2) Commercial Profit > And Its Characteristics

< We saw in Book Two that the *pure* functions of capital in the circulation sphere create neither value nor surplus-value. These functions are the operations which the capitalist must undertake firstly in order to realise the *value* of his commodities and secondly in order to transform that value back into commodities. They are the operations by which the capitalist effects the metamorphosis of commodity capital, C′ – M – C, and the act of buying and selling. Quite the reverse: it was shown that the time required for these operations sets *limits* to the formation of value and surplus-value, *objectively* as far as the commodities are concerned and subjectively as regards the capitalist. What applies to the metamorphosis of commodity capital as such is naturally not changed in any way when a part of this capital assumes the form of *commodity-dealing capital* and the operations which effect the metamorphosis of commodity capital appear as the special business of a particular set of capitalists, or as the exclusive function of one part of money capital. The metamorphosis of commodity capital C′ – M – C consists of the sale and purchase of commodities > by the *producer* of the commodities (i.e., the industrial capitalist), < and if these operations are not able to create any value or surplus-value for the industrial capitalist, *the same* operations cannot possibly do so when they are performed by other persons instead of him. Moreover, if we consider > the *money capital* that the industrial capitalist must constantly have at his disposal (particularly when we consider *the total industrial capital*) < if the reproduction process is not to be interrupted by the process of circulation but rather to be continuous, then if this money capital creates neither value nor surplus-value > (it is in fact itself only a form of *circulating* capital) < it cannot acquire such properties if, instead of being put into circulation by the industrial capitalist, it is always put into circulation by a another set of capitalists, to perform the same functions. (The extent to which mercantile capital can be *indirectly* productive is something we have already indicated in part in section one and we shall go into this in somewhat more detail later > in section three, with a very brief glance at the subdivisions of mercantile capital.)

< *Commodity-dealing capital*, therefore, stripped of all the heterogeneous functions that may be linked to it, such as warehousing, transporting/carrying, retailing/*dividing*, and restricted to its true function of buying in order to sell, creates neither value nor surplus-value (but simply mediates their *realisation* and with this also the actual exchange of the commodities, their transfer from one hand to another, *the actual metabolic process*.) And yet, since the circulation phase of capital forms just as much a phase in the reproduction process as does production, the capital that functions independently in the circulation

process must yield the average profit just as much as the capital that functions in the various branches of production. If mercantile capital were to yield a higher average percentage of profit than industrial capital, a part of industrial capital would change into mercantile capital. If it yielded a lower average percentage of profit, the opposite process would take place. > A part of mercantile capital would change into industrial capital. < No species of capital finds it easier to change its function, its destiny.

Since mercantile capital does not itself produce any surplus-value, it is clear that the surplus-value that accrues to it in the form of the average profit forms a portion of the surplus-value > or surplus labour < produced by the *productive capital* as a whole. The question now is this: *how* does mercantile capital attract the part of the surplus-value or profit produced by productive capital that falls to its share?

It is a mere *semblance* that mercantile profit is just a *supplement, a nominal* increase in the *price* of commodities above their *value*.

It is clear that the merchant can obtain his profit only from the *price* of the commodities he sells, and also that this profit which he |252| makes on the sale of his commodities must be equal to the *difference between the selling and the buying price*, or the *excess of the selling price of the commodities above their buying price*.

It may well happen that the *additional costs* (*costs of circulation*) go into the commodity after its purchase and before its sale, and it is equally possible > that it may be sold before these additional costs go into the commodity. These costs are greater than 0 or equal to 0. If they are greater than 0, it is clear that the difference between the sale price and the purchase price – which is the same as the excess of the sale price over the purchase price – does not represent profit alone. (If we call the purchase price P, the sale price P′, the costs K, and the *difference* or the excess of the sale price over the purchase price D, then $P' - P = D$. If we call the profit p, the profit, p, $= P' - K - P$, or $p = P' - (K + P)$. If $K = 0$, $D = p$; the difference equals the profit. But if K is greater than 0, clearly $D - K = p$, or the difference minus the additional cost equals the profit. To simplify the analysis, we first assume that $K = 0$. Later on, we shall look at the situation when K is greater than 0.)

< For the productive capitalist, the difference between the sale price and the purchase price of his commodities is equal to the difference between their price of production and their cost price, or, if we consider productive capital as a whole, it is equal to the difference between the *value* of these commodities and their *cost price for the capitalists*, which can be further resolved into the *excess* of the *total quantity* of labour realised in them over the quantity of *paid* labour realised in them. Before the commodities that the industrial capitalist

bought are thrown onto the market again as saleable commodities, they pass through the production process in which the component of their price that is to be realised later as profit is *produced*. The situation with the commodity dealer is different. He has commodities in his possession only as long as they are in their circulation process. He simply continues the *sale* of them begun by the productive capitalist, the realisation of their price, and so he does not make them undergo any intervening process in which they might absorb new surplus-value. Whereas the productive capitalist realises the surplus-value (or profit) that has already been produced, the merchant or commodity-dealer does not just have to *realise* his profit in and through circulation, he also has to *make* it. This appears to be possible only because he sells commodities which were sold to him by the productive capitalist at their *prices of production*, or, if we take commodity capital as a whole, at their *values*, at *more than* their prices of production, making a *nominal addition* to their prices; looking at this again from the point of view of commodity capital as a whole, he sells them at *more than* their value and pockets the difference between their nominal value and their real value, in a word he sells them *dearer* than they are.

The form of this addition is very simple to understand. Say for instance that an ell of linen costs 2 shillings. If I am to make 10 percent profit on re-selling it, I must add one tenth to its price, and so I sell the ell at 2s. $2\frac{2}{5}$d. The difference between its actual price of production and its sale price is then $2\frac{2}{5}$d., and this is a profit of 10 percent on 2 shillings. In fact I sell the ell of linen to its buyer at a price that is really the price of $1\frac{1}{16}$ ells. Or, and this comes to the same thing, it is just as if I had sold the buyer only $\frac{10}{11}$ of an ell for 2 shillings and kept $\frac{1}{11}$ for myself. In fact I can buy back $\frac{1}{11}$ of an ell with the $2\frac{2}{5}$d., if we take the price per ell at 2s. $2\frac{2}{5}$d. This would simply be an *indirect way* of sharing in the surplus-value and the surplus product by making a *nominal increase in the prices* of the commodities.

This is the realisation of mercantile profit – by an addition to the prices of commodities – as it presents itself at first sight, |253| and in fact the whole idea that profit derived from a nominal increase in commodity prices, or by selling them *above* their value, arises from the viewpoint of mercantile capital.

When we look more closely, however, we soon see that this is *a mere illusion*. And, assuming the predominance of the capitalist mode of production, this is not the way *commercial profit* is realised. (What we are dealing with here is always the average, and not individual cases.) Why do we assume that the merchant can only realise a profit of for example 10 percent on his commodities by selling them at 10 percent *above* their price of production? Because we have assumed that the producer of those commodities, the industrial capitalist (and it is he, as the personification of productive capital, who always figures as *the producer* vis-à-vis the outside world) has sold them to the merchant at their price of production. If the *purchase prices* that the merchant pays for commodities are equal to their prices of production, and in the last analysis therefore to their *values*, so that the *production price*, and in the last instance the *value* of the commodities represents the *cost price* to him, then in fact the *excess* of his *sale price* over his *purchase price* – and this difference forms the only source of his profit – must be an excess of its commercial price over its production price, and in the last analysis the merchant sells all commodities *above* their values. But why did we assume that the industrial capitalist sold commodities to the merchant at their *prices of production*? Or rather, what was *presupposed* in this assumption? That *mercantile capital* (and here we are still dealing with this only as commodity-dealing capital) does not > take part alongside the other capitals < in establishing the *general rate of profit*. In explaining the general rate of profit we necessarily proceeded from this assumption, firstly because mercantile capital as such did not yet exist for us, and secondly because the average profit, and therefore the general rate of profit, had necessarily to be developed as an equalisation of the *profits* of the *surplus-values* that are *actually* produced by productive capitals of the different spheres of production. In connection with mercantile capital, on the other hand, we are dealing with a kind of capital that takes a share in profit without participating in producing it. It is therefore necessary to correct, or rather to *supplement* (complete) our earlier presentation (in Chapter Two).

Let us assume that the total productive capital advanced during the year is 720c + 180v, and that s′ is 100 percent. The product is then 720c + 180v + 180s. If we call this product or the commodity capital produced C, its *value* or *price of production* (the two coincide, if we consider not this or that description of commodities, but their totality) = £1,080 and the rate of profit on the total capital of 900 = 20 percent. This 20 percent, as explained already, is the *average rate of profit*, since here we are calculating surplus-value not on this or that capital of a particular composition, but rather on the total productive capital with its average social composition. So C = £1,080 and the rate of profit = 20 percent. But we are now going to assume that besides this productive capital of £900 there is also a mercantile capital of £100, taking the same proportionate share of profit according to its size. According to our assumption, this is one-tenth of a total capital of 1,000. It thus takes a one-tenth share in the total surplus-value of 180, which is 18. > (180 being the total surplus to be divided.) < In fact, therefore, the profit to be divided among the remaining nine-tenths of the total capital is now only 180 – 18 = 162, and $^{162}/_{900} = ^{18}/_{100}$ = 18 percent. Thus the price at which C is sold to the commodity dealers by the owners of this productive capital of 900 is 720c + 180v + 162s = 1,062. If the merchant adds to his capital of 100 the average profit of 18 percent, he sells the commodities at 1,062 + 18 = £1,080, that is to say at their price of production, or, taking the commodity capital as a whole, at their actual |254| *value*, although he only makes his profit in and through circulation and only by the *excess* of his sale price over and above his purchase price. Nevertheless, he does not sell the commodities *above* their value, or, more precisely, *above* their price of production, because he has bought them at *less than* their value, or *below* their price of production from the industrial capitalists.

Mercantile capital thus makes a determining contribution to the establishment of the general rate of profit according to the proportion it forms in the total capital. If the *average rate of profit* is 18 percent, as in the case we are considering here, it would be 20 percent if one-tenth of the total capital were not mercantile capital and the *general* rate of profit were not consequently reduced from 20 to 18, or by one-tenth. We thus obtain a more precise and more accurate definition of the *production price*. By 'production price' we still mean, as before, the price of the commodity, which is equal to its *cost* (the value of the constant and variable capital it contains) *plus the average profit* on that. But the average profit is now determined differently. It is determined by the total profit that the total productive capital produces; but it is not calculated just on this total productive capital alone, so that, if this is 900 as above, and the profit is 180, the average rate of profit would be $^{180}/_{900} = {}^{20}/_{100}$ = 20 percent; it is calculated, rather, on the total *productive and commercial capital* together, so that if 900 is productive and 100 mercantile capital, the average rate of profit = $^{180}/_{1000} = {}^{18}/_{100}$ = 18 percent. The price of production is therefore k (the cost) + 18 percent, instead of k + 20 percent. The average rate of profit already takes into account the part of the aggregate profit that accrues to mercantile capital. The real value, or production price, of the total commodity capital is therefore k + p + c (where c = the commercial profit). The *price of production*, or the price at which the industrial capitalist sells as such, is therefore less than the real production price of the commodity, or, if we consider all commodities together, the price at which the industrial capitalist class sells them are less than their value. > Since the *price of production = cost + average profit* (calculated according to the average rate of profit), and since the average profit is less than the real profit produced by *productive* capital, calculated on the value of that productive capital, it is clear that the price of production (= cost + average profit) must be less than the real price of the commodity. In the above case, therefore, 900 (cost) + 18 percent of 900, or 900 + 160 profit, is less than 900 cost + 180 profit, that is to say the 20 percent the capital of 900 really produces, calculated on that sum of 900. < Now since the merchant sells at 110 commodities that cost him 100, he still adds 18 percent; but because the commodities he has bought at 100 are worth 110, he does not sell them above their value > (the same is true if he sells at 100 commodities which cost him $90\frac{1}{11}$). We want to keep the expression *price of production* for the more exact sense just developed. It is then clear that the *productive capitalist's profit* = the excess of the *price of production* of the commodity over its *cost price*, and that, as distinct from this *industrial* profit, the *commercial* profit = the excess of the *sale price* over the *production price of the commodity*, which is its *purchase price* for the merchant; but the *real price* of the commodity = its *production price* + *the mercantile profit*. Just as industrial capital only realises profit, which is contained already in the value of the commodity as surplus-value, the mercantile capitalist only does so because the *whole of the surplus-value* or *profit* is not yet realised in the price of the commodity as realised by the industrial capitalist.[4] The selling price of the merchant thus stands above the buying price, not because *it is above* the total value, but because the *buying price* is below the total value.

|255| Thus mercantile capital is involved in the equalisation of surplus-value that forms average profit, therefore, even though it is not involved in the production of that surplus-value. The average rate of profit therefore already takes account of the deduction from surplus-value which falls to mercantile capital, in other words the merchant's deduction from the profit of productive capital. > The production price of the commodity, formed by adding together the costs + the average profit, is equal to the buying price of the commodity for the merchant, thus it is less than its real price.

< It follows from the preceding remarks:

(1) The bigger mercantile capital is *in comparison* with productive capital, the smaller the rate of industrial profit, and vice versa.

(2) It was shown in Chapter One that the *rate of profit* is always expressed in a *smaller* rate than the rate of actual surplus-value, that is it always *underestimates* the exploitation of labour. In the above case, for example, we have 800c + 100v + 100s, a rate of surplus-value of 100 percent, expressed in a rate of profit of only 20 percent. This difference is still greater in so far as the *average profit* itself, including as it does the proportional surplus going to the mercantile capital, appears even smaller, in the above case 18 percent instead of 20 percent.

4 Bellers [1699, p. 10]. In the *Morning Star* (1 December 1862) a Manchester manufacturer laments as follows: '*Deduct* from the *gross produce* the wages of labour, the rent of land, the interest of capital, the cost of raw material, and the *gains of the agent, merchant, or dealer*, and what remained was *the profit of the manufacturer*, the Lancashire resident, the occupier, on whom *the burden of maintaining the workmen for so many partakers in the distribution of the gross produce* is thrown'.

The average *rate of profit* for the directly exploiting capitalist thus makes the *rate of profit* appear smaller than it actually is.

Assuming that all other circumstances remain the same, the *relative size* of commercial capital (though retail traders, a hybrid species, form an exception) will be in inverse proportion to the rapidity of its turnover, hence in inverse proportion to the overall vigour of the reproduction process.

In the course of scientific analysis, the formation of the *general rate of profit* appears to proceed from the productive capitals and the competition between them, being only later rectified, supplemented and modified by the intervention of mercantile capital. In the course of historical development the situation is exactly the reverse. It is commercial capital which first determines the prices of the commodities more or less according to their *values*, and it is in the sphere of the reproduction process that a general rate of profit is first formed. Mercantile profit originally determines industrial profit. It is only when the capitalist production has come to prevail, and the producer himself has become a mere merchant, that mercantile profit is reduced to the aliquot part of the surplus-value falling due [to] it as an aliquot part of the total social capital employed in the work of reproduction.

We have seen, precisely in looking at the supplementary equalisation of profits brought about by the intervention of mercantile capital, that no additional element goes into the value of the commodity for the purchaser's money *capital* while the addition to the price which goes to make up the sale price and thereby forms his profit is equal to the portion of the commodity's value that productive capital has not included in the *production price* of the commodity.[5] > The productive capitalist has left this out, and handed over to the merchant the job of adding this subsequently, as his work in the formation of price. < The case of this money capital is similar to that of the industrial capitalist's fixed capital. In so far as it is not consumed, its value does not constitute an element of the commodity's value. In the price the merchant pays for the commodity capital, he replaces its production price, M, in money. His *sale price*, determined in the way analysed above, $= M + \delta M$, with δM expressing the addition to the commodity's price determined by the general rate of profit. When he sells the commodity, therefore, he receives back the original money capital he advanced for its purchase and this δM as well. What we see here is simply that his money capital is nothing more than the *commodity capital* of the productive capitalist turned into *money capital*, which can no more affect the value of this commodity capital than if the latter were sold directly to the final consumer

5 [Marx added the word 'capital' here. Translator]

instead of to the merchant. In fact he merely anticipates (presumes) the final consumer's payment. But this is correct only if, as we have so far assumed, K = 0, or that the merchant |256| does not have to advance any other capital, circulating or fixed, in the process of commodity metamorphosis, buying and selling, apart from the money capital he had to advance to buy the commodity from its producer. This is not the case, however, as we saw in discussing the costs of circulation (Book Two, Chapter I.3).[6] And these costs of circulation represent in part costs that the merchant has to > reimburse to < other agents of circulation, and in part costs that arise directly from his specific business.

> We now consider the case where K is greater than 0. <

< Whatever kind of circulation costs these may be, whether they arise from the business of the merchant pure and simple and belong therefore to the merchant's specific circulation costs, or whether they represent charges arising from belated production processes that are inserted within the circulation process, such as dispatch, transport, warehousing, etc., they always require on the part of the merchant, besides the money capital advanced in the purchase of commodities, an additional capital that is advanced in purchase and payment for these means of circulation. In so far as this cost element consists of circulating capital, it goes into the *sale price* of the commodity completely, *as an additional element*, while in so far as it consists of fixed capital, it goes in purely in proportion to its *waste*; but in so far as these are purely commercial costs of circulation, this element forms only a nominal value and not a real addition to the value of the commodity. Whether circulating or fixed, however, this entire additional capital goes into the *formation of the general rate of profit*. > But we must not include this twice in our calculations. If we regard warehousing, carrying, etc., as particular spheres of productive capital, they are included in the £900 which was advanced as productive capital in the above example. We therefore retain the equation 720c + 180v + 160s = 1,060, including in this 1,060 the items of the cost of circulation which are not purely commercial.

< |257| The purely *commercial* costs of circulation (excluding therefore the costs of dispatch, transport and warehousing, etc.) are the costs of the process of buying and selling that are necessary to realise the *value* of the commodity, to transform it from commodity into money or from money into commodity > (or to exchange them with one another) < to facilitate the *exchange process*. (In this connection we ignore completely any eventual production processes that continue during the act of circulation and can exist quite separately from

6 [Volume II, Chapter Six, as finally published. Translator]

commerce as such; as for instance the transport industry proper and the dispatch of goods can be completely separate from trade, as branches of industry, and actually are so. Goods for purchase and sale may also be kept in docks > or auction rooms < with the *costs* arising from this figuring only as costs for the merchant himself. All this is to be found in the wholesale trade proper, where commercial capital appears in its purest form, hardly mixed up at all with other functions. The driver, the mariner and the railwayman are not 'merchants'.) We have already noted earlier that these operations break down into accounting, book-keeping, marketing, correspondence, etc. The *constant* capital required for this consists of offices, paper, postage, etc. (The other circulation costs such as forwarding charges, transport costs and the advance payment of customs duties can in part be seen as advances by the merchant for the purchase of the *commodities* with the result that they enter into their *purchase price*; > or, in so far as he for example maintains a warehouse, he combines another function with his original function as a merchant. If a merchant stores his commodities on the docks, in auction rooms or in general warehouses, this business of warehousing and storage does not concern him, to the extent that it is a separate business; the costs of this enter into the price of the commodity as a given element.) < The other costs are reducible to *variable capital*, that is to say capital advanced for the employment of mercantile wage-labourers.

All these costs are incurred not in the *production* of the commodities' use-value, but rather in the *realisation* of their value, > or the transformation of money back into commodities. < They are *pure* costs of circulation. They do not come into the immediate production process, but they do come into the circulation process, hence into the *production process as a whole*, in other words the *reproduction process*.

The only part of these costs that concerns us at this point is that laid out in *variable capital*. (Also to be investigated here are, firstly, how the law that only *necessary labour* goes into the value of the commodity applies in the *circulation process*, secondly, how *accumulation* appears [*erscheint*] in the case of commercial capital, and thirdly how commercial capital functions in the *actual* overall process of reproduction.)

(These costs arise from the *economic form* of the product as a *commodity*.)

If the labour-time that the productive capitalists, > the producers, < themselves lose in selling their commodities directly to one another – objectively speaking the commodities' circulation time – does not add any value to these commodities, it is clear that this labour-time does not change its character by being undertaken by the *merchant* instead of the productive capitalist. The transformation of commodities into money, and money into commodities (means of production) is a necessary function of capital and therefore a *necessary operation* for the capitalist, who is in fact simply personified capital, capital endowed with its own consciousness and will. But these functions neither increase value nor create surplus-value. The merchant, by performing these operations and carrying on the functions of capital in the circulation sphere after the productive capitalist has ceased to do this, simply takes the place of the productive capitalist. The labour-time > (or labour in general) < that these operations cost is being employed on necessary operations in the reproduction process of capital, but it does not add any extra value. If the merchant did not perform these operations (and so did not > apply the labour and < spend the labour-time they require) he would not be using his capital as a *circulation agent* of productive capital; he would not be continuing the function that the productive capitalist has abandoned, and hence would not share as a *capitalist*, in proportion to the capital he advanced, in the general profit produced by the class of productive capitalists. > This is the explanation for the phenomenon that < the merchant capitalist does not need to employ *any* wage-labourers in order to *share in the surplus-value*, and to valorise the capital he has advanced as capital. If his business and his capital are small, he may himself be the only worker employed. He is paid by the part of the profit that accrues to him from the difference between the *purchase price* of the commodities and their *real price of production*. |258| On the other hand, in this case, if the capital advanced by the merchant is small, the *profit* he realises may not be any greater than the *wage* of a better-paid skilled worker; it may even be less. And in point of fact, functioning alongside him are the direct *commercial* agents of the productive capitalists, who receive the same or a greater income, whether in the *form of a wage* or a share in the profit made on each sale (*commission*, etc.) In the one case the merchant pockets the *mercantile profit* as an independent capitalist; in the other case the direct employee of the industrial capitalist is paid a part of the *mercantile profit* in the form of either a wage or a share in the profit of the *industrial + mercantile profit* of the productive capitalist, whose direct agent he is. But in all these cases – although the income the *circulation agent* receives may *appear* to him as a simple wage, as payment for the work he has performed, and although, where it does not take this form, the size of his profit may still only be equivalent to the wage of a better-paid worker – his income still derives solely from the *mercantile profit*. This results from the fact that his labour is not *value-creating* labour.

The fact that the operation of circulation is prolonged means for the productive capitalist (1) a personal loss of time, in so far as he is prevented from performing his own function as director of the production process, and (2) an extended stay of his product, in its money or commodity form, in the circulation process, a process in which it is not valorised and in which the immediate process of production is interrupted. To prevent this process from being interrupted, either production must be cut back or additional money capital must be advanced, so that the production process can continue on *the same* scale. In each case, what this amounts to is that he either makes a *smaller* profit, > because he has a *smaller* portion of the capital continuously in the production process < or he has to advance an additional amount of money capital in order to make *the same* profit. This is just the same as if the merchant replaces him. Instead of the productive capitalist spending more time on the circulation process, the merchant spends this time; instead of his being forced to advance additional capital for circulation, the merchant advances it; or, what comes to the same thing, whereas previously a substantial portion of his capital is constantly washing around the circulation process, now the merchant's capital is altogether cooped up in it; and instead of making *a smaller profit*, he now had to abandon a part of his profit to the merchant. In so far as commercial capital remains confined to the limits within which it is necessary, the distinction is simply that this *division of capital's functions* enables less time to be devoted exclusively to the circulation process, and less capital advanced for it, so that the reduction in the *total profit* which shows itself in the form of *mercantile profit*, is less than it would be otherwise. If, in the above example, 720c + 180v + 180s, the productive capitalist is left with a profit of 160 or 18 percent instead of 180 or 20 percent, owing to the 100 of merchant's capital, this might perhaps be 200 without the *independence* of the operations of commercial capital, and we should then have an advance by the productive capitalist of 720c + 180v + 180s as before, but in addition 150 as a consequence of the circulation process, making 1,050 in all. The surplus-value of 180 on the 1,050 would then represent a rate of profit of $17\frac{1}{7}$ percent.[7]

If the productive capitalist now advances – apart from the additional capital needed to buy commodities, etc., before his commodity capital, which is still in circulation, has been transformed afresh into money – still further capital (office expenses and the wages of commercial workers) in order to *realise the value* of his commodity, that is to pass through the circulation process, this forms *additional capital* but it does not form *surplus-value*. It must be replaced out of the commodities' value, for a portion of these commodities must again be bought and reconverted into office costs, etc. (such expenses as are spent upon, and necessary for, the circulation of commodities), but no additional surplus-value is formed thereby. As far as the total social capital is concerned,

7 [Marx's figure here was changed by Engels to $16\frac{4}{11}$, although it is in fact correct. Translator]

what this amounts to is that a part of this capital is required for secondary operations that do not enter into the *valorisation process*, and that this part of the social capital has constantly to be reproduced for this purposes. In this way, the *rate of profit* for both the individual capitalists (and the whole class of productive capitalists) is reduced, a result which follows from every injection of additional capital made to put the same mass of variable capital into movement. > This *increase in the value of the commodities* is here just as disadvantageous as an increase in value resulting from a fall in the productivity of labour.

< |259| If these additional costs – along with the business of circulation itself – are taken over from the productive capitalist by the commercial capitalist, there is still a reduction in the rate of profit, but to a lesser degree, and by a different route. What happens now is that the merchant advances more capital, M + ΔM (ΔM here = the cost of circulation, K, disregarding the M which is directly laid out in buying and selling) instead of M, and therefore the sum of the total mercantile profit rises, hence mercantile capital enters together with productive capital into the equalisation of the average rate of profit on a greater scale, hence the *average profit* falls. In the above example, let a further additional capital of 50 be advanced for K, apart from the 100 mercantile capital. The *productive capital* was 720c + 180v + 180s, which was then reduced to 162 because 100 was added for merchant's capital; so that then the *average profit* was 18 percent instead of 20. Now a further 50 is added, and the average profit falls to $17\frac{1}{7}$ percent. > But now, at 17 $\frac{1}{7}$ percent on his capital of 150, the merchant gets a profit of $25\frac{5}{7}$. < The productive capitalist sells the commodities for 900 + $154\frac{2}{7}$ = $1054\frac{2}{7}$, and the merchant sells them for 1,130. (1,080 + 50 for expenses he has to recover). It must be assumed that the *division* between mercantile and productive capital, involves a *concentration of mercantile costs* and a consequent *reduction* in them.

The question now arises as to the position of the commercial *wage-labourers* employed the merchant capitalist, in this case the dealer in commodities.

From one point of view, a commercial employee of this kind is a wage-labourer like any other. Firstly, in so far as his labour is bought with the merchant's variable *capital*, not with money that he spends as revenue; it is bought, in other words, not for a personal service but for the purpose of valorising the capital advanced in it. *Secondly*, in so far as the value of his labour, and therefore his wage, is determined, like that of all other wage-labourers, by the production and reproduction costs of this *particular* labour-capacity, not by the product of his labour.

But there is necessarily the same difference between him and the workers directly employed by productive capital as there is between productive capital and mercantile capital, and consequently between the industrial capitalist and the merchant. Since the merchant, being simply an agent of circulation > or a mere functionary of circulating capital < produces neither value nor surplus-value (for the additional value that he adds to the commodities by his K comes down to the addition of previously existing value, although here the question forces itself on us: how does he *maintain* the value of this *constant* capital?) the mercantile workers he employs in these *same* functions cannot possibly create *surplus-value* for him directly. Here, just as with the productive workers, we assume that wages are determined by the value of labour-capacity, hence that the merchant does not enrich himself by a *deduction from wages*, so that in reckoning his costs he does not put down an advance for labour that he *only* pays in part. In other words, he does not enrich himself by cheating his clerks, etc.

The problem that arises in connection with these mercantile workers is by no means that of explaining how they *directly* produce *profit* for their employers, even though they do not directly produce *surplus-value* (of which profit is simply a transformed form). This question has in fact already been resolved by the general analysis of mercantile profit. Just as productive capital makes its profit by *selling* labour that is already contained and realised in the commodity, labour for which |260| it has not paid an equivalent, so *mercantile capital* makes a profit by not paying productive capital *in full* for the *unpaid labour* contained in the commodity (in the commodity, in so far as the capital laid out to produce it functions as an aliquot part of the total productive capital), but only paying a part of it but selling in turn the *unpaid* part which is still contained in the commodity.

Mercantile capital's relationship to surplus-value is different from that of productive capital. The latter produces surplus-value by the direct exploitation of labour, the direct appropriation of alien labour. The former appropriates a portion of this surplus-value by *transferring* it from the productive capital to itself.

It is only by way of its function in the *realisation of values* that mercantile capital functions as capital in the reproduction process, and therefore draws its dividends – as functioning capital – from the surplus-value created by the total capital. For the individual merchant the *mass of his profit* depends on the amount of capital that he can employ in this process, and the greater the *unpaid labour* of his clerks, the more capital he can employ in buying and selling. The very function by virtue of which the merchant capitalist's money is capital is performed in large measure by his workers. Their *unpaid labour*, even though it does not *create* surplus-value, does create *for him* the ability to *appropriate surplus-value*, which, as far as this capital is concerned, gives exactly the same result, it is therefore a source of profit *for it*. Otherwise the business of commerce could never be conducted on a large scale, *in the capitalist manner*.

Just as *unpaid labour* directly creates *surplus-value* for productive capital, so also does the unpaid labour of the commercial wage-labourer create a *share in that surplus-value* for mercantile capital.

The difficulty is rather as follows:

Since the labour (and the labour-time) of the merchant himself is not value-creating labour (although it procures him a share in the surplus-value already produced by productive capital) what is the situation with the *variable capital* he lays out on the purchase of mercantile labour-capacity (commercial labour-power)? Should this variable capital be included in M as K, part of the cost of the outlay of commercial capital the merchant has advanced? *If not*, this would appear to contradict the law of the equalisation of the rate of profit, and what capitalist would advance £150 if he could reckon only £100 of it as capital advanced? *If it is included*, this would seem to contradict the very nature of mercantile capital, since this kind of capital does not function as capital by setting alien labour in motion, in the manner of productive capital, but rather by itself working, that is to say itself performing the functions of buying and selling, and it is only for this purpose and in this way that it transfers to itself part of the surplus-value created by the productive capital. >

There are two ways in which we can get to the heart of the matter here. *Firstly*, by assuming that every merchant functions alone, without commercial workers, for the purely commercial part of his business; and *secondly*, by investigating the relationship the productive capitalist, the manufacturer for example, has with the mercantile part of his business, not only with the merchant who works on commission, but with the clerks, book-keepers, etc., who form the commercial *appendage* to his real workshop, his factory, etc.

NB. (We shall first be able to look at the *particular form of accumulation* of *mercantile capital* when we have drawn *money-dealing capital* into the investigation as well as *commercial capital*.)

< (The following points have therefore to be investigated: the *merchant's variable capital*; the law of *necessary labour* in circulation; how the work of the merchant *maintains* the value of his constant capital; the role of commercial capital in the overall reproduction process; and finally the *division* into commodity capital and money capital on the one hand and into commercial capital and money-dealing capital on the other.)

|261| If every merchant possessed only the amount of capital that he was personally able to turn over by his own work, there would be an infinite fragmentation of *commercial capital*, > and this disproportion < this fragmentation

would necessarily increase with the progress of the capitalist mode of production and in the same measure, since the productive capital would produce on a larger and larger scale and would operate with larger and larger quantities. To the same extent as capital was centralised in the sphere of production, it would be decentralised in the sphere of circulation. The purely *commercial* business of the productive capitalist > (and therefore his purely commercial expenditure) < would be infinitely expanded, in as much as he would have to deal with 100 or even 1,000 different merchants. The result would be the loss of a large part of the advantage that derives from the *autonomous position* of mercantile capital; and besides the purely commercial costs, the other costs of circulation (those of packing, dispatch, etc.) would also grow. These would be the direct effects for *productive capital*. Let us now consider commercial capital; in the first place, how *commercial work proper would be affected*. It takes no more time to *reckon* with large figures than with small. It takes ten times longer to make ten purchases of £100 than one purchase of £1,000. It takes ten times as much correspondence work, paper and postage to write to ten small merchants as to one big one. The *precise division of labour* to be found in commercial offices, where one person keeps the books, another the cash-box, a third writes letters, this one buys, another sells, that one travels, etc., spares a tremendous amount of labour-time, so that the number of workers involved in wholesale trade is in no way proportionate to the comparative *scale* of the transactions. > *This is the case, because in trade, much more than in industry, the same function costs the same amount of labour-time, whether performed on a small or a large scale*. This applies to reckoning, buying, book-keeping, corresponding, marketing, etc. Whether a courier brings one letter or 100 to the post, or whether a clerk pays duties for £100 worth of commodities or for £10,000 worth at the customs office, or whether a few items or many are parcelled up, the costs do not grow in the same proportion as the scale of activities. < Thus concentration historically appears in commerce earlier than in the productive workshop. There are also the expenses for constant capital. A hundred small offices cost infinitely more than a single big warehouse, etc. Transport costs – which enter into the merchant's business at least as *costs to be advanced* – also grow with fragmentation.

The productive capitalist would have to spend more labour and incur greater circulation costs on the commercial side of his business. *The same commercial capital* would require *many more workers* (namely the small merchants themselves) for the performance of its functions, and besides this a *larger commercial capital* would be required to turn over *the same commodity capital* > (on account of the growth in the costs of circulation and in the constant capital of the many small merchants).

< If we call the commercial capital directly invested in the buying and selling of commodities M, and the *variable capital* ΔM, M + ΔM is smaller than the commercial capital M would be if a part of it were not invested in ΔM.

But we have still not come to the end of our difficulties.

The price at which the commodities are sold must be sufficient to pay the average profit on M + ΔM. This is already explained by the fact that M + ΔM is always a reduction on the original M. But this sale price must also be sufficient both to replace ΔM itself, besides the additional profit on ΔM; and to pay the wage, in fact therefore to replace the merchant's variable capital, = ΔM. It is this last point that creates the difficulty. Does ΔM form a new component of the price, or is it simply a part of the *profit* made with M + ΔM, which, as far as the commercial employees are concerned, appears only as *wages*, and, as far as the merchant is concerned, as *simply a continuation of his variable capital?* In the latter case, the profit which the merchant makes on the capital he had advanced, M + ΔM, = M′, is equal to p (the profit on M′ or on the part of this profit which he calculates *as such*) + ΔM, which he pays out in the form of wages.

|262| It all boils down to finding the limits of ΔM.

We must first define the problem precisely. Let us call the capital directly laid out on the purchase and sale of commodities M, the constant capital utilised for this function K and the variable capital that the merchant lays out ΔM.

As to M, its replacement presents no difficulty at all. It is only the realised *buying price* (for the merchant) or the *price of production* for the manufacturer. The merchant pays this price, and once he has sold the commodity in turn he receives back M as a portion of his sale price. In addition to this he receives the profit on M, as already explained. > But this M does not enter into the price of the commodity. < Say a commodity costs £100, and the profit on it is 10 percent. The commodity is then sold at £110, > which is equal to 100C + 10P. < The commodity still costs 100 as before, so that the commercial capital of 100 only adds 10 to it.

If we now take K, this is equal to (although in fact it is *less than*) the portion of constant capital that the producer would need for selling and buying; this would however form an additional part of the constant capital he uses directly in production. Nevertheless, this must be constantly replaced from the price of the commodity, or, and this is *the same thing*, a corresponding part of the commodity must constantly be spent, and, from the point of view of the total social capital, produced and reproduced. This part of the constant capital advanced would have the same restrictive effect on the *rate of profit* as does the mass of constant capital directly invested in production. In as much as the industrial capitalist leaves the commercial part of his business to the merchant he does not need to advance this portion of capital. Instead of him, it is the *merchant who advances it.* (This is as yet only a nominal advance, for the merchant neither produces nor reproduces the constant capital he uses. His production therefore appears as his own business, or at least as part of the business of certain productive capitalists, who thereby play the same role as those who supply *constant* capital to those who produce *the means of subsistence.*) The merchant thus receives firstly the replacement for this constant capital, and secondly the profit on it. The profit of the productive capitalist is therefore reduced. But because of the concentration and economy that results from the division of labour, this reduction is *less* than it would be if he had to advance the capital himself. The reduction in the rate of profit is less, because the amount of capital advanced in this way is smaller.

Formerly, the *sale price* consisted of M + K + the *profit on M + Kc.* After our previous remarks, this part of the sale price presents no difficulty. But now we also have ΔM, or the *variable capital* advanced by the merchant.

The sale price now becomes M + K + ΔM + the profit on M + K + the profit on ΔM.

M only replaces the purchase price, but it does not add anything to this price besides the profit on M. K not only adds the profit on K, but also K itself, but K + the profit on K, the part of the production costs advanced in the form of constant capital + the resulting reduced average profit, would be greater in the hands of the productive capitalist than those of the commercial capitalist. The *reduction in the average profit* appears in this way, that the full average profit is calculated after the deduction of M + K from the productive capital advanced, but that the *deduction from the average profit* for M + K is paid to the merchant, with the result that it appears [*erscheint*] as the *profit of a special capital,* commercial capital.

|263| But the situation is different with ΔM + the profit on ΔM, or, in the case given here, ΔM + $\frac{1}{10}$ ΔM, since we have assumed a profit rate of 10 percent > whereby we leave turnover time out of account and calculate the 10 percent on the sale of the mass of commodities. < And here is the real difficulty.

What the merchant buys with ΔM, according to our assumption, is merely *commercial labour,* hence labour necessary to facilitate the functions of capital circulation (C – M and M – C.) But *commercial labour* is the labour that is always necessary for a capital to *function as commercial capital,* for it to mediate the transformation of commodities into money and money into commodities. It is labour that *realises values* but does not create any values. And only in so far as a *capital* performs these functions – hence its possessor performs these operations, this labour, with his capital – does this capital function as *commercial* capital and therefore take part in regulating the *general rate of profit*, by drawing its dividends from the total profit. In ΔM + the profit on ΔM, however, it seems that first the labour is *paid* (since it comes to the same thing whether the productive capitalist pays the merchant for his *own* labour or for that of his employees) and secondly the *profit* on the payment for this labour that the merchant himself would have had to perform. Commercial capital *receives* firstly the repayment of ΔM and secondly the profit on it; this arises because it *firstly* gets paid for the labour through which it functions as commercial capital, and *secondly* gets paid the profit because it functions as capital, that is to say because it performs labour that is paid to it in *profit*, it receives in its capacity as functioning capital. This is therefore the question we have to resolve.

Let us take M = 100, ΔM = 10 and the rate of profit = 10 percent. We put K equal to 0 so as to avoid unnecessarily reintroducing an element of the purchase price that does not belong here and has already been dealt with. The purchase price would then be 100M + 10 (profit on M) + 10ΔM + 1 (profit on ΔM) = 121.

But if the merchant did not lay out this ΔM on wages – since ΔM is paid simply for commercial labour, hence for labour *needed to realise the value of the commodity capital* which productive capital put on the market – matters would stand as follows: to buy or sell commodities for 100 the merchant gives up his time in the transactions of buying and selling, and we shall suppose that this is the whole time at his disposal. The commercial labour represented by ΔM, or 10, if it is not paid as wages but rather by way of profit, will have as a prerequisite another commercial capital of 100, since 10 percent of this is 10, or ΔM. This second 100M would not enter into the price of the commodity additionally, but the 10 percent would do so. Therefore two capitals of 100 each, 200 altogether, would buy commodities for 200 + 20 = 220.

Since commercial capital is nothing at all but the form in which a part of the productive capital functioning in the circulation process *has become autonomous*, all questions relating to it must be resolved in this way: the problem must at the outset be put in the form in which the phenomena peculiar to commercial capital do not yet appear independently but are still in direct connection with productive capital. Productive capital, with an *office* instead of a *workshop*, functions continuously in the circulation process. And this is where the ΔM that is at issue here must first of all be examined

From the outset, the *office* is always infinitesimally small in comparison with the industrial workshop. Yet it is clear none the less that as the scale of production is expanded, the commercial operations that have to be carried out on behalf of the productive capital, both to sell the available product in the form of commodity capital and to transform the money thus obtained back into means of production, and to keep accounts for the whole process, will also increase. (The setting of prices, the drawing up of accounts and the conduct of correspondence are all part of this.) The more the scale of production grows, the greater > (even if by no means in the same degree) < is the labour and other circulation costs involved |264| in the *realisation of value and surplus-value* (the commercial operations of productive capital.) It is therefore necessary to employ commercial wage-labourers who make up the office properly so called. The expenditure on this, even though it is incurred in the form of *wages*, is distinct from the *variable capital* laid out in the purchase of the productive workers. It *increases* the outlays of the productive capitalist, the mass of capital he has to advance, without directly increasing the *surplus-value*. For this is an *outlay* which is paid for labour employed simply in *the realisation* of values already created. Just like other outlays of the same kind, *this too* reduces the *rate of profit*, because C grows but not s. For example, C grows from C to ΔC, so that instead of rate of profit of $\frac{s}{C}$ we get a smaller rate of profit of $\frac{s}{C + \Delta C}$. The productive capitalist therefore attempts to keep these circulation costs to a minimum, just as he does his outlay on constant capital. (Economies on this.) Productive capital therefore does not behave towards its commercial employees as it does towards its productive wage-labourers. The more of the latter are employed, all other circumstances remaining the same, the more massive is production and the greater the surplus-value or profit. Conversely, however, the greater the scale of production and the greater the value and therefore surplus-value to be realised (the greater the commodity capital produced), the more do office expenses grow in absolute terms (even if not relatively), thus providing the occasion for a kind of division of labour. The extent to which profit is the prerequisite for these outlays is shown among other things by the way that, as commercial salaries increase, a part of these is often paid as a percentage of the profit. *It lies in the nature of the situation* that a labour that consists simply in *intermediary operations*, involving partly the calculation of values, and partly their *realisation*, depends on the *magnitude of the values produced and to be realised*, that a labour of this kind functions not as the *cause* of the *respective magnitudes and amounts of values*, as does directly productive labour, but rather as a *consequence* of them. (It is the same with the other costs of circulation. If there is much to be weighed, measured, packed and transported, there must be *plenty* there in the first place. A multiplication of the work of packing and transporting, on the other hand, does not multiply the *commodities* that are the objects of this activity.)

The commercial worker does not produce surplus-value directly. But the price of his labour is determined by the *value of his labour-capacity* (what it costs to produce it), while the *exercise of this labour-capacity*, the exertion, expenditure of energy and wear and tear it involves, is no more limited by the value of his labour-capacity than it is in the case of any other wage-labourer. His wage therefore does not stand in any necessary relationship to the amount of profit that he helps the capitalist to realise. What he costs the capitalist and what he brings in for him are different quantities. What he brings in is a function not of any direct creation of surplus-value but of his assistance in reducing the cost of realising surplus-value, in so far as he performs part of his *labour unpaid*. The commercial worker proper belongs to the better-paid class of wage-labourer; he is one of those whose labour is skilled labour, above-average labour. His wage, however, has a tendency to fall, as the capitalist mode of production advances, even in relation to average labour. Firstly, because of the *division of labour* within the mercantile sphere: this means that only a one-sided development of capacity need be produced and that part of the cost of producing this capacity to labour is free for the capitalist, since the worker's skill is developed by the function itself, and all the more quickly, the more one-sided the function becomes with the division of labour. Secondly, because basic skills, knowledge of commerce, etc., are reproduced ever more quickly, easily, generally and cheaply, the more the capitalist mode of production adapts teaching methods, etc., to practical purposes. The general extension of popular education permits this variety of labour to be recruited from classes which were formerly excluded from it, and accustomed to a lower standard of living. (This also increases competition.) With a few exceptions, therefore, the labour-capacity of these people is devalued with the advance of capitalist production; their salary falls, while their working ability increases. > The ancillary materials of their labour, such as the account books and accountancy techniques necessary for commercial activity, are also perfected.

< The capitalist increases the number of these workers, if he has more value and profit to realise. The increase in this labour is always an effect of the increase in surplus-value, and never a cause of it.

|267| A certain duplication consequently takes place. On the one hand the functions of commodity capital and money capital (and consequently also of commercial capital) are *general formal determinations* of productive capital. On the other hand, *special capitals* (and consequently also peculiar sets of capitalists) are exclusively engaged in these functions; and these functions thus develop into special spheres for the valorisation of capital.

The aspect of *productive capital* that pertains to circulation consists not only in its continuous presence [*Dasein*] as commodity capital and money capital, but also in the *commercial office* alongside the *workshop*. But with mercantile capital this *has acquired autonomy*. For the latter, the commercial office forms its only workshop. The part of capital applied in the form of circulation costs appears much greater in the case of the large-scale merchant than in the case of the industrialist, because besides the specific mercantile offices which are associated with every productive workshop, the *part of the productive capital* which would have had to be employed in this way by the whole class of productive capitalists is now concentrated in the hands of individual merchants. By taking over the job of ensuring that the functions of circulation continue, they also take over the costs that arise from this.

To productive capital the costs of circulation appear as *expenses*, which they are. To the merchant they appear as the source of his profit, which – on the assumption of a general rate of profit – stands in proportion to the size of these costs. Investment in these circulation costs is therefore productive investment as far as mercantile capital is concerned. *For it*, therefore, the commercial labour that it buys is also directly productive.

|268| (3) The Turnover Of Mercantile Capital.[8] Prices.

The *turnover* of productive capital is the unity of its production and circulation times and consequently embraces the entire reproduction process. The turnover of *commercial capital*, in contrast, since it is in fact nothing but the movement of commodity capital that has become autonomous, represents only the first phase of the *commodity's metamorphosis*: C – M, as the *reflux movement of a special capital*. This is M – C, C – M, from the merchant's point of view, the turnover of commercial capital. The merchant transforms his money into commodities (he buys); then he transforms these same commodities back into money (he sells), and so on in constant repetition. > (If we consider commercial capital as a whole, as mediating the C – M – C of productive capital, a merchant buys C, and then in turn sells it. For him this represents M – C – M; but for the productive capitalist the sale of C is the first phase in C's metamorphosis. Another merchant sells C′ (which is in turn M – C′ – M for him) and for the productive capitalist this represents M – C′, the second metamorphosis of the commodity. The same merchant can buy commodities for the former productive capitalist, and he can sell commodities for the latter.) < Within circulation, the metamorphosis of productive capital always presents itself as C – M, M – C′; the money obtained from the sale of C is used in order to buy C′; this is the actual exchange of C for C′, and the same sum of money changes hands twice here. Its movement mediates the exchange of C for C′. In the merchant's case,

8 [Mercantile capital is a synonym for commercial capital. Editor]

however, the process is M – C, C – M′. The same commodity changes hands twice; it mediates the return of the money to him.

If, for example, the merchant's capital is £100, and he uses it to buy commodities to the value of £100, later selling these commodities for £110, his capital (or portion of capital) of £100 has thereby passed through a *turnover*, and the *number* of turnovers during the year depends on how often this movement of M – C – M′ is repeated.

We are completely leaving aside here the *costs* that may be involved in the > difference (ΔM) which, in M – C – M′ (M – C – M + ΔM), distinguishes M′ from M, where, therefore, the additional amount = the commercial profit + the cost of replacing the capital that has been consumed, < since these costs in no way affect the form we are concerned to analyse here.

There is thus a complete analogy here between the *number of turnovers* of a given commercial capital and the repetition of the circuits of money as a simple *means of circulation*. Just as the same sovereign, circulating 10 times, buys 10 times its value in commodities, so the same money capital, belonging to the merchant, £100 for example, buys 10 times its value in commodities, or realises a total commodity capital of 10 times its value, £1,000. But there is a difference, and it is this: with the circulation of money as means of circulation, the same piece of money passes through different hands, and this is how it repeatedly performs the same function and how the velocity of the circulation substitutes for the *quantity* of currency. In the merchant's case, however, the same money capital, irrespective of the pieces of money of which it is composed, repeatedly buys and sells commodity capital to the amount of its value and hence repeatedly returns to the same owner as M + ΔM, returning to its starting-point as value plus surplus-value. This is what *characterises* its turnover as a *turnover of capital*. It constantly withdraws more money from circulation than it puts in. It goes without saying, of course, that as the turnover of commercial capital accelerates (and this is also where the function of money as *means of payment* predominates, under a developed credit system) the same quantity of money also circulates more quickly.

The repeated turnover of commodity-dealing capital, however, is never anything more than a repetition of buying and selling; whereas the repeated turnover of productive capital expresses the periodicity and renewal of the entire reproduction process (including the process of consumption). For commercial capital, in contrast, this is simply an external condition. Productive capital must constantly put commodities on the market and withdraw them from it again, if the rapid turnover of commercial capital is to remain possible. If the reproduction process is generally slow, so is the turnover of commercial capital. Now commercial capital certainly facilitates > and accelerates < |269| the turnover of productive capital, but it only does this in so far as it cuts down the latter's *circulation time*. It has no direct effect on the *production time*, which also forms a limit to the time of circulation[9] of productive capital. This is its first barrier. Secondly, however, quite apart from the limit formed by reproductive consumption, this turnover of commercial capital is ultimately limited by the speed and volume of consumption, since the whole of the portion of commodity capital that goes into the consumption fund depends on this.

Now, leaving aside completely the turnovers within the world of commerce, where one merchant after the other sells the same commodity, a kind of circulation which may present a very flourishing appearance in periods of speculation, commercial capital first of all *abbreviates* the phase C – M for productive capital. *Secondly*, given the modern credit system, it has a large part of the society's total money capital at its disposal, so that it can repeat its operations before it has definitively made a sale, and in this connection it is immaterial whether Merchant No. 1 is selling directly to the final consumer or whether there are 12 other merchants between the two, > Merchant No. 12 having the job of definitively selling to the consumer. *Thirdly*, < given the tremendous elasticity of the reproduction process, which can always be driven beyond any given barrier, he finds no barrier in production itself, or only a very elastic one. Apart from the separation of C – M and M – C, which follows from the nature of the commodity, a *fictitious demand* is therefore created. Despite the *autonomy it has acquired*, the movement of commercial capital is never anything more than the movement of productive capital within the sphere of circulation. But by virtue of this *acquired autonomy*, its movement is – within certain limits – independent of the reproduction process and its barriers, and hence it also drives this process beyond its own barriers. This inner dependence in combination with external autonomy drives commercial capital to a point where the *inner connection* is forcibly re-established by way of a *crisis*.

This explains the phenomenon that crises do not first break out and are not first apparent in the retail trade, which has to do with immediate consumption, but rather in the sphere of wholesale trade, as well as *banking*, which places the money capital of the entire society at the wholesalers' disposal.

The manufacturer may actually sell to the exporter, and exporter to > an importer < and the importer to the manufacturer, and the manufacturer to the wholesaler, etc. But at some particular imperceptible point the commodity lies unsold (or it may also be that the total stocks of all producers, etc., are in excess supply). It is precisely then that consumption is generally at its

9 [Marx wrote 'time of revolution'. Translator]

highest level, partly because one productive capitalist sets a series of others in motion, partly because the workers these employ, being fully occupied, have more than usual to spend. > Apart from this impact on the working class (and on the capitalists themselves, whose income increases, and also that of all those set in motion by the productive classes) < there is, as we have already seen, a constant circulation between one constant capital and another (even leaving aside the accelerated accumulation) which is entirely independent of individual consumption in so far as it never enters into this, although it is definitively limited by it, since the production of constant capital never takes place for its own sake but simply because more of it is needed in those spheres of production whose products do enter into individual consumption. This can continue quite happily for a considerable period of time, stimulated by prospective demand, and in those branches of industry business proceeds very briskly, as far as both merchants and productive capitalists are concerned. The crisis occurs as soon as the returns of those merchants who sell far afield (or who have accumulated stocks at home) become so slow and sparse that the banks press for payment or other merchants do, whose bills have fallen due. And then we have the crash, putting a sudden end to the apparent prosperity.

The superficiality [*Äusserlichkeit*] and the irrational character [*Begriffslosigkeit*] of commercial capital's turnover is still greater in so far as the turnover of the same commercial capital can mediate the turnovers of very different productive capitals at the same time or in succession.

> But there is one more important circumstance to consider.

|270| It needs to be remarked in advance that < not only can the *turnover of commercial capital* mediate the turnovers of various *different* productive capitals; it can also mediate the *opposing* phases of commodity capital's metamorphosis. > For the producer of linen, M – C represents C – M, the sale of his commodity. C – M on the part of the merchant who, for example, sells the linen to the bleacher, represents M – C for the latter. < Here, therefore, the turnover of the same merchant's capital – in actual fact the same C – M, the realisation of the linen – represents two opposite acts by two different productive capitalists. To the extent that the merchant does eventually sell his commodity for productive consumption his C – M represents the M – C of one productive capital and his M – C always represents the C – M of another productive capital.

If, as in the present chapter, we leave aside K, the portion of capital that the merchant advances besides the sum laid out on the purchase of commodities, we must of course also leave aside ΔK, the additional profit that he makes on this additional capital. This is the strictly logical and mathematically correct way of looking at things, if it is a question of seeing how profit and the turnovers of mercantile capital affect prices.

If the production price of 1lb. of sugar is £1, with £100 the merchant can buy 100lb. of sugar. If this is the amount he buys and sells in the course of a year, and the average annual rate of profit is 15 percent, h will add £15 to this £100, and 3 shillings to each £1, the production price of 1lb. Thus he will sell the sugar at £1 3s. a lb. If the production price of 1lb. of sugar falls to 1 shilling, then with his £100 the merchant will now buy 2,000lb., and sell each 1lb. at 1s. 1⅘d. The annual profit on the capital of £100 laid out in his sugar trade will still be £15, as before. It is simply that he has to sell 100lb. in one case and 2,000lb. in the other. The level of the price of production, whether high or low, has nothing to do with the rate of profit;[10] but it has a decisive effect on the *aliquot part of the sale price* of each 1lb. of sugar that goes to form commercial profit; in other words the addition to the price that the merchant makes on a certain quantity of the commodity (the product). If the production price of a commodity is low, so is the sum that the merchant advances in its purchase price, namely the purchase price he advances for a *given quantity*, and so too, at a given rate of profit, is the amount of profit he makes on a given quantity of this cheaper commodity. Alternatively, and this comes to the same thing, he can buy a larger amount of this cheaper commodity with a given capital, for example £100, and the overall profit of £15 which he makes on his £100 is then distributed in small fractions over the individual constituents of this mass of commodities. And vice versa. This depends completely on the higher or lower productivity of the productive capital with whose commodities he conducts his trade. If we ignore those cases where the merchant is a monopolist and also monopolises production, as was the case for instance with the Dutch East India Company, nothing could be more ridiculous than the prevailing conception that it depends on the merchant whether he wants to sell many commodities at a low profit on the individual commodity, or a few commodities at a high profit. The true *limits* to his sale price are, on the one hand, the *production price* of the commodity, over which he has no control; and, on the other hand, the average *rate of profit*, over which he has just as little control. (The only thing he has to decide, though the size of his available capital and other circumstances

10 'Profit, on the general principle, is always the same, whatever be price; keeping its place like an incumbent body on the swelling or sinking tide. As, therefore, prices rise, a tradesman raises prices; as prices fall, a tradesman lowers prices' (Corbet 1845, p. 15.) Here, as in general in this text, Corbet refers only to ordinary commerce, not to *speculation*. An examination of speculation, as of everything related to the subdivisions of commercial capital, falls outside the area we are concerned with. 'The profit of trade is a *value added to capital* which is independent of price, the second (speculation) is founded on the *variation* in the *value of capital* or in *price* itself'. (Corbet 1845, p. 127.)

play a part here too, is whether he wants to deal in expensive commodities or cheap ones.) The attitude of the merchant therefore depends entirely on the degree of development of the *capitalist mode of production*, and not on his own wishes. The old Dutch East India Company, as a purely commercial company having a *monopoly of production*, could imagine that it might still pursue, under completely changed conditions, a method that corresponded at most to the beginnings of capitalist production.[11]

The following circumstances foster the popular prejudice mentioned above, which, moreover, like all false ideas about profit, etc., arose from taking the viewpoint of commerce alone and from commercial preconceptions: firstly, phenomena of competition, which pertain simply to the *division of commercial profit* among the individual merchants, the shareholders in the total commercial capital, for example when one merchant sells more cheaply than another, so as to drive his competitor from the field.

|271| Secondly, if production prices fall as a result of increases in the productivity of labour, and if sale prices therefore fall as well, demand often rises still more quickly than supply, and with it market prices, or, in other words, the sale prices yield more than the average profit.

Thirdly, a merchant may reduce the sale price (and this means nothing but a reduction in the usual profit that he adds to the production price), in order to turn over a larger capital in his business, and to do it more quickly. All these are matters that pertain simply to competition among the merchants themselves.

(We have already shown in considering *value* in Book One, Chapter Seven, that a high or low level of commodity prices determines neither the mass of surplus-value that a given capital produces nor the rate of surplus-value; even though according to the relative quantity of the commodities that a given capital produces, the price of the individual commodity and therefore also the part of that price that forms surplus-value, will be higher or lower. The unit prices of commodities are determined, in so far as they correspond to values, by the total quantity of labour realised in them. If only a little labour is realised in many commodities, the price of the individual commodity will be low and so will be the surplus-value contained in it. But how the labour realised in a commodity is divided into paid and unpaid labour, and what proportion of the commodity's price therefore represents surplus-value, has nothing to do with this total quantity of labour, hence nothing to do with the price of the commodity. The

11 An economist of Professor Roscher's calibre can still imagine, in Leipzig, that it was reasons of 'good sense and humanity' that produced the change in sale prices, and that this was not the result of a revolution in the mode of production itself. [Roscher 1858, p. 192.]

rate of surplus-value does not depend on the absolute *magnitude of the surplus-value* > contained in the price of the individual commodity < but rather on its *relative magnitude*, its relationship to the wages that went into the commodity in question. Hence the rate may be high even though the absolute amount of surplus-value in each individual commodity is small. The magnitude of this absolute amount does not depend on the division of the labour into paid and unpaid, but rather on its productivity.

As far as the commercial sale price is concerned, the production price is a given, *external* assumption.

The level of commercial commodity prices at an earlier period was due (1) to the high level of production prices, in other words the low productivity of labour, and (2) to the absence of a general rate of profit, since commercial capital drew to itself a far higher proportion of the surplus-value than would have accrued to it in conditions of a general mobility of capital. The ending of this situation, therefore, is in both respects the result of the development of the capitalist mode of production.)

Turnovers of commercial capital are longer or shorter in various branches of trade, and the number of turnovers in the year is thus greater or smaller. Within the same branch of trade, the turnover is quicker or slower in different phases of the economic cycle. There is, nevertheless, *an average* number of turnovers, which is discovered by experience.

We have already seen that the turnover of commercial capital differs from that of productive capital. (This follows from its very nature, since a *partial turnover*, a *phase* in the turnover of *productive capital* appears as a *complete turnover of an independent commercial capital*.) It stands also in a different relationship to the determination of profit and price.

As far as productive capital is concerned, its turnover expresses on the one hand the periodicity of reproduction and therefore depends on the amount of commodities put on the market over a certain period of time. On the other hand, the circulation time also forms a limit, even if one capable of extension, which may have a more or less constricting effect on the formation of value and surplus-value, because it has an impact on the scale of the production process. Thus the turnover exerts its determining function on the mass of surplus-value annually produced and therefore on the *formation of the general rate of profit*.

The average *rate of profit*, on the other hand, is a given magnitude as far as mercantile capital is concerned. Mercantile capital does not have a direct effect on the creation of profit (surplus-value) and it enters as a determining element into the formation of the general rate of profit only in so far as it draws its dividends from the mass of profit that productive capital produces, according to the proportion that it forms in the total capital.

The greater the number of turnovers made by a productive capital – under the conditions developed in Book Two, Chapter Two – the greater is the *mass of profit* that it |272| forms. Now it is true that the *establishment of a general rate of profit* means that this *total profit* is divided among the various capitals not according to the ratio in which they directly participate in its production, but rather according to the aliquot parts that they form in the total capital, in other words in proportion to the *size of the capitals*. But this does not alter the essence of the matter. The greater the number of turnovers of the total capital, the greater the *mass of profit*, the mass of surplus-value produced every year, and the greater *as a result* the rate of profit.

It is different with commercial capital. For commercial capital the *rate of profit* is a given magnitude, determined on the one hand by the *mass of profit that productive capital produces*, and on the other hand by the *relative size of the commercial capital*, or its quantitative proportion to the *total capital*, to the sum of the capital advanced in the processes of production and circulation. The *number of its turnovers*, however, has a determining effect on its *relationship to the total capital*, or the *relative magnitude* of the *commercial capital* needed for circulation, since it is clear that the *absolute size* of the necessary commercial capital stands in *an inverse* ratio to the *rapidity of its turnover*; its relative magnitude, however, or the share that it forms in the total capital, is given by its absolute magnitude, all other circumstances remaining the same. Say that the total capital is £10,000; then, if the commercial capital is one-tenth of this, it is £1,000; if the total capital is £1,000, one-tenth of this is £100. In this respect its *absolute* magnitude varies, although its *relative magnitude* remains the same, varying with the *magnitude of the total capital*. Here, however, we take its *relative magnitude*, as given, say one-tenth of the total capital. But its *relative* magnitude is itself determined by the turnover. Given a rapid turnover, its absolute size may be £1,000, for example, in the first case, and £100 in the second case, so that its relative size is one-tenth. With a slower turnover, its absolute size may be £2,000 in the first case and £200 in the second. Its relative magnitude would have grown from one-tenth of the total capital to one-fifth. > Thus 10 percent in the first case, and 20 percent in the second. < Circumstances that shorten the average turnover of commercial capital, such as the development of means of transport, for example, reduce the absolute magnitude of this commercial capital > (all other circumstances remaining the same) < and hence raise the general rate of profit. And vice versa. (The developed capitalist mode of production, compared with earlier conditions, has a double effect on commercial capital; the *same amount of commodities* are turned over with a smaller amount of *actually functioning* commodity capital; while on account of the *more rapid turnover* of this commercial capital and the greater speed of the reproduction process on which it depends, the ratio of commercial capital to productive capital is reduced.) On the other hand, with the development of the capitalist mode of production all production becomes *commodity production*, and hence the whole of the product comes into the hands of agents of circulation, in which connection it may also be added that in an earlier mode of production, under which production was carried out on a smaller scale, quite apart from the mass of products that were directly consumed in kind by the producers themselves and the mass of services that were performed in kind too, a very large proportion of the producers sold their commodities directly to the ultimate consumers or worked to their personal orders. Thus although commercial capital is *larger* in earlier modes of production in proportion to the commodity capital which it turns over:

(1) it is *smaller absolutely*, because a disproportionately smaller part of the entire product is produced as a commodity and therefore has to go into circulation as commodity capital and fall into the hands of the merchants; it is smaller because the commodity capital is smaller.

(At the same time, however, it is relatively *larger* > in earlier modes of production < not only on account of its slower rate of *turnover* and in proportion to the *mass of commodities* it turns over. It is also larger because the *price of this mass of commodities*, and also therefore the commercial capital that has to be advanced for it, is higher as a result of the lower productivity of labour compared with capitalist production, so that the *same value* is expressed in a *smaller* amount of commodities.)

(2) not only is a *greater mass of commodities* produced on the basis of the capitalist mode of production (in which connection the reduced value of *the same* mass of commodities must be taken into account), but *the same* mass of products, for example corn, forms a *greater mass of commodities*, that is to say it comes into commerce. |273| (This is true for all capital that is invested in circulation, as in for example in shipping, railways, telegraphs, etc.)

(3) However, and this is an aspect to be discussed when we come to '*competition among capitals*', *non-functioning or only semi-functioning commercial* capital also grows with the progress of the capitalist mode of production, with the increased ease of entry into the retail trade, with speculation, and with a plethora of capital. However, taking the *magnitude* of the commercial capital in relation to the total capital as given, the differences in turnover between various branches of commerce do not affect the size of the total profit that accrues to the commercial capital, nor do they affect the general rate of profit. The merchant's profit is determined not by the *mass of commodity capital* that he turns over but rather by the *amount of money capital that he advances in order*

to mediate that turnover. If the general annual rate of profit is 15 percent and the merchant advances £100, then, if his capital turns over once a year, he will sell his commodities at £115. If his capital turns over five times a year, he will sell a commodity capital of £100 every fifth part of a year for £103, and over the whole year, therefore, he will sell a commodity capital of £500 for £515. This gives him, as before, an annual profit of £15 on the capital of £100 he has advanced. If this were not the case, commercial capital would yield a far higher profit than productive capital, in relation to the number of its turnovers, and this would contradict the law of the *general rate of profit*.

> There are therefore two differences between commercial and productive capital:

< (1) The number *of turnovers* of commercial capital in various branches of commerce has a direct effect on the commercial *prices* of commodities. The level of the commercial price supplement, that is to say the aliquot part of the commercial profit on a given capital that is added to the production price of the individual commodity, stands in *inverse* proportion to the number of turnovers or the speed of the turnover of the commercial capital in the various different branches of production. If a mercantile capital of £100 turns over five times a year, it adds to the same value of commodity capital only a fifth of the price increase that another mercantile capital, able to turn over only once a year, adds to a commodity capital of the same value.

The way that sale prices are affected by the (average) turnover time of capitals in various branches of commerce can be reduced to the principle that, in proportion to the velocity of the turnover, the *same mass of profit* that is determined by the *general* annual *profit rate* for a given amount of commercial capital – determined independently, that is, of the particular character of that capital's commercial operations – is distributed differently over commodity masses of the same value, adding for example $^{15}/_{5}$ = 3 percent when it turns over five times a year, as against $^{15}/_{1}$ = 15 percent when it turns over only once. > In the first case, therefore, the *sale price* of a mass of commodities of £100 is raised by 3, in other words by 3 percent, or by a fraction of 33⅓; in the second case by 15 percent, or by a fraction of 6⅔ of its value.

< Thus the same percentage of the annual profit on commercial capitals in different lines of business raises the *sale prices* of the commodities in question by quite different percentages, calculated on the values of these commodities, in direct proportion to the differences in their turnover times.

As far as productive capital is concerned, on the other hand, its turnover time has no effect on the *magnitude of the value* of the individual commodities produced, although it does affect the *mass* of the *values* (and the surplus-values) that a given capital produces in a given time, because it affects the mass of labour exploited. This is concealed and *appears* as something different as soon as we look at *production prices*, but that is simply because the production prices of various commodities diverge from their values, according to the laws already developed. Taking the production process as a whole, and looking at the total mass of commodities produced by productive capital, one at once finds confirmation of the general law.

|274| Thus, while a close consideration of the influence of turnover time on value formation in the case of productive capital leads back to the general law and basis of political economy, namely that the values of commodities are determined by the labour-time contained in them, the influence of the turnovers of commercial capital on commercial prices exhibits phenomena which seem *directly*, that is to say in the absence of a very far-reaching analysis of the intermediate stages of the process, to presuppose a purely arbitrary determination of prices, namely a determination simply by the fact that capital has made up its mind to make a certain amount of profit per year. It seems, in particular, as if the *circulation process as such* determines the prices of commodities, through the influence of the turnover, and that this is, within certain limits, independent of the process of production.

All superficial and topsy-turvy views of the overall process are derived from consideration of commercial capital and from the notions that the movements peculiar to it give rise to in the minds of the agents of circulation.

(As the reader will have realised in dismay, the analysis of the *real, inner* connections of the *capitalist production process* is a very intricate thing and a work of great detail; it is a task of science to reduce the merely phenomenal movement to the actual inner movement. Accordingly, it will be completely self-evident that, in the minds of the agents of capitalist production and circulation, *notions* must necessarily form about the laws of production that diverge completely from these laws and are merely the *expression in consciousness* of the apparent movement. The notions of a merchant, a stock-exchange speculator or a banker are necessarily quite upside-down. The notions of the manufacturers are falsified by the acts of circulation to which their capital is subjected, by the equalisation of the general rate of profit, and so on.[12] Competition, too, necessarily plays in their minds a completely upside-down role. If

12 The following observation, if very naive, is at the same time quite correct: 'The fact that one and the same commodity can be obtained from different sellers at very different prices also very often has its basis in an incorrect calculation.' (Feller and Obermann 1859, p. 451.) This shows how the determination of price becomes *purely theoretical*, in other words abstract.

the *limits of value and surplus-value are given*, it is easy to perceive how the competition between capitals transforms values into prices of production and still further into commercial prices, transforming surplus-value into *average profit*. But without these *limits*, there is absolutely no way of seeing why competition should reduce the general rate of profit to one limit rather than another, to 15 percent instead of 1,500 percent. It can at most reduce it to *one* level. But there is no principle contained in it that can determine this level itself.)

(2) From the standpoint of mercantile capital, therefore, > (as opposed to that of productive capital) – < turnover itself *appears* to *be the determinant of price*. On the other hand, while the speed of productive capital's turnover, in so far as it enables a given capital to exploit more labour (or less) has a determining and delimiting effect on the *mass of profit* and therefore on the *general rate of profit*, mercantile capital is faced with a *rate of profit* > within the year < which is *externally* given, and this rate's inner connection with the formation of surplus-value is completely obliterated. If *the same* productive capital, all other circumstances remaining the same, turns over four times a year instead of twice, it *produces* twice as much surplus-value and therefore twice as much profit. The differing turnover time in different branches of commerce, however, does manifest itself inversely, in the following way, that the *profit* made on the turnover of a certain commodity capital stands in *inverse* proportion to the number of turnovers of the money capital that turns over this commodity capital. In particular, 'quick returns and small profits' appears to the shopkeeper as a *principle* which he follows on principle.

It is readily apparent, of course, that this law applies only to the turnovers of mercantile capital within a particular line of business, and, leaving aside the mutually compensatory alternation of quicker and slower turnovers, holds only for the average turnover made by the whole of the mercantile capital invested in this particular branch. The capital of A, invested in the same branch as B, may make more or less than the average number of turnovers. In this case, the others may make less or more. This in no way affects the turnover of the total mass of mercantile capital invested in this branch. But it is of decisive importance for the individual merchant or retailer. In such a case he makes |275| a *surplus profit*, just as industrial capitalists make surplus profits if they produce under more favourable conditions than the average. If competition compels it, he can sell more cheaply than his 'friend of commerce' or 'mercantile brother', without reducing his profit below the average. (If the conditions that enable him to have a quicker turnover can themselves be purchased, as for example the location of his sales outlets, he may pay *extra rent* for this, in other words a part of his surplus profit may be transformed into rent.)

(4) Money-Dealing Capital

The purely *technical movements* that money undergoes in the circulation process of *productive capital*, and, we can now add, *commodity-dealing capital* (since this takes over part of the circulation process of productive capital as *its own specific* movement) – these movements, as the function of a *special* capital, which practices them, and them alone, as its specific operations, transform this capital into *money-dealing capital*. A part of the productive capital (and now more directly also of commodity-dealing capital) exists throughout not only in the money form, as money capital in general, but as money capital which is involved in these technical functions. A particular part of the total capital now separates off and becomes autonomous in the form of *money capital*, its capitalist function consisting exclusively in the performance of these operations for the entire class of industrial and commercial capitalists. Just as in the case of commodity-dealing capital, a part of the productive capital present in the circulation process in the form of money capital separates off and performs these operations of the reproduction process for the whole of the remaining capital. The movements of this money capital are thus simply movements of a *now independent part* of *productive capital* in the course of its reproduction process > (while commodity-dealing capital itself occupies this position in relation to productive capital).

< It is only when, and to the extent that, *capital* is newly invested (this is also the case with *accumulation*) that the *money form* of capital or capital in its money form appears as the *starting point* and the *concluding point* of the movement. But for any capital that is already in its process, both the *starting point* and the *concluding point* appear simply as *points of transition*. In as much as productive capital, between its emergence from the sphere of production and its re-entry into it, has to pass through the same metamorphosis C′ – M – C, M is in fact, as was already shown in connection with the circulation of the commodity as such, simply the end result of one phase in this metamorphosis, after which it becomes the starting point of its opposite, complementary phase. (With commercial capital too, although for it C – M always presents itself as M – C – M, yet for it too, as soon as it is actually in operation, the actual process is always the continuous one of C – M – C.) Commercial capital, however, goes through the acts C – M and M – C simultaneously. That is, it is not just that one capital is in the C – M stage while the other is in the stage M – C, but rather that the same capital is always buying and selling *at the same time*. On account of the continuity of the production process it is always in both stages *simultaneously*. While one part of the capital is being transformed into money, so as later to be transformed back into commodities, the other part is simultaneously

being transformed into commodities, so as later to be transformed back into money.

Whether the money functions here as means of circulation or means of payment depends on the form of the commodity exchange. In both cases, the capitalist always has to make payment to many people and receive money in payment from many people. This merely *technical operation* of monetary payment and receipt itself constitutes work, and, in so far as the money functions as means of payment, it makes it necessary for accounts to be drawn up and balanced. This work is a *cost of circulation*. It is not value-creating labour. The amount of this work is *reduced* because it is carried out for the *capitalist class* as a whole by a special department of agents or capitalists.

|276| A certain section of capital must always be present as a hoard, as a reserve of means of purchase and payment, or unoccupied capital in the money form, waiting to be utilised, and a part of the capital constantly returns in this form. On top of the taking in and paying out of money, and bookkeeping, the hoard itself has to be *kept safe*, which is again a special operation. In fact the hoard is constantly dissolved into means of circulation and means of payment, and reformed from money received from sales and payments that have fallen due; and it is this constant movement of the section of capital that exists as money dissociated from the capital function itself, this *technical* operation, which gives rise to special work and costs: *costs of circulation*.

The division of labour brings it about that these technical operations required by the functions of capital are performed as far as possible for the capitalist class as a whole by a particular division of agents or capitalists, as their exclusive functions, and concentrated in their hands. There is here a twofold division of labour, as with commercial capital. It becomes a special business, and because it is performed as a special business for the monetary mechanism of the entire class, it is concentrated and undertaken on a large scale; so that we find a further division of labour within this special business, both a division into various branches independent of one another, and the development of the workplace within these branches (large offices with a division of labour into the payment of money, the receipt of money, the settlement of balances, the safe keeping of money) separated from the acts that make these technical operations necessary and make the capital advanced in these functions into money-dealing capital.

The various operations whose achievement of an autonomous position as special businesses gives rise to the money trade arise out of the various characteristics of money itself and its functions, which capital therefore also has to perform in the form of money capital.

I have already shown how money in general developed originally from the exchange of commodities (exchange of products) between different communities.[13]

Dealing in money, therefore, first develops out of international trade. As soon as *different national coinages* exist, merchants who buy in foreign countries have to convert their own local coins into foreign currency and vice versa, or else convert coins of various kinds into uncoined pure silver (or gold) as world money. Hence the *exchange business*, which should be viewed as one of the spontaneous bases of the modern money trade.[14] From this there developed *exchange banks*, in which silver (or gold) functions as world money – now known as *bank* or *commercial money*, as distinct from currency. *Exchange transactions*, even if in this case they only involved providing notes for payment to

---

13 In Marx 1859, pp. 26–8.] [English: MECW 29, 1987, pp. 289–91.]

14 'The great differences among coins as regards their weight and standard, and imprints stamped on them by the many princes and cities that had minting rights, always made it necessary, in businesses where settlement in one particular form of coin was needed, to make use of the *local* currency. In order to make payments in bar, merchants who travelled to a foreign market provided themselves with uncoined pure silver, or even gold. Similarly, they exchanged the local coins they received for uncoined silver and gold when they set out on the return journey. Exchange dealing, the conversion of uncoined previous metal into local coin and vice versa, therefore became a very widespread and profitable business'. (Hüllmann 1826, pp. 437–8.) '*Exchange banks* do not owe their name … to *exchange in the sense of bills of exchange, but rather to the exchange of different kinds of money*. Long before the establishment of the Amsterdam Exchange Bank in 1609 there were already *money-changers* and *exchange businesses* in the trading cities of the Netherlands, and even *exchange banks* > (See Mees 1838 [as quoted in Vissering]) < … The business of a money-changer was to exchange the many different kinds of coin that were brought into the country by foreign traders for the current legal tender … The orbit of their activity gradually widened … They became the cashiers and bankers of their day. But the Amsterdam government saw a danger in the combination of cashier activity with exchange activity (*Mees*), and so as to combat that danger, it decided to establish a big institution which would undertake both exchange and cashier business on behalf of the public authority. This was the celebrated *Amsterdam Exchange Bank of 1609. The exchange banks of Venice, Genoa, Stockholm and Hamburg* similarly owe their origin to the continuous need to convert different varieties of money. Out of all these, the Hamburg bank is the only one still in existence today, since the need for an institution of this kind is still felt in this trading city, having as it does no coinage of its own … > Thus there arose a distinction between *bank money*, which is the currency in which the bank itself settles its accounts, and *cash money*, which is the form of money in daily circulation'. < (Vissering 1860, pp. 247–8.)

travellers from a money-changer in one country to one in another, had already developed in Rome and Greece out of the specific business of money-changing.

Trade in gold and silver as commodities (raw materials for the production of luxury goods) forms the spontaneous basis of the *bullion trade*, the trade that mediates the functions of money as world money. These functions, as previously explained, are of two kinds. The first is to facilitate circulation back and forth between the various national spheres of circulation, for the settlement of international payments, as well as the movement of capital loaned at interest, and the second is to enable movement from the sources of the production of precious metals onto the world market, and the distribution of this supply between the various national spheres of circulation. In England, for example, *goldsmiths* still functioned as bankers for the greater part of the seventeenth century. Here we shall completely ignore the way that the settlement of international payments develops further in the *exchange business*, etc., together with everything related to dealings in securities, in short we shall ignore all the specific forms of the credit system, with which we are not yet concerned.

As world money, national money discards its local character; one national money is expressed in another, and in this way they are all reduced to their gold or silver content. Since both these commodities circulate as world money, they have to be reduced in turn to the ratio between their values, which is constantly changing. The money-dealer makes it his own special business to carry on this intermediary function.

Money-changing and the *bullion trade* are thus the original forms of the money business and arise from the double function of money: as national coin and as world money.

The capitalist production process (and *trade* in general too), even where production is not yet carried on in the capitalist manner, leads to the following results: *firstly, the accumulation of money as a hoard*, in this case as the part of capital that must always be available in the money form, as a *reserve fund of means of purchase and payment. This is* |277| the first form of the hoard, as it reappears in the capitalist mode of production and generally comes into being with the development of commercial capital, at least for the use of this capital. In both cases this applies as much to international circulation as to domestic. This hoard is in constant flux, constantly spilling out into circulation and returning from it. The *second form* of the hoard is that of idle capital temporarily unoccupied in the money form, together with newly accumulated money capital that has not yet been invested. The functions that this hoard formation itself makes necessary start with its storage, book-keeping, etc.

Secondly, however, and linked with this, is the expenditure of money in buying, and its receipt from selling, paying and the receipt of payments, settlement of payments, etc. To start with, the money-dealer does all this as a simple *cashier* for merchants and industrial capitalists.[15]

Money-dealing is fully developed, even if still in its first beginnings, as soon as the functions of *lending and borrowing*, and *trade on credit*, are combined with its other functions. We shall deal with this in the next chapter, when we examine *interest-bearing capital.*

(The bullion trade itself – the transfer of gold or silver from one country to another – is simply the result of the commodity trade, determined by the rate of exchange, which expresses the state of international payments and the rate of interest in various markets. The bullion dealer as such only transmits the results.)

In considering money and how its movements and formal characteristics develop out of simple commodity circulation, we saw (in Book One, Chapter One) that the movement of the quantities of money circulating as means of

---

15 'The institution of cashier has perhaps nowhere kept its original and independent character in so pure a form as in the trading cities of the Netherlands' (on the origins of the cashier business in Amsterdam see Luzac 1782). 'Its functions overlap to a certain extent with those of the old Amsterdam Exchange Bank. The cashier receives a certain sum of money from the merchants who make use of his services, opening a 'credit' for them in his accounts; they also send him their claims for payment, which he collects for them and credits them with; on the other hand he makes payments against their drafts ('cashiers' letters') and debits the sums involved to their current account. For these entries and payments he makes a small charge, by which he gains an appropriate wage for his labour, entirely based on the number of turnovers taking place between the parties involved. If there are payments to be settled between two merchants, both of whom use the same cashier, these are adjusted very simply by entries on both accounts, while the cashiers settle their reciprocal claims among themselves every day. *The cashiers' business properly so called consists in this making of payments*; it excludes industrial undertakings, speculation and the opening of overdrafts; for the rule here must be that the cashier does not permit any payment over and above their credit by the clients who have opened an account with him'. (Vissering 1860, pp. 243–4.) *On the cashiers' associations in Venice*: 'Because of Venice's needs, and its peculiar geography, which made it more troublesome to carry cash around than in other places, the merchants of this city set up cashiers' associations with appropriate safeguards, supervision and management. The members of these associations subscribed certain sums on which they drew drafts for their creditors, whereupon the sum paid was deducted from the debtors' account on the page of the book set aside for that purpose, and the sum with which the creditor was credited was added to his account. Such were the first beginnings of the so-called *girobanks*. These associations are certainly old. But to push their origin back as far as the twelfth century is to confuse them with the State Loan Institution set up in 1171'. (Hüllman 1826, pp. 453–4.)

purchase and payment is determined by the volume and speed of the *metamorphosis of commodities*; and this metamorphosis, as we know now, is itself simply an aspect of the reproduction process as a whole. As far as obtaining the money material (gold and silver) from its source of production is concerned, this is reducible to direct commodity exchange, exchange of gold and silver as a commodity against other commodities, and is thus just as much an aspect of commodity exchange as obtaining iron or other metals. As far as the movement of precious metals on the world market is concerned, however (we ignore here such movements as express the pumping out of capital > from one country to another, < a transfer which also takes place in the form of commodity capital) this is as completely determined by international commodity exchange as the movement of money as a means of domestic purchase and payment is determined by domestic commodity exchange. (The export and import of precious metals from one national sphere of circulation to another, in as much as this is caused simply by the devaluation of a national currency, or by bi-metallism, lies outside monetary circulation proper and is merely a correction of aberrations brought about by arbitrary state decrees.) As far as the formation of hoards is concerned, finally, in so far as this represents a reserve fund of means of purchase and payment, whether for domestic or foreign trade, and is also merely a form of temporarily idle capital, in both cases this formation is simply a necessary precipitate of the circulation process.

Monetary circulation as a whole is a mere *result* of commodity circulation, in its volume, its forms and its movements, and from the capitalist standpoint commodity circulation itself represents simply the circulation process of capital (including the exchange of capital for revenue and of revenue for revenue, in so far as the expenditure of revenue is realised in retail trade). In the same way, it is completely self-evident that *money-dealing* does not just mediate the mere result and form of appearance of commodity circulation, that is the circulation of money. This *monetary circulation itself*, as a moment of commodity circulation, is for money-dealing a *given*. The latter's mediatory role is confined, instead, to its *technical operations*, which it concentrates, reduces and simplifies. Money-dealing does not form hoards, but it supplies the technical means for hoard formation, in so far as this is *voluntary* (and not the expression of unoccupied capital or of a disturbance in the reproduction process), thus *reducing it to its economic minimum*; since the reserve fund of means of purchase and payment, if managed on behalf of the capitalist class as a whole, does not need to be as great as if each capitalist had to administer his fund separately. The money trade does not buy *precious metals*, but only mediates their distribution after the commodity trade has bought them. Money-dealing mediates the settlement of accounts, in so far as money functions as means of payment, and by the mechanism it creates for these settlements it reduces the quantity of money these require; but it determines neither the relationship nor the volume of these mutual payments. The bills and cheques, for example, which are exchanged for one another in banks and clearing-houses derive from businesses > which are themselves completely |278| independent of those houses < and are the results of already given operations, so that all that is involved here is a better technical settlement of these results. In so far as money circulates as means of purchase, the volume and number of purchases and sale is completely independent of money-dealing. The latter can only abbreviate the *technical operations* that accompany these transactions and thereby also reduce the quantity of ready cash needed for their turnover.

Money-dealing in the pure form in which we are considering it here (that is to say, separately from the credit system) thus only bears on the technical side of one aspect of commodity circulation, namely monetary circulation and the various functions of money that arise from it.

This distinguishes money-dealing quite fundamentally from dealing in commodities, which mediates the metamorphosis of commodities and commodity exchange, even though it allows this process of commodity capital to appear as the process of a special capital separate from industrial capital. If therefore commodity-dealing commercial capital displays a special form of circulation, M – C, C – M, where it is the commodity that changes place twice and brings about the reflux of money, as opposed to C – M, M – C, where it is money that changes hands twice and mediates commodity exchange, no such special form can be seen in the case of money-dealing capital.

To the extent that money capital is advanced by a special section of capitalists in this technical mediation of monetary circulation – this capital representing on a diminished scale the additional capital which the merchants and the industrial capitalists would otherwise have to advance for this purpose themselves – there we also have the general form of capital M – M′. The fact that M is advanced means that the person advancing it receives M + ΔM. But the mediation between M and M′ involves only the technical moments of the metamorphosis and not its > conceptual [*begrifflich*] < moments.

It is self-evident that the mass of money capital with which the money-dealers are concerned is the circulating money capital of the merchants and the industrial capitalists, and that the operations the money-dealers perform are simply the operations of the merchants and industrialists, mediated by the former.

It is equally clear that their profit is simply a deduction from surplus-value, since they are dealing only with values already realised (even if realised only in the form of claims for payment).

Just as with commodity trade, here too we find a duplication of functions. For one section of the technical operations connected with money circulation must be performed by the commodity dealers and producers themselves. >

5)[16]

< The special form in which money is accumulated by commercial capital will not be considered until the next chapter. >

6)

< From what has already been developed, it should be clear enough that nothing could be more absurd than to treat *merchant's capital*, whether in the form of commodity-dealing capital or that of money-dealing capital, as a special branch of *productive capital*, in the same way as mining, agriculture, stock-raising, manufacture, the transport industry, shipping, etc., are particular spheres of investment > and therefore form branches of productive capital brought into existence by the social division of labour. < Even the simple observation that every productive capital, when it is in the circulation phase of its reproduction process, performs exactly the same functions as commodity capital and money capital, which appear as the exclusive functions of merchant's capital in its two forms, would put a stop to this crude conception. In commodity-dealing capital and money-dealing capital, rather, the *distinctions* between productive capital as such and the same capital in the sphere of circulation attain *an autonomous position* in the following way: the specific forms and functions that capital temporarily assumes in the latter case come to appear as independent forms and functions of particular *kinds* of capital that have separated off and become completely confined to this sphere. The *transformed form* of productive capital, and the *material* distinctions between productive capitals applied in different ways as a result of the nature of different branches of production (different use-values) are poles apart from one another.

Besides the crude fashion in which economists always treat distinctions of form, since they are in actual fact interested only in the material side, there are in the case of the vulgar economist two further reasons for this confusion:

---

16 [Engels converted the rest of Marx's Chapter Four into his Chapter 20, 'Historical Material on Merchant Capital'. Editor]

Firstly, his inability to explain the characteristic features of mercantile profit; *secondly*, his apologetic endeavour to derive the forms of commodity capital and money capital, and consequently commodity-dealing and money-dealing capital, *forms* which arise from the specific form of the capitalist mode of production |279| (which presupposes as its initial basis the circulation of commodities, and hence of money), as forms which necessarily arise from the *production process as such*.

If commodity-dealing capital and money-dealing capital were distinct from wheat cultivation only in the same way as this is distinct from stock-raising and manufacture, it would be as clear as day that production in general and capitalist production in particular were completely the same, and in particular that the distribution of the social product among the members of society, whether for industrial or individual consumption, must be effected just as eternally by merchants and bankers as the consumption of meat must be by stock-raising and that of articles of clothing by their manufacture.[17]

The great economists, such as Smith, Ricardo, etc., focused their attention on the basic form of capital, capital *as productive capital*, and in fact treated circulation capital only in so far as it is itself a phase in productive capital's

---

17 The wise Roscher [1858, p. 103] has cleverly worked out that if certain features characterise trade as a mediation between producers and consumers, 'one' (he?) must equally well be able to characterise production itself as a mediation of consumption (*between whom?*). From this it naturally follows that commercial capital is a part of productive capital, just like industrial or agricultural capital, etc. Thus because one can say that man can only mediate his consumption by production (and he has to do this even without a Leipzig education), or that labour is necessary for the appropriation of nature (which you can if you like call '*mediation*'), it follows as a matter of course that a *social* 'mediation' that arises from a specific *social* form of production – precisely because it is a mediation – has the same absolute character of necessity, the same status. It seems that the term 'mediation' settles everything. Besides, merchants are not mediators between producers and consumers (we ignore here for the time being those consumers who do not produce), but rather mediate the exchange of products between these producers), but rather mediate the *exchange of products between these producers*; they are simply intermediaries in an *exchange* which would still proceed in thousands of cases even without them. > 'The peasant sells for example butter in the market. With the money he receives for this he buys English linen goods, German agricultural implements, French cognac, American tobacco, Cuban sugar, Javan coffee, and perhaps some China tea. He has sold his butter to the butter merchant, and bought the things he needs from the shopkeeper. But these two were merely intermediaries in the exchange. In point of fact the exchange consisted in this, that he brought the products of his labour onto the world market and received in return for them the products of the labour of dozens of other people'. (Vissering 1860, pp. 16–17.) <

reproduction process. They were therefore perplexed by *mercantile capital* as a special variety of capital. The principles governing profit, value formation, etc., cannot be applied directly to mercantile capital. They therefore in fact entirely ignored it. They only refer to it in passing, as a *variety* of productive capital. Where they deal with it specifically, as Ricardo does in connection with foreign trade, they seek to demonstrate that it creates *no value* (and consequently also no surplus-value). But what holds for foreign trade holds also for commerce within a country.

> 7) < Up to now we have considered *merchant's capital* from the standpoint of the capitalist mode of production and within its limits. And yet not only trade, but also *trading capital*, is older than the capitalist mode of production, and is in fact the oldest historical mode in which *capital* has an independent existence.

Since we have already seen that money-dealing and the capital invested in it needs nothing more for its development than the existence of large-scale trade in general, and subsequently of commodity-dealing capital, it is only this latter which we have to deal with now.

Because commercial capital is confined to the circulation sphere, and because its sole function is to mediate the exchange of commodities, no further conditions are needed for its existence – leaving aside undeveloped forms that arise from barter – than are necessary for the simple circulation of commodities and money. Or, one might say that precisely the latter is *its* condition of existence. Whatever mode of production is the basis on which the products circulating have been produced – whether it is the primitive community, slave production, small peasant and petit-bourgeois production, or capitalist production – their character as commodities is in no way altered thereby, and as commodities that have to go through the exchange process and the changes of form that accompany it. The extremes between which commercial capital mediates are given, as far as it is concerned, just as they are given for *money* and its movement. The only thing necessary is that these *extremes* should be present as *commodities*, whether production is over its whole range commodity production or whether it is merely the surplus from producers who work to satisfy their own direct needs that is put on the market. Commercial capital simply mediates the movement of these extremes, the commodities, as *preconditions already given* to it.

The *extent* to which production goes into trade and passes through the hands of merchants depends on the mode of production, and it reaches a maximum with the full development of the capitalist mode of production, where the production is produced simply as a commodity and not at all as direct means of subsistence. On the other hand, whatever mode of production is the basis, trade promotes the generation of a surplus product designed to go into exchange, so as to increase the consumption or the hoards of the producers (which we take here to mean the *owners* of the products). It thus gives production a character oriented more and more towards exchange-value.

|280| The metamorphosis of commodities, their movement, consists (1) materially, in the exchange of different commodities for one another, and (2) formally, in the transformation of commodities into money, selling, and the transformation of money into commodities, buying. And the function of commercial capital is reducible to these functions, the exchange of commodities through buying and selling. Commercial capital thus simply mediates the exchange of commodities, though it should be understood right from the start that this is not just an exchange between the immediate producers. In the case of the slave relationship, the serf relationship, and the relationship of tribute (to the extent that communities come into consideration) it is the slave-owner, the feudal lord or the state which receives the tribute, that is the owner of the product and therefore its seller. The merchant buys and sells for many people, sales and purchases are concentrated in his hands, and in this way buying and selling cease to be linked to the direct need of the buyer (as merchant).

But whatever the social organisation of the spheres of production whose commodity exchange the merchant mediates, his wealth always exists as *money wealth* and his money always functions as capital. Its form is always M – C – M′;[18] money, the independent form of exchange-value, is the starting-point, and the increase of exchange-value the independent purpose. Commodity exchange itself, and the operations that mediate it – separated from production and performed by non-producers – becomes simply a means of increasing wealth, and not just wealth, but wealth in its general social form as *exchange-value*. The driving motive and determining purpose here is the transformation of M into M + ΔM; the M – C and C – M′ that mediate the act M – M′ appear simply as transitional moments in this transformation of M into M + ΔM. This M – C – M′, as the characteristic movement of commercial capital, is distinguished from C – M – C, commodity trade between the producers themselves > which is directed at the *exchange of commodities*, < that is to say the exchange of products (use-values) as its ultimate purpose.

18 See the passage from Turgot quoted previously. [Marx quoted a passage on this subject from Turgot 1844, p. 45, in Book Two, later published as Volume II of *Capital*; English version: Marx 1978, p. 416, n. 1. Translator]

The less developed production is, the more monetary wealth is concentrated in the hands of merchants and appears in the specific form of mercantile wealth.

Within the capitalist mode of production – that is to say, once capital has taken control of production itself and given it a completely altered and specific form – *commercial capital* appears simply as capital in a *particular function*. In all earlier modes of production, commercial capital rather appears as *the* function of capital *par excellence*, and the more so, the more production is directly the production of the means of subsistence.

Thus there is no problem at all in understanding why commercial capital appears as the historic form of capital long before capital has subjected production itself to its sway. Its development to a certain level is itself a *historical* prerequisite for the development of the capitalist mode of production (1) as the prerequisite for the concentration of monetary wealth, and (2) because the capitalist mode of production presupposes production for trade, that is to say on a mass scale rather than for the individual customer, for a buyer who does not buy for the satisfaction of his own personal needs, but rather concentrates in his act of purchase the acts of purchase of many people. On the other hand, every development in commercial capital gives production a character oriented ever more to exchange-value, transforming products more and more into commodities. Even so, this development, taken by itself, is insufficient to explain the transition from one mode of production to the other, as we shall soon see in more detail.

Within the capitalist mode of production, commercial capital is demoted from its earlier separate existence to become a *particular moment* of capital investment in general, and the equalisation of profits reduces its profit rate to the general average. It now functions simply as the agent of productive capital. The particular social conditions that form with the development of commercial capital no longer play a determining part here; on the contrary, where commercial capital predominates, obsolete conditions obtain. This is true even *within* the same country, where for example purely trading cities exhibit a far greater analogy with past conditions than manufacturing towns.[19]

---

19 Mr. W. Kiesselbach (in Kiesselbach 1860) is in fact still living in a mental world where commercial capital is *the* form of capital as such. He does not have the slightest idea of the modern meaning of capital, any more than Herr Mommsen does when he speaks of 'capital' and the rule of capital in his *Roman History*. In modern English history, the actual merchant estate and the trading cities also appear to be politically reactionary and in league with the landed and financial aristocracies against industrial capital. Compare

|281| The independent and preponderant development of capital in the form of commercial capital is equivalent to the absence of any subjection of production to capital, in other words to the development of capital on the basis of a social form of production that is foreign to it and independent of it. The *independent* development of commercial capital thus stands in inverse proportion to the *general economic development* of society.

|283a| If independent mercantile wealth is the prevailing form of capital, this means that the *circulation process has attained independence* vis-à-vis its extreme, and these are the exchanging producers themselves. These extremes remain separate from the circulation process, and this process from them. Here the product becomes a commodity through trade. It is trade that develops products into the form [*Gestaltung*] of commodities; not the produced commodities whose movement constitutes trade. Capital as capital, therefore, appears first of all in the circulation process. In this circulation process, money develops into capital. It is in circulation that the product first develops as an exchange-value, as commodity and money. Capital can be formed in the circulation process, and must be formed there, before it learns to master its extremes, the various spheres of production between which circulation mediates. The circulation of money and commodities can mediate spheres of production with the most diverse organisation, which in their internal structure are still oriented principally to the production of use-values. When the circulation process becomes independent in this way, as a process in which the *spheres of production are linked together by a third party*, this expresses a double situation. On the one hand, that circulation has still not mastered production, but is related to it simply as its *given* precondition. On the other hand, that the production process has not yet absorbed circulation into it as a mere moment. In capitalist production, on the contrary, both these things are the case. The production process is completely based on circulation and circulation is a mere moment and a transition phase of production, simply the realisation of a product produced as a commodity and the replacement of its elements of production produced as commodities. The form of capital that stems directly from circulation – commercial capital – now appears simply as one of the forms of capital in its movement of reproduction.

|281| This law appears particularly clearly in the history of the *carrying trade*, > (trade between intermediaries) < as conducted by the Venetian, Genoans,

for example the political role of Liverpool and Manchester. The complete domination of industrial capital has been acknowledged by English mercantile capital and by the moneyed interest only since the abolition of the duties on corn.

Dutch, etc., where the major profit was made not by supplying the particular products of their own country, but rather by mediating the exchange of products between communities which were undeveloped commercially – and in other economic aspects – and by exploiting both the producing countries.[20] Here we have commercial capital in its pure form, quite separate from the extremes, the spheres of production, between which it mediates. This is one of the main sources from which it is formed. But this monopoly of the carrying trade, and the trade itself, declines with the progress of the economic development of the peoples originally exploited by it from both sides, whose lack of development was the *basis of its existence*. In connection with the carrying trade, this appears not only as a decline in one particular branch of trade, but also as a decline in the supremacy of the exclusively trading peoples and in their commercial wealth in general, which rested on the basis of this carrying trade. This is simply a particular form in which the subordination of commercial capital is expressed with the progressive development of the capitalist mode of production. As for the manner and form in which commercial capital operates where it dominates production directly, a striking example is given not only by colonial trade in general (the so-called *colonial system*), but quite particularly by the operations of the former Dutch East India Company.

Since the movement of commercial capital is M – C – M′ > (or M – C, C – M + ΔM) < the first profit to be made (*for* the merchant) is made by acts which proceed within the circulation process itself, hence must be made in the two acts of purchase and sale. It is realised, secondly, in the final act, the act of sale, hence as *profit upon expropriation*.[21] At first appearance, a pure and independent commercial profit seems impossible as long as products are sold at their values.[22] |284| 'Buy cheap and sell dear' is the law of commerce, not the exchange of *equivalents*. The concept of *value* is involved here in so far as the various commodities are all values and therefore money; from the qualitative

---

20 Cf. Book III of Adam Smith: 'The inhabitants of trading cities, by importing the improved manufactures and expensive luxuries of richer countries, afforded some food to the vanity of the great proprietors, who eagerly purchased them with *great quantities of the rude produce of their own lands*. The commerce of a great part of Europe in those times, accordingly, consisted chiefly in the exchange of their own rude, for the manufactured produce of more civilised nations'. (Smith 1802, pp. 454–5.) > *The manufacture of luxuries, established by merchants*, is 'the offspring of foreign commerce'. (Smith 1802, pp. 456–7 [Smith 1999, p. 504].) *Here the merchant directly becomes an industrialist*. <

21 [In English in the original. 'Expropriation' is used here by Marx to mean 'the act of giving up one's property'. Translator]

22 Opdyke? [Opdyke 1851]

point of view, they are equal expressions of social labour. But *in value* their *magnitudes* are not equal. The *quantitative relationship* in which products exchange is at first completely accidental. They assume the commodity form in so far as they are in some way *exchangeable*, that is to say expressions of *the same thing*. Continued exchange, and accordingly continued reproduction, increasingly tends to abolish this accidental character. At the outset, however, this does not occur for the producers and consumers but rather for the mediator between the two, the merchant, who compares money prices and pockets the difference. It is through this movement that the *equivalence* is established.

Commercial capital, in the first instance, is simply the mediating movement between extremes it does not dominate and prerequisites it does not create.

Just as money does not arise from the simple form of commodity circulation, C – M – C, as merely a measure of value and means of circulation, but also arises as an absolute form of the commodity and therefore of wealth, as a hoard, making its conservation and accumulation into an end in itself, so also, from the mere circulation form of commodity capital, M – C – M', do money and the hoard develop into something that is maintained and increased merely by alienation [*Veräusserung*].

The trading peoples of antiquity were like the gods of Epicurus, existing in the *intermundia*,[23] or rather, they were like the Jews, existing in the pores of Polish society. The *carrying trade* of the first independent, large-scale and highly developed trading peoples and cities rested on the barbarism of the producing peoples between which they acted as intermediaries.

In the stages that preceded capitalist society, it was trade that prevailed over industry; in modern society it is the reverse. Trade naturally reacts back to a greater or lesser extent on the communities between which it is pursued; it subjects production more and more to exchange-value, by making consumption and existence more dependent on sale than on the direct use of the product. In this way it dissolves the old relationships. It increases monetary circulation. It no longer just takes hold of surplus production, but gradually gobbles up production itself and makes entire branches of production dependent on it > (on the luxury materials brought in from outside). < This solvent effect, however, depends very much on the nature of the producing community.

> *Steuart*: 'Trade is an operation, by which the wealth, or work, either of individuals, or of societies, may be exchanged by a set of men called merchants,

23 [The interstices between different worlds, which was where the ancient Greek philosopher Epicurus located the gods. Marx had used this analogy before. See Volume I of *Capital*; English version: Marx 1976, p. 172. Translator]

for an equivalent, proper for supplying every want, without any interruption to industry, or check to consumption'. (Steuart 1770, p. 166.) 'While wants continue simple and few, a workman finds time enough to distribute his work: when wants become more multiplied, men must work harder; *time becomes precious*; hence trade is introduced with the merchant as middleman between workmen and consumers'. (Steuart 1770, p. 171.) 'The *collection*' (of the products) '*into a few hands* is the introduction of trade'. 'The consumer does not buy in order to sell again; the merchant buys and sells merely with a view to gain'. (Steuart 1770, p. 175) 'The most simple of all trade is that which is carried on by *bartering the necessary articles of subsistence*'. (ibid.) 'When reciprocal wants are supplied by barter, there is not the smallest occasion for money; this is the |285| most simple of all combinations. When wants are multiplied, bartering becomes more difficult; upon this *money* is introduced. This is the common price of all things; it is a proper equivalent in the hands of those who want. This operation of buying and selling is a little more complex than the former'. Hence (1) *barter;* (2) *sale;* (3) *commerce*. The merchant must now be brought in. 'What before we called wants, is here represented by the consumer; what we called industry, by the manufacturer; what we called *money, by the merchant* ... This operation' (of buying and selling) 'is' (now) 'trade; it relieves both parties of the trouble of transportation and adjusting wants to wants, or wants to money; the *merchant represents by turns the consumer, the manufacturer, and the money*. To the consumer he appears as the whole body of manufacturers; to the manufacturers as the whole body of consumers; and to the one and the other class his credit supplies the use of money'. (Steuart 1770, pp. 177–8.) 'Merchants are supposed to buy and sell not by necessity, but with a view to profit'. (Steuart 1770, p. 201.)

< |281|[24] It [commercial profit] not only appears as *fraud*[25] and cheating but to a large extent does derive from this. > However much this *continues* to be true in individual cases, it does not affect the averages. With undeveloped modes of production, in contrast, < apart from the fact that commercial capital exploits the difference between production prices in various countries (and in this connection it acts to equalise commodity values and to set them) commercial capital is able to appropriate for itself a preponderant part of the *surplus product*: partly by acting as middleman between peoples (communities) whose production is still basically oriented towards use-value, so that the sale of that

24 [Marx repeated this page number in his manuscript. Translator]

25 Franklin, as quoted in Book One, Chapter One. [Franklin 1836, p. 376, quoted in Volume I of *Capital*; English version: Marx 1976, p. 267.]

part of their product that in some way or other steps into circulation, and thus the sale of products at their value in general, is of subordinate importance for their economic organisation; and partly because in those earlier modes of production the principal proprietors of the surplus product with whom the merchant trades, the slaveholder, the feudal landlord, and the state (for example the oriental despot) represent the consumption wealth which the merchant sets out to trap, as Adam Smith correctly perceived in relation to the feudal epoch.[26] Commercial capital, when it holds a dominant position, is thus in all cases a system of plunder,[27] just as its development in the trading peoples of both ancient and modern times is directly bound up with violent plunder, piracy, the taking of slaves and subjugation in general (in colonies). So it was in Carthage and Rome, and later on with the Venetians, Portuguese, Dutch, etc.

|282| The development of trade and commercial capital always gives production a growing orientation towards exchange-value (and at the same time also towards its multiplication, differentiation and expansion). (It also renders it cosmopolitan, developing money into world money.) Trade always has, to a

26 [This note simply repeats the earlier quotation from Adam Smith, given above on p. 434. Translator]

27 Luther: 'Now there is a great complaint among the merchants about the nobles, or robbers, because they have to trade with great danger, and are liable to be imprisoned, beaten, taken hostage or robbed. If they were to suffer such things for the sake of justice, the merchants would be saints ... But since the same great injustice and unchristian thieving and robbing are committed by merchants the whole world over, even against one another, is it any wonder that God has arranged things so that such great wealth unjustly made should again be lost or robbed, and the merchants themselves beaten about the head or imprisoned? ... And the princes should see to it that such unjust dealing is punished with due penalty, and take care that their subjects should not be so shamefully abused by merchants. Because they fail to do so, God uses knights and robbers as his devils to punish the injustice of the merchants, just as he plagued Egypt and plagues the whole world with devils, or destroys it through enemies. He thus sets one rogue against the other, without in this way implying that knights are lesser robbers than are merchants, although merchants daily rob the whole world, while a knight may rob one or two people once or twice a year ... Heed the words of Isaiah: your very rulers are confederate with thieves. For they hang the thieves who have stolen a guilder or half a guilder, but they mingle with those who rob the whole world and steal more surely than any others, so confirming the proverb that big thieves hang little thieves. Or, as the Roman senator Cato said, "Mean thieves lie in dungeons and in the stocks, while public thieves go about in gold and silk". What will God's final word be? He will do as he said to Ezekiel; he will amalgamate princes and merchants, one thief with another, like lead and iron, as when a city burns down, leaving neither princes nor merchants'. (Martin Luther in his work on usury, issued in the year 1524) [Luther 1589, p. 296.]

greater or lesser degree, a solvent effect on the pre-existing organisations of production, which in all their various forms are principally oriented to use-value. but how far it leads to the dissolution of the old mode of production depends first and foremost on the solidity and inner articulation of this mode of production itself. > (We shall come back to this point immediately.) < And what *results from* this process of dissolution, i.e., what *new mode of production* arises in place of the old, does not depend on trade, but rather on the character of the old mode of production itself. In the old world, the *world of antiquity*, the influence of trade and the development of commercial capital always produced the result of a *slave economy*; (depending on the point of departure it could also result in the transformation of a patriarchal slave system oriented towards the production of direct means of subsistence into one oriented towards the production of surplus-value > in agriculture the establishment of a plantation system, etc.) < In the modern world, on the other hand, its outcome is the *capitalist mode of production*. This shows that these *results* are themselves conditioned by quite other circumstances than the development of commercial capital.

It lies in the nature of the case that as soon as specifically urban industry separates off from agriculture, its products are in and for themselves commodities, so that their sale requires the mediation of trade. The dependence of trade on urban development is to this extent self-evident, as is the conditioning of the latter on trade. The degree to which industrial development goes hand in hand with these processes is, however, dependent on entirely different circumstances. For example, in ancient Rome, in the late republican era, commercial capital developed to a higher level than ever before in the ancient world, without any kind of progress in the development of crafts; whereas in Corinth and other Greek cities of Europe and Asia Minor a high level of craft development went hand in hand with the development of commercial capital. On the other hand, in diametrical opposition to urban development and its conditions, the commercial spirit and the development of commercial capital are often characteristic of wandering, *nomadic* peoples.

There can be no doubt – and this very fact has led to extremely false conceptions – that the great revolutions which took place in trade in the sixteenth and seventeenth centuries, along with the geographical discoveries of that epoch, and which rapidly advanced the development of commercial capital, were a major factor in promoting the transition from the medieval, feudal mode of production to the modern, capitalist mode. The sudden expansion of the world market, the multiplication of commodities in circulation, the race among the European nations to seize the products of Asia and the treasures of America, the colonial system, all these made a fundamental contribution towards shattering the feudal barriers to a new mode of production. And yet the modern mode of production in its first period, that of manufacture, developed only where the conditions for it had been created in the Middle Ages. Compare Holland with Portugal, for example.[28] And whereas in the sixteenth century (and in part still in the seventeenth century) the sudden expansion of trade and the creation of a new world market had an overwhelming influence on the defeat of the old mode of production and the rise of the capitalist mode,[29] this happened in reverse on the basis of the capitalist mode of production, once it had been created. The world market itself forms the basis for this mode of production. On the other hand, the immanent need that this has to produce on an ever greater scale drives it to the constant expansion of the world market, so that now it is not trade that revolutionises industry, but rather industry that constantly revolutionises trade. Moreover, commercial supremacy is now linked with the greater or lesser prevalence of the conditions for large-scale industry. Compare England and Holland, for example. The history of Holland's decline as the dominant trading nation is the history of the > dependency of commercial capital on productive capital < and its subordination to it.

The obstacles that the internal solidity and articulation of earlier national modes of production oppose to the solvent effect of trade are strikingly apparent in England's commercial relationships with India and China. There the broad basis of the mode of production is formed by the union between small-scale agriculture and domestic industry, on top of which we have in the Indian case the form of self-sustaining communities.[30] In India the English applied their direct political |283| and economic power, as masters and landlords, to destroying these small economic communities.[31] In so far as English trade has

28 The predominant role of the basis laid > for the development of trade by the *influence* of < fishing, manufacture and agriculture for Holland's development, quite apart from other circumstances, was already being discussed by the writers of the eighteenth century. See Massie for example [Massie 1750, p. 60: 'In Holland the great labour required to drain their land makes their necessity to trade greater than in any other part of the habitable world'.]

29 As against the earlier conception that underestimated the scope of Asiatic, ancient and medieval trade, it has now become the fashion to overestimate its significance and extent to an extraordinary degree. The best antidote to this view is to consider and contrast English exports and imports today with those at the start of the eighteenth century. And yet these were already incomparably greater than those of any earlier trading people. (See Anderson.) [Anderson 1764, p. 261.]

30 > It can be seen from Abel, etc., that in China too this was the original form, based on a communism which arose spontaneously (although this was itself formed in the course of a long historical process). [*Arbeiten* 1858.] <

31 More than in the case of any other nation, the history of English economic management in India is a history of mistaken and really stupid (in practice infamous) economic exper-

had a revolutionary effect on the mode of production in India, this is simply to the extent that it has destroyed spinning and weaving, which form an age-old and integral part of this unity of industrial and agricultural production, through the cheapness (and the underselling) of English commodities. In this way it has torn the community to pieces. Even here, their work of dissolution is succeeding only very gradually. These effects are felt still less in China, where no assistance is provided by direct political control. The great economy and saving of time that results from the *direct* connection of agriculture to manufacture presents a very stubborn resistance here to the products of large-scale industry, whose prices include the overhead expenses of the circulation process with which they are everywhere perforated.[32] In contrast to English trade, *Russian* trade leaves the economic basis of Asiatic production quite untouched.

The transition from the feudal mode of production takes place in two different ways. The producer may become a *merchant* and a *capitalist*, in contrast to the agricultural natural economy and the guild-bound handicraft of medi-

---

iments. In Bengal they created a caricature of large-scale English landed property; in the more south-eastern areas they created a caricature of peasant smallholdings. In the West they did all they could to transform the Indian economic community with common property in the soil into a caricature of itself.

32 > Mitchell (Elgin Blue Book). Now for the commentary – taken from a letter, written at Hong Kong, and signed 'W.H. Mitchell' (pp. 246–7 of the Blue Book relating to Lord Elgin's special mission to China and Japan, published in 1859, above mentioned [*Correspondence* 1859]). Mr. Mitchell says: 'A coat (to suit a working Chinaman) must contain at least three times the weight of raw cotton which we put into the heaviest goods we export to China: that is to say it would be three times as heavy as the heaviest drills and domestics we can afford to send out here: no doubt we could supply this country with goods as heavy and durable as their own, or as they require them, but whether we could do so as cheaply as they produce them for themselves, will presently appear. The best mode of illustrating the question will be by a single example taken from the province with which I am best acquainted, that of Fuh-Kien, and I would beg to direct the particular attention of the Board of Trade to the beautiful and simple economy of it, an economy which renders the system literally impregnable against all the assaults of foreign competition. So far back as 1844, I sent musters of this native cloth, of every quality, home to England, with the prices specified, and my correspondents assured me they could not produce it in Manchester at the rates quoted, much less lay it down here'. After describing the mode of manufacture at some length, Mr. Mitchell reminds Sir G. Bonham, to whom his letter is addressed, that Fuh-Kien is a province in which cotton does not grow, and ends that part of his subject by saying: 'So much for the cheap production of native cloth in the Southern provinces: *a fortiori* must the same reasoning apply to the Northern, where the staple grows at the threshold of the homestead'. [The whole of this note is a newspaper cutting Marx attached to page 283 of his manuscript.] <

eval urban industry. This is the really revolutionary way. Alternatively, however, the *merchant* may take direct control of production himself. But however frequently this occurs as a historical transition – as for example with the English clothier of the seventeenth century, who brought weavers who were formerly independent under his control, selling them the wool they had to work up, and buying their product[33] – it cannot bring about a revolution in the old mode of production by itself, but rather preserves and retains it as its own precondition. Until recently, for example, the manufacturer in the French silk industry, and the English hosiery and lace industries too, was a manufacturer only in name. In reality he was merely a merchant, who kept the weavers working in their old, fragmented manner, and only exercised control as a merchant: it was a merchant they were really working for. This method always stands in the way of the genuinely capitalist mode of production and disappears with its development. Without revolutionising the mode of production, it simply worsens the conditions of the direct producers, transforms them into mere wage-labourers and proletarians under worse conditions than those directly subsumed [*subsumiert*] under capital, and appropriates their surplus labour on the basis of the old mode of production. Somewhat modified, the same relationship is to be found in some parts of the manufacture of furniture carried on in London in the craft manner.

Cabinet-making is an extensive feature of the district of London known as Tower Hamlets. > Here there is a division of labour in the sense that < the whole of furniture production is divided into very many separate, mutually independent branches. One firm just makes chairs, another tables, a third chests and so on. But these firms themselves are conducted more or less on a handicraft basis, by one master with a few journeymen. Despite this, production is on too large a scale to work directly for private clients. The buyers are the proprietors of the furniture stores. On Saturday the master goes to these stores and sells his products, with as much haggling over the price as there is in a pawnshop of an advance on some item or other. These masters need their weekly sale simply to buy more raw material for the coming week and to pay wages. Under these conditions they are really only middlemen between the merchant and their own workers. The merchant is the real capitalist and pockets the greater part of the surplus-value. Things are similar in the transition to manufacture from branches that were formerly pursued as handicrafts or as sidelines to rural industry. > Thus the merchants are described in Lyon, Nottingham, etc., as *the manufacturers*, although those middlemen only exploit the workers in

---

33 > Tuckett [1846, p. 137.] <

a direct fashion. This forms a transition to manufacture or even to large-scale industry (see now *hosiery* for example) and < it depends on the technical development of the small owner-operated establishment. > Where it already rests on machines which are of a handicraft-like character – or on machines which are kept within the limits of handicraft operation – there is a transition to large-scale industry.

< The transition can take three forms: (1) the merchant becomes an industrialist directly; this is the case with crafts that are founded on trade, that is on foreign materials, luxury industries, where the merchants import both raw materials and workers from foreign parts, as they were imported into Italy from Constantinople.

(2) The merchant makes the small masters into his middlemen, or even turns the immediate producer into his middleman. He allows the producer to stay nominally independent and leaves his mode of production unchanged.

(3) The industrialist becomes a merchant and produces directly *on a large scale* for the market.

|283a| In the Middle Ages, the merchant was simply someone who *'transferred' commodities*, as Poppe correctly put it, whether these were produced by *members of guilds* or by peasants.[34] The merchant becomes an industrialist, or rather he has craftsmen, and small producers (particularly rural ones), doing the work on their own account. Alternatively, the producer becomes a merchant. Whereas before the clothier gradually received his wool from the merchant in small portions and worked for the merchant, now he buys the material himself. The conditions of production go into the production process as commodities that he has himself bought. And instead of producing for the individual merchant or for particular customers, the clothier now produces for the entire world of commerce. The producer is himself a merchant. Commercial capital now performs the circulation process and nothing more. Originally, trade was the precondition for the transformation of guild and rural domestic craft production and feudal agricultural production into capitalist production. Now it develops the product into a commodity, partly by creating a market for it, partly by supplying new commodity equivalents and new raw and ancillary materials for production, and thereby opening new branches of production which are based on trade from the very beginning, both on production for the market and on conditions of production that derive from the world market > (instead of being local or national). < As soon as manufacture becomes somewhat stronger, and still more so large-scale industry, it creates a

34 [Poppe 1807, p. 70. Translator]

market for itself and uses its commodities to *conquer* it. Trade now becomes the servant of industrial production, for which the constant expansion of the market is a condition of existence. An ever more extensive mass production swamps the existing market and thus works steadily towards its own expansion, breaking through its barriers. What restricts this mass production is not trade (in as much as this only expresses existing demand), but rather the scale of the functioning capital and the development of the productivity of labour. The industrial capitalist is constantly faced with the world market; he compares and must constantly compare his own cost prices, not only with market prices at home, but with those of the whole market of the world. In a previous epoch, this comparison was almost exclusively the concern of the merchant estate and thus ensured commercial capital its mastery over productive capital.

|283| The first scientific, theoretical treatment of the modern mode of production – the *mercantile system* – necessarily proceeded from the superficial phenomena of the circulation process, as these acquire autonomy in the movement of commercial capital. Hence it only grasped the semblance [*Schein*] of things. This was partly because commercial capital is the first independent mode of existence of capital in general, and partly on account of the overwhelming influence that commercial capital exercised in the period when feudal production was first overthrown, the period of the rise of modern production. The genuine science of modern economics begins only when one passes from the circulation process to the production process. Interest-bearing capital, too, is admittedly also an age-old form of capital. But we shall *see later on* why mercantilism did not take this as its basis, but rather engaged in polemics with it.[35] >

35 [See below, manuscript pages 398 and 402. Translator]

The Division of Profit Into Interest and Profit of Enterprise. (Industrial or Commercial Profit). Interest-Bearing Capital

(1) [Interest-Bearing Capital]

On our first consideration of the *general rate of profit* > and the *average rate of profit* that corresponds to this < (Chapter Two of this book) we didn't yet have the average rate of profit before us in its finished form, since the equalisation that produced it still appeared simply as an equalisation of the *productive capitals* invested in different spheres. This was supplemented in the last chapter, where we discussed the participation of commercial capital in equalisation (as well as mercantile profit). The general rate of profit or the average profit were then presented within more closely defined limits than before. In the further course of our analysis it is to be understood that when we speak of the *general rate of profit* or the *average profit* this is in the latter sense, hence exclusively with respect to the finished form of the average rate. Since in this version the average rate is the same for industrial and mercantile capital, it is also no longer necessary to make a distinction between industrial and commercial profit, to the extent that we are now dealing only with this average profit. Whether capital is invested industrially in the sphere of production or commercially in that of circulation, it yields *the same annual average profit*.

On the basis of the capitalist mode of production, money (i.e., money taken as the *independent expression* of a sum of value, whether this actually exists in money or in commodities) can be transformed into capital, and through this transformation it is turned from a given, fixed value into a *self-valorising* value, capable of increasing *its own value*. It becomes a producer of profit, i.e., it enables the capitalist to extract > from the workers < and to appropriate for himself a certain quantity of unpaid labour, surplus product and surplus-value. In this way the money receives an additional use-value, besides the *use-value* it possesses *as money*, namely the ability to function as *capital*. Its use-value here consists precisely in the *profit* that it produces when transformed into capital. In this capacity of *potential* capital, as a means for the production of profit, it becomes a *commodity*, but a commodity of a special kind. Or, and this comes to the same thing, *capital as capital* becomes a *commodity*.[1]

Let us take the average annual rate of profit as 20 percent. Under average conditions, then, and with the average level of intelligence and activity appropriate to the intended purpose, a sum of value of £100, expended as capital, will yield a profit of 20 percent. Thus a man who has £100 at his disposal holds in his hands the power of making this £100 into £120, and thus producing a profit of £20. He holds in his hands a *potential* capital of £100. If this man makes over his £100 for a year to someone else, who actually does use it as capital, he gives him the power to produce £20 of profit, a surplus-value that costs him nothing and for which he does not pay any equivalent. If the second man pays the proprietor of the £100 a sum of £5, say, at the end of the year, i.e., *a portion of the profit produced*, what he pays for with this is the use-value of the £100, the use-value of its capital function, the function of producing a profit of £20. The part of the profit paid in this way is called *interest*, which is thus nothing but a particular name, a special title, for a *part of the profit* which the functioning capitalist has to pay to the owner of the capital |287|, instead of pocketing it himself.

It is clear that the possession of this £100 gives its owner the *power* to demand an *interest*, in other words a certain part of the profit that his capital produces. If he did not give the other person the £100, the latter would be unable to produce the profit of £20, and unable to function at all as a capitalist.[2]

It is nonsense for Gilbart to speak here of 'natural justice' (see note 2). The *justice of transactions* between the agents of production consists in the fact that these transactions arise from the relations of production as their natural consequence. The legal forms in which these economic transactions appear as *voluntary actions* of the participants, as the expressions of their *common will* and as contracts that can be enforced on the individual parties by the power of the state, are mere forms that cannot themselves determine this content. They simply express it. The content is *just* when it corresponds to the mode of production and is adequate to it. It is *unjust* as soon as it contradicts it. Slavery, for example, is *unjust* on the basis of the capitalist mode of production; so is cheating on the quality of commodities, etc.

---

1 A few passages could be quoted here in which the economists see matters in this way: '*You*' (the Bank of England) 'are very large dealers in the *commodity of capital*?' (*Report on the Bank Acts*, 1857, answer no. 1194.)

2 'That a man who borrows money with the intention of making a profit on it, should give *a part of the profit* to the lender is a self-evident principle of natural justice'. (Gilbart 1834, p. 163.) [Marx's version, given here, differs slightly from the original. Translator]

The £100 produces a profit of £20 by functioning as capital, whether industrial or mercantile. But the *sine qua non* of its ability to function as capital is that it is actually *spent* as capital, that the money is laid out on the purchase of means of production (in the case of industrial capital) or of commodities (in the case of mercantile capital). To be spent, however, it must first be available. If A, the owner of the £100, either spent it for his private consumption or treated it as a hoard, it could not be *spent* as capital by B, the functioning capitalist. B does not spend *his own* capital, but that of A; yet he cannot spend A's capital unless A wishes this. In point of fact, therefore, it is A who originally spends the £100 as capital, even though his function as a capitalist is entirely restricted to this act of expenditure. As far as the £100 is concerned, B functions as a capitalist only because A turns the £100 over to him, and hence spends it *as capital.*

Let us first consider the characteristic *circulation of interest-bearing capital.* The second thing to investigate would then be the specific way in which it is *sold as a commodity*, namely *being lent*, instead of being *sold.*

First. The starting-point is the money that A advances to B. (This can occur either with or without security. The first form, however, is mainly characteristic of the ancient world, with the exception of advances on commodities or papers such as bills of exchange, etc. These particular forms do not concern us here. What we have to deal with is interest-bearing capital in its ordinary form.) In B's hands, the money really is transformed into capital, going through the movement $M - C - M'$ and then returning to A as M', in other words as $M + \Delta M$, ΔM represents the interest. (The capital may remain in B's hand for a protracted period, during which he pays interest at specific intervals > and only returns the capital, with the final interest instalment, after a long time has elapsed. < This case too we leave aside for the sake of simplification.)

The movement is thus $M - M - C - M' - M'$.

What appears in *duplicate* here is (1) the expenditure of the money as capital, and (2) its reflux as realised capital, as M' or $M + \Delta M$.

In the movement of mercantile capital, $M - C - M'$, the same commodity changes hands twice, or several times > (if numerous merchants stand between the first seller and the final buyer); < but each time the *same* commodity changes place in this way it displays a metamorphosis, a purchase or sale of the commodity, no matter how often this process might be repeated before its definitive sale.

In $C - M - C$, on the other hand, we have a double change of place > (change of hands) < by the same money, but one which displays the complete metamorphosis of the commodity, this being first |288| transformed into money, and then out of money again into another commodity.

With interest-bearing capital, in contrast, M's first change of place is neither a moment of metamorphosis nor a moment of the reproduction of capital. This begins only the second time it is spent, in the hands of the functioning capitalist, who uses it to pursue trade or transforms it into productive capital. M's first *change of place* here expresses nothing more than its transfer or making over from A to B; (a transfer which takes place under certain legal forms and provisions).

This *double* expenditure of the money as capital, the first time as a simple transfer from A to B, is matched by its double return. As M' or $M + \Delta M$, it returns from the movement cycle to the functioning capitalist B. B then *transfers* it, > hands it back, < to A, but with a part of the profit as well, as realised capital, $M + \Delta M$, where ΔM does not amount to the whole profit, but simply the part of the profit that is interest. It flows back to B as he has paid it out, as functioning capital, but as the property of A. For its return movement to be complete, B has to transfer it again to A. Besides the capital sum, however, B has also to surrender to A a *part of the profit* he has made on this capital sum, under the name of *interest*, since A has given the money to him only as capital, i.e., as *value* that is not just maintained in the course of its movement, but creates a *surplus-value* for its owner.

(It remains in B's hands only as long as it is functioning capital. And on its return {after the prescribed interval has elapsed} it ceases to function as capital. As capital that is no longer functioning, however, it must again be transferred from the hands of B to those of A, who has not ceased to be the capital's legal owner during the whole period of its alienation [*Entäusserung*] to B.)

The form of *lending* which is characteristic of this commodity, of *capital as commodity*, can incidentally be found in other transactions, in place of the form of *sale*. This form of lending results from the characteristic that *capital* steps forth as a *commodity*, in other words it results from the fact that *money as capital* becomes a commodity.

> We need to make a distinction here.

< We have already seen that capital functions in the circulation process as *commodity capital* and *money capital*. In neither of these forms, however, does *capital as capital* become a commodity.

Once productive capital has been transformed into commodity capital, it must be placed on the market and sold as a commodity. Here it functions simply as a commodity. The capitalist appears simply as the seller of a commodity and the buyer as the buyer of a commodity. As a commodity, the product must realise its value in the circulation process. For this reason, it is quite immaterial here whether this commodity is bought by a consumer as means of subsistence or by a capitalist as means of production, as a component of capital. >

In its real function, < in the act of circulation, the commodity capital functions simply as a *commodity*, not as *capital*. It is commodity capital as distinct from a simple commodity, (1) because it is already pregnant with surplus-value, so that the realisation of its value is at the same time the realisation of surplus-value; though this does not alter its simple existence as a commodity, as a product with a definite price; and (2) because this function it has as a commodity is a moment of its reproduction process as capital, and hence its movement as a commodity, when placed in relation to the process as a whole, is at the same time its movement as capital. It does not become capital *by the act of selling* > *or the metamorphosis of the commodity* itself < but only through the *connection* between its fate, or its movement as a commodity, with its total movement as capital.

As *money capital*, likewise, it actually operates simply as *money*, i.e., as means of purchase for commodities (the means of production). The fact that this money is also money capital, a form of capital, is not the result of the act of purchase, the actual function it performs here as money, but rather of the way in which this act is connected with the overall movement of capital, or, more precisely, because this act of purchase it performs as money introduces the capitalist production process.

|289| In so far as it actually functions, however, and actually plays its role in the process, commodity capital is active here only as *commodity*, and money capital only as *money*. In no individual moment of the metamorphosis, taken by itself, does the capitalist sell the *commodity* to the buyer *as capital*, even though it represents capital for him; nor does the buyer dispose of his money as capital to the *seller*. In both cases the *commodity* is simply sold as a commodity, and money simply as money, it is given out as a means of purchase, i.e., the commodity is purchased with it.

It is only by putting together the whole of the process, with the point of departure appearing simultaneously as the point of return, only in $G - G'$ (or $C - C'$ > if one proceeds from the commodity as the starting-point) < that capital emerges in the *circulation process* as *capital*. (In the production process it emerges as capital through the subordination of the worker to the capitalist and the production of surplus-value.) But here the mediation has disappeared. What does exist is M' or $M + \Delta M$ (whether this value sum increased by ΔM exists in the form of money, commodities or means of production, > fixed capital, etc.) < a sum of money equal to that originally advanced plus an excess over this, the realised surplus-value. And precisely at this point of return, where the capital exists as realised capital, as *valorised value*, in this form – in so far as it is taken as a point of repose, imaginary or real – the capital *never* enters circulation but rather appears as withdrawn from circulation, as the result of the entire process.

In so far as it is spent again, it is never alienated to a third party *as capital* but rather sold to him as a simple commodity or transformed into a commodity simply as money. It is never alienated in its circulation process as *capital*, but only as commodity or money, and here this is its only *existence for others*. Commodity and money are capital here not because commodities are turned into money and money into commodities, not in their actual relationships, either to the capitalist himself (considered subjectively) or as moments of the reproduction process (considered objectively). It is not in the *process of circulation* that capital exists as *capital* but only in the *production process*.

With interest-bearing capital the situation is different, and this is precisely what constitutes its specific character.

The owner of money who wants to valorise his money as interest-bearing capital parts with it to someone else, puts it into circulation, makes it into a *commodity* **as capital**; as capital not only for himself but also for others. It is not simply capital for the person who alienates it, but it is made over to the other person *as capital*, as *value* that possesses the *use-value* of creating surplus-value, profit; > it is therefore handed over to him as capital, i.e., as a value that *maintains itself* in the movement and, after it has performed its function, < *returns to* the person who originally gave it out, in this case the money's owner. That is, it is removed from him only during a certain interval, only temporarily stepping out of the possession of its owner into the possession of the functioning capitalist. It is neither paid out nor sold, but simply *lent, loaned out*; it is only alienated on condition that it is, first, returned to its starting-point after a definite period of time, and *second*, returned as realised capital, so that it has realised its *use-value* of producing surplus-value.

Since the commodity is lent out as *capital*, it can be lent either as *circulating capital* or *fixed capital. Money* can be lent in both forms; it is lent as fixed capital, for example, if it is repaid in the form of an annuity, so that a portion of the capital always returns together with the interest. Certain commodities, such as houses, machines, etc., can be lent only as fixed capital, by the nature of their *use-value*. But all loan capital, whatever form it might have, and no matter how its *repayment* might be modified by the nature of its use-value, is always simply a special form of money capital. For what is lent here is always a definite sum of money, and it is on this sum that the interest is reckoned. If what is lent is neither money nor circulating capital, it is also paid back in the way that fixed capital returns. The lender receives both a periodic interest and a part of the used-up value of the fixed capital itself, an equivalent for the depreciation over this period. And at the end of the loan's term, the unused portion of the fixed capital is returned in kind. If the loaned capital is circulating capital, it similarly returns to the lender in the general mode of return of circulating capital.

The *manner of its return* is thus determined in each case by the actual cyclical movement of capital as it reproduces itself and its specific varieties. But for loan capital, the return takes the form of a *repayment*, because the advance, the alienation of the loan capital, has the form of a *loan*.

In this chapter we shall be dealing only with *money capital proper*, from which the other forms of loan capital are derived.

The capital lent out returns in a double sense. In the reproduction process it returns to the functioning capitalist, and then its return is repeated once again as a transfer to the lender, the money capitalist, as a *repayment* to its real proprietor, a return to its legal starting-point.

In the actual process of circulation, capital always appears as commodity or money, and its movement is reducible to a series of purchases and sales. In short, the circulation process is reducible to the metamorphosis of commodities. It is different when we consider the reproduction process as a whole. If we proceed from money (and it is the same thing if we proceed from the commodity, for we are then proceeding from its *value*, and thus viewing it too in the guise of money), a certain sum of money is given out and it returns after a given period > both the original sum of money and an excess over this, < an increment. What returns is > an increased sum of money < the replacement for the original value advanced, plus a surplus-value. It has been maintained and increased in the course of a certain cyclical movement. But money that is lent as capital is hired out precisely as a sum of money that is maintained and increased, a sum which returns with an addition after a certain period and can go through the same process again and again. It is not given out as money or as a commodity, hence it is neither exchanged for a commodity when it is advanced as money nor sold for money when it is advanced as a commodity. It is rather given out as *capital*. The reflexive relationship in which capital presents itself when we view the capitalist production process as a whole and a unity, and in which capital appears as money breeding money, is here simply embodied in it as its character, its capacity, without the *intervening mediating movement*. And it is in this capacity that it is alienated.

Lending appears to Proudhon as an evil, because it is not *selling*. A loan made at interest 'is the ability to *sell the same object over and over again*, and always to receive the same price afresh, *without ever ceding ownership over the thing one has sold*'. (Bastiat 1850, p. 9.)[3] The object (such as money, a house, etc.) does not change its owner, as it does in buying and selling. But he does not see that when

3 [The words Marx quotes here were written not by Proudhon but by Charles-François Chevé, editor of *La Voix du Peuple*, who wrote the first letter in this collection. Translator]

money is given out (as in the case of interest-bearing capital) *no equivalent* for it is received in return. It is true that in any act of buying and selling, in fact whenever an exchange process takes place, the *object* is given away. One always 'cedes ownership over the thing one has sold'. But the *value* is not given away. What is given away when a sale takes place is the commodity, but not its *value*, for this is returned in the form of money (or, and this is here just another form of money, a *bill*, an entitlement to payment). On purchase, money is given away, but not its *value*, which is replaced in the form of commodities. Throughout the reproduction process, the productive capitalist keeps *the same* value in his hands, but |290| in different forms.

In so far as *exchange* takes place, i.e., the exchange of objects, there is no change in value. The capitalist in question always keeps the same value in his hands. While the capitalist is producing *surplus-value*, no exchange takes place, and by the time it does take place the surplus-value is already contained in the commodities.

As soon as we consider not the isolated acts of exchange but rather the overall circuit of capital, M – C – M′, what happens is that a definite sum of value is constantly advanced, and this sum of value plus the surplus-value or profit is withdrawn from circulation. (The mediation of this process, however, is not visible in the simple acts of exchange alone. And it is precisely this process of M *as capital* which the interest of the lending capitalist is based on and from which it derives.)

'In point of fact', says Proudhon, 'the hat-maker who sells hats ... receives in return *their value*, neither more nor less. But the lending capitalist ... not only receives back the whole of his capital, he receives *more than this capital, more than he puts into the exchange. On top of his capital*, he receives *an interest*'. (Bastiat 1850, p. 69.)

Here the hat-maker represents the productive capitalist in contrast to the lending capitalist. Proudhon has evidently not managed to penetrate the secret of how the productive capitalist can sell commodities at their *values* (the adjustment to prices of production is a matter of indifference in *his* way of conceiving the question), and by that very act obtain a *profit* over and above the capital he has put into the exchange. Let us assume that the price of production of 100 hats is £115 and that this price happens to be equal to the *value* of the hats (hence the capital that produces the hats is of average social composition). If the profit is 15 percent, the maker realises a profit of £15 by selling the commodities at their value of £115. To him they cost only £100. If he has produced them with his own capital, he pockets the entire excess of £15; if with borrowed capital, he has possibly to give up £5 of this as interest. This in no way affects the *value of the hats*, but simply the *distribution* of the surplus-value already contained in the hats among different people. And since the *value* of the hats is not affected by the payment of interest, the following nonsensical remarks by Proudhon are entirely without justification: 'Since, in trade, the *interest on capital* is added to the worker's *wages to make up the price of the commodity*, it is impossible for the worker to buy back the product of his own labour. To live by working is a principle that involves a contradiction, under the rule of interest'. (p. 105.)[4]

How little Proudhon has understood the nature of capital is shown by the following sentence, in which he describes the movement of capital in general in terms of the specific movement of interest-bearing capital:

'Since, through exchange, money capital always returns to its source with an accumulation of interest, reinvestment, if always done by the same hand, enables the same individual to draw a continual profit'. (p. 154.)

What still remains a puzzle to him in the specific movement of interest-bearing capital?

The categories: buying, price, alienation of goods, and the > superficial < and immediate form in which *surplus-value* appears here; in fact it is the phenomenon that here *capital* has become a *commodity as capital*, that selling has been transformed into lending, and price into a share in the surplus profit.

The *return of capital* to its starting-point is always the characteristic movement of capital in its overall process. This is by no means something exclusively characteristic of interest-bearing capital. What distinguishes interest-bearing capital is the *superficial* form of the return, separated off from the mediating circuit.

The lending capitalist parts with his capital, *transfers* it to the productive capitalist, *without receiving an equivalent*, but this handover is in no way an act of the actual circulation process of capital; it introduces the circulation, on the part of the productive capitalist. This first change of place of the money does not express any act of metamorphosis, neither a purchase nor a sale. Ownership is not surrendered, since no exchange takes place and no equivalent is received. The return of the |291| money from the hands of the productive capitalist to those of the lending capitalist simply supplements the first act in which the

---

4 'A house', 'money', etc., should therefore not be lent as '*capital*' but rather as 'commodities ... at cost price'. (Bastiat 1850, pp. 43, 44.) Luther stands somewhat above Proudhon. He already knew that profit-making is independent of the form of lending or buying: 'They turn *buying* also into *usury*. But this is too much to bite off all at once. We must confine our attention for the time being to dealing with usury in lending, and when we have set this right (after the day of judgement) we shall go on to give *usury in buying* its lesson too'. (Luther 1540.)

capital has been given out. Advanced in the money form, the capital returns to the productive capitalist again in the money form. But since the capital did not belong to him when he gave it out, it cannot belong to him on its return. (The reproduction process cannot possibly transfer the capital into his *property*.) He therefore has to give it back to the lender. The initial act which transfers the capital from the lender to the borrower is a legal transaction which has nothing to do with the actual circulation and production process of capital, but simply *introduces* it. The repayment, which transfers the capital that has returned from the borrower to the lender again, is a second legal transaction, the complement to the first; the one introduces the real process, the other is a subsequent act after that has been completed. The point of departure and point of return, the lending out of the capital and its recovery, thus appear as arbitrary movement mediated by legal transactions, which take place before and after the real movement of capital and have nothing to do with it as such. It would make no difference to this real movement if the capital belonged to the productive capitalist, and therefore returned to him alone as *his property*. In the first introductory act, the lender hands over his capital to the borrower. In a second, subsequent and concluding act, the borrower gives this capital back to the lender. In so far as the transaction between these two is concerned (we leave aside for the time being the interest, in so far as we are dealing simply with the *movement of loaned capital* between lender and borrower) these two acts, which are separated by a longer or shorter *interval* (during which the real movement of capital takes place), encompass the whole of the movement. And this movement, namely the act of giving out of a sum of value on condition of repayment > to a third person, who is obliged to return this sum of value after a certain period of time, this giving away on condition of receiving back < is the general movement of *lending and borrowing*, this specific form of a solely conditional alienation of money or commodities.

The characteristic movement of capital in general is the return of money to the capitalist. This *return of capital* to its point of departure receives in the case of interest-bearing capital a completely superficial form, separated from the real movement whose form it is. A hands over his money, not as money but rather as capital. The money does not produce a change in the capital. It simply changes hands. Its actual transformation into capital is accomplished only in the hands of B. But for A it has become capital simply by having been given to B. The actual return of the capital from the production and circulation process takes place for B. For A, however, the return takes place in the same form as the alienation > (as a simple repayment). The money moves from B's hands back into those of A. < The giving out or lending of money for a certain time, and repayment of this with interest (surplus-value) is the entire form of the movement attributable to interest-bearing capital as such. The real movement of the money lent out as capital is an operation which lies *beyond* the transactions between borrowers and lenders. In this operation *this mediation is obliterated*, invisible and not directly involved. Capital as a special kind of commodity also has a *form of alienation peculiar to it*. Here, therefore, the return does not appear as a consequence and result of a definite series of economic processes, but rather as a consequence of a special legal contract between buyer and seller. The period of the return depends on the real production process; in the case of interest-bearing capital, its return as capital *seems* to depend simply on the contract between lender and borrower. And so the return of the capital, in connection with this transaction, no longer appears as a result determined by the production process, but rather as if the capital lent out had never lost the form of money. Of course, these transactions are determined by the real returns. But this does not *appear* in the transaction itself. (It is also by no means always the case *empirically*. If the *real return* does not take place at the right time, the borrower must look to see what other sources of help he can draw on to fulfil his obligations towards the lender.) The mere form of capital – money that is given out as a sum, A, and returns within a certain period as a sum A + $^1/_x$ A, without any other mediation besides this temporal interval > between the giving out and the return payment < – is the irrational [*begriffslose*] form of the real movement.

In the real movement of capital, the return is a moment in the circulation process. Money is first transformed into means of production; it becomes a commodity as a result of the production process; by the sale of the commodity it is transformed back into money, and in this form it returns to the hands of the capitalist who first advanced the capital in its money form. But in the case of interest-bearing capital the return, like the giving out, is simply the result of a legal transaction between the owner of the capital and a third[5] person. > It therefore also appears, as far as the relations between the moneyed capitalist and the productive capitalist go, as no more than a loan of money (a giving out or alienation of money) and a repayment of the money that has been borrowed (its return). < Everything that happens in between is obliterated.

But because money advanced as capital has the property of returning to the person advancing it, to the person who has transformed it into capital, expended it, because M – C – M′ is the immanent form of the capital movement, for this very reason the owner of money can lend it as *capital*, as something which possesses the property of returning to its source and *maintaining* (and

5 [Engels altered this to 'second'. Translator]

increasing) *itself as value in the movement* it undergoes. He gives it out as *capital* because, after being employed as capital, it returns to its starting-point, hence it can be *returned to* the lender after a certain period precisely because it flows back to him personally.

The *lending of money* as capital – the possibility of giving it out on condition of its repayment after a certain period – depends on the assumption that the money really is applied as capital and really does flow back to its starting-point. The real *cyclical movement of money as capital* is therefore the assumption behind the legal transaction by which the borrower of the money has to return it to the lender. (If the borrower does not apply it as capital, that is his affair. The lender lends it as *capital*, and as capital it has to pass through the functions of capital, which include the circuit of money and its return to its starting-point.)

The acts of circulation $M - C$ and $C - M'$, in which capital functions *as money* or *as commodity*, are simply intermediary processes, particular moments of its overall movement. As capital, it passes through the movement $M - M'$. It is advanced as money (or *a sum of value* in any form) and returns as a sum of value. The lender of money does not spend this on purchasing a commodity, or, if the sum of value exists in commodities, he does not sell these in exchange for money; he rather advances it *as capital*, as $M - M'$, as money (value), which returns again to its starting-point after a definite period has expired. Instead of using it to buy or sell, therefore, he *lends* it. This *lending* is therefore the appropriate form for *its alienation as capital*, instead of as money or as a commodity. (It by no means follows from this that *lending* cannot also be a form for transactions that have nothing at all to do with the capitalist process.)

|292| Up to now we have only considered the *movement* of the loaned capital between its owner and the productive capitalist. We must now turn to the investigation of *interest*.

The lender gives his money out as *capital*; the commodity he alienates to someone else *is capital*, and this is why it returns to him. > It is not *sold*, but only *lent* for a certain period of time. < But the mere return of the sum of value would not be a *return* of this sum *as capital*, but a simple *repayment of a sum of value previously loaned*. In order to return as capital, the sum of value advanced must not only have maintained itself in the movement, but *valorised itself*, it must have increased its value, so as to return with a surplus-value, as $M + \Delta M$, where this ΔM is *interest*, or that part of the profit (average profit) which does not remain in the hands of the functioning capitalist, but falls rather to the moneyed capitalist.

To say that it is alienated by him as *capital* means that it has to be returned to him as $M + \Delta M$. (Later on, we shall still have to consider the form in which *interest* returns in the meantime, but *without* the capital.)

What does the moneyed capitalist give to the borrower, the productive capitalist? What does he actually *alienate* to him? It is only the act of *alienation* [*Veräusserung*] that makes the lending of money the alienation of *money* as *capital* or, in other words, the *alienation of capital itself* as *a commodity*.

It is only through this process of *alienation* that the lender of money > – in the form of moneyed capital – < gives out the *commodity* in his possession as *capital* to someone else.

What is alienated in the case of ordinary *sale*? Not the *value* of the commodity sold, for this only changes its form. It exists ideally in the commodity as its *price* before it is really transferred to the hands of the seller in the form of *money*. The same value and the same magnitude of value here undergo only a change of form. At one point they exist in the commodity form, at another point they exist in the money form. What is *really* alienated by the seller (and thus transferred to the individual or productive consumption of the buyer) is the *use-value* of the commodity, the commodity as use-value.

What then is the *use-value* that the moneyed capitalist *alienates* for the duration of the loan and makes over to the productive capitalist, the *borrower*?

It is the use-value that money receives through the fact that it can be transformed into *capital*, can function *as capital*, and can therefore produce in its movement a definite surplus-value – the *average profit* (anything more or less than this quantity appears here as merely accidental > and external to the function of capital as capital), in addition to its quality of *maintaining* and < conserving its original amount of value.

It is this use-value that money has as capital – the capacity to produce the average profit – that the moneyed capitalist *alienates* to the productive capitalist for the period *of the loan*, the period during which he places the capital loaned at the latter's disposal.

The position of the money loaned in this way is to a certain extent analogous with the position of labour-capacity vis-à-vis the productive capitalist. (But the latter *pays* the value of the labour-capacity, whereas he simply *repays* the value of the loaned capital.) The *use-value* of labour-capacity for the productive capitalist is that it produces more value (profit) when being consumed than it itself possesses and costs. This excess *exchange-value* is its use-value for the productive capitalist. And the use-value of the money capital advanced similarly appears as a capacity to establish and increase *exchange-value*.

|293| In actual fact the moneyed capitalist *alienates* a *use-value*, and for this reason what he gives out is given out as a *commodity*. To this extent the analogy with the *commodity* as such is complete. Firstly, it is a *value* transferred from one hand to another. In the case of the usual commodity, the commodity as such, both buyer and seller retain in their hands the *same* value that they

alienated, only in a different form; the one in the commodity form, the other in the money form. The *difference* in the case of the loan is that in this transaction the moneyed capitalist is the only one who gives out value; but he preserves this by the *repayment*. In this loan transaction, only one party receives *value*, since only one party gives value out. Secondly, one party *alienates* a real use-value, and the other party *receives* and consumes it. As *distinct from* the commodity as such, this use-value it itself *exchange-value*, it is the excess of *value* over its original magnitude that results from the use (of the money as capital). Thus use-value is the *profit*.

The use-value of the money lent out is its ability to function *as capital* and, as such, to produce *average profit* under average circumstances.[6]

What then does the productive capitalist *pay*, and what therefore is the *price* of the capital lent out? 'That which men pay as interest for the use of what they borrow' is '*a part of the profit it*' (the borrowed money) 'is *capable of producing*'.[7]

What the buyer of an ordinary commodity *buys* is *its use-value*: what he *pays* is its *exchange-value*. What the borrower of the money buys is likewise its *use-value as capital* (the use); but what does he *pay* for this? Certainly not its price or value, as with other commodities. The value does not change its form between lender and borrower, as it does between buyer and seller, so that this value exists at one point in the form of money, and at another in the form of a commodity. The identity between the value given out and that received back is displayed here in a completely different way. The *sum of value* (the money) is given out without an equivalent and returned > repaid < after a certain period of time. > It is only in this way that the lender recovers the same value as he gave up, since < he in fact remains the owner of this value throughout, even after it has been transferred from him to the borrower. > (This difference in the relationship is also apparent in the case of simple commodity exchange: < here the money is always on the side of the buyer; but with lending the money is on the side of the seller. It is he who gives the money away for a certain time, and it is the buyer of the capital who receives it as a commodity. But this is possible only in so far as the > money functions as capital and is therefore *advanced*.) < The borrower borrows the money as *capital*, as *self-valorising value*. But it only

6 'The equitableness of taking interest depends not upon a man's making or not making *profit*, but upon its' (the borrowed money's) 'being capable of producing profit, if rightly employed …' (Massie 1750, p. 49.)

7 Ibid. Also in the same work: 'Rich people … instead of employing their money themselves … let it out to other people *for them to make profit of*, reserving for the owners a *proportion of the profit* so made' (pp. 23–4).

becomes capital *in itself*, just like any capital at its starting-point, at the moment when it is first advanced. It is only by its use that it is valorised and *realised* as *capital*. But it is as realised capital that the borrower has to pay it back, hence as *value plus surplus-value* (interest); and the latter can only be a part of the profit he has realised. Only a part, and not the *whole*. For the use-value for the borrower is that it produces a profit *for him*. Otherwise no *alienation of use-value* would have taken place on the part of the lender. But the *whole of the profit* cannot fall to the borrower either. Otherwise he would have paid nothing for the alienation of the use-value, and he would have returned to the lender the money advanced merely as money and not as capital, *realised capital*, for it is realised capital only as M + ΔM.

Both lender and borrower give out the same sum of money as capital. But it is only in the hands of the latter that it functions as capital. The profit is not doubled by the double existence of the same sum of money as capital for two persons. It can only function as capital for both of them through a *division of the profit*. The part that falls to the lender is called *interest*.

|294| The entire transaction takes place, according to our assumption, between two kinds of capitalist, the moneyed capitalist and the productive capitalist.

It must never be forgotten that *capital as capital* is a commodity here, and that the commodity we are dealing with is *capital*. All the relationships that appear here, therefore, would be *irrational*, from the standpoint of the *simple commodity*, or even from the standpoint of capital in so far as it functions as *commodity capital* in the overall process. *Lending* and *borrowing*, instead of *selling* and *buying*, is there a distinction proceeding from the specific nature of the commodity, which is capital. Similarly the fact that what is paid here is interest instead of the *price* of the commodity. If interest is spoken of as the *price* of money capital, this is an *irrational* form of price, which completely contradicts the concept of the *price* of a commodity.[8] Capital manifests itself as capital

---

8 Here, *price* is reduced to its purely abstract form, completely lacking in content, as simply a particular sum of money that is paid for something which somehow or other figures as a use-value, whereas according to its concept price = the exchange-value of this use-value expressed in money. 'The term *value*, when applied to currency, has three several meanings … (2) *currency, actually in hand … compared with the same amount of currency to be received upon a future day*'. For its value 'is measured by the rate of interest, the rate of interest being determined by the ratio between the amount of loanable capital and the demand for it'. (Torrens 1847, pp. 5–6.) (*Interest* as the *price of capital* is a completely irrational expression right from the start. Here a commodity has a double value, first a *value* and then a *price* that is different from this value, although price is the monetary expression of value.) Money capital

by its *valorisation*; the *degree* of this valorisation expresses the quantitative extent to which it is realised *as capital*. The surplus-value or profit produced by it – the rate or level of this – can only be measured in comparison with the *value* of the capital advanced. And so the greater or lesser valorisation of interest-bearing capital is also measurable only by comparing the amount of interest (the part of the total profit falling to it) with the value of the capital advanced. If price thus expresses the value of a commodity, interest expresses the *valorisation* of moneyed capital, and therefore appears as the *price* the lender is paid for it.

We see from this how absurd it is from the very outset to try to apply the simple relationships of exchange mediated by money, the relationship of buyer and seller, to this phenomenon directly. The basic assumption is precisely that money functions *as capital* and *therefore* can be made over to someone else as capital (in itself).

Capital itself appears here as a commodity in so far as it is offered on the market and the *use-value of money as capital* really is alienated. Its use-value however is itself to produce a profit.

The value of money or commodities as *capital* is not determined by their value as money or commodities but rather by the quantity of surplus-value that they 'produce' for their possessor. The product of capital is profit. On the basis of capitalist production, the difference between money spent as money and money advanced as capital is simply a difference in *application*. Money (or a commodity) is capital *in itself* (just as labour-capacity is labour *in itself*). For

---

is at first nothing more than a *sum of money*, or the value of a certain quantity of commodities assessed as a *sum of money*. If a *commodity* is lent as capital, that is only the disguised form of a sum of money. For what is *lent* as capital is not a certain number of pounds of cotton, but rather a certain amount of money that exists in the form of cotton as the cotton's value. The *price* of capital therefore relates to it as a sum of money, even if not as currency, as Mr. Torrens thinks. How, then, is a sum of value to have a price besides its own price, besides the price that is expressed in its own money form? Price, after all, is the value of the commodity as distinct from its use-value (and this is also the case with *market price*, whose distinction from value is not *qualitative* but merely *quantitative*, bearing exclusively on the magnitude of value). A price that is qualitatively distinct from value is a contradiction in terms. 'The ambiguity of the term *value of money* or of the currency, when employed indiscriminately as it is, to signify both *value in exchange* for commodities, and *value in use of capital*, is a constant source of confusion'. (Tooke 1844, p. 77.) Tooke fails to see the main 'confusion' here (which in fact lies in the thing itself) namely that *exchange-value* as such (interest) comes to be the *use-value* of capital > (capital is thereby identified with labour-capacity, the use-value of which is exchange-value). <

(1) money can be transformed into the conditions of production, and is already, just as it is, simply an abstract expression of the conditions of production, their existence as *value*, and (2) the objective elements of wealth in themselves possess their property of being *capital* because their antithesis – wage-labour – which makes them capital is present as the basis of social production. The antithetical social determination of *objective wealth* vis-à-vis labour is expressed in *capital ownership as such*, quite apart from the process itself. This one moment, then, separated from the capitalist production process itself, whose constant result it is, and as whose constant result it is also its constant prerequisite, is expressed in this way, that money, and likewise commodities, are in themselves *latent* capital, that they can be sold as *capital*, and that in this form they give control of the labour of others, and are therefore self-valorising value. (They give a claim to the appropriation of the labour of others.) Here it also emerges clearly that *this relationship* is the title and the means to the appropriation of the labour of others, and not any kind of labour that the capitalist is supposed to offer as an equivalent.

Capital further appears as a commodity in so far as the division of profit into interest and profit proper is governed by supply and demand, hence by competition, just like the market prices of commodities. But here the *distinction* is just as striking as the analogy. If supply and demand coincide, the market price of the commodity corresponds to its price of production, i.e., its price is then governed by the inner laws of capitalist production, independently of competition, since fluctuations in supply and demand explain nothing but divergences between market prices and prices of production. (These divergences are mutually compensatory, so that over certain longer periods the average market prices are equal to the prices of production.) As soon as they coincide, these forces cease to have any effect > in one direction or another, they paralyse one another, and the immanent determination of prices then emerges as the law of the individual case as well; market price then corresponds to price of production in its immediate existence (and not merely as an average of all market price movements). The price of production, for its part, is governed by the immanent laws of the mode of production itself. If supply and demand coincide, their effect ceases, and wages are equal to the value of labour-capacity. It is different, though, with interest on moneyed capital. Here competition does not determine divergences from the law, for there is no *law* of distribution other than that dictated by competition, because, as we shall go on to see, there is *no natural rate of interest*. What is called the natural rate of interest means rather the rate established by free competition. There are no *natural limits* to the rate of interest. Where competition does not just determine divergences and oscillations, hence where it ceases to determine anything, in a situation of equilibrium between antagonistic forces, what is to be determined is in itself lawless and arbitrary. (But more about this in section two.)

In the case of interest-bearing capital, everything appears in a superficial manner [*äusserlich*]; the advance of capital as a mere transfer from lender to borrower; its return as realised capital, as a mere re-transfer (repayment) with interest from the borrower to the lender. In the same way, the feature [*Bestimmung*] which is immanent in the capitalist mode of production, that the rate of profit is determined not simply by the ratio of the profit to the capital value advanced, but also by the length of the turnover time, > in which the profit is realised; < in other words the profit yielded by productive capital in particular periods of time. This too appears superficially in the case of interest-bearing capital, in such a way that a certain |295| interest appears to have been paid to the lender for a certain time-interval.

With his customary insight into the inner connections of things, the Romantic, Adam Müller, says this:

'In determining the *price* of things, no one asks about *time*; in determining interest, *time* is the most important factor'. (Müller 1809, p. 138.)

He *does not see* how *labour-time* and *circulation time* come into play in determining the *prices* of commodities, and how it is precisely in this way that the rate of profit is determined for a given period of turnover of capital, while interest is determined precisely by this determination of profit for a given period. His wisdom here, as always, lies in the way that he sees clouds of dust on the surface and pretentiously proclaims this dust to be something mysterious and significant.

(2) Division of Profit. Rate of Interest. The Natural Rate of Interest

(The subject of this section {like all we shall have to say about credit later} can by no means be treated in detail here. It is clear, however, 1, that competition between lenders and borrowers, and the resulting short-term oscillations in the money market, fall outside the scope of our discussion, 2, that to examine the circuit the rate of interest describes during the industrial cycle requires a prior examination of that cycle itself, which equally cannot be dealt with here, and 3, that the same applies to the greater or lesser equalisation of interest on the world market. All we are concerned to develop here is, on the one hand, the form of interest-bearing capital and on the other hand the way interest acquires autonomy vis-á-vis profit.)

Since interest is simply a part of profit, a part which (on the basis of our previous assumption) the functioning capitalist has to pay to the moneyed capitalist, the *maximum limit of the interest* appears to be the *profit* itself, in which case the share that accrues to the functioning capitalist would be zero. Leaving aside special cases (where the interest actually may be greater than the profit, but then cannot be paid *out of* the profit), we might perhaps consider the maximum limit of interest as the whole profit minus the part of it reducible to wages of superintendence, which we shall examine later. The *minimum rate* of interest is completely impossible to determine. It could fall to any level, however low. But counteracting circumstances set in again and again, which cause it to rise beyond this minimum level.

'The relation between the sum paid for the use of capital and the capital expresses the *rate of interest* as measured in money'. (*The Economist*, 22 January 1853.)

'The *rate of interest* depends: (1) upon *the rate of profit*; (2) upon the *proportion* in which *the entire profit* is *divided* between lender and borrower'. (ibid.) Since 'that which men pay as interest for the use of what they borrow' is 'a part of the profits it is capable of producing, *this interest must always be governed by those profits*'.[9]

We shall start by assuming a *fixed proportion between the total profit and the part of it* paid to the moneyed capitalist *as* ***interest***. On this supposition it is clear that the interest will rise or fall with the total profit, and the latter is determined by the *average rate of profit* (and the variations in this average rate of profit). If the average rate of profit is 20 percent, for example, and the interest is a quarter of the profit, the interest rate will be 5 percent. If the rate of profit is 16 percent the interest rate will be 4 percent and so on. (In the first case, the interest could rise to 8 percent and the industrial capitalist would still make the same profit as before with a rate of profit of 16 percent, with the interest at 4 percent, namely 12 percent. If the interest were to rise to 6 or 7 he would still retain a greater part of the profit than where the average rate of profit was 16 percent and the interest 4 percent.) (If interest were a *constant* portion of the average profit, it would follow that the higher the *general rate of profit*, the greater the |296| *absolute difference* between the total profit and the part of the total profit accruing to the functioning capitalist, and *vice versa*. A fifth of 10 is 2; the difference between the *total profit* and the *profit* after deduction of the interest = 8. A fifth of 20 is 4; the difference is 20 − 4 = 16. A fifth of 25 is 5; the difference is 25 − 5 = 20. A fifth of 30 is 6; the difference is 30 − 6 = 24. A fifth of 35 is 7; the difference is 35 − 7 = 28. The different interest rates of 4, 5, 6, and 7 percent would here always express no more than one-fifth, or 20 percent, of the

9 Massie 1750, p. 49.

total profit. If *rates of profit* vary, *different rates of interest* may express the same aliquot parts of the *total profit* or the same *percentage share* in it. With *interest* such a *constant* proportion, the *industrial* profit (the difference between the total profit and the interest) would be greater, the higher the *general rate of profit* and vice versa.)

All other circumstances remaining the same (or, which comes to the same thing, supposing a more or less *constant* ratio between interest and the whole profit) the functioning capitalist will be able and willing to pay a higher or lower interest in direct proportion to the level of his *rate of profit*.[10] Since we have seen that the level of the profit rate stands in an inverse proportion to the development of capitalist production, it follows that the higher or lower rate of interest in a country stands in the same inverse proportion to the level of industrial development – to the extent that the differences in the rate of interest express actual *variations in the rate of profit*. We shall see later on that this need by no means always be the case. In this sense one can say that interest is regulated by *profit*, and more precisely by the *general rate of profit*. And this kind of regulation applies even to its average.

At all events, the average rate of profit should be considered as the *ultimate regulating limit* of interest.

We shall immediately go on to consider more closely the circumstance that interest is to be related to the *average profit*.

{Where a given whole – such as profit – is to be divided between two people, the first thing that matters is of course the *size* of the whole to be divided, and this, the magnitude of *profit*, is determined by the average rate of profit.}

Once the *general rate of profit*, in other words the magnitude of the *profit* on a capital of a given size, say 100, has been *assumed as constant, as given*, the *variations in the interest* will evidently vary in inverse proportion to the part of the profit that remains to the functioning capitalist, to the extent that he operates with borrowed capital; > or, in other words, they will vary in the proportion to which these two sorts of capitalist, the functioning and the moneyed capitalist, divide between themselves the surplus-value or surplus product (the product in which unpaid labour is materialised). < And the circumstances that determine the magnitude of the profit to be divided are very different from those that determine its distribution among these two kinds of capitalist, and often operate in completely opposite directions.

10 'The natural rate of interest is governed by the *profits of trade* to particulars'. (Massie 1750, p. 51.)

NB. (The course of this section suggests that it is better, before the laws governing the distribution of profit are investigated, to develop first of all the way in which the *quantitative* division becomes a *qualitative* one. Nothing more is needed to make the transition from the previous section to this one > – since the average rate of profit and the average profit have been given by what was developed earlier – < than to equate interest to a portion of this profit that has not been determined more closely.)

If we consider the turnover cycles in which modern industry moves – state of quiescence, growing animation, prosperity, overproduction, crisis, stagnation, quiescence, etc. – (cycles which it falls outside the scope of our argument to analyse further) we find that a low level of interest generally corresponds to periods of prosperity or extra profits, a rise in interest comes between prosperity and its reversal, but that a maximum of interest up to extreme heights of usury corresponds to the crisis.[11] From summer 1843 onwards there was a period of marked prosperity. The rate of interest, which in spring 1842 was still 4½ percent, fell in |297| spring and summer 1843 to 2 percent.[12] In September it even fell to 1½ percent,[13] then, during the crisis of 1847, it rose to 8 percent and more. >

(Of course, low interest can also be accompanied by stagnation, and rising interest {even if the rise is only moderate} can be accompanied by growing animation.)

(In order to find the average rate of interest it is necessary to calculate, 1, the average rate of interest during its variations over the cycles of turnover, and 2, the *rate of interest* on investments made for a lengthy period.)

< The rate of interest reaches its highest level during crises, when *people have to borrow in order to pay*, no matter what the cost. > (We shall look at this form later on.)[14]

---

11 > 'In the *first period*, immediately after a pressure, money is abundant without speculation; in the *second period*, money is abundant and speculations abound; in the *third period*, speculation begins to decline and money is in demand; in the *fourth period*, money is scarce and a pressure arrives'. (Gilbart 1849, p. 149.)

12 > [Thomas] Tooke explains this 'by the *accumulation of surplus capital* necessarily accompanying the scarcity of profitable employment for it in previous years, by the release of hoards, and by the revival of confidence in commercial prospects'. (Tooke 1848, p. 54.)

13 > Gilbart 1849, p. 166.

14 Since the rise in interest corresponds to a fall in the price of securities, this is at the same time a very suitable opportunity to get hold of such interest-bearing securities at spot prices, and in the regular course of events these securities are bound to reach at least their average price (and above) as soon as the rate of interest falls again. > These crises allow

< But there is also a tendency for the rate of interest to fall, independently of fluctuations in the rate of profit, for three reasons:

1 'Were we even to suppose that capital was never borrowed with any view but productive employment, I think it very possible that interest might vary without any change in the rate of *gross* profits. For as a nation advances in the career of wealth, a class of men springs up and increases more and more, who by the labours of their ancestors find themselves in the possession of funds sufficiently ample to afford a handsome maintenance from the interest alone. Very many also who during youth and middle age were actively engaged in business retire in their latter days to live quietly on the interest of the sums they have themselves accumulated. This class, as well as the former, has a tendency to increase with the increasing riches of the country, for those who begin with a tolerable stock are likely to make an independence sooner than they who commence with little. Thus it comes to pass, that in old and rich countries the amount of national capital belonging to those who are unwilling to take the trouble of employing it themselves, bears a larger proportion to the whole productive stock of the society, than in newly settled and poorer countries.[15] How much more numerous in proportion to the population is the class of *rentiers* in England! As the class of *rentiers* increases, so also does that of lenders of capital, for they are one and the same. > Therefore from this cause alone interest must have a tendency to fall in old countries'.[16]

< 2 The development of the credit system, the ever-growing control this gives to industrialists and merchants over all the money savings of all classes of society through the mediation of the bankers, as well as the progressive concentration of these savings on a mass scale, so that they can function as money capital, must also lead in this direction. (See later.)

As far as the determination of the *rate of interest* is concerned, > which Ramsay calls the *rate of net profit*, < he says that it 'depends partly upon the rate of *gross profits*, partly on the proportion in which these are separated

---

the bankers 'to reinvest their capital in depreciated stocks, in anticipation of the collapse which decreases their private securities, reduces the rate of interest to a minimum'. (Roy 1864, p. 100.) During the crisis of 1847 'an old customer of a banker was refused a loan upon a £200,000 bond; when about to leave to make known his suspension of payment, he was told there was no necessity for the step, under the circumstances the banker would buy the bond at £150,000'. (Roy 1864, p. 80.)

15 ['Districts' in Ramsay's original text.]

16 Ramsay 1836, pp. 201–2.

into profits of capital and those of enterprise. This proportion again depends upon the *competition between the lenders of capital and the borrowers*; which competition is *influenced*, though by no means *entirely regulated*, by the rate of gross profit expected to be realised.[17] And the reason why competition is not exclusively regulated by this cause is because on the one hand many borrow without any view to productive employment; and, on the other, because the *proportion of the whole national capital to be lent varies with the riches of the country independently of any change in gross profits*'.[18]

The prevailing *average rate of interest* in a country, as distinct from the constantly fluctuating market rate, *cannot be determined by any law*. There is *no natural rate of interest* of this kind, therefore, in the sense that there is for example a natural rate of profit or a natural rate of wages.[19] The coincidence between demand and supply means nothing at all here, even taking the average rate of profit as given. Where this formula is resorted to in other cases (and this is then correct for practical purposes) it serves as a formula for finding basic rules (the 'regulating limits', or the 'limiting magnitudes') which are independent of *competition* and indeed, on the contrary, *determine* it. Specifically, it is a formula for those caught up in the practice of competition, in its manifestations and in the ideas that develop out of these. With it they can arrive at some idea, even if still a superficial one, of the inner connection of economic relations that presents itself within competition. It is a method of getting from the variations that accompany competition to the limits of those variations. This is not the case with the *average rate of interest*. |298| There is no reason at all why the average conditions of competition, of equilibrium between lender and borrower, should give the moneylender an interest of 3, 4, 5, percent, etc., on his capital, or alternatively *a certain percentage*, 20 percent or 50 percent, *of the gross profit*. Where, as here, it is competition *as such* that decides, the determination is inherently *accidental, purely empirical*, and only pedantry or

17 Since the rate of interest is determined by and large by the average profit rate, extraordinary swindling can very often go together with a low rate of interest. For example the railway swindle [of 1844]. The Bank of England's interest rate (the Bank Rate) was only raised to three percent on 16 October 1844.

18 Ramsay 1836, pp. 206–7.

19 Massie was already entirely correct when he remarked: 'The only thing which any man can be in doubt about on this occasion is *what proportion of these profits do* of right *belong to the borrower*, and what *to the lender*; and this there is no other method of determining than by the opinions of borrowers and lenders in general; for right and wrong, in this respect, are only what common consent makes so'. (Massie 1750, p. 49.)

fantasy can seek to present this accident as something *necessary*.[20] Nothing is more amusing in the Parliamentary Reports for 1857 and 1858 on currency and banking (the *titles* of these need to be checked) than to listen to the directors of the Bank of England, London and country bankers, and professional theorists when they chatter back and forth about the '*real* rate *produced*', without getting any further than such commonplaces as for example that 'the price paid for the *use of loanable capital* should vary with the supply of such capital', that 'a high rate and a low profit could not *permanently* exist', and other such platitudes.[21] Custom, legal tradition, etc., are just as much involved in the determination of the average rate of interest as is competition itself (in so far as this average rate exists not only as an average number but as an actual magnitude). > The discussion of these matters therefore belongs in the *section on competition*. < (An average rate of interest must be assumed in many legal disputes, where interest has to be reckoned and *adopted* as legal.) If we go on to ask why the limits of the average interest rate cannot be derived from general laws, the answer simply lies in the nature of interest. It is merely a part of the average profit. The same capital appears in a double capacity, as loanable capital in the hands of the lender, and as industrial or commercial capital in the hands of the functioning capitalist. But it functions only once, and produces *profit* only once. In the production process itself, the character of capital as *loanable* does not play

20 > See for example Opdyke, Arnd, etc. < Opdyke 1851, pp. 86–7, makes a most unsuccessful attempt to explain the general phenomenon of a five percent rate of interest in terms of eternal laws. But incomparably more naive is Herr Karl Arnd, in a book he published in 1845. Here we may read: 'In the natural course of the production of goods, there is only *one* phenomenon which seems to regulate to some extent the rate of interest, at least in fully developed countries: this is the ratio by which the volume of timber in European forests increases through its annual growth. This growth takes place, *quite independently of their exchange-value*' (how strange it is that the trees arrange their growth 'independently of their exchange-value'!) 'in the ratio of 3 or 4 to 100. *Accordingly, therefore*' (since the growth of trees is quite independent of their exchange-value, however much their exchange-value may depend on their growth) 'we should not expect a reduction below the level which it' (the rate of interest) 'has at present in the richest countries'. (Arnd 1845, pp. 124–5.) This deserves to be known as the 'primordial forest rate of interest', and in the work we have quoted its discoverer makes another remarkable contribution to 'our science' as the 'philosopher of the dog tax'. (Arnd 1845, pp. 420–1.)

21 The Bank of England raises and lowers the *bank rate* according to the inflow and outflow of bullion (although always of course with an eye to the rate that prevails outside the bank), 'by which gambling in discounts, by anticipation of the alterations in the bank rate, has now become half the trade of the great heads of the money centre'. (Namely, the London money market.) (Roy 1864, p. 113.)

any role. How the two parties who have claims on this profit actually *share* it between them is as it stands a *purely empirical* fact, pertaining to the realm of chance, just as the respective shares in the common profit of a business partnership are distributed among its various members. With the division between surplus-value and wages, on which the determination of the profit rate essentially depends, two quite different elements are involved, labour-capacity and capital. It is the functions of two independent variables which set limits to one another, and the quantitative division of the value produced emerges from the qualitative distinction. We shall see later on that the same thing takes place with the division of surplus-value between rent and profit. With interest, there is nothing of the kind. Here, on the contrary, the *qualitative* distinction proceeds from the purely quantitative division of the *same piece of surplus-value*, as we shall immediately go on to see.

3 'The price of *commodities* fluctuates continually; they are all made for different uses; the *money* serves for all purposes. The commodities, even those of the same kind, differ according to quality; *hard cash* is always of the same value, or at least *is assumed to be so. Thus it is* that the *price of money*, which we designate by the term interest, has a *greater stability and uniformity* than that of any other thing'.[22] > This is our friend Steuart's explanation.

< From what has already been developed, it follows that there is no *natural rate of interest*, but if on the one hand the *average* or *middling rate of interest* (as distinct from the constantly fluctuating market rates of interest), cannot be given limits by a general law, since what is involved is simply a distribution of the gross profit between two persons who possess capital under different titles, the *rate of interest, conversely*, whether it is the average rate or the *market rate at the time*, appears as something quite different from the general rate of profit, which is a *uniform, definite and palpable* magnitude. The rate of interest is related to the profit rate in the same way as the *market price* of a commodity is related to its *value*.

In so far as the *rate of interest* is determined by the *rate of profit*, this is always through the *general rate of profit* and not through the specific rates that may prevail in particular branches of industry, still less by the extra profit that the individual capitalist might make in a particular sphere of business.[23] The

---

22 Steuart 1789, p. 27.

23 'This *rule of dividing profits* is not, however, to be applied particularly to every lender and borrower, but to lenders and borrowers in general ... remarkably great and small gains are the reward of skill and the want of understanding, which *lenders have nothing at all to do with*; for as they will not suffer by the one, they ought not to benefit by the other. What has been said *of particular men in the same business is applicable to particular sorts*

general rate of profit in fact *appears* therefore as an empirical fact in the *average rate of interest*, although the latter is not a pure and reliable expression of the former.

|299| It is certainly true that the *interest rate* itself is always different according to the class of security provided by the borrowers, but for these classes it is uniform. This distinction, therefore, does not militate against the *fixed and uniform character of the rate of interest.*

In every country, the *middling rate of interest* appears over long periods as a *constant magnitude*, because the *general rate of profit* changes only in the long run, despite constant change in the particular rates of profit, a change in one sphere being offset by an opposite change in another. And the relative *constancy* of the profit rate is reflected in the more or less constant character of the *middling rate of interest* (the *average, or common, rate of interest*).

As far as the constantly fluctuating market rate of interest is concerned, this is a fixed magnitude at any given moment, just like the market price of commodities, because on the money capital all loanable capital confronts functioning capital as an *overall mass*; in other words the relationship between the supply of loanable capital on the one hand, and the demand for it on the other, is what determines the *market price* of interest at any given time. This is all the more true, the more the development and associated concentration of the *credit system* gives loanable capital a *general social character*. The *general rate of profit*, on the other hand, only ever exists as a tendency, as a movement of equalisation between particular rates of profit. The competition between capitalists – which is itself this movement of equalisation – consists here in their withdrawing capital from those spheres where profit is below the average for a long period, and injecting it into spheres where it is above this level; or, alternatively, in their dividing additional capital between these spheres in varying proportions. There is a constant variation in the injection of capital into these different spheres.

We have seen that although it is a category absolutely different from the commodity, interest-bearing capital becomes a *commodity sui generis* for which

---

of business; if the merchants and tradesmen employed in any one branch of trade get more by what they borrow than *the common profits* made by other merchants and tradesmen of the same country, the extraordinary gain is theirs, though it required only common skills and understanding to get it; and not the lenders', who supplied them with money '... for the lenders would not have lent their money to carry on any branch of trade upon lower terms than would admit of paying so much as the *common rate of interest*; and therefore they ought not to receive more than that, whatever advantages may be made by their money'. (Massie 1750, pp. 50–1.)

reason interest, its price, > is in turn entirely distinct from the market *price* < which, as in the case of the commodity, is fixed at any given time by demand and supply. The market rate of interest, although in constant flux, thus appears at any given moment as every bit as *fixed* and *uniform* as the momentary market price of any commodity. The moneyed capitalists supply this commodity, and the functioning capitalists *buy* it; they constitute the demand for it. This process of fixing the rate by supply and demand does not apply to the equalisation that produces the general rate of profit. If the prices of commodities in one sphere are below or above their price of production (and in this connection we ignore the fluctuations connected with the industrial cycle, or those that simply bear on the individual business), an equalisation takes place by the expansion or contraction of production, i.e., an increase or decrease in the quantity of commodities that these industrial capitals put on the market, mediated by the immigration or emigration of capital with respect to these particular spheres of production. It is the equalisation brought about in this way, whereby the average market prices of commodities are reduced to their prices of production, that corrects divergences between the particular rates of profit and the general or average profit rate. This process never appears and never can appear as if productive or mercantile capital as such were a *commodity* vis-à-vis a *buyer*, in the way that interest-bearing capital is. To the extent that it *does appear* it appears only in the fluctuations and equalisations that reduce the market prices of *commodities* to their production prices; not as the direct establishment of an average profit. The *general rate of profit* is determined in fact by the surplus-value that the total capital produces, by the ratio of this surplus-value to the value of the producing capital, and by competition, but only in so far as this is the movement through which the capitals invested in particular spheres of production seek to draw equal dividends from this surplus-value in proportion to their relative size. The general rate of profit, in other words, is determined in ways which are quite different from and far more complicated than those which determine the *market rate of interest*. The latter is directly determined by the relation between supply and demand, and is therefore not a palpable and given fact in the way that the interest rate is. The particular profit rates in the various spheres of production are themselves more or less a matter of guessing; but in so far as they do show themselves, |300| it is not their *uniformity* that is apparent but rather their *variation*. But the *general rate of profit* itself simply *appears* as the *minimum limit* of profit, not as an empirical form of the *actual profit rate*.

In stressing this distinction between the *interest rate* and the *profit rate*, we have so far left aside the following two factors: (1) the historical pre-existence of interest-bearing capital and the existence of a general rate of interest handed down by tradition; (2) the far stronger direct influence that the world market exerts on the establishment of the interest rate, independently of the conditions of production in a single country, as compared with its influence on the profit rate.

It becomes a general property of any sum of money of £100 that it will yield 2, 3, or 5 percent. The average profit does not appear as a directly given fact, but rather as the average result of an equalisation of the oscillations between contradictory tendencies. With the interest rate it is different. It is in its *universality* a fact which is fixed every day, a fact which even serves industrial and mercantile capital as a presupposition and an item in their operating calculations. Meteorological reports do not show the level of the barometer and thermometer any more precisely than stock-market reports show the level of the interest rate, not for this capital or that, but rather for the *capital that is to be found on the money market, i.e., capital that is loanable.*

On the money market it is only lenders and borrowers who face one another. The commodity has the same form – *money*. All particular forms of capital, arising from their investment in particular spheres of production or circulation, are obliterated here. It exists in the undifferentiated, self-identical form of independent value, of money. Competition between particular spheres now ceases; they are all thrown together as *borrowers of money*, and capital confronts them all in a form still indifferent to the specific manner and mode of its application. Here capital really does emerge, in the pressure of *the demand for it*, as *the common capital of the class*, whereas productive capital appears like this only in the movement and competition between the particular spheres. (?)[24] Money capital (capital on the money market), on the other hand, really does possess the form in which it is distributed among the capitalist class as a common element among these various spheres, irrespective of its particular application, according to the production requirements of each particular sphere. On top of this, with the development of large-scale industry money capital emerges more and more, in so far as it appears on the market, as not represented by the *individual* capitalist, the proprietor of this or that parcel of the mass of capital on the market, but rather as a concentrated and organised mass, placed under the control of the bankers as representatives of the social capital in a quite different manner to real production. The result is that, as far as the form of demand goes, capital for loan is faced with the entire weight of a class, while, as far as supply goes, it itself appears *en masse* as loan capital.

24 [This question mark appears without explanation in the original manuscript. Translator]

These are some of the reasons why the *general rate of profit* presents a blurred and hazy picture compared with the *sharply defined rate of interest*, which although its level fluctuates always confronts the borrowers as fixed and given, because it fluctuates in the same way for them all. In the same way, changes in the value of money do not prevent it from having the same value in relation to every commodity, and the market prices of commodities fluctuate daily, although this does not prevent them from being quoted every day in the reports. It is just the same with the rate of interest, which is quoted just as regularly as the *price* of money. This is because capital itself is offered here as a *commodity* – namely money. To establish its price is therefore to establish its *market price*, just as with all other commodities; and so the rate of interest always presents itself as a *general rate of interest*, as so much for so much money, as quantitatively determined. The *rate of profit*, on the other hand, can vary even within the *same* sphere, with the *market prices of the commodities remaining the same*, according to the different conditions in which the individual capitalists produce the same commodity; for the profit rate on a particular capital is not determined by the market price of the commodity, but rather by the *difference between market price and cost price*. And these various rates of profit, firstly within the same sphere and then within the *various different spheres*, can be equalised only through the process of constant fluctuations.

(*A form of credit which demonstrates the point*. We know that when money functions as *means of payment* instead of *means of purchase*, the *commodity is alienated* first and its *value* realised only later. If payment takes place only after the *commodity* has been re-sold, this *sale* does not appear as a consequence of the *purchase*, but rather it is by the *sale* that the *purchase* is realised. The sale becomes a means of purchase.) *Secondly, certificates of debt* (bills, etc.) become means of payment for the creditor. Thirdly, money is replaced by the *settlement of outstanding debt certificates*.

3. Interest and Profit of Enterprise

Interest originally appears, originally is, and remains in reality, nothing but a *part of the profit*, i.e., the surplus-value, > (the *unpaid labour* appropriated by capital) < which the functioning capitalist, whether industrialist or merchant, must pay to the owner and lender of capital in so far as the capital he uses is not his own but *borrowed*. If he simply uses his own capital, there is no such *division of the profit*; it belongs to him completely. In fact, in so far as the owners of capital use it themselves in the reproduction process, they do not compete together to determine the *interest rate*, and it is clear here already how the category of interest – which is impossible without the establishment of a rate of interest – lies outside the movement of productive capital as such.

'The *rate of interest* may be defined to be that proportional sum which the lender is content to receive, and the borrower to pay, for a year, or for any longer or shorter period, for the use of a *certain amount of moneyed capital* ... When the *owner of capital employs it actively in reproduction*, he does not come under the head of *those capitalists, the proportion of whom*, to the *number of borrowers, determines the rate of interest*'.[25] It is in fact only the *division of capitalists* into moneyed capitalists and industrial capitalists that transforms a part of the profit into *interest* and creates the category of interest at all; and it is only the competition between these two kinds of capitalist that creates the *rate of interest*.

(As long as a capital is functioning in the reproduction process, supposing it to belong to the industrial capitalist, so that no condition of repayment to any lender whatever exists, what he has at his disposal as a private individual is simply the *profit*, which he can spend as revenue. As long as his capital functions as capital, it belongs to the reproduction process. Certainly he is its owner, but this ownership does not enable him, as long as he uses it as capital for the exploitation of labour, to dispose of it in any other way. It is just the same with the moneyed capitalist. As long as his capital is lent out and operates as moneyed capital, bringing him interest, a part of the profit, he cannot dispose of the principal. This is apparent as soon as he lends for example for a year or more, receiving interest at certain dates *without the return of his capital*. But even the return of the capital makes no difference here. If he receives it back, he must always lend it out afresh if it is to operate as capital for him, in this case moneyed capital. As long as it is in his hands, it does not bear any interest and does not operate as capital; and once it does bear interest and operate as capital, it is no longer in his hands. Hence the possibility of lending capital |301| in perpetuity. The following remarks by Tooke are therefore completely false. He says:

'Mr. Bosanquet observes: "Were the rate of interest reduced as low as 1 per-cent, *capital borrowed would be placed nearly on a par with capital possessed*"'. (Bosanquet 1842, p. 73.)

Tooke then makes the following incidental comment:

'That a capital borrowed at that, or even a lower rate, should be considered nearly on a par with capital *possessed*, is a proposition so strange as hardly

25 Tooke 1838, pp. 355–6.

to warrant serious notice, were it not advanced by a writer so intelligent, and, on some points of the subject, so well informed. Has he overlooked the circumstance, or does he consider it of little consequence, that there must, by the supposition, be *a condition of repayment?*'[26] If interest were zero, the productive capitalist who had borrowed capital would be *on a par* with one working with *his own* capital. That is to say, both would pocket the same average profit, and their capital, whether it was borrowed or their own, would operate as capital only by producing a profit. The repayment requirement would make no difference here. The closer the rate of interest comes to zero, if it falls to 1 percent, for example, the more is borrowed capital placed on a par with possessed capital. If moneyed capital is to continue to exist as moneyed capital, it must always be lent out afresh, and indeed at the prevailing rate of interest, say 1 percent, and always to the same class of industrial and mercantile capitalists. As long as these function as capitalists, the distinction between the one who operates with borrowed capital and the one who operates with possessed capital, is simply that one has to pay interest and the other does not. One pockets the whole profit, P, while the other only pockets P – I, profit minus interest; the closer I is to zero, the closer P – I is to P, hence the more are both capitals on a par with one another. One has to pay back his capital and borrow anew; but the other, as long as his capital is to function, must similarly advance it afresh each time to the production process, and he has no control over it that is independent of this process.)

The question that now arises is this. How does this *purely quantitative division of profit into gross*[27] *profit and interest* turn into a *qualitative* distinction? In other words, how does it happen that even the capitalist who simply uses his own capital, and no borrowed capital, classes part of his gross profit under the special category of interest and takes particular account of it as such? And how, therefore, does it subsequently happen that *all* capital, whether borrowed or not, is *distinguished* as *interest-bearing capital* from itself in its function as capital bringing a gross profit?

We must recognise that not just any chance *quantitative* division of profit turns into a *qualitative* one in this way. For example, some productive capitalists enter into a partnership to pursue a particular business and divide the profit among themselves on the basis of legally established contracts. Others carry on their business without partners, each on his own account. Capitalists of the latter sort do not reckon their profit under two categories, one part as individual

26 Tooke 1844, p. 80.

27 [Engels changed 'gross' to 'net'. Translator]

profit, the other as company profit for a *partnership that does not exist*, > in the manner of the productive capitalist who only works with capital he has borrowed, regarding part of it as the interest for the capital he has *not borrowed*. < Here, therefore, the quantitative division does not turn into a qualitative one. There is a quantitative division when the owner happens to consist of several legal persons; there is no such division when this is not the case.

In order to answer this question, we must pause a little longer to consider the real starting-point of interest formation, i.e., we must proceed from the assumption that the moneyed capitalist and the productive capitalist actually do come face to face, not just as legally separate persons but as persons who play quite different roles in the reproduction process, or in whose hands the same capital really does go through a double and completely different movement. The one simply lends the capital, the other applies it productively.

|302| For the productive capitalist working with borrowed capital, the *gross profit* breaks down into two parts, the *interest* that he has to pay to the lender, and > *gross profit minus the interest* or < the *excess of the gross profit over and above the interest*, which forms his *own* share in the profit. If the general rate of profit is given, this latter part is determined by the rate of interest; if the rate of interest is given, it is determined by the rate of profit. Besides, however much the gross profit, the actual value magnitude of the total profit, may diverge from the average profit in any individual case, the part that belongs to the functioning capitalist is determined by the *interest*, since interest is fixed by the general rate of interest (leaving aside any special legal stipulations), *anticipated, presupposed*, before the production process begins, hence before its results, the gross profit, has been obtained. We have seen that the specific and characteristic product of capital is *surplus-value*, and, more precisely defined, *profit*. But for the capitalist working with borrowed capital, the part of the profit that remains to him after interest is paid is not *profit*, but *profit minus* interest > the part of the profit that remains over after the interest has been paid. < It is *this part of the profit*, therefore, that necessarily appears to him as the product of capital *in its actual functioning*; and this really is the case *for him*, since he represents capital only as *functioning* capital. He is its personification in so far as it functions, and it *functions* in so far as it is productively[28] invested in industry or trade, and he performs through his use of it the operations prescribed by the line of business in which he is employing his capital. Unlike the *interest* which he has to pay to the lender out of the gross profit, the remaining part of the profit which accrues to him necessarily assumes the *form of industrial or com-*

28 [Engels replaced 'productively' with 'profitably'. Translator]

mercial profit, or, to describe it with a German expression which embraces both these things, it has the shape of *profit of enterprise* [*Unternehmungsgewinn*]. If the gross profit is equal to the average profit, the *size* of this profit of enterprise is determined exclusively by the *rate of interest*. If the gross profit diverges from the average profit, the difference between it and the average profit, after interest is deducted, is determined by all the conjunctures that give rise to such a temporary divergence, whether in the profit rate in one particular sphere of production as opposed to the general profit rate, or in the profit made by an individual capitalist in a certain sphere as opposed to the average profit in that sphere. We have seen that the *rate of profit*, within the *production process* itself, does not depend only on the *surplus-value* but on many other factors besides. It depends for example on the purchase prices of the means of production, on methods that are more productive than the average, on economising on constant capital, and so on. And, quite apart from the price of production, it also depends on the state of the trade cycle, and in each individual business deal it depends on the greater or lesser cunning and perseverance of the capitalist, whether he sells above or below the production price and thereby appropriates a greater or lesser share of the total surplus-value *within the circulation process*. In each case, however, the *quantitative* division of the gross profit is *transformed* here into a *qualitative* one, and this is all the more so in that the *quantitative* division itself depends on *what* is to be divided, how the active capitalist looks after his capital and what gross profit it yields him as functioning capital, i.e., as a result of his functioning as an active capitalist. We assume here that the functioning capitalist is *not the owner* of the *capital*. > Quite the opposite. < Property in capital is represented in relation to him by the lender, the moneyed capitalist. The *interest* that he pays to the lender appears therefore as the *part of the gross profit* that accrues to *property in capital* as such. In contrast to this, the part of the profit that falls to the active capitalist, as *profit of enterprise*, appears to derive exclusively from the operations or functions that he performs with the capital in the reproduction process, especially therefore the functions that he performs as an entrepreneur in industry or trade. In relation to him, therefore, interest appears as the mere fruit of property in capital, of capital in itself, abstracted from the reproduction process of capital in so far as it 'does not work', does not function; whereas profit of enterprise appears to him as the fruit, > not of *capital in itself*, of *property in capital*, < but as the fruit of the *functions* he performs with it, as the fruit of capital's *process*, a process that appears to him now as his own activity, in contrast to the *non-activity* and the non-intervention of the moneyed capitalist in the production process. This qualitative separation between the two parts of gross profit, as a result of which *interest* |303| is the *fruit of capital in itself*, *of property in capital* without reference to the production process, while *profit of enterprise* is the fruit of capital *in process* and hence of the active role that the employer of capital plays in the reproduction process – this *qualitative* separation is in no way merely the subjective conception of the moneyed capitalist on the one hand and the productive capitalist on the other. It rests on *objective facts*, for the *interest* flows towards the moneyed capitalist, the lender, who is simply the *owner of the capital* and thus represents nothing but *property in capital* before the production process and outside the production process; while *profit of enterprise* flows to the purely *functioning* capitalist, who is not the *owner of capital*.

But once the merely *quantitative* division of gross profit between two different persons with different legal titles to the *same* capital and hence to the profit it produces, turns into a *qualitative* division for the productive capitalist, in so far as he acts with borrowed capital, and for the moneyed capitalist, in so far as he does not apply his capital himself, one part of the profit appears in and of itself as the fruit that accrues to capital in *one capacity*, as interest, while the other part appears as a specific fruit of capital in an *opposite capacity*, and hence as *profit of enterprise*; the one being the simple fruit of *property in capital*, the other being the fruit of the *mere functioning* and *process of capital*, as the fruit of capital in process, or of the *functions* that the productive capitalist exercises. This mutual ossification and autonomisation of the two parts of the gross profit, as if they derived from two essentially separate sources, must now be fixed for the entire capitalist class and the total capital. This is true irrespective of whether the capital applied by the active capitalist is borrowed or not, or whether or not the > capital appropriated by the < moneyed capitalist is used by him or not. The *profit on any* capital, and thus also the *average profit* based on the equalisation of capitals among themselves, breaks down or is divided into two *qualitatively* distinct, mutually autonomous and independent parts, *interest* and *profit of enterprise*, which are both determined by specific laws. The capitalist who works with *his own* capital, as well as the one working with *borrowed* capital, divides his gross profit into interest that accrues to him as *owner*, as lender of his own capital to himself, and *profit of enterprise*, which accrues to him as a functioning capitalist. It becomes a matter of indifference, as far as this *division* is concerned > (from the *qualitative* point of view) < whether the capitalist really does have to share with another or not. The person who employs the capital, even if he works with his own capital, breaks down into two people, the mere owner of capital and its user; his capital itself, with respect to the categories of profit that it yields, breaks down into owned capital, capital outside the production process, which yields an *interest in itself*, and *capital in the production process*, which yields *profit of enterprise* as capital in process.

Interest is now established in such a way that it does not appear as a division of the gross profit irrespective of production, which takes place only 'incidentally' when the industrialist operates with the capital of others. Even when he operates with his own capital, his *profit* is divided into *interest* and *profit of enterprise*. In this way the merely *quantitative* division becomes a *qualitative* one; it takes place independently of the industrialist's ownership or lack of ownership of his capital, which is an accidental circumstance. We are not concerned here simply with two quantities of profit distributed to different people, but with two specific categories of profit, which stand in different relationships to capital, hence have a relationship to different characteristics of capital.

It is now very easy to see *the reasons why* this division of gross profit into *interest* and *profit of enterprise*, once it becomes a qualitative > division for the productive capitalists who work with borrowed capital, < receives this character of a qualitative division for the total capital and the capitalist class as a whole.

|304| These reasons are as follows:

Firstly, there is the simple *empirical* circumstance that the majority of productive capitalists operate both with their own and borrowed capital, even if in different ratios, and that the ratio between their own and the borrowed capital changes from one period to another.

Secondly, the transformation of a part of the gross profit into the form of interest transforms its other part into *profit of enterprise*. This latter is in point of fact only the antithetical form that the excess of gross profit over interest assumes as soon as the latter exists as a category of its own. The general question of how gross profit is differentiated into interest and profit of enterprise comes down simply to the question of how a part of the gross profit is *generally*[29] ossified and autonomised as *interest*. Historically, however, interest-bearing capital exists as a ready-made form handed down, and hence *interest* as a *ready-made form of the surplus-value produced by capital*, long before the capitalist mode of production and the conceptions of capital and profit corresponding to it come into existence. In the popular mind, therefore, *moneyed capital*, interest-bearing capital, is still seen as capital *as such*, counting as capital *par excellence*. Hence we have on the other hand, and prevailing down to Massie's time, the notion that it is money as such that is paid for in interest. The circumstance that loan capital yields *interest* whether it is itself actually applied as capital or not – if for example it is only borrowed for consumption – confirms the conception that this kind of capital is quite independent. The

29 [In English in the original. Translator]

best proof of the independent form that interest assumes as against profit, and interest-bearing capital against productive capital, in the earliest periods of the capitalist mode of production, is that only in the middle of the eighteenth century was it *discovered* (by Massie and after him by Hume) that interest is just one part of the gross profit, and that it actually needed to be *discovered* in this way.

Thirdly, whether the productive capitalist operates with his own capital or with borrowed capital in no way alters the fact that the class of moneyed capitalists confronts him as a special kind of capitalist, moneyed capital as an autonomous kind of capital, and interest as the *separate form of surplus-value* that corresponds to this specific capital. From the *qualitative* point of view, interest is the surplus-value supplied by capital as simple ownership, which *capital yields in itself*, even if its owner remains outside the reproduction process. It is therefore surplus-value yielded by capital in separation from its process. From the *quantitative* point of view, the part of the profit that forms interest seems to be related not to industrial and commercial capital as such but rather to *moneyed capital*, and the rate of this part of the surplus-value, the *rate of interest*, confirms this relationship. This is *firstly* because the rate of interest – despite its dependence on the general rate of profit – is separately determined, and *secondly* because it appears, just like the market price of commodities, as something *hard and fast*, for all its changes: a *palpable* and always *given relationship* as opposed to the intangible rate of profit. If all capital were to be found in the hands of industrial capitalists, there would be no interest and no rate of interest. The independent form that the *quantitative* division of the gross profit assumes produces this *qualitative* distinction. If we compare the productive capitalist with the moneyed capitalist, he is distinguished simply by *profit of enterprise*, that is, the surplus of gross profit over average interest, which the *rate of interest* causes to appear as an empirically given quantity. If we compare him on the other hand with the productive capitalist who operates with his own instead of borrowed capital, the latter is only distinguished from him as a *moneyed capitalist* in that he pockets the interest himself instead of paying it out. From both sides, the part of the gross profit which is distinct from interest itself > as *profit of enterprise* < appears to him as a surplus-value that capital yields in and of itself and which it would therefore yield even |305| without its productive application. For the individual capitalist this is in practice correct. He has the choice between lending his capital out as interest-bearing capital (whether it already exists as moneyed capital from the start or he needs first to transform it into moneyed capital) or valorising it himself as productive capital. Taken *generally*, i.e., when we apply it to the whole social capital, as is done by some vulgar economists and even presented as the basis of profit, this is of course quite absurd. It is utter nonsense to suggest that all capital could be transformed into moneyed capital without the presence of people to buy and valorise the means of production, which is the form in which the great mass of capital exists – in fact it is the whole of capital, leaving aside the part that exists in monetary form. Concealed in this idea, moreover, is the still greater nonsense that capital could yield *interest* on the basis of the capitalist mode of production without functioning as productive capital, i.e., without creating *surplus-value*, of which interest is simply one part, in other words that the capitalist mode of production could proceed on its course without capitalist production. If an inappropriately large number of capitalists sought to transform their capital into moneyed capital, the result would be a tremendous fall in the value of the capital they had turned into money and a tremendous fall in the rate of interest; a section of the capitalists would immediately be disabled from living on their interest and thus compelled to turn themselves back into productive capitalists. But, as we have said above, for the individual capitalist this is a *fact of life*. Even if he operates with his own capital, therefore, he necessarily considers the part of his average profit which is equal to the average interest as the offspring of his *capital as such*, leaving aside the production process; and in contrast to this part that is given a separate existence as *interest*, he considers the excess of the gross profit over and above this as simply *profit of enterprise*.[30]

Fourthly,[31]

|306| We have seen, therefore, that the part of the profit which the functioning capitalist has to pay to the mere owner of the capital borrowed is *transformed* into the separate form for a part of the profit that all capital yields *as such*, whether borrowed or not, under the name of *interest*. How large this part is depends on the average rate of interest. Its origin is evident only in the way that the functioning capitalist, in so far as he is the owner of his own capital, does not compete – at least not actively – in determining the rate of interest. The *purely quantitative* division of profit between two people with different legal titles to it has been transformed into a *qualitative distinction* that appears

30 > The superficial conception of the contrast between *interest* and *profit of enterprise*: 'Profit = remuneration for the productive employment of savings; *profit properly so called* is the remuneration for the *agency* [*of*] *superintendence during this productive employment*'. (*Westminster Review*, January 1826, p. 107.) Here, therefore, interest is the remuneration for the employment of money *as capital*; it therefore arises from capital as such, which is remunerated for its quality of being capital. As against this, industrial profit arises from the function of capital as capital 'during this productive employment', i.e., in the production process itself. <

31 [Marx did not add anything to this word. Translator]

to arise from the very nature of capital and profit. For, as we have seen, as soon as a part of the profit generally assumes the form of *interest*, the difference between the average profit and the interest, or the part of profit over and above the interest, is transformed into a form antithetical to interest, that of *profit of enterprise*. *Both* of these forms, interest and profit of enterprise, exist only in their antithesis. Thus they are neither of them related to the *surplus-value*, of which they are simply parts, under different categories, titles or names. Instead, they are related to one another. It is because one part of profit has been turned into *interest* that the other part appears in the form of *profit of enterprise*.

(By *profit* here we always mean the average profit, since the divergences from this either between individual capitalists or between capitalists in different spheres of production – hence the variations in the *distribution* of the *average profit* or *surplus-value* that fluctuate back and forth in the competitive struggle – are quite immaterial to us here. This applies throughout the present investigation.)

Interest, then, is the *net profit*[32] yielded by property in capital as such, whether to the mere *lender*, who remains outside the reproduction process, or to the owner of the capital, who himself employs it productively. Yet it does not yield him this net profit in so far as he is a functioning capitalist but rather as a moneyed capitalist, the lender of his own capital as moneyed capital, interest-bearing capital, to himself as functioning capitalist. Just as the transformation of money (value in general) into capital is the constant *result* of the capitalist production process, so its existence as capital is in the same way the constant *presupposition of this process*. That is to say, through its ability to be transformed into means of production it always commands *unpaid* labour and hence transforms the production and circulation process of commodities into the *production of surplus-value* for its possessor. Interest therefore simply expresses the fact that value in general – *objectified* labour in its general social form – value that assumes the form of means of production in the actual production process, confronts living labour-capacity (labour-power) as an *autonomous* power and is the means of appropriating *unpaid* labour, and that it is this power in that it confronts the worker as the *property of another person*. On the other hand, however, this antithesis to wage-labour is *obliterated* in the form of *interest*; for interest-bearing capital *as such* does not have wage-labour as its opposite but rather *capital* > *to the extent that it is functioning*; < it is the *capitalist actually functioning* in the reproduction process whom the lending capitalist directly confronts, and not the wage-labourer who is expropriated from the means of

32 Ramsay describes interest as 'net profit'. (Ramsay 1836, p. 193.)

production precisely on the basis of capitalist production. *Interest*-bearing capital is capital as *property* as against capital as *function*. But to the extent that capital does not function, it does not exploit workers and does not come into opposition with labour.

On the other hand, *profit of enterprise* does not form an antithesis with *wage-labour* but rather with *interest*.

Firstly, taking the average profit as given, the rate of profit of enterprise is determined not by wages but rather by the *rate of interest*. It is either high or low in *inverse* proportion to the latter.[33]

|307| Secondly, the functioning capitalist derives his title (claim) to *profit of enterprise*, and thus profit of enterprise itself, not from his *ownership of capital* but rather from the function of capital as opposed to the capacity in which it exists only as inert property. This emerges as a direct and existing antithesis as soon as he operates with *borrowed* capital, where interest and profit of enterprise accrue to two different persons. Profit of enterprise arises from the function of capital in the reproduction process, hence as a result of the operations and activity by which the functioning capitalist mediates these functions of industrial and commercial capital. But it is no sinecure to be a representative of functioning capital, unlike the case with interest-bearing capital. On the basis of capitalist production, the capitalist directs both the production process and the circulation process. The exploitation of productive labour costs > labour <, whether he does this himself or has it done in his name by others. In opposition to interest, therefore, his profit of enterprise presents itself to him as independent of his property in capital and rather as the result of his functions as non-owner – as a *worker*. He inevitably gets the idea into his brainbox, therefore, that his profit of enterprise, very far from forming any antithesis with wage-labour and being only the unpaid labour of others, is rather itself a *wage*, the 'wages of superintendence of labour', a higher wage than that of the ordinary wage-labourer, (1) because it is more complex labour, and (2) because he pays the wages to himself. That his function as a capitalist consists in producing *surplus-value*, i.e., *surplus labour*, in the most economical conditions possible, is completely forgotten in the face of the antithesis that interest accrues to the capitalist even if he does not perform any function as capitalist, but is simply the owner of capital; whereas profit of enterprise accrues to the functioning capitalist even if he is not the owner of the capital with which he functions. In the face of the antithetical form of the two parts into which

33 'The profits of enterprise depend upon the net profits of capital, not the latter upon the former'. (Ramsay 1836, p. 214.)

profit and thus *surplus-value* divides, it is forgotten that both are simply parts of *surplus-value* and that such a division can in no way change its nature, its origin and its conditions of existence. In the actual process, the functioning capitalist represents capital against the wage-labourers as the property of others and the moneyed capitalist, as represented by the functioning capitalist, participates in the exploitation of labour. That it is only as the representative of the means of production towards the workers that the active capitalist can exercise his function, can have the workers work for him or can have the means of production function *as capital*, is something that is forgotten in the face of the opposition between the function of capital in the reproduction process and mere ownership of capital outside the reproduction process. In point of fact, the form that the two parts of *profit*, i.e., *surplus-value* assume as interest and profit of enterprise does not express any relationship with labour, because this relationship exists only between labour and *profit*, or rather *surplus-value*, as the *sum* of these two parts, their *whole* and their *unity*. The ratio in which profit is divided, and the different legal titles by which this division takes place, *already assume profit* and presuppose its existence. If the capitalist is the actual *owner* of the capital with which he functions, he pockets the entire profit or surplus-value; for the worker it is all the same whether this is what the capitalist does or whether he has to pay one part to a third party as the legal proprietor. The *basis for the division of the profit* (the surplus-value) between two kinds of capitalist is thus transformed imperceptibly into the *basis of existence of the profit* or surplus-value to be divided, which *capital* derives as such from the reproduction process quite apart from any later division. From the fact that interest confronts profit of enterprise, and vice versa, but neither confronts labour, it follows: that *profit of enterprise plus interest*, i.e., *profit*, and consequently *surplus-value*, is derived – from what? From the *antithetical form* of its two parts! But *profit* is *produced* before this division takes place, and before there can be any talk of it.

Interest-bearing capital proves itself as such only in so far as the money lent really is transformed into capital and produces a surplus, of which interest is one part. This does not by itself rule out that the bearing of interest might be its inherent property, independent of the production process. Labour-capacity, for instance, proves its value-creating property only if it is activated and realised in the labour process; but this does not exclude it from being potentially in itself already value-creating activity as a capacity, and as such it does not just arise from the process but is rather presupposed by it. It is bought as the ability to create value. It can be bought by someone without their having it work productively. The same applies to capital. It is the business of the borrower whether or not he uses it as capital, and thus really does activate its inherent property of producing surplus-value within the process of production. What he pays for in both cases is surplus-value *as such*, surplus-value contained in the commodity as a potentiality.

Since the aspect of *capital's specific social determination* in the capitalist mode of production – capital ownership (as the capacity to command the labour of others) – becomes fixed, with interest appearing as the part of surplus-value that capital produces in this connection, the other part of the surplus-value, *profit of enterprise*, necessarily appears as if it does not derive from capital as capital, but rather from the *production process* independently of its *specific social determination*, which indeed has already obtained its particular mode of existence in the form of interest on capital. The production process, however, when separated from capital, is simply the *labour process* in general. The industrial capitalist, as distinct from the owner of capital, is not an agent of capital's functioning but a functionary separate from capital, a simple instrument of the labour process in general, a *worker*, and indeed *someone who works for a wage*. Interest in itself expresses precisely the existence of the *conditions of labour as capital*, in their social antithesis to labour and their metamorphosis into personal powers vis-à-vis labour and over labour. Interest represents mere ownership of capital as a means of appropriating the product of other people's labour. But it represents this character of capital as something that falls to it outside the production process itself and is by no means the result of its specific character. It presents it not in direct antithesis to labour but quite the reverse, with no relationship to labour at all, merely as a relationship between one capitalist and another. Thus as a capacity that is external and indifferent to the actual relationship between capital and labour. In *interest*, therefore, the particular form of profit in which the *antithetical character* of capital acquires an autonomous expression, it does so in such a way that this antithesis is completely obliterated therein; it completely abstracts from the antithesis. Interest is a *relationship* between capitalists, not between capitalist and worker. On the other hand, this *form of interest* gives the other part of profit the *qualitative form* of *profit of enterprise*, and subsequently of *wages of superintendence*. The particular functions which the capitalist has to perform as such, and which fall to his part precisely as distinct from the workers and in opposition to them, are presented as simply *functions of labour*. He creates surplus-value not because he works *as a capitalist* but rather because, leaving aside his character as a capitalist, he also *works*. This part of surplus-value is therefore no longer surplus-value at all, but rather its opposite, the equivalent for labour performed. Since the estranged [*entfremdet*] character of capital, its antithesis to labour, is shifted outside the actual process of exploitation, this process of exploitation itself appears as simply a labour process, in which the functioning capitalist simply performs work which *differs* from that done by the *workers*. As labour, the labour of exploiting is identical with the labour being exploited. The labour of exploiting is identified with the labour that is exploited. The social form of capital devolves upon *interest*, but interest expressed in a *neutral and indifferent form*; the *economic function of capital* devolves on profit of enterprise, but with the specifically capitalist character of this function removed.

|308| Exactly the same thing takes place in the consciousness of the capitalist as with the *grounds of compensation* discussed previously (in Chapter Two of this book) with respect to the equalisation of the average profit. These grounds of compensation, which have a determining role in the distribution of surplus-value, are turned in the capitalist's way of conceiving things into *grounds for the emergence* of profit and for a (subjective) *justification* of the existence of profit itself.

The notion that *profit of enterprise* is a *wage for the superintendence of labour*, which arises from the antithesis between this profit and *interest*, finds further support in the fact that one *part of the profit* can actually be separated off as *wages*, and really does separate off; or rather, a part of wages, conversely, on the basis of the capitalist mode of production, appears as an *integral component of profit*. As Adam Smith already established, this part presents itself in its pure form as independent and completely separate both from profit in general (as the *sum of interest* and *profit of enterprise*), and also from the part of profit that remains behind as the so-called profit of enterprise, and serves to pay the *wages of a general manager* in those branches of business where the scale, etc., permits sufficient division of labour for a special salary to be paid to a general manager.

> Before we proceed any further, one remark should be added:

If *interest-bearing* capital did not take on an independent shape as a *special form of capital* through the fact that a special kind of capitalist lived exclusively on interest and remained outside the actual reproduction process, the *rate of interest* would not exist; i.e., a part of the profit would not acquire a *quantitative* determination and a *fixed magnitude* in the form of interest. Moreover, there would not develop out of this *quantitative* determination a *qualitative* difference, because, as shown previously, this difference only arises from the *quantitative* separation. There would exist no standard by which to measure a part of the profit as a mere valorisation of property in capital – i.e., the simple antithesis between objective wealth and labour. Profit would therefore not be divided into two parts and these two parts would therefore not take on the independent and contrasting forms of interest and profit of enterprise. But the ossification and autonomisation of both parts vis-à-vis one another makes the actual state of affairs appear in inverted form in the mind. Profit (which is itself already a transformed form of surplus-value) does not appear as the *presupposed unity*, the sum total of unpaid labour, which is divided into interest and profit of enterprise. Instead of this, interest and profit of enterprise appear as independent magnitudes, which form profit, *gross profit, when added together*. Since the relation to surplus-value, and therefore the real relationship of capital to wage-labour, has now been extinguished in each of these parts, considered separately, so also does this apply to profit itself, to the extent that it presents itself as a mere addition, as a supplementary quantity of these given magnitudes which have been determined independently and are apparently *presupposed* to it.

< The work of supervision and management necessarily arises where the direct production process takes the form of a socially combined process, and does not appear simply as the isolated labour of separate producers.[34] But it is of a double nature. On the one hand, in all labour where many individuals cooperate, the interconnection and unity of the process is necessarily represented in a governing will, and in functions that concern not the detailed work but rather the workplace and its activity as a whole, as with the conductor of an orchestra. This is a productive labour that has to be performed in every combined mode of production.

On the other hand (quite apart from the commercial department) this *work of supervision* necessarily arises in all modes of production that are based on the *opposition* between the worker as direct producer and the proprietor of the means of production. The greater this opposition, the |309| greater the role that this *work of supervision* plays. It reaches its highest level in the *slave system*.[35] But it is also necessarily immanent in the capitalist mode of production, since here too the production process is at the same time a process of the *consumption of labour-capacity by the capitalist*. In despotic states, similarly, the work of supervision and all-round intervention of the government involves both aspects: the performance of those general tasks that arise from the nature of all communities, and the specific functions that arise from the *opposition* between the government and the mass of the people.

---

34 '*Superintendence* is here' (in the case of the peasant proprietor) 'completely dispensed with'. (Cairnes 1862, pp. 48–9.)

35 'If the nature of the work requires that the workmen' (that is to say, the slaves) 'should be dispersed over an extended area, the number of overseers, and, therefore, *the cost of the labour which requires this supervision*, will be proportionately increased'. (Cairnes 1862, p. 44)

With the writers of antiquity, who had the slave system in mind, we find in their theory (and this was also the case in practice) that the two aspects of the *labour of superintendence* coincide as inseparably as they do with the modern economists, who view the capitalist mode of production as the absolute mode. On the other hand, as I shall show straight away with an example, the apologists of the modern slave system know just as well how to use the *labour of superintendence* as a ground for justifying slavery as other economists do as a ground for the system of wage-labour.

The *villicus* of Cato's time:

'At the head of the slave-worked estate [*familia rustica*] stood the manager [*villicus*, from *villa*], whose job it was to take and spend, buy and sell; he received his instructions from the master, and gave both orders and punishments in his absence ... The manager of course had more freedom than the other slaves. The Magonian books advise that he should be permitted to marry and raise children, as well as keeping his own money; Cato said that he should be married to the female manager. He alone had any prospect of obtaining his freedom, as a reward from the master for good behaviour. The other slaves all formed a common household ... Every slave, including the manager himself, received his necessities at the master's expense at definite intervals and in fixed amounts, and had to make do with this ... The quantity depended on the work, so that the manager, for instance, whose work was lighter than that of the other slaves, received a smaller ration than they did'.[36]

Aristotle: 'For the master' (the capitalist) 'as such is concerned not with the acquisition of slaves' (the ownership of capital, which gives him the power to buy labour) 'but with the use of them' (the use of wage-labourers in the production process). 'There is nothing great or wonderful about this science; for the master need only know how to order that which the slave must know how to execute. Hence anyone who is in a position which places him above the toil of supervision has a *steward* [επίτροπος] who assumes this *honour*, while he is able to occupy himself with public affairs, or philosophy'.[37]

What Aristotle is saying, in blunt terms, is that *domination*, in the economic domain as well as the political, imposes on those in power the *function of dominating*, which means, in the economic domain, that apart from buying and selling (which is the job of the *villicus*) they must know how to consume labour-capacity. And he adds that this *labour of superintendence* is not a matter

---

36 Mommsen 1856, pp. 809–10. [In English: Mommsen 1894, pp. 68–70.]

37 Aristotle 1831, Book 1, Chapter 7. [In English: Aristotle 1920, p. 37.]

of very great moment, which is why the master leaves the 'honour' of this drudgery to an overseer, as soon as he is wealthy enough.

|310| The *labour of superintendence and direction*, in so far as it is not a particular function arising from the nature of all combined social labour, but arises rather from the opposition between the owner of the means of production and the owner of mere labour-capacity – whether the latter is bought along with the worker himself, as in the slave system, or alternatively the worker sells his own labour-capacity, so that the production appears at the same time as a process of the consumption of labour by capital – this function, arising from the servitude of the direct producer, is made into a justification of *that relationship* itself, and the exploitation and appropriation of the worker's unpaid labour is presented as the wage due to the owner of capital. This has never been done more effectively than by a defender of slavery in the United States, a lawyer by the name of [Charles] O'Conor, at a meeting in New York on 19 December 1859, under the banner of '*Justice to the South*'. 'Now, gentlemen', he said amidst tremendous applause, 'to that condition of bondage the negro is assigned by nature. He has the strength and is potent to labour; but the nature which created the power, denied him both the intellect to *govern*, and the *willingness to work*. (Applause.) Both were denied him! And that nature which deprived him of the will to labour, *gave him a master to coerce that will*, and to make him a useful servant in the clime in which he was capable of living, *both for himself and for the master who governed him*. I maintain that it is not injustice to leave the negro in the position in which nature placed him, to give him *a master to govern him* ...; nor is it depriving him of any of his rights to *compel him to labour in return*, to *afford to that master a just compensation for the labour and the talent employed in governing him, and rendering him useful to himself* and to the society in which he lives'.

The wage-labourer, like the slave, must have a master, to make him work and govern him. And once this relationship of domination and servitude is assumed, it is quite in order for the wage-labourer to be compelled to produce his own wages, and, on top of this, the *wages of superintendence*, a compensation for the work of dominating and supervising him, in order 'to afford to that master a just compensation for the labour and talent employed in governing him and rendering him useful to himself and to the society in which he lives'!

The *labour of superintendence and direction*, in so far as it arises from the antithetical character of the relationship, the domination of capital over labour (and is therefore common to all modes of production which, like the capitalist one, are based on class opposition) is also directly and inseparably linked, on the basis of the capitalist mode of production, with the productive functions that all combined social labour assigns to particular individuals as their special work. The *wages* of an επίτροπος, or manager, or *régisseur* (as he was known in feudal France) become completely separated from profit and even take the form of *wages* for skilled labour, as soon as the business is conducted on a sufficiently large scale for such a manager to be paid, even though the productive capitalists are still a long way from 'pursuing public affairs or philosophy'.

Mr. Ure has already noted that it is not the industrial capitalists but the industrial managers who are 'the soul of our manufacturing system'.[38] As far as the mercantile side of the business goes, > any comment would be superfluous, < as the nature of mercantile profit was already examined in the previous chapter.

The *wages of superintendence* (in the case of both the mercantile and the industrial manager) appear as completely separate from profit (as distinguished from interest)[39] |311| both in the workers' *cooperative factories* and in bourgeois[40] *joint-stock companies*. The separation of the *wages of superintendence* from profit, which in other cases appears accidental, is here a *constant* factor. In the case of the cooperative factory, the *antithetical* character of the *labour of superintendence* disappears, since the manager is *paid* by the workers

---

38 Ure 1836, p. 68. Here this Pindar of the manufacturers also testifies that most of the latter do not have the slightest understanding of the machines they employ.

39 Capitalist production has itself brought it about that the labour of direction is readily available, quite independently of the ownership of capital. It has therefore become superfluous for this labour of direction to be performed by the *capitalist*. A music director need in no way be the owner of the instruments in his orchestra, nor does it form part of his function as a conductor that he should have anything to do with the 'wages' of the other musicians. Cooperative factories provide the proof that the capitalist has become just as superfluous as a functionary in production as he himself, from his superior vantage-point, finds the landlord to be. In so far as the work of the capitalist does not arise from the production process as a *capitalist* process, i.e., does not come to an end with capital itself; in so far as it is not a name for the function of exploiting the labour of others; in so far therefore as it arises from the form of labour as *social* labour, from the circulation, etc., it is just as independent of capital as is this form itself, once it has burst out of its capitalist shell. To say that this labour, as *capitalist labour*, is necessarily the function of the capitalist means nothing more than that the vulgarian cannot conceive of the existence of these forms, developed in the womb of the capitalist mode of production, in separation from, and freed from, their antithetical character. Vis-à-vis the moneyed capitalist, the productive capitalist is a worker, but *his work is that of a capitalist*, i.e., an exploiter of the labour of others. The *wage of this labour* is exactly equal to the quantity of others' labour appropriated, in other words it depends directly upon the degree of exploitation, not on the *degree of exertion* that this exploitation costs to the capitalist, and which he may pay to a general manager.

40 [Engels changed this word to 'capitalist'. Translator]

instead of representing capital in confrontation with them. *Joint-stock companies* in general (developed with the credit system) have the tendency to separate this *labour of superintendence* more and more from the *possession of capital*, whether one's own or borrowed; just as with the development of bourgeois society the judicial or administrative functions, for example, became separate from *landed property*, with which they were bound up in feudal times. But since on the one hand the functioning capitalist confronts the mere owner of capital, the moneyed capitalist (and with the development of credit this *moneyed capital* itself takes on a *social* character, and is loaned out by persons *other than* those who own it directly); and on the other hand the *mere manager*, who does not possess capital under any title, either by loan or in any other way, takes care of all the *real functions* that fall to the functioning capitalist as a functioning capitalist, there remains only the *functionary*, and the *capitalist* vanishes from the production process as a superfluous individual.

From the published accounts of the cooperative factories in England we can see that – after deducting the *wages of the manager*, which form a part of the variable capital laid out, just like the wages of the other workers – their *profit* was greater than the *average*, even though they sometimes paid a much higher interest than private factories did. > It was seen earlier (in Chapter One of this book) that, assuming a given level of surplus-value, the rate of profit may rise or fall for reasons which are independent of the rate of surplus-value, and the cause of the < higher profit was in all these cases a greater economy in the use of constant capital. What is important for us in this conception is that here the *average profit* (= interest + profit of enterprise) presents itself palpably and *in actual fact* as a magnitude completely separate from the *wages of superintendence*. Since profit here was higher than average, *profit of enterprise* was also higher than elsewhere.

The same fact is apparent in certain capitalist joint-stock undertakings, for example the joint-stock banks. The London and Westminster Bank paid an annual dividend of 30 percent in 1863, the Union Bank of London paid 15 percent, as did the London Financial and others.[41]

The confusion between profit of enterprise and the *wages of superintendence* originally arose from the antithetical form that the surplus of profit over interest assumes in opposition to that interest. It was developed further with the

41 In addition to the *wages of the managers*, the *interest* paid to depositors is also deducted from the total profit. The high profit is explained here by the small proportion of the paid-up capital in relation to deposits. For example, in 1863 the London and Westminster Bank had a paid-up capital of £1,000,000 and deposits of £14,540,275, while the Union Bank of London had a paid-up capital of £600,000 and deposits of £12,384,173.

apologetic intention of presenting profit not as surplus-value – unpaid labour – but as the *capitalist's own wage*. The socialists then raised the demand that profit should be reduced in *practice* to what it claimed to be in *theory*, namely a mere *wage of superintendence*. And the socialists' demand made things very uncomfortable for the euphemistic theory as soon as, on the one hand, the wage of superintendence found its specific level and its market price, just like any other wage, with the formation of a numerous class of commercial and industrial managers,[42] and, on the other hand, actually fell, just like wages for skilled labour in general, with the reduction in the cost of producing labour-power with special training which is brought about by development in general.[43] With the development of cooperation on the part of the workers, and of joint-stock companies on the part of the bourgeoisie, the last pretext for confusing profit of enterprise with the wages of superintendence was pulled away from beneath their feet, and *profit* came to appear in practice what it undeniably was in theory, mere *surplus-value* (value for which no equivalent has been paid, realised unpaid labour), hence the functioning capitalist *really* exploits labour and the fruits of his exploitation, if he operates with borrowed capital, are divided into *interest* and *profit of enterprise*, the surplus of the profit over the *interest*.[44]

---

42 'Masters are labourers as well as their journeymen. In this character their interest is precisely the same as that of their men. But they are also either capitalists, or the agents of the capitalist, and in this respect their interest is decidedly opposed to the interest of the workmen'. (Hodgskin 1825, p. 27.) 'The wide spread of education among the journeyman mechanics of the country diminishes daily the value of the labour and skill of almost all masters and employers by increasing the number of persons who possess their peculiar knowledge'. (Hodgskin 1825, p. 30.)

43 'The general relaxation of conventional barriers, the increased facilities of education, tend to bring down the wages of skilled labour instead of raising those of the unskilled'. (Mill 1849, p. 479.)

44 On the basis of capitalist production, a new swindle with the *wages of superintendence* develops, in that, over and above the actual manager a lot of extra directors step forth, and they in fact make the idea of *superintendence* a mere pretext for plundering the shareholders and enriching themselves. Very nice details of this are to be found in Evans 1845. What bankers and merchants gain by the direction of eight or nine companies may be seen from the following illustration: 'The private balance sheet of Mr. Timothy Abraham Curtis, presented to the Court of Bankruptcy when that gentleman failed, exhibited an income *under the head of directorship* of between £800 and £900 a year. Mr. Curtis having been associated with the Courts of the Bank of England and East India House, it was considered quite a plum for a public company to acquire his services in the boardroom'. (Evans 1845, pp. 81–2.) 'A directorship returns at least £1 1sh. for attendance on each weekly

|312| 4. The The Externalisation of Surplus-Value and the Capital Relation in General in the Form of Interest-Bearing Capital[45]

In interest-bearing capital, the *capital relation* reaches its *most externalised* and *fetishised* form. Here we have M – M′, money that produces more money, self-valorising value, without the process that *mediates* the two extremes. In *commercial capital,* M – C – M′, at least the general form of capital's movement is present, even though this takes place only in the circulation sphere, so that profit appears as merely *profit upon expropriation*.[46] Nevertheless, it represents a process, the unity of opposing phases, a *movement* that breaks down into two opposing phases, the purchase of commodities and their sale. This is obliterated in M – M′, the form of interest-bearing capital. If £1,000 is lent out by a capitalist, for example, and the interest rate is 5 percent, the value of the £1,000 as capital = £1,050 (= C + $^{C}/_{i}$, where C = capital and i = the rate of interest). The value of £1,000 as capital is £1,050. In other words, capital is not a simple quantity. It is a *relation of quantities*, a ratio between the principal as a given value, and itself as surplus-value. And as we have seen, *capital* presents itself *in this way*, as this directly self-valorising value, for all productive capitalists, whether they function with their own or with borrowed capital.

M – M′. Here we have the original starting-point of capital, money, and the formula M – C – M′, reduced to its two extremes M and M′, money that creates more money (namely M = M + ΔM). This is the original and general formula for capital reduced to a meaningless abbreviation. > (A *shortened* formula.) < It is capital in its finished form, the unity of the production and circulation processes, and hence capital yielding a definite surplus-value in a specific period of time. In the form of interest-bearing capital, capital appears immediately, without its being mediated by the processes of production and circulation. > In commercial capital profit *appears* to arise from the *exchange* (and therefore it is profit upon expropriation), hence it appears to result in any case from a *social relation* and not from a *thing* [*Ding*]. In capital and interest, < capital appears as a mysterious and self-creating source of interest, of its own increase. The thing (money, commodity, value) is now capital as a thing, and capital appears as a mere thing; the overall result of the processes

board day'. (Evans 1845, p. 81.) The proceedings of the bankruptcy courts show that these *wages of superintendence* stand in an inverse ratio to the real superintendence actually exercised by these nominal directors.

45 [Engels changed this title to 'Interest-Bearing Capital as the Superficial Form of the Capital Relation' of his Chapter 24. Editor]

46 [See note 21 of Chapter Four for Marx's use of this word. Translator]

of production and circulation appears as a property inherent in the thing itself, and it is up to the possessor of money, i.e., of the commodity in its ever-exchangeable form, whether he wants to spend it as money or hire it out as capital. In interest-bearing capital, therefore, this *automatic fetish* is elaborated into its pure form, self-valorising value, money that makes (breeds) money, and in this form it no longer bears any marks of its origin. The social relation is consummated in the relationship of a thing (money) to itself.

Instead of the *actual* transformation of money into capital, we have here only the form of this *devoid of content*. As in the case of *labour-capacity*, the use-value of money is that of creating *exchange-value*, a greater *exchange-value than is contained in itself*. Money exists δυνάμει [potentially] as *self-valorising value* of this kind, and as such it is lent, this being the form of value for this particular commodity. Thus it becomes as completely the property of money to create value, to yield interest, as it is the property of pear trees to produce pears. And it is as this interest-bearing thing that the money-lender sells his money. Nor is that all. The actually functioning capital, as we have seen, presents itself in such a way that it yields *interest* not as functioning capital, but rather as *capital in itself*, as moneyed capital.

There is yet a further distortion. Whereas interest was simply a *part of the profit*, i.e., the surplus-value, extorted from the worker by the functioning capitalist, it now appears as if *interest* is, on the contrary, the specific fruit of capital, the original thing, while profit, now transformed into the form of *profit of enterprise*, appears as a mere accessory, a trimming, added in the production and circulation process. The *fetish character of capital* and the *representation of this capital fetish* is now complete. In M – M′ we have the irrational form of capital, the misrepresentation and objectification [*Versachlichung*] of the relations of production, at its highest power: the interest-bearing form, the simple form of capital, in which it is presupposed to its own reproduction process; the *ability of money or a commodity* to valorise its own value – the capital mystification in its most glaring form.

|313| For the vulgar economist, who wants to present capital as an independent source of wealth, of value creation, this form is of course a godsend, a form in which the source of profit is no longer recognisable and in which the result of the capitalist production process – separated from the process itself – obtains an autonomous existence.

It is only in moneyed capital that capital becomes a commodity, whose self-valorising quality has a *fixed price* as expressed in the prevailing rate of interest.

As *interest-bearing capital*, and moreover in its immediate form of *interest-bearing money capital* (the other forms of interest-bearing capital, which do not concern us here, are derived from this form and presuppose it), capital obtains its pure fetish form, M – M′ being the *subject*, a thing for sale. Firstly, by way of its continuing existence as *money*, a form in which all capital's determinations are dissolved and its real elements are invisible. Money is in fact the very form in which the distinctions between commodities as different use-values are obliterated, and hence also the *distinctions between productive capitals*, which consist of these commodities and the conditions of their production; it is the form in which capital exists as autonomous exchange-value. In the real process of capital the money form is an evanescent form. On the money market capital always exists in this form. *Secondly*, the surplus-value it creates, here again in the form of money, appears to accrue to it as such. Like the growth of trees, the generation of money [τόκος][47] seems a property of capital in this form of money capital.

In interest-bearing capital, the movement of capital is abbreviated. The mediating process is omitted, and a capital of 1,000, for example, is characterised as a thing that in itself is 1,000 and in a certain period is transformed into 1,100, just as wine in the cellar improves its use-value after a given period of time. Capital is now a thing, but the thing is capital. The money is now 'as if by love possessed'.[48] As soon as it is lent, or else available to the reproduction process (in so far as it yields *interest* to the functioning capitalist as its owner, separate from industrial profit), interest accrues to it no matter whether it is asleep or awake, at home or on its travels, by day or by night. In interest-bearing capital, therefore (and all capital is money capital in its value expression, or is now taken as the expression of money capital), the pious wish of the hoarder is realised.

It is this *ingrown existence* of *interest* in money capital as a thing (which is how the production of surplus-value by capital appears here) that Luther was so concerned with in his naively blustering attack on usury. After he explains that *interest* may be demanded if the failure to repay a loan at the specified date causes the lender certain expenses that he has to pay, or if he missed the opportunity for a profitable bargain (he gives the example of the purchase of a garden), he continues: 'Now that I have lent you this (100 guilders), you have caused me to suffer double *damage*, since *here I cannot pay and there I cannot buy*, and therefore suffer loss in both directions. This is called *duplex interesse, damni emergentis et lucri cessantis* [Twofold compensation, for the loss incurred and the gain missed] … On hearing that Hans has suffered a loss

47 [This can mean both 'offspring' and 'interest'. Translator]
48 [The well-known quotation from Goethe's *Faust*. Translator]

with the 100 guilders he lent, and that he demands fair compensation for this, they rush in and charge *on each 100 guilders a double reimbursement*, namely for the cost of the payment and the inability to buy the garden, *just as if the 100 guilders had had two losses grown on to it naturally*, so that *wherever they have 100 guilders available they put them out and count two losses on top of that, although they haven't suffered any loss at all* ... That is why you are a usurer, taking damages from your neighbour's money for a supposed loss which in fact no one caused you, and which you can neither prove nor *calculate*. The lawyers call damages of this kind *non verum, sed fantasticum interesse* [not true but imaginary damages]. A loss which each dreams up for himself ... It will not do to say that the losses |314| might have been incurred, because I was *neither able to pay nor make a purchase*. That would be a case of *ex contingente necessarium* [making an accident into a necessity], making something out of nothing, and making what is uncertain into something completely sure. Surely usury of this kind would devour the whole world in a few years ... If the lender meets with misfortune *accidentally*, through no fault of his own, he must be recompensed, but in deals of this kind it is the reverse. There they scheme to profit at the expense of their needy neighbours, seeking to nourish their greed and get rich, to be lazy and idle and live in luxury on the *labour of other people*, without care, danger or loss. To sit by my stove and let *my 100 guilders gather wealth for me in the country*, and yet *keep it safe in my purse* because it is *only a loan*, without any danger or risk – my dear friend, who wouldn't like that?'[49]

The conception of capital as value that reproduces itself, by virtue of its innate quality as a perennial and growing value – the 'hidden quality' of the scholastics – led up to the amazing fancies of Dr. Price, which leave far behind the fantasies of the alchemists; fancies which Pitt took quite seriously, and which he made the basis of his financial policy in his legislation on the sinking fund.[50]

'Money bearing compound interest increases at first slowly. But, the rate of increase being continually accelerated, it becomes in some time so rapid, as to mock all the powers of the imagination. One penny, put out at our Saviour's birth to 5 percent compound interest, would, before this time, have increased to a greater sum than would be obtained in 150 millions of earths, all solid gold. But if put out to simple interest, it would, in the same time, have amounted to no more than seven shillings and four pence half-penny. Our

---

49 Luther 1540.

50 [Established by the English prime minister William Pitt the Younger in 1786. Marx discussed the sinking fund briefly in an article published on 7 May 1858 (MECW 15, 1986, p. 513.) Translator]

government has hitherto chosen to improve money in the last, rather than the first of these ways'.[51]

He flies still higher in his 1772 book, *Observations on Reversionary Payments*: 'A shilling put out to 6 percent compound interest at our Saviour's birth' (presumably in the Temple of Jerusalem) 'would ... have increased to a greater sum than the whole solar system could hold, supposing it a sphere equal in diameter to the diameter of Saturn's orbit'.[52] 'A state need never therefore be under any difficulties; for, with the *smallest* savings, it may, in as little time as its interest can require, pay off the *largest* debt'.[53] What a charming theoretical introduction to the English national debt!

Price was simply dazzled by the enormous numbers resulting from geometrical progression. Since he viewed capital as a self-acting automaton, without any regard for the conditions of reproduction and labour, *as a mere number that increases by itself* (just as Malthus saw human beings in his own geometrical progression), he could imagine that he had found the law of its growth in the formula $s = c\,(1 + i)^n$, where s = the sum of capital and compound interest, c = the capital advanced, i = the rate of interest (expressed in aliquot parts of 100), and n = the number of years for which the process continues.

---

51 Price 1772 (1), p. 19. This is his naively clever point: 'It is borrowing money at simple interest, in order to improve it at compound interest'. (Hamilton 1814, p. 133.) According to this, borrowing would be the most secure means of enrichment for private individuals too. But if I borrow £100 at an annual interest of 5 percent, for example, I have to pay 5 percent at the end of the year, and assuming that this advance is for 100 million years, in the meantime I still have only £100 to lend out each year, and similarly £5 to pay at the end of each year. This process never enables me to lend out £105 simply by having borrowed £100. How would I then be able to pay the 5 percent? By a new loan, or, if I am the state, by taxation. If, however, the industrial capitalist borrows money and has to pay 5 percent as interest out of a profit of say 15 percent, he might consume 5 percent (although his appetite grows with his income) and capitalise 5 percent. In other words, 15 percent profit is already presupposed, if 5 percent interest is to be regularly paid. If the process continues, the profit rate will fall, say from 15 percent to 10 percent, > because, in contrast to the constant capital, the variable capital declines, hence the profit rate also declines. < But Price completely forgets that the interest of 5 percent presupposed a rate of profit of 15 percent, and he lets this rate continue with the accumulation of capital. He does not have to concern himself with the *real* process of accumulation at all, but only to lend money out, for it to return to him at compound interest. Where this comes from is quite immaterial to him, since this is the innate quality of interest-bearing capital.

52 Price 1772 (2), p. xiii.

53 Price 1772 (2), pp. xiii–xiv, 136. To be checked in the notebook [Marx's comment – Translator].

Pitt took Dr. Price's mystification quite seriously > in a speech of 1792 in which he proposed an increase in the amount of money to be devoted to the sinking fund.

< 'In 1786 the House of Commons resolved unanimously that £1,000,000 should be raised for public purposes'.[54] According to Price, whom Pitt believed, nothing could be better than to tax the people with a view to 'accumulating' the sum raised by those taxes, and thus spiriting away the national debt by the mystery of compound interest. > Hence taxes for the sinking fund or fund for amortisation. < 'That resolution of the House of Commons was soon followed by a bill drawn up by Pitt, which provided for the accumulation of a quarter of a million pounds sterling, until, with the expired annuities, the fund should have grown to £4,000,000 a year'. (Chapter XXXI of the Act of 26 George III.) In his speech of 1792, in which he proposed to increase the sum devoted to the sinking fund, Pitt adduced machines, credit, etc., among the reasons for England's commercial pre-eminence, but he said that 'the most widespread and enduring cause was *accumulation*. This principle, he said, was now completely developed in the work of Adam Smith, that genius, etc. ... and this |315| accumulation > of capitals < was to be accomplished by reserving at least a portion of the annual profit for the purpose of increasing the principal, which was to be employed in the same manner the following year, and which thus would yield a continued profit'.[55] By way of Dr. Price, therefore, Pitt transformed Adam Smith's theory of accumulation into the enrichment of a nation by accumulation of debts, and thus arrived at the comforting progress towards an infinity of loans, loans to pay loans with, etc.

We already find with Josiah Child, the father of modern banking, that '£100 put out at 10 percent for 70 years, adding interest on interest, would produce £102,400'.[56]

How far Dr. Price's conception has unwittingly been taken over by modern economics is shown by the following quotation from *The Economist*:

'*Capital*, with *compound interest on every portion of capital saved, is so all engrossing, that all the wealth in the world from which income is derived has long ago become the interest on capital* ... all rent (of land) is *now* the payment of interest on capital previously invested in the land'.[57]

---

54 Lauderdale 1808, p. 176.

55 Lauderdale 1808, pp. 178–9.

56 Child 1754, p. 115.

57 *The Economist*, 19 July 1851. > (This passage should be compared with Luther's view: 'Therefore there is no greater enemy of man on this earth (except the devil) than a

All wealth that can ever be produced belongs to capital in its capacity as interest-bearing capital, and everything that it has received up till now is only a first instalment for its 'all engrossing' appetite. By its own inherent laws, all surplus labour that the human race can ever supply belongs to it, *Moloch*.

Finally, the following rigmarole from the 'Romantic', Müller:

'Dr. Price's tremendous growth of compound interest, or of the self-accelerating forces of human beings, presupposes an undivided or uninterrupted and uniform arrangement for several centuries, if it is to produce these tremendous effects. As soon as capital is broken up into individual branches, which start to grow independently, the entire process of the accumulation of forces begins afresh. Nature has distributed over a career of some twenty to twenty-five years the progression of force that is the average lot of *each individual worker*. After this period has elapsed, the worker abandons his career and must now transfer the capital obtained through compound interest on labour to a new worker, in most cases dividing it among several workers or children. The latter must first learn to activate and apply the capital that falls to them before they can actually draw compound interest from it. Moreover, a tremendous amount of the capital bourgeois society obtains, even in the most energetic communities, is accumulated only gradually over long years, and not directly applied to the expansion of labour. Rather, once a substantial sum has been collected, it is transferred to another individual, a worker, a bank or the state, in the form of a *loan*. The recipient of this, then, in so far as it is he who actually sets the capital in motion, *draws compound interest from it*, and can easily require the lender to content himself with simple interest. Finally, the law of consumption, greed and waste reacts against that tremendous progression in which the forces of men and their products might increase, if the law of production or thrift alone prevailed'.[58]

---

money-grabber and usurer, *for he wants to lord it over all men*. Turks, mercenaries and tyrants are also bad men, yet they must let the people live, and confess that they are bad, and enemies, and do, indeed they must, occasionally show pity to some people. But a usurer and a money-grabber *would have the whole world* perish of hunger, thirst, misery and want, so far as in him lies, so that he may have all to himself' ('all the wealth in the world') 'and so that *every one may receive from him as from a God and be his serf for ever*. This is what makes him glad, this is what refreshes his blood. And, at the same time, he can wear sable cloaks, golden chains, rings and gowns. He can wipe his mouth and be taken for a worthy, pious man, and be celebrated as someone who is more merciful than God himself, and more loving than the Mother of Gold, and all the holy saints'.) (Luther 1540.) <

58 Müller 1809, vol. 3, Berlin, pp. 147–9.

It would be impossible to babble a greater amount of hair-raising nonsense than this in so few lines. Not to mention the comical confusion of worker with capitalist, or the value of labour-capacity with the interest on capital, and so on, the receipt of compound interest is simply explained, among other things, by saying that capital is 'lent out' and it '*then*' brings in 'compound interest'.

Our Müller's procedure is characteristic of the Romantics in every detail. Its content consists of everyday prejudices, skimmed from the most superficial appearance of things. This false and trivial content is then 'elevated' and rendered poetic by a mystificatory mode of expression.

|316| The accumulation process of capital may be conceived as an accumulation of compound interest in so far as the part of the profit (surplus-value) which is transformed back into capital, i.e., which serves to absorb new surplus labour, may be called interest. However:

1. Leaving aside all accidental circumstances, a large part of the existing capital is constantly being more or less *devalued* in the course of the reproduction process, because the value of the commodities is determined not by the labour-time originally taken by their production, but rather by the labour-time that their reproduction takes, and this steadily decreases as the social productivity of labour develops. At a higher level of development of social productivity, therefore, all existing capital, instead of appearing as the result of a long process of > 'capital saved' (what a stupid expression!) < appears as the result of a relatively short reproduction period.[59]

2. As was shown in Chapter Three, the rate of profit decreases in proportion to the growing accumulation of capital and the accompanying rise in the productivity of social labour, this being expressed precisely in the relative decrease in the proportion of variable capital to constant capital. In order to produce the same rate of profit, therefore, if the constant capital set in motion by a worker increases ten-fold, the > surplus-value < would have to increase ten-fold as well, and very soon the total labour-time, even the full twenty-four hours of the day, would not be sufficient, even if it were entirely appropriated by capital. Price's progression depends on the idea that the rate of profit does not decline, as does every idea of this 'all engrossing capital, with compound interest'.[60]

---

59 See Mill and Carey, and Roscher's uncomprehending commentary on them [Roscher's commentary on Mill and Carey is on pp. 77–9 of Roscher 1858.]

60 'It is clear, that no labour, no productive power, no ingenuity, and no art, can answer the overwhelming demands of compound interest. But all saving is made from the revenue of the capitalist, so that actually these demands are constantly made, and as constantly

The identity of surplus-value and surplus labour sets a qualitative limit to the accumulation of capital: the *total working day*, the present development of the productive forces and of the *population*, limits the number of working days that can be exploited simultaneously. But if surplus-value is conceived in the irrational [*begriffslos*] form of interest, the limit is only *quantitative*, and mocks all the powers of the imagination.

Interest-bearing capital, however, displays the conception of the *capital* fetish in its consummate form, the idea that ascribes to material wealth (in the fixed form of money, moreover) the power of producing surplus-value in geometrical progression through some innate quality, as a pure automaton, so that this accumulated product of labour, as *The Economist* believes, has long since discounted the whole of the world's wealth for all time to come, as belonging to it, and falling due to it, by right. Past labour is seen as pregnant in and of itself with a portion of present or future *living surplus labour*. We know, however, that in actual fact the *preservation* and thus also the reproduction of the value of the products of past labour is *only* the result of their contact with living labour; and, secondly, that the command that the products of past labour exert over living surplus labour lasts only as long as the *capital relation*, the specific social relation in which past labour confronts living labour.

|317| 5. Credit. Fictitious Capital

It lies outside the scope of our plan to give an analysis of the credit system and the instruments this creates for itself, such as credit money, etc. Only a few points will be emphasised here, points which are necessary for the characterisation of the capitalist mode of production in general. In this connection we shall simply be dealing with commercial credit. The connection between commercial credit's development and the development of state credit remains outside our consideration.

I have already shown how the function of money as *means of payment* develops out of simple commodity circulation, so that a relationship of creditor and debtor is formed > between the producers and the traders of commodities.[61] <

---

the productive power of labour refuses to satisfy them. A sort of balance is, therefore, constantly struck'. (Hodgskin 1825, p. 23.)

61 Marx 1859, pp. 121–2 [English: MECW 29, 1987, pp. 371–3]. Tooke has the following to say about credit in general: 'Credit, in its most simple expression, is the confidence which, well or ill-founded, leads a person to entrust another with a certain amount of capital, in money or in goods, computed at a value in money agreed upon, and in each case payable at the

With the development of trade and the capitalist mode of production, which produces only for circulation, this *spontaneous basis* for the credit system is expanded, generalised and elaborated. By and large, money now functions only as means of payment, i.e., commodities are not sold for money, but for a written *promise to pay* at a certain date. All such promises can be subsumed under the general category of *bills of exchange*. Until they expire and are due for payment, these bills themselves circulate as means of payment, and they form the actual commercial money.[62,63] To the extent that they ultimately cancel each other

---

expiration of a fixed term. In the case where the capital is lent in money, that is, whether in banknotes, or in a cash credit, or in an order upon a correspondent, an addition for the use of the capital of so much upon every £100 is made to the amount to be repaid. In the case of goods the value of which is agreed in terms of money, constituting a sale, the sum stipulated to be repaid includes a consideration for the use of the capital and for the risk, till the expiration of the period fixed for payment. *Written obligations of payment* at fixed dates mostly accompany these credits, and the *obligations or promissory notes after date being transferable*, from the means by which the lenders, if they have occasion for the use of their capital, in the shape whether of money or goods, before the expiration of the term of the bills they hold, are mostly enabled to borrow or to buy on lower terms, by having their own credit strengthened by the names on the bills in addition to their own'. (Tooke 1844, p. 87.) > 'Every transaction, of what nature soever, which is not arranged by payment in money on the spot, is strictly a *credit* or *time bargain* ... These bargains are the rule in the commercial system, and cash bargains the exception'. (*The Currency Theory* 1845, p. 29.) <

62 Leatham. 'I find ... the amount for the whole of the year of 1839 ... to be £528, 493, 842' (he assumes that foreign bills of exchange make up about a fifth of the total) 'and the amount of bills out at one time in the above year to be £132,123,460'. (Leatham 1840, pp. 55–6.) 'The bills of exchange are a component of the currency greater in amount than all the rest put together'. (Leatham 1840, pp. 3–4.) 'This enormous superstructure of bills of exchange rests (!) upon the base formed by the amount of banknotes and gold, and when, by events, this base becomes too much narrowed, its solidity and very existence is endangered'. (Leatham 1840, p. 8.) 'If I estimate the whole currency and the amount of the liabilities of the Bank and the country bankers, payable on demand, I find a sum of £153 million, which, by law, can be converted into gold ... and the amount of gold to meet this demand is only £14 million'. (Leatham 1840, p. 11.) 'The bills of exchange cannot be placed under control, except by preventing the abundance of money, and low rate of interest or discount, which create a part of them, and encourage their great and dangerous expansion. It is *impossible* to decide what part arises out of *bona fide* transactions, such as actual bargain and sale, or what part is fictitious, and mere accommodation paper, i.e., where one bill is drawn to take up another running, in order to raise a fictitious capital, by creating so much currency. In times of abundance, and cheap money, this I know reaches an enormous amount'. (Leatham 1840, pp. 43–4.)

63 > 'All other forms of credit' (*bills of exchange*, and cheques to the extent that they do not themselves serve for the *liquidation* of reciprocal claims, or circulate like notes instead of

out by the balancing of debts and claims, they function absolutely as money, even though there is no final transformation into money proper. As these reciprocal advances by producers and merchants form the *real basis* of credit,[64] so

---

money) 'merely change the *office of money* from that of transferring the ownership of the property of commodities sold, to that of *liquidating the obligations which represent them*'. (Opdyke 1851, pp. 323–4.) 'There are even some cases where a party liquidates the claim of his creditors with the note of his debtor, or where he employs it in the purchase of goods. In these and similar expedients, *credit is a substitute for money*'. (ibid.) 'By means of these bills (their discounts) the tradesman is enabled to give credit and to extend his business without requiring any addition to his capital'. (Gilbart 1834, p. 152.) 'Deposits are money only to the extent that they are capable of transferring property from hand to hand *without the intervention of money*'. (Bosanquet 1842, p. 82.) 'A deposit can be created without banknotes or coins. For example, a banker opens a cash account of £60,000 based on title deeds, etc., which afford him a guarantee. He enters £60,000 into his deposits. The metal and paper portion of the currency remains unaltered in amount, but the *power of purchase* is apparently increased to the extent of £60,000'. (Gilbart 1834, p. 83.) < 'An average amount of payments to the extent of upwards of £3,000,000 is settled through the Clearing House every day of business in the year, and the daily amount of money required for this purpose is little more than £200,000'. (Gilbart 1834, p. 86.) '*Bills of exchange* are undoubtedly currency, independent of money, in so far as they transfer property from hand to hand by means of endorsements'. (Gilbart 1834, pp. 92–3.) > (To the extent that the bills are not finally paid in bar, they must pass through the Clearing House and be cancelled out against the deposits.) < 'It may be assumed that upon an average there are two endorsements upon every bill in circulation, and ... each bill performs two payments before it becomes due. Upon this assumption it would appear that by endorsement alone property changed hands, by means of bills of exchange, to the value of 2 times 528 million, or £1,056,000,000, more than £3,000,000 per day, in the course of the year 1839. We may therefore safely conclude that deposits and bills of exchange together perform the functions of money, by transferring property from hand to hand without the aid of money, to an extent daily of not less than £18,000,000'. (Gilbart 1834. p. 93.)

64 'In every country, the greater part of credit transactions take place within the orbit of industry ... The producer of raw material advances his product to the manufacturer who processes it, and receives from him a promise to pay on a certain date. The latter, after completing his share of the work, advances his product in turn to another manufacturer who is to process it further, on similar conditions, and in this way credit extends ever further, from one person to another, right through to the consumer. The wholesaler makes advances of commodities to the retailer, while he himself receives these from the manufacturer or an agent. Everyone borrows with one hand and lends with the other, sometimes money, but *far more frequently products*. There is thus an *incessant exchange of advances* in industry, which combine and intersect each other in all directions. The development of credit is nothing more than the multiplication and growth of these reciprocal advances, and this is the true seat of its power'. (Coquelin, 1842, p. 797.)

their instrument of circulation, the bill of exchange, forms the basis of credit money proper, the *circulation of banknotes*, etc. These are not based on monetary circulation (whether of metallic or government paper money) but rather on the circulation of *bills of exchange*.

The other aspect of the credit system involves the *development of the money trade*, which naturally advances in tandem with the development of trade in commodities in the capitalist mode of production in general.

We saw in the previous chapter how the maintenance of a reserve fund for merchants, etc., the technical operations of receiving and paying out money, international payments, and hence the bullion trade as well, are concentrated in the hands of the *money-dealers*. On the basis of this trade in money, and attaching itself to it, the other side of the credit system also develops: the management of *interest-bearing capital* or moneyed capital as the special function of the money-dealers. The borrowing and lending of money becomes their special business. They appear as middlemen between the real lender of money capital and its borrower. To put it in general terms, the business of banking consists from this aspect in concentrating *money capital for loan* in large masses in the bank's hands, so that, instead of the individual lender of money, it is the bankers as representatives of all lenders of money who confront the reproductive capitalists. They concentrate the moneyed capital in their hands as its general managers. On the other hand, they concentrate the borrowers vis-à-vis all the lenders, in so far as they borrow for the entire world of trade. (They make their profit in general by borrowing at lower rates than those at which they lend.) A bank represents on the one hand the centralisation of moneyed capital, or the lenders, and on the other hand the centralisation of the borrowers.

The loanable capital the banks have at their disposal accrues to them in two ways. On the one hand they are the cashiers of the productive capitalists, and the moneyed capital which every producer and merchant keeps as a reserve fund or which flows to them as payment is concentrated in their hands. These funds thus become moneyed capital, which is available for loan. In this way the reserve fund of the commercial world is restricted to the necessary minimum, because it is concentrated *as a communal fund*, and one part of the money capital, which would otherwise be dormant in reserve, is lent out and functions as interest-bearing capital. On the other hand, however, their loan capital is formed from the deposits made by the moneyed capitalists, who hand over to them the job of lending it out. With the development of the banking system, and particularly once they pay interest on deposits, the money savings and the temporarily unoccupied money of all classes are also deposited with them. Thus small sums which otherwise would not have been able to function as moneyed capital are combined together into great masses and in this way form a monetary power. This collection of small amounts, as a particular function of the banking system, must be distinguished from the banks' function as middlemen between the actual money capitalists and the lenders.[65] Finally, revenues that are expected to be consumed only gradually are also deposited with the banks.[66]

Lending is effected (we are dealing here only with commercial credit proper) by *discounting bills of exchange* – transforming them into money before their due date – and by *advances* of various kinds: direct advances on personal credit, as with the Scottish banks;[67] loans against interest-bearing paper, government paper and stocks of all sorts; and particularly also advances against bills of lading, dock warrants and other certified *titles to the ownership of commodities*, as well as overdrafts on deposits, etc.[68]

65 [Engels changed 'lenders' to 'borrowers'. Translator]

66 Tooke. 'The business of bankers ... may be divided into two branches. One branch of the bankers' business is to collect capital from those who have not immediate employment for it, and to distribute or transfer it to those who have. This is a *circulation of capital*. The other branch is to receive deposits of the incomes of their customers and to pay out the amount as it is wanted for expenditure by the latter in the objects of their consumption ... This is a circulation of currency ...' (Tooke 1844, pp. 36–7) 'A concentration of capital on the one hand and the distribution of it on the other, from that branch which is employed in administering the circulation for local purposes of the district'. (Tooke 1844, p. 37.)

67 > *Advances of the Scottish banks in notes.* <

68 *On swindling in the East India trade, by means of bills of exchange and loans on bills of lading.* Bills were not drawn here because commodities had been bought and sold, but rather commodities were bought and sold in order to gain possession of something that could be discounted and converted into money. > This is how it was done: 'The East India trade has been one huge system of credit. If goods were bought in Manchester, by a house in London, they were paid for by bills at six months' date, and, as soon as shipped, an advance was obtained again by a bill at six months for a large part of the first cost by the consignee' (the receiver of the goods, the factor) 'who, again, in his turn, not infrequently drew upon the house in India, against the bills of lading when transmitted. < The shipper and the consignee were thus both put in possession of funds, months before they actually paid for the goods; and, very commonly, these bills were renewed at maturity, on pretence of affording time for the returns in a 'long trade'. Moreover, losses by such a trade, instead of leading to its contraction, led directly to its increase. The poorer men became, the greater need they had *to purchase, in order to make up, by new advances*, the capital they had lost on the past adventures. *Purchases* thus became, not a question of supply and demand, but the most important part of the *financial* operations of a firm labouring under difficulties. But this is only one side of the picture. What took place in reference to the export of goods at home, was taking place in the purchase and shipment of produce abroad. Houses in

|318| Now the credit that the banker gives can be provided in *various forms*, e.g., in bankers' bills,[69] bank credits, cheques,[70] etc., and finally in *banknotes*.

India, who had credit to pass their bills, were purchasers of sugar, indigo, silk, or cotton – not because the prices advised from London by the last overland mail promised a profit on the prices current in India, but because *former drafts upon the London house would soon fall due*, and must be provided for. What was so simple as to purchase a cargo of sugar, pay for it in bills upon the London house at 10 months' date, transmit the *shipping documents* by the overland mail; and, in less than two months, the goods on the high seas, or perhaps not yet passed the mouth of the Hoogly, were *pawned in Lombard Street* – putting the London house in funds eight months before the drafts against those goods fell due. And all this went on without interruption or difficulty, as long as bill brokers had abundance of "money" at call, to *advance on bills of lading* and *dock warrants*, and to discount, without limit, the bills of India houses drawn upon the eminent firms in Mincing Lane'. (*Manchester Guardian*, 24 November 1847.)

69 > See the trickery engaged in by [Samuel Jones] Loyd and Co. 'It is the usual course, whenever money becomes tight, that the bankers will get their customers to take a bill upon London. (902). That acts as a currency? Yes: the man must go and rediscount that if he wants banknotes. (903). That operates to the bank as a privilege of coining? For a time; it is a species of payment that Jones Loyd and Co. adopted from immemorial when there was a period of pressure. (904). Then their drafts increase during a period of pressure? It has always been the case when money is worth more than five percent ... (905) They were the medium by which banknotes could be obtained more easily ... (907) The banker gives a bill easier to discount than the bill he took from the party ... (911) These bills from Jones Loyd and Co were of use before they were discounted. If a man could not have money, he took instead a bill from Jones Loyd and Co. (992). Those bills very frequently passed through 20 or 30 hands. (4636)'. 'I was told of innumerable cases in which parties having their bills discounted accepted, in lieu of Bank of England notes, drafts on London. (4637). Would you not say that that was rather an evasion and contravention of the Act of 1844? It is a substitution. There were drafts of 21 days (upon the bankers in London) payable to the party or order'. (*Committee on Commercial Distress*, 1848. [*First Report* 1848]) <

70 Fullarton. All these forms are '*transferable claims*', or rather instruments by which claims are made transferable. 'There is scarcely any shape into which credit can be cast, in which it will not at times be called to perform the *functions of money*; and whether that shape be a banknote or a bill of exchange, or a banker's cheque, the process is in every essential particular the same, and the result is the same'. (Fullarton, 1845, p. 38.) > According to MacCulloch, 'but for the expedients resorted to for the purpose of economising the currency, a *circulation of 200 millions at the very least* would be required to perform the functions now performed by 50 or 60 millions of banknotes and gold'. (Quoted by Fullarton 1845, p. 46.) 'The statistics periodically published by *the Bank of France* show the extent to which money is economised *within its own walls* by means *of cheques* ... during the quarter ended 31 December 1840, the transactions completed by means of

A banknote is nothing more than a bill on the banker, payable to its possessor and substituted by the banker for private drafts. This last form of credit seems especially striking and important to the layman, firstly because this kind of credit money emerges from commercial circulation into general circulation and functions here as money; also because in most countries the major banks that issue notes are a peculiar mishmash between national banks and private banks and actually have the government's credit behind them, their notes being more or less legal tender; and secondly because it is evident here that what the banker is dealing in is *credit* itself, since the banknote merely represents a circulating token of credit. But the banker also deals with credit in all other forms, even if he advances money deposited with him in cash, etc.[71] In actual

---

specie, *notes* and *transfers* from one account to another (the transfers operating by means of cheques upon current account) [were as follows]: by *specie*: 221,432,200 francs; by *notes*: 1,049,240,000 francs; by *transfers*: 1,742,897,700 francs. The proportions were therefore 58 percent for *transfers*, 35 percent for *notes* and 7 percent for *specie*'. (*The Currency Theory* 1845, pp. 40–1.)

'Banknotes are the small change of credit'. (*The Currency Theory*, p. 51.) As far as the exchange of notes between bankers is concerned (the Scottish banks exchange twice a week, through their agents in Edinburgh), the author says: 'It is not customary ... for issuing banknotes in any part of the world ... to re-issue the promissory notes of their neighbours; and, so long as a note is not issued, it can signify ... very little to any but the parties, whether it is returned to the issuer or locked up in the drawer of an accidental holder'. (*The Currency Theory*, note on p. 95.)

71 > Loyd. 'The banker, who is the go-between, who receives deposits on the *one* side, and applies, entrusting them in the *form* of capital'. (3763). Answer of Loyd (Overstone.) (*Report on Bank Acts*, 1857.) 'The proposition which the banker makes ... to the public is this: "I will exchange my *credit* for your *capital*, but you must allow me the use of your capital *without interest*, and yet pay me interest for the use of my credit"'. (Raguet 1840, note, p. 204.) < 'The trading capital of a bank may be divided into two parts: the *invested capital* and the *banking capital*' (which has been borrowed). (Gilbart 1834, p. 117.) 'There are three ways of raising a banking or borrowed capital. First, by receiving deposits; secondly, by the issuing of notes; thirdly, by the drawing of bills. If a person will lend me £100 for nothing, and I lend that £100 to another person at four percent interest, then, in the course of a year, I shall gain £4 by the transaction. Again, if a person will take my "*promise to pay*" and bring it back to me at the end of the year, and pay me four percent for it, just the same as though I had lent him 100 sovereigns, then I shall gain £4 by that transaction; and again, if a person in a country town brings me £100 on condition that, twenty-one days afterwards, I shall pay the same amount to a person in London, then whatever interest I can make of the money during the twenty-one days, will be my profit. This is a fair representation of the operations of banking, and of the way in which a banking capital is created by means of deposits, notes and bills'. (Gilbart 1834, p. 118.) 'The profits of

a banker are generally in proportion to the amount of his banking or borrowed capital ... To ascertain the real profit of a bank, the interest upon the invested capital should be deducted from the gross profit, and what remains is the banking profit' (ibid.) 'The *advances of bankers* to their customers are made with other people's money'. (Gilbart 1834, p. 146.) 'Precisely those bankers who do not issue notes create a banking capital by the discounting of bills. They render their discounts subservient to the increase of their deposits. The London bankers will not discount except for those houses who have deposit accounts with them'. (Gilbart 1834, p. 119.) 'A party who has had bills discounted, and has paid interest on the whole amount, must leave some portion of that amount in the hands of the banker *without interest*. By this means the banker obtains more than the current rate of interest on the money actually advanced, and raises a banking capital to the amount of the balance left in his hands'. (Gilbart 1834, pp. 119–20.)

Economising on reserve funds, deposits, cheques: 'Banks of deposit', by means of the transfer of titles, 'economise the use of the circulating medium and enable a large amount of transactions to be settled with a small amount of money. The money thus liberated is employed by the banker in *making advances*, by discount or otherwise, to their customers. Hence the principle of *transfer* gives additional efficiency to the deposit system'. (Gilbart 1834, pp. 123–4.) 'It matters not whether the two parties, who have dealings with each other, keep their accounts with the same banker or with different bankers; for the bankers exchange their cheques with each other at the clearing house ... The deposit system might thus, by means of transfers, be carried to such an extent as wholly to supersede the use of a metallic currency. Were every man to keep a deposit account at a bank, and make all his payment by cheques, money might be superseded, and cheques become the sole circulating medium. In this case, however, it must be supposed that the banker has the money in his hands, or the cheques would have no value'. (Gilbart 1834, p. 124.)

> On the *organisation of the banks*: (1) *branches* (2) *agencies*, with regard to the country bankers. < 'Each country banker employs a London agent to pay his notes and bills and, on the other hand, to receive sums that may be lodged by parties residing in London for the use of parties residing in the country'. (Gilbart 1834, p. 127.) 'Each banker [accepts] the notes of others, but never re-issues them. In all larger cities they come together once or twice a week and exchange their notes. The balance is paid by draft on London > payable on demand; or the London agent of the one party is directed to pay the amount to the London agent of the other party'. (Gilbart 1834, p. 134.)

Banking and speculation. < 'It is the object of banking to give facilities to trade, and whatever gives facilities to trade gives facilities to *speculation*. Trade and speculation are in some cases so nearly allied, that it is impossible to say at what precise point trade ends and speculation begins ... Wherever there are banks, capital is more readily obtained, and at a cheaper rate. The cheapness of capital gives facilities to speculation, just in the same way as the cheapness of beef and of beer gives facilities to gluttony and drunkenness'. (Gilbart 1834, pp. 137–8.)

'As banks of circulation always issue their own notes, it would seem that their discounting business was carried on exclusively with this last description of capital' > (raised by the

fact, banknotes are simply the small change of wholesale trade, and the deposit is always the main thing as far as the banks are concerned. See for example the Scottish banks.[72]

Special *credit instruments*, like special forms of banks, need not be considered in any more detail for our present purpose.

---

notes themselves) < 'but it is not so. It is very possible for a banker to issue his own notes for all the bills he discounts, and yet nine tenths of the bills in his possession shall represent real capital. For, although in the first instance the banker's notes are given for the bill, yet these notes may not stay in circulation until the bill becomes due. The bill may have three months to run, the notes may return in three days'. (Gilbart 1834, p. 172.)

> *Cash credit. Overdrawing.* < 'The overdrawing of a cash credit account is a regular matter of business; it is, in fact, the purpose for which the cash credit has been granted … Cash credits are granted not only upon personal security' > (where the individual enters a bond, an obligation) < 'but also upon the security of the Public Funds'. (Gilbart 1834, pp. 174–5.)

> *Loans on commodities.* < 'Capital advanced, by way of loan, on the securities of merchandise, would produce the same effects as if advanced in the discounting of bills. If a party borrows £100 on the security of his merchandise, it is the same as though he had sold his merchandise for a £100 bill, and got it discounted with the banker. By obtaining this advance he is enabled to hold over this merchandise for a better market, and avoids a sacrifice which, otherwise, he might be induced to make, in order to raise the money for urgent purposes'. (Gilbart 1834, pp. 180–1.)

72 *Deposits*: 'It is unquestionably true that the £1,000 which you deposit at A to-day may be re-issued tomorrow, and form a deposit at B. The day after that, re-issued from B, it may form a deposit at C … and so on to infinitude, and that the same £1,000 in money may thus, by a succession of transfers, multiply itself into a sum of deposits absolutely indefinite. *It is possible*, therefore, that *nine tenths of all the deposits in the United Kingdom* may have no existence *beyond their records* in the books of the bankers who are respectively accountable for them … Thus in Scotland, where the currency has never exceeded three millions sterling, the deposits in the banks are 27 millions sterling … Unless a general run on the banks were to take place, the same £1,000 would, if sent back upon its travels, *cancel* with the same facility a sum equally indefinite. As the *same* £1,000, with which you cancel your debt to a tradesman to-day may cancel his debt to the merchant tomorrow, the merchant's debt to the bank the day following and so on without end; so the same £1,000 [may] pass from hand to hand and from bank to bank, and cancel any conceivable sum of deposits'. (*The Currency Theory* 1845, pp. 62–3.)

> If a bank gives out 'notes' drawn on its 'depositors', this is clearly nothing but a change in the *form* of the bank's liabilities, from the form of deposits, payable on demand, to the *form of notes, payable on demand.* <

[Supplementary Material][73]

> |319| *The distribution of capitals in the different branches of trade by the discount of bills.*

'Every branch of trade is liable to fluctuations' dependent on demand and supply. 'Hence capital undergoes a perpetual transfer from the production of those articles for which there is less demand, to the production of those articles for which there is a greater demand. But in what way is this transfer effected? Is it by a manufacturer leaving one employment for another? No. The manufacturer in the declining trade will reduce his capital, while the manufacturer in the prosperous trade will augment his capital; and the transfer of capital from one trade to the other is effected chiefly by bills of exchange. The manufacturer who has sold a lesser quantity of commodities will have fewer bills for his banker to discount; the other, having sold a greater quantity of commodities, has more bills for discount. The banker's capital, which he employs chiefly in the discount of bills, is thus easily transferred from one branch of manufacture to another, in exact proportion to the circumstances of the respective parties'. (Gilbart 1834, pp. 153–4.)

'Long bills encourage speculation' (Gilbart 1834, p. 156).

Payment in bills of exchange instead of cash. < In the last week of April 1847, the Bank of England advised the Royal Bank of Liverpool that their 'discounts with them' would have to be 'diminished by a half, as they ran off. This announcement operated with peculiar hardship on this account, that the payments into Liverpool had latterly been much more in bills than in cash; and the merchants who generally brought to the Bank a large proportion of cash |320| with which to pay their acceptances, had latterly been able to bring only bills which they had received for their cotton and other produce, and that increased very rapidly as the difficulties increased ... The acceptances ... which the Bank had to pay for the merchants, were acceptances drawn chiefly upon them from abroad, and they have been accustomed to meet those acceptances by whatever payment they received for their produce ... The bills that the merchants brought ... in lieu of cash, which they usually brought ... were of various dates, and of various descriptions; a considerable number of them were bankers' bills, of three months' date, the large bulk being cotton bills'. (*First Report* 1848, p. 26.) (Cited according to the page numbers entered in the British Museum.) 'These bills of exchange were bankers' bills, accepted by London

73 [Title added by the MEGA editors. Editor]

bankers, and by merchants in every trade, Brazilian, American, Canadian, West Indian … The merchants did not draw upon each other; but the parties in the interior, who had purchased produce from the merchants, remitted these bills on London bankers, or bills on various parties in London, or bills upon anybody' (*First Report* 1848, p. 27). 'The announcement of the Bank of England caused a reduction of the maturity terms of bills drawn against sales of foreign products, frequently extending to over three months' (*First Report* 1848, pp. 26–7).

In the spring of 1847 (*April*) 'almost all mercantile houses had begun to starve their business more or less for *investments in railways* … by taking part of their commercial capital for railways' (*First Report* 1848, pp. 41–2). 'Loans were made on railway shares at a high rate of interest, eight percent for example, by private individuals, by bankers and by fire offices' (*First Report* 1848, p. 66). 'Loans to so great an extent by commercial houses to railways induced them to lean too much upon banks by the discount of paper, whereby to carry on their commercial operations' (*First Report* 1848, p. 67).

Question 207: 'Should you say that the railways calls had had a great effect in producing the pressure which there was in April and October? I should say that they had had hardly any effect at all in producing the pressure in April; I should imagine that up to April, and up, perhaps, to the summer, they had increased the power of bankers in some respects rather than diminished it; for the expenditure had not been nearly so rapid as the calls; the consequence was, that most of the banks had rather a large amount of railway money in their hands in the beginning of the year. In the summer that melted gradually away, and on the 31 December it was materially less. One cause of the pressure in October was the gradual diminution of the railway money in the bankers' hands; between the 22 April and the 31 December the railway balances in our hands were reduced one third; and the railways calls have also had this effect strongly throughout the Kingdom; they have been gradually draining the deposits of bankers > and the amount of credit balances in the banks' (*First Report* 1848, pp. 43–4).

< The same was said by Samuel Gurney (questions 1754 and 1755): 'During the year 1846 … there had been a considerable demand for capital for railways, *but it did not increase the interest. There was a condensation of small sums into large masses*, and *those large masses were used in our market*; so that, upon the whole, the effect was to throw more money into the money market of the city than to take it out'.

> Adam Hodgson, director of the Royal Bank of Liverpool, quoted earlier, says that the Bank of England 'in fact created an *obstruction in the way of the usual convertibility of bills of exchange*' (*First Report* 1848, p. 43).

He explains the very *low rate of interest* at present by 'the almost perfect destruction of commerce, and the almost *total want of means of employing money*' (*First Report* 1848, p. 45).

Bills the reserve of bankers. Hodgson says: < 'It has been our habit to keep at least nine tenths of all our deposits, and all money we have of other persons, in our bill case, in bills that are falling due from day to day ... so much so, that during the time of the run, the bills falling due were almost equal to the amount of the run upon us day by day' (*First Report* 1848, p. 53).

Speculative bills. Cotton bills. 5092. 'Who were those bills (against sold cotton) generally accepted by? By produce brokers: a person buys cotton, and places it in the hands of a broker, and *draws upon that broker*, and gets the bill discounted'. 5094. 'And they are taken to the banks at Liverpool, and discounted? Yes, and in other parts besides ... I believe if it had not been for the accommodation thus granted, and principally by the Liverpool banks, cotton would never have been so high last year as it was by one and a half pence or two pence a pound'.

600. 'You have stated that a vast amount of bills were put in circulation, drawn by speculators upon cotton brokers in Liverpool; does that system extend to your advance on acceptances upon colonial and foreign produce as well as on cotton? It refers to *all kinds of colonial produce*, but to cotton most especially'.

601. 'Do you, as a banker, discourage ... that description of paper? We do not; we consider it a very legitimate description of paper, when kept in moderation ... Bills of this kind are frequently renewed'.

The main forms of swindling in the East Indian market (and in the Chinese market) in 1847.

Charles Turner (*Liverpool merchant in the East India trade*): 'We are all aware of the events which have taken place as regards the *Mauritius trade* and other trades of that kind. The brokers have been in the habit ... *not only of advancing upon goods after their arrival* to meet the bills drawn against those goods, which is perfectly legitimate, and upon the *bills of lading* ... but ... they have advanced upon the produce before it was shipped, and in some cases before it was manufactured. I, for example, had bought bills in Calcutta to the extent of six or seven thousand pounds; the proceeds of the bills went down to Mauritius to help in the growth of sugar; those bills came to England, and above half of them were protested; for when the *shipments of sugar came forward*, instead of being held to pay those bills, it had been mortgaged to third parties > to pay previous engagements < before it was shipped, in fact almost before it was boiled' (*First Report* 1848, p. 78).

'The manufacturers now insist that the goods for the East Indian market must be paid for in cash, but that does not amount to much, because if a buyer has any credit at all in London, he can draw upon the house, and get the bill discounted; he goes to London, where discounts now are cheap; he gets the bill discounted, and *pays cash to the manufacturer* ... It takes twelve months, at least, for the shipper of goods to get his return from India ... A man with ten or fifteen thousand pounds would go into the Indian trade; he would open a credit with a house in London, to a considerable extent, giving that house one percent; he, drawing upon the house in London, on the understanding that the proceeds of the goods that go out are to be returned to the house in London, but it being perfectly understood by both parties that the man in London is to be kept out of a cash advance; that is to say the bills are to be renewed till the proceeds come home. The bills were discounted at Liverpool, Manchester, or London ... many of them lie in the Scotch banks' (*First Report* 1848, p. 79). 786. 'There is one house which failed in London, the other day, and in examining their affairs a transaction of this sort was proved to have taken place; there is a house of business at *Manchester*, and another at *Calcutta*; they opened a credit account with a house in London to the extent of £200,000; that is to say, the friends of this house in Manchester, who consigned goods to the East India house from Glasgow and Manchester, had the power of drawing upon the house in London to the extent of £200,000; at the same time, there was an understanding that the corresponding house in Calcutta was to draw upon the London house to the extent of £200,000; with the proceeds of those bills sold in Calcutta, they were to buy other bills, and remit them to the house in London, to take up the first bills drawn from Glasgow ... Thus £600,000 of *bills would have been created* upon that transaction'. 971. 'At present, if a house in Calcutta purchase a cargo, and give their own bills of lading home to this country, those bills of lading which are sent home immediately become available to them in Lombard Street for advances, and they have eight months' use of the money before their correspondents are called upon to pay'.

|*321*| *Accumulation of moneyed capital and its influence on the rate of interest.*

'In England there has taken place a steady accumulation of *surplus wealth, which has a tendency ultimately to assume the form of money*. On the other hand, next in urgency perhaps to the desire to acquire money is the wish to part with it again for some species of investment that shall yield interest or profit; for money itself, as money, yields neither. Unless, therefore, concurrently with this ceaseless influx of surplus capital, there is a gradual and sufficient extension of the field for its employment, we must be subject to *periodical accumulations of money*, seeking investment, of more or less volume, according to the movement of events. For a long series of years, the grand absorbent of the surplus wealth of

England was our public debt ... As soon as in 1816 it had reached its maximum and no longer operated as an absorbent, a sum of at least 27 millions per annum was necessarily driven to seek other channels of investment. What was more, various return payments of capital were made ... *Schemes*, which require for their completion *great masses of capital*, and serve, from time to time, to carry off the surplus of unemployed capital ... and in this country at least are absolutely necessary to carry off those periodical accumulations of the surplus wealth of the community which find no outlet through the ordinary channels of investment [were almost totally absent]' (*The Currency Theory* 1845, pp. 32–4). The same author says, about the year 1845: 'Within a very recent period *prices* have sprung upwards from the lowest point of depression ... Consols touch par ... The bullion in the vault of the *Bank of England* has for months exceeded in amount the treasure held by this establishment since its institution. Shares of every description range at prices on the average wholly unprecedented, and *interest* has declined to rates which are all but nominal ... [These are] *evidences that another heavy accumulation of unemployed wealth exists at this hour in England*, that another period of speculative excitement is at hand' (*The Currency Theory* 1845, p. 36).

'Although the *import of bullion* is no sure sign of gain upon the foreign trade of the country, yet, in the absence of any explanatory cause, it does *prima facie* represent a portion of it' (Hubbard 1843, pp. 40–1). 'Suppose, then, that at a period of steady trade, fair prices ... and full currency, a deficient harvest should give occasion for an import of corn, and an export of gold to the value of five millions. The circulation' (?) 'would of course be reduced by the same amount. An equal quantity of the circulation might still be held by individuals, but the deposits of merchants at their bankers, the balances of bankers with their money-broker, and the reserve in their till, will all be diminished and the immediate result of this reduction *in the amount of unemployed capital* will be a rise in the rate of interest, for example from 4 percent to 6 percent. Trade being in a sound state, confidence will not be shaken, but *credit* will be more highly valued' (Hubbard 1843, p. 42).

'But imagine that *all prices fall*. The superfluous currency returns to the bankers in increased deposits, the abundance of unemployed capital lowers the rate of interest to a minimum, and this state of things lasts until either a return of higher prices or a more active trade call the dormant currency into service, or until it is absorbed by investments in foreign stocks or foreign goods' (Hubbard 1843, p. 68).

As a result of the famine of 1846–7 large imports of food were necessary. This caused 'the imports of the country to be very largely in excess over its exports ... Hence a considerable drain upon the banks and an increased application to the discount brokers and other parties for the discount of bills; they began to scrutinise the bills more closely ... The facilities of houses then began to be very seriously curtailed, and the weak houses began to fail. Those houses which relied entirely upon their credit went down. This increased the alarm that had been previously felt and the *bankers and others, finding that they could not rely with the same degree of confidence that they had previously done upon turning their bills and other money securities into banknotes*, for the *purpose of meeting their engagements*, still further curtailed their facilities, and in many cases refused them altogether; *they locked up their banknotes*, in many instances, for the purpose of meeting their own engagements; they were afraid of parting with them. Alarm and confusion increased daily' and without Russell's letter[74] '*universal bankruptcy* would have been the issue' (*Report from the Secret Committee* 1857, pp. 74–5). Charles Turner, the Liverpool East India merchant mentioned earlier, testified as follows: 'Some houses had large means, but not *available*. The whole of their capital was locked up in estates in the Mauritius, or indigo factories, or sugar factories. Having incurred liabilities to the extent of five to six hundred thousand pounds sterling they had no *available assets to pay their bills*, and eventually it proved that *to pay their bills they were entirely dependent upon their credit*' (*Report from the Secret Committee* 1857, p. 81).

Question 1664. Samuel Gurney, London billbroker, stated: 'At present (1848) there is a *limitation of transaction* and a *great superabundance of money*'. 1763. 'I do not think it was owing *to the want of capital*; it was owing to the alarm' (the *difficulty of getting notes*) 'that existed that the rate of interest got so high'.

In 1847 at least £9,000,000 was paid abroad for food (£7,500,000 from the Bank of England and £1,500,000 from other sources) (*Report from the Secret Committee* 1857, p. 204). 'The public stocks in the country and canal and railway shares had already by 23 October 1847 been depreciated to the amount of £114,752,225' (*Report from the Secret Committee* 1857, p. 288). Morris, the governor of the Bank of England, was questioned by Lord Bentinck (3846): 'Are you not aware that all property *invested in stocks and produce of every description was depreciated* in the same way; that raw cotton, raw silk, unmanufactured wool were sent to the continent at the same depreciated price, and that sugar, coffee and tea were sacrificed as at forced sales?' He replied: 'It was inevitable that the country should make a considerable sacrifice for the purpose of meeting the efflux of bullion which had taken place in consequence of the large

74 [The prime minister at the time, Lord John Russell, wrote to the Bank of England in October 1847 suspending the Bank Act of 1844. Translator]

importation of food'. 3848. 'Do not you think it would have been better to trench upon the £8,000,000 lying in the coffers of the Bank than to have endeavoured to get the gold back again at such a sacrifice? No I do not'. Now for the commentary on this heroism. Disraeli examines W[illiam] Cotton, a director and former governor of the Bank of England (4356). Disraeli: 'What was the rate paid to the Bank proprietors in 1844? It was seven percent for the year. 4357. And the dividend for 1847? Nine percent. 4338. Does the Bank pay the income tax for its proprietors in this year? It does. 4359. In 1844? It did not. 4360. Then *this act has worked very well for the proprietors*. 4361. The result is, that since the passing of the act, the dividend of the proprietors has been raised from seven percent to nine percent, and the Income Tax, that previously to the Act was paid by the proprietors, is now paid by the Bank? It is so'.

Hoarding by the bankers. 4605. (Mr. Pease). 'As the bank was obliged still to raise its rate of interest, everyone seemed apprehensive; country bankers increased the amount of bullion in their hands (1847), and increased the amount of notes, and many of us who were in the habit of keeping, perhaps a few hundred pounds of gold and banknotes, immediately laid up thousands in our desks and drawers, as there was an uncertainty of discounts, and about our bills being current in the market, *a general hoarding ensued*'. 4691. 'Then, whatever may have been the cause during the last 12 years, the result has been rather in favour of the Jew and the money dealer, than the *productive class* generally'.

> *Value of capital*. 4777. 'As regards the *value of capital*, it is a *question of discredit*, and not a *question of scarcity*'.

Ease of credit (*abundance of money*). 4886. (Evidence of [Robert] Gardner, Manchester spinner, manufacturer and merchant.) 'I consider that the distress arose first from the *abundance of money*, or rather *of confidence*, and the *great facility with which we could get discounts*; almost any description of bills that had six or eight months to run could be done with great ease at three and three and a half percent, and all former experience has proved that when ever that is the case it produces the opposite effect'. 5080. 'The *production*' (manufacturing) 'is fallen off one third in the year 1847'.

< How much the money-dealer takes advantage of times of pressure is clear from Thomas Tooke's evidence (5451): 'In the hardware districts of Warwickshire and Staffordshire, a great many orders for goods were declined to be accepted in 1847, because the rate of interest which the manufacturer had to pay for discounting his bills more than absorbed all his profits'.

> (It is very easy to see how bills of exchange can operate without the intervention of money: A has to pay a bill to B, gives him a draft upon his banker; B pays that draft to his banker and the two bankers exchange the drafts with

each other, they cancel them out.) (The process is still simpler when both A and B have the same banker.)

Circulation, money, capital. 'It is clear that only that portion of coin or money which is at any time in the hands of the public, employed in performing the exchange of commodities, is entitled to be deemed *circulation*, while all the *coin or bullion*, lying in the hands of bankers or merchants, seeking an opportunity for profitable investment is *capital* – *capital* may be *withdrawn from the circulation*, either permanently, by the introduction of an economising principle; or temporarily, at *particular periods of the year*, when less circulation is required'. (*The Economist*, 1845, p. 238.) 'Nor is the process changed in any way because deposits are for short periods, and always at the command of depositors; for, if they are withdrawn by one, they are replaced by another, |322| and the *general average does not vary much*'. (ibid.)

< 3635. 'You' (addressing the idiotic [George] Norman, Director of the Bank of England) 'stated that you consider that *the rate of interest* depends, *not upon the amount of notes*, but upon *the supply and demand of capital*. Will you state what you include in '*capital*', besides notes and coin? I believe that the ordinary definition of '*capital*' is commodities or services used in production'. 3636. 'Do you mean to include all commodities in the word '*capital*', when you speak of the *rate of interest?* All commodities used in production'. 3637. 'You include all that in the word "*capital*" when you speak of the rate of interest? Yes. Supposing a cotton manufacturer to want cotton for his factory, the way in which he goes to work to obtain it is, probably, by getting an advance from his banker, and with the notes so obtained he goes to Liverpool and makes a purchase. What he really wants is the cotton; he does not want the notes or the gold, except as a means of getting the cotton. Or he may want the means of paying his workmen; then again, he borrows the notes, and he pays the wages of the workmen with notes; and workmen, again, require food and lodging, and the money is the means of paying for those'. 3638. '*But interest is paid for the money?* It is, in the first instance; but take another case. Supposing he *buys the cotton on credit*, without going to the Bank for an advance, then the difference between the ready-money price and the credit price at the time at which he is to pay for it is *the measure of the interest*. Interest would exist if there was no money at all'. (*Report of the Select Committee on Bank Acts* 1857.)

This complacent twaddle is entirely worthy of this pillar of the Currency Principle! First the discovery, worthy of a genius, that banknotes or gold are means of buying something > (he forgets the numbers) 'and that people do not borrow them for their own sake. And what is the *interest rate* supposed to be governed by on this assumption? By the supply and demand of commodities. All we knew about this until now was that it governed the market prices of the commodities. But quite different rates of interest are compatible with the same market prices. Now a further cunning twist. He is faced with the correct remark, 'But interest is paid for the money', which of course implies the question: What does the interest that the banker receives without in any way dealing in commodities have to do with those commodities? And do not manufacturers receive the same rate of interest for money they put out in completely different markets, hence in markets in which there is a quite different relationship between the 'supply and demand' of the 'commodities used in production'. This awe-inspiring blockhead replies that if the manufacturer buys cotton on credit 'then the difference between the ready-money price and the credit price at the time at which he has to pay for it is *the measure of the interest*'. Quite the opposite. The existing rate of interest, the regulation of which it is the task of our friend Mr. Norman to explain, is the *measure of the difference between the ready-money price* and *the credit price* at the time at which he is to pay for it'. First of all, the cotton is for sale at its cash price. This is determined by the market price, which is itself governed by the state of demand and supply. Say that the price is £1,000. This concludes the transaction between the manufacturer and the cotton broker, as far as buying and selling is concerned. But now there is a second transaction as well. This is between lender and borrower. The value of £1,000 is advanced to the manufacturer in cotton, and he has to pay it back in money, say in three months' time. The interest on £1,000 for three months, as determined by the market rate of interest, then forms the extra charge over and above the ready-money price. The price of the cotton is determined by supply and demand. But the price for the loan of the *value of the cotton* for three months, for the £1,000, is determined by the rate of interest. And this circumstance, that the cotton itself is transformed in this way into money capital, proves to Mr. Norman that 'interest would exist if there was no money at all'. It there were no money at all, there would certainly not be a general rate of interest.

The first thing to note is the vulgar conception of 'capital' as 'commodities used in production'. In so far as these commodities figure as 'capital', they express their *value as capital*, as distinct from their *value as commodities*, in the *profit* that is made from their productive or mercantile transformation. And the *rate of profit* certainly always has something to do with the market price of the commodities bought and their 'supply and demand', though it is also determined by quite different factors. And there is no doubt that the rate of profit forms a general limit to the rate of interest. But what Mr. Norman is supposed to tell us is just how this limit is determined. And it is determined by the *supply and demand of moneyed capital* as distinguished from other forms of capital. Mr. Norman could now be asked further: how is the demand and supply of *moneyed capital determined*? There is no doubt that there is a secret connection between the supply of real capital and the supply of moneyed capital, and it is equally clear that the productive capitalists' demand for moneyed capital is determined by the circumstances of actual production! Instead of talking about this, he offers the wise remark that the demand for moneyed capital is not identical with the demand for money as such; and this only because he, Overstone and the other currency prophets always have at the back of their minds a bad conscience about the way they are seeking through artificial legislative interference with the currency to make 'capital' as such and to raise the rate of interest!

Now to Lord Overstone's calculations, in which he tries to explain why he takes '10 percent' for his 'money' because 'capital' is so scarce in the country. > (These quotations are all from the report of the 1857 Committee.)[75]

< '3653. *The fluctuations in the rate of interest* arise from one of two causes: an alteration in the *value of capital*' (Stop! The value of capital, generally speaking is the *rate of interest*. Hence an alteration *in the rate of interest arises from an alteration in the rate of interest*! The value of capital, as we have already shown, never means anything else in theory. Or else, if Lord Overstone understands by value of capital the *rate of profit*, this penetrating thinker comes back to the assertion that the interest rate is regulated by the rate of profit!) 'or an *alteration in the amount of money* in the country; all great fluctuations of interest, great, either in their duration or in the extent of the fluctuation, may be distinctly traced to *alterations in the value of capital*; more striking practical illustrations of that fact cannot be furnished than the rise in the *rate of interest in 1847*, and during the last two years' (1855 and 1856?) 'the minor fluctuations in the rate of interest which arise from an alteration in the quantity of money are small both in extent and in duration. They are frequent, and the more frequent they are, the more effectual they are for accomplishing their destined purpose' (namely to enrich bankers like Overstone. Mr. S. Gurney expressed himself very naively on this before the House of Lords in 1848: '1324. Do you think that the great fluctuations in the rate of interest which have taken place in the last year are advantageous or not to bankers and dealers in money? I think they are advantageous to dealers in money. All fluctuations in trade are advantageous to the knowing man'. '1325. May not the banker suffer eventually from the high rates of interest, by impoverishing his best customers? No, I do not think it has that effect perceptibly'.) (*Voilà ce que parler veut dire.*)[76]

---

75 [*Report on the Bank Acts* 1857. Translator]

76 ['This is what you call spilling the beans!' Translator]

We shall return to the question of how the *rate of interest* is influenced by the quantity of money. But it must be noted that already Overstone has committed yet another *quid pro quo*. In 1847 the demand for moneyed capital increased for various reasons. (Before October there was no worry about the 'quantity of money'.) (Dearer corn, rising cotton prices, the unsaleability of sugar on account of excessive imports, railway speculation, the flooding of foreign markets with cotton goods, East Indian speculation, etc. All these things led to an increase in the demand for moneyed capital, i.e., for credit and money, for very varied reasons, such as overproduction and underproduction, etc.) The increased demand for moneyed capital had its origins in the actual production process. But whatever the cause, it was the *demand for moneyed capital* that made its value increase, and therefore made the *value of capital* increase. If Mr. Ex-Loyd[77] is trying to say that the value of moneyed capital rose because it rose, that is correct. But if by 'value of capital' he means a rise in the rate of profit as a cause of the rise in the rate of interest, this immediately proves to be false. The demand for moneyed capital, and thus the *value of capital*, can rise even though profit is falling; as soon as the relative supply of moneyed capital falls, its *value* rises. What Mr. Ex-Loyd is trying to prove is that the crisis of 1847, and the high rate of interest that accompanied it, had nothing to do with the 'quantity of money' present, i.e., with the provisions of the 1844 Bank Act which he inspired; although it actually did have something to do with it, as soon as the fear of exhaustion of the Bank's reserve – a creation by Loyd – added monetary panic to the October crisis. But this is not the point in question here. A pressure for moneyed capital was present, |323| brought about by the size of the operations, proceeding from a disturbance in the reproduction process which resulted from the harvest failure, the speculation, the excessive import of sugar, etc. What people who had bought corn at 120 shillings per quarter lacked, when the price fell to 60 shillings, was the 60 shillings reduction in credit for this. It was not a want of notes that prevented them from converting the *old value* into money. The same with those who had imported too much sugar, when its value sank to the depths. The same lack was felt by the gentlemen who had tied up their 'floating capital' in railways and relied on borrowing to conduct the 'legitimate' part of their business. All of this pressure on moneyed capital is expressed, in Loyd's view, in a 'moral sense' of the enhanced 'value of his money', and this enhanced value of moneyed capital corresponded directly to the *depreciated money value* of real capital. (Commodity capital, etc.) The *value of capital* in one form rose, because the value of capital in the other form

77 [Lord Overstone]

fell. Mr. Ex-Loyd, however, tries to identify these two types of *value of capital* by counterposing both of them to a lack of 'circulation', a lack of money. The same amount of moneyed capital, however, can be lent out with very different quantities of the medium of circulation.

Let us take his own example of 1847. The official Bank Rate was as follows: January, 3 to 3½ percent; February, 4 to 4½ percent; March, generally 4 percent; April (panic), 4 to 7½ percent; May, 5 to 5½ percent; June, mostly 5½ percent; July, 5 percent; August, 5 to 5½ percent; September, 5 percent, with minor variations of 5¼, 5½ and 6 percent; October, 5, 5½ and 7 percent; November, 7 to 10 percent; December 7 to 5 percent.

In this case, interest rose because profits declined and the value of commodities > (as expressed in the *price* of commodities) < fell enormously. So if Mr. Ex-Loyd says on this basis that the rate of interest rose in 1847 because the *value of capital* rose, he can only mean by the value of capital the value of moneyed capital, and this is the *rate of interest*. But later on he gives the game away and identifies the value of capital with the *rate of profit*. (Ex-Loyd was in addition to this unaware that part of the high interest paid in 1856–7 was a symptom that the kind of credit-jobbers were abroad who paid interest not out of their profits but out of other people's capital.)

(But he assumed, a few months before the crisis of 1857, that 'trade was essentially sound'.)

'3722. That idea of the profits of trade being destroyed by a rise in the rate of interest is most erroneous. In the first place, a rise in the rate of interest is seldom of any long duration; in the second place, if it is of long duration, and of great extent, it is really a *rise in the value of capital*, and why does the *value of capital* rise? *Because the rate of profit is increased*'. (Here, then, we finally learn what the 'value of capital' means. Besides, the rate of profit can remain high for a long period, even though profit of enterprise falls and the rate of interest rises, so that interest comes to swallow up the greater portion of the profit.)

'3724. The rise in the rate of interest has been in consequence of the great increase in the trade of the country, and the great rise in the rate of profits; and to complain of the rise in the rate of interest as being destructive of the two things which have been its own cause is a sort of logical absurdity which one does not know how to deal with'.

This is about as logical as if he had said: 'The rise in the rate of profit has been in consequence of the speculative rise in the prices of commodities, and to complain of the rise in the prices of commodities as being destructive etc'. Only for a usurer enamoured of his high rate of interest is it 'illogical' that a thing can be destructive of the things which are its cause. The greatness of the Romans was the cause of their 'conquests', and it was their conquests which destroyed their 'greatness'. Wealth is the cause of luxury, and luxury is destructive of wealth. > What a 'simpleton'! < There is no better sign of the idiocy of the present time than the respect that the 'logic' of this millionaire, this dunghill aristocrat, has inspired throughout England! Moreover, if a high rate of profit and the expansion of trade can be the cause of a *high interest rate*, this in no way means that a high interest rate is the cause of high profits. And the question is precisely whether this high interest persisted (as it actually turned out during the crisis) after the high rate of profit had gone the way of all flesh.

'3718. With regard to a great rise in the rate of discount, that is a circumstance entirely arising from the increased value of capital, and the cause of that increased value of capital I think any person may discover with perfect clearness. I have already alluded to the fact that during the thirteen years this Act has been in operation, the trade of this country has increased from £45,000,000 to £120,000,000. Let any person reflect upon all the events which are involved in that short statement; let him consider the *enormous demand upon capital* for the purpose of carrying on such a gigantic increase of trade, and let him consider at the same time that the natural source from which that *great demand should* be supplied, namely, the *annual savings* of this country, has for the last three or four years been consumed in the unprofitable expenditure of war. *I confess that my surprise is, that the rate of interest is not much higher than it is; or, in other words, my surprise is, that the pressure for capital to carry on these gigantic operations, is not far more stringent than you have found it to be*'.

What a strange jumble of words from the logical usurer!

Here he is again with his '*increased value of capital*'! The fellow seems to imagine that on the one hand there was this *enormous expansion of the reproduction process*, hence an *accumulation of real capital*, and that on the other hand there was a '*capital*', for which an 'enormous demand' arose 'for the purpose of carrying on such a gigantic increase of trade!' But wasn't this gigantic increase itself the increase in capital, and if it created a 'demand', did it not create at the same time the 'supply', and did it not also increase the supply of 'moneyed capital'? If the rate of interest rose to a very high level, this was simply because the demand for moneyed capital grew still more quickly than the supply, which means, in other words, that with the expansion of real production, the 'carrying on' of the latter expanded on the basis of the credit system? Without that, the real expansion would not coincide with the increasing demand for 'accommodation', and this is evidently what the banker understands by 'the enormous demand'. It is certainly not the expansion of the *demand for capital* that pushed the value of the export trade up from £45 million to £120 million. And what does Mr. Ex-Loyd mean, moreover, when he says that the 'annual saving of this country' consumed by the Crimean war form 'the natural source from which that giant demand should have been supplied'? Firstly, how then did England accumulate from 1792 to 1815, which was a war of quite a different order from the puny little Crimean one? Secondly, when the natural source was dried up, from what source was the capital supplied? As is well known, England did not take out any loans from foreign countries. If there was an 'artificial' source as well as the 'natural' one, it would certainly be the method most favoured by a nation to use the 'natural' source in war and to apply the 'artificial' source in trade. But if only the old moneyed capital was available, could its efficiency be doubled by a high rate of interest? Mr. Ex-Loyd evidently believes that the nation's 'annual savings' (which were however 'consumed' in this case) are simply transformed into moneyed capital. But if there was no real accumulation [involving a rise in production], what would be the good of an accumulation of moneyed claims upon that production?

The rise in 'the value of capital' resulting from a high rate of profit is lumped together by Ex-Loyd with the increase resulting from the *demand for moneyed capital.* This demand may arise from causes completely independent of the rate of profit. He himself adduces as an example that in 1847 it rose as a result of the diminution of real capital. His language varies: sometimes he speaks of the 'value of real capital', sometimes of the 'value of moneyed capital'.

|324| The following passage is a further demonstration of the fellow's dishonesty and meanness, as well as his narrow banker's standpoint, to which he gives a didactic emphasis:

3728. 'You have stated that the rate of discount is of no material moment you think to the merchant; will you be kind enough to state what you consider the ordinary rate of profit?' Mr. Loyd declares it 'impossible' to give an answer > in order not to get entangled in unpleasant numerical questions.

< 3729. 'Supposing the average rate of profit to be, say, from 7 to 10 percent, a variation of from 2 to 7 or 8 percent in the rate of discount must naturally affect the *rate of profit*, must it not?' (The question itself confuses the *rate of profit of enterprise* with the *rate of profit*, and overlooks the fact that the rate of profit is the common source of both of them. The rate of interest may not disturb the rate of profit, although it will the commercial or industrial profit.) The reply: 'In the first place, parties will not pay a rate of discount which seriously interrupts their profits; they will discontinue their business rather than do that'. (*If they can*, without ruining themselves. As long as their profits are high, they pay the discount rate, because they wish to, and when it is low, they pay it because they have to.) 'What is the meaning of discount? Why does a person discount a bill? ... Because he wants to obtain the command of a greater quantity of capital'. (Hold it there! Because he wants to *anticipate* the return in money of his engaged capital, and not come to a standstill. Because he wants to meet

payments due. He requires a *greater quantity of capital* only if the business is going well, or if he is speculating with someone else's capital, even when business is bad. Discounting is in no way merely a means for *expanding his business*. > As he gives credit in order to make a profit, he wants to take profit from the money lender in order to carry on his business.) < 'And why does he want to obtain the command of a greater quantity of capital? Because he wants to employ that capital; and why does he want to employ that capital? because it is profitable to him to do so; it would not be profitable to him to do so *if the rate of discount destroyed his profit*'.

(This self-satisfied logician *assumes* that bills are discounted only in order to expand a business, and that the business is expanded because it is profitable. The first assumption is false. The ordinary businessman discounts his bills to anticipate the money from his capital and in this way keep the reproduction process flowing; not to expand his business or 'to raise' surplus capital by way of discount, but rather to compensate for the credit he gives with the credit he takes. And if he discounts to 'expand' his business on credit, leaving aside speculative prospects, he is a credit swindler who is doing it to cover one squalid deal with another, and not to raise profits but to get his hands on other people's capital.)

After Mr. Loyd has identified discounting in this way with the appropriation of a 'surplus quantity of capital' (instead of with the conversion of bills, which represent capital, into money) he immediately retracts his statement as soon as the thumbscrews are applied.

'3730. Merchants being engaged in business, must they not for a *certain period* carry on their operations in despite of any *temporary increase* in *the rate of discount?*' > Instead of answering this, the usurer sneers: < 'There is no doubt that in any particular transaction, if a person can get his command of capital at a low rate of interest rather than at a high rate of interest, taken in *that limited view of the matter*, that is convenient to him'. But for Ex-Loyd it is an 'extended view of the matter' when he always understands by 'capital' only his banker's capital, and therefore regards the man who discounts the bill as a man 'without capital', because his capital exists in the commodity form, or the money form of his capital is a bill which Mr. Loyd converts into another money form.

3732. 'With reference to the Act of 1844, can you state what has been about the average rate of interest in proportion to the amount of bullion in the bank; would it be a fact that when the amount of bullion has been about £9,000,000 or £10,000,000, the rate of interest has been six or seven percent and that when it has been £16,000,000 the rate of interest has been, say, from three to four percent?' (The questioner is trying to compel him to explain the rate of interest, as influenced by the mass of bullion in the bank, on the basis of the rate of interest as influenced by the 'value of capital'.) 'I do not apprehend that that is so ... but if it is, then I think we must take still more stringent measures than those adopted by the Act of 1844, because if it be true that the greater the store of bullion, the lower the rate of interest, we ought to set to work, according to that view of the matter, to increase the store of bullion to an indefinite amount, and then we should get the interest down to nothing'.

Mr. Cayley, undisturbed by this bad joke, continues:

'3733. If that be so, supposing that £5,000,000 of bullion was to be restored to the Bank, in the course of the next six months the bullion would then amount say to £16,000,000, and supposing that the rate of interest was thus to fall to three or four percent, how could it be stated that that fall in the rate of interest arose from a great decrease of the trade of the country? I said that the recent rise in the rate of interest, not that the fall in the rate of interest, was closely connected with the great increase in the trade of the country'. (But what Cayley said was this: if a rise in the rate of interest, together with a contraction of bullion, is a sign of an increase in business, then a fall in the rate of interest, together with an expansion of bullion, must be a sign of a decrease in trade, > thus showing that Ex-Loyd's remark leads to absurd consequences.)

< '3736. I observed your Lordship to say that *money* was the instrument for obtaining *capital*'. (This is precisely what is nonsensical, to see it only as an instrument: it is a *form* of capital.) 'Under a drain of bullion, is not the great strain, on the contrary, for *capitalists to obtain money?* No. *It is not the capitalists*, it is *those who are not capitalists who want to obtain money*; and why do they want to obtain money? ... Because through the money they obtain *the command of the capital of the capitalist* to carry on the business, of the persons *who are not capitalists*'. Here he explains in so many words that manufacturers and merchants are not capitalists, and the *capital of the capitalist* is moneyed capital.

'3737. Are not the parties who draw bills of exchange capitalists? The parties who draw bills of exchange may be, or may not be, capitalists'. Now he is stuck.

The question is then asked whether the bills of exchange the merchants draw do not represent the goods they have sold or shipped. He denies that these bills represent the value of commodities in the same way as banknotes represent bullion. This is rather impudent. (3740, 3741.)

'3742. Is not his [the merchant's] object to get money? No. Getting money is not the object in drawing the bill; *getting money is the object in discounting the bill*'. (Drawing the bill is transforming commodities into a form of credit money, just as discounting the bills is transforming this credit money into a different form (if this is banknotes). But here Mr. Loyd concedes that the object of discounting is *getting money*. Previously he had claimed that discounting was not to convert capital from one form into another, but to raise *surplus capital*.)

'3743. What is the great desire of the mercantile community, under a pressure of panic, such as you state to have occurred in 1825, 1837 and 1839; is their object to get possession of capital or of the legal tender? Their object is to get the command of capital to carry on their business'. (Their object is to obtain *means of payment* for bills on themselves that fall due, on account of the shortage of credit that has set in, and at the same time not to have to unload their commodities below their price. > If their securities are worthless < or they do not have any capital at all, of course they obtain capital with these means of payment, since they obtain *value* without an equivalent. The demand for *money as such* always consists simply to obtain convertibility for *value* out of the form of the commodity or bill (creditor's claim) into the form of money. Hence, even aside |325| from crises, the great distinction between raising capital through discounts and converting monetary claims from one form into the other.)

'3744. Will you be good enough to describe what you actually mean by the term '*capital*'? Capital consists of various commodities, by the means of which trade is carried on; there is fixed capital, and there is circulating capital. Your ships, your docks, your wharves etc. are fixed capital; your provisions, your clothes etc. are circulating capital'. > (What deep insight into 'capital'! And is it not shameless on the part of the discounters, who, in times of money pressure, are unable to sell their provisions and clothes, to want provisions and clothes, and even docks and wharves!)

< '3745. Is this country oppressed under a drain of bullion? Not in *any rational sense of the word*'. (And now comes the old Ricardian > shit) ... < 'In the natural state of things, the money of the world is distributed amongst the different countries of the world in certain proportions, those proportions being such that under that distribution the intercourse between any one country and all the other countries of the world jointly will be an intercourse of barter; but disturbing circumstances will arise to affect that distribution, and when those arise a certain portion of *the money of any given country* passes to other countries'.

'3746. Your Lordship now uses the term "*money*". I understood you before to say that it was a *loss of capital?* That what was a loss of capital?

3747. The export of bullion? *No*, I did not say so. If you treat bullion as capital, no doubt it is a loss of capital; it is parting with a certain proportion of those *precious metals* which constitute the *money of the world*.

3748. I understood your Lordship to say that an *alteration in the role of discount* was a mere sign of an alteration in the value of capital? I did.

3749. And that the *rate of discount generally alters* with the *state of the store of bullion* in the Bank of England? Yes; but I have already stated that the fluctuations of the rate of interest which arise from *an alteration in the quantity of money*' (what he therefore means here is the quantity of bullion) 'in a country are very small'.

'3750. Then, does your Lordship mean that there is *a less capital* than there was, when there is a more continuous yet *temporary increase in the rate of discount* than usual? Less, in one sense of the word. The *proportion* between capital' (just a moment ago it was money or bullion) (and before that it was the 'high rate of profit', coming from the extension, not the contraction of trade or capital) 'and the demand for it has altered; it may be by an increased demand, not by a diminution of the quantity of capital'.

'3751. What is the capital which you particularly allude to? That depends entirely *upon what the capital* is *which each person wants*. It is the capital which the country has at its command for conducting its business, and when that business is doubled there must be a great increase in the demand for the capital with which it is to be carried on'. (This lousy banker first doubles business activity and then the demand for the capital to carry it on with. All he ever has in mind is his 'business friend' who raises 'a greater quantity of capital' from Mr. Loyd 'to double his business'.) '*Capital is like any other commodity*' (according to Mr. Loyd capital is precisely the totality of commodities and nothing different from them) 'it will vary in its price' (hence commodities change their prices twice, once as commodities and then as capital) 'according to the supply and demand'.

'3752. The changes in the rate of discount are generally connected with the changes in the amount of gold which there is in the coffers of the Bank. Is it that capital to which your Lordship refers? No'.

'3753. Can your Lordship point to any instance in which there has been a large store of *capital* in the Bank of England connected with a high rate of discount? The Bank of England is not a place for the *deposit of capital*, it is a place for the *deposit of money*'.

'3754. Your Lordship has stated that the rate of interest depends upon the amount of capital; will you be kind enough to state what capital you mean, and whether you can point to any instance in which there has been a large store of bullion in the Bank, and at the same time a high rate of interest? It is very probable' (Aha!) 'that the *accumulation of bullion* in the Bank may be coincident with a low rate of interest, because a period in which there is a diminished demand for capital' (namely moneyed capital: 1844 and 1845 were times of prosperity) 'is a period during which, of course, the *means or instrument through which you command capital may accumulate*'.

'3755. Then you think that there is no connection between the rate of discount and the amount of bullion in the coffers of the Bank? There may be a connection, but there is not a connection of principle' (although his Bank Act of 1844 made it a principle of the Bank of England to regulate the rate of interest according to the quantity of bullion in its possession) 'there may be a coincidence of time'.

'3758. Do I rightly understand your Lordship to say, that the difficulty of merchants in this country, under a state of pressure, in consequence of a high rate of discount, is in getting *capital*, and not in getting *money?* You are putting two things together which I do not join in that form; their *difficulty is in getting capital*, and their *difficulty also is in getting money*. The difficulty of getting money, and the difficulty of getting capital, is *the same difficulty* taken in two *successive stages of its progress*'. Now the fish is caught again. The first difficulty is to discount a bill (or make a loan on a security.) It is a difficulty of converting capital, or a commercial representative of capital, into money. And this difficulty is expressed, disregarding other things, in the *high rate of interest*. But once the money has been received, where is the second difficulty? If it is only a question of paying, is there any difficulty in paying away money? And if it is a question of buying, who ever heard that in such times of pressure there existed any difficulty *in buying*? And in any case, assuming that this refers to the particular case of an increase in the price of corn, cotton etc., this difficulty would still not present itself in 'the *value* of the money', i.e. the rate of interest, but rather in the price of the commodity; and this difficulty is already solved in that our man now has the money he needs to buy it with.

'3760. But a higher rate of discount is an increased difficulty of getting money? It is an increased difficulty of getting money, but it is not *because you want to have the money*' > (just like someone who does not sell his commodities because he wants to play with his money. What a wise saying!) < 'it is only *the form*' (and this form goes into the banker's pocket) 'in which the increased *difficulty of getting capital*' > (even if this means that *commercial borrowing* has become more difficult, it is only an increased demand for money, or credit capital) < 'presents itself according to *the complicated relations of a civilised state*'. (!) > (Humbug!)

< 'Reply to question 3763: the banker is the go-between who receives deposits on the one side, and on the other applies those deposits, *entrusting* |325a| them, *in the form of capital*, to the hand of persons etc'

Here we finally have what *he* means by capital. He transforms money into *capital* by 'entrusting it' (a euphemism for 'lending it') out at interest. >

Discount Rate of the Bank of England. Bullion. Notes

1844

Notes held by public	*Reserve*	*Bullion*	*Minimum rate of interest*
7 Sept. £20,176,000	8,175,000	15,209,000	2½%
28 Dec. £19,123,000	9,077,000	14,878,000	

Until the end of 1844 the rate of interest generally remained at 2½%. The maximum rate never rose above 3%. The *aggregate* circulation (apart from the Bank of England) in England and Wales: September 1844: £7,496,859, December 1844: £7,529,401.

1845

Notes held by public	*Reserve*	*Bullion*	*Minimum rate of interest*
4 Jan. £19,669,000	8,418,000	14,802,000	2½%
1 Nov. £22,047,000	5,220,000	13,855,000	
29 Nov.	8,992,719	13,237,000	
1 Dec. £20,595,000	5,946,000	13,067,000	
31 Dec.£19.857.000	6,915,000	13,326,000	

The aggregate monthly circulation of country banks in January was £7,486,316. In December (and also in November) we found 3% as a minimum rate of interest and 5% as a maximum. In November bullion was falling. It was £13,855,000 on 1 November, and £13,237,000 on 29 November. At the beginning of December it was £13,067,000 and at the end it went back up to £13,326,000. At the beginning of January (4 January) private deposits amounted to £8,037,320. At the beginning of November they were £9,099,737.

1846

Notes held by public	*Reserve*	*Bullion*	*Minimum rate of interest*
3 Jan. £20,257,000	6,419,000	13,281,000	3½%

The rate of interest varied however. It rose to 5% and also fell occasionally to 3¼%. Bullion varied over the year between 14 and 13 million. The other securities were between 12½ and 23 million. Private deposits were £8,380,465. Private securities were £16,262,593.

1847

Notes of public	*Reserve*	*Bullion*	*Rate*	*Other securities*	*Private deposits*
2 Jan. £20,031,000	8,227,000	14,952,000	3%	15,071,820	7,903,959
16 Jan. £20,679,000	6,546,000	13,949,000	3½%	14,450,711	10,339,726
10 Apr. £20,403,000	2,833,000	9,867,000	5%	18,136,377	11,257,744
17 Apr. £20,243,000	2,558,000	9,330,000		17,111,001	10,004,699

From January until April the minimum rate was 4%. In April it fluctuated between 5 and 7%. It rose to 8% in October. By then the reserve was something over £1,000,000 and bullion was over £8,000,000.

1848

Notes of public	*Reserve*	*Bullion*	*Rate*	*Other securities*	*Private deposits*
1 Jan. £17,925,000	7,866,000	12,404,000	5%	16,989,221	8,523,108
29 Jan. £19,142,000	7,640,000	13,390,000	4%	14,321,905	10,768,087
17 June £17,377,000	9,975,000	14,169,000	3½%	11,148,869	9,157,381
4 Nov. £18,554,000	8,243,000	13,408,000	3%	10,805,561	10,795,395

1849

Notes of public	*Reserve*	*Bullion*	*Rate*	*Other securities*	*Private deposits*
6 Jan. £17,250,000	10,985,000	15,025,000	3%	10,825,470	8,814,702
24 Nov. £17,999,000	11,571,000	16,380,000	2½%	9,660,032	9,456,116

1850

Notes of public	*Reserve*	*Bullion*	*Rate*	*Other securities*	*Private deposits*
5 Jan. £18,257,000	12,011,000	17,020,000	2½%	11,691,026	9,735,268
28 Dec. £18,574,000	9,778,000	14,964,000	3%	14,459,608	9,147,039

1851

Notes of public	*Reserve*	*Bullion*	*Rate*	*Other securities*	*Private deposits*
4 Jan. £19,037,000	9,236,000	14,830,000	2½%	15,181,698	9,480,319
6 Sept. £19,363,000	8,344,000	14,290,000	3%	13,193,878	8,121,431

1852

Notes of public	*Reserve*	*Bullion*	*Rate*	*Other securities*	*Private deposits*
3 Jan. £19,285,000	11,707,000	17,558,000	2½%	12,214,222	9,371,117
10 Apr. £21,208,000	11,526,000	19,245,000	2%	11,225,844	13,992,932
14 Aug. £22,953,000	12,667,000	21,926,000	2%	10,740,159	13,088,533
24 Dec. £22,226,000	11,846,000	20,749,000	2%	14,135,952	12,264,343

1853

Notes of public	*Reserve*	*Bullion*	*Rate*	*Other securities*	*Private deposits*
8 Jan. £23,361,000	9,809,000	19,766,000	2½%	15,025,553	14,310,648
22 Jan. £23,474,000	9,444,000	19,405,000	3%	14,170,745	13,727,637
4 Jun. £23,423,000	8,367,000	18,254,000	3½%	14,632,359	12,902,839
3 Sept. £22,466,000	7,697,000	16,500,000	4%	14,546,194	11,017,313
17 Sept. £22,422,000	6,977,000	15,862,000	4½%	16,740,682	11,053,973
1 Oct. £22,773,000	6,259,000	15,613,000	5%	12,339,083	11,885,565

1854

Notes of public	*Reserve*	*Bullion*	*Rate*	*Other securities*	*Private deposits*
7 Jan. £21,348,000	7,801,000	15,831,000	5%	16,736,409	12,744,634
13 May £21,144,000	4,713,000	12,589,000	5½%	15,144,039	10,587,010
2 Dec. £19,617,000	7,627,000	13,870,000	5%	13,710,468	9,759,246

1855

Notes of public	*Reserve*	*Bullion*	*Rate*	*Other securities*	*Private deposits*
6 Jan. £19,682,000	7,307,000	13,667,000	5%	15,481,228	9,981,364
7 Apr. £19,812,000	8,580,000	15,079,000	4½%	13,655,995	11,396,875
16 June £19,536,000	11,814,000	18,061,000	3½%	12,399,704	13,307,714
8 Sept. £20,142,000	7,526,000	14,270,000	4%	16,637,227	10,970,353
15 Sept. £19,713,000	7,397,000	13,698,000	4½%	17,388,784	11,146,762
29 Sept. £20,173,000	6,195,000	12,939,000	5%	19,915,763	11,437,955
6 Oct. £20,292,000	5,473,000	12,279,000	5½%	19,791,293	10,837,643

The 5½% indicated under 6 October continued during the month. In November and December the rate rose to 6% for loans of 60 days and under, and for loans of over 60 days and under 95 days it was 7%. On 29 December £18,701,000 was held in notes by the public, £5,964,000 in *reserve* and £10,820,000 in *bullion.*

|325b|

1856

Notes by public	Reserve	Bullion	Rate	Other securities	Private deposits
5 Jan. £18,901,000	5,520,000	10,537,000	6–7%	19,871,874	12,607,840
2 Feb. £19,122,000	5,412,000	10,706,000	ditto	18,216,497	13,807,258
1 Mar. £18,935,000	5,493,000	10,600,000	ditto	19,490,762	13,918,279
5 Apr. £19,445,000	4,470,000	10,057,000	ditto	19,711,720	13,918,279
10 May £19,943,000	3,691,000	9,779,000	ditto	15,297,277	10,613,914
24 May £19,332,000	5,082,000	10,559,000	6%	15,377,046	11,472,481
31 May £19,554,000	5,687,000	11,385,000	5%	14,042,418	10,745,271
28 June £19,515,000	7,389,000	13,074,000	4½%	14,803,958	9,810,045
4 Oct. £20,926,000	3,776,000	10,784,000	5%	21,582,464	10,323,552
11 Oct. £20,543,000	3,521,000	10,140,000	6–7%	21,049,117	9,848,912
8 Nov. £20,239,000	3,151,000	9,530,000	6–7%	18,626,428	9,652,655
6 Dec. £19,195,000	5,151,000	10,486,000	6½%	17,389,715	9,297,193
20 Dec. £18,513,000	5,864,000	10,514,000	6%	17,654,460	9,493,093

The fellows gave out 1,847 *dividends* of 9% instead of 7% as previously, as well as two bonuses of 1% each. And in 1857 they raised the dividends to 11%.
(See the *Report from the Select Committee on Bank Acts,* 1857, Part Two [Appendices 6, pp. 62–7; 13, pp. 114–35; 14, pp. 136–47; and 15, p. 150])

< After Mr. Ex-Loyd has previously said that the change in the rate of discount, consequent on the change in the bullion amount (or quantity of money) was only *coincidental,* but the two were not essentially connected, he repeats:

'3805. When the *money* in the country is diminished by a drain, its value increases, and the Bank of England must conform to that alteration in the *value of money* (therefore in the value of money *as capital,* because its value in the correct sense remains the same) which is meant by the technical term of raising the *rate of interest*'.

'3819. I never confound the terms' (of money and capital, because he never distinguishes them). > (It would be just as possible to quibble over capital and commodity, in so far as the latter is a form of capital and in so far as it is merely a commodity when being bought and sold.)

< '3834. The very large *sum* which had to be paid' (for corn in 1847) '*which was in point of fact capital*, for the supply of the necessary provisions of the country'.

'3841. The variations in the rate of discount have no doubt a very close relation to the state of the reserve, because the state of the reserve is the indicator of the increase or the decrease of the quantity of money in the country; and in proportion as the money in the county increases or decreases, the value of that money will increase or decrease, and the bank rate of discount will conform to the change'.

'3842. There is an intimate connection between them' (the state of bullion and the reserve). Here he explains the changes in the rate of interest in terms of changes in the 'quantity of money'. > This is a lie, < because the reserve can decline because the money in the country increases. This is the case if the public accepts more notes and there is no decline in the bullion. But then the rate of interest rises, because the banking capital of the Bank of England is then limited by the Act of 1844. He cannot speak of this, because owing to the changes brought about in the accounting system by the Act of 1844 the two departments have almost nothing to do with each other. > On 10 May 1856, for example, the value of the *notes* in the hands of the public was £19,943,000, of the reserve £3,691,000, and of *bullion* £9,779,000. Total money: £29,722,000, made up of notes (except the reserve) and bullion.

On 11 October 1856, when interest was between 5, 6 and 7% (depending on the number of days), the notes in the hands of the public amounted to £20,543,000, the reserve £3,521,000 and the bullion £10,141,000. Total money: £30,683,000.

< '3859. *A high rate of profit* will always create a *great demand for capital*; a great demand for capital will *raise the value of it*'. Here at last we have his connection between the 'high rate of profit' and 'demand for capital'. Now for example in 1844–5 there was a high rate of profit in the cotton industry, because cotton was cheap and its price did not increase. Hence the value of capital (and according to Loyd's earlier remarks capital is what every person needs in his business), i.e., the *cotton*, did not become dearer for the spinners. Now the high rate of profit may have caused some manufacturers to borrow *money* in order to expand their businesses. Thus their demand for 'moneyed capital' would rise, but not for anything else.

'3889. Bullion may or may not be money, just as paper may or may not be a banknote'.

'3896. Do I correctly understand your Lordship, that you give up the argument which you used in 1840, that the fluctuations in the notes out of the Bank of England ought to conform to the fluctuations in the amount of bullion? I give it up so far as this – that now with the means of information which we possess, the notes out of the Bank of England must have added to them the notes which are in the banking reserve of the Bank of England'. (This is superlative. The arbitrary stipulation that the Bank print as many paper notes as it has in bullion, plus £14,000,000 more, naturally means that its note issue fluctuates with the fluctuation of its bullion. But since the present 'means of information which we possess' show clearly that the mass of notes that the Bank can print (and which the Issue Department transfers to the Banking Department) – that this *circulation*, according to the fluctuation of bullion, between the two departments of the Bank of England, does not determine the fluctuations in the circulation outside its doors, it follows that the latter now becomes completely immaterial, and this circulation between the two departments, whose difference from the real circulation is *shown by the reserve*, becomes all-important.) (It is important only because the reserve, as a consequence of the Act of 1844, indicates how close the Bank is to the legal maximum of its issue, and how much the depositors can obtain from the Banking Department.)

> '3944. Will you have the goodness to inform the Committee what you regard as the reserve of the Bank of England? That amount of the notes issued by the Issue Department which is not elsewhere than in the Bank of England'.

< The following is a brilliant example of the fellow's roguishness and bad faith:

'4243. Does the quantity of capital, do you think, oscillate from month to month to such a degree as to alter its value in the way exhibited of late years in the oscillations in the rate of discount? The relation between the demand and supply of capital may undoubtedly fluctuate, even within short periods ... if France tomorrow put out a notice that she wishes to borrow a very large loan, there is no doubt that it would immediately cause a great alteration in the *value of money*, that is to say in *the value of capital* in this country. 4245. If France announces that she wants suddenly ... thirty millions' worth of *commodities*, there will be a great demand for those commodities. There will be a great demand for *capital* to use the more scientific and simpler term. 4246. The *capital* which France would wish to buy with her loan is one thing, and the money with which she buys it is another; is it the money which alters in value or not? We seem to be reviving the old question, which I think is more fit for the chamber of a student than for this committee room'. > And with this he sneaks out of the room.

[The Role of Credit in Capitalist Production][78]

< |326| The *general observations* we have so far been induced to make concerning the credit system are as follows:

I. The necessity of its formation, to facilitate the *equalisation of the rate of profit*, or the movement of this equalisation, on which the whole of capitalist production depends.

II. The reduction in circulation costs.

1. A major cost of circulation is money itself, in so far as it is *itself value*. And this is economised on in three ways by credit.

A. In that money is completely dispensed with in a large number of transactions.

B. In that the circulation of the metallic or paper currency is accelerated.[79] (This partly coincides with what will be said under 2 below. On the one hand the acceleration is *technical*: i.e., with the > *real* circulation of commodities or the amount of business transactions < remaining the same, a smaller quantity of banknotes performs the *same* service. This is connected with the technique of banking. On the other hand, credit accelerates the velocity of the metamorphosis of commodities, and *therefore* the velocity of monetary circulation.)

C. In that gold money is replaced by paper.

---

78 [Title added by the MEGA editors. Editor]

79 'The average of notes in circulation at the Banque de France during the year 1812 was 106,538,000 francs; in 1818: 101,205,000 francs, whereas the *movement* of the currency, or the annual aggregate of disbursements and receipts upon all accounts was, in 1812, 2,837,712,000 francs; in 1818, 9,665,030,000 francs. The activity of the currency in France, therefore, during 1818, as compared with its activity in 1812, was in the proportion of three to one. The great regulator of the velocity of circulation is credit ... This explains why a severe pressure upon the money market is generally coincident with a *full* circulation'. (*The Currency Theory* 1845, p. 65.) 'Between September 1833 and September 1843 nearly 300 issue banks were added to the total throughout Great Britain; the result was a reduction in the circulation of two and a half million: it was £36,035,244 at the end of September 1833 and £33,518,554 at the end of September 1843'. (*The Currency Theory* 1845, p. 53.) 'The prodigious activity of Scottish circulation enables it, with £100, to effect the same quantity of monetary transactions, which in England it requires £420 to accomplish' (op. cit., p. 55). (This last point refers only to the technical side of the operations.)

2. *Acceleration, through credit,* of the various phases of circulation or commodity metamorphosis, then an acceleration of the metamorphosis of capital and hence an acceleration of the overall reproduction process. (On the other hand, credit also allows the acts of buying and selling to take a longer time, and hence serves as a basis for speculation.) Contraction of the reserve fund, which can be viewed in two ways: on the one hand as a reduction in the currency, and on the other hand as restriction of the part of the capital which must always be in existence in the form of money.[80]

III. *The formation of joint-stock companies*. This involves:

1. A tremendous expansion in the scale of production, and enterprises which would be impossible for individual capitals; at the same time, enterprises that were previously *governmental* become *social*;

2. Capital, which is inherently based on a social mode of production and presupposes a social concentration of the means of production and of labour-powers, now receives the form of *social capital* (capital of directly associated individuals) as opposed to *private capital*, and its enterprises appear as social enterprises as opposed to private ones. This is the abolition [*Aufhebung*] of capital as private property *within* the confines of the capitalist mode of production itself.

3. The transformation of the actually *functioning capitalists* into mere *managers* (of other people's capital) and of the *owners of capital* into mere property-owners, mere *moneyed capitalists*, even if the dividends they draw include both interest and profit of enterprise, i.e., the *total profit* (for the manager's salary is or should be simply the wage for a certain kind of skilled labour, finding its level in the labour market like all other sorts of labour) is still drawn only in the form of interest, i.e., as a mere *reward for capital ownership*, which is now as completely separated from its function in the actual production process as this function, in the person of the manager, is from capital ownership. Profit thus appears (and no longer just the part of it, the *interest*, which obtains its justification from the *profit* of the borrower) as simply the appropriation of other people's surplus labour, arising from the transformation of the means of production into capital, i.e., from their estrangement [*Entfremdung*]; from their opposition, as the property of another, vis-à-vis the actual producers, which includes all individuals from the manager down to the lowliest wage-labourer. In joint-stock companies, the function is separated from capital ownership, so

80 'Before the establishment of the banks ... the *amount of capital* withdrawn for the *purposes of currency* was greater, at all times, than the actual circulation of commodities required'. (*The Economist*, 1845, p. 238.)

labour is also completely separated from ownership of the means of production and the surplus labour. This result of capitalist production in its highest development is a necessary point of transition towards the transformation of capital back into the property of the producers, but no longer as the private property of individual producers, but rather as their property as associated producers, as directly social property. It is furthermore a point of transition towards the transformation of all functions formerly bound up with capital ownership in the reproduction process into *simple* functions of the associated producers, into social functions. Before we go on, the following economically important fact must be noted. Since *profit* here simply assumes the form of interest, enterprises that *merely yield an interest* are possible, and this is one of the reasons that delay the *fall in the general rate of profit*, since these enterprises, where the constant capital stands in such a tremendous ratio to the variable, do not necessarily go into the equalisation of the general rate of profit. This is the *abolition of the capitalist mode of production within the capitalist mode of production*, and hence it is a self-abolishing contradiction, which presents itself *prima facie* as a mere point of transition to a *new* mode of production. It presents itself as such a contradiction even in appearance. It establishes *monopolies* in certain spheres and hence provokes *state intervention*. It reproduces a *new financial aristocracy*, a new pack of parasites in the guise of company promoters and directors (merely *nominal* managers); an entire system of swindling and cheating with respect to the issue of shares and dealings in shares. It is private production unchecked by private ownership.|327| Apart from the joint-stock system – which is an abolition of capitalist private industry on the basis of the *capitalist system* itself, and which destroys private industry to the same degree that it spreads and takes over new spheres of production – credit offers the individual capitalist or reputed capitalist an absolute command over *other people's capital* and *other people's property*, within certain limits (and, through this, command over other people's labour.)[81] It is disposal over social capital, rather

81 See for example the list of bankruptcies for 1857 in *The Times*, and compare the 'personal' assets of the bankrupts with their 'liabilities'. 'The truth is that the power of purchase by persons having capital and credit is much beyond anything that those who are unacquainted practically with speculative markets have any idea of'. (Tooke 1844, p. 79.) 'A person having the repute of capital enough for his regular business, and enjoying good credit in his trade, if he takes a sanguine view of the prospect of a rise of price of the article in which he deals, and is favoured by circumstances in the outset and progress of his speculation, may effect purchases to an extent perfectly enormous compared with his capital'. (Tooke 1844, p. 136.) 'The manufacturers, merchants, bankers etc. carry on operations much

than his own, that gives him command over social labour. The actual capital that someone possesses, or their 'reputed capital', now becomes the basis of a superstructure of credit. (This is especially the case in wholesale trade, and the greater part of the national wealth passes through this trade.) All standards of measurement, all explanatory reasons that were still more or less justified within the capitalist mode of production now vanish. What the trader on credit *risks* is social property, not his own. Equally absurd now is any talk about *saving*, since what is demanded now is that others should save on his behalf; while his luxurious style of living makes it derisory to talk of *abstinence*. Conceptions that still had a certain meaning at a less developed stage of capitalist production now become completely meaningless. Success and failure lead in both cases to the concentration of capital, and *therefore to expropriation*, on the most enormous scale. Expropriation now extends from the immediate producers to the small and medium capitalists themselves. This expropriation is the starting-point of the capitalist mode of production, the goal of which is to carry it through to completion, and even, in the final analysis, to expropriate all individuals from the means of production – which, with the development of social production, ceases to be means of private production and products of private industry, and can only remain means of production in the hands of the associated producers, hence their social property, just as they are their social product. But within the capitalist system itself this expropriation takes the *antithetical* form of the appropriation of social property by a few; and credit gives these few ever more the character of simple adventurers. Since ownership now exists in the form of shares, its movement and transfer become simply the result of stock-exchange dealings, where little fishes are gobbled up by sharks, and sheep by ravening wolves. In the joint-stock system, there is already a conflict with this old form, but the joint-stock system itself, *within* its capitalist limits, leads to a renewed development of the opposition between the character of wealth as something social and wealth as a private affair. The *cooperative factories* run by workers themselves are, within the old form, the first examples of the emergence of a new form, although they naturally reproduce, and they must reproduce, in all cases, in their present organisation, all the defects of the existing system. But the opposition between capital and labour is abolished here *within* the factories, even if at first only in the form that the workers in association are their own capitalist, i.e., they use the means

---

beyond those which the use of their own capital alone would enable them to do ... Capital is rather the foundation upon which a good credit is built than the limit of the transactions of any commercial establishment'. (*The Economist*, 1847, p. 1333.)

of production to valorise their own labour. These factories show how, at a certain stage of development of the material forces of production, and of the social forms of production corresponding to them, a new mode of production develops and is formed naturally out of the old one. Without the factory system that arises from the capitalist mode of production, cooperative factories could not develop. Nor could they do so without the credit system that has grown out of the same mode of production. This credit system, since it forms the principal basis for the gradual transformation of capitalist private enterprises into capitalist joint-stock companies, presents in the same way the means for the gradual extension of cooperative enterprises on a more or less national scale. Capitalist joint-stock companies as much as cooperative factories should be viewed as forms of transition from the capitalist mode of production to the *associated* one, except that in one case the opposition is abolished in a negative way and in the other in a positive way.

Up till now we have considered the development of the credit system, and the *latent* abolition of capital ownership contained within it, principally in relation to productive capital. In what follows we shall go over to considering *interest-bearing* capital as such (both the impact of the credit system on it and the form that it assumes in this connection). With respect to this, in general, a few more specifically economic comments remain to be made.

But first of all this:

If the credit system appears as the principal lever of overproduction and excessive speculation in commerce, this is simply because the reproduction process, which is elastic by nature, is now forced to its extreme limit; and this is because a great part of the social capital is applied by those who are *not its owners*, and who therefore *undertake risks* in quite a different way from owners who, when they function on their own behalf, anxiously weigh up the limits of their private capital. This only goes to show how the *valorisation* of capital founded on the *antithetical* character of capitalist production permits the real, free development of the productive forces only up to a *certain point*, which the credit system constantly breaks through.[82] Hence the credit system accelerates the material development of the productive forces and the creation of the world market, |328| which is > up to a certain degree – until the material foundations of the new mode of production have been established – < the *historic task* of the capitalist mode of production. At the same time, credit accelerates the violent outbreaks of this contradiction, crises, and with these the elements of dissolution of the old mode of production.

---

82 Chalmers 1832.

The credit system has a dual character immanent in it: on the one hand it develops the driving force of the capitalist mode of production, enrichment by the exploitation of other people's labour, into the purest and most colossal system of swindling and gambling, and the exploitation of social wealth by a few; on the other hand it constitutes the form of transition towards a new mode of production. It is this dual character that gives the principal spokesmen for credit, from Law through to Isaac Péreire, their nicely mixed character as both swindlers and prophets.

The distinction between *circulation* and *capital*, as made by Tooke and Wilson, in which connection the distinctions between means of circulation as coin, money, money capital and interest-bearing capital (or *moneyed capital*, as the English put it) are lumped together haphazardly, comes down to two things:

1)

Circulation I is circulation of coins (money), in so far as it mediates the *expenditure of revenue*, hence the commerce between individual consumers and *retail traders*, a category in which we include all merchants who sell to the *consumer* (to the individual consumer as distinguished from the productive consumer or producer.) Here money circulates in the function of *coin*, even though it constantly *replaces capital*. A certain part of the money of a country is always devoted to this function, however, although this quantity consists of constantly changing constituent parts > of the total money in circulation. < On the other hand, in so far as money mediates the *transfer of capital*, whether as *means of purchase* (means of circulation) or *means of payment*, it is *capital*. Thus it is neither the function of means of purchase nor that of means of payment which distinguishes it from coin; for money can also function as *means of purchase* between dealers and dealers, in so far as they buy things from each other with cash, and it can even function between dealer and consumer as *means of payment* if credit is given, the revenue being consumed first and only paid for afterwards. The difference is that in the second case this money does not just *replace capital* for one party (the *seller*), but is also spent as *capital* by the other party (the *buyer*). The distinction is in fact not one between the *money form* of revenue and the *money form* of capital, but between *circulation* and *capital*, for a definite quantity of money *circulates* to mediate the transactions between the dealers, just as it does in the first function. Confusions of various kinds are now brought into the picture:

1. through confusing functional characteristics,

2. through bringing in the question of the overall quantity of money circulating in both the different functions, and

3. through bringing in the question of the *relative proportions* of the *quantities of currency* in the two functions, and hence in the two spheres of the reproduction process. To deal first with number 1, the confusion is already present in Tooke's expression, that money is *circulation* (currency) in one form and *capital* in the other form.[83] In so far as money serves for one or the other of these functions, whether for realising revenue or for transferring capital, it functions in buying or selling or in payment, as means of purchase or payment, and in the broad sense of the term as *means of circulation*. The further characteristic that it may have in the *accounts* of its spender or receiver, that it represents either capital or revenue for him, alters absolutely nothing here, and this too can be shown *in two ways*. Although the kinds of money circulating in the two spheres are different, the same piece of money, for instance a £5 note, moves from one sphere to the other and performs both functions in turn; this is unavoidable simply because the retail trader can give *his* capital its money form only in the form of the coin that he receives from his buyers. We can assume that small change proper > constantly remains in the possession of the grocer; < he constantly uses it to give change and constantly receives it back again from his customers in payment. But he also receives *money*, i.e., coin, in the metal that is a measure of value, hence in England > half or whole < sovereigns or banknotes, particularly banknotes of lower denominations, such as five pound and ten pound notes. He deposits these gold coins and notes with his banker every day of the week, and he pays for his purchases with cheques on his bank deposit. But the same sovereigns, half sovereigns and notes are just as constantly withdrawn from the bank by the public as a whole in their capacity as consumers, as the money form of their revenue, either directly or indirectly, and thus they constantly flow back to the grocer, for whom they realise a part of his capital afresh plus revenue. |329| (This last circumstance is important, and is completely overlooked by Tooke. Only in so far as money is *laid out* as money capital, at the beginning of the process, does capital value exist as such. The commodity contains capital plus surplus, hence it is capital with its source of revenue incorporated into it.)

---

83 [See the quotation from Tooke on p. 317 of Marx's manuscript, note 66 (at p. 504). Translator]

Secondly, however, for the grocer himself, the currency replaces *his capital*, it represents his capital in its monetary form.

To transform the distinction between circulation as circulation of revenue and as circulation of capital into a distinction between *circulation* and *capital*, is a piece of nonsense. This kind of jargon derives from the fact that Tooke simply adopts the point of view of the *issuing banker*, who provides the banknotes. The portion of his banknotes which is continuously in the hands of the public (even if this always consists of different individual banknotes) and functions as *means of circulation* costs him nothing apart from paper and printing costs. The notes are circulating certificates of indebtedness (bills of exchange) made out in his own name, which bring in money to him and thus form a means of valorising his capital. But they are not the same as *his capital* (which may be his own or borrowed). And this is the origin of the distinction between *circulation* and *capital*, which has nothing to do with defining the concepts as such, let alone Tooke's suggested definition.

The particular character of money – whether it functions as the money form of revenue or of capital – does not at first affect its character as *means of circulation*. It retains this character whether it performs one function or the other. If the money appears as the money form of revenue, however, it functions more as a means of circulation in the strict sense (coin, means of purchase), on account of the fragmentation of these purchases and sales, and because the majority of the revenue spenders, the workers, can buy relatively little on credit; while in the world of trade and commerce, where the circulating medium is the money form of capital, money functions principally as *means of payment*, partly on account of concentration and partly on account of the prevailing credit system. But the distinction between money as *means of payment* and money as *means of purchase* (medium of circulation) is a distinction within money itself, not a distinction between *money* and *capital*. If more copper and silver circulates in the retail trade, and in the wholesale trade more gold, this does not make the distinction between silver and copper on the one hand and gold on the other into a distinction between *circulation* and *capital*.

On number 2, in so far as money circulates, whether as means of purchase or means of payment – irrespective of which of the two spheres it circulates in, and quite independently of its function of turning revenue or capital into gold or into silver – the laws developed earlier in considering simple commodity circulation are valid for the *quantity* of money circulating. In both cases the *amount of money in circulation*, the amount of *currency*, is determined by the same factors, namely the *velocity of circulation*, i.e., the number of times the same function of means of purchase and payment is repeated by *the same* piece of money in a given period of time; the *mass* of simultaneous sale and purchases, or payments; the *sum of the prices* of the commodities circulating; and finally the *payment balances* that have to be settled at the same time. Whether the money functioning in this way represents capital or revenue for those who pay it and receive it is absolutely without any bearing on the matter. Its quantity is determined by its function as means of purchase and payment.

On number 3, although the two spheres of circulation have an *inner* connection, since on the one hand the amount of revenue to be spent expresses the scale of consumption, while on the other hand the amount of capital circulating in production and trade expresses > the general *state* of the business, < the sale and speed of the reproduction process, *the same* factors have different effects, and even work in *opposite* directions on the *quantity* of money circulating in the two functions or the two spheres, or the *quantity of circulation*, as the English bankers describe the amount of currency. And this gives a new occasion for Tooke's nonsensical distinction between *circulation* and *capital*. (The fact that the fellows who support the currency theory confuse two disparate things is in no way an adequate reason for presenting this as a conceptual distinction.)

In *times of prosperity*, of great expansion, when the reproduction process exhibits rapidity and energy, the workers are fully employed. In most cases there is also a rise in wages, which to some extent balances the fall in wages *below* the average level in the other phases of the commercial cycle. In addition to this, revenues grow significantly and consumption rises. This phase is also accompanied by a rise in the prices in different branches, etc., > (as well as a rise in the cash outlays for the payment of customs dues etc.)

< There is also a growth in the *quantity* of the *currency*, but only within *certain* limits, since the greater velocity of circulation limits the growth in the quantity of the currency. In so far as the part of the revenue that consists of wages is always originally advanced in the form of *variable capital*, and indeed in the money form, the section of capital requires more money for its circulation in times of prosperity. But we must not count this twice; |330| firstly as money needed to circulate the variable capital and secondly as money needed to circulate the workers' revenue. The money paid to the workers as wages is spent in the retail trade and returns with more or less weekly regularity to the banker in the deposits of the shopkeeper, after it has mediated all kinds of intermediate transactions in smaller circuits. In times of prosperity the *return* of money is easy for the productive capitalists, and so their need for monetary accommodation is not increased by their having to pay more in wages, and to use more money for the circulation of their variable capital.

As far as concerns the circulation needed for transfers of capital, that is to say transfers simply between the capitalists themselves, this period of prosperity is at the same time a period of elastic and easy credit. The velocity of this circulation is regulated directly by credit, and the amount of the circulating medium required to settle payments (and even to make cash purchases) undergoes a relative decline. It may expand in absolute terms, but it always decreases relatively, compared with the expansion of the reproduction process. A larger mass of payments, on the one hand, is settled without any intervention of money; on the other hand, given the great vigour of the process, there is a quicker movement of the same quantities of money, whether in the function of means of purchase or means of payment. The same amount of money mediates the returns of a greater number of individual capitals.

On the whole, the currency appears to be 'full' in such periods, although Division II contracts, while Division I expands.

(The returns express the transformation of commodity capital back into money, M – C – M′, as we saw when considering the circulation process. Credit makes the return independent of the actual return, whether we are dealing with the productive capitalist or with the merchant. Each of them sells on credit; his commodity is thus alienated before it is transformed back into money for him, hence before it returns to him in the money form. On the other hand, each of them buys on credit, and thus the value of his commodity has been transformed back for him either into productive capital or commodity capital before this value has actually been transformed into money. But in such times of prosperity the returns are available before the bill falls due and the time for payment arrives. The grocer is certain to pay the wholesaler, the latter the producer, and the producer the importer, etc. The *appearance* of rapid and certain returns always persists for a certain period of time after the reality has come to an end, by virtue of the *credit* that has already been given, since the credit returns stand in for the real returns. The banks start to scent danger as soon as their clients deposit more bills of exchange with them than money. See the evidence of the Liverpool bank director.)[84]

In the *period of adversity*, the opposite is the case. Circulation number I *contracts*. (Prices fall, wages and the quantity of transactions also fall, etc.) With the decline in credit, the need for *monetary accommodation* increases, a point which we shall immediately go into in more detail.

But first of all, I must repeat what I remarked earlier: 'In periods of expanding credit, the velocity of monetary circulation increases more quickly than the

84 [As quoted below, on p. 370 of Marx's manuscript. Translator]

prices of commodities, whereas in periods of falling credit the prices of commodities fall more slowly than the velocity of circulation'.[85]

There can be no doubt at all that with the decline in credit which goes together with a stagnation in the reproduction process, the *amount of circulation* required for number I declines, whereas that for number II increases. It remains to be investigated, however, how far this is identical with the assertions of Fullarton and others to the effect that:

'A *demand for capital on loan* and a demand for additional circulation are quite distinct things, and not often found associated'.[86]

It is clear from the outset that in the first case, where the *quantity of the circulating medium* must grow, there is a growing demand for it. But it is equally clear that if a manufacturer draws more out of the wealth he has deposited with a banker in sovereigns or notes because he has to spend more capital in the money form, it is not his *demand for capital* that is growing but only his demand for this particular *form* of expending his capital. This demand relates only to the technical form in which he *casts* his capital into circulation. In just the same way, given the differential development of the credit system, the same *variable capital*, for example, the same *amount of wages*, |331| requires a greater quantity of currency in one country than in another; in England, for example, more than in Scotland, in Germany more

---

85 Marx 1859, pp. 83–4 [English version: MECW 29, 1987, p. 340.]

86 Fullarton 1845, p. 82. 'It is a great error, indeed, to imagine that the demand for *pecuniary accommodation*' (that is, for the loan of capital) 'is identical with a demand for additional means of circulation, or even that the two are frequently associated'. (Fullarton 1845, p. 97.) That 'a demand for pecuniary accommodation' need in no way be identical with a 'demand for gold' (which Wilson, Tooke and the others call *capital*) can be seen from the following evidence of Mr. Weguelin, Governor of the Bank of England:

'The discounting of bills to that extent' (namely one million a day for three successive days) 'would not reduce the *reserve* unless the public demanded a greater amount of active circulation. The *notes issued on the discount of bills* would be returned through the medium of the bankers and through deposits. Unless these transactions were for the purpose of exporting bullion, and unless there were an amount of internal panic which induced people to lock up their notes, and not to pay them into the hands of the bankers, the reserve would not be affected by the magnitudes of the transaction'. > (Mere change in the form of the liabilities, etc.) < (*Report on the Bank Acts*, 1857, evidence, No. 241.)

'The Bank may discount a million and a half a day, and that is done constantly, without its reserve being in the slightest degree affected, the notes coming back as *deposits*, and no other alteration taking place than the *mere transfer from one account to another*'. (*Report on the Bank Acts* 1857, No. 500.) The notes serve here merely as means for the *transfer of credit*.

than in England. For farmers, in another example, *the same capital* (active in the reproduction process) requires different amounts of money to perform its functions > in different seasons. But the opposition that Fullarton makes is incorrect.

It is not the amount of the *demand for loans* that distinguishes the period of prosperity from the period of adversity, but rather the *facility* with which this demand for loans is satisfied. It is in fact precisely the tremendous development of the credit system, and therefore also the demand and supply of loans, during the period of prosperity, which brings about the pressure that occurs during the period of adversity. Thus it is not a difference in the *quantitative extent of the demand for loans* that characterises the two periods!

As we have noted before, the two periods are distinguished in the first place by the fact that in the period of prosperity it is the demand for *circulation* (currency) between dealers and consumers, and in the period of adversity it is the demand for *circulation* for the transactions between capitalists which predominates. In the period of reaction the first declines while the second increases.

What determines the views of Fullarton and others is the phenomenon that at such times, while the securities in the hands of the Bank of England increase, its note circulation declines, and vice versa.[87] The volume of securities expresses

87 It is important to set down the whole of the passage from Fullarton here, because it also demonstrates what he understands by '*capital*'. < 'A very slight examination of the Parliamentary Returns may convince any one, that the *securities* in the Bank of England fluctuate more frequently in an opposite direction to its circulation than in concert with it, and that the example, therefore, of that great establishment furnishes no exception to the doctrine so strongly pressed by the country bankers, to the effect that no bank can enlarge its circulation, *if that circulation* be *already adequate to the purposes to which a banknote currency is commonly applied*; but that *every addition to its advances*, after that limit is passed, *must be made from its capital*, and supplied by the *sale of some of its securities in reserve*, or by *abstinence from further investment in such securities*'. > (So what does Fullarton mean by 'capital' here? It is when the bank can no longer make advances *in promises to pay*, which of course cost it nothing. But with what does it make these advances? With the proceeds from the *sale of securities in reserve* ('securities in reserve' are understood to be government paper, share certificates and other interest-bearing paper). And what does it sell these securities for? For money, gold or banknotes (in so far as the latter are legal tender, as those of the Bank of England are). What it advances, therefore, is in all circumstances *money*. But this money now represents a part of its capital. If it advances gold, this is self-evident. If notes, then these notes now represent capital, since the bank has parted with a real value in exchange, the interest-bearing papers. In the case

the *volume of pecuniary accommodation*, of discounted bills of exchange > (and loans against easily convertible securities. Sometimes the Bank *lends* against long bills, makes advance on them; this happened in 1847 with the bills associated with the East India trade.)

Since the Bank of England makes all loans and discounts in its own notes, we need to ask what becomes of these notes? The situation is different for the private banks, because in such cases they can replace their own notes with Bank of England notes.

< To start with, if the 'demand for pecuniary accommodation' arises out of an adverse balance of payments, and, consequently, a drain of bullion, the matter is very simple. > The bills are discounted against banknotes. < The banknotes are exchanged against bullion and the bullion is exported. It is the same thing as if the Bank had paid bullion directly, without the mediation of notes, as it does in discounting bills of exchange. A rising demand of this kind – and in certain cases it reaches seven to ten million pounds sterling – naturally does not add a single five pound note to the country's internal circulation. If it is said that the bank advances *capital* in this case and not *the means*

---

of the private banks, the notes that accrue to them by the sale of securities can only be Bank of England notes, since others are not accepted in payment for securities. But if it is the Bank of England itself, then those of its own notes that it retains cost it capital, i.e., interest-bearing paper. Besides, it thereby withdraws its own notes from circulation. > (It can only reissue the same notes again or replacements for them if the *maximum level* of their circulation has not been reached. < If it reissues these notes again they now represent capital.) > But how they can get into this position of selling their securities is something we must investigate later. For private bankers, the additional phrase '*or by abstinence from further investment in such securities*' has no other meaning than that they are now unable to invest the Bank of England notes or gold they would otherwise have invested in such securities. They themselves cannot buy *securities* with their own notes. The Bank of England, if it is compelled to sell securities in order to get back its own notes or to get back gold, cannot of course buy securities with its notes. < In all these circumstances, the word *capital* is used only in the banking sense, where it means that the banker is forced to lend more than just his credit.) ... 'On the 3rd. January 1837, when the resources of the Bank were strained to the uttermost to sustain credit and meet the difficulties of the money market, we find its *advances on loan and discount* carried to the *enormous sum of £17,022,000*, an amount scarcely known since the war, and almost equal to the entire aggregate issues which, in the meanwhile, remain unmoved at so low a point as £17,076,000! On the other hand, we have on the 4th. of June 1833 a circulation of £18,892,000 with a return of private securities in hand, nearly if not the very lowest on record for the last half century, amounting to no more than £972,000!' (Fullarton 1845, pp. 97–8.)

of circulation, this has a double meaning. Firstly, that it does not advance *credit* but *real value*, a part of its own capital or the *capital* deposited with it. Secondly, that it advances money not for internal circulation but rather for international circulation, *world money*, and in this case the money must always exist in its form as hoard, in its *metallic embodiment*; in the form in which it is not only the form of value but is equal to the value whose money form it is.

Even though this gold now represents *capital*, banking capital or commercial capital, whether for the Bank, the exporting merchant or the bullion dealer, the demand does not arise for it as *capital*, but rather as the absolute form of *money* capital. It arises in the very same moment as the foreign markets are flooded with unrealisable English *commodity capital*. What is demanded is not capital as capital but rather capital as *money*, in the form in which *money* is a commodity on the general world market; and this is its original form as precious metal. The drain of gold is therefore not '*a mere question of capital*' as Fullarton, Tooke, etc., say. It is rather a question of *money*, > although this is money with a specific function. That it is *not* a question of 'internal circulation', as the currency fellows think, does not mean, as Fullarton and co. think, that it is a mere '*question of capital*'. It is a question of money < in the form in which money is an *international means of payment*. 'Whether ... *capital* is transmitted in merchandise or in specie, is a point which in no way affects the nature of the transaction',[88] but it very much affects the circumstance whether a drain takes place or not. It is 'transmitted in specie' because it cannot be 'transmitted in merchandise', or not without a very major loss. The anxiety that the modern banking system has when faced with a 'drain of bullion' goes beyond anything that the Monetary System ever dreamed of, even though for it bullion was the only true measure of wealth. Let us take for example the following reply by the Governor of the Bank of England, [James] Morris, to a question from the parliamentary committee: |332| 3846: 'When I spoke of the depreciation of stocks and fixed capital, are you not aware that all property invested in stocks and produce of every description was depreciated in the same way; that raw cotton, raw silk, and unmanufactured wool were sent to the continent at the same depreciated price, and that sugar, coffee, and tea were sacrificed as at forced sales? It was inevitable that the country should make a considerable sacrifice for the purpose of meeting the efflux of bullion which had taken place in consequence of the large importation of food'. 3848: 'Do you not think it would have been better to trench upon the £8 million lying in the coffers of the

88 Fullarton 1845, p. 131.

Bank than to have endeavoured to get the gold back again at such a sacrifice? No, I do not'.[89] Here *gold* is taken as the only true wealth.

(Tooke's discovery that 'with only one or two exceptions, and those admitting of satisfactory explanation, *every remarkable fall of the exchange*, followed by a drain of gold, that has occurred during the last half-century, has been coincident throughout with a comparatively low state of the circulating medium, and vice versa' {Fullarton 1845, p. 121} shows that these drains of gold take place in most cases as the 'signal of a collapse already commenced', as 'an indication of *overstocked markets*, of a *cessation of the foreign demand for our productions*, of *delayed returns*, and as the necessary sequel of all these, of *commercial discredit*, manufactories shut up, artisans starving, and a general stagnation of industry and enterprise'. {Fullarton 1845, p. 129} This is also of course the best refutation of the currency people's contention that 'a full circulation' drives out bullion and 'a low circulation' attracts it. > For us, however, the passage is particularly noteworthy as it shows the influence of bullion. < On the other hand, although it is generally in periods of prosperity that a full bullion reserve *is present*, this treasure is always built up in the quiescent and stagnant period that follows the storm.)

But if we leave aside for now the drains of bullion (the whole wisdom about which amounts to the statement that the demand for *international means of circulation and payment* is different from the *demand* for *internal means of circulation and payment* {which is why it goes without saying that 'the existence of a drain does not necessarily imply any diminution of the internal demand for circulation' (Fullarton 1845, p. 112)}, and that the *sending abroad* of precious metals > (putting them into international circulation) < is not the same as putting notes or coin into internal circulation (in any case I have already shown previously that the *movement of the hoard*, which is set aside as a reserve fund for international payments, has in and of itself nothing to do with the movement of money as means of circulation). However, there is a certain complication involved here, in that this reserve fund > serves at the same time as a guarantee of the convertibility of notes and deposits, i.e., that < the *various functions of the hoard*, which I developed from the nature of money – its function as a reserve fund of *means of payment* (for payments that fall due at home); as a *reserve fund* for currency; and finally as a *reserve fund* for world money – are all imposed upon a *single reserve fund*.

89 *First Report* 1848. > The [distress] of the Bank was of course somewhat alleviated by the fact that in 1847, as also in 1857, it did excellent business as a result of the crisis, and its dividends rose above 9 percent in the first case, and 11 percent in the second. <

It follows from this that in certain circumstances an internal drain may be combined with an external drain. Apart from this, an additional function is imposed, > which by no means follows from the nature of the other functions the hoard has to perform in its quality of a reserve fund < namely it has to serve as a *fund guaranteeing convertibility*, in countries where the credit system and credit money are developed. On top of all this, finally, we have (1) the concentration of the national reserve fund in a single principal bank, and (2) its reduction to the minimum possible level. Hence Fullarton's lament: 'And one cannot contemplate the perfect silence and facility with which variations of the exchange usually pass off in continental countries, compared with the state of feverish disquiet and alarm always produced in England whenever the treasure in the Bank seems to be at all approaching to exhaustion, without being struck with the great advantage in this respect which a metallic currency possesses'. (Fullarton 1845, p. 143).) But if we leave aside drains of bullion, |333| how can a bank such as the Bank of England increase its securities (i.e., the amount of its pecuniary accommodation) without increasing its note issue?

All notes *outside the bank's premises*, whether circulating, or dormant in private hoards, are, in respect to the bank itself, in *circulation*, i.e., not held by the bank. The bank's notes issued against securities must therefore flow back to it again, in order not to increase the amount of circulation. This reflux can take place in two ways.

Firstly, the bank pays notes to A against securities; A uses these to pay B for a bill of exchange that falls due; and B deposits the notes again with the bank. The issue of these notes is thus at an end, but the loan remains. ('The loan remains, and the currency, if not wanted, finds its way back to the issuer') (Fullarton 1845, p. 97.) > What the bank advanced to A was not *capital*, but *notes*; < but the same notes have now returned to it; while it is a debtor to B for the sum of value expressed in these notes, and B therefore has at his disposal a corresponding part of the bank's capital. > From the point of view of its ledger, the transaction amounts to an advance of the capital to A. But the ledger's point of view does not affect the nature of the transaction. And that is, that what A needed was not *capital*, but the '*means of payment*' to B, and that the note the bank issued has functioned as *means of payment*, and that the pressure for pecuniary accommodation is by no means a demand for capital, but a *demand* for *means of payment*, although in the last resort the bank cannot satisfy the demand by adding to the quantity in circulation a number of notes to that value, but only by becoming indebted to B to a certain amount of value, hence placing the advance on the account of its own capital.

< *Secondly*. A pays to B, and either B himself or C, the person to whom he again pays these notes, uses the notes to pay bills due to the bank, directly or

indirectly. In this case the bank is paid with its own notes. Since the transaction is completed in this way (until A's repayment to the bank) > it cannot be said that the bank has in any sense advanced capital. It has advanced notes, which serve A as *means of payment* to B, and which serve B as means of payment to the bank. For A, however, what is at stake here is *capital* (in the sense of being a *sum of value* invested in business) in so far as he later has to pay to the bank the money that returns to him, hence a part of his capital; in which connection it is a matter of complete indifference to him whether he pays the money back in gold or in notes, since *he* (unlike the bank) must sell off commodity capital of whatever kind, and pay to the bank the income from whatever sale he makes, having received an equivalent amount of gold or notes of the same denomination. The gold or notes are for him the *value expression* of capital.[90]

< In the case of private banks of issue, the distinction is that if their notes neither remain in local circulation nor return to the banks in the form of deposits or for the payment of bills falling due, these notes come into the possession of people to whom they must return gold or Bank of England notes in exchange for them. In this case the advance of their notes actually represents an advance of Bank of England notes, or, and this is the same thing for them, of gold, hence of their *banking capital*. The same thing is true when the Bank of England itself – and this applies to all banks whose note issue is subject to a legal maximum – has to sell public securities in order to withdraw its own notes from circulation and to issue them again; here its own notes now represent a part of its *externalised* [*veräussertes*] *banking capital*.

Even if circulation were purely metallic, there could be at the same time (1) a drain of gold which empties the treasury, and (2) since the bank's principal requirement for gold is simply to make payments (to settle past transactions), its advances on securities could greatly increase, but return to it in the form of deposits or in the repayment of bills falling due, so that on the one hand the bank's overall reserves would decrease, while on the other hand the same sum that it formerly had as an owner would now be a sum for which it was in debt to its depositors, and finally the total quantity of the circulating medium would decline.

It has so far been assumed that the advances are made in notes and involve at least a temporary increase in the note issue, even if this immediately vanishes again. But this is not necessary. Instead of paper notes, the bank can open

---

90 [Engels described this paragraph as 'incomprehensible' and he redrafted it completely for the published edition. The Engels version is in Fernbach 1981, pp. 587–8. Translator]

a credit account for A, so that A, as its debtor, becomes an imaginary depositor. He pays his creditors with cheques on the bank, and the recipient of these cheques pays them again to his banker, who exchanges them in the *Clearing House* against the cheques drawn on him. In this case there is no intervention of notes at all, and the entire transaction is confined to one in which the bank settles its own debt with a cheque drawn on itself, its actual compensation consisting in its claim against A. In this case the bank has advanced to A part of its *banking capital*, in the form of a part of its own claim as a creditor.

In so far as this pressure for pecuniary accommodation is pressure upon capital, it is only pressure on *banking capital*; capital from the standpoint of the banker; namely as a demand for *gold* (in the case of a bullion drain), *Bank of England notes* (the notes of the national banks), which a private banker can only obtain by buying them with an equivalent, so that they represent capital for it. Or finally it might be a demand for *public securities* (government bonds and other interest-bearing papers) which have to be flogged off if gold or notes are to be obtained. (These securities, however, if they are *government bonds* are capital |334| only for the person who has bought them, to whom they represent his *purchase price*, the capital he has invested in them. They are not capital in themselves, but simply the *claims of a creditor*; if they are *mortgages*, they are simply claims on future rents, and if they are *stocks* of some other kind, they are simply property titles which give the holder a claim to the receipt of future surplus-value. None of these things is *capital*; they do not constitute any component of productive capital and are also in themselves not *values*.) By similar transactions, money, etc., that belongs to the bank can be transformed into deposits, so that the bank becomes a debtor instead of an owner of them, and holds them under a different title. Important as this is *for the bank itself*, it in no way affects the amount of capital stored in the country, or even the money capital. *Capital* here figures simply as *money capital* > and, with the exception of *money*, < as a mere *title to capital*. This is very important, since pressure of this kind upon banking capital and its relative scarcity in respect to the demand for it is confused with a diminution of real capital, which in such cases overstocks the markets.

Now, therefore, we have two explanations for the increase in securities held by the bank (or the growing pressure of monetary accommodation) and the simultaneous reduction or stagnation in the total amount of currency: (1) the drain of bullion; and (2) the demand for money simply as *means of payment*, where > it is issued only temporarily < or where the transaction takes place by way of book credit, and no notes at all are issued. The payments are thus mediated simply by a credit transaction, and the sole purpose of the monetary transaction is the settlement of those payments. It is a peculiarity of money that where it functions simply in settlement of payments (and in times of crisis people borrow in order to make a payment, not in order to buy; to settle past transactions, not to start fresh ones) its actual circulation is simply a vanishing magnitude, even when this settlement does not take place entirely by credit operations, without any intervention of money; that therefore a tremendous mass of these transactions can take place, along with a great pressure for monetary accommodation, without any expansion in the circulation. The simple fact that the Bank of England's circulation remains at the same level, or even declines – 'a low currency' – together with a large pecuniary accommodation, > as indicated by the expansion of the securities < is in no way a prima facie proof, as Fullarton, Tooke and so on would like to claim, owing to their incorrect view of the 'question of capital', that the circulation of money (notes) in its function as means of payment does not increase and expand. Since the circulation of notes as means of purchase *declines*, its circulation as *means of payment* can increase, and the total sum of notes in circulation, which equals the sum of the notes functioning as means of purchase and means of payment, can remain static, or even decline. In their eyes, the circulation of banknotes as *means of payment* is *not* circulation.

If circulation as means of payment were to increase to a higher degree than circulation as means of purchase declined, the total circulation would grow, although the quantity of money functioning as means of purchase would experience a significant decline. And this actually does happen at certain points in the crisis. Since Fullarton and the others do not understand that the *circulation of notes* as *means of payment* is the characteristic feature of such times of pressure, they treat this phenomenon as accidental. 'With respect, again, to those examples of eager competition for the possession of banknotes, which characterise seasons of panic and which may sometimes, as at the close of 1825, lead to a sudden, though only temporary, enlargement of the issues, even while the efflux of bullion is still going on; these, I apprehend, are not to be regarded as among the natural or necessary concomitants of a low exchange; the *demand in such cases* is not *for circulation*' (this should read circulation as a means of purchase) 'but for hoarding, a demand on the part of alarmed bankers and capitalists, which arises generally in the last act of the crisis, after a long continuation of the drain, and is the precursor of its termination'.[91]

---

91 Fullarton 1845, p. 130. > 4605. 'As the Bank' (of England) 'was obliged still to raise its rate of interest, everyone seemed apprehensive; country bankers increased the amount

< We have already discussed (under the rubric of '*means of payment*') how in the case of an *interruption* in the chain of payments, money reverts from its merely ideal form into the material and also absolute form of value vis-à-vis commodities. This interruption itself is in part the effect, in part the cause, of the collapse of credit and the circumstances that accompany it: overstocked markets, depreciation[92] of commodities, interruption of production, etc.

It is clear, however, that Fullarton, etc., transform the distinction between money as '*means of purchase*' and money as '*means of payment*' into a false distinction between 'currency' and 'capital'. And at the bottom of this again lies the narrow-minded banker's conception of 'circulation'.

---

of bullion in their hands, and increased their amount of notes, and many of us who were in the habit of keeping perhaps a few hundred pounds of gold and banknotes immediately laid up thousands in our desks and drawers, and as there was an uncertainty about discounts, and about our bills being current in the market, a general hoarding ensued'. (*First Report* 1848.) What appears as *circulation* for the national bank, therefore, is the dispersal of hoards from the centre to the periphery. At such times, it is the custom among some of the more speculative London moneylenders to produce an artificial dearth of notes:

'On one occasion an old, grasping banker in his private room raised the lid of the desk he sat over, and displayed to a friend rolls of banknotes, saying with intense glee that there were £600,000 of them, they were held to make money tight, and would all be let out after three o'clock on the same day. This circumstance happened ... within the actual month of the lowest circulation in 1839'. (Roy 1864, p. 81.)

'The supply of *capital* (!) has increased, and the demand for accommodation has diminished. The usual desire to provide against every emergency, and which stimulated the inquiry at the close of last week, has resulted, as ordinarily, in the public having endeavoured to secure larger sums than in reality were necessary for their wants; and having fully supplied themselves, they are glad to place their balances out at deposit, risking the chance whether they will have to take them up or not ... Some very curious rumours are current of the means which have been resorted to in order to *create a scarcity of banknotes* ... Questionable as it would seem to suppose that any trick of the kind would be adopted, the report has been so universal that it really deserves mention'. (*The Observer*, 24 April 1864.)

1653. Samuel Gurney, London billbroker, states: 'There was a general demand upon us for the money, which was deposited in our hands on the part of our country friends in October last' (1847) 'from all parts of the country'. [*First Report* 1848] <

92 [This word is in English in the original. Translator]

|335| 2)[93]

We must now take a closer look at what banking capital consists of.

We have just seen how Fullarton, etc., transform the distinction between money as 'means of circulation' and money as 'means of payment' (also as 'world money' as far as the drains of bullion are concerned) into a distinction between '*circulation*' (*currency*) and '*capital*'.

The special role that 'capital' plays here means that the amount of attention enlightened economics devoted to insisting that 'money' was not capital is paralleled by this banker's economics, which tries just as assiduously to insist that money is in fact capital *par excellence*.

In the further course of our investigations, we shall show that 'money capital' is confused in this context with '*moneyed capital*', in the sense of '*interest-bearing capital*', although in the first sense capital is always 'money capital', as distinct from its proper forms, namely 'commodity capital' and 'productive capital'.

It might still be asked what is lacking in such times of pressure, 'capital', or 'money' in its capacity as '*means of payment*'? And this is a well-known controversy.

At first, in so far as the pressure is demonstrated by a 'drain of bullion', it is clear that what is demanded is the international means of payment. But money in its capacity as international means of payment is gold in its metallic reality, as itself a *valuable substance* (*an amount of value*). It is also 'capital', but capital not as *commodity capital*, by rather as *money capital*, capital not in the form of a commodity but rather in the form of money (and, moreover, of money in the pre-eminent sense of the term, in which it exists as a commodity on the general world market). There is no opposition here between the demand for money (as means of payment) and the demand for capital. The opposition is rather between capital in its money form and in its commodity form; and the form in which it is required here, and has to function, is its *money form*.

Apart from this demand for bullion, it cannot be said that in such times of pressure there is in any sense at all a deficiency of '*capital*'. (Under extraordinary circumstances, such as a rise in grain prices, a cotton famine, etc., this can be the case; but these are by no means necessary or regular concomitants of such times of pressure; and the existence of such a lack of capital, therefore, cannot be inferred *prima facie* from the existence of a pressure for monetary accommodation.) On the contrary. Markets are overstocked, and '*commodity*

93 [Title added by the MEGA editors. Editor]

capital' inundates the market. Hence it is not in any case a '*lack of commodity capital*' that causes the pressure. We shall return to this question after we have dealt with the other points.

Banking capital consists of (1) cash, in the form of gold or notes; (2) securities. These latter may again be divided into two parts: *commercial securities* (bills) which are floating, and the discounting of which is the specific business of the banker; and *other securities* (public securities, such as consols,[94] exchequer bills and other securities) and stocks of all kinds, in short interest-bearing papers, which are essentially different from bills of exchange (perhaps also *mortgages*). Apart from these, which are its *real components*, banking capital can be divided into the invested capital of the banker himself and the *deposits* (which form his banking capital, or borrowed capital). Notes must be added here, in the case of issuing banks. We shall leave these entirely out of account to start with. > As far as the deposits are concerned, we shall look at them (and also at the *notes*) more closely later on, but for the present they remain outside our consideration. < It is clear enough that the actual components of banker's capital – money, bills of exchange, securities – are not affected by whether this money, these bills or these securities represent his own capital, or capital he has borrowed, i.e., *deposits*. The subdivisions remain the same whether he pursues his business *exclusively* with *his own* capital or conducts it entirely with capital which has been *deposited* with him.

a) The *form of interest-bearing capital* makes any definite and regular monetary revenue appear as the '*interest*' on a capital, whether it actually derives from a capital or not. The money income is first transformed into '*interest*', and with the interest we then have the 'capital' from which it derives.

The matter is simple. Say that the average rate of interest is 5 percent per year. A capital of £500 would thus (provided it is lent out, or transformed into interest-bearing capital) bring in £25 a year. Hence every fixed annual income of £25 is seen as the interest on a capital of £500. Yet this is and remains a purely illusory notion, except on the assumption that the source of the £25, whether this is a mere title of ownership or claim to a debt, or whether it is an actual element of production, such as a piece of land for example, is directly *transferable*, or takes on a form in which it is 'transferable'. As examples, on one side and on the other, let us take the national debt and wages. The state |336| has to pay its creditors a certain sum of 'interest' each year for the capital it has borrowed. (The creditor cannot recall his capital from the debtor but can

94 [Consolidated Annuities, British government securities consolidated in 1751 into a single stock. Translator]

only sell his claim, his title of ownership.) The capital itself has been consumed, spent by the state. It no longer exists. What the state's creditor possesses is (1) the state's *promissory note* for, say, £100; (2) this promissory note gives him a claim on the state's annual revenue, i.e., the proceeds of the year's taxation, to a certain amount, say 5 percent; (3) he is free to sell this promissory note to anyone he likes. If the rate of interest is 5 percent (and assuming the state's creditworthiness is good), and other circumstances remaining the same, owner A can sell the note for £100 to B; since it is the same thing for B, the buyer, whether he lends out £100 at 5 percent per year or assures himself of an annual tribute of £5 from the state by paying out £100.

But in all these cases, the *capital* from which the state's payment is regarded as an offspring (interest) is *illusory*; it is *fictitious capital*. It is not only that the sum that was lent to the state no longer has any kind of existence. It was never destined to be spent as *capital*, to be invested, and yet only by being invested as capital could it have been transformed into self-maintaining value. As far as the original creditor A is concerned, the share of the annual taxation he receives represents interest on his capital, just as does the share of the wealth of the spendthrift that accrues to the usurer, although in neither case has the money been laid out as capital. The possibility of selling the state's promissory note represents for A the possible *return* or *repayment of the principal sum*. As far as B is concerned, from his own private standpoint his capital has been invested as interest-bearing capital. In actual fact he has merely taken the place of A, and bought A's claim on the state. No matter how many times these transactions take place, the capital of the national debt remains purely *fictitious*, and the moment these promissory notes become unsaleable, the illusion of this capital disappears. Nevertheless, as we shall soon see, this *fictitious* capital has its own characteristic movement.

(With interest-bearing capital, any *sum of value* appears as capital as soon as it is not spent as revenue; namely as the *main amount, the principal*, in contrast to the actual or possible interest it can bear.)

Moving on from the *capital of the national debt*, where a *negative quantity* appears as capital – interest-bearing capital always being the mother of every insane form, so that *debts*, for example, can appear as *commodities* in the mind of the banker[95] – we shall now consider *labour-capacity*. Here wages are conceived as *interest*, and hence *labour-capacity* as the *capital* that yields this interest. If the wage for a year is £50, say, and the rate of interest is 5 percent, one annual *labour-capacity* is taken as equal to a *capital* of £1,000. Here the

95 > See Roy 1864. <

absurdity of the capitalist's way of conceiving things reaches its climax, in so far as instead of deriving the valorisation of capital from the exploitation of labour-capacity, they explain the productivity of labour-capacity inversely, by declaring that labour-capacity itself is that mystical thing, interest-bearing capital. In the second half of the seventeenth century (with Petty, for example) this was a favourite notion, but it is still used today, in all seriousness, by vulgar economists, and especially by German statisticians.[96] Two inconvenient circumstances, however, militate against this unthinking notion: *firstly*, the fact that the worker has to *work* in order to receive this '*interest*', and *secondly*, the fact that he cannot turn the *capital value* of his labour-capacity into a financial gain by means of a '*transfer*' to someone else. On the contrary, the annual *value* of his labour-capacity is equal to his average annual wage, and his labour has to replace its buyer with this value itself plus the surplus-value that is its valorisation. Under the slave system the worker does have a *capital value*, namely his *purchase price*. And if he is hired out, the hirer must replace the annual depreciation, or the wear and tear of the capital, plus the interest.

The formation of *fictitious capital* is known as *capitalisation*. Any regular, periodic income can be capitalised by reckoning it up, on the basis of the average rate of interest, as the *amount* that a capital lent out at this interest rate would yield. For example, if the annual income in question is £100 and the rate of interest is 5 percent, £100 would be the annual interest on £2,000, and this imagined |337| £2,000 is then taken as the *capital value* of the legal title (the title of ownership) to the annual £100. For the person who buys this title of ownership, the annual income of £100 does actually represent conversion of the capital he has invested into interest at 5 percent. In this way, all connection with capital's actual process of valorisation is lost, right down to the last trace, confirming the notion that capital automatically valorises itself.

Even when the *promissory note* – the *security* – does not represent a purely *illusory* capital, as it does in the case of national debts, the *capital value* of this security is still a pure illusion. We have already seen how the credit system produces associated capital. Securities > represent < titles to the ownership of this capital, but the *shares* in railway, mining, shipping companies, etc., represent real capital, namely capital invested and functioning in these enterprises, or the

96 'The worker has a *capital value*, which is found by considering the monetary value of his annual service as a payment of interest ... if the average daily wage is *capitalised* at a rate of four percent, we make the *average value of an agricultural worker of the male sex* to be 1,500 thalers in German Austria, the same in Prussia, 3,750 thalers in England, 2,000 thalers in France, and 750 thalers in Russia proper'. (Reden 1848, p. 434.)

sum of money that was advanced by the shareholders to be spent in these enterprises as capital. (They can of course also simply be fraudulent.) But the capital does not exist twice over, once as the *capital value* of the ownership titles, the *shares*, and then again as the *capital* actually invested, or to be invested, in the enterprises in question. It exists only in the latter form, and the share is nothing but an *ownership title* to the surplus-value which this capital is to realise. A may sell this title to B, and B to C, etc. These transactions have no essential effect on the matter. A or B has then transformed his title into capital, but C has transformed his capital into a mere ownership title to the surplus-value expected from this share capital.

The independent movement of the *values* of these *ownership titles*, whether those of government bonds or those of shares, strengthens the illusion [*Schein*] that they constitute real capital besides the capital or claim to which they may give title. They become *commodities*, their prices having a specific movement and determination. Their *market values* receive a determination differing from their *nominal values*, without any change in the *value* of the actual capital (even if its *valorisation* does change). On the one hand, their market values fluctuate with the level and security of the receipts to which they give a legal title. If, for example, the *nominal value* of a share, i.e., the sum advanced which the share originally represents, is £100, and the enterprise yields 10 percent instead of 5 percent, its market value rises to £200, in other words it doubles, since, when capitalised at 5 percent, it now represents a fictitious capital of £200. Someone who buys it for £200 gets 5 percent on his capital investment. The opposite is the case when the revenue from the enterprise declines. Market value is partly *speculative*, since it is determined not just by the actual revenue but rather by the anticipated revenue, which has to be calculated in advance. But if we take the *valorisation* of the actual capital to be *constant*, or, where no such capital exists, as in the case of national debts, if we assume that the annual yield is *fixed by law*, the *prices* of these *securities* rise and fall in *inverse* proportion to the *rate of interest* > (to the variations in the rate of interest). If the interest rate rises from 5 percent to 10 percent, a *security* that ensures a yield of £5 now represents a capital of only £50. If the interest rate falls from 5 to 2½ percent, a security that yields 5 percent rises from £100 to £200. Its value is always the equal to the capitalised yield, i.e., the yield as reckoned on an illusory capital at the existing rate of interest. In times of pressure on the money market, therefore, these securities fall in price for two reasons: first, because the rate of interest rises, and second, because they are thrown onto the market in massive quantities, to be realised in money. This fall in price occurs irrespective of whether the yield these securities ensure for their owner is *constant*, as in the case of government bonds, or whether the *valorisation of the real capital* that they represent may possibly be affected by the disturbance of the reproduction process, as in the case of railways, coalmines, etc. Once the storm is over, these securities rise again to their former level, in so far as the undertakings they represent have not come to grief or turned out to be fraudulent. Their depreciation in a crisis is a means of concentrating monetary wealth.

In so far as the rise (appreciation) or fall (depreciation) of these securities is independent of the movement in the value of the real capital that they represent, the wealth of a nation is just as great afterwards as before. 'The public stocks in the country and canal and railway shares had already by the 23rd of October 1847 been depreciated in the aggregate to the amount of £114,752,225'.[97] As long as their depreciation was not the expression of a real standstill in production and in railway and canal traffic, or of the abandonment of genuine undertakings, or a squandering of capital in enterprises which produced no result, the nation was not a farthing poorer by the bursting of these bubbles of nominal money capital.

|338| All these securities actually represent nothing but '*accumulated claims upon production*'. Their money or capital value either does not represent capital at all, as in the case of national debts, or is regulated independently of the *real capital value* they represent.

In all countries of capitalist production, there is a tremendous amount of so-called *interest-bearing capital* or *moneyed capital* in this form. And an *accumulation* of *money capital* means for the most part nothing more than an accumulation of these 'claims upon production', and an accumulation of the market price (of the illusory capital value) of these claims.

One portion of banker's capital is invested in these so-called *interest-bearing securities*. This is itself a part of the reserve capital and does not function in the banking business proper. The most important portion consists of bills of exchange, i.e., promises to pay issued by productive capitalists or merchants. For the money-lender, these bills are interest-bearing paper, i.e., when he buys them, he deducts *interest* for the period that they still have to run. How much is deducted from the sum the bills of exchange represent thus depends on the rate of interest at the time.[98] >

---

97 [James] Morris, Governor of the Bank of England, evidence in the *First Report* 1848 [reply to question 3800].

98 > The bills of exchange become '*discountable articles*, i.e. articles which there is an opportunity of *converting*, at any time, into money; such a discount or deduction from the amount of the bill or note as is *equal to the interest upon it*, during the period which it has to run, being paid as the *price of conversion*'. (Thornton 1802, p. 26.) <

< The final portion of the banker's 'capital' consists of his *money reserve* (in gold or notes). Deposits, unless fixed in place for a longer period by contract, are always at the command of the depositors. They are in a state of perpetual fluctuation.[99] But if they are withdrawn by one depositor, they are replaced by another, so that 'the general averages do not vary much'.

The reserve funds of the banks, in countries of developed capitalist production, always express the average amount of money existing as a *hoard*, and a part of this *hoard* itself consists of *paper*, mere drafts on gold, which have no *value of their own*. The greater part of banker's capital is therefore purely fictitious and consists of *claims* (bills of exchange and public securities) and shares (property titles, drafts on future revenues). It should not be forgotten here that the *money value of this capital*, as represented by these papers in the banker's tills, is completely *fictitious*, even in so far as they are drafts on *assured revenues* (as with public securities) or ownership titles to actual capital (as with shares), their money value being determined differently from the value of the *actual capital* they represent; or, where they represent only a claim to revenue and *not* capital at all, the *claim to the same revenue* is expressed in a constantly changing *fictitious money capital*. Added to this is the fact that this fictitious banker's capital represents to a large extent not *his own* capital but rather that of the public which *deposits* with him, whether with interest or without.

Deposits are always made in money (gold or notes). Except for the *reserve fund* (which contracts or expands according to the needs of actual circulation), these deposits are in fact always either in the hands of productive capitalists and merchants, serving to discount their bills of exchange and to make loans to them on that basis; or else they are in the hands of dealers in securities (stockbrokers), or in the hands of private persons who have sold their *securities*, or in the hands of the government (in the case of treasury bills and new loans > some of which are kept by the bankers as security). < The *deposits* themselves play a double role. On the one hand, as already mentioned, they are lent out as interest-bearing capital and are thus not to be found in the banks' tills, figuring instead in their books as credits held by the depositors against the bankers. On the other hand, they function as mere *memoranda* of credits, in so far as the reciprocal claims of the > merchants (and in general, of the < owners of deposits) are settled by drawing on their deposits and cancelled out against each other. (It is completely immaterial in this connection whether the

---

99 > 'The merchants' money, whether it be in the hands of the bank or the bankers, is perpetually fluctuating, although its amount is always very considerable'. (Steuart 1789, p. 228.) <

deposits are with *the same* banker, so that he can cancel the various accounts against each other, or with different banks, which exchange their cheques on each other and pay the difference.)

With the development of interest-bearing capital and the credit system, all *capital* seems to be *duplicated*, and at some points *triplicated*, by the various ways in which the same capital, or even the same claim, appears in various hands in different forms. The greater part of this 'money capital' is purely fictitious. For example, with the exception of the reserve fund, deposits are never more than credits with the banker, and never exist as real deposits. In so far as they are used for bank transfers, they function as capital for the bankers, after the latter have *lent them out*. The bankers pay each other reciprocal drafts on these non-existent deposits by balancing the credits against each other.

|339| In relation to the role that money plays in the lending of capital,[100] Adam Smith says:

'Even in the moneyed interest, however, the money is, as it were, but the deed of assignment, which conveys from one hand to another those capitals which the owners do not care to employ themselves. Those capitals may be greater, in almost any proportion, than the amount of the money which serves as the instrument of their conveyance; *the same pieces of money* successively serving for many different loans, as well as for many different purchases. A, for example, lends to W a thousand pounds, with which W immediately purchases of B a thousand pounds' worth of goods. B, having no occasion for the money himself, lends the identical pieces to X, with which X immediately purchases of C another thousand pounds' worth of goods. C, in the same manner, and for the same reason, lends them to Y, who again purchases goods with them of D. In this manner, the same pieces, either of coin or of paper, may, in the course of a few days, serve as the instrument of three different loans, and of three different purchases, each of which is, in value, equal to the whole amount of these pieces. What the three moneyed men, A, B, and C, assigned to the three borrowers, W, X, and Y, is the power of making those purchases. In this power consist both the value and the use of the loans. The stock lent by the three moneyed men is equal to the value of the goods which can be purchased with it, and is three times greater than that of the money with which the purchases are made. Those loans, however, may be all perfectly well secured, the goods purchased by the different debtors being so employed, as in due time to bring back, with a profit, an equal value either of coin or paper. And as the *same pieces*

100 [Engels reversed this phrase. Translator]

of money can *thus* serve as the *instrument* of different loans to three, or for the same reason, to thirty times their value, so they may likewise successively serve as the *instrument* of repayment'. [Smith 1999, Book II, chapter IV, p. 452.]

Since the same piece of money can make several different purchases, depending on the velocity of its circulation, it can by that very fact be the instrument for different loans, for purchases move it from one hand to another, and a loan is simply a transfer from one hand to another that is not mediated by any purchase. For each seller, the money represents the transformed form of his commodity; nowadays, when every commodity is expressed as a capital value, the money in its various loans successively represents different capitals, which is simply a different way of putting the previous statement that it can successively realise different commodity values. Money also serves, as a means of circulation, to transfer real capitals from one hand to another. In a loan, it is not transferred from one hand to another as a means of circulation. As long as it remains in the lender's possession, it is not a means of circulation in his hands but the value-existence of his capital. And it is in this form that he transfers it to someone else in a loan. If A had lent money to B, and B to C, without any purchases intervening, the *same money* would not represent three capitals but only one, just one *capital value*. How many capitals it actually does represent depends on how often it functions as the value form of various different commodity capitals.

What Adam Smith says about loans in general applies equally to deposits, this being simply a particular name for loans that members of the public make to the bankers. The same *pieces of money* can serve as the instrument for any number of deposits.

'It is unquestionably true that the £1,000 which you deposit at A today may be re-issued tomorrow, and form a deposit at B'. > This is only possible in two cases. Either the depositor takes the £1,000 away from A, in order to deposit them with B. Then the £1,000 represent only a *single* deposit, which is with B instead of A. Or A issues the £1,000 in discounting a bill of exchange or in paying cheques drawn on him (as long as they are not from the depositor of the £1,000) and then the recipient can in turn deposit the £1,000 with another banker (in the case of discounting this must take place through a purchase or be mediated through a payment to a third party, since no one discounts a bill in order to deposit the money thus obtained). < 'The day after that, reissued from B, it may form a deposit at C ... and so on to infinitude; and the same £1,000 in money may, thus, by a succession of transfers, multiply itself into a sum of deposits absolutely indefinite. It is possible, therefore, that nine tenths of all the deposits in the United Kingdom may have no existence *beyond their records in the books of the bankers* who are respectively accountable for them ... Thus in Scotland, where currency has never exceeded £3,000,000, the deposits are £27,000,000. Unless a run on the banks be made, the same £1,000 would, if sent back upon its travels, cancel with the same facility a sum equally indefinite. As the same £1,000 with which you cancel your debt to a tradesman today may cancel debt to the merchant tomorrow, the merchant's debt to the bank the day following, and so on without end; so the same £1,000 may pass from hand to hand, and bank to bank, and cancel any conceivable sum of deposits'. (*Currency Theory* 1845, pp. 62, 63.)

Just as everything in this credit system appears in duplicate and triplicate, and is transformed into a mere phantom of the mind, so this also happens to the '*reserve fund*', where one might finally expect to lay hold of something solid.

[James] Morris, Governor of the Bank of England, says this: 'The *reserves* of the private bankers are in the hand of the Bank of England in the *form of deposits*. A drain of gold would, in the first instance, appear as an operation upon the Bank of England; but it would also be acting upon the reserves of the bankers, in as much as it is a withdrawal of a portion of the reserves which they have in the Bank of England. It would be acting upon the reserves of all the bankers throughout the country'. (*First Report* 1848 [3639, 3642.]) Ultimately, therefore, what these 'reserve funds' actually boil down to is the 'reserve fund' of the Bank of England. But this reserve fund, too, has a double existence. The 'reserve fund' of the Banking Department is equal to the excess of notes that the Bank is authorised to issue over and above the notes that are actually in circulation. The legal maximum note issue is £14,000,000 (the amount for which no bullion reserve is required, this being the state's debt to the Bank of England) plus the number of notes which equals the bullion reserve of the Bank. So if this reserve is also £14,000,000, the bank can issue £28,000,000 in notes, and if 20 million are already in circulation, the reserve fund of the Banking Department is £8,000,000. This £8,000,000 in notes is then (legally) the banking capital the Bank of England has at its disposal, and at the same time the reserve fund for its deposits. Should a drain of bullion take place, reducing the metal reserve by £6,000,000, for example – for which an equal sum in notes would have to be destroyed – the Banking Department's reserve would fall from £8,000,000 to £2,000,000. On the one hand, the Bank would increase its interest rate very sharply; on the other hand the bankers who had deposited with it, as well as the other depositors, would see the reserve fund for their own credits with the Bank take a sharp drop. In 1857 London's four largest joint-stock banks threatened that if the Bank of England did not obtain a 'government letter' suspending the Bank Act of 1844, they would call in their deposits and bankrupt the Banking Department. Thus it is possible for the Banking Department to go bankrupt, as in 1847, when there are still as many millions as you care to mention lying in the Bullion Department (in 1847 there were 8 millions), as a guarantee of the convertibility of the notes in circulation. Though this is in turn an illusion.

|340a| > *Concerning deposits and reserve funds. Billbrokers.* < 'That large portion' (of deposits) 'however, for which the bankers have themselves no immediate demand, passes into the hands of the billbrokers, who give to the banker in return commercial bills already discounted by them for persons in London and in different parts of the country, as a security for the sum advanced by the banker. The billbroker is responsible to the banker for payment of this money at call: and such is the magnitude of these transactions that Mr. Neave, the present Governor of the Bank, stated in evidence: "We know that one broker had 5 millions, and we are led to believe that another had between 8 and 10 millions; there was one with 4, another with 31/2, and a third above 8. I speak of deposits with brokers"'. (*Report on the Bank Acts* 1858, p. 5, section 8.) 'The London billbrokers ... carried on their enormous transactions *without any cash reserve*; relying on the run off of their bills falling due, or in extremity, on the power of obtaining advances from the Bank of England on the security of bills under discount'. (*Report on the Bank Acts* 1858, p. 17.) 'Two billbroking houses in London suspended payment in 1847; both afterwards resumed business. In 1857 they suspended again. The liabilities of one house in 1847 in round numbers: £2,683,000 with a capital of £180,000; the liabilities of the same house in 1857 were £5,300,000, the capital ... probably not more than a quarter of what it was in 1847. The liabilities of the other firm were between £3,000,000 and £4,000,000 at each period of stoppage, with a capital not exceeding £45,000'. (*Report on the Bank Acts* 1858, p. xxi, section 52.)

|340| 3)[101]

The only difficult questions in connection with the credit system, which we are now approaching, are as follows:

Firstly: the *accumulation* of money capital as such. How far is it, and how far is it not, indicative of a genuine *accumulation of capital*, i.e., reproduction on an expanded scale? Is the phenomenon of the so-called *plethora of capital*, an expression used only of moneyed capital, simply a particular expression of over*production*, or does it form a separate phenomenon alongside this? Does

101 [Title added by the MEGA editors. Editor]

such an oversupply of moneyed capital coincide with the presence of stagnant sums of money (coin/bullion or notes) so that it is expressed in a greater *quantity of money*?

Secondly: to what extent does a pressure of money express a want of real capital? To what extent does it coincide with a want of money as such, a want of means of payment?

In as much as we have so far considered the *specific form of the accumulation of monetary wealth*, this comes down to the accumulation of '*claims of property on labour*'. The accumulation of *capital* in the form of the national debt, means nothing more than a *growth in the number of state debts* and therefore of a class of *state creditors* with a prior claim to take certain sums from the taxes.[102] (Moreover, the very fact that an accumulation of debts can *appear* as an accumulation of capital constitutes the culmination of the distortion involved in the credit system. > We shall need to come back to this point later on.) < These promissory notes which were issued for a capital originally borrowed but now spent, these paper duplicates of annihilated capital, function for their private owners as capital in so far as they are *saleable commodities* and can therefore be transformed back into capital.

The ownership titles to joint-stock companies, railways, etc., are genuinely titles to real capital. Yet they give no control over this capital. The capital cannot be withdrawn. They only give a legal title to a share of the surplus-value that is produced by this capital. But these titles similarly become *paper duplicates* of the real capital (as if a bill of lading simultaneously acquired a value *alongside* the cargo it refers to). They become nominal representatives of non-*existent capitals*. For the actual capital exists as well, and in no way changes hands when these duplicates are bought and sold. They become forms of interest-bearing capital because not only do they assure certain revenues but the capital values invested in them can also be repaid by their sale. In so far as the accumulation of these securities expresses an accumulation of railways, mines, etc., it

---

102 'The public funds are no more than an *imaginary capital*, which represents that portion of the annual revenue which is set aside to pay the debt. A capital of equal size has been frittered away; this gives the loan its denominator, but it is not this which is represented by the public fund, for the capital no longer exists anywhere. New wealth, however, must arise from labour and from industry; an annual portion of this wealth is assigned in advance to those who have lent the wealth which has been destroyed. This portion will be taken in taxes from those who produce wealth, and given to the state's creditors, and, according to the customary proportion between capital and interest in the country, an imaginary capital is assumed of sufficient size to yield the annual income which these creditors are due to receive'. (Sismondi 1827, pp. 229–30.)

expresses an expansion of the actual reproduction process, just as the expansion of a tax list on movable property, for example, indicates an expansion of this property itself. But as duplicates that can themselves be *exchanged as commodities*, and hence themselves circulate as *capital values*, they are illusory, and their values can rise and fall quite independently of the actual capital to which they are titles. Their values have a necessary *tendency to rise* with the *fall in the rate of interest*, in so far as this is a simple result of the tendential fall in the rate of profit, independently of the specific movements of moneyed capital, so that this imaginary wealth, which according to its value expression gives each person his aliquot share of a definite original nominal value, expands in the course of the development of the capitalist mode of production.

Profits and losses, and also the concentration of these property titles, are by the nature of the case more and more the result of *gambling*, which now appears in place of *labour* as the original source of capital ownership, as well as taking the place of the direct use of force. This kind of imaginary money wealth makes up a considerable part not only of the money wealth of private individuals, but also of *banking capital*, as we have already demonstrated.

One point which we mention here only to discard it from our consideration is that the accumulation of money capital might also be taken to mean the accumulation of wealth in the hands of bankers (professional money-lenders) as intermediaries between the private lenders and the public (state) and those borrowers engaged in the process of reproduction; for the entire immense extension of the credit system, and *credit* as a whole, is exploited by the bankers as *their private capital*. These fellows possess their capital and revenue permanently in the *money form* or in the form of direct claims to money. The accumulation of wealth by this class may proceed in a very different way from that of accumulation properly so called; but it proves in any case that they pocket a good portion of the wealth.

|340a| To circumscribe the question before us within narrower limits: government bonds, shares and other securities of all kinds are all *spheres of investment* for loanable capital, for capital that is destined to bear interest. They are forms for lending it out (for investing it). But they are not themselves the *moneyed capital* which has been invested in them. On the other hand, in so far as credit plays a direct role in the reproduction process, what the industrialist or merchant needs when he wants to have bills discounted or to take out a loan is neither shares nor government stock. What he wants is *money*. (That is why he pawns or flogs off those securities when he can procure the money in no other way.) It is the accumulation of this *loanable capital* we have to deal with here, and, moreover, the direct accumulation of loanable 'moneyed' cap-

ital. What is involved here is not the lending of houses, machines or other fixed capital. Nor is it the advances that industrialists and merchants make to each other within the ambit of the reproduction process, although we shall have to come back to this point. What we are concerned with here is exclusively the *money loans* that are made by the bankers as intermediaries to the industrialists and merchants.

> It is clear from the outset that < not *every accumulation* or increase in *moneyed capital* (loanable capital) indicates a genuine accumulation of capital or an expansion of the reproduction process. > Every disturbance of the reproduction process (once the immediate impact of the crisis has passed) not only *lessens* the *demand* for moneyed capital and makes it relatively redundant, it also *increases* its supply and therefore its absolute magnitude. After every crisis, therefore, when the reproduction < process has undergone a contraction (after the crisis of 1847, for example, production in the English industrial districts was cut by a third), when commodity prices stand at their lowest point, and when the entrepreneurial spirit is crippled, there is a low *rate of interest*, which in this case simply indicates an increase in *moneyed capital* owing to the *contraction and paralysis of productive capital*. It is self-evident that less *means of circulation* are required with lower commodity prices, a smaller number of transactions and a contraction in the capital laid out on wages; that after foreign debts have been liquidated, partly by a drain of bullion and partly by bankruptcies, no money is required to act as 'world money'; and finally that the business of discounting bills of exchange (etc.) itself declines along with the number and amount of these bills. It is also clear that the demand for *moneyed capital* declines, whether for means of circulation or means of payment, or in the form of capital to be invested 'anew', and it therefore becomes *relatively* redundant.[103] But the *supply* of moneyed capital also undergoes a positive increase in such circumstances.

---

103 'At present' (after the crisis of 1847) 'there is a limitation of transactions and a great superabundance of money.' (*First Report* 1848, no. 1664.) The rate of interest was very low on account of the 'almost perfect destruction of commerce, and the almost total want of means of employing money'. (*First Report* 1848, p. 45.) Evidence of Adam Hodgson, Director of the Royal Bank of Liverpool.

The nonsense that these gentlemen concocted to explain the situation (and Hodgson, moreover, is one of the best of them) can be seen from the following sentence: 'The pressure' (in 1847) 'arose *from a real diminution of the moneyed capital of the country*.' It arose 'partly from the necessity of paying in gold for imports from all parts of the world, and partly from the absorption of floating into fixed capital'. (*First Report* 1848, p. 63.) It is impossible to see how the 'absorption of floating into fixed capital' is supposed to reduce the 'moneyed capital of the country', since in the case of railways, for example, which were the main concern at that time, no gold or paper is used to make railway tracks, and the money for railway shares, in so far as it is deposited for calls, functions just like all other money deposited with the bankers, and in fact increases the loanable moneyed capital, as I shall show later on. The money that was actually spent on construction circulated throughout the country as means of purchase and payment. It is only in so far as articles of fixed capital are not exportable, because no disposable capital is obtained by way of returns for articles exported, including returns in bullion, that money capital can be affected. But English export goods, too, were at that time overstocked and unsaleable on foreign markets at that time. For the merchants and manufacturers in Manchester etc., who had tied up a part of their normal working capital in railway shares (and had also taken out loans on that basis) were dependent on borrowed capital to conduct their business, their 'floating capital' really had been fixed. But it would have been the same thing if they had invested the capital belonging to their business, but withdrawn from it, in mines, for example, instead of railways, even though the products of mining are themselves 'floating capital' – iron, copper etc. (The real reduction in circulating capital as a result of a shortfall in corn and cotton was of course an occurrence that had nothing to do with the railway swindle.) 'Almost all mercantile houses had begun to starve their business more or less for investment in railways' (*First Report* 1848, p. 42). 'Loans to so great an extent by commercial houses to railways induced them to lean too much upon joint stock and private banks by the discount of paper, whereby to carry on their commercial operations' (the same Hodgson, *First Report* 1848, p. 67). 'In Manchester there have been immense losses in consequence of the speculation in railways' (Robert Gardner, Manchester spinner, manufacturer and merchant, evidence, no. 4884).

Apart from the colossal degree of swindling and simultaneous saturation of the market in the East India trade, there were other reasons why even very wealthy firms in this sector went bust: 'They had large means, but not available. The whole of their capital was locked up in estates in the Mauritius, or indigo factories, or sugar factories. Having incurred liabilities to the extent of £500,000–£600,000, they had no available assets to pay their bills, and eventually it proved that to pay their bills they were entirely dependent on their credit' (Charles Turner, Liverpool East India merchant, evidence, no. 730.)

Then Gardner again (no. 4872): 'Immediately after the China treaty, so great a prospect was held out in the country of a great extension of our commerce with China, that there were many large mills built with a view to that trade exclusively, in order to manufacture that class of cloth which is principally taken for the China market, and our previous manufactures had the addition of all those'. 4874: 'How has that trade turned out? Most ruinous, almost beyond description; I do not believe that of the whole of the shipments that were made in 1844 and 1845 to China, above two-thirds of the amount have ever been returned; in consequence of tea being the principal article of repayment and of the expectation that was held out, we, as manufacturers, fully calculated upon a great reduction in the duty on tea'. There follows the characteristic credo of the English manu-

|341| *Credit* as *Regulator of the Velocity of the Currency*. 'The great regulator of the velocity' of circulation 'is credit'. This is the explanation as to why 'a severe pressure upon the money market is generally coincident with a *full* circulation'. (*The Currency Theory* 1845, p. 65.) This is to be understood in two senses. Firstly, all economical methods of circulation are based upon credit. But secondly, take, say, a £500 note. A uses it today to pay for a bill of exchange on B, B deposits it the same day with his banker, the latter discounts the bill of exchange with it on C, C pays it to his banker, the banker gives it to a billbroker on call, etc. The velocity with which the note circulates, serves for purchases or payments, is facilitated here by the velocity with which it returns and again in the form of deposits to somebody, and then in turn passes to somebody else in the form of loans. The economical approach appears in its highest form in the clearing house, where there is *nothing more than an exchange of bills*, and the predominant function of money is as means of payment. But the existence of these *bills* depends upon *the credit* which the *producers, merchants etc. advance to each other*. If this credit grows less, the amount of bills (particularly long bills) is reduced, and therefore there is also a reduction in the efficacy of this method of transfer. And this *economy*, which rests on the suppression of money in the transactions, and which rests entirely on the function of money as means of payment, this resting in turn on credit (leaving aside the higher or lower level of development of the technique of concentrating these payments) can only be of two kinds: reciprocal payment obligations, represented by bills of exchange or by drafts, are either cancelled out by *one and the same banker*, who simply transfers the debt from the account of one person to the account of another, or

---

facturer, naively expressed: 'Our *commerce with no foreign market is limited by their power to purchase* the commodity, but it *is limited in this country by our capability of consuming that which we receive in return for our manufactures*'. (The relatively poor countries with which England trades can of course *pay for* every possible amount of English commodities, but unfortunately rich England cannot *assimilate* the products sent in return.) 4876. 'I sent out some goods in the first instance, and the *goods sold at about 15 percent loss*, from the full conviction that the price at which my agents could purchase tea would leave so great a profit in this country as to make up the deficiency > in the sale of goods there, < but instead of profit I lost in some instances 25 and up to 50 percent'. 4877. 'Did the manufacturers generally export on their own account? Principally: the *merchants*, I think, very soon saw that the thing would not answer, and they rather encouraged the manufacturers to consign them than take a direct interest themselves'. In 1857, on the other hand, it was chiefly the merchants who had to cough up (i.e., to go bankrupt), as this time the manufacturers left them to overimport goods into foreign markets 'on their own account'.

the bankers settle their obligations between each other.[104] The concentration of £8,000,000 to £10,000,000 of bills in the hands of a billbroker, such as Samuel Gurney for example, is one of the main methods of extending the scale of this settlement of accounts. This economy in scale raises the efficacy of the currency, to the extent that now a much smaller quantity of currency is required to balance out the accounts.

The *velocity of money as means of circulation* (which also allows it to be used more economically) depends entirely on the flow of purchases and sales (or also the way the payments interlock, where they occur sequentially in their money form). But this velocity is mediated by credit. A coin, G, can only turn over five times as a pure means of circulation, without the intervention of credit, if A, its original possessor, buys from B, B buys from C, C buys from D, D from E, and E from F; if, therefore, its transfer from one hand to the next is

104 > 985. 'In 1831 a £5 note remained out 115 days, and now it remains out only 70 days. Now, if the *average amount of circulation is the same*, it is clear that there is a much *greater activity of circulation*'. (*Report on the Bank Acts* 1857.)

Average Number of Days a Note of each Class remains in Circulation

	£5	£10	£20 to £100	£200 to £500	£1000
1792	–	236	209	31	22
1818	148	137	121	18	13
1831	115	80	44	14	13
1844	82	70	34	13	12
1845	80	72	35	12	9
1846	79	71	34	12	8
1847	74	67	32	10	7
1848	71	64	31	11	10
1849	71	66	32	11	10
1850	75	68	32	11	9
1851	73	66	31	10	9
1852	73	65	32	12	10
1853	75	62	28	10	9
1854	73	63	31	10	8
1855	72	61	30	10	7
1856	70	58	27	9	7

< (See the papers handed over by Mr. [Matthew] Marshall, Chief Cashier of the Bank of England, in *Report on the Bank Acts* 1857, Part II, Appendix, pp. 300 and 301.)

mediated through actual purchases and sales. But if B deposits the money with his banker and the latter gives it out in discounting C's bill of exchange, C buys from D, D deposits it with his banker and the latter loans it to E, who buys from F, the *velocity of money as a mere means of circulation* (means of purchase) is mediated through various credit operations – B's deposit with his banker, the banker's discount for C, D's deposit with his banker, and the banker's discount for E. It is therefore mediated through four credit operations. Without these credit operations the same coin would have had to perform five acts of purchase one after the other during the given time period. The fact that it changed hands as a deposit and in a discount, without the mediation of actual buying and selling, has increased the speed with which it moves from hand to hand in the course of actual sales and purchases.

(We saw earlier that the same note may form a deposit for several different bankers. It can also form different deposits with the same banker. With the note G, which A has deposited, he discounts B's bill of exchange, B pays C, C deposits the same note with the very banker who gave it out in the first place. It has therefore now formed two deposits with him.)

< Commercial credit (i.e., the credit that capitalists involved in the reproduction process give each other) forms the basis of the *credit system*. Its representative is the *bill of exchange*, a promissory note or document of deferred payment. Each person gives credit with one hand and receives credit with the other hand. We shall start by completely ignoring *banker's credit*, which is an entirely separate and essentially different element. In so far as these bills of exchange continue to circulate among the merchants themselves as means of payment, by endorsement from one to another, but without the intervention of any discounting, all that happens is the transfer of the claim from A to B, and absolutely nothing in the relationship is changed. One person simply takes the place of another, > (although even in this case the liquidation of debts can take place without the intervention of money. < Say that spinner A has to pay a bill to cotton broker B, and the latter to the importer. If the same importer who imports cotton also exports yarn > {or if, and this comes down to the same thing, the exporter of yarn receives a bill of exchange on the importer of cotton as the place of payment in America} the exporter can pay the spinner with the |342| bill of exchange on the importer of cotton, the importer of cotton can pay the exporter with a bill on the cotton broker, and the cotton broker and the spinner can exchange their bills with each other, if their reciprocal debts are equal, or pay a balance in addition if they are unequal. < The entire transaction then simply mediates the exchange of cotton and yarn. The exporter simply represents the spinner and the cotton broker represents the cotton grower.)

Two things should be noted about this circuit of purely commercial credit:

Firstly, the settlement of these reciprocal claims depends on the return of the capital, i.e., it depends on C – M, which is simply deferred. If the spinner has received a bill from the clothier, the clothier will be able to pay when the goods he has on the market have in the meantime been sold. If the speculator in corn has given a bill of exchange on his factor, the factor will be able to pay the money after the corn has been sold at the expected price, etc. These payments thus depend on the fluidity of reproduction, i.e., of the production and consumption process. But since the credits are reciprocal, the ability of each person to pay depends at the same time on the ability of another person to pay; for, when drawing a bill, the drawer must have counted either on the return of capital in the own business or on a return in the business of a third party who has to pay him a bill in the intervening period. Leaving aside the expectation of a return, payment is only possible by means of reserve capital, which the person drawing the bill has at his disposal, in order to meet his obligations in case returns are delayed.

Secondly, this credit system does not obviate the need for cash payments. For a start, a large proportion of expenses must always be paid in cash – wages, taxes, etc. But if for example B, who accepts a bill from C in lieu of immediate payment, has himself to pay a bill that falls due to D before the former bill falls due to him, he must also have cash for this. Furthermore, the balancing out of the bills of exchange in this circle of reproduction (particularly in the case of the actual producers of commodities) must always undergo interruptions. We have seen when examining the reproduction process how the producers of constant capital exchange part of their constant capital with one another. In this case, the bills may more or less balance. The same thing happens when production is on an ascending curve, and the cotton broker draws on the spinner, the spinner on the manufacturer, the latter on the exporter, the exporter in turn on the importer (perhaps again an importer of cotton) and so on. But the circuit of transactions and the consequent doubling back of the claims do not take place in all cases. It does not take place, for example, between the spinner and the coal supplier and the machine-builder. The spinner never makes counter-claims on the machine-builder in the course of his business, since his product, yarn, never becomes an element in the machine-builder's reproduction process. The claims of the latter type must therefore be settled in cash.

The limits of this commercial credit, considered by itself, are (1) the wealth of the producers and the merchants, i.e., the reserve capital at their disposal in case of a delay in returns; and (2) these returns themselves. They may be delayed in time, or commodity prices may fall in the meantime, or again the commodities may temporarily become unsaleable as a result of a glut on the market. The longer bills run for, the greater the reserve capital needed and the greater the possibility that returns may be diminished or delayed as a result of a change in commodity prices in the meantime; and the greater the possibility for an excess of supply on the market > since this comes to the surface much later. < Returns are that much less certain, moreover, the more the original transaction was inspired by speculation on a rise or fall in commodity prices. It is clear, however, that with the increase in the productivity of labour and therefore the growth of production on a large scale, (1) markets expand and become further removed from the place of production, (2) credits have to be prolonged, and (3) the speculative element must come more and more to dominate transactions. Large-scale production throws the entire product in the arms of commerce, and it is impossible for the nation's capital to double, so that commerce would be in a position by itself to [buy and] sell the whole national product with its own capital. Credit is thus indispensable here, a credit that grows in volume with the growing value of production and grows in duration with the increasing size and distance of the markets. A reciprocal effect takes place here. The development of the production process expands credit, while credit in turn leads to an expansion of productive and mercantile operations.

If we consider this credit in separation from banker's credit, it is evident that it grows with the scale of productive capital itself. Loanable capital and reproductive capital are identical here; the capitals lent are either *commodity capitals* destined for consumption ultimately, or *commodity capitals* destined to enter as elements into the constant portion of *productive capitals* (to replace them). So what appears here as *loaned* capital is always capital that |343| exists in a *certain phase* of the reproduction process, but is transferred from one hand to another, > without being mediated by definitive purchases and sales. < Cotton, for instance, is transferred to the spinner against a bill of exchange, the yarn is transferred to the clothier against a bill of exchange, the cloth is transferred into the hands of the retailer or the exporter against a bill of exchange. It passes from the hands of the exporter into those of a merchant in the East Indies against a bill of exchange, and let us assume that the merchant sells it and buys indigo for it, and so on. During this transfer from one hand to another, the cotton is undergoing its transformation into cloth, and the cloth is finally exchanged for indigo, which once again enters into the reproduction process. The different phases of the reproduction process are mediated here by credit. The spinner has not paid for the cotton, the manufacturer has not paid for the yarn, nor the merchant for the cloth, etc. In the first act of the process, the commodity cotton passes through the various phases of its production, and this transfer is mediated by credit. But once the cotton has received its final form as a commodity the subsequent transfers are merely transfers of the same commodity capital through the hands of various merchants, who finally sell it to the consumer, buying other commodities in exchange, which enter in turn either into consumption or into the reproduction process. There are thus two phases to be distinguished here: in the first phase credit mediates the successive phases in the production of the article in question; in the second phase it simply mediates the transfer from the hands of one merchant into those of another – the act C – M. But here too at least the commodity is permanently engaged in the act of circulation, hence in a phase of the reproduction process.

What is lent out here, therefore, is never *unoccupied capital*, but rather capital that must change its form in the hands of its owner, capital that exists in a *form* in which it is simply *commodity capital* for him, i.e., capital that must be transformed back and in the first instance at least converted into money. (It is the metamorphosis of the commodity that is mediated here by way of credit; not only C – M, but also M – C and the actual production process.)

A large amount of credit within the reproductive circuit (leaving aside banker's credit) does not signify a lot of *unoccupied* capital which is offered for loan and seeks profitable investment, but rather a *high level of employment* of capital in the reproduction process. What credit mediates here is therefore (1) as far as the productive capitalists are concerned the transition of productive capital from one phase into another, the connection of spheres of production that belong together and mesh into one another; (2) as far as the merchants are concerned, the transfer of commodities from one hand to another until their definitive sale for money or their exchange with another commodity.

> (We saw earlier that apart from fixed capital, which is unconsumed, though applied to production, the consumers by no means have to replace the whole of the capital laid out in production, since a part of the constant capital is replaced by natural processes, and another part is replaced by exchange between the producers of the constant capital. But when the part which represents their income and their variable capital is no longer replaced by sale to the productive consumers of their capital, whose own transactions depend on sale to the consumer, this process naturally comes to a halt even among the producers of constant capital.)

< (The maximum of credit is the same thing here as the fullest employment of productive capital, i.e. the utmost employment of the latent reproductive power, without any regard to the limit of consumption. This limit of consumption is extended by the stretching of the reproduction process itself; on the one hand this increases the consumption of revenue by workers and reproductive capitalists, while on the other hand it is itself identical with the stretching of productive consumption.)

As long as the reproduction process remains fluid, so that returns are assured, this credit persists and extends, and its extension is based on the extension of the reproduction process itself. As soon as stagnation occurs, as a result of delayed returns, overstocked markets or a fall of prices, a surplus of productive capital is available, but in a form in which it cannot accomplish its functions. There is a great deal of unsaleable commodity capital. There is a great deal of unsaleable fixed capital. And in addition the fixed capital is in part unemployed as a result of the stagnation in reproduction. Credit contracts, (1) because this capital is 'unemployed', i.e., it is stuck in one of the phases of reproduction; it cannot complete its metamorphosis; (2) because confidence in the fluidity of the reproduction process has collapsed; (3) because the demand for this commercial credit declines. > The clothier who restricts his production and has a mass of unsold cloth around his neck does not need to buy yarn on credit; < the merchant does not need to buy any cloth on credit, and so on.

|344| So if there is a disturbance in this intensification and expansion of the reproduction process, there is also a lack of credit; it gets harder to obtain goods on credit (although the demand for cash payment or the *cautious* approach to selling characterises the phase of the industrial cycle that follows the panic). In the crisis itself, since everyone has goods to sell and cannot sell, yet *must sell in order to pay*, the quantity of capital blocked in its reproduction process, though not of unoccupied capital to be invested, is precisely at its greatest when the lack of credit is also most acute (and hence the rate of discount is at its highest). The capital is in fact massively unemployed, since the reproduction process is obstructed. Factories stand idle, raw materials pile up in the storehouses, finished products remain on the market as commodities without shifting. Nothing could be more mistaken, therefore, than to ascribe such a situation to a *lack of productive capital*. It is then that there is a *surplus* of productive capital, partly in relation to the normal, then contracted scale of reproduction, and partly in relation to the paralysis of consumption. (Let us conceive the whole society as composed simply of productive capitalists and wage-labourers. Let us also leave aside those changes in price which prevent large portions of the total capital from being replaced in their average proportions, and which, in the overall context of the reproduction process as a whole, particularly as developed by the credit system, must constantly bring about momentary situations of stagnation. Let us likewise ignore the fraudulent and speculative transactions promoted by the credit system. In this case, every crisis would be explicable only in terms of a disproportion in production between different branches, and a disproportion between the consumption of the capitalists themselves and their accumulation. But as things actually stand, the replacement of the capitals invested in production depends to a large extent on the consumption capacity

of the *non-productive classes*, while the consumption capacity of the workers is restricted partly by the laws governing wages and partly by the fact that they are employed only as long as they can be employed at a profit for the capitalist class. The ultimate reason for all real crises always remains the poverty and restricted consumption of the masses, in the face of the drive of capitalist production to develop the productive forces as if only the absolute consumption capacity of the society set a limit to them.)

The only case in which we can speak of a genuine lack of productive capital (at least in developed capitalist countries) is that of a general harvest failure, affecting either the staple foodstuffs or the principal raw materials for industry.

But on top of this commercial credit we have moneyed credit proper. Advances made by industrialists and merchants to each other fuse together with advances of money made to them by bankers and money-lenders. In the discounting of bills of exchange the advance is purely nominal. A sells his yarn for a bill of exchange, but he discounts this bill. In actual fact he advances his banker's credit, and the banker in turn advances the money capital of his depositors, who consist of the industrialists and merchants themselves, though also including workers (by means of savings banks) as well as the recipients of ground-rents and other unproductive classes. For each individual, then, the need for reserve capital is circumvented, as is dependence on the actual returns. On the other hand, however, the situation is so much complicated by bill-jobbing, and by the sale of commodities simply in order to be able to draw bills of exchange, that the appearance of a very solid business with brisk returns can persist for a while even when the returns have in actual fact long been made at the expense of swindled money-lenders and swindled producers. This is why business always seems almost exaggeratedly healthy immediately before a crash. The best proof of this is provided by the *Reports on the Bank Acts* issued in 1857 and 1858, in which all the bank directors and merchants, in short a whole committee of people, congratulated each other on the prosperity and soundness of business just one month before the crisis broke out (August 1857).[105] Lord Overstone, who was one of the witnesses who gave evidence to the 1857 Committee, took the lead in this orgy of self-congratulation.

---

105 > 'Report proposed by Mr. Cayley, no. 11: "that trade was considered indisputably sound by the witnesses of last year"' (1857 {*Report on the Bank Acts* 1858}). < Incidentally, it is particularly striking how [Thomas] Tooke again falls victim to the illusion when writing as a historian, in his *History of Prices* [1838, pp. 241–2]. Trade is always sound and the campaign is proceeding successfully until the alarm bells suddenly start to ring.

> The quantity of loanable moneyed capital – unemployed moneyed capital seeking for profitable investment – is at its greatest after a crisis, when the reproduction process has undergone a contraction and the amount of reproductive capital has therefore fallen to some extent (in so far as it consists in stocks of commodities), but a part of the fixed capital is not fully employed. The money usually devoted to commercial discounts accumulates in the money centres; prices fall, workers lose their employment; the circulating medium therefore declines in quantity. Returns from abroad start to come in partially in the form of bullion, because the low level of prices and the lack of entrepreneurial spirit cripple imports. In this situation, therefore, no one can maintain that interest rates are low because of a superabundance of capital. What has happened is a contraction of productive capital and, as against this, an expansion, partly relative and partly absolute, of capital in its moneyed form.

|345| A large part of the money, the function of which was the payment of wages and more generally the expenditure of income (in England at present this amounts to about £50,000,000), is itself now transformed into loanable capital. The same is true in part of the bullion returns, which normally did not form part of the hoards of Western countries, but rather were constantly on the move from the sources of production in the Western industrial countries to the East in exchange for Asiatic products. Since business, apart from being in its shrunken state, is now conducted cautiously and on short bills, the usual business returns flow in smoothly and there is therefore little opportunity for discount and loans.

< An expansion of moneyed capital arising from the fact that, as a result of the spread of banking (see the example of the Ipswich bank, where in the few years immediately prior to 1857,[106] the farmers' deposits quadrupled) what was

---

106 > 'Trade stagnates after a panic. The money usually devoted to commercial discount *accumulates* in the money centres; prices fall, from the disemployment of labour; the rate of interest declines to two or perhaps one and a half percent: this low rate by degrees tempts at the same time the cupidity of the adventurer and the owner of money – of the borrower and the lender. Every species of domestic enterprise employs labour; unemployment [employment?] increases; wages rise; consumption is extended; prices rise. This is the period of prosperity, of profit to the employer, of plenty to the workmen. Higher prices encourage imports, at the same time that they stimulate competition among adventurers, and money ... rises in value proportionally, still not too high for profit. But this rise of prices discourages the export trade; exports diminish; the balance of trade becomes against us; the screw turns; discount is difficult; confidence is shaken; pressure is converted into panic, and then comes the collapse'. [The source of this quotation is not known.] <

formerly a private hoard or a reserve of coin is now always transformed for a certain period into *loanable capital*, no more expresses a *growth in productive capital* than did the growing deposits in the London joint-stock banks once these began to pay interest on deposits. As long as the scale of production remains the same, this expansion simply gives rise to a superabundance of loanable moneyed capital as compared with productive capital. Hence a low rate of interest.

If the reproduction process has again reached the flourishing stage that precedes the stage of over-exertion, commercial credit expands greatly, and this in turn actually forms the 'sound' basis for a steady flow of returns and an expansion of production. In this situation the rate of interest is still low, even if it has risen above its minimum. This is actually the only point in time at which it may be said that a low rate of interest, and hence a relative abundance of loanable capital, coincides with an actual expansion of productive capital. The regular flow of the returns, combined with an expansion of *commercial* credit, ensures the supply of loanable capital despite the increased demand and keeps the interest rate at its existing level. But now the jobbers start to enter the picture to a perceptible degree, operating without reserve capital, or in some cases without any capital, and therefore relying entirely on moneyed credit. Added to this is the great expansion of fixed capital in all its forms and the opening of new enterprises, etc. Interest now rises to its average level.

It reaches its maximum again as soon as the reproduction process is paralysed and, save for the exceptions mentioned earlier, there is a superabundance of *unoccupied productive capital*.

By and large, therefore, the movement of moneyed capital (as expressed in the rate of interest) runs in the opposite direction to that of productive capital. When the rate of interest arrives at its average level, the mid-point which is equidistant from its minimum and its maximum, this expresses a combination of abundant loanable capital with a big expansion of productive capital. When the rate of interest is low but above its minimum, this expresses the same combination, when it coincides with 'improvement' and 'growing confidence' after the crisis. But at the beginning of the industrial cycle a low rate of interest coincides with a contraction of productive capital, and at the end of the cycle a high rate of interest coincides with a superabundance of productive capital. The low rate of interest that accompanies the 'improvement' phase expresses the fact that commercial credit only needs a small amount of moneyed credit, since it still stands on its own two feet.

A feature of this cycle is that, once the first impulse has been given, the same story must reproduce itself periodically. In the state of quiescence, production falls below the level it attained in the previous cycle and for which the real basis has now been laid. In the phase of prosperity – the middle period – it develops further on this basis. In the period of overtrading the productive forces are stretched to their limit, even beyond the capitalist barriers to the production process.

The reason for the lack of 'means of payment' in the period of crisis is self-evident. The convertibility of bills of exchange has replaced the metamorphosis of the actual commodities, and all the more so at such a time when one group of firms is operating purely on credit. Arbitrary bank legislation (such as that of 1844–5) may worsen these monetary crises. But no kind of legislation can abolish the crises themselves. It is self-evident that when the whole process rests on credit, a credit crisis, involving a lack of the means of payment, must break out if credit is withdrawn and only cash payment is accepted. The entire crisis must therefore present itself on the face of it as a crisis of credit and money. But in fact it does not[107] just involve the 'convertibility' of bills of exchange into money. An immense quantity of these bills represent purely fraudulent transactions, which now come to light and are exploded; as well as unsuccessful speculations conducted with other people's capital, and finally commodity capitals which have either depreciated or represent returns which can no longer be achieved. The whole artificial system of forced expansion of the reproduction process cannot be cured by now allowing one bank, for example the Bank of England, to give all the swindlers the capital they lack in paper money and to buy all the depreciated commodities at their nominal values. Moreover, everything here appears upside down, since in this paper world the real price and its real elements are nowhere to be seen, but all one sees is bullion, notes, bills (convertibility) and securities. This distortion is particularly evident in centres such as London, where the monetary business of the entire country is concentrated; it is less apparent in the centres of production.

/345/ It should also be remarked in passing, in connection with the superabundance of productive capital, that commodity capital is at the same time *money capital*, i.e., a certain sum of value expressed in the commodity's price, > or a *sum of money* in which its exchange-value is expressed. < As a use-value it is a certain quantity of objects, and these are present in excess. But as money capital it is subject to constant expansion and contraction. In the months immediately preceding the crisis, and during the crisis, the commodity capital contracts in its capacity as money capital. It represents less money

107 [Engels removed this word. Translator]

capital for its owner and for his creditors (also as security for bills of exchange and loans) than at the time when > the purchases and sales, < and the discounts and loans made with it as security, were concluded. If this is the meaning of the contention that the money capital of a country is 'lessened' in times of pressure, all this amounts to is the statement that commodity prices have fallen. (Such a collapse of prices only balances out their earlier inflation.) (The incomes of the unproductive classes and of those who live on fixed incomes remain for the most part stationary during the price inflation that goes hand in hand with overproduction and overtrading. Their capacity to consume thus undergoes a relative decline, and with it also their ability to replace the portion of the total production that would normally enter into their consumption. Even if their demand remains the same nominally, it still declines in real terms.) > What follows the crisis in reality is: (1) a restriction of production, and (2) a fall in prices. The restriction of production lessens the amount of commodity capital coming onto the scene and the fall in prices expands the market for the same quantity of use-values. < As regards the question of exports and imports, it should be noted that all countries are successively affected, and that it is then apparent that they have all, with a few exceptions, exported and imported too much, hence the balance of payments is against them all, so that the root of the problem is not the balance of payments at all. England, for example, suffers from a drain of bullion. It has imported too much. But at the same time every other country is overstocked with English commodities. They too have imported too much, or been made to import too much. (There is a distinction, however, between the country that exports on credit, and those that do not, or on a smaller amount of credit. The latter then import on credit; and this is only not the case when exports are made on consignment.) The crisis may break out first of all in England, the country that gives the most credit and takes the least, because the balance of payments is against it, even though the balance of trade is in its favour. (This fact is partly to be explained by the credit given by England and partly by the lending of capital abroad, which means that a large quantity of returns flows back to England in addition to trading returns in the strict sense.)

(Sometimes the crisis breaks out first of all in America, the country that takes the most credit for trade and capital from England.) The crash in England, preceded and accompanied by an efflux of bullion, settles England's balance of payments, partly by bankrupting its importers (on which more below), partly by driving part of its commodity capital abroad at low prices, and partly by the sale of foreign securities, and the purchase of English ones, etc. Now another country enters the line of fire. The balance of payments was temporarily in its favour; but now the normal interval between the balancing of payments and the balancing of trade is abolished, or cut short, by the crisis. The same situation then repeats itself here. England now has |346| an influx of bullion, the other country an efflux. What appears in one country as excessive importing appears in the other as excessive exporting (here we are not referring to dearths, etc., resulting from a harvest failure but rather to a general crisis). In other words a general overproduction takes place, facilitated by credit and the general inflation of prices that accompanies this. > The crisis breaks out first of all in the country which has the balance of payments against it (to be distinguished from the *balance of trade*; the balance of payments is only the *immediate* situation of the balance of trade, which has to be liquidated at once, or within a definite interval.) This country will in normal circumstances be England or the United States, i.e., either the country which gives the greatest credit and receives the least in return, or the country which receives the greatest credit, and gives the least in return. The crisis strikes here and liquidates the immediate balance of payments. This then gives the signal 'balance of payments' to another nation and the same phenomena are repeated there, such as efflux of bullion, etc. The pressure of the country in which the crisis first broke out (leaving aside the impact of the state of the English or the American money market, of credit, and of the total amount of commodities present on the world market as a whole) accelerates the approach of the due date for the balance of payments of other countries, hence a general crisis. Whereas the due dates for the balance of payments and the balance of trade are normally separated for different nations, they are now forced together so that they occur at the same time, just as, within the country in crisis, all payments now have to be made simultaneously.

< In 1857 the crisis broke out in the United States. This led to an efflux of bullion from England to America. But as soon as the American bubble burst, the crisis spread to England, and there was an efflux of bullion from America to England. Similarly between England and the Continent. In times of general crisis the balance of payments is against every nation (at least the commercially influential nations), but always against each in succession, like a volley of infantry fire, as soon as the sequence of payments reaches it; and once the crisis has broken out in England, for example, this sequence of dates is condensed into a very short period. It is then evident that all these countries have simultaneously overexported (i.e., overproduced) and overimported (i.e., overtraded), and that in all of them prices were inflated and credit overstrained. In every case the same collapse follows. The simple phenomenon of an export of bullion then affects each of them in turn, and shows by its very universality (1) that it is simply a phenomenon of the crisis and not its basis, and (2) that the sequence in which this export of bullion affects different countries simply

indicates when their turn has come to settle their account with heaven, and when the due date for the crisis has come for them and its latent elements have burst forth in their own case.

It is characteristic of the English economic writers – and the economic literature worth mentioning since 1830 principally boils down to writings about currency, the credit system and crises – that they consider the export of bullion, etc., in short the turn of the exchange rates in times of crisis, simply from the *English standpoint*, as a purely national phenomenon, and resolutely close their eyes to the fact that if their bank raises the interest rate in times of crisis, all other European banks do the same thing, and that if they raise a cry of distress about an efflux of bullion today, this is echoed tomorrow in America and the day after that in Germany and France.

In 1847 'the engagements running upon this country' (for the most part for corn) 'had to be met'. 'Unfortunately *they were met to a great extent by failures* in 1847' (wealthy England made sure it was well-nourished by bankrupting the continental nations) 'but to the extent to which they were not met by failures, they were met by the exportation of bullion'. (*Report on the Bank Acts*, 1857, no. 1218.) Thus in so far as a crisis in England is *intensified* by the banking legislation, this is also in times of dearth a means of cheating the corn-exporting nations, first of their food, and then of the money for their food. A ban on the *export of corn* in times such as these, in the case of nations which are themselves suffering, to a greater or lesser extent, from a dearth of corn, is thus a very rational means to employ against this plan by the Bank of England to 'meet engagements' for corn imports 'by failures'. It is then far better that the corn exporters and growers should lose a part of their profit for the benefit of their own country than that they should lose their capital for the benefit of England.

|347| It can be concluded from what has been said here that commodity capital loses its capacity to represent *money capital* in the crisis (and generally in times of pressure). The same is true of fictitious capital, *interest-bearing paper*, in so far as this itself circulates as money capital on the stock exchange. As the interest rate rises, its price falls (quite apart from the absence of credit), and this compels the holders of this paper to unload it onto the market on a massive scale, in order to obtain money. In the case of public shares, their price falls partly because of a decline in the revenues on which they are claims, partly because of the fraudulent character of the enterprises they represent. This fictitious money is enormously reduced during crises, and with it the power of its holders (the bankers, merchants, etc.) to raise money with it in the market. The reduction in the *money denomination* of these securities has however nothing to do with the real capital they rep-

resent, although it has a great deal to do with the solvency of their holders.

'Extensive fictitious credits have been created by means of accommodation bills, and open credits, great facilities for which have been afforded by the practice of joint stock country banks discounting such bills and rediscounting them with billbrokers in the London market, upon the credit of the bank alone, *without reference to the quality of the bills* otherwise'. (*Report on the Bank Acts*, 1858, p. 54.)

> |346| A part of the accumulated moneyed capital is in fact nothing but an expression of productive capital. For example, when around the year 1857 England invested £80,000,000 in American railway enterprises, etc., these were almost entirely financed by the export of English products, for which the Yankees did not have to pay anything in return. In order to send this money over, they bought bills of exchange on America, for which the Yankees did not have to pay in England (they did not have to send any returns).

< But the question we need to deal with here is how far a superabundance of moneyed capital – or rather the *accumulation of capital* in the form of loanable moneyed capital – coincides with genuine accumulation.[108]

The transformation of money into *moneyed capital* (i.e., loanable moneyed capital) is a far simpler matter than the transformation of money into productive capital. But we must distinguish here between two different things:

(1) the mere transformation of money into moneyed capital;

(2) the transformation of capital or revenue into money that is transformed into moneyed capital.

It is only the latter point which can involve a positive accumulation of moneyed capital, related to the genuine accumulation of productive capital.

Let us look first at point (1). We have already seen how an accumulation (a superabundance) of moneyed capital can take place which is connected with productive accumulation only relatively, i.e., it stands in inverse proportion to it. This is the case in the two phases of the industrial cycle, firstly at the time when productive capital has contracted, at the beginning of the cycle that follows the crisis, and secondly at the time when improvement sets in, but commercial credit still exerts very little pressure on moneyed credit. In the first case the money capital that was formerly employed in active business appears as *unemployed moneyed capital*; in the second case it appears as employed at very low terms, because now the productive capitalist dictates

108 [This is the beginning of Engels's Chapter 31 entitled 'Money Capital and Real Capital: II (Continuation)'. Editor]

to the moneyed one. The *superabundance of moneyed capital* expresses in the first case the stagnation of productive capital, and in the second case the relative independence of commercial credit from moneyed credit (resting on the fluidity of returns, short commercial credits, and operations predominantly conducted with one's own capital.) The people who work with the credit capital of others have not yet entered the fray, and the people who work with their own capital have not yet extended their activities into anything like pure credit operations. In the first case, the superabundance of moneyed capital expresses the exact opposite of genuine accumulation. In the second case it coincides with the renewed expansion of the reproduction process; it accompanies it without causing it. Although the superabundance of moneyed capital is already decreasing, this is only in relative terms, in proportion to the level of demand. In both cases the expansion of the accumulation process proper is promoted, because the low rate of interest, which coincides in the first case with low prices, and in the second case with improving prices, increases the portion of the profit that is transformed into profit of enterprise. This is all the more so when interest rises to its average level at the height of the time of prosperity, when it has admittedly risen but not in proportion to profit. > The previous relative abundance of moneyed capital (or its growth, which is a merely temporary expression of stagnation, just as hoard-formation is in general) can in this way, as a circumstance which promotes genuine accumulation, be one of the situations which leads to a real increase of moneyed capital.

< We have seen on the other hand that an accumulation of moneyed capital may take place without any genuine accumulation merely through an *expansion of the banking system*, a saving on the currency reserve, or even a saving on private individuals' reserve funds or means of payment, which are in this way transformed into loanable capital for short periods. This is why this loanable capital is also known as *'floating capital'*. (*Report on the Bank Act* 1857, question 501: 'What do you mean by "floating capital?" "It is capital applicable to loans of money for short periods" says Mr. Weguelin, Governor of the Bank of England'. 502: 'Bank of England notes ... country banks' circulation, and the amount of coin which is in the country'. 503. 'It does not appear from the Returns before this committee that there is any very great *variation in the active circulation*, if by floating capital you mean active circulation?'. {Though it is a very major distinction as to who it is that advances the active circulation, the *lender* or the reproductive capitalist himself.} |347| 'I include in floating capital the *reserves of the bankers*, in which there is a *considerable fluctuation*'. In other words, a major fluctuation takes place in the portion of deposits which the bankers have not lent out again but which figures rather as, for the most

part, the *reserve* of the Bank of England. The same gentleman finally says that floating capital may be – bullion (503).) It is quite priceless how all the categories of political economy take on a different form in this credit gibberish of the money market. There, 'floating capital' is the expression for 'circulating capital' (which is of course something completely different), *money* is 'capital', and 'bullion' is 'capital' and notes are 'circulation' and capital is 'a commodity' and 'debts' are commodities and 'fixed capital' is money invested in securities that are difficult to convert. This 'floating capital' is only lent out for short periods (and thus should only be used for short-term discounting). It is constantly flowing back and forth. If one person withdraws it, someone else puts it in. The amount of loanable moneyed capital (and here we are not referring at all to loans invested for years, but rather to loans invested in deposits and securities) thus actually grows quite independently of genuine accumulation.

'The joint-stock banks of London ... have increased their deposits from £8,850,774 in 1847 to £43,100,724 in 1857 ... The evidence given to your Committee leads to the inference that of this vast amount a large part has been derived from *sources not heretofore made available for this purpose*; and that the practice of opening accounts and depositing money with bankers has extended to numerous classes who did not formerly employ *their capital* (!) in that way. It is stated by Mr. Rodwell, the chairman of the Association of Private Country Bankers, and delegated by them to give evidence to your Committee, that in the neighbourhood of Ipswich this practice has lately increased *fourfold* among the farmers and shopkeepers of that district; that almost every farmer, even those paying only £50 per annum rent, now keeps deposits with bankers. The aggregate of these deposits of course finds its way to the employments of trade, and especially gravitates to London, the centre of commercial activity, where it is employed first in the discount of bills, or in other advances to the customers of the London bankers. That large portion, however, for which the bankers themselves have no immediate demand, passes into the hands of the billbrokers, who give to the bankers in return commercial bills already discounted by them for persons in London and in different parts of the country'. (*Report on the Bank Acts*, 1858, p. v.)

In fact, therefore, as far as the transactions between those bankers and the billbrokers go, the former *rediscount* the bills already discounted by the billbrokers; but, in point of fact, a great mass of the bills discounted by the billbrokers were already originally *rediscounted* by them and with the same money with which the banker rediscounts the broker's bills, the latter rediscounts other bills.

The following passage from *The Economist* sheds an interesting light on this *rediscounting*, and on the facilities which the purely technical increase in *loanable moneyed capital* provides for credit swindles:

'For some years past' (moneyed!) 'capital has accumulated in some districts of the country more rapidly than it could be used, while, in others, the means of employing' (moneyed) 'capital have increased more rapidly than the capital itself. While the bankers in the purely agricultural districts throughout the kingdom found no sufficient means of profitably and safely employing their deposits in their own districts, those in the large mercantile towns, and in the manufacturing and mining districts, have found a larger demand for capital than their own means could supply. The effect of this relative state of different districts has led, of late years, to the establishment and rapid |349| extension of a new class of houses in the distribution of capital, who, though usually called billbrokers, are in reality bankers upon an immense scale. The business of these houses has been to receive, for such periods, and at such rates of interest as were agreed upon, the surplus capital of bankers in those districts where it could not be employed, as well as *the temporarily unemployed moneys of public companies and extensive mercantile establishments*, and advance them at higher rates of interest to bankers in those districts where capital was more in demand, generally by *rediscounting* the bills taken from their customers; > as well as to merchants, in large sums, in most cases giving and taking such securities as were deemed satisfactory.[109] < And in this way Lombard Street has become the great centre in which the transfer of spare capital has been made from *one part of the country*, where it could not be profitably employed, to *another*, where a demand existed for it, as well as between individuals similarly circumstanced. At first these transactions were confined almost exclusively to borrowing and lending on *banking securities*. But as the capital of the country rapidly accumulated, and became more economised by the establishment of banks, the funds at the disposal of these "discount houses" became so large that they were induced to make advances first on *dock warrants of merchandise*, and then on *bills of lading, representing produce not even arrived in this country*, though sometimes, if not generally, secured by bills drawn by the merchant upon his broker. This practice rapidly changed the whole character of English commerce. The facilities thus afforded in Lombard Street gave extensive powers to the brokers in Mincing Lane, who on their part ... offered the full advantage of them to the import-

109 > It is not the convertibility of the securities into money which is the knottiest problem in crises, but the circumstance that these securities have ceased to be securities for the money that is expected to be received from a discount or a loan. <

ing merchant; who so far took advantage of them that, whereas twenty-five years ago the fact that a merchant received advances on his bills of lading, or even his dock warrants, would have been fatal to his credit, the practice has become so common of late years that it may be said to be now the general rule, and not the rare exception as it was twenty-five years ago. Nay, so much further has this system been carried that *large sums have been raised in Lombard Street on bills drawn against the forthcoming crops of distant colonies*. The consequence of such facilities being thus granted to the importing merchants led them to extend their transactions abroad, and to invest their "*floating*" capital with which their business had hitherto been conducted, in the most objectionable of all fixed securities – *foreign plantations* – over which they could exercise little or no control. And thus we see the direct chain of credit through which the "capital" of the country, *collected in our rural districts*,[110] and in small amounts in the *shape of deposits in country banks*,[111] and centred in Lombard Street for employment, has been, first, made available for *extending operations in our mining and manufacturing districts* by the *rediscount of bills to banks in those localities*; next, for granting greater facilities for the importation of foreign produce by *advances upon dock warrants and bills of lading*, and thus *liberating* the *"legitimate" mercantile capital* of houses engaged in the foreign and colonial trade, and inducing to its most objectionable advances on foreign plantations'.[112]

We have already seen how major public enterprises, like railways, etc., can temporarily increase 'loanable capital' > in the intervening period, when deposits have been made upon 'calls' but have not yet been used up for their specific purpose. (See page 320, '207' and Samuel Gurney, 1742.)[113]

---

110 > This is what *The Economist* was writing in 1847. By 1857 things had progressed further. Now the spare cash, etc., 'collected in London' was placed at the disposal of the billbrokers and bankers. <

111 This is the 'nice' way to devour credits. The 'rural' depositor imagines that he is making a deposit with his 'banker', and he also imagines that when the banker makes loans, it is to private individuals with whom he is acquainted. He has not the least idea that that banker puts his 'deposit' at the disposal of a London billbroker over whom he cannot exercise the smallest influence.

112 *The Economist* 1847, p. 1334.

113 [This refers back to the quotation from p. 207 of *First Report* 1848, on page 320 of Marx's manuscript, see above, and to Samuel Gurney's answer to question no. 1742 in the same report. Translator]

|348| It has already been shown, in our consideration of simple money circulation, that if the velocity of circulation and an economical use of the means of payment are assumed, the quantity of money really circulating is simply determined by the prices of the commodities and the number of transactions. The same law applies to the circulation of notes.[114]

Yearly Averages of (Bank of England) Notes with the Public. The figures in the following list should be multiplied by 1,000.

Year	Notes of £5 and £10	% of total circ.	Notes of £20 to £100	% of total circ.	Notes of £200 to £1,000	% of total circ.	Total
1844	9,263	45.7	5,735	28.3	5,253	26.0	20,241
1845	9,698	46.9	6,082	29.3	4,942	23.8	20,722
1846	9,918	48.9	5,778	28.5	4,590	22.6	20,286
1847	9,591	50.1	5,498	28.7	4,066	21.2	19,155
1848	8,732	48.3	5,046	27.9	4,307	23.8	18,085
1849	8,692	47.2	5,234	28.5	4,477	24.3	18,403
1850	9,164	47.2	5,587	28.8	4,646	24.0	19.398
1851	9,362	48.1	5,554	28.5	4,557	23.4	19,473
1852	9,839	45.0	6,161	28.2	5,856 maximum	26.8	21,856
1853	10,699 maximum	47.3	6,393 maximum	28.2	5,541 second highest	24.5	22,653
1854	10,565	51.0	5,910	28.5	4,234	20.5	20,709
1855	10,628	53.6	5,706	28.9	3,459	17.5	19,793
1856	10,680	54.4	5,645	28.7	3,323	16.9	19,648
1857	10,659	54.7	5,567	28.6	3,241	16.7	19,467

(*Report on the Bank Acts* 1858, p. 69.)

'The whole amount of banknotes has actually diminished since 1844' (*Report on the Bank Acts* 1858, p. 70).

114 [Engels relocated this important paragraph to his Chapter 33 (Marx 1981 [Engels], p. 655). Editor]

The smaller banknotes, £5 and £10, which enter most into the retail transactions of the country, increased in number, as shown by the above list, from 9,263,000 in 1844 to 10,699,000 in 1853. This occurred 'concurrently with the increase of the gold circulation'. (*Report on the Bank Acts* 1858, p. 4.) There was a fall in the number of notes of higher denominations, on the other hand. The notes from £200 to £1,000 declined from 5,865,000 in 1852 to 3,241,000 in 1857. This represents a fall of 2,624,000. The explanation is as follows:

'On 8 June 1854, the private bankers of London admitted the joint stock banks to the arrangements of the clearing-house, and shortly afterwards the final clearing was adjusted in the Bank of England. The daily clearances are effected by transfers in the accounts which the several banks keep in that establishment. In consequence of the adoption of this system, the large notes which the bankers formerly employed for the purpose of adjusting their accounts are no longer necessary'. (*Report on the Bank Acts* 1858, p. 7.)

Question 947. 'Whatever measures you resort to, the amount of the notes of the public, you say, remains the same; that is somewhere about £20,000,000?' Answer of Mr. [Sheffield] Neave, Governor of the Bank of England: 'In ordinary times, the uses of the public seem to want about £20,000,000. There are special periodical moments when, through the year, they rise to another £1,000,000 or £1,500,000. I stated, that if the public wanted more, they could always take it from the Bank of England'. 948: 'You stated that during the panic the public would not allow you to diminish the amount of notes. Can you account for that? In moments of panic, the public have, as I believe, the full power to help themselves as to notes; and of course, as long as the Bank has a liability, they may use that liability to take the notes from the Bank'. 949: 'Then there seems to be required, at all times, somewhere about £20,000,000 of legal tender? £20,000,000 of notes with the public; it varies. It is £18,500,000, £19,000,000, £20,000,000 and so on; but, taking the average, you may call it from £19 million to £20 million'.

Mr. Slater (of the firm of Morrison, Dillon and Co., which was then one of the largest firms of the metropolis) has this to say: 'To prove how little of real money, that is of Bank of England notes and gold, enters into the operations of trade, it may be interesting, as well as conclusive on that point, to refer to the analysis of a continuous course of commercial transactions, extending over several millions yearly, and which may be considered as a fair example of the general trade of the country. The proportions of receipts and payments are reduced to the scale of £1,000,000 during the year 1856, and are as follows:

Receipts		*Payments*	
In bankers' drafts and mercantile bills of exchange payable after date	£553,596	Bills of exchequer payable after date	£302,674
In cheques on bankers, etc. payable on demand	£357,715	Cheques on London bankers	£663,672
In country bankers' notes	£9,627		
Total	£900,938	Total	£966,346
In Bank of England notes	£68,554	In Bank of England notes	£22,743
In gold	£28,089	In gold	£9,427
In silver and copper	£1,486	In silver and copper	£1.484
In post office orders	£933		
Total	£99,062	Total	£33,654
Sum Total	£1,000,000	Sum Total	£1,000,000

(*Report on the Bank Acts* 1858, p. lxxi.)

According to this, less than 7 percent of the *money received* was in Bank of England notes, and up to 3 percent was in gold and silver. Of the payments made, 2 percent was in Bank of England notes, and 1 percent was in gold and silver. In contrast, about 90 percent of the payments *received*, and nearly 97 percent of the payments made, consisted of the *portion of the currency* formed of the credit and capital of the traders themselves'. (ibid.)

|349| Before we go over to (2)[115] two more points need to be made. First, that < the volume of *loanable capital* is completely different from the *quantity of circulation*. By *quantity of circulation*, here, we mean the sum of all notes and bullion, etc. A part of this quantity forms the bankers' *reserve*, and this is subject to change. > Second, that after every period of crisis, the highest level reached in the previous industrial cycle becomes the basis or the lower level in the subsequent cycle.

115 [This is the section entitled 'Transformation of Capital or Revenue into Money that is Transformed into Loan Capital'. See above, p. 346 of the manuscript. Translator]

|350| On the second point: < the *real or declared value* of the produce and manufactures exported from the United Kingdom was £40,396,300 in *1824*, a year of prosperity. It then fell below this sum, fluctuating between £35 million and £39 million. In *1834*, another year of prosperity, it rose above the 1824 level to £41,649,191 and in *1836* it attained a new maximum of *£53,568,571*.

In *1837* it fell to £42 million (higher than in 1824) and then fluctuated between £50, 51, 52, and 53 million (but not in this order). In 1844 it reached *£58½ million* (far more than the maximum of 1836), and in *1845* it was £60,111,082. It then fell to £57 million in 1846 and fluctuated between £58 million (almost £59 million) in 1847, £52 million (almost £53 million) in 1848, rose to £63½ million in 1849, reached almost £99 million in 1853, and fell in 1854 to somewhat over £97 million. In 1855 it was £95½ million, in 1856 it was £115,826,948 and in 1857 it reached a maximum of £122 million. In 1858 it fell to £116 million, but already by 1859 it had risen again to £130 million. In 1860 it was £135 million (almost 136), in 1861 it was £125 million (higher than in 1857) and in 1863 it was roughly £146½ million.

> But the above-mentioned law is shown even more clearly when we consider the *official* value, which only indicates the *quantity* of exports, as opposed to their 'real or declared value'. (In particular it is less apparent before 1844 in the latter form.)

We shall therefore look first at the operation of the law from 1844 onwards as indicated by the real or declared value, and then at the period from 1827 to 1840 as indicated by the *official value*.

	£	
1836 *Maximum*	53,368,572	
1844 Prosperity year of the new *cycle*	58,584,292	
1845 *Maximum*	60,111,082	
1846	57,786,876	
1847	58,842,377	(higher than 1844)
1848 *The year that followed the crisis*	52,849,025	
1849	63,596,025	(already above the *1845* maximum)
1850	71,367,885	
1851	74,448,722	
1852	78,076,854	
1853	98,933,781	
1854	97,184,726	

	£	
1855	95,688,085	
1856	115,826,948	
1857 (*Crisis*)	122,066,107	
1858 *The year after the crisis*	116,608,756	(higher than the year before the crisis)
1859	130,411,529	
1860	135,842,817	

This law is still more apparent in the earlier period, because the *official value*, or *quantity*, shows it much more clearly than the *real value*.

	Official value (£)	*Real value* (£)	*British and Irish produce and manufactures*
1824	48,735,551	40,396,300	This was the highest level reached (in quantity) up to that date.
1825	47,166,020	38,877,385	
1826	40,965,735	31,536,723	
1827	52,219,280	37,181,335	This is already significantly higher (as to quantity) than the maximum of 1824, but it is the *minimum*, compared to the following years.
1828	52,797,455	36,812,756	
1829	56,213,041	35,842,623	
1830	61,140,864	38,271,597	
1831	60,683,933	37,164,372	
1832	65,026,702	36,450,594	
1833	69,989,939	39,667,347	
1834	73,831,550	41,649,191	Year of prosperity
1835	78,376,731	47,372,270	
1836	85,229,837	53,368,571	Maximum reached in the phase 1824–36. (Almost twice the 1824 figure.)
1837	72,548,047	42,070,744	*Year of crisis* (or after it)
1838	92,459,231	50,060,970	
1839	97,402,726	53,233,586	
1840	102,714,060	51,406,430	

< The same thing could of course also be shown for imports, which indicate the expansion of the market, but here we are concerned only with the scale of production.

|351| On the first point, on 12 November 1857 (the day of the issue of the Treasury Letter),[116] 'the entire reserve of the *Bank of England* was only £580,751 (including London and all its branches); their *deposits* at the same time amounting to £22,500,000; of which near six and a half million belonged to London bankers'. (*Report on the Bank Acts* 1858, p. lvii.) > In 1864 the deposits in nine London banking institutions alone were £67,377,556 (as against a reserve fund of £649,982 and a paid up capital of £4,615,695.) (See the *Return* {1865?} on Overstone's motion in 1864.) This *Return* needs to be examined in general in order to compare the *amount of the deposits* with the *amount of circulation at that time*.[117] (The deposits alone were perhaps three times as large as the banknote circulation of the Bank of England.)

< *Variations* in the rate of interest (setting aside those taking place over longer periods, or the differences between interest rates in different countries; the first kind being conditioned by variations in the general rate of profit, the second by differences in profit rates and the development of the credit system) depend on the quantity of moneyed capital available (all other circumstances, such as confidence, etc., *remaining the same*). They depend, that is to say, on the quantity of capital lent in the form of money, in coin and notes; *as distinct from productive capital*, which is lent, as such, by means of commercial credit among the reproductive agents themselves.

But the *volume* of this moneyed capital is still different from and independent of the *quantity of money in circulation*.

If £20 is lent five times in the course of a day, for example, a moneyed capital of £100 would have been lent, and this would equally mean that this £20 had functioned at least four times > (with the exception of the first lender) < as means of purchase or payment; for if the same amount of money were lent to five people, without the mediation of purchase and payment, so that it did not represent the transformed form of capital (commodities, including labour-capacity as well) at least four times, it would simply constitute five debts of £20 owed by the recipients.

In countries where the credit system is highly developed we can assume that all moneyed capital, i.e., all moneyed capital available for loan, exists in the *form of deposits* with bankers and money-lenders. This at least holds good

116 [The letter which suspended the operation of the Bank Act of 1844. Translator]

117 [It is not known which *Return* Marx is referring to here. Translator]

for business as a whole. > (Incidentally, it should be noted in addition, in relation to what we said earlier, that < in times of prosperity, before speculation properly so called sets in (new enterprises, etc.) credit is easy and confidence is strong. When such is the case, *transfers of credit* perform the greater part of the functions of circulation without the intervention of banknotes.)

The very possibility of *large-scale deposits* while the *amount of the means of circulation* > (including bullion and coin) < *is relatively small* depends entirely on (1) the number of purchases and payments that *the same piece of money* performs; and (2) the number of times it returns to the bank as a *deposit*, so that its repeated function as means of purchase and payment is mediated by its *transformation into a deposit*. A shopkeeper, for instance, may deposit £100 a week with his banker in money; the banker uses this to pay out a part of the manufacturer's deposit; the latter pays this to his workers, and they use it to pay the shopkeeper. The shopkeeper then makes a fresh deposit with it, and so on. The £100 deposited by the shopkeeper has thus served firstly to pay out a deposit of the manufacturer's, secondly to pay the workers, thirdly to pay the shopkeeper himself, and fourthly to deposit a second instalment of his moneyed capital; for at the end of twenty weeks, assuming that he did not have to draw on this money himself, he would have deposited £2,000 in the bank, using the same £100.

The extent to which this moneyed capital is *unoccupied* is shown only in the ebb and flow of the *bankers' reserve funds*.[118]

Here, in point (2), we are considering the *accumulation of moneyed capital*, in so far as this does not express a stagnation in the flow of commercial credit, or a saving either on the currency or on the reserve money capital of the agents engaged in reproduction.

---

118 This is why Mr. Weguelin, the Governor of the Bank of England in 1857, concludes that the *bullion* in the Bank of England is the only 'reserve capital'.

'Practically, I think, the *rate of discount* is governed by *the amount of unemployed capital* which there is in the country. The amount of unemployed capital is *represented* by the reserve of the Bank of England, which is practically a *reserve of bullion*. When, therefore, the bullion is drawn upon, it *diminishes the amount of unemployed capital in the country*, and consequently raises the value of that which remains'. (*Report on the Bank Acts* 1857, no. 1258.)

'The reserve of bullion in the Bank of England is, in truth, the central reserve, or hoard of treasure, upon which the whole trade of the country is carried on ... it is upon that hoard or reservoir that the action of the foreign exchanges always falls'. (*Report on the Bank Acts* 1857, no. 1364.)

Leaving aside these two exceptions, an accumulation of moneyed capital may arise through an exceptional *influx of bullion*, as happened in 1852 and 1853 as a result of the Australian and Californian discoveries. This gold was deposited in the Bank of England. The depositors accepted notes in return, which were not directly deposited with bankers by the people to whom the gold belonged. In this way, there was an extraordinary *increase in circulation*.[119] The Bank tried to valorise these deposits by reducing its discount rate to two percent.

|352| All moneyed capitalists accumulate directly in the money form, whereas we have seen that the real accumulation of the productive capitalists occurs through an increase in the elements of reproductive capital itself. The development of the credit system and the tremendous concentration of moneyed concerns must therefore already accelerate in and of itself the accumulation of moneyed capital, as a form separate from genuine accumulation. This development of moneyed capital is therefore a result of genuine accumulation, since it is the consequence of the development of the reproduction process, and the profit that forms the source of accumulation for these moneyed capitalists is simply a deduction from the surplus-value that the reproductive agents extract (as well as an appropriation of part of the interest on the savings *of other people*.) Moneyed capital accumulates at the same time at the expense of the reproductive capitalist classes. In the adverse phases of the industrial cycle, for instance, the rate of interest may rise so high that it swallows up the whole of the profit for a certain length of time.[120] At the same time, the prices of public and other securities fall. This is the moment at which the moneyed capitalists invest in these depreciated securities on a massive scale, as it will soon go up again in the later phases, and even rise above its normal level. They will then sell it off, thereby appropriating a part of the public's moneyed capital. The securities that are retained yield a higher interest, since they were bought below their price. But all the profit which the moneyed capitalists make, and which they convert back into capital, they first transform into loanable 'moneyed capital'. Thus we already have an accumulation of moneyed capital, as distinct from genuine accumulation – even if this accumulation is the latter's offspring – when we simply consider the *moneyed capitalists* (bankers, etc.) themselves. This is the accumulation carried out by this

---

119 *Report on the Bank Acts 1857*, no. 1329 (Weguelin's evidence).

120 *Report on the Bank Acts 1857*, no. 1353 (Newmarch). In the course of six months of 1853, £22–£23 million of bullion piled up in the Bank of England.

particular class of capitalist. And it must grow with each extension of the credit system, since it accompanies the genuine expansion of the reproduction process.

If the rate of interest is low, this depreciation of *moneyed capital* falls principally on the depositors and not on the banks. (Before the recent development of joint-stock banking, three-quarters of all bank deposits did not receive any interest.)

As far as the monetary accumulation of the remaining class of capitalist is concerned, we disregard here the part that is invested in interest-bearing paper and accumulates in this form. We shall simply consider the portion that is placed on the market as 'moneyed', loanable capital.

Here we have firstly the section of *profit* that is not spent as revenue, being rather designed for accumulation, but for which the reproductive capitalists concerned do not have any immediate employment in their own businesses. This profit exists directly in *commodity capital*, making up a portion of its value. If the *commodity capital* is not then transformed back into its elements of production by which we mean not only its *value portion* which is the same as the original capital, but also a part of the profit (we leave aside here for the time being the merchant, whom we shall examine more specifically later on), it must > be realised in money and < exist for a certain period in the money form. Its amount rises with the volume of the capital itself, even given a declining rate of profit. The part to be spent as revenue is gradually consumed, but in the meantime it constitutes *moneyed capital* as a deposit with the banker. And so even the growth of the part of the profit spent as revenue is expressed in a temporary *accumulation of moneyed capital*, which is however constantly repeated. The same thing applies to the other part, the part which is destined for *accumulation*. With the development and organisation of the credit system, the rise in revenue (the rise in the consumption of the reproductive capitalist) is expressed as an *accumulation of moneyed capital*. And this holds good for all revenues, in so far as they are only gradually consumed, hence rent, the higher forms of wages, the income of the unproductive classes, etc. > (Apart from the case of the productive capitalists, < all these revenues assume for a time the *form of money revenue*, and can therefore be converted into deposits and thereby into moneyed capital.) It is true of all revenue, whether destined for consumption or for accumulation, that as soon as it exists in whatever kind of money form it is a portion of the value of the commodity capital that is transformed into money, and is therefore the expression and result of genuine accumulation, though not itself productive capital. If a spinner has exchanged his commodity for cotton, save for the part that forms revenue and is exchanged for money, the actual existence of his productive capital is the yarn that has passed into the possession of the clothier or into private consumption > (depending on the type of yarn in question) < and this yarn, moreover, whether it serves for reproduction or for consumption, is the existence of both capital value and of the surplus-value contained in it. The amount of surplus-value transformed into money depends on the amount of surplus-value contained in the yarn. But as soon as it is transformed into money, this money is simply the value existence of that surplus-value. And as such it becomes an element of *moneyed capital*. No more is needed for this than that its transformation into a deposit (if it has not already been lent out by its owner). If it is to be transformed back into productive capital, on the other hand, > the extent to which it is transformed depends on the price and the massiveness of the elements of reproduction.

|352A| The Confusion

> The impact of the *banking reserve*, as constituted by the Act of 1844, on the variations in the rate of discount. (*Report on Bank Acts* 1857, nos. 1357, 1358 and 1366.)

< *Bill Circulation and Banknote Circulation.* There is 'no connection between the variations in the amount of bill circulation and the variations in the banknote circulation ... the only result ... pretty uniform ... that whenever *there is any pressure upon the money market*, as indicated by a rise in the rate of discount, then the volume of the bill circulation is very much increased, and vice versa'. (no. 1426. [William] Newmarch) >

Difficulties encountered by the Bank of England in increasing its discount business by lowering the rate of interest. (nos. 1468–71.)

Effects of a rise in the rate of discount.

No. 1476. 'The mere arithmetical amount of increased charge occasioned is ... very greatly exceeded by the apprehension attending a monetary panic'.

No. 1477. 'It is a moral effect produced by the apprehension that capital will not be forthcoming to conduct operations which are in progress to a conclusion? Yes, and that calculations and transactions which have been entered into upon the assumption that no change would take place in the rate of discount will be disturbed'. (Question put by [Thomas] Weguelin to the witness Newmarch)

< No. 1563. ([James] Wilson's question) 'The circulation of a banker, so far as it is kept out upon the average, is *an addition to the effective capital* of that banker, is it not? Certainly'. (Evidence of Newmarch.)

No. 1564 (The same pair): 'Then whatever profit he derives from that circulation is *a profit derived from credit*, and not *from a capital which he actually possesses?* Certainly'. >

Nos. 1568–72. *How bills endorsed by country bankers circulate.*

The bankers also raise *credit capital* by paying with bills *endorsed* by them, by issuing *drafts* (in return for cash) which run for twenty-one days and by issuing notes.

No. 1573 (Newmarch): (The country bankers send their cash to the London billbrokers for interest, and from the latter they receive as securities bills of exchange already discounted. They then issue these bills of exchange in *payment*, endorsing them.) 'The great operations of credit through the country banker are performed in that way by bills of exchange' (which circulate) 'taken out of the banker's portfolio, and endorsed by him, and passed over to merchants and others, and then paid away'.

Drain of bullion abroad on account of the (mercantile) *balance of payments* as a *means for investing* English *capital in foreign enterprise* and *also for carrying on foreign expenditure* (wars, etc.) (Newmarch, no. 1702.)

< Savings are made on circulation, *in addition to banking facilities*. The '*introduction of better modes of communication, penny postage, telegraph*, economise the necessity for the circulating medium' (no. 1741).

No. 1747. 'In Scotland and Ireland, where the smaller denomination of circulation consists of paper, the circulation has increased by about 31 percent, while the circulation of notes in England has remained stationary'.

No. 1749. 'The entire note circulation of the *United Kingdom is £39,000,000*'.

No. 1752. *The average circulation of banknotes in Scotland, 1834*: £3,120,000; *1844*: £3,020,000; *1854*: £4,050,000. >

Exchange. No. 1797 (Newmarch): 'I do not think that that part of the expenditure which is sent out in the form of commodities affects the computation of the exchange; we know perfectly well that the computation of the exchange between two countries is affected, one might say, solely by the quantity of obligations or bills offering in one country, as compared with the quantity offering in the other country against it'.

No. 1802. 'An adverse exchange with one country necessarily produces a favourable exchange with another'.

No. 1804 (Wilson): 'The effect of making railways in India, whether you send bullion, or whether you send materials, would be the same upon the capital market here in increasing the value of capital as if the whole was sent out in bullion?' (Newmarch, in reply) 'In the one case the £6,000,000' (invested there) 'would be returned immediately; in the other case it would not be returned so rapidly'.

Under *cross examination* by Sir Charles Wood (no. 1818 onwards), Newmarch is completely at a loss to explain what use '*inconvertibility*' is from his and Tooke's standpoint (i.e., if notes were issued on mercantile securities.)

No. 1868 (Sir Charles Wood): 'Then do you consider all banknotes beyond the two thirds of bullion held in reserve *as so much capital added to the capital of the country?* Those banknotes are generally so much added to the available capital of the country, because they effect an economy to that amount in the instrument of exchange, which but for those banknotes must be represented by coin'.

No. 1889 (Newmarch): 'The amount of funds constantly employed in the London money market may be described as something like £120,000,000'.

No. 1896 (Newmarch): 'The effect' (of a low rate of discount) 'is to debase gradually the quality of the securities upon which advances are made, and to produce, sooner or later, a violent rebound'.

< No. 1938. Sir Charles Wood again puts Newmarch in difficulties by asking him 'how will the *exchange* with that country' (Turkey) 'be ... affected, supposing the trade with Turkey to be in an ordinary state of equilibrium, by the export of warlike stores to the Crimea?' >

|352b| No. 1947 (the chairman, [Edward] Cardwell): 'A banknote is a promise to pay on demand?'

No. 1948. 'If the state were to confer upon a private individual the privilege of issuing promises to pay which he was not bound to pay, it would in fact confer on that private individual a power of committing a fraud?'

No. 1959 (Newmarch): 'So far from its being a necessary effect of the introduction of inconvertible paper to produce excess, we know it to be a fact that after the Bank restriction had been in force two years, the accumulation in the Bank of England was so large as to induce the Bank's directors to give formal notice under the statute to the government that they were prepared to resume cash payments'.

No. 1961. 'In order to give support to this peculiar tale', Cardwell assumes that 'the government pays ... inconvertible paper, and does *not* receive inconvertible paper in payment to itself'.

Nos. 1988 onwards: Completely incorrect theory of Newmarch concerning the *exchangeable value* of gold when there is a purely metallic circulation. He considers that the value would then be determined by the total quantity of gold in the country, whether in the shape of coin, plate or metal. No. 1991. Sir F[rancis] Baring asks: 'The exchangeable value of gold and prices rise according to the quantity of gold in the country' (in whatever shape)? This shows Newmarch up as an idiot.

< No. 2031 onwards: Mr. John Stuart Mill makes a splendid fool of himself, with his belief that the Act of 1844 checked over-speculation. This wiseacre had the good luck to make his comments on '*the 12th. day of June 1857*'. Four months later his wisdom after the fact would have looked even more ridiculous. The donkey actually congratulates 'the Bank Directors' and 'the commercial public generally' because they 'understand much better than they did the nature of a commercial crisis' (no. 2031).

No. 2066. Wiseacre Mill thinks that £1 notes are issued as 'advances made to manufacturers or others who pay wages ... the notes do or may get into the hands of labourers and others who expend them for consumption, and *in that case the notes do constitute in themselves a demand for commodities*, and may for some time tend to promote a rise of prices'. Does Mr. Mill assume that the manufacturers will pay higher wages because they are paying them in £1 notes instead of gold sovereigns? Or does he believe that if the manufacturer receives his discount in £100 notes and exchanges this for sovereigns, these 'wages' would produce less 'demand' than if they were paid originally in £1 notes? And does the jackass not know that in some mining districts wages are or were paid in local notes, even if notes of £5 together for several workers? Does this diminish their power of demand? Or does this bletherer think the bankers will then lend more money to the manufacturers? >

Exchange.

No. 311. 'An *adverse exchange* means nothing more than the number of bills upon this country exceeding the number of bills which this country has drawn upon other countries'.

No. 976 (Wilson): 'The whole demand for bullion, beyond the ordinary circulation of the country, is to meet a foreign drain when it arises'.

No. 1363. 'The reserve of bullion of the Bank of England is, in truth, the central reserve or hoard of treasure upon which the whole trade of the country is carried on ... All the other banks in the country look to the Bank of England as the central hoard or reservoir from which they are to draw their reserve of coin; and it is upon that hoard or reservoir that the action of the foreign exchanges always falls'.

No. 2172. 'Then the operation' (when the rate of interest is high) 'would be, that foreign capitalists would be attracted by the low price of securities, not by the high rate of discount here? The two always come together'. No. 2171 (Mill): 'If Rothschild bought securities' the people who receive the money would 'discount or send their money to bankers by whom it would be employed in discounts'. The exchange would be rectified in this way. This also occurs in part through a reduction in imports, and, where the drain of bullion results from a sudden demand (for corn, etc.), an increase in exports. One should not forget that transactions between countries do not cease for one moment.

< No. 2176 (Mill): 'When there is a state of commercial difficulty ... [there is a] considerable fall in the price of securities, both private and public ... railway shares for instance fall very much ... Foreigners send over to buy railway shares in the country, or English holders of foreign railway shares sell their foreign railway shares abroad ... so that much transfer of bullion is prevented'.

No. 2182 (Mill): 'A large and rich class of bankers and dealers in securities, through whom the equalisation of the rate of interest and *the equalisation of commercial pressure between different countries* usually takes place ... is always on the look out to buy securities which are likely to rise ... the place for them to buy securities will be the country which is sending bullion away'. Nos. 2183: 'These investments took place to a very considerable extent in 1847, to a sufficient extent to have relieved the drain considerably'.

< No. 2400 (Hubbard): 'The effect of the export of bullion ... has no reference whatever to the prices of commodities. But it does have an important effect upon the price of securities, because *as the rate of interest varies* the *value of the commodities which embodied that interest* is necessarily powerfully affected'. He demonstrates with a list that from 1834 to 1843 and from 1845 to 1856 the movement of prices was quite independent of changes in the amount of bullion exported and the rate of interest. On the other hand, there was a close connection between the *movement of bullion* 'which, in fact, is the *representative of our uninvested capital* and the *rate of interest*'. Hubbard gives the price movements of the following commodities: cotton, cotton yarn, cotton cloth, wool, woollen cloth, flax, linen, indigo, iron bars, tin plates, copper, tallow, sugar, coffee and silk.

No. 2402 (Hubbard): 'In 1847 a very large amount of American securities were retransferred to America and Russian securities to Russia, and other continental securities were transferred to those places from which we drew our supplies of grain'.

> (See the *summary of the list on the next page*.)

|352c| *Hubbard's List, abbreviated.*

< From 1834 to 1843

Year	*Periods of comparison*	*Bullion in the bank (£)*	*Market rate of discount*	*Prices of 15 main articles*		
				Rose	Fell	Did not vary
1834	1 March	9,104,000	2¾			
1835	1 March	6,274,000	3¾	7	7	1
1836	1 March	7,918,000	3¼	11	3	1
1837	1 March	4,077,000	5	5	9	1
1838	1 March	10,471,000	2¾	4	11	
1839	1 September	2,684,000	6	8	5	2
1840	1 June	4,571,000	4¾	5	9	1
1840	1 December	3,642,000	5¾	7	6	2
1841	1 December	4,873,000	5	3	12	
1842	1 December	10,603,000	2½	2	13	
1843	1 June	11,566,000	2½	1	14	

From 1844 to 1853

Year	*Periods of comparison*	*Bullion in the bank (£)*	*Market rate of discount*	*Prices of 15 main articles*		
				Rose	Fell	Did not vary
1844	1 March	16,162,000	2¼			
1845	1 December	13,237,000	4½	11	4	
1846	1 September	16,366,000	3	7	8	
1847	1 September	9,140,000	6	6	6	3
1850	1 March	17,126,000	2½	5	9	1
1851	1 June	13,705,000	3	2	11	2
1852	1 September	21,853,000	1¾	9	5	1
1853	1 December	15,093,000	5	14	0	1

Hubbard's comment on this is: 'As in the 10 years between 1834 and 1843, so also between 1844 and 1853, movements in the bullion of the Bank were invariably accompanied by a decrease or increase in the loanable value of money advanced on discount; and the variations in the prices of commodities in this country exhibit an entire independence of the amount of circulation as shown in the fluctuation in bullion at the Bank of England'. (*Report on Bank Acts 1857*, part 2, appendix, pp. 290 and 291.)

Since the demand for, and the supply of, commodities regulates their market prices, it is clear how wrong Overstone is to identify the demand for moneyed capital (as indicated in the discount; one ought rather to speak of variations in supply) with the demand for 'real capital'. In reality he is now merely hiding his old shit that commodities are regulated by variations in currency under the phrase that variations in the discount rate are variations in the demand for 'real capital' (as distinguished from money capital). In actual fact this is the old rubbish that the movements of bullion, by making the quantity of currency in the country greater or less, affect the prices of commodities. 'Unless the value of money is brought into action in the question of cost, or in the question of supply and demand, those variations in the rate of interest leave prices totally unaffected'. (If there were a drain of bullion and prices fell, the value of the exports of the bullion-exporting country would fall {according to the currency theory} and the value of its imports would rise, just as prices rise in the country to which the bullion is going.)

No. 2545. 'There are great quantities of European securities ... which have a European currency in all the different money markets, and those bonds, as soon as their value is affected, in one market, as much as to be reduced by 1 or 2 percent, are immediately purchased for transmission to those markets where their value is still unimpaired'.

No. 2565. 'Are not foreign countries ... in debt to the merchants of this country? Very largely'. No. 2566: 'Therefore, the encashment of those debts might be sufficient to account for a very large accumulation of capital in this country? In 1847, the ultimate restoration of our position was effected by our striking off so many millions previously due by America, and so many millions due by Russia to this country'.

No. 2572. 'In 1847 the exchange between this country and St. Petersburg was very high. When the government letter came out, authorising the Bank to issue ... the stipulation was ... discount at 8 percent. At that moment, with the then rate of discount here, it was a profitable operation to order gold to be shipped from St. Petersburg to London, and on its arrival to lend it at 8 percent up to the maturity of the 3 months' bill drawn against the purchase and shipment of gold'. No. 2573: 'In all bullion operations there are many points to be taken into consideration; there is the rate of exchange, and the rate of interest which is available for the investment during the period of the maturity of the bill'. >

Quantity of money.

No. 2614. (This is related just to the *quantity of circulation.*) 'It is usually to replace a contraction in the external circulation which is taking place through the action of the revenue. I find at the end of each quarter, that the action of the revenue is to throw into the reserve of the Bank of England a considerable portion of the note circulation as well as of the gold circulation of the country; and it is at those periods that the advances are most active, and the consequence of those advances is to return to the public for the purpose of carrying on their operations the notes and gold which have been brought in through the action of the revenue'. < No. 2844: 'When the rate of discount is highest, the Bank is the cheapest place to go, and when it is lowest the billbrokers are the cheapest parties'. >

|352d| No. 3295. 'An export of gold might take place ... because gold was at a premium in other countries where it was required'. (Wilson)

< The reciprocal transfer of commodities:

No. 4330. Evidence of [Nathaniel] Alexander (East Indian merchant): 'In my own business at the present moment, if I lay out 6s. in Manchester I get 5s. back in India; if I lay out 6s. in India, I get 5s. in London'. (Proof that the Indian market is overstocked with Manchester goods and the London market is overstocked with Indian goods.) No. 4331: 'The consequence is, that I am at a standstill at the present moment in my own business'.

The *history of the drain of silver* from France to Asia (which England had in part to replace with gold) shows at the same time that *silver* (which is here equivalent to gold) was sent instead of commodities, not because the latter's prices had risen in the country which produced them, but because they had fallen in the country which imported them: they were depreciated through being overimported. (According to the currency fellows an export of this kind would lead to a fall in the prices of these commodities in England and a rise in India.)

No. 4337. 'Is the drain for China or for India? You send the silver to India, and you buy opium with a great deal of it and all this goes on to China to lay down funds for the purchase of the silk; and the state of the markets in India' (in spite of the accumulation of silver there) 'makes it a more profitable investment for the merchant to lay down silver than to send piece goods or British manufactures'. No. 4338: 'In order to obtain the silver ... [there is a] great drain from France'. No. 4344: 'Instead of bringing in silk from France and Italy, we are sending it there in large quantities, both from Bengal and from China'.

> No. 4348. The drain of 1847 had come to an end by October 1847. No. 4349. In December [1847] the bullion of the Bank of England increased from £8 million to £12 million. No. 5075: If the rate of interest were lower in England than on the Continent [there would be a] 'tendency for bills upon London to come here earlier and to be realised by discount in the London market, and the proceeds to be remitted in coin'. No. 5076: 'By that means the bankers upon the Continent would *anticipate* at an earlier period *their demands upon London?* They would

discount their bills'. No. 5078: 'He would not keep his English bills' (this is a Hamburg banker speaking) 'if he could convert them at 5½ while he could discount bills in Hamburg at 7½'.

(With the development of *interest-bearing paper* the mercantile and general means of raising money on loans increase, and with this facility the demands upon the money market [also increase]. Railway debentures, for example, are largely held by bankers. [No. 5120]: 'You may lend money upon London and North Western Stock with 20 percent margin' {on the nominal value}. 'It is a very good security'. All these marketable papers are mercantile means of raising loans, and these loans are determined by the discount rate.)

The *balance of payments* is independent of the *balance of trade* to the extent that it does not depend solely on the level of reciprocal debt (leaving aside *loans* to foreigners, commercial or political, which do not constitute *counter-claims* but merely a claim to future interest and repayment) but also on the due date for payment of those debts.

< The very growth of exports, for more or less every country, but particularly for the country that gives credit, presents itself as an increasing demand on the *internal money market*, which is, however, only felt as such in times of pressure.

No. 5126. 'When there is an increase of foreign trade, is it not the case that *consignments* of British manufacturers abroad are generally represented by *bills* drawn by the manufacturers upon the *shippers* [to be repaid] at considerably distant dates? Yes'.

No. 5127. 'Is it not frequently the case that an understanding exists that those bills are to be redrawn from time to time?' [Chapman's reply] 'This is a thing which they keep from us; we should not admit any bill of that sort ... I dare say it is done, but I cannot speak to a thing of the kind'. (The 'innocent' Chapman!)

No. 5129. 'If there is a large increase of the exports of the country, as there was last year, of £20,000,000 in one year, will not that naturally lead to a great demand for capital for the *discount of bills representing those exports?* No doubt'.

No. 5130. 'Inasmuch as this country gives credit, as a general rule, to foreign countries for all exports, it would be *an absorption of a corresponding increase of capital for the time being?* This country gives an immense credit; but then it *takes credit for its raw material*. We are drawn upon from America always at 60 days, and from other parts at 90 days. On the other hand we give credit; if we send goods to Germany we give two or three months'.

No. 5131. Wilson asks Chapman whether, 'with regard *to the importation of raw materials and produce, bills are not already drawn* upon England simultaneously with shipment from abroad, and do they not even accompany the *bills of lading?*' Chapman believes that this is the case, but knows nothing of these 'mercantile' affairs.

No. 5133. With regard to the goods which are sent *to* the United States, Chapman says that matters are arranged like this: 'The goods are *symbolised* in transit. > Those bills are not drawn directly upon America; they are drawn upon the great American bankers here (in London) at four months, and are remitted for by their houses abroad to meet those engagements'.

No. 5134. The shipper of goods here for America drawn upon a great American house in this country. No. 5135: 'The correspondent who has ordered those goods must place the American house here in funds by the time the bill becomes due'.

< No. 5136. Wilson's question: 'As a general rule, are not the more remote transactions conducted by the merchant, who waits for his capital until the goods are sold? There may be houses of great private wealth who can afford to lay out *their own capital*, and *not take any advance upon the goods*; but the most part are *converted into advances* by the *acceptances* of some well-known established houses, > whose acceptances the parties making the advances are willing to take'.

< '5137. Those houses are resident … either in London or Liverpool, or elsewhere'.

'5138. Therefore, it makes no difference whether *the manufacturer lies out of his money*,[121] or whether *he gets a merchant* in London or Liverpool to advance it; *it is still an advance in this country?* Precisely. *The manufacturer in few cases* has anything to do with it' (but in 1847 it was in large part the rule). 'A man dealing in manufactured goods, for instance at Manchester, will |352e| buy his goods and ship them through a house of respectability in London; when the London house is satisfied that they are all packed according to the understanding, he *draws upon this London house for six months*' (or longer!) 'against these goods to China or India, or wherever they are going; then the *banking world* comes in and discounts that bill for him; so that, *by the time he has to pay for those goods*' (to pay the manufacturer) 'he has the money all ready by the discount of that bill'.

'5139. Although he has the money, the *banker* is lying out of the money? The banker has the bill; the banker has bought the bill; he uses his banking capital in that form, namely in discounting commercial bills'.

'5140. Still, *that forms part of the demand upon the money market in London?* No doubt; it is the substantial occupation of the money market and of the Bank of England. The Bank of England are as glad to get these bills as we are, because they know them to be good property'.

---

121 [Lies out of his money = remains unpaid. An accepted locution, used in the original text of the *Report*. Translator]

'5141. In that way, as the export trade increases, the demand upon the money market increases also? As the prosperity of the country increases, we' (the Chapmans!) 'partake of it'.

'5142. Then when these various fields for the employment of capital increase suddenly, of course the natural consequence is that the rate of interest is higher? No doubt about it'.

In 5143 Chapman 'cannot quite understand, that under our great exports we have had such occasion for bullion'.

In 5144 the worthy Wilson asks: 'May it not be that we give *larger credits upon our exports than we take credits upon our imports?* I rather doubt that point myself. If a man accepts against his Manchester goods sent to India, you cannot accept for less than ten months. We have to pay America for his cotton ... some time before India pays us; but still it is rather refined in its operation'.

'5145. If we have had an increase, as we had last year, of £20 million in our exports of manufactures, we must have had a very large increase of imports of raw material previously to that' (and in this way *over-exports* are already identified with *over-imports*, and overproduction with over-trading) 'in order to make up that increased quantity of goods? No doubt. 5146. We should have to pay a very considerable balance, that is to say, *the balance would run against us during that time*, but in the long run, with America ... the exchanges are in our favour, and we have been receiving for some time past large supplies of bullion from America'.

> '5147. But though the balance may be on our side, which only shows that we send more to America than we receive from America, at the same time ... as far as regards the employment of capital ... we are' (who? by whom? does he mean the producer and the merchant?) 'paid for our goods long before we receive payment for them'.

< In 5148 Wilson asks the arch-usurer Chapman whether he does not consider his high interest rate as a token of great prosperity and 'high profits'. Chapman, evidently astonished by the naiveté of this sycophant, naturally confirms this, but is honest enough to make the following qualification: 'There are some who cannot help themselves; they have engagements to meet, and they must fulfil them, whether profitable or not; but, for a continuance, it would indicate prosperity'. (Both men forget that it might indicate, as it did in 1857, that the knights errant of credit are abroad, people who can pay high rates of interest because they pay out of other people's pockets (though in this way they help to determine the rate of interest for everyone), and meanwhile they can anticipate the profits. At the same time, precisely this can really be a very profitable business for manufacturers, etc. The system of advances makes the returns completely deceptive. This also explains the fol-

lowing, which needs no explanation as far as the Bank of England is concerned, because when interest rates are high it discounts at a lower rate than the others:)

'5156. I should say', says Chapman, 'that our discounts, taking the present moment, when we have had for so long a high rate of interest, *are at their maximum*'. (This was said just a few months before the crash of 1857.) '5157: In 1852' (when the interest rate was low) 'they were not nearly so large'. (Because at that time business was in fact much sounder.) >

'5159. If there was a great flood of money in the market ... Bank rate being so low, we should get a decrease of bills ... In 1852 there was a totally different phase of things. The exports and imports of the country were as nothing compared to the present. 5161. Under this high rate of discount, our discounts are *as large as* ... in 1854' (when the rate of interest was between 5 and 5½ percent).

Reserve.

'4926. The note reserve is the difference between the total amount issued and the amount which the Bank is entitled to issue.

4928. The note reserve in the Bank is dependent upon the total amount of bullion and the quantity in the hands of the public.

4929. Then you may say, in general terms, that the note reserve in the Banking Department is dependent upon the bullion in the Issue Department'. (This is not *completely* correct. [If] the quantity in the hands of the public is assumed to be constant, it depends upon the variations in the bullion; [but if] the amount of bullion is assumed to be given [and constant], it depends upon the variations in the quantity in the hands of the public.)

'4994. As *the bullion goes out it cancels so* [and so] *many notes, and that of itself has an effect upon the money market*'.

< '5046. One section of the community knows nothing of the other; one is the manufacturer, for instance, who exports to the Continent, or imports his raw commodity; he knows nothing of the man who deals in bullion'. >

'5054. If we let money be at 4 and 3 percent, and contractors for railroads, or whatever the things may be, are allowed to enter into those things with foreigners, they must be carried through'.

< '5057. You quite agree that there is no mode by which you can modify the demand for bullion, except by raising the rate of interest? When our bullion falls to a certain point, we had better sound the tocsin at once'. >

|352f| *The quotations on this page are from the Secret Committee of the House of Lords on Commercial Distress, 1857.*[122]

---

122 [Marx is referring here to the *Report from the Secret Committee of the House of Lords*

< 2996 (Tooke): 'In April 1847 there was a panic, of comparatively short duration, not attended with commercial failures of importance. *Pressure in October* [was] more intense than at any period in April ... [there was] an almost unparalleled amount of commercial failures'.

2997 (Tooke): 'In April, the rates of exchange, *principally with America* ... entailed the necessity of exporting a considerable quantity of gold in payment for the unusually large importations from thence; only by a most violent effort did the Bank succeed in raising the exchanges and stopping the efflux of bullion'.

2998 (Tooke): 'In October ... the exchanges [were] in favour of this country'.

3000 (Tooke): 'The turn of the exchanges began in the third week of April'. 3001: 'They fluctuated in July and August; after the beginning of August they were constantly in favour of this country'.

3003 (Tooke): 'The drain of bullion after August arose from a *demand for internal circulation*'.

'3010. The greater fluctuations in the interest rate in 1847 as compared with 1837 and 1839 were due solely to the separation of the Bank into two departments'.

3015 (Tooke): 'The safety of banknotes was affected neither in 1825 nor in 1837 and 1839. 3022. The demand for gold in 1825 was aimed only at filling the vacuum created by the complete discredit of the £1 notes of the country banks; this vacuum could be filled only by gold, until such time as the Bank of England also issued £1 notes'. (In November and December 1825 there was no demand for [gold for] foreign export.)

3028 (Tooke): 'In point of discredit at home as well as abroad ... a failure in paying the *dividends and deposits* would be of far greater consequence ... than the suspending the payment of banknotes'.

3035 (Tooke): 'Would you not say that any circumstance which had the effect of ultimately endangering *the convertibility of the note* would be one likely to add serious difficulty in a moment of commercial pressure? *Not at all*'. >

3040 (Tooke): 'The banks' (the Bank of England, and the Scotch, Irish and country banks) 'had almost twice as much gold in 1847 as when the drain of bullion commenced in 1839'.

< 3058 (Tooke): 'In the course of 1847 ... *an increased issue* ... might have contributed *actually to replenish the coffers of the Bank*, as it did in 1825'.

---

appointed to inquire into the causes of the distress which has for some time prevailed among the commercial classes, etc., 28 July 1848, reprinted London, 1857. Translator]

> 3118 (Tooke): 'The tendency of a great reduction in the rate of interest would be to force capital abroad, and that would end in an exportation of the precious metals'.

1116 (Samuel Gurney): As a result of the 'distrust' after the panic of April 1847, banknotes were hoarded. 'The amount of notes in the hands of the public' was 'nearly £21,000,000 ... and at least from £4 million to £5 million were locked up and inoperative'.

Gurney denies the effect of the railways on the crisis of 1847.

'1253. There is the loose and floating money, and there is the money that requires permanent investment, and there is a wide difference between the value of the one and the value of the other. I have no hesitation in saying that the value of Consols was much lower in consequence of the railways and their bonds; and so with Exchequer Bills; but the floating money of Lombard Street was not lower in consequence. 1260. It had the effect of concentrating a vast number of small sums, and these large sums came into our market'.

1761 ([George Carr] Glyn): 'The stock of the bullion in the Bank had been reduced by the export of gold to the Continent in the early part of the year (1847); but in November and December the demand upon the Bank was for an *internal drain*, which internal drain was met by an *issue of notes*'.

1788 (Glyn): 'You can always tell whether it is a demand for export? 1789. Yes, from the fact of the exchanges being against this country'.

1843 (*Drain of bullion during favourable exchanges*): 'Did not the bullion go out last year (1847) up to the middle of September? Very likely. There was an *export of bullion to Hamburg after the exchange had turned in our favour* arising from this fact: the rate of interest at Hamburg had risen very high indeed, and it was immediately checked by the export of bullion from this country: it was only £200,000'.

1956 (A[lexander] H[enry] Wylie, Liverpool merchant, particularly connected with the American trade and owner of a firm in New Orleans):

The cotton in Liverpool (seven-eighths of all the stocks in Great Britain) is imported on account of *merchants residing there*, or on *account of the spinner*, who goes direct to the mill 'and does not come into the Liverpool market. The great bulk is imported on the *account of the merchant in Liverpool*, or on the *account of the merchant or planter in America*; but this last is the smaller interest. 1958. Between the merchant and the consumer, the business is generally transacted in Liverpool through a broker'. (The *brokerage* is half a percent on the amount of the sale.) '1960. Until the cotton is taken out for consumption, it remains at the risk and the charge of the importing merchant'.

'1963. The *cotton begins to come in quantity*' (to Liverpool) '*at the commencement of the year*. The American Cotton Statements date from the first of September of each year, and the receipts into the cotton ports are generally over by the month of June or July at the latest. The period between those months, our months of import, or, speaking roundly, the first six months of the year, are months of import and consumption, and the last six months are exclusively months of consumption. 1964. With regard to taking out cotton for consumption ... it is a process which goes on from week to week throughout the year. 1966. If ... my house in New Orleans purchased cotton there for shipment to me in Liverpool, they would have to pay cash for it to the planter or his agent. 1967. Between the importer and the merchant in the cotton states it is ... a cash transaction, and almost always before delivery'. 1968. 'As between the *importing merchant* and the *manufacturer*' the latter 'has the option of paying at ten days less the discount; but generally the payment is made by a *banker's bill at three months*'. 1971. 'If it' (the interval before the cotton has been sold to the manufacturer) 'lasts longer, the *broker intervenes with an advance*. 1972. The house at New Orleans draws ... at *60 days'* sight. 1973. But if that credit be placed against the duration of the voyage, it is generally absorbed, so that the cotton is paid for by the time it arrives in Liverpool, or is placed upon the market. 1985. The import of cotton from the East Indies is paid for by bills at *a longer term*'. (The import from the East Indies and other quarters represents about a quarter of that from the United States.) The following data are important for the crisis of 1847:

Stocks of Cotton in Great Britain

31 December 1845	1,055,000 bales
31 December 1846	545,000 bales
31 December 1847	451,000 bales (no. 1979)

|352g| 1988 (Wylie). The total import of cotton to Great Britain was:

1845	1,858,000 bales
1846	1,243,000 bales
1847	1,233,000 bales

'1992. What has been the effect of that continued *short supply* upon the price of cotton in this country in the last three years? The price of cotton rose considerably *at the close of 1846* and the *beginning of 1847*. We saw that the consumption of cotton was going on at such a rate that it was not only eating up all the import of each year, but was seriously trespassing upon the stock; and if the consumption of cotton of 1847 had been equal to the consumption of the preceding year, *the year would have closed with less than a week's supply of cotton in Great Britain*'.

'1993. The trade in the years 1844, 1845, and part of 1846 was so remunerative to the *spinner* that the extension of mills and machinery was pushed to a degree not warranted by the supply of the raw material, and that *almost all our markets, whether at home or abroad, became glutted with goods in the year 1846* ... The additional mills (March 1845) *in course of erection or contracted for* at Preston were equal in extent to six hundred horse power'.

< '1994. At the close of 1845 there was no trade that was more remunerating, and in which there were such large profits. The stock of cotton in 1845 was large, and good useful cotton could be bought at 4d. per pound, and from such cotton good second 40s. mule twist was made at an expense not exceeding a like amount, say at a cost of 8d. per pound in all to the spinner. This yarn was largely sold and contracted for in September and October 1845 at 10½d. and 11½d. per pound, and in some instances the spinners realised a profit equal to the first cost of cotton'. '1996. The trade continued to be remunerative until the *beginning of 1846*'. > '1998. His' (the *manufacturer's*) 'profits began sooner and fell off earlier than those of the spinner. Perhaps they might be dated from the opening of the China trade. 1997. The diminution of the profits was gradual'.

'2000. In Great Britain the consumption rose as follows:

1842	1,193,000 bales
1843	1,388,000 bales
1844	1,426,000 bales
1845	1,566,000 bales
1846	1,559,000 bales

Stocks of Cotton at Liverpool, 3 March

	1848	1847	1846	1845	1844
American:	156,930	311,190	558,630	530,450	430,119
Other Ports:	144,140	156,100	258,950	243,350	198,923
Total:	301,070	467,290	817,580	773,800	627,042
Price of 'Fair Orleans':	5d.	7d.	4⅝d.	4⅞d.	6¼d.

< In March 1844 the stock of cotton was more than double what it is this day [3 March 1848], and yet the price then was 1¼d. per pound dearer. > We have not had so small a stock as we now hold since 1840, at which time cotton was 2d. per pound dearer than it is today'.

< This exposes the self-interest in Ex-Loyd's wisdom that money is 'dear' because *capital* is 'scarce'. Owing to the high interest (panic, etc.) cotton prices were driven far below the level corresponding to the supply. The result of this was on the one hand a tremendous decline in imports in 1848 and on the other hand a decline in production in the United States, hence a rise in cotton prices in 1849. (According to him, the reason why commodities were too dear was that there was too much money in the country. > The imbecile!)

< 2002. 'The late decline in the condition of the cotton manufactories is not to be ascribed to the want of raw material, as the *price* [seems to have been] lower though the stock of the raw material is very much diminished'. But Mr. Ex-Loyd conveniently confuses the price (*value*) of a commodity with the *value of money* (i.e., interest).

> 2006. 'The price of cotton ... advanced from September 1846 to January 1847. It then remained pretty steady until the end of April, when there was a pressure upon the money-market, which drove many holders into the market, and there was then a temporary depression of a very serious nature, nearly 2d. per pound. But there was a recovery from this depression, and in July prices were higher than in the preceding January. The most serious decline commenced in September or October, and continued till the close of the year'.

2008. As a result of the money pressure, 'all the merchants became sellers at once'. 2010. 'The manufacturer of course must have obtained considerable advantage from that? I do not think he did; for the importer is also the exporter, and if the means of a merchant as an importer are curtailed, so are his capabilities as an exporter'. 2011. 'In the export of manufactured goods? Yes'. 2013. 'This pressure came upon the manufacturer simultaneously with the importer of cotton, so as to oblige him also to bring his goods to market to meet his engagements'.

2014. 'I cannot conceive anything more unwise than to interfere with the regular course of any trade, especially one of so much importance as cotton. The result is now shown in the reduction of the stock, which is now so small that the union of a few capitalists might stop the industry of Lancashire'.

2016. 'The *demand for corn* stimulated very largely the *orders for goods in America*; certainly so at the beginning of the year (1847); but when the pressure in the money market occurred *the direct demand became limited*, and the trade took another form, *many merchants and manufacturers on this side ship-*

ping and sending their goods out merely as a means of raising money'. 2017. 'Has it been much the practice of manufacturers to send out their goods, not in consequence of orders but upon speculation, for the purpose of *getting advances* upon the goods so sent out? Largely so, to all quarters'.

2018. 'Are you of opinion ... that stocks of British goods have largely accumulated in the ports of the United States, and that sales have been effected there at very ruinous prices? The export trade to the United States was not larger than the United States could have taken off, if *it had been distributed throughout the year*; but there was so much suddenly thrown into the United States, sent absolutely for the purpose of sale and realisation, that the trade was completely disorganised and disarranged'.

2020. 'The fall in the price of manufactured goods in America was fully equal to the fall in the price of the raw material in this country'.

2021. 'At the close of the year, yarn was sold in Manchester at the price for which the cotton out of which it was spun had been bought in the preceding July'.

2023. 'The price of a good second 40 s. mule twist was 10½d. per pound in January (1847); it varied little until July, and then commenced a gradual decline; in October the same yarn fell to 9½d., and continued to decline until it touched 7¾d. at the close of the year'. < 2026. Wylie says: 'These principles' > (asserted by the currency fellows, the upholders of the Acts of 1844 and 1845) < [seemed to me to be] '*of a nature that would give an artificial high value to money, and an artificial and ruinously low value to all commodities and produce*'.

(Talk about centralisation! The credit system, centring on the quasi-national banks and the great money-lenders and usurers around them, is one enormous centralisation, and gives this class of parasites a fabulous power, not only to decimate the productive capitalists periodically, but to interfere. This is the most dangerous power of interference with real production, since this lot know nothing of, and have nothing to do with, production.) (The acts of 1844 and 1845 are a demonstration of the growing power of these bandits, added to whom are the financiers and stockjobbers.)

> 2051. 'Almost all sales of goods' (in October 1847 and subsequent months) 'were forced sales; indeed a sale of produce or property was the only means left of raising money, the *customary banking facilities* not existing'.

2097. Now Wylie speaks about the *export of manufactures* by Liverpool exporters. He reads out a letter from the 'most eminent merchant in Liverpool', who says < 'Inasmuch as bills at four months, which is the regular course of drafts from the manufacturing towns on merchants and bankers for the purchase of goods going to the United States, could not be discounted except at great sacrifice, the execution of orders was checked to a great extent, until after the government letter of 25 October' [which suspended the 1844 Bank Act], 'when those four months' bills became discountable'.

> 2098. 'The ordinary course of that transaction is for the house shipping at Liverpool to be drawn upon at four months by the manufacturer? Yes, that is, by the purchaser or his agent'.

< 2012. 'In October last [October 1847] there was scarcely an American buyer purchasing goods here who did not at once curtail his orders as much as he possibly could; and when our *advices of the dearness of money reached America, all fresh orders ceased*'.

2134. 'The two cases of corn and sugar were special. The corn market was affected by the prospects of the harvest, and *sugar* was affected by the *immense stocks and imports*'.

2163. 'Much' [of our indebtedness to America] 'was liquidated by forced sales of consigned goods, and I fear that much was cancelled by failures here'.

2196. 'Interest of 70 percent was paid in October last on the London Stock Exchange'.

> 2273. [Sir William] Brown (representing the biggest firm in Liverpool): 'When it' (the Bank of England) 'raised the rate of interest, it might have discounted freely before the letter of 25 October was issued, because the money was not then withdrawn from the Bank to go into new operations but to pay running engagements, so that the notes that went out at one door would come in at another'.

2300 (Brown). 'What was the cause which led to the adverse exchange with America in 1847? We were importing, largely from America, provisions to supply the wants of the people. Bills were plentiful, and being plentiful they fell to 6 percent. Then it became our interest to send gold out, from the rise of interest on the part of the Bank of England. They sympathised so much with us in the United States (for we cannot make a movement in money matters but they almost always respond to it), that the value of money rose so much that it *decreased mercantile operations*, with our decreased import of bread stuffs, and made bills less plentiful, so that they rose to 10 and 11 percent; and then it became necessary to perform a different operation, and to bring the gold this way instead of sending it out'.

2301. 'Had the *rise of interest* ... any considerable effect in checking the manufacturing production in Lancashire? It so far checked it that it diminished the export of goods. We are not the owners of the goods. We act chiefly as bankers ... Mr. A in the United States goes to my brother, my partner in America, and states that he wants to import £1,000 or £2,000 value of goods. They look into the credit of the house, and if they are satisfied a *credit* is opened with us. The order goes to the manufacturing districts, to some individual who is authorised by us, when the goods are ready, to draw upon us for the amount of this credit. When we found that the rate of interest was considerably increased, we thought we saw a storm approaching, and we immediately wrote to our friends not to grant new credits ... We at the same time applied to some of those parties who held credits upon us in this country, and wished them to use as small an amount as possible'.

2304. 'We had several applications from parties who had credits upon ourselves and others, who stated they were not able to execute their orders, in consequence of not *being able to make their bills convertible*'.

2326. 'It is impossible to raise the interest of money here to any extent without raising it in the United States'.

2342. 'The quantity of cotton that comes to Liverpool at various times is sometimes so great that without accommodation ... on the part of the broker to the merchant, or by the banker to the holder of cotton, it would be impossible to hold that stock which is necessary for the general consumption of the country; and the advance in price created by this mutual accommodation helps to keep up the price in the United States, or elsewhere ... so as to give a remunerative price to the planter, and enables us to get a supply. But latterly the price has not been kept up sufficiently'.

|352i| < (James Morris, Governor of the Bank of England.) 137. (Although the rate of exchange was favourable, after August 1847): '2,200,000 sovereigns went out into the country in consequence of the internal demand, > and therefore the bullion in the Bank decreased, although the importation had taken place'.

< 147. 'The large number of persons employed upon railways last year > was one cause of a very largely increased gold circulation in the country ... < also the circumstance of the bankers wishing to provide themselves with gold in times of distress was another cause'.

[John Horsley] Palmer, director and ex-Governor of the Bank of England: 684. 'During the whole period from the middle of April 1847 to the day of withdrawing the restrictive clause in the Act of 1844 the foreign exchanges were in favour of this country'.

> (A real crash took place in 1825, after the drain of bullion had ceased. In 1839 there was a drain of bullion without a crash. In 1847 the drain of bullion ceased after April, but the crash was in October. In 1857 the (external) drain had ceased by the beginning of November, yet the crash took place in November.)

(Before the crisis of 1857, in October, the Bank of England placed £1,000,000 of silver at the disposal of the East India Company (obtained from France by exchanging a million in gold). In addition to this, during the crisis the Act of 1845 made a drain of gold to Scotland and Ireland necessary.)

On 28 February 1837 there were £3,900,000 to £4,000,000 of bullion in the possession of the Bank. After the Act of 1844 the Bank would have been left with only £650,000 in the reserve. With the Act of 1844 (830) 'it would have been impossible, in the winter of 1836, when the Northern and Central Bank failed, to support that bank, or to assist the American houses in 1837'. 836. 'The pressure in 1837 was chiefly confined to the American trade'.

838 (Palmer). Some directors of the Bank proposed in 1837 'to make money dear and commodities cheap, by which the foreign payment would be accomplished'.

897. 'The export trade (for India and China) has, for some time past, principally been carried on for the account of the manufacturers; and, in order to give time for the returns from the East, the merchants who have been the principal parties carrying on that trade have given their acceptances for short periods – three months or six months – and with an understanding that the bills, when they fell due, should be renewed for a further period, so as to give time for the return of the proceeds from India. That was the course ... when there was money pressure ... in the autumn of 1847. The banks, from the discredit then existing, refused to renew the description of bills referred to, which threw the advance upon many of the exporting merchants, whose capital was not equal to sustain the demand upon them. I believe such to have been the principal cause of the East India failures'.

900. 'It is difficult to say ... in what form or mode the export trade will be carried on to the extent of the demands of India till further *money capital* is found by the merchants of this country to supply the *place of that credit* by which it has been hitherto principally conducted'.

906. 'The establishment of an artificial limitation of the power of the Bank under the Act of 1844, instead of the ancient and natural limitation of the Bank's powers, namely the actual amount of its specie, tends to create artificial difficulties, and therefore an operation upon the price of merchandise that would have been unnecessary but for the provisions of the Act'.

950. 'In the period of the railway deposits there was *no increase of circulation*, but a very large increase of securities, which arose from the large increase of *deposits by the notes paid into the hands of the Bank in the first instance*. The amount of notes in circulation, and the securities held by the Bank, have no necessary relative proportion'.

968. 'You cannot, by the working of the Act of 1844, materially reduce the bullion by foreign demand, under ordinary circumstances, below £9,500,000. It would then cause a pressure upon prices and credit, which would occasion

such an advance in the exchange with foreign countries as to increase the import of bullion, and to that extent add to the amount in the Issue Department'.

996. 'Under the limitation that you are now subject to, you have not the command of *silver* to an extent that you require at a time when silver would be required for an action upon the foreign exchanges'.

999. 'What was the *object* of the regulation restricting the Bank as to the amount of silver to one fifth? I cannot answer that question'.

The object was to make *money dear*; the same object as, apart from the currency principle, the division into two departments, and the obligation of the Scotch and Irish banks to have gold backing for the issue of notes beyond a prescribed extent. This produced a decentralisation of the national treasure, disabling it from correcting unfavourable exchanges in its entirety. This applies to all these provisions: that the Bank of England is not allowed to issue *notes* to a greater value than £14,000,000 except backed by gold; that the Banking Department must be administered as a conventional bank, depressing the rate of interest in times of plenty, and raising it in times of pressure; the limitation of silver, the principal means of correcting exchanges with the Continent and Asia; and the regulations regarding the Scotch and Irish banks, which never want the gold for export, and are forced to keep it for an illusory convertibility of notes. In fact, the Act of 1844 produced the first run for gold on the Scotch banks (1857). Then the failure to make any distinction between the *external* and the *internal* demand for gold. (The constant fluctuations in the merchant rate of interest.) With regard to silver, Palmer says this (992): 'The Bank could only purchase silver when the exchange was in favour of the country'. 994. 'The Bank can never purchase silver by an issue of notes in times of an unfavourable rate of foreign exchange'. 1003. 'The only object in holding a considerable amount of the bullion in silver is to facilitate making the foreign payment so long as the exchanges are against the country'. 1004. '*Silver* is a *commodity* which, *being money* in every other part of the world, is therefore the most direct commodity ... for the purpose; except as regards the United States. The United States have latterly taken gold alone'.

|352j| 1018. 'Then are the Committee to understand that it is your opinion that in cases of pressure, unaccompanied by a state of the exchanges which draws the bullion from you, it is not expedient for the Bank to exceed the old rate of interest of five percent? Certainly'.

1019. 'If the Bank had not raised its interest above five percent, would it have been able to discount all the first-class bills presented to it? Not with a reserve of £3,000,000'.

1020. 'Without the Act of 1844 ... there would have been no difficulty in meeting such a demand'.

1022. 'Under the Act of 1844, in the position in which the Bank was placed in October, there was *no rate of interest* which the Bank could have charged to houses of credit which they would have not been willing to pay to carry on their payment' (and this *high interest* was precisely the object of the 1844 Act).

1029. 'The great distinction which I wish to draw is between the action of the rate of interest upon a foreign demand and an advance in the rate for the object of checking a demand upon the Bank during a period of internal discredit'.

1023. Before the Act of 1844 'when the exchanges were in favour of the country, and positive panic and alarm existed through the country, there was no limit put upon the issue, by which alone that state of distress could be relieved'.

1059. 'About £75,000,000 was invested in railways in 1846 and 1847'. 1063. 'In 1845 and 1846, which was the great time of the railway speculation, the interest of money was not above 3 or 3½ percent. During the principal part of 1845 it was under 3 percent'. 1064. 'I do not know how a *low rate of interest*' (this is Palmer speaking) 'shows a *diminished demand for commercial capital*'. 1065. 'Or rather, did the railways not create a *scarcity of capital* in those years?'

1060. 'The investment in railways appears to have affected *the value of other kinds of fixed capital*, such as insurance stocks, canal stocks, and property of that nature. It likewise may have affected, to a certain degree, a portion of the trading community, who may have been forced to abstract from their commercial capital part of their funds to pay up railway calls. Still I do not believe that it has been the cause of any material mischief to the present time. It has principally raised *the value of money* invested in railway debentures and stocks, which has tended to increase the difficulties of the directors in raising the money which they require to carry on their works'.

< 3375 ([Primrose William] Kennedy, the manager of one of the Scottish banks): 'Was there anything that you can call a circulation of gold in Scotland previously to the passing of the Act of 1845? None whatever'. 3376. 'Has there been any additional circulation of gold since? None whatever; *the people dislike gold*'.

> 3446 (When questioned about whether they could not reduce the amount of currency by raising the rate of discount, he replied): 'During the whole of the year 1847 the rate of interest we allowed upon deposits and the rate of interest we charged was higher than at any previous period; it was higher than in the year 1846; but during the whole of 1847, when we were endeavouring by those means to protect ourselves – not with the view of diminishing our currency –

it was larger in amount in every month of that year than it had been during the whole of 1846, which was a year of comparative ease. So that I conceive that as long as there are internal transactions requiring notes or gold to perform them, bankers must, either through the demands of their depositors, or in one shape or another, furnish as much currency as those transactions require'. 3448. 'Do you mean to say that the Banks in Scotland have no means of restricting their transactions? They can restrict the transactions, but they cannot control the currency'.

3450. As a result of the Act of 1845, about £1,000,000 of useless money was retained in the banks of Scotland.

3549. 'The practice of paying *interest upon their deposits* by the banks in Scotland of course brings the notes back to them as quickly as they can come when not wanted for daily purposes? The practice of allowing interest upon deposits induces parties immediately to pay in their money that they do not require for their daily use for expenditure for small transactions'.

3550. 'Does not the practice of the banks in allowing cash credits act in a similar manner in inducing parties to pay up as quickly as possible? Of course the more they pay in, the less interest they have to pay upon their advances'.

3578 (Evidence of [James Andrew] Anderson, manager of the Union Bank of Scotland): 'The system of exchanges between yourselves prevents any overissue on the part of any one bank? Yes. There is a more powerful preventive than the system of exchanges ... the universal practice in Scotland of keeping a bank account; everybody who has any money at all has a bank account, and puts in every day the money which he does not immediately want, so that at the close of the business of the day there is scarcely no money out of the banks except what people have in their pockets' (this in fact has absolutely nothing to do with the question, but it does indeed ensure the currency of the notes of every bank throughout the whole of Scotland).

< 3588. 'The only pressure upon the Bank of England by the banks in Scotland for gold was for foreign exchanges? It was; and *that is not relieved by holding gold in Edinburgh*'.

3590. 'Having the same amount of securities in the Bank of England' (or in the private banks of London) 'we have the same power that we had before of making a drain upon the Bank of England'.

> 3595. 'Has the circulation authorised by the Act been exceeded generally since the passing of that Act? It has been exceeded very generally'.

3596. 'Particularly at two periods of the year, at the Two Terms times? Yes'. 3598. The reason for this expansion of the circulation: 'Payment of rent and wages. The amount of expansion in the country is greater than in the town. The expansion at the Ayr Bank was larger than in Glasgow. In the whole country it expands generally from three millions to four; an increase of about a third'. 3599. 'How soon do those notes come back again into the banks? They begin to come back about a fortnight after the term day'. 3600. 'Not more than a month elapses till it is considerably reduced'.

III (Continued from p. 598)[123]

< The massive nature of the sum of money which has to be transformed back into capital in this way is the result of the massive scale of the reproduction process; but considered *for itself*, as moneyed capital, it is not itself a *sum of reproductive capital.*

The most important thing in our presentation so far is the point that the expansion of that *portion of revenue* that is destined for consumption (and in this connection we ignore the worker, since his revenue = the variable capital) presents itself first of all as an *accumulation of money capital.* There is thus an element in the *accumulation of money capital* that is essentially separate from the genuine accumulation of productive capital; for the portion of the annual product allotted to consumption is in no way *capital.* A part of it replaces *capital*, i.e., the constant capital of the producers of provisions, but in so far as it really is transformed into capital, it exists as the *natural form* of the revenue of the producers of the constant capital. The same money that represents revenue, that serves simply to mediate consumption, is constantly transformed into loanable '*moneyed capital*'. In as much as this money represents wages, it is at the same time the money form of variable capital; and in as much as it replaces the constant capital of the producers of the means of consumption, it is the money form of their constant capital, and it serves for the transfer of the elements of the constant capital that need to be replaced. But neither in one form nor the other does it in itself represent accumulation, although its volume grows with the scale of the reproduction process. But at the same time it temporarily performs the function of loanable '*moneyed capital*', i.e., of money capable of being loaned. In this respect, therefore, the accumulation of *moneyed capital* must always reflect a greater accumulation of capital than is actually taking place, in so far as the process of individual consumption appears in its mediation and expansion through money as an *accumulation of moneyed*

123 [Here Marx returns to his discussion of the 'accumulation of moneyed capital', which was broken off at p. 598; p. |352| Marx's manuscript. This is the beginning of Engels's Chapter 32 entitled 'Money Capital and Real Capital: III (Conclusion)'. Translator]

capital. Hence it supplies the money form for genuine accumulation, for money that initiates new capital investments.

The *accumulation of moneyed capital* partly represents nothing more than the fact that all the money whose form reproductive capital takes on in its process > leaving aside the direct exchange of its real elements < assumes the form, not of money the *reproductive agents* advance, but of money that they borrow; so that in actual fact the advance of money that must occur in the reproduction process appears as an advance of *borrowed* money. In fact one party lends another the money that he needs in the reproduction process. But this takes the form that the *banker* lends the money to the *reproductive agents*, > while the latter hand over the balance of the money capital they require to the public, to which they themselves belong. < It is also an expression of the fact that disposal over this capital passes entirely into the hands of the bankers as intermediaries.

> (Two forms of the *accumulation of money capital* still need to be distinguished from the transformation of revenue back into capital. < Capital is 'liberated', for example, by a fall in the prices of raw material or other elements of production. If the capitalist cannot directly expand his reproduction process, one part of his money capital is freed from its function in the circuit and transformed into loanable *moneyed capital*. Secondly, there is a return in *gold* or *silver*, particularly in the case of the merchant. > This is the worst form of return for him, since when the return is in the form of a commodity he can still make a profit on the price of the commodity, firstly by selling the initial commodity, and then by selling the returned commodity, whereas gold or silver, the commodities which constitute the material of the country's money, only realise their value, and are only capable of being transformed into a particular quantity of the country's money (a quantity determined by the extent of their own value). If now there are interruptions, < so that the merchant can only begin a new series of business transactions later, the money represents for him simply a *hoard*, unoccupied capital. But at the same time it directly represents an accumulation of loanable '*moneyed capital*'. In the first case, the accumulation of moneyed capital expresses the repetition of the reproduction process under more favourable conditions, the genuine release of a portion of capital previously *tied up*, hence giving the reproduction process the power to expand with the same monetary means. In the second case there is simply an interruption in the flow of transactions. In both cases money is transformed into *moneyed capital*, representing an *accumulation of it*, and it has the same impact on the money market and the rate of interest, although the two cases have a diametrically opposed relationship to the genuine accumulation process. Finally, the accumulation of moneyed capital is effected by the group of people who have

safely made their profits and withdrawn from the reproduction process. The greater the profit made in the course of the industrial cycle, the greater the number of these 'retiring greengrocers'. In this case, therefore, the accumulation of moneyed capital expresses on the one hand a genuine accumulation (in its relative volume); on the other hand it simply expresses the degree to which reproductive capitalists are transformed into moneyed capitalists.)

|354| As far as the other portion of the profit is concerned, which is not destined to be consumed as revenue, this is transformed into *moneyed capital* only if it cannot be directly used to expand business in the sphere of production in which the profit has been made. This can happen for two reasons: either because this sphere is saturated and no more capital is required; or because before it can function as capital, the accumulation must first attain a certain volume, determined by the appropriate proportions for the investment of new capital in this particular business. It is therefore firstly transformed into *moneyed capital* and serves to expand production in other spheres. Taking all other circumstances as equal, the amount of profit destined for transformation back into capital will depend on the amount of profit made and hence on the expansion of the reproduction process itself. But if this new accumulation comes up against difficulties in its application, owing to a lack of spheres of employment > (so that the sole result is that the reproductive capital applied pays interest at a lower rate) < this *plethora of moneyed capital* proves nothing more than the *barriers of the capitalist production process*. The resulting credit swindles demonstrate that there is no *positive* obstacle to the employment of this surplus capital, but rather an obstacle set up by its own *laws of valorisation*, by the barriers within which capital can valorise itself as capital. A plethora of moneyed capital as such does not necessarily signify overproduction, or even a want of spheres of employment for capital.

> Apart from this it should be borne in mind that < the accumulation of moneyed capital simply means that *money* is precipitated as loanable money > (or takes on the form of loanable money). < This process is very different from a genuine transformation into capital; it is simply the accumulation of money in a form in which it can be transformed into capital, > capital not available in and for itself. < As we have shown, however, this accumulation can express elements that are very different from genuine accumulation. With genuine accumulation constantly expanding, this expanded accumulation of money capital can be in part its result, in part the result of elements that accompany it but are quite different from it > (and possibly antagonistic to it, a point we leave aside here). < The very fact that the accumulation of moneyed capital is augmented by these elements that are independent of genuine accumulation, even if they accompany it, must lead to a constant plethora of the moneyed

capital at certain phases of the cycle, and this plethora develops alongside the development of the credit system. Hence there develops at the same time a need to drive the production process beyond its capitalist barriers; overtrading, overproduction, and excess credit. This must always happen, however, in forms which bring about a rebound.

As far as the accumulation of money capital from rent, wages, etc., goes, it is unnecessary to go into this here. The only element to be stressed is that as the division of labour progresses with the advance of the capitalist mode of production, the business of *genuine saving* and *abstinence* (by hoarders), in so far as this supplies elements of accumulation, is left to those who receive the minimum of such elements, and often enough lose what they have saved, as workers do when banks collapse. For on the one hand the productive capitalist does not 'save' his capital himself but rather disposes of the savings of others in proportion to the size of his capital; while on the other hand the moneyed capitalist makes the savings of other people into his 'capital' and converts the credit that the reproductive capitalists give to each other, and the public gives to them, into a source of his own private enrichment. The final illusion of the capitalist system, as to capital being the offspring of saving and labour, crumbles into dust. Not only does profit consist in the appropriation of other people's labour, but also the capital with which this labour of others is exploited consists of other people's property, which the moneyed capitalist puts at the disposal of the productive capitalist, and through which he in turn exploits the latter.

We still need to say something about *credit capital*.

(How often the same *piece of money* can figure as *moneyed capital* > in other words to how great an amount < depends entirely on the following: (1) how often it realises *commodity values* in sale or in payment, as well as how often it realises *revenue*. > This revenue can itself |355| be nothing other than a part of the *value of the commodity*, whether this part is laid out in *wages* {productive or unproductive} or it *realises* the surplus-value which the seller himself or some third person (the money-lender, or the landlord, or the state) is to spend. < How often it comes into someone else's hands as *realised* value, whether that of capital or of revenue, clearly depends therefore on the scale and volume of the real transactions; (2) economy in payments and the development and organisation of the credit system; (3) the linkage and speed of action of credits, so that if the money is precipitated at one point as a deposit, it is immediately sent out again as a loan.)

Even on the assumption that the form in which the *moneyed capital* exists is simply that of *money* (gold or silver, i.e., the commodity whose material serves as a measure of value) a large portion of this *moneyed capital* is necessarily always merely fictitious, i.e., a title to value, just like value tokens. > A has sold his commodity or his labour, and received M for it, *money*. To the extent that this money must function in the metamorphosis of capital it is not transformed into moneyed capital but rather exchanged by its owner for the elements of reproduction. In so far as it serves immediately for the realisation of revenue, it is paid out as currency and < cannot therefore be transformed into moneyed capital (at least, not into moneyed capital for its owner). But in so far as it is transformed into moneyed capital, and the same money repeatedly represents moneyed capital, it is clear that it only exists at one point as metallic money; at all other points it exists simply in the form of a *claim* to capital. The *accumulation of these claims*, on our assumptions, arises from a genuine accumulation, i.e., from the transformation of the value of commodity capital, etc., into money; and yet the *accumulation of these claims* or titles as such is still different both from the genuine accumulation from which it arises and from the future accumulation (the process of production) which is mediated by the lending of money.

On the face of it, moneyed capital always exists in the form of money.[124] Later on it exists as a *claim upon money*, since the money in which it originally

124 See *Report on Bank Acts* 1857. '4516. As a banker do you deal in capital or in money? We deal in money. 4517. How are the deposits paid into your bank? In money. 4518. How are they paid out? In money. 4519. Then can they be called anything else but money? No'. (Evidence of [John] Twells, banker.)

Overstone shows a persistent confusion between 'capital' and 'money'. 'Value of money' for him also means interest, but determined by the quantity of money; and interest is supposed to be the 'value of capital', as determined by the demand for productive capital and by the profit that this yields.

'4140. The use of the word "*capital*" is very dangerous'. '4148. The export of bullion from this country is a diminution of *the quantity of money* in this country, and a diminution of the quantity of money in this country must of course create a pressure upon the *money market* generally' (not, therefore, upon the *capital* market). '4112. As the money goes out of the country, the *quantity* in the country is diminished; that diminution of the quantity remaining in the country produces an increased *value of that money*' (What this originally means in his theory is an increase in the relative value of money as money, as compared to the value of commodities, brought about by a contraction in circulation; hence where this increase in the value of money = a fall in the value of commodities. But since in the meantime it has been incontrovertibly demonstrated even for him that the quantity of money in circulation does *not* determine prices, it is now the reduction in money as currency that is supposed to increase its value as interest-bearing capital, as moneyed capital, and hence the rate of interest.) 'And that increased value of what remains stops the exit of money, and is kept up until it has brought back that quantity of money which is necessary to restore the equilibrium'.

existed now functions, as soon as it has been lent out, as the real money form of capital, money capital, in the hands of the borrower. For the lender it has been transformed into a *claim upon money*, into an ownership title. The same quantity of money can therefore represent very different quantities of moneyed capital. Whether it is realised capital or realised revenue it becomes nothing but money by the *simple act of lending it out*, by its transformation into a deposit, if we consider the general form in the developed credit system > and in so far as we are dealing with commercial loans. < The *deposit* is *moneyed capital* for the depositor. But in the hands of the banker it may only be *potential moneyed capital*, lying idle in his till, instead of in that of its owner.[125] > There are now two questions to be answered: *firstly*, how is a relative increase or reduction in moneyed capital, in short its temporary or more lasting accumulation, related to the accumulation of productive capital? And *secondly*, how is this related to the *quantity of money* available in the country, in whatever form?

Looking first at the longer term < the class of moneyed capitalists grows as real material wealth increases, firstly because there is an increase in the number of retired greengrocers, who live on interest, and secondly, because the credit system develops, which means an increase in the number of *bankers* > (and also financiers, but we are disregarding public credit here).

---

125 This is where the confused notion comes in, that both things are 'money', the deposit as a claim, and the deposited money in the banker's possession.

'4531. You have parted with your £5,000 of notes to somebody else? Yes. 4532. Then he has £5,000 in deposits? Yes. 4533. And you have £5,000 of deposits left? Exactly. 4534. He has £5,000 in money, and you have £5,000 in money? Yes. 4535. But it is nothing but money at last? No' (evidence of Twells, the banker, before the *1857 Committee*). The confusion arises in part from this: A, who has deposited the £5,000, can draw on it, and can dispose of it just as if he still had it. To this extent, it functions for him as *potential* money. But in all these cases, he destroys his deposit to the extent that he draws on it. If he withdraws actual money and his money has already been lent again, he is paid not with his own money, but rather with the money someone else has deposited. If he pays a debt to B with a cheque on his banker, B deposits this cheque with his banker, and if A's banker has cheques, the money that A deposited has performed money functions twice: firstly in the hands of the person who received the money that A has deposited; and secondly in the hands of A himself. In the second function, there is an adjustment of claims (the claim of A on his banker and claim of the latter on B's banker) without the *intervention of money*. Here the deposit has a double effect as money, namely first as actual money and then as a claim to money. Mere claims upon money > (which are not in turn themselves satisfied out of the actual deposits of others) < can only perform the second function through the balancing out of claims.

< NB. With the development of moneyed capital the *volume of interest-bearing paper*, public effects and so on, also expands, as explained already. At the same time, however, so does the demand for moneyed capital, since the *jobbers* who speculate in this paper play a major role in the money market. If all purchases and sale of this paper were *bona fide* transactions, it would be correct to say that they could have no effect on moneyed capital, since if A sells his paper, he withdraws just as much money as B puts into paper. Even then, however, in view of the fact that the paper certainly exists, but the capital that it originally represented does not (at least not as moneyed capital), a new demand for moneyed capital of this kind is always created. But at all events it is then moneyed capital which was previously at the disposal of B, and now is at A's disposal.

'4886. Do you consider that it is a correct description of the causes which determined the rate of discount, to say that it is fixed by the quantity of capital in the market which is applicable to the discount of mercantile bills, as distinguished from other classes of securities? No. I think that the question of interest is affected by all convertible securities of a current character; it would be wrong to limit it simply to the discount of bills, because it would be absurd to say that when there is a great demand for money upon consols, or even exchequer bills, as has ruled very much of late, at a rate much higher than the commercial rate, our commercial world is not affected by it; it is very materially affected by it'.

|356| '4890. When sound and current securities, such as bankers acknowledge to be so, are in the market, and people want to borrow money upon them, it certainly has its effect upon commercial bills; for instance, I can hardly expect a man to let me have money at five percent upon commercial bills, if he can lend his money at the moment at six percent upon consols, or whatever it may be; it affects us in the same manner; a man can hardly expect me to discount bills at five and a half percent if I can lend my money at six percent'.

'4892. We do not talk of investors who buy their £2,000 or £5,000 or £10,000 as affecting the money market materially. If you ask me as to the rate of interest upon consols, I allude to people who deal in hundreds of thousands of pounds, who are what are called jobbers, who take large portions of loans, or make purchases in the market, and have to hold that stock till the public take it off their hands at a profit; the men therefore want money'. > (Evidence of Chapman, managing director of the firm of Overend, Gurney and Co., to the *Select Committee on Bank Acts, 1857*.) < With the development of the credit system, concentrated money markets are created, as in London, which are at the same time the major seats of dealings in these securities.

The bankers put massive amounts of the public's moneyed capital at the disposal of these most damnable rogues, and so the brood of gamblers multiplies.

> We shall wait until later to investigate Overstone's jumble of phrases.

< We have already shown in dealing with interest-bearing capital that the average interest over a period of several years is determined, all other circumstances remaining the same, by the average *rate of profit*, and not by *profit of enterprise*, which is no more than profit minus interest.

Also mentioned already, and to be investigated further below, is the fact that the *variations in commercial interest* – the interest calculated by the money-lenders for discounts and loans within the business of commerce – also show a phase in the course of the industrial cycle in which on the one hand the rate of interest rises above its minimum and on the other hand reaches the average medium level (a rate of interest which then directly precedes its rise above the medium level).

Two things should be noted here, however:

Firstly, if the interest rate remains high for a long period of time (and here we are speaking of the interest rate in a particular country, such as England, where the average rate of interest is given for a relatively long period and is also expressed in the interest paid for more fixed investments – what we might call private interest), this is *prima facie* evidence that the *rate of profit* during this period is also high, but it does not necessarily prove that the *rate of profit of enterprise* is high. (Capitalists who work predominantly with their own capital realise the above-mentioned high *rate of profit*, since the interest they pay to themselves is only a matter of accounting.) The possibility of a high rate of interest of longer duration – we are not referring here to the phase of actual pressure on the money market – is given by the high rate of profit. It is possible however that this high rate of profit, after deducting the high rate of interest, leaves behind nothing more than a *low rate of profit of enterprise*. The latter may contract, while the high rate of profit continues. This is possible because enterprises once embarked on must be continued. In this phase, operations are conducted largely with credit capital (other people's capital) and the high rate of profit may well be speculative and prospective, > with the high interest being paid for the present at the expense of other people's capital. < It is possible to pay interest at a high rate with the high rate of profit but a declining profit of enterprise. It can be paid – and this is partly the case in periods of speculation – not out of profits but out of the borrowed capital itself, and this situation can last a good while.

Secondly, to say that the demand for moneyed capital and hence the interest rate rises because the *rate of profit* is high is not the same as saying that the *demand for (productive) capital* rises and that the rate of interest is high *for this reason*.[126]

> |357| To the extent that moneyed capital is demanded, not in order to *make payments*[127] (we need to pay special attention to this point; it is most important for the rise in the value of moneyed capital) < but in order to make purchases, and to transform moneyed capital into productive capital. And then it is demanded either by the productive capitalist or by the merchant. The productive capitalist invests it in the means of labour (raw materials, accessories and machinery) and in labour-capacity.

The rising demand for labour can never be in itself a reason for a rising rate of interest (as determined by the rate of profit). *Higher wages* are never a cause of higher profit, although, taking particular phases of the industrial cycle, they may be one of its results. > This can therefore be ruled out of consideration from the outset. < The demand for labour may increase because the exploitation of labour is proceeding under particularly favourable conditions, but the rising demand for labour and hence for variable capital does not in and for itself increase *profits*. It rather reduces them in proportion. Yet the demand for variable capital may increase, and thus also the demand for moneyed capital, and this may increase the rate of interest. The market price of labour-capacity then rises above its average value and at the same time the rate of interest rises, because the demand for moneyed capital rises in these conditions. An increased demand for labour raises the price of this commodity just like any other, raising its *price*, but not raising *profits* (which depend precisely and principally on the relative cheapness of this commodity) … At the same time, however, under the conditions we have assumed, this demand raises the *rate of interest* by increasing the demand for moneyed capital. If the moneyed capitalist, instead of lending out money, were to transform himself into a productive capitalist, the fact that he has to pay more for labour would not in and of itself increase his profit but rather lead to a proportionate reduction in it. The combination of circumstances may still be such that his profit rises nevertheless, but this is never because he pays more for labour. The latter circumstance, however, in as much as it increases the demand for moneyed

126 'Money upon the Stock Exchange is, generally speaking, cheaper than it is elsewhere', said [James Morris], the then Governor of the Bank of England, in evidence before the *Secret Committee of the House of Lords* (*Report of the Secret Committee* 1857, no. 219.)

127 > In times of crisis prices are to a considerable degree inflated by speculation, resulting from the exaggerations of credit. It is then impossible to keep these prices up by supporting the holders of, or speculators in, those commodities. The bubble must burst. <

capital, is sufficient to raise the interest rate. If the level of wages rises, for whatever reason, in a conjuncture which is otherwise unfavourable, the rise in wages causes the profit rate to fall, and the rate of interest to rise, to the extent that the wage rise increases the demand for moneyed capital.

Leaving aside labour, what Overstone calls the 'demand for capital' consists simply of the demand for commodities. The demand for commodities raises their *price*, whether this demand rises above the average, or the supply falls below the average. If the productive capitalist or the merchant now has to pay £150, for example, for the quantity of commodities for which he formerly paid £100, he would have to borrow £150 instead of £100, and would therefore have to pay £7½, at a 5 percent rate of interest, instead of the previous £5. The amount of interest he has to pay rises because of the rise in the amount of capital borrowed. > If the rate of interest is given, as it is at every moment, the man who borrows £100,000 does not pay a higher rate of interest than he who borrows £1,000 (he probably pays a lower rate) although the former pays £5,000 a year in interest and the latter only pays £50.

< (Overstone's entire aim is to present the interests of the moneyed and the productive capitalists as *identical*, while his Bank Act is precisely calculated to exploit the *difference* between these interests for the benefit of moneyed capital.)

It is possible that the demand for commodities, in the case where their supply has fallen below the average, absorbs no more moneyed capital than before. The same sum, and perhaps a smaller one, has to be paid for their overall value, but a smaller quantity of use-value is received for this sum. In this case the demand for moneyed capital remains *the same*, hence the rate of interest will not rise, although the demand for commodities (cotton for example) has risen in relation to their supply, and the commodities' price has therefore risen as well. The rate of interest can only be affected when the *total demand for moneyed capital grows*. > We have just seen that this does not necessarily happen if there is simply a fall in supply.

< The supply of an article may, however, fall below its average level (as is the case with a dearth of cotton, corn, etc.) while the demand for moneyed capital grows, because there is speculation that prices may rise still higher, and one means of making them rise is to withdraw a part of the supply temporarily from the market. In order to clear the debts incurred on the commodities without selling them, money is obtained by means of bill of exchange operations. In this case the demand for moneyed capital grows, and the rate of interest may rise (it often does not rise) in order artificially to reduce the *supply* of commodities to the market. The rise in the rate of interest then expresses an artificial reduction in the supply of commodity capital.

|358| On the other hand, the demand for an article may increase because its supply has increased, and the article stands below its average price. In this case, the demand for moneyed capital may remain the same or even fall, because more commodities are to be had with the same sum of money. There could also be a speculative redemption[128] of stocks, partly to use the opportunity for productive purposes, partly in view of a possible later rise in prices. In this case the demand for moneyed capital could grow, and would thus be the expression of an excess supply of the elements of productive capital.

(All we are considering here is the *demand* for moneyed capital, in respect to the demand and supply of commodity capital. We have already explained earlier how the state of the reproduction process affects the *supply* of moneyed capital.)

By cunningly identifying moneyed capital with capital in general Overstone seeks to use the trivial statement that the market rate of interest is determined by the supply of, and the demand for, (moneyed) capital to transform the usurer into the only 'capitalist' and to turn his capital into the only capital.

In times of pressure, the demand for moneyed capital is a demand for the *means of payment* and nothing else (it is not a demand for money as a means of purchase). The interest rate can then rise very high, whether real capital is abundant or wanting. (The demand for means of payment is simply a demand for *convertibility* into money, in so far as the merchants and producers are able to offer good security; it is a *demand for moneyed capital*, in so far as these fellows have no *bona fide* source from which to make their payments: the advance of the means of payment therefore gives them not only the *money form*, but also the *equivalent* that they lack for payments, in whatever form this might be. This is the point at which both sides are simultaneously right and wrong in times of pressure. Those who say that there is simply a *lack of means of payment* either have in mind the owners of *bona fide* securities or else they are fools who believe it is the duty of a bank, or a power possessed by a bank, to transform every bankrupt swindler into a solvent character by means of paper tokens. Those who say that there is simply a *lack of capital* are either merely quibbling, since in such times *inconvertible* capital abounds (as a result of over-importing and overproduction), or they are alluding only to those credit-jobbers who actually are put in a position where they can no longer obtain other people's capital to operate with and then demand that they should not only help them pay for the capital lost but also enable them to continue their swindling.)

---

128 [Engels replaced this word with 'formation'. Translator]

It is the foundation of the bourgeois production process that *money* confronts *commodities* as an autonomous form of value, or that exchange-value must obtain an autonomous form in money, and this is possible only if one particular *commodity* becomes the material in whose value all other commodities are measured, this thereby becoming the *universal commodity*, the commodity *par excellence*, in contrast to all other commodities. This must show itself in two ways, particularly in developed capitalist nations, which replace money to a great extent either by credit operations or by credit money. In times of pressure, when credit contracts or dries up altogether, *money* suddenly confronts commodities absolutely as the only means of payment and the true existence of *value*. Hence the general depreciation of commodities [which makes it difficult] to transform them into money, i.e., into their own purely fantastic form. Secondly, however, credit money is itself only *money* in so far as it absolutely represents real money as to its value. With the efflux of bullion, its *convertibility* into money becomes problematic, i.e., its identity with gold. Hence we get forcible measures, raising the rate of interest, etc., in order to make sure of this convertibility. This can be more or less intensified by erroneous legislation, based on incorrect theories of money and forced upon a nation by the interest of dealers in money such as Overstone. But the basis of it is provided by the basis of the mode of production itself. A depreciation of credit money (not to speak of a complete loss of its monetary character, which is in any case purely imaginary) would destroy all the existing relationships. The value of commodities is thus sacrificed in order to ensure the fantastic and autonomous existence of this value in money. In any event, a money value is only guaranteed as long as money itself is guaranteed. That is why many millions' worth of commodities have to be sacrificed for a few millions in money. This is unavoidable in bourgeois production and forms one of its particular charms. In earlier modes of production, this does not happen, because given the narrow basis on which these move, neither credit nor credit money is able to develop. As long as the *social* character |359| of labour appears as the *monetary existence* of the commodity and hence as a *thing* outside actual production, monetary crises, independent of real crises or aggravating them, are unavoidable. It is evident on the other hand that as long as a bank's *credit* is not undermined, it can alleviate the panic in such cases by increasing its credit money, whereas it increases the panic by contracting credit. The entire history of modern industry shows that bullion would be required solely for settling international trade, where its equilibrium is undermined, if production at home were properly organised. (The suspension of cash payments which is resorted to in extreme cases shows that gold coin is not required for domestic use.)

It would be ridiculous to say of two individuals that they both have an unfavourable *balance of payments* in their dealings with each other. If they are both debtors and creditors to each other, it is clear that when their claims do not balance, one of them must be the debtor to the other for the remainder. With *nations* this is by no means the case. And this fact is recognised by all economists when they say that the *balance of payments* may be favourable or unfavourable for a country, even though the *balance of trade* must ultimately balance out. The balance of payments is distinct from the balance of trade in that it is that particular balance of trade which must be settled at a particular *date*. The effect of crises, then, is to compress the difference between the balance of payments and the balance of trade into a *short period of time*; and the specific conditions that develop in nations affected by a crisis, and hence by the arrival of this date of payment, already involve a contraction of this kind in the settlement period. Firstly the shipment of bullion abroad; then the forced selling of goods sent on consignment; the export of commodities in order to sell them off cheaply or obtain money advances on them at home; the rise in interest rates, the fall in the value of securities, the recall of credit, the forced selling of foreign securities, the attraction of foreign capital to invest in these depreciated securities, the decline in the import of foreign commodities, and finally bankruptcy, which settles a whole series of claims. (Metal is also still sent to the bankrupt country, because drafts on it are uncertain and payment in metal is the most secure method.) Added to this is the fact that > nations consist of millions of different people, so that what affects one group does not affect another, etc., < and that in relation to Asia all nations are generally debtors simultaneously, either directly or indirectly. Once these various factors exert their effect on the other countries involved, these too experience an export of bullion, i.e., their payments fall due, and the same phenomenon is repeated.)

In the case of commercial credit, interest, as the difference between the credit price and the cash price, is involved in the price of a commodity only in so far as bills of exchange have a longer term than usual ('long bills'). In other cases this is not so. And this is explained by the fact that each person takes this credit from one direction and extends it in another. But in so far as discounting is involved here in this form, it is not governed by this commercial credit, but rather by the *money market*.

If the demand for moneyed capital (the rate of interest) and the supply of commodities (their relative supply) were identical, then according to whether we considered various different commodities or *the same* commodity at different stages, interest would have to be both high and low. In 1844 the Bank of England's interest rate fluctuated between 4 percent (from January to September) and 2½ to 3 percent (from November to the end of the year). In 1845 it was 2½, 2¾, and 3 percent from January to October, and between 3 and 5 percent during the final months of the year. The average price of fair Orleans cotton was 6¼d. in 1844 and 4⅞d. in 1845. On 3 March 1844 the Liverpool cotton stock was 627,042 bales, and on 3 March 1845 it was 773,800 bales. To judge from the low price of cotton, the rate of interest should have been low in 1845, which was in fact the case for the greater part of that year. But to judge from the yarn it should still have been high, for prices were relatively high and profits absolutely so. 'In 1845 ... good useful cotton could be bought at 4d. per pound, and from such cotton good Second 40s. mule twist was made at an expense not exceeding a like amount, say at a cost of 8d. per pound in all to the spinner. The yarn was largely sold and contracted for in September and October 1845 at 10½d. or 11½d. per pound, and in some instances the spinners realised a profit equal to the first cost of the cotton'. (*Report from the Secret Committee* 1857, no. 1994.)

|360| The whole matter can be brought to the test in this way:

The demand for and supply of loanable 'capital' would be identical with the demand for and supply of capital in general (although this last phrase is absurd; for the producer or the merchant, commodities are a form of his capital, but he never demands capital as capital, but always a particular commodity, a *commodity* as such; he buys and pays for it as a *commodity*, whatever part it may play as capital in the movement of *his* capital); if there were no money-lenders and instead of them the lender owned machines, raw material, etc., and lent these out or hired them (as houses are rented now) to the productive capitalists who were themselves the owners of a portion of these things. In conditions such as these, the supply of loanable capital would be identical with the supply of the elements of production for the productive capitalist, and of commodities for the merchant. But it is clear that the division of profit between lender and borrower would then be completely dependent, in the first place, on the *ratio* in which this capital is borrowed and in which it is the property of the person employing it.

According to Mr. Weguelin (the Governor of the Bank of England) the rate of interest is determined by: 'the amount of unemployed capital' (*Report on Bank Acts* 1857, 252.) 'The rate of interest is merely an index of the amount of unemployed capital seeking investment' (271). Later this unemployed capital is called 'floating capital' (485), and it turns out to be 'Bank of England notes' (in reserve) 'country banks circulation, and the amount of coin which is in the country' (502) and later 'bullion' (503) in the bank. Thus the same Weguelin says that the Bank of England exerts great influence on the rate of interest in times 'when, in fact, we *are holders of the greater portion of the unemployed capital*'

(1198), whereas according to Mr. Ex-Loyd (see above) the Bank of England is 'no place for capital'.[129] Further on the same Weguelin says: 'I think the rate of discount is governed by *the amount of unemployed capital* which there is in the country. The amount of unemployed capital is *represented* by the reserve of the Bank of England, which is practically *a reserve of bullion*. When, therefore, the bullion is drawn upon it *diminishes the amount of unemployed capital in the country*, and consequently raises the value of that which remains'.

> 'The alterations' (in the rate of discount) 'since 1844 have been some 60 in number, whereas the alterations prior to 1844, in the same space of time, certainly did not amount to a dozen'. (1358, evidence of William Newmarch.) < 'The Bank is obliged to depend for the solvency of its Banking Department upon what it can do to replenish the reserve in that department; and therefore as soon as it finds that there is any drain in progress, it is obliged to look to the safety of its reserve, and to commence contracting its discounts, or selling securities'. (2102, evidence of John Stuart Mill.) (Taking the Banking Department by itself, the *reserve* is a reserve for *deposits* only. According to people like Overstone, the Banking Department should simply act as a banker, without regard to the 'automatic' note issue. But in times of real pressure the institution keeps an eye on the bullion, independently of the reserve of the Banking Department.) >

[The Confusion. Continued from p. 622][130]

> *What the Bank gives with one hand it receives with the other one* (as far as the quarterly payment of dividends to the state's creditors is concerned): 'A certain proportion of those dividends go into the hands of bankers, and are again immediately made available for commercial purposes, and re-enter again into the deposits of the Bank or pay off the loans made by the Bank previously to the dividends'. (*Report on Bank Acts* 1857, no. 39.)

'241. The *discounting of bills* to that extent (one million a day for three successive days) would not reduce the reserve unless the public demanded a greater amount of active circulation. The notes *issued on the discount* of bills would be returned through the medium of the bankers and through deposits. Unless the transactions were for the purpose of exporting bullion, and unless there were an amount of internal panic which induced people to lock up their

---

129 [Answer 3253, on page |324| of Marx's manuscript. Translator]

130 [Continued from p. |352j| of Marx's manuscript. Editor]

[bank]notes, and not to pay them into the hands of the bankers, as is usually the case, the reserve would not be affected by the magnitude of the transactions'.

'500. The Bank may discount a million and a half in a day, and that is done constantly, without its *reserve* being in the slightest degree affected, the *notes coming back as deposits*, and no other alteration taking place than the mere transfer from one account to another'.

This is in complete contrast to the behaviour of the hoarder: '2408. Nobody will keep a note if he can help it; a note kept is so much lost to every person who keeps it. Persons keep only what they really require for the operations of paying, and in the case of bankers as a protection to their reserve'.

'2626. The amount of advances does not necessarily affect the bullion; if the amount of advances takes place with reference to internal purposes, the bullion may be very little affected by it'.[131]

Circulation (the issuing of banknotes) and *deposits* are, to that extent, the same thing. In both cases there is profit, derived from the fact that in the one case not all the deposits are drawn out and in the other case not all the notes are sent in for payment.

Rate of Interest and Amount of Circulation. < Under the Bank Restriction Act[132] there was an excess of currency, and the rate of interest was always far higher than since the resumption of cash payments. It later fell sharply with reduced banknote issues and rising exchanges. In 1822, 1823 and 1832 general circulation was low, and the rate of interest was also low. In 1824, 1825 and 1836 circulation was high, and the rate of interest rose. In summer 1830 circulation was high and there was a low rate of interest. Since the gold discoveries currency circulation throughout Europe has expanded, and the interest rate has risen. |361| The rate of interest, therefore, does not depend on the amount of currency in circulation.

> *Depreciation during the crisis.* According to a paper issued by the House of Lords in 1848 there was between February 1847 and 23 October 1847 a depreciation of government securities of £93,824,217, of dock shares of £1,094,714, of canal shares of £252,574, and of railway shares of £19,579,820 (as a result of the general contraction of credit).

131 Hubbard, meanwhile, has some wonderful notions: '2629. The Bank Act, by putting a strong and distinct limitation to the *issue* of *credit paper* in this country, has *converted that credit paper into capital*'. He wisely adds that this is only true: 'so far as regards the owners of that privilege' (2667).

132 [The Bank Restriction Act of 1797 suspended the Bank of England's obligation to make cash payments. It remained in force until 1820. Translator]

< The only one of the witnesses before the 1857 Committee on the Bank Acts who provides us with any insight into the state of affairs in the country is the London banker [John] Twells (a sort of 'Birmingham man').[133] '4488. How do you think that the Act of 1844 has operated?' Twells replies, in July 1857: 'If I were to answer you as a banker, I should say that it has operated exceedingly well, for it has afforded a rich harvest to bankers and capitalists of all kinds. But it has operated very hardly to the honest industrious tradesman who requires steadiness in the rate of discount, that he may be enabled to make his arrangements with confidence ... it has made money-lending a most profitable pursuit for them'.

'4489. It enables the London joint stock banks to return from 20 to 22 percent to their proprietors'.

'4490. Little tradesmen and respectable merchants who have not a large capital' are very much pinched. 'I observe such an amazing quantity of their acceptances unpaid. They are always small, perhaps ranging from £20 to £100, a great many of them are unpaid, and go back unpaid to all parts of the country, which is always an indication of suffering amongst ... little shopkeepers'.

The same Twells declares (4494) that trade is now unprofitable. His subsequent remarks are important, since he saw the latent presence of the crisis when none of the idiots suspected anything.

'4494. Things keep their prices' in Mincing Lane, but 'we sell nothing'. '4495. A Frenchman sends £3,000 worth of goods to a broker in Mincing Lane to sell them at a certain price. The broker cannot obtain this price. He informs the Frenchman. The Frenchman says he would lose money below that price. Then the broker assists him with £1,000, the Frenchman drawing a three-month bill of exchange on the broker for £1,000, with the goods as security. Three months later the bill expires, and the broker is no nearer selling than he was before. He then has to pay this £1,000 bill, and though he has security for the £3,000, he cannot make it available; then he is in difficulties, and that is how one person pulls down another'.

'4496. With regard to the large exports ... where there is a depressed state of trade at home, it necessarily forces large exportation'.

'4497. Do you think that the home consumption has diminished? Very much indeed ... immensely ... the shopkeepers are the best authorities'.

---

133 [A supporter of the 'Birmingham School' of 'little shilling men', who advocated reducing the gold content of the coinage and issuing paper currency not backed by a bullion reserve. Translator]

'4498. Still the importations are very large, does that not indicate a large consumption? It does, if you can sell; but many of the warehouses are full of these things; in this very instance which I have been relating, there is £3,000 worth imported which cannot be sold'.

The same banker: 'When money is dear ... *capital* ... is cheap' (4514).

The same again: 'Others are going in to a very great extent, carrying on a prodigious trade in exports and imports, to an extent far beyond what their capital justifies them in doing; there can be no doubt at all of that. These men may succeed; they may by some lucky venture get large fortunes and put themselves right. That is very much the system in which a great deal of trade is now carried on. Persons will consent to lose 20, 30 and 40 percent upon a shipment; the next venture may bring it back to them. If they fail in one after another, then they are broken up; and that is just the case which we have often seen recently; mercantile houses have broken up, without one shilling of property being left' (4616).

'4791. I should have very great difficulty in explaining to you, unless I could have the pleasure of showing you the books, how much higher the profits are now than they used to be formerly. When *interest* is low, from excessive issues, we have large deposits; when interest is high, we get the advantage in that way'.

'4794. When money is at a moderate rate, we have more demand for it; we lend more; it operates in that way. When it gets higher we get more than a fair proportion for it; we get more than we ought to do'.

> *Quantity of money. Chapman's evidence*. '4868. If the money coming from the dividends into the hands of the public is not counteracted by repayment of loans to the Bank, large sums become unoccupied; and it is better worth the while of the persons receiving those dividends to take a lower rate of discount than to keep their money unemployed, and therefore we get very much below the Bank then'.

Artificial scarcity of banknotes. Chapman's evidence. '4963. I have also no hesitation in saying that I do not think it is a proper condition of things that the money market should be under the power of any individual capitalist, such as does exist in London, to create a tremendous scarcity and pressure when we have a very low state of circulation out. That is possible ... There is more than one capitalist who can withdraw from the circulating medium £1,000,000 or £2,000,000 of notes' (for example by selling public securities) 'if they have an object to attain by it'. >4967 illustrates 'that sudden withdrawal of notes'.

< It should never be forgotten that although a fairly permanent sum of £19,000,000 to £20,000,000 in notes is ostensibly in the hands of the public, the part of these notes that is actually circulating, on the one hand, and the part that lies *unemployed* as a reserve with the bankers, on the other, are both constantly

and substantially changing. If the reserve is large, it is said from the standpoint of the money market that the circulation is full, precisely when the actual circulation is low; and if the reserve is small (hence the actual circulation is full) the money market calls it low, i.e., only a small amount exists as unemployed money capital. A genuine expansion or contraction of circulation independent of the state of business – one in which the amount that the public needs remains the same – is only to be found for technical reasons. For example at the payment date of taxes notes (and coins) flow into the Bank of England in more than their customary measure, and in fact circulation contracts, irrespective of the need for it. Conversely, when dividends are paid out on the national debt. In the former case, loans are taken out from the bank to obtain means of circulation. In the latter case, the rate of interest charged by the private bankers falls on account of the temporary growth in their reserves. This has nothing to do with the absolute amount of circulation, but it is simply a decision by the party that *issues* the notes, for whom it represents an issue of loanable capital, | 362 | and who therefore pockets the profit from this issue.

In the one case there is simply a temporary displacement of the circulating medium, which the Bank of England adjusts by making short-term loans at low interest shortly before the due date for the payment of dividends; the surplus notes paid out in this way then fill the gaps that the payment of taxes gives rise to, while their repayment to the Bank brings back the surplus notes the payment of the national debt has placed with the public.

In the other case a low or full circulation is never more than a different distribution of the same mass of circulation between means of circulation actually circulating and deposits, i.e., the instrument of loans.

On the other hand, if for example an influx of bullion leads to an increase in the number of notes given out by the Bank of England in return, these help the business of discounting outside the Bank and flow back in the repayment of loans, > while the fresh discounts occur outside the Bank's precincts, < so that the absolute volume of notes in circulation is only temporarily increased.

If the circulation is full, on account of an expansion of business (which is also possible with relatively low prices) the rate of interest may be relatively high on account of the demand for moneyed capital that results from rising profits and a growth in business enterprise. If it is low, on account of a contraction of business, or also on account of a greater ease of obtaining credit, the rate of interest may be low even if prices are high. (See Hubbard.)[134]

134 [See above, pages 352b and 352c of Marx's manuscript. Translator]

The absolute quantity of circulation has a determining effect on the rate of interest only in periods of pressure. In this case, either the demand for a full circulation is merely a demand for hoarding (apart from the reduced velocity with which the money circulates, and with which *the same* money is constantly converted into loanable capital), on account of the *lack of credit*, as in 1847, when the government letter [suspending the 1844 Bank Act] did not lead to any expansion in the circulation. Or else more means of circulation may really be required under these circumstances, in the way that the circulation really did grow for some time after 1857 subsequent to the government letter of that year.

In other cases, the absolute quantity of circulation has no effect on the rate of interest, since, firstly, taking the economy and velocity of circulation as constant, it is determined by the price of commodities and the volume of transactions (one of these elements generally counteracts the effect of the other) and also by the state of credit, although it does not conversely determine the latter; and since, secondly, prices and interest do not stand in any necessary relationship to each other.

The distinction between the issue of means of circulation and the lending of capital is best shown in connection with the actual reproduction process. In examining that process, we saw how the various components of production are exchanged for one another.[135] > But the exchange is mediated through money. < For example, variable capital consists in practice of the provisions of the working men, a portion of their own product. But it is paid out to them bit by bit in money. This the capitalist has to advance, and it depends very much on the organisation of the credit system whether he can pay out the new variable capital again the next week with *the old* money that he paid out the week before. It is similar in the acts of exchange between the various categories of capital (for example the constant capital and the capital existing in the means of subsistence). The money for their circulation must, however, be advanced by one or both of the exchanging parties. It then remains in circulation, but returns time and again, after completing its exchange, to the person who advanced it, since for him it forms an outlay of surplus capital (over and above his productive capital). When the credit system is developed, so that money is concentrated in the hands of the bankers, it is they who advance it (at least nominally). This advance is only related to the money in circulation. It is an advance of circulation, not an advance of the capitals it circulates.

---

135 [A reference to the discussion in what became Part Three of Volume II of *Capital*. Translator]

'5062. There may be times when the notes in the hands of the public, though they be very large, are not to be had'. (The money is there; but everyone takes good care not to transform it into loanable 'money'. Everyone tries to keep it safely with himself.)

> *23 October 1856*. Notes in the hands of the Bank of England: £2,550,740; notes in the hands of the public: £21,155,000 (extremely full); bullion: £9,231,000. (But this was when a bullion drain was in progress.) Rate of interest: 6½ percent. By *30 November* the amount of bullion had fallen to £8,914,000. (The above-mentioned rate of interest was created by the demand for bullion to send abroad.)

'5035. There was a great demand for bullion for the French market and the continental market? Certainly; to supply our China and India demands, we had to go to France for it'.

'5043. If the money' (banknotes, with the rate of interest high) 'was required it would be wanted for the *settlement of previously contracted engagements* which were falling due from day to day'. See also 5042: 'No person can trade anew upon ten percent'.

5099 (examination of [Samuel] Gurney, chief billbroker of London) < 'The country bankers in rural districts send up their unemployed balances to yourselves and other houses? Yes. 5100. And, on the other hand, the Lancashire and Yorkshire districts require discounts from you for the use of their trade? Yes'.

'5101. Then by that means the *surplus money* of one part of the country is made available for the demands of another part of the country? Precisely so'.

> 5105. For his money at call, Chapman likes to have neither securities, nor Exchequer Bills, nor 'anything of a *fluctuating* character'. He prefers (5106) good commercial bills, which fall due every day in certain proportions.

< A particularly amusing aspect of Chapman's evidence is how these fellows actually view the public's money as their own property and believe it is their duty to ensure the permanent convertibility of their bills of exchange. The questions and answers show great naïveté.

The legislature, it seems, has a duty to ensure the permanent 'convertibility' of the bills accepted by the major firms. (The Bank of England must, they say, be obliged to discount them without exception.) The year 1857, incidentally, saw the bankruptcy of three such billbrokers, to the tune of some £8 million, though they had relatively no capital of their own!

'5177. Do you mean by that that you think that they ought to be discountable on compulsion, in the same way that a Bank of England note is now exchangeable against gold by compulsion?' [Yes] '5178. Is not the engagement of Messrs. Baring an engagement to pay a certain sum of money when the bill is due? That is perfectly true; but Messrs. Baring, when they contract that engagement, and every other merchant who contracts an engagement, never dream that they are going to pay it in sovereigns; they *expect that they are going to pay it at the clearing house*'. '5180. Do you think that there should be any machinery contrived by which the public would have a right to claim money before that bill was due by calling upon somebody to discount it? No, not from the acceptor; but if you mean by that that we are not to have the possibility of getting commercial bills discounted, we must alter the whole constitution of things'. > '5181. I am talking about the *expediency of making a bill of exchange discountable by compulsion?* It ... should be convertible'. < '5182. Then you think that it ought to be convertible into money, exactly in the same way that a Bank of England note ought to be *convertible* into money? Most decidedly so, under certain circumstances'. '5184. Then you think that the provisions of the currency should be so shaped that a bill of exchange of undoubted character ought at all times to be as readily exchangeable against money as a banknote? I do'.

|363| '5185. You do not mean to say that either the Bank of England or any individual should by law be compelled to exchange it? I mean to say this, that in framing a bill for the currency, we should make *provision to prevent the possibility of an inconvertibility of the bills of exchange* of the country arising'. This is the *convertibility of the bill of exchange* against the *convertibility of the banknote*.

'5190. The money-dealers of the country only, in point of fact, represent the public'. (Just as Mr. Chapman did later before the Assizes in the Davidson case. See *The Great City Frauds*.)[136]

> Chapman then comments poetically (5195) that, in a certain 1839 case which involved his pigsty, 'there was no interruption to the *ebb and flow of the banking money*'.

Quantity of money. < '5196. During the *quarters*' (when the dividends are paid) 'it is absolutely necessary that we should go to the Bank of England. When you abstract from the circulation £6 million or £7 million of revenue in *anticipation* of the dividends, somebody must *be the medium of supplying that* in the intermediate time'. (In this case the question at issue is the *supply of money*, not the supply of *capital*, or moneyed capital.)

> *Panic*. < '5169. Everybody acquainted *with our commercial circle* must know that when we are in such a state that we find it impossible to sell Exchequer bills, when India bonds are perfectly useless, when you cannot discount the first commercial bills ... great anxiety on the part of those whose business renders them liable to pay the circulating medium of the realm on demand, which is

136 [This is a reference to the report of the Davidson case in Laing 1856. Translator]

the case with all bankers. Then the effect of that is to make every man double his reserve. Just see what the effect of that is throughout the country, that every country banker, of whom there are about 500, has to send up to his London correspondent to remit him £5,000 in banknotes. Taking such a limited sum as that as the average, which is quite absurd, you come to £2,500,000 taken out of the circulation. How is that to be supplied?'

Those private capitalists, etc., who have money, on the other hand, do not want to let go of it whatever the interest rate, for, as Chapman puts it, they say: 'We would rather have *no interest at all* than have a doubt about our getting the money in case we require it'. (5195).

'5173. Our system is this: that we have £300,000,000 of liabilities which may be called for at a single moment to be paid in the coin of the realm, and that coin of the realm, if the whole of it is substituted, amounts to £23,000,000, or whatever it may be; is that not a state which may throw us into convulsions at any moment?'

Here the credit system suffers an inversion, and turns into the monetary system.

Apart from the domestic panic during crises, we can speak of the *quantity of money* only with regard to bullion, 'the money of the world'.

The same Chapman, speaking of the year 1847: 'The primary cause of the derangement of the money market no doubt was *in the quantity of money* which was required to regulate our exchanges, in consequence of the extraordinary importations of the year'. (5218.)

Firstly, this hoard of world market money was at that time reduced to its minimum; secondly, it served at the same time as a guarantee of the convertibility of credit money. It thus combined two completely different functions, although both of these arise from the nature of money, since real money is always world market money, and credit money always depends on world market money.

In 1847, without the suspension of the Bank Act of 1844, '*the clearing houses could not have been settled*'. (5221)

> '5223. If we had each of us agreed to pay with *bills of exchange*, how far that might have settled it I cannot say'.

< Even so, the fellow did have some inkling of the impending crisis:

'5236. There are certain conditions of the money market (*and the present is not very far from it*) where money is exceedingly difficult, and recourse must be had to the Bank'.

'5239. With reference to the sums which we took from the Bank on the Friday, Saturday and Monday, the 19th. 20th. and 22nd. of October 1847, we should only have been too thankful to have got the bills back on the Wednesday following; the money reflowed to us directly the panic was over'.

Chapman believes (5274) that the 'bills of exchange running on London amount at any one time to ... from £100 million to £120 million'. (This does not include local bills.) > To this must be added the deposits on call.

< '5287. Whereas in October 1856, the amount in the hands of the public ran up to £21,155,000 there was an extraordinary difficulty in obtaining money; *notwithstanding that the public held so much, we could not touch it*'. This was due to the 'anxiety' felt 'in certain concerns, in consequence of what happened to the Eastern Bank' in March 1856.

5290 and 5291. As soon as the panic is over 'all bankers *deriving their profits from interest* begin to employ the money immediately'.

5302. Chapman explains the alarm over the decreasing reserve of the Bank of England not from fear for the deposits, but rather because 'all those who are responsible for paying large sums of money on demand know very well that they may be driven to the Bank in case of a tightness of the market'.

It is very pleasant, incidentally, to observe how the reserve vanishes as an *actual amount*. The bankers keep a minimum for their current business with the Bank of England (or with themselves). The billbrokers hold the 'loose banking money of the country' without a reserve. And all the Bank of England has to set against its liabilities for deposits is simply the reserves of the bankers and others, besides public deposits. It allows these reserves to fall to the lowest point, for example to £2 million. Apart from this £2 million in paper, therefore, the entire swindle has *no* reserve other than bullion in times of pressure (and these periods reduce the reserve, because notes are paid out again in bullion and cancelled). Hence the influence of every reduction in the bullion reserve is a further drain of bullion.

'5306. If there should not be currency to settle the transactions at the clearing house, the only next alternative which I can see is to meet together, and to make our payments in first-class bills, bills upon the Treasury, and Messrs Smith, Payne[137] and so forth'.

'5307. Then, if the government failed to supply you with a circulating medium, you would create one for yourselves? What can we do? The public come in, and take the circulating medium out of our hands; it does not exist'.

'5308. You would only then do in London what they do in *Manchester every day of the week*? Yes'.

137 [In fact Smith, Payne & Smiths, a leading private bank in London at the time. Translator]

> *Capital and Money*. < Chapman has a quite splendid answer [to the question] put to him by [Edward] Cayley (a 'Birmingham man')[138] in relation to Overstone's conception of *capital*:

|364| '5315. It has been stated before this committee that in a pressure like that of 1847, men are not looking for *money*, but are looking for *capital*; what is your opinion in that respect? I do not understand it; *we only deal in money*; I do not understand what you mean by it'.

'5316. If you mean' (by commercial capital) 'the quantity of money which a man has of his own in his business, if you call that *capital*, it forms, in most cases, *a very small proportion of the money* which he wields in his affairs *through the credit which is given him by the public*'. (Through the *medium of such fellows as Chapman*!)

'5339. Is it the want of property that makes us give up our specie payments? Not at all ... It is not that we want property, but it is that we are moving under a highly artificial system; and if we have an immense superincumbent demand upon our currency, circumstances may arise to prevent our obtaining that currency. Is the whole commercial industry of the country to be paralysed? Shall we shut up all the avenues of employment?'

'5338. If the question should arise whether we should maintain specie payments, or whether we should maintain the industry of the country, I have no hesitation in saying which I should drop'.

As to the *hoarding* of banknotes 'with a view to aggravate the pressure', > see the same Chapman, in 5358 and 5383. '5387. The Act of 1844 ... affords such an opportunity'.

'4864. We think that it is our natural business to go to the Bank during the quarters when the public money goes into the Bank; somebody must supply that vacuum, and it is our natural business to do it'.

< 5508. (Examination of [Edward] Capps) 'Then, upon the whole ... you think that the present system' (the Act of 1844) 'is a somewhat adroit scheme for bringing the *profits of industry* periodically into the *usurer's bag*? I think so. I know that it has operated so in the building trade'.

> See house building in London for an example of *how the credit system* helps to transform a small-scale mode of production into a large-scale mode of production.

(*Report on Bank Acts* 1857, pp. 507, 508 and 509.)

The amount of loanable capital depends not only on the quantity it possesses in itself but on the *state of credit*. When the state of credit is bad, firstly,

138 [See above, note 133. Translator]

the industrialists lend less to each other, and secondly, some of the idiots who provide the moneyed capital for the bankers get nervous, and refuse to 'lend' under any conditions whatever.

It is necessary to distinguish between *fictitious capital* (interest-bearing papers) and the *credit capital* constituted by *banknotes, banker's drafts*, etc. (where, in other words, someone makes *credit* itself into a commodity in which he trades.)

|365| *The Import and Export of Bullion*

Unfortunately, imports of bullion and specie did not start to be registered in the United Kingdom (at the Custom House) until *November 1857*.

Total annual import of gold and silver (bullion and specie), in £.

1858	1859	1860	1861	1862	1863
29,493,190	37,070,156	22,978,196	18.747,045	31,656,476	30,030,794

Total annual export of gold and silver (bullion and specie), in £.

1858	1859	1860	1861	1862	1863
19,628,876	35,688,803	25,534,768	20,811,648	29,326,191	26,544,040

Excess of imports over exports:

9,864,876	1,381,353			2,330,285	3,486,754

Excess of exports over imports:

		2,556,572	2,064,603		

Thus the total *excess of imports over exports* = 17,062,706
and the total *excess of exports over imports* = 4,621,175
Overall excess of imports = 12,441,531.

The figures on exports and imports have been taken from a Blue Book, *Statistical Abstract* 1865.

If we now first compare the *relative excess of imports over exports*, or vice versa, with the *bullion in the Bank of England* (although a maximum of one-fifth of this is silver; in our later calculations we shall look at the figures for gold alone).

1858	1859	1860	1861	1862	1863
Excess of imports over exports:					
9,864,876	1,381,353			2,330,285	3,486,754
Excess of exports over imports:					
		2,556,572	2,064,603		

Average bullion in the Bank for each year:

1858	1859	1860	1861	1862	1863
17,847,750	17,928,750	15,239,750	13,009,250	16,342,750	14,556,500

As a whole, the variations in the quantity of bullion in the Bank of England are a fairly approximate representation of the movement in the total import and export of bullion. Nevertheless, there are also significant divergences between the two sets of figures.

1858 and 1859
The *excess of imports in* 1859 was £1,381,353, thus the quantity of bullion in the Bank of England (if it varied completely *identically* with this figure) would have to be 17,847,750 + 1,381,353 = 19,229,103, but it is in fact *£1,300,353 less than this.* This difference is to be explained either by its greater use as material for luxury goods, or the entry of a part of the excess quantity into internal circulation as gold or silver coin. The latter figure therefore needs to be subjected to a comparison.

1859 and 1860
The *excess of exports over imports* in 1860 was £2,556,572. The quantity of bullion should therefore have been 17,928,750 – 2,556,572 = 15,372,178; but it is £132,428 less than this, an insignificant divergence.

1860 and 1861
The *excess of exports over imports in 1861* was £2,064,603. The quantity of bullion should therefore have been 15,239,750 – 2,064,603 = 13,175,147; but it is £165,897 less, again an insignificant divergence.

1861 and 1862
The *excess of imports over exports in 1862* was £2,330,285. The quantity of bullion should therefore have been 13,009,250 + 2,330,285 = 15,339,535, but it is *£1,003,215 greater*. This *larger* figure therefore represents not just an influx of bullion but the transformation of previously circulating gold (or silver) currency into a store of wealth.

1862 and 1863
The *excess of imports over exports in 1863* was £3,486,754. The quantity of bullion should therefore have been 16,342,750 + 3,486,754 = 19,829,504, but is £5,279,004 *too small*. This is a *very considerable divergence*, and represents a decline of £1,792,250 in bullion as compared with 1862.

We therefore arrive at these results: if we look at the *excess of import over export of bullion in 1859 as compared with 1858* the increase of bullion in the Bank was £1,300,353 less than the excess.

When 1862 is compared with 1861, the increase of bullion in the Bank is £1,003,215 *more* than the excess.

When 1863 is compared with 1862, there is an *absolute reduction of bullion in the Bank* of £1,792,250 despite a *significant excess* of imports, as compared with the expected excess of £5,279,004.

(Incidentally, a large part of the bullion could have been exported by *emigrants*. Their exports do not figure in these lists. But this has nothing to do with the balance of trade.)

|366| In contrast to the above, *when we compare 1860 with 1859 we find* an excess *of exports over imports*, but the fall in bullion is £*132,428 less* than the fall we should expect.

Equally, when *1861 is compared with 1860* the fall is £*165,897 less* than expected.

Where exports increase, the fall in the quantity of bullion in the Bank follows the actual reduction very closely.

Where imports increase, there are very large divergences, and indeed, in 1863 there is even a divergence in the opposite direction.

We now have to take into consideration that we are speaking of *total bullion*, without distinguishing between gold and silver, whereas the Bank of England is only allowed to hold one-fifth of its bullion in silver.

Total imports of gold:

1858	1859	1860	1861	1862	1863
22,793,126	22,297,698	12,584,684	12,163,937	19,903,709	19,142,685

Total exports of gold:

12,567,040	18,081,139	15,641,578	11,238,372	16,011,963	15,303,279

Excess of imports over exports:

1,226,086	4,216,559		925,565	3,891,746	3,839,386

Excess of exports over imports:

		3,056,894			

If the movement of gold alone had been considered, the increase of bullion would have had to be much more pronounced in all years, with the exception of *1860*, and in 1861 there would have been, not a reduction, but an increase of bullion.

But now we come to silver:

Total imports of silver:

1858	1859	1860	1861	1862	1863
6,700,064	14,772,458	10,393,512	6,583,108	11,752,772	10,888,129

Total exports of silver:

7,061,836	17,607,664	9,893,190	9,573,276	13,314,228	11,240,761

Excess of imports over exports:

		500,322			

Excess of exports over imports:

331,772	2,835,206		2,990,168	1,561,456	352,632

Comparing 1859 with 1858 and subtracting the excess of exported silver from the excess of imported gold:

there is an *excess* of 1,381,353

Comparing 1860 with 1859 and subtracting the excess of imported silver from the excess of exported gold:

there is a reduction of 2,556,572

Comparing 1861 with 1860 and subtracting the excess of exported silver from the excess of imported gold:

there is a reduction of 2,064,603

Comparing 1862 with 1861 and subtracting the excess of exported silver from the excess of imported gold:

there is an increase of 2,330,285

Comparing 1863 with 1862 and subtracting the excess of exported silver from the excess of imported gold:

there is an increase of 3,486,734.

With the exception of 1860 there is a constant excess of silver export over silver import.

But how is it possible constantly to export more silver than is imported, without exchanging gold for it in order to make up the balance? Would this not then appear as an *export of gold*?

The situation is simply this, that £2,835,206 of the silver bullion reserve has been exported. This has to be replaced by gold, and thus the only excess that remains is the £1,381,853 excess of gold.

If we compare 1860 with 1859, the amount of silver has increased by £500,322. If we subtract this from the excess of exported gold, there remains a reduction of £2,556,572.

From 1861 onwards there is a constant reduction in silver. But what is the *source* of this excess of silver exports over imports?

We shall (perhaps) have to come back to this silver question. (Of course, if one assumes that there is *a supply of silver on the market*, or that it can be obtained from other sources than the Bank of England, everything would be simple.)

If we compare 1859 with 1858, the average bullion in the Bank of England (compared with the average bullion present in 1858) shows an increase of £81,000. This is £1,300,353 less than the total annual average excess of bullion. The *excess* of bullion imports over exports itself amounts to £1,381,353. Almost the whole of this excess, therefore, apart from the £81,000, is not indicated in the Bank of England's bullion figures. But we find an excess of *coined* gold, comparing 1859 with 1858, of £1,418,486. This circumstance alone would permit one to conclude that more of the imported gold has entered into internal circulation. (Even if everything had passed through the hands of the Bank of England, this *average* annual amount of bullion would not need to increase, if the greater part of it were withdrawn for internal circulation.) We also find that the number of *people who emigrated*, comparing 1859 with 1858, rose by 6,460. (This is admittedly a small number.)

However that may be, it is evident from what we have said that the *rise and fall of the amount of bullion* in the Bank of England, irrespective of the fact that it does not exactly square with the real import and export of bullion, is by no means determined just by the relationship between the *import and export of commodities*, but much more by the *relationship between the import and export of bullion* itself, since both processes continue uninterruptedly, and what *appears* as an *increase* or a *reduction* in the bullion in the Bank only reflects the *predominance of one balance or the other in the movement of these oscillations from side to side.*

|367| The following table will make this point clearer. Unfortunately it can only start in 1858 (after the month of November 1857) because that was when the import of bullion started to be recorded.

The Import and Export of Gold, in £ (Import from other countries to England, Export from England to other Countries)

	1858	1859	1860	1861	1862	1863
Russia						
Import from	1,448,129	2,070,066	165,488	557,353	756,842	904,532
Export to	0	96,818	1,573	0	1,797,973	2,707,857
Hanse Towns						
Import from	1,490,850	351,317	26,417	364,394	422,020	185,658
Export to	101,920	423,963	22,067	15,410	30,374	1,080,944
Denmark						
Import from	0	0	0	0	0	0
Export to	0	5,712	0	0	0	0
Holland						
Import from	43,014	16,705	7,675	6,584	43	114,267
Export to	13,996	317,222	10,329	242	68,018	4.374

The Import and Export of Gold, in £ (cont.)

	1858	1859	1860	1861	1862	1863
Belgium						
Import from	89,127	11,256	25,402	515,250	7,948	16,084
Export to	198,957	188,447	118,808	5,047	249,893	19,075
France						
Import from	654,001	936,546	341,177	2,504,493	91,980	187,546
Export to	10,530,095	14,902,469	10,400,604	998,304	6,356.200	3,502,829
Portugal						
Import from	125,872	77,923	2,522	8.730	5,995	1,544
(Azores and Madeira)						
Export to	127,067	395,567	602,145	336,921	967,445	638,755
Spain and Canaries						
Import from	16,863	7,116	7,595	6,826	12,344	5,098
Export to	60,307	345,558	755,022	647,556	1,392,654	1,054,144
Gibraltar						
Import from	32,029	5,191	5,094	18,192	8,318	9,842
Export to	0	109,946	144,906	53,014	105,470	52,695
Malta						
Import from	31,470	8,056	21,513	9,454	4,053	485
Export to	0	109,946	144,906	53,014	105,470	52,695
Turkey						
Import from	35,906	146,020	1,924	27,830	427	98,430
Export to	655,802	3,002	109	494	1,124,096	35,534
Egypt						
Import from	1,221,985	167,694	12,322	15,509	3,709	16,359
Export to	131,286	613,264	1,301,886	796,495	1,919,621	3,473,682
West Coast of Africa						
Import from	110,679	97,079	91,131	78,272	99,922	69,606
Export to	missing	missing	missing	missing	missing	missing

	1858	1859	1860	1861	1862	1863
British Possessions in South Africa						
Import from	11,405	8,847	17,893	8,878	9,038	4,824
Export to	64,500	7,301	50,619	133,360	0	159,211
Australia						
Import from	9,064,763	8,624,566	6,719,000	6,331,225	6,704,753	5,995,368
Export to	0	0	29,592	0	0	19,469
Mauritius						
Import from	0	0	0	0	0	0
Export to	107,323	631	0	0	0	0
East Indies						
Import from	0	0	0	0	0	0
Export to	0	0	0	0	0	0
China						
Import from	0	0	0	0	0	0
Export to	0	0	0	0	0	0
British Columbia						
Import from	3,668	0	7,000	4,785	11,088	12,509
British North American Provinces						
Import from	150	116,902	25,636	51,261	51,767	34,633
Export to	3,945	26,248	9,003	631,576	283,380	129,092
United States						
Import from	4,502,464	7,909,342	3,917,755	38,434	9,731,434	7,520,682
Export to	135,382	9,999	1,724,008	7,297,887	36,670	39,924
Brazil						
Import from	1,382,653	401,368	183,007	664,929	269,902	63,881
Export to	289,404	97,660	357,099	20,286	408,769	1,681,025

The Import and Export of Gold, in £ (cont.)

	1858	1859	1860	1861	1862	1863
Mexico, South America and the West Indies						
Import from Mexico alone	2,465,357	1,337,332	996,951	935,307	1,631,464	3,896,554
Export to	0	0	0	239	14,999	122,445

|368| With silver we shall only compare import and export where there are significant differences:

Import and Export of Silver

	1858	1859	1860	1861	1862	1863
Hanse Towns						
Import	180,130	1,035,149	393,300	79,988	1,473,518	686,359
Export	556,739	856,252	375,312	318,558	213,622	383,981
Holland						
Import	6,132	370,712	2,496	130,289	163,836	420,804
Export	668,025	29,401	124,584	348,438	357,022	216,982
Belgium						
Import	556,347	1,521,176	569,854	314,189	1,069,952	954,709
Export	29,212	68,982	92,607	187,318	84,527	192,230
France						
Import	2,079,204	6,365,852	3,698,019	689,522	2,202,972	1,256,724
Export	390,552	481,902	914,742	1,052,737	849.463	1,258,155
Mexico, South America except Brazil, and the West Indies						
Import	2,943,169	3,363,01	4,518,097	5,047,612	6,242,068	6,651,506
Export	0	0	0	634	0	27
United States						
Import	309,308	1,763,639	874,827	28,249	332,728	626,842
Export	67,185	4,343	3,212	84,066	858	14,271

	1858	1859	1860	1861	1862	1863
Egypt, coin chiefly for China, etc.						
Import	1,470	7,616	2,088	2,496	2,205	1,727
Export	1,651,175	4,045,982	1,936,926	1,021,660	3,806,34	2,586,309
Egypt, bullion chiefly for India						
Export	3,437,675	11,957,285	6,187,310	6,258,179	6,903,865	6,229,439
Egypt, total export						
	5,088,850	16,003,267	8,124,236	7,279,839	10,710,209	8,815,748

Total of Gold and Silver (Bullion and Specie. Imports and Exports)

	1858	1859	1860	1861	1862	1863
Russia						
Import	1,448,283	2,070,066	169,109	557,353	764,554	912,486
Export	0	122,287	1,673	0	1,855,401	2,707,857
Hanse Towns						
Import	1,670,980	1,386,466	419,717	444.382	1,895,538	872,017
Export	658,659	1,280,215	397,379	333,968	243,996	1,462,925
Holland						
Import	49,146	387,417	10,171	136,873	163,879	535,071
Export	682,021	346,623	134,913	348.680	425,040	221,356
Belgium						
Import	645,474	1,532,432	595,256	829,439	1,077,900	970,793
Export	288,169	257,429	211,415	192,375	344,420	211.305
France						
Import	2,733,205	7,302,398	4,039,196	3,194,015	2,294,952	1,444,270
Export	10,920,647	15,384,371	11,315,346	2,051,041	7,205,663	4,750,984
Portugal,						
Import	467,882	331,322	255,603	127,360	97,021	59,164
Export	127,067	395,567	602,476	337,562	970,267	638,755

Total of Gold and Silver (Bullion and Specie. Imports and Exports) (cont.)

	1858	1859	1860	1861	1862	1863
Spain						
Import	47,921	10,168	11,715	37,100	22,692	8,942
Export	60,307	346,352	756,064	650,246	1,398,078	1,058,826
Turkey						
Import	44,185	155,208	3,228	30,990	2,935	98,558
Export	653,802	3,054	109	494	2,029,121	35,534
Egypt						
Import	1,223,455	175,310	14,410	18,005	5,914	18,086
India and China						
Export	5,220,136	16,616,531	9,426,122	8,076,334	12,629,830	12,289,430
Australia						
Import	9,066,289	8,627,854	6,719,857	6,331,828	6,705,036	5,995,441
Export	395	103	29,720	0	0	21,382
***Mexico*, South America and the West Indies**						
Import	5,408,526	4,700,345	5,515,048	5,982,919	7,873,532	10,548,060
Mexico alone						
Export	0	0	0	873	14,999	122,472
Brazil						
Import	1,425,514	423,161	190,219	732,938	357,746	162,384
Export	415,795	197,062	524,312	169,813	452,392	1,731,037
United States						
Import	4,811,772	9,672,981	4,792,582	66,683	10,064,162	8,147,524
Export	202,567	14,342	1,727,220	7,381,953	37,528	54,195

|369| (*House of Lords. Committee. 1848.*)[139]

139 [*Report from the Secret Committee* 1857. Translator]

(Continued from page 646; from p. |364| of Marx's manuscript)

3008 (Tooke): 'Whenever there exist motives to enterprise, whether in the shares of joint stock companies or in investments of any kind at home or abroad, *a low rate of interest* tends very considerably to promote and extend the tendency to speculation'.

3094 (Tooke): 'The Bank has *the power* (*not* to extend the amount of notes in the hands of the public) *but* ... to reduce the amount of notes in the hands of the public, not however without a very violent operation'.

3099 (Tooke [gives an example of when the Bank extended its advances without issuing more banknotes].) < 'In 1835, when the Bank made use of the West India deposits and of the loan from the East India Company in *extended advances to the public*. At that time the amount of notes in the hands of the public was actually rather diminished ... the same discrepancy [was observable] in 1846 at the time of the payment of the *railway deposits* into the Bank; the *securities* were increased to *about thirty millions*, while [there was] no perceptible effect upon the *amount of notes* in the hands of the public'.

> 3100 (Tooke): 'At that period whatever the bank received in the shape of deposits and invested in securities, in the shape of discounts or otherwise, was taken from one portion of commerce and transferred to another? Precisely'.

3101 (Tooke): 'If a merchant discounts bills to the amount of £10,000 ... in the great majority of cases he receives simply the power of drawing upon the Bank, he passes his cheque accordingly; that cheque he sends to his banker, and the banker *sets it off either against his acceptances held by the Bank*, or puts it to its *deposit accounts there*'.

3104 (Tooke): 'The *quantity of paper* representing the precious metals in the hands of the public has nothing to do with the *value of the paper* as compared *with the precious metals themselves*'.

Exchange.

3107 (Tooke's evidence.) The rise in the rate of interest encourages investments from abroad in English securities. At the same time 'foreign securities are sent from this country to be realised abroad. The same cause induces a *contraction of mercantile credit* given by merchants of this country to merchants abroad. It induces also the transmission of commodities which otherwise would not have been exported, that is, they *are in such cases sent as a means of drawing against* without reference even to prices; and it checks importation. In short ... it forces *capital in its more compendious and ready form, that is in gold*, into this country instead of allowing it to be got out'.

3122 (Tooke): 'During speculative periods or rising prices the buyers or operators *are always in very good credit*, and the operation is generally independent of any *immediate* banking operation'.

The influence of the Bank of England on the rate of discount.

3132 (Tooke): 'Dealing on so very large a scale with its own capital, and the deposits from the government revenue, and the Exchequer balances, it may cause a very considerable temporary *variation*, distinct from what would be the ordinary market rate'.

Quantity of Notes.

1137 (Samuel Gurney): 'We never apply to the Bank for money except when there is a short supply of banknotes in Lombard Street, and the *notes are actually wanted*'.

1139 (the same): 'When we apply to the Bank for money it is *because the bankers are short of banknotes*. The cheque which we draw on the Bank and pay into our own bankers or other bankers *is immediately turned into notes*'. 1140. 'While one banker has a surplus and another wants it, we adjust it between them. It is when there is a short supply on the whole that we take money from the bank, and it immediately becomes diffused in banknotes in Lombard Street'.

1143 (the same): 'The temptation of a *high rate of interest* in a very small degree only, if at all, neutralises the effect of alarm'.

1262 (the same): 'When a panic exists a man does not ask himself what he can get for his banknotes, or whether he shall lose one or two percent by selling his Exchequer bills, or three percent. If he is under the influence of alarm he does not care for the profit or loss, *but makes himself safe* and allows the rest of the world to do as they please'.

1297 (the same): 'It' (*silver*) 'at once *becomes money* when sent to a foreign country'.

1306 (the same): 'When the interest came up … to that high rate of above eight percent, it could only be paid by persons who were pressed for the purpose of meeting their engagements. 1310. People were forced to make good existing engagements, but they took care to make no new ones'.

1324 (the same): 'Do you think that the great fluctuations in the rate of interest … are advantageous or not to the bankers or dealers in money? < I think they are advantageous to dealers in money. All fluctuations in trade are advantageous to the knowing man'.

> 1344 (*Quantity of money*): 'We never apply to the Bank, unless the amount of circulating medium in the City is below the requirements, then we become in a large degree the agents in getting it from the Bank. If the supply of circulating medium is adequate we never go near them'.

1514 (Loyd): 'Pressure, and a high rate of interest, *caused by the want of sufficient capital*, cannot be relieved by an extra issue of banknotes'.

1588 (the same): '*Credit* is a *means of obtaining another man's capital*'.

1589 (the same): 'An interruption to credit is an interruption to the facility of so borrowing other people's capital as to carry on trade'.

1604 (the same): 'In fact the high rate of interest and the depression of the manufacturing interests was the necessary result of the diminution of the national capital, applicable to manufacturing and trading purposes'. (He naturally raves about *high interest*.)

|370| 1650. With railways, says [George Grenfell] Glyn, 'there is a saving in the expense of transit. But I look more at the actual saving in the *amount of capital which was formerly locked up in the stocks of retail traders* which has been decreased from the increased facility of obtaining supplies'.

1654 (Glyn). In 1845 and 1846 there was a great increase in the number of Railway Bills granted. 1655. The interest rate was low. 'If the transfer from floating capital to fixed had been felt ... it would be felt now, inasmuch as the Railway Calls have gone on'.

1665 (the same): 'It still had the effect of causing a greater importation of food to the extent of the high wages which they' (the labourers) 'received for railway work as compared with what they would have had from agricultural employment, or from the workhouse, and that is considerably more'.

1709 (the same): 'Under circumstances of great pressure upon the country, it' (the Bank of England) '*commands* the rate of interest. 1710. Whenever the discounts of the private bankers or brokers become comparatively limited, they fall upon the Bank of England, and then it ... has the power *commanding* the market rate'.

1721 (the same): In October 1847 'there was an *actual hoarding* on the part of the public, and to a considerable extent'.

1729 (the same): 'It' (the power of the bank of making advances) 'did not prevent the failure of houses which ought to have failed, nor will it ever, unless they make *advances upon improper securities*. But the fear in October 1847 was not for insolvent but for solvent houses'.

1736 (the same): '*It*' (the Government Letter suspending the Bank Act) 'produced the *same effect* as if the Bank *had made an issue*; because *it brought out the hoards of notes, and they went into circulation*'.

2308 ([Sir William] Brown of Liverpool): 'In 1847 the lowest rate of interest was 3¼ percent, and the highest was 10 percent, showing a difference of 6¾ percent. But I should add to that that this does not give an accurate view of what the *interest of money was in 1847*, because persons frequently paid a commission in addition to this *which made it amount to 10, 20 or 30 percent*, depending upon the length of time that the bill had to run, and the pressure for money at the moment'.

The *sanctity* and *inviolability of the bullion reserve* (under the Act of 1844) is treated far less seriously than it is by hoarders.

2311 (Brown): 'This money' (in the Issue Department) 'might as well have been thrown into the sea from any use that it was of the time, there being no power of employing any of it without violating the act of Parliament'.

2444 ([James] Lister, Managing Director of the Union Bank, Liverpool): 'There was an undue *extension of credit* … because a man transferred property from business into railways and was still anxious to carry on the same extent of business. He probably first thought that he could sell the railway shares at a profit and replace the money in his business. Perhaps he found that could not be done, and he then got credit in his business where he formerly paid in cash. There was an extension of credit from that circumstance'.

2500. 'Were those bills … upon which the banks had sustained a loss by holding them principally bills upon corn or bills upon cotton? … They were bills upon all kinds of produce, corn and cotton and sugar, all foreign produce of all descriptions. There was scarcely anything, perhaps with the exception of oil, that did not go down'.

2506. 'A broker who accepts a bill will not accept it without a good margin as to the value' (of the produce for which it is drawn.)

2512. 'There are two kinds of bills drawn against produce; the first is the original bill drawn abroad upon the merchant who imports it. In consequence of the steamers, the bills which are drawn against produce frequently fall due before the produce arrives. The merchant, therefore, when it arrives, if he has not sufficient capital, has to pledge that produce with the broker till he has time to sell that produce. Then a new species of bill is immediately drawn by the merchant in Liverpool upon the broker, upon the security of that produce, lodged in the warehouses in Liverpool, bonded or free. Then it is the business of the banker to ascertain from the broker whether he has the produce, and to what extent he has advanced upon it. It is his business to see that the broker has property to protect himself if he makes a loss'.

2516. 'We also receive bills from abroad. There are foreign bills. A man buys a bill abroad on England, and sends it to a house of England; we cannot tell whether that bill is drawn prudently or imprudently, whether it is drawn for produce or for wind'.

2519. 'Is there anything on the face of the bill to show on what account it is drawn? No, not necessarily'.

2533. 'You said that almost every kind of foreign produce was sold at a great loss. Do you think that that was in consequence of undue speculation in that produce? It arose from a very large import, and there not *being an equal consumption* to take it off. It appears *that consumption fell off a great deal*'. 2534. 'In October ... produce was almost unsaleable'.

Quantity of notes.

2645 (Samuel Gurney): 'At the end of October 1847 there were £20,800,000 of notes in the hands of the public. At that period there was great difficulty in getting possession of banknotes in the money market. This arose from the alarm of not being able to get them in consequence of the restriction of the Act of 1844. At present' (October 1848) 'banknotes in the hands of the public [amount to] £17,700,000, but ... it *is much beyond what is required.* There is no banking house or money dealer in London but what has a larger amount of banknotes than they can use'. 2650. 'The amount of banknotes ... out of the custody of the Bank of England affords a totally insufficient exponent of the active state of the circulation, without taking into consideration likewise ... the state of the commercial world and the state of credit'. 2651. 'The feeling of surplus that we have under the present amount of circulation in the hands of the public arises in a large degree from our present state of great stagnation. In a state of high prices and excitement of transaction, £17,700,000 would give us a feeling of restriction'.

|371| 2844 ([Charles] *Wright*, banker, of Nottingham): 'Any excess of circulation' (on the part of the Bank of England) 'will go into the *deposits*, and thus assume a *different name*'.

2930. 'During the alarm it requires twice as much circulation as in ordinary times, because the circulation is hoarded by bankers and others'.

3195. ([William] Cotton, director and ex-Governor of the Bank of England): In 1847 'there was a large, and I think very indiscreet extension of trade beyond the capital the parties had to carry it on, in the corn trade, in consequence of the profits which had resulted from the first importations of corn. In the India trade there was a larger extent of trade carried on than was justified by the amount of capital, and which had been supplied by renewing bills. There was also a very large amount, far beyond what the parties were justified in appropriating, on fixed securities in the Mauritius trade. After the failure of one or two houses it appeared that credit had been stretched to a most unreasonable extent, larger than I ever recollect'.

3199. (On the *India trade.*) 'The system had increased during the years 1845 and 1846 of manufacturers exporting through merchants in London, and drawing upon them bills of exchange of a certain date, and engaging to renew those bills; it was therefore not the capital of the house which was exporting, but the capital of others, borrowed on discount by the manufacturers, and most extensive advances were made to houses in India for indigo, sugar and other works'.

3238. 'Would that' (namely the influx from a country where the interest was low into a country where the interest was high) 'produce under general circumstances ... an *average rate of interest* over the civilised portion, say of Europe? It does *not produce an average rate of interest*, because one country may be differently circumstanced to another; the interest may be high in one country, and low in another; but *still if it was higher than ordinary* in one country, and *lower than ordinary* in another, it would cause an influx of the precious metals from the country where it was lowest to that where it was highest'. But it would not produce '*an equal rate of interest* all over the world'.

Quantity of notes. 3252. 'Do you think that the amount of reserve which bankers and commercial men feel it prudent and necessary to maintain for the satisfaction of their engagements, by keeping out of the active market of circulation and of commerce a certain amount of money, has a tendency to raise the rate of interest? I think if that amount was put into the market it would have a tendency to lower the rate of interest'. 3253. 'If it is forced out of the market, must it not have a tendency to *raise* the rate of interest? If parties lock up their money ... the consequence is that its value will rise'.

3920. ([Sir Archibald] Alison): 'At the two terms of Whitsuntide and Martinmas all the great payments – such as rents of lands and houses, as well as interest upon bonds and other payments – are made due'. (*In Scotland.*)

Influence of prosperity and distress on the quantity of banknote circulation in Ireland. Evidence of M. Donnell (Governor of the Bank of Ireland) to the *House of Lords Committee* 1848 [1857], nos. 4173–81. Compare [Robert] Murray (Manager of the Provincial Bank of Ireland), nos. 4246–9, 4252–3, 4266, 4278 and the *Papers* [attached to the *Report of the Secret Committee* 1857], pp. 461–2.

Profits of the big banks. < 'The following summary of the profits derived by the Bank of England from 1797 to 1817 was produced before the Lords' Committee during the latter year upon the resumption of cash payments:

Bonuses and increased dividends	£7,451,136
New stocks divided amongst the proprietors	£7,276,500
Increased value of capital	£14,553,000,

making in all, on a capital of £11,642,400 a gain of £29,280,636 in nineteen years'. (Hardcastle 1843, p. 120.)

'If we calculate the total profits of the Bank of Ireland' (which also suspended cash payments in 1797), 'since the suspension upon the principle applied to the Bank of England by the Lords' Committee, we shall find the result nearly as follows:

Annual dividends as per returns to 1821:	£4,736,085
Declared bonuses	£1,225,000
Surplus assets	£1,214,800
Increased value of shares (capital)	£4,185,000
Total gains on a capital of £3,000,000	£11,360,885'.

(Hardcastle 1843, pp. 363–4)

|372|[140] With respect to the *hoarding of notes* in times of pressure, we should note that the *hoarding* of precious metals repeated here is the same as it occurs in the most primitive stages of society, in times of disturbance.

The Act of 1844 is interesting in its effects in so far as it seeks to transform all the country's precious metal into *a medium of circulation*; it seek to equate an efflux of bullion with a contraction of the currency and an influx of bullion with an expansion of the currency. When put to the test, the opposite was proved. With a single exception, which we shall mention immediately, the quantity of Bank of England notes in circulation since 1844 has never reached the maximum that the Bank was authorised to issue. And the crisis of 1857 demonstrated that in certain circumstances this maximum is insufficient. Between 13 and 30 November 1857, a daily average of £488,830 above the maximum was in circulation. (The statutory limit at that time was £14,475,000 plus the amount of bullion in the cellars of the Bank.) (*Report on the Bank Acts* 1858, p. ix.)

The following remarks should be made, in relation to the efflux and influx of bullion:

Firstly, the *ebb and flow of bullion between the countries that do not produce gold and silver* should be distinguished from the *flow of gold and silver from their sources of production* to various other countries, and the distribution of this surplus bullion among the latter.

Before the mines of Russia, California and Australia had an impact the supply for the non-producing countries since the beginning of this century was only sufficient for the replacement of worn out coins, the customary provision of luxury materials and the export of silver to Asia.

Since that time, however, the export of silver to Asia has grown extraordinarily, with the *Asian* trade of America and Europe. The silver exported from Europe was largely replaced by the additional gold. Further, a portion of the

140 [This is the beginning of Engels's Chapter 35 entitled 'Precious Metals and the Rate of Exchange'. Editor]

gold newly imported was absorbed by the domestic money circulation. It was estimated that up to 1857 about £30 million worth of gold had been added to England's domestic circulation. Moreover, the *average level* of bullion reserves has increased since 1844 for all the central banks of Europe (and Yankee land). (The growth of domestic money circulation also means that after the panic, in the subsequent period of stagnation, bank reserves already grow more quickly as a result of the greater quantity of gold currency withdrawn from domestic circulation and immobilised.) Finally, the consumption of gold and silver for luxury articles has risen during the recent period owing to the increase in wealth.

Secondly, there is a constant export and import trade between the countries that do not produce gold and silver; the *same country* both constantly imports and constantly exports bullion. It is only the *preponderance* of one movement or the other, in one direction or the other, that determines whether, on the whole, bullion is exported or imported, since these movements, which simply oscillate and often run parallel, to a large extent neutralise each other. But for this very reason, people *overlook* the fact that the two movements are constantly in action, and the overall parallelism between them, as far as their result is concerned. The matter is always conceived as if the export or import of bullion is the expression of the import and export relationship of commodities, whereas it also expresses a relationship between the export and import of bullion itself.

Thirdly, the preponderance of exports over imports, or vice versa, can be broadly measured by the *increase or decrease in the bullion reserves of the central banks*. This measurement's degree of precision depends of course first and foremost on how far the bullion stockpiled in the so-called national bank represents the whole of the *national hoard*. But even assuming that this is the case, the measurement is still not exact, since in certain circumstances an additional import of bullion may be absorbed by internal circulation and the growing luxury use of gold and silver; and also since an internal drain of gold coin can take place without any additional import, and hence there could be a diminution of the bullion reserve without an accompanying increase in its export.

|373| *Fourthly*, an export of bullion takes the form of a 'drain' if the movement of decline *continues* for a long period, so that the decline presents itself as a *tendency* of the movement. This happens if the impact of this decline on the *quantity* of bullion is so pronounced that it depresses the reserve significantly below its average level, until it approaches the *average minimum* of the reserve. The minimum is a more or less *arbitrary* magnitude, since it is determined by the regulations imposed by the Bank Acts, with regard to the necessary reserve for the convertibility of notes, etc.

Fifthly, the *function of the reserve fund, the bullion reserve of the Bank*, a function that is not the sole determinant of its *formation*, since the fund can grow simply through the fact that external and internal trade is paralysed, is threefold: (i) it is a reserve fund for international payments, in fact a *reserve fund of world money*; (ii) it is a *reserve fund for domestic coin circulation*, which expands and contracts; and (iii) (and this is connected with the *banking* function and has nothing to do with the function of money simply as money) it is a reserve fund for the payment of deposits and the convertibility of notes. It can therefore, as an international fund, also be affected by the *balance of payments*, whatever the reasons determining this and whatever their relationship to the balance of trade. It may also be affected by the expansion or the contraction of the domestic coin currency. Its third function – as a guarantee fund – does not admittedly determine the spontaneous movement of the bullion reserve, but it still has a double effect. If notes are issued to replace the gold coin in domestic circulation (and also therefore silver coin where silver is the measure of value), the second function of the reserve fund disappears. And a part of the gold that has served for this purpose will now permanently find its way abroad. In this case, there is no internal drain of bullion nor, therefore, is there any expansion of the bullion reserve by the immobilisation of a part of the circulating coin. Moreover, if a minimum bullion reserve must be maintained for the payment of deposits and the convertibility of notes, this affects the kind of impact a bullion drain has; it affects the portion of the reserve which the bank seeks to maintain by force or the portion it might seek to get rid of as a useless hoard. With a purely metallic circulation and a centralised banking system, the bank would similarly have to treat its hoard as a guarantee for the payment of its deposits, and drain of bullion could lead to the same panic as in Hamburg [in 1857].

Sixthly, with the possible exception of 1837, the real *crisis* has always broken out only *after the exchanges have turned*, i.e., once the import of bullion has the upper hand again over its export. > This is how it happened in 1825, 1847 (where the turn took place after April) and in 1857 (where the turn came at the beginning of November). The drain of bullion, which in April 1847, for instance, caused an independent monetary panic, is therefore never anything more than the precursor of a crisis, and has reached the turning point before the crisis breaks out. In 1839 there was a considerable drain of bullion (for corn) without either a crisis or a monetary panic (although there was much commercial distress.)

< *Seventhly*, as soon as the *general crises* have burned out, the bullion (leaving aside the influx of surplus bullion from the producing countries) is again distributed in the proportions in which it previously existed as a *hoard* in the

various countries, *in a state of equilibrium*. All other circumstances remaining the same, the relative size of the hoard in each country is determined by that country's role in the world market. It flows out of a country that has a greater share than normal, and into another; these movements of ebb and flow simply restore its original distribution among the different national hoards (although this redistribution is mediated by the effect of the different agencies already mentioned in dealing with the turn of the exchanges.) As soon as normal distribution is re-established – from this moment on – there is first a growth, and then again a drain.

Eighthly, drains of bullion are usually the symptom of a change in the circumstances of foreign trade, and this change is in turn an indication that conditions are again approaching a crisis.

Ninthly, the balance of payments may be in favour of Asia and against Europe and America.

> |374| If the Bank of England were a bank which did not issue banknotes but only metallic means of circulation, the effect of 'an *influx of bullion*' would be:

'first, to increase the deposits, and correspondingly the reserve of bullion; second, to increase the *securities*, and, if discounts were not required, by *advances on stock* at a low rate of interest; and third, by the establishment of a low rate of interest ultimately to promote more active business, and to increase the circulation through advances on bills'.

While the effect of 'an *efflux of bullion*' would be: 'first, to draw upon the reserve of coin in the Bank (by discounting more bills), which the Bank held over and above the quantity required to protect their deposits; second, to draw upon the deposits held by the bank, which could only be done, partly by a reduction of securities, and partly by reduction of the coin in hand; and third, as a consequence of these measures, and other causes, to contract trade and reduce the circulation'. (*The Economist*, vol. 5, 1847, p. 521.)

'The *Scottish* banks keep unemployed balances of cash with their London agents', for example with Jones, Loyd and Co., who keep them in the Bank of England. This gives the Scottish banks 'a command to that extent over the bullion of the Bank of England' which is 'always on the spot where it is required ... to meet foreign payments' (ibid.)[141]

---

141 *On the movement back and forth of gold as a result of the Act of 1845:* 'Since the bill of 1845 for Scotland a large drain of the coin of the Bank of England has taken place of late, to supply a mere contingent demand in Scotland, which may never occur ... Since that period, therefore, there has been a large sum uniformly locked up in Scotland, and another considerable sum constantly travelling back and forward between London and Scotland. If a period arrives, when a Scottish banker expects an increased demand for *his* banknotes, a

< *Imports of bullion* take place principally at two moments. In the first phase of *low interest rates*, which follows the crisis and is the expression of the contraction of production; and in the second phase, when the rate of interest rises, but has not yet reached its *average* level. This is the phase in which returns are brisk, *commercial* credit is high, and therefore the demand for *moneyed capital* does not grow in proportion to the expansion of production. In both of these phases, where *moneyed capital* is relatively abundant, the surplus influx of capital (gold and silver), which exists in a form in which it can initially *only* function as moneyed capital, has a significant impact on the rate of interest and thereby on the entire business climate.

On the other hand, a *drain*, that is to say a continuous and quantitatively extensive movement of the *export of bullion*, sets in, and its onset is itself the expression of the fact that the returns are no longer brisk, that markets are overstocked, and that the apparent prosperity is only kept going by *credit*, hence that a certain pressure upon moneyed capital already exists and therefore the rate of interest has reached at least its *average* level. Under these circumstances, the effect of a continued withdrawal of capital, in a form in which it functions directly as *moneyed capital*, is therefore significant. This must have a direct impact on the rate of interest. But the rise in the rate of interest, instead of restricting credit transactions, expands them, and leads to a strain on all its resources.[142] This period therefore precedes the crash.

The reasons just adduced mean that it is not the mere *quantity* of bullion (whether it is *imported* or *exported* bullion) that operates *as such*, but that

---

box of gold is brought down from London; when this period is past, the same box, generally unopened, is sent back to London'. (*The Economist*, 23 October 1847.)

142 Examination of Newmarch, 1520: 'The volume of bills in circulation increases with the rate of interest? It seems to do so'. 1522: 'In quiet ordinary times the ledger is the real instrument of exchange; but when any difficulty arises; when, for example, under such circumstances as I have suggested, there is a rise in the bank-rate of discount ... then the transactions naturally resolve themselves into drawing bills of exchange, those bills of exchange being not only more convenient as regards legal proof of the transaction which has taken place, but also being more convenient in order to effect purchases elsewhere, and being pre-eminently convenient as a means of credit by which capital can be raised'. (*Report on the Bank Acts* 1857.)

Added to this is the fact that as soon as (under generally menacing circumstances) a rise in the bank-rate of discount occurs – which at the same time offers the prospect or the probability of a limitation's being introduced at the Bank of the term of the bills of exchange admitted to discount – the fear arises that this will mount to a crescendo. Everyone, therefore, and the credit-jobber above all, seeks to discount the future and to have as many means of credit as possible at his disposal at the given moment.

this *firstly* has its effect by way of the *specific character* of the bullion as *moneyed capital* while secondly it acts as the feather which when added to the weight already on the scales is enough to tip the balance to one side; it has this effect because it intervenes in circumstances where anything extra on one side or the other is sufficient to give the *decisive impulse*. Were it not for these reasons, it would be completely impossible to understand how a drain of bullion of, say, between five and eight million pounds sterling, and that is the limit of our experience up to now, could exert any significant effect. This amount of capital is of a more or less infinitesimal magnitude in comparison with the total volume of production in England.[143] But it is precisely the development of the credit and banking system, tending on the one hand to impress all moneyed capital into the service of production (or, which comes to the same thing, to transform all money income into capital) and, on the other hand, to reduce the monetary reserve, as compared with the functions it has to perform, to its minimum, that creates this sensitivity of the whole machinery. At less developed levels of production, an outflow or an addition to the reserve over and above its average amount is a matter of relative indifference. And in any case even a quantitatively significant drain of bullion is relatively without effect, if it does not take place under the above-mentioned circumstances.

|375| The explanation we have given has ignored those cases in which the drain of bullion arises as a result of harvest failures, etc. Here, a major and sudden disturbance in the balance of production, as expressed in the drain of bullion, obviates the need for any further explanation > (in fact the matter is self-explanatory.) < The effect is all the greater, the more a disturbance of this kind coincides with a period when the production process is working at *high pressure*.

We have also ignored the function of *bullion* as a guarantee for the convertibility of banknotes and as the *pivot* of the entire credit system. The central bank is the pivot of the credit system, and the *bullion reserve* is the pivot of the bank.[144] The collapse of the credit system into the monetary system is a

143 See for example Weguelin's ridiculous response when he says that an outflow of £5 million in bullion is that much capital less, and seeks to use this to explain phenomena that do not occur even with infinitely greater rises in price, or depreciations, contractions and expansions of real capital. On the other hand, the attempt to explain these phenomena as direct symptoms of an expansion or contraction in the *mass* of real capital (looked at from the point of view of its material elements), is no less ridiculous.

144 1364 (Newmarch): 'The reserve of bullion in the Bank of England is, in truth ... the central reserve or hoard of treasure upon which the whole trade of the country is carried on. *It is*

necessary development, as I have already shown in connection with '*means of payment*'.[145] Both Tooke and Loyd concede that the utmost sacrifice of real wealth is necessary in order to maintain the *metallic basis*. The dispute simply turns on a plus or a minus and on the more or less rational way of coping with something unavoidable.[146] A certain quantity of *metal* that is insignificant in comparison with production as a whole is acknowledged as the *pivot* of the system. Hence, on top of the terrifying illustration of this 'pivotal character', the beautiful theoretical dualism. As long as it examines *capital* in its professional capacity, enlightened economics looks down on gold and silver with the utmost disdain, as being the most indifferent and useless form of capital. As soon as it deals with banking, however, this aspect of things is turned on its head, and it becomes capital *par excellence*, for whose preservation every other form of capital and labour have to be sacrificed. But in what way are gold and silver distinguished from other forms of wealth? Not by magnitude of value, for this is determined by the quantity of labour materialised in them. But rather as autonomous incarnations and expressions of the *social* character of wealth. The *social* existence that it has appears as *something beyond*, as a thing, object or commodity outside and alongside the *real* elements of social wealth. *Credit*, being a social form of wealth, displaces money and usurps its position. It is confidence in the social character of production that makes the money form of products appear as something merely evanescent and ideal, as a mere notion. But as soon as credit is shaken, and this is a necessary phase in the cycle of modern industry, all real wealth is supposed to be *actually* transformed into *money*, into gold and silver, a crazy demand, but one that necessarily grows out of the system itself. And the gold and silver that is supposed to satisfy these immense claims amounts in all to a few millions in the vaults of the bank.[147] A drain of bullion, therefore, shows most strikingly by its effects that production is not really subjected to *social* control, as a *social process*, and that the *social* form of

---

a kind of pivot, upon which the whole trade of the country is made to turn; all the other banks in the country look to the Bank of England as the central hoard or reservoir from which they are to draw their reserve of coin; and it is upon that hoard or reservoir that the action of the foreign exchanges always falls'.

145 [In Marx 1859, pp. 126–7. English version: MECW 29, 1987, pp. 376–7. Translator]

146 'Practically, then, both Mr. Tooke and Mr. Loyd would meet an additional demand for gold … by an early … contraction of credit by raising the rate of interest, and restricting advances of capital …' But Loyd's illusions lead him to impose burdensome and even dangerous 'restrictions and regulations'. (*The Economist*, vol. 5, 1847, p. 1418.)

147 See the passage in Chapman. [No. 5057 of Chapman's evidence to the 1857 Committee. Marx quoted this passage earlier, on page 352e of the manuscript.]

wealth exists alongside wealth itself as a *thing*. The bourgeois system does have this in common with earlier systems in so far as these are based on commodity trade and private exchange. But it is only with this system that the most striking and grotesque form of this absurd contradiction and paradox arises, because (1) in this system production for direct use-value, for the producer's own use, is most completely abolished, so that wealth exists only as a *social* process expressed in the intertwinement of production and circulation; and (2) with the development of the credit system, the bourgeois system constantly strives to abolish this metallic barrier, which is both a material and an imaginary barrier to wealth and its movement, while time and time again hitting its head against it.

It is demanded that all bills of exchange, etc., be simultaneously and immediately convertible into bank money, and all the bank money convertible into gold (commodities too).

> |376| (Newmarch also adds *paper* to this list. See Appendix.) 1426: 'The result is that it appears by these figures that there is no connection between the variations in the amount of bill circulation and the variations in the banknote circulation'. (1857).

1494. Newmarch: 'We know quite well that *changes in the rate of discount move in cycles*; and that if you have a very low rate of discount in consequence of capital being abundant and cheap, an alteration would take place in *the quality of the bills admitted to discount*, and there would be in consequence a large extension of the transactions and trade of the country. That large extension ... sooner or later, produces a rise in the state of discount, and it may or may not (generally it has done so) *produce an efflux of treasure* ... < Judging from experience, it is very unlikely that the efflux of treasure arising from any oscillation in the foreign trade will proceed beyond £3 million or £4 million'. >

1499. Evidence of Newmarch. 'As a large amount of treasure has been exported out of this country it must have been in payment of importations into this country?' He answers in the affirmative, and adds: 'or in payment of *obligations incurred by this country on behalf of other countries*. Take for example the Eastern trade; it is quite well known that a very large part of the balance which has been paid in bullion in the first instance immediately by this country, has not been exclusively on account of this country; that the transmission of treasure to the East represents the payment of debts arising out of imports of silk and tea, not merely into the United Kingdom, but also into France, and other parts of Europe and the United States ... The large remittances of treasure that have taken place to India' (in so far as they were *not* destined for China) 'have not been for the discharge of mercantile debts due from this country to India, but for the purpose of placing in India English capital, to be expended there in the construction of railways'.

1504. Evidence of Newmarch. 'A considerable amount of silver has been sent out to the East merely as an *exchange operation*; it has not been carried out either for the payment of balances or for investment in railways, but ... merely as an operation on the exchanges'. 1505. 'To be invested in bills drawn upon this country? Yes'.

1506. 'Those bills are drawn against produce shipped to this country? Generally speaking, they are'.

1509. At the close of 1853 [there was] considerable apprehension in the public mind. In *September* the Bank of England raised its discount on three occasions ... In the early part of *October* (1853) ... [there was] a considerable degree of apprehension and alarm in the public mind ... [which was] relieved before the end of November, and almost wholly removed, in consequence of the arrival of nearly £5 million of treasure from Australia. Similarly, in the autumn of 1854, by the arrival in October and November of nearly £6 million of treasure. Ditto, in similar circumstances, in 1855, by the arrival in September, October and November of a total of nearly £8 million; and then at the close of 1856 ... the same occurrence. 'In truth' says Newmarch, 'I might appeal to the observation almost of any member of the Committee, whether *the natural and the complete solvent* to which we have got into the habit of looking for any financial pressure, is *not the arrival of a gold ship*'.

1650 and 1651 (Newmarch): 'The *country circulation*, of which we have now returns for the last twenty years' (that was in 1857, now there are returns for almost thirty years) 'has observed a peculiar cycle in every one of those years. It is high in one month ... low in another month, and in a certain other month occurs a medium point. This occurs year by year ... cycles regulated by peculiarities of trade, or of the seasons, such as the harvest, and a variety of other things which uniformly create a greater demand for money at one particular period than at another'.

|377| *Drains of bullion*. 1702 (Newmarch): 'You may have a drain of bullion ... either on purely mercantile grounds, that is, where the imports have exceeded the exports' (as from 1836 to 1844 mainly for corn; similarly in 1847) 'or ... in order to provide the means of investing English capital in some foreign enterprise' (as to the East in 1857, in consequence of the investment of English capital in Indian railways, etc.) 'or ... for the purpose of carrying on a foreign expenditure, as in 1854 and 1855, in consequence of the Commissariat expenditure in the Crimea'.

Circulation. 1749 (Newmarch): 'The entire circulation of banknotes in the United Kingdom is, in round figures, £39 million'. 1747 ([James] Wilson): 'In

Scotland and Ireland, where the smaller denomination of circulation consists of paper, the circulation has increased by about 31 percent, *while the circulation of notes in England has remained stationary*'.

1750. 'The circulation of gold in that portion of the United Kingdom where £1 notes do not circulate is £70 million'.

< *Exchanges with Asia*. The following points are important, firstly because they show how England, when its exchange[148] with Asia is adverse, has to draw upon other countries whose imports from Asia are mediated through English middlemen as far as the monetary transactions go. Secondly, however, because here again Mr. [James] Wilson makes the foolish attempt to identify the impact of an *export of bullion* on the exchanges with the impact of an *export of capital* in general on the rate; the export in both cases being not a means of purchase or payment but an export for investment. It goes without saying, to start with, that if so and so many million pounds are sent to India, to be invested there in railways, whether they are sent in bullion or in rails is simply a *difference in form*, the same amount of capital being transferred in each case from one country to another; this transfer, moreover, does not go into the calculation of ordinary mercantile transactions, and the exporting country does not expect any other return for it than the subsequent *annuities* (from the revenue of the railways, etc.) This drain of bullion, because it is bullion (directly moneyed capital and the basis of the entire monetary system) will not necessarily, under all circumstances, have a direct effect on the *money market* of the bullion-exporting country (hence on its *rate of interest*), but it will in this case. It also has a *direct effect on the exchanges*. In particular, bullion is sent in payment only in so far as the bills of exchange that are offered on the London money market, on India for example, are insufficient to make these extra remittances. There is thus a surplus of demand for bills of exchange upon India, and so the *exchange* temporarily turns against England, not because it is in debt to India but rather because it has to send extra money to India, hence there is a greater pressure upon all means of liquidating that extra debt. (In the long run, such an export of bullion must have the effect of increasing Indian demand for English commodities, because it directly increases India's capacity to consume European goods. If however the capital is dispatched in the form of rails, etc., it cannot have any influence on the *exchanges*, since India does not have to make any return payment for these. And it does not need to have any influence whatever on the money market. Wilson seeks to postulate an effect of this kind on the basis of the fact that extra outlays such as

148 [Engels altered 'exchange' to 'rate of exchange'. Translator]

these lead to an extra demand for monetary accommodation, and thus affect the rate of interest. This *may well be* the case; but as a general assertion it is sheer rubbish. Wherever the rails may be sent and laid, whether on English soil or on Indian, they represent nothing but a certain expansion of English production in a certain department. To maintain that an expansion of production, within very large limits, cannot take place without creating a rise in the rate of interest, is utter foolishness. The monetary accommodation, i.e., the amount of transactions in which credit operations are involved, may grow; but these operations can increase while the *given rate of interest* remains the same. This was in fact the case in England during the railway mania [of the 1840s]. The rate of interest did not rise. And it is evident that as far as real capital is concerned, in this case commodities, the effect on the money market is exactly the same whether these commodities are destined for consumption abroad or at home. There could only be a distinction if England's capital investment in foreign countries checked the *commercial* exports (exports bringing a return) which would otherwise have taken place, or in so far as these investments were already a symptom of an overstraining of credit, etc.) > (*Turn the page.*)

|378| 1786. Newmarch thinks that the balance of the exchanges was in favour of England and against India between 1851 and 1855. In 1851 English exports to India were £7,420,000, while the funds drawn from India to the East India company for their own expenditure amounted to £3,200,000. Together, the total export from the United Kingdom to India was £10,620,000. In 1855 exports were £10,350,000 and India House drafts were £3,700,000, making the total export of the United Kingdom £14,050,000. In 1855 the total real value of imports from India was only £12,670,000; this makes a balance of £1,380,000 in favour of the United Kingdom. <

1787. But, says Wilson, 'the *exchanges* are affected also by *indirect* trade. Thus exports from India to Australia and North America, effected by means of drafts upon London, have the same result as if the goods came directly from India to England'.

1788, 1789. If India and China are taken *together* the balance would be for India and against England (China being a debtor to India generally, and England to China, the sums involved going on to India by this detour.)

1791. That idiot Wilson then asks whether the 'effect upon the exchanges' would not be the same whether the invested capital went 'in the form of coin' or 'rails and locomotives'.

1792 (Newmarch): 'As far as regards the immediate operation on the bullion market, the investments of the £12 million would only be operative as far as bullion was required to be sent out for actual money disbursements'.

1797. Weguelin asks: ‘If *no return* is made for this iron, how can it be said to affect the exchanges?’ Newmarch replies: ‘I do not think that that *part of the expenditure which is sent out in the form of commodities affects the computations of exchange* … the computation of the exchange between two countries is affected, one might say, *solely by the quantity of obligations or bills offering in one country*, as compared with the quantity offering in the other country against it; that is the rationale of the exchange. The £12 million for India was in the first place subscribed in this country. If the nature of the transaction was such that the whole of that £12 million was required to be laid down in Calcutta, Bombay and Madras in treasure … this sudden demand … would very violently operate upon the price of silver and upon the exchange, just the same as if the India Company were to give notice tomorrow that their drafts were to be raised from £3 million to £12 million. But half of this £12 million is spent in buying commodities in this country, iron rails and timber, and other materials for building carriages and stations … It is an expenditure in this country of the capital of this country for a particular kind of commodity to be sent out to India, and there is an end of it’.

1798 (Weguelin). ‘But the production of that iron, etc., produces a large *consumption of foreign articles* which might affect the exchange? Certainly’.

1799. Wiseacre Wilson then offers the opinion that the iron largely represents labour, and this (its *value*) consists for the most part of ‘*imported articles*’ consumed by the workers. > 1800. Therefore, if the iron and the locomotives are sent abroad to pay for those imported articles, you would be able to balance the exchange.

< 1801. ‘It would have the effect of *turning the exchanges against this country* if you sent abroad the articles which were produced by the consumption of the imported articles without receiving any remittance for them either in the shape of produce or otherwise?’ > Now Newmarch gives an example of the kind of logic these fellows are fond of: < ‘That principle’ he says ‘is exactly what took place in this country during the time of the great railway expenditure. For three, four or five years, you spent £30 million on railways, nearly the whole of which went in the payment of wages. For three years you employed a larger population in constructing railways, and locomotives, and carriages, and stations, than you employed in the whole of the factory districts. The workers bought tea, sugar, spirits and other foreign commodities; these commodities were imported’. > And what was the consequence of this? Was it as claimed by Mr. Wilson? To turn the exchanges? Quite the contrary. < ‘It was a fact that during the time this great expenditure was going on the *foreign exchanges between this country and other countries were not* materially deranged. *There was no efflux of bullion*. On the contrary, *there was rather an influx*’.

1802 (Newmarch): 'I agree with the principle that no one country can have permanently against itself an adverse state of exchange with all the other countries with which it deals; an adverse exchange with one country necessarily produces a favourable exchange with another'.

But Wilson, that dunce, insists (1802) that the extra shipment of ores and locomotives must 'affect the *exchanges* with India', adding the triviality that 'the *transfer* of capital' would be 'the same whether it was sent in one form or another'. Newmarch replies to this (1803) that 'the obligation' would be the same, and Wilson then draws a false conclusion from this (1804), asking him whether 'the effect would be the same *upon the capital market*' (in general) 'here in *increasing the value of capital* as if the whole was sent out in bullion?' > Blockhead! < If iron prices did not rise, this was in any case a proof that the value of the rail capital had not increased. What he is talking about is the value of moneyed capital – interest. > He is trying to smuggle this in. One can see how the fellow mixes everything up. His *economic* doctrine keeps preying on his mind. < He would like to identify *moneyed capital* with capital in general. The effect on the money market in England is simply that, firstly, £12 million was subscribed for Indian railways. Well! This is a matter which has nothing to do with the exchanges, nor has it anything to do with the *destiny* of the £12 million. If the money market is easy, it need not produce any effect at all (as for example in 1844 and 1845). If the money market is already somewhat strained, the rate of interest could be affected, but only in the sense of an *increase*, and according to Wilson's theory this would have a favourable effect on the *exchanges* for England, i.e., it would check the tendency to export bullion; if not to India, then at least elsewhere. Here Mr. Wilson immediately jumps from one thing to another. Under number 1802 it was the 'exchanges' which were supposedly affected; then under number 1804 it was 'the value of capital'. These are two very different things. The rate of interest may have an effect on the exchanges, and the exchanges may have an effect on the rate of interest. But the rate of interest may remain constant while the *exchanges* vary, and the *exchanges* may remain constant while rates of interest vary. The reason why Wilson 'jumps around' in this way is that it prickles him that there should be a difference in the effect of the mere 'form' in which capital is sent abroad, i.e., that the *difference in the form* of the capital is of such importance, and indeed that this applies to its money form, something which very much contradicts enlightened economics! Newmarch answers Wilson one-sidedly, in so far as he does not give him any warning that he was previously speaking about 'exchanges' and now talks of the 'rate of interest'. This is what Newmarch says (showing his *vacillation* in his answer to question 1804): 'No doubt if there is a demand for £12 million to be raised, *it is immaterial* as regards *the general rate of interest* whether that £12 million is required to be sent in bullion or in materials. I think, *however*' (a fine transition, this 'however', when he intends to say the exact opposite) '*it is not quite immaterial*' (it is immaterial, but, however, it is not immaterial!) 'because in the one case the £6 million would be returned immediately; in the other case it would not be returned so rapidly. Therefore it would make *some*' (how very specific!) 'difference whether the £6 million was expended in this country or wholly sent out of it'. Is this supposed to mean that the £6 million would be *returned* immediately? In so far as this £6 million is replaced, it exists in rails, locomotives, etc., that are sent to India, from where they do *not* return, but their *value* returns very slowly, whereas the £6 million in bullion might well return very quickly in kind. In so far as the £6 million was spent on wages, it has been consumed, but the money in which it was advanced continues to circulate in the country just as before, or else forms a reserve. The same applies to the profits of the rail producers and the portion of the £6 million which replaces their constant capital. The ambiguous word 'return' is thus used by Newmarch simply to avoid saying directly |379| that the money remains in the country, and that in so far as it functions as *moneyed capital*, the difference for the money market (apart from the fact that circulation might have swallowed up more coin) is simply that it is spent on A's account instead of B's. *Investment* of this kind in foreign countries can only affect the exchanges (but not exchanges with the country in which it is invested) if it is transferred in *commodities* instead of in bullion, to the extent that the production of these commodities required an *extra import of other foreign commodities*. And *this* kind of production is not liable to liquidate that extra demand. The same is true with any export on credit, whether for investment or for merely commercial purposes. Moreover, this extra demand may also call forth a reciprocal extra demand for English goods, for example from the colonies or the United States.

Newmarch previously said [1786] that English exports to India were *greater* than imports, as a result of the East India Company's drafts. Sir Charles Wood cross-examines him on this point > and, considered as Wood is, rather sharply. < This excess of English exports over Indian imports is brought about, in point of fact, by an *Indian import*, for which England pays no equivalent: the drafts of the East India Company (now the Government of India) dissolving into a tribute levied upon India. In 1855, for example, English imports from India came to £12,670,000; English exports to India were £10,350,000. A balance of £2,250,000 in India's favour. 'If that was the whole state of the case, that £2,250,000 would have to be remitted in some form to India. But then come the advertisements from the India House. The India House advertise to this effect, that they are *prepared to grant drafts on the various presidencies* in India to the extent of £3,250,000'. (This amount is for the *charges connected* with the *home establishment* of the East India Company and the dividends to be paid to the proprietors of the East India stock in England.) 'And that not merely liquidates the £2,250,000 which arose out of the course of trade, but it presents £1,000,000 of surplus'. (1917. Newmarch.)

Wood says (1922): 'Then the effect of those India House drafts is not to increase the exports to India, but *pro tanto* to diminish them?' (That is to say, to diminish their necessity, the imports from India remaining the same.) Mr. Newmarch explains this by saying that the English export *'good government'* in return for the £3,700,000. (1925.) Wood, who as Minister for India was quite aware of the 'sort of good government' exported by the English, offers this correct and ironic rejoinder (1926): 'Then the export which you state is caused by the East India drafts, is an export of good government, and not of produce'. England exports a good deal of 'good government' in this way, and also receives remittances of capital invested in foreign countries (thus receiving imports quite independently of the ordinary course of commerce, in the form of tribute, in part in return for 'good government', in part in return for capital invested in the colonies and elsewhere. For this tribute it does not have to pay an equivalent in produce.) It is therefore clear that the *exchanges* are not affected, if England consumes this tribute without exporting anything in return. It is also clear that the *exchanges* are not affected when it re-invests this tribute in foreign expenditure, for example by sending gunpowder to the Crimea (thus consuming it productively abroad rather than unproductively at home). Besides, as to the imports from abroad, as far as they enter into England's revenue – and they must of course be paid either as tribute, in which case no equivalent is needed, or paid for by exchange in return for this unpaid tribute, or in the ordinary course of commerce – England can either consume them or re-invest them as capital. Neither the one nor the other affects the exchanges, and wiseacre Wilson overlooks this point. Whether it is foreign or home produce which forms *a portion of the revenue* – the latter case simply presupposing the exchange of home produce for foreign produce – the *consumption* of this revenue, productive or unproductive, in no way affects the *exchanges*, even if it does affect the volume of reproduction. The following extracts should be judged accordingly.

|380| 1934. Wood asks Newmarch how the sending of war supplies to the Crimea could affect the exchange with Turkey. Newmarch replies: 'I do not see that the mere transmission of *warlike stores* would necessarily affect the exchanges, but *certainly* the *transmission of treasure* would affect the exchange'. (Here, therefore, he distinguishes between *moneyed capital* and *other capital.*) But now Wilson asks:

(1935): 'If you make an export of any article to a great extent, for which there is to be no corresponding import' (Mr. Wilson forgets that in the case of England there are many imports for which there never was an export {except in the shape of 'good government' or capital formerly exported}; in any case these are imports that do not enter into the regular *commercial* movement; but are exchanged, for instance, with American produce, and the fact that American produce is exported without an import alters nothing in the situation, that the *value of these imports* may be consumed without an *equivalent* drain from abroad; they have been obtained without export, and they may be spent without entering into the commercial balance) 'you do not discharge the *foreign debt* you have created by your imports' (but if you have paid beforehand for that import, say by the credit given to foreign countries, *no debt* is created by it, and the question is quite independent of the international balances; it resolves into productive or unproductive expenditure, whether the things so exported are foreign or domestic products) 'and therefore you must by that transaction affect the exchanges by not discharging the foreign debt, by reason of your export having no corresponding imports? Yes'. (The kernel of Wilson's argument is that every export without an import is an import without an export; since foreign imported articles do enter into the production of the article exported. The assumption is that any such export either creates or is founded upon an unpaid import, a foreign debt. This is wrong, even leaving aside the following two circumstances: (1) England gets certain imports *gratuitously*, and pays no equivalent for them, for instance Indian imports. It may exchange them for American imports, and export these without import; in any case, as far as the *value* is concerned, it has only exported something that cost it nothing. And (2) it may have paid for *imports* (American ones, for instance) which form surplus capital; if these are consumed unproductively, in gunpowder, this does not create a debt to America and does not affect the exchanges with America. > But let us leave this aside.) We saw earlier when examining the process of reproduction that, on the one hand, the profits of the capitalists who produce products which enter into revenue (as consumables), and can themselves be consumed or be reconverted into capital, and, on the other hand, the revenues of the capitalists and the workers (a part of which can be taken through taxes), in short the whole of the consumable product, comes down to *revenue*, and is therefore consumable. Whether a part of this is consumed in kind, or it is previously exchanged for foreign produce before it is consumed; whether, moreover, the part of the product of the capitalists who produce constant capital which represents revenue is exchanged for home or foreign produce, for example for the elements of war supplies, does not change the situation in any way. It does not affect the foreign *exchanges*. It only affects the scale of reproduction. To the extent that it is only *revenue*, which is expended in war supplies for the Crimea, it affects only the character (the value in use) of the returns received by England, but not the *exchange*. < That duffer Newmarch contradicts himself in questions 1934 and 1935, and Wood draws attention to this in question 1938. Newmarch loses his temper > and tries to sneak out.

|381| *Balance with Asia.*

1918 (Newmarch): 'When you combine India and China, when you bring into account the transactions between India and Australia, and the still more important transactions between China and the United States, the trade being a triangular one, and the adjustment taking place through us ... then it is true that the *balance of trade was not merely* against this country, but *against France* and *against the United States*'.

The Bank of England's influence.

<1889 (Newmarch): 'I have satisfied myself that the amount of funds constantly employed in the money market may be described somewhat like £120 million; and of that £120 million a very considerable proportion, something like 15 or 20 percent, is wielded by the Bank of England'. >

In numbers 1866, 1867 and 1868 Newmarch considers two-thirds of the banknotes issued by country bankers and the Bank of England beyond the third held in bullion to be like the 'creation of so much capital', because 'coin to that extent is saved'. The banker's profits may for that reason not be greater than the profits of other capitalists. The fact remains the same, however, that the banker derives a *profit* from this national economising on coin. The fact that this appears as *private profit* by no means shocks the bourgeois economists, for whom profit is in general the same as the appropriation of national labour.

1823. Newmarch is unable to say in what respect from his point of view the *convertibility* (the reflux) of notes adds anything to the *limitation* of the notes issued.

In the following phrases, *The Economist* endeavours to identify a *superabundance of moneyed capital* (a low rate of interest) with a *superabundance of capital in general*:

< 'No doubt, however, such *abundance of capital* as is indicated by *large stocks of commodities of all kinds, including bullion*' (there may be a large influx of bullion, accompanied by a contraction of production, as always after a crisis; in the following phase bullion may flow in from countries that merely produce bullion; the influence of the other commodities in this period is balanced out by exports) 'would necessarily lead not only to *low prices of commodities* in general, but also to a *lower rate of interest for the use of capital*'. (Why? The low price of cotton, for example, enables the spinner to make high profits. Why then is the interest rate low? Certainly not because the profit that can be made with

borrowed capital is high. But purely and simply because under the conditions indicated, the *demand for moneyed capital does not grow* in proportion to this profit, hence it has a *different* movement from that of real capital. What *The Economist* wants to prove here is precisely the *opposite*: that its movement is identical with that of real capital.) 'If we have a stock of commodities on hand, which is sufficient to serve the country for two years to come, a command over those commodities would be obtained for a given period at a much lower rate than if the stocks were barely sufficient to last us two months'. (Here, firstly, it is assumed that there is an *overstocking* of the home market, quite apart from the absurd supposition that there are stocks for two years in advance.) This would lead to a fall in prices. As a result less would have to be paid for a bale of cotton. But this in no way means that the money needed to purchase a bale of cotton would be *cheaper* to borrow. That depends on the state of the money market. If it is cheaper to borrow, this is only because *commercial* credit is such that the influence on it of monetary credit *is less* than usual. These overstocked imports are *means of subsistence*, raw materials or accessory materials. A low price for all of these *raises profits*. How could a low price reduce *interest* unless it was as a result of the *antagonism* rather than the identity, between an abundance of real capital and the demand for monetary accommodation? In such circumstances, the *merchant* can lend more easily to the *industrialist*; because of this easing of *commercial credit* the industrialist needs less *monetary credit*; hence the rate of interest can be low. This low rate of interest has nothing to do with the *import of bullion*, though the two phenomena may be concomitant, and the same causes that lead to low prices for imports may also lead to an excess of imported bullion. If the *import market* were really overstocked, this would mean a decline in demand for imports, which would be inexplicable given the *low* prices, unless it were due to a *contraction in production*; but this would again be inexplicable given the excess of imports at *low* prices. Nothing but absurdities, in order to show that a *fall in prices* equals a *fall in interest*. The two things may be concomitant. But then they express a movement of *productive capital* and *moneyed capital* in opposite directions (they do not express their *identity*.) 'All loans of money, in whatever shape they are made, are simply a transfer of *command over commodities* from one to another. Whenever, therefore, commodities are abundant, the interest of money must be low, and when they are scarce, the interest of money must be high'.[149] (Why? If commodities are cheap, I need, say, £1,000 to buy a

149 ['A reply to further remarks on the proposed substitution of one pound notes for gold', in *The Economist*, no. 195, 22 May 1847, p. 574. Translator]

certain quantity of them, instead of £2,000. But perhaps I now buy for £2,000 double the quantity of commodities I bought before, expanding my business by advancing, or, respectively, borrowing the real capital. On both occasions I spend £2,000. My demand on the money market remains *the same*, even though my demand on the commodity market rises with the fall in commodity prices. But if my demand decreases as prices fall, i.e., if my production does *not* expand with the fall in commodity prices, which would contradict all the laws put forward by *The Economist*, the demand for *moneyed capital* would fall, although *profit* would increase; this increased profit would however create a demand for moneyed capital. A low level of commodity prices, moreover, may arise for three reasons. Firstly, from a lack of demand. In that case, the rate of interest is low because production is paralysed, not because commodities are cheap, the cheapness being simply an expression of this paralysis. Or else because the supply is too large in relation to the demand. This may be the case because of a crisis (overstocking of markets, etc.) and may coincide with a *high* rate of interest. Or it may be because the *value* of commodities has fallen, hence the same demand can be satisfied at a lower price. Why should the rate of interest fall in this last case? Because profit grows? If it is because less moneyed capital is needed to obtain *the same* real capital, this simply proves that profit and interest stand in an *inverse* proportion to each other. In any case, the general thesis put forward by *The Economist* is wrong. Low money prices and a low rate of interest are not identical. Otherwise, the interest rate would be lowest in the poorest countries, where the money prices are lowest, and highest in the richest countries, where the money prices of agricultural products are highest.)

|382| Generally speaking, *The Economist* concedes that if the value of money falls, this has no influence on the rate of interest. £100 still yields £105; if the £100 is worth less, so too is the £5 of interest, and vice versa. The ratio is not affected by a rise or fall in the value of the original sum. Considered as value, a bale of cotton is always equal to a certain sum of money. If its value rises, it is equal to a greater sum of money. If it is £2,000, 5 percent is £100; if it is £1,000, 5 percent is £50. But this in no way affects the *interest rate*. > Similarly with a *fall in its value*. The element of truth in all this is simply that more monetary accommodation is required when £2,000 is needed to buy the same quantity of commodities than when only £1,000 is needed. All this shows, however, is that the ratio between profit and interest is an inverse one. For profit grows with the cheapening of constant and variable capital, and interest falls. However, the *converse* can also be the case. This happens frequently in the cotton industry. Cotton may be cheap, for example, because there is no demand for yarn and cloth; it can be relatively dear because there are large profits to be made in

spinning and weaving. On the other hand, profits on spinning, etc., may be high because the price of cotton is low. Hubbard's list shows that the interest rate and the prices of commodities pursue movements that are completely independent of each other; while the movements of the interest rate are precisely adapted to the movements of bullion (the movements of the exchanges). 'Whenever, therefore, commodities are *abundant*, the interest of money must be low'. Precisely the opposite happens during crises; commodities are present in excess, they cannot be converted into money, and *therefore* the rate of interest is *high*; on the other hand, there is a great demand for commodities and hence easy returns, but at the same time a rise in the prices of commodities, and a *low* rate of interest on account of these easy returns. 'When they' (the commodities) 'are scarce, the interest of money must be *high*'. (In the period of quiescence after the crisis the opposite phenomenon again occurs. Commodities are scarce in absolute terms, but not in relation to demand, and the interest rate is low.) 'As commodities become abundant, the number of sellers, in proportion to the number of buyers, increases, and, in proportion as the quantity is more than is required for immediate consumption, so must a larger portion be *kept for future use*. Under these circumstances, the terms on *which a holder becomes willing to sell* for a future payment, or *on credit*, become lower than if he were certain that his whole stock would be required within a few weeks'. (*The Economist*, 1847, vol. 5, p. 574.) > This depends on the circumstances. < If there is overstocking of the imported commodities, or stock in general, *the rate of interest* may rise, i.e. the demand for moneyed capital may rise, with the intention of holding on to it, without putting it onto the market. If may fall, because the amount of *commercial credit* is greater in comparison with the demand for monied credit.

> If a quantity of money, for example £20 million, is sent abroad, it is only represented by the *imported* commodities as long as they retain the same price. If their price falls, *part of the money returns in the form of bullion*. In this case, the *import of bullion* expresses the fall in the price of the imported commodities, the raw materials and colonial goods, a fall which follows the enhancement of their price.

We need to distinguish two phases in the growth in bullion imports. The first phase is one of simple *excess*, as a result of a previous excess export of bullion. Here the *increase in imports* simply restored the *old equilibrium*. The second phase is an import of bullion *beyond this point of equilibrium*. What this expresses, then, is nothing other than that the prices of manufactured products are again rising in proportion to the raw material and the elements of variable capital, since these have both risen previously as a result of the reduction in their production, and now fall again as a result of the stimulus which has been given to their production precisely through the increase in their price.

<*Bills and banknotes.* 'Notes payable *on demand* can never be kept out in excess, because the excess would always return to the bank for payment, while *bills at two months* may be issued in great excess, there being no means of checking the issue till they have arrived at maturity, when they may have been replaced by others. For a people to admit the safety of the circulation of bills payable only *on a distant day,* and to object to the safety of a circulation of paper payable *on demand,* is, to us, perfectly unaccountable.' (*The Economist,* 1847, vol. 5, p. 575.)

Exchanges. The Economist mentions the rapid effect on the *exchanges* in 1847 which resulted from the increase in the interest rate and other pressure on the money market. But it should not be forgotten that despite the turn of the exchanges, bullion continued to flow out until the *end of April*; this was only replaced by an ascending movement from May onwards.

'On 1 January 1847 the bullion in the bank amounted to £15,066,691, the rate of discount was 3½ percent, the rate of exchange on Paris was 25.75, on Hamburg 13.10, on Amsterdam 12.3¼. On 5 March bullion had fallen to £11,595,535, the rate of discount had risen to 4 percent, but the rate of exchange fell to 25.67½ in Paris, 13.9¼ in Hamburg, and 12.2½ in Amsterdam. The drain of bullion continues'.

	Bullion discount		*Highest exchanges – three months*		
			Paris	*Hamburg*	*Amsterdam*
20 March	£11,231,630	4%	25.67½	13.9¾	12.2½
3 April	10,246,410	5%	25.80	13.10	12.3½
10 April	9,867,053	(great scarcity of money)	25.90	13.10½	12.4½
17 April	9,329,941	5½%	26.02½	13.10¾	12.5½
24 April	9,213,890	*Pressure*	26.05	13.12	12.6
1 May	9,337,716	*Great Pressure*	26.15	13.12¾	12.6½
8 May	9,588,759	*Greatest Pressure*	26.27½	13.15½	12.7¾

(Despite the turn in the exchanges the drain continues; its probable destination being the United States.)

In 1847 the total export of gold, silver, bullion and specie from the United Kingdom was £8,602,597.

Of this, there went to the	*United States*	3,226,411
	France	2,479,892
	Hanse Towns	958,781
	Holland	247,743.

'We thus see' (says *The Economist*, 1847, vol. 5, p. 954) 'how rapid and striking was the effect of a rise in the rate of interest, and the pressure which ensued in correcting an adverse exchange, and in turning the tide of bullion back to this country. This effect was produced *entirely independently of the balance of trade*. A higher *rate of interest caused a lower price of securities*, both foreign and English, and induced large purchases to be made on foreign account, which increased the amount of bills to be drawn from this country, while, on the other hand, the high rate of interest and the difficulty of obtaining money was such that the demand of those bills fell off, while their amount increased' > (so great was the difficulty in negotiating bills). < 'For the same cause, *orders for imports were countermanded*, and *investments of English funds abroad were realised and brought home* for *employment here*. Thus, for example, we read in the *Rio de Janeiro Price Current* of 10 May: "Exchange has experienced a further decline, principally caused by a pressure on the market for remittance of the proceeds of large sales of government stock, on English account". Capital belonging to this country, invested in public and other securities abroad, when the interest was very low here, was thus again brought back when the interest became high'.

> |*383*| ***Foreign and Home Drain.***
'A demand for money in ordinary times, and a demand for it in periods of panic, are diametrically different. The one is for money to be put into circulation; the other, for money to be taken out of it'. (Joplin 1836, pp. 81–2.) 'When want of confidence prevails, twice the amount of currency becomes necessary to conduct the same operations, at the same scale of prices as before' (Joplin 1836, p. 92.)

< *England's Balance of Trade*. India alone has to pay up to £5 million in tribute for 'good government', interest on British capital, etc., not counting the sums sent home each year by public servants as a part of their income, and by English merchants as part of their profits, for investment at home. *Large remittances* are continuously and constantly made from *every British colony* for the same reasons. Most banks in Australia, the West Indies and Canada are conducted with British capital, the dividends being paid in England. England also possesses many foreign securities (European and American, North and South), on which it receives interest. On top of this there is its participation in foreign railways, canals, etc. These remittances are almost entirely made in

products over and above the annual amount of English exports. Only a small sum, in contrast, can be set off against this to cover the foreign owners of English securities and the consumption of English residents abroad.

The question as to how this affects the *balance of trade* and the *exchanges*, is 'at any particular moment, *one of time*'. 'Practically speaking ... England gives long credits upon her exports, while the imports are paid for in ready money. At particular moments this difference of practice has a considerable effect on the exchanges. At a time *when our exports are very considerably increasing*, as in 1850, a continual increase of investment of British capital must be going on, *beyond the amount remitted*, to the extent of the increase, whatever that may be. In this way, remittances of 1850 may be made against goods exported in 1849. But if the exports of 1850 exceed those of 1849 by £6 million, the practical effect must be that more money is sent abroad, by that amount, than is returned in the same year. And in this way an effect is produced on the exchanges and the rate of interest. When, on the contrary, our trade is depressed after a commercial crisis, and when our exports are much reduced, the remittances due for the past years of larger exports greatly exceed the value of our exports; the exchanges become correspondingly in our favour, capital rapidly accumulates at home, and the rate of interest becomes less'. (*The Economist*, 11 January 1851, p. 30.)

Foreign exchanges can vary:

(1) as a result of a temporary *balance of payments*, whatever may be the causes determining this; these may be purely commercial, they may involve investment, or political expenditure;

(2) as a result of a devaluation of money in one country, either of coins or of banknotes, which leads to a change in the *nominal rate of exchange*. This change is purely nominal. If £1 subsequently represented only half as much money as before, it would be reckoned at 12½ francs instead of 25 francs, etc.;

(3) when exchanges take place between countries, one of which uses silver as 'money', the other gold, the rate of exchange is dependent on the relative fluctuations in the value of these two metals, since such fluctuations obviously alter the parity between the two. An example of this was in 1850, when the *foreign exchanges* were against England, even though its exports rose enormously. There was still *no efflux of bullion*, for all that. It was the effect of a temporary rise in the value of silver as compared with gold. (See *The Economist*, 30 November 1850, pp. 1317–19.)

Exchange rate parity for £1 is: 25 francs 20 centimes in Paris, 13 marks and 10½ schillings in Hamburg and 11 florins and 97 cents in Amsterdam. In proportion as the exchange rate on Paris rises above 25 francs 20 centimes, it becomes more favourable for the English debtor to France or for the purchaser of French commodities. In both cases less sterling is needed > to achieve the desired aim. < In more distant countries, where bullion is not so easy to come by, when bills of exchange are scarce and insufficient for the purpose of making remittances, the natural effect is to raise the prices on the spot of such produce as is usually shipped to England, by creating a greater demand for the purpose of effecting remittances. This is often the case in India. (An *unfavourable* rate of exchange, and even a drain of gold, *may* occur in England if there is a very great abundance of money, a low rate of interest, and English securities are at a high price.)

In the course of 1848, England received large quantities of *silver* from *India*, as a result of the difficulty in obtaining bills of exchange, owing to the crisis of 1847 and the great lack of credit in which the trade had become entrapped. Once the silver arrived it soon made its way to the Continent (where there was much hoarding in the year 1848). In 1850 the state of the Indian rate of exchange made it profitable for the silver imported in 1848 to return back to India. > There was therefore much demand in India for this silver.

|384| Ricardo makes the following two assertions:

(1) that the *rate of interest* may rise because the prices of commodities are depressed; hence in this case the *value of moneyed capital* rises because there is a superfluity of *real capital*, and

(2) that the *rate of interest* may fall temporarily as a result of an *increase in the quantity of money*. (Since the discoveries in Australia, etc., the impact of this has been precisely the opposite: *a rise in the* (average) *rate of interest* is generally associated with an increase in the quantity of money, owing to the immense impulse received from this by production as a whole.)

'When the *market prices* of goods *fall* from an abundant supply, from a diminished demand, or from a rise in the value of money, a manufacturer naturally accumulates an unusual quantity of finished goods, being unwilling to sell them at very depressed prices. To meet his ordinary payments, for which he used to depend on the sale of his goods, he now endeavours to *borrow on credit*, and is often obliged to give an increased rate of interest'. (Ricardo 1821, p. 350.)

'If by the discovery of a new mine, by the abuses of banking, or by any other cause, the quantity of money be greatly increased, its ultimate effect is to raise the prices of commodities … but there is always an interval, during which some effect is produced on the rate of interest' (ibid.)

The bankers justify the *profit* they make by issuing *banknotes* with the argument that on the average they do not make any more profit from the capital they have invested than other capitalists. There is, however, absolutely no reason why private persons should make a profit from 'national' saving. < Between 1797 and 1815 the Bank of England, whose banknotes only have any credit because of the state, demanded payments from the state (i.e., the public), in the form of interest on loans, in return for the power the state gives to it of issuing banknotes. Could there be anything crazier than that? >

Banknotes and transferable deposits.

'If the ordinary balance kept by one individual with his banker were £1,000, and he were compelled to reduce it to £500, the money thus withdrawn from his account would be paid by him to other parties, who would pay it into their account with their bankers, so that what was taken out of one bank would be placed with another. The bankers, therefore, find that the aggregate of the balances deposited with them is not materially affected by the fluctuations in the accounts of individuals ... If we deposit one hundred pounds with a bank which issues notes, when we draw it out again the banker does not give us the money we deposited with him ... but gives us his own notes instead. We pay them to our creditor, and by receiving the notes he obtains a claim to the hundred pounds instead of us. Now if this person had an account with the same banker, and instead of one hundred pounds of the banker's notes, we had given him a cheque for one hundred pounds, precisely the same purpose would have been answered. The banker would charge our account with one hundred pounds, and give his account credit for that sum; but instead of holding the money in banknotes, which give him a command of the deposit in the hands of the banker that the notes represented, he would hold it in deposit at the credit of his own account, which he could either draw out in notes, or pay over to any other person by *cheque* in the same manner. Thus a *transferable deposit* and *a banknote* are *equally* money. And although the London bankers do not issue their own notes, the money deposited with them renders them, in fact, the greatest banks of circulation in the kingdom'. (Joplin 1844, pp. 38–9.)

|385| *Rate of Exchange*.

The tendency of the rate of exchange, in so far as its variations are caused by an excess of debt or credits, or the relative abundance or scarcity of bills upon the market, is always to return to *equality*. Hence 'if the premium were equal to the expense [of transmitting specie from London to New York] gold might be transmitted from London to New York but bullion would *not* be sent by the merchant as a remittance *if consumable commodities* of British produce could be sold with a profit on the American market, for in the latter case the seller of a bill in London would obtain, not only the *premium on his bill of exchange*, but *a profit on the commodities* which he exported ... The double inducement thus held out by an adverse exchange necessarily *forces* the *exportation* of commodities from the country to which it is adverse, and restricts the importation of commodities from the country to which it is favourable'. (Stirling1846, pp. 260–1.)

The dignity of a banker.

< Gavin Mason Bell, a Scottish bank manager, writes as follows: 'Banking establishments are religious and moral institutions. How often has the fear of being seen by the watchful and reproving eye of his banker deterred the young tradesman from joining the company of riotous and extravagant friends? What anxiety he has to stand well in the estimation of his banker, always to appear respectable! The banker's frown has more influence on him than the discouragements and moral lectures of his friends. Has he not trembled to be supposed guilty of deceit or the slightest mis-statement, lest it should give rise to suspicion, and his accommodation be in consequence restricted or discontinued? The advice of his banker is of more importance to him than that of his priest'. (Bell 1840, pp. 46–7.) >

Money for transfer of capital and realisation of income.

'Money is employed to perform two operations essentially distinct ... As a medium of exchange between dealers and dealers, it is the instrument by which *transfers of capital* are effected; i.e., the exchange of a certain amount of capital in money for an equal amount of capital in commodities. But money employed in the *payment of wages*, and in purchase and sale between dealers and consumers, is *not capital* but *income*; that portion of the income of the community which is devoted to daily expenditure. It circulates in constant daily use, and is that alone which can with strict propriety be termed *currency*. Advance of capital depends entirely on the will of the bank and other possessors of capital – for borrowers are always to be found, but the amount of currency depends on the wants of the community, among whom the money circulates, for the purposes of daily expenditure'. (Kinnear 1847, pp. 3–4.)

< 'On 18 September 1846 the circulation of the Bank of England was £20,900,000 and the bullion £16,273,000; on 5 April 1847 the circulation was £20,815,000 and the bullion £10,246,000. Hence despite the export of six millions of gold there was no contraction of the currency of the country'. (Kinnear 1847, p. 5) >

|390| *The amount of circulation in Scotland, for example.*

Evidence of P.W. Kennedy, manager of the Ayrshire Joint Stock Bank: 'In a report of 1840 from the *Glasgow Chamber of Commerce* it is stated that the first return of the circulation was made in Scotland in 1825. Everyone knows the extraordinary advance which Scotland made between that period and 1840. For instance, in the former of those years she manufactured 55,000 bales of cotton, in the latter 120,000 bales. In 1826, the produce of the iron furnaces was 33,500 tons, in 1840 about 250,000 tons. In 1826 the banking capital of Scotland was £4,900,000, in 1840 about £10,000,000. Yet, with all this progress in industry and wealth, the circulation of notes, which in 1825 varied from £3,400,000 to

£4,700,000, was between £2,960,000 and £3,670,000 in 1829, and in the first three months of 1840 it was £2,940,000'.

Evidence of H.W. Hobhouse (a banker at Bath): 'The country circulation is found to decrease and expand in correspondence with the amount of business transacted at different periods of the year. In this respect its variations are of a uniform and general character. It decreases half a million every year from spring to the summer quarter and expands again by degrees towards autumn and Christmas'. ('Evidence on Banks of Issue', in *Second Report* 1841.)[150]

Tooke 'discovers', following Fullarton, that with the exception of 1839 a drain always coincides with low circulation. But this was not the case in 1847 (railway workers in England, wages paid by the government in Ireland and high corn prices at the same time, yet both an external drain and an internal drain for circulation). Nor was it the case in 1857.

The Bank of England's screw. < 'As soon as the Bank of England puts on the screw *all purchases for foreign exportation* immediately cease' > (this was partially confirmed by the evidence of [Sir William] Brown before the House of Lords' Committee in 1848). < 'The exporters wait until prices have reached the lowest point of depression, and then, and not till then, they make their purchases. But when this point has arrived the exchanges have been rectified – gold ceases to be exported before that lowest point of depression has arrived. Purchases of goods for exportation may have the effect of bringing back some of the gold which has been sent abroad, but they come too late to prevent the drain'. (Gilbart 1840, p. 35.) 'Another effect of regulating the currency by the foreign exchanges is that it leads in seasons of pressure to an enormous rate of interest'. (Gilbart 1840, p. 40.) 'The cost of rectifying the exchanges falls upon the productive industry of the country, while during the process the profits of the Bank of England are actually augmented in consequence of carrying on her business with a less amount of treasure'. (Gilbart 1840, p. 52.) >

Banknotes and bills of exchange. 'What do the banks do? Instead of limiting themselves, as the private bankers do, to inscribing their signature as guarantors to the notes they receive, and then returning them into circulation, they withdraw them, keep them in their vaults, and *in their place they put into circulation other notes they themselves have created with their sole signature on them*'. (Coquelin 1842, p. 810.) 'And in order to save the payee from having to endorse the notes later when they want to hand them over to other people, they pronounce them payable to the bearer' (Coquelin 1842, p. 811.) 'The *banknote* does not replace *money*, it replaces *commercial paper*' (Coquelin 1842, p. 812.)

---

150 [Quoted by Marx from Bell 1842, pp. 106 and 22. Translator]

|391| *Bubble Companies*: 'Mining, railway schemes etc. … the gain to be secured solely through an … advance of price' (Corbet 1841, p. 210). 'Many of these undertakings held out to the public are never intended to be carried into execution, at least by the original projectors; the sole object with whom being merely to get the *shares up to a premium*, when they sell out before a call or a heavy call is made … almost the sole scope of the puffing, delusion and gambling is when the company is about to be formed' (ibid.)

Scottish Banks. Cash Credit. Hardcastle. Notebook XVI. (31).[151]

Credit and Money. 'An increase of purchases on credit does not require, until a future period, a corresponding increase of money to pay for it' (Opdyke 1851, p. 325).

A rise in the rate of interest: '[Its] *immediate effect* … is always an increased demand for discount, especially if any suspicion exists that a further rise will take place … merchants and bankers make an effort to *increase their reserves of cash*; the latter in the shape of banknotes or deposits in the Bank of England, the former in the shape of deposits with their bankers. For this purpose, bankers dispose of securities, consols, and exchequer bills, and merchants a large amount of their bills at hand, so the demand for money is not checked, but immediately raised' (*The Economist*, 22 January 1853, p. 85).

Bills and banknotes.

< 'The reduction of the amount of the note circulation uniformly increases the amount of the bill circulation. The bills are of two classes – *commercial bills* and *bankers' bills* … when money becomes scarce, the moneylenders say "draw upon us and we will accept". And if a country banker discounts a bill for his customer, instead of giving him cash he gives him his own draft at twenty-one days upon his London agent. These bills serve the purpose of a currency' (Gilbart 1840, p. 31).

The monetary system is essentially Catholic, the credit system essentially Protestant. 'The Scotch hate gold'. As paper, the monetary existence of commodities has a *purely social* existence. It is *faith* that brings salvation. Faith in money value as the immanent spirit of commodities, faith in the mode of production and its predestined disposition, faith in the individual agents of production as mere personifications of self-valorising capital. But the credit system is no more emancipated from the monetary system as its basis than Protestantism is from the foundations of Catholicism.

> |392| *Banknotes and their convertibility*.

---

151 [Marx refers here to Notebook XVI of his 'London Notebooks 1850–53', which contains on pages 31–3 extracts from Hardcastle 1843. Translator]

< |393| (6) Pre-Bourgeois Relations

Interest-bearing capital, or, as we might describe it in its archaic form, *usurer's capital*, belongs, together with its twin brother, *merchant's capital*, to the antediluvian forms of capital which were in existence long before the capitalist mode of production and are present in the most diverse economic formations of society.

Usurer's capital requires nothing more for its existence than that at least a portion of the product is transformed into commodities and that money in its various functions develops concurrently with the trade in commodities.

The development of usurer's capital is bound up with that of *merchant's capital*, and particularly with that of money-dealing capital.

In ancient Rome, from the latter phases of the republic onwards, although manufacture stood at a much lower level than the average for the ancient world, merchant's capital, money-dealing capital and usurer's capital were developed to their highest point (within the ancient form).

We have already seen how hoard formation necessarily arises along with money. But the professional hoarder only becomes serious when he transforms himself into a usurer.

The merchant borrows money to make a profit with it, to use it as capital (to lay it out). Even in the earlier forms, therefore, the money-lender confronts him in precisely the same way as the modern capitalist. This specific relationship was even perceived by the Catholic universities. 'The universities of Alcalá, Salamanca, Ingolstadt, Freiburg im Breisgau, Mainz, Cologne and Trier successively acknowledged the legitimacy of *interest on commercial loans*. The first five of these approvals are deposited in the consular archives of the city of Lyons, and are printed in the appendix to the *Traité de l'usure et des intérêts* by Bruyset-Ponthus, Lyons'.[152]

In all forms whether the slave economy (not patriarchal slavery, but rather that of the later phases of the Greco-Roman era) exists as a means of enrichment, and where money is thus a means for appropriating other people's labour by the purchase of slaves, land, etc., money can be valorised as capital and comes to bear interest precisely because it can be invested in this way.

The characteristic forms, however, in which *usurer's capital* exists in phases prior to the capitalist mode of production are twofold: firstly, *usury* by leading money to extravagant magnates, essentially to *landed proprietors*; and secondly, *usury* by lending money to small producers who possess their own conditions

152 Augier 1842, p. 206.

of labour, a category which includes artisans but refers quite specifically to *peasants*, since under the conditions where this mode of production prevails the peasant class must form the great majority > of these small-scale self-sustaining producers.

< I say '*characteristic* forms'. The same forms recur on the basis of the capitalist mode of production, but without determining its character. In the latter case they are not the '*characteristic*' forms of interest-bearing capital.

Both of these things, the ruin of the rich landed proprietors through usury and the bleeding dry of the small-scale producers, lead to the formation and concentration of large money capitals. But the extent to which this process abolishes the old mode of production (as was the result in modern Europe) and establishes the capitalist mode of production depends entirely on the level of historical development and the conditions that this provides.

|394| *Usurer's capital*, as the characteristic form of interest-bearing capital, corresponds to the predominance of *small-scale production*, a self-employed peasantry, and so on. Where, as in the developed capitalist mode of production, the conditions of labour and the product of labour confront the worker as *capital*, he does not have to borrow any money in his capacity as a *producer*. When he does borrow, this is out of personal need, as at the pawnshop. When, on the other hand, he is the proprietor (in reality or nominally) of his conditions of labour and his product, it is as a *producer* that he relates to interest-bearing capital (the money-lender's capital), which confronts him as usurer's capital. Professor Newman puts the matter in a superficial way when he says that the banker is respected, while the usurer is hated and despised, because the former lends to the rich and the latter to the poor.[153] He overlooks the fact that a difference between two social modes of production and the social arrangements corresponding to them is involved here, and the question cannot just be resolved into the contrast between rich and poor. Rather, the usury that acts upon the poor producer goes hand in hand with the usury that exploits the rich landed proprietor. As soon as the usury of the Roman patricians had completely ruined the Roman plebeians, the small farmers, this form of exploitation came to an end and the petty-bourgeois economy was replaced by a pure slave economy.[154]

In the form of *interest*, the usurer can in this case swallow up everything *in excess of* the producers' wages (their most essential means of subsistence). This

153 > The banker 'differs from the old usurer … in that he lends to the rich and seldom or never to the poor. Hence he lends with less risk, and can afford to do it on cheaper terms, and for both reasons he avoids the popular odium which attended the usurer'. (Newman 1851, p. 44.) <

154 > Compare Mommsen 1856, p. 832. < [English translation: Mommsen 1894, pp. 98–9.]

interest later appears as profit or rent. It is therefore quite absurd to compare the *level of this interest*, in which *all* surplus-value save that which accrues to the state is appropriated, with the [modern] *rate of interest*, where interest, or at least the normal interest, forms only *one part of that surplus-value*. This is to forget that the wage-labourer produces and must give up to the capitalist who employs him profit, interest and rent, in short the entire surplus-value. (Carey makes this absurd comparison in order to show the great advantage for the worker of the development of capital and the accompanying fall in the interest rate.)[155] If the usurer, not content with extracting his victim's surplus labour, gradually obtains the title of ownership to his conditions of labour themselves – land, house, etc. – and consistently sets out to *expropriate* him in this way, it still should not be forgotten that the complete *expropriation of the worker* from his conditions of labour is not a result towards which the capitalist mode of production tends, but rather the *given presupposition* from which it proceeds. The wage-slave is just as much excluded by his position as the slave proper from being a debt slave, at least in his quality as producer; he can only become so in his quality as a consumer. *Usurer's capital*, in this form in which it actually appropriates all the surplus labour of the *direct producer*, without altering the mode of production; and in which it is immanently determined by the producers' ownership or possession of their conditions of labour (and the isolated production corresponding to this), and in which labour is not directly subsumed by capital, which therefore does not confront it as industrial capital, this usurer's capital *impoverishes* the mode of production, cripples the productive forces instead of developing them, and at the same time perpetuates these lamentable conditions in which the *social productivity of labour* is not developed at the cost of the worker himself, as it is in the capitalist mode of production.

Usury thus works on the one hand to ruin ancient and feudal wealth and property. On the other hand, it also ruins small peasant and petty bourgeois production, in short all forms in which the producer still appears as the owner of his means of production.

|395| In the capitalist mode of production, the worker is *not the owner* of the conditions of production, of the land that he tills; of the raw material he works up, etc. This alienation of the conditions of production from the producer, however, corresponds here to a real change in the mode of production itself. The tool becomes a machine; the workers are brought together in a workshop, etc. The mode of production itself no longer permits the fragmentation of

155 [Carey 1835, pp. 112–13. Translator]

the instruments of production that is linked with small-scale property, any more than it permits the isolation of the workers themselves. In capitalist production, usury can no longer *divorce* the conditions of production from the producer, since they are already divorced from him.

Where the means of production are fragmented, usury *centralises* monetary wealth. It does not change the mode of production, but clings on to it like a parasite and throws it into misery. It sucks it dry, drains it of all strength, and forces reproduction to proceed under ever more frightful conditions. Hence the popular hatred of usury, particularly in the ancient world, where the producer's ownership of his conditions of production was at the same time the basis for political relations, for the independence of the citizen.

As long as slavery prevails, or surplus labour is consumed by the feudal lord and his retainers, the mode of production still remains the same if the lord falls prey to usury; it simply becomes harsher for the workers. The indebted slaveholder or feudal lord squeezes more out of them because more is squeezed out of him. Ultimately he may be completely replaced by the usurer, who himself becomes a landowner, etc., as did the members of the equestrian order in ancient Rome. The old exploiter, whose exploitation was more or less an instrument of political power, is replaced by a coarse, money-grubbing upstart. But the mode of production itself remains unchanged.

Usury only has a revolutionary effect on all pre-capitalist modes of production in so far as it destroys and dissolves the forms of ownership which provide a firm basis for the articulation of political life and whose constant reproduction in the same form is a necessity for that life. In Asiatic forms, usury can persist for a long while without leading to anything more than economic decay and political corruption. It is only where and when the other conditions for the capitalist mode of production are present that usury appears as one of the means of formation of this new mode of production, by ruining the feudal lords and small-scale production, and as a way of centralising the conditions of labour as capital.

'In the Middle Ages, there was *no general rate of interest* in any country. The strictness of the priests in adhering to church law meant a lack of secure judicial institutions for enforcing the payment of loans. All the higher was the interest rate in individual cases. This was due to the *low monetary circulation* and the need to make most payments in cash, as well as the lack of development of the system of bills of exchange. There was therefore a great deal of variation in the attitude to interest and the concept of usury. In Charlemagne's time it was considered usurious to take 100 percent in interest. At Lindau am Bodensee in 1344 some local burghers took 216⅔ percent. In Zürich the town council fixed 43⅓ percent as the legal interest. In Italy, 40 percent had to be paid on occasion, though from the twelfth century to the fourteenth the rate did not usually exceed 20 percent. Verona settled on 12½ percent as the lawful rate of interest. The Emperor Frederick II fixed a rate of 10 percent, but this was only for the Jews. He did not wish to decree a rate for Christians. 10 percent was already customary in the Rhineland in the thirteenth century'. (Hüllmann 1827, pp. 55–7)

[Usurer's capital is] exploitation by capital, without capital's mode of production. This relationship also recurs within the bourgeois economy in backward branches of industry, or those that are struggling against the transition to the modern mode of production. In comparing the English rate of interest with the Indian, for example, we must not take the Bank of England's interest rate but rather that charged, for instance, by people lending, for example, weaving frames to small producers in domestic industry (see the example below).

Usury is historically important in contrast to wealth devoted entirely to consumption, as being itself a *process giving rise to capital.* Usurer's capital and mercantile wealth bring about the formation of a monetary wealth independent of landed property.

|396| The less developed the character of the product as a commodity, the less exchange value has taken command of production in its whole breadth and depth, the more does *money* appear as wealth as such, wealth proper, wealth in general, as against its restricted form of appearance in use-values. *Hoard formation* depends on this. Leaving aside money as world money and as hoard, it is particularly in the form of *means of payment* that it emerges as the absolute form of the commodity. And it is particularly its function as means of payment that develops *interest*, and with it money capital. What wealth wants to facilitate its extravagance and corruption is money as money, as the *general power of purchasing*. (Also for paying debts.) What the small-scale producer needs money for above all is for *payment.* (*Taxes* also play a part here.) In both cases money is needed as money. On the other hand, it is only in *usury* that hoard formation becomes a reality for the first time and fulfils its dreams. What is sought from the owner of the hoard is not capital but rather money as money; but through interest he transforms this money hoard, as it is in itself, into capital – into a means by which he takes partial or complete command of surplus labour, and in this way of a portion of the conditions of production themselves, even if these nominally still confront him as someone else's property. Usury seems to live in the pores of production, like the gods in Epicurus's metaphysical system. It is all the more difficult to get money, the less the commodity form has become the general form of the product. The usurer therefore does not come up against any barrier except the incapacity of those in need of money to pay or their capacity to resist.

In small peasant and petty-bourgeois production, money is used principally as *means of purchase* when the worker loses his conditions of production through accidents, or some extraordinary dislocation (the worker being still their owner in these modes of production), or at least when they are not replaced in the ordinary course of *reproduction*. Means of subsistence and raw materials belong among these conditions of production. A *rise in their price* can make it impossible to replace them from the proceeds of the product, just as simple harvest failure can prevent the peasant from replacing his seed corn in kind. > Here are some *examples*. < The same wars through which the Roman patricians ruined the plebeians, forcing them into war services which prevented them from reproducing their conditions of labour, and hence *pauperised* them (and *pauperisation*, the curtailment or loss of the conditions of reproduction is the prevailing form here), filled the stores and vaults of the former with plundered copper, the money of that epoch. Instead of providing the plebeians directly with the commodities they needed – corn, horses, etc. – they lent them this copper, which was of no use to themselves, and made use of the situation to extort enormous and usurious levels of interest, thereby making the plebeians into their debt slaves and their prisoners. The German peasants under Charlemagne were similarly ruined by wars, so that nothing remained for them but to exchange the position of debtor for that of serf. We know for example that in the Rumanian lands, etc., famine led free men to sell themselves as slaves to the rich. This is enough said in regard to general '*turning points*'. When considered in detail, the preservation or loss of the producers' conditions of production depends on a thousand accidental circumstances, and each such accident or loss means pauperisation, and is a point at which the parasite of usury can seize hold. The peasant only needs one of his cows to die and he is thereby rendered incapable of repeating his reproduction on the previous scale. At that point usury enters the picture.

Means of payment. This is the proper, principal and specific terrain of usury. Any monetary obligation that falls due at a certain time – tribute, tax, etc. – brings with it the need for payment in money. Large-scale usury is associated with tax farmers from ancient Rome right through to modern times. With the development of trade, purchase and payment become separate in time. Money has to be provided by a particular date. The separation of purchase and payment is demonstrated clearly even now by the modern money crises.

The same usury we are discussing becomes a major means of extending the need for money as means of payment, since it drags the producer deeper and deeper into debt, and destroys his customary means of payment in that the interest burden itself makes his level of production inadequate. Here usury springs from money as *means of payment*, and broadens this function of money, its most specific terrain.

|397| *The credit system* develops as a *reaction against usury*.

But this should not be misconstrued, nor by any means taken in the sense of the ancient writers, the Fathers of the Church, Luther or the socialists.

It means neither more nor less than the *subordination* of interest-bearing capital to the conditions and requirements of the *capitalist mode of production*. In the modern credit system, interest-bearing capital has by and large been made adequate to the conditions of the capitalist mode of production. *Usury* as such not only continues to exist, but in nations of developed capitalist production it is freed from the limits that former legislation had always placed on it. Interest-bearing capital appears as (merely takes on the form of) usurer's capital vis-à-vis persons and classes, or in conditions where borrowing in the sense appropriate to the capitalist mode of production does not and cannot occur; where borrowing results from individual need, as at the *pawnshop*; where borrowing is for extravagant consumption; or where the *producer* is a *non-capitalist producer*, a small peasant, an artisan, etc., hence where the direct producer is still the proprietor or the possessor of his own conditions of production; finally where the capitalist producer himself operates on so small a scale that his situation approaches that of those self-employed working men.

What distinguishes *interest-bearing capital*, in so far as it forms an essential element of the capitalist mode of production, from *usurer's capital* is in no way the nature or character of this capital itself. It is simply the changed conditions under which it functions, and hence also the totally transformed figure of the borrower who confronts the money-lender. Even where a man without means obtains credit, whether as an industrialist or as a merchant, it is given in the expectation that he will function as a capitalist, will use the capital borrowed to appropriate unpaid labour. He is given the credit as a *potential capitalist*. And this fact, so very much admired by the economic apologists, that a man without wealth but with energy, ability, steadfastness and business acumen can transform himself into a capitalist in this way – just as the commercial value of each person is always assessed more or less correctly in the capitalist mode of production – much as it constantly drives an unwelcome series of new soldiers of fortune onto the field alongside and against the various individual capitalists already present, actually reinforces the rule of capital itself, widens its basis and enables it to recruit ever new forces from the lower strata of society; just as the fact that in the Middle Ages the Catholic Church recruited its forces from the best brains of the nation, without regard to status, birth or wealth, was a major means of reinforcing the rule of the hierarchy and suppressing the laity. The more a ruling class is able to absorb the ablest people from the lower classes, the more solid and dangerous is its domination.

Instead of issuing anathemas against interest-bearing capital in general, the initiators of the modern credit system proceed in the opposite way, by *explicitly recognising it*.

We are not referring here to the reaction against usury, which sought to protect the poor from it, as in the case of the *Monts de Piété* set up in 1350 at Salins in Franche-Comté and later at Perugia and Savona in Italy, in 1400 and 1479. These are noteworthy only because they display the irony of history, which turns pious wishes into their very opposite when they are realised. A conservative estimate for the interest that the English working class pays to the pawnshops, those offshoots of the *Monts de Piété*, would be 100 percent.[156] Nor do we have in mind the credit fantasies of such men as Dr. Hugh Chamberlen or John Briscoe,[157] who tried to emancipate the English aristocracy from usury in the last decade of the seventeenth century by way of a *Land Bank* using paper money based on landed property.[158]

|398| The credit associations set up in the twelfth and fourteenth centuries in Venice and Genoa arose from the need of maritime trade and the wholesale trade based on it to emancipate itself from the domination of old-fashioned usury and from the monopolists of money-dealing. If the actual banks that were founded in these urban republics were at the same time institutions for public credit, from which the state received advances against taxes which were yet to be raised, it should not be forgotten that the merchants who set up these associations were themselves the top dogs in those states. They had

156 'It is by frequent fluctuations within the month, and by pawning one article to relieve another, where a small sum is obtained, that the premium for money becomes so excessive. There are about 240 licensed pawnbrokers in the metropolis, and nearly 1,450 in the country. The capital employed is supposed somewhat to exceed a million pounds sterling; and this capital is turned round thrice in the course of a year, and yields each time about 33⅓ percent on an average; according to which calculation, the inferior orders of England pay 100 percent annually for the temporary loan of a million, exclusive of what they lose by goods being forfeited.' (Tuckett 1846, p. 114.)

157 [Chamberlen 1695; Briscoe 1696. Translator]

158 Even in the very titles of their works, they gave as their main purpose 'the general good of landed men, the great increase of the value of land', the exemption of the 'nobility, gentry etc. from taxes, enlarging their yearly estates etc.' Only the usurers would lose from this, these worst enemies of the nation, who had caused the nobility and the yeomanry more damage than an invading French army could have done.

an equal interest in emancipating their governments and themselves from usury[159] and, at the same time, placing the state more firmly under their own subordination. When it was decided to set up the Bank of England, the Tories objected that banks were republican institutions. Flourishing banks existed in Venice, Genoa, Amsterdam and Hamburg. But who ever heard of a Bank of France or Spain?

The Bank of Amsterdam (1609) was not a milestone in the development of the modern credit system, any more than that of Hamburg (1619). It was simply a bank for deposits. The cheques the bank issued were in actual fact simply receipts for the coined or uncoined precious metal deposited with it and circulated only with the endorsement of their recipients. But in Holland commercial credit and dealing in money did develop along with trade and manufacture, and by the course of development itself, interest-bearing capital became subordinate to industrial and commercial capital. This was already evident from the *low level of the interest rate*. > (*Quantitatively*.) < In the seventeenth century, however, Holland served as the model country of economic development, just as England does today. The monopoly of old-fashioned usury, based on poverty, was thrown overboard there automatically.

Right through the eighteenth century there resounds the cry for a *forcible* reduction in the interest rate, with reference being made to Holland. Legislation proceeds in the same direction; the aim being to subordinate interest-bearing capital to commercial and industrial capital, instead of the reverse. The leading spokesman of this approach is Sir Josiah Child, the father of normal English private banking. He declaims against the monopoly of the usurers in the same way as Moses and Son [who were dealers in ready-made clothes] attack the monopoly of the bespoke tailors. This Josiah Child is also the father of English stock-jobbing. As autocrat of the East India Company, he defends its monopoly in the name of free trade. Against Thomas Manley (*'Interest of Money Mistaken'*)[160] he says, for example: 'As the champion of the timid and

---

159 The rich goldsmiths, for example (the forerunners of the bankers) made King Charles II pay interest rates of 20 to 30 percent on loans. 'This profitable business induced the goldsmiths to become increasingly lenders to the King, to anticipate all the revenue, to take every grant of Parliament into pawn as soon as it was given; also to outvie each other in buying and taking to pawn bills, orders and tallies so that in effect all the revenue passed through their hands'. (Francis 1848, p. 31.) 'The erection of a bank had been suggested several times before that. It was at last a necessity'. (Francis 1848, p. 38.) 'The bank was a necessity for the government itself, sucked dry by usurers, in order to obtain money at a reasonable rate, on the security of parliamentary grants'. (Francis 1848, pp. 59–60.)

160 [Manley 1668. Translator]

trembling bands of usurers, he erects his main batteries at that point which I have declared to be the weakest … He emphatically denies that the low rate of interest is the cause of wealth and vows that it is merely its effect' (Child 1754, p. 120). 'If it is commerce that enriches a country, and if a lowering of interest increases commerce, a lowering of interest or a restriction of usury is doubtless a fruitful and principal cause of the wealth of a nation. It is not at all absurd to say that the same thing may be simultaneously a cause under certain circumstances, and an effect under others' (Child 1754, p. 155). 'The egg is the cause of the hen, and the hen is the cause of the egg. The lowering of interest can therefore cause an increase of wealth, and the increase of wealth can cause a still greater lessening in interest' (Child 1754, p. 156). 'I am *the advocate of industry* and my opponent pleads in favour of idleness and inactivity' (Child 1754, p. 179).

This *violent* struggle against usury – this endeavour to subordinate interest-bearing capital to industrial capital – is only the prelude to the organic creations that these conditions of the capitalist mode of production establish in the form of the modern banking system, which on the one hand robs usurer's capital of its monopoly, since it concentrates all dormant money reserves together and places them on the money market, while on the other hand restricting the monopoly of the precious metals themselves by creating credit money.

|400| Usury, just like trade, *exploits given relations of production* but does not create them; both usury and trade are related to them in a merely external way. Usury seeks directly to maintain these relations of production, so as to be able to exploit them over and over again; it is conservative, and simply makes the relations of production more wretched. The less the conditions of production enter as commodities in to the process and emerge from it as commodities, the more does their creation out of *money* appear as a special act. The less production as a whole depends on circulation, the more does usurer's capital flourish.

To say that *monetary wealth* develops as a special kind of wealth means, as far as usurer's capital is concerned, that it possesses all its claims in the form of *monetary claims*. It develops in a country all the more, the bulk of production is confined to services in kind, etc., in other words to use-values.

On interest in the Middle Ages.

'In the Middle Ages the population was purely agricultural. Under such a government as was the feudal system there can be but little traffic, and hence but little profit. Besides, in an agricultural country a person seldom wants to borrow money except he be reduced to poverty or distress'. Henry VIII limited interest to 10 percent, James I to 8 percent, Charles II to 6 percent, Anne to 5 percent. 'In those times, the lenders … had, in fact, though not a legal, yet an actual monopoly, and hence it was necessary that they, like other monopolists, should be placed under restraint. In our times, it is the rate of profit which regulates the rate of interest. In those times, it was the rate of interest which regulated the rate of profit. If the money-lender charged a high rate of interest to the merchant, the merchant was obliged to charge a higher rate of profit on his goods. Hence a large sum of money would be taken from the pockets of the purchasers to be put into the pockets of the money-lenders' (Gilbart 1834, pp. 163–5.)

(Usury, by its double effect, is a powerful means for creating the preconditions for industrial capital. Firstly, it always forms an independent hoard of monetary wealth, alongside the class of merchants, and secondly it appropriates the conditions of labour, by ruining the owners of the old conditions of labour.)

Luther on usury.

'I have heard it said that 10 gulden are now taken annually at each Leipzig fair. That is 30 gulden on every 100; some add the Neuenburg fair, thus making 40 gulden on every 100. Whether this is true, I do not know. For shame! What the devil will be the end of this? … If someone who has 100 florins at Leipzig takes 40 per year, this means that he has gobbled up a peasant or a burgher over the year. If he has 1,000 florins, he takes 400 each year and gobbles up a knight or a rich nobleman. If he has 10,000 florins he takes 4,000 a year and gobbles up a rich count. If he has 100,000, as must be the case with the big dealers, he takes 40,000 a year and has gobbled up a great and rich prince. If he has 1,000,000 he takes 400,000 and gobbles up a great king. And to do this he does not suffer any danger, either to his body or his goods; he does not work, but sits by his stove and bakes apples; in this way a mean robber could sit at home and gobble up the whole world in ten years' (Luther 1589, pp. 312–13.)

'Fifteen years ago I wrote against usury, when it had already spread so widely that I could not hope for any improvement. Since that time it has become so arrogant that it is no longer *content to be classed as vice, sin or shame*, but has itself praised as a pure virtue and honour, as if it is acting out of great love for people and doing a Christian service. What will help and deliver us now that shame has become honour and vice virtue? > It was with good reason that Seneca the Younger wrote *"Deest remediis locus, ubi, quae vitia fuerunt, mores fiunt"* [There is no remedy to be had in a place where what were previously vices have now become normal conduct]'. (Luther 1540.)

'Thus Squire Usurer says: My dear fellow, as things are at present, I do my neighbour a great *service* in that I lend him a hundred at five, six, ten. And he thanks me for such a loan as a very special favour. He does indeed beg me for it and he pledges himself freely and willingly to give me five, six, ten gulden in a hundred. Should I not be able without extortion to take this interest with a good conscience? ... Extol yourself, put on finery and adorn yourself ... but whoever takes more or better than he gives, that is usury, and the name for it is not *service* but *wrong* done to his neighbour, just like stealing and robbing. All is not *service* and benefit to a neighbour that is called *service* and benefit. For an adulteress and an adulterer do one another great service and pleasure. A horseman does a fire-raiser a great and noble service by helping him to rob on the highway, and to attack the people and the land. The Papists do our people a great service in that they don't drown, burn and murder all of them, or let them all rot in prison, but let some live and only drive them out or take from them what they have. The devil himself does his servants great, immeasurable services ... To sum up, the world is full of great, excellent and daily service and benefit ... The poets write about a Cyclops called Polyphemus, who promised Ulysses that he would do him an act of friendship, namely, that he would eat his companions first, leaving Ulysses to the last.[161] This would indeed have been a service and a good favour. These days, nobles and commoners, peasants and burghers, diligently perform and practice services and good deeds of this kind ... They wipe their mouths and say: Yes, one must have what one must have; I perform a service by letting people have my things, although I might and could keep them for myself ... The sons of men are now so holy that no one can practise usury, be covetous or be wicked. The world has become holy and nothing else, *everyone serves his fellow-man*, nobody does anyone any harm ... But if this is the kind of service he does, he does it for the devil himself, although a poor, needy man requires such a service, and must indeed accept that it is a service or a favour not to be gobbled up completely' (ibid.)

'Therefore there is no greater *enemy of man* on this earth (after the devil) than a skinflint and a usurer, because *he wants to be God over all men*. Turks, soldiers and tyrants are also bad men, yet they must let the people live, and confess that they are bad, and enemies, and do (indeed they must) now and then show mercy to some people. But a usurer and money-grubber is one who would have the whole world perish of hunger and thirst, misery and want, so far as he is capable of this, so as to have all to himself, and so that *everyone may receive from him as from a God and be his serf for ever*. This is what gladdens his heart, and refreshes his blood. And at the same time he can strut around in sable cloaks, gold chains, rings, and gowns; he can wipe his mouth and be deemed and taken for a worthy and pious man ... Pious usurer! ... He is as

161 [Homer, *Odyssey*, Book IX, Verses 369–70. Translator]

despicable in his life … as is the Pharisee who fasts twice a week and is not as other men are' (ibid.)[162] (See also Luther 1555.)

|401| < 'Jews, Lombards, usurers and extortioners [were] our first bankers, our primitive traffickers in money, their character little short of infamous … They were joined by the London goldsmiths. As a body … our primitive bankers [were] a very bad set, they were griping usurers, iron-hearted extortioners' (Hardcastle 1843, pp. 19, 20).

> Where trade was well developed, as in the Italian cities (particularly maritime trade), the credit system was present early on. In Holland, for example. It can be said that the development of the credit system kept pace everywhere with the growth of maritime trade and of overseas markets. Here interest is regulated by profit. (Quite apart from the establishment of banks in Venice, Genoa, Barcelona, etc., and later in Holland). < 'The example provided by Venice was quickly imitated; all maritime cities, and all cities everywhere which had made a name for themselves by their independence and their trade, founded the first banks. The return of their ships, which was often delayed, led unavoidably to the custom of giving credit, which was strengthened still further in the wake of the discovery of America and the trade there'. (This is an important point.) 'The chartering of ships made *large advances* necessary, as was already true in antiquity in the case of Athens and Greece. In 1308 the Hanseatic city of Bruges possessed an insurance company'. (Augier 1842, pp. 202, 203.)

The extent to which *lending to landed proprietors*, and thus to the wealthy in general for consumption, was still the prevalent form even in England in the last third of the seventeenth century, before the development of the modern credit system, can be seen from the writing of Sir Dudley North, among others. North was not only one of the leading English merchants, but also one of the most important theoretical economists of his time.

'The moneys employed at interest in this nation, are not near the tenth part, *disposed to trading people*, wherewith to manage their trades; but are for the most part lent for the supplying of luxury, and to support the expense of persons who, though great owners of land, yet spend faster than their lands bring in; and being loath to sell, choose rather to mortgage their estates'. (North 1691, pp. 6, 7.)

In Poland in the *eighteenth century*: 'Warsaw had a large business in bills of exchange, but one that was principally based on and oriented towards the usury of its bankers. In order to obtain money, which they could lend to extravagant magnates at 8 percent and more, they sought and obtained an open

162 [Quoted from: Luke 18: 11–12. Translator]

exchange credit abroad, i.e., a credit which did not have any commodity trade as its basis, but which the foreign drawee would continue to accept as long as the remittances from these exchange dealings did not fail to come in. They paid heavily for this with the bankruptcy of men like Tepper and other well respected Warsaw bankers' (Büsch 1808, p. 233).

The Advantages for the Church of Prohibiting Interest. 'The taking of interest had been banned by the Church, but not selling property to extricate oneself from need. It was not even forbidden to transfer property to the money-lender for a definite period, until repayment, so that the money-lender not only found his security in this, but could also enjoy compensation for the money he had lent in having the use of this property ... The Church itself, or the communities and pious bodies associated with it, drew great advantage from this, especially at the time of the Crusades. This brought a very great part of the nation's wealth into the possession of the so-called 'dead hand' of the Church, especially since Jews were barred from practising usury in this way, it being impossible to conceal the possession of such fixed pledges ... Without the ban on interest, the Churches and the monasteries would never have been able to get so rich' (Büsch 1808, p. 55).

|402| Just as in this case with Child, opposition to usury can be found in all English writings on banking in the last third of the seventeenth century and the beginning of the eighteenth (Law):[163] the demand for the emancipation of trade and industry (and of the state) from usury. Also illusions about the miraculous effect of credit, of the removal of the monopoly held by precious metals and their replacement by paper, etc. The Scot William Paterson, founder of the Bank of England and the Bank of Scotland, is very much Law the First.[164]

---

163 [John Law, Scottish economist and financier, advocated the unlimited issue of banknotes without gold or silver backing, and set up a bank in France on this basis, which collapsed in 1720. Translator]

164 'All the goldsmiths and pawnbrokers set up a howl of rage' against the Bank of England. (Macaulay 1855, p. 499.) 'During the first ten years the Bank had to struggle with great difficulties; foreign feuds; its notes were at a heavy discount ... The goldsmiths' (in whose hands the trade in precious metals served as the basis of a banking business) 'were jealous of the Bank, because their business was diminished, their discounts were lowered, and their transactions with the government had passed to their opponent'. (Francis 1848, p. 73.) From the very outset, the banker can make cheaper advances than the private capitalist > (quite apart from the profit he makes on banknotes, etc.) < and the private usurer > partly because of the scale on which he conducts his business, the economies on capital, his overall understanding of the relations of production of all those who conduct commerce and industry, and particularly because of the extraordinarily low ratio in which his private

Even before the foundation of the Bank of England, a plan for a '*National Bank of Credit*' had already been drawn up in 1683, one of its objects being the following: 'that tradesmen, when they have a considerable quantity of goods, may, by the help of this bank, deposit their goods, by raising a credit on their own dead stock, employ their servants, and increase their trade, till they get a good market instead of selling them at a loss'.[165] 'After much trouble, this *Bank of Credit* was established at Devonshire House, in Bishopsgate Street. Its object, as we have related, being principally to advance money to tradesmen and manufacturers, on the security of goods. Three fourths of the value was lent on these, and bills for their amount given to the depositor. In order to render them current, an appointed number of persons in each trade were formed into a society to regulate commercial concerns. Any individual possessed of such bills might therefore obtain from this company goods or merchandise with as much ease as if they offered current coin. The bank of credit does not appear to have flourished. The machinery was too complicated, and the risk of depreciation in the value of manufactures was too great'.[166]

If we concentrate on the real content of these writings, which were the theoretical accompaniment to the formation of the modern credit system in England and helped to promote it, we find nothing in them but the demand for the subjugation of interest-bearing capital and *loanable* means of production in general to the capitalist mode of production, as one of its conditions. If we

capital stands to the capital lent out and profitably exploited. < 'It is possible for them' (the bankers) 'to provide the industrialist with his tools more cheaply, i.e., *at lower interest*, than the landowners and capitalists could do this, since the latter could more easily make mistakes in their choice of borrower'. (Bazard 1831, p. 202.) But the author himself adds in a footnote: 'The advantage that was supposed to follow from the intervention of the banker between the idle capitalists and the *travailleurs* is often outweighed, and even destroyed, by the opportunity our *disorganised* society offers for egoism to hold sway, in the various forms of fraud and charlatanry; the bankers often intervene between the *travailleurs* and the idle capitalists simply to exploit both sides, to the detriment of society as a whole'. (Ibid.) The word '*travailleur*' stands here for the *capitaliste industriel*. It is wrong, incidentally, to view the resources that the modern banking system has at its disposal simply as the resources of the idle capitalists. In the first place, these resources include the portion of capital that industrialists and merchants keep temporarily unoccupied in the money form (as a money reserve or as capital still to be invested), hence this is idle capital, but not the capital of the idle; secondly, they include that portion of everyone's revenues and savings that is permanently or temporarily set aside for accumulation. And both of these are essential to the character of the banking system.

165 [Francis 1848, pp. 39–40. Translator]

166 [Francis 1848, pp. 40–1. Translator]

just look at the phrases used, the way they coincide, right down to the very words, with the banking and credit illusions of the Saint-Simonians is often astonishing.[167]

It must never be forgotten, however, firstly that *money* (in the form of precious metal) remains the foundation from which the credit system can *never* break free, by the nature of the case. Secondly, that the credit system has the monopoly of the social means of production (in the form of *capital* and *landed property*) in the hands of private individuals as its *presupposition*, and that it is itself an immanent form of the *capitalist mode of production*, and, on the other hand, functions as a vehicle for developing it into its last possible form.

The *banking system*, by its formal organisation and centralisation, is the most artificial and elaborate product brought into existence by the capitalist mode of production.[168] Hence the tremendous power an institution such as the Bank of England has over trade and industry, even though their actual movement remains completely outside its orbit and it behaves quite passively towards them. Such a bank, however, supplies the form of a general book-keeping and distribution of the means of production on a social scale, even if only the form. We have seen that the average profit of the individual capitalist, or of any particular capital, is determined not by the surplus labour this capital exploits but by the quantity of social surplus labour that the total capital exploits, from which each particular capital draws its dividends as being only a proportional part of the total capital. This 'social' character of capital is

167 Just as for the Physiocrats, the 'cultivateur' does not mean the actual working peasant, but rather the 'fermier', or big farmer, so Saint-Simon's 'travailleur' is not the 'ouvrier', or worker, but the industrial and commercial capitalist, and this usage is still current with his disciples. 'A *travailleur* [worker] needs helpers, supporters, *ouvriers* [workers]; he puts them to work, and their labour is productive'. (Enfantin 1831, p. 104.) It should by no means be forgotten that it was only in his last work, *Le Nouveau christianisme*, that Saint-Simon directly emerged as a spokesman for the working class and declared its emancipation to be the final goal of his endeavours. All his earlier writings are in fact simply a glorification of modern bourgeois society against feudal society, and of the industrialists and bankers against the marshals and jurists of the Napoleonic era. How different this is from the contemporary writings of Owen! Even for his followers, as the passage quoted above shows, the industrial capitalist remains the *travailleur par excellence*. If one reads his writings critically, it is no surprise that the reality of his credit and banking dreams turned out to be the *Crédit Mobilier*; a form of institution which incidentally could come to such prominence only in a country like France, where neither the modern credit system nor large-scale industry was sufficiently developed. In England and America this kind of thing would have been impossible.

168 This was already noted in 1697 (*Some Thoughts* 1697.)

mediated and completely realised only by the full development of the credit and banking system. On the other hand this development also goes further. It places all available and even potential capital of the society that is not already actively committed at the disposition of the industrial and commercial capitalists, so that neither the lender |403| nor the user of this capital are its 'owners' or producers. It thereby abolishes the *private character* of capital and thus *inherently* bears within it, though only *inherently*, the abolition of capital itself.

Through the banking system, the distribution of capital is removed from the hands of the private capitalists and usurers and becomes a *special business*, a social function. At the same time, however, the banking system becomes the most active means for driving capitalist production beyond its own barriers, and one of the most effective vehicles for crises and swindling.

By substituting various forms of *circulating credit* for *money*, the banking system shows further that the latter is in actual fact nothing but a special expression of the *social* character of labour and its products, which, as antithetical to the basis of private production, must however always present itself in the final analysis as a thing, as a particular commodity alongside other particular commodities. Finally, there can be no doubt that the credit system will serve as a powerful lever in the course of the transition from the capitalist mode of production to the mode of production of *associated labour*; but only as one element in connection with other large-scale organic changes in this mode of production itself. On the other hand, illusions about the miraculous power of the credit and banking system, in the socialist sense, arise from complete ignorance about the capitalist mode of production and about the credit system as one of its forms. As soon as the means of production cease to be transformed into capital (which also means the abolition of private property in land) credit as such no longer has any means, something which even the Saint-Simonians have realised, incidentally.[169] On the other hand, as long as the capitalist mode

---

169 'The purpose of credit is this: in a society where some people *possess* tools for industry without the ability or the will to use them, while other people, who are industrious, do not *possess* the instruments of labour, to make it as easy as possible to transfer these instruments from the hands of the former, the owners, to those of the latter, the people who know how to use them. Let us note that according to this definition *credit is a result of the manner in which **property** is constituted*'. (Enfantin 1831, p. 45.) Thus credit disappears together with this constitution of property. [It is further said that] 'they' (the banks of today) 'consider themselves destined to follow the movement *initiated by transactions outside their own domain*, but not to provide the impulse for these themselves; in other words, the banks play the role of capitalists for the *travailleurs* to whom they advance

of production persists, interest-bearing capital persists as one of its forms, and in fact forms the basis of the credit system. Only that same '*sensational writer*' (Proudhon) who wanted to allow commodity production to continue while abolishing *money*[170] was capable of dreaming up the enormity of a *crédit gratuit* [interest-free credit], that pious wish arising from the petty-bourgeois standpoint. > This sort of thing is the natural territory of all the windbags and makers of empty projects.

< We have seen that *merchant's capital* and *interest-bearing capital* are the oldest forms of capital. But it lies in the very nature of the matter that *interest-bearing capital* should appear to the popular mind as the form of capital *par excellence*. In merchant's capital we have a mediating activity, whether this is interpreted as fraud, labour or in any other way. In interest-bearing capital, on the other hand, the self-reproducing character of capital, self-valorising value, the production of surplus-value, appears as a purely occult quality. Hence it also happens that even some political economists, particularly in countries where industrial capital is not yet fully developed, as in France, cling to interest-bearing capital as the basic form and see ground-rent, for example, as simply another form of this, since here too it is the form of *lending* that is dominant. In this way the internal articulation of the capitalist mode of production is completely misconceived, and it is entirely overlooked that the land, just like capital, is only hired out to capitalists. Instead of money, means of production can of course be loaned in kind, in the shape of machines, business premises, etc.

---

capital' (Enfantin 1831, p. 98.) The *Crédit Mobilier* is already latent in the idea that the banks themselves should take over this leadership, and display their excellence 'by the number and usefulness of the *firms they control* and the *work they have promoted*' (Enfantin 1831, p. 101.) In the same way, Constantin Pecqueur demands that the banks (called by the Saint-Simonians a 'general system of banks') should govern production. Pecqueur is always a Saint-Simonian, even if far more radical. He wants 'the credit institution ... [to] govern *the entire movement of national production*'. 'Just try to create a national credit institution which will advance resources to people of talent and merit, but no property, without binding these borrowers together *compulsorily* in a close solidarity in production and consumption, but rather, on the contrary, in such a way that they themselves determine what they exchange and produce. In this way you will only achieve what the private banks already do achieve, anarchy, a disproportion between production and consumption, the sudden ruin of some and the sudden enrichment of others; so that your institution will never do more than produce a sum of benefit *equally* balanced by a sum of misfortune borne by others ... You will simply have provided the wage-earners whom you assist with the means to compete with one another, just like their bourgeois masters do now'. (Pecqueur 1842, pp. 433, 434.)

170 Marx 1859, p. 64. [In English: MECW 29, 1987, p. 323.]

But in this case these represent a certain sum of money, and if, apart from the interest, a portion is paid for wear and tear, this arises from the use-value, the specific natural form, of these elements of capital. The decisive question, here again, is whether they are lent to the immediate producers, which presupposes the *non-existence* of the capitalist mode of production, at least in the sphere in which this takes place, or whether they are lent to industrial capitalists, which presupposes precisely that the basis is the capitalist mode of production. It is still more irrelevant and senseless to bring in here the renting of houses, etc., for individual consumption. It is clear that the working class is swindled in this form too, and to an enormous extent; but the workers are equally exploited by the petty trader who supplies them with the means of subsistence. (This is a secondary exploitation, which proceeds alongside the original exploitation that takes place directly within the production process itself.)

|404| The distinction between *selling* and *lending* here is completely immaterial and formal, and as already shown, appears *fundamental* only for those who are in complete ignorance of the real context.

> (It would be better to place the comparison between usurious rates of interest in India and England under *similar conditions* in my critique of Carey.)

∴

At present (October 1865) the Bank of England is conducting operations against the internal drain (raising the rate of interest). The rate of interest was at 7 percent on 11 October 1865, and the Bank issued the following report of the state of affairs at that date:

Notes issued:		26,606,340
Reserve in the Banking Department:		4,294,145
Notes in circulation, therefore:		22,312,195
Gold Coin and Bullion (Issue Department):		11,956.340
Reserve in the Banking Department:		780,006
Total of Bullion:		12,736,346
Reserve of Banking Department,	*Notes:*	4,294,145
	Bullion:	780,006
Total Reserve:		5,074,151

Private Securities (Bills, etc.)		24,086,476
Deposits	*Public:*	7,228,737
	Private:	13,506,498
Total		20,735,235

Exchanges: favourable. At the end of *September* the bank raised the rate of discount from 4 to 4½ percent. At the beginning of October it raised it to 5 percent, some days later to 6 percent, and on 7 October to 7 percent.

|406| < CHAPTER SIX

The Transformation of Surplus Profit into Ground-Rent

(a) Introduction

The analysis of *landed property* in its various historical forms lies outside the scope of the present work. We are concerned with it only in so far as a portion of the *surplus-value* that capital produces falls to the share of the landowner. We assume therefore that agriculture, just like manufacturing, is dominated by the capitalist mode of production, i.e., that agriculture is pursued by capitalists, who, > looked at in material terms, < are distinguished from other capitalists simply by the element in which their capital and the wage-labour that it sets in motion are invested. As far as we are concerned, the farmer produces corn, etc., just as the manufacturer produces yarn. The assumption that the capitalist mode of production has taken control of agriculture implies also that it dominates all spheres of production and bourgeois society, so that its preconditions, such as the free competition of capitals, their transferability from one sphere of production to another, an equal level of average profit, etc., are also present in their full development. The form of landed property with which we are dealing is a *specific* historical form, a form *transformed* by the intervention of capital and the capitalist mode of production, whether the original form was that of feudal landed property or agriculture pursued as a livelihood, in which latter case possession of the land and the soil appears as one of the conditions of production for the immediate producer, or at least as the most advantageous condition, the condition for *his* mode of production to flourish. If the capitalist mode of production always presupposes the expropriation of the workers from the conditions of their labour, in agriculture it presupposes the expropriation of the rural workers from the soil and their subjection to a capitalist who pursues agriculture for the sake of profit. It is thus completely immaterial for our presentation if it is objected that other forms of property and agriculture have existed or still exist besides this one. This reproach can affect only those economists who treat the capitalist mode of production on the land and the form of landed property corresponding to it not as historical categories but as *eternal* ones.

Our own reason for considering the modern form of landed property is simply that we need to consider all the specific relationships of production and exchange that arise from the investment of capital on the land. Without this, our analysis of capital would not be complete. We therefore confine ourselves exclusively to the investment of capital in agriculture proper, i.e., in the production of the main plant crops on which a population lives. We can in fact say wheat specifically, since this is the major means of sustenance for modern nations (nations of developed capitalism). (Instead of agriculture, we might equally well have taken *mining*, since the laws are the same.) It is one of Adam Smith's great services |407| that he showed how the ground-rent for capital applied to the production of products which are not general *means of subsistence*, for example industrial crops (for industrial materials), independent stock-raising, etc., is determined by the ground-rent yielded by capital invested in the production of the main means of subsistence.[1] In fact no further progress has been made in this connection since his time. What we should have to keep in mind as a restriction or addition belongs to the independent treatment of landed property, and not here. We shall therefore deliberately not deal with landed property in so far as this is not related to land devoted to wheat production. Instead, we shall simply refer to it here and there for purposes of illustration.

For the sake of completeness it should be noted that what we understand here by land also includes *water*, etc., in so far as this has an owner and appears as an accessory to the land.

Landed property presupposes that certain persons enjoy the *monopoly* of disposing of particular portions of the globe as exclusive spheres of their private will to the exclusion of all others.[2] Once this is given, it is a question of develop-

1 [Marx discussed this aspect of Adam Smith's work *The Wealth of Nations* in the 1861–63 Manuscripts. See Notebook XII, page 627, of these manuscripts, in English in MECW 31, pp. 564–5. Translator]

2 Nothing could be more curious than Hegel's development of private property in land. Man as a person must give his will *actuality* as the soul of external nature, and hence take possession of this nature as his private property. If this is the distinguishing mark of '*the*' person, of man as person, it would follow that a man must be a landowner if he is to realise himself as a person. Free private property in land – a very *modern* historical product – is for Hegel not a particular *social* relation, but rather a relationship *between man as 'person' and 'nature'*, the 'absolute *right of appropriation* which man has over all "things"'. (Hegel, 1840, § 44 [English: Knox 1967, p. 41].) It is, first of all, clear that the individual person cannot maintain himself as a proprietor by his 'will' alone, vis-à-vis the will of someone else who similarly wants to give himself corporeal actuality in the same fragment of the globe. Quite other things than the 'good' will are needed for this. Moreover, there is absolutely no way of seeing where the 'person' sets a limit to the realisation of his will, whether the existence of his will is

ing the *economic value* of this monopoly, in other words *valorising it* on the basis of the capitalist mode of production. The *legal* power of these persons to use and misuse certain portions of the globe is not in itself decisive, for the use of this power depends entirely on economic preconditions, which are independent of their wills. The legal conception itself means nothing more than that the landowner can behave in relation to the land just as any commodity owner can with his commodities; and this idea – the legal notion of free private landed property – arises in the ancient world only at the time of the dissolution of the organic bonds of society, and in the modern world only with the development of the capitalist mode of production. In Asia, it has simply been imported here and there by Europeans. In the section on primitive accumulation[3] we saw how this mode of production presupposes on the one hand that the direct producers are freed from the position of mere appendages of the soil (in the form of bondsmen, serfs, slaves, etc.) and on the other hand the expropriation of the mass of the people from the land. To that extent, the monopoly of landed property is a *historical precondition* for the capitalist mode of production and remains its permanent *foundation*, as with all previous modes of production based on the exploitation of the masses in one form or the other. But the form of *landed property* which greets the capitalist mode of production at the start does not correspond to this mode. The form that does correspond to it is only created

---

realised in an entire country or in a whole heap of countries. Here Hegel comes unstuck completely. 'Taking possession is always piece-meal in type; I take into possession no more than what I touch with my body. But here comes the second point: external objects extend further than I can grasp. Therefore, whatever I have in my grasp is linked with something else'. (Hegel 1840, §55, addition 34 [English translation, Knox 1967, p. 238].) But this something else is connected in turn with something else again, so that the limit as to how far my will has to pour out into the soil as soul completely vanishes. Hegel goes on to say: 'If I am in possession of something, the intellect immediately draws the inference that it is not only the immediate object in my grasp which is mine but also what is connected with it. At this point *positive law* must enact its statutes, since *nothing further on this topic can be deduced from the concept*'. (Hegel 1840, §55, addition 34 [English translation, Knox 1967, p. 238].) This is an extraordinarily naive confession for the Concept [*Begriff*] to make, and it proves that the Concept, which makes the great blunder right from the start of taking a quite particular legal notion of landed property which belongs to bourgeois society as absolute, 'grasps' nothing of the actual forms [*Gestaltungen*] of this landed property. At the same time, this discussion involves an admission that with the changing needs of social and economic development '*positive law*' can and must change its provisions.

3 [This refers back to the part of the manuscript which became *Capital* Volume I, Part 8. Translator]

by the capitalist mode of production itself, through the subjection of agriculture to capital; and in this way feudal landed property, clan property or small peasant property is transformed into the *economic* form corresponding to this mode of production, however diverse the legal forms of this may be. It is one of the great results of the capitalist mode of production that on the one hand it transforms agriculture from a merely empirical set of procedures, mechanically handed down and practised by the most undeveloped part of society into a conscious scientific application of agronomy, in so far as this is at all possible within the conditions of private property;[4] that on the one hand it completely detaches landed property from relations of lordship and servitude, while on the other hand it completely separates the land as a *condition of labour* from landed property and the landowner, for whom, moreover, this land represents nothing but a certain money tax that his monopoly permits him to extract from the industrial capitalist, the farmer. It undoes the connection to such an extent that the landed proprietor can spend his entire life in Constantinople, while *his own* landed property remains in Scotland. Landed property thus receives its *purely economic form* by the stripping away of all its former political and social

4 Quite conservative agricultural chemists, such as [James Finlay Weir] Johnston (!) for example, admit that private property places insuperable barriers on all sides to a genuinely rational agriculture. So too do writers who are professed defenders of the monopoly of private property across the globe, such as M. Charles Comte, for instance, in a two-volume work which has the defence of private ownership as its special purpose. 'A people', he says, 'cannot attain the degree of well-being and power that their nature grants them unless *each part of the land that sustains them receives the destiny that stands most in harmony with the general interest.* In order to give their riches a substantial development, a single will, and above all an enlightened one would have had to take in hand, if possible, the disposal of each individual piece of its territory, and make each portion contribute towards the prosperity of all the others. But the existence of such a will ... would be incompatible with the division of the land into private holdings ... and with [maintaining] the guarantee of each proprietor's ability to dispose of his wealth in an almost absolute manner' [Comte 1834, p. 228]. Johnston, Comte, etc., in considering the contradiction between property and a rational agronomy, are simply thinking of the cultivation of the land of a single country as a whole. But the way that the cultivation of particular crops depends on fluctuations in market prices and the constant changes in cultivation associated with these price fluctuations, as well as the entire spirit of the capitalist mode of production, which is directed towards the *most immediate* monetary profit, stand in contradiction to agriculture, which has to concern itself with the whole range of permanent conditions of life required by interconnected human generations. A striking example of this is provided by the *forests*, which are managed in the common interest – and even then only to a limited extent – solely in those rare cases when they are *not* private property but are subject to state administration.

embellishments and admixtures that are denounced as uselessly and absurdly superfluous by the industrial capitalists themselves, and by their theoretical spokesmen, in the heat of their struggle with landed property, as we shall see later. The rationalisation of agriculture, on the one hand, which enables it to be pursued for the first time on a *social* scale, and the reduction of landed property to an absurdity, on the other – these are |408| the great services rendered by the capitalist mode of production. These historical services, just like its other historical advances, were purchased first of all through the complete impoverishment of the immediate producers.

Before we come on to our subject itself, a few preliminary observations are still needed, to guard against any misunderstandings.

The presuppositions for the capitalist mode of production are thus as follows: the direct cultivators (the actual cultivators) are *wage-labourers*, employed by a capitalist, the *farmer*, who pursues agriculture simply as a particular field of exploitation of capital, as an investment of his capital in a particular sphere of production. At certain specified dates, e.g., annually, this farmer-capitalist pays the landowner, the proprietor of the land he exploits, a contractually fixed sum of money (just like the interest fixed for the borrower of money capital), for permission to employ his capital in this particular field of production. This sum of money is known as *ground-rent*, irrespective of whether it is paid for agricultural land, building land, mines, fisheries, forests, etc. It is paid for the entire period for which the landowner has contractually lent the land to the farmer, rented it to him. Ground-rent is thus the form in which landed property is economically realised, valorised. We have together here, moreover, and confronting one another, all three classes that make up the economic framework of modern society – the wage-labourers, the people who function as capitalists and the landowners.

Capital may be fixed in the earth, incorporated into it, both in a more transient way, as is the case with improvements of a chemical kind, application of fertilizer, etc., and, more permanently, as with drainage ditches, the provision of irrigation, the levelling of land, farm buildings, etc. I have elsewhere used the expression '*la terre-capital*' to denote capital incorporated in the earth in this way.[5] This is one of the categories of fixed capital. The *interest* on the capital

5 Marx 1847, p. 165 [MECW, 6, 1976, p. 205]. There I make the distinction between *terre-matière* [land as matter] and *terre-capital* [land as capital]. 'The very fact of applying further outlays of capital to land already transformed into means of production increases land as capital without adding anything to land as matter, that is, to the extent of the land ... Land as capital is no more eternal than any other capital ... Land as capital is fixed capital; but fixed capital gets used up just as much as circulating capital.' (ibid.)

incorporated into the earth and the improvements that are thereby made to the soil as an instrument of production *may* form a portion of the rent that is paid by the farmer to the landowner,[6] but it does not constitute ground-rent proper, which is paid for the use of the soil as such, whether this is in its natural state or has been cultivated. In a systematic treatment of landed property, which lies beyond our present scope, this portion of the landowner's income would be presented in detail. Here a few words on the subject must be sufficient. The more temporary capital investments that are involved in the ordinary production process in agriculture are *all made without exception* by the farmer himself. These investments, and even simply cultivation if it is conducted in any kind of rational way – i.e., if it cannot just be reduced to brutal exhaustion of the soil, as was the case for instance with the former slave-holders of South America, against which however the landowning gentlemen insure themselves by clauses in their contracts – improve the soil,[7] increase its product and transform the earth from a mere raw material into earth-capital. A cultivated field is worth more than an uncultivated one of the same natural quality. Even the more permanent fixed capital incorporated into the earth, which is used up over a longer period, is in large measure the work of the farmer and in certain spheres often exclusively so. But as soon as the lease stipulated in the contract has expired – and this is one of the reasons why the landowner seeks to shorten the term of the lease to a minimum, as the capitalist mode of production develops – the improvements made to the land fall to the landowner as his *property*, as an inseparable accident of the substance, the land. When the new lease contract is concluded, the landowner adds interest on the capital incorporated into the earth to the ground-rent proper, whether he leases the land again to the farmer who made the improvements or to another farmer. His rent thus swells; or, if he plans to sell the land – and we shall go on to see how its price is determined – its value has now risen. He does not sell just the land, but rather the improved land, the capital incorporated into the earth, which has cost him nothing. This is one of the secrets – quite apart from the movement of ground-rent as such – |409| of the increasing enrichment of the landowners, the constant rise in their rents and the growing monetary value of their estates as economic development progresses. Thus they put away in their own private purses the result of a social development achieved without their participation –

6 I say '*may* form' because in certain circumstances this interest is governed by the law of ground-rent and may therefore disappear, for instance when there is competition from new lands of great natural fertility.

7 See James Anderson and [Henry Charles] Carey.

fruges consumere nati.[8] But this is at the same time one of the *greatest obstacles to a rational agriculture*, since the farmer avoids all improvements and outlays which are not expected to give a return within the duration of his lease; and we find this denounced as an obstacle over and over again, both in the last century by James Anderson, the true originator of the modern theory of rent, who was also a practising farmer and for his time a significant agronomist, and in our own day by the opponents of the way landed property in England is at present constituted.[9]

This process still does not appear so clearly in agriculture proper as in the use of land for *building houses* (and building in general). A very great part of the land used for building in England is not sold as freehold but leased by the landlords for ninety-nine years, 'or a less time' if possible, for building purposes. When the contractual term has expired, the buildings fall to the landlord, together with the land itself. 'They' (the tenants) 'are bound to deliver up the house at the expiration of the lease, in good tenantable condition, to the great landlord, after having paid an exorbitant ground-rent up to the expiration of the lease. No sooner is the lease expired, than the agent or surveyor will come and examine your house, and see that you put it into good repair, and then take possession of it, and annex it to his lord's domains. The fact is, that if this system is permitted to be in full operation for any considerable period longer,

8 ['They are born to consume the earth's fruits'. From Horace, *Epistles*, I.2, line 27. Translator]

9 A.A. Walton has this to say on the subject: 'All the efforts of the numerous agricultural associations throughout the country must fail to produce any very extensive or really appreciable results in the real advancement of agricultural improvement, so long as such improvements mean in a far higher degree increased value to the estate and rent-roll of the landlord, than bettering the condition of the tenant farmer or the labourer. The farmers, generally, are as well aware as either the landlord or his agent, or even the president of the Agricultural Association, that good drainage, plenty of manure, and good management, combined with the increased employment of labour, to thoroughly cleanse and work the land, will produce wonderful results both in improvement and production. To do all this, however, considerable outlay is required, and the farmers are also aware that however much they may improve the land or enhance its value the landlords will, in the long run, reap the principal benefit, in higher rents and the increased value of their estates ... They are shrewd enough to observe what those orators' (landowners and their agents speaking at 'agricultural dinners') 'by some singular inadvertence, omit to tell them – namely, that the lion's share of any improvements they may make is sure to go into the pockets of the landlords in the long run ... However much the former tenant may have improved the farm, his successor will find that the landlord will always increase the rent in proportion to the increased value of the land from former improvements'. (Walton 1865, pp. 96–7.)

the whole of the house property in the kingdom will be in the hands of the great landlords, as well as the land. The whole of the West End of London, north and south from Temple Bar, may be said to belong to about *half a dozen great landlords*, all let at enormous rents, and where the leases have not quite expired, they are fast falling due. The same may be said either more or less of every town in the kingdom. Nor does this grasping system of exclusion and monopoly stop even here. Nearly the whole of the dock accommodation in our seaport towns is by the same process of usurpation in the hands of the great leviathans of the land'.[10] Under these conditions it is clear that when the last census for England and Wales (the census of 1861, published in 1863) gave the number of house-owners as 36,032, out of a population of 20,066,224, the proportion of owners to the number of houses and the population would shrink tremendously if the big proprietors were put on one side and the small ones on the other.

The example of property in houses (property in buildings) is important: (1) because it clearly shows the distinction between *ground-rent* proper and the *interest* on the fixed capital incorporated into the land, which can form an addition to ground-rent. The interest on the buildings, as on the capital that the farmer incorporates into the soil in the case of agriculture, accrues to the industrial capitalist, the builder or the farmer, for the duration of the lease, and has in and of itself nothing to do with the ground-rent that has to be paid each year on specified dates for the use of the land; (2) because it shows how, in the case of land, the capital of others incorporated into it ultimately falls to the share of the landlord, > in so far as he does not sell the houses together with the land, < and the interest on this swells his rent.

|410| Some writers, partly acting as advocates for landed property against the attacks of the *bourgeois* economists, and partly in an effort to transform the capitalist system of production into a system of 'harmonies' instead of antitheses, as for example Carey, have sought to present ground-rent, the specific economic expression of landed property, as identical with interest. In this way, the opposition between landowners and capitalists would be abolished. The converse method was applied at the inception of the capitalist mode of production. At that time landed property still passed in the popular mind as the original and respectable form of private property, whereas interest on capital was denounced as usury. Sir Dudley North, John Locke, etc., therefore asserted that the interest on capital was a form analogous to ground-rent, just as Turgot derived a justification of interest from the existence of ground-rent. Quite

10 Walton 1865, pp. 92–3.

apart from the fact that ground-rent can and does exist without the addition of any interest on the capital incorporated into the soil, the above writers forget that the landowner not only receives *interest* on *other people's* capital in this way, without its costing him anything, but he gets other people's capital itself for nothing into the bargain. The justification for landed property, as that for all other forms of property of a particular mode of production, is that the mode of production itself has a *historical* (transitory) necessity, and so too therefore do the relations of production and forms of property that arose from it. As we shall see later on, however, landed property is distinguished from the other forms of property by the fact that at a certain level of development it appears to be a superfluous nuisance even from the standpoint of the *capitalist mode of production.*

Ground-rent may also be confused with interest in another form, and its specific character thus misconceived. Ground-rent presents the appearance of a *certain sum of money* that the landowner draws each year from leasing out a piece of the earth. We have already seen how any particular money income can be *capitalised,* i.e., can be considered as the interest on an imaginary capital. If the average interest is five percent, for example, an annual ground-rent of £200 may be viewed as the interest on a capital of £4,000. It is the *ground-rent as capitalised* in this way that forms the *purchase price* or *value of the land,* a category that is *prima facie* irrational, in the same way that the price of labour is irrational, since the earth is not the product of labour, and thus has *no value.* On the other hand, however, a genuine relation of production lies hidden within this irrational form. If a capitalist buys a piece of land for £4,000 that yields an annual rent of £200, he draws the average annual interest of five percent on the £4,000 in just the same way as if he had invested this capital in interest-bearing securities or had lent it out directly at five percent interest. There is a valorisation of a capital of £4,000 at five percent. On this assumption he would have replaced the purchase price of his property in twenty years by the receipts from it. In England, therefore, the purchase price of landed estates is reckoned at so and so many 'years' purchase', which is simply another expression for the capitalisation of the ground-rent. It is in actual fact not the purchase price of the land, but rather that of the ground-rent which it yields, reckoned according to the prevailing rate of interest. This capitalisation of the rent, however, presupposes the rent itself, whereas the rent cannot be conversely derived and explained from its own capitalisation. The presupposition from which we have to proceed is rather the rent's *existence,* which is independent of the sale.

It therefore follows that, taking the ground-rent as a *constant* magnitude, the price of land will rise or fall in inverse ratio to the rate of interest. If the standard rate of interest were to fall from five to four percent, an annual ground-rent of £200 would represent the annual valorisation of a capital of £5,000 instead of one of £4,000, and so the price of the same piece of land would rise from £4,000 to £5,000, or from twenty years' purchase to twenty-five. In the converse case, the converse would hold. |411| This movement in the price of land is governed simply by the rate of interest and is independent of the movement of ground-rent itself. But since we have seen that the rate of profit has a tendency to fall as social development proceeds, and so too therefore does the rate of interest, in as much as this is governed by the profit rate; and since we have also seen that even leaving aside the rate of profit, the interest rate has a tendency to fall as a result of the growth of money capital for loan, it follows that the price of land has a *tendency to rise*, independently of the movement of ground-rent and the price of the products of the soil, of which ground-rent is one part.

The confusion between ground-rent itself and the form of interest that it assumes for the *purchaser* of the land – a confusion that is based on complete ignorance of the nature of ground-rent – cannot fail to lead to the most peculiar and incorrect conclusions. Since landed property is seen in all older countries as a particularly superior form of property, and the purchase of land moreover as a particularly secure capital investment, the rate of interest at which ground-rent is bought generally stands somewhat lower than is the case with other long-term capital investments, so that the buyer of land may receive, say, only four percent of his purchase price, while he would otherwise receive five percent for the same capital; or, and this comes to the same thing, he pays more capital for the ground-rent than he would for the same annual money income in other investments. M. Thiers, in his generally abysmal pamphlet entitled *la Propriété* (it is the printed text of the speech he delivered against Proudhon in the French National Assembly in 1848), concludes from this that ground-rent is low, whereas all that this shows is the high level of its purchase price.

The fact that the capitalised ground-rent presents the appearance of the price or value of the land, so that the earth is bought or sold just like any other commodity, provides some apologists with a justification for landed property; the buyer has paid an equivalent for it, as with any other commodity, and the greater part of landed property has changed hands in this way. The same justification would then apply also to slavery, since for the slaveowner who has paid cash for his slaves, the product of their labour simply represents the interest on the capital invested in their purchase. To derive a justification for the existence of ground-rent from a purchase and sale is nothing more than justifying its existence in terms of its existence.

Important as it is for the scientific analysis of *ground-rent* – i.e., the autonomous, specific economic form of landed property on the basis of the capitalist mode of production – to consider it in pure form and free from all the admixtures that blur and falsify this category, it is just as important for understanding the practical effects of landed property, and even for a theoretical insight into a mass of facts that contradict the concept and nature of ground-rent and yet appear as its *modes of existence*, to know the elements from which these obscurities in the theory arise.

In practice, everything that the farmer pays to the landowner in the form of the lease-price for permission to cultivate the soil appears as *ground-rent*. Whatever the components out of which this tribute has been put together, and whatever the sources from which it might derive, it has in common with ground-rent proper that the monopoly to a piece of the earth enables the so-called landowner to exact a tribute, to put a price on it. What this has in common with ground-rent proper is that it determines the price of land, which, as shown above, is nothing but the capitalised revenue from the lease of the land.

We have already seen that the interest on capital incorporated into the soil may form an exotic component of the ground-rent of this kind, a component that must form an addition to the total rental of a country that grows continuously as economic development progresses. But, leaving aside this interest, it is possible for the lease-price to include either partly, or in certain cases entirely, such as when ground-rent proper is completely absent and the land thus actually valueless, a hidden deduction from average profit, |412| normal wages, or both together. This part, whether of profit or of wages, appears here in the shape of *ground-rent* because instead of accruing to the industrial capitalist or the wage-labourer, which would be normal, it is paid to the landowner in the form of the lease-price. Economically speaking, neither part forms ground-rent; but in practice it forms income for the landowner, an economic valorisation of his monopoly, just as much as genuine ground-rent does, and it has the same effect in determining the price of land.

We are not referring here to the conditions in which *ground-rent*, the mode of landed property corresponding to the capitalist mode of production, has a formal existence even though the capitalist mode of production itself does not exist, the tenant farmer himself is not an industrial capitalist, and his manner of farming is not a capitalist one. This is how it is in *Ireland*, for example. Here the tenant farmer is generally a small peasant. What he pays the landowner for his lease often absorbs not only a portion of his profit, i.e., his own surplus labour, to which he has a right as the owner of his own instruments of labour, but also a portion of the normal wage, which he would receive for the same amount of labour under other conditions. The landowner, moreover, who does nothing at all here to improve the soil, expropriates from him the small capital which he incorporates into the soil for the most part by his own labour, just as a usurer would do in similar conditions. Only the usurer would at least risk his own capital in the operation.[11]

We say nothing of the exceptional conditions in which, even in countries where the capitalist mode of production prevails, the landowner can extort a high rent which bears no relation to the product of the soil, as for example with the leasing of small plots of land to *factory workers* in the English manufacturing districts, either for little gardens or for amateur cultivation in their spare time.[12]

What we are talking about here is agricultural rent in countries where the capitalist mode of production is developed. Among English farmers, for example, there is a number of small capitalists who are destined or compelled to apply their capital in agriculture, as farmers, owing to their upbringing, training, tradition, competition and other circumstances. They are forced to be content with a smaller than average profit and to part with a portion of this to the landowner in the form of rent. This is the only condition on which they are permitted to invest their capital on the land, in agriculture. Since landowners everywhere exert a major influence on legislation, and in England even a predominant one, this influence can be exploited to cheat the entire class of farmers. The Corn Laws of 1815, for instance – a tax on bread by their own admission imposed on the country in order to ensure the idle landowners the continuance of rent receipts that had grown abnormally during the Anti-Jacobin War[13] – had the effect, apart from a few years of exceptionally good harvests, of keeping the prices of agricultural products above the level to which they would have fallen under a system of free corn import. But they did not have the result of keeping prices at the levels decreed as *normal* by the legislating landowners, in the sense that these prices formed the legal limit for the import of foreign corn. Leasehold contracts were none the less concluded under the impression

11 It is this continuing robbery that forms the subject of the dispute over the 'Irish Tenants' Rights Bill'. What is demanded in this case is essentially that the landowner who gives a tenant farmer notice to quit should be forced to compensate him for the improvements he has made to the land or the capital he has incorporated into it. Lord Palmerston's usual cynical reply to this is: 'The House of Commons is a house of landed proprietors'. [Marx wrote about Irish tenants' rights in an article for the *New York Daily Tribune*, published on 11 July 1853. See 'The Indian Question – Irish Tenant Right', in MECW 12, 1979, pp. 157–62. Translator]

12 From the *Reports of the Inspectors of Factories*. [Marx meant to refer to *Public Health Report* 1865, pp. 10, 11, 212 and 249.]

13 Parry etc. [Parry 1816, p. 100; MECW 34, 1994, pp. 320–1.]

of these normal prices. As soon as the illusion collapsed, a new law was passed with new normal prices, which were as much the expression of landed property's greedy imagination as the old ones had been. The farmers were cheated in this way from 1815 right up to the 1830s. Hence during the whole of this era the constant theme was '*agricultural distress*'. Hence one saw during this period the expropriation and ruin of an entire generation of farmers and their replacement by a new class of capitalists.[14]

A far more general and important fact, however, is the reduction of wages below their normal average for agricultural labourers properly so-called, so that a *part of the worker's wage* is deducted from him, to form a component of the lease-price and thus accrue to the landowner instead of the agricultural day-labourer under the *guise of ground-rent*. This is the general rule in England and Scotland, for example, with the exception of a few favourably situated counties. The reports of the proceedings of the Parliamentary *Committees of Inquiry* into the level of wages paid in England before and after the introduction of the Corn Laws – up till now the most valuable contribution to the history of wages in the nineteenth century, and almost unexploited, besides being at the same time a pillory which the English aristocracy and bourgeoisie erected for themselves – proved convincingly and beyond all doubt that the high rents and corresponding rise in land prices during the Anti-Jacobin War were due in part quite simply to a deduction from wages and the forcing down of them even below the physical minimum, i.e., to the payment to the landowner of a part of the normal wage of labour. Various circumstances had made this operation possible, among others the depreciation of money and the manipulation of the Poor Laws in the country districts, at the very same time as the incomes of the farmers rose enormously and the landowners enriched themselves fabulously.[15] Indeed, one of the principal arguments in defence of the Corn Laws, on the part of the farmers as well as the landowners, was that it would be physically impossible to lower the wages of the agricultural day-labourers *any further*. This situation has not fundamentally altered, and in England, as in all the European countries, a part of the normal wage still goes into ground-rent just as before. When the Earl of Shaftesbury, then Lord Ashley, one of the philanthropic aristocrats, who was extraordinarily moved by the condition of the

14 See the *Prize Essays* [*Three Prize Essays* 1842]. Meanwhile the Corn Laws still held prices up to an artificially high level. This favoured the better-off farmers. They profited from the stationary condition in which the protective tariff kept the great mass of farmers, who, with or without good reason, placed their faith in the exceptional average price.

15 *The Economist* [Marx did not complete this reference.]

English factory workers, threw himself into the Ten Hours agitation as the workers' parliamentary spokesman, the representatives of the industrialists took their revenge by publishing some statistics about the wages of agricultural labourers in some villages that belonged to him. These statistics showed clearly that a portion of the ground-rent received by this philanthropist consisted simply of the plunder that his tenants extracted from the wages of those labourers. The industrialists' publication is also interesting in as much as the facts it contains are worthy of a place alongside the worst of the revelations of the Committees of 1814 and 1815.[16] Whenever circumstances compel a temporary rise in the wages of agricultural labourers, the cry resounds from the farmers that the raising of wages to their normal level, such as obtains in other branches of industry, is impossible and would inevitably ruin them without a simultaneous reduction in ground-rent. It is thereby *admitted* that in the name of ground-rent the farmers make a deduction from wages and hand this over to the landowner. Between 1849 and 1859, for instance, agricultural wages rose in England in consequence of a combination of overwhelming circumstances, such as the exodus from Ireland, which cut off the supply of agricultural labourers from there; the exceptional absorption of the agricultural population by manufacturing industry; the wartime demand for soldiers; an exceptional emigration to Australia, California and other parts of the United States; and other reasons that we shall not go into any further here. At the same time, with the exception of the bad harvests of 1854–6, average cereal prices fell by more than 16 percent during this period. The farmers clamoured for a reduction in rents. In some cases they did obtain this. By and large, however, their demand did not meet with success. They took refuge |414| in a reduction of production costs, including the massive introduction of steam-engines and new machinery, which partly replaced horses and drove these out of economic use, but partly also entered into competition with the agricultural labourers, and thus brought about an artificial surplus population among them, hence a fresh fall in wages. And all this happened despite an overall relative decline in the agricultural population during this decade, compared with the growth in the total population, and even an *absolute* decline in the agricultural population in some purely agricultural districts.[17] [Henry] Fawcett, at that time Professor of Political Economy at Cam-

---

16 [The reference here is to 'Wages of Agricultural Labourers (From the Morning Chronicle)' in *The Economist*, 29 March 1845 (Marx 1976, p. 832). Translator]

17 See a paper read in 1859 by Mr. John C[halmers] Morton at the London Society of Arts on 'The Forces used in Agriculture'. Mr. Morton gives here the returns from bills and other authentic documents, which he collected from about one hundred farmers residing in twelve Scottish and thirty-five English counties.

bridge, spoke in the same terms to the Social Science Congress on 12 October 1865: 'The labourers were beginning to emigrate, and the farmers were already beginning to complain that they would not be able to pay such *high rents* as they have been accustomed to pay, because labour was becoming dearer in consequence of emigration'. Here an appreciation of land is thus directly identified with a depreciation of wages. And in so far as the high level of land prices is conditioned by this factor which swells rents, a high price of land is identical with a low price of labour. 'The *lease-price* rises' (in France) 'because the prices of bread, wine, meat, vegetables and fruit rise, while the price of labour remains stationary. If the elderly go through their fathers' accounts, which takes us back approximately one hundred years, they will find that at that time the price of a working day in rural France was exactly the same as it is today. The price of meat, however, has tripled since then ... Who is the victim of this revolution? Is it the rich man, the owner of the farm, or the poor man who works it? ... The rise in rents is the sign of a public disaster' (Rubichon 1837, p. 101).

We must further keep in mind, in considering the *forms of appearance* of ground-rent, i.e., of the lease-price that is paid to the landowner under the heading of *ground-rent* for the use of the soil, whether for productive purposes or for purposes of consumption, that the *prices* of things which have no *value* in and for themselves,[18] i.e., they are not the product of labour, like land, or at least cannot be reproduced by labour, such as antiques etc., may be determined by quite fortuitous combinations of circumstances. For a thing to be sold, it simply has to be capable of being monopolised and alienated.

The example of rent as a result of deduction from average profit on the one hand and from average wages on the other.

It has been noticed that in many districts '*rent* for large farms' is 'smaller than for smaller ones', because 'the competition is usually greater for the latter than for the former, and as few small farmers are able to *turn their attention to any other business* than that of farming, their anxiety to get a suitable occupation leads them in many instances to *give more rent* than their judgment can approve of'. (John L. Morton, land agent, agricultural engineer, etc., 1858, p. 116.)

|415| The same Morton, however, indicates that this distinction is diminishing in England, > which he explains by referring to the greater and greater influx of men 'who have made their capital in commercial or manufacturing business' (ibid.) < 'I believe', he adds, 'that *emigration*, precisely among the class of small

---

18 > See Wakefield. [A reference to Edward Gibbon Wakefield's idea of setting an 'artificial price' for uncultivated land in the Colonies. See Marx 1976, p. 938. Translator] <

farmers, has much to do with it'. > This situation, says Morton, is now 'changing rapidly [and there are more offerers for large than for small farms]'. Thus 'Mr. Grey, of Dilston in Northumberland, states that for five farms he let in 1855, he had offers [as follows]:

1st.	At a *rental* of £2,000	10 offers,
2nd.	1,305	6 offers,
3rd.	1,050	7 offers,
4th.	256	6 offers,
5th.	180	2 offers'. (Ibid.)

< Morton also gives an example where the rent evidently includes a deduction from the wage of the farmer himself and hence still more certainly of the men he employs. This is the case with farms of under 70 to 80 acres, which cannot keep *two pairs* of horses – two plough teams. 'Unless he' (the tenant) 'works with his own lands as laboriously as any labourer, his farm will not keep him. If he entrusts the performance of his work to workmen, while he continues merely to observe them, the chances are that at no distant period he will find he is unable to pay his rent' (Morton 1858, p. 118). Morton concludes from this that 'unless the tenants in the district are very poor' the minimum for a farm should be 70 acres, 'so that the tenant can keep two or three horses' (ibid.)

Here is a sample of the extraordinary wisdom of Monsieur L[éonce] de Lavergne (*Membre de l'Institut* et *de la Société de l'Agriculture*): in his *Économie rurale de l'Angleterre* (quoted from the English translation, Lavergne 1855), he makes the following comparison of the annual benefits derived from cattle, which *labour* in France *but not in England* (where they are replaced by horses):

France		**United Kingdom**	
Milk	£4 million	Milk	£16 million
Meat	£16 million	Meat	£20 million
Work	£8 million		
Total	£28 million	Total	£36 million.[19]

19 [Lavergne 1855, p. 42. Translator]

But in this case the higher product is simply because, as he himself points out, milk in England is as dear again as in France, while he assumes the same price for meat in both countries (Lavergne 1855, p. 35). The English milk product would thus be reduced to £8 million and the total product to £28 million, as in France. It is a bit much for Monsieur Lavergne to take into account at the same time both the quantities produced and the *differences in price*, so that, if England produces certain articles *dearer* than France, this appears as an example of English agricultural superiority, whereas at most it means a bigger profit for farmers and landlords.

The following passages from his work show that M. Lavergne is not only acquainted with the economic successes of English agriculture, but also *shares* the *prejudices* of English farmers and landlords:

'One great drawback attends cereals generally ... they exhaust the soil which bears them' (Lavergne 1855, p. 48). M. Lavergne not only believes that other crops do *not* do this; he believes that fodder and root crops (artificial grass and roots) *enrich* the soil: 'Forage plants derive from the atmosphere the principal elements of their growth, *while they give to the soil more than they take from it*; thus both directly, and by their conversion into animal manure, contributing in two ways to repair the mischief done by cereals and exhausting crops generally; one principle, therefore, is that they should at least *alternate with these crops*; in this consists the Norfolk rotation' (Lavergne 1855, pp. 50 and 51.)

No wonder then that M. Lavergne, believing these fairy stories of the English country mind, should also believe that the wages of English agricultural labourers have lost their previous abnormality since the repeal of the Corn Laws in 1848. See what was already said on this subject in Book One, Chapter Five,[20] > where we examined the average price or minimum and the average of wages. < We may also quote what Mr. John Bright said in his speech in Birmingham on 13 December 1865. After speaking of the 'five million families who are entirely *unrepresented* [in Parliament]', he continued: 'There is among them one million, or rather more than one million, in the United Kingdom, who are classed in the unfortunate list of paupers. There is another million just above pauperism, but always in peril lest they should become paupers. Their condition and prospects are not more favourable than that. Now look

---

20 [This refers to a chapter on the accumulation of capital in a part of the 1863–65 Manuscript that has not been preserved. But the elements of it later became *Capital*, Volume I, Chapter Twenty-Five, Section 5.e (pp. 828–53 in the English translation, 1976). Translator]

to the ignorant and lower strata of this portion of the community. Look to their abject condition, to their poverty, to their suffering, to their utter hopelessness of any good. Why, in the United States – even in the Southern States during the reign of slavery – every negro had an idea that there was a day of jubilee for him. But to these people – to this class of the lowest strata in this country – I am here to state that there is neither the belief of anything better nor scarcely an aspiration after it. Have you read a paragraph which lately appeared in the newspapers about John Cross, a *Dorsetshire* labourer? He worked six days in the week, had an excellent character from his employer for whom he had worked twenty-four years at the rate of eight shillings per week. John Cross had a family of seven children to provide for out of these wages in his hovel ... for a feeble wife and an infant child. He took – legally I believe he stole – a wooden hurdle of the value of sixpence. For this offence he was tried before the magistrates and sentenced to fourteen or twenty days' imprisonment ... I can tell you that many thousands of cases like that of John Cross are to be found throughout the country, and especially in the South, and that their condition is such that hitherto the most anxious investigator has been unable to solve the mystery as to how they keep body and soul together. Now cast your eye over the country and look at these five millions of families and the desperate condition of this stratum of them. Is it not true that the unenfranchised nation may be said to toil and toil, knowing almost no rest? Compare it with the ruling class – but if I do I shall be charged with communism ... But compare this great toiling |416| and unenfranchised nation with the section who may be considered the governing classes. Behold its weariness – for there is weariness among them, but it is the weariness of satiety – and see how they rush from place to place, as it were to discover some new pleasure' (*Morning Star*, 14 December 1865.)

We shall go on to show how *surplus labour* and hence *surplus product* in general are confused with *rent*, this specific, *quantitatively and qualitatively determined portion of the surplus product* (at least on the basis of the capitalist mode of production). The *indigenous* basis of surplus labour as such, i.e., a natural condition without which this is impossible, is that nature provides the necessary means of subsistence – whether in products of the land, animal or vegetable, or in fisheries, etc. – with the application of an amount of labour-time that does not swallow up the entire working day. This *indigenous productivity of agricultural labour* (and here we include simple gathering, hunting, fishing, stockraising) is the basis of all surplus-value; just as *all* labour is originally first directed towards the production or the getting hold of food (its appropriation). (Animals also provide pelts for warmth in cold climates; there are also natural cave-dwellings, etc.)

The same confusion between surplus product and ground-rent is expressed in a different way by Mr. Dove, for example.[21] Originally, agricultural labour and manufacturing labour are not separate; the second is an appendage of the first. The *surplus labour* (and the *surplus product*) of the agricultural family, clan or commune, etc., comprises both agricultural and industrial labour. The two go hand in hand. (How would agriculture be possible, without agricultural implements? Weaving, spinning, etc., are agricultural side-occupations.) We have already shown that just as the labour of the individual worker breaks down into necessary and surplus labour, so the *total labour of the working class* can be divided in such a way that the part that produces the entire means of subsistence needed by the working class (including the means of production required for the production of those means of subsistence) performs the *necessary labour* for the society. The labour performed by the whole remaining part of the working class can be considered as *surplus labour*, but the necessary labour in no way includes *just* agricultural labour; it also includes the labour that produces all other products that > satisfy the remaining primary needs < (it produces all the products that necessarily enter the worker's average consumption). Some, moreover, perform *only necessary labour*, because others perform *only surplus labour*, and vice versa. This is simply a division of labour between them. It is the same with the division of labour between agricultural and industrial workers in general. The purely manufacturing character of one section's labour is matched by the abstractly agricultural labour of the other. (This abstract agricultural labour is by no means of *natural and spontaneous origin*, but is rather itself a product of *social development*, and it corresponds to a definite stage of production.) Just as a part of the agricultural labour is realised in products that either serve purely for luxury or form the raw materials for manufacturing, but in no way go into *foodstuffs*, at least not foodstuffs for the masses, so on the other hand a part of manufacturing labour is realised in products that serve as necessary means of consumption for agricultural and non-agricultural workers alike. It is wrong to conceive this manufacturing labour – from the social standpoint – as surplus labour. It is in part just as much 'necessary' labour as is [the necessary portion of] agricultural labour. It is also simply the *autonomised* form of a part of the labour that was previously linked and entwined with agricultural labour, and it is a necessary complement to agricultural labour in its 'pure' form. (Considering this from the physical aspect, 500 mechanised weavers, for example, produce a far higher degree of *surplus cloth* than one, i.e., much more than is required for their own clothing.)

21 [Dove 1854, pp. 264 and 273. Translator]

|417| There are three major errors which obscure the analysis of ground-rent and are to be avoided in dealing with it.

(1) The confusion between the various *forms of rent* which correspond to different levels of development of the social production process.

Whatever the specific form of rent may be, what all its types have in common is the fact that the appropriation of *rent* is the economic form in which *landed property* is realised, and that ground-rent in turn presupposes landed property, the ownership of particular pieces of the globe by particular individuals – whether the proprietor is a person representing the community, as in Asia, Egypt, etc.; whether this landed property is simply an accidental accompaniment of the property that certain persons have in the persons of the immediate producers, as in the systems of serfdom and slavery; whether it is pure private property that non-producers have in nature, a simple ownership title to land; or finally, whether it is a relationship to the land which, as with colonists and small peasant proprietors, appears as directly implied, given their isolated and not socially developed labour, in the appropriation and production of the products of particular pieces of land by the direct producers.

This *common character* of the different forms of *rent* – as the economic realisation of *landed property*, the legal fiction by virtue of which various individuals have exclusive possession of particular parts of the globe – leads people to overlook the distinctions.

(2) All *ground-rent* is *surplus-value* and *surplus labour* (in its more undeveloped form of *rent in kind* it is still a direct *surplus product*). Hence the error that the rent corresponding to the capitalist mode of production, which is always an *excess over and above the profit*, i.e., over and above a portion of commodity value that itself consists of *surplus-value* (surplus labour) – that this particular and specific component of *surplus-value* can be explained simply by explaining the general conditions of existence for surplus-value and profit. These conditions are, first, that the direct producers must work for more *time* than is required to produce and reproduce their own labour-power, to reproduce themselves. They must perform some kind of *surplus labour*. That is the *subjective* condition. But the *objective* condition is that the natural conditions are such that *a part of their available labour-time* is sufficient to reproduce and maintain them as producers; in other words that the production of their necessary means of subsistence does not consume their entire labour-power. Natural fertility sets one limit here, as a point of departure or basis. The development of the social productivity of their labour sets the other limit. Looked at more closely, since the production of *foodstuffs* is the very first condition of their life and of any production at all, the labour employed in this production, i.e., *agricultural* labour in the broadest economic sense, must be sufficiently fruitful to

prevent the entire available labour from being absorbed in the production of foodstuffs for the immediate producers, so that agricultural surplus labour and hence an agricultural surplus product are possible. To take this further, the total agricultural labour – necessary and surplus – of one section of society must be sufficient to produce the necessary foodstuffs for the entire society, i.e., also for the non-agricultural workers; this great *division of labour* between cultivators and manufacturers must be possible, and similarly that between the cultivators who produce foodstuffs and those who produce raw materials, vegetable or animal. Although the labour of the direct producers of foodstuffs, taken by itself, breaks down into necessary and surplus labour, in relation *to society* it thus represents *only* the *necessary* labour required for the production of foodstuffs. The same thing is the case, incidentally, with any division of labour *within society*, as distinct from the division of labour within the individual workshop. It is the labour *necessary* for the production of particular articles – for the satisfaction of a particular social need for particular articles. If this division is proportional, the products of the different groups will be sold at their values (later on, at the prices of production) or at prices which are modifications of these values, which are however determined by general laws. This is in fact the *law of value* as it makes itself felt, not in relation to the individual commodities or articles but rather to the total products at a given time of particular *spheres of social production* autonomised by the division of labour; so that not only is no more labour-time spent on each individual commodity than necessary, but out of the total social labour-time only the proportionate quantity *needed* is devoted to the *various groups* of commodity. *Use-value* remains a condition. But whereas in the case of the individual commodity this use-value depends on its satisfying in and of itself a social need, in the case of the mass social product it depends on its adequacy to the *quantitatively specific social need* for each particular kind of product and therefore on the proportional division of labour between these various spheres of production in accordance with these social needs, which are quantitatively circumscribed. (This point should be introduced in connection with the distribution of capital between the various spheres of production.) The *social need*, i.e., the use-value measured on a *social* scale, here appears decisive for the *quota of total social labour-time* that falls to the share of the various particular spheres of production. But this is simply the same law that is already exhibited by the individual commodity, i.e., that its *use-value* is the precondition of its exchange-value. It is a point that bears on the relation between necessary and surplus labour only in as much as an imbalance in this proportion means that the commodity value, and therefore also the surplus-value contained in it, cannot be realised. For example, the proportion of cotton goods produced may be too high even though the labour-time realised in this total product is simply that needed under the given conditions. But too much of society's overall labour has been spent on this particular branch, and so a portion of the product is relatively useless. The total product is therefore sold as if only the necessary proportion had been produced. This *quantitative barrier* to the *quota of social labour-time* devoted to the various particular spheres of production is simply a further developed expression of the law of value in general; even though *necessary* labour-time takes on a different meaning here. Only such and such a quantity of this is *necessary* for the satisfaction of the social need. The limit in this case is brought to light through the *use-value*. Under the given conditions of production, society can spend only *so much* of its total labour-time on one particular kind of product.

But the subjective and objective conditions of surplus-value and surplus labour in general have nothing to do with the particular form, whether this is profit or rent. They apply to surplus-value as such, whatever particular form this may assume. They therefore do not explain *rent*.

(3) A particular *peculiarity* which arises very clearly with the *economic valorisation of landed property*, that is to say the development of *ground-rent*, is that its *amount* > (irrespective of who receives it) < is in no way determined by the action of its recipient, but rather by a development of social labour which is independent of him and in which he plays no part. This is why something that is *common* to all branches of production and their products on the basis of commodity production, and to capitalist production in particular, which is *commodity production* in its entirety, is easily conceived as a peculiar property of rent (and of the product of agriculture in general).

The value of rent (and with it the value of land) rises in the course of social development, as a result of the labour of the whole of society. Not only does the market and demand for agricultural products grow, but also the demand for the land itself grows directly, since it is a condition of production competed for by all possible branches of business, including non-agricultural ones. More precisely, rent, and with it the value of land (confining ourselves simply to *agricultural rent* proper) develops along with the *market* for the products of the land and hence along with the *growth in the non-agricultural* |417a| *population*; it increases with their needs and their demand both for *foodstuffs* and for *raw materials*. It lies in the nature of the capitalist mode of production that it constantly reduces the agricultural population in relation to the *non-agricultural* population, because *here* [in industry] the growth of constant capital in relation to variable is linked with an *absolute* growth in variable capital (even if a *relative* decline in relation to constant); while *there*, in agriculture, the variable capital required for the cultivation of a particular piece of land declines *absolutely* and therefore grows only in so far as new land is cultivated, which however presupposes in turn a still greater growth in the non-agricultural population.

In actual fact, however, the same thing happens not just to the products of agriculture but to all other products produced on the basis of *commodity production* and its absolute form, the *capitalist mode of production.*

These products are *commodities*, use-values which possess an exchange-value, and particularly one that *can be realised*, converted into money, only and exclusively to the extent to which other commodities form an equivalent for them and other products confront them as *commodities* and as values; to the extent, therefore, to which they are not produced as direct means of subsistence for their producers themselves but as *commodities*, as products which only become use-values > for their producers < by being transformed into exchange-value (money), by their alienation. The market for these commodities develops by way of the social division of labour; the *separation* between different productive labours transforms their respective products reciprocally into commodities, into equivalents for one another, making them serve one another reciprocally as *markets*. This is in no way something peculiar to the products of agriculture.

Rent can develop as *money-rent* only on the basis of commodity production, and particularly of capitalist production, and it develops to the same extent to which *agricultural production* becomes commodity production, i.e., the extent to which *non-agricultural production* undergoes an independent development in relation to it; for it is to this extent and only to this extent that the product of agriculture becomes a commodity and a value. To the same extent that commodity production and hence the *production of value* develops with capitalist production, so too there develops the production of *surplus-value* and *surplus product*. But in the same measure as the latter develops, there develops in landed property the ability to *capture a growing portion of this surplus-value* by way of its monopoly of the earth and hence to raise the value of its rent and the price of the land itself. It is the capitalist himself who has the active function in the development of this surplus-value and surplus product. The landowner has only to seize a portion of the surplus product and the surplus-value that increases without any effort on his part. This is the *peculiarity* of his position, not the fact that the value of the agricultural products, and hence of the land itself, is constantly growing as the market for these expands, demand increases and with it the world of commodities that confronts the products of agriculture – in other words the number of *non-agricultural* commodity producers and the scale of non-agricultural commodity production. Since this happens without his assistance, however, it appears to the landowner as something unique that the mass of value, the mass of surplus-value, and the transformation of a portion of this surplus-value into rent depends on the social production process, on the development of commodity production in general. That is why Dove, for example, would like to explain rent on this basis.[22] He says that rent does not depend on the size of the agricultural product but rather on its *value*; this however depends on the size and productivity of the non-agricultural population. But it is also true to say for any other product that it only develops as a commodity in part with the volume and in part with the diversity of the *series of other commodities* that form equivalents for it. We have already shown this in our general presentation of value. On the one hand, the exchangeability of a product depends entirely on the multifariousness of the different commodities that exist outside it. On the other hand, |417b| the *quantity* in which it can itself be produced as a commodity depends in turn on this exchangeability.

No producer, neither the manufacturer nor the cultivator, considered in isolation, produces a *value* or a commodity. Their product becomes a value and a commodity only in a specific social context. *Firstly*, in so far as it appears as an expression of *social labour*, and therefore *their own labour-time* appears as part of the general *social labour-time*; *secondly*, where this social character of their labour appears as a *social character* impressed on their product, in its money character and its general *exchangeability* as determined by its price.

Thus if, *on the one hand*, instead of explaining rent, it is surplus-value or in a still more blinkered conception surplus product in general that is being explained, then, *on the other hand*, the blunder is committed of ascribing a character that applies to all products as *commodities* and values exclusively to the products of agriculture. The superficiality is heightened when a retreat is made from the general determination of value to the *realisation* of a particular commodity value. A commodity can realise its *value* only in the process of circulation, and whether and to what extent it does realise this depends on the market conditions at the time.

Thus it is not peculiar to rent that agricultural products *develop as values*, i.e., that they confront other commodities as commodities themselves and that the non-agricultural products confront them as commodities, nor that they develop as *particular* expressions of *social labour*. What is peculiar is that with the conditions in which agricultural products develop as values (commodities), and the conditions of realisation of their values, *landed property* also develops the *power* to appropriate a growing part of these values created without its assistance, and a growing part of the surplus-value is transformed into rent.

---

22 [Dove 1854, p. 279. Translator]

|418| (c) Absolute Ground-Rent

> (*Differential rent* should be treated before this section, under b), and in examining absolute ground-rent, under c), we presuppose this prior treatment.

The transition from differential rent to absolute rent is to be made in the following way:

< In our analysis of differential rent, we proceeded from the premise that the worst land pays *no ground-rent*, or, to put it more generally, land pays ground-rent only when the *individual production price* of its product is *below* the production price that governs the market, giving rise to a *surplus profit* that is transformed into rent. The first thing to note here is that the law of differential rent, as differential rent, is entirely independent of the correctness or incorrectness of that premise.

If we call the general production price that governs the market P, then, for the product of the worst type of land, P coincides with its individual (real) production price; i.e., the *price* of the product pays for the constant and variable capital consumed in the course of production plus the average profit (= profit of enterprise plus interest.) Rent here is zero. The individual production price of the next better type of land, land of the second class, (II) = P′ and P is greater than P′, i.e., P pays for more than the actual production price of the product of land in Class II. Now let $P - P' = \delta$; δ, the excess of P over P′, is thus the surplus profit made by the farmer in Class II. This is transformed into rent, to be paid to the landowner. For the third class of land, let the actual production price be P″, so that $P - P'' = 2\delta$; this 2δ is now transformed into rent. Similarly, for the fourth class the individual production price is P‴, and $P - P''' = 3\delta$, transferred into rent, and so on. Let us now assume that the premise of zero rent for land in the first class, Class I, the price of its product being P + 0, is incorrect. Instead, say that it pays a rent, = r. Two things then follow.

Firstly, the price of the product of Class I land would not be governed by its *price of production*, but would contain a *surplus* over and above this; it would be P + r. For, assuming the capitalist mode of production in its normal condition, i.e., assuming that the surplus r that the farmer pays to the landowner is neither a deduction from wages nor from the average profit of capital, he can pay it only by selling his product *above* its price of production, so that it would yield him a *surplus profit* if he did not have to part with this surplus to the landowner in the form of rent. The governing market price of the total product on the market from all types of land would then not be the price of production that capital generally yields in all spheres of production, i.e., a price equal to the outlays plus the average profit, it would be this production price plus the rent, P + r rather than just P. For the price of the product of Class I land always represents the limit of the governing general market price, the price at which the *total product* can be supplied, and to this extent it governs the price of this total product.

Secondly, however, in this case, even though the general price of the product of the land would be basically modified, the law of differential rent would not in any way be thereby abolished. For if the price of the product of Class I, and therefore the general market price, was P + r, the price for Classes II, III, IV, etc., would be P + r too. But since for Class II, $P - P' = \delta$, $(P + r) - (P' + r)$ would also $= \delta$; and similarly for Class III, $P - P'' = (P + r) - (P'' + r) = 2\delta$; for Class IV, $P - P''' = (P + r) - (P''' + r) = 3\delta$, etc. The differential rent would thus be the same as before, and would be governed by the same law, even though the rent contained an element independent of this law and underwent a general rise together with the price of the product. It follows from this that whatever the rent on the least fertile types of land might be, not only is the law of differential rent independent of it, but the only way to grasp the true character of *differential rent* itself is to set the rent for Type I land at zero. Whether it really is zero, or greater than zero, is immaterial as far as the differential rent is concerned, and does not need to be taken into account.

The law of differential rent is thus unaffected by the result of the following analysis.

If we now investigate more closely the basis of the assumption that the product of the poorest land, Type I, pays no rent, we get the following result. If the market price of the product, say corn, reaches such a level that an additional advance of capital invested in Type I land pays the customary *price of production*, i.e., yields the customary average profit on the capital, this condition is sufficient *for the investment of additional capital* on Type I land.[23] That

23 It should be noted here that even in this case the market price must be higher than the production price of Class I. For as soon as the additional supply is obtained, the relationship of demand and supply is evidently changed. Formerly the supply was not sufficient, whereas now it is sufficient. The price must therefore fall. In order to fall, it must have stood higher than the production price of Class I. But the less fertile character of Class I land that has been newly cultivated means that the price does not fall again as low as it was when the production price of Class II governed the market. The production price of Class I sets a limit for a relatively permanent rise in the market price, and not just a temporary one. If on the other hand the land newly brought into cultivation is more fertile than the Class I land that formerly governed the price, and yet is only sufficient to cover the additional demand, the market price remains unchanged. But the analysis of whether the worst class of land pays a rent coincides in this case too with the question under discussion in the text, for here too the assumption that the Class I land does not pay any rent would be explained by the fact that the *market price* is just sufficient for the

is to say, this condition is sufficient for the capitalist to invest new capital at the customary profit and to valorise it in the normal way. To the extent that he has to decide as a capitalist, the capitalist farmer on Type I land *can* cultivate under these conditions. The condition for the valorisation of capital as capital on Type I land is now present. But it in no way follows from the premise that capital could now be invested by the farmer on Type I land under the average valorisation conditions of capital > if he had *no* rent to pay < that this land in Type I is now immediately at the farmer's disposal > as a *field of application* for his capital. < The fact that the farmer could valorise his capital at the customary profit if he paid *no* rent is |420| absolutely no reason for the landowner to lease out *his* land to the farmer for nothing, and to be so philanthropic to his client as to extend him a *crédit gratuit*.[24] This assumption would involve *abstracting from landed property, abolishing landed property*, whose very existence is a *barrier* to the investment of capital and its unrestricted valorisation on the land – a barrier that in no way collapses in the face of the farmer's reflection that the level of corn prices would enable him to obtain the customary profit on his capital by exploiting Type I land, as long as he did not pay any rent, i.e., if he could actually treat landed property as non-existent. Differential rent *presupposes* precisely the *monopoly of landed property*, landed property as a barrier to capital, for otherwise the surplus profit would not be transformed into ground-rent and would not accrue to the landlord instead of to the farmer. And landed property remains such a barrier even where rent in the form of differential rent disappears, i.e., on Type I land. If we consider the cases where capital investment on the land can take place *without payment of rent*, in a country of capitalist production, we shall find that they all involve a *factual* – if not also a legal – *abolition of landed property*, an abolition that can occur only under very special conditions of an accidental nature.

Firstly, if the landowner is himself a capitalist or the capitalist himself a landowner. In this case he *can cultivate his land himself*, as soon as the market price has risen sufficiently to obtain the *price of production* from land which at present belongs to Type I, i.e., to replace the capital advanced plus the average profit. And why? Because as far as he is concerned landed property does not set any barrier to the investment of his capital. He can treat the land as a simple natural element and let his decision be determined exclusively by considering the valorisation of his capital, by using capitalist considerations. Such

capitalist farmer to cover the capital applied plus the average profit; in short, the market price provides him with the price of production of his commodities.

24 [Interest-free credit, as advocated by Proudhon and his followers. Translator]

cases do exist in practice, but only as exceptions. Just as the capitalist cultivation of the land assumes a separation between functioning capital and landed property, so it generally rules out *self-cultivation* by the landed proprietor. We can see immediately that this is purely accidental. If an increased demand for corn requires the cultivation of a greater extent of Type I land than is to be found in the hands of self-cultivating proprietors, i.e., if one part of it has to be *leased* in order to be cultivated at all, this hypothetical abolition of the barrier that landed property places to the investment of capital immediately falls to the ground. It is an absurd contradiction to start from the separation between tenant farmer and landowner, and between capital and land, which corresponds to the capitalist mode of production, and thus to assume the reverse as a general rule, i.e., to assume that the landowner is a *self-cultivator*, wherever, and to the extent that, capital would draw no *rent* from cultivating the land if there were *no landed property* existing independently vis-à-vis capital. (See the passage on rent of mines in Adam Smith.)[25] This abolition of landed property is accidental. It may occur or it may not.

|421| *Secondly. The contents of a lease* may include *particular pieces of land* that pay *no rent* at the given level of market prices, and are therefore rented out *for nothing*, though they are not viewed in this light by the landowner, since what he has his eye on is the *total rental* of the land leased and not the particular rent of individual component parts. In this case, the rent paid by the farmer for the investment of his capital disappears as far as these non-rent-bearing pieces of his farm are concerned, and with it landed property as a barrier to the application of capital, and this is moreover by contract with the landowner himself. But the only reason why he pays no rent for these pieces of land is that he does pay rent for the land to which they are an accessory. In this case, the combination presupposed is precisely one in which he does *not* need to resort to the worst land, land of Type I, as an *independent* and new *source of production* in order to make up the missing supply. Instead, this land of Type I simply forms an element of the farm inseparable from the better type of land. But the case that is to be investigated here is precisely that in which tracts of Type I land are farmed independently and have therefore to be *independently leased out* under the general preconditions of the capitalist mode of production.

Thirdly. A farmer may invest extra capital on his existing leasehold property even though at the existing market prices the additional product obtained in this way simply yields him the price of production, the customary profit, and does not enable him to pay an additional rent. Thus for one part of the capital

---

25 [See below, page 441 of Marx's manuscript. Translator]

invested on the land he does pay ground-rent, for the other part he does not. But we can see from the following analysis how little this solves the problem. If the market price (and also the fertility of the soil) enables him to obtain a surplus yield with the additional capital, which, like the old capital, yields him a surplus profit as well as the price of production, then he pockets this profit himself for the duration of the lease. And why? Because as long as the tenancy lasts (contractually), the *barrier that landed property* places to the investment of his capital in the land has been removed. Yet the mere fact that in order to secure this surplus profit he must take on additional worse land and lease it separately shows irrefutably that the investment of additional capital on the old land is not sufficient to produce the increased supply that is needed. The one assumption rules out the other. Now one could say that the rent of the worst type of land, Type I, is itself a differential rent compared with the land cultivated by its own proprietor (even though this occurs only as a chance exception), or with additional capital investment on the old leaseholds that do not yield any rent. This however would be a differential rent that did not arise from the differing fertility of different types of land and therefore did not presuppose that Type I land paid no rent and that its product was sold at the price of production. Moreover, whether additional capital investments on the same leasehold land yield rent or not is as completely immaterial in determining whether the land in Type I that is newly taken on pays rent or not, as it is immaterial, for example, for investment in a new and independent factory, whether another manufacturer in the same branch of production invests a part of his capital in interest-bearing paper because this cannot be completely valorised in his own business; or whether he makes extensions to his factory that do not yield him the full profit, though they do yield more than the interest. As far as he is concerned, this is a secondary matter. But any new enterprise must yield the average profit, and it is set up on this expectation. Additional capital investments |422| on the old leasehold properties, moreover, and the additional cultivation of new land of Type I, set *barriers* to each other. The limit up to which additional capital can be invested on the same leasehold under less favourable conditions of production is given by the competing new investments on Type I land; on the other hand, the rent that this type of land can yield is limited by the competing additional capital investments on the old leaseholds.)

But none of these prevarications solves the problem, which, put simply, is as follows. Let us assume that the market price for the products of the soil is sufficient for portions of Type I land to be taken into cultivation and for the capital invested to obtain the *production price* of the products from these new fields, i.e., the replacement of the capital that has been consumed plus the average profit. Let us assume, therefore, that the conditions for a normal *valorisation of capital on Type I land* are present. Will this suffice? Can this capital then really be invested? Or must the market price rise high enough for even the worst land to yield a rent? In other words, does the monopoly of landed property place a barrier to the investment of capital that would not be present from capital's own standpoint without the existence of this monopoly? The very terms of the question itself show how, if for example there are additional capital investments on old leaseholds that yield no rent at the prevailing market price but simply the average profit, this in no way solves the problem of whether capital can now be invested on Type I land which would similarly yield the average profit but no rent. This is precisely the question. It is clear from the need to take new land into cultivation that the additional capital investments which yield no rent do not satisfy the demand. If the additional cultivation of land of Type I is undertaken only in so far as this yields *rent*, i.e., yields more than the price of production, no more than two cases are possible. Either the market price must rise so far that even the *final additional capital investments on the old leaseholds* yield *rent*, whether this surplus profit is pocketed by the farmer or the landlord. This rise in price (and yield of rent from the final additional capital investments) would then be the result of the impossibility of cultivating land of Type I *unless rent is obtained* thereby. For if the price of production, the yield of the average profit pure and simple, was sufficient to induce cultivation, the price would not have risen so high and new lands would already have come into competition as soon as they yielded these prices of production and no more. The additional capital investments on the old leaseholds that yielded no rent would then be faced with competition from the capital investments on land of Type I that likewise yield no rent. Or, alternatively, the final capital investments on the old leaseholds yield no rent, but the market price has still risen high enough for land of Type I to be taken up and to yield rent. In this case, the additional capital investment that yielded no rent was possible only because the land of Type I could not be cultivated until the market price allowed it to pay rent. In the absence of this condition, it would already have been cultivated, at a lower price level, and those later investments of capital on the old leaseholds that need the *high market price* to yield the customary profit without rent could not have taken place. Given the high market price, they yield only the average profit. At a lower price, which would have occurred when the price of production allowed land of Type I to be cultivated, these investments would not have yielded this profit and so they could not have taken place at all under this condition. The rent of Type I land would thus form a differential rent compared with these capital investments on the old leaseholds that yield *no* rent, but the fact that it yields a differential rent of this kind is simply the result of its not being available for cultivation at all unless it yields a rent; i.e., unless there is a need for this rent which is not determined by any difference in the types of land and which places a barrier to the possible investment of additional capitals on the old leaseholds. In both cases |423| the rent of Type I land would not be the result of a rise in corn prices, but the opposite of this: the fact that the worst soil has to yield a rent for cultivation to be possible at all would be the reason why corn prices rise to the point at which this condition can be fulfilled.[26]

Whenever we say that Type I land pays *no rent* – on the assumption that the corn price is governed by the price of production – we mean *rent* as a specific category. If the *lease-price* paid by the farmer involves a deduction from the normal wages of his workers or from his own normal average profit, he does not pay any rent as an independent component of the price of his commodity distinct from wages and profit. We have already noted that this constantly happens in practice. In so far as agricultural wages in a country are generally depressed below the normal average level, so that there is a deduction from wages, with a part of the wage regularly going into rent, this is not an exceptional case for the farmer on the worst land. His price of production already includes these low wages as a constituent item, and so the sale of the

26 Differential rent has the peculiarity that here landed property seizes only the surplus profit that the farmer himself would otherwise pocket, and under certain circumstances does pocket for the duration of his tenancy. Here landed property simply causes the transfer of a portion of the commodity price that arises without any effort on its part (rather as a result of the determination by competition of the production price governing the market), a portion reducible to surplus profit, from one person to the other, from the capitalist to the landowner. Landed property is not in this case a cause that creates this component of price or the rise in price that it presupposes. But if the worst Type I land cannot be cultivated – even though its cultivation would yield the price of production – until it yields a surplus over and above this production price, a rent – landed property is the creative *basis* of this rise in price. Landed property has created this rent itself. Nothing is altered in this if, as in the second case examined here, the rent now paid by Type I land forms a differential rent compared with the final additional capital investment on old leaseholds that only pays the price of production. For the fact that Type I land cannot be cultivated until the governing market price has risen high enough to let it yield a rent is the sole basis here for the rise in the market price to a point which, while it pays the final capital investments on the old tenancies only their price of production, still pays a price of production that also yields a rent for land of Type I. The fact that this land must pay rent at all is the cause which works here to create a differential rent between Type I land and the final capital investments on the old leasehold farms.

product at its price of production does not enable the farmer of this land to pay a rent. The landlord can even lease out his land to a worker who is content to pay him, in the form of *rent*, everything, or the greater part of it, that the sale price yields him over and above his wages. In none of these cases is a genuine *rent* paid, even though a *lease-price* is. Where relations corresponding to the capitalist mode of production exist, however, rent and lease-price must coincide. This is precisely the normal relationship which is to be examined here.

If our problem is not solved by the cases considered above, i.e., those in which capital investments can be made on the land in the capitalist mode of production without yielding rent, still less is it solved by making reference to *colonial conditions*. (In speaking here of colonies, we refer always to colonies proper, agricultural colonies.) What makes a *colony* a colony is not just the amount of fertile land to be found in its natural condition. It is rather the circumstance that this land has *not been appropriated*, it has *not* been subsumed under *landed property*. This makes all the difference between the old countries and the colonies as far as land is concerned: the legal or factual *non-existence of landed property*, as Wakefield[27] correctly notes, a fact already discovered long before him by Mirabeau, the Physiocrat,[28] and other early economists. It is completely immaterial here whether the colonists appropriate the land directly or whether they merely pay the state a tax in return for a valid legal title, under the guise of a nominal land price. It is also immaterial that colonists already settled may be the legal owners of the land. Here, landed property actually forms no barrier to the investment of capital, or of labour without capital; the seizure of part of the land by colonists already established does not prevent the newcomers from making new land into a field of investment for their own capital |424| or their labour. > Even in colonies *grants* of big uncultivated estates to particular individuals as their private property constitute a burdensome restriction on colonisation (since they restrict the field of employment) and if this were done on a large scale it would destroy the colony's character as a colony, and it would still do nothing to establish the conditions enjoyed by countries of ancient civilisation there, as Wakefield has correctly remarked.[29] (This point did not prevent the same Wakefield from advocating the estab-

---

27 [Wakefield 1833, pp. 122–82.]

28 [See *L'Ami des Hommes*, Paris, 1756, by Victor Riqueti, Marquis de Mirabeau (1715–89), the Physiocratic writer, father of Count Mirabeau, who played an important part in the early years of the French Revolution. Translator]

29 Wakefield 1833.

lishment of an artificial land price in the colonies.)[30] < Thus if we want to investigate how landed property affects the prices of its products, and rent, in cases where it restricts the land as a field of employment for capital to be invested, it is completely absurd to refer to free bourgeois colonies where neither the capitalist mode of production exists in agriculture nor the form of landed property corresponding to it, indeed where landed property does not exist at all in practice. (This is what Ricardo does, for example, in his chapter on *rent*.[31] He starts by saying that he intends to analyse the effect of the appropriation of land on the value of its products, but immediately goes on to take the colonies as his illustration, assuming that land there is in a relatively elementary state and its exploitation *not* impeded by the monopoly of landed property.)

Legal ownership of the land, by itself, does not give the proprietor any ground-rent. It certainly does give him the power, however, to withdraw his land from cultivation until economic conditions permit a valorisation of it that yields him a surplus, whether the land is used for agriculture proper or for other productive purposes such as building, etc. He can neither increase nor reduce the absolute quantity of this field of employment, but he can affect the quantity of it on the *market*. It is a characteristic fact, therefore, and one which Fourier already noted, that in all civilised countries a relatively significant portion of the land always remains uncultivated.[32]

Assuming then that demand requires the taking up of new land which is, say, less fertile than that previously cultivated, will the owner of this land lease it for nothing just because the market price of its product has risen high enough for capital investment to pay the farmer the price of production and thus yield him the *customary profit*? By no means. The capital investment must yield him a rent. He leases only when a lease-price can be paid. The market price must therefore have risen above the price of production, to P + r, so that a rent can be paid to the landowner. Since by our assumption landed property does not bring anything without being leased, unleased land being economically worthless, a small rise in the market price above the price of production is sufficient to bring new land of the poorest kind onto the market.

The question now arises whether it follows from the *ground-rent of the poorest land*, which cannot be derived from any difference in fertility, that the price of its product is necessarily a *monopoly price* in the customary sense, or a price that includes rent in the form of a *tax*, levied in this case by the landowner

30 [See Marx 1976, pp. 938–9. Translator]

31 [Ricardo 1821, pp. 53–4. Translator]

32 [Fourier 1829, p. 402. Translator]

rather than the state? It is obvious that this tax has its given economic limits. |425| It is limited by additional capital investments on the old leaseholds, by competition from foreign agricultural products (we are assuming free trade), by competition between landed proprietors within the country, and finally by the needs of the consumers and their ability to pay. But this is not what is involved here. The question is whether the rent that is paid by the poorest land goes into the price of its product, which by our assumption is what governs the general market price, in the same way as a *tax* goes into the price of the commodity on which it is levied, i.e., as an element *independent* of its value.

This by no means follows *necessarily*, and it is asserted only because the distinction between the *value* of commodities and their *price of production* has as yet not been understood.

We have already seen that the *price of production* of a commodity is not at all identical with its *value*, although the production prices of commodities, when considered in their totality, are governed only by their total value, and although the movement of production prices for commodities of different kinds, all other circumstances remaining the same, is determined exclusively by the movement of their values. It has been shown that the production price of a commodity may stand *above* or *below* its value, and will only coincide with it in exceptional cases. But the fact that agricultural products are sold *above* their price of production by no means proves that they are also sold *above* their value; just as the fact that industrial products are sold on average at their *price of production* does not show that they are sold *at their value*. It is possible for agricultural products to be sold *above* their price of production and *below* their value, just as many industrial products yield their *price of production* only because they are sold *above* their value.

The relationship of a commodity's *price of production* to its *value* is determined exclusively by the *proportion* between the *variable* part of the capital with which it is produced and the *constant* part, or, in other words, by the organic composition of the capital producing it. If the composition of capital in one sphere of production is lower than that of the *average social capital*, i.e., if its variable component, that laid out on wages, is greater, in comparison with the average social capital, than its constant component, that laid out on the objective conditions of labour, the value of the commodity it produces must stand *above* its price of production. That is to say, such a capital produces more surplus-value, given the same exploitation of labour, and therefore more profit, than an equally large aliquot part of the average social capital, because it applies more living labour. The *value* of its product therefore stands *above* its price of production, since this price of production is equal to the capital that has been consumed, its cost of production, plus the average profit, and the average profit is *lower* than the profit (the produced profit) contained in this commodity. The *surplus-value* produced by the average social capital is less than the surplus-value produced by a capital of this lower composition. The reverse is true if the capital invested in a particular sphere of production is *higher* in composition than the average social capital. The *value* of the commodities it produces then stands *below* their price of production, which is generally the case with the products of the most highly developed industries.

|426| If the capital in a particular sphere of production has a *lower* composition than the *average social capital*, this is firstly only a different expression for the fact that the *productivity of social labour* in this particular sphere of production stands below the average level of its development; for the level of productivity attained is expressed in the relative preponderance of the constant portion of capital over the variable, or in the steady decline of that component of a given capital laid out on wages. If the capital in a particular sphere of production has a *higher* composition, on the other hand, this expresses a level of development of the productivity of social labour which stands higher than the average.

Leaving aside actual artistic works, which are excluded from our subject by the very nature of the case, it is self-evident that different spheres of production, according to their technical characteristics, require differing proportions of constant and variable capital, and that living labour must play a greater part in some and a smaller part in others. In *extractive industry*, for example, which should be sharply distinguished from agriculture, raw material completely disappears as an element of the constant capital, and even ancillary materials play a significant role only very occasionally. > (From the economic point of view one can identify the ancillary material with the raw material.) < In the mining industry, however, the other part of constant capital, which consists of fixed capital and so on, does play a significant role. Even so, here too, as for example in the iron industry, we can measure the progress of industry by the relative growth in constant capital in comparison with variable.

If the composition of capital in agriculture proper is *lower* than the social average, this is *prima facie* an expression of the fact that in countries of developed capitalist production, agriculture has not progressed to the same extent as manufacturing industry. > It has progressed *relatively* less than manufacturing industry. (This therefore refers not to the progress of agriculture but to its *degree* of progress.) < Leaving aside all other *economic* conditions, which have a partially determinant effect, facts of this kind are explicable simply in terms of the earlier and more rapid development of the mechanical sciences, and especially of their application, compared with the later and in part still very recent development of chemistry, geology and physiology, and their application to agriculture in particular. It is also an indubitable and long-known fact[33] that advances in agriculture are themselves always expressed in a relative growth in the constant portion of capital as against the variable. Whether the composition of agricultural capital is *lower* than the *social average* in a specific country where the capitalist mode of production predominates, as in England for example, is a question which can be settled only by statistical investigation and into which it would be superfluous to go in detail for our purposes. In any case, it still holds theoretically that it is only on this premise that the *value* of agricultural products can rise above their *price of production*; i.e., that the *surplus-value* produced in agriculture by a capital of a given size, or, and this comes to the same thing, by the *surplus labour* that it sets in motion and commands (hence also the total living labour applied), is greater than for a capital of the same magnitude of the socially average composition |427| > (for the magnitude of the capital consumed in the course of production {or the actual cost of production} is immaterial in establishing the price of production. It is equal to K + P′, where K, the cost price, is variable, but P′ always expresses the same proportional surplus-value {proportional to the capital advanced}).

< This assumption is therefore sufficient as far as the form of rent we are examining here is concerned, and it is a necessary assumption for this rent to arise. Where this hypothesis is inapplicable, the form of rent corresponding to it also disappears.

The fact, however, that there is a surplus in the *value* of agricultural products over and above their price of production would by no means be sufficient *in itself* to explain the existence of a *ground-rent* independent of differences in fertility between different types of land or successive investments of capital on the same land, in short of a rent conceptually distinct from differential rent, which can therefore denote as *absolute rent*. A whole number of manufacturing products are characterised by a *value above their price of production*, without thereby yielding a surplus over and above the average profit, a surplus profit that could be transformed into rent. The existence and the concept of the *price of production* and the *general rate of profit*, which includes this, rest on the fact that commodities are *not* sold at their values. The *prices of production* arise from an adjustment of commodity values under which, after the reimbursement of the respective capital values consumed in the various spheres of production, the total surplus-value is distributed not in the proportion in which it is pro-

33 See for example Dombasle and R. Jones. [Dombasle 1828, pp. 301–7; Jones 1831, p. 227. Marx discussed these works in his 1861–63 manuscripts. In English: MECW 31, 1989, pp. 259–60 and MECW 33, 1991, pp. 330–1. Translator]

duced in the individual spheres of production > (or, in other words, not in the proportion in which the capitals of the various spheres of production set surplus labour in motion), < and hence contained in their product, but rather in proportion to the size of the capitals advanced. It is only in this way that an *average profit* arises, and a *production price* for commodities can be arrived at, the characteristic element of which is this average profit. It is the constant tendency of capitals to bring about, by competition, this *equalisation* in the distribution of the surplus-value that the total capital produces, and to overcome all obstacles to it. It is therefore their tendency only to tolerate such surplus profits as arise, under whatever circumstances, not from the differences between the values of commodities and their prices of production, but rather from the general price of production governing the market and the individual production prices deriving from this; surplus profits which therefore do not arise between two different spheres of production but rather within each sphere of production, so that they do not affect the *general production prices* of the different spheres, i.e., the general rate of profit, but rather presuppose the *transformation of value into price of production.*

This equalisation of surplus-value, however, depends as already explained on the continuously changing proportionate distribution of the total social capital between the various spheres of production; on a continuous immigration and emigration of capitals; on their transferability from one sphere to another; in short, on their free movement between these various spheres of production as so many available fields of employment for the independent parts of the total social capital. It is |428| assumed in this connection that no *barriers*, or at least only accidental and temporary ones, prevent the competition of capitals, for example in a sphere of production where the *value* of commodities stands *above their price of production* or where the *surplus-value* produced stands above the *average profit*, from reducing value to price of production and thereby distributing the excess surplus-value of this sphere of production among all the spheres of production exploited by capital in due proportion. If the opposite occurs, if capital comes up against an alien power which it can overcome only partly or not at all, a power which restricts its investment in particular spheres of production, allowing this only under conditions that completely or partially exclude the above-mentioned general equalisation of surplus-value to give an average profit, it is clear that in these spheres of production a *surplus profit* will arise, from the excess of commodity value above its price of production, which is transformed into *rent* and as such can become autonomous vis-à-vis profit. And it is as an alien power and a barrier of this kind that landed property confronts capital over its investment in the land, or that the *landowner* confronts the *capitalist.*

Here landed property is the barrier that does not permit any new capital investment on formerly uncultivated or unleased land without levying a toll, i.e., demanding a rent, even if the land newly brought under cultivation is of a kind which does not yield any differential rent, and which if it had not been for landed property could have been cultivated already with a smaller rise in the market price, so that the governing market price would have paid the tiller of the worst land only his *price of production*. But as a result of the barrier that landed property sets up, the market price must rise to a point at which the land can pay a *surplus over the price of production*, i.e., a rent. Since however the *value* of the commodities produced by agricultural capital stands *above* their price of production on our assumption, this rent forms the excess of the *value* above the *price of production*, or a *part* of this excess (except for one case that will be examined straight away). Whether the rent is equal to the whole difference between the value and the price of production, or only to a greater or lesser part of the difference, depends entirely on the state of supply in relation to demand and on the extent of the area newly brought into cultivation. As long as the rent is not *equal* to the excess of the value of the agricultural products over their price of production, one part of this surplus always goes into the general equalisation and proportionate distribution of all the surplus-value among the various individual capitals. As soon as the rent is *equal* to the excess of the value over the price of production, this entire part of the extra surplus-value (the excess of surplus-value over and above > the part of surplus-value measured in line with < the average profit) would be withdrawn from the process of equalisation > and proportionate distribution of the surplus-value or surplus labour among the capitals of the various spheres of production. < But whether this absolute rent is equal to the whole extra value over and above the price of production, or only to a part of this, agricultural products are always sold at a *monopoly price*, not because their price stands above their *value*, but rather because it is equal to their *value*, or is in an intermediate position between their value and their price of production. These products have a monopoly because their value is not levelled down to their price of production as it is with other industrial products whose values stand above the general price of production. Since one part of the value and price of production is in fact an empirically given constant, namely |429| the *cost price*, the capital = K consumed in the course of production, the distinction lies in the other part, the variable part, the *surplus-value* which as an element of the price of production = P, the profit, i.e., the total surplus-value reckoned on the social capital and on each individual capital as an aliquot part of this, but which in the *value* of the commodity is equal to the actual surplus-value which this particular capital has produced > (which depends on the quantity of surplus labour it sets in motion), < forming an integral part of the commodity value it has created. If the value of a commodity is above its price of production, the price of production = K + P, and its value = K + P + δ, so that P + δ = the surplus-value contained in it. The difference between the value and the price of production, (K + P + δ) – (K + P) is thus δ, the excess of the surplus-value produced by this capital over the surplus-value allotted to it by the general rate of profit. It follows from this that the price of agricultural products can stand above their price of production without reaching their value. It also follows that up to a certain point there can be a continuous rise in the prices of agricultural products before their price has reached their value. It equally follows that it is only as a result of the monopoly of landed property that the excess value of agricultural products over their price of production at a particular moment can come to be their general market price. It finally follows that in this case it is not the rise in the product's price that is the cause of the rent but rather the rent that is the cause of the rise in its price. If the price of the product from the worst land = P + r, all the differential rents will rise by corresponding multiples of r, since by our assumption P + r becomes the governing market price.

If the average composition of the non-agricultural social capital were C^{85} V^{15} and the rate of surplus-value 100 percent, the price of production would be 115. If the composition of the agricultural capital were C^{75} V^{25}, the value of its product and the governing market value would be 125, given the same rate of surplus-value. If the agricultural and non-agricultural products balanced out to give an average price, the total [surplus] value would be 15 + 25 = 40, which amounts to 20 percent on a capital of 200. The product of each would be sold at 120. Given an equalisation of production prices, therefore, the production prices, hence the average market prices of the non-agricultural products, would rise and those of the agricultural products fall. If the agricultural products were sold at their full value, they would > rise by the whole surplus-value of 10, < and the industrial products would stand 5 lower than if this equalisation took place. If market conditions do not permit agricultural products to be sold at their full value, at the total surplus over their price of production, the effect lies between the two extremes: industrial products would be sold somewhat above their value, and agricultural products somewhat above their price of production.

Although landed property can drive the price of the products of the soil above their price of production, it does not depend on landed property, but rather on the general state of the market, how far the market price rises above the price of production and towards the value, and to what extent, therefore, the surplus-value produced over and above the given average profit in agriculture is either transformed into rent or goes into the general equalisation of surplus-value that settles the average profit.

In any case, this absolute rent, arising from the excess *value* over and above the *price of production*, is simply a part of the agricultural *surplus-value*, the transformation of this surplus-value into rent, its seizure by the landowner; just as differential rent arises from the transformation of *surplus profit* into rent, its seizure by landed property, at the general governing *price of production*. These two forms of rent are the only normal ones. Apart from this, rent can derive only from a genuine *monopoly price*, which is determined neither by the price of production of the commodities nor by their value, but rather by the demand of the purchasers and their ability to pay, consideration of which therefore belongs to the theory of competition, where the actual movement of market prices is investigated.

|430| If all the land of a country that is suitable for agriculture were leased out – assuming the capitalist mode of production, and normal conditions everywhere – there would be no land that did not yield rent, but there could be capital investments, particular portions of capital invested on the land, that did not yield rent; for once the land is leased out, landed property ceases to operate as an absolute barrier to the capital investment needed. It continues to operate as a relative barrier even then, in so far as the reversion to the landowner of the capital incorporated into the soil sets the farmer very definite barriers. In this case, though, all rent would be transformed into a differential rent determined not by differences in the quality of the soil but rather by the difference between [the surplus profit arising after] the final capital investment on the land and the rent that would be paid for the lease of land of the worst class. Landed property operates as an absolute barrier only in as much as any permission to use land as a field of employment for capital requires that a tribute be paid to the landowner. Once this permission has been given, the landowner can no longer place any absolute barrier to the quantitative level of capital investment on a given piece of land. In the case of the building of houses, for example, a barrier is always imposed by the property of a third party in the land on which the house is to be built. But once this land is leased for house-building purposes, it depends on the lessee of the land whether he plans to erect a large house on it or a small one.

If the average composition of agricultural capital were the same as that of the average social capital, or even higher, the result would be the disappearance of absolute rent in the sense developed above, namely a rent that is different both from differential rent and from rent depending on an actual monopoly price. This is because the value of the agricultural product would then not stand above its price of production, and agricultural capital would not set more labour in motion, and would thus not realise more surplus labour than non-agricultural capital. The same thing would happen if, with the progress of agriculture, the composition of agricultural capital became equalised with that of the average social capital.

At first sight it may seem a contradiction to assume that on the one hand the composition of the agricultural capital becomes higher, with its constant part growing vis-à-vis its variable part, while on the other hand the price of agricultural products rises high enough to enable new and worse land than previously to pay a rent, which in this case could derive only from an excess of the market price over the value and the price of the product, in other words could derive only from a monopoly price for the product.

|431| A distinction needs to be made here.

We started to consider the formation of the rate of profit, we saw that capitals which are, technologically speaking, of similar composition, i.e., set the same amount of labour in motion in proportion to machinery and raw material, may still be composed differently because of the *differing values* of their constant capital components. The raw material or machinery may for example be dearer in one case than in the other. In order to set the same amount of labour in motion (and this was necessary, on our assumption, to work up the same amount of raw material), a larger capital would have to be advanced in one case than in the other, since with a capital of 100, for example, I cannot set in motion the same amount of labour if the raw material that has to be purchased out of the 100 costs in the one case 40 and in the other case 20. But we should immediately see, if the price of the dearer raw material sinks down to the level of that of the cheaper one, that these capitals are none the less similar in their technological composition. The value ratio between variable and constant capital would then be the same, although no change had taken place in the technological proportion between the living labour applied and the quantity and nature of the condition of labour required. A capital of lower organic composition, on the other hand, considered simply in terms of its value composition, could in appearance rise to the same level as a capital of higher organic composition, simply by an increase in the value of its constant parts. If we take for example a capital composed as $C^4 V^1$, because it used a great deal of machinery and raw material in relation to living labour-power, and another capital of $C^1 V^4$, which uses a lot of living labour, little machinery and little and cheap raw material in relation to labour-power, so that a simple rise in the value of the raw material and ancillary materials could equalise its composition, so that out of the 100, four-fifths would be constant capital and one-fifth variable capital, the fourfold labour-power would still have to be set in motion, as before, in order to work on the same amount of raw material. Capitals of the same organic composition can thus have a differing value composition, and capitals of the same value composition (in percentage terms) can stand at varying levels of organic composition, displaying various different levels of development of the social productivity of labour. Thus the mere fact that agricultural capital now stood at the same level by value composition |432| would not prove that the social productivity of labour was equally highly developed. All it could show would be that its own product, which again forms part of its conditions of production, is dearer, or that ancillary material such as fertiliser, which used to be obtained locally, now have to be carried a long way.

Leaving this aside, however, we still have the particular character of agriculture to consider.

Assume that labour-saving machinery, chemical aids, etc., take a greater share in the process > (and also the reduction in the amount of labour needed to sow a given quantity of seed, perhaps by means of sowing machines, so that there are more seeds per worker) < assume therefore that the constant capital grows technologically, not just in value but in quantity, in its proportion to the amount of labour-power applied, in the case of agriculture (as with the mining industry) this is not just a matter of an increase in the *social* but also in the *natural productivity* of labour, which depends on the productivity of the soil (it depends on the *natural conditions* of labour). It is possible for the increase in the social productivity of agriculture simply to compensate for a decline in natural productivity, or not even to do this much – and this compensation can only be effective for a certain period – so that despite the technical development, the product does not become cheaper but is simply prevented from becoming dearer. It is also possible, in a situation of rising corn prices, for the absolute amount produced to decline, but this affects capital that consists for the most part of machinery (or also of cattle), where only the depreciation has to be replaced. The variable capital, meanwhile, the capital laid out in wages, always has to be replaced completely from the product, and here the decline in the absolute amount of product is accompanied by a relative increase in the surplus product.

But it is also possible that, as agriculture progresses, only a moderate rise in the market price above the average will be needed for poorer land which, given a lower level of assistance from industrial aids, would have required a greater rise in the market price, to be cultivated and also to yield a certain amount of rent.

The fact that in stock-raising, for example, the amount of labour-power applied is on the whole very small compared with the constant capital existing in the livestock themselves, could be taken as a decisive objection to the contention that agricultural capital, in percentage terms, sets more labour-power in motion than does non-agricultural capital of the average social composition. It should be noted here, however, that in explaining rent we take as the initial determinant that section of agricultural capital which produces the decisive cereal foodstuffs and thus the major means of subsistence for all civilised peoples. Adam Smith has already shown (and this is one of his services to our understanding of the matter) that the rents |433| in stock-raising and in the general average of all capital invested on the land that does not go into the production of the main means of subsistence, such as corn for instance, are subject to a completely different price-determination. Prices here are determined by the fact that the price of the product of land which is used, say, as an artificial pasture for cattle, but which could equally well be turned into arable land of a certain quality, has to rise high enough to yield the same rent as equally good arable land; in this case, therefore, the rent of the corn-growing land is a determining factor in the price of cattle, so that Ramsay was correct to note that in this way the price of cattle is artificially raised by rent, by the economic expression of landed property, and thus by landed property itself.[34]

'By the extension, besides, of cultivation, the unimproved wilds become insufficient to supply the demand for butcher's meat. A great part of the cultivated lands must be employed in rearing and fattening cattle; of which the price, therefore, must be sufficient to pay, not only the labour necessary for tending them, but the rent which the landlord, and the profit which the farmer, could have drawn from such land employed in tillage'.[35] 'The cattle bred upon the most uncultivated moors, when brought to the same markets, are, in proportion to their weight or goodness, sold at the same price as those which are reared upon the most improved land. The proprietors of those moors profit by it, and raise the rent of their land in proportion to the price of their cattle' (Smith).[36] In this case too, therefore, the differential rent as distinct from the corn rent, is in favour of the inferior land.

Absolute rent explains certain phenomena which at first sight make rent appear to be due to a mere monopoly price. Take for instance the owner of a woodland that exists without any human action, i.e., not as the result of afforestation, in Norway for example, and append it to Adam Smith's example. If he is paid a rent by a capitalist who has timber felled, perhaps to meet a demand from England, he is paid a greater or lesser rent in timber over and above the profit on the capital advanced. This seems in the case of this purely

---

34 Ramsay 1836, pp. 278–9. [Quoted by Marx in MECW 33, 1991, p. 283. Translator]

35 [Here there should be introduced a] *quotation from an earlier writer, in which the relationship between meat and corn is discussed.* [Marx refers here to Price 1803, p. 149, quoted by him in the 1861–63 manuscript, MECW 34, 1994, p. 255. Translator]

36 [Smith 1776, p. 185. Translator]

natural product to be a simple monopoly surcharge. In actual fact, however, the capital here consists almost solely of variable capital laid out on labour, which therefore sets more surplus labour in motion than another capital of the same size. The value of the timber thus contains a greater excess |434| of unpaid labour, or surplus-value, than the product of capitals of higher composition. The average profit can thus be paid from the timber, while a significant excess accrues to the owner of the woodland in the form of rent. We may assume, conversely, that given the ease with which the felling of timber can be extended, and this production thus very rapidly increased, the demand would have to rise very considerably to make the price of timber equal to its value, so that the entire excess of unpaid labour (over and above the part that falls to the share of the capitalist as average profit) would accrue to the proprietor in the form of rent.

We have assumed that land newly brought into cultivation is of inferior quality to the worst of the land previously cultivated. If it is better, it bears a differential rent. Here, however, we are investigating precisely the case where rent does not appear as differential rent. There are only two possible alternatives at this point. Either the land newly taken up is worse than, or it is just as good as, the land previously cultivated. We have already investigated the position where it is worse. What we now have to investigate is where it is just as good. Equally good land, and even better, can be newly cultivated as agriculture develops just as much as worse land can, as we have already shown in the case of differential rent. *Firstly*, because in the case of differential rent (and *rent in general*, since even in the case of *non-differential rent* the question still always arises of whether the fertility of the land on the one hand, and its location on the other, permit it to be cultivated at all at the governing market price, with profit and rent; > whether the market price is high enough always depends on these two conditions of fertility and location), < two factors operate in opposite directions. Sometimes they counterbalance each other and sometimes one outweighs the other. A rise in market price (assuming that > the means of cultivation remain the same, and that mechanical progress or progress of another kind does not form a new element which did not previously fall into the balance in favour of an extension of cultivation, assuming, in one word, that < the cost price of cultivation has not fallen) may bring into cultivation more fertile land which was previously excluded from competing by its location. Or else, in the case of less fertile land, it may increase the advantage of location so much that this balances the low yield. Alternatively, even if the market price does not rise, the location can allow better land to join the competition by way of improved means of communication, as we have seen on a large scale with the prairie states of North America. Even in countries which have long been civilised, this is constantly the case, if not on the same scale as in the colonies, where, as Wakefield correctly notes,[37] location is decisive. Thus firstly the contradictory effects |435| of location and fertility, and the variability of the location factor, which is constantly balanced out, bringing about constant, admittedly progressive, changes, which also tend to balance out, alternatively bring equally good, better or worse tracts of land into competition with those previously cultivated.

Secondly. The development of natural science and agronomy > leads to changes in the understanding of the fertility of different types of soil, and the attitude towards it. This fertility itself in fact alters, in line with changes in the *means* of valorising it which are at the society's disposal. (We entirely leave out of account here that different plants are subject to wide variations in fertility. Here we are concerned only with the main sources of food.) Fertility would only be constant if the *means* of valorising it were immediately and simultaneously available, discovered or created. < In the recent past, for example, light varieties of soil, which were previously considered inferior, have risen to the first rank in France and the eastern counties of England.[38] On the other hand, land which was considered poor not on account of its general chemical composition but because mechanical and physical obstacles stood in the way of its cultivation was turned into good land as soon as the means for overcoming these obstacles were discovered.

Thirdly. In all countries of old-established civilisation, old historical and traditional conditions, in the form of Crown lands, common lands, etc., have withheld great stretches of land from agriculture in a purely arbitrary manner. > These lands are gradually coming under cultivation. < If one contemplates the history of the Enclosure Acts in England, and the history of the common lands which they successively brought under cultivation (a process which is continuing), nothing appears more ridiculous than the fantastic idea that this process was directed by a modern agricultural chemist on the model of Herr von Liebig, and that certain fields were marked off for cultivation on account of their chemical properties and others were excluded.

Fourthly. Leaving aside the fact that the level of population and capital reached at any given time sets a certain limit to the extension of agriculture in a country, though this limit can in turn be stretched, the decision as to whether more or less new land is taken into cultivation depends in a given situation not only on accidental factors, which have a temporary influence on market prices,

---

37 [Wakefield 1833, pp. 214–15. Translator]

38 See Passy [1854, p. 515.]

such as a series of favourable or unfavourable seasons, but also on the overall condition of the capital market and the business conjuncture in that country. In some periods the possibility that uncultivated land may yield the farmer an average profit – whether he pays rent or not – will not suffice to draw additional capital towards agriculture. At other times, when capital is abundant, it streams into agriculture even without a rise in market prices, as long as the normal conditions are fulfilled. Better land than that previously cultivated is in fact only excluded from competition by the element of location, or by previous barriers to the valorisation of its peculiar features which have not yet been broken through, |436| (failure of agronomy to break through the barriers, for instance) or by a lack of mechanical means or else for accidental reasons. We have only to deal therefore with kinds of land which are just as good as those last cultivated. > Leaving aside the above-mentioned capital and credit conditions < there always exists a distinction between the new land and that last cultivated in the shape of the varying cost of ploughing up, and it depends on the level of market prices and the situation of the market as a whole whether this is undertaken or not. Once this land actually does come into competition, the market price falls back again to its previous level, so that the new land will bear *the same* rent as the old land; > since its fertility is the same, on our assumption. < The hypothesis that it will bear no rent is demonstrated by its supporters by assuming what should actually be proved, namely that the last land did not bear any rent. One could prove in the same way that the last houses to be built yield no rent besides simple interest on the buildings, even if they are rented out. The fact of the matter is that they yield rent even before they bring in house rent, for they often stand empty for a long while. Just as successive capital investments on one piece of land *can* yield a *proportionate* surplus product, and hence the same rent, so *can* fields of the same quality as those last cultivated yield the same product at the same cost. It would otherwise be incomprehensible how fields of the same quality are ever brought under cultivation *successively* and not all at once, or indeed why any are at all, since the first would draw after it the competition of all the others. The landowner is always ready to draw a rent, i.e., to receive something for nothing, but capital requires certain conditions in order to fulfil his wish. The mutual competition of plots of land depends not on the landowner's intention to have them compete but rather on the availability of capital to compete on new fields with the old.

Since agricultural rent proper is simply a monopoly price, this rent can only be small, just as absolute rent can only be small in normal conditions, whatever the excess value of the product over its production price may be. The essence of absolute rent consists in this: equally large capitals produce different *amounts* of surplus-value in different spheres of production according to their differing average composition, given an equal rate of surplus-value or equal exploitation of labour. |437| In industry these different amounts of surplus-value are equalised to give the average profit or are divided uniformly between the individual capitals as aliquot parts of the total social capital. Whenever industry needs land, whether for agriculture or for the extraction of raw materials, landed property blocks this equalisation process for the capitals invested on the land and captures a portion of the surplus-value which would otherwise go into the equalisation process, giving a general rate of profit. Rent then forms a part of the value of commodities, in particular of their surplus-value, which simply accrues to the landowners, who extract it from the capitalists, instead of to the capitalist *class*, who have extracted it from the workers. It is assumed in this connection that agricultural capital sets more labour in motion than an equally large portion of non-agricultural capital. The extent of this gap, or whether it exists at all, depends on the relative development of agriculture and industry. By the nature of the case, this difference must decline with the progress of agriculture, unless the ratio in which the variable part of the capital declines vis-à-vis the constant part is still greater in industrial capital than in agricultural. This absolute rent plays a still more important role in extractive industry proper, where one element of constant capital, raw material, completely disappears, and where, with the exception of branches for which the portion consisting of machinery and other fixed capital is very significant, the lowest composition of capital invariably prevails. Precisely here, where rent seems to derive from a monopoly price alone, extraordinarily favourable market conditions are required for the commodities to be sold at their *value* or for rent to equal the entire excess of surplus-value in a commodity over and above its price of production. This is the case for example with rent for fishing grounds, quarries, natural forests, etc.[39]

Wherever rent exists, differential rent always appears and always follows the same laws as it does in agriculture.[40] Wherever natural forces can be monopolised and give the industrialist who makes use of them a surplus profit, whether it be a waterfall, a productive mine, fishing grounds or a well-situated building site, the person indicated as the owner of these natural objects, by virtue of his title to a portion of the earth, seizes this surplus profit from the capital

39 Ricardo gives an extraordinarily superficial account of this point. See his passage on Adam Smith. [Ricardo 1821, pp. 53–5. Marx discussed this passage in the 1861–63 manuscript. See MECW 31, 1989, pp. 465–73. Translator]

40 [This is the beginning of Engels's Chapter 46 entitled 'Rent of Buildings. Rent of Mines. Price of Land'. Editor]

in question in the form of rent. As far as land for building is concerned, Adam Smith has discussed how the basis of its rent, as with all |438| non-agricultural land, is governed by agricultural rent proper.[41] > With the possible exception of the rent paid for *mines*, in view of the evident exploitation of increases in population and production on the part of the lazy parasites who own the land, < this non-agricultural rent is characterised first by the preponderant influence that *location* exerts here on the differential rent (differential rent is very important, for example, in the case of *vineyards*); and secondly by the palpable and complete passivity displayed by the owner, whose activity consists simply in exploiting the progress of social development, towards which he does not contribute and in which he risks nothing, unlike the industrial capitalist; and finally by the prevalence of a monopoly price in many cases, and particularly the most shameless exploitation of poverty (for poverty is a more fruitful source for house-rent than the mines of Potosi were for their owners).[42] The tremendous power this gives landed property when it is combined together with industrial capital in the same hands enables capital practically to exclude workers engaged in a struggle over wages from the very earth itself as their dwelling-place.[43] (Here one section of society demands a tribute from the other for the right to *inhabit* the earth, just as in landed property in general the proprietors demand the right to exploit the earth's surface, its bowels, and air above, and thereby the maintenance and development of life.) The rise in population, and the consequent increase in the need for housing, is not the only factor that must necessarily increase the rent on buildings. So too does the development of *fixed* capital, which is either incorporated into the earth or strikes root in it, like all industrial buildings, railways, factories, storehouses, docks, etc., which rest on it. It is impossible, even with Carey's determination, to confuse house-rent, in as much as this is interest on the capital invested in the house, with rent of land pure and simple, particularly when, as in England, the landowner and the speculative builder are completely different people. Two elements come into consideration here: on the one hand the exploitation of the earth for the purpose of reproduction or extraction, on the other the *space* that is required as an element for any production and any human activity. On both counts landed property demands its tribute. The demand for building land raises the value of land as space and foundation, while at the same time there is

---

41 Adam Smith [1776, pp. 202–7.]

42 Laing and Newman [Laing 1844, p. 150; Newman 1851, pp. 129–30.]

43 *Crowlington strike.* [A reference to the expulsion of coalminers from their houses during the strike of 1865, not in 'Crowlington' but in Cramlington, Northumberland. Translator]

a growing demand for those elements of the earth's physical constitution that serve as building material.[44]

For the same reasons, in cities that are experiencing rapid growth, particularly where building is carried on with industrial methods, as in London, |439| it is the *ground-rent* and not the *house* that forms the real object of speculation. (This passage we quote is also interesting because it shows how building has turned into a capitalist trade.)[45]

Report on the Bank Acts 1857. (Examination of Mr. Edward Capps, builder.) > He says here (5413): 'You must build houses now ready for the market, the same as a bootmaker must make boots, or a stocking manufacturer must make stockings or any other article. People do not now, generally speaking, order houses to be built so much as they did in those days'; (the days of his childhood) 'but if they want houses they go round and select those which are most suitable for them. Therefore builders find it just as necessary in the present day to have their commodities ready for the market as any other persons carrying on any other branch of business; it was not so much so formerly'.

'5414. With regard to speculative building, the change has been more of this nature. Formerly, forty years ago, what houses were built upon speculation were built out of the savings and profits of builders upon their ordinary jobbing business' (namely the business they did to order) 'and it answered very well at that day. Builders conducted their transactions with very great moderation and prudence; they always had three or four houses upon the stocks, just to keep their men in constant employment, their main reliance being on their ordinary business. But now the system of building is quite altered in that respect. A man can do no good by doing business in that way; he must go and take a large plot of ground, and he must perhaps engage to lay out twenty or fifty times the amount of his own capital upon it; and if he can get through his undertaking before any crash comes, if he can run up a lot of structures (and many of them are very flimsy, I am sorry to say, at the present day), he may make a good slice of money, but he is liable to be pulled up very suddenly by a failure in the finances, from the uncertainty of our present monetary system'.

'5415. Then at present the general practice is to build upon a large scale, relying upon a demand for houses |440| when they have been built? Yes, and

---

44 'The paving of the streets of London has enabled the owners of some barren rocks on the coast of Scotland to draw a rent from what never afforded any before'. (Smith 1776, pp. 204–5.)

45 [Marx summarised this passage in what later became *Capital* Volume II. In English: Marx 1978, Chapter 12, pp. 311–12. Translator]

raising money upon mortgage as the buildings proceed. Almost the whole of Belgravia and Tyburnia, and the countless thousands of villas round London are built upon that principle'. (There is no risk at all involved here for the landowning gentlemen. Either they sell the ground as freehold, and anticipate the rent by including it in the price, or they have the building itself as security.)

'5417. Then, in general, the materials are paid for, but the money is borrowed? The money is borrowed; the man must have some capital to begin with. I might take a piece of ground requiring a capital of £50,000. I could commence a speculation of that kind probably with not more than £1,000 or £1,500, just enough to start with'.

< '5435. I think a man who wishes to rise in the world can hardly expect to rise by following out a fair trade, > what is called a jobbing trade, he will not make sufficient profit out of it. < It is necessary for him to add speculative building to it, and that must be done not on a small scale; > it must be done on a large scale, < for the builder makes very little profit out of the buildings themselves; he makes the principal part of the profit *out of the improved ground-rents*. Perhaps he takes a piece of ground, and agrees to give £300 a year for it; by laying it out with care, and putting certain descriptions of buildings upon it, he may succeed in making £400 or £450 a year out of it, and his profit would be the *increased ground-rent* of £100 or £150 a year rather than the profit of the buildings which > he puts upon the ground; that < in many instances, he scarcely looks at all'.

|441| The actual rent of mines is determined exactly as is agricultural rent. 'There are some' (mines) 'of which *the produce* is barely sufficient to pay the labour, and replace, together with its ordinary profits, the stocks employed in them. They afford profit to the undertaker of the work, but no rent to the landlord. They can be wrought advantageously by nobody but the landlord, who, being himself the undertaker of the work, gets the ordinary profit of the capital which he employs in it. Many coalmines in Scotland are wrought in this manner, and can be wrought in no other. *The landlord will allow nobody else to work them without paying some rent, and nobody can afford to pay any*'. (Adam Smith.)[46]

It is necessary to distinguish whether the rent flows from a monopoly price, because a monopoly price for the products (or for the land itself) exists independently of it, or the products are sold at a monopoly price because of the existence of a rent. By monopoly price here we mean any price determined simply by the desire and ability of the buyer to pay, independently of the price of the product as determined by general price of production and value. A vine-

46 [Smith 1776, p. 207. Translator]

yard, for example, bears a monopoly price if it produces wine which is of quite exceptional quality but can be produced only in relatively small quantities. By virtue of this monopoly price, the wine-grower whose excess over the value of his product is determined purely and simply by the wealth and the preference of fashionable wine-drinkers can realise a substantial surplus profit. This surplus profit, which in this case flows from a monopoly price, is transformed into rent and accrues in this form to the landowner by virtue of his title to the portion of the earth endowed with these special properties. Here, therefore, the monopoly price creates the rent. Conversely, the rent would create the monopoly price if corn were sold not only above its price of production but also above its value, as a result of the barrier that landed property opposes to the *rent-free* investment of capital on uncultivated land.

(The fact that it is only the title a number of people have to property in the earth that enables them to appropriate a part of society's *surplus labour* |442| as tribute, and in an ever-growing measure as production develops, is concealed by the circumstance that the capitalised rent, i.e., precisely this capitalised tribute, appears as the price of land, which can be bought and sold just like any other item of trade. For the buyer, therefore, his claim to rent does not appear as something obtained *for nothing*, without the labour, risk or the entrepreneurial spirit of capital, but rather as the return for his equivalent. Rent seems to him, as we have already noted, simply as interest on the capital with which he has purchased the land, and with it the claim to rent. In exactly the same way, it appears to the slaveowner who has bought a black slave that his property in the slave is created not by the institution of slavery as such but rather by the purchase and sale of this commodity. But the purchase does not produce the title; it simply transfers it. The title must be there before it can be bought, and neither *one* sale nor a series of sales, their constant repetition, can create this title. It was entirely created by the relations of production. Once these have reached the point where they have to be sloughed off, the material source, the economically and historically justified source of the title that arises from the process of the social production of life, ceases to exist, and with it all transactions based on it. From the standpoint of a higher socio-economic formation, the private property of particular individuals in the earth will appear just as absurd as the private property of one man in another man. Even an entire society, a nation, or all simultaneously existing societies taken together, are not the *owners* of the earth. They are simply its *occupiers*, its *beneficiaries*, and they have to bequeath it in an improved state to the succeeding generations as *boni patres familias* [good heads of the household].)

> It has been seen < (and here we disregard all fluctuations due to competition, all speculation in land, and even small-scale property, where the earth

forms the main instrument of the producers and must therefore be bought by whatever the price) that:

(I) The *price of land* may rise without an increase in *rent*, namely

1 merely through a *fall in the rate of interest*, which has the effect that rent is sold at a higher price, and so capitalised rent, the price of land, increases;

2 because of a growth in the *interest* on the *capital incorporated* into the land;

(II) The price of land may rise because the *rent* increases.

The rent may increase because the *price of the product of the land* rises, in which case the *rate of differential rent* always rises, whether the rent on the worst cultivated land is high, low or non-existent. By the *rate* of differential rent we mean the *ratio* between the *part of surplus-value* that is transformed into *rent*, and the *capital advanced* to produce the agricultural product. This is different from the *ratio* between the surplus product and the total product, for the total product does not include the part of the constant capital advanced which has not been consumed in the product but continues to exist alongside it. It is implied in this, however, that on those types of land that bear a differential rent a growing portion of the product is transformed into excess surplus product. > (We shall examine this point more closely in the section on differential rent.) < On the worst land, it is the rise in price of the product of the land that creates rent for the first time and hence creates the price of land.

But rent can also grow without any rise in the price of the agricultural product. This can remain constant or even decline.

If it remains *constant*, this is only possible (leaving aside monopoly prices) for one of two reasons. Either (1) because new lands of better quality are cultivated along with *equally large capital investments* on the older lands, which however are sufficient only to meet the increased demand, so that the governing market price remains unchanged. In this case, the price of the older lands does not increase, but the price of land newly taken up rises above that of the older land;

Or (2) because with the relative yield remaining the same, and the market price too, the *amount of capital exploiting* the land increases. Thus even if the rent remains the same in proportion to the capital advanced, it might double in *amount*, say, because the capital itself has doubled. Since there is no fall in the price, the second capital investment yields a surplus profit just as much as the first, which is similarly transformed into rent once the term of the tenancy expires. The *amount of rent* rises here because the *amount of rent-producing capital* rises. The contention that different successive capital investments on the same stretch of land can produce a rent only in so far as their yield is uneven, and *therefore* a *differential rent* arises, amounts to saying that if two capitals of £1,000 each are invested on two *equally productive fields*, |444| only one of them can yield rent, even when these two fields belong to the better class of land which does yield a differential rent. (The sum of *rental income*, the *total ground-rent* of a country, therefore grows with the amount of *capital invested*, with the extension of cultivation, in short, without necessitating a rise in the price of the individual unit of land or in the rate or even the mass of rent. This can even be combined with a *fall* in the rent on individual holdings.) To deny this, would be to maintain that capital investments made *successively* on two different pieces of land *alongside one another in the same location* would obey two different laws, although we can derive *differential rent* from an *identical* law in both cases, namely from differences in the productivity of capital investment both on *the same* field and on *different* fields. The only modification here which is overlooked is that when successive capital investments are applied to land in different locations, they come up against the *barrier of landed property*, which is not the case with successive capital investments on *the same* land. This is the reasons for the check which these different forms of investment exert on each other. There is no difference in the capital involved here. If the composition of capital remains the same, and similarly the rate of surplus-value, the *rate of profit remains unaltered*, so that with twice the capital there is twice the amount of profit. The *rate of rent* also remains the same under these conditions. If a capital of £1,000 yields a rent of x, then under the conditions assumed here one of £2,000 yields a rent of 2x, > and 2x: 2,000 = x: 1,000. < But in relation to the area of land, which remains unchanged, since by our assumption double the amount of capital is at work on *the same* field, the result of the rise in the *mass of rent* is a rise in its *rate* as well. The same acre which brought in a rent of 50 now brings in a rent of 100, say. The total rate of rent has thus doubled.[47] The proportion of one part of the surplus-value, the money rent (for money is the independent

---

47 It is one of the services of Rodbertus, whose important text on rent we shall return to in Book Four, that he developed this point. The first mistake he makes, however, in connection with capital, is to see the growth in profit as always expressing a growth in capital, so that the ratio remains the same as the mass of profit rises. But this is wrong, since even if the exploitation of labour remains the same, the profit rate may still rise as the composition of capital changes, precisely because there is a fall in the proportionate value of the constant capital as compared with the variable. Secondly, he makes the mistake of treating the proportion of money rent on a piece of land of a definite size, one acre for example, as if this had been the general premise of classical economy in its analyses of the rise and fall of rent. This again is incorrect. Classical economics always treated the rate of rent, in as much as it considered rent in its natural form, in relation to the product, and in as much as it considered rent as money rent it treated it in relation to the capital advanced, since these are in fact the *rational* expressions.

expression of value), to the land is as it stands absurd and *irrational*; for it is incommensurable quantities that are measured against each other here, a particular *use-value* on the one hand, a piece of land of so and so many square feet, and *exchange-value*, in particular *surplus-value*, on the other. All this means in actual fact is that, under the given conditions, the ownership of these square feet of land enables the landowner to seize a certain amount of |445| unpaid labour, which capital has realised by rooting in the soil like a pig in potatoes. *Prima facie*, however, the expression is as if one were to speak of the ratio of a £5 note to the diameter of the earth > or some other heavenly body. But these *irrational* forms in which certain economic relationships *appear* and are grasped in practice are of no concern to the practical bearers of those relationships in their everyday dealings; since they are accustomed to operating within these forms, they do not think there is anything peculiar about them. A complete contradiction holds nothing at all mysterious for them. In forms of appearance that are estranged [*entfremdet*] from their inner connection and, taken in isolation, are absurd, they feel as much at home as a fish in water. What Hegel says about certain mathematical formulae applies here too: what ordinary human understanding finds irrational is in fact rational, and what it finds rational is irrational.[48,49] (Since *vulgar economics* actually does nothing more than interpret, systematise and turn into apologetics the notions of agents trapped within bourgeois relations of production, it should not surprise us that precisely in the estranged *form of appearance* of economic relations that involves these *prima facie* absurd and complete contradictions – and all science would be superfluous if the form of appearance [*Erscheinungsform*] of things directly coincided with their essence [*Wesen*] – precisely here vulgar economics feels completely at home, these relationships appearing all the more self-evident to it the more their inner connections remain hidden, and the more they are comprehensible to the ordinary mind. Thus it does not have the slightest suspicion that the trinity from which it proceeds, *land – rent, capital – interest, labour – wages* or *price of labour*, consists of a conflation of three things which is *prima facie* impossible to perform. First we have the *use-value* of land, which has no value, and the exchange-value *rent*; here, then, a social relation, conceived as a thing, is placed in a proportionate relationship with nature; what we have here are

48 [Hegel 1830, para. 231.]

49 [From here to the end of this paragraph (in parentheses) is Engels's third fragment at the beginning of his Chapter 48 ('The Trinity Formula'). As discussed in the Introduction (pp. 50–1), this fragment was intended by Marx to go at the *beginning* of his Chapter Seven ('Revenue and Its Sources') and thus was misplaced by Engels. Editor]

two incommensurable magnitudes. Then *capital – interest*. If capital is conceived as a certain sum of value with its independent expression in money, it is *prima facie* nonsense that a value should have more value than it is worth. This form, capital – interest, is precisely the form in which any mediation [*Vermittlung*] disappears, and capital is reduced to its most general formula, but for this reason also it is a formula that is absurd and inexplicable. This is precisely the reason why the vulgar economist prefers the formula *capital – interest*, with its occult quality of a value that is unequal to itself, to the formula *capital – profit*, as here we already get somewhat closer to the actual capital-relation. Then again, disturbed by the feeling that four is not five and hence 100 shillings cannot possibly be 110 shillings, he flees from capital as value to the material substance of capital; to its use-value as one of labour's *conditions of production*, i.e., machinery, raw material, etc. It is then possible, instead of the incomprehensible first relationship, in which 4 = 5, to construct this time a completely *incommensurable* relationship between a *use-value*, a thing, on the one side of the equation, and a specific social relation of production, surplus-value, on the other; as in the case of landed property. As soon as this *incommensurability* is attained, everything becomes clear to the vulgar economist, and he feels no need for any further reflection. For he has reached exactly what is 'rational' to the bourgeois mind. Finally, *labour – wages, the price of labour*, is an expression which, as shown earlier,[50] absolutely contradicts the concept of value and equally therefore that of price, this being in general only a specific expression of value; so that 'price of labour' is as irrational as a yellow logarithm. The vulgar economist, though, is exceedingly satisfied here, since he has now reached the profound insight of the bourgeois, that he pays money for labour, and the very contradiction between this formula and the concept of value relieves him from the obligation of understanding the latter.)

|446| As far as the land area itself is concerned, a rise in the *amount* of rent is thus expressed in the same way as a rise in the *rate of rent*, hence the embarrassment when the conditions that would explain the one case are absent in the other.

The price of land can rise even if the price of its product declines.

In this case, the differential rent (and therefore the price of land) may have increased by a further *differentiation*. Or, if this is not the case, increased productivity of labour may have led to a fall in the price of specific quantities of the product, such as for example a bushel, while at the same time the number of bushels has increased more than their price has fallen. Assume that one

50 [In Marx 1976, pp. 675–82. Translator]

quarter, or 8 bushels, costs 60s. If 16 bushels were produced instead of 8 on the same acreage, with the same capital (the cost of a bushel was previously 7½ s.) and the bushel costs 5s., then the quarter would cost 40s., which is a considerable fall in price. 16 bushels would now cost 16 × 5 = 80, so that the value of the product of the same capital on the same acreage would have risen by a third = 33⅓ percent, although the price of a bushel has fallen from 7½ to 5. (The way in which this is possible even though the product is not sold above its price of production or its value will be examined when we consider differential rent.)

(In actual fact, it is possible in only two ways. Either poor land is withdrawn from competition, but the price of the better land rises if the differential rent grows, so that the general improvement has had an *uneven* effect on the different types of land; or the same price of production on the worst land {and the same value, if absolute rent is paid} is expressed in a larger amount of product, owing to increasing labour productivity. The product still represents the same value as before, but the price of its |447| aliquot parts has fallen, while their number has increased. If the same capital is applied, this is impossible; for in that case the same value is always expressed in any portion of the product. It is possible, however, if an extra capital is invested for gypsum, guano, etc. The condition is, that the price of the individual bushel, even though it does fall, does not fall in the same ratio as the number of bushels increases.)

|446| III. These various conditions for a rise in rent, hence either in the price of land in general or in that of particular types of land, may in part compete with each other, in part exclude each other, and it can be that they only take effect in turns.

But it follows from the above discussion that a rise in the price of land does not in itself mean a rise in rent, and that we cannot conclude that a rise in rent, which always brings with it a rise in the price of land, will always mean an increase in its products.[51]

Instead of returning to the actual natural causes for the exhaustion of the land, which incidentally were unknown to any of the economists who wrote about differential rent, on account of the backward state of agricultural chemistry in their time, they resort to the superficial conception that there is a limit to the amount of capital which can be invested in a particular field *for reasons of space*. The *Edinburgh Review*, for example, counters Richard Jones by saying that the whole of England cannot be fed by cultivating Soho Square.

51 For an actual case of a fall in land prices combined with a rise in rent, see Passy [1854, p. 516.]

This is seen as a particular disadvantage of agriculture, but precisely the opposite is the case. Here successive capital investments can be made to bear fruit just because the earth itself functions as an instrument of production, which is not the case with a factory, where it functions only as the foundation, the site, the spatial base of operations – or at least this is the case only to a very limited extent. It is certainly possible to concentrate a great productive installation in a small space, compared with fragmented handicraft production; and this is what modern industry does. But once the level of productivity is given, a certain space is always required, and building upwards is only possible to a certain degree > (without multiplying the costs involved). If this were not the case, why would the manufacturer be forced to extend his factory, or to build a second building next to the first one? < The fixed capital invested in machines, etc., is not improved by use; on the contrary, it depreciates. Here too, particular improvements are possible as a result of new discoveries, > steam boilers can be improved, etc., < but taking the development of productivity as given, machinery can only deteriorate. When productivity develops rapidly, the whole of the old machinery must be replaced by a more advantageous kind, and it is therefore lost. The advantage enjoyed by the earth is that successive capital investments on it are possible without the loss of the earlier ones, and this at the same time implies the possibility of a difference in yield between these successive capital investments.

|448| It is necessary to clarify the exact nature of the difficulty faced by modern economics, as the theoretical expression of the capitalist mode of production, in its treatment of ground-rent.[52] What this difficulty is, has still not been understood even by a large number of contemporary writers, as is shown by each fresh attempt to give ground-rent a 'new' explanation. The novelty in this case almost always consists in a regression to standpoints long since superseded. The difficulty is not one of explaining the *surplus-value* produced by agricultural capital and the *surplus product* that corresponds to it. This question is solved by analysis of the surplus-value produced by productive capital in general, whatever the sphere in which it has been productively invested. The difficulty consists rather in showing how, after the equalisation of surplus-value between the various capitals to give the *average profit*, whereby they receive a share in the total surplus-value produced by the social capital in all spheres of production together that corresponds and is proportionate to their relative sizes > (or to the aliquot part they form in the total social

52 [This is the beginning of Engels's Chapter 47 entitled 'The Genesis of Capitalist Ground Rent'. Editor]

capital); < in showing how, after this equalisation, after the distribution of all the surplus-value that there is to distribute has apparently already taken place, there is still an *excess* part of this surplus-value left over, a part which capital invested on the land pays to the landowner in the form of ground-rent, and where it comes from. Quite apart from the practical motives which goaded the modern economists to investigate this question, as spokesmen for industrial capital against landed property – motives which we shall indicate in more detail in the chapter on the history of ground-rent[53] – the question was of decisive interest for them as theorists. To concede that the phenomenon of rent for capital invested in agriculture stemmed from a particular effect of the sphere of investment itself, from the earth's crust or certain properties pertaining to it, would be to renounce the very concept of value itself, i.e., to abandon any possibility of scientific knowledge in this area. Even the simple perception that rent is paid out of the *price* of the agricultural product – which is true even when it is paid in kind, if the farmer is to extract his price of production from it – showed the absurdity of explaining the *excess* of this *price* over and above the customary price of production, i.e., the *relative dearness* of agricultural products, in terms of the extra natural productivity of agricultural industry over the productivity of other branches of industry, because, on the contrary, the more productive labour is, the cheaper each aliquot part of its product, since the greater the amount of use-value in which *the same* quantum of labour, i.e., *the same value*, is represented.

|449| The whole difficulty in analysing rent thus consisted in explaining the *excess* of agricultural profit over *average profit*; not surplus-value as such, but rather the *extra surplus-value* specific to this sphere of production; i.e., not even the '*net product*', but rather the excess of this '*net product*' over the '*net product*' of our branches of industry. The average profit itself is a product, formed by a process of social life proceeding under quite particular historical relations of production, a product which, as we have seen, presupposes very far-reaching mediations. If we are to speak of an excess over the *average profit*, this average profit must first be established as a *measure* and, as is the case in the capitalist mode of production, as the overall *regulator* of production. Thus in forms of society where it is not yet capital that performs this function of extracting all > surplus-value (or < surplus labour) and appropriating it for itself, at least in the first instance – where capital has not yet subsumed society's labour

53 [Marx intended to produce a fourth volume of *Capital* on the history of economic theory, the first draft of which is contained in the 1861–63 manuscripts. In English, see MECW 31, 1989, pp. 344–58 for the history of the theory of ground-rent. Translator]

or has done so only sporadically – there can be no question at all of *rent* in the modern sense, of rent as an *excess* over and above the *average profit*, i.e., over and above the proportionate share of each individual capital in the total surplus-value that the total capital produces. It shows the naiveté of M. Passy (on which more below) that he speaks of rent in the most primitive conditions as already a surplus over and above *profit* – a historically determined *social* form of surplus-value which, according to M. Passy, can exist on a natural basis even *without* any society.[54]

For the early economists, who were only just beginning to analyse the capitalist mode of production, which was, moreover, in their time still undeveloped, the analysis of rent presented either no difficulty at all or else a difficulty of a quite different kind. Petty, Cantillon,[55] and all those other writers who stand closer to the feudal period assume that *ground-rent* is the *normal form of surplus-value*, while profit for them is still lumped indiscriminately together with wages or at most appears as a portion of this surplus-value extorted from the landowner by the capitalist. They therefore base themselves on a state of affairs in which, firstly, the agricultural population is still the overwhelming majority of the nation, and, secondly, the landowner still appears as the person who appropriates in the first instance the excess labour of the immediate producers by way of his monopoly of landed property. In addition to this, landed property still appears as the main condition of production. Nothing could be more alien to them than a way of posing the question which proceeded from the standpoint of capitalist production, and sought to investigate |450| how landed property manages to extract again from capital a part of the surplus-value that capital has produced (i.e., extorted from the immediate producers) and in the first instance already appropriated.

With the Physiocrats, the difficulty is of quite another kind. As the first *systematic* interpreters of capital, they try to analyse the nature of *surplus-value* in general. For them this analysis coincides with the analysis of *rent*, the only form in which surplus-value existed for them. *Rent-bearing* or *agricultural* capital, therefore, is for them the only capital that produces surplus-value, and the agricultural labour that it sets in motion is the only labour giving rise to surplus-value, i.e., quite correctly from the capitalist standpoint the only truly *productive labour*. They quite rightly regard the production of surplus-value as the determining element. Apart from other services, which we shall discuss

---

54 [Passy 1854, p. 511. Translator]

55 [Petty 1667, pp. 23–4; Cantillon 1756, pp. 175–7. Translator]

later on,[56] theirs is the great merit of returning from commercial capital, which operates only in the sphere of circulation, to productive capital, in contrast to the supporters of the Mercantile System, which was, in its crude realism, the actual vulgar economics of the day, and which, with its practical interests, entirely swamped the beginnings of scientific analysis conducted by Petty and his successors. > (In relation to our critique of the Mercantile System it should be borne in mind that we are concerned only with < its conceptions of capital and surplus-value.) We have already noted[57] that the Monetary System correctly proclaims that production for the world market and the transformation of the product into a commodity, hence into money, is the precondition and requirement for capitalist production. In its continuation as the Mercantile System, it is no longer the transformation of commodity value into money that is decisive, but instead the production of surplus-value, albeit from the irrational standpoint of the circulation sphere, and at the same time in such a way that this surplus-value is expressed in surplus money, in a favourable balance of trade. But it is also the characteristic feature of the self-interested merchants and manufacturers of that time, and belongs to the period of capitalist development that they represent, that the transformation of feudal agricultural societies into industrial societies, and the resulting industrial struggle of nations on the world market, involves an accelerated development of capital which cannot be obtained in the so-called natural way by only compulsory means. It makes an enormous difference whether the national capital is transformed into industrial capital gradually and slowly, or this transformation is accelerated over time by the taxes they impose through protective duties, which rest in fact on the landlords, the yeomanry and the artisans, by the accelerated expropriation of independent direct producers, and by the forcibly accelerated accumulation and concentration of capital, in short by the accelerated establishment of the conditions of capitalist production. It also makes an enormous difference in the capitalist and industrial exploitation of the *nation's natural productive power*. The national character of the Mercantile System is therefore not just cant when its spokesmen refer to it. On the pretext of being concerned only with the wealth of the nation and the sources of assistance for the state, they declare in fact that the interests of the capitalist class, and of enrichment in general, are the ultimate purpose of the state, and they proclaim their support for bourgeois society as against the old supernatural state. At the same time,

---

56 [Marx is referring forward to the proposed Volume IV. Translator]

57 [In *A Contribution to the Critique of Political Economy, Part One*, Chapter 2, Section C. English: MECW 29, 1987, pp. 389–91. Translator]

however, they show their awareness that the development of the interests of capital and the capitalist class, of capitalist production, has become the basis of the nation's power and predominance in modern society.

|451| The Physiocrats were also correct to say that in fact all production of surplus-value, and thus also every development of capital, rested on the productivity of agricultural labour as its natural foundation. If men are not even capable of producing more means of subsistence in a working day, and thus in the narrowest sense more agricultural products, than each worker needs for his own reproduction, if the daily expenditure of the worker's entire labour-power is only sufficient to produce the means of subsistence indispensable for his individual needs, there can be no question of any surplus product or surplus-value at all. A level of productivity of agricultural labour which goes beyond the individual needs of the worker is the basis of all society, and in particular the basis of the capitalist mode of production, which releases an ever-growing part of society from the direct production of the means of subsistence, transforming them, as Steuart says, into 'free hands',[58] and making them available for exploitation in other spheres.

But what should we say of contemporary economic writers such as Daire,[59] Passy, etc., who, now that classical economics has run its course, when it is actually on its deathbed, repeat the most primitive ideas about the natural conditions of surplus labour and hence surplus-value in general, believing themselves to have said something new and striking about ground-rent, long after this ground-rent has been explained as a *particular form* and *specific portion of surplus-value*? It is precisely characteristic of vulgar economics that what in a now superseded stage of development was new, original, profound and justified is repeated at a time when it is flat, incorrect and stale. It thereby acknowledges that it does not even have an inkling of the problems with which classical economics was concerned. It confuses these with questions that are put forward only at a lower state of development of bourgeois society. It is just the same with its incessant and self-satisfied chewing over of Physiocratic notions about free trade. These have long since lost any and every theoretical interest, even if they may be still of some practical interest to some state or other.

In a genuine natural economy, where no part of the agricultural product, or only a very small part, enters into the circulation process, and this is itself only a relatively insignificant part of that product of the product that represents the

58 [Steuart 1770, pp. 31, 48, 151, 153, and 396. Translator]

59 [Daire 1847, and Marx's comments in MECW 30, 1988, p. 362. Translator]

landowner's revenue – as for example in many ancient Roman latifundia, as also in the manors of Charlemagne's time, and more or less throughout the Middle Ages (see Vinçard)[60] – the whole of the product and surplus product of estates by no means consisted simply of the products of agricultural work. It equally included the products of industrial work. The existence of domestic handicrafts and manufacture as an ancillary pursuit to agriculture, which is the basic activity, is the condition for the mode of production on which this natural economy rests, both in European antiquity and medieval times and still today in the village communities of India, |452| where their traditional form of organisation has not yet been destroyed. The capitalist mode of production completely abolishes this connection, a process which can be studied on a large scale particularly during the last third of the eighteenth century in England. People who had grown up in more or less semi-feudal societies, such as Herrenschwand,[61] for example, still considered this separation of agriculture and manufacture as a foolhardy social venture, an incomprehensibly risky mode of existence, at the end of the eighteenth century. And even in those agricultural economies of ancient times which show the greatest similarities with the capitalist rural economy, namely Carthage and Rome, the appropriate analogy is with a plantation economy rather than with the form really corresponding to the capitalist mode of exploitation.[62] There is a formal analogy, though one which also appears to be completely deceptive in all essential points for someone who has understood the capitalist mode of production (unlike Herr Mommsen,[63] who discovers the capitalist mode of production as soon as a monetary economy appears). Even such a formal analogy is to be

---

60 [Vinçard 1846. Translator]

61 [Marx was aware of the views of Jean Herrenschwand, a Swiss economist who wrote in the eighteenth century, through the summary by Joseph Garnier (Garnier 1853, p. 951). Translator]

62 Adam Smith emphasises how in his time (and this is still true for our own, as far as the plantation economy > of the United States < is concerned) rent and profit are still not always separate, since the landowner is also the capitalist, as Cato for instance was on his estates. This separation, however, is precisely the precondition for the capitalist mode of production, the whole idea of which is in any case entirely contradictory to the basis of slavery.

63 In his *History of Rome*, Mommsen uses the word '*capitalist*' not at all in the sense of modern economics and modern society, but rather in the manner of a popular notion which persists on the Continent – though not in England or America – where an antiquated view of the matter continues to be held long after it has ceased to exist. [See Mommsen 1894, p. 66, n. 2.]

found nowhere in mainland Italy in ancient times, but only perhaps in Sicily, since this served as an agricultural tributary for Rome, its agriculture being essentially designed for export. Here one can find farmers in the modern sense.

An incorrect conception of the nature of rent has been handed down to modern times, a conception based on the fact that rent in kind still survives from the Middle Ages, in complete contradiction to the conditions of the capitalist mode of production, partly in the tithes paid to the Church, and partly as a curiosity in old contracts. The impression is thus given that rent arises not from the *price* of the agricultural product but from its *quantity*, i.e., not from social relations but from the earth itself. We have already shown how, even though surplus-value is expressed in a surplus product, it is not true conversely that any surplus product in the sense of a mere increase in the quantity of the product represents a surplus-value. It can represent a deduction from value. Otherwise the cotton industry would have had to show an enormous surplus-value in 1866 compared with 1846, even though the price of yarn had fallen. Rent may grow enormously as a result of a series of bad harvests, since the price of corn rises, even though this surplus-value is expressed in an amount of dearer wheat which is growing smaller in absolute terms. Conversely, a series of good years may lead to a fall in rent because the price falls, even though the lower rent is expressed in a greater amount of cheaper wheat. The first thing to note about rent in kind, then, |453| is that it is simply a tradition brought over from another mode of production, which survives, as a ruin of its former existence, while its contradiction with the capitalist mode of production is shown by the way that it disappeared automatically from private contracts and, where legislation could intervene, as with the tithes, was forcibly abolished as an incongruity.[64] Secondly, however, where it continued to exist on the basis of the capitalist mode of production, it was nothing more, and could be nothing more, than an expression of money rent in medieval guise. Say that a quarter of wheat stands at 40s. Out of this one quarter, one part must replace the wages contained in it and be sold so as to advance these again; another part must be sold in order to pay the part due as taxes. Seed corn and a certain amount of manure are themselves involved in reproduction as commodities, wherever the capitalist mode of production and the division of social labour associated with it are developed, and so replacements for these must be bought; a further part of the quarter must be sold to supply money

64 [This refers specifically to Britain, where the Tithe Commutation Act (1836), passed in 1836, commuted those Church tithes which were still levied in kind into money payments. Translator]

for this. In as much as they do not actually have to be bought, > do not really enter into the metamorphosis of < commodities, but are taken from the product in kind, to go once more as conditions of production into its reproduction – which happens not only in agriculture, but in many branches of production that produce constant capital – they are entered into the books in money of account, and deducted as constituents of the cost price. The wear-and-tear of machinery and fixed capital in general must be replaced in money. Finally, there is the profit, which is reckoned on the sum of those expenses that are expressed in real money or in money of account. This profit is represented by a particular part of the gross product, determined by its *price*. The part that then remains forms the rent. If the contractual product-rent is greater than this residue as determined by the price, it does not form rent but is a deduction from profit. Simply by virtue of this possibility, product-rent, which does not follow the constant price of the commodity, and can therefore come to either more or less than the actual rent, and which can form a deduction not just from profit but from the components required to replace the capital, is [antiquated and] ripe for removal. This product-rent, in fact, in so far as it is rent not simply in name but in actual fact, is determined exclusively by the excess of the *price* of the product over its *cost of production*. It simply takes this variable magnitude as a constant one. But it is such a homely[65] idea that the product first suffices in kind to feed the workers, then to leave the capitalist farmer more food than he needs, and that the surplus over and above that forms the *natural* rent. It would be just the same with a calico producer who manufactures 200,000 ells of cloth. This is not only sufficient to clothe his workers, and to more than clothe his wife, all his offspring and himself, it also leaves him calico to sell and finally to pay a hefty rent in kind. It is such a simple matter! We deduct the production costs of the 200,000 ells, and a surplus of calico must remain over as rent. But what an > artificial and < naive idea it is to deduct production costs of, say, £15,000 from the 200,000 ells, without knowing the sale price of calico; to deduct money from calico, an exchange-value from a use-value, and then to determine the surplus calico in terms of pounds sterling! It is worse than squaring the circle, which is at least based on the concept of limits, in which straight lines and curves merge together. But this is M. Passy's recipe. We deduct money from calico before the calico is transformed into money, either in the mind or in actuality! The surplus is the rent, which however should be treated 'naturally' (see for example Karl Arnd),[66] and not with diabolical 'sophistries'!

65 [In English. Translator]

66 [Arnd 1845, pp. 125–37 and 461–2. See also MECW 30, 1988, pp. 356–7. Translator]

It is foolishness such as this, the deduction of the production costs, i.e., the production price, from so and so many bushels of wheat, the subtraction of a sum of money from a cubic measure, which is the logical conclusion of this whole 'natural development' of rent!

|454| If we consider ground-rent in its simplest form, *labour rent*, where the direct producer devotes one part of the week, with tools that belong to him either legally or in practice (the plough, the draft animals, etc.), to land that is in practice his own, and works the other days of the week for the landlord on his estate, gratuitously, the situation here is still completely clear: rent and surplus-value are identical. *Rent* and not profit is the form in which the *unpaid surplus labour* is expressed. > (Compare what was said about this form in Book I, Chapter 2.)[67] The extent to which the worker (a 'self-sustaining serf') can obtain a surplus over > his indispensable means of subsistence, hence a surplus over < what we in the capitalist mode of production would call *the minimum amount of wages*, depends, assuming all other circumstances remain the same, on the extent (the length) of his statute-labour. This *surplus* over and above the necessary means of subsistence, which is the germ of *profit* in the capitalist mode of production, is thus entirely determined by the level of *ground-rent*, which here not only *is*, but *appears* as *unpaid surplus labour* – labour for the 'proprietor' of the conditions of production, which here coincide with the land itself, or, in as much as they are distinct from it, count merely as an accessory to it. That the serf's product must be sufficient in this case to replace his *conditions of labour* as well as his subsistence is a situation that remains *the same* in *all* modes of production, since it is not a result of this *specific form* but rather a natural condition for all continuing and *reproductive* labour in general, of any continuing *production* that is always at the same time *reproduction*, i.e. also reproduction of its own conditions of operation. It is clear, too, that in all forms where the actual worker himself remains the '*possessor*' of the *means of production* and the *conditions of labour* needed for the production of his own means of subsistence, the property relationship must appear at the same time as a direct *relationship of domination and servitude*, and the direct producer therefore as an unfree person, whose unfreedom may however undergo a progressive attenuation from serfdom with statute-labour down to a mere tribute obligation. The direct producer in this case is on our assumption in possession of his own means of production, the objective conditions of labour needed for the realisation of his labour and the production of his means of subsistence; he pursues his agriculture *independently*, as well

---

67 [See Marx 1976, pp. 344–8. Translator]

as the rural-domestic industry associated with it. This independence is not abolished when, as in India for example, these self-sustaining peasants form among themselves a more or less natural community of producers, since what is at issue here is independence *vis-à-vis* the nominal landlord. Under these conditions, the surplus labour for the nominal landowner can only be extorted from them by *extra-economic* compulsion, whatever form this might assume.[68] This differs from the slave or plantation economy in that the slave works with conditions of production that do not belong to him, and does not work independently. Relations of personal dependence are therefore necessary, in other words personal unfreedom, in whatever degree, and being chained to the land as its accessory – *bondage* in the true sense. If there are no private landowners but it is the state (as in Asia) which confronts them |455| *directly* as simultaneously landowner and sovereign, *rent* and *tax* coincide, or rather there does not exist any tax distinct from this form of ground-rent. Under these conditions, the relationship of dependence does not need to possess any *harsher* form, either politically or economically, than that which is common to all subjection to this state. Here the state is the supreme landlord. Sovereignty here is landed property concentrated at the national level. But for this very reason there is no private landed property, though there is both private and communal possession and usufruct of the land.

The specific *economic* form in which unpaid surplus labour is pumped out of the *direct producer* determines the relationship of domination and servitude, as this grows directly out of production itself and reacts back on it in turn as a determinant. On this is based the entire configuration of the economic community arising from the actual relations of production, and hence also its specific political form. It is in each case the direct relationship of the owners of the conditions of production to the immediate producers – a relationship whose particular form naturally corresponds always to a certain level of development of the type and manner of labour, and hence to the development of its social productivity – in which we find the innermost secret, the hidden basis of the entire social edifice, and hence also the political form of the relationship of sovereignty and dependence, in short, the specific form of state in each case. This does not prevent the same economic basis – the same in its major conditions – from displaying endless variations and gradations in its appearance, as the result of innumerable different empirical circumstances, natural condi-

68 When a country was conquered, the first thing for the conqueror was always to take possession of the people. (Cf. Linguet, and also Möser.) [Linguet 1767, p. 309; Möser 1820, pp. 164–7.]

tions, racial relations, historical influences acting from outside, etc., and these can only be understood by analysing these empirically given conditions.

As regards *labour rent*, the most simple and primitive form of rent, this much is self-evident: here rent is the original form of *surplus-value* and coincides with it. On the other hand, it needs no further analysis here that surplus-value coincides with *the unpaid labour of others*, since this still exists in its visible, palpable form, the labour of the direct producer for himself being still separate both in time and space from his work for the landed proprietor, with the latter appearing directly in the brutal form of *forced labour* for another person. Likewise, the 'property' the land has of yielding a *rent* is reduced here to a palpably open secret, for the same nature that delivers rent also includes |456| the *human labour-power* that is chained to the land, and the *property relationship* that *forces* its owner to *exert* and *activate* this labour-power beyond the degree that would be required to satisfy his own indispensable needs. The rent consists in the direct appropriation by the landowner of this extra expenditure of labour-power; for the direct producer does not pay any further rent on top of this. In this case, where surplus-value and rent are not only identical, but the surplus-value still palpably takes the form of surplus labour, the *natural conditions* or *limits* of rent are immediately evident, *because* they are the limits of *surplus labour in general*. The direct producer must (1) have sufficient labour-power, while (2) the natural conditions of his labour, in the first instance the land to be worked, must be fruitful enough, i.e., the *natural productivity* of his labour must be great enough to allow him the possibility of *surplus* labour over and above the labour needed to satisfy his own indispensable needs. It is not this possibility that creates rent; only *compulsion* makes the possibility a reality. The possibility itself, however, is bound up with subjective and objective natural conditions. Here, too, there is nothing at all mysterious. If labour-power is meagre and the natural conditions of labour scarce, the amount of surplus labour is also small; but so too then are (1) the needs of the producers, (2) the relative number of landed proprietors to whom this surplus labour accrues, and finally (3) the surplus product in which this weak quantity of surplus labour is realised for the small number of landed proprietors.

Finally, it immediately follows from labour rent that, assuming all other circumstances to be constant, it depends entirely on the *scale* of the *surplus* or the *forced labour* whether and how far the direct producer is capable of improving his own situation, enriching himself, producing a surplus over and above his indispensable means of subsistence, or, to anticipate > by introducing a category which does not yet belong here, but applies to a much later mode of production, < whether and how far he can produce some kind of *profit* for himself, i.e., a surplus over and above the minimum of the wage he also himself produces > (to use a category which is also often anticipated here and wrongly so). < Rent here is the normal and so to speak legitimate form of *surplus labour*, which absorbs everything, and far from being an *excess* over and above *profit*, i.e., in this case above some other kind of surplus over wages, not only the size of such a *profit*, but even its very existence, all other circumstances remaining the same, depends on the *size of the rent*, i.e. of the surplus labour that has compulsorily to be performed for the proprietor.

|457| Some historians have expressed their amazement that when the direct producer is not a proprietor but only a possessor, all his surplus labour in fact belonging *de jure* to the landowner, it is still possible for this villein or serf to develop independent means of his own or, relatively speaking, to become wealthy. It is evident, however, that in the aboriginal and undeveloped conditions on which this social relation of production and the mode of production corresponding to it are based, *tradition* must play a predominant role. It is also evident here as always that it is in the interest of the dominant section of the society to sanctify the existing situation as a *law*, and to fix the limits consecrated by custom, usage and tradition as *legal* limits. Even ignoring any other factors, this happens automatically as soon as the constant reproduction of the basis of the existing situation, the relationship underlying it, assumes in the course of time a regular and ordered form; and this regulation and order is itself an indispensable aspect of any mode of production that is to become solidly established and free from mere accident or caprice. It is precisely the form in which it is socially established, and hence the form of its relative emancipation from mere caprice and accident. It can attain this form in stagnant and stationary conditions, both of the production process and of the relations that correspond to it, simply by reproducing itself, which will happen automatically. Once the reproduction of these relations of production has continued for a certain length of time, it is reinforced as a tradition and sanctified as a social rule, order and law. > If we assume that, for example, the amount of statute-labour on the proprietor's estate is originally two or three days a week, we must assume that this surplus labour, since its form < depends on the undeveloped condition of all labour's social productive powers, since it depends on the crudeness of the mode of labour itself, *by its nature* takes up a relatively far smaller part of the total labour of the direct producers than in more developed modes of production, and in the capitalist mode of production in particular. Two days of statute-labour a week, for example, persist as a constant quantity, regulated by customary or written law. But the *productivity* of the remaining days of the week |458| that the direct producer has at his disposal is a *variable* quantity, which must develop as he progresses in experience, just as the new needs with which he becomes familiar, the expansion of the market for his product, and the grow-

ing security he has that this portion of his labour-power is at his disposal will spur him to increased exertions. It should not be forgotten in this connection that the use of this labour-power is by no means confined to agriculture but also includes rural domestic industry. This provides the possibility of a certain degree of economic development, dependent of course on favourable circumstances, innate racial characteristics and the capacity of the latter to develop and change.

Produce rent. Economically speaking, the transformation of *labour rent* into *produce rent* does not change the nature of ground-rent at all. This consists, in the forms we are dealing with here, in the fact that ground-rent is the only dominant and *normal form of surplus-value* or *surplus labour*; which is expressed in turn in its being the only surplus labour or surplus product which the direct producer who finds himself in *possession* of the conditions of labour needed for his own reproduction has to provide for the *owner* of the one condition of labour that includes everything else at this stage, the land; while on the other hand it is only the land that confronts him as the *property of another person*, a condition of labour that has *become independent of him*, and is personified in the landowner. But while produce rent is the dominant and furthest developed form of ground-rent, it always remains more or less accompanied by survivals of the earlier form, i.e., rent to be paid directly in labour, statute-labour, whether the proprietor be a private person or the state. This form of rent presupposes a higher cultural level on the part of the immediate producer, i.e., a higher stage of development of his labour and of society in general; and it distinguishes itself from the preceding form by the fact that surplus labour is no longer performed in its natural form, i.e., no longer under the direct supervision and compulsion of the landlord or his understrappers.[69] Rather, the immediate producer, driven on by the force of circumstances instead of direct compulsion and by legal requirements instead of by the whip, is himself responsible for performing this surplus labour. *Surplus production*, in the sense of production over and above the indispensable needs of the immediate producer, and within a field of production that actually belongs to him, on the land that he himself exploits (instead of, as in the previous situation, on the landlord's estate *alongside* and *outside* his own) has here already become the self-evident rule. In this relationship, |459| the immediate producer has the use of more or less his entire labour-time, even if one part of this labour-time, originally more or less the whole *surplus* part of his labour-time, continues to belong for free to the landowner, although the latter no longer receives this directly, in its own

69 [In English. Translator]

natural form, but rather in the natural form of the product in which it is realised. The burdensome interruption of labour for the landowner, which was a more or less constant feature of statute-labour, depending on the way this was regulated (compare for example what was said earlier about the *corvée* in the Danubian Principalities)[70] now disappears > (in the case of pure produce rent), < or is at least reduced to a few brief intervals in the year where certain statutory obligations persist alongside produce rent. The work of the producer for himself and his work for the landowner are no longer palpably separate in time and space. This produce rent, in its pure form, even though relics of it may be handed down to more developed modes and relations of production, still presupposes a natural economy, i.e., it presupposes that the economic conditions are produced entirely or at least in the main by the economic unit itself, being directly replaced and reproduced out of its gross product. It also presupposes the union of rural domestic industry and agriculture; the surplus product which forms rent is the product of this combined agricultural-industrial family labour, whether the produce rent includes a greater or smaller amount of industrial products, as was frequently the case in the Middle Ages, or whether it is paid simply in the form of agricultural products proper. In this form of rent, the produce rent in which surplus labour is expressed need by no means take up the entire excess labour of the rural family. On the contrary, the producer has a greater room to manoeuvre, compared with labour rent, to gain time for excess labour on products that belong to him, just like the product of that labour which satisfies his indispensable needs. In this form, too, greater differences arise in the economic situation of the individual direct producers. There is at least the possibility available for this, and the possibility for the direct producer of obtaining the means whereby he may in turn exploit the labour of others. Yet this does not affect our discussion of the pure form of rent, as we cannot embark hereon the endlessly varied combinations in which the specific forms of rent may be combined, adulterated and amalgamated. The form of produce rent, bound up with a particular type of product and of production itself; the connection indispensable to it between agriculture and domestic industry; and the almost total self-sufficiency that the peasant family thereby obtains, its almost complete independence from the market and from |460| the movement of production and of the history of that part of society outside itself, in brief, the character of natural economy as such, all make this form eminently suitable as a basis for those static conditions of society we can see in Asia for example. Here, as in the earlier form of labour rent, *ground-rent* is the *normal*

---

70 [See Marx 1976, pp. 344–8. Translator]

form of surplus-value, and therefore of surplus labour, i.e., of the *entire excess labour* that the direct producer must perform *for nothing*, in actual fact therefore *compulsorily*, for the owner of his most essential condition of labour, the land – even if this compulsion no longer confronts him in its previous brutal form. *Profit*, if we may incorrectly give this name in anticipation to that *fraction* of the excess of his labour over and above the necessary labour which he appropriates for himself, so little determines *produce rent* that it rather grows up behind its back, meeting a natural limit in the level of the *produce rent*. The latter may be so high as seriously to endanger the reproduction of the conditions of labour, the means of production themselves, making the expansion of production more or less impossible, and reducing the direct producers to the *physical minimum* of the means of subsistence. This is particularly the case when this form is found in existence and exploited by a conquering trading nation, as by the English in India for example.

Money rent. What we mean by money rent is not the industrial or commercial ground-rent based on the capitalist mode of production, which is merely an excess *over* the average profit, but the ground-rent that arises simply from a formal transformation of produce rent, > hence proceeds from the basis of the latter < just as that was itself simply transformed labour rent. Instead of the product itself, the direct producer now has to pay his landowner (whether the state or a private person) the price of this. An excess product in its natural form is no longer sufficient, it has to be transformed from this natural form into the money form. Although the direct producer still continues to produce at least the greater part of his needs, his means of subsistence, himself, a portion of his product must now be transformed into a *commodity* and be produced as a commodity. The character of the entire mode of production is thus more or less changed. It loses its independence, its separation from any social context. > It becomes dependent on market conditions. < What now becomes decisive is the proportion of production costs, which now include greater or smaller monetary expenditures; or at least the excess of the part of the gross product to be transformed into money over and above the part that must serve on the one hand again as means of production and on the other hand as direct means of subsistence. The basis of this type of rent, however, though it is now approaching its dissolution, remains *the same* as for the produce rent that formed its starting-point. The direct producer is still the hereditary or otherwise traditional possessor of the land, who has to provide for the landowner, as the proprietor |461| of this most essential condition of production, an *excess of compulsory labour*, i.e., unpaid labour provided without an equivalent, in the form of the surplus product transformed into money. (Property in agricultural equipment and other movable items, which are distinct from the land itself, is already transformed in the earlier forms into the property of the direct producers, first of all simply in practice but later also in law, and this is still more of a premise for the form of money rent.) The transformation of produce rent into money rent that takes place at first sporadically, then on a more or less national scale, presupposes an already more significant development of trade, urban industry, commodity production in general and therefore monetary circulation. It also presupposes that products have a market price and are sold more or less approximately at their *values*, which in the earlier forms by no means needs to be the case. In the eastern part of Europe we can still see something of this transformation going on today. How little it can be accomplished without a certain development of labour's social productive power is attested to by various failed attempts under the Roman Empire to make this transformation, followed by a regression to rent in kind, after which the attempt was made to transform into money rent at least the part of this rent existing as a state tax. The same difficulty of transition was shown for example under the *ancien régime* in France by the amalgamation and adulteration of money rent through the addition of residues of its earlier forms.

But *money rent* as a transformed and contrasting form of produce rent is the final form of the type of ground-rent we have been considering here, while being at the same time the *form of its dissolution*, namely *ground-rent as the normal form of surplus-value* and the unpaid *surplus labour* which has to be performed for the owner of the conditions of production. In its pure form, this rent, just like labour rent and produce rent, does not represent any excess over and above profit. In its concept it includes profit. In so far as profit arises alongside it *in practice* as a particular part of surplus labour, the money rent, like rent in its earlier forms, is still the *normal limit* to this profit, which can develop only in proportion to the possibility of exploiting that labour, whether a person's own excess labour or that of others, which remains after the surplus labour expressed in money rent has been paid. If a profit really does arise alongside the rent, it is not the profit that sets a limit to rent, but inversely rent which sets a limit to profit. As we have already said, however, *money rent* is at the same time the form of dissolution of the *ground-rent* we have so far been dealing with here, which coincides with surplus-value and surplus labour – ground-rent as the normal and dominant form of surplus-value.

|462| If we leave aside all intermediate forms, such as that of the small peasant farmer, money rent must lead either to the transformation of the land into free *peasant property* or to the form characteristic of the *capitalist mode of production*, rent paid by the farmer-capitalist.

With money rent, the traditional relationship fixed by customary law between the landowner > (whether this is the state or a private proprietor) <

and his vassal, who *possesses* and *exploits* one part of the land, is necessarily transformed into a contractual relationship, a purely monetary relationship determined by fixed rules of positive law. The possessor of the land virtually becomes a *mere tenant*. On the one hand this transformation is utilised, where general conditions of production are suitable, for the expropriation by stages of the old peasant possessor and installation in his place of a capitalist farmer; on the other hand it allows the former possessor to buy himself out of his obligation to pay rent and leads to his transformation into an independent peasant farmer, with full ownership in the land he cultivates.

The transformation of rent in kind into money rent, moreover, is not only necessarily accompanied, but even anticipated, by the formation of a class of non-possessing day-labourers, who hire themselves out for money. During the period of its development, when the new class still appears only sporadically, > and before its maturity, when it enters the picture on a national scale, < the custom necessarily takes shape, among the better-off rent-paying peasants, of exploiting agricultural labourers on their own account, just as in the feudal period the wealthier peasant serfs already kept serfs of their own. In this way, it gradually becomes possible for them to build up a certain amount of capital, and to transform themselves into future capitalists. Among the old possessors of the land, producing for themselves, this provides a seed-bed for the nurturing of capitalist farmers, whose development is conditioned by the development of capitalist production, not just in the countryside but in general, and who advance particularly rapidly when, as in England in the sixteenth century, they are aided by such particularly favourable conditions as the progressive depreciation of money at that time, which, given the traditionally long terms of tenancy contracts, inevitably enriched them at the landowners' expense.

Moreover, once rent takes the form of money and the relation between cultivator and landlord becomes a contractual relation – a transformation which is only possible given a certain relative level of development of the world market, trade and manufacture – land inevitably starts to be leased to capitalists, who were formerly outside rural limits and who now transfer to the land, and to the rural economy, capital that has been obtained in the town, together with the capitalist mode of production, which has already been developed in the towns, namely the production of the product of the soil as a mere commodity, and a mere means to the appropriation of surplus labour. As a general rule, this form can emerge only in those countries that dominate the world market during the period of transition from the feudal to the capitalist mode of production. With the intervention |463| of the capitalist farmer between the landlord and the actual cultivator of the soil, all relationships that arose from the old rural mode of production are torn asunder. The farmer becomes the real boss of these cultivators and the real exploiter of their surplus labour, while the landowner stands in a direct relationship only to this capitalist farmer, and a mere monetary and contractual relationship at that. The *nature of rent* changes thereby, not only as a matter of fact and fortuitously, as happened in part in some places during the prevalence of the previous forms, but rather normally, as its acknowledged and dominant form. From the normal form of surplus-value and surplus labour, it is reduced so as to become the excess of this surplus labour over and above the *part of it* that is appropriated by the exploiting capitalist in the form of profit; the entire surplus labour, both profit and excess over profit, is now directly extracted by him, received in the form of the total surplus produce and turned into money. It is now only an excess part of this surplus-value which he extracts by virtue of his capital, by the direct exploitation of the agricultural worker, that he hands over to the landlord as rent. How much or how little he parts with in this way is determined on average, as a limit, by the average profit that capital yields in the non-agricultural spheres of production and by the non-agricultural prices of production that this governs. Rent has now been transformed from *the normal form* of surplus-value and surplus labour into an excess over the part of surplus labour that is claimed by capital as a matter of course and normally – an excess peculiar to one sphere of production, the agricultural sphere. Instead of *rent*, the normal form of surplus-value is now *profit*, and rent now counts as an independent form only under special conditions, not a form of surplus-value in general but of a particular offshoot of this, *surplus profit*. It is unnecessary to go into any further detail as to how this transformation corresponds to a gradual transformation in the mode of production itself. This already results from the fact that it is now normal for this capitalist farmer to produce the agricultural product as a commodity, and that while formerly only the excess over his means of subsistence was transformed into a commodity, now a relatively minute part of these commodities is directly transformed into his own means of subsistence. It is no longer land, but capital, that has now directly subsumed even agricultural labour under itself and its productivity.

|464| The average profit and the price of production governed by it are formed outside the rural situation, in the orbit of urban trade and manufacture. The profit of the peasant who owes rent does not enter into this equalisation process, for his relationship to the landlord is not a capitalist one. In so far as he makes a profit, realising an excess over and above his necessary means of subsistence, whether by his own labour or by exploiting the labour of others, this happens behind the back of the normal relationship, other factors being equal, it is not the level of this profit that determines the rent, but this profit is conversely determined by the rent as its limit. The high rate of profit in the

Middle Ages was not due simply to the low composition of capital, in which the variable element, the part laid out on wages, was predominant. It was a result of the fraud committed against the countryside, the appropriation of a part of the landowner's rent and of the income of his vassals. The countryside may have exploited the town politically in the Middle Ages, wherever feudalism was not broken through by exceptional urban development as in Italy, but the town everywhere and without exception exploited the countryside economically through its monopoly prices, its system of taxation, its guilds, its direct commercial trickery and its usury.

One might imagine that the very entry of the capitalist farmer into agricultural production would already provide proof that the price of agricultural products, which had always paid a rent in some form or other, would have to stand above the production price of manufactured goods, at least at the time when they entered production; either because they reached the level of a monopoly price, or because they rose to their value, and their value actually does stand above the average price of production governed by the average profit. For if this were not so, the capitalist farmer, given the prevailing prices for agricultural products, could not possibly first realise the average profit from the price of these products and then pay out of this same price a further excess above this profit in the form of rent. One might conclude from this that the general rate of profit guiding the capitalist farmer in his contract with the landlord was formed without taking rent into account, and that as soon as this general rate comes to govern rural production he thus finds this excess in existence and pays it to the landlord. It is in this traditional manner that Mr. Rodbertus explains things, for example.[71] However:

Firstly. This entry of capital into agriculture as an independent and leading power does not take place everywhere all at once, but rather gradually and in particular branches of production. At first it does not take hold of agriculture proper, but rather branches of production such as stock-raising and particularly sheep farming, whose main product, *wool*, is first to offer a market price permanently in excess of its price of production, in conditions of the rise of industry; this is not equalised until later on. That was the case in England during the sixteenth century.

|465| *Secondly*. Since capitalist production sets in only sporadically at first, this provides absolutely no grounds to object to the assumption made here that it first of all takes hold of those farms which can on the whole pay a differential rent as a result of their special fertility or particularly favourable location.

71 [Rodbertus 1851, pp. 81–100; see also MECW 31, 1989, pp. 289–97. Translator]

Thirdly. Even assuming that the prices of agricultural products do stand above their prices of production when this mode of production gets underway, which in fact presupposes an increasing weight of urban demand, as was undoubtedly the case in England in the last third of the seventeenth century, it is still true that once the new mode of production has extended beyond the mere subsumption of agriculture under capital and the improvement in agriculture necessarily bound up with this development, and a reduction in production costs has set in, this will be balanced by a reaction, a fall in the price of agricultural products, as occurred in England in the first half of the eighteenth century.

Thus rent as an excess above the average profit cannot be explained in this traditional way. Whatever the empirically given historical circumstances under which it may first arise, once it has struck root rent can occur only under the modern conditions previously discussed.

We should finally note in connection with the transformation of rent in kind into money rent that the capitalised rent, the *price* of land, and therefore its alienability [*Veräusserlichkeit*] and actual alienation, now becomes an important aspect; and that not only can the former rent-payer transform himself in this way into an independent peasant proprietor, but also urban and other holders of money can buy plots of land with a view to leasing them either to peasants or to capitalists, and enjoying the rent as a form of interest on their capital thus invested. This factor, too, helps to promote the transformation of the former mode of exploitation, or the relationship between the owner and the actual cultivator of the land, and of rent itself.

|466| We have now reached the final point in our *development of ground-rent through its different stages*.

In all these forms of ground-rent – labour rent, produce rent, money rent (as simply a transformed form of ground-rent) – the rent-payer is always taken as the actual exploiter and possessor of the land, whose *unpaid surplus labour* goes directly to the landlord. Even in the last form – money rent – in so far as this is *pure*, i.e., simply the transformed form of produce rent, this is not only a possible case, it is so in actual fact.

As a transitional form from the original form of rent to capitalist rent, we can take the *system of métayage*, or *share-cropping*, in which the tenant farmer provides, besides his labour (he may in turn additionally employ workers or not), a part of the operating capital, the landlord providing not only the land but a further portion of capital (e.g., livestock), and the product being divided between share-cropper and landowner in definite proportions, which vary in different countries. The farmer, here, has insufficient capital for full capitalist cultivation. The share that the landlord receives, on the other hand, does not have the pure form of rent. It may include interest on the capital he advances, and a surplus rent on top of this. It may absorb the entire surplus labour of the farmer, or leave him a greater or smaller share of this. Rent here, however, no longer appears as the *normal* form of *surplus-value* in general; for on the one hand the share-cropper, whether he applies his own labour or that of others, is supposed to have a claim to one part of his produce, not in his quality of labourer, but of possessor of part of the instruments of production, as his own capitalist. On the other hand, the landlord claims his part not exclusively on [the basis of] his ownership of land, but as lender of capital.[72]

One can consider the system which originally existed in the Romanian principalities, for example, as an original form of independent peasant economy. This itself constitutes a transition to the lower forms of ground-rent. Here, one part of the land belongs to the individual peasants and is cultivated by them independently. Another part is cultivated in common and forms a surplus product, which serves partly to meet the communal expenses, and partly as a reserve in case of harvest failures, etc. The two latter parts of the surplus product are gradually usurped by state officials and private individuals, and the originally free peasant proprietors are thus transformed into people who owe compulsory labour services or produce rent, while the usurpers of the common land transform themselves into *proprietors*, not only of the usurped common land but of the parcels of land of the actual cultivators as well.

|467| We do not need to go into any further detail here as regards the *slave economy* (which also passes through a number of gradations from patriarchal slavery to the actual plantation system) or the *estate economy*, in which the landowner cultivates his own estate, possessing all the instruments of production and exploiting his land using workers, whether free or unfree, who are paid either in kind or with money. Here the landowner coincides with the owner of the instruments of production, i.e., with the direct exploiter of the workers who are also numbered among the instruments of production. There is therefore no separation between rent and profit, the different forms of surplus-value. The entire *surplus labour* of the workers, which is expressed here in the surplus product, is *extracted* from them *directly* by the landowner, as the proprietor of all the instruments of production, of which the direct producers also form a part, in the original form of the system. Where the capitalist conception prevails, as on the North American plantations, this entire surplus-value is conceived as *profit*; where the capitalist mode of production does not exist itself, and the conception corresponding to it has not been transferred over from the

72 Cf. Buret [1843], Tocqueville [1856], Sismondi [1827, pp. 189–203. Translator]

countries of capitalist production, it appears as *rent*. In neither case does this form offer any difficulty. The landowner's income, the *available surplus product* he appropriates, whatever name we might give to it, is here the normal and prevailing form in which the entire unpaid surplus labour is directly appropriated, and landed property forms the basis for this appropriation.

Small-scale peasant ownership. Here the cultivator is also the free proprietor of his land, which appears as his main instrument of production, and as the indispensable field of employment for his labour and his capital. No *lease-price* is paid in this form; thus rent does not appear as a separate form of surplus-value, even if, in countries where the capitalist mode of production is otherwise developed, it does present itself as *surplus profit*, by comparison with other branches of production, though as surplus profit which falls to the cultivator, as does the entire yield of his labour.

Like its earlier forms, this form of landownership presupposes that the agricultural population has a great numerical preponderance over the urban population, hence that even if the capitalist mode of production is otherwise dominant it is only developed in relative terms and therefore the concentration of capitals is also confined to narrow limits in the other branches of production, and a fragmentation of capitals prevails.

By the nature of the case, a predominant part of the agricultural product must be consumed here by the peasants themselves; i.e., an overwhelming part of their product must serve as direct means of subsistence, with only the excess over and above this going into trade with the towns as a commodity.

|468| No matter how the average market price of agricultural products is governed here, there must evidently be a *differential rent*, an excess portion of the price of the commodity, for the better or better-located lands, just as there is in the capitalist mode of production. > (When this form exists in states of society where no market prices at all have yet developed, this differential rent appears in the shape of an excess *surplus product*.) < It is simply that the cultivator whose labour is realised under more favourable natural conditions pockets this himself. In this form, the *price of the land* in fact makes up an element of the peasant's production costs, since, as this form develops further, either the price of land is computed at a certain monetary value in dividing up an inheritance, or, as a holding or its constituent parts constantly changes hands the land is bought by the peasant himself (for the most part with money raised through a mortgage). Where the *price of land*, which is nothing but *capitalised rent*, is an element assumed in advance, and the rent therefore seems to exist independently of any *differentiation* in the land's fertility and location – precisely here, in this form, it is to be assumed in the average case that there is *no absolute rent*, i.e., that the worst soil does not pay any rent; for absolute rent assumes either

a realised *excess value of the product* above its *price of production* or an *excess* monopoly price for the product above its value. But since the rural economy here is largely one of agriculture for direct subsistence, with the land being an indispensable field of employment for the labour and capital of the majority of the population, the governing market price of the product only reaches its value under extraordinary conditions; one can assume that this value stands above the price of production, on account of the preponderance of the element of living labour, although this difference between the value and the price of production will in turn be limited by the lower composition of non-agricultural capital in countries where a smallholding economy prevails. The smallholding peasant's exploitation is not limited by the *average profit* on capital, in as much as he is a small capitalist; nor is it limited by the *need for a rent*, in as much as he is a landowner. The only absolute barrier he faces as a petty capitalist is the wage that he pays himself, after deducting his actual expenses. He cultivates his land as long as the price of the product is sufficient for him to cover this wage; and he often does so down to the physical minimum of wages. As far as his *quality as a landowner* is concerned, as the proprietor of his land he does not face any *property barrier*, since this can present itself only in opposition to a capital and a labour separate from it, by imposing an obstacle to its application. The *interest* on the price of land is a *barrier*, however, as it generally has to be paid over to a third party, the mortgagee. But this interest can indeed be paid out of the part of the surplus labour that under capitalist conditions would form the *profit*. The rent anticipated in the *price of land* and the interest paid on it, therefore, can be no more than a part of the surplus labour of the peasant over and above the labour indispensable for his own subsistence, but this surplus labour does not have to be realised in a *portion of commodity value* equal to the entire *average surplus profit*, and still less in an *excess* above the surplus labour realised in the average profit, i.e., a surplus profit. The rent may be a deduction from the average profit or even the only *part* of this that is realised. In order for the peasant smallholder to cultivate his land or to buy land to cultivate, therefore, it is not necessary, as in the normal capitalist mode of production, for the *market price* of the agricultural product to rise high enough to yield the *average profit*, and still less an excess over and above this *average profit* that is fixed in the form of *rent*. Thus it is not necessary for the market price to rise either to the value of his product or to its price of production. This is one of the reasons why the price of corn in countries where small-scale ownership predominates is *lower* than in the countries of the capitalist mode of production. A portion of the surplus labour performed by those peasants working under the least favourable conditions is presented to society for nothing and does not contribute towards governing the price of production or forming value generally. This lower price of corn is therefore a result of the poverty of the producers and by no means of the productivity of their labour.

|469| This form of free smallholding ownership by peasants who farm their land themselves, as the dominant, normal form, constitutes the economic basis of society in the best periods of classical antiquity, while we find it among modern peoples as one of the forms that emerge from the dissolution of feudal landed property. Examples are the yeomanry in England, the peasant estate in Sweden and the French peasants. (We are not speaking here of the *colonies*, since there the independent cultivator develops under different conditions.)

The free ownership of the peasant who farms his land himself is evidently the most normal form of landed property for small-scale cultivation, i.e., for a mode of production in which possession of the land is a condition for the worker's ownership over the product of his own labour, and in which, whether he is free or a dependent proprietor, the cultivator always has to produce his means of subsistence himself, independently, as an isolated worker with his family. Ownership of land is just as necessary for the complete development of this activity as is ownership of the instrument of labour for the free development of the handicraftsman's trade. It forms here the basis for the development of personal independence. It is a necessary transition point in the development of agriculture itself.

The causes of its decline show its limitations. These are: the destruction of rural domestic industry, its normal complement, by the development of large-scale industry; the gradual impoverishment and exhaustion of the soil which has been subjected to this form of cultivation; the usurpation of communal property by large landowners, this communal property always forming a second complement to the smallholding economy and being the only thing which makes possible the upkeep of livestock; the competition of large-scale agriculture, whether in the form of plantations or the capitalist form. Improvements in agriculture also contribute to this, by leading to a fall in the prices of agricultural products, while also requiring greater expenditures and more abundant objective conditions of production, as in England in the first half of the eighteenth century.

The agricultural smallholding, by its very nature, rules out the development of the productive powers of social labour, the social concentration of capitals, stock-raising on a large scale or the progressive application of science.

Usury and the tax system must always impoverish it. The outlay of capital in the price of land withdraws this capital from agriculture. Incessant fragmentation of means of production and isolation of the producers themselves. Tremendous wastage of human labour. The progressive deterioration of the conditions of production and the increase in price of the means of production is a necessary law of small-scale landowning. The disastrous effect of good seasons for this mode of production.[73]

|470| One particular evil of small-scale agriculture, where this is combined with the free ownership of land, arises from the way the cultivator lays out *capital* in *purchasing the land.* (The same applies to the transitional form in which the owner of a large estate lays out capital first to buy land and then again to cultivate it himself as his own farmer.) Given the mobile character land acquires as a mere commodity, changes in possession multiply,[74] so that with each new generation, and each division of an inheritance, the land forms a new *capital investment*, i.e., from the peasant's standpoint it is land that he *has bought*, or it becomes such. The *price of land* here forms a predominant element of the (individual) *overhead cost of production*, or the *cost price* of the product for the individual producer.

The *price of land* is nothing but rent, *capitalised* and thus *anticipated.* If agriculture is pursued on a capitalist basis, so that the landowner simply receives the annual rent and the farmer pays nothing for the land besides this, it is obvious that the capital which the landowner himself invests in purchasing land, though for him it is an interest-bearing capital investment, has nothing at all to do with the capital invested in agriculture itself. It forms part neither of the fixed capital (investment capital) functioning here nor of the circulating capital (enterprise capital);[75] it procures a title for the purchaser to receive the annual rent, but it has absolutely nothing to do with the *production* of that rent. The buyer of the land simply hands the capital over to the person selling it, and the seller thereby renounces his property in the land. Thus this capital no longer exists as *capital* for the buyer; he no longer has it; it therefore does not form

73 See the King of France's speech, in Tooke [Marx refers here to a speech by Napoleon III in 1854, quoted in Tooke and Newmarch 1857, pp. 29–30. Translator]

74 See Mounier [1846, pp. 102, 118, and 189] and Rubichon [1837, pp. 23–4.]

75 Maron [1859] proceeds from an incorrect assumption by his opponents. He assumes that the capital invested in the purchase of land is 'investment capital' and simply challenges the respective definitions of the concepts investment capital and operating capital, i.e., fixed capital and circulating capital. His completely schoolboyish ideas about capital in general, even if they are excusable for a non-economist, given the general condition of German 'national economics', conceal from him that this capital is *neither* investment capital nor operating capital. In the same way, the capital that someone invests on the stock exchange in the purchase of shares or government paper is by no means actually 'invested' in any branch of production, even if it appears as a *capital investment for him* personally.

part of the capital he can invest in the land itself in any way at all. Whether the landowner has bought the land dearly or cheap, or even got it for nothing, by no means affects the capital that the farmer invests in agriculture and changes nothing in the rent. The only thing that changes is whether this rent appears to him as interest or not, or as a higher or lower interest.

Take the case of the slave economy, for example. The price that is paid here for the slave is nothing but the *capitalised* surplus-value or profit that is to be extracted from him. But the capital paid in purchasing the slave does not form part of the capital by which profit, surplus labour, is extracted from him. On the contrary. It is capital which the person who conducts his business with the slave has alienated, it is a deduction from the capital which he has at his disposal in actual production. It has ceased to exist for him, just as the capital invested in the purchase of land has ceased to exist for agriculture. The best proof of this is that it comes into renewed *existence* for him, the slaveowner or the landowner, only when he *sells* the slave or the land again. But then the same relationship is set up for the buyer. The fact that he has bought the slave by no means enables him immediately to exploit him. He is only able to do this by putting further capital into the slave economy itself.

|471| The same capital does not exist twice over, first in the hands of the seller of the land and then in the hands of its buyer. It passes from the buyer to the seller, and that is the end of it. The buyer now has no capital, but a piece of land instead. The fact that the rent obtained from the actual investment of capital on this piece of land is now reckoned by the new landowner as interest on capital that he has not invested on the land but has parted with in order to obtain it, does not change the economic nature of the land factor in the slightest, any more than the fact that someone has paid A £1,000 for three percent stocks (government bonds) has anything to do with the capital from whose revenue the interest on the national debt is paid.

In actual fact, what is paid over in the purchase of land, just like the money spent on the purchase of government bonds, is only *potential* capital, just as any *sum of value* is *potential* capital on the basis of the capitalist mode of production. What was paid for the land, just as for government bonds or any other bought commodities, is a *sum of money*. This is *potential* capital, because it can be transformed into capital. It depends on the use made of it by the seller whether the money he receives really is transformed into capital or not. For the buyer, it can no longer function as such, any more than any other money he has definitively spent. It functions in his accounts as interest-bearing capital, since he reckons the income he receives – as rent from the land or as revenue he receives from the state – as *interest* on the money that it cost him to purchase the title to this revenue. He can realise it as capital only by reselling it. But then someone else, the new buyer, steps into the same relationship as the former was in before; no change of hands can transform the money spent in this way into actual *capital* for the spender.

In the case of small-scale landed property, the illusion is still more strongly reinforced that land has a *value* of its own and thus goes into the production price of the product as capital, just like a machine or cotton. But we have seen that there are only two cases in which rent and hence capitalised rent, the *price of land*, can go into the price of the agricultural product as a determining factor. Firstly, if the value of the agricultural product stands above its price of production, as a result of the composition of agricultural capital – a capital which has nothing in common with capital laid out on the purchase of land – and market conditions enable the landowner to valorise this difference. Secondly, if there is a monopoly price. And these conditions obtain least of all in the case of small-scale agriculture and landed property, since it is precisely here that a large part of production is designed to satisfy the producer's own needs, and proceeds without being governed by the general rate of profit. This is because here, more than under any other conditions, the *lease-price* constitutes a part of the profit and even a deduction from wages, which is then only nominally *rent*, not a category to be distinguished from wages and profit.

Thus the expenditure of money capital on the purchase of land is not an investment of agricultural capital. It proportionately reduces the capital which the cultivators have at their disposal in their actual sphere of production. It proportionately reduces the scale of their means of production and hence contracts (and worsens) the economic basis of reproduction. It subjects the cultivator to usury, since in this sphere there is always less actual credit. It is a constraint on agriculture, even when the purchase of large estates is involved. It in fact contradicts the capitalist mode of production, for there |472| the indebtedness of the landowner, whether his estate is inherited or bought, is on the whole immaterial. Whether he pockets the rent himself or has to pay it over to a mortgagee does not affect the cultivation of the property leased.

We have seen that once the ground-rent is given, the price of land is governed by the rate of interest. If this is low, the price of land is high, and vice versa. In normal conditions, therefore, a high price of land and a low rate of interest go together, so that if the peasant has to pay a high price for land when the interest rate is low, the same low rate of interest will also procure him his operating capital at favourable terms of credit. In actual fact, though, things are different when smallholding predominates. Firstly, the general laws of credit do not apply to the peasants, since they presuppose that the producers are capitalists. Secondly, where smallholding predominates (we are not referring here to colonies) and the smallholding peasant forms the backbone of the nation, the formation of capital, and thus reproduction, is relatively weak. Still weaker is the formation of money capital, i.e., loanable capital, in the sense we have previously developed. The latter assumes the concentration of capital and the existence of a class of rich, idle capitalists.[76] Thirdly, where landownership forms condition of life for the greater part of the producers, as it does here, and a necessary field for their outlay of capital, the price of land will rise independently of the rate of interest and often in inverse proportion to it, because the demand for landed property will outweigh the supply. Being sold in this case in parcelled lots, the land fetches a far higher price than when sold in large estates, since the number of small buyers is large and the number of large buyers is small.[77] All these reasons lead to a rise in the price of land, even at a relatively high rate of interest. The relatively low interest that the peasant draws from the capital he lays out on the purchase of land[78] contrasts with the high rate of interest he himself has to pay to the creditors who issued his mortgage. The Irish system shows the same thing, only in another form.

An element that is foreign to production as such, the *price of land*, can thus rise here to a level which makes production impossible.[79]

If the *price of land* plays such a role, if the purchase and sale of land, the circulation of land as a commodity, develops to this extent, this is the practical result of the development of the capitalist mode of production, in as much as here the *commodity* becomes the general form of every product and of all instruments of production. On the other hand, this takes place only where the capitalist mode of production is developed to a limited extent and does not yet display all its characteristic features; because it precisely depends on a situation where agriculture is no longer – or not yet – subjected to the capitalist mode of production, but is rather subjected to a mode of production taken over from forms of society that have disappeared. The drawbacks of the capitalist mode of production, with its dependence of the producer on the *money price* of his product, are thus combined here with the drawbacks

---

76 Massie [1750, pp. 23–4.]

77 *Bandes Noires etc.* Rubichon. (Newman ?). [The *bandes noires* were speculative companies set up in France at the beginning of the nineteenth century to buy land previously confiscated during the French Revolution and then to divide it up and resell it at a profit. See Rubichon 1837, pp. 129–30 and Newman 1851, pp. 180–1. Translator]

78 Mounier [1846, pp. 267–73 and 295–7.]

79 Dombasle. [Mathieu de Dombasle 1828, pp. 301–7. See also MECW 31, 1989, pp. 259–60. Translator]

that arise from its *incomplete* development. The peasant becomes a merchant and an industrialist without the conditions which enable him to produce his product as a commodity.

The conflict between the *price of land* as an element of the cost price for the producer and as a *non-element* of the price of production for the product (even when rent is a determining factor in the price of the agricultural product, the capitalised rent which is *advanced* for twenty years or more never is) is just one of the forms expressing the contradiction between the private ownership of land and a rational agriculture, the normal social use of the land. On the other hand, |473| *private ownership of land*, and thus the expropriation from the land of the direct producers, is a fundamental condition of the capitalist mode of production.

Here [in the case of small-scale agriculture] the *price of land*, as a form and result of private property in land, appears as a barrier to production itself. In the case of large-scale agriculture and large-scale landed property resting on the capitalist mode of operation, *property* similarly appears as a barrier, since it restricts the farmer in the productive investment of capital, which ultimately benefits not him but the landowner. In both forms, instead of a conscious and rational treatment of the land as permanent communal property, as the inalienable condition for the existence and reproduction of the chain of human generations, we have the exploitation and squandering of the powers of the earth (not to mention the fact that exploitation is made dependent not on the level of social development reached but rather on the accidental and unequal conditions of the individual producers). In the case of small-scale ownership, this results from a lack of the resources and scientific knowledge needed to apply the social productive powers of labour. In the case of large-scale landed property, it results from the exploitation of these resources for the most rapid possible enrichment of the farmer and the proprietor. In both cases it results from dependence on the market price.

All criticism of small-scale landownership is ultimately reducible to criticism of *private property* as a barrier and obstacle to agriculture. So too is all counter-criticism of large landed property (leaving aside political considerations, etc.) This barrier and this obstacle which all private property in land places to agricultural production and the rational treatment, maintenance and improvement of the land itself, develops in various different forms, and in quarrelling over the specific forms of the evil its ultimate root is forgotten.

It is a presupposition of small-scale landownership that the overwhelming majority of the population is agricultural and that isolated labour predominates over social labour; wealth and the development of reproduction, therefore, both in their material and their intellectual aspects, are ruled out under these circumstances, and with this also the conditions for a rational agriculture; large-scale landownership, on the other hand, reduces the agricultural population to a constantly decreasing minimum and confronts it with a constantly growing industrial population conglomerated together in large towns; in this way it produces conditions that provoke an irreparable rift in the interdependent process of social metabolism, a metabolism prescribed by the natural laws of life itself. The result of this is a squandering of the vitality of the soil, and trade carries this devastation far beyond the bounds of a single country.[80]

While small-scale landownership creates a class of vandals standing half outside society, combining all the crudeness of primitive social forms with all the torments and misery of civilised states, large-scale landed property undermines labour-power in the final sphere to which its inborn natural energy flees, and where it is stored up as a reserve fund for renewing the vital power of the nations, on the land itself. Large-scale industry and industrially pursued agriculture go hand in hand. If they are originally distinguished by the fact that the former lays waste and ruins labour-power and thus the natural power of man, whereas the latter does the same to the natural power of the soil, they link up in the later course of development, since the industrial system applied to agriculture also debilitates the workers there, while industry and trade for their part provide agriculture with the means of exhausting the soil.

|474| (b) **Differential Rent**

In our analysis of rent we intend to proceed first of all from the assumption that products that pay a ground-rent – which means that a part of their surplus-value and therefore also a part of their total price is reducible to rent – are sold just like all other commodities at their *prices of production* (for our present purpose we need consider only agricultural and mining products), i.e., that they are sold at prices which are equal to their cost elements (the value of the constant and variable capital consumed) plus a profit determined by the *general rate of profit*, which is calculated on the total capital advanced, whether consumed or not. We assume that the average sale prices of these products are equal to their prices of production. The question then arises of how a ground-rent can develop on this assumption, i.e., how a portion of profit can be transformed into ground-rent, so that a part of the commodity price thus accrues to the landowner.

---

80 Liebig [1862 (1), pp. 292–302.]

To demonstrate the general character of this form of ground-rent, we assume that the factories in a country are powered predominantly by steam-engines, but a certain minority rely on *natural waterfalls* instead. We assume that the production price in the branches of industry first mentioned is 115 for a quantity of commodities for which a capital of 100 is consumed. The 15 percent profit is calculated not just on the consumed capital of 100 but on the total capital that is applied in the production of this commodity value. This production price, as we explained earlier, is determined not by the *individual cost price* of any one individual producer (manufacturer), but rather by the price that it costs on average > to place a certain quantity of commodities on the market < under the average conditions for capital in that whole sphere of production. It is in fact the market price of production; the average market price as distinct from its oscillations. It is always in the form of the *market* price, and moreover in the form of the *governing market price*, or the *market price of production*, that the nature of the commodity's *value* presents itself, its character being determined not by the labour-time *needed* by a certain individual producer to produce a certain quantity of a commodity or a certain number of individual commodities, but by the *socially* necessary labour-time required under the average social conditions of production to produce the *total socially required quantity* of the species of commodity available on the market.

Since the specific numerical relations are completely immaterial here, we shall further assume that the cost price of the factories that are driven by water-power comes to only 90 instead of 100. Since the production price of the great mass of goods that govern the market is 115, with a profit of 15 percent, the factories that drive their machines with water-power will also sell at 115, i.e., at the market price as governed by the average price. Their profit will amount to 25 instead of 15; the governing price of production enables them to make a surplus profit of 10 percent, not because they sell their commodities *above* the price of production but because they sell them *at* that price, because their commodities are produced, or their capital functions, under exceptionally favourable conditions, conditions that stand above the average level prevailing in this sphere.

|475| Two things are immediately evident here:

Firstly, the *surplus profit* of those producers who use natural water-power as their motive force behaves first of all just like *any other* surplus profit (this category has already been developed in our presentation of the price of production) which is not the chance result of transactions in the circulation process, or accidental fluctuations in the market price. This surplus profit is thus similarly equal to the *difference* between the *individual price of production* of these favoured producers and the *general* social *price of production* in the sphere of production as a whole, which is what governs the market. This difference is equal to the excess of the general production price of the commodity over its individual production price. The two governing limits of this > difference or this < excess are on the one hand the *individual cost price* and hence the individual production price, and on the other the *general production price*. The value of the commodities produced by water-power is lower because a smaller amount of labour is required for their production, i.e., less labour enters in the objectified form, as a portion of the constant capital. The labour applied here is *more productive*, its individual productivity being greater than that of the labour employed in the majority of factories of the same type. Its greater productivity is expressed in the way that it needs a smaller quantity of constant capital to produce the same amount of commodities, a smaller quantity of objectified labour than the others. This greater individual productivity of the labour applied reduces the value, and therefore the production price (because this is here the cost price) of the commodity. (Less labour is also required, because no labour is required for heating, etc.) For the manufacturer, this presents itself in the following way, that the *cost price* of the commodity for him is less. He has less objectified labour to pay for, and less living labour-power needs to be applied (hence less wages need to be paid). Since the cost price of his commodity is less, so too is his individual production price. His cost price is 90 instead of 100. And so his individual production price is also only $103\frac{1}{2}$ instead of 115 (100: 115 = 90: $103\frac{1}{2}$. > And $103\frac{1}{2}$ + 10, which is the extra profit, = 113 + $\frac{10}{5}$ = 115.) < The difference between his individual production price and the general one is determined by the difference between his individual cost price and the general one. This is one of the magnitudes that set limits to his surplus profit. The other is the *general price of production*, in which the general rate of profit is one of the governing factors. If coal becomes cheaper, the difference between his individual cost price and the general one declines, and so therefore does his surplus profit. If he had to sell the commodity at its individual value, > or the production price determined by its individual value, < the difference would disappear. It is the result on the one hand of the fact that the commodity is sold at its *general market price*, the price at which competition balances the individual prices, and on the other hand of the fact that the greater individual productivity of the labour that he sets in motion does not benefit the workers, but, like the productivity of labour in general, their employer, i.e., it presents itself as the productivity of capital.

Since one limit to this extra profit is the level of the *general price of production* (and the *general rate of profit* is a factor in this) the surplus profit can arise *only* from the *difference* between the general and the individual production prices, and hence from the difference between the *individual* and the *general rate of profit*. An excess *over and above* this difference would presuppose the sale of the product *above* the price of production governed by the market, and not *at* that price.

|476| *Secondly*, the *surplus profit* of the manufacturer who uses natural water-power as his motive force instead of steam has not so far been distinguished in any way from all other surplus profit. All *normal* surplus profit, i.e., surplus profit not brought about by accidental business transactions or fluctuations in the market price, is determined by the difference between the *individual production price* of the commodities produced by this particular capital and the *general production price* which governs the market prices of commodities for capital right across this sphere of production, or, in other words, the market prices of commodities for the total capital invested in this sphere of production.

But now comes the rub.

To what circumstances does the manufacturer in the present case owe his surplus profit, > the difference between his individual rate of profit and the general rate of profit, < the excess yielded to him by the production price which is governed by the general rate of profit?

In the first instance, he owes it to a *force of nature*, the motive force of water-power which is provided by nature itself and is not itself the product of labour, unlike the coal that transforms water into steam, which has value and must be paid an equivalent, i.e., costs something. It is a *natural agent of production*, and no labour has gone into creating it.

But that is not all. The manufacturer who operates with the steam-engine also applies natural forces which cost him nothing, but which make labour more productive, and, in so far as they cheapen the production of the means of subsistence the workers require, increase surplus-value and hence profit; which are therefore just as much monopolised by capital as are the natural social forces of labour, which arise from cooperation and so on. The manufacturer pays for the coal, but not for the ability of water to change its aggregate state and transform itself into steam, nor does he pay for the elasticity of the steam, etc. This monopolisation of natural forces, i.e., of the heightening of labour-power brought about by natural forces, is common to all capital that operates with steam-engines. It may increase the part of the product of labour that is transformed into surplus-value as against the part that is transformed into wages. In so far as it does this, it increases the *general rate of profit* but it does not create any surplus profit, for this consists precisely in the excess of individual profit over and above the average profit. If the application of a *natural force* does in this case create *surplus profit*, this cannot arise solely from the fact that the increased productivity of labour is due here to the use of a natural force. Further modifying factors must come into play.

Conversely, the simple application of natural forces in industry may affect the *level of the general rate of profit* through its impact on the amount of labour required to produce the means of subsistence. But it does not in and of itself create any *divergence* from the general rate of profit, and it is precisely a divergence of this kind that we are dealing with now.

Moreover, the surplus profit that an individual capital in a *particular sphere of production* might otherwise realise – for divergences in the rate of profit between particular spheres of production are constantly balanced out to give the *average rate of profit* – arises, apart from merely accidental divergences, from a reduction in the cost price, i.e., in production costs, which is due either to the fact that capital is applied on a *greater than average scale*, so that the overhead costs of production are reduced, while the general causes of a rise in labour productivity, such as cooperation, division of labour, etc., can operate to a greater extent and with more intensity, because over a more extensive field; or else to the fact that, apart from the |477| scale of the functioning capital, better methods of work, new inventions, improved machines, and chemical trade secrets are employed, in short it is due to the application of new, improved and above-average means and methods of production. The reduction in the cost price, and the surplus profit which flows from this, arise here from the manner and form in which the functioning capital is invested. They arise either from its concentration in exceptionally large amounts in a single hand – something that is cancelled out as soon as equally large amounts of capital are employed as an average – or from the circumstance that capital of a particular size functions in a particularly productive way – and this circumstance ceases to operate as soon as the exceptional manner of production becomes the general rule, or is overtaken by one still more advanced.

The reason for the surplus profit in this case thus originates from the *capital* itself (under which we include the labour that it sets in motion). It might be a difference in the magnitude of the capital applied or a more efficient application of it; and nothing inherently prevents all the capital in the same sphere of production from being invested in the same way. Competition between capitals actually tends to the contrary, it tends to cancel out these distinctions more and more; the determination of *value* by socially necessary labour-time asserts itself through a cheapening of commodities and a compulsion to produce all commodities under the same favourable conditions.

It is different with the *surplus profit* of the manufacturer who makes use of the waterfall. The increased productivity of the labour he applies arises neither from the *capital* and *labour* themselves nor from the simple application of a natural force distinct from capital and labour but incorporated into the capital. It arises from the greater *natural* productivity of a labour linked with the use of a natural force, but a natural force that is not available to all capital in the same sphere of production, as is for example the elasticity of steam; its use therefore does not automatically occur as soon as capital is invested in this sphere. What is used is rather a *monopolisable* natural force which, like the waterfall, is available only to those who have at their disposal *particular pieces of the earth's surface* and their appurtenances. It does not at all lie within capital's power to call into being this *natural condition* of greater labour productivity, in the way that any capital can transform water into steam. The condition in question is found in nature only at certain places, and it is not bound up with products that labour can produce such as machines, coal, etc., hence it cannot be produced by laying out a specific amount of capital. It is, instead, bound up with a particular natural constitution of the ground, of particular parts of the ground. The manufacturers who possess waterfalls exclude those who do not possess them from employing this natural force, because land is limited, and this is even more the case for land endowed with water-power. (It cannot, however, be ruled out that although the number of natural waterfalls in a country is limited, the amount of water-power that industry can use may still be increased. A waterfall can be artificially channelled to give it the necessary motive power; a water-wheel can be improved in order to use as much of this water-power as possible; where the ordinary type of wheel is not suited to the supply of water, turbines can be used; > so that though the number of natural waterfalls cannot be increased, it is still possible to increase the number utilisable by industry within a given country.) < Possession of this natural force forms a monopoly in the hands of its owner, a condition of higher productivity for the capital invested, which cannot be produced by capital's own production process;[81] the natural force which can be monopolised in this way is always attached to the earth. > (Thus sunlight itself can be monopolised.) These natural forces |478| remain in the hands of the manufacturers who possess them. < They do not belong to the general conditions of the sphere of production in question nor to those of its conditions that are generally reproducible. If we now imagine that these waterfalls, together with the land on which they are located, are in the hands of subjects who are accepted as the proprietors of those portions of the globe, as *landowners*, then these people are in a position to prevent the application of capital to the waterfall and its utilisation by capital. They can

81 On *extra profit*, see the *Inquiry* (against Malthus). [*An Inquiry* 1821, pp. 105–9.]

either allow this use or refuse it. But capital cannot create a waterfall from its own resources. The *surplus profit* that arises from this use of the waterfall thus arises not from the *capital* but rather from the use by capital of a monopolisable and monopolised *natural force*. Under these conditions, the surplus profit is transformed into a *ground-rent*, i.e., it accrues to the owner of the waterfall. If the manufacturer pays the latter £10 per year for the waterfall, his profit comes to £15, 15 percent on the £100 which is now the amount of his production costs. And he is still in a position just as good as the other capitalists in his sphere of production who operate with steam. > (In one respect he is better off, since he saves on the outlay for a steam-engine and can therefore work with a smaller amount of capital.) < Nothing is altered if the capitalist owns the waterfall himself. He still draws the surplus profit of £10 not as a capitalist but as the owner of the waterfall; and for the precise reason that this excess arises not from his capital as such, but rather from his power to dispose of a *natural force* that is limited in scope, separable from his capital, and monopolisable. It is transformed into *ground-rent*.

Firstly, it is clear that this rent is always a *differential rent*, for it does not contribute to determining the general *production price* of the commodity, but takes this as given. It always arises from the difference between the individual production price of the particular capital which has the monopolised natural force available to it and the *general production price* for capital invested in the sphere of production in question.

Secondly, this ground-rent does not derive from any *absolute rise* in the productivity of the capital applied or of the labour it appropriates, which can only ever reduce the value of commodities; it arises rather from the greater *relative* returns from certain particular capitals invested in a sphere of production, as compared with those capital investments that are excluded from the exceptional, favourable conditions of productivity which have been created by nature. If, for example, the use of steam guaranteed an overwhelming advantage which would not occur if water-power were used, even though coal has value and water-power does not, and this advantage more than compensated for that fact, water-power would not be used and could not produce any surplus profit, hence no rent either.

Thirdly, the *natural force* in question is not the source of the surplus profit but simply a *natural basis* for it, because it is the *natural basis* of the exceptionally increased productivity of social labour. Use-value is absolutely the natural bearer of *exchange-value*, but it is not its cause. If the same use-value could be obtained without labour, it would have no exchange-value, > but it would retain as before its *natural* usefulness as a use-value. < On the other hand, however, a thing cannot have exchange-value without having *use-value*, i.e., without being a natural bearer of labour of this kind. If the various different values did not balance out into production prices and the various individual production prices into a general production price that governs the market, a rise in labour productivity resulting from the use of a waterfall would simply *lower* the prices of the commodities produced with the waterfall without raising the portion of profit contained in those commodities, just as increased labour productivity in general would not be transformed into surplus-value if capital did not appropriate as its own the productive power, natural and social, of the labour applied.

|480| *Fourthly, landed property* in the waterfall has in and of itself nothing to do with the creation of the portion of surplus-value (profit) and hence of the price of the commodity that is produced with the aid of the waterfall. This surplus profit exists even if there is no landed property, if for example the land on which the waterfall is located can be used by the manufacturer as unclaimed land. Thus landed property does not create the portion of value that is transformed into surplus profit; rather it simply enables the landowner, the proprietor of the waterfall, to entice this surplus profit out of the manufacturer's pocket and into his own. It is not the cause of this profit's creation, but rather of its transformation into the form of *ground-rent*, hence of the appropriation of this portion of profit or commodity price by the landowner or the waterfall-owner.

Fifthly, it is clear that the *price of the waterfall*, hence the price that the landowner would receive if he sold it to another landowner (a third party) or to the manufacturer himself, does not at first go directly *into the production price of the commodities concerned*, even though it does go into the manufacturer's individual cost price, for rent arises in this case from the *production price* of those commodities of the same kind that are produced by steam-engines, which is determined independently of the waterfall. Moreover, the *price of the waterfall* is altogether an irrational expression which conceals a real economic relationship. The waterfall, like the earth in general and every natural force, has no *value*, since it represents no objectified labour and hence no *price*, this being in the normal case nothing but value expressed in money. Where there is no value, there is by that very fact nothing to be expressed in money. The price in this case is nothing but *capitalised rent*. Landed property enables the proprietor to *lay hold of* the difference between the individual profit and the average profit; the profit acquired in this way, which is renewed every year, can be *capitalised* and then *appears* as the price of the natural force itself. If the surplus profit that the use of the waterfall yields to the manufacturer is £10 per year and the average interest is five percent, this £10 per year represents the interest on a capital of £200; and this capitalisation of the annual £10 that the waterfall empowers its owner to extract from the manufacturer then appears as the *capital value* of the *waterfall itself*. The fact that the waterfall does not itself have value but that its *price* is simply the reflection of the surplus profit extracted, calculated in the capitalist way, is immediately evident in the way that the price of £200 simply expresses the product of the surplus profit of £10 multiplied by twenty years, whereas, if circumstances remain otherwise the same, the same waterfall actually enables its owner to seize hold of this annual £10 for an indefinite time, thirty or a hundred years, while on the other hand, if a new method of production that cannot make use of water-power lowers the cost price of the commodities produced by steam from £100 to £90, the surplus profit would disappear, and the rent and the price of the waterfall along with it.

Now that we have established the general concept of differential rent in this way, we turn to considering this rent in agriculture itself. (What will be said of agriculture applies on the whole to mining as well.)

|481|[82] The following statement by Ricardo is completely correct: '*Rent*' (i.e., *differential* rent; he assumes that no rent exists besides differential rent) 'is always the difference between the produce obtained by the employment *of two equal quantities of capital and labour*'. (Ricardo 1821, p. 59.) 'On the *same quantity of land*', he ought to have added, as far as *rent of land* and not surplus profit in general is concerned.

Surplus profit, in other words, if produced in normal conditions and not created accidentally by transactions during the circulation process, 'is always obtained by two equal quantities of capital and labour' and this surplus profit is transformed into *rent* if two equal quantities of capital and labour with unequal results are employed on the same *quantities of land*. > In considering *ground-rent* it is not sufficient simply to say that < surplus profit arises from the unequal results of equal quantities of capital employed. Capitals of different size could also be employed in the different investments, and this is even the general assumption; but equal *proportionate* parts, for example £100 of each, give unequal results; i.e., the rate of profit > of *equal quantities* of capitals of different sizes < is then unequal; this is the general precondition for the *existence* of *surplus profit* in any sphere of employment [of capital] whatever. The second aspect is the *transformation* of this surplus profit into the form of the *rent of land* (rent in general, as a *form* distinct from profit); it is always necessary

82 [This is the beginning of Engels's Chapter 39 ('The First Form of Differential Rent'). Editor]

to investigate when, how and under what circumstances this transformation takes place.

Ricardo is also correct when he makes the following statement (as far as *differential rent* is concerned):

'Whatever diminishes the inequality in the produce obtained on the same or on new land tends to lower rent; and whatever increases that inequality, necessarily produces an opposite effect, and tends to raise it' (Ricardo 1821, p. 74).

These causes, however, do not include only the general ones of *fertility* and *situation*, but also (1) the distribution of taxes, according to whether this has a uniform or a divergent effect; the latter is always the case when taxation is not centralised, as it is in England, and the tax is levied on the *land* and not on the *rent*; (2) *inequalities* that result from differences in the development of agriculture in different parts of the country (since this branch of industry, on account of its traditional character, is more difficult to equalise than is manufacture); and (3) inequalities in the way capital is divided among the farmers. As the capitalist mode of production in agriculture is in fact the last step of capitalist production altogether, the transformation of the peasant into a wage-labourer, these inequalities are greater here than in any other branch of industry.

After these preliminary remarks, I intend to start by summarising very briefly the way the particular features of *my* development differ from that of Ricardo, etc.

|482| We start by considering the unequal results of unequal quantities of capital applied to different lands of the same area (or, to be more precise, the results calculated on *equal acreages* of *different cultivated* lands).

The two general causes of these unequal results, which are independent of capital, are (1) *fertility*, and (2) the *location* of the land. (The latter is decisive in the case of *colonies*, and decisive everywhere for the sequence in which lands can be *successively* brought into cultivation.) (In dealing with point (1) we shall have to discuss what is meant by the *natural fertility* of the land, and the *different* aspects this involves.) It is also clear that these two different bases for differential rent, fertility and location, can operate in opposite directions. A piece of land may be very well situated but of very low fertility, and vice versa. > Only the initial circumstances count. < This is an important fact, since it explains why it is possible to proceed from better soil to worse as well as the other way round in the gradual process of bringing the soil of a whole country into cultivation. It is clear, finally, that the progress of social production in general has on the one hand a *levelling* effect on location as a basis for differential rent, since it creates local markets and improves location by creating *means of communication and transport*; while on the other hand it increases *differences in the local situation of areas of land*, by separating agriculture from manufacturing and by the formation of great centres of production, leading to the relative depopulation of the countryside.

First of all, however, we shall leave aside this *point of location* and simply consider *natural fertility*. Apart from large-scale climatic aspects and so on, *differences in natural fertility* consist in differences in the *chemical composition of the soil*, i.e., variations in the amount of *nutrient elements* for the *plants* it contains. However, assuming the same *chemical composition* and in this sense the *same natural fertility* of two areas of land, their actual effective fertility will differ according to how far these nutrient elements occur in > a more or less < readily assimilable *condition/form*, and can be directly used as plant foodstuffs. Thus the extent to which the same natural fertility can be obtained on soils that are naturally *equally fertile* depends in part on the *chemical* development of agriculture and in part on its *mechanical* development. Even though *fertility* is an objective property of the soil, it thus always involves an economic *relation*, a relation to the given chemical and mechanical level of agricultural development, and therefore *changes* with this level of development. By *chemical* means (e.g., the use of certain liquid fertilisers on stiff clayey soil, or the calcination of heavy clayey soil) and by *mechanical* means too (e.g., special ploughs for heavy soil) it is possible to remove obstacles which made soils of equal fertility less productive in practice. (Drainage, too, comes under this heading.) The *sequence* followed in bringing different types of soil into cultivation may also be changed in this way, as it was for instance between light sandy soil and heavy clayey soil at one period of English agricultural development. This further shows how *historically* – in the successive course of cultivation – the sequence can go just as much from more fertile to less fertile soil as the reverse. The same thing can happen as a result of artificially induced improvements in the composition of the soil or > simply through a change in farming methods. The same result, finally, can come about through a < change in the hierarchy of soil types when various subsoil conditions come into play, once the subsoil also begins to be ploughed and turned over into top layers. This is brought about partly by the use of new agricultural methods (such as the cultivation of fodder grasses) and partly by mechanical means, which either turn the subsoil into the top layer or mix the two together, or else cultivate the subsoil without turning it up.

|483| All these influences on the *differential fertility* of different prices of land boil down to the fact that as far as *economic* fertility is concerned, the level of *labour productivity*, in this case the ability of agriculture directly to make the fertility of the soil *available* – an ability that varies with different stages

of development – is just as much a factor in the so-called *natural fertility* of the soil as its *chemical composition* and *richness* (leaving aside other *natural* properties).

We thus assume a *given level of agricultural development*. We further assume that the hierarchy of soil types is calculated in relation to this level of development, as is of course always the case with *simultaneous capital investments* on different lands. The differential rent can then exhibit an increasing or decreasing series, for although the *series is given* for the totality of lands actually cultivated, these have always been *formed* by a successive movement.

Assume four types of soil, A, B, C, and D. Assume further that the price of a quarter of wheat is £3, or 60 shillings. Since the rent here is simply *differential rent*, this price of 60 shillings a quarter is equal to the production costs on the worst soil, i.e., it is equal to the *capital* plus the *average profit*.

Let A be this worst soil, giving 1 quarter = 60 shillings for an outlay of 54⁶⁄₁₁ shillings; i.e., a profit of 10 percent, since 110: 60 = 100: 54⁶⁄₁₁. (Hence a profit of 5⁵⁄₁₁ shillings.)

Let B yield 2 quarters, sold at 120 shillings for the same outlay. (This would result in a profit of 65⁵⁄₁₁, or a surplus profit of 60 shillings {= 5⁵⁄₁₁ + 60 shillings.})

Let C yield 3 quarters, sold at 180 shillings for the same outlay. (This would result in a surplus profit of 120 shillings, and a total profit of 125⁵⁄₁₁.)

Let D yield 4 quarters = 240 shillings = surplus profit of 180 shillings.

We should then have the following sequence:

TABLE I

Type of soil	*Capital*	*Profit*	*Product*	*Produce rent*	*Money rent*
A	54⁶⁄₁₁s. or £2.14⁶⁄₁₁s.	5⁵⁄₁₁s.	1 qr,	0	0
B	54⁶⁄₁₁s. or £2.14⁶⁄₁₁s.	65⁵⁄₁₁s.	2 qr.	1 qr.	£3 or 60s.
C	54⁶⁄₁₁s. or £2.14⁶⁄₁₁s.	125⁵⁄₁₁s.	3 qr.	2 qr.	£6 or 120s.
D	54⁶⁄₁₁s. or £2.14⁶⁄₁₁s.	185⁵⁄₁₁s.	4 qr.	3 qr.	£9 or 180s.
Total			10 qr.	6 qr.	£18

The respective rent would be, for D, 185⁵⁄₁₁ – 5⁵⁄₁₁ s. or the difference between D and A; for C, 125⁵⁄₁₁ – 5⁵⁄₁₁ s. or the difference between C and A; for B, 65⁵⁄₁₁–

$5\frac{5}{11}$s. or the difference between B and A; while the total rent for B, C, and D = 6 quarters = 6 × 60 = 360 s. or £18, which is the sum of the differences between D and A, C and A and B and A.

|484| This *series*, which represents a given product in a given condition, can just as well occur, *considered abstractly* (and we have already explained why this can also be the case in reality) as a *decreasing* series (i.e., descending from D to A, from the more fertile soil to soil that is progressively less fertile) and as an *increasing* series (rising from A to D, from the less fertile to the more fertile soil). Finally, it may rise and fall alternately, as for example from D to C, C to A and A to B.

> If we first follow the *series* in reverse sequence, we find that the process in the decreasing series is as follows: the price per quarter gradually rises from 15 shillings to £3 (60 shillings). Once the 4 quarters produced by D (which we may consider as millions of quarters) are no longer sufficient, the wheat price rises to the level at which the missing supply can be obtained from C. That is, the wheat price would have to rise to 20 shillings per quarter, and the same process is repeated between C and B, and B and D. As a result the wheat price per quarter rises from 14 to 20, from 20 to 30 and from 30 to 60 shillings, four times the original price. The rent for D is thus first 5 shillings per quarter, and 10 shillings for two quarters; then 15 shillings per quarter for D and so on.

If the profit rate for D was originally 10 percent, his profit would be only $5\frac{5}{11}$ shillings, but this would represent more corn when the price of corn is 15 shillings than when it is 60 shillings. But since the corn goes into wages, and a portion of each quarter must replace wages, while another part replaces constant capital, the surplus-value would therefore be higher under this assumption, and so too, other circumstances remaining the same, would the rate of profit. (The question of the rate of profit will have to be specially investigated in more detail.)

If the sequence went the opposite way, so that the process began with A, then as soon as new agricultural land had to be taken into cultivation, the price per quarter would rise above 60 shillings; but since the supply needed would come from B, a supply of two quarters, it would fall again to 60 shillings; for while B produces at 30 shillings per quarter, it sells at 60 shillings, since its supply is only just sufficient to meet the demand. A rent is thus formed for B which comes initially to 60 shillings, and similarly for C and D; still on the assumption that even though they supply at 20 shillings and 15 shillings per quarter respectively the market price remains 60 shillings, since the supply of the one quarter that A provides is needed to satisfy the total demand. In this case, the rise in demand above the supply that was satisfied first by A, and then by A and B, would not have meant that B, C and D could successively be cultivated, but rather that the overall cultivated area would be extended, and it might so happen that the more fertile lands came under cultivation only later.

In the *first sequence*, rents rise with the *increase in price* and the *rate of profit* declines. This decline could be partially or completely paralysed by counteracting circumstances, *a point we shall go into in more detail later*; it must not be forgotten that the general rate of profit is not determined by the *surplus-value* in *all* spheres of production. It is not agricultural profit that determines industrial but the reverse. But more on this later, too.

In the second sequence, the rate of profit on the capital invested remains the same. The mass of *profit* is represented by less *corn*, but the relative price of corn compared with other commodities will have *risen*. It is just that the increase in profit, instead of flowing into the pockets of the [farming] industrialists, and presenting itself as a growing *profit*, separates off from profit in the form of rent. The price of corn, however, remains stationary under the assumption made here.

|485| *The development and growth of differential rent remains the same*, both when prices remain the same and when they rise and both when there is a continuous progression from worse soil to better and when there is a continuous regression from better soil to worse.

We formerly assumed (1) that the price rises in the one sequence, and remains stationary in the other; and (2) that there is a continuous progression from better soil to worse, or conversely from worse soil to better.

But let us assume that the demand for wheat rises from the original 10 quarters to 17 quarters, and further that the worst soil, A, is displaced by another patch of ground which yields one and a third quarters for a production cost of 60 shillings ($54\frac{6}{11}$ s. costs plus 10 percent profit or $5\frac{5}{11}$ s.), its production price per quarter of wheat thus being 45 shillings; or else that the old soil, A, has been improved as a result of rational cultivation, or has been cultivated more productively while the costs remained the same, by the introduction of clover, for example; let us further assume that the soil types B, C and D continue to supply the same amount of product as before, but that new types of soil come into cultivation: A′ with a fertility between A and B, and B′ and B″ with fertilities between B and C. In that case, the following phenomena would occur:

Firstly, the *production price* of a quarter of wheat, or its governing market price, would fall from 60s. to 45s., or by 25 percent.

Secondly, there would be at the same time a progression from more fertile to less fertile soil and from less fertile soil to more fertile. Soil A′ is more fertile than A, but less fertile than B, C and D that were cultivated previously; and B′ and B″ are more fertile than A, A′ and B but less fertile than C and D. The sequence would thus take on a criss-cross pattern. The progression would not be towards soil that was absolutely less fertile compared with the formerly most fertile soil types C and D; on the other hand it would not be to absolutely more fertile soil, but simply to soil that was relatively more fertile compared with the previously least fertile A, or to A and B.

Thirdly, the rent on B would have fallen > by a third of a quarter, < and similarly the rent on C and D, but the total rental (in corn) would have risen from 6 quarters to $7\frac{2}{3}$; the amount of cultivated and rent-bearing land would have increased, and the total product would increase from 10 quarters to 17. The profit, if it remained the same for A, would have risen, expressed in corn; but the rate of profit itself might have risen, since there has been an increase in relative surplus-value. (In that case, wages and thus the outlay on variable capital would have fallen, and so too therefore would the total outlay.) The total rental in money would have fallen from 360 shillings to 345 shillings. > If, on the other hand, we had assumed that A, with a production price of 60, produced only $1\frac{1}{4}$ quarters, but left the rest of the surplus production unchanged, the total excess would have been $7\frac{1}{3}$ quarters, so that, with the price of the quarter at 48 shillings, the $7\frac{1}{3}$ quarters would cost 368 shillings. The rental would thus have risen by 8 shillings, although the price of corn had fallen from 60 to 48.

< We can now draw up the new sequence, as follows:

> |486| TABLE II

Type of soil	*Capital (shillings)*	*Production price per qr.*	*Profit*	*Product*	*Corn rent*	*Money rent*
A	$54\frac{6}{11}$	45s.	$5\frac{6}{11}$	$1\frac{1}{3}$ qr,	0	0
A′	$54\frac{6}{11}$	36s.	$20\frac{5}{11}$	$1\frac{2}{3}$ qr.	$\frac{1}{3}$ qr.	15s.
B	$54\frac{6}{11}$	30s.	$35\frac{5}{11}$	2 qrs.	$\frac{2}{3}$ qr.	£1.10s.
B′	$54\frac{6}{11}$	$25\frac{5}{7}$s.	$50\frac{5}{11}$	$2\frac{1}{3}$ qrs.	1 qr.	£2.5s.
B″	$54\frac{6}{11}$	$22\frac{1}{2}$s.	$65\frac{5}{11}$	$2\frac{2}{3}$ qrs.	$1\frac{1}{3}$ qr.	£3
C	$54\frac{6}{11}$	20s.	$80\frac{5}{11}$	3 qrs.	$1\frac{2}{3}$ qr.	£3.15s.
D	$54\frac{6}{11}$	15s.	$125\frac{5}{11}$	4 qrs.	$2\frac{2}{3}$ qrs.	£6
Total				17 qrs.	$7\frac{2}{3}$ qrs.	£17.5s.

< Finally, if only the soil types A, B, C and D are cultivated, as before, but their productivity has risen in such a way that A produces 2 quarters instead of 1; B, 4 quarters instead of 2; C, 7 quarters instead of 3; and D, 10 quarters instead of 4, the total production will rise from 10 quarters to 23. If we assume that the

demand will absorb these 23 quarters as a result of a rise in population and a fall in price, we arrive at the following result:

> TABLE III

Type of soil	*Capital (shillings)*	*Production price per qr.*	*Profit*	*Product*	*Corn rent*	*Money rent*
A	$54\frac{6}{11}$	30s.	$5\frac{5}{11}$	2 qrs.	0	0
B	$54\frac{6}{11}$	15s.	$65\frac{5}{11}$	4 qrs.	2 qrs.	£3
C	$54\frac{6}{11}$	$8\frac{4}{7}$	$155\frac{5}{11}$	7 qrs.	5 qrs.	£7.10s.
D	$54\frac{6}{11}$	6	$245\frac{5}{11}$	10 qrs.	8 qrs.	£12
Total				23 qrs.	15 qrs.	£22.10s.

< The numerical ratios are as arbitrary here as in the other tables, but the assumptions are entirely rational.

|487| The first and major assumption is that the improvement in agriculture has differing effects on different types of soil and in this case has a greater effect on the better soil types C and D than on A and B. Experience shows that this is the general rule, even if the opposite case is also possible, that the improvement has a greater effect on worse soils than on better. (In that case the rent on the latter would fall instead of rising.) With the *absolute growth* in the fertility of all types of soil, the table also presupposes a *growth in the higher relative fertility* of the better soil types C and D, hence a growth in the difference in products from the same capital investment and therefore a *rise in differential rent*.

The second assumption is that total demand keeps pace with the *growing total product*. *Firstly*, it is not necessary to consider the growth as happening suddenly; series III can be considered as arising gradually. *Secondly*, it is wrong to maintain that the consumption of the necessary means of subsistence does not grow when this becomes cheaper. The repeal of the Corn Laws in England[83] has proved the opposite, and the contrary conception arose only through the fact that major sudden variations of the harvest, themselves due simply to *seasonal changes*, produce a sudden disproportionate rise or fall in corn prices. This is not the case, however, when the growth in consumption results from

83 See Newman. [Newman 1851, p. 158.]

a fall in the governing production price itself. *Thirdly*, part of the grain can be consumed in the form of spirits or beer > so that some of the fields which were previously sown to wheat now bear barley. < And the growth in consumption of these two articles is by no means confined within narrow limits. *Fourthly*, these matters also depend in part on population growth; and in addition one may bear in mind that a country is also involved in exports, as England still was in the first half of the eighteenth century > (and for a certain length of time after that), < so that the demand is not governed by the limits of national consumption alone. Finally, the increase in the production of wheat, for example, may have the effect that *wheat* becomes the staple foodstuff of the mass of the people, instead of rye or oats, which also leads to a growth in the market for that cereal, while the reverse case may also arise with a decline in the product and an increase in its price.

On these assumptions, therefore, series III gives the result that the price per quarter falls from 60 to 30 shillings, i.e., by 50 percent, while production grows from 10 to 23 quarters, compared with series I, hence by more than 100 percent; the rent on land of type B remains the same, while on soil C it rises by 25 percent and on D by 33⅓ percent, the total rental thus rising from £18 to £22½, i.e., by 25 percent.

A comparison of the above tables I, II and III (in which series I should be taken twice, rising from A to D and falling from D to A) and which can be interpreted either as representing *given* distinctions with a given state of society (e.g., *alongside each other* in three different countries) or as succeeding each other at *various times* in the development of the same country, gives the following results:

(1) The *sequence*, when *complete*, always appears a *decreasing* one, whatever the *course of its formation* might have been, for, in considering rents, one will always first proceed from the soil that bears the maximum rent and only come last to that which yields no rent.

(2) The *production price* of the worst soil that yields no rent is always the governing market price, although, considering Table I, where it is taken as a rising sequence, the market price would remain *stationary* only if ever better land were cultivated.[84]

---

84 > It should be remarked in addition here that if we take series I in ascending order, < the *price of the corn produced on the best soil* is the governing one, in so far as the extent to which soil A remains the price-governing soil depends on the quantity produced on the best soil. If B, C and D produce more than is demanded, A ceases to govern the price. Storch [1815, pp. 78–9] has a vague notion of this when he makes the best type of soil the governing type. In this way, *American* grain prices govern *English* ones.

|488| (3) The differential rent arises from the difference in the *natural fertility* of soil types that is *given* for the level of development of agriculture found in existence at the time (leaving aside here the *location*), i.e., it arises from the limited extent of the best lands and from the fact that the same capital has to be applied to *unequal* types of soil, which thus yield unequal products for the same capital. > This situation is thus different from that in industries where it is possible to fulfil the demand for additional machines of equal or greater productivity; or at least, in agriculture such machines cannot be delivered *to the extent* that they put all inferior machines out of work.

< (4) The existence of a *differential rent* and a *graduated differential rent* can be based just as well on a declining scale, in a progression from better soil to worse, as on an ascending scale, in a progression from worse soil to better; or it can arise in an alternating criss-cross pattern. (The former case may be formed by a progression either from D to A or from A to D. The latter involves both kinds of movement.)

(5) According to its *mode of formation*, differential rent can develop along with a stationary, rising or falling price of the agricultural product. In the case of a falling price, the total production and the total rental may rise, so that rent is formed on land which previously did not bear rent, even though the worst soil, A, has been displaced by *better* soil, or has itself been improved, and although there is a fall in the rent on other, better, types of soil, and even on the best types. This process can also be linked with a fall in the total rental (in money). Finally, in the case of falling prices, owing to a general *improvement* in cultivation, so that both the product of the worst soil and its price fall, rent on a portion of the better types of soil may remain the same or fall, while rising on the best types of soil. This is because the *differential rent* on any soil, compared with the worst soil, depends on the price of wheat, per quarter for example, if the difference in the *quantity produced* is given. But when the price is given, it depends on the *difference in the amount produced*, and in the case of an increasing absolute fertility of *all* soil, that of the better types of soil rises *relatively* more than that of the inferior soils. Given a price of 60s., therefore (Table I), the rent on D is determined by its differential product as compared with that of A, hence by the excess of 3 quarters; the rent is therefore 3 × 60 = 180s. or £9, but the rent on D (Table III), where the price of a quarter is 30s. (hence half as large), is determined by the amount of D's excess product over A, which is 8 quarters, but 30 × 8 = £12.[85]

85 > See on this the passage from *The Economist*. ['Relations of landlord and tenant. Letter to

< With this we can abandon the *first erroneous conception of differential rent* (as seen in West, Malthus and Ricardo),[86] which assumed a necessary progression to ever worse soil, or an ever declining agricultural fertility. As we have seen, differential rent can arise with a progression to ever better soil; it can arise if a better soil takes the lowest place instead of that which was formerly the worst; it can be linked with a progressive advance in the productiveness of agriculture. Its only precondition is the *inequality of land types*, and, as far as the development of productivity comes into consideration, it assumes that the rise in the absolute fertility of the total acreage does not exclude > differences *in the relative fertility* of different plots of land < but either increases them, leaves them as they were or lessens them. > It does not balance them out.

< From the *beginning until the middle of the eighteenth century* there was a steady fall in grain prices, alongside a simultaneous growth in rents (taking the period as a whole), in the total rental, in the extent of land cultivated, in the population, and in agricultural production. This corresponds to Table I, combined with Table II in an upward direction, but in such a way that the worst soil, A, is either improved or taken out of cultivation (which does not mean that it cannot be used for other *agricultural* or *industrial* purposes). All this happened despite the falling price of gold and silver.

From the *beginning of the nineteenth century* (this date should be indicated more precisely) *until 1815*, there was a continuous rise in grain prices, with a steady growth in rent, rental, the extent of the land cultivated, the population and agricultural production. This corresponds to Table I in a downward direction. (References should be introduced here indicating the cultivation of *inferior* lands at this time.)

In the time of Petty and Davenant, there are complaints by landlords about improvements and the enclosure of common lands; *a fall in rents* on better lands, and a rise in the total *rental* by the extension of rent-bearing land.[87]

(Further references to be given on these three points; similarly on the *differences in fertility* between different sections of cultivated land in one country.)

In connection with differential rent in general, it should be noted that the *market value* is always above the *total production price for the overall quantity produced.*

---

the Editor of *The Economist* from a landlord and farmer', in *The Economist*, London, No. 381, 14 December 1850, p. 1379. Translator]

86 [West 1815, p. 98; Malthus 1815, p. 39; Ricardo 1821, pp. 53–75. Translator]

87 [Petty 1699, p. 230; Charles Davenant, *Discourses on the Publick Victuals, Part 2*, London, 1698, pp. 26–8; analysed by Marx in MECW 31, 1989, pp. 343–4. Translator]

Let us take Table I for instance. The total product of 10 quarters costs 600 shillings = £30, since the market price is determined by the production price of A. The *actual production price*, however, is:

for A 1 qr = £3; 1 qr = £3
for B 2 qrs = £3: 1 qr = £1.10s.
for C 3 qrs = £3; 1 qr = £1
for D 4 qrs = £3; 1 qr = 15s.

Total 10 qrs = £12
Average: 1 qr = £1.4s.

The real production price of the 10 quarters is exactly £12; they are sold for £30, 250 percent too dear.

The real average price for 1 quarter is £1.4s. The market price is £3, similarly 250 percent too much.

This is determination by a *market value* brought about by competition on the basis of the capitalist mode of production; it is competition that produces a false social value. This results from the law of *market value* to which agricultural products are subjected. > It results from the *social* determination of market value which is based on the exchange value of the product. < It does not arise from the *soil* and the differences in its fertility. If we imagine that the capitalist form of society has been abolished and that society is an association, the 10 quarters would represent a quantity of social labour-time contained in £12. Society would therefore not purchase this product at two and a half times the actual labour-time contained in it; the basis for a class of landowners would thereby disappear. This would have the same effect as a cheapening of the product to the same amount by foreign imports. Correct as it is to say that – keeping to the present mode of production, but assuming that differential rent accrued to the state – the prices of agricultural products would remain the same, all other circumstances remaining the same, it is still wrong to say that the *value* of these products would remain the same if capitalist production were replaced by association. The fact that commodities of the same kind have an identical *market price* is the way in which the social character of value is realised on the basis of the capitalist mode of production, and in general of production depending on individual commodity exchange. Where society, considered as a consumer, pays too much for agricultural products, this is a minus for the realisation of labour-time in agricultural products, but it now forms a plus for one part of society, the owners of the land.

|490| A *second circumstance*, important for what will be presented in the next section as differential rent II, is as follows:

It is not only the rent per acre that is involved here, or in general the distinction between *production price* and *market price*, or between *individual* and *general* production price per acre; what is also important is *how many acres* of each type of soil are under cultivation. Here the importance of this has a direct bearing only on the *size of the rental*, i.e., the total rent for the whole cultivated area; though it serves for us at the same time as a transition to our discussion of a rise in the *rate of rent*, even when prices do not rise, or there is no increase in the differences in the relative fertility of the soil types when prices fall. *Let us take Table I.*

	Cost of production	*Product*	*Rent in corn*	*Rent in money*	*Acres*
A	60s. = £3	1 qr.	0	0	1
B	60s. = £3	2 qrs.	1 qr.	£3	1
C	60s. = £3	3 qrs.	2 qrs.	£3	1
D	60s. = £3	4 qrs.	3 qrs.	£9	1
Total	£12	10 qrs.	6 qrs.	£18	4

(Capital advanced = 218 5/11 s. = slightly over £10.8s., say £10.)

If we now assume that the number of acres of the *same* classes of land under cultivation doubles, we get:

TABLE IA

	Cost of production		*Product*	*Produce rent*	*Rent in money*	*Acres*
A	£3 an acre;	£6 for 2 acres	2 qrs.	0	0	2
B	ditto	ditto	4 qrs.	2 qrs.	£6	2
C	ditto	ditto	6 qrs.	4 qrs.	£12	2
D	ditto	ditto	8 qrs.	6 qrs.	£18	2
Total:	£24		20 qrs.	12 qrs.	£36	8

(Capital advanced = over £20.)

We shall now take two further cases, the first being one in which production expands on the worst land and extends greatly on land type B, and the second where it falls relatively on the worst land and increases on the better types of land.

TABLE IB

	Cost of production		*Product*	*Rent in corn*	*Rent in money*	*Acres*
A	£3 an acre;	£12 for 4 acres	4 qrs.	0	0	4
B	ditto	ditto	8 qrs.	4 qrs.	£12	4
C	ditto	ditto	6 qrs.	4 qrs.	£12	2
D	ditto	ditto	8 qrs.	6 qrs.	£18	2
Total:	£36		26qrs.	14 qrs.	£42	12

(Capital advanced: = over £30.)

and now finally:

TABLE IC

	Cost of production		*Product*	*Rent in corn*	*Rent in money*	*Acres*
A	£3 an acre.	1 acre = £3	1 qr.	0	0	1
B	ditto	2 acres = £6	4 qrs.	2 qrs.	£6	2
C	ditto	5 acres = £15	15 qrs.	10 qrs.	£30	5
D	ditto	4 acres = £12	16 qrs.	12 qrs.	£36	4
Total:	£36		36 qrs.	24 qrs.	£72	12

(Capital advanced: £30.)

|491| *Firstly*, in all these cases, I, Ia, Ib, Ic, the rent per acre remains the same; for the product of the same quantity of capital on each acre of *the same* type of soil is in fact unchanged. > In each of the tables, and in comparing one table with another, < we simply assume what is the case in any country at a particular point in time, i.e., that the various types of soil share the total cultivated area in

a definite ratio; and what is always the case in two countries compared together, or in the same country at *different* points in time, namely that the *ratio in which* the total cultivated area is divided between them changes.

If we compare Ia with Ib, we see that when the cultivation of land in all four classes grows in the same proportion, a doubling of the number of acres in cultivation doubles the total production and similarly the corn and money rent.

If, however, we compare Ib and Ic respectively with I, in both cases we have a tripling of the area under cultivation. In both cases this rises from 4 acres to 12, but in Ib, classes A and B take the major share in the growth, A bearing no rent and B the smallest differential rent; i.e., of the 8 acres newly cultivated, 3 each fall into classes A and B, a total of 6, while only 1 each, a total of 2, fall into C and D. In other words, three quarters of the increase (three quarters of 8 = 6) takes place on A and B and only one quarter on C and D. On this assumption, the tripling of the expanse under cultivation in Ib compared with I does not involve a tripling of the product, for the product rises only from 10 to 26 quarters, > whereas it would have had to rise to 30 quarters for the increase in production to correspond with the increase in acreage. < On the other hand, since a substantial part of the growth took place on A, which does not yield any rent, and of the growth on the better lands the major part took place on class B, the corn rent therefore rises only from 6 to 14 quarters and the money rent from £18 to £42, > looked at from the point of view of the total rental.

< If we instead compare Ic with I, a case in which the land which does not pay rent does not increase its extent at all, while land that yields the minimum rent exhibits only a weak increase, the major part of the growth taking place on C, the second best land, with a considerable increase on the best land, D, as well, we find that with the tripling of the cultivated area production has risen from 10 to 36 quarters, i.e., by more than three times (almost quadrupling in fact); the corn rent has risen from 6 to 24 quarters, or quadrupled, and the money rent has also quadrupled, from £18 to £72.

In all these cases, the price of the agricultural product remains stationary, in the nature of things; in each case the *rental* grows with the expansion of cultivation, as long as this does not take place exclusively on the worst lands, which pay no rent. But this growth *varies*. To the extent that the expansion takes place on the better types of soil, so that the quantity produced does not just grow in proportion to the expansion of the land cultivated, but more steeply, the corn and money rent grows. To the extent that the worst soil and the adjacent categories of land take the principal share of the increase (which assumes that the worst soil is a *constant* category), the total rental does not rise in proportion to the expansion of cultivation. Thus, given two countries in which land A, which yields no rent, is of the same quality, the *rental* stands in *inverse* proportion to the aliquot part of the total cultivated area composed by the worst and less good soil types, and hence also in inverse *proportion* to the quantities produced by *identical capital investments* on equal areas. The proportion between the *amount of the worst cultivated soil and that of the better and the best* and the total area of a country thus has an effect on the total rental which is opposite to the effect that the relation between the *quality of the worst cultivated soil and that of the better and the best* has on the *rent* per acre, and hence, with other circumstances remaining the same, also on the total rental. The *confusion between these two aspects* has given rise to all kinds of confused objections against differential rent.

|492| > The *total rental* therefore grows simply as a result of the extension of cultivation, which leads to the employment of more capital and labour upon the land.

< But the most important point is this. Even though, on our assumptions, the ratios between *rents* on the various types of soil, reckoned on a per acre basis, remain the same, and so too therefore does the *rate of rent*, considered in regard to the capital laid out on each acre, the following phenomenon presents itself:

If we compare Ia with I – the case in which the acreage cultivated increases *proportionately*, along with the capital invested in it – we find that, just as the total production has grown in proportion to the increased land area cultivated, i.e., both have *doubled*, so the same is the case with the rental. It has risen from £18 to £36, just as the number of acres has risen from 4 to 8.

If we take the total area of 4 acres, the overall rental comes to £18, i.e., an *average rent*, taking into account also the soil that bears no rent. *A landowner who owned the entire 4 acres could calculate it in this way*, for example, and that is how the *average rent* for an entire country is statistically reckoned. The total rental of £18 is produced by applying a capital of £10. The ratio between these two figures is the *rate of rent*, which in this case is 180 percent.

The same *rate of rent* per acre occurs in Ia, where 8 acres have been cultivated instead of 4, but where all types of soil have shared in the increase in the same proportion. The proportions are the same. An *average rent* for the 8 acres of £4.10s. and a rate of rent of 180 percent for the capital laid out of £20.

If we consider Ib, on the other hand, where the increase took place principally on the two inferior soil types A and B, we have a rent of £42 for 12 acres. This gives an *average rent per acre* of $^{42}/_{12}$ = £3½. And if we calculated the ratio between the total capital laid out of £30 and the rent of £42, we reach a rate of rent of 140 percent. The *rate of rent*, reckoned per acre, has therefore fallen from £4.10s. to £3.10s., and in proportion to the capital it has fallen from 180 percent to 140 percent.

(If the expansion of cultivation in case Ib had taken place simply on soil A, we would have 9 acres of A, 1 of B, 1 of C and 1 of D. The total rental would still be £18, giving an average rent per acre on these 12 acres of £1.10s. and £18 of rent on a capital of £30 laid out gives a rate of rent of 60 percent. The *average rent* both per acre and in relation to the capital laid out would have sharply declined, while the total rental would not have grown.) With a growth in the total rental from £18 to £42, > and a rise in the rent on all classes of land, because there has been an increase in the acreage cultivated on all classes of land < there is thus a fall in the *average rate of rent*, both per acre and reckoned on the capital invested; similarly, production has grown, but not proportionately. This takes place even though the rent on all soil types remains *the same*, whether reckoned per acre or on the capital invested. It takes place because three-quarters of the increase occurs on soil A (which bears no rent) and soil B (which bears only a minimal rent.)

|493| Let us finally compare Ic with I and Ib. If we do this, we find that, compared with I, the acreage has tripled, and so has the capital laid out. The *average rent per acre*, however, is £6 (£72 on 12 acres), whereas it was only £4.10s. in case I. The rate of rent on the *capital laid out* (£72: £30) is 240 percent instead of 180 percent. There is still greater difference in the product, which has risen from 10 quarters to 36 quarters. Compared with Ib, where the total acreage under cultivation, the capital applied and the differences between the types of soil cultivated all remain the same, though differently distributed, the product is 36 quarters instead of 26 quarters, an increase of a third, the *average rent per acre* is £6 instead of £3.10s., hence almost twice as much, and the *rate of rent* on an equal total capital advanced is 240 percent instead of 140 percent.

> It can be seen from this demonstration that, whether one takes the different conditions in Tables I, Ia, Ib and Ic as *existing simultaneously alongside one another* in different countries, or as successive situations in *the same* country, and, given the following assumptions – a *stationary price of grain*, because the yield on the worst, rent-free land remains the same; the *same differences* in fertility between the various categories of soil cultivated; an equal respective product therefore from *equal capital investment* on equal aliquot parts, acres, of the area cultivated in each class of soil; and finally a constant ratio between the rent per acre on each type of soil and an equal rate of rent on the capital invested in each piece of land of the same kind – on these assumptions, we get the following results: firstly, the *rental* always grows with an expansion of the cultivated area and therefore with an increased capital investment, except for the case when the entire growth falls on the rent-free soil; secondly, however, both the *average rent per acre* (*total rental* divided by the *total area of the cultivated land*) and the average *rate of rent* (total rental divided by the *total capital*

invested) may vary very significantly; and even if both move in the same direction, they may still move in different proportions. If we leave aside the case where the growth takes place simply on the rent-free soil A, we find that the *average rent per acre* and the *average rate of rent* on the capital invested in agriculture depend on the *proportionate shares* that the various classes of soil make up within the total cultivated area; or, and this comes to the same thing, they depend on the way in which the total capital applied is distributed over the soil types of different fertility. Whether much land is cultivated or only a little, so that the total rental is larger or smaller (except for the case where the growth is solely on A), the average rent per acre or the *average rate of rent* on the capital applied remains *the same* as long as the proportions in which the different types of soil participate in the total acreage remain constant. Despite a rise in the total rental as cultivation extends and more capital is invested, and even a considerable rise, the *average rent* per acre and the *average rate of rent* per capital fall, if the proportion of rent-free lands, and those that only bear a small differential rent, is greater or grows *in relation to* the better land, which yields a higher rent. Finally, the *average rent* per acre and the *average rate of rent* on capital rises when the better lands constitute a relatively larger part of the total area and therefore relatively more capital investment falls to their share.

|494| If we thus consider the *average rent* per acre of the total cultivated land, which is what is generally done in statistical works, since either different countries are compared at the same time or different periods in the history of the same country, we see that the *average level of rent per acre*, and hence also the total rental, corresponds to a certain extent (without being identical; in fact the proportion tends to increase) not to the *relative* but to the *absolute* fertility of agriculture in a country, i.e., it corresponds to the quantity of products that are supplied on average by a given area. For the greater the share of the total area constituted by the better types of soil, the greater is the volume of products from the same capital investment and the same land area; and the greater, too, is the *average rent per acre*. And conversely. Thus rent appears as determined not by the ratio of differential fertility, but rather by the absolute fertility, which would refute the law of differential rent. That is why certain phenomena are denied, or else the attempt is made to explain them in terms of *non-existent* distinctions in average grain prices and the differential fertilities of lands under cultivation, phenomena whose actual basis is simply that the *proportion of the total rental, either to the total area of land cultivated or to the total capital invested in the soil* – given the same fertility for rent-free soil and hence equal production prices, and given the *same differences* between the various soil types – is not determined only by the rent per acre or the *rate of rent* on capital but just as

much by the *relative proportion* of each soil type to the total acreage under cultivation; or, and this comes to the same thing, by the *distribution* of the total capital applied *among the various types of soil*. Until now, this circumstance has been completely overlooked, in a quite striking fashion.

It still shows, and this is important for the further course of our investigation, that the relative level of *average rents per acre*, and the average *rate of rent*, or the average ratio of the total rental to the total capital invested in the soil, may *rise* or *fall* even though prices, the difference in fertility of the lands under cultivation and the *rent per acre* or the *rate of rent for the capital invested per acre* in each actual rent-bearing soil category, or for all actually rent-bearing capital, all remain the same, simply through an *expansion* of the cultivated area.

II)[88] Until now, we have considered differential rent only as the result of *differences in the productivity* of equal capital investments on *equal land areas* of different fertility, so that *differential rent* was determined by the difference between the yield of *capital* invested on the worst land, which did not bear rent, and that of capital invested in better land. In this case we had capital investments in different land areas alongside one another, so that each new investment of capital corresponded to a more extensive cultivation and an expansion of the cultivated area. But, after all, *differential rent* as such was simply the result of the varying productivity of *equal capitals* when invested on the land. Can it make a difference, then, whether *sums of capital* are invested *successively* in time on *the same* piece of land with varying productivity, or invested *alongside one another* on different pieces of land, as long as we assume that the results are the same?

|495| It cannot be denied, first of all, that as far as *the formation of surplus profit* is concerned, it is all the same whether [i] £3 in production costs spent on an acre of land A yields 1 quarter, so that £3 is the production price of 1 quarter and its governing market price, while on an acre of land B £3 spent on production costs yields 2 quarters, and therefore a surplus profit of £3, £3 on an acre of land C yields 3 quarters and a surplus profit of £6, and £3 on an acre of land D yields 4 quarters and a surplus profit of £9; or whether [ii] the same result is obtained by the application of this £12 in production costs or £10 of capital in the same sequence to *one and the same* acre and giving the same results. In each case, there is a capital of £10, with successive portions of £2.10s. being invested, whether these are invested side by side on 4 acres

88 [This is the beginning of Engels's Chapter 40 ('The Second Form of Differential Rent'). Editor]

of differing fertility, or successively on *one and the same* acre, in such a way that, because of the *varying product*, one of these capitals of £2.10s. yields no surplus profit, while the other portions give a surplus profit, each in proportion to the difference between its yield and that of the investment on rent-free land.

The *surplus profits* and the varying rates of surplus profit for different portions of capital value are formed in a uniform way in both cases. And rent is nothing but a *form* of this surplus profit, surplus profit in fact forming its substance. None the less, the second method does give rise to certain difficulties as regards the transformation of surplus profit into rent, that change in form which involves the transfer of surplus profits from the capitalist farmer to the proprietor of the land. Hence the stubborn resistance of the English farmers to any official agricultural statistics. Hence the struggle between them and the landlords when it comes to establishing the actual results of their capital investment.[89] In any case, the *rent* here is fixed when the farms are leased, and the subsequent surplus profits accrue to the farmer as long as the tenancy contract lasts. Hence the farmers' battle for long tenancies, and conversely the increase in 'tenancy at will' contracts resulting from the superior power of the landlords.

It is clear from the start, therefore, that even if it makes no difference as far as the law of *surplus profit formation* is concerned whether *equal capitals are invested alongside* each other on equal-sized tracts of land with unequal results or whether they are invested *successively on the same piece of land*, it still makes a significant difference for the *transformation of surplus profits into ground-rent*. In the latter case, the limits of this transformation are both narrower and more unstable. Hence in countries where agriculture is *intensive* (and what this means economically speaking is simply the concentration of capital on the same piece of land instead of its distribution over adjacent tracts) the job of the *valuer*, as Mr. Morton explains it in his *Resources of Estates*, comes to be a very important, complicated and difficult profession. In the case of more permanent improvements, the artificially inflated differential fertility of the land coincides with its new natural fertility when the lease expires, and hence the assessment of *rents* coincides with the assessment of varying fertility between types of land in general. In so far as the formation of surplus profit is determined on the other hand by the amount of working capital, the *level of rent* for a working capital of given size is added to the *average rent* for the land, so as to ensure that the new farmer has sufficient capital to continue cultivation in the same intensive manner.

---

89 Morton [1858, pp. 126–9 and 151–62.]

|496| The following additional points have still to be made, in relation to the first form of differential rent, considered in section I, although they also apply in part to the second form.

Firstly. We have seen how the *average rent* per acre or the average rate of rent on capital may rise with the extension of cultivation, given stationary prices and an unchanged differential fertility of the lands being cultivated. As soon as all the land in the country is appropriated, and capital investment on the land, agriculture and population have all reached a certain level – factors that are all taken for granted once the capitalist mode of production becomes dominant and takes control of agriculture too – the price *of the uncultivated* land of various qualities (assuming only *differential rent*) is determined by the price of land of equivalent quality and location that *is under cultivation*. The price is the same, roughly speaking, after the deduction of the additional cost of ploughing up new land, even though this land does not bear *any rent*. Admittedly, the price of land is nothing but *capitalised rent*. But even in the case of cultivated lands, it is only future rents that are paid for in their price, e.g., twenty years' rent is paid *en bloc*, if the determining interest rate is 5 percent. As soon as the land is sold, it is sold as rent-bearing land, and the prospective character of the rent (which is considered here as the fruit of the soil, something that it is only in surface appearance) does not distinguish the uncultivated land from the cultivated. The *price* of uncultivated land, like its rent, which is what this compressed formula represents, is purely illusory as long as this land is not actually being valorised. But it is determined *a priori* in this way, and becomes a reality as soon as buyers are found. Thus if the actual *average rent* in a country is determined by its actual average annual rental and the ratio of this rental to the total cultivated area, the *price* of the uncultivated portion is determined by the price of the cultivated part, and is therefore simply a reflection of the capital investment in the cultivated lands and its impact there. Since, with the exception of the worst land, all types of soil bear rent (and this rent, as we shall go on to see in the case of the second form of differential rent, rises with the amount of capital and the corresponding intensity of cultivation), a nominal price is thereby formed for the uncultivated portions of land, so that these too become a commodity, a source of wealth for their owner. This explains at the same time why the price of land rises for the entire area, even for uncultivated land.[90]

Land speculation (in the United States for example) depends on this reflection which capital (and labour) cast on the land.

---

90 Opdyke [1851, pp. 88–98.]

Secondly. All advances in the extension of *cultivation* takes place either towards *worse* soil or on the *various* given types of soil in different proportions, according to their characteristics. An advance towards *worse soil*, of course, is never chosen by preference; taking the capitalist mode of production as given, it can only be the result of rising prices, and in any mode of production only the result of necessity. But this point does need to be somewhat modified: bad soil may be relatively preferred to better on account of its *location*, which is decisive for every extension of cultivation in new countries. Another reason may be that, although the soil in a certain region may on the whole be fertile, better and worse soil may be closely intermingled in some places, so that the inferior soil has to be cultivated simply because of its proximity to the better soil. If the inferior soil forms enclaves within the better soil, the better soil gives it the advantage of *location* as against more fertile land that is not yet part of the cultivated area or is about to become so.

The state of Michigan, for example, was one of the first Western states to *export corn*. Its soil on the whole is poor. But its proximity to the state of New York and its water routes via the Lake of Ontario and the Erie Canal gave it at first an initial advantage over the states further west, though these were more fertile by nature. The example of this state, in comparison with the state of New York, also shows us the transition from better soil to worse. The soil of New York state, and particularly its western part, is much more fertile, particularly for the cultivation of wheat. Rapacious methods of cultivation made this fertile soil infertile, and then the Michigan soil started to appear more fertile.

'In 1838, wheaten flour was shipped at Buffalo *for* the West, and the wheat region of New York, with that of Upper Canada, were the main sources of supply. Now, after only twelve years' (since 1846) 'an enormous supply of wheat and flour is brought from the West, along Lake Erie, and shipped upon the Erie Canal for the East, at Buffalo and the adjoining port of Blackrock ... The effect of these large arrivals from the Western States – which were unnaturally stimulated by the European famine of 1847 ... has been to render wheat less valuable in western New York, to make the wheat culture less remunerative, and to turn the attention of the New York farmers more to grazing and dairy husbandry, fruit culture, and other branches of rural economy, in which they think the North-West will be unable so directly to compete with them'.[91]

> In this case, then, the exhaustion of the fertile soil of New York meant that the soil of Michigan, etc., was now the more fertile. <

91 Johnston 1851, pp. 220–23.

Thirdly. It is false to assume that the soil in those colonies and other new countries that can export corn at *cheaper prices* is therefore necessarily of greater natural fertility.[92]

[Johnston adds]: 'We are accustomed to attach the idea of *great natural productiveness*, and of boundless tracts of rich land, to those new states from which come the large supplies of wheat that are annually poured into the port of Buffalo, > and which vex the New York and New England farmers by the effect upon the prices of the staple article of vegetable food'.[93]

< This depends first of all on economic conditions. The entire population of a state such as this, e.g., Michigan, begins by being almost exclusively engaged in agriculture, and particularly in the mass crops which alone can be exchanged for industrial goods and tropical products. Their entire surplus product thus appears *in the shape of corn* (or wheat). This fundamentally distinguishes the colonial states founded on the basis of the modern world market from those of earlier times, and particularly those of antiquity. They receive ready-made, through the new circumstances, products that they would under other circumstances have to produce themselves, such as clothing, tools, etc. It is only on this basis that the Southern states of the Union could make cotton into their principal product. It is the division of labour on the world market that permits this. Thus if, considering their newness and their relatively small population, they *appear* to produce a very large surplus product, this is not due to the fertility of their soil or the productiveness of their labour, but rather to the *one-sided* form of this labour and thus of the surplus product in which it is expressed.

In addition to this, relatively infertile soil which is cultivated for the *first time*, and which has never been touched by agriculture before, has accumulated so much in the way of easily assimilated plant nutrients, at least in its top layers, that it will yield harvests for quite a long period without any fertiliser, even if cultivated *in a superficial fashion*. (In the Western prairies, a further factor is that scarcely any clearing costs are incurred, since nature has already made the land arable.) In less fertile regions of this kind the surplus comes not from the high *fertility of the soil*, i.e., from the *yield per acre*, but rather from the *great acreage* that can be cultivated in a superficial manner, since this land costs the cultivator nothing, or at least only an infinitesimal amount compared with the older countries. This is true for example where share-cropping is practised, as

---

92 In this case grain is not only sold *below* its value, but also below its *price of production*, i.e., below the production price determined by the *average rate of profit* in the older countries.

93 Johnston 1851, p. 223.

in parts of New York, Michigan, Canada, etc. |498| A family cultivates say 100 acres superficially and although the product per acre is not large, the product of 100 acres provides a considerable surplus for sale. On top of this, cattle, etc., can be grazed almost cost-free on natural pasture, without any need for artificial meadows. The decisive thing here is not the *quality* of the soil but its *quantity*. The possibility of this *superficial* cultivation is of course more or less rapidly exhausted in inverse proportion to the fertility of the new soil and in direct proportion to the export of its product. In countries where agriculture is older, the property relations, which determine the price of uncultivated land by reference to that of cultivated land, make any such kind of extensive farming impossible.[94]

We can see from the following example that this does not mean, as Ricardo imagines, that this land is necessarily very fertile, or that only soil types of the same fertility are cultivated. In the state of Michigan, 465,000 acres were sown to wheat in 1848, to produce 4,739,300 bushels, or an average per imperial acre of 10$\frac{1}{5}$ bushels; this is less than 9 bushels if seed-corn is deducted. Here are the results for 29 counties:

2 counties gave an average of 7 bushels per acre, 3 gave 8, 2 gave 9, 7 gave 10, 6 gave 11, 3 gave 12, 4 gave 13, 1 gave 16, and 1 gave 18.[95]

As far as practical agriculture is concerned, *higher fertility* of the soil is the same thing as a *greater availability, a greater ease of access*, to that fertility. Availability may be greater with a naturally poor soil than with soil that is naturally rich, and this is the *kind of soil* which the cultivator will take up first, and if capital is wanting, he will be compelled to take it up. > Nothing could be more ridiculous, therefore, than the course of events postulated by Ricardo, etc.

< *Finally*. The extension of cultivation to larger areas (apart from the case just considered, in which resort has to be had to a *worse soil* than that formerly cultivated), on the various soil types from A to D, for example, and therefore the cultivation of more acres of B and C, by no means depends on a previous rise in grain prices, any more than the annual expansion of a manufacturer of cotton twist, for instance, depends on a continuous rise in the price of yarn. Even though a major rise or fall in market prices does have an effect on the scale of production, there is still, apart from this – and even given average prices,

---

94 'And yet such a country will *give excellent first crops*, even of wheat, and will supply to those who skim the first cream off the country a large surplus of this grain to send to market'. (Johnston 1851, p. 224.)

95 Johnston 1851, p. 225.

whose level neither forms a *check* on production nor gives it an *exceptional spur* – the same perpetual relative *overproduction* in agriculture |499| > as in all other branches of production conducted in the capitalist fashion, < which is inherently identical with *accumulation*, and which in the case of other *modes of production* is directly caused by an increase in population, and in the colonies by continuing immigration. Demand grows steadily, and with this in prospect new capital is continually invested in new land; even though this happens for different crops and according to particular circumstances. The formation of new capitals brings this about automatically. But as far as the individual capitalist is concerned, he measures the scale of his production by the capital he has available, to the extent that he can gain a clear view of this himself. What *he* has in mind is to take as big a share of the market as possible. If there is overproduction, he blames it on his competitors, not on himself. The individual capitalist can extend his production just as much by *personally* appropriating a greater aliquot share of the *given market*, as by expanding *the market* itself.

In considering differential rent II, the following points should now be stressed:

Firstly. Its *basis* and *point of departure*, not only *historically* but as far as concerns its *movement* at any *given* point in time, is differential rent I, i.e., the *simultaneous cultivation alongside one another* of *lands* of different fertility and location, the *simultaneous application alongside one another* of different components of the total agricultural capital to *different tracts of land*.

Regarded historically, this is self-evident. In *colonies*, the colonists need only invest a little capital; the main agencies of production are labour and the soil itself. Each individual family head tries to hew out of the rough an independent field of employment for himself, hence separately from the other colonists. In agriculture proper, this must always be the case, also in all non-capitalist modes of production. In the case of sheep-farming and stock-raising in general as an independent branch of production, there is a more or less communal exploitation of the land, and this exploitation is extensive in character from the outset. The capitalist mode of production develops out of earlier modes of production in which the means of production are either in law or in fact the property of the cultivator himself, in other words a situation where agriculture is pursued as a kind of handicraft. By the nature of things, it is only gradually, starting from this basis, that the means of production become concentrated and transformed into capital vis-à-vis the immediate producers. > (Credit also plays a role in this concentration.) < Where the capitalist mode of production first takes on its characteristic form is in sheep-farming and stock-raising; but this is not the concentration of capital on a relatively small land area, but rather production on a larger scale; the saving of production costs is achieved by the keeping of horses, etc., and not in fact by the use of more capital on the same land. It follows from the natural laws of farming, moreover, that given a certain level of agriculture and the corresponding exhaustion of the soil, capital, which in this sense is synonymous with means of production already produced, becomes the decisive element in the cultivation of the soil. As long as the cultivated land forms a relatively small portion in relation to the uncultivated land and the soil's natural resources are not exhausted (as is the case when stock-raising and meat-consumption predominate, in the period when they *first* appeared, which *preceded* the predominance of agriculture proper and the consumption of vegetables), the capitalist mode of production contrasts with peasant production particularly by the *amount of land* that is cultivated under one capitalist, and thus also by the extensive use of capital on a greater area.

It must therefore be borne in mind at the outset that *differential rent I* is the historical basis and starting-point from which development takes place. On the other hand, the movement of *differential rent II* at any given moment occurs only on an area that in turn forms the variegated basis for different rent I.

|500| *Secondly*. In the case of differential rent in form II, the variation in fertility is supplemented by *differences in the distribution of capital* (and access to credit) among the farmers. In manufacture proper, a specific minimal scale of business is soon formed in each branch of industry, and accordingly a minimum capital without which a particular business cannot be successfully conducted > (weaving, for instance, differs from spinning in the minimum required). < Also formed in each branch of industry is a *normal average amount* of capital above this minimum, which the great bulk of producers must and do have at their disposal. Anything above this can form extra profit; anything below it does not receive even the average profit. The capitalist mode of production takes hold of agriculture only in a slow and uneven manner, as we can see in the case of England, the classical land of the capitalist mode of production in this sector. In so far as there is no free import of corn, or the volume and consequent effect of this is restricted, the market price is determined by those producers who work on inferior soil, i.e., producers whose conditions of production are less favourable than the average. A large part of the total capital applied in agriculture, which stands at its disposal, is to be found in their hands.

(It is true that the peasant, for example, devotes *a great deal* of labour to his small parcel of land. But this labour is isolated, and deprived of the objective social and material conditions of productivity; it is denuded of them.)

The effect of this factor is that the genuinely capitalist farmers are in a position to appropriate a portion of the surplus profit; this would disappear, at least as far as the present point is concerned, if the capitalist mode of production were as uniformly developed in agriculture as in manufacture.

Let us start by considering simply the formation of *surplus profit* in the case of differential rent II, without troubling ourselves yet about the conditions under which this surplus profit can be transformed into *ground-rent*.

It is then clear that *differential rent II* is simply a different expression of *differential rent I*, and it is the same thing as far as its nature is concerned. The differing fertility of different types of land *affects* differential rent I only in so far as it means that capitals invested on the land give *unequal* results or products, either for the same size of capital or when taken *proportionately*. It can make no difference to this differing fertility or its product, and hence to the formation of differential rent for the more fruitfully invested portions of capital, whether this inequality marks different capitals invested successively on the same piece of land or whether the capitals are invested on several pieces of land of different types. In both cases it is the *land* which shows *differing fertility* for the same capital investment, but now *the same* land does for *a capital* invested successively in different portions what in differential rent I is done by different kinds of land for different capitals of equal size, each forming part of the total social capital.

|501| If *the same capital* of £10, which in Table I was invested by different farmers in the form of independent capitals of £2.10s. on one acre each of the four land types A, B, C and D, were instead to be invested successively on one and the same acre of D, so that the first investment yielded 4 quarters, the second 3 quarters, the third 2 quarters and the last 1 quarter (or alternatively in the inverse sequence), the price of £3 per quarter for the wheat supplied by the least fruitful portion of the capital would not yield any differential rent, though it would determine the production price as long as it is necessary to supply wheat whose production price is £3. And since we assume capitalist production, so that the price of £3 includes the *average profit* that any capital of £2.10s. yields, the three other portions of £2.10s. each will therefore yield *surplus profits*, according to the *difference of their product* [from the product of the least fertile land], since this product is sold not at its price of production but rather at the price of production of the least fruitful investment of £2.10s., an investment that yields no rent and in which the price of the product is governed by the general law of production prices. The formation of surplus profits would be the same as in Table I.

It should be remarked straight away here that differential rent II has differential rent I as its presupposition. The minimum product that a capital of

£2.10s. yields, i.e., what it yields on the worst land, is here taken as 1 quarter. Let us assume, therefore, that the farmer of land type D spends, besides the £2.10s. that yields him 4 quarters and for which he pays 3 quarters in differential rent, a further £2.10s. on the same land which only yields him 1 quarter, just like the same capital on the worst land A. This would then be a capital investment which *bore no rent*, since he would only obtain the average profit. There would be no surplus profit to transform into rent. On the other hand, however, this declining product of the second capital investment on D would not have any *effect on the profit rate*. It would be the same as if £2.10s. were newly invested on a further acre of type A, something that could not affect the surplus profit in any way, or, accordingly, the differential rent for the land types A, B, C and D. For the farmer, the additional investment of £2.10s. on D would have been just as advantageous as we assumed the investment of the original £2.10s. on the acre of D to have been, even though that yielded 4 quarters. Let him make two further capital investments of £2.10s. each, the first giving him an additional product of 3 quarters, the second an additional product of 2 quarters. A further *decline* would then have occurred, compared with the yield of the first investment of £2.10s. on D, which gave 4 quarters, hence a surplus profit of 3 quarters. But this would simply be a decline in the *level of surplus profit* and would affect neither the average profit nor the governing *production price*. This would be the case only if the *surplus production* which yields these *falling surplus profits* threw acre A out of cultivation because the amount of surplus product cast onto the market for this reason rendered the production of A superfluous. In that case the *declining* yield of the additional capital investment on acre D would be combined with a fall in the production price, e.g., from £3 to £1.10s., if acre B became the non-rent-bearing land that precisely governed the market price. The product of D would now be 4 + 1 + 3 + 2 = 10 quarters, whereas it was formerly 4 quarters. The price per quarter, however, as governed by B, would have fallen to £1.10s. The difference between D and B would be 10 − 2 = 8 quarters, which at £1.10s. per quarter is £12, whereas the money rent on D was formerly £9. This should be borne in mind. On a *per acre* basis, the level of *rent* would have risen by a third, or 33⅓ percent, despite the declining rate of surplus profit on the two additional capitals of £2.10s. It is only in the case where the demand for corn grows in such a way that the *market price* rises above the production price of A, so that the surplus product on A, B or any other *class* of land could only be supplied at a higher price than £3 – it is only in this case that a rise in the *production price* and the *governing* market price would be combined with a decline in the product of an additional capital investment on any one of the classes A, B, C or D. In so far as this continued for a prolonged period and did not lead to the cultivation of *additional* land of type A (of at least A's quality), with other factors also not bringing a supply at a lower rate, wages would rise, other things being equal, and, all other circumstances remaining the same, the profit rate would fall to that extent. It would be a matter of indifference in this case whether the increased demand was satisfied by drawing in worse land than A or by additional capital investment, whether on D itself, or on any of the other types of land. The differential rent would rise in combination with a falling rate of profit.

From this we can see the very complicated combinations to which differential rent always gives rise, and particularly when Form II is taken together with Form I, whereas Ricardo for instance deals with the matter quite one-sidedly and 'in simple terms'. One can have, for example, a *fall* in the *governing market price* and at the same time a *rise in rent* on the more fertile lands, per acre, so that both the absolute product and the absolute surplus product increase. (In the case of differential rent I in a downward series the *relative* surplus product can grow, hence also the rent per acre, even though the *absolute surplus product* per acre remains *constant* or even declines.) At the same time, however, the yield of *successive capital investments* on the same soil declines, even though a major part of these capital investments are applied to the more fertile lands. From one point of view – as far as the *product* and *production price* are concerned – the productivity of agriculture has risen. From another point of view (the yield of the land itself) it has *declined*, since there is a decline in the *rate of surplus profit* and the *surplus product per acre* in proportion to the various capital investments on *the same* land.

Given a *declining yield* for successive capital investments, differential rent II would necessarily involve an *increase in the production price* and an absolute decline in productivity only if those capital investments could take place only on the worst land, land of type A. In this case, every decrease in productivity would involve a decline in the product per acre, while on the better types of land it would only lead to a decline in the *excess surplus product*.

It is in the very nature of the case, however, that with the development of intensive cultivation, i.e., successive capital investments *on the same soil*, these investments take place predominantly on the better types of land, or at least to a higher degree. (Here we are not referring to the permanent improvements by which bad land is transformed into better land.) The declining yield of successive capital investments must therefore act principally in the manner described. The better land is selected because it offers the better prospect that the capital applied to it will bring in a profit; i.e., it contains a *greater quantity* of the *natural elements* of fertility, and all that is needed is to make these available.

When *rich farming* emerged in England after the repeal of the Corn Laws, a large amount of what was formerly wheat-growing land was turned over to other uses, converted into pasture for cattle, etc., while the fertile tracts suitable for wheat were drained, etc. The capital for wheat cultivation was concentrated more closely on those lands.

In this case – and here all possible surplus rates *between the highest surplus profit of the best land and the product of land of type A* involve not just a *relative* but an *absolute* increase in the surplus product per acre – the newly formed surplus profit (and potential rent) does not represent a portion of the *earlier average profit turned into rent* (a portion of the product which formerly represented average profit), but rather additional *surplus profit*, which, instead of retaining this form, now presents itself as rent.

|502| A *single* case, in which the declining yield of capitals subsequently added to the types of land already under cultivation can subsequently lead to a rise in the price of production, a fall in the rate of profit and the formation of increased differential rent – for in this case the differential rent will rise on all types of land, just as if worse land than A now governed the market price – was treated by Ricardo as the only case, the normal case, and he reduced the whole formation of differential rent to this.

This would also be the case if only type A land was cultivated and successive capital investments on it did not involve a proportionate increase in production.

Here, therefore, differential rent I is completely lost sight of in dealing with differential rent II.

With the exception of this case, where there is insufficient supply from the types of land cultivated, so that the market price is continuously above the price of production either until new and additional worse land is taken into cultivation or until the total product of the additional capital invested on the various types of land can only be supplied at a higher production price than prevailed before – with the *exception of this case*, the proportionate decline in the productivity of additional capitals leaves the governing production price and the profit rate unaffected.

[Three further cases are then possible.]

(a) If the *additional capital* on any of the land types A, B, C or D yields only the profit rate as determined by the production price of A, no surplus profit would be formed, and so there would be no potentiality for *rent*, any more than there would be if additional land A had been brought under cultivation.

(b) If the additional capital yields a *higher* product, new *surplus profit* (potential rent) is obviously formed, if the governing price remains the same. But this is not necessarily the case, not if this additional supply throws land A out of cultivation, and therefore out of the series of competing land types. The profit rate would rise if this were combined with a fall in wages or if the cheaper product were an element of constant capital. If the additional capital displayed its increased productivity on the best land types, C and D, the extent to which the *formation of increased surplus profit* (and therefore increased rent) was combined with the fall in price and the rise in the rate of profit would depend completely on the *magnitude* of the increasing productivity, and the amount of *capital newly added.* (The rate of profit can also rise without a fall in wages, through a cheapening of the elements of constant capital.)

(c) If the *additional capital investment* occurs in combination with *declining surplus profits*, but in such a way that its product leaves a surplus over and above the product of the same capital on land A, then, under all circumstances, if the increased supply does *not* force land A out of cultivation, there is a new formation of surplus profits, which may take place on D, C, B and A simultaneously. If on the other hand the worst soil, A, is driven out of cultivation, the governing production price falls, and whether the surplus profit expressed in money, and hence the differential rent, rises or falls depends on the ratio between the reduced price per quarter and the reduced number of quarters forming the surplus profit. In any case, however, we have here the peculiar phenomenon that the *production price* can fall together with declining surplus profits, instead of having to rise, as it would seem at first sight.

|503| These additional capital investments combined with *decreases* in yield correspond completely to the case in which four new independent capitals of £2.10s. each are invested on *types of land* whose fertility lies between A and B, B and C, and C and D, respectively yielding 1½ quarters (less than B, more than A), 2⅔ quarters (more than B, less than C) and 3½ quarters (more than C, less than D). *Surplus profits* and potential rents would be formed on all these types of land for all four additional capitals, even though the rate of surplus profit, compared with the rate for the same capital investment on better land in each case, would have fallen. And it would not make any difference whether these four capitals were invested on D, etc., or were distributed between D and A.

We come now to a basic distinction between the two forms of *differential rent, I and II.*

Given a constant production and constant differences, the *average rent* per acre may rise with the total rental in the case of differential rent I, and so may the *average rate of rent on capital.* But the average is merely an abstraction. The actual level of rent, per acre or reckoned on capital, *remains* the same under these assumptions.

Under the same assumptions, however, the *level of rent measured per acre* may rise, even though the *rate of rent, measured on the capital laid out*, remains the same.

Assume that production doubles by the investment of a total of £20 on A, B, C and D, instead of the £10 made up by investing £2.10s on each of them, relative fertility *remaining the same*. This would be just the same as if 2 acres of each of these types of land were cultivated instead of 1 acre, with costs remaining the same. The profit rate would remain the same, and so would its proportion to the surplus profit or rent. But if A now bears 1 quarter, B 4 quarters, C 6 quarters and D 8 quarters, the production price remains £3 per quarter, since this increase is due not to a doubled yield on the same capital, but to the same proportionate yield on a doubled capital. The 2 quarters from A would now cost £6, just as formerly 1 quarter cost £3. Profit on all four types of land would have doubled, but only because the capital laid out has doubled. But the rent would have doubled in the same proportion; it would be 2 quarters for B instead of 1 quarter, 4 quarters for C instead of 2 quarters and 6 quarters for D instead of 3 quarters; and the money rents for B, C and D would accordingly be £6, £12 and £18 respectively. The *money rent* per acre would have doubled just as the product per acre has doubled, and so too would the *land price* in which this money rent is capitalised. > Since the acreage has not increased, the produce rent for B, C and D for the same amount of land would have doubled, as also would the money rent. < Reckoned in this way, the level of the *corn and money rent* rises, and with it the price of land, because the yardstick by which it is measured, the acre, is a piece of *land* of *constant* size. No change has taken place, however, in the proportionate magnitude of the rent, calculated on the capital invested (and the rent on capital itself is to be calculated as a *rate of rent*). The total money rent of £36 is related to the capital of £20 that has now been laid out as the money rent of £18 was related to the capital previously laid out of £10. The same thing applies to the ratio of the money rent for each kind of land to the capital laid out on it; on C, for example, we have £12 rent to £5 capital, as we formerly had £6 to £2.10s. capital. No new differences arise here between the capitals laid out, but new surplus profits do arise, merely because the additional capital is invested on some rent-bearing types of soil, or on all of them, giving the same proportionate product. If the doubled investment were to be made only on C, for example, the differential rent between C, B and D would remain the same when reckoned on capital; for if the differential rate on C has doubled, so too has the capital invested.

This makes it clear that with the *production price*, the *differences* between types of land and the rate of profit remaining the same, and hence the same *rate of surplus profits* or *rent* (measured on capital) the level of both *produce rent* and *money rent* per acre can rise, and with it the price of land.

The same thing can occur in the case of *declining rates of surplus profit* and hence of rent, i.e., with a declining productivity of additional (supplemental) applications of capital, which still however *bear rent*. If the additional portions of capital on B, C and D of say £2.10s each, as before, were not to double the product but instead B were to yield only 3½ quarters, C 5 quarters and D 7 quarters, the differential rent on B for the second £2.10s. portion of capital would only be ½ quarter instead of 1 quarter, on C 1 quarter instead of 2 quarters and D 2 quarters instead of 3 quarters.

The proportion between rent and capital for the first investment was as follows for B: rent £3: capital £2.10s. > (The numbers were different, but we leave this as it is for convenience.) < It is now £2.10s.: £2.10s and the same ratio applies to all the other categories of land. Despite the fall in the rate of relative productivity and therefore in the rate of surplus profit reckoned on capital, *produce and money rent* would have risen from 1 quarter to 1½ quarters for B (£3 to £4.10s.), from 2 quarters to 3 quarters for C (£6 to £9) and from 3 quarters to 5 quarters for D (£9 to £15). In this case the *differences for the additional capitals* would have *declined*, compared with the *capital* invested on A, and the *production price* would have remained the same, but the rent per acre and hence the *price* of land per acre would have risen.

|504| We now proceed to show the results (the combinations) of *differential rent II*, which does however presuppose as its basis differential rent I.

A.) *Constant Price of Production* (this implies that the market price continues to be governed by the capital invested on the worst land, A.)[96]

I. If the *additional capital invested* on any of the rent-bearing types of land B, C and D is only as productive as the same capital on land A, i.e., if at the governing price of production it yields only the average profit and thus no surplus profit, the effect on rent is zero. Everything remains as it was before. It is the same as if a number of acres of quality A, the worst land, had been added to the area previously cultivated.

II. On each different type of land, *additional capitals* produce *extra products in proportion to their size*; i.e., the *volume of production* grows, according to the specific fertility of each type of land, *in proportion to the amount of extra capital.*

96 [This is the beginning of Engels's Chapter 41 ('Differential Rent II – First Case: Price of Production Constant'). Editor]

TABLE I

Type	Acres	Capital advanced	Profit	Cost of production	Rate of profit	Product per acre	Surplus profit	Rate of surplus profit	Corn rent	Money rent
A	1	£2.10s.	10s.	£3 per qr.	20%	1 qr.	0	0	0	0
B	1	£2.10s.	10s.	£1.10s. per qr.		2	£3	120%	1 qr.	£3
C	1	£2.10s.	10s.	£1 per qr.		3	£6	240%	2 qrs.	£6
D	1	£2.10s.	10s.	15s. per qr.		4	£9	360%	3 qrs.	£9
Total	4	£10	£2	£12 (altogether)		10 qrs.	£18	180% (average)	6 qrs.	£18

Let us now assume that the *investment of capital* on all four types of land is doubled, and the product rises *proportionately*. We should now have:

TABLE II

Type	Acres	Capital advanced	Profit	Cost of production	Rate of profit	Product per acre	Surplus profit	Rate of surplus profit	Corn rent	Money rent
A	1	£5	20s.	£3	20%	2 qrs.	0	0	0	0
B	1	£5	20s.	£1.10s.		4	6	120%	2 qrs.	£6
C	1	£5	20s.	£1		6	12	240%	4 qrs.	£12
D	1	£5	20s.	15s.		8	18	360%	6 qrs.	£18
Total	4	£20	£4			20 qrs.	£36	180% (average)	12 qrs.	£36

It is unnecessary here for the capital investment on all types of land to double, as in Table II. The law is the same whenever the capital is doubled on one or more of the rent-bearing types of land, whether it is type D or any other. It is also not necessary for the capital investment to increase in *equal proportions* on all types of land. > It may increase x times on one and y times on the rest, for instance. < All that is required is simply that *production* on *each type of land* should increase in the same ratio as capital, in other words *proportionately*.

Here, rent rises simply as a result of increased capital investment on the land and in proportion to this increase of capital. This *increase in the product* and in rent *proportionately to the extra capital*, as a result of and in proportion to increased capital investment, is just the same, as far as the amount of product and rent is concerned, as if the *cultivated area of the better types of land* had increased and these were cultivated with the same capital investment as the same types of land were previously. In the case of Table II, for example, the result would remain the same if > instead of 3 acres an additional 6 acres, 2 each for the respective types of land B, C and D, had been put under cultivation.

< This case also has the underlying assumption that there has been no *improvement*, no *more fruitful* application of capital, but simply an even and constant application of *more* capital in the same area with the same result as before.

Here all *proportionate* ratios remain the same. However, if we consider not the proportionate differences but the *purely arithmetical* ones, the *differential rent* on the various types of land can alter. Let us assume for example that the extra capital has been invested solely on B and D. The difference between D and A is then 7, as against 3 before; between B and A it is 3 as against 1 before, and between C and B it is minus 1 instead of plus 1. But this *arithmetical difference*, which is decisive in the case of *differential rent I*, in so far as it expresses the difference in productivity for the same capital investment, is here quite immaterial, since it is simply the result of different *further investment* or non-investment of capital, given a constant *difference* for each equal portion of capital on the various lands.

|505| III

The *extra capitals* bring forth an extra product > in proportion to the surplus product of the *portions of capital first invested* < and thus form surplus profits, though at a *declining rate*, and not in proportion to the *increase in their size*.

TABLE III

Type	Acres	Capital advanced	Profit	Cost of production	Rate of profit	Product per acre	Surplus profit	Rate of surplus profit	Corn rent	Money rent
A	1	£2.10s.	10s.	£3 per qr.	20%	1 qr.	0	0	0	0
B	1	£2.10s.	20s.	£1.10s. per qr.		2	£3	120%	1 qr.	£3
		£2.10s.		£2		1½	£1.10s.	60%	½ qr.	£1.10s.
Total for B		£5		£3.10s.		3½	£4.10s.	90%	1½	£4.10s.
C	1	£2.10s.		£1 per qr.		3	£6	240%	2 qrs.	£6
		£2.10s.	20s.	£1.10s.		2	£3	120%	1 qr.	£3
Total for C		£5		£2.10s.		5	£9	180%	3 qrs.	£9
D	1	£2.10s.		15s. per qr.		4	£9	360%	3 qrs.	£9
		£2.10s.		17½s. per qr.		3½	£7.10s.	150%	2½ qrs.	£7.10s.
Total for D		£5	20s.	£1.12⁴⁄₇s. per qr.		7½	£16.10s.	255%	5½ qrs.	£16.10s.
Overall totals		£17.10s.	£3.10s.	£21 per 17 qrs.		17	£30	175%	10 qrs.	£30[97]

It is once again immaterial whether the extra investments – the investments made the second time around on *the same* land – fall uniformly on the various types of land or not; whether the declining production of surplus product proceeds in equal or unequal proportions; whether the additional capital investments all fall on *the same* rent-bearing type of land; or whether they are distributed, uniformly or not, on rent-bearing lands of different quality. All these factors are immaterial for the laws to be developed here. The only assumption is that extra capital investments on any of the rent-bearing land types yield surplus profit, but in *declining* proportion to the increase in capital. In the examples given in the above table, the limits of this decline lie between 3 quarters, or £9, which is the rent on the first capital investment of the best land,

97 The total surplus profit of £30 is made up of £18 on the first class and £12 on the second class; the average rate of surplus profit is 180% on the first class and 110% on the second class; the produce rent is 6 quarters on the first investment, and 4 quarters on the second investment; finally the money rent is £18 on the first class and £12 on the second class.

D, and 1 quarter, or £3, which is the product of the same capital investment on the worst land, A. The product of the best land on the investment of the original capital forms the maximum limit, and the product of the worst land, A, which bears no rent and gives no surplus profit, forms the minimum limit of the product that the successive capital investments on any of the land types yielding surplus profit actually yield in a situation of a *decline* in productivity from successive capital investments. While case II implies that new plots of land of the *same quality* as the better types are added to the cultivated area, and that the quantity of one or more of the cultivated land types increases, case III implies that additional plots of land are cultivated whose degree of fertility varies between D and A, between that of the best land and that of the worst. If the successive capital investments take place exclusively on land D, they can encompass the existing differences between D and A, as well as those between D and C and between D and B. If they all take place on land C, they can encompass only the differences between C and A and C and B; if on B, then only the differences between B and A.

But the *law* is that the *rent* on all these types of land grows absolutely, even if not in proportion to the additional capital invested. > If the rate of decline of the surplus product is given, the rent increases on a piece of land in proportion to the quantity of capital successively invested, the quantity of excess capital; if the amount of capital is given, the rent declines in proportion to the rate of decline in the productivity of the excess capital.

|506| < The *rate of surplus profit* declines, in relation both to the extra capital and the total capital invested on the land; but the *absolute amount of surplus profit* increases; just as the falling rate of profit on capital in general is usually combined with an increasing absolute mass of profit. The average surplus profit for the capital investment on B, for example, is now 90 percent on the capital, while for the first capital investment it was 120 percent. The total surplus profit, however, increases from 1 quarter to 1½ quarters, and from £3 to £4.10s. The total rent taken by itself – and not in relation to the doubled sum of capital advanced – has risen absolutely, > as is shown by the phenomenon that the corn rent rises from 1 quarter to 1½ quarters and the money rent from £3 to £4.10s. < The differences in the rents from the different types of land and their relationship to one another may change in this case; but this *change in their differences* is here the *result* and not the *cause* of the comparative increase in rents.

IV

The case in which the extra capital investments are bound up with *rising rates of surplus profit* requires no further analysis. It is self-evident that on this assumption rents per acre rise, and in a higher ratio than the extra capital, wherever the extra investments have taken place. In this case, the *extra capital investment* is combined with *improvement*. This includes the case in which a *small influx* of extra capital produces *the same* or a *greater* effect than the previous addition of a larger amount. This case is not entirely *identical* with the earlier one, and this is a *distinction* which is important for all capital investments. If for instance 100 gives a profit of 10, when applied in a particular form, and 200 a profit of 40, the profit has risen from 10 percent to 20 percent, and in this respect it is the same as if 50, applied in a more effective way, gave a profit of 10 instead of 5. (We assume here that the profit is bound up with a proportionate increase in the product.) But the difference is that in the one case I have to double the capital, while in the other I produce the doubled effect with the same capital as before. It is certainly not the same whether I produce (a) the same product as before with half as much *living and objectified labour*, (b) *double* the previous product with *the same* labour, or (c) use *twice as much labour* (capital) to produce a *proportionately higher* product, say four times the amount. In the first case labour is set free – in either living or objectified form – and can be applied elsewhere: the *power of disposition* over labour and capital is increased. The *setting free* of capital (and labour) is in itself an increase in wealth, and it has exactly the same effect as if this extra *capital* were obtained by *accumulation*, but it saves on the work of accumulation. > The difference can also be shown in this way: if in case (a) I continued to work with the same capital, I obtain the same result as in (b); but in (b) I do not obtain the same result as in (a). It is assumed here that in order to *double* the product I *must* apply the *same quantity of labour and capital* as I did before. In (a) the product has in fact been *quadrupled* in proportional terms, if I use the same amount of labour (instead of half as much labour), and when I use double the amount there will be an eight-fold increase in the product. Case (c) is related to case (b) exactly as case (b) is related to case (a). Even so, it is relatively unfavourable, and still more unfavourable when compared with (a). Case (c) can only occur when *double the amount of capital* (double the amount of labour) is available or is withdrawn from other areas where it was applied until then. For the *determination of value* the situation is exactly the same.

< Let us assume that a capital of 100 has produced a product of 10 ells. Say that this capital contains as much constant capital as it does living labour and profit. The cost of an ell is therefore 10. If I can then produce 20 ells with the

same capital of 100, the cost of an ell falls to 5. If on the other hand I can produce 10 ells with a capital of 50, the cost of an ell is still 5 and a capital of 50 has been set free, in so far as the former supply of the commodity is still sufficient. If I have to invest a capital of 200 to produce 40 ells, the cost of an ell is similarly 5. There is no difference in the determination of value (or that of price) any more than there is a difference in the quantity produced in proportion to the capital advanced. But in case (a) capital is released; in case (b) extra capital is spared, given that twice the amount of production is required; and in case (c) the increased product can be obtained only by a growth in the capital advanced, although not in the same proportion as if productivity had remained constant and the same extra product had had to be supplied at that same level of productivity. (This all belongs in Chapter One of Book Three.)

Considered from the standpoint of capitalist production, if we have regard to the cost price and not the formation of surplus-value, it is always cheaper to employ constant capital rather than variable. A saving in costs on the element that creates surplus-value, labour, does the capitalist the same service as a rise in surplus-value itself, as long as the governing production price remains the same. This presupposes in fact the development of credit and the superabundance of loanable capital that corresponds to the capitalist mode of production. Say I employ on the one hand an additional constant capital of £100, this £100 being the product of five workers over a year; and, on the other hand, £100 of variable capital. If the rate of surplus-value is 100 percent, the value that the five workers have created is £200; the value of the £100 of constant capital, however, is £100, while as capital it is perhaps £105, if the rate of interest is 5 percent. The same sums of money, quantities of value, express very different values when their products are considered.

> The *value of £100* in constant capital and £100 in *variable* capital advanced to production is expressed in *completely different proportions* in the *product*. < Another factor, as far as the cost of commodities from the capitalist's standpoint is concerned, is the further distinction that of the £100 constant capital, in so far as this is invested not in *raw material* but in machinery, etc., only the wear-and-tear goes into the value of the commodity, whereas the £100 for wages must be *completely* reproduced in it.

In the case of *colonists* and self-sustaining producers, who mostly have no access to *capital*, or only at high interest rates, the portion of the product that represents *wages* is their *revenue*, whereas for the capitalist it is a *capital advance*. They therefore consider this *labour cost* as the *proceeds of their labour*, which is the most important thing for them. As far as their *extra labour* is concerned, after this labour cost is deducted, it is always realised in an *excess* product, and whenever they can sell it and valorise it (or directly make use of it themselves) they consider it as something which has cost them *nothing*, as it has not cost any *objectified labour*. It is only the expenditure of objectified labour which is seen by them as an *alienation* [*Entäusserung*] of wealth. They naturally seek to sell at as high a price as possible; but even a sale below the *value* and below the *cost of production* still seems to them like a *profit* (as long as this profit is not anticipated by any indebtedness, mortgages, etc.)

For the capitalist, on the other hand, the outlay of both *constant* capital and *variable* is an advance of *capital*. The relatively greater advance of constant capital reduces the *cost price*, other things being equal, as it also reduces the value of the commodities. Hence although *profit* arises simply from the *surplus labour*, i.e., simply from the employment of *variable capital*, it can seem to the individual capitalist that living labour is the most expensive element in his production costs, which should be reduced to the smallest possible level. This is simply a *capitalistically* distorted form of the correct position, that the relatively greater application of *past labour*, as compared with *living labour*, > means a saving in the latter and a more plentiful supply of it. < This is how everything appears from the standpoint of competition: *falsely*.

|507| Assuming *stable production prices*, the extra capital investments can be made with *constant, increasing* or *decreasing productivity* on the better lands, i.e., on all land from B upwards. On A itself this would only be possible, on our assumptions, either with productivity unchanged, in which case the land would continue to bear *no* rent, or productivity *increases*; one part of the capital invested on land of type A would then bear rent, the other not. But it would be impossible on the assumption of a *decline in A's productivity*, for in that case the production price would not remain constant, but would *rise*. Under all these circumstances, however, i.e., whether the surplus product brought in is *proportionately* above or below this proportion – and thus whether the *rate of surplus profit* on the capital remains constant, rises or falls as the capital grows – the *surplus product* and the *surplus profit* per acre corresponding to it *grows*, and so too, therefore, potentially, does the rent, in corn and money. The growth in the simple *mass* of surplus profit or rent, reckoned per acre, i.e., reckoning the *growing* mass by a *constant yardstick*, and here therefore by a definite quantity of land, is expressed as a growth in the *proportion*. The *rent, or the level of rent*, reckoned per acre, thus grows under these conditions simply as a result of the *increase* in the capital invested on the land. And this takes place, moreover, with production prices remaining the same, and irrespective of whether the productivity of the extra capital remains the same, decreases or increases. The latter factors modify the degree to which the *level of rent* per acre grows, but not the fact that it does grow. This is a phenomenon *which*

is peculiar to differential rent II and distinguishes it from *differential rent I*. If the additional capital investments were made alongside one another spatially, on new additional land of the appropriate quality, instead of temporally, in succession, on the same land, the *amount* of the rental would have grown, and so would the *average rent* of the overall cultivated area, as shown earlier, but not the *level of rent* per acre. With the result remaining the same, as far as the amount and value of total production and the surplus product are concerned, the concentration of capital on a more restricted area increases the level of rent per acre, whereas under the same conditions its *dispersion over a greater area*, all other things remaining the same, could not produce this effect. The more the capitalist mode of production develops, however, the more the concentration of capital on the same area increases, so that the rent per acre rises. Hence in two countries where production prices are identical, and the differences between land types are also identical, and the same amount of capital is invested, but in one country this happens more in the form of *successive* investments on *the same land*, and in the other country more in the form of *parallel* and coordinated investments on *a greater amount of land*, the rent per acre and therefore the price of land would be *higher* in the first country and lower in the second, even though the *total rental* in both countries was the same. This difference in levels of rent could thus be explained neither in terms of a difference in the natural fertility of the land types nor in the amount of labour applied, but exclusively in terms of the different kinds of capital investment.

(In speaking of a *surplus product* here, we mean the *aliquot portion of the product* in which the *surplus profit* is expressed. Generally, however, we take *surplus product* to mean the portion of the product in which the *total surplus-value* is expressed, or in particular cases, the *average profit*. The specific meaning that this term obtains in the case of rent-bearing capital can give rise to misunderstandings, as we saw previously).

|508| B)[98] *Falling Price of Production*

The price of production may *fall* if additional applications of capital take place while productivity *remains constant, falls or rises*, > i.e., with a constant, a falling or a rising *rate* of productivity. >

98 [This is the beginning of Engels's Chapter 42 ('Differential Rent II – Second Case: Price of Production Falling'). Editor]

I. *Falling Price of Production with the Productivity of Additional Capital Investment Remaining Constant. Rate of Surplus Profit (the rate of surplus profit changes as the surplus profit itself changes)*

In this case, the *product* from the various types of land, corresponding to their respective quality, grows to the same *extent* as does *the capital invested on the land.* This implies, given that the differences between types of land remain the same, a *growth in production* and also a growth in surplus profit proportionate to the growth in capital investment. This case, therefore, rules out any impact on differential rent of a surplus investment of capital on land type A. On this land, the rate of surplus profit is zero; it therefore remains zero, since it is assumed that the productivity of the extra capital and hence the rate of surplus profit remains *constant.* > It also excludes any further application of capital to A, whether this leads to an increase or a decrease in productivity.

< Under these assumptions, therefore, the governing production price can only fall when the governing factor ceases to be the production price of A, the latter's place being taken by the next best land, B, or some other land that is better than A; i.e., capital is withdrawn from A – or even from A and B, if the production price of land C becomes the governing one – so that all inferior land drops out of the competition between wheat-growing lands. The condition for this, under the given assumptions, is that the *extra* product of the *additional capital investments* satisfies the demand, and hence the production of the inferior land, A, etc., is superfluous to the supply required.

Let us therefore take Table II, above, but assume that instead of 20 quarters, 18 quarters now satisfies the demand. A would drop out; B, with its production price of 30s. per quarter, would become the price-governing land. The differential rent then assumes the following form:

TABLE IV

Acres	*Capital advanced*	*Profit*	*Production cost*	*Rate of profit*	*Product per acre*	*Surplus profit*	*Rate of surplus profit*	*Corn rent*	*Money rent*
B 1	£5	20s.	£1.10s.	20%	4 qrs.	0	0	0	0
C 1	£5	20s.	£1		6 qrs.	£3	60%	2 qrs.	£3
D 1	£5	20s.	15s.		8 qrs.	£6	120%	4 qrs.	£6
Total	£15	£3	21⅔s.		18 qrs.	£9	60%	6 qrs.	£9

The total rent, therefore, compared with Table II, would have fallen from £36 to £9, and in corn from 12 quarters to 6 quarters, although the total production has fallen only by 2 quarters, from 20 to 18 quarters. The rate of surplus profit, reckoned on the capital, would have fallen to a third of its former level, from 180 percent to 60 percent. > The productivity of the various capital investments on B, C and D would have remained *the same*.

< The decline in corn and money rent thus corresponds to a fall in the *production price*. Compared with Table I, however, there is simply a decline in the money rent; the corn rent in both cases is 6 quarters, but in one case the money rent amounts to £18, and in the other case to £9. > On land C the money rent was previously £6 and it is now £3, but < the corn rent has remained the same as in Table I, namely 2 quarters, > and the same is true of land type D.[99]

< In fact, the product of A has been driven out of the market by the additional production obtained from the uniformly operating additional capital, and land A is thus excluded as a competing agent of production, as a result of which a new *differential rent I* has been formed, in which the better land B plays the same role as the inferior land A did before. B's rent therefore disappears, although *nothing has changed in the differences* between B, C and D because of the investment of additional capital. The part of the product that is transformed into rent therefore *falls*.

> (If we compare the position of land type D in tables I and IV, we see a rise in *corn rent* on D, for in Table I it is only 3 quarters, while in Table IV it is 4 quarters, although the money rent falls from £9 to £6. The corn rent of D in Table I is 3 quarters, hence over ⅓ of the total product of 10; in Table IV, on the other hand, the corn rent is only 1 less than ¼ of the total product of 18. But since the total product is larger (18 > 10), less than ¼ of 18 is more than ⅓ of 10. Or if we take the product of D alone, instead of the total product, we find that in Table I there is a product of 4 quarters and a *corn rent* of 3 quarters, hence ¾ of the product; while in Table IV the product of D is 8 quarters and the rent of 4 quarters forms only ½ of this. But half of 8, 8/2, is greater than ¾ × 4.)

< If the above result – the satisfaction of the demand with the exclusion of A – had been brought about by the investment of *more than* twice the capital on C or D or both of these, things would have taken a different course. In that case, we should have:

99 [This appears to contradict the data presented in Tables I and IV. Translator]

TABLE IVA

Acres	*Capital advanced*	*Profit*	*Production cost*	*Rate of profit*	*Product per acre*	*Surplus profit*	*Rate of surplus profit*	*Corn rent*	*Money rent*
B 1	£5	20s.	£1.10s.	20%	4 qrs.	0	0	0	0
C 1	£7.10s.	30s.	£1		9 qrs.	£7.10s.	60%	5 qrs.	£7.10s.
D 1	£5	20s.	15s.		8 qrs.	£6	120%	4 qrs.	£6
Total	£17.10s.	£3.10s.	21⅔s.		21 qrs.	£13.10s.	90%	9 qrs.	£13.10s.

Here the product on C has risen from 6 quarters in Table IV to 9 quarters, the surplus product from 2 quarters to 3 quarters, the money rent from *£3 to £7.10s.* In Table II it was £12, but in Table I, before the second capital investment it was only £6. It has fallen in comparison with Table II and risen in comparison with Table I. As far as the total rent is concerned, the *corn rent* has risen, compared with I, and fallen, compared with II. The money rent has fallen compared with both I and IV.

|509| If a third capital investment of £2.10s. has been applied to land B this would certainly have altered the amount of production, but it would have left the rent unaffected, since the successive capital investments are assumed not to produce any difference on *the same* type of land, and land B does *not* yield rent.

If we assume, on the other hand, that the third capital investment takes place on D instead of on C, we arrive at Table IVb, as follows:

TABLE IVB

Acres	*Capital advanced*	*Profit*	*Production cost*	*Rate of profit*	*Product per acre*	*Surplus profit*	*Rate of surplus profit*	*Corn rent*	*Money rent*
B 1	£5	20s.	£1.10s.	20%	4 qrs.	0	0	0	0
C 1	£5	20s.	£1		6 qrs.	£3	60%	2 qrs.	£3
D 1	£7.10s.	£1.10s.	15s.		12 qrs.	£12	120%	8 qrs.	£12
Total	£17.10s.	£3.10s.	21⅔ s.		22 qrs.	£15	90%	10 qrs.	£15

Here the total product is 22 quarters, more than double that of Table I, although the capital advanced is only £17.10s. as against £10, i.e., less than double. The total product is also 2 quarters larger than that in Table II (where the product was 2 [0] quarters) even though in the latter case the capital advanced was greater than in Table IVb, namely £20, as opposed to £17.10s.

On land D, the *corn rent* > is more than twice as large as in Table I. It < has increased from 3 quarters to 8 quarters, and the money rent is a third larger, namely £12 instead of £9. The corn rent is a third larger than in Table II, namely 8 quarters instead of 6, and the money rent is smaller, £12 instead of £18.

Taking the total rents, the *corn rent* in Table IVb is 10 quarters, greater than that in Table I, 6 quarters, and that of Table IVa, 9 quarters. It is smaller than that of Table II, which was 12 quarters. The *money rent* in Table IVb is £15, which is greater than that of Table IVa, £13.10s., and smaller than those of Table I, which was £18, and Table II, which was £36.

In order for the total rental under the conditions of Table IVb to be the same as in Table I, even though the rent on B has disappeared, we must have a further rent of £3 a quarter for the surplus produce; 12 quarters at £1.10s. a quarter is the new production price (£18), and 6 quarters at £3 a quarter is £18. The relative size of the surplus capital required for this will vary according to whether we invest it on C or D, or divide it between the two.

On C, the additional capital yields 2 quarters of surplus product, which = 33⅓ s., and the profit of 20 percent on this is 6⅔s., hence the price of production = £2, or £1 per quarter. On D, the additional capital for 2 quarters = 25s., and the profit of 20 percent is 5s., hence the price of production = 30s., or 15s. per quarter.

|510| TABLE IVC

Acres	*Capital advanced*	*Profit*	*Rate of profit*	*Product per acre*	*Surplus profit*	*Rate of surplus profit*	*Corn rent*	*Money rent*
B 1	£5	20s.	20%	4 qrs.	0	0	0	0
C 1	£6.13⅓s.	26⅔s.		8 qrs.	£6		4 qrs.	£6
D 1	£7.10s.	30s.		12 qrs.	£12		8 qrs.	£12
Total	£19.3⅓s.	£3.16⅔s.		24 qrs.	£18		12 qrs.	£18

And then if the surplus capital required to produce 2 quarters is added to D, we get:

TABLE IVD

Acres	*Capital advanced*	*Profit*	*Rate of profit*	*Product per acre*	*Surplus profit*	*Rate of surplus profit*	*Corn rent*	*Money rent*
B 1	£5	20s.	20%	4 qrs.	0	0	0	0
C 1	£5	20s.		6 qrs.	£3		2 qrs.	£3
D 1	£8.15s.	35s.		14 qrs.	£15		10 qrs.	£15
Total	£18.15s.	£3.15s.		24 qrs.	£18		12 qrs.	£18

The total money rent would be less than half of what it was in Table II, where the excess capital was invested at *unchanged* prices of production. The most important thing is to compare the above tables with Table I.

We find that the total money rental remains the same, £18, despite a fall of a half in the production price, from £3 to 30s. a quarter, while the *corn rent* has doubled, namely from 6 quarters to 12 quarters (necessarily so, because £1 *now* buys twice as much corn as it did previously). The rent on B has disappeared; on C it has remained *the same* in Table IVc, and *fallen by half* in Table IVd, while on D it has risen in Table IVc from £9 to £12 and in Table IVd from £9 to £15. *Production* has risen from 10 quarters to 24 quarters, almost by two and a half times, and profit has risen from £2 to £3.5s. The total capital investment has risen in one case (Table IVc) from £10 to £19.3$\frac{1}{13}$ s., hence it has not quite doubled, and in the other case (Table IVd) it has fallen a long way short of doubling, rising from £10 to £18.15s.

The *total money rent*, reckoned on the capital advanced, is in Table IVd almost 100 percent of it, in Table IVc it is somewhat less, but in Table I it is 180 percent of it. It has thus fallen by more than 80 percent. The *average money rent per acre* has risen. Its previous average, in Table I, was £4.10s. per acre over 4 acres. Now it is £6 on 3 acres. Its average on the rent-bearing lands was formerly £6 per acre and is now £9. The average money rent, or the *money value of the rent per acre has also risen*, and it now represents twice *as much corn product* as it did before; but the 12 quarters of corn rent are now less than half of the total product of 24 quarters, whereas in Table I the 6 quarters of rent made up six-tenths of the total product of 10 quarters. Thus even though the rent has fallen, taken as an *aliquot part of the total product*, and similarly if reckoned as a percentage of the capital advanced, its *money value* reckoned per acre has risen, and its product value still more. If we take land D, where changes in rent have taken place, the production costs laid out amount to £10.10s. and the capital laid out is £8.15s.

The money rent is £15. In Table I the capital laid out was £2.10s. and the production costs were £3; money rent was £9. Thus the production costs have risen threefold, and the capital outlay fourfold. In Table IVd, the money rent of £15 for D is not quite one and a half times the production costs, and not quite twice the capital outlay. Yet the *money rent* per acre is two-thirds greater, £15 instead of £9. In Table I the corn rent of 3 quarters is $\frac{3}{4}$ the total product of 4 quarters; in IVd a rent of 10 quarters is $\frac{5}{7}$ D's total product of 14 quarters: > the first named ratio is $\frac{21}{28}$, the second is $\frac{20}{28}$. < This shows how the money value and the corn value of the rent per acre can increase, even though this forms a smaller aliquot part of the total yield and has fallen in relation to the capital advanced.

In Table I, the value of the total product is £30; the total rent is £18, more than half of this. In Table IVd, the value of the total product of 24 quarters is £36, of which the rent at £18 is exactly one-half.

The reason why, despite the fall of the price per quarter from £3 to £1.10s., hence a fall of 50 percent, the money rent remains the same and the corn rent doubles, is that the price of corn, now £1.10s. per quarter, is multiplied by *such an increased number of quarters* (in other words, so many more surplus quarters are produced) that it amounts to as much as the previous corn price of £3 multiplied by 6 quarters (£1.10s. × 12 quarters = £3 × 6 quarters). In other words, surplus production has increased in the same proportion as the corn price has fallen; the latter has fallen by 50 percent and the former has increased by 100 percent. But in order to bring about this result, total production must grow almost two and a half times, under the conditions we have set, and capital investment on the better types of land must more than double. All other circumstances remaining the same, the proportion in which the latter must grow depends on how the *extra* capital investment is divided between the better and the best types of land, assuming here that the productivity of capital on each type of land grows *in proportion* to its amount.

If the fall in the price were less, less *extra* capital would be required to produce *the same money rent.* If a *greater supply* were needed to drive A out of cultivation – and this depends not only on A's product but on the *proportionate* share that A has in the total cultivated area – if therefore a greater *quantity of extra capital* were also required on the land of better quality than A, the money rent and the corn rent would have grown still further, other things being equal, even though both disappeared on the land of type B.

|511| > The reason why the invested capital is not *entirely* twice the former amount, although the productivity of the respective additions of capital has

remained the same on all the land types, is that ¼ of the former total capital of £10, namely £2.10s., is no longer present. £7.10s. is left. Twice this is £15. On top of this, £3.15s. have been added to D, which makes £18.15s. altogether. The capital on land types B, C and D has more than doubled, but this is not a doubling of the old capital of £10, but of the old capital less £2.10s., in other words a doubling of £7.10s. < If the capital that disappeared from A had been £5, > as in Table II, the same situation would have arisen as when the extra capital was entirely devoted to D, as in Table IVd. < The two tables to be compared in this case would be II and IVd.

The total product would have grown from 20 quarters to 24 quarters. The money rent would only be half as large, £18 instead of £36; the corn rent would be the same, at 12 quarters. > But the £18 on a capital of £18.15s. would be 104⅙ percent; whereas £36: £20 = 180 percent.

If a surplus product of 24 quarters = £36 could be produced on D with a capital of £17.10s. (which would represent the same percentage of 104⅙ percent) the total production in Table IVd would be 36 quarters instead of the 20 in Table II, and the money rent would remain the same. But the total capital would now be £10 + £17.10s. = £27.10s., whereas the capital in Table II was £20. The total capital advanced would only have risen by a little more than a third; but production would have almost doubled; < the *corn rent* would have doubled, the money rent would have remained the same. Thus if the price falls as a result of the investment of excess money capital on the lands yielding higher rent, i.e., all except A, while productivity remains the same, the total capital will have a tendency not to grow in the same proportion as production and corn and money rent as compared with the former situation. The same law is also apparent in the way that the capital advanced must be applied in greater proportions to C than to D; a greater proportion of it must be applied to the land bearing less rent than to the land bearing more rent. This is simply for the following reason. In order for the money rent to remain the same or to rise, a definite additional quantity of surplus product must be produced, and the greater the fertility of the lands yielding surplus product, the less capital this requires. If the differences between B and C, and C and D, were still greater, still less extra capital would be needed. The specific proportion depends (1) on the ratio in which the price falls, thus on the difference between B and A; (2) on the ratio of the differences between the better types of land, from B upwards; and (3) on the amount of extra capital invested on this lands.

|512| We see in fact that this law expresses nothing more than was already developed in dealing with A: if the *production price* is given, whatever its level might be, the rent *can* rise as a result of extra capital investment. For the result of the exclusion of A from cultivation is a new *differential rent I*, with B now as

the worst land and £1.10s. a quarter as the new production price. This is as true of Table IV as it is for Table II. It is the same law, simply that B is taken as the starting-point instead of A, and the production price as £1.10s. instead of £3.

This is important here only for the following reasons: in so far as such and such a quantity of extra capital was needed to withdraw capital from land of type A and make up the supply without it, it has been demonstrated that depending on the conditions this may be accompanied by a rising, a falling or a stable *rent per acre*, if not on all lands, at least on some, and for the average of *cultivated* lands. We have seen that corn rent and money rent do not behave in the same way.

> For example:

Table I:	corn rent = 6 qrs. and money rent = £18
Table IV:	corn rent = 6 qrs. and money rent = £9
Table IVa:	corn rent = 9 qrs. and money rent = £13.10s.
Table IVb:	corn rent = 10 qrs. and money rent = £15
Table IVd:	corn rent = 12 qrs. and money rent = £18.

With falling production prices the corn rent must double for the money rent to rise again to its previous level.

But at the same time, this corn rent of 6 quarters is represented in a smaller money rent of £9, and when the corn rent has risen by half, to 9 quarters, the money rent is £13.10s.

< It is only tradition, however, that still gives corn rent any role. One might just as well prove that a manufacturer could buy far more of his own yarn with profit of £5 than he could formerly with a profit of £10. This does show, however, that while money rents are falling, the landowning dogs can still make significant *gains*, as producers of the raw materials and manufactures of which money rents form a part.

II. *A Falling Price of Production accompanied by a Fall in the Rate of Productivity of the Extra Capital Investment*

Nothing new is involved here except that the *production price* can also fall, as in the case last considered, if the *extra capital investments* on better types of land than A make A's product superfluous and hence cause capital to be withdrawn from A, or if A is applied to the production of a different crop. This case has already been exhaustively discussed. We have shown that the *corn and money rents per acre* can grow, decline or remain the same. > It goes without saying that since here the excess quarters cost more, have a greater money value, a smaller capital investment is required to bring about the same result (although from the point of view of the product there is greater growth in the capital applied). Compare for example Table III (from page 505) and Table I (from page 504), as follows:

TABLE I

Type	Acres	Capital advanced	Profit	Cost of production	Rate of profit	Product per acre	Surplus profit	Rate of surplus profit	Corn rent	Money rent
A	1	£2.10s.	10s.	£3 per qr.	20%	1 qr.	0	0	0	0
B	1	£2.10s.	10s.	£1.10s. per qr.		2	£3	120%	1 qr.	£3
C	1	£2.10s.	10s.	£1 per qr.		3	£6	240%	2 qrs.	£6
D	1	£2.10s.	10s.	15s. per qr.		4	£9	360%	3 qrs.	£9
Total	4	£10	£2			10 qrs.	£18	180% (average)	6 qrs.	£18

If we now assume that the 16 quarters supplied by B, C and D, with a declining *rate of productivity* is sufficient to remove A from competition, Table III now becomes as follows:

TABLE III[100] (*modified*)

Acres	*Capital advanced*		*Profit*	*Production cost*		*Product per acre*		*Total*	*Corn rent*	*Money rent*
	1	2		1	2	1	2			
B 1	£2.10s.	£2.10s.	£1	£1.10s.	£2	2 qrs.	1½ qrs.	3½ qrs.	0	0
				total: £3.10s.						
C 1	£2.10s.	£2.10s.	£1	£1	£1.10s.	3 qrs.	2 qrs.	5 qrs.	1½ qrs.	£2.12½s.
				total: £2.10s.						
D 1	£2.10s.	£2.10s.	£1	15s.	17½s.	4 qrs.	3½ qrs.	7½ qrs.	4 qrs.	£7
				total: £1.12½s.						
Total	£15		£3					16 qrs.	5½ qrs.	£9.12½s.

100 [This corresponds to Table V in Engels's published version. Translator]

Here, with a declining *rate of productivity* on the extra capitals and a varying decline on the different types of land, the governing production price has fallen from £3 to £1.15s. The capital investment has risen by half, from £10 to £15. The money rent has fallen by almost a half, from £18 to £9.12½s., but the corn rent by only a twelfth, from 6 quarters to 5½ quarters. The total product has risen from 10 quarters to 16 quarters, or to 160% of its previous level. The corn rent is somewhat over a third of the total product. The capital advanced stands in a ratio of £15: £9.12½ s. to the money rent, whereas the previous ratio was 10:18. > Production would only need to be increased by less than £8.10s. for the money rent to be equal in both cases.

< |513| III. *A Falling Price of Production accompanied by a Rising Rate of Productivity for the Extra Capital.*

This is distinguished from B I, above, page 508, in which the *price of production* falls while the *rate of productivity remains the same*, simply by the fact that if a given surplus is necessary to remove A from cultivation, this happens more quickly in the present case.

Both when the productivity of the additional capital investments is falling and when it is rising, the effect of this process can be *uneven*, according to how the *investments* are distributed over the different types of land. Depending on whether this varying effect tends to even out the differences or to intensify them, the differential rent on the better types of land will fall or rise, and so too, therefore, will the total rental, as was already the case with *differential rent I*. Moreover, everything depends on the size of the capital that is displaced with A, as well as on the *relative amount of capital which has to be advanced*, given rising productivity, to supply the excess product that is to meet the demand.

The only point worth investigating here, and this takes us back directly to the analysis of how this differential profit is transformed into differential rent, is this:

In the first case (A, above, page 504), where the *production price remains the same*, the excess capital that might be invested on land A is a matter of indifference for the *differential rent* as such, since now as before land A bears no rent, the price of its product remaining the same and continuing to govern the market.

In the second case (B I, above, page 508), where the *production price falls* and the *rate of productivity* remains the same, land A necessarily drops out, and still more so in B II (page 512) (falling production price with a falling rate of productivity), since otherwise the excess capital on land A would necessarily increase the production price. Here, however, where the production price falls because the *productivity of the extra capital* rises, this additional capital can be invested as well on land A as on the better types of land.

We shall assume that an extra capital of £2.10s. invested on land A produces 1⅕ quarters instead of 1 quarter.

TABLE V[101]

Acres	Capital	Profit	Rate of profit	Product per acre (qrs.)	Total product (qrs.)	Corn rent	Production price per qr.	Money rent. surplus profit
A 1	£5	20s.	20%	1 + 1⅕	2⅕	0	£2.14⁶⁄₁₁s.	0
B 1	£5	20s.		2 + 2⅖	4⅖	2⅕	£1.7³⁄₁₁s.	£6.¹⁄₁₁s.
C 1	£5	20s.		3 + 3⅗	6⅗	4⅖	18²⁄₁₁s.	£12
D 1	£5	20s.		4 + 4⅘	8⅘	6⅗	13⁷⁄₁₁s.	£18
Total	£20	£4		10 + 12	22	13⅕		£36

This table should be compared with Tables I and II. In Table II the *doubled capital investment* is combined with *constant* productivity, in proportion to the capital invested.

Here we have assumed a fall in the governing production price. If it were to remain constant at £3, the worst land, which *previously did not bear any rent*, would now yield a rent without drawing into cultivation any even worse land; the reason for this is that *productivity* would have increased on land A, but only for a portion of the capital, and not for the original capital. > The first quarter *cost* £3 to produce; the next quarter cost only £2.10s., or 50s. Instead of this the quarter is now sold at the average price of both quarters; less than £3 and more than the £2.14⁶⁄₁₁ s. it cost to produce the quarter with the second portion of capital. < Since the rate of *productivity* grows with the extra capital investment, this implies an *improvement*, which may consist in the application of *more* capital as such to each acre (more fertiliser, more mechanised labour, etc.) or even in the fact that it is only with this extra capital that a qualitatively different and more productive investment of capital can be brought about. In both cases, a product of 2⅕ quarters is obtained for an outlay of £5 of capital per acre, whereas with half this capital investment, £2.10s., the product was

101 [Table VI in the published version. Translator]

only 1 quarter. Leaving aside transitory market conditions, the product of land A could continue to be sold at a *higher production price*, instead of at the *average* price, only if a significant area of class A land continued to be cultivated with a capital of only £2.10s. per acre. But as soon as the new proportion of £5 per acre, and hence this *improved* mode of operation, became universal, the *governing production price* would have to fall to £2.15s. The distinction between the two *portions of capital* would disappear, and then an acre which was cultivated with a capital of only £2.10s. per acre would be abnormal and would cease to be cultivated according to the new conditions of production. The *distinction* would no longer be between the products of different portions of capital on the same acre, but rather between a *satisfactory* total capital investment per acre and an *unsatisfactory* one. From this we can see, *firstly*, that when a large number of farmers have an insufficient amount of capital in their possession (it has to be a large number, otherwise they would be compelled to sell *below* their production price), this has just the same effect as the *differentiation of types of land* themselves in a diminishing series. The *poorer type of agriculture* on worse soil increases the rent on the better soil; it can even create *a rent* on better cultivated land of the same quality, which this would not otherwise yield. We see, secondly, how differential rent, in so far as it arises from successive investments of capital on *the same* total area, is actually reduced to an average in which the effects of the different capital investments can no longer be recognised or distinguished. They do not produce *rent* on the worst lands, but rather (1) turn the average price of the total product, say on an acre of A, into the new governing price, and (2) present themselves as changes in the *total amount* of capital per acre required under the new conditions for satisfactory cultivation of this land, > and not as the distinct results of individual successive capital investments, in which case the smaller original capital outlay would have had the decisive impact. < The same is true then with the differential rents of the better types of land. Their differential rent is determined by the difference between the average product of the type of land in question and the product of the worst land, in a situation where an increased investment of capital has now become normal.

No land yields any product (wheat, for example) without a capital investment. This is true even in the case of simple differential rent, *differential rent I*. When it is said that 1 acre of A, the land that governs the production price, yields such and such a product at this price or that, and that the better types of land, B, C and D, yield some particular *differential product*, and hence, at the governing price, some specific amount of ground-rent, this always assumes that a *definite amount of capital* is applied, namely that considered normal under the given conditions of production, just as in industry a *certain minimum of capital* is required to make it possible to produce |513a| commodities at their price of production.

Where this *minimum* changes as a result of successive investments of capital on the same land in connection with *improvements*, this is a gradual process. As long as a certain number of acres of A, for example, do not receive this extra working capital, *rent* on the better cultivated acres of A is generated because the production price has *remained constant*, while the rent on all the better types of land, B, C and D is thereby increased. But as soon as the new type of cultivation has spread sufficiently on an average to become normal, the rent for the rent-bearing lands falls again, and the portion of land type A that does not possess the average working capital must sell *below its individual production price*, hence below the average level of profit.

With a *falling* production price, this occurs when surplus productivity remains *the same* or even when it *declines*, because as a result of increased capital investment the *necessary* product is provided by the better types of land and A's working capital, for instance, is withdrawn and A no longer competes in the production of *this* particular product, wheat for example. The *amount of capital* that is then applied *on average* to the better land B, which now governs the price, is now established as *normal*; and in speaking of the *varying fertility* of the tracts of land, we assume that this is the new normal quantity of capital applied *per acre*.

It is clear on the other hand that this average capital investment (for example £8 per acre in England *before* 1848 and £12 per acre *after* 1848) is what provides the standard when rent contracts are drawn up. For the farmer who spends more than this, the *surplus profit is not* transformed into rent. Whether this happens when the lease expires will depend on the competition of those farmers who are in a position to make the same extra outlay. We are not referring here to *lasting* improvements to the land, which continue to provide an increased product with the same outlay of capital or even a declining outlay. Although these are the product of *capital*, they function just like natural differences in the quality of the soil.

We can see therefore that *differential rent II* involves an element that does not develop as such in the case of *differential rent I*, since this can persist independently of any change in the *normal capital investment* per acre. On the one hand the results of different capital investments on land type A are blurred, their product appearing as an average product per acre. On the other hand, there is a change in the *normal minimum*, or the *average quantity of capital outlays* per acre, so that this change appears as a *property of the soil*. Finally, there is a distinction in the way the *surplus profit* is transformed into the form of *rent*.

Table V also shows that, > with the rise in the product from 10 to 22 quarters, as compared with Table I, *before* the additional investment of capital, and as compared with Table II, where there is an additional investment of capital which is equally large and productivity that remains *constant*, < the *corn rent* in one case more than doubles, and in the other case rises to 1⅕ quarters, while the *money rent* in one case also more than doubles, but in the other case only rises to a very slight extent, by 6/11 s. It would have grown significantly either if the extra capital had been directed more to the better types of land > (to B, C and D more than to A, and to D more than to C, and to C more than to B) < or alternatively if the governing average price per quarter on A had stood higher, so that the fructifying effect of the additional capital investment of A had been less (always assuming *the same* preconditions).

> If it were to be assumed that < the rise in fertility as a result of the extra capital had a differing effect on the different types of land, this would give rise to changes in their differential rents.

What has been proved in any case is that when the *production price falls* as a result of a rise in *surplus productivity*, resulting in turn from an increase in capital investment – i.e., as soon as this productivity grows in a higher ratio than the capital itself increases – the rent per acre for a capital investment of double the quantity might not just double, *per acre*, but *more than* double.

It could also fall, if the production price were to fall much lower as a result of a rapid growth in productivity on land A.

> The calculation in the above table (Table V) is wrong. Under the conditions we have set, the *money rent* must remain the same (compared with Table II) or it must *double* as compared with Table I, i.e., it must act as if the *capital investment* were doubled, with *price* and productivity both *constant*. The *corn rent*, in contrast, will increase along with the productivity.

As far as the money rent is concerned, it is the same as if productivity had increased *equally* on all types of land with an *unchanged level of capital investment*. In Table I, for example, if the productivity of the land doubled. The differential yield, in quarters, rises in the same proportion as the price of production falls. The number of quarters grown rises in the same proportion as the price of the quarter falls. Thus the product and the money rent remain the same. This must have entirely the same impact in this case. The price of production falls, but the amount of surplus product from the second round of capital investment grows in the same proportion. Let us take the first case in *differential rent I, table I*, and double the productivity of the same capital investment,

TABLE I (*modified*)

Acres	Capital advanced	Profit	Cost of production	Rate of profit	Product per acre	Surplus profit	Corn rent	Money rent
A 1	£2.10s.	10s.	£3 per 2 qr.					
			£1.10s. per qr.	20%	2 qrs.	0	0	0
B 1	£2.10s.	10s.	15s. per qr.		4 qrs.	£3	2 qrs.	£3
C 1	£2.10s.	10s.	10s. per qr.		6 qrs.	£6	4 qrs.	£6
D 1	£2.10s.	10s.	7½s. per qr.		8 qrs.	£9	6 qrs.	£9
Total	£10	£2			20 qrs.	£18	12 qrs.	£18

Land type B sells a quarter twice as cheaply, but it sells twice as many quarters as land type A, and the same goes for C and D. Neither the corn rent nor the money rent is affected in this case. Let us now take the case we wish to investigate.

|514| TABLE VI

(1) Acres	(2) Capital 1	2	(3) Profit	(4) Rate of profit	(5) Product per acre 1	(6) 2	(7) Total	(8) Price of production (per qr.)	(9) Corn rent	(10) Money rent
A 1	£2.10s.	£2.10s.	£1	20%	1 qr. +	3 qrs.	4 qrs.	£1.10s.	0	0
B 1	£2.10s.	£2.10s.	£1		2 qrs. +	6 qrs.	8 qrs.	15s.	4 qrs.	£6
C 1	£2.10s.	£2.10s.	£1		3 qrs. +	9 qrs.	12 qrs.	10s.	8 qrs.	£12
D 1	£2.10s.	£2.10s.	£1		4 qrs. +	12 qrs.	16 qrs.	7½s.	12 qrs.	£18
Total	£20		£4		40 qrs.		40 qrs.		24 qrs.	£36

Thus the corn rent does not remain the same as it did when there was a doubling of fertility with *the same* capital outlay.

The explanation emerges when we look at heading (5), product per acre. In all types of land the product of the second round of capital investment is *three times greater* as a proportion of the *original product*, not as a proportion of the total product of A. The total product of A = 4 quarters, that of B = 8 quarters, C = 12 and D = 16, and 4: 8: 12: 16 = 1: 2: 3: 4, which was the original series.

They have all quadrupled. But in column (6) the product of the extra capital is only *tripled*. The series is 3: 6: 9: 12 = 1: 2: 3: 4. The corn rent has doubled as compared with Table II, because the same money value is represented by a double corn value. Column (5) gives as the difference 1 quarter + 2 quarters + 3 quarters = 6 quarters, which with a doubled capital investment combined with *constant* productivity gives 12 quarters. (See Table II on page 504.) With double the fertility and *the same* capital the same series would give 2 quarters + 4 quarters + 6 quarters, making in all 12 quarters as before. Thus for the first series column (5) gives a difference of 6 quarters; but for the second series column (6) gives 3 quarters + 6 quarters + 9 quarters = 18 quarters. This comes to the same thing as if, in Table I (modified), the *doubled fertility* had been accompanied by a simultaneous doubling of the capital investment. The corn rent would then also be 24 quarters and the money rent £36. The corn rent is doubled as compared with Table II on page 504 because here the total product of every type of land is doubled with a doubling of the capital investment. Here, however, the total product has tripled.

The money rent would rise under these conditions if, provided the proportionate impact of the additional capital was the same on each of the different types of land, the *amount of capital* had more than doubled and was concentrated more on the better than the inferior types of land, or if the additional fertility magnified the differences between the different types.

Let us assume that the additional capital investments on B and C, for example, did not increase productivity in the same proportion as they did on A, so that the proportionate differences declined, and that there was no growth in the product corresponding to the fall in the price. In that case the rent on D would rise, the rents on B and C would fall, the total money rent would fall and the corn rent would rise.

TABLE VII

Acres	Capital 1	Capital 2	Profit	Product per acre 1	Product per acre 2	Product per acre Total	Price of production (per qr.)	Corn rent	Money rent
A 1	£2.10s.	£2.10s.	£1	1 qr. +	3 qrs.	4 qrs.	£1.10s.	0	0
B 1	£2.10s.	£2.10s.	£1	2 qrs. +	2½ qrs.	4½ qrs.	£1.6⅓s.	½ qr.	15s.
C 1	£2.10s.	£2.10s.	£1	3 qrs. +	5 qrs.	8 qrs.	15s.	4 qrs.	£6
D 1	£2.10s.	£2.10s.	£1	4 qrs. +	12 qrs.	16 qrs.	7½s.	12 qrs.	£18
Total	£20		£4	10 qrs. +	22½qrs.	32½qrs.		16½ qrs.	£24.15s.

The money rent, finally, would rise if, given the same *proportionate rise in fertility*, more additional capital was applied to the better lands than to A, or if the additional capital investments on the better lands acted with an increased productivity. In both cases the differences would grow.

> Thus the *money rent* always remains the same with *falling production prices as a result of increased fertility with increased capital investment*, if the *additional capital* is distributed *evenly* among the types of land of different fertility, and *the investment itself* acts proportionately on the different types of land according to the *commercial* difference between them. The corn rent rises. For the money rent it is the same as if the capital investments on the different types of land had increased proportionately while the prices *remained unchanged.*

< The *money rent* falls if the improvement resulting from extra capital investment reduces the differences, either all or some, by having more effect on A than on B and C. > The fall is greater, the less additional fertility there is on the better types of land. < Whether the corn rent rises, falls or remains stationary depends on the degree of unevenness in this effect.

The *money rent* rises, and the *corn rent* with it, either if more capital is added to the rent-bearing land than to A, in conditions where the proportionate differences in the additional fertility remain the same, and more capital is added to the lands of higher rent than to those of lower rent, or if, given the *same* additional capital, the fertility on the better and best lands grows more than on A. Indeed, in the latter case, the rent rises in relation to the degree to which the increase in fertility is greater in the superior categories of land than in the inferior ones.

|515| Under all circumstances, however, the *rent* rises relatively if the *increased fertility*, the increased productivity, is the result of a new addition of capital and not simply of increased fertility while the *capital investment remains constant.* This is the absolute point of view, and it shows that here, as in all earlier cases, the rent per acre, and now the higher *rent per acre* (as in the case of *differential rent I*, the rent over the whole cultivated area – the level of the *average rental*) is the result of increased capital investment on the land, whether this functions with a *constant* rate of productivity in a situation of constant or falling prices, with a *declining rate of productivity* in a situation of constant or falling prices, or with an *increasing rate of productivity* in a situation of falling prices. (For our assumption of a *constant price* with a constant, falling or rising rate of productivity for the extra capital, and a *falling price* with a *constant, falling or rising rate of productivity*, can be reduced to the assumption of a *constant rate of productivity* for the excess capital in a situation of constant or falling price, a *falling rate of productivity* in a situation of constant or falling

price and a *rising rate of productivity* with constant or falling price.) Although the rent may remain stationary or even fall in all these cases, it would fall further if the *additional* application of capital (in otherwise unchanged conditions) were *not* the condition for higher fertility. The *additional capital* is then always the cause of the *relatively* high level of rent, although this may have fallen in absolute terms.

C) *Rising Price of Production*:[102] {(*Rent should be discussed* under the following headings:

A 1. The *concept of differential rent* as such. The example of water-power. Then the transition to agricultural rent proper.
A 2. *Differential rent I*, arising from the varying fertility of different tracts of land.
A 3. *Differential rent II*, arising from successive capital investments on the same land. This should be *divided further* into:
  (a) differential rent with the *price of production stationary*,
  (b) differential rent with the *price of production falling*,
  (c) differential rent with the *price of production rising*,
  and (d) *the transformation of surplus profit into rent*.
A 4. The influence of this rent on the *rate of profit*.
B. *Absolute rent*.
C. *The price of land*.
D. *Final considerations on ground-rent*.)}

We now have the following general results from considering differential rent as a whole:

Firstly. The *formation of surplus profits can occur* in various ways. It can occur on the basis of *differential rent I*, i.e., on the basis of the investment of the total agricultural capital on an acreage consisting of types of land of differing fertility. Or *the variation in the surplus productivity* of *successive* capital investments on *the same* land (what is meant here by 'surplus productivity' is *greater productivity* {for example in quarters of wheat} than the same capital investment produces on the worst type of land, A, though the worst type of land is not to be taken as the worst type of land altogether but the land that governs the *price of production*), the *transformation of surplus profits into rent*, hence their transfer from farmer to proprietor, always presupposes as

102 [There is only a title for this third case. Engels himself wrote his Chapter 43 on this subject. Editor]

its initial condition that the *various actual individual prices of production* (i.e., those which are independent of the general production price that governs the market price) which the partial products of the individual successive capital investments have are equalised in advance to give an individual *average price of production*. The *excess of this general production price of the product* of an acre over the *individual average production price* forms and measures the rent *per acre*. In the case of *differential rent I* the differential results can be distinguished in and for themselves, because they take place on different areas of land, outside and alongside one another, given a capital outlay per acre that is taken as normal, and the normal cultivation corresponding to it. In the case of differential rent |516| II they must first be made *distinguishable*, they must in fact be transformed back into differential rent I, and this can only be done in the manner indicated.

Let us take Table III, for instance, on page 505.

For the first capital investment of £2.10s., land B yields 2 quarters per acre, and for the second capital investment *of equal size* it yields 1½ quarters; a total of 3½ quarters on *the same* acre. We cannot tell from this 3½ quarters, which all grows on the same land, how much is the product of the first capital investment and how much is the product of the second. It is in fact the product of the total capital investment of £5, and the fact of the matter is simply that a capital of £2.10s. yielded 2 quarters, while one of £5, and not £4, yields not 4 quarters but 3½. (It would be exactly the same if the £4 were to yield 3½ quarters, so that the yields of the two capital investments were equal, or even 5 quarters, so that the second capital investment produced an excess of 1 quarter over the first investment.) The production price of the first 2 quarters is £1.10s. per quarter, and that of the subsequent 1½ quarters is £2 per quarter. The 3½ quarters together therefore cost £6 (their *individual* production price). This is the *production price* of the total product, and makes an average of $34\frac{2}{7}$s. or £1.$14\frac{2}{7}$ s. per quarter. For the general production price of £3, as determined by land of type A, this gives a surplus-value [profit] per quarter of $25\frac{5}{7}$ s., and thus for the 3½ quarters a surplus-value [profit] of £4.10s., or 90s. Given an average production price for B of $34\frac{2}{7}$ s. per quarter, this is expressed in 1½ quarters. > Or one could have done the calculation in this way: the individual production price of B's 3½ quarters = £6. The sale price or general production price = £10.10s. The *surplus profit* = £4.10s. But the average price of the quarters produced on B = $34\frac{2}{7}$ s. Hence the £4.10s. are the expression of 1½ quarters. < B's surplus profit is thus expressed in an aliquot part of B's product, the 1½ quarters that forms the rent expressed in corn and is sold at £4.10s., according to the general production price. But, *conversely*, the excess product on an acre of B over that of an acre of A does not in itself represent surplus profit and hence surplus product. For example, the acre of B produces 3½ quarters, the acre of A only 1 quarter. The excess product on B is thus 2½ quarters, but the surplus product is only 1½ quarters, for twice as much capital is applied on B as on A, so that the production costs here are double. If there were a similar investment of £5 on A, and the rate of productivity remained the same, its product would be 2 quarters instead of 1 quarter; the actual surplus product would be found not by comparing 3½ with 1 but by comparing 3½ with 2, hence it would not be 2½ quarters but only 1½. Moreover, if B had made a third capital investment, of £2.10s., yielding only 1 quarter, so that the quarter cost £3, as it did on A, its sale price of £3 would only cover the cost of production, yielding no more than the average profit, but no surplus profit, and therefore nothing that could be transformed into *rent*. In itself, the product per acre, compared with the product per acre of land A, indicates neither whether it is the product of the same capital investment or a greater one, nor whether the *excess product* simply covers the production price or whether it is a result of the higher productivity of the excess capital.

Secondly. Given a *declining surplus productivity* of the extra capital investments, whose *minimum limit* (as far as the formation of new surplus profit is concerned) is the capital investment that simply covers the *production costs*, i.e., that produces a quarter of wheat as expensively as the *same* capital investment would on an acre of land A, for £3 on our assumption, it results from our previous argument that the *minimum limit* at which > (ignoring the prior *rise* in the production price without which the extra capital investment would not have taken place to that extent) < the total capital investment on an acre of B would form no more rent is that to which the *individual average production price* of the product per quarter would fall on the better land *below* the *production price* on land A.

If *capital investments are added* to land B which only pay the production price but yield no *surplus profit*, thus form no new *rent*, then although this increases the individual average production price per quarter, it does not affect the *surplus profit* formed by the better capital investments, which eventually affect the *rent*. For the average production price always remains *below* that of A, > whatever the multiple of the capital investments added in this way < and if the surplus per quarter declines, the number of quarters increases in the same proportion, so that the surplus remains constant.

In the case indicated above, the first two capital investments on B, of £5 each, produce a yield of 3½ quarters, i.e., a corn rent of 1½ quarters, or a surplus profit of £4.10s., on our assumption. If a third capital investment of £2.10s. is now added, which only produces 1 quarter, and whose individual production price of £3 therefore coincides with the governing general production price, the total production price of the 4½ quarters will be £9. Hence the average price per quarter = 40s. of £2. B's average production price per quarter has thus risen from 34²⁄₇ s. to £2. This gives a surplus of £1 per quarter, compared with the governing price of land A, whereas the previous surplus was 25⁵⁄₇ s. per quarter. But £1 × 4½ = £4.10s., just as previously £1.5⁵⁄₇ s. × 3½ was £4.10s.

If we assume that instead of making one additional capital investment of £2.10s., which produces the extra quarter only at its general production price, the cultivator of land B made two such investments, the product would be 3½ quarters, which cost £6 (for the first two capital investments) and 3 quarters which cost £9. Altogether this would be 6½ quarters at a cost of production of £15. The average price per quarter would have risen again from £1 to £2⁴⁄₁₃. The surplus per quarter, compared with the governing production price of land A, would have fallen from £1 to £⁹⁄₁₃. But this surplus of £⁹⁄₁₃ would not be multiplied by 6½ quarters instead of 4½. And (£1 × 4½) = 4½ and (£⁹⁄₁₃ × 6½ or ¹³⁄₂) = ⁹⁄₁₃ × ¹³⁄₂ = ⁹⁄₂ = 4½.

The first thing that follows from this is that no increase in the price of the product (its *governing production price*) takes place or is needed to call into existence additional capital investments on the better land, even up to the level at which the additional capital completely ceases to provide surplus profit and *just* continues to yield the *average profit*. It also follows from this that the *total surplus profit* per acre remains the same here, no matter how much the *average price* falls; however small the *average surplus* becomes, it can never disappear, and must, when multiplied by the number of quarters produced per acre, always leave the total surplus unchanged. In order that the *average production price per acre* on B, namely £3, may fall[103] to the general production price, *additional capital* must be added, the product of which has a *higher production price* than the average. But we shall see that even that is not sufficient by itself to *reduce* the average price per quarter on B to £3, *the general production price.*

|518| Let us assume that production on land B is as follows:

1. *3½ quarters as before as a production price of £6*; two *capital investments* of £2.10s. each, which both form *surplus profits*, but of *decreasing* size.
2. *1 quarter at £3*; one *capital investment* in which the *individual* production price would be equal to the governing general production price.
3. *1 quarter at £4*; one *capital investment* in which the average production price per quarter is a third or 33⅓ percent higher than the general production price.

103 [Engels changed this to 'rise'. Translator]

We should then have 5½ quarters per acre at £13, for a capital investment of £10; four times the original capital investment, but not quite three times the proportionate product of the first capital investment.

5½ quarters at £13 gives an average price per quarter of £$2\frac{4}{11}$, hence a *surplus of £$\frac{7}{11}$ per quarter*, which can be transformed into rent. 5½ quarters sold at the governing price of £3 = £16.10s. After deducting the production cost of £13, there remains a surplus profit or rent of £3.10s., which would represent $1\frac{25}{52}$ quarters at the present average production price per quarter on land B. The money rent would have fallen by £1, the corn rent by about ½ quarter, yet despite the fact that the fourth extra capital investment on B produces not only no surplus profit, but *less* than the average profit, there is still *surplus profit* and *money rent* as before, reckoned on the *total capital investment.*

If we assume that not only this fourth capital investment, but the third, too, produces at over the governing production price in this way, > while the second capital investment produces at a price which coincides with the governing price, < the total production would be 3½ quarters at £6 plus 2 quarters at £8, which makes a total of 5½ quarters for a production cost of £14. The average price per quarter would be £$2\frac{6}{11}$. This would leave a surplus of $\frac{5}{11}$ per quarter ($\frac{2}{11}$ less than previously). The total price at £3 per quarter would be £16.10s. Subtracting £14 leaves £2.10s., or 50s. for rent. > The *money rent* would have fallen by £2 instead of £1. < The corn rent, however, would now be $\frac{55}{56}$ of a quarter, not quite a whole quarter. > *The average price of the quarter on land B rises here* because there has been double the *amount of capital investment* at the price of £3, which is *higher* than the governing production price. The total product must be increased by 1 quarter.

The same result would have emerged if the *proportionate reduction* of productivity for the third capital investment had been still *greater*. For example, with 3½ quarters at £6, 1 quarter at £6, and 4½ quarters at £12, the average for 1 quarter is £2⅔, and the surplus per quarter is £⅓. Taken over 3 quarters, this is £1, which is somewhat under ½ quarter under the governing average price on land B.

|519| < This shows us, at all events, that the rent on the better lands need not disappear with *additional capital investments* whose product costs *more than* the general price of production, but need only *decline*, this decline being in proportion on the one hand to the *aliquot part* that this relatively unproductive capital forms of the total capital outlay, and in proportion on the other hand to the *decline in its productivity* > or the *rise* of its individual production price *above* the general production price. < The average price of its product would still always stand *below* the governing price and would thus still leave a surplus profit which could be transformed into rent.

Let us now assume that the *average price* for a quarter produced on land B coincides with the *general production price.* > Since the portion of the capital which only yields average profit, i.e., where the individual and the general production price coincide, makes no difference to the situation in this case, we shall leave it out of account.

	Average price per quarter
3½ qrs. at £6	34 2/7s. = £1.14 2/7s.
1½ qrs. at £6	1 qr. = £4
1 qr. at £6	1 qr. = £6
Total of 6 qrs.	1 qr. = £3

Capital outlay	*Profit*	*Rate of profit*	*Surplus*	*Qrs.*	*Surplus qrs.*
1 £2.10s.	10s.	20%	£3	2	1
2 £2.10s.	10s.	20%	£1.10s.	1½	½
3a £3⅓	13⅓s.	20%	loss	1½	loss
3b £1⅔	6⅔s.	20%	loss	1½	loss
4 £5	£1	20%	loss	1	loss
Total £15	33	20%	0	6	0

In this case the farmer sells each quarter at its individual *price of production*, and hence sells the total number of quarters at their *average production price* per quarter, which coincides with the *general* production price of £3 per quarter. He therefore continues to make a profit of 20%, or £3, on the £15 of capital. But the rent has disappeared. Where does the surplus go when the individual production price of each quarter is equalised with the general price of production in this way?

The surplus profit on the first £2.10s. was £3; on the second £2.10s. it was £1.10s.; the total surplus profit on this third of the capital advanced, i.e., on £5, was £4.10s. = 90%.

The third capital investment of £5 not only yields no surplus profit, but its product of 1½ quarters, sold at the *general price of production* of £3, brings a loss of £1.10s. > A loss of £1.10s. on an investment of £5 gives a loss of 30% on this second part of the capital advanced.

< On the *fourth capital investment, finally*, which is also £5, the product of

1 quarter, sold at the general price of production, brings a loss of £3. > A loss of £3 on an investment of £5 gives a loss of 60% on this final part of the total capital advanced.

Thus a third of the £15 gives a surplus profit of 90%, and two thirds of the £15 give a *loss* of 30 + 60, in other words 90%. 90 − 90 = 0.

< The surplus profits and the losses cancel out. The rent therefore vanishes. In fact, however, this is possible only because the elements of *surplus-value* that formed *surplus profit* or *rent* now go into the *formation of the average profit*. The farmer makes this average profit of £3 on the £15, or 10s. on £2.10s. at the expense of the rent.

> In forming the *total price* of £18 for 6 quarters, the farmer calculates that £6 is the individual production price of the first $3\frac{1}{2}$ quarters; the production price of the next $1\frac{1}{2}$ quarters is £6; and the production price of the last 1 quarter is also £6. In order to make an average profit he would have to sell these $2\frac{1}{2}$ quarters at £12, hence at £$4\frac{4}{5}$ a quarter; if he sold at the *general production price* he would sell them at a loss of £4.10s. The first $3\frac{1}{2}$ quarters, on the other hand, at their individual *production price*, cost him £6, which is $34\frac{2}{7}$ s. per quarter; by selling them at £6 he sells them at £4.10s. below the general production price. The surplus profit, which previously formed rent, now covers the loss; he can sell 1 quarter which cost him £6 to produce at £3 because he sells the other quarters, which cost him only £1.10s. to produce, at £3.

< The establishment of equality between the *individual average production price* of a quarter on B and the *general production price* on A, which governs the market price, presupposes that the amount by which the *individual price of the product of the initial capital investments* stands below the general production price is counterbalanced more and more, and finally cancelled, by the amount by which the *product of the later capital investments* stands above the general production price. During this process what appears as *surplus profit* as long as the quarters produced by the initial capital investments are sold by themselves gradually becomes a part of *their* average production price, and thereby goes into forming an average profit, until it is completely absorbed by the latter. > Thus, if the average price of the 6 quarters finally became £18, the *average production price* of each of those quarters would be £3. But the *average price* of the first $4\frac{1}{2}$ quarters, considered separately, was only $34\frac{2}{7}$ s. If they had been sold individually at £3 per quarter (the governing price of production) this would produce a rent of £4.10 s. If they are sold now for £3, this produces *no* rent |520|, since they now cost £3 per quarter as aliquot parts of the 6 quarters (profit included).

< If, instead of £15 capital, only £5 is laid out on B and the extra $2\frac{1}{2}$ surplus quarters can be produced because $2\frac{1}{2}$ acres more of A are under cultivation

with a capital investment of £2.10s. per acre, then additional capital laid out would amount only to £6¼, hence the total outlay on A and B for the production of these 6 quarters would be only £11¼ instead of £15. The 6 quarters would still be sold together for £18, as before, but the *capital outlay would have diminished by £3¾.*

It would be a different matter if in order to produce the extra 2½ quarters it were necessary to resort to worse land than A, to A^{-1} and A^{-2}, with a resulting production price per quarter for 1½ quarters on land A^{-1} of £4, and for the final quarter on A^{-2} of £6. In that case, £6 would be the governing production price per quarter. The 3½ quarters from B would be sold for £21 instead of for £10.10s., which would give a money rent of £15 instead of £4.10s., and a corn rent of 2½ quarters instead of 1½ quarters. On A, similarly, the 1 quarter would now yield a rent of £1 = ⅙ of a quarter. One final remark needs to be made before we discuss this point further:

The *average price of a quarter* on B is equalised and coincides with the general production price of £3 per quarter governed by A, as soon as the one-third of the total capital that produces the additional 1½ quarters is offset by the two-thirds of the total capital that produces the *deficiency* (minus quantity) of 1½ quarters. > (Namely 2½ quarters instead of 4.) < How soon this equalisation is reached, or how much capital must be invested on B with deficient productivity for it to be reached, depends, taking the surplus productivity of the first capital investments as given, on the relative underproductivity of the capitals later applied, compared with an equally large capital investment on the poorest land, A, or on the *individual* production price of the product of this investment, compared with the general, governing price of production.

Here are further points that arise from the foregoing:

Firstly. As long as the *additional capitals* are invested on the same land with surplus productivity, even if this is *decreasing*, the *absolute corn and money rent per acre* rises, even if it declines relatively, in proportion to the capital advanced (i.e., the *rate of surplus profit*). The minimum limit here is formed by that additional capital which *yields only the average profit*, or for whose product the *individual* production price *coincides with the general one*. The production price remains *the same*, under these conditions, as long as the increased supply does not make production from the poorer types of land superfluous. (Even with a falling price, these additional capitals still produce a *surplus profit*, although it is quantitatively less than before because the new governing production price is less than the old one.)

Secondly. The mere investment of additional capital which produces only the average profit, i.e., whose surplus productivity = 0, does not alter in any way the amount of surplus profit and hence rent that is formed. The individual average price per quarter rises on the better types of land through this investment; the excess per quarter declines, but the number of quarters over which this reduced excess is distributed increases, in such a way that the product of the two remains the same.

Thirdly. Additional capital investments for which the *individual* production price of their products stands *above* the *general* production price, so that their surplus productivity is not just zero but less than zero, a negative quantity, i.e., a productivity less than that of the same capital investment on the price-governing land A, |521| bring the *individual average price per quarter* of the total product of the better land ever closer to the general production price, and thus reduce the *difference* between the two, which forms the *surplus profit* or rent, in the same proportion. More and more of what would form surplus profit or rent goes into the formation of the average profit. Nevertheless, the total capital invested on an acre of B continues to yield a *rent* (surplus profit), even if this *declines* with the increasing amount of capital of *deficient productivity* and with increases in the *level* of this underproductivity. In this case, the rent per acre falls in absolute terms as capital grows and production increases, and does not just fall relatively to the growing size of the capital invested, as it does in the second case.

The rent can disappear only if the *individual average production price* of the total product on the better land, B, coincides with the general price of production, i.e., if the entire surplus profit of the earlier and more productive capital investments has been used to form the *average profit.*

The limit to the fall in the rent per acre is the point at which this *ceases, disappears*. But this point is not reached when the extra capital investments start to produce with *deficient productivity*, but only when the *extra investment of deficiently productive portions of capital* becomes so great that its effect cancels out the surplus productivity of the *initial capital investments*, so that the productivity of the total capital invested comes to be equal to that of the capital on A, and hence the *individual average price* per quarter on B becomes equal to that on A.

Even in this case, as we have shown, the *price of production*, £3 per quarter, remains the same, despite the disappearance of the rent. > The *surplus profit* from the initial capital investments in fact exactly balances out the negative profit on the later investments. < It is only *beyond this point* that the *price of production* has to rise, as the result of the increase either in the *degree* to which the extra capital's productivity is deficient, or in the *amount* of extra capital of *the same* deficient productivity. If, for example, 2½ quarters were produced on the same land at £4 per quarter instead of 1½ quarters, the result would be as follows:

1. With 2½ quarters produced at £4 a quarter

Capital invested	*Product*	*Cost of production*
£5	3½ qrs.	£6
£8⅓	2½ qrs.	£10
£5	1 qr.	£6
£18⅓	7 qrs.	£22

In this case, the quarter would cost £3⅐ to produce, hence it would stand ⅐ above the general price of production, which would have to rise.

2. With 1½ quarters produced at £4 a quarter

Capital invested	*Product*	*Cost of production*
£5	3½ qrs.	£6
£5	1½ qrs.	£6
£10	2 qrs.	£12
£20	7 qrs.	£24

In this case, the average production price per quarter would rise to £3³⁄₇, hence the governing production price of £3 would have to rise at least to £3³⁄₇.

|522| Thus *extra capital* with *deficient productivity* and even capital with *increasingly deficient productivity* could still be applied for a long while before the individual average price per quarter on the better lands became equal to the general price of production, i.e., before the complete disappearance of the excess of the latter over the former, and hence of surplus profit and rent.

Even in this *case*, moreover, the extinction of rent on the better types of land would mean only that the *individual average price per quarter* of the product from those better types would coincide with the *general price of production*; no rise in this general price would yet be required.

In the above example, taking the better land B, which however is lowest in the series of better or rent-bearing types of land, 3½ quarters were produced by a capital of £5 with *surplus productivity* and 2½ quarters by a *capital of £10 with deficient productivity,* > (which in part itself declines almost twofold in comparison with the governing capital on A) < making a total of 6 quarters, i.e., 7⁄12 of the total product produced by the better invested capitals and 5⁄12 of the total product produced by the portions of capital with deficient productivity. And it is only at this point that the individual *average production price* of the 6 quarters rises to £3 per quarter, coinciding therefore with the general production price of £3 per quarter.

Under the law of *landed property*, however, the extra 5⁄12 of the total product could not have been produced in this way, at £3 per quarter, except in the case where the extra 2½ quarters could be produced on 2½ new acres of type A land. Case 2 (page 520) in which the *extra capital* only produces at the *general price of production* would have formed the minimum limit. Below this, *extra capital investment* on the same land would have to cease.

If the farmer has to pay, say, £4.10s. rent for the first two capital investments of £5, every capital investment which produces a quarter for sale at *below* £3 could only produce it at the cost of a deduction from his profit. In the case of deficient productivity, equalisation of the *individual average price of his quarter* is thereby prevented.

Let us take this case in connection with the previous example (on page 519) where the production price of £3 per quarter on land A governs the production price for land B.

Capital outlay on 1 acre of B		*Profit*	*Rate of profit*	*Surplus profit*	*Qrs. per acre*	*Cost of production*	*Money rent*	*Sale price*
1 First Outlay	£2.10s.	10s.	20%	£3	2	£1.10s. per qr.	£3	2 qrs. = £6
2 Second Outlay	£2.10s.	10s.	20%	£1.10s.	1½	£2 per qr.	£1.10s.	1½ qrs. = £4½
3 Third Outlay	£5	£1	20%		1½	£4 per qr.		1½ qrs. = £4½
4 Fourth Outlay	£5	£1			1	£6 per qr.		1 qr. = £3
Total	£15				6			£18

The *production costs* of the 3½ quarters from the first two capital investments amount to *£3 per quarter* for the farmer, since he has to pay a rent of £4.10s., i.e., the difference between his *individual* production price and the general production price. For him, therefore, the surplus in the price of the product of the first two capital investments, or the *individual average price* of the quarters which the first two capital investments have produced, cannot serve to balance the deficit suffered on the products of the third and fourth capital investments. The 1½ quarters from capital investment number 3 cost the farmer £6, profit included; but he can only sell for £4.10s., taking the *general production price* to be £3 per quarter. He would therefore lose not only the *whole of his profit*, but a tenth of his capital of £5, namely 10s. His *loss on profit and capital* for the third investment would come to £1.10s., and for the fourth investment £3 (£1 profit and £2 capital), together making £4.10s., exactly as much as *the rent* for the better capital investments, whose *individual average price*, however, cannot go into the *individual average production price* of B's *total product* as a compensating factor at a capital outlay of £15, under the given conditions.

If it were necessary for the third capital investment to produce its extra 1½ quarters, the governing market price would have to rise to £4 per quarter. As a result of this, the rent on B would rise for the first and second capital investment, a rent would be formed on A > and an *increase in the governing market price* would have to take place, an increase from 3 to 4, by one-third, or 33⅓%.

Thus although the *differential rent* is only a *formal transformation of surplus profit into rent*, which simply enables the landowner to transfer the surplus profit from the farmer to himself, it becomes plain that the *successive employment of capital*, on the *same* soil, or what comes to the same thing, the increase of the capital employed upon the same soil, tends rather to find its *limit* in this transference, given a *declining rate* of productivity and a *constant production price*; in fact it comes up against a more or less artificial *barrier*, a result of the merely *formal* transformation of surplus profit into *ground-rent* which is a consequence of landed property. The *rise in the general price of production* which becomes necessary here, where the limit is narrower than elsewhere, is in this case therefore not only the basis for the rise in differential rent. In addition to this, the existence of *differential rent* as *rent* is at the same time the basis for the rise in the price of production, and for the need for an earlier and more rapid rise in the latter, in order to guarantee the supply of the surplus product.

|523| The following should also be noted.

The price of production could not rise to £4, as above, thanks to the *extra capital* on land B, if land A were to supply the extra product at £3, or at anything *less than £4*; or if newer and poorer land than A, A^{-1} for instance, came into competition, with a price of production that was above £3 but below £4. We thus see how *differential rent I* and *differential rent II*, while the first is the basis of the second, at the same time place *limits* on each other, leading sometimes to *successive investments of capital* on the *same piece of land*, and sometimes to *capitals invested side by side*, i.e., to new investments of capital on new additional land. (These limits have a similar effect as limits in other cases, such as where better land is taken up.)

Successive capital investments on the poorest land, land of type A. (Differential rent on the poorest land, land of type A.)

Let us assume that the demand for corn is rising and the supply can only be satisfied by *successive capital investments* with deficient productivity on the rent-bearing lands, by additional capital investment on land A, also with declining productivity, or by *capital investment* on new lands even poorer than land A.

Let us take land B as representative of the better land.

The extra capital investment requires a rise in the *market price* above the former governing production price of £3 per quarter in order to make possible the extra production of 1 quarter on land B. (This quarter may represent 1 million quarters, and each acre 1 million acres.) On C and D, etc., the best types of land, there may also be a surplus product, but only with *declining surplus productivity*. If the 1 quarter on B can be produced more cheaply by additional capital investment than 1 quarter on A by the same investment of capital, or by descending to land A^{-1}, which can only produce at £4 per quarter, for example, whereas the extra capital investment on A could produce at, say, £3.15s. per quarter, the extra capital on B would govern the *market price*.

A would have produced 1 quarter as before at £3, B, also as before, would have produced 2 quarters at £3 and $1\frac{1}{2}$ quarters also at £3, making together $3\frac{1}{2}$ quarters at an *individual production price* of £6. > Let there now be an extra £4 in production costs on B ($3\frac{2}{3}$ capital and $\frac{1}{3}$ profit according to the old rate of profit, or $3\frac{7}{11}$ capital and $\frac{3}{11}$ profit if the rate of profit had *fallen* to 10 percent as a result of the rise in the price of corn); the old production costs would remain the same on the other tracts of land, but the £3 of production costs would not be divided in the proportion £2.10s. capital and 10s. profit but rather in the proportion £$2\frac{8}{11}$ capital + £$\frac{3}{11}$ profit; this is simply a different distribution of the production costs. The variable capital would have risen in value, and the profit would have fallen correspondingly. The first $3\frac{1}{2}$ quarters on land B would cost £10.10s., of which £6 would cover the production costs and £4.10s, would form surplus profit and be paid as rent. As a result of the rise in the market price above £3, the additional quarter could not be produced on B, because it could be produced on A for £3.15s. < Let us assume therefore that the cost of production on B rises for the additional quarter to £3.10s. > (which, at the *old profit rate*, is divided between $64\frac{5}{6}$ s. capital and $5\frac{1}{6}$ s. profit, making an additional capital investment of £3.$4\frac{5}{6}$ s.) < In this case the product of land

B, which has risen from 3½ quarters to 4½ quarters, would be sold at £15.15s. The production costs of the first 3½ quarters form a deduction of £6 from this sum, and those of the final quarter a further deduction of £3.10s., making a total deduction of £9.10s. Rent would be £6.5s., as against only £4.10s. before. In this case, the acre of A would also yield a rent of 10s.; but it would not be the worst land, A, but the better land, B, which governed the production price of £3.10s. It is assumed here of course that there is no new accessible land of quality A and as well situated as that already cultivated, but that either a *second capital investment* would be needed on the stretch of A already cultivated, albeit at a still higher cost of production, or it would be necessary to have recourse to the still worse type of land, A^{-1}. As soon as *differential rent II* comes into effect, by way of successive capital investments, the *limits to the rising production price* can be governed by better land, and the *worst land*, the basis for *differential rent I*, can then bear rent. In this case, then, all cultivated land would bear rent in the sense of simple *differential rent*. We should then have the following table:

Acres	Capital investment	Profit	Product per acre	General production price	Individual production price	Corn rent	Money rent
A 1	£2.10s.	10s.	1 qr.	£2.10 per qr.	£3	⅐qr.	10s.
B 1	(1)£2.10s.		2 qr.				
	(2)£2.10s.		1½qr.				
	Governing						
	(3)£3.4⅚s.	£1.5⅙s.	1 qr.			$1\frac{11}{14}$qr.	£6.5s.
			(Total: 4½qrs.)				
C 1	(1)£2.10s.	£1	3 qrs.				
	(2)£2.10s.		2½ qrs.		£$1\frac{1}{11}$	3½ qrs.	£12.5s.
			(Total: 5½ qrs.)				
D 1	(1) £2.10s.	£1	4 qrs.				
	(2) £2.10s.		3½ qrs.		16s.	5½ qrs.	£19.5s.
			(Total: 7½ qrs.)				
Total	£20.14⅚s.	£3.15⅙s.	18½ qrs.				

> (If it were assumed, as in the previous calculation, that the cost of production was *the same for every capital investment* as for the product of the worst land,

so that the cost of production on C and D was £16 and not £12, and the capital investment was not £5 but £6.9$\frac{2}{3}$ s., this would show how the corn rent diminishes on C and D as well. The governing capital investment is £3.10s.; but the surplus product on C and D is £2.10s. for each portion of investment. If only £2.10s. were invested on B, the surplus product would not be 1 quarter but only $\frac{5}{7}$ of a quarter at 50s., which makes 70s., or £3.10s. per quarter. The difference does not emerge clearly because the 1 extra quarter on B is due to the greater capital investment on B. The following table is intended to make this clear:)

|524|

Acres	*Capital investment*	*Profit*	*Product per acre*	*Total*	*Corn rent*	*Money rent*
A 1	£2.10s.	10s.	1 qr.	1 qr.	$\frac{1}{7}$ qr.	10s.
B 1	(1) £2.10s,	£1.15$\frac{1}{6}$	2 qr.		$1\frac{11}{14}$ qr.	£6.5s.
	(2) £2.10s.		$1\frac{1}{2}$ qr.			
	(3) £2.10s, + 14$\frac{5}{6}$s.		$\frac{5}{7}$ + $\frac{2}{7}$ qrs.			
C 1	(1) £2.10s.	£1	3 qr.	$5\frac{1}{2}$ qr.	$3\frac{11}{14}$ qrs.	£13.5s.
	(2) £2.10s.		$2\frac{1}{2}$ qr.			
D 1	(1) £2.10s.	£1	4 qr.	$7\frac{1}{2}$ qr.	$5\frac{11}{14}$ qrs.	£20.5s.
	(2) £2.10s.		$3\frac{1}{2}$ qr.			
Total	£20.14$\frac{5}{6}$s.	£4.5$\frac{1}{6}$s.		$18\frac{1}{2}$qr.	$11\frac{7}{14}$ qrs.	£40.5s.

< The corn rent must increase once the *governing production price* of corn rises, i.e., once an increase takes place in the price of a *quarter of corn* from the price-governing land or in the level of the price-governing capital investment on one of the land types. It is the same as if all types had become less fertile and produced only $\frac{5}{7}$ of a quarter for a capital investment of £2.10s. The extra corn that they produce with the same capital investment is transformed into *surplus product*, representing *surplus profit* and hence *rent*. If we assume that the profit rate remains unchanged, the farmer can buy less corn with his profit. The profit rate may remain the same if wages do not rise – either because they are pressed down to the physical minimum, i.e., below the normal value of labour-power; or because the *working day is prolonged* or made *more intensive* and hence the *profit rate* in the non-agricultural branches of industry, which is what governs

agricultural profit, remains the same, if it does not rise; or because, although the same capital is invested in agriculture, it includes more of the constant and less of the variable type.

We have now dealt with the first way in which rent can arise on the poorest land, A, without bringing into cultivation still worse land; namely the way in which it originates from the difference between its individual price of production, which was formerly the governing one, and the new, higher price of production at which the last bit of extra capital supplies the extra product needed on better soil but with *deficient productivity*.

|525| If the extra corn had to be supplied by land A^{-1}, which can only supply at £4 per quarter, the rent of A would rise to £1 per acre. In that event, however, A^{-1} would take the place of A as the worst cultivated land, and A^{-1} would enter into the series of rent-bearing types of land as its lowest member. Differential rent I would have been affected. This is a case which therefore lies outside a discussion of *differential rent II*, which arises from the varying productivity of successive capital investments on the same stretch of land.

But differential rent can still arise on land of type A in *two other ways*, apart from the one we have already indicated.

Firstly, with a constant price – any given price, even one that has *fallen* in comparison with the one previously prevailing – if the additional *capital investment* leads to surplus productivity, which must *prima facie* always be the case up to a certain point, particularly on inferior land.

Secondly, however, if the productivity of successive capital investments on land A declines.

It is assumed in both cases that the increased production is required by the state of demand.

Here, though, from the standpoint of differential rent, a particular difficulty presents itself on account of the law previously developed, i.e., that it is always the *individual average price of production of each quarter of corn* within the total production or the total outlay of capital that is decisive. In the case of land A, however, unlike the better types of land, there is no *production price* given outside itself, such as would restrict the *equalisation between the individual production price and the general one* > for the new capital investment. < For the individual production price of the product of land A is precisely the *general production price* that governs the market price.

Assume:

(1) *The productivity of successive capital investments is rising*. 3 quarters instead of 2 quarters can be produced on 1 acre of A with a capital advance of £5, and at a cost of production therefore of £6. The first capital investment of £2.10s. supplies 1 quarter, the second 2 quarters. In this case, > £5 of capital or

< £6 in production costs yields 3 quarters, so that the *average* cost is £2 per quarter; if these 3 quarters are then sold at this average price, £2 per quarter, land A continues to bear no rent, all that has happened is that the basis of *differential rent II* has changed. £2 has become the governing production price instead of £3; a capital of £2.10s. now produces an average of 1½ quarters on the poorest land instead of 1 quarter, and this is now the official yield for all superior types of land when £2.10s. is invested. A part of their former surplus product goes from now on into forming their necessary product, just as a part of their surplus profit goes into the formation of the average profit. If we now examine how things stand for the better types of land, however, where the average calculation in no way affects the absolute surplus, since for these soils the *general production price* is a given barrier to capital investment, the 1 quarter from the first capital investment costs £3 and the 2 quarters from the second investment cost only £1.10s. each. A *corn rent of 1 quarter* and a *money rent of £3* thus arise on A, even though the 3 quarters are still sold at their old price of £9. If there is then a third capital investment of £2.10s., with the same productivity as the second |526| > the average price would now be: £3 for 1 quarter; £3 for the next 2 quarters; and £3 for the last 2 quarters. < Thus a total of 5 quarters would be produced for £9. The average price per quarter would be £1⅘ = £1.16s. The average price would have fallen again, not because of a new rise in the productivity of the third capital investment, but rather because of the addition of a new capital investment with the *same surplus productivity* as the second. Instead of causing an *increase* in the rent, as would be the case with the rent-bearing land types, the successive capital investments of equal surplus productivity on *land A* would cause a proportionate fall in the *price of production*, and with it in the differential rent on all other types of land (all other circumstances remaining the same). If, however, the first capital investment, which produces 1 quarter at a production cost of £3, sets the governing price for all the rest, the 5 quarters would be sold at £15, £3 per quarter, and the differential rent for the later successive capital investments on land A would amount to £6. Additional surplus capital per acre of land A, whatever the form in which it is applied, would here be an improvement, while the additional capital would also have made the original capital more productive. It would be nonsense to say that half of the capital had produced 1 quarter, and the other half had produced 2 quarters. £6 per acre would produce 3 quarters, while £3 would only produce 1 quarter. Whether or not a rent arises here – a surplus profit – would depend entirely on the circumstances. Normally, the governing price of production would have to fall. This is the case when improved but more costly cultivation of land A is undertaken only because it also takes place on the better types of land, hence there is a general revolution in agriculture, so that now, when we speak of the

natural fertility of land A, we assume that it is obtained with £6 or £9 instead of with £3. This would particularly be the case if the majority of the cultivated fields of land type A, which provide the bulk of the supply, are transferred to this new method. But if the improvement initially affected only a small portion of the acreage of land A, this better cultivated part of land A would supply a surplus profit which the landlord would quickly reach out to turn completely or in part into *rent*, and fix it as such. In this way, if demand kept pace with the increase in supply, and to the extent that the whole area of land A was gradually transferred to the new method, rent could gradually form on all land of type A, and the surplus production would be completely or partially confiscated, according to market conditions. The establishment of equality between land A's *production price* and the *average price* of its product in conditions of increased capital outlay might in this way meet an obstacle through the *fixing* of the *surplus profit* of this increased capital outlay in the form of rent. In that case, as we saw previously on the better lands (in conditions of declining productivity), it would again be the *transformation of surplus profit into ground-rent*, i.e., the intervention of landed property, that raised the *production price*, instead of the *differential rent* being simply the result of differences between the *individual* production price and the *general* one. For land A this would prevent the two prices from coinciding because it would prevent the production price from being governed by A's *average* production price; a higher production price than necessary would be maintained, and rent created accordingly. Even with the free import of corn from other countries, the same result could be obtained or maintained, by compelling the farmer to turn such land as was capable of competing in corn cultivation without yielding rent, at the price of production governed by conditions abroad, to other uses, e.g., to pasture sheep on it. The result of this would be that only rent-bearing land – i.e., only land whose individual *average* price of production per quarter was less than that determined by conditions abroad – was used for the cultivation of grain. It should generally be assumed that the *production price* would *fall*, though not |527| to the *average price*. It would stand higher than this, but below the production price of A, the worst land under cultivation, so that competition from new land of type A would be excluded (or restricted).

(2) *The productivity of the successive capital investments is declining.*

Assume that land A^{-1} can only produce each additional quarter at £4, whereas land A can do this at £3.15s: less dear, but 15s. dearer than the quarter produced by the first capital investment, which produced £2.10s. at £3.

In the latter case the price of the two quarters would be £6.15s; i.e., an average price per quarter of 67½ s., or £3.7½ s. The production price would rise, but only by 7½ s., whereas if additional capital was applied to *new* land, which produced at £3.15s., it would rise by a further 7½ s. (and thereby cause an additional proportionate rise in all other differential rents).

The production price per quarter of land A would thus be equalised with its average production price per quarter with an increased capital investment, and it would be the governing price. It would therefore yield no rent, because no surplus profit arose from it.

But if this quarter produced by the second capital investment were sold at £3.15s., land A would now yield a rent of 15s., and this would happen on all other acres of A, on which no extra capital investment had been made, and which therefore continued to produce at £3 per quarter. As long as there are still uncultivated parts of land A, the price can rise only temporarily to £3.15s. per quarter. The competition of new tracts of land A would keep the price of production down to £3 until all parts of land A which were in no less favourable a situation and were able to produce at less than £3.15s. a quarter were exhausted. This is the assumption we should like to make, although when one acre of a certain type of land bears rent, the landlord will not lease out another acre except under the same conditions as previously.

It depends once more on the extent to which the second capital investment on land A has become general whether the production price is equalised to the average price or the individual production price of the second capital investment of £3.15s. becomes the governing one. The latter is the case only when the landlord has the time to *fix as rent* the surplus profit that was made before the *demand* was satisfied at a price *of £3.15s.*

On the declining productivity of the soil when successive capital investments are made.

Liebig should be consulted on this question.[104] We have seen that successive declines in surplus productivity always increase the rent per acre when the price of production is constant, and that the rent may increase even when the price is falling.

The following general point should be noted, however:

From the standpoint of the capitalist mode of production, there is always a relative *increase in the price* of products if, in order to obtain the same product, an *outlay* must be made that was previously *unnecessary*. For the *replacement of capital* consumed in the course of production does not simply mean the replacement of *values* expressed in particular means of production. *Natural elements* which go into production as agents without costing anything, whatever role they might play in production, do not go in as *components*

104 [Liebig 1862 (2), pp. 146–7. Translator]

of capital, but rather as a free natural power of capital., i.e., a free natural power of labour. If a natural power of this kind, therefore, which *originally* cost nothing, > has to be *replaced by human labour, by human activity*, in the further course of production, < a new and additional element goes into the capital. A relatively greater capital investment is thus needed in order to obtain *the same* product. All other circumstances remaining the same, production becomes *more expensive*. >

|528| <CHAPTER SEVEN>

The Revenues (Income) and Their Sources

1) The Trinity Formula. 4) Relations of Production and Distribution. 2) On the Analysis of the Production Process. 3) The Illusion of Competition. 5) Classes

<1 The Trinity Formula>

(Compare page 445 of this book.[1] The passage should be transferred here.)

< The capitalist process of production is a specific *social* form of the production process in general, which is both a production process of the material conditions of existence for the members of society, for human life altogether, and a process, proceeding in specific historical and economic relations, relations of production, which reproduces these relations of production themselves and with this the *whole range* of bearers of this process of production, their material conditions of existence and their relations of production and reproduction, i.e., the specific economic form of their society, because the totality of these relationships which the bearers of this production have towards nature and each other, the relationships in which they produce, is *society*, viewed according to its economic structure. This production process proceeds under specific material conditions, which are however also the bearers of specific social relations which individuals enter into in the process of reproducing their life. Those conditions, like these social relations, are on the one hand the *presuppositions* of the capitalist production process, and on the other hand its *results* and *creations*. They are both produced and reproduced by it. We have seen that *capital*, in the social production process appropriate to it – and the capitalist is simply personified capital, he functions within the production process simply as the bearer of capital – pumps out a certain quantum of *surplus labour* from the direct producers or workers, surplus labour which it receives without an equivalent and which by its very nature always remains *forced labour*, however much it appears as the result of free contractual agreement. This surplus labour is expressed in a *surplus-value*, and this surplus-value exists in a *surplus product*. (*Surplus labour* in some form must always remain, as labour beyond the extent of given needs. It is just that in the capitalist system, as in the slave system and

1 [445 is the page in Marx's manuscript; see pp. 766–7 in this book. Editor]

so on, it has an antagonistic form and it is complemented by the pure idleness of one section of society. A certain quantum of surplus labour is required as insurance against accidents and for the progressive extension of the reproduction process that is needed to keep pace with the development of needs and the progress of population > which from the capitalist standpoint is called *accumulation.* < It is one of the civilising aspects of capital that it extorts this surplus labour in a manner and in conditions that are more advantageous to social relations and to the creation of the elements of a new and higher formation than was the case under the earlier forms of slavery, serfdom, etc. Thus on the one hand it leads towards a stage at which compulsion and the monopolisation |529| of social development (with its material and intellectual advantages) by one section of society at the expense of another disappears; on the other hand it creates the material means and the nucleus for relations that permit the *surplus labour* to be combined, in a higher form of society, with a greater reduction of the overall time devoted to material labour. For, according to the development of labour productivity, surplus labour can be large when the total working day is short and relatively small when the total working day is long. If the necessary labour-time is 3 hours and surplus labour also 3 hours, the total working day is 6 hours and the rate of surplus labour is 100 percent. If the necessary labour-time is 9 hours and the surplus labour 3 hours, the total working day is 12 hours and the rate of surplus labour only 33⅓ percent. *Secondly*, however, it depends on the productivity of labour, etc., how much use-value is produced in a given time, and therefore in a given surplus labour-time. The real wealth of society and the possibility of a constant expansion of its reproduction process therefore does not depend on the length of surplus labour, but rather on its productivity and on the more or less abundant conditions of production in which it is performed. In fact the realm of freedom begins only when labour determined by necessity and external expediency comes to an end; it lies by its very nature beyond the sphere of material production proper. Just as the savage must wrestle with nature to satisfy his needs, to maintain and reproduce his life, so must civilised man, and he must do so in all forms of society and under all possible modes of production. This realm of natural necessity expands with his development, because his needs do too; but the productive forces to satisfy these expand at the same time. Freedom, in this sphere, can consist only in this, that socialised man, the associated producers, govern their metabolic interaction with nature rationally, bringing it under their collective control instead of being dominated by it as a blind power; accomplishing this metabolism with the smallest expenditure of energy and in conditions most worthy and appropriate for their human nature. But this always remains a realm of necessity. The true realm of freedom, the development of human powers as an end in itself, begins beyond it, though it can only flourish with this realm of necessity as its basis. The reduction of the working day is the basic prerequisite.) This *surplus-value* (or surplus product) of which we are speaking is divided among the capitalists as dividends in proportion to the quota of social capital that belongs to each of them (if we ignore accidental fluctuations in distribution and consider simply the law governing them, their regulating limits). In this form, surplus-value appears as the *average profit* that accrues to capital, an average profit that is divided in turn into *profit of enterprise* |530| and interest and can accrue under these two categories to different sorts of capitalist. This appropriation and distribution of *surplus labour*, or rather *surplus-value* and the *surplus product* which it represents, meets with a barrier in *landed property*, > in other words the proprietors of the land. < Just as the functioning capitalist pumps out surplus labour from the worker, and thus surplus-value and surplus product in the form of *profit*, so the landowner pumps out a part of this surplus-value or surplus profit in turn from the capitalist in the form of *rent*, according to the laws developed earlier. If we speak here therefore of *profit* as the share of surplus-value that accrues to capital, what we mean is an *average profit* (equal to profit of enterprise plus interest) that is already less than the total profit > (which is identical with the total surplus-value) < because of the deduction of rent; the deduction of rent is presupposed. The *profit* of capital (profit of enterprise plus interest) and *ground-rent* are therefore nothing but particular components of *surplus-value*, categories in which this surplus-value is distinguished according to whether it accrues to capital or landed property; designations which do not affect its essence in any way. Added together they form the sum of the *total surplus-value*. Capital directly pumps from the workers the surplus labour that is expressed in surplus-value and surplus product. It can be considered in this sense as the *producer* of surplus-value. Landed property has nothing to do with the actual production process. Its role is restricted to transferring a part of the surplus-value produced from capital's pocket into its own. On the other hand, the landowner does play a part in the capitalist production process, not only by the pressure that he exerts on capital, and not simply by the fact that large landed property is a premise and condition of the capitalist mode of production > because of its expropriation of the workers from their conditions of labour < but also, and particularly, because he appears as the personification of one of the essential conditions of production.

The *worker*, finally, as owner and seller of his *personal labour-power*, receives under the name of *wages* a part of the product; in this there is expressed the *portion of his labour* that we call *necessary labour*, i.e., labour necessary for the maintenance and reproduction of this labour-power, whether the conditions of this maintenance and reproduction are poorer or richer, more favourable or less favourable.

Disparate as these relations may otherwise appear, they have one thing in common: capital yields profit to the capitalist, year in and year out; |531| land yields ground-rent to the landowner; and labour-power, under normal conditions, and as long as it remains usable > and does not have to be replaced by fresh labour-power, < yields wages to the worker. These three components of the total value annually produced, and the portions of the annually produced total product corresponding to them, can be consumed by their respective owners each year, and the sources of their reproduction will not run dry. (We leave accumulation aside here at first.) They appear as fruits of a perennial tree for annual consumption, or rather the fruits of three trees; they constitute the annual incomes of the capitalists, the landowners and the workers, *income* or *revenues*, distributed by the functioning capitalist, as the person who directly pumps out surplus labour and makes use of labour in general. To the capitalist capital, to the landowner land, and to the worker labour-power, or rather his labour itself (since he sells labour-power only in its actual externalisation, and the *price of labour-power*, as shown earlier, is necessarily expressed on the basis of the capitalist mode of production as the *price of labour*) – these appear as the three *distinct sources* of their specific revenues: profit, ground-rent and wages. And they actually are so in the sense that capital for the capitalist is a perpetual machine that pumps out surplus labour, land for the landowner is a permanent magnet for attracting a part of the surplus-value pumped out by capital and finally labour is the constantly self-renewing condition and means for the worker to obtain a part of the value he has produced and hence a portion of the social product measured by this portion of value, his necessary means of subsistence, under the heading of wages. They are also sources of revenue in the sense that capital fixes one portion of the value of a year's labour and hence of its product in the *form of profit*, landed property fixes another part in the *form of rent*, and wage-labour a third portion in the *form of wages*, and that it is precisely by this transformation that these portions are converted into the revenues of the capitalist, the landowner and the worker, without creating the substance itself that is transformed into these various categories. The distribution rather presupposes this substance as already present, i.e., the total value of the annual product, which is nothing other than materialised [*materialisierte*] social labour. But it is not in this form that the matter presents itself to the agents of production, the bearers of the *various functions* in the production process, but rather in a distorted form. Why this happens we shall see in the further course of our analysis. *Capital, landed property* and *labour* appear to these agents of production as three different and independent sources, from which there arise three different components of the annually produced value (and hence of the product in which it exists); from these sources, therefore, there arise not only the different *forms* of this value as revenues which accrue to particular factors of the social production process, but this value itself arises, and with it the substance of these forms of revenue.[2]

|470| *Capital – profit* (profit of enterprise plus interest), *land – rent, labour – wages*. This is the trinity form which encompasses all the mysteries of the social production process.

Since it is *interest*, as shown already, that appears as the specific and characteristic product of capital, with profit of enterprise appearing in contrast to this as a wage independent of capital, this first trinity form can be reduced to a more precise expression:

Capital – interest, land – rent, labour – wages, where profit, the form of

surplus-value specifically characteristic of the capitalist mode of production, is fortunately set aside, > removed from the scene, reduced to nothing.

< If we now look more closely at this economic trinity, we find, firstly, that the ostensible sources of the wealth annually available belong to completely disparate spheres and do not have the slightest analogy with each other. They are related to each other as much as legal fees, beetroot and music are.

Capital, land, labour! But capital is not a thing, it is a definite *social* relation of production pertaining to a particular historical formation of society, a socially determined relation, which takes the form of a thing, and gives this thing a specific social character! Capital is not the material, produced means of production or the instrument of labour. It is the means of production as *transformed* into capital, these being no more capital in themselves than gold and silver are money. Capital is the means of production *monopolised* by a particular section of society, it is the products and conditions of activity of labour-power which have *become autonomous* vis-à-vis this living labour-power and are personified in capital through this antithesis! It is not only the workers' products which are transformed into independent powers, the products as masters and buyers of their producers, but the *social powers* > which also, in the < *form* of this labour, also confront them as *properties* of their product! Here, therefore, we have a definite *social* form, albeit at first sight a very mysterious form, of one of the social factors which produces a historically specific social process of production! And now, side by side with this, *land*, inorganic nature in its

2 [The next five paragraphs are Engels's fragment #1, which he relocated to the beginning of his Chapter 50 ('The Trinity Formula'); see pp. 39–40 of the Introduction. Editor]

utterly primeval wildness, *rudis indigestaque moles*.[3] *Value* is *labour*. So *surplus-value* cannot be earth. The land's *absolute fertility* does nothing but let a certain quantum of labour give a larger amount of product, conditioned by the natural fertility of the soil. The *differences* in the soil's fertility have the effect that the same amounts of labour and capital, i.e., *the same* value, are expressed in differing quantities of agricultural products, so that these products have *different individual values*. The equalisation of these individual values to give market values has the effect that 'the advantages of fertile over inferior land … are transferred from the cultivator, or consumer, to the landlord' (Ricardo 1821, p. 62). Lastly, as the third in the league, a mere spectre – *labour*, which is nothing but an abstraction, and, taken by itself, cannot exist at all, or, if we take what is actually meant here, the entire productive activity of man, through which his metabolic interchange with nature is mediated. But this is not only divested of any social form and specific character, but even in its mere natural existence, independent of society, it is lifted right out of society altogether and defined as the externalisation and confirmation of life both for a man who is not yet social and for a man who is subject to some kind of social determination![4]

|471| *Capital – interest, landed property, private property over the earth* (and indeed private property of a modern type, corresponding to the capitalist mode of production) – *rent, wage-labour – the wages of labour!*

This is the form in which there is supposed to be a connection between the sources of revenue! *Wage-labour* and *landed property*, like *capital*, are historically specific social forms; one of labour, the other of the *monopolised* earth. Both are in fact forms which correspond to capital and belong to the same economic formation of society! > (The really correct formula is *capital – profit* (profit of enterprise and interest), landed property – rent, wage labour – wages of labour.)

< The first thing that strikes one about this formula is that alongside *capital*, the form of an *element of production* (a condition of labour) belonging to a specific mode of production, a specific historical shape of social production processes, alongside an element of production amalgamated with and presented in a specific social form, we have classed the *earth*, on the one hand, and *labour* on the other, two elements of the real labour process, which are material elements of any process of production, and have nothing to do with its social forms. > It is the same as if one were to list among different kinds of human being bankers (capitalists), negroes, xxxxx, etc.

3 [Ovid, *Metamorphoses*, Book 1, 7, 'An unformed, shapeless mass'. Translator]

4 [This is the end of Engels's fragment #1 and the next four paragraphs are Engels's fragment #2. Editor]

< *Secondly*. In the formula *capital – interest, earth – rent, labour – wages*, capital, earth and labour appear respectively as sources of *interest* (instead of profit), *rent*, and *wages* as their products or fruits – one the basis, the other the result; one the cause, the other the effect – and moreover in such a way that each individual source is related to its *product* as something extruded from it and produced by it. All three forms of income, interest (instead of profit), rent and wages are so many portions of the product's *value*, or, expressed in money, certain portions of money, of *price*. The formula capital-interest is certainly the most irrational formula for capital, but it is a formula for it. But how is the earth to have a *value*, how can it create a socially specific quantum of labour, and the particular *portion of value* of its own products that forms *rent* at that? The earth, for example, is active as an agent of production in the production of a use-value, a *material product*, say *wheat*. But it has nothing to do with producing the *value of the wheat*. In as much as value is expressed in wheat, the wheat is considered simply as a certain quantum of materialised social labour, this labour being quite indifferent to the particular material in which it is expressed or to the particular use-value of this material. It does not contradict this that (1) all other circumstances remaining the same, whether wheat is cheap or dear depends on the earth's productivity. The productivity of agricultural labour is linked to natural conditions, and according to their productivity the same quantum of labour is expressed in a larger or smaller number of products or use-values. The magnitude of the quantum of labour expressed in one bushel depends on the number of bushels that the same quantum of labour supplies. The quantity of product that the value represents depends here on the earth's productivity; but this value is given, and is independent of this distribution. Value is expressed in use-value, and use-value is a condition for the creation of value; but it is foolish to contrapose a use-value, the earth, on the one hand, and *value* on the other, > as its product < and a *particular portion of value* at that! (2) The.[5]

|532| *Differential rent* is bound up with the relative fertility of different land, i.e., with properties that > are inherent in (or < arise from) the land as such. But in as much as it depends *firstly* on the differing *individual* values of the products of different types of land, it is simply the characteristic already mentioned; while in as much as it depends, secondly, on the governing *general market value*, which is different from these individual values, this is a social law brought about by competition which has nothing to do either with the land or with the various degrees of its fertility.

5 [The manuscript breaks off at this point; end of Engels's fragment #2. Editor]

It might appear as if at least in *labour – wages of labour* a rational relationship was expressed. But this is just as little the case as with *land – rent*. In as much as labour is value-forming and is expressed in the value of commodities, it has nothing to do with the distribution of this value among the different categories. And as far as its specific social character as *wage-labour* goes, it is not this that is value-forming. We have repeatedly shown that *wages* or the *price of labour* is simply an irrational expression for the *value or price of labour-power*; and the particular social conditions in which this labour-power is sold have no bearing on labour as a general agent of production. Labour naturally creates, is also represented in, that value component of the commodity which as wages forms the price of labour-power. But it is not represented in it any more than it is in the portions that form rent or profit. Altogether, when we have labour as value-forming in mind, we are not considering it in its concrete shape as a condition of production, but rather in terms of a *social* characteristic that is different from that of *wage-labour*.

Even the expression *capital – profit* is incorrect here. If capital is conceived in the only connection in which it produces *surplus-value*, namely in its relationship to labour, in the compulsion which it exerts on labour-power (i.e., on the wage-labourer himself), this surplus-value comprises not only profit (profit of enterprise plus interest) but also *rent*, i.e., the entire and *undivided surplus-value*. Here, on the contrary, as a source of revenue, it is placed in connection only with that part which accrues to the capitalist. This is not the total *surplus-value* it extracts, but simply the part it extracts for the capitalist. The context disappears even more once the formula is transformed into *capital – interest*.

If we start by considering the disparity between the three sources, we find secondly that their *products*, > their *issues, their offspring*, < the revenues, all belong to *the same* sphere, that of value. However, this is cancelled out (this *relationship* not only *between incommensurable* magnitudes, but also between quite *heterogeneous, unconnected* and *incomparable* things) by the fact that capital, like the *earth* and *labour*, is considered simply from the standpoint of its *material* substance, i.e., as produced *means of production*, in which connection abstraction is made both from capital as a *relation* to the worker and from capital as *value*

|533| *Thirdly*. In this sense, therefore, the formula *capital – interest (profit), earth – rent, labour – wages* presents a uniform and symmetrical incongruity. In fact, since it is not that *wage-labour* appears as a socially specific form of labour, but rather that all labour appears as *wage-labour* by nature (or presents itself like this to those trapped within capitalist relations of production) the *determinate and specific social* forms which the objective *conditions of labour* – the produced *means of production* and the *earth* – assume vis-à-vis wage-labour

(as they in turn presuppose *wage-labour*) coincide directly with the *material* existence of these conditions of labour, or with the shape that they generally possess in the actual labour process, independent of any specific social form, even independent of any social form of this whatever. The form of conditions of labour that are *alienated* from labour, *made independent of it* and *transformed*, the *produced means of production* being transformed into *capital* and the *earth* into private property, *monopolised* earth, this form therefore coincides with the existence and function of the *produced means of production* and the *earth* > in the labour process, < the production process in general. Those means of production are in and for themselves, by nature, *capital*. In other words, capital is nothing but a mere economic name for those means of production; and similarly the earth is in and for itself, by nature, the earth as *monopolised* by a certain lot of landlords. Just as the products become an independent power vis-à-vis the producers in capital and the capitalist – who in actual fact is nothing but capital personified – so *land is personified* in the landowner, he is the land similarly standing up on its hind legs and asserting its independence, claiming in the shape of the landlord its part of the values produced by its help, so that it is not the land that receives the portion of the product needed for reproduction, but instead the landlord who receives a portion of this product to be sold off and wasted. It is clear that capital presupposes that labour is wage-labour. It is just as clear, however, that once you proceed from labour as wage-labour, so that it appears self-evident that wage-labour coincides with labour in general, *capital* and the *monopolised earth* must also appear as the *natural* form of the conditions of labour vis-à-vis labour in general. It now appears as the natural form of the means of labour that they should be capital, as a *purely material* [*dinglich*] character which arises from their function in the labour process in general. Capital and > the means of labour < thus become identical expressions. Likewise land and land *monopolised* by private property become identical expressions. The means of labour as such, being capital by nature, thus become the source of profit in the same way as the earth as such becomes the source of rent.

|534| Labour as such, in its simple characterisation as purposive productive activity, is related to the means of production not in their characteristic social form but rather in their material substance, as the material and means of labour in which they are distinguished from one another only materially, as use-values, the earth as non-produced means of labour, the others as produced. If labour and wage-labour thus coincide, so too do the particular social form in which the conditions of labour confront labour, and their own material existence. The *means of labour* are then *capital* as such, while the *earth* as such is *landed property*. The formal autonomy these conditions of labour acquire vis-à-vis labour,

the particular form of this autonomy they possess > vis-à-vis wage-labour, < is then a property inseparable from them as things, as material conditions of production, an immanently ingrown feature (or quality) that necessarily falls to them as elements of production. Their specific social character in the capitalist production process is an innate material character natural to them, which belongs to them as elements in the production process. It must then appear that it is both the respective share of the earth as the original field of employment of labour, the realm of natural forces, the arsenal of all objects of labour which is present in advance, and the other respective share of the produced means of production (instruments of labour, raw material, etc.) in the production process as such, which are expressed in the respective shares that fall to them as capital and landed property, or rather to their social representatives in the form of profit (interest) and rent, just as the worker's share appears to him in wages as the share of his labour in the production process. Rent, profit and wages thus appear to grow out of the roles that the earth, the produced means of production and labour play in the real labour process, considering their labour process simply as proceeding between man and nature. It is clear, furthermore, and it is only the same thing again in a different form, that the product in which the *worker's* labour presents itself for him as *his* income, his revenue, is simply the *wage*, the *portion of value* (and hence of the social product measured by this value) that represents his wage. If wage-labour coincides with labour in general, *wages* must coincide with the product of labour, and the *portion of value* that wages represent must coincide with the value created by labour in general. But in this way the other portions of value, profit and rent, confront wages just as independently and must arise from sources of their own that are specifically distinct from labour and independent; they must arise from the collaborating elements of production to whose owners they accrue, i.e., profit from the material elements of capital (the means of production) and rent from the earth, or *nature*, as represented by the landowner.[6]

|535| Landed property, capital and wage-labour are therefore transformed from sources of revenue in the sense that capital attracts from the capitalist a portion of the surplus-value which it extracts from labour, in the form of *profit*; the proprietorship of the earth attracts another part to the landowner in the form of *rent*, and labour gives the worker the final portion of value that is still available in the form of the *wage*, in other words from sources by virtue of which one part of the value is transformed into the *form of profit*, a second into the *form of rent* and a third into the *form of wages* – into real sources from which

6 Roscher [1858, p. 394.]

these portions of value themselves *arise*, together with their respective portions of the product, in which they exist or into which they can be converted, the *value* of the *product itself* therefore arising from these as its ultimate source.[7]

We have already demonstrated, in connection with the simplest categories of the capitalist mode of production,[8] the *commodity* and *money*, the mystificatory character that transforms the social relations for which the material elements of wealth serve as bearers in the course of production into properties of these things themselves (*commodities*), and still more explicitly transforms the relation of production itself into a thing (*money*). All forms of society participate in this distortion, in so far as they involve commodity production and monetary circulation. In the capitalist mode of production, however, where capital is the dominant category and forms the dominant relation of production, this bewitched and distorted world develops much further. If we view capital first in the immediate process of production, as an extractor of surplus labour, this relationship is still very simple; the real connection impresses itself on the bearers of this process (the capitalists) themselves, and is still in their consciousness. The fierce struggle over the limits of the working day shows this in a striking way. But even within this immediate sphere, the sphere of the immediate process between labour and capital, the matter does not rest at this simple stage. With the development of relative surplus-value and the veritable, specifically capitalist mode of production, involving the growth of the productive forces of social labour, these productive forces and the social context of labour in the immediate labour process are shifted from labour to capital. Capital thereby already becomes a very mystical being, since all the productive forces of social labour appear attributable to it, and not to labour as such, as a power springing forth from its own womb. Then the *circulation process* intervenes. All sections of capital, even agricultural capital, have to pass through > the material and formal changes of this process |536| < to the same degree > as the specifically capitalist mode of production develops. < In this sphere, the conditions of the original production of value fall completely into the background. Even in the immediate production process, the capitalist is active also

7 'Wages, profit and rent are the three *original* sources of all revenue, as well as of all *exchangeable value*'. (Smith 1776, p. 63.) > The statement is a tautology in this form. Wages, profit and rent are the three original forms of revenue. To say that these are the *original sources* of revenue means to say that revenues arise from revenues. < 'Thus the *causes of material production* are at the same time *the sources of the original revenues that exist*'. (Storch [1815, p. 259.])

8 [This is where Engels added the key misleading phrase 'and commodity production in general'; see pp. 40 of the Introduction. Editor]

as commodity producer, as manager of commodity production. The production process thus presents itself to him by no means as just the simple production process of surplus-value. Whatever the surplus-value capital has pumped out in the immediate production process and realised in commodities, the value and surplus-value contained in these commodities must first be realised in the circulation process. Both the restoration of the values advanced in production, and, in particular, the surplus-value contained in the commodities, seem not to be realised in circulation but actually to arise from it. This appearance [*Schein*] is reinforced by two circumstances in particular: firstly *profit upon alienation*,[9] which depends on the cheating, cunning, expertise and talent > of the buyer and the seller < and a thousand and one market conjunctures; then the fact that a second determining element enters here besides labour-time, i.e., *circulation time*. Even though this functions only as a negative limit on the formation of value and surplus-value, it appears to be just as positive a ground as labour itself, and it also appears to involve a determination independent of labour that arises from the nature of capital. [In Book Two] we had of course to present this circulation sphere only in relation to the new determinations of form it produces, to demonstrate the further development of the form of capital that takes place in it. In reality, however, this sphere is the sphere of competition, which is subject to accident in each individual case, where therefore the inner law that prevails through the accidents and governs them is visible only when these accidents are combined in large numbers, hence it is invisible and incomprehensible to the individual agents of production themselves. Further, however, the actual production process, as the unity of the immediate production process and the circulation process, produces new forms [*Gestaltungen*] in which the threads of the inner connection get increasingly lost, the relations of production become independent of each other and the components of value ossify into independent forms.

The transformation of surplus-value into profit is just as much determined by the circulation process as by the process of production. Surplus-value in the form of profit is no longer related to the portion of capital laid out on labour, which is where it derives from, but rather to the total capital. The profit rate is governed by its own laws, which permit it to vary while the rate of surplus-value remains the same, and even require this variation. All this conceals |537| the true nature of surplus-value more and more, concealing therefore the real mechanism of capital. This happens still more with the transformation of profit into average profit and of values into prices of production, the governing aver-

9 [Marx wrote 'expropriation' here. Translator]

ages of market price. A complex social process intervenes here, the equalisation of capitals, which cuts the relative average prices of commodities loose from their values, and the average profits in the various spheres of production from the actual exploitation of labour by the particular capitals involved (quite apart from the individual capital investments in each particular sphere of production). The average price of commodities not only seem to differ from their value, i.e., from the labour realised in them, but they actually do differ, and the average profit of a particular capital differs from the surplus-value this capital has extracted from the workers employed by it. Now the value of commodities appears directly only in the influence of the changing productivity of labour on the rise and fall of prices of production; on their movement, not on their final limits. Profit now appears as determined only secondarily by the direct exploitation of labour, in so far as, given > the existence of governing < market prices that are seemingly independent of this exploitation, it permits the capitalist to realise a profit which diverges from the average level. *Normal average profit* itself seems immanent in capital independently of exploitation; abnormal exploitation or even average exploitation under exceptionally favourable conditions seems only to determine divergences from average profit, and not this average profit itself.

The division of profit into profit of enterprise and interest (not to speak of the intervention of commercial profit and money-dealing profit, which are founded on the circulation sphere and seem to derive entirely from this, and not from the production process itself) completes the autonomisation of the *form* of surplus-value, the ossification of its form as against its substance, its essence. One portion of profit, in contrast to the other, separates itself completely from the capital-relation as such and presents itself as deriving not from the function of exploiting wage-labour > (which is naturally inseparable from the activity of management) < but rather from the wage-labour of the capitalist himself. As against this, interest then seems independent both of the wage-labour of the worker and of the capitalist's own labour; it seems to derive from capital as its own independent source. If capital originally appeared on the surface of circulation as the capital fetish, value-creating value, it now presents itself once again in the shape of interest-bearing capital as its most estranged [*entfremdet*] and peculiar |538| form. That is why the form 'capital – interest', as a third in the series after 'earth – rent' and 'labour – wages', is much more consistent than 'capital – profit', since profit still retains a memory of its origin which in interest is not simply obliterated but actually placed in a form diametrically opposed to this origin.

Finally, alongside capital as an independent source of surplus-value, there appears landed property, as a limit to the average profit, which transfers a portion of the profit (surplus-value) to a category that neither works itself nor directly exploits workers, and cannot even, like interest-bearing capital, spew out edifying rationalisations about the risk and sacrifice involved in lending capital. Because in this case one part of the surplus-value seems directly bound up not with social relations but with a natural element, the earth, the form of alienation and ossification of the various parts of surplus-value is complete, the inner connection completely dissolved and its source completely buried, precisely through the assertion of their autonomy vis-à-vis each other by the various relations of production which are bound up with the different material elements of the production process. Capital – profit (or better still, capital – interest), land – rent, labour – wages, this economic trinity as the connection between the components of value and wealth in general and its sources, completes the mystification of the capitalist mode of production, the reification [*Verdinglichung*] of social relations, and the immediate coalescence of the material relations of production with their historical and social specificity: the bewitched, distorted and upside-down world haunted by Monsieur le Capital and Madame la Terre, who are at the same time social characters and mere things. It is the great merit of classical economics that it swept away this false appearance and deception, this autonomisation and ossification of the different social elements of wealth vis-à-vis one another, this personification of things and reification [*Versachlichung*] of the relations of production, this religion of everyday life, by reducing interest to a part of profit and rent to the surplus above the average profit, so that they both coincide in surplus-value, and by presenting the circulation process as simply a metamorphosis of forms, and finally in the immediate process of production reducing the value and surplus-value of commodities to labour. Yet even its best representatives remained more or less trapped in the world of illusion [*Schein*] their criticism had dissolved (nothing else is possible from the bourgeois standpoint). They all therefore fell more or less into inconsistencies, half-truths and unresolved contradictions. It is also quite natural, on the other hand, that the actual agents of production themselves feel completely at home in these estranged and irrational forms of capital – interest, land – rent and labour – wages, for these are precisely |539| the forms [*Gestaltungen*] of appearance [*Schein*] in which they move, and with which they are involved every day. It is equally to be expected, therefore, that vulgar economics, which is nothing more than a didactic and more or less doctrinaire translation of the everyday notions of the actual agents of production, giving them a certain comprehensible arrangement, finds the *natural* basis of its fatuous self-importance established beyond all doubt precisely in this trinity, in which the entire inner connection is obliterated. This formula also corresponds to the interests of the dominant classes, since it preaches the natural necessity and justification of their *sources of income* and erects this into a dogma. (In presenting the *reification of the relations of production* and their *autonomisation* vis-à-vis the agents of production themselves, we shall not go into the form and manner in which these connections appear to them as *natural laws*, governing them irrespective of their will, in the form that the world market and its conjunctures, the movement of market prices, > the periods of credit, < the cycles of industry and trade and the alternation of epochs of prosperity and crisis appears as a *blind necessity* asserting its control over them. We refrain from discussing these questions because the actual movement of competition, etc., lies outside our plan, and we only need to present the internal organisation of the capitalist mode of production in its ideal average, so to speak.)

In earlier forms of society, the economic mystification comes in principally in connection with money and interest-bearing capital. It is excluded by the very nature of the case, firstly, where production is predominantly for use-value, for the producers' own needs; and secondly, where, as in ancient and medieval times, slavery or serfdom forms the broad basis of social production. In the latter case, the dominance of the conditions of production over the producers is concealed by the visible relations of domination and servitude, which appear as direct driving forces of the production process. In oriental communities (where an indigenous communism prevails) and even in the urban communities of the ancient world, it is the actual community and its conditions that presents itself as the basis of production, the reproduction of this community being production's ultimate goal. Even in the guild system of the Middle Ages, neither capital nor labour appear unrestrained; their connections are determined by the system of corporations and the relationships this involves, as well as by the corresponding ideas of professional obligation, craftsmanship, etc. Only in the capitalist mode of production …

(2) [On the Analysis of the Production Process][10]

|540| For the analysis that follows in this section we can ignore the distinction between value and price of production, since this disappears whenever we are concerned with the *value* of labour's total annual product, i.e., the value of the product of the *total social capital*.

Profit (which is profit of enterprise plus interest) and *rent* are nothing but characteristic forms assumed by particular portions of the *surplus-value* in

10 [Title added by the MEGA editors. Editor]

commodities. The size of the *surplus-value* sets a *quantitative* limit to the parts into which it can be divided. Average profit plus rent is therefore equal to surplus-value. (It is possible for a part of the surplus labour and hence surplus-value contained in commodities not to go directly into the equalisation that gives the average profit, so that a part of the value of the commodities is not expressed at all in their price. But, firstly, this is compensated for by a rise in the rate of profit, if the commodity sold below its value forms an element of constant capital, or else by the expression of profit and rent in a larger product, if this commodity enters into the part of value consumed as revenue, as an article of individual consumption. Secondly, it is cancelled in the average movement. In any case, even if a portion of surplus-value not expressed in the *price* of the commodity is omitted from the process of price formation, the sum of average profit plus rent can in its *normal* form never be *greater* than the total surplus-value, though it can be *less*. This *normal* form assumes a wage corresponding to the value of labour-power. Thus even *monopoly rent*, in so far as it is not a *deduction from wages* and does not form a special category, must always indirectly form part of surplus-value. Even if it is not a part of the excess price over and above the production costs of the actual commodity of which it itself forms a component, as in the case of differential rent, or an excess part of the surplus-value in the commodity of which it forms a component over and above its own portion of surplus-value as measured by the average profit (as in the case of absolute rent) it is still a part of the surplus-value of other commodities, i.e., those which are exchanged against this commodity with a monopoly price. The sum of average profit and ground rent can never be greater than the quantity of which these are parts, and this quantity is already given before the division takes place. Whether the entire surplus-value of the commodities, i.e., all the surplus labour they contain, is realised in their price or not is therefore immaterial as far as we are concerned here. In actual fact, the surplus-value is not completely realised, for this reason: since the amounts of socially *necessary* labour required for the production of a given commodity are constantly changing owing to the constant changes in the productivity of labour, one section of commodities is always produced under abnormal conditions and the commodities must *therefore* be sold below their *individual* value. At all events, profit plus rent equals the entire *realised* surplus-value (surplus labour), and for our present purposes the realised profit and rent are realised surplus-value, i.e., the total surplus-value that enters into the prices of the commodities, and thus in practice *all* the surplus-value that forms a component of this price.)

|541| *Wages*, on the other hand, which are the third characteristic form of revenue, are always equal to the variable component of capital, i.e., the

component that is laid out not on instruments of labour but on the purchase of living labour-power, on the payment of workers. > The *value* of the wage is always measured by the *value* of the variable capital. < (The labour paid in the expenditure of revenue is itself paid for from wages, profit or rent, and thus does not form any portion of the value of those commodities with which it is paid. So it does not come into consideration for the analysis of commodity value and the components into which this is divided.) It is the materialisation of that portion of the workers' total working day in which the value of variable capital and hence the price of labour is reproduced; the portion of commodity value in which the worker reproduces the value of his own labour-power or the price of his labour.

The worker's total working day is divisible into two parts. One part is that in which he performs the quantum of labour needed to reproduce the value of his own means of subsistence: the paid part of his total labour, which is the part *necessary* for his own maintenance and reproduction. The entire remaining part of the working day, the entire excess quantum of labour he performs beyond the labour realised in the value of his wages, is *surplus labour, unpaid labour*, which is represented in the *surplus-value* of his total commodity production (and thus in the excess quantity of commodities), surplus-value which is divisible in turn into differently named portions, *profit* (profit of enterprise plus interest) and rent.

The total *portion of commodity value*, therefore, in which the total labour that the worker adds during a day or a year is realised, the total value of the annual product that this labour creates, breaks down into the value of wages, profit and rent. For this total labour breaks down into necessary labour, by which the worker creates the portion of the product's value with which he is paid himself, i.e., wages, and *unpaid surplus labour*, by which he creates the portion of the product's value that represents surplus-value and that is subsequently divided into > (bifurcates into) < profit and rent. Besides this labour, the worker performs no other, and besides the total value of the product, which assumes the form of wages, profit and rent, he creates no other value. The value of the annual product in which the labour he has newly added during the year is represented is equal to wages or to the value of the variable capital, plus surplus-value. The latter in turn takes on the forms of profit and rent.

|542| Thus the total portion of the annual product's value which the worker creates in the course of the year is expressed in the annual *sum of value* of the three revenues, the value of wages, profit and rent. It is evident, therefore, that the value of the constant portion of capital is *not* reproduced in the *annually created product value*, for wages are equal simply to the variable

portion of capital advanced in production, while rent and profit are equal to the surplus-value, the *excess value* produced over and above the total value of the capital advanced, i.e., the value of the constant capital plus the value of the variable capital.

It is completely immaterial for the problem to be solved here that one part of the surplus-value which has been transformed into the form of profit and rent is not consumed as revenue but serves for accumulation. The part of this that is saved as an accumulation fund serves towards forming new, additional capital, but not towards replacing the old capital, whether the component of the old capital laid out on labour-power or that laid out on means of labour. A double problem arises here. On the one hand, the value of the annual product in which these revenues – wages, profit and rent – are consumed contains in it a portion of value equal to the value of the *constant* portion of capital that has gone into it > (and it is all one whether this product enters into individual consumption, into productive consumption or into accumulation; so as to simplify matters we can regard the revenues as entering in their entirety into individual consumption.) < It contains this portion of value on top of the portion of value reducible to wages and the portion reducible to profit and rent. Its value therefore = wages + profit + rent + C, with C standing for the constant portion of its value. How then is the value annually produced, which is simply wages + profit + rent, to buy a product whose value is (wages + profit + rent) + C? How can the value annually produced buy a product that has a higher value than itself?

If on the other hand we ignore the portion of constant capital which has not gone into the product and so continues to exist after the annual commodity production, though with a reduced value; > (we can thus abstract entirely here from < *fixed capital*, the part of *constant capital* that is applied but not consumed) we find that the constant capital advanced in the form of raw and ancillary materials has gone completely into the new product, while one part of the means of labour has been used up completely, and another used up partially, in other words only part of its value has to be consumed in production. The part |543| of the constant capital that has been used up completely in production must be replaced in kind. Taking all other factors as unchanged, and particularly the productivity of labour, the same amount of labour is required to replace it as before, i.e., it must be replaced by an equivalent > (considered from the point of view of exchange-value.) If this does not happen, reproduction itself cannot take place on the old scale.

< But who is to perform this labour, and who does perform it?

As far as the first problem is concerned – who is to pay for the *constant* portion of value contained in the product, and with what – it is assumed that the value of the constant capital that has been used up in production reappears as a part of the product's value. This does not contradict the premises of the second problem. For we have already shown right at the beginning of our work (Book I, Chapter Three, in the section on the labour process and the valorisation process)[11] that when new labour is added, even though it does *not* reproduce the old value but just makes an *addition* to it, only creating additional value, the old value is still preserved in the product; and that this happens not by virtue of the value-creating characteristic of labour, i.e., > viewed purely in terms of its quantity, < but rather through its function as real, productive labour. No additional labour was needed, therefore, to perpetuate the value of the *constant* element in the product on which the revenue, i.e., the total value *created* during the year, is spent. But *fresh, additional labour is needed* to replace the constant capital consumed during the previous year in kind (and in value), since without this replacement no reproduction is possible at all.

All newly added labour is expressed in the value newly created in the course of the year, which in turn goes entirely into the three revenues, wages, profit and rent. On the one hand, therefore, there is *no* excess social *labour* left over for the replacement of the *constant capital consumed*, which has to be reproduced partly both in kind and in value, and partly simply in value (just for the wear-and-tear of the fixed capital, > not for its complete displacement). < On the other hand, the value annually created by labour, which breaks down into the three forms of wages, profit and rent, and is spent in these forms, seems *insufficient* to *pay for* or to *buy* the constant component of capital, which the annual product must contain on top of the value of the revenues.

|544| We can see that the problem posed here was already solved when we dealt with the reproduction process (in Book II, [Part] 3.) We come back to it here firstly because there *surplus-value* was not yet developed in its forms of revenue – *profit* (profit of enterprise + interest) *and rent* – and hence could not yet be dealt with in these forms; and secondly because it is precisely in connection with the form of wages, profit and rent as *revenues* that an incredible blunder has run through the analyses of all political economists since Adam Smith.

In Book II, > in dealing with the reproduction process, < we divided all capital into two great classes: [Department Two][12] which produces products which

---

11 [Published as Volume I, Chapter 7. Translator]

12 [In Marx's manuscript, Department II ('Class II') produces means of production and

serve directly as means of individual consumption, and [Department One] which produces the means of production necessary for the production of these products, in other words constant capital. (The fact that certain products may serve both for personal satisfaction and as means of production, such as horses, corn, etc., in no way undermines the absolute validity of this division. It is in fact not a hypothesis but simply the expression of a fact. Let us take a country's annual product. *One part* of this product goes into individual consumption, whatever may be its ability to serve as means of production. It is the product on which wages, profit and rent are spent. This *product* is the *product* of a specific department of the social capital. It is possible that this *same capital* also produces products belonging to Department One. In as much as it does this, it is not the portion of this capital *consumed* in the *product* of Department Two which produces the products of Department One. This whole product, which enters individual consumption, and on which revenue is spent, is the *existence of the capital consumed in it* + the excess produced. It is thus the product of a capital invested simply in the production of *means of consumption*. In the same way, > the second part of the annual product [Department One] < which serves as means of reproduction (raw material and instruments of labour), whatever capacity this product might otherwise have, by its particular nature, to serve as means of consumption, is the product of a capital invested simply in the production of means of production. By far the majority of the products that form constant capital exist in a material form in which they cannot go into individual consumption. In as much as they might do so, as a peasant for instance could eat his seed-corn or slaughter his draught oxen, the economic barrier facing him makes it exactly the same as if this part did exist in a non-consumable form.)

|545| > Let us call one class Class I, the other II. < We abstract in both cases from the *fixed part* of the capital which continues to exist both in kind and in value, independently of the annual product of the two departments.

In Department II, on whose products wages, profit and rent are spent, i.e., revenues consumed, the *product* itself, from the point of view of its value, consists of three components. One component is equal in value to the portion of constant capital consumed in production; a second component is equal in value to the variable portion of capital advanced, that spent on wages; finally, a third component is equal to the surplus-value produced, i.e., profit + rent. The component of Department II's product, the value of the constant capital,

---

Department I produces means of consumption. We have followed Engels, and tradition, in reversing this order. Translator]

can be consumed neither by the capitalists and workers of Department II, nor by the landowners. It forms no part of their *revenue* but must be replaced in kind, and for this to be done it must be sold. The two other components of this product, on the other hand, are equal to the value of the revenues produced in this department, wages + profit + rent.

In Department I, the product formally consists of the same components. But here the part that forms revenue, wages + profit + rent, in other words the variable capital + the surplus-value, is consumed not in the natural form of the products of this Department I but rather in the products of Department II. The value of the revenues in Department I must therefore be consumed in the part of the product of Department II that forms the constant capital of II that is to be replaced. The part of Department II's product that has to replace its constant capital is consumed in its natural form by the workers, capitalists and landowners in Department I. These spend their revenues on this product II. The product of Department I, on the other hand, in so far as it represents the revenue of Department I, is productively consumed in its natural form by Department II, whose constant capital it replaces in kind.

Finally the portion of constant capital in Department I which needs replacing is in fact replaced from the products of Department I itself, which consist precisely of raw material, ancillary materials and instruments of labour, partly by exchange products from the capitalists of Department I themselves, partly by the ability of one section of these capitalist of Department I to use their own products again as means of production. If Department II consists of 400c + 100v + 100s = 600 altogether, and Department I consists of 800c + 200v + 200s = 1,200, then in II 200 is consumed by the producers and proprietors as revenue: this leave 400. This is consumed by the workers, capitalists and rent-receivers of Department I, who take 400. The consumed product of II is consumed as revenue by I, and the revenue part of I which consists of non-consumable products is consumed as constant capital by II, i.e., it is productively consumed by II. All that remains is to work out the fate of the 800 left from I. This is replaced out of the product of 1,200, or rather out of 1,200 – 400, for 400 of the 1,200 have been converted into the constant capital for II. It should be noted that the figures here are completely arbitrary, so that the correspondence between the value of Department I's revenue and Department II's constant capital also seems arbitrary. It is important, however, to bear in mind that in so far as the reproduction process proceeds *normally* and with other circumstances remaining the same (leaving aside accumulation) the sum of wages, profit and rent in Department I must be equal in value to the constant portion of capital in Department II. Otherwise Department II cannot replace its constant capital, nor can Department I convert its revenue from non-consumable into consumable form.

|546| The *value of the annual commodity product*, therefore, just like the *value* of the commodity product of a particular capital investment or the *value of any individual commodity*, can be broken down into *two components*: component A, which replaces the value of the constant capital advanced, and component B, expressed in the *form of revenue* as *wages, profit and rent*. Component B *contrasts* with component A in so far as, all other circumstances being assumed equal, this (1) never assumes the form of revenue, and (2) always returns in the form of *capital*, and indeed in constant capital. The other component, B, however, has its internal distinctions as well. > Two parts of it – profit and rent – do admittedly form components of the value of the *product*, and of *capital*, to the extent that the latter exists in the *form of commodity capital*, capital that is pregnant with surplus-value (although this surplus-value only manifests itself in the *final price* at which the product is *sold* to the ultimate consumers, whether individual or productive). They do not, however, form any part of the capital *advanced for production*. < What profit and rent have in common with wages is that all three are forms of revenue. Yet they are basically distinguished by the fact that profit and rent represent surplus-value, i.e., *unpaid labour*, and wages represent *paid labour*. The *portion of the product's value* that represents paid wages, i.e., replaces wages – and if reproduction proceeds on the same scale and under the same conditions it is transformed back into wages – returns first of all as *variable capital*, as a component of the capital that has to be advanced once more for reproduction. This component has a double function. It exists firstly in the form of capital, being exchanged as such for labour-power. In the hands of the worker it is transformed into the revenue (means of subsistence) that the worker draws from the sale of his labour-power; then, as revenue, it is consumed. This double process is demonstrated by the way it is transacted through monetary circulation. Variable capital is advanced in money, paid out in wages. This is its first function as capital. It is replaced by labour-power and transformed into the externalisation of this labour-power, into labour. This is the process as far as the capitalist is concerned. Secondly, however, the workers use this money to buy a portion of their commodity product, which is measured by this money and is consumed by them as revenue. If we imagine a situation without monetary circulation, one part of the worker's product is already in the hands of the capitalist in the form of variable capital. He advances this part as capital, giving it to the worker in exchange for new labour-power, while the worker consumes it as revenue, either directly or by exchanging it for other commodities. Thus the portion of the product's value destined to be transformed in the course of reproduction into *wages*, into *revenue for the worker*, returns first of all to the capitalist in the form of *capital*, *variable capital* to be precise. It is an essential condition for the repeated repro-

duction of labour as *wage-labour*, of the instruments of production as *capital* and of the production process itself as a *capitalist* process, that it should return in this form.

|547| So as not to get entangled in useless difficulties, we must distinguish *gross output* and *net output* from *gross income* and *net income*.

The *gross output* (= *gross product*) is the entire product reproduced. With the exception of the portion of fixed capital which is applied but not consumed, the value of the gross output or gross product is equal to the value of the capital advanced and consumed in production, constant capital and variable, plus the surplus-value, which breaks down into profit and rent. Or, if we consider not the product of the individual capital but rather the total social capital, the gross output is equal to the material elements forming the constant plus the variable capital, plus the material elements of the surplus product, in which profit and rent are represented.

The *gross income* is the *portion of value*, and the part of the *gross product* or *gross output* measured by this, which remains over after deducting the *portion of value*, and the part of the total production measured by it, which replaces the *constant capital* advanced and consumed in production. Gross income, therefore, is equal to *wages* (or the part of the product > which replaces the variable capital and is < destined to become the workers' income again) plus *profit* plus *rent*. Net income, on the other hand, is the surplus-value (and hence the *surplus product*) that remains after wages are deducted, and so it expresses in fact the surplus-value that capital realises and has to share with landed property, and therefore the *surplus product* measured by this.

We have now seen that the *value* of each individual commodity, and the *value* of the total commodity product of each individual capital, can be divided into two parts: one which simply replaces constant capital, *and another* which, although a fraction of it returns as variable capital, i.e., also returns in the form of capital, is destined nevertheless to be transformed completely into *gross income* and to assume the form of *wages, profit* and *rent*, the sum of these three being what constitutes gross income. We have also seen that the same thing happens with respect to the *value* of the total annual product of a society. Thus the only distinction between the product of the individual capitalist and that of society is that from the standpoint of the individual capitalist net income is different from gross income, since wages are included in the latter while they are excluded from the former. Considering the income of the society as a whole, national income consists of wages plus profit plus rent, i.e., the gross income. But this too is an abstraction, since the whole society, on the basis of the capitalist mode of production, is considered from the capitalist standpoint and hence views as net income only those incomes reducible to profit and rent.

|548| Such fantasies as those of Monsieur Say, on the other hand, to the effect that the entire gross product of a nation is reducible to net output, or is not distinct from this, in other words that this distinction ceases to obtain from the standpoint of the nation as a whole, are simply the necessary expression, the final expression, of the absurd dogma that has pervaded the whole of political economy since Adam Smith, namely that the *value of commodities* can ultimately be broken down into wages, profit and rent.[13]

It is extremely easy of course, in the case of the individual capitalist, to see that one part of his product must be transformed back into capital (ignoring the expansion of reproduction, or accumulation), and indeed not into variable capital, > which is destined to return to the worker as his income, and therefore to be converted into the form of revenue, < but into *constant* capital, which can never be transformed into income. Simply to look at the production process makes this obvious. The difficulty begins only when the production process is considered as a whole, on a large scale. On the one hand we have an undeniable practical fact. The value of the *entire part of the product* that is consumed as revenue, in the form of wages, profit and rent (and it is quite immaterial here whether it is consumed individually or productively), actually disappears *completely*, on analysis, into the sum of value formed from wages plus profit plus rent, i.e., into the *total value* of the three revenues, although the value of this part of the product, just like the part that does *not* go into revenue, contains a *portion of value* which is equal to the value of the constant capital contained in it, so that it is *impossible, prima facie*, for it to be limited by the value of the revenue. On the other hand, we have an equally undeniable theoretical contradiction – and the easiest though fraudulent solution to the problem is to claim that it is only from the standpoint of the individual capitalist that *commodity*

---

13 Ricardo makes the following very good observation about the unthinking Monsieur Say: 'Of net produce and gross produce M. Say speaks as follows: "The whole value produced is the gross produce; this value, after deducting from it the cost of production, is the net produce". (Vol. II, p. 49.) There can then be no net produce, because the cost of production, according to M. Say, consists of rent, wages and profits. In page 508 he says: "The value of a product, the value of a productive service, the value of the cost of production, are all then similar values, whenever things are left to their natural course". Take a whole from a whole, and nothing remains'. (Ricardo 1821, p. 512, note.) As we shall see later on, however, Ricardo never argued against Adam Smith's erroneous analysis of 'natural price' [in Smith 1776, vol. 1, ch. 7], his resolution of this into the value sum of the revenues. It didn't worry the former, and he assumed its correctness in his analyses to the extent that he 'abstracted' from the constant portion of commodity value. He thus fell from time to time into the same way of conceiving the problem.

value appears to contain a further *portion of value* distinct from that existing in the form of revenue. Here, all further reflection is rendered unnecessary by the mere phrase that what appears as revenue for one person forms capital for another. How, if the value of the entire product can be consumed in the form of revenue, the old capital *can* be replaced, and how the value of the product of each individual capital can be equal to the value sum of the three revenues plus the constant capital, while the combined *value sum* of the products of all capitals added together equals the value of the three revenues plus 0, all this can only appear as an insoluble riddle, and must |549| be *explained* by alleging that analysis is incapable of catching hold of the simple elements of price and must instead make do with a vicious circle and an infinite regress, so that what appears as constant capital is reducible to wages, profit and rent, but the commodity values in which wages, profit and rent are expressed are determined in turn by wages, profit and rent, and so on *ad infinitum*.[14]

The fundamentally false dogma that the *value of commodities* can ultimately be reduced to *wages, profit and rent* is thus expressed in the assertion that the *consumer* has ultimately to pay the *total value* of the total product; or that the monetary circulation between producers and consumers must ultimately be equal to the monetary circulation between the producers themselves; these assertions are all as false as the fundamental principle on which they are based.

The problems that lead to this false and *prima facie* absurd analysis can be summarised as follows:

(1) The basic relationship of constant and variable capital is not understood, and so neither is the nature of surplus-value and with it the entire basis of the

14 'In every society the price of every commodity finally resolves itself into some one or other, or all of those three parts' (viz., wages, profit, rent) ... 'A fourth part, it may perhaps be thought, is necessary for replacing the stock of the farmer, or for compensating the wear and tear of his labouring cattle, and other instruments of husbandry. But it must be considered that the price of any instrument of husbandry, such as a labouring horse, is itself made up of the same three parts; the rent of the land upon which he is reared, the labour of tending and rearing him, and the profits of the farmer who advances both the rent of this land, and the wages of this labour. Though the price of corn, therefore, may pay the price as well as the maintenance of the horse, the whole price still resolves itself either immediately or ultimately into the same three parts of rent, labour' (he should say wages) 'and profit'. (Smith 1776, pp. 60–1.) We shall show later on how Adam Smith himself feels the contradiction in this evasion and its unsatisfactory character, for it is nothing more than an evasion for him to send us from pillar to post, even though he never indicates the actual capital investment into which the price of the product is 'ultimately' resolved into these three parts alone without further analysis.

capitalist mode of production. The value of each partial product of capital, each individual commodity, includes a portion of value which equals constant capital, and a portion of value which equals variable capital (which is transformed into wages for the worker), and a portion of value which equals surplus-value (which is in turn later further separated into the forms of profit and rent). How then is it possible for the worker with his wages, the capitalist with his profit, and the landowner with his rent, to buy *commodities* that contain not only one of these components but all three, and how is it possible for the value sum of wages, profit and rent, i.e., the three sources of income taken together, which are to buy the *commodities which are to enter into the total consumption* of the recipients of these incomes, to contain a further additional value component on top of these three, i.e., constant capital? How can a value of four be bought with a value of three?[15] We have given an analysis of this in Book Two, Chapter Three.

15 Proudhon declares his inability to understand this in a narrow-minded formula: 'The worker cannot buy back his own product', because the interest contained in it is added on to the 'cost price to himself'. But does M. Eugène Forcade show any more understanding? 'If Proudhon's objection were correct', he says, 'not only would it apply to the profits of capital; it would eliminate the very possibility of industry. If the worker is compelled to pay 100 for something for which he has only received 80, if his wages can buy back only the value he has put into a product, this amounts to saying that the worker cannot buy anything, that wages cannot buy anything. For the cost price always contains something more than the wages of the worker, and the sale price always contains something more than the profit of the entrepreneur, for example the price of the raw material, which is often paid abroad ... Proudhon has forgotten the continual growth of the national capital, he has forgotten that this growth takes effect for all the workers, both the entrepreneurs and the labourers'. (Forcade 1848, pp. 998–9.) Here we have the optimism of bourgeois thoughtlessness in the most appropriate form of its wisdom. First M. Forcade believes that the worker could not survive if he did not receive a higher value than that which he produces, while conversely the capitalist mode of production would be impossible if he really did receive the value he produces. Secondly, he correctly generalises the problem that Proudhon expressed only from a restricted point of view. The price of a commodity contains an excess not only on top of wages but also on top of profit, i.e., the constant portion. So the capitalist too, on Proudhon's argument, could not buy the commodity back with his profit. But how does Forcade solve this riddle? By a meaningless phrase – the *growth of capital*. Thus the constant growth of capital is to mean among other things that while the political economist finds it *impossible* to *analyse price* for a capital of 100, it is *superfluous* to analyse price for a capital ten times greater. What would we think of a chemist who, when asked how it is that the soil's product contains more carbon than the soil itself, replied: this comes from the constant growth of agricultural

(2) It is not understood how and in what way labour, while it adds new value, also preserves old value in a new form, *without* producing this value afresh.

(3) There is no understanding, either, of the reproduction process as it presents itself not from the standpoint of the individual capital but from that of the total capital, in other words of how, firstly, the product in which wages and surplus-value are realised, in short *the whole of the value* created by all *the labour newly added in the course of the year*, can be realised |550| and expended and replace its *constant value portion* and still *simultaneously* be reducible to a *value* defined simply by revenues; and of how, secondly, the *constant* capital consumed in production can be replaced materially and in value by a new capital, although the *total sum of newly added labour* is realised only in wages and surplus-value, and is exhaustively expressed in the sum of these two.

This is the main difficulty, the analysis of reproduction and the relationship of its various components, both in their material character and in their value

(4) But there is still a further problem, which becomes yet more difficult once the different components of surplus-value appear in the form of revenues which are independent of each other. This is that the firm determinations of revenue and capital change places and shift, so that they seem to be only relative determinations pertaining to the standpoint of the individual capitalist, and seem to vanish altogether when the total production process is in view. For instance, the revenue of the workers and capitalists in the department that produces constant capital replaces the constant capital of the capitalist class, which produces the means of consumption, both in value and materially. This problem can be 'evaded' with the notion that what is revenue for one is capital for another, so that these definitions have nothing to do with the actual distinctions in the components of commodity value. Further, commodities that are ultimately destined to form the material elements of revenue expenditure, i.e., means of consumption, pass through various stages in the course of the year, e.g., cotton, yarn, cloth. At one stage they form part of constant capital, at another they are consumed individually and go entirely into revenue. It is possible to imagine, therefore, as Adam Smith did, that constant capital is merely an *apparent* element of commodity value, which disappears in the overall context. There is also an exchange of variable capital for revenue. With his wage, the worker buys the portion of commodities that forms his revenue. He thereby returns to the capitalist the money form of the variable capital. Some of the

---

production? > It seems that the 'respectable' desire to express one's satisfaction with bourgeois relationships takes precedence over any desire for truth and any enthusiasm for scientific investigation!

products forming constant capital, finally, are replaced in kind or by exchange between the producers of the constant capital itself, a process that seems to have nothing to do with the consumers. When this is overlooked, the illusion arises that the consumers' revenue replaces the entire product, including the constant portion of value.

|551| (5) Apart from the confusion produced by the transformation of values into prices of production, a further confusion derives from the *transformation of surplus-value* into two separate, mutually independent forms of revenue related to the various elements of production, into profit and rent. It is forgotten that the *values of commodities* are the basis and that the decomposition of this *value* into particular components, and the further *development of these value components* into *forms of revenue*, their *transformation* into relations that the various owners of the different agents of production have to these *particular value components*, their distribution among these owners according to particular categories and titles, alters absolutely nothing in the value determination and its law, although the equalisation of profit, i.e., the distribution of the total surplus-value among the various capitals and the obstacles that landed property in part places in the way of this (in absolute rent) gives rise to *governing average prices* for commodities ('the necessary price') that diverge from their individual values. This again affects only the addition of surplus-value to the various commodity prices; it does not abolish surplus-value itself, nor the total value of commodities as the source of these various price components.

This is the *quid pro quo* which we shall discuss in the following section, and it is necessarily connected with the *illusion* [*Schein*] that value arises from its own components. Firstly, in other words, the various value components of commodities receive independent forms in the *revenues* and are related to the particular material elements of production as their sources, instead to the value of the commodities as their single source. They are indeed related to the elements of production, but not as *components of value*, rather as revenues, as value components *accruing* to these particular categories of agents of production, the worker, the capitalist and the landowner. It is possible then to imagine that the *process happens in reverse*, these components of value, instead of arising from the decomposition of commodity value, actually give rise to it by coming together. This then leads to a splendid vicious circle, in which the value of commodities arises from the value sum of wages, profit and rent, while the value of wages, profit and rent is determined in turn by the value of commodities, etc.[16]

16 'The circulating capital invested in materials, raw materials and finished products is itself composed of commodities, whose necessary price is formed from the same elements, in

If we consider the normal state of reproduction, we see that only a part of the freshly added labour is applied to the production and hence the actual replacement of constant capital, namely the part which replaces the constant capital that has been used up in the production of means of consumption, of commodities that form the material elements of revenue. |552| This is balanced by the fact that the constant portion of Department II costs no *additional labour*. But the constant capital that is *not the product of freshly added labour* (taking the reproduction process as a whole, thus including the equalisation of Departments I and II), although the product could *not* be produced without it, is exposed during the reproduction process, in its material aspect, to accidents and dangers that may decimate it, > such as harvest failures, conflagrations and shipwrecks. < It may also depreciate in value as a result of a change in the productivity of labour, > though this only applies to individual capitalists. < One part of the *profit* accordingly serves as an insurance fund, and thus also a part of the *surplus-value* (and therefore also of the *surplus product*) in which the freshly added labour is expressed. And the nature of the problem is not changed in any way by whether this insurance fund is managed by insurance companies as a separate business or not. This is the *only part* of the revenue that is neither consumed as such nor serves necessarily as an accumulation fund. Whether it actually does serve as such a fund, or simply offsets a shortfall in reproduction, is a matter of chance. This is also the only part of surplus-value and the surplus product, and thus of *surplus labour*, leaving aside the part serving for *accumulation*, i.e., for the expansion of the reproduction process, that would have to continue in existence after the abolition of the capitalist mode of production. In this situation, of course, the part regularly consumed by the direct producers would not remain confined to its current minimum level. Apart from surplus labour for those who cannot yet participate in production on grounds of age, or can no longer do so, there would be no other surplus labour, labour for the maintenance of those who do *not* work.

If we think of the beginnings of society, we find that no produced means of production are yet in existence, hence there is no *constant capital*, whose value goes into the product and has to be replaced in kind from the product on the same scale, in the course of reproduction, to an extent determined by its value.

---

such a way that it would be an unnecessary repetition to count this part of the circulating capital as one of the elements of the necessary price'. (Storch 1815, p. 140.) Among these elements of circulating capital, Storch includes the constant portion of value. (The *fixed* capital is simply circulating capital in a different form.) 'It is true that the worker's wages as well as the portion of the entrepreneur's profit that consists of wages – if one considers these as a portion of means of subsistence – is similarly composed of commodities bought

But in this case nature directly provides means of subsistence that do not first need to be produced. Thus it also gives the savage, who has only a few needs to satisfy, the *time*, if not to use the means of production not yet in existence for new production, then – besides the labour that it takes to appropriate the means of subsistence given ready-made by nature – to transform other natural products into means of production, such as a bow, a stone knife, etc. This process in the case of the savage completely corresponds, taking simply the material aspect, to the transformation of surplus labour back into new capital. In the process of accumulation, we still have the continued utilisation of excess labour for the production of capital, and the fact that all new capital arises from *profit*, *rent* or other forms of *revenue*, i.e., from surplus labour, leads to the false idea that *all commodity value* arises from a revenue.[17]

---

at the current price, which themselves include wages, capital-rents, ground-rents and profits of enterprise ... this observation only goes to prove that it is *impossible to resolve the necessary price into its simplest elements*' (ibid., note). In his polemic against Say (Storch 1824) he does show that he understands the absurdity of the conclusion which follows from the false analysis of commodity value that resolves it just into revenue, and he does correctly point out the ridiculous character of this result, from the standpoint of a nation rather than that of the individual capitalist. But he does not himself take a single step further in his analysis of the 'necessary price', which, as he explained earlier in his *Cours d'économie politique*, is impossible to resolve into its actual elements instead of a false infinite regress. 'It is apparent that the value of the annual product can be divided on the one hand into capital, on the other into profit, and that each of these portions of value of the annual product will regularly buy the products that the nation needs, both to maintain its capital and to replace its consumption stock' (Storch 1824, pp. 134–5) ... 'Can they' (a self-sustaining family) 'live in their barns or stables, eat up their seed-corn and animal fodder, slaughter their draught cattle for clothes, and amuse themselves with their agricultural implements? According to M. Say's doctrine, all these questions have to be answered in the affirmative'. (Storch 1824, pp. 135–6.) 'Once it is conceded that the revenue of a nation is equal to its gross product, i.e. that no *capital* has to be deducted, it must also be conceded that the nation can consume the entire value of its annual product unproductively, without doing the slightest damage to its future revenue'. (Storch 1824, p. 147.) 'The products that make up a nation's capital are not consumable'. (Storch 1824, p. 150.)

17 The entire problem arises from the way that all freshly added labour, in so far as the value it creates is not reducible to wages, appears as *profit*, conceived here as the general form of surplus-value, i.e., as a value that costs the capitalist nothing, so that it certainly does not have to replace anything advanced, any capital. This value exists therefore in the form of additional available wealth, i.e., from the standpoint of the individual capitalist in the form of his revenue. But this newly created value can be *consumed as well productively as it can individually*, as *capital* as well as *revenue*. Its natural form already dictates that it must in

|553| This transformation of profit back into capital rather shows the opposite on closer analysis, i.e., it shows that the additional labour – which always takes the form of revenue – serves not to maintain or reproduce the old capital value but rather to create new and additional capital, in so far as it is not consumed as revenue.

We see, moreover, that one part of the freshly added labour is constantly absorbed in the reproduction and replacement of the constant capital consumed, even if this freshly added labour can be *completely* resolved into revenues – wages, profit and rent. It is overlooked in this connection, however, (1) that the value component of the product of this labour is not the product of the freshly added labour but constant capital that was already in existence and has been used up; hence that part of the product in which this value component is expressed is not transformed into revenue but replaces the means of production of this constant capital in kind; (2) that the value component in which this freshly added labour is actually expressed is *not* consumed in kind as revenue but rather replaces the *constant capital* in another sphere, where it exists in a natural form in which it can be consumed as revenue, even if this is *not* exclusively the product of freshly added labour.

For reproduction to continue to proceed on the same scale, each element of constant capital must be replaced (at least in efficacy if not in quantity) by a new item of *the same* kind. If the productivity of labour remains the same, this replacement in kind involves the replacement of the same *value* that the constant capital had in its old form. But if the productivity of labour rises, so that the same material elements can be reproduced with less labour, a *smaller* value component of the product can replace the constant part fully in kind. The surplus can then go towards forming new additional capital, > or it can give a greater amount of the product a form in which it can be consumed < or the surplus labour can be reduced. If, on the other hand, the productivity of labour declines, a part of the surplus product must go into replacing the old capital instead of functioning as before as surplus product.

If we make abstraction from the specific economic form and consider it simply from the standpoint of the formation of new means of production > (new objective conditions of labour) < the transformation of profit (or rent, or any kind of surplus-value) back into capital shows that there is always a situation in which the worker spends additional labour on producing means of pro-

part be consumed productively. It is also clear that the labour added each year creates both *capital* and revenue, as is then shown also in the process of accumulation. But the portion of the working day used for the creation of new capital (i.e., in our analogy the part of the

duction, on top of that spent in obtaining his immediate means of subsistence. The transformation of profit into capital is nothing more than the use of a part of the additional labour to form new and additional means of production. If this happens in the form of the transformation of *profit* into *capital*, it simply means that it is not the worker but the capitalist who has the surplus labour at his disposal. If this surplus labour must first go through a stage in which it appears as *revenue* (whereas in the case of the savage, for example, it appears as labour immediately directed to the production of the means of production), it simply means that this labour, or its product, has first been appropriated by a *non-worker*. What is actually transformed into capital is not *profit* as such. In relation to capital, the transformation of surplus-value simply means that the surplus-value and surplus product are not individually consumed by the capitalist, > that he does not spend the value in question < as revenue. What is really transformed in this way is *value*, objectified labour, and the product in which this value is directly expressed, or for which it is exchanged, after prior conversion into money. Even if profit is transformed back into capital, it is not this specific *form* of surplus-value, *profit*, that forms the source of the new capital. Surplus-value, in this connection, is simply transformed from one form into the other. But it is not this *formal transformation* that makes it into capital. It is the commodity and its value that now function as capital. But it is completely immaterial for the objectification of this labour, for value itself, that the *value* of the commodity is *not paid* – and it is only in this way that it becomes surplus-value.

|554| The whole misunderstanding is expressed in various forms. One form, for instance, is that the *commodities* which *constant capital* consists of themselves contain elements of wages, profit and rent. Or that what is revenue for one person is capital for another, and that these are therefore simply *subjective* relationships. Thus the spinner's yarn contains a value component that represents profit for him. If the weaver buys the yarn, he realises the spinner's profit,

---

working day that the savage spends not in appropriating the fruit, but rather in shaping the wooden implement with which he appropriates the fruit) then becomes invisible, because the entire product of the surplus labour presents itself first of all in the form of *profit*, a characteristic which in fact has nothing to do with this surplus product itself, but simply bears on the monetary relationship between the capitalist and the surplus-value he pockets. In actual fact, the surplus-value that the worker creates can be divided into revenue and capital, i.e., into means of consumption and *additional* means of production. But the *old constant capital* (apart from the part that is *damaged*, i.e., *destroyed* to that extent, hence not reproduced, and insurance is there to take care of such disturbances of the reproduction process) is not reproduced by the freshly added labour (viewed in terms of its *value*).

but as far as the former is concerned the yarn is simply part of his constant capital.

In addition to what we said previously about the relation between revenue and capital, we should note here that what goes into the weaver's capital with the yarn, as a constituent element considered in value terms, is the *value of the yarn*, the *value of the commodity*. How the components of this value might be reducible for the spinner into capital and revenue, in other words into paid and unpaid labour, is a matter of complete indifference for determining the value of the commodity itself (apart from modifications deriving from *average profit*). Always lurking in the background is the idea that profit, and the surplus in general, is an *excess over and above the value of the commodity*, made in fact by a surcharge, by mutual cheating, and by profit upon expropriation.[18] But since the production price of the commodity is paid, or even its value, so too are those value components of the commodity that appear to their seller in the form of revenue. (*Monopoly prices* are not at issue here.)

Secondly, it is quite correct that the commodity components which constant capital consists of are reducible like all other commodity value to value components that could be resolved for their producers and the owners of the means of production into wages, profit and rent. But as we have already shown in our analysis [in Book One] this by no means prevents one part of the commodity product of each capital from exclusively representing the constant capital component, another the variable capital component and a third the surplus-value.

Storch puts forward what is also the opinion of many other people when he says: 'The saleable products that make up the national revenue must be considered by political economy in two different ways: as values, in relation to individuals; and as goods, in relation to the nation; for the revenue of a nation is not assessed like that of an individual, according to its value, but rather according to its utility, or according to the needs which it can satisfy' (Storch 1824, p. 19.)

Firstly, it is a *false abstraction* to treat a nation whose mode of production is based on value, and which, moreover, is organised on a capitalist basis, as a unified body simply working for national needs.

Secondly, even after the capitalist mode of production has been abolished, *social* production will remain, and the *determination of value* will still prevail in the sense that the *regulation of labour-time* and the *distribution of social labour* among the various branches of production will become more essential than ever, as well as the keeping of accounts on this.

18 ['Expropriation' is in English in the original. Translator]

(3) The Illusion [*Schein*] of Competition

We have shown that the value of commodities, or the price of production governed by their total value, can be resolved into:

(1) A value component that replaces *constant capital* or represents *past labour*, which entered into the commodity in the form of means of production; in short, the *value* or price at which these means of production went into the commodity's production process. We are referring here not to the individual commodity but always to *commodity capital*, i.e., the form which the product of capital takes over a definite period of time, e.g., annually, and of which the *individual* commodity forms only one element. > The *individual commodity* can be divided into identical components as a portion of the *commodity product* of capital.

< (2) The *value component of variable capital* that measures the income of the worker and is transformed for him into *wages*, wages therefore which the worker has reproduced in this variable component; in short, the value component which represents the *paid portion* of the *labour freshly added* to the first, constant portion in the production of the commodity.

(3) The *surplus-value*, i.e., the value component of the commodity product in which the *unpaid labour* or *surplus labour* is expressed. This last value component again assumes those independent forms that are at the same time *forms of revenue*; the forms of *profit* on *capital* (*interest* on capital as such, and *profit of enterprise* on capital as functioning capital), and *ground-rent*, which falls to the owner of the land which is playing its part in the actual production process. Components (2) and (3), taken together, are the *value component* that always assumes the revenue forms of *wages* (this only after it previously had the form of *variable capital*), *profit* and *rent*. This is distinguished from the constant component (1) by the fact that it *contains* the whole of the value in which there is objectified the *labour freshly added* to that constant part, the means of production of the commodity. If we leave aside the constant component of value, it is correct to say that the value of a commodity, in so far as this represents freshly added labour, is always *reducible* to three elements, *wages*, *profit* and *rent*,[19] which constitute the three forms of revenue, while the respective value magnitudes, i.e., the aliquot parts that these form of the total value, are determined by different, specific laws that have already been developed. It would be wrong, however, to say, conversely, that the value of wages, the rate of profit and

19 [Engels turned the paragraph which begins on page 574 of Marx's manuscript into a footnote at this point. Translator]

the rate of rent are *independent constituent elements of value*, with the *value of the commodity*, minus its constant component, arising from their *combination*; in other words it would be wrong to say that these form *constituent components* of commodity value or of the price of production.[20]

The distinction can readily be seen.

Assume that the value produced by a capital of 500 is 650, namely 400c + 100v + 150s. The 150s breaks down again into 75 *profit* and 75 *rent.* > (Hence 30 percent on 500, 15 percent of which is profit + interest, 15 percent rent.) < We shall further assume, in order to avoid needless difficulties, that this capital is of average composition, so that its production price and its value coincide. This is the case whenever the product of this individual capital can be treated as the product of a part of the total capital corresponding to it in size. Here wages, as measured by the variable capital, make up 20 percent of the capital advanced; the surplus-value, reckoned on the total capital, makes up 30 percent, i.e., 15 percent profit and 15 percent rent. |556| The total value component of the commodity in which the *freshly added labour* is objectified is 250, independently of its division, respectively, into wages, profit and rent. The proportionate relationship between these components shows that the labour-power which was paid for with £100 has supplied a quantum of labour expressed in a sum of money (in pounds sterling, say) of 250. We can see from this that the worker has performed one and a half times as much surplus labour as he has labour for himself. With a working day of 10 hours he would be working 4 hours for himself and 6 hours for the capitalist (4: 6 = 100: 150). The labour of the workers who are paid £100 is expressed therefore in a money value of £250. Apart from this value of £250, there is nothing left to be shared between worker and capitalist, or capitalist and landowner. It is the total value freshly added to the value of the means of production, which was £400. The commodity value of £250 thus produced, and determined by the amount of labour objectified in it, sets the limit to the dividends that the worker, capitalist and landlord can draw from this value in the form of revenue – wages, profit and rent.

Let us assume that a capital of the same organic composition, i.e., the same proportion between living labour-power applied and constant capital

20 'It will be sufficient to remark, that the same general rule which regulates the value of raw produce and manufactured commodities, is applicable also to the metals; their value depending not on the rate of profits, nor on the rate of wages, nor on the rent paid for mines, but on the total quantity of labour necessary to obtain the metal, and to bring it to market'. (Ricardo 1821, p. 77.)

set in motion > (on the assumption that the value of that constant capital also remains the same) < is forced to pay £150 instead of £100 for the same labour-power, and that profit and rent are also divided in different proportions. We should then have 400c + 150v + 100s, and the 100s breaks down now into 45 *profit* + 55 *rent.* In this case, since it is assumed that the variable capital of 150 sets in motion the same amount of labour as the 100 did previously, the newly produced value would still be 250 and the value of the total product would continue to be 650. But the rates of wages, profit and rent, i.e., the proportion in which the newly produced total value was divided, would be very different. So too would be the total capital advanced, even though it only sets in motion the same amount of labour. Wages would make up $27\frac{3}{11}$ percent of the capital advanced, profit $8\frac{2}{11}$ percent, and rent 10 percent on this capital, so that the total surplus-value would be somewhat more than 18 percent. > (The new division into $363\frac{7}{11}$ constant capital, $136\frac{4}{11}$ variable capital and $90\frac{24}{33}$ surplus-value corresponds to a surplus-value of a little over 18 percent.) < The increase in wages would alter the unpaid part of the total labour, and with it the total surplus-value. The worker would have worked 6 hours of the 10-hour working day for himself and only 4 hours for the capitalist. The proportions of profit and rent would also be different, and the diminished surplus-value would be divided in a changed proportion between capitalist and landowner. Finally, since the value of the constant capital has remained unaltered while the value of the variable capital advanced has risen, the diminished surplus-value would be expressed in a still further reduced gross *rate of profit,* by which we mean here the ratio of the total surplus-value to the total capital advanced.

These *changes* in the value of wages, the rate of profit and the rate of rent, whatever the effect of the inherent laws governing the proportions between these parts, could take place only within the limits set by the newly created commodity value of 250. (The only exception would be if rent created a monopoly price for the commodity. This would in no way affect the law, but simply make it more complicated to examine it. For if we are dealing in this case simply with the product itself, it is only the division of the surplus-value that would vary; while if we are considering its relative value vis-à-vis other commodities, the only difference would be that one part of the surplus-value would be transferred from these to our specific commodity.)

|557| We can see the situation from the following example:

	c	v	s	Rate of profit	Rate of surplus-value	Value of product	To be distributed as revenue
First case	400	100	150	30%	150%	650	250
Second case	400	150	100	c. 18%	66⅔%	650	250

In the second case, a capital of 500 would be divided as follows:

	c	v	s	Rate of profit	Rate of surplus-value	Value of product	To be distributed as revenue
	363 7/11	136 4/11	c. 90	c. 18%	66⅔	590	226

Thus the surplus-value, firstly, falls by a third of its former amount, from 150 to 100. The rate of profit falls by somewhat more than a third, from 30 percent to around 18 percent. If it fell by only a third it would fall to 20 percent. It falls *somewhat more* than the *surplus-value,* because the diminished surplus-value has to be reckoned against an increased total capital advanced. But it does not fall in *the same* proportion as the *rate of surplus-value,* > which falls from 150 percent to 66⅔ percent, because the differences between the *rates of profit* are determined by the proportions 150: 400 + 100 and 100: 400 + 150, or 150: 500 and 100: 550, whereas the differences between the *rates of surplus-value* are determined by the proportions 150: 100 and 100: 150.

< The *rate of profit* falls more than the *actual* absolute *surplus-value,* but it falls less than the *rate of surplus-value.*

It is also evident from the above that the values and quantities produced remain the same if the same *amount of labour* is still applied as before, even though the *capital advanced* has expanded as a result of the increase in its variable component. This *expansion of the capital advanced* would also be very evident for a capitalist opening a new business (a fresh capital investment), but, *taking reproduction as a whole,* it means nothing more than that a greater part of the *value newly created* by the freshly added labour is transformed into *wages,* and therefore first of all into *variable capital,* instead of into *surplus-value* and *surplus product.* The *value of the product* thus remains the same, since it is limited by the figure of 250, which represents the freshly added labour. This product, if it itself went back into constant capital, would still represent the same amount, with the same magnitude of value, i.e., the same amount of constant capital would retain the same value. The situation would be different if *wages* rose, not because the worker would keep a *greater part* of his own labour, but because the productivity of labour would have declined, allowing him to keep a greater part of his own labour as a result. In this case, the *total value* in which the same labour was expressed, i.e., paid and unpaid labour, would remain *the same*; but this quantity of labour would be expressed in a diminished product, hence the *price of each part of the product* would rise, since each part represented more labour. The increased wage of 150 would represent a product no greater than 100 did before; the diminished surplus-value of 100 would now represent only two-thirds of the former product, 66⅔ percent of the product that was previously expressed in 100. In this case, the constant capital would also become more expensive, in so far as this product entered into it. But that would not be the result of the increase in wages, but rather the increase in wages would result from the fact that the commodity had become more expensive as a result of the diminution in productivity of the same amount of labour. The illusion [*Schein*] arises that the rise in wages has made the product dearer; but here this is not the *cause* but the *consequence* of a change in the commodity's value resulting from the diminished productivity of labour.

If, on the other hand, the *value* of the means of production applied by the same amount of labour rises or falls (and assuming otherwise identical circumstances, in which the same amount of labour applied is expressed in the figure 250), it follows that the *value of the product*, of the same volume of products, will rise or fall by the same amount. 450c + 100v + 150s gives a product value of 700 for what had a value of 650 previously, while 350c + 100v + 150s gives a product value of 600 for what had a value of 650 previously.

Thus, if the capital advanced for putting the same amount of labour in motion grows or declines, the value of the product rises or falls, conditions being otherwise identical, as long as the increase or decrease in the capital advanced derives from a change in the value magnitude of the constant capital component. It remains *unchanged*, on the other hand, if the increase or decrease in the capital advanced derives from a change in the value magnitude of the *variable component of the capital*, with labour productivity remaining the same. As far as constant capital is concerned, the increase or decrease in its value is not compensated for by any movement in the opposite direction. In the case of variable capital, assuming that the productivity of labour remains the same, the increase or decrease in its value is compensated for by a movement in the opposite direction on the part of surplus-value, so that there is no change in the value of the variable capital plus the surplus-value, hence the value freshly added to the means of production by labour and expressed in the product also remains unchanged.

If the increase or decrease in the variable capital or wages is the result of a rise or fall in commodity prices, i.e., of a decrease or increase in the productivity of the labour applied in that capital investment, this does affect the value of the product. But in this case the rise or fall in wages is not the cause but the consequence.

If in the above example we were to replace 400c + 100v + 150s with 400c + 150v + 100s, and to assume that the rise in variable capital from 100 to 150 was the result of a decline in labour productivity not in this particular branch, e.g., the cotton industry, but rather in agriculture, which provides the workers' means of sustenance, the value of the product would remain unchanged. The value of 650 would still be expressed in the same amount of cotton yarn as before.

The following point also emerges from what we have developed here: if the reduction in the outlay on constant capital is the effect of economy, etc., in branches of production whose products go into the workers' consumption, this could lead to a *reduction* in wages just as could a direct increase in the productivity of the labour applied, because it would cheapen those commodities and hence increase surplus-value. In this case the rate of profit would rise for two reasons: on the one hand because the value of the constant capital would have declined, and on the other hand because surplus-value would have increased. In considering the transformation of surplus-value into profit, we assumed that wages did not fall but remained constant, since we were concerned there to investigate the fluctuations in the rate of profit *independently* |558| of changes in the rate of surplus-value. The laws developed there, however, are *general* ones, and apply also for capital investments where the products do *not* go into the consumption of the workers, so that changes in the value of the product are without influence on wages.

The *value freshly added each year by new labour* to the means of production or the constant component of capital can be separated out and resolved into the different revenue forms of wages, profit and rent; this does not change anything in the *limits of the value* itself, the *sum of value* that is divided between these different categories. In the same way, a change in the ratio of these individual portions among themselves cannot affect their sum, which is a *given amount*. > The autonomisation of the categories is itself a merely *formal autonomisation* and the change in the proportions between these *portions of value* leaves the *value* which is divided in the same way as a < given figure of 100 always remains the same whether it is divided into 50 + 50, or 20 + 70 + 10, or 50 + 25 + 25. The value component of the product that is broken down into these revenues is determined, just as the constant value component of the capital is, by the *value of the commodities*, i.e., by the relative quantity of labour materialised in them. What is given first, therefore, is the mass of commodity values to be divided into wages, profit and rent, i.e., the absolute *limit* to the sum of value portions in these commodities. *Secondly*, as far as the individual categories themselves are concerned, their average and governing limits are similarly given. *In this delimitation, wages form the basis*. In this respect they are governed by a natural law; this minimum limit is given by the physical minimum of means of subsistence that the worker must receive in order to maintain his labour-power and make it permanent (reproduce it). It is therefore given by a *definite amount of commodities*. The value of these commodities is determined by the labour-time required for their reproduction, hence by the portion of labour *freshly added* to the means of production, in other words by the *portion of the working day* that the worker requires in order to produce and reproduce an equivalent for the value of these necessary means of subsistence. If his average means of subsistence come to 6 hours of average labour per day, he must spend on average some 6 hours of his daily labour working for himself. The *actual value* of his *labour-power* diverges from this *physical minimum*; it differs according to the level of social development (and also varies with differences in climate); it depends not only on physical needs but also on historically developed social needs, which become second nature. In each country, however, this *governing average wage* is a given quantity at any given period. The value of all other revenues thus has a limit. This is always equal to the value represented by the total working day (which coincides here with the average working day, since we are dealing here with the total amount of labour set in motion by the total social capital), minus the part of it realised in wages. Its limit is therefore given by the limit of the value representing unpaid labour, i.e., by the amount of this unpaid labour. If the part of the working day that the worker needs to reproduce the value of his wage has its ultimate barrier in the *physical minimum* of this wage, the other part of the working day, in which surplus labour is expressed, i.e., the *value component* that expresses surplus-value, has its barrier in the *physical maximum of the working day*, i.e., in the total physical quantity of labour-time the worker can provide if he is to maintain and reproduce his labour-power. Since what we are dealing with here is the distribution of the *value* in which the total labour freshly added each year is expressed, the *working day* can be taken as a *constant* quantity, and it is assumed to be so however much or little it may depart from its physical maximum. We thus have an absolute limit for the value component that |559| forms surplus-value and can be broken down into profit and ground-rent; this is determined by the excess of the unpaid portion of the working day over its paid portion, i.e., by the value component of the total product in which *this surplus labour* is realised. If we call the surplus-value whose limits are thus determined profit, when it is calculated on the total capital advanced, as we have already done, this profit, considered in its absolute amount, is equal to the surplus-value, i.e., it is just as regularly determined in its limits as the latter is. It is the ratio between the total surplus-value and the total social capital advanced in production. If this capital is 500 (it can be millions) and the surplus-value 100, the absolute limit to the *rate of profit* is 20 percent. The division of the social profit among the capitals applied in the various different spheres of production which is measured by this rate produces *prices of production* which diverge from commodity value and which are the actual averages governing market prices. But this divergence from value abolishes neither the determination of prices by values nor the *limits imposed on profit* by the laws we have developed. The value of a commodity, instead of being equal to the capital consumed in it plus the surplus-value it contains, is now equal to the capital, C, consumed in it plus the surplus-value that falls to it by virtue of the general rate of profit, say 20 percent, on the total capital advanced for its production, whether the capital is consumed or simply applied. This surcharge of 20 percent, however, is itself determined by the surplus-value created by the total social capital, and its proportion to the value of this capital; and that is why it is 20 percent and not 10 percent or 100 percent. Therefore the transformation of values into prices of production does not abolish the limits to profit but rather simply alters its distribution among the various particular capitals of which the social capital is composed, distributing it across them evenly, in proportion as they form value components of this total capital. Market prices rise above these governing production prices or fall below them, but these fluctuations balance each other out. If one contemplates price lists over a prolonged period, and ignores those cases in which the actual value of a commodity alters as a result of a change in labour productivity, as well as cases in which the production process is disturbed by natural or social disasters, it is surprising both how narrow the limits of these divergences are and how regularly they are balanced out. The same rule of governing averages is found here as the one Quételet demonstrated in connection with social phenomena.[21]

If the adjustment of commodity values to prices of production does not meet with any obstacles, *rent* is reduced to *differential rent*, i.e., it is restricted to the cancellation of the *surplus profits* that the governing prices of production would give to one section of capitalists, these now being appropriated by the

---

21 [Quételet 1848. Translator]

landowners. Thus *rent* has its definite value limits here in the divergences among the individual rates of profit that are produced when production prices are governed by the general rate of profit. If landed property places obstacles in the way of this adjustment of commodity values to prices of production, and appropriates an *absolute rent,* this is limited by the excess of the *value* of agricultural products over and above their prices of production, i.e., by the excess surplus-value contained in them over and above the profits that capitals receive by virtue of the general rate of profit. This *difference* then fixes the limit of the rent, which continues to form simply a specific portion of the given surplus-value contained in the commodities.

|560| Finally, if the equalisation of surplus-value to average profit in the various spheres of production meets with obstacles in the form of artificial or natural monopolies, and particularly the monopoly of landed property, so that a *monopoly price* can be enforced, higher than both the price of production and the value of the commodities this monopoly affects, this does not mean that the limits fixed by commodity value are abolished. A *monopoly price* for certain commodities simply transfers a portion of the profit made by the other commodity producers to the commodities with the monopoly price. Indirectly, there is a local disturbance in the *distribution* of surplus-value among the various spheres of production, but this leaves the *limits* themselves unaffected. If the commodity with the monopoly price is part of the workers' necessary consumption, it increases > the *value* of < wages and thereby reduces surplus-value, as long as the workers continue to receive the *value of their labour-power*. It could reduce the wage itself > (although its value would remain the same) < but only if it previously stood above the physical minimum. In that case, the monopoly price is paid through a deduction from real wages (i.e., a deduction from the amount of use-values the worker receives for the same amount of labour) and is paid out of the *profit* of other capitalists. The limits within which a monopoly price affects the normal regulation of commodity prices are firmly determined and can be precisely calculated.

Just as the division of the commodity value newly added and completely reducible to revenue finds its given and governing limits in the proportion between necessary and surplus labour, wages and surplus-value, so the division of this surplus-value itself into profit and ground-rent finds its limits in the laws governing the equalisation of the profit rate. > As far as *interest* and *profit of enterprise* are concerned < the *average profit* itself sets the limit for both of them. It sets the given amount of value they have to share, and there is no more than this for them to share. The *specific ratio* of this division is *accidental* here, i.e., it is determined exclusively by relations of competition. Whereas in other cases market prices cease to diverge from the average prices which govern them when demand and supply match each other, and the effect of competition is abolished, here this is the only determining factor. And why? Because a factor of production, capital, has to share the *portion of surplus-value accruing to it* between two owners of this same factor of production. But if the division of average profit has in this case no determining limit as imposed by the laws we have developed, that does not abolish this limit as a portion of commodity value; as little as when two partners in a company share their profit unequally, because of different external circumstances, this in any way affects the limits of this profit.

Thus if the *portion of commodity value* representing or expressing *labour freshly added* to the value of the means of production breaks down into different portions, which assume mutually independent shapes in the form of *revenues*, this does not in any way mean that wages, profit and ground-rent are now to be considered as the *constituent elements*, with the governing price (natural price, necessary price) of *commodities* itself arising from their *combination* or *sum*; so that it would not be the commodity value, after deduction of the constant value component, that was the original unity and breaks down into these three components, but the price of each of these three components was rather determined independently, and the *commodity's price* originated only from the addition of these three independent magnitudes. In actual fact commodity value is the *quantitative premise*, the sum total value of wages, profit and rent, whatever their relative magnitudes may be. In the false conception considered here, however, wages, profit and rent are three independent amounts of value, whose total produces, limits and determines the total amount of commodity value.

|561| It is evident from the start that if wages, profit and rent constituted the *price of commodities*, this would necessarily hold good both for the constant portion of commodity value and for the other portion in which variable capital and surplus-value are represented. This constant part can therefore be left out of consideration here, since the value of the commodities it consists of would likewise break down into the sum of the values of wages, profit and rent. As already noted in section 2,[22] this view also involves a denial of the existence of such a constant value component.

It is also evident that any concept of value would vanish here. All that was left would be the idea of *price*, in the sense that a certain amount of money is paid to the owners of labour-power, capital and land. But what is money? Money is not a thing but a particular form of value, so that it again presupposes

22 [See above, page 548 of the manuscript. Translator]

value. What is said, therefore, is that a certain amount of gold or silver is paid for those 'elements of production', or that they are mentally equated with this amount. But gold and silver are themselves commodities like all others (and enlightened economics is proud of its ability to recognise this). The price of gold and silver is thus also determined by wages, profit and rent. So we cannot determine wages, profit and rent by equating them with a certain quantity of gold and silver, for the value of this gold and silver, as the equivalent in which they are to be assessed, is precisely supposed to be determined by wages, profit and rent independently of gold and silver, i.e., independently of the value of *any* commodity, which is precisely their product. To say that the value of wages, profit and rent consists in their being equal to a certain amount of gold and silver is thus simply to say that they are equal to a certain amount of wages, profit and rent.

Let us first take *wages*, for even from this angle it is necessary to start from labour. How then is the governing price of wages determined, the price around which the market price oscillates?

By the demand for, and supply of, labour-power, it will be said. But what demand for labour-power are we talking about? *The demand from capital.* The demand for labour is thus equal to the *supply of capital.* To speak of the supply of capital we must first of all know what capital is. What does capital consist of? Let us take its simplest manifestation: money and commodities. But money is simply a form of commodity. So it consists of commodities. The value of commodities, however, is determined in the first instance, on the present assumption, by the price of the labour producing them, wages. Wages are presupposed here, and treated as a constituent element of the *price of the commodity.* > The *price of labour* is therefore presupposed as a constituent element of the price.

< This price must then be determined by the proportion of labour on offer to capital. > The price of capital itself is equal to the price of the commodities of which it consists. < Capital's demand for labour is equal to the supply of capital. The supply of capital is equal to the supply of a sum of commodities of a given price and this price is in the first instance regulated by the price of labour, the price of labour being equal in turn to the portion of commodity price which constitutes variable capital and is handed to the worker in exchange for his labour. > But the price of the commodities which make up capital is itself determined in the first instance by the price of labour.

Capital's demand is equal to its supply. Its supply is the supply of a particular quantity of commodities part of which have the task of forming the price of labour, and have to be spent as *wages.* < But the price of these commodities, of which the capital consists, is determined by wages, profit and rent. The determination of wages cannot start from capital, for the value of capital is itself determined by wages.

Moreover, it is no use bringing in competition. Competition makes the market price of labour rise or fall. But assume that the demand for and supply of labour match each other. How are wages determined then? By competition? But we have just presupposed that competition ceases to be a determinant, that its effect is abolished by the establishment of an equilibrium between its two counteracting forces. And our intention is precisely to find the *natural price* of wages, i.e., a price of labour which is not governed by competition, but on the contrary governs competition.

|562| Nothing remains, then, but to determine the *necessary price* of labour by reference to the worker's necessary means of subsistence. But these means of subsistence are commodities, and they have a price. The *price of labour* is thus determined by the *price of the necessary means of subsistence*, and the price of the means of subsistence, like that of all other commodities, is determined in the first instance by the *price of labour*. So the price of labour, > as determined by the price of the means of subsistence, < is determined by the price of labour. > The price of labour is determined by itself. < In other words, we do not know how the price of labour is determined. > (We do not know what *price* is in general. For price is in the first instance a certain sum of money. This sum of money, however, is equal to the *price* of the commodities it can buy. What then is the price of these commodities?) < Labour always has a *price* here, since it is considered as a commodity. Thus in order to speak of the price of labour, we must know what *price* in general is, > irrespective of the price of this *particular* commodity. (In order to determine the *price* of the commodity, we determine the *prices* of *definite*, specific commodities.)

< Let us assume, however, that the *necessary price of labour* is determined in this delightful way. What about the *average profit*, then, the profit of any capital in normal conditions? The price of the commodity is now = W, i.e., = the wage embodied in it. The average profit must be determined by an *average rate of profit*, > i.e., a certain proportion to the first element in the price of the commodity, which is W, wages. < Is this determined by competition between the capitalists? But this *competition* already assumes the existence of profit. It assumes different rates of profit and hence different profits, whether in the same branch of production or in different branches. Competition can act on the profit rate only by acting on the prices of commodities. Competition can only bring it about that producers *within* the same sphere of production sell their commodities at *the same* price, and that within different spheres of production they sell their commodities at prices which give them *the same* profit, the same proportionate surcharge to the price of the commodity that

has initially been determined by wages. Hence competition can only even out inequalities in the rate of profit. In order to even out *unequal* rates of profit, *profit* must be presupposed as an element of commodity price. Competition does not create profit from nothing. It can raise or lower it, but it does not create the level that is present as soon as this equalisation has taken place. And in so far as we speak of a *necessary* rate of profit, we precisely want to know the *rate of profit* independently of the movement of competition, we want to know the rate which actually governs competition. The average rate of profit appears when there is a balance of forces between the competing capitalists. Competition can produce this equilibrium, but not the *rate of profit* which then emerges. For what reason, when the forces are in balance, is the general *rate of profit* 10 percent, or 20 percent or even 100 percent? Because of competition. But, conversely, competition has abolished the causes that produced divergences from the rates of 10, 20 or 100 percent. It has brought about commodity prices at which each capital yields *the same* profit. But the *level of this profit* is independent of competition. All competition does is persistently reduce all divergences to this level. One person competes with another, and competition forces him to sell his commodity at the same price as the next man. But why is this price 10, or 20, or 100?

There is nothing left for it, then (since competition has to take on itself the burden of explaining all the irrationalities of the economists, whereas it was actually their job to explain competition) but to declare that the *rate of profit* and hence *profit itself* is a surcharge, determined in an incomprehensible way, on the price of the commodity, which is determined by wages. The only thing competition tells us is that this *rate of profit* must be at *a given* level. But we already knew that when we spoke of the general rate of profit and the 'necessary price' of profit.

It is completely unnecessary to repeat this absurd process for ground-rent.

|563| We can already see that if the process is carried through in any consistent way, it makes profit and rent appear as mere surcharges, determined by incomprehensible laws, on top of a commodity price determined in the first place by *wages*.

If we ignore the fantastic idea of a profit and rent created by *circulation*, i.e., profit and rent as price components arising from *sales* – and the circulation sphere can never yield anything that was not previously put into it – the matter simply comes down to the following:

Say that the price of a commodity as determined by wages is 100, the rate of profit 10 percent on wages, and the rent 15 percent on wages. The commodity price as determined by the sum of wages, profit and rent is then 125. The surcharge of 25 cannot derive from the sale of the commodity. For if everyone who sells to someone else sells what cost 100 at 125, it is the same thing as if they had all sold at 100. The operation must therefore be considered independently of the circulation process.

If the three elements of the commodity price are divided within the commodity itself, and this commodity now costs 125 (and it makes no difference here if the capitalist first sells at 125 and only later pays the worker 100, himself 10 and the landlord 15), the worker receives ⅘ = 4 × 25 = 100 of the value and the product. The capitalist receives ⅒ of what the worker receives, or 2⁄25 of the product, and the recipient of rent 3⁄25. Since the capitalist sells at 125 instead of 100, he gives the worker only ⅘ of the product in which his labour is expressed. It would be the same thing, therefore, if he gave the worker 80 and kept back 20, with 8 of this accruing to him (2⁄25 of *the product*) and 12 to the recipient of rent (3⁄25 of the product). He has then sold the commodity at its value, since in actual fact the price surcharges are independent of the commodity's value, which on this assumption is determined by wages. It emerges by way of this detour, therefore, that the term 'wages' in this conception, = 100, is equal to the value of the product, i.e., to the sum of money in which this particular amount of labour is expressed; but that this *value* is different again from real wages, = 80, and hence leaves a surplus of 20. It is simply that this situation is now brought about by a nominal surcharge to the price. Thus if wages were 110 instead of 100, profit would have to be 11 and ground-rent 16½, i.e., the price of the commodity would be 137½. This would leave the proportions quite unaltered. But since the division is always obtained by a nominal surcharge of a certain percentage on wages, the price rises and falls with wages. First wages are posited as equal to the value of the commodity, and then they are again separated from the value of the commodity. In fact, however, all this irrational detour has achieved is to bring us back to the determination of the value of the commodity by the amount of labour contained in it, while the value of wages is determined by the price of the necessary means of subsistence and the excess of the value over and above wages constitutes profit and rent.

|564| The dissolution of commodity *values* after the deduction of the value of the means of production used up in producing them, hence the dissolution of this *presupposed quantity of value* – a quantity which is determined by the quantity of labour used up in producing the commodity product – into three component parts, which take the shape of autonomous forms of revenue all independent of each other, namely wages, profit and ground-rent – so that for example if this value = 100, wages = x, profit = z and ground-rent = y, 100 is broken down into x + z + y, however their relative magnitudes may change – this dissolution is represented on the immediately visible surface of capitalist production, and hence in the consciousness, and the ideas, of the

agents trapped within it, in a *distorted* fashion, namely as if the price of the commodity were determined by the value magnitudes of wages, profit and rent, which are governed independently of each other, and as if the magnitude of the commodity's own value only results from the *sum* of these independently determined quantities; so that the commodity value is not given as 100 (minus the value of means of production used up in it), this 100 then being divided up into x + z + y, but the converse, x, y and z are each given and determined independently, and it is only from the *sum* of these quantities, which may be greater or less than 100, the commodity's *constituent elements*, that the *magnitude* of the commodity's own *value* results.

This *quid pro quo* is necessary:

Firstly, because the commodity's value components confront each other as independent revenues, which are related *as such* to three completely separate agents of production, labour, capital and the earth, and appear therefore to arise from these. Property in labour-power, capital and the earth is the reason why these different value components of the commodity fall to their respective proprietors, transforming them therefore into their *revenues*. But value does not arise from a *transformation* into revenue, it must rather already be in existence before it can be transformed into revenue and assume this form. The opposite appearance is necessarily reinforced all the more in as much as the relative size of these three parts is determined by different kinds of laws, their relationship with the value of the commodities, and limitation by this, being also by no means indicated on the surface.

Secondly, we have seen that a general rise or fall in wages, by causing the general rate of profit to move in the opposite direction, other things being equal, alters the production prices of various commodities, raising some and making others fall, depending on the average composition of capital in particular spheres of production which produce particular commodities. In some spheres of production, therefore, '*experience*' shows that the average commodity price rises because wages have risen and falls because they have fallen. What is not 'experienced' is the secret regulation of these changes by a commodity value independent of wages. If the change in wages is local, on the other hand (taking place only in particular spheres as a result of specific circumstances), there may be a *nominal* rise in the price of these commodities, > corresponding to the specific rise in wages. < This rise in the relative value of one kind of commodity, in relation to others for which wages remain unchanged, is then simply a reaction to the local disturbance of the uniform distribution of surplus-value over the various spheres of production, a means of adjusting the particular rates of profit to the general rate. 'Experience' here again shows the determination of the price by wages. What is experienced in both of *these* cases is how wages have determined commodity prices. What is not experienced is the hidden basis of this relationship. Moreover, the average price of labour, i.e., the value of labour-power, is determined by the > value < of the necessary means of subsistence. If this rises or falls, so does the price of labour. Thus what is experienced here once again is the connection between wages and the price of commodities; but the cause may present itself as an effect, and the effect as a cause, as is also the case with the movement of market prices, where a rise in wages above their average corresponds to the rise in market prices above prices of production characteristic of periods of prosperity, while the subsequent fall in wages below their average corresponds to the fall in market prices below prices of production. Given the link between production prices and commodity values and leaving aside the oscillating movement of market prices, experience ought always on the face of it to confirm that when wages rise the profit rate falls, and vice versa. But we have seen that the profit rate may be determined, independently of wage movements, by movements in the value of constant capital; so that wages and the rate of profit may rise or fall in the same direction, instead of in inverse directions. If the rate of surplus-value directly coincided with the rate of profit, this case would not occur. Even if wages rise as a result of a rise in the price of the means of subsistence, the rate of profit can remain the same, or rise, as a result of greater intensity of labour or a lengthening of the working day. All these '*experiences*' confirm the *illusion* produced by the *independent, distorted* form of the value components, as if the value of commodities was determined either by wages alone, or by wages and profit together. As soon as this seems to be the case for *wages*, i.e., as soon as the *price of labour* seems to coincide with the *value created by labour*, it is self-evidently the case also for profit and rent. Their prices must then be governed independently of labour and the value created by it.

|565| *Thirdly*, let us assume that the values of commodities, or the prices of production that are only in appearance independent of these, always coincide directly at the phenomenal level with market prices, instead of simply operating as the governing average prices through continuous compensations for the constant fluctuations in market prices, > i.e., the way they rise above or fall below the average level. < Let us further assume that reproduction always takes place under the same unchanging conditions, i.e., that the productivity of labour remains *constant* for all elements of capital. Let us finally assume that the value component of the commodity product that is formed in each sphere of production by adding a new quantum of labour, i.e., a newly produced value, to the value of the means of production, always breaks down in the same proportions into wages, profit and rent, so that the wages actually paid, the profit actually realised and the actual rent, always coincide directly with, respectively,

the value of the labour-power, the portion of the total surplus-value distributed between > each independent portion of the total capital < (each independently functioning portion of the total capital) and the limits to which ground-rent is normally confined on this basis. > In the real movement, on the other hand, the opposite takes place. Just as the market prices of commodities oscillate around their production prices, so does the market price of labour oscillate around the value of labour-power, and in the same way the market rate, or the actual level, of profit and the price of a lease oscillates around the normal average profit and the normal rent.

< Under these assumptions, then, with the values of commodities constant, and *appearing to be so*, with the *value component* of the commodity product that is reducible to revenue forming a constant quantity and always presenting itself as such, and finally with this given and constant portion of value always breaking down in the same proportions into wages, profit and rent – even on these assumptions the real movement would *necessarily* appear in a *distorted form*; not as the dissolution of a value magnitude *given in advance* into three revenues, three parts which take on forms of revenue which are independent of each other, but conversely as the *formation* of this value magnitude as the *sum* of the component elements of wages, profit and ground-rent, taken as determined independently and separately. The reason why this *illusion* [*Schein*] would necessarily arise is that in the real movement of individual capitals and their commodity product what happens is not that the value of the commodity appears as the premise of its dissolution but, on the contrary, the components into which it can be dissolved function as the *premises* for its value.

We saw at the outset that the *cost price* of a commodity appears to each capitalist as a given quantity and constantly presents itself as such in the actual production process. But the cost price is equal to the value of the constant capital, the means of production that have been advanced plus the value of labour-power, although this presents itself to the agents of production in the irrational form of the *price of labour*, so that *wages* too appear as the worker's revenue. The average price of labour is a given magnitude, since the *value of labour-power*, like that of any other commodity, is determined by the labour-time necessary for its reproduction. But as far as the *component of commodity value* that resolves into wages is concerned, this does not arise from the fact that it assumes the form of *wages* – that the capitalist *advances* the wage to the worker > (an advance which, as shown earlier, is itself merely the *phenomenal form* of the worker's respective share in his own product) – < but rather from the fact that the worker produces an equivalent corresponding to his wages, > or the price of his labour, which corresponds in fact to the price or value of his labour-power, < i.e., that one part of his daily or yearly labour produces the value contained in the price of his labour-power. Wages, however, are *agreed* by contract, > and, at least in law, paid, < before the value equivalent corresponding to them is produced > by the freshly added labour. < And |566| since they are a *price element* whose magnitude is given before the commodity and its value are produced, a component of the *cost price*, wages appear not as a part separated off from the total value of the commodity in an independent form, but rather the reverse, as a given magnitude that determines the total value in advance, i.e., as a *formative element of price or value*.

Average profit plays a role in the *price of production* similar to that played by wages in the commodity's *cost price*, for the price of production is equal to the cost price plus the average profit on the capital advanced. This average profit has a practical bearing in the mind and accounting of the capitalist himself as a regulating element, not only in so far as it determines the transfer of capital from one sphere of investment into another, but also for all sale and contracts involved in a reproduction process extending over a prolonged period. But in so far as it has this practical bearing, it is a magnitude *fixed in advance*, which really is independent of the value and surplus-value produced in any particular sphere of production, and even more independent, accordingly, of each individual capital investment in any of these spheres. Instead of being the result of a division in value, it rather presents the *appearance* [*Erscheinung*] of a magnitude independent of the value of the commodity product, given in advance of the commodity's *production process* and itself determining the average price of the commodity, i.e., it presents the appearance of a *formative element of value*. Surplus-value, moreover, as a result of the separation of its various parts into forms which are completely independent of one another, appears as a premise of the commodity's *value formation in a far more concrete form*. One part of the average profit, in the form of interest, confronts the functioning capitalist from an independent position as an element already *presupposed* in the production of commodities and their value. Much as the amount of interest may fluctuate, it is at any given moment and for any single capitalist a given magnitude, which for him, the individual capitalist, enters into the *cost price* of the commodities he produces. The same can be said of *ground-rent*, in the form of the contractually agreed lease-money paid by the agricultural capitalist, > and in the form of *house rent*, or, in the case of other entrepreneurs, the rent they pay for the ground on which their factory buildings rest, and for the space in which the production process takes place, which is to a greater or lesser degree a fixed cost for every enterprise. < These constituents, into which surplus-value can be resolved, since as elements of the cost price they are given for the individual capitalist, therefore *appear* in inverted form, as the *formative elements of surplus-value*, forming one portion of commodity prices in the way that wages form the other.

The secret reason why these products of the dissolution of commodity value constantly appear as the *premises* of value formation itself is simply this, that the *capitalist mode of production*, like every other, constantly reproduces not only the material product but also the socio-economic relations that form it, its *formal economic determinants*. Its result thus constantly appears as its premise, and its premises as its results. And it is this constant reproduction of the same relationships which the individual capitalist *anticipates* as self-evident, as an indubitable fact. As long as capitalist production continues, one part of the labour newly added is constantly resolved into wages, another into profit (interest and profit of enterprise) and the third into rent. This is *assumed* in the contracts between the proprietors of the various different agencies of production, and the assumption is correct, however much the relative quantitative proportions may fluctuate in each individual case. The specific shape in which the value components confront each other is *presupposed* because it is constantly reproduced, and it is constantly reproduced because it is constantly presupposed.

But experience and appearance also show that *market prices* – and it is only under the impact of market prices that the value determination actually becomes apparent to the capitalist – are by no means dependent on these anticipations as regards their level; they are not affected by whether interest or rent is fixed high or low. Market prices are constantly changing, and their average for longer periods |567| is precisely what gives rise to the respective averages of wages, profit and rent, as the *constant* quantities that therefore ultimately govern market prices.

It seems very simple, on the other hand, to make the following reflection: if wages, profit and rent are *formative elements of value*, because they appear as presupposed in value production, and are presupposed for the individual capitalist in the cost price and the price of production, then the *constant capital component*, whose value enters as a given element in every individual sphere of production, is also a value-forming element. But this constant capital component is nothing but a sum of commodities and hence commodity values. We would thus reach the absurd tautology that commodity value forms commodity value, or is the cause of commodity value.

If the capitalist had any interest at all in considering this – and what he considers as a capitalist is determined exclusively by his own interests, and his self-interested motives – he is taught by experience that the product he himself produces goes into other spheres of production as a constant capital component, while products from these other spheres go into his own product as constant capital components. Since for him, therefore, as far as his new production goes, additional value seems in appearance to be *formed* by the magnitudes of wages, profit and rent, this must also apply to the constant component that consists of the products of other capitalists, and therefore the price of the constant capital component, and with it the *total value* of the commodities, can be reduced in the last instance, ultimately, even if in a way that cannot entirely be fathomed, to the sum of value that results from the addition of independent value-forming elements governed by different laws and originating from different sources, namely wages, profit and rent.

Fourthly, it is a matter of complete indifference to the individual capitalist whether commodities are sold at their values or not. Therefore he is also indifferent to value determination itself. Right from the start, this is something that goes on behind his back, by virtue of relations independent of him, since it is not *values* but rather *prices of production* differing from them that form the governing average prices in each sphere of production. Value determination as such interests and affects the individual capitalist, and capital in any particular sphere of production, only in so far as the diminished or increased amount of labour that is required with the rise or fall in the productivity of the labour producing the commodities in question enables him in the one case to make an extra profit at the existing market prices, while in the other case it compels him to increase the prices of his commodities, since more wages, more constant capital, and hence also more interest, fall to the share of each unit product or individual commodity. This interests him only in so far as it raises or lowers his own production costs for the commodity, i.e., in so far as it places him in an exceptional position.

Wages, interest and rent, on the other hand, appear to him as *limits which govern* not only the price at which he can realise the portion of profit that accrues to him as a functioning capitalist, the *profit of enterprise*, but also the price at which he has to sell his commodity if continuing reproduction is to be possible. It is a matter of complete indifference to him whether he realises the value and surplus-value contained in the commodity on its sale or not, as long as he extracts from the price the customary profit of enterprise, or a greater profit, above the cost price as individually given for him by wages, interest and rent. Apart from the constant capital component, therefore, *wages*, interest and *rent* appear to him as the *limiting* elements to the price of the commodity, hence as the elements which determine and *create* it.

|568| If he manages to drive wages down below the value of labour-power, for example, i.e., below their normal level, or to obtain capital at a lower rate of interest and pay a lease-price below the normal level of rent, he does not at all mind selling his product below its value, or even below its price of production,

hence parting with a portion of the *surplus labour* contained in the commodity for nothing. The same thing applies to the constant capital component. If an industrialist can purchase raw material, for instance, at less than its price of production, > whether he sells it at less than its price of production in the finished product is not important to him. < His profit of enterprise can remain *the same*, and even grow, as long as the *excess* of the commodity price above the elements of it that must be paid for, replaced by an equivalent, remains the same or grows. But on top of the value of the means of production that enter into his production process at given prices, it is precisely wages, interest and rent that go into this production at limiting and governing *prices*. These prices therefore appear to him as the elements determining the *prices of his commodities*. Profit of enterprise, from this standpoint, appears either as determined by an *excess* of market price, > or rather by the relationship between *given* market prices and *market prices* < resulting from chance relations of competition, over the immanent value of commodities as determined by the above-mentioned elements of price; or, in so far as it is itself included in the market price as a determinant element, it appears as being itself dependent on competition among buyers and sellers.

Both in competition between the individual capitalists and in competition on the world market, given and presupposed amounts for wages, interest and rent go into the account as constant and governing quantities; constant not in the sense that they do not change, but rather in that they are given in any one particular case and constantly set the limit for the ever-fluctuating market price. In competition on the world market, for example, it is exclusively a question of whether, with the given levels of wages, interest and rent, the commodity can profitably be sold at or below the given general market price, i.e., whether it can be sold to realise an appropriate profit of enterprise.

If wages and the price of land are low in one country but interest on capital is high, because the capitalist mode of production is not fully developed, while in another country wages and the price of land are nominally high whereas the interest on capital is low, a capitalist in the first country will use more land and labour and a capitalist in the second country relatively more capital. In calculating how far competition between the two is possible, these factors are determining elements. Experience shows here in theory, and the self-interested calculations of the capitalist show in practice, that commodity prices are determined by wages, interest and rent, i.e., by the prices of labour, capital and land, and that these price elements are in fact the governing elements of *price formation*.

There still of course remains one element that is not assumed in advance but results from the *market price* of commodities, namely the excess over the cost price, into which wages, etc., enter as constituent elements. This element appears in each individual case as determined by competition, and in the average case by the average profit, which is again governed by the same competition, only over longer periods.

|569| *Fifthly*, on the basis of the capitalist mode of production, it is so completely obvious a step to split up the *value* in which the freshly added labour is expressed into the revenue forms of *wages*, *profit* and *ground-rent* that this method is used even where the conditions of existence for these forms are absent *prima facie*. (Not to speak of past historical periods, of which we gave examples in dealing with ground-rent.) That is to say, everything is subsumed under them, by way of analogy.

If an independent worker labours for himself and sells his own product – we may take as an example a small peasant, since in this case all three forms of revenue can be used – he first of all > works for himself and sells his own product < so that he is considered as his own employer (capitalist), employing himself as a worker, and as his own landowner, using himself as his own farmer. He pays himself wages as a worker, lays claim to profit as a capitalist and pays himself rent as a landowner. Once the capitalist mode of production and the relationships corresponding to it are assumed as the general social basis, this subsumption is correct in as much as he does not have *his labour* to thank but rather his possession of the means of production – which in this case always have the form of *capital* – > because this is a form which has become autonomous vis-à-vis labour – < to thank for the fact that he is in a position to appropriate his own surplus labour. Furthermore, in as much as he produces his product as a commodity and is therefore dependent on its *price* (and even if he is not, this price can be estimated) the amount of surplus labour he can *valorise* is not dependent on its own magnitude but rather on the *general rate of profit*; and likewise the possible excess above the quota of surplus-value determined by the general rate of profit is again not determined by the amount of labour he performs, but rather can be appropriated by him only because he is the owner of the land. Because a form of production that does not correspond to the capitalist mode of production can be subsumed under its forms of revenue (and to a certain degree rightly) the illusion [*Schein*] that relationships that correspond to the capitalist mode of production are the natural relationships under any mode of production receives yet further reinforcement.

If however wages are reduced to their general basis, namely that portion of the product of his labour which goes into the worker's own individual consumption; if this share is freed from its capitalist limit and expanded to the scale of consumption that is on the one hand permitted by the existing productivity of society (i.e., the social productivity of his own labour as social labour) and on the other hand required for the full development of individuality; if surplus labour (and therefore also surplus product) is reduced to the degree needed under the given conditions of production, both to form an insurance and reserve fund and to ensure the constant expansion of reproduction in the degree determined by social requirements; if, finally, both (1) the necessary labour, and (2) the surplus labour are taken to include the amount of labour that those capable of work must always perform for those members of society not yet capable, or no longer capable, of working – i.e., if both wages and surplus-value, > necessary labour and surplus labour, < are stripped of their specifically capitalist character – then nothing more of these forms remains than those foundations that are common to all social modes of production.

This kind of subsumption, incidentally, is also characteristic of modes of production previously dominant, for example the feudal one. Relations of production that in no way corresponded to it, standing completely outside it, were subsumed under feudal relationships; e.g., the *tenures in common socage* (as opposed to the *tenures on knight's service*), which only involved *pecuniary* obligations and were feudal only in *name*.[23]

|570| (4) Relations of Production and Distribution

The value newly added in a year by freshly added labour (hence also the part of the annual product in which this *value* is expressed, and which can be > bought with it or < extracted and separated from the total product) can be divided, as we have shown, into three parts, which in terms of revenue take on three different forms, forms that express one part of this value as belonging or accruing to the owner of labour-power, one part as accruing to the owner of capital and a third part as accruing to the owner of landed property. These are thus relations or forms of distribution, for they express the relationships in which the total value newly produced is distributed among the owners of the various agencies of production.

In the customary view, these *relations of distribution* appear to be *natural relations*, relations arising from the nature of all social production, from the laws of *human production pure and simple*. It cannot be denied, of course, that precapitalist societies display other *modes of distribution*, but these are then explained as undeveloped, incomplete and disguised, not reduced to their

23 > Neale 1860, p. 22. <

purest expression and highest form, modalities of these natural relations of distribution with a different hue.

The only bit of truth in this conception is this: once any kind of social production is assumed (e.g., that of the indigenous Indian communities or the more artificially developed communism of the Peruvians) it is always possible to distinguish between the portion of labour whose product is directly consumed individually by the producers and their dependants, and – leaving aside the portion for productive consumption – a further portion of labour that is always surplus labour, whose product always serves to satisfy general social needs, no matter how that surplus product is distributed and whoever functions as the representative of those social needs. The identity of the different modes of distribution thus comes down to the fact that they are identical if we *abstract* from their distinctions and specific forms and just cling to > (fix on to) < their unity in contrast to what distinguishes them.

A more developed, and a more critical, awareness concedes the *historically developed character of these relations of distribution*,[24] but holds all the more firmly to the supposedly constant and *unhistorical character* of the *relations of production* themselves, as arising from human nature.

The scientific analysis of *the capitalist mode of production* proves the contrary, it proves that this is a mode of production of a particular kind and a specific historical determinacy; that like any other particular mode of production it assumes a given level of social productive forces and of their forms of development as *its historical precondition*, a condition that is itself the historical result and product of a previous process and from which the new mode of production proceeds as its given foundation; that the relations of production corresponding to this specific and historically determined mode of production – relations into which men enter in their social life-process, i.e., in the creation of their social life – have a specific, historical and transitory character; and that finally the so-called |571| *relations of distribution* are essentially identical with those *relations of production*, the obverse of the same coin, so that they both share the same historically transitory character.

In dealing with the *relations of distribution*, it is usual to start from the alleged fact that the annual product is divided into wages, profit and ground-rent. But, expressed in this way, the statement is wrong. The product is divided into *capital* on the one hand and *revenues* on the other. One of these revenues, wages, only ever assumes the form of a revenue, the revenue of the worker, after it has previously confronted the same worker in the form of *capital*. The

24 Mill 1844 [pp. 132–3.]

confrontation between the produced conditions of labour and the products of labour all together as *capital*, and the direct producers, gives the material conditions of labour right from the start a *specific social character* vis-à-vis the workers, and hence sets up a specific relationship which the workers enter into, in production itself, with the owners of these conditions of labour and with each other. The transformation of these conditions of labour into capital also involves the expropriation of the direct producers from the land, and hence a specific form of landed property.

If one part of the product were not transformed into capital, the other would not assume the forms of wages, profit and rent.

On the other hand, if the capitalist mode of production presupposes this specific social form of the conditions of production, it constantly reproduces it as well. It not only produces the material products, but constantly reproduces the relations of production in which these are produced, and with them also the corresponding relations of distribution.

It may be said, incidentally, that *capital* (and landed property, which this includes as its antithesis) itself already presupposes a *distribution*; it presupposes the expropriation of the workers from the conditions of labour, the concentration of these conditions in the hands of a minority of individuals, the exclusive ownership of the land by other individuals, in short, all the relations that were developed in the section on *'Primitive Accumulation'*.[25] But this *distribution* is completely different from what is understood by relations of distribution when a historical character is claimed for these, in contrast to the relations of production. What is meant under this rubric are the different titles to the part of the product that falls to individual consumption. The relations of distribution referred to above, on the other hand, are the foundation of particular social functions which are ascribed to specific agents of production within the relation of production itself, as distinct from the direct producers. They give the actual conditions of production, and their representatives, a specific social quality. They determine the whole character and movement of production.

Two characteristic traits mark the capitalist mode of production from the start.

Firstly, it produces its products as *commodities*. The fact that it produces commodities does not in itself distinguish it from other modes of production; but the fact that the dominant and determining character of its product is that it is a *commodity* certainly does. This means, first of all, that the worker himself appears only as a seller of commodities, and hence as a *free wage-labourer*. Thus

25 [In what later became Volume I, Part Eight, of *Capital*. Translator]

labour generally appears as *wage-labour*. It is unnecessary after the argument already developed to demonstrate once again how the relationship of capital and wage-labour determines the whole character of the mode of production. The principal agents of this mode of production itself, the *capitalist* and the *wage-labourer*, are as such simply embodiments and personifications, specific social characters that individuals assume in the social production process, products of these specific social relations of production.

The character of the product as a commodity (1), and the character of the commodity as the product of capital (2), already include all the relations of circulation, i.e., a specific social process which products must pass through and in which they assume specific social characters; they equally include specific relationships between the agents of production, determining the valorisation of their product and its transformation back into either means of subsistence or means of production. But even leaving this aside, these two characters give rise to the entire determination of value, the |572| regulation of total production by *exchange-value*, i.e., this quite specific form of value in which labour counts only as *social* labour. On the other hand the distribution of this social labour and the reciprocal complementation of its products, their metabolism, and their subjugation to and insertion into the social mechanism, are left to the accidental and reciprocally counteracting motives of the individual capitalist producers. Since these confront one another only as commodity owners, each trying to sell his commodity as dear as possible (and seeming to be governed only by caprice even in the regulation of production), the inner law operates only by way of their *competition*, their alternating pressure on each other, which is how divergences are mutually counterbalanced. It is only as an inner law, as a *natural law* vis-à-vis the individual agents, that the law of value operates here and that the social balance of production asserts itself in the midst of accidental fluctuations.

What is also implied already in the *commodity*, and still more so in the commodity as the *product of capital*, is the reification [*Verdinglichung*] of the social determinations of production and the subjectification [*Versubjektivierung*] of the material bases of production which characterise the entire capitalist mode of production.

The second thing which particularly marks the capitalist mode of production is the *production of surplus-value* as the direct object and determining motive of production. Capital essentially produces capital, and it does this only as long as it produces surplus-value. In dealing first with relative surplus-value and then with the transformation of surplus-value into profit, we have seen how a mode of production peculiar to capitalism is based on this – a particular form of development of the social productive powers of labour, but as powers of capital that have asserted their autonomy vis-à-vis the worker, thus directly opposing his own development. Production for value and surplus-value involves, as we went on to show, a tendency (a rule, a norm) to reduce the labour-time needed to produce a commodity, i.e., to reduce the commodity's *value* below the existing social average at any given time > in the *production process*; (and simultaneously, in the circulation process, to sell the commodity where possible above its value); to reduce it to the lowest possible level, and in particular to *reduce the cost price* to the minimum.

< The authority that the capitalist assumes in the immediate production process, as personification of capital, the social function he dons as manager and ruler of production, is essentially different from the forms assumed by authority on the basis of production with slaves, serfs, etc.

Although on the basis of the capitalist mode of production the *social* character of their production confronts the mass of the direct producers in the form of a governing authority of the utmost severity, and the social mechanism of the labour process has received here a completely hierarchical articulation – though this authority accrues to its bearers only as the personification of the conditions of labour vis-à-vis labour itself, not as political or theocratic rulers as it did in earlier forms of production – the most complete anarchy reigns among the bearers of this authority, the capitalists themselves, who confront one another simply as owners of commodities, and within this anarchy the social interconnection of production prevails over individual caprice only as an overwhelming natural law.[26]

Let us consider, moreover, the so-called *forms or relations of distribution* themselves. The wage presupposes wage-labour, profit presupposes capital. These specific forms of distribution thus presuppose specific social characters for the conditions of production and specific social relations for the agents of production. The specific relation of distribution thus simply expresses the historically determined relation of production.

Let us take profit, for example! This specific form of surplus-value is the presupposition for the process of renewed formation of the means of production in the *form of capitalist accumulation*. It is therefore a relationship governing reproduction, even if it appears to the individual capitalist that he could consume the whole of the profit as revenue. There are limits to this, however, which he encounters already in the form of the insurance and reserve fund, the law of competition, etc., and which prove to him in a practical way that profit is not

---

26 [Engels added part of page 574 of the manuscript to the text at this point. See below, note 28. Translator]

simply a category appertaining to the distribution of the product for individual consumption. The entire capitalist production process, moreover, is governed by the prices of products. But the governing prices of production are themselves governed in turn by the equalisation of the rate of profit and the distribution of capital among the various spheres of social production which is appropriate to that equalisation. Thus profit appears in this case as the principal driving force not just of the products' distribution but also of their actual production, because it determines the distribution of capitals and of labour itself among the various spheres of production. |573| The division of profit into profit of enterprise and interest appears simply as a distribution of the same revenue! But this division arises first of all from the development of capital as self-valorising, surplus-value-producing value, a specific social configuration of the dominant production relation. It develops from within itself the credit system, etc., and with this the whole shape of production. In interest, etc., the ostensible forms of distribution go into the price as determining elements of production!

It might appear for *ground-rent* that this is a form of distribution pure and simple, since landed property as such performs no function in the production process, or at least no normal function! But the fact that (1) rent is limited to the excess over and above the average profit, and (2) the landlord has been reduced from guide and master of the production process and the entire process of social life to a mere leaser-out of land, a usurer in land and a mere recipient of rent, is a *specific historical result* of the capitalist mode of production. It is a historical precondition for this mode of production that the soil has to receive the form of landed property. And it is a product of the specific character of this mode of production that landed property takes on forms which permit the capitalist mode of operation in agriculture. It is possible to give the name of rent to the landowner's income in other forms of society. But this is essentially different from rent as it appears in this mode of production.

The so-called *relations of distribution*, therefore, correspond to and arise from historically particular and specific social forms of the production process and of the relationships which men enter into among themselves in the process of reproducing their human life! The historical character of these relations of distribution is the historical character of the relations of production, and they simply express one side of these. > But the forms of production and distribution find expression in the same way. The bourgeois < (capitalist) distribution is different from those forms of distribution that arise from other modes of production, and every form of distribution vanishes along with the particular form of production that it arises from and belongs to.

The view that considers *only* the relations of distribution to be historical, and not the relations of production, is simply the perspective of a criticism of bourgeois economics that has made a start but is still imprisoned within the latter's views. It is also based on a confusion and identification of the social production process with the *simple labour process*, as the solitary savage would have to perform it without the aid of any kind of *social* development. In so far as the labour process is a simple process between man and nature, its simple elements remain common to all social forms of its development. But each particular historical form of this process further develops the material foundations and social forms. Once a certain level of maturity has been attained, the particular historical form is shed and makes way for a higher form. The sign that the moment of such a crisis has arrived is that the contradiction and antithesis between, on the one hand, the relations of distribution, hence also the specific historical form of the relations of production corresponding to them, and, on the other hand, the productive forces, productivity and the development of the agencies of production, gains in breadth and depth! A conflict then sets in between the material development of production and its social form.[27]

|574| > The following addition should be made to section 3:

< In connection with the division into *wages, profit and ground-rent* of the *value* added to the constant capital component, it is self-evident that these are *components of value*. They can of course be imagined as existing in the immediate product in which this value is expressed, i.e., in the product that the workers and capitalists in a particular sphere of production, e.g., cotton-spinning, have directly produced, say in yarn. In fact, however, they are no more and no less expressed in this product than in any other kind of commodity, any other component of material wealth of *the same* value. In practice we find that wages are paid in *money*, i.e., the pure expression of value, and similarly interest and rent. For the capitalist, in fact, the transformation of his product into the pure value expression is very important; this is already assumed in connection with distribution. Whether these *values* are transformed back into the same product, the same commodity, from whose production they derived, whether the worker buys back a part of the product he directly produced or buys the product of other labour has nothing to do with the essence of the matter. Herr Rodbertus gets quite needlessly worked up over this subject.[28]

> The following addition should be made to section 4:

---

27 See the essay on competition and cooperation (1832?). [Fernbach added the following editorial footnote: 'Apparently *A Prize Essay on the Comparative Advantage of Competition and Cooperation*, London, 1834'. Editor]

28 [Engels moved this paragraph back to section 3, page 554 of the manuscript. See above, note 18. Translator]

< It is only because labour is presupposed in the form of wage-labour, and the means of production in the form of capital – hence only as a result of this specific form of these two essential agencies of production – that one part of the value (of the product) presents itself as *surplus-value* and this surplus-value presents itself as *profit* (rent), as the gain of the capitalist, as additional available wealth belonging to him. And it is only because it presents itself as *his profit* that the new additional means of production, designed for the expansion of reproduction and forming a portion of the product, present themselves as new additional *capital*, and the expansion of the reproduction process in general presents itself as a *process of capitalist accumulation*.

Even though the form of labour as *wage-labour* is decisive for the shape of the entire process and for the specific mode of production itself, it is not *wage-labour* that is the determinant of value. What matters in the determination of value is the overall social labour-time, the total amount of labour which society has at its disposal and whose relative absorption by the different products determines, as it were, their respective social weight. But the particular form in which social labour-time plays its determining role in the value of commodities coincides with the form of labour as wage-labour, and the corresponding form of the means of production as capital, in so far as it is on this basis alone that *commodity production* becomes the general form of production.[29]

|575| (5) **Classes**

The owners of nothing but labour-power, the owners of capital and the landowners, whose respective sources of income are wages, profit and ground-rent – in other words wage-labourers, capitalists and landowners – form the three great classes of modern society based on the capitalist mode of production.

It is undeniably in England that this modern society and its economic articulation is most widely and most classically developed. Even there, though, this class articulation does not emerge in a pure form. Here too, intermediate and transitional stages always conceal the boundaries (though incomparably less so in the countryside than in the towns). We have seen how it is the constant tendency and law of development of the capitalist mode of production to divorce the means of production ever more from labour and to concentrate fragmented means of production more and more into large groups, i.e., to transform labour

29 [Engels moved these two paragraphs back into section 4. See above, note 25. Translator]

into wage-labour and the means of production into capital. And this tendency also corresponds to the independent divorce of all landed property from capital and labour,[30] or the transformation of all landed property into the form of landed property corresponding to the capitalist mode of production.

The next question to be answered is: 'What makes a class?' And this arises automatically from answering another question: 'What makes wage-labourers, capitalists and landowners the formative elements of the three great social classes?'

At first sight, it is *the identity of their revenues and revenue sources*. For these are three great social groups whose components, the individuals forming them, live respectively from wages, profit and ground-rent, from the valorisation of their labour-power, their capital and their landed property.

From this point of view, however, doctors and government officials, for example, would also form two classes, as they belong to two distinct social groups, the revenue of each group's members flowing from its own source. The same would hold true for the infinite fragmentation of interests and positions into which the division of social labour splits not only workers but also capitalists and landowners – the latter, for instance, are divided into vineyard-owners, field-owners, forest-owners, mine-owners, fishery-owners, etc.

---

30 Friedrich List observes correctly: 'The predominance of *owner-management* on large estates simply indicates inadequate civilisation, and a lack of means of communication, local industry and wealthy cities. That is why we find it all over Russia, Poland, Hungary and Mecklenburg. It was formerly predominant in England too, but with the arrival of trade and industry these estates were broken up into medium-sized farms and leased out'. (List 1842, p. 10, note.)

APPENDIX

Location of Passages of Text Not Included by Engels in the Published Version of *Capital* Volume III

In the present translation passages included by Engels are placed within angled brackets, < >. Passages falling outside these brackets were either not included by Engels or modified very substantially by him.

The following list gives three sets of page number references: to the present translation, to the MEGA edition, MEGA$^{(2)}$ II.4.2 and to Marx's original manuscript.

Translation	MEGA Edition	Marx
Chapter 1		
49–92	7–59	1–37
95	61	38
100–50	66–116	42–73
158–73	125–40	78–90
179–99	145–64	94–108
202–10	167–75	111–19
223–4	185–7	126–7
235	198	133
247	209	153
Chapter 2		
256	221	161
257–65	223–9	162–6
266-7	232–3	167–8
273	239–40	172
310–11	274–6	197–8
317–18	282–3	202b
Chapter 3		
325	290–1	207
333–4	299–300	213–14
338–9	303	216

(cont.)

Translation	MEGA Edition	Marx
345	311	221
349–53	314–18	223–6
361	326	232
368–71	333–6	238–9
374–5	339–40	242
Chapter 4		
379–80	345	245
384	349	248
390	356	252
393–4	359–60	254–5
395–6	362–3	256–7
402–3	368–9	260–1
409–10	375–6	268
415	380	271
430	395	279
434–5	403–4	281
440–1	407–8	283–5
Chapter 5		
464–5	434–5	297
481	449	306
485–6	454–5	308
466	466	315
500	469–70	317
505–6	473–4	318
509	476	319
511	478	320
514	482	321
525	492	325
528–33	494–500	325a, 325b
545–6	512	331
551	515–16	333
552	518	334
560	525	338
563	527	339

Translation	MEGA Edition	Marx
568	532	340
571–2	534	341
575	538	343
577–8	541	344–5
579–86	544–8	345–7
592–3	554–5	350
598–602	561–5	352a, 352b
603–5	567–9	352c
609	571	352e
610–19	573–80	352f, g, h and i
619–20	582–3	352j
626–7	587–9	355
630–1	591–2	357
636–7	597–8	360
637	600	361
639	602	361
646–60	606–19	364–71
668	623	374
672–7	626–9	376–8
680–2	634–5	380–1
684	638	382
686–92	640–5	383–91
703–6	657–9	400–1
711–12	664	404
Chapter 6		
727–8	681–2	415
748	702	427
757	711	435
700–2	715–16	438–40
769	723	447
812	767	485–6
815	770	488
840–3	796–8	505–6
846–7	801–2	508
852–3	806	511
854	808	512

(cont.)

Translation	MEGA Edition	Marx
860–2	813–15	513–14
870–1	822	519–20
876–8	827–9	523–4
Chapter 7		
905	860	546
927–8	882–3	561–2
932–3	888	565

Bibliography

1 References for Introduction by Fred Moseley

Arthur, Chris 1997, 'Against the Logical-Historical Method: Dialectical Derivation versus Linear Logic', in *New Investigations of Marx's Method*, edited by Fred Moseley and Martha Campbell, New Jersey: Humanities Press.

Bellofiore, Riccardo and Roberto Fineschi, 'Introduction', in *Re-reading Marx: New Perspectives after the Critical Edition*, edited by R. Bellofiore and R. Fineschi, London: Palgrave.

Engels, Frederick 1970 [1859], Review of K. Marx, *A Contribution to the Critique of Political Economy*, in Marx 1972.

——— 1981a [1894], Preface to *Capital*, Volume III, by Karl Marx, New York: Random House.

——— 1981b [1894], Supplement to *Capital*, Volume III, by Karl Marx, New York: Random House.

Fine, Ben 1983, 'A Dissenting Note on the Transformation Problem', *Economy and Society*, 12, 4: 520–25.

Hecker, Rolf 2009, 'Marx's Manuscripts of *Capital*, Volume II in the MEGA', in *Re-reading Marx: New Perspectives after the Critical Edition*, edited by R. Bellofiore and R. Fineschi, London: Palgrave.

Heinrich, Michael 1989, 'Capital in General and the Structure of Marx's *Capital*', *Capital and Class*, 38: 63–79.

——— 1996–7, 'Engels' Edition of the Third Volume of *Capital* and Marx's Original Manuscript', *Science and Society*, 60: 452–67.

——— 2007, 'On Karl Marx's *Das Kapital. Kritik der politischen Ökonomie, Dritter Band* (MEGA II/15)', *Historical Materialism*, 15: 195–210.

Inwood, Michael 1992, *A Hegel Dictionary*, Oxford: Blackwell Publishers.

Marx, Karl 1971 [1861–3], *Theories of Surplus Value*, Volume 3, Moscow: Progress Publishers.

——— 1972 [1859], *A Contribution to the Critique of Political Economy*, New York: International Publishers.

——— 1973 [1857–8], *Grundrisse*, Middlesex, England: Penguin Books.

——— 1977a [1867], *Capital*, Volume I, New York: Random House.

——— 1977b [1863], 'Results of the Immediate Process of Production', in Marx, *Capital*, Volume I, New York: Random House.

——— 1978 [1885], *Capital*, Volume II, New York: Random House, edited and published by Frederick Engels; cited as Marx 1978 [Engels].

——— 1981 [1894], *Capital*, Volume III, New York: Random House, edited and published by Frederick Engels; cited as Marx 1981 [Engels].

——— 1981 [1856–9], *Letters*, in *Marx-Engels Collected Works*, Volume 40, New York: International Publishers.

——— 1985 [1860–4], *Letters*, in *Marx-Engels Collected Works*, Volume 41, New York: International Publishers.

——— 1987 [1864–8], *Letters*, in *Marx-Engels Collected Works*, Volume 42, New York: International Publishers.

——— 1988 [1868–70], *Letters*, in *Marx-Engels Collected Works*, Volume 43, New York: International Publishers.

——— 1989a [1861–3], *Economic Manuscript of 1861–63*, in *Marx-Engels Collected Works*, Volume 31, New York: International Publishers.

——— 1989b [1861–3], *Economic Manuscript of 1861–63*, in *Marx-Engels Collected Works*, Volume 32, New York: International Publishers.

——— 1991 [1861–3], *Economic Manuscript of 1861–63*, in *Marx-Engels Collected Works*, Volume 33, New York: International Publishers.

——— 1992 [1864–5], *Ökonomische Manuskripte 1864–65*, in *Marx/Engels Gesamtausgabe*, Section II, Volume 4.2, Berlin: Dietz.

——— 1995 [1883–6], *Letters*, in *Marx-Engels Collected Works*, Volume 47, New York: International Publishers.

——— 2004, *Das Kapital: Kritik der Politischen Ökonomie, Dritter Band*, in *Marx/Engels Gesamtausgabe*, Section II, Volume 15, Apparat, Berlin: Dietz.

Moseley, Fred 1995, 'Capital in General and Marx's Logical Method: A Response to Heinrich's Critique', *Capital and Class*, 56: 15–48.

——— 2002, 'Hostile Brothers: Marx's Theory of the Distribution of Surplus-value in Volume 3 of *Capital*', in *The Culmination of Capital: Essays on Volume 3 of Capital*, edited by G. Reuten and M. Campbell, London: Palgrave.

——— 2009, 'The Development of Marx's Theory of the Distribution of Surplus-Value in the *Manuscript of 1861–63*', in *Re-reading Marx: New Perspectives after the Critical Edition*, edited by R. Bellofiore and R. Fineschi, London: Palgrave.

——— 2011, 'The Whole and the Parts: The Early Development of Marx's Theory of the Distribution of Surplus-value in the *Grundrisse*', *Science and Society*, 75, 1: 59–73.

——— 2016, *A Macro-Monetary Interpretation of Marx's Logic in* Capital *and the End of the 'Transformation Problem'*, Leiden: Brill.

Müller, M.J., J. Jungnickel, B. Lietz, C. Sander, and A. Schnickmann 2002 [1992], 'General Commentary to Marx's Manuscript of *Capital*, Book 3 (1864/65)', *International Journal of Political Economy*, 32, 1: 14–34.

Murray, Patrick 2002, 'The Illusion of the Economic: The Trinity Formula and the "religion of everyday life"', in *The Culmination of Capital: Essays on Volume Three of Marx's 'Capital'*, edited by M. Campbell and G. Reuten, London: Palgrave.

Ramos, Alejandro 1998, 'Value and Price of Production: New Evidence on Marx's Transformation Procedure', *International Journal of Political Economy*, 28: 4.

Reuten, Geert 1997, 'The Notion of Tendency in Marx's 1894 Law of Profit', in *New Investigations of Marx's Method*, edited by F. Moseley and M. Campbell, New Jersey: Humanities Press.

——— 2002, 'The Rate of Profit Cycle and the Opposition between Managerial and Finance Capital: A Discussion of *Capital III*, Parts Three to Five', in *The Culmination of Capital: Essays on Volume 3 of Capital*, edited by G. Reuten and M. Campbell, London: Palgrave.

——— 2009, 'Marx's General Rate of Profit Transformation: Methodological and Theoretical Obstacles – an Appraisal based on the 1864–65 Manuscript of *Das Kapital III*', in *Re-reading Marx: New Perspectives after the Critical Edition*, edited by R. Bellofiore and R. Fineschi, London: Palgrave.

Roth, Regina 2002, 'The Author Marx and His Editor Engels: Different Views on Volume 3 of *Capital*', *Rethinking Marxism*, 14, 2: 59–72.

——— 2009, 'Karl Marx's Original Manuscripts in the Marx-Engels-Gesamtausgabe (MEGA): Another View *Capital*', in *Re-reading Marx: New Perspectives after the Critical Edition*, edited by R. Bellofiore and R. Fineschi, London: Palgrave.

Saad-Filho, Alfredo 1993, 'A Note on Marx's Analysis of the Composition of Capital', *Capital and Class*, 50: 127–46.

Vollgraf, Carl Erich and Jürgen Jungnickel 2002 [1994], 'Marx in Marx's Words: On Engels's Edition of the Main Manuscript of Book 3 of *Capital*', *International Journal of Political Economy*, 32, 1: 35–78.

Wolff, Richard, Antonio Callari and Bruce Roberts 1984, 'A Marxian Alternative to the "Transformation Problem"', *Review of Radical Political Economics*, 16, 2–3: 115–35.

2 Parliamentary Reports and Other Official Publications

Census of England and Wales, 1861, Volume II, London, 1863.

Coal Mine Accidents. Abstract of a Return to an Address of the Hon. the House of Commons, dated 3 May 1861. Ordered by the House of Commons to be printed, 6 February 1862, London, 1862.

Comptes Rendus Hebdomadaires des Séances de l'Académie des Sciences, par MM. les Secrétaires Perpétuels, Paris, 1862.

First Report from the Secret Committee on Commercial Distress, with the minutes of evidence. Ordered, by the House of Commons, to be printed, 27 July 1848, London, 1848.

Programme du Congrès International Statistique, tenu à Paris le 10 Sept. 1855, Paris, 1856.

Public Health. Sixth Report of the Medical Officer of the Privy Council, with Appendix, 1863, London, 1864

Public Health. Reports of the Medical Officer of the Privy Council. Seventh Report, 1864, London, 1865.

Report addressed to Her Majesty's Principal Secretary of State for the Home Department, relative to the Grievances Complained of by the Journeymen Bakers; with Appendix of Evidence. Presented to Both Houses of Parliament by Command of her Majesty, London, 1862.

Report from the Secret Committee of the House of Lords appointing to inquire into the causes of the distress which has for some time prevailed among the commercial classes. Ordered by the House of Commons to be printed, 28 July 1848, London, 1857.

Report from the Select Committee on Bank Acts; together with the proceedings of the committee, minutes of evidence, appendix and index. Ordered by the House of Commons to be printed, 30 July 1857, London 1857.

Report from the Select Committee on the Bank Acts; together with the proceedings of the committee, minutes of evidence, appendix and index. Ordered by the House of Commons to be printed, 1 July 1858, London 1858.

Reports of the Inspectors of Factories to Her Majesty's Principal Secretary of State for the Home Department for the half-year ending:
31st October 1845 London 1846 (1)
30th April 1846 London 1846 (2)
31st October 1846 London 1847
31st October 1847 London 1848
31st October 1848 London 1849 (1)
30th April 1849 London 1849 (2)
31st October 1849 London 1850 (1)
30th April 1850 London 1850 (2)
31st October 1850 London 1851 (1)
30th April 1851 London 1851 (2)
31st October 1852 London 1852
30th April 1853 London 1853
31st October1853 London 1854 (1)
30th April 1854 London 1854 (2)
31st October 1855 London 1856 (1)
30th April 1856 London 1856 (2)
31st October 1856 London 1857 (1)
30th April 1857 London 1857 (2)
30th April 1858 London 1858 (1)
31st October 1858 London 1858 (2)
30th April 1859 London 1859
31st October 1859 London 1860 (1)
30th April 1860 London 1860 (2)
31st October 1860 London 1860 (3)
30th April 1861 London 1861

31st October 1861 London 1862 (1)
30th April 1862 London 1862 (2)
31st October 1862 London 1863 (1)
30th April 1863 London 1863 (2)
31st October 1863 London 1864 (1)
30th April 1864 London 1864 (2)
Second Report from the Select Committee on Banks of Issue, Ordered by the House of Commons to be printed, 15 June 1841, London, 1841.
Statistical Abstract for the United Kingdom, No. 12: From 1850 to 1864, London, 1865.

3 Works by Named or Anonymous Authors

Anderson, Adam 1764, *A historical and chronological deduction of the origin of commerce, from the earliest accounts to the present time*, Volume 1, London.
Arbeiten der Kaiserlich Russischen Gesandtschaft zu Peking über China, sein Volk, seine Religion, seine Institutionen, socialen Verhältnisse etc., translated from Russian by Carl Abel and F.A. Meckelburg, Volume 1, 1858, Berlin.
Aristotle 1831, *De Republica*, Berlin.
——— 1920, *Aristotle's Politics*, translated by B. Jowett, Oxford.
Arnd, Karl 1845, *Die naturgemässe Volkswirthschaft gegenüber dem Monopoliengeist und dem Communismus, mit einem Rückblicke auf die einschlagende Literatur*, Hanau.
Augier, Marie 1842, *Du Crédit Public et de son histoire*, Paris.
Babbage, Charles 1832, *On the Economy of Machinery and Manufactures*, London.
——— 1833, *Traité sur l'économie des machines et des manufactures, trad. de l'anglais*, Paris.
Bastiat, Frédéric and Pierre-Joseph Proudhon 1850, *Gratuité du crédit. Discussion entre M. Fr. Bastiat et M. Proudhon*, Paris.
Bazard, Saint-Amand 1831, *Doctrine de Saint-Simon. Exposition. Première Année, 1828–1829*, 3rd. edn., Paris.
Bell, Gavin Mason 1840, *The Philosophy of Joint Stock Banking*, London.
——— 1842, *The Country Banks and Currency*, London.
Bellers, John 1699, *Essays about the Poor, Manufactures, Trade, Plantations, and Immorality*, London.
Bosanquet, James Whatman 1842, *Metallic, Paper, and Credit Currency, and the means of regulating their quantity and value*, London.
Briscoe, John 1696, *A Discourse on the Late Funds of the million-act, lottery-act and Bank of England*, 3rd. edn., London.
Buret, Antoine-Eugène 1843, *Cours d'économie politique*, Brussels.
Büsch, Johann Georg 1808, *Theoretisch-Praktische Darstellung der Handlung in ihren mannichfaltigen Geschäften*, 3rd. edn., Volume 2, Hamburg.

Cairnes, John Elliot 1862, *The Slave Power*, London.

Cantillon, Richard 1756, 'Essai sur la nature du commerce en général', in *Discours politiques*, Volume 3, Amsterdam.

Carey, Charles 1835, *Essay on the Rate of Wages*, Philadelphia.

Chamberlen, Hugh 1695, *A Proposal for Erecting a General Bank. Which may be fitly called the Land Bank of England*, London.

Cherbuliez, Antoine 1841, *Richesse ou pauvreté. Exposition des causes et des effets de la distribution actuelle des richesses sociales*, 2nd. edn., Paris.

Child, Josiah 1754 [1669], *Traités sur le commerce et sur les avantages qui résultent de la réduction de l'intérêt de l'argent; avec un petit traité contre l'usure par Thomas Culpeper. Trad. de l'anglais*, Amsterdam and Berlin.

Comte, Charles 1834, *Traité de la propriété*, Volume 1, Paris.

Coquelin, Charles 1842, 'Du Crédit et des Banques dans l'Industrie', *Revue des deux mondes*, 4th. Series, 31: 776–827.

Corbet, Thomas 1841, *An Inquiry into the Causes and Modes of the Wealth of Individuals; or the principles of trade and speculation explained*, London.

Correspondence relative to the Earl of Elgin's special missions to China and Japan, 1857–1859. Presented to the House of Commons by command of Her Majesty, in pursuance of their address dated July 15, 1859, 1859, London.

The Currency Theory Reviewed in a letter to the Scottish people on the menaced interference by government with the existing system of banking in Scotland. By a banker in England, 1845, Edinburgh.

Daire, Eugène 1847, *Mémoire sur la doctrine des Physiocrates*, Paris.

Davenant, Charles 1698, *Discourses on the Publick Victuals, Part 2*, London.

Dove, Patrick Edward 1854, *The Elements of Political Science in Two Books, Book Two: On Doctrine*, Edinburgh.

Dureau de la Malle, Adolphe 1840, *Économie politique des Romains*, Volume 1, Paris.

Enfantin, Barthélemy-Prosper 1831, *Économie politique et politique. Religion saint-simonienne*, Paris.

An Essay, in answer to the question, whether does the principle of competition, with separate individual interests, or the principle of united exertions ... form the most secure basis for the formation of society, 1834, London.

Evans, David Morier 1845, *The City, or the Physiology of London Business; with Sketches on Change, and at the Coffee Houses*, London.

Feller, Friedrich E., and Dr. Carl G. Obermann 1859, *Das Ganze der kaufmännischen Arithmetik*, 7th. edn., Leipzig.

Forcade, Eugène 1848, 'La guerre du socialisme. II. L'économie politique révolutionnaire et sociale', *Revue des Deux Mondes*, 18: 24.

Fourier, Charles 1829, *Le nouveau monde industriel et sociétaire, ou invention du procédé d'industrie attrayante et naturells distribuée en séries passionnées*, Paris.

Francis, John 1848, *History of the Bank of England, its times and traditions*, Volume 1, London.

Franklin, Benjamin 1836 [1769], 'Positions to be Examined, Concerning National Wealth', in *The Works of Benjamin Franklin. With note and a life of the author.*, edited by J. Sparks, Volume 2, Boston.

Fullarton, John 1845, *On the Regulation of Currencies*, 2nd. edn., London.

Garnier, Joseph 1853, 'Herrenschwand', in *Dictionnaire de l'économie politique*, Volume 1, Brussels.

Gilbart, James William 1834, *The History and Principles of Banking*, London.

——— 1840, *An Inquiry into the Causes of the Pressure on the Money Market during the year 1839*, London.

——— 1849, *A Practical Treatise on Banking*, 5th. edn., Volume 1, London.

Greg, Robert Hyde 1837, *The Factory Question and the Ten Hours Bill*, London.

Hamilton, Robert 1814, *An Inquiry into the Rise and Progress of the National Debt of Great Britain*, 2nd. edn., Edinburgh.

Hardcastle, Daniel Jun. 1843, *Banks and Bankers*, 2nd. edn., London.

Hegel, Georg Wilhelm Friedrich 1830, *Enzyclopädie der Philosophischen Wissenschaften im Grundrisse, Erster Teil, Die Wissenschaft der Logik*, 3rd. edn., Berlin.

——— 1840 [1821], *Grundlinien der Philosophie des Rechts*, 2nd. edn., Berlin.

Hodgskin, Thomas 1825, *Labour Defended Against the Claims of Capital; or, the unproductiveness of capital proved, by a labourer*, London.

Hubbard, John Gellibrand 1843, *The Currency and the Country*, London.

Hüllmann, Karl Dietrich 1826, *Städtewesen des Mittelalters*, Volume 1, Bonn.

——— 1827, *Städtewesen des Mittelalters*, Volume 2, Bonn.

An Inquiry into those Principles respecting the Nature of Demand and the Necessity of Consumption, lately advocated by Mr. Malthus, from which it is concluded, that taxation and the maintenance of unproductive consumers can be conducive to the progress of wealth, 1821, London.

Johnston, James Weir 1851, *Notes on North America, agricultural, economical and social*, Volume 1, London.

Jones, Richard 1831, *An Essay on the Distribution of Wealth, and on the Sources of Taxation*, London.

——— 1833, *An Introductory Lecture on Political Economy. delivered at King's College, London, 27 February 1833. To which is added a syllabus of a course of lectures on the wages of labour*, London.

Joplin, Thomas 1844, *Currency Reform: Improvement not Depreciation*, London.

——— 1836, *An Examination of the Report of the Joint Stock Bank Committee*, London.

Kiesselbach, Wilhelm 1860, *Der Gang des Welthandels und die Entwicklung des europäischen Völkerlebens im Mittelalter*, Stuttgart.

Kinnear, John Gardiner 1847, *The Crisis and the Currency*, London.

Knox, Thomas Malcolm 1967 [1952], *Hegel's Philosophy of Right, translated with notes*, Oxford.

Laing, Samuel 1844, *National Distress; its causes and remedies*, London.

Laing, Seton 1856, *A New Series of the Great City Frauds of Cole, Davidson & Gordon*, London.

Lauderdale, James Maitland 1808, *Recherches sur la nature et l'origine de la richesse publique, et sur les moyens et les causes qui concourent à son accroissement*, Paris.

Lavergne, Léonce de 1855, *The Rural Economy of England, Scotland and Ireland*, Edinburgh, London.

Leatham, William 1840, *Letters on the Currency*, 2nd. edn., London.

Lefrançois, Éduard (n.d.), *Notions de mécanique générale, Pt.2*, Brussels.

Liebig, Justus von 1862 (1), *Die Chemie in ihrer Anwendung auf Agricultur und Physiologie*, 7th. edn., Part 1, Brunswick.

——— 1862 (2), *Einleitung in die Naturgesetze des Feldbaues*, Brunswick.

Linguet, Simon-Nicolas-Henri 1767, *Théorie des lois civiles, ou principes fondamentaux de la société*, Volume 1, London.

List, Friedrich 1842, *Die Ackerverfassung, die Zwergwirthschaft und die Auswanderung*, Stuttgart.

Luther, Martin 1540, *An die Pfarrherrn, wider den Wucher zu predigen. Vermahnung*, Wittenberg.

——— 1555, *Eyn Sermon auf das Evangelium von dem reichen Mann and armen Lazaros*, Wittenberg.

——— 1589, 'Von Kauffshandlung und Wucher', in Martin Luther, *Der Sechste Teil der Bücher des Ehrnwürdigen Herrn Doctoris Martini Luther*, Wittenberg.

Luzac, Elie 1782, *Hollands Rijkdom, III*, Leyden.

Macaulay, Thomas Babington 1855, *The History of England from the accession of James the Second*, Volume 4, London.

Macnab, Henry Grey 1821, *Examen impartial des nouvelles vues de M. Robert Owen*, Paris.

Malthus, Thomas Robert 1815, *An Inquiry into the Nature and Progress of Rent*, London.

——— 1820, *Principles of Political Economy*, London.

——— 1827, *Definitions in Political Economy*, London.

——— 1836, *Principles of Political Economy*, 2nd. edn., London.

[Manley, Thomas ?] 1668, *Interest of Money Mistaken, or a treatise proving that the abatement of interest is the effect and not the cause of the riches of a nation*, London.

Maron, Hermann 1859, *Extensiv oder Intensiv?*, Oppeln.

Marx, Karl 1847, *Misère de la Philosophie. Réponse à la Philosophie de la misère de M. Proudhon*, Paris, Brussels.

——— 1859, *Zur Kritik der politischen Oekonomie. Heft 1*, Berlin.

——— 1885, *Das Kapital. Kritik der politischen Oekonomie. Bd. 2. Buch 2: Der Cirkulationsprocess des Kapitals*, edited by Friedrich Engels, Hamburg.

——— 1976 [1890], *Capital. A Critique of Political Economy. Volume 1*, translated by Ben Fowkes, London: Penguin Books.

——— 1978 [1885], *Capital. A Critique of Political Economy. Volume 2*, translated by David Fernbach, London: Penguin Books.

Massie, Joseph 1750, *An essay on the governing causes of the natural rate of interest; wherein the sentiments of Sir William Petty and Mr. Locke, on that head, are considered*, London.

Mathieu de Dombasle, Christophe-Joseph-Alexandre 1828, 'Des baux à portage de fruits', in *Annales Agricoles de Roville*, by C.J.A. Mathieu de Dombasle, Book 4, Paris.

MECW 1976, 6, London: Lawrence and Wishart.

MECW 1979, 12, London: Lawrence and Wishart.

MECW 1986, 15, London: Lawrence and Wishart.

MECW 1987, 29, London: Lawrence and Wishart.

MECW 1988, 30, London: Lawrence and Wishart.

MECW 1989, 31, Moscow: Progress Publishers.

MECW 1989, 32, London: Lawrence and Wishart.

MECW 1991, 33, London: Lawrence and Wishart.

MECW 1994, 34, London: Lawrence and Wishart.

Mees, Willem Cornelis 1838, *Proeve eener geschiedenis van het Bankwezen in Nederland*, Rotterdam.

MEGA 1980, II.2, *Ökonomische Manuskripte und Schriften 1858–1861*, Berlin: Dietz Verlag.

MEGA 1978, II.3.3, *Zur Kritik der Politischen Ökonomie (Manuskript 1861–1863), Text. Teil 3*, Berlin: Dietz Verlag.

MEGA 1979, II.3.4, *Zur Kritik der Politischen Ökonomie (Manuskript 1861–1863), Text. Teil 4*, Berlin: Dietz Verlag.

MEGA 1980, II.3.5, *Zur Kritik der Politischen Ökonomie (Manuskript 1861–1863), Text. Teil 5*, Berlin: Dietz Verlag.

MEGA 1982, II.3.6, *Zur Kritik der Politischen Ökonomie (Manuskript 1861–1863), Text, Teil 6*, Berlin: Dietz Verlag.

Mill, John Stuart 1844, *Essays on Some Unsettled Questions of Political Economy*, London.

——— 1849, *Principles of Political Economy*, 2nd. edn., Volume 1, London.

Möser, Justus 1820, *Patriotische Phantasien*, Part 4, Berlin.

Mommsen, Theodor 1856, *Römische Geschichte*, 2nd. edn., Volume 1, Berlin.

——— 1894, *The History of Rome*, translated by W.P. Dickson, Volume 3, London.

Morton, John Lockhart 1858, *The Resources of Estates: being a treatise on the agricultural improvement and general management of landed property*, London.

Mounier, L. 1846, *De l'agriculture en France d'après les documents officiels. Avec des remarques par Rubichon*, Volume 1, Paris.

Müller, Adam Heinrich 1809, *Die Elemente der Staatskunst*, Volumes 2 and 3, Berlin.

Neale, Charles 1860, *Two Lectures on the History and Conditions of Landed Property*, Oxford.

Newman, Francis William 1851, *Lectures on Political Economy*, London.

Newman, Samuel Philips 1835, *Elements of Political Economy*, Andover and New York.

North, Dudley 1691, *Discourses upon Trade*, London.

Observations on Certain Verbal Disputes in Political Economy particularly relating to value and to demand and supply, 1821, London.

Opdyke, George 1851, *A Treatise on Political Economy*, New York.

Parry, Charles Henry 1816, *The Question of the Necessity of the Existing Corn Laws*, London.

Passy, Hippolyte-Philibert 1854, 'De la rente du sol', in Charles Coquelin (ed.), *Dictionnaire de l'économie politique*, 2nd. edn., Volume 2, Paris.

Pecqueur, Constantin 1842, *Théorie nouvelle d'économie social et politique*, Paris.

Petty, William 1667, *A Treatise of Taxes and Contributions*, London.

——— 1699, *Several Essays in Political Arithmetick*, London.

Poppe, Johann Heinrich Moritz 1807, *Geschichte der Technologie seit der Wiederherstellung der Wissenschaften bis an das Ende des achtzehnten Jahrhunderts*, Volume 1, Göttingen.

Price, Richard 1772 (1), *An Appeal to the Public on the Subject of the National Debt*, London.

——— 1772 (2), *Observations on Reversionary Payments*, 2nd. edn., London.

——— 1803, *Observations on Reversionary Payments*, 6th. edn., London.

Quételet, Adolphe 1848, *Du système social et des lois qui le régissent*, Paris.

Raguet, Condy 1840, *A Treatise on Currency and Banking*, 2nd. edn., Philadelphia.

Ramsay, George 1836, *An Essay on the Distribution of Wealth*, Edinburgh and London.

Reden, Friedrich von 1848, *Vergleichende Kulturstatistik*, Berlin.

Ricardo, David 1821, *On the Principles of Political Economy*, London.

Rodbertus, Karl Heinrich 1851, *Sociale Briefe an von Kirchmann. Dritter Brief: Widerlegung der Ricardo'schen Lehre von der Grundrente*, Berlin.

Roscher, Wilhelm 1858, *Die Grundlagen der Nationalökonomie*, 3rd. edn., Stuttgart, Augsburg.

Roy, Henry 1864, *The Theory of the Exchanges. The Bank Charter Act of 1844. The abuse of the metallic principle to depreciation*, London.

Rubichon, Maurice 1837, *Du mécanisme de la société en France et en Angleterre*, 2nd. edn., Paris.

Say, Jean-Baptiste 1817, *Traité d'économie politique, ou simple exposition de la manière dont se forment, se distribuent et se consomment les richesses*, 3rd. edn., Volume 1, Paris.

Schoedler, Friedrich 1852, *Das Buch der Natur, die Lehren der Physik, Astronomie, Che-*

mie, Mineralogie, Geologie, Physiologie, Botanik und Zoologie umfassend, 6th. edn., Brunswick.

Sismondi, Jean-Charles-Léonard Simonde de 1827, *Nouveaux principes de l'économie politique ou de la richesse dans ses rapports avec la population*, 2nd. edn., Volume 2, Paris.

Smith, Adam 1802, *Recherches sur la nature et les causes de la richesse des nations, trad. par Germain Garnier*, Volume 3, Paris.

——— 1999 [1776], *The Wealth of Nations, Books I to III*, London: Penguin Books.

Some Thoughts of the Interest of England. By a lover of commerce, 1697, London.

Steuart, James 1770, *An Inquiry into the Principles of Political Oeconomy: being an essay on the science of domestic policy in free nations*, Volume I, Dublin.

——— 1789, *Recherches des principes de l'économie politique, ou essay sur la science de la police intérieure des nations libres*, Volume 4, Paris.

Stirling, Patrick James 1846, *The Philosophy of Trade*, Edinburgh.

Storch, Henri 1815, *Cours d'économie politique*, Volume 2, St. Petersburg.

——— 1824, *Considérations sur la nature du revenu national*, Paris.

Thornton, Henry 1802, *An Enquiry into the Nature and Effects of the Paper Credit of Great Britain*, London.

The Three Prize Essays on Agriculture and the Corn Law. Published by the National Anti-Corn Law League, Manchester and London, 1842.

Tocqueville, Alexis de 1856, *L'Ancien Régime et la révolution*, 2nd. edn., Paris.

Tooke, Thomas 1838, *A History of Prices, and of the state of circulation, from 1793 to 1837*, Volume 2, London.

——— 1844, *An Inquiry into the Currency Principle, the connection of the currency with prices, and the expediency of a separation of issue from banking*, 2nd. edn., London.

——— 1848, *A History of Prices, and of the state of the circulation, from 1839 to 1847*, London.

———, and William Newmarch 1857, *A History of Prices from 1792 to the present time*, Volume 6, London.

Torrens, Robert 1821, *An Essay on the Production of Wealth*, London.

——— 1847, *On the Operation of the Bank Charter Act of 1844 as it affects commercial credit*, 2nd. edn., London.

Tuckett, John Debell 1846, *A history of the past and present state of the labouring population, including the progress of agriculture, manufactures and commerce*, Volume 1, London.

Turgot, Anne-Robert-Jacques 1844 [1769], *Réflexions sur la formation et la distribution des richesses*, Paris.

Ure, Andrew 1836, *Philosophie des manufactures, ou économie industrielle de la fabrication du coton, du lin et de la soie etc.*, Volume 1, Brussels.

Vinçard, Pierre-Denis 1846, *Histoire du travail et des travailleurs en France*, Volume 1, Part 2, Paris.

Vissering, Simon 1860, *Handboek van Praktische Staathuishoudkunde, Deel 1*, Amsterdam.

Wakefield, Edward Gibbon 1833, *England and America, vol. 2*, London.

Walton, Alfred Armstrong 1865, *History of the Landed Tenures of Great Britain and Ireland*, London.

West, Edward 1815, *Essay on the application of capital to land, with observations shewing the impolicy of any great restriction of the importation of corn*, London.

Abbreviations

MECW	Karl Marx Frederick Engels Collected Works
MEGA	Karl Marx Friedrich Engels Gesamtausgabe (Second Edition)

Index

www.ingramcontent.com/pod-product-compliance
Ingram Content Group UK Ltd.
Pitfield, Milton Keynes, MK11 3LW, UK
UKHW021854100926
8556IPUK00020B/1214

9 781608 466900